Health Care Needs Assessment

The epidemiologically based needs assessment reviews

Second Edition

Volume 2

Edited by

Andrew Stevens
Professor of Public Health
Department of Public Health and Epidemiology
University of Birmingham

James Raftery
Professor of Health Economics
Health Services Management Centre
University of Birmingham

Jonathan Mant
Senior Clinical Lecturer
Department of Primary Care and General Practice
University of Birmingham

and

Sue Simpson
Research Fellow
Department of Public Health and Epidemiology
University of Birmingham

RADCLIFFE PUBLISHING

OXFORD • SAN FRANCISCO

Radcliffe Publishing Ltd
18 Marcham Road
Abingdon
Oxon OX14 1AA
United Kingdom

www.radcliffe-oxford.com
Electronic catalogue and worldwide online ordering facility.

British Library Cataloguing in Publication Data

A catalogue record for this book is available from the British Library.

ISBN 1 85775 891 9 (volume 1)

ISBN 1 85775 892 7 (volume 2)

ISBN 1 85775 890 0 (set)

Typeset by Advance Typesetting Ltd, Oxford
Printed and bound by TJ International Ltd, Padstow, Cornwall

Contents: VOLUME 1

Contents: VOLUME 2

Preface

This book is the second edition of the *Health Care Needs Assessment Reviews*, first published in 1994. The objective of the first edition was to produce definitive assessments of the 'need' for health services of a typical health authority's population by individual disease or health problem. This was undertaken for 20 key topics. Each topic was dealt with under a standard protocol designed by the editors. Authors were asked to include: (i) a statement of the problem (disease); (ii) sub-categories of the problem meaningful to commissioners of health care; (iii) information on incidence and prevalence of the problem; (iv) a description of current services available to address the problem and their costs; (v) a summary of what is known about the effectiveness and cost-effectiveness of the main services; and (vi) recommendations and quantified models of care. The authors were also invited to give their opinion on suitable outcome measures and audit methods which might be used to monitor services and to indicate any research requirements arising from the review of needs assessment.

The same protocol has been used in this second edition, but the content has been updated. The evidence base of health care has moved on, new technologies and practices for tackling health problems have been introduced and the structure of the UK's health services has changed. In April 2002, 302 primary care trusts replaced 99 health authorities and 481 primary care groups in England, with similar changes in Scotland and Wales. The responsibilities of primary care trusts, however, specifically those to do with planning and commissioning services to meet the needs of their population, remain very similar to those of health authorities.

This second edition updates the 20 topics included in the original version. It is accompanied by a second series, published in 1997, covering a further eight topics (accident and emergency departments; child and adolescent mental health; low back pain; palliative and terminal care; dermatology; breast cancer; genitourinary medicine services; and gynaecology). A third series is in preparation. This will include adult critical care; black and minority ethnic groups; continence; dyspepsia; hypertension; obesity; peripheral vascular disease; pregnancy and childbirth; and prison health.

Each chapter has been reviewed by the editors and by external anonymous peers. The chapters are the work of individuals or groups of authors chosen for their expertise in the topic area. Authors work to the standard protocol but with freedom of emphasis according to the topic. As such, chapters do not necessarily reflect the professional consensus or the views of the sponsors of this project and should not be regarded as setting an obligatory norm. Rather the chapters present the evidence and arguments on which commissioners of health care might base their decisions.

The editors wish to acknowledge the contributions of Anne Kauder, Mike Dunning and Graham Winyard, who all helped devise the original project and steer it into its present form, of Graham Bickler and of other steering group members for their advice over the years. We would also like to thank the many external experts who have reviewed the individual chapters and whose comments have helped to contribute to the value of the needs series.

Andrew Stevens
James Raftery
Jonathan Mant
Sue Simpson
May 2004

List of contributors

Dima Abdulrahim
Advisor
National Treatment Agency
Email: Dima.Abdulrahim@nta-nhs.org.uk

John R Ashton
Regional Director of Public Health
Government Office for the North West
Email: John.R.Ashton@doh.gsi.gov.uk

Ameet Bakhai
Senior Fellow and Cardiology Specialist Registrar
Clinical Trials and Evaluation Unit
Royal Brompton Hospital
Email: a.bakhai@cteu.org

Roger Beech
Senior Lecturer
Director of Research
Centre for Health Planning and Management
Keele University
Email: r.beech@keele.ac.uk

Tim J Bowker
Associate Medical Director
British Heart Foundation, and
Consultant Cardiologist
St Mary's Hospital, Paddington, and
Honorary Senior Lecturer
National Heart and Lung Institute
Imperial College London
Email: bowkert@bhf.org.uk

Carol Brayne
Professor of Public Health Medicine
Department of Public Health and Primary Care
University of Cambridge
Email: cb105@medschl.cam.ac.uk

Christopher CH Cook
Professorial Fellow
St Chad's College
University of Durham
Email: c.c.h.cook@durham.ac.uk

Brian Cooper
Honorary Research Fellow
Section of Old Age Psychiatry
Institute of Psychiatry
Email: spjubco@iop.kcl.ac.uk

Chris Cullen
Professor of Clinical Psychology
Department of Psychology
Keele University
Email: c.cullen@keele.ac.uk

Jill Dawson
Reader in Health Services Research
School of Health and Social Care (OCHRAD)
Oxford Brookes University
Email: jdawson@brookes.ac.uk

Jenny Donovan
Professor of Social Medicine
Head of Health Services Research
Department of Social Medicine
University of Bristol
Email: jenny.donovan@bristol.ac.uk

Heather Farrar
Consultant in Public Health
Bournemouth Teaching Primary Care Trust

Ray Fitzpatrick
Professor of Public Health and Primary Care
Division of Public Health and Primary Health Care
Institute of Health Sciences
University of Oxford
Email: raymond.fitzpatrick@nuf.ox.ac.uk

John Fletcher
Consultant Public Health Physician
Oxford City Primary Care Trust
Email: john.fletcher@post.harvard.edu

Kevin Fox
Consultant Cardiologist and Honorary Senior Lecturer
National Heart and Lung Institute
Imperial College London
Email: k.fox@imperial.ac.uk

Mark Goldman
Chief Executive
Birmingham Heartlands and Solihull NHS Trust
Email: mark.goldman@heartofwmids.nhs.uk

Martin C Gulliford
Senior Lecturer
Department of Public Health Sciences
King's College London
Email: martin.gulliford@kcl.ac.uk

David Hall
Professor of Community Paediatrics
Institute of General Practice
University of Sheffield
Email: d.hall@sheffield.ac.uk

Matthew Hickman
Senior Lecturer
Centre for Research in Drugs and Health Behaviour
Division of Primary Care and Population Health Sciences
Imperial College London
Email: m.hickman@imperial.ac.uk

Peter Hill
Honorary Consultant in Child and Adolescent Psychiatry
Department of Psychological Medicine
Great Ormond Street Hospital for Children
Email: strandend@dial.pipex.com

Shane Kavanagh
Director of Health Economics
Johnson & Johnson Pharmaceutical Services
Beerse
Belgium
Email: skavanag@psmbe.jnj.com

Kornelia P Kotseva
Senior Clinical Research Fellow
National Heart and Lung Institute
Imperial College London
Email: k.kotseva@imperial.ac.uk

Don Lavoie
Deputy Regional Manager, London
National Treatment Agency
Email: don.lavoie@nta-nhs.org.uk

Paul Lelliott
Director
The Royal College of Psychiatrists Research Unit
London
Email: plelliott@cru.rcpsych.ac.uk

Mary W Lyons
Senior Lecturer
Centre for Public Health
Faculty of Health and Social Sciences
Liverpool John Moores University
Email: M.Lyons@livjm.ac.uk

Jonathan Mant
Senior Clinical Lecturer
Department of Primary Care and General Practice
University of Birmingham
Email: j.w.mant@bham.ac.uk

John Marsden
Senior Lecturer in Addictive Behaviour
Division of Psychological Medicine
Institute of Psychiatry
King's College London
Email: J.Marsden@iop.kcl.ac.uk

David Melzer
Clinical Senior Research Associate
Department of Public Health and Primary Care
University of Cambridge
Email: dm214@medschl.cam.ac.uk

David E Neal
Professor
Oncology Department
Addenbrooke's Hospital
Cambridge
Email: den22@cam.ac.uk

Rebecca R Neal
Clerk
House of Lords
London

Katherine Pearce
Consultant in Public Health Medicine
Cambridge and Huntingdon Health Authority

Wendy Phillips
Consultant in Communicable Disease Control
South Yorkshire Health Protection Service
Email: wendy.phillips@doncastereastpct.nhs.uk

James Raftery
Professor of Health Economics
Health Services Management Centre
University of Birmingham
Email: j.p.raftery@bham.ac.uk

Siân Rees
Senior Policy Advisor
Mental Health Services Branch
Department of Health
London
Email: sian.rees@doh.gsi.gov.uk

Paul Roderick
Senior Lecturer in Public Health Medicine
Health Care Research Unit
University of Southampton
Southampton General Hospital
Email: pjr@soton.ac.uk

Alison Salt
Consultant Paediatrician
Wolfson Centre
Institute of Child Health
London

Hugh Sanderson
Consultant in Public Health
Central South Coast Cancer Network
Hampshire and Isle of Wight Strategic Health Authority
Email: hugh.sanderson@hiowha.nhs.uk

Simon Scott
Lead Commissioner, Substance Misuse
Brighton and Hove City PCT
Email: simon.scott@bhcpct.nhs.uk

Sue Simpson
Research Fellow
Department of Public Health and Epidemiology
University of Birmingham
Email: s.l.simpson.20@bham.ac.uk

Stephen Spiro
Professor of Thoracic Medicine
The Middlesex Hospital, London

Sarah Stewart-Brown
Professor of Public Health
Division of Health in the Community
Warwick Medical School (LWMS)
University of Warwick
Email: sarah.stewart-brown@warwick.ac.uk

Andrew Stevens
Professor of Public Health
Department of Public Health and Epidemiology
University of Birmingham
Email: a.j.stevens@bham.ac.uk

John Strang
Director and Professor of the Addictions
National Addiction Centre
Institute of Psychiatry
King's College London
Email: j.strang@iop.bpmf.ac.uk

John R Thompson
Professor of Ophthalmic Epidemiology
Department of Ophthalmology
University of Leicester
Email: john.thompson@le.ac.uk

Derick Wade
Professor and Consultant in Neurological Rehabilitation
Oxford Centre for Enablement
Email: derick.wade@dial.pipex.com

Andrew R Walker
Robertson Centre for Biostatistics
University of Glasgow
Email: A.Walker@stats.gla.ac.uk

Sarah Walters
Senior Clinical Lecturer
Department of Public Health and Epidemiology
University of Birmingham
Email: S.Walters@bham.ac.uk

Derek J Ward
Specialist Registrar in Public Health
Public Health Directorate
South Worcestershire Primary Care Trust
Email: djward@btinternet.com

Richard Wilson
Senior Public Health Information Specialist
South Birmingham Primary Care Trust
Moseley Hall Hospital
Email: Richard.Wilson@SouthBirminghamPCT.nhs.uk

John K Wing
Retired

Rhys Williams
Professor of Clinical Epidemiology
The Clinical School
University of Wales Swansea
Email: D.R.R.Williams@swansea.ac.uk

Simon Winner
Consultant Physician
Department of Clinical Geratology
Radcliffe Infirmary, Oxford
Email: simon.winner@geratology.ox.ac.uk

David A Wood
Garfield Weston Chair of Cardiovascular Medicine
National Heart and Lung Institute
Imperial College London
Email: d.wood@imperial.ac.uk

Denise Young
Greater Glasgow Health Board

Date of acceptance for publication

11 Varicose Veins and Venous Ulcers*

Sue Simpson and Paul Roderick

1 Summary

Introduction/statement of the problem

Chronic venous disease is the most common vascular condition to affect the lower limb. It covers a wide range of conditions which can be broadly categorised as varicose veins, chronic venous insufficiency and venous ulcers. Venous disease is associated with a large burden of ill-health and it consumes a substantial amount of NHS resources. In the UK each year roughly half a million people consult their general practitioners about varicose veins and associated symptoms. Varicose veins are one of the most common conditions seen in surgical clinics, they make up a significant part of the elective surgery workload and they are responsible for a large proportion of patients on surgical waiting lists in NHS hospitals. Venous ulcer care is a major component of community nursing services. Venous disease has been a Cinderella area of health care, in terms of both research and treatment, though this situation is changing. Moreover, this situation has raised important questions about what conditions the NHS should treat.

Whilst there is lay recognition that a varicose vein is a tortuous twisted vein, a standard definition has not yet been agreed. In addition, the exact pathophysiology surrounding the development of varicose veins remains controversial. Most varicose veins are primary (i.e. arising *de novo*), and whilst there are some recognised predisposing factors, structural abnormalities and abnormal haemodynamic effects which may influence their development, there is no agreement on which of these is the main cause of veins becoming varicose.

Venous ulcers are located at the severe end of the spectrum of chronic venous disorders of the leg. A chronic venous ulcer can be defined as an area of discontinuity of epidermis, persisting for 4 weeks or more and occurring as a result of venous hypertension (increased pressure) and calf muscle pump insufficiency. Venous hypertension is the undisputed initiating factor in venous ulcer development but a detailed understanding of the aetiology of venous ulcers is lacking, not least information on the natural history of varicose veins in relation to venous ulcers.

There appears to be a high degree of acceptance of symptoms of venous disorders of the leg among affected persons, but for around a third of people they do present a significant problem. Symptoms reported by patients presenting with varicose veins include aching pain, tiredness/feelings of heaviness, throbbing, itching and swelling in the lower limbs. Not all varicose veins are associated with symptoms. Cosmetic dissatisfaction with the appearance of varicose veins is probably universal, although the impact it

---

* This is an update of a chapter included in the first edition by M Robbins, SJ Frankel, K Nanchahal, J Coast and MH Williams.

has on an individual and his or her lifestyle will be a matter of personal outlook. Few studies of function or quality of life have been carried out for venous disorders of the leg. Those that exist report that patients with varicose veins have a reduced quality of life compared with the general population and that those with venous leg ulcers have a poorer quality of life than age-matched controls.

The management of venous disorders is thought to represent between 1% and 3% of total health care expenditure. In the UK in 2000–01, 107 020 people were admitted to hospital for operations for varicose veins of the lower limb. The management of leg ulcers comprises a significant portion of the workload of community and hospital nurses, general practitioners, dermatologists, surgeons and physicians involved in the care of the elderly. Each ulcer costs around £2000–4000 per annum to treat and the total cost to the National Health Service in 1995 was estimated at £600 million.

Recurrence of varicose veins after treatment is a significant problem to the health service. This occurs in 20–80% of cases treated for primary varicose veins, depending on the definition of recurrence used, length of follow-up and the initial treatment. The rate of occurrence increases with time, with an estimated recurrence rate of around 50% up to 5 years. Approximately 20% of varicose vein surgery is for recurrent disease. Recurrence may be due to inadequate assessment and initial surgery and to the development of new varicose veins. Venous ulcers take time to heal; up to 50% of venous ulcers may be present for 7 to 9 months, between 8% and 34% may be present for more than 5 years, and about 70% of patients have recurrent ulcers.

Sub-categories

No universally accepted classification of chronic venous disease has been agreed and of those classifications that exist, few have been based on objective measurements of abnormal venous pressure/flow. The classification systems used most widely are those developed by Widmer in 1978, Porter in 1988 and the CEAP (clinical signs, etiologic classification, anatomic distribution and pathophysiologic dysfunction) classification presented by the American Venous Forum in 1995. None of these have been formally validated.

The sub-categories to be used in this chapter are as follows:

- **mild discretionary:** asymptomatic, cosmetic/mild discomfort or swelling
- **severe non-discretionary:** severe pain/swelling, skin change (lipodermatosclerosis) without ulcer
- **venous ulcer:** chronic ulceration (healed and active).

Prevalence/incidence

The population distribution of varicose veins has to be put in a context of uncertainty. The many studies that consider the prevalence of varicose veins and venous disorders are difficult to interpret, as:

1   the method of measurement/assessment of varicose veins varies greatly, including the validity of the questionnaires used
2   the comparability is limited by the varying definitions of varicose veins used
3   much of the epidemiological data relates to highly selected groups rather than a cross-section of the general population. The nature of many of the populations studied renders most of these studies of limited value in determining levels of service requirement in the UK.

The prevalence of venous-related oedema and skin changes is not well documented but there is a large number of studies on the prevalence of leg ulceration. Venous ulcers are the commonest cause of leg ulceration. However, as with the studies on varicose veins, the variations between definitions and methodology employed in these studies make it difficult to give a definitive prevalence figure.

The best available data representative of the UK population are from the Edinburgh vein study, carried out between 1994 and 1996. Incorporating the results of this study into the sub-categories defined in the previous section, a prevalence of varicose veins and chronic venous insufficiency (CVI) has been estimated (*see* Table 1). These values underestimate the population prevalence, as the Edinburgh study only included 18- to 64-year-olds and venous disease is commoner in older age groups. In addition, there are no data available on non-Caucasians.

Table 1: Estimated prevalence of varicose veins and CVI (in a population aged 18–64 years).

Sub-category		Estimated prevalence (%)	
		Male	Female
A	Mild discretionary*	40	31
B	Severe non-discretionary†	8	7
C	Venous ulcer‡	1	1

* Based on the prevalence of trunk varices (Grade 1) and CVI (Grade 1).
† Based on the prevalence of trunk varices (Grade 2–3) and CVI (Grade 2).
‡ VU is both healed and active ulceration (the latter about 0.1–0.25%).

Whilst many risk factors for varicose veins have been postulated (including age, pregnancy, ethnicity, family history, obesity, occupations requiring prolonged standing or sitting, lack of dietary fibre, use of constricting corsets and sitting posture for defecation), the evidence linking most factors to varicose vein development is limited. Age is the most important, but recent studies have not found significant gender differences and an association with obesity seems to be confined to females. If the link with obesity is real, the prevalence of varicose veins could increase with the rising levels of obesity in the UK population.

Services available

Primary prevention

The scope for primary prevention is limited. Specific measures that have been suggested include weight control, reducing the amount of standing, greater physical activity and prophylaxis against deep vein thrombosis (DVT) (e.g. in surgical patients). The use of compression stockings after an acute DVT has been shown to reduce the incidence of CVI and venous ulcer which can occur as a post-thrombosis complication.

Presentation

Many people with varicose veins will choose not to seek any medical advice. People who do go to their general practitioner are primarily concerned about the cosmetic appearance of their veins or present with symptoms associated with varicose veins. Concern about the future course of the veins is also a common underlying reason. Symptoms draw attention to varicose veins but it has been found that varicose veins may not be the cause of the symptom. Women are more likely to consult their GP with varicose veins than men.

The National Institute for Clinical Excellence has published a guide to appropriate referral from general practice to specialist services for varicose veins. The guide emphasises that most varicose veins require no treatment and state that the key role of primary care is to provide reassurance, explanation and education.

Assessment

An initial diagnosis of varicose veins is usually made up of the signs observed by the general practitioner and the symptoms reported by the patient. However, the accuracy of clinical examination in identifying the site of incompetence is poor. Whether a diagnosis of varicose veins then becomes a referral for treatment and/or further assessment at an outpatient clinic depends upon the severity of the signs and symptoms, the likelihood of complications, patient preferences and the supply of treatment options. There is no single test available to provide answers to the many questions that need to be asked to decide if and how to treat varicose veins and other venous disorders of the leg. For this reason a number of specialised investigations have evolved over the years and include non-invasive methods (continuous-wave Doppler ultrasound, duplex scanning, plethysmography, near-infra-red spectroscopy) and invasive methods (phlebography/varicography, foot venous pressure measurements, ambulatory venous pressure). Each technique of investigation has its own advantages and disadvantages, and out of the series of tests available in the vascular laboratory, several methods will measure the same thing. Whatever the method used, the interpretation is open to inter-observer variation and can be expensive and time-consuming. The duplex method has become the investigation of choice, especially for recurrent disease, post-DVT disease, and for CVI or venous ulcer. In the UK it would be unusual for any patient to undergo any test other than a duplex outside a research protocol.

Treatment

The general indications for treatment of varicose veins are to prevent complications related to venous disease, to relieve symptoms and to improve the appearance of the leg. However, there is no national consensus as to which varicose veins should be treated based on site of incompetence, severity, etc. and as to which types of treatment to be offered (*see* below).

Pharmacotherapy

A variety of medications are available for the relief of various individual symptoms, such as heaviness, discomfort, itching, cramps, pain and aching, and swelling.

Compression therapy

Compression is the mainstay of venous ulcer treatment. It acts to reduce vein calibre, capillary filtration and venous reflux and improves venous pumping. These effects increase venous return, improve lymphatic drainage and decrease oedema. Materials used for compression include elastic and inelastic bandages, and elastic stockings. There are many ways of applying compression, such as single layers of bandaging, multiple layers of bandaging, compression stockings or a combination of bandages. Intermittent pneumatic compression is an alternative method.

Sclerotherapy

Sclerotherapy is the injection of an irritant solution into an empty vein, resulting in an endothelial reaction, fibrosis and complete venous destruction. Compression usually accompanies sclerotherapy. Its importance in the sclerotherapy process, the strength of compression and the length of time for which it is applied vary and depend on the technique used. As a mode of treatment, sclerotherapy has been variably popular in Europe and the USA.

Echosclerotherapy

Echosclerotherapy is a modification of sclerotherapy which involves injection of a sclerosing agent into a vein under ultrasound guidance and therefore in real proximity to the leakage point.

Surgical management

The basis of surgery is to ligate (tie off) any incompetent venous connections and/or to strip out (remove) any varicose veins.

The types of operation available to treat varicose veins include:

- phlebectomies (avulsions) of varicosities, ligation of tributaries and local excision of tributaries
- flush ligation of the sapheno-femoral junction, also called high saphenous ligation
- stripping of the long saphenous vein
- sapheno-popliteal junction ligation, also called short saphenous ligation
- stripping of the short saphenous vein (but avoided by most surgeons)
- ligation of the medial lower leg communicating veins
- ligation of other communicating veins (i.e. gastrocnemius, lateral calf, Hunterian and miscellaneous veins)
- operations on recurrent varicose veins.

New technologies and other treatments

Continuous-wave laser systems, such as carbon dioxide lasers and argon lasers, have been tested for their effects on leg veins. Some laser systems show promise as alternative or complementary therapies for telangiectasias. Whilst compression therapy is the main venous ulcer therapy, various other interventions including electrical stimulation, laser therapy and ultrasound have been used in addition to, or in replacement of, compression where the latter is contraindicated. New therapies for varicose veins include radio-frequency ablation and the use of a laser probe to close off the long saphenous vein under ultrasound control.

Configuration of services

Day-case surgery

Day-case surgery for varicose veins has been shown to be economic, safe and effective and to reduce waiting time for surgery. It is now widely accepted as the most appropriate way to treat many patients who need common surgical procedures, and there has been a national drive to increase the percentage of varicose veins dealt with as day cases. However, day-case surgery is disliked by a proportion of patients and in the private sector varicose vein surgery is very rarely carried out as a day case. Patients for whom day surgery may be unsuitable include those with extensive varicosities, those needing open calf perforator surgery, those requiring post-operative bed rest for venous ulcers, and those with pre-existing medical conditions.

Waiting lists

Increasing pressure on surgical resources in terms of inpatient beds and operating-theatre availability has led to increasing waiting lists for varicose veins. A number of waiting-list initiatives have demonstrated that varicose vein waiting lists can be significantly reduced. Waiting for an operation can result in deterioration in the clinical condition of the patient and considerable morbidity for the patient while they wait.

Management of venous ulcers

There is wide variation in the management of venous leg ulcers with types of care including hospital inpatient care, hospital outpatient clinics, primary care clinics and home visits. The introduction of community ulcer clinics has been shown to significantly improve leg ulcer healing and reduce costs by about £150 000 per 250 000 population per annum.

Current service provision

Data on current service provision are based on hospital episode data from NHS hospitals in England (HES data) from 1990–91 to 2000–01. There were 45 216 main operations for varicose veins in NHS hospitals in England in 2000–01. The rate of surgical treatment for varicose veins increased after 1990–91 until 1995–96 when there were 121 operations per 100 000 population. Since then the rate has declined and is now back at 1990 levels with a rate of 92 per 100 000 population in 2000–01. The rates for treatment for varicose veins are highest amongst females between 35 and 64 years of age. The most notable trend is that the proportion of operations for varicose veins carried out as day surgery has increased considerably, from 19% of operations in 1990–91 to 55% of operations in 2000–01. Other important trends are the increase in waiting times for varicose vein operations and the noticeable decrease in length of stay for those patients admitted as inpatients. There are no routine data on the indications for surgery or on surgery for recurrent disease with which to evaluate the appropriateness of outcomes of surgery.

Similarly, there are no routinely collected data on elective hospital treatment carried out in England and Wales by the independent sector. However, one study found that surgery performed in independent hospitals accounted for 24% of the ligation or stripping operations for varicose veins in England and Wales in 1997–98, and the number of privately-funded operations accounted for 21% of these operations.

As venous ulcers are largely managed in outpatient clinics, there are limited routine data on workload, processes or outcomes of care.

Effectiveness

The effectiveness of the different forms of management for varicose veins and venous ulcers can be assessed by the amount of reduction in the presenting symptoms and signs, and in the long term by the volume of need for further treatment, including that for recurrent disease. The effectiveness of different types of treatment still remains unclear. This is reflected in the large variation in the balance of treatment types between countries (e.g. in drugs, sclerotherapy and surgery). A Task Force on Chronic Venous Disorders of the Leg was established in September 1993 with the purpose of comprehensively evaluating this area of medicine. One of its mandates was to critically review existing scientific evidence on the diagnosis and treatment of the condition. The results of their evaluation are reported in Section 6. Where more current effectiveness data have been identified this information has been included. The Cochrane Peripheral Vascular Disease Group is co-ordinating systematic reviews of many aspects of venous disease management.

Models of care/recommendations

Key features of a venous disease service appear to be as follows:

1 appropriate referral of patients in whom varicosities are presented or suspected (*see* NICE referral advice)
2 availability of appropriate diagnostic assessment tests and staff trained in their use – this includes not only Doppler but also ideally duplex ultrasound
3 trained junior surgical staff and supervision of inexperienced surgical trainees by consultants
4 maximal use of day surgery – wherever possible, varicose vein treatment should be provided in a day-care setting
5 consideration of the opening of elective treatment centres following the model established in South Wales evaluated by Harvey *et al.* – such centres reduced waiting times and increased the volume of varicose vein surgery
6 community venous ulcer clinics with appropriately trained nurses and an optimal flow of patients.

2 Introduction/statement of the problem

Venous disease is the most common vascular condition to affect the lower limb.[1] The term 'chronic venous disorders of the leg' covers a wide range of conditions, including asymptomatic incompetence of venous valves, venous symptoms, telangiectases, reticular veins, varicose veins, oedema, skin changes and leg ulceration. These can be broadly categorised into varicose veins, chronic venous insufficiency (CVI) and venous ulcers. The relationship between these conditions in the general population is illustrated in Figure 1.

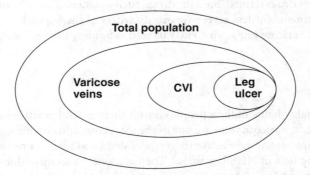

Figure 1: The relationship between varicose veins, chronic venous insufficiency and leg ulceration in the population. *Source*: Callam, 1999.[1]

This chapter addresses varicose veins of the lower limbs but excludes those that may arise as a complication of pregnancy and the puerperium. Varicose veins may be primary or secondary (usually associated with past venous thrombosis affecting the deep and communicating veins).[2] The chapter will also consider other chronic venous disorders of the leg since:

- there is no clear definition of what constitutes a varicose vein

- there is often no differentiation between varicose veins and other more or less severe venous disorders of the leg (especially when considering prevalence and service provision in the literature)
- it is generally believed that varicose veins can progress to venous ulcers
- venous ulcers are an important health problem.

The relevant ICD disease codes and OPCS operation codes can be found in Appendix 1.

An interpretation of the evidence concerning appropriate levels of NHS provision of treatment for varicose veins and other venous disorders of the leg is presented. The broad questions addressed in this analysis are as follows.

- How common are varicose veins and what are the symptoms and complications associated with them?
- What scope is there for the primary prevention of varicose veins?
- When should diagnostic assessment be used and which is the best method?
- Which type of surgery should be used to treat varicose veins to alleviate symptoms and reduce the extent of recurrence? What is the place of other therapies?
- How has varicose vein treatment expanded and what is the current level?
- Is day surgery suitable for varicose vein surgery, and what categories of patient should have day surgery?
- How can the large waiting lists associated with varicose vein surgery be reduced?
- How should services for venous disorders be organised?
- What level and content of provision should a commissioning body accommodate?

Health care needs can be defined in terms of the individual's capacity to benefit from treatment. The problem faced by commissioning authorities when considering treatments for varicose veins and associated conditions is in defining the level of particular treatments that should be provided to permit such benefits to be experienced. The question is therefore not simply whether individuals may benefit, but which individuals with which categories of morbidity should be provided with which specific forms of care. In the light of publicity over new drugs termed 'lifestyle' drugs, such as sildenafil, a decision as to whether the NHS should be funding treatments for less severe venous disorders of the leg such as telangiectases, reticular veins and asymptomatic varicose veins, which may be seen as funding cosmetic surgery, will be questioned.

Varicose veins

In the UK each year roughly half a million people consult their general practitioners about varicose veins and associated symptoms.[3] Varicose veins are one of the most common conditions seen in surgical clinics; they make up a significant part of the elective surgery workload and are responsible for a large proportion of operations on waiting lists in NHS hospitals.[4] The independent sector reduces some of this burden, being responsible for around 24% of surgery for varicose veins.[5] Although it has been suggested in the past that there is a low level of interest in varicose veins in the medical profession,[6] and that operations for varicose veins are seen as low priority and are often performed by the least experienced member of the surgical team, often without supervision,[3] there has been considerable change in the last decade, with varicose veins now being taken on increasingly by interested vascular surgeons.[7]

A standard definition of what constitutes a varicose vein has not yet been agreed. The *Oxford Medical Dictionary* defines them as 'veins that are distended, lengthened and tortuous'.[8] Porter described varicose veins as dilated, palpable subcutaneous veins generally larger than 4 mm.[9] The World Health Organization (WHO) defines them as 'saccular dilatation of the veins which are often tortuous'.[10] However, these definitions, if taken literally, could be restrictive and unhelpful to a commissioner of health care, who will be faced with conditions that the definition would exclude but which are often referred to under the umbrella heading of varicose veins or, more broadly, venous disease. This is discussed further in the section on sub-categories.

In the absence of a precise definition of varicose veins, it is important to understand broadly what varicose veins are and what causes them. Again, this is the subject of much debate.

Anatomy

Venous blood from the skin and subcutaneous fat in the legs is returned to the heart through veins working against gravity. These veins contain valves to prevent a back-flow of blood. There are three types of vein in the lower limbs, and two of these are important when considering venous disease.

- **Deep veins:** These are the venae comitantes to the tibial arteries – the popliteal, tibial and femoral veins and their tributaries. These veins are found beneath the fascia within the fascial compartments. Almost 90% of all venous blood leaves the legs by the deep veins.[11] The blood is under high pressure due to the effects of the calf and foot muscle pump.
- **Superficial veins:** These drain the skin and subcutaneous fat and are situated beneath the skin in the superficial fascia. They include the long and small saphenous veins and their tributaries. The blood is normally under lower pressure than in the deep system due to the protective effect of one-way valves which are in the perforating veins connecting superficial and deep systems. If these valves become incompetent, pressure rises in the superficial system.

Some venous blood drains towards the deep venous system through perforating veins or via the long or short saphenous veins which join the deep system at the sapheno-femoral junction in the groin and the sapheno-popliteal junction behind the knee. It can also drain directly into the deep venous system or bypass the deep system entirely and enter the pelvis.[12] The deep veins carry more blood at a higher pressure than the superficial veins.

Blood is moved from the leg to the heart primarily by the pumping action of the leg muscles, i.e. by muscular compression. The deep veins are subjected to intermittent pressure both at rest and during exercise from pulsations of the adjacent arteries and contractions of the surrounding muscles, which compress the veins and force blood up the limbs towards the heart. As the muscles surrounding the deep veins relax, the pressure within the deep vein lowers temporarily. This causes venous blood to be drawn from the superficial veins into the deep veins, in turn lowering the superficial venous pressure. Competent valves are required to prevent reflux, and to protect the superficial veins and capillaries from a sudden rise in venous pressure when the muscles contract.

Aetiology

In basic terms, the three components of the venous system of the limb – deep veins, superficial veins and perforating veins – work together. Dysfunction of any of these results in dysfunction of the other two.[11] However, although varicose veins have been recognised for centuries, the exact pathophysiology surrounding the development of varicose veins remains controversial. The vast majority of varicose veins arise de novo (i.e. are primary). A minority are secondary to obstruction, e.g. pelvic tumours or post-deep vein thrombosis (DVT). Varicose veins do have some recognised predisposing factors, structural abnormalities and abnormal haemodynamic effects which may influence their development.[13]

Predisposing factors

Predisposing factors for varicose veins are difficult to establish due to the interplay of environmental and genetic elements. Family history of varicose veins, increasing age, female sex (though this is now questioned), parity, ethnicity and occupation may all be factors in the development of varicose veins. A case also exists for the role of height, weight, smoking (though the evidence is weak) and tight underclothes. Aggravating factors such as a fibre-depleted diet (leading to constipation) and long hours spent standing and sitting have been emphasised, and a recurring hypothesis is that adoption of the 'industrial lifestyle' is the major predisposing factor for development of varicose veins. These risk factors will be discussed further in Section 4.

Structural abnormalities

Valvular deficiency

One school of thought is that varicose veins occur when the valves in the veins are incompetent, i.e. they fail to prevent blood returning to the direction from which it has come, resulting in reflux.[14,15] This leads to enlargement of the vein (in length and width) and tortuosity. The location of incompetence varies. DVT is a common mechanism for the destruction of valves in the deep and perforating veins.[11] DVT is estimated to precede the development of varicose veins in as many as 25% of patients,[16] though more information is needed on the association between DVT and varicose veins.

Valvular incompetence in the superficial veins has been said to contribute to 80% of venous disorders.[17] Although valves in varicose veins are stretched and do become atrophic,[18] some believe this to be secondary to the disease process and at present there appears to be little evidence overall to suggest a role for an inherent valvular abnormality as the main cause of primary varicose veins.[13]

Vein wall abnormalities

A number of studies now support the hypothesis that a change in the vein wall precedes valvular incompetence.[18–22] The suggestion that varicose veins are caused by abnormal collagen metabolism has been the subject of much dispute, and changes in elastin content and an increase in smooth muscle in the vein wall as the cause of varicose veins have been suggested.[13] A study in 1992 found a significantly reduced vein wall elasticity and an increased arterial flow in high-risk limbs compared with normal limbs but no corresponding increase in the incidence of valvular incompetence.[23] This study therefore suggests that the role of the venous valves in the development of varicose veins is secondary to changes in the elastic properties of the vein wall and the rate of arterial flow. However, another study of the wall structure and composition of varicose veins with reference to collagen, elastin and smooth muscle content suggested that varicose veins are a dynamic response to venous hypertension and are not thin-walled structures.[24]

Haemodynamic effects

It is thought that increased and irregular blood flow in the veins causes them to become dilated. In addition, the role of arteriovenous fistula in the development of varicose veins was thought to be a contributory aetiological factor. However, very few believe this and the evidence for these theories is limited and inconclusive.[13]

Chronic venous insufficiency/venous ulcers

CVI is manifested by lower limb oedema and lipodermatosclerosis, i.e. skin changes such as pigmentation, atrophy and eczema. It arises secondary to venous hypertension. The high pressure leads to oedema, and leakage of protein has local inflammatory effects.

A chronic venous ulcer can be defined as an area of discontinuity of epidermis, persisting for four weeks or more and occurring as a result of venous hypertension and calf muscle pump insufficiency.[25] It is easily recognised when it is situated in the 'gaiter' region near the medial malleolus (the protuberance at the lower end of the tibia), and occasionally adjacent to the lateral malleolus (the protuberance at the lower end of the fibula). It has a shallow base with a flat margin and the surrounding skin has features of long-standing venous hypertension, i.e. haemosiderin pigmentation, atrophie blanche, eczema, and dilated venules over the instep of the foot.[26]

Venous ulcers are located at the severe end of the spectrum of chronic venous disorders of the leg (*see* Figure 1). Because of this they occur more often in subjects with other forms of venous diseases such as varicose veins and skin changes.[27] Venous leg ulceration has been reported to account for 70–95% of all leg ulcers,[26,28] and 20–50% of these are said to be a consequence of varicose veins.[29,30] However, there is a general lack of data explaining the way varicose veins develop into venous ulcers, and at what point treatment could be advised as being prophylactic rather than remedial.

Venous hypertension is the undisputed initiating factor in venous ulcer development. More severe venous incompetence is associated with a higher risk of ulceration. The higher the venous pressure, the greater the risk, whether incompetence involves the deep or superficial venous system.[31] The reasons why venous ulcers go on to develop is still an area of debate, but there are three main theories (*see* Box 1).

An important determinant of venous ulcers is the venous hypertension that can arise after deep vein thrombosis, especially if it extends above the knee. Brandjes *et al.* have shown that wearing a compression stocking can reduce the incidence of the post-thrombotic limb.[32] This condition commonly occurs after DVT; in the Brandjes study of DVT it occurred in 60% of the control arm within 2 years.

Box 1: Events which cause venous ulceration – three theories. *Source*: Adapted from Hollinsworth, 1998.[297]

- **Fibrin cuff:**[33] Excessive venous pressure causes large molecules of fibrinogen to leak out into superficial tissues because capillary walls are only one epithelial cell thick. Fibrinogen is then polymerised into fibrin cuffs around capillaries, which prevents oxygen and nutrients from diffusing out from the capillaries, leading to cell death and ulceration.
- **White cell trapping:**[34] Venous hypertension causes white blood cells to become trapped and accumulate in the capillaries of dependent legs (legs which are allowed to hang down in the dependent position for long periods). This leads to capillary occlusion, and the release of proteolytic enzymes and toxic metabolites, which result in local ischaemia and ulceration.
- **A combination of mechanisms:**[35] A cascade of events is initiated by venous hypertension. White blood cells release cytokines which stimulate other cells to synthesise fibrin cuffs. These cuffs inhibit the development of new blood vessels and deprive superficial tissues of oxygen and nutrients, leading to tissue damage and ulceration.

More recently, thrombophilia is being investigated as a risk factor for chronic venous ulceration, with a review of the literature concluding that patients with chronic venous ulceration appear to have a prevalence of thrombophilia much higher than the general population but similar to post-DVT patients.[296] One study investigating the prevalence of thrombophilia in patients with chronic venous leg ulceration found that 41% of these patients had thrombophilia.[79] This rate was 2 to 30 times higher than the rate in the general population but was similar to that reported for patients with DVT. However, in patients with chronic venous ulceration, thrombophilia did not appear to be related to a history of DVT, a pattern of reflux or severity of disease.

The impact of chronic venous disorders of the leg

Impact on health and quality of life

There appears to be a high acceptance of symptoms of venous disorders of the leg among affected people.[36] In around two-thirds of patients who have varicose veins the condition is medically insignificant, i.e. it is seen by the patient as insufficiently important to mention spontaneously in health questionnaires, despite being diagnosable on clinical examination. This acceptance could be put down to the fact that varicose veins are such a widespread disease and in most patients are only a slowly progressing condition.[37] For the remaining patients, varicose veins do present a significant problem,[38] one of which may be concerns about the future impact of the disease.

Symptoms reported by patients presenting with varicose veins include aching pain, tiredness/feelings of heaviness, throbbing, itching and swelling in the lower limbs. The relationship between the visible severity of varicose veins and symptoms is, however, weak. Cosmetic dissatisfaction with the appearance of varicose veins is probably universal, although the extent to which it distresses an individual and affects his or her lifestyle will be a matter of personal outlook.

Varicose veins can sometimes be complicated by haemorrhage and thrombophlebitis. The presence of varicose veins is a risk factor for venous thrombosis during abdominal and pelvic major surgery. The role of thromboprophylaxis in varicose vein surgery is uncertain – these patients are generally younger than major surgery patients, are at risk of bleeding post-operatively, and compression methods cannot be easily applied (at least to the operated limb).

Women are more likely to consult their doctor for varicose veins than men. A study in Edinburgh found that only 10% of men reported a previous doctor's diagnosis of varicose veins, compared with 17% of women. This was despite the fact that these men on examination were subsequently found to have a significantly higher prevalence of lower limb varices than women.[39]

Few studies of function or quality of life have been carried out for venous disorders of the leg. Biland and Widmer reported that 10% of patients with varicose veins were unable to work and 25% demonstrated reduced well-being.[40] Smith *et al.*, using the Aberdeen Questionnaire, found that patients with varicose veins have a reduced quality of life compared with the general population and that this is significantly improved at 6 weeks by operating on them.[41] People with leg ulcers have a poorer perceived quality of life than age-matched controls, mainly because of pain and odour.[42] Studies of patients with venous ulcers in the UK have shown high levels of depression, pain and isolation, with very considerable gains from effective treatment.[43] In some severe cases, venous ulcers may lead to long-term entry into care in nursing or residential homes.[44]

Socio-economic impact

The management of venous disorders is thought to represent between 1% and 3% of total health expenditure, with this estimate not including some supplies, cosmetic products and social costs, such as lost productivity.[27]

In the UK in 2000–01, 107 020 people were admitted to hospital for operations for varicose veins of the lower limb (Hospital Episode Statistic [HES] data).[45] In a study carried out in 1992 in five countries (the UK, France, Spain, Italy and Germany),[38] medical costs of venous disorders as estimated from the total amount of resources used annually for ambulatory care (doctors and nurses, drugs purchased and hospital costs) added up to £300 million for the UK. In Germany, around 2% of all people with varicose veins deemed themselves unfit to work for several weeks each year because of complaints related to the condition.[37] Venous disease also creates longer-term costs in disability and dependence on State-funded invalidity pensions.[44] Invalidity costs stemming from venous disease were 0.4% of the total in the UK in 1992.[38]

The management of leg ulcers comprises a significant portion of the workload of community and hospital nurses, general practitioners, dermatologists, surgeons and physicians involved in the care of the elderly. Each ulcer costs around £2000–4000 per annum to treat,[46] and the total cost to the National Health Service in 1995 was estimated at £600 million per annum.[25] There is also a considerable cost to the patient[47] and carers.

Recurrence following treatment

Recurrent varicose veins are a significant problem, with recurrence reported as occurring in 20–80% of cases treated for primary varicose veins, although this depends on the definition of recurrence employed, the length of follow-up and the initial treatment.[48] The rate of occurrence increases with time. Juhan *et al.* assumed a recurrence rate of around 50% up to 5 years.[49] Approximately 20% of varicose vein surgery is for recurrent disease.[50] The average time between the first and second operation ranges from 6 to 20 years.[48] The reasons commonly cited for recurrence include inadequate assessment, incomplete or inadequate surgery, neovascularisation and the subsequent development of reflux from the deep to superficial venous systems.[51–55] Surgery for recurrent varicose veins is technically more demanding and prolonged.[56]

Venous ulcers are chronic and recurrent.[2] Up to 50% of venous ulcers may be present for 7 to 9 months, between 8% and 34% may be present for more than 5 years, and between 67% and 75% of patients have recurrent ulcers.[57,58] Venous ulcers are the most common type of lower limb ulcer, followed by arterial and neuropathic ulcers. They are commonest in the gaiter area above the ankle.[63]

3 Sub-categories

A classification of varicose veins that is of operational use to commissioning authorities is clearly important. However, there is a lack of a clear and universally accepted classification of varicose veins that is easy to use in practice.[59] There are a number of classification systems for varicose veins that are widely used, but they are usually incorporated into classifications of venous disease and are based on clinical severity (*see* Table 2). Few classification systems use objective measurements.

Widmer's classification[60] presented in 1978 is commonly used but is related only to the clinical appearance of the limb. It has been used in clinical studies of treatments of venous disorders but its validity has never been formally assessed.[27] A committee chaired by Porter in the USA[9] described classifications by anatomic region, clinical severity, physical examination and functional assessment. Again, although this classification has been used in many studies on diagnosis and treatment, it has not been formally validated.[27] The most recent classification system to be published is the CEAP classification presented by the American Venous Forum in 1995. This is based on clinical signs, aetiologic classification, anatomic distribution and pathophysiologic dysfunction (CEAP) (*see* Appendix 2). It was developed to provide a comprehensive, objective classification that could be promoted worldwide.

The ease of application of the CEAP classification and its validity have yet to be formally assessed.[27] However, there has already been some criticism of it.[62] The fact that it is all-encompassing has been deemed unnecessary from a clinical point of view, and also that it has attempted to classify on more than one extreme. In addition, its use for epidemiological research has been questioned, as it describes an individual patient and would therefore give rise to many subgroups.[37] It has been suggested that a working classification of chronic venous disease relating to valvular incompetence and/or obstruction

Table 2: Classification of varicose veins and chronic venous disease of the leg.

Author	Class	Definition
Widmer (1978)[60]		*Varicose veins*
	1	*Hyphenwebs*: intradermal venectasis
	2	*Reticular varices*: dilated tortuous veins, not belonging to the main trunk or its major branches
	3	*Trunk varices*: dilated, tortuous trunks of the long or short saphenous vein and their branches of the first or second order. Each category is graded 1–3 according to the degree and extent of tortuosity and prominence.
		Chronic venous insufficiency Categorised into grades I, II and III according to the presence of dilated subcutaneous veins, skin changes and ulceration.
Porter (1988)[9]	0	Asymptomatic
	1	Mild, i.e. mild to moderate ankle swelling, mild discomfort, and local or generalised dilation of subcutaneous veins. Usually superficial veins only.
	2	Moderate, i.e. hyperpigmentation of the skin, moderate brawny oedema, and subcutaneous fibrosis. There is usually prominent local or regional dilatation of the subcutaneous veins.
	3	Severe, i.e. chronic distal leg pain associated with ulcerative or pre-ulcerative skin changes, eczematoid changes, and/or severe oedema. Usually involves the deep venous system with widespread loss of venous valvular function and/or chronic deep vein obstruction.
'CEAP' (1995)[61] – Clinical classification	0	No visible or palpable signs of venous disease
	1	Telangiectases or reticular veins (also called spider veins/thread veins/star bursts/matted veins)
	2	Varicose veins
	3	Oedema
	4	Skin changes ascribed to venous disease (e.g. pigmentation, venous eczema, lipodermatosclerosis)
	5	Skin changes (as defined above) in conjunction with healed ulceration
	6	Skin changes (as defined above) in conjunction with active ulceration

alone is required.[62] A proposal for two basic classifications has been put forward by Darke and Ruckley:[62]

1 an index of severity based on symptomatology (this is an adaptation of the CEAP clinical classification) and ulceration which is a guide to deciding priorities of need
2 a classification of simple morphology that can be related to treatment options (*see* Table 3).

The VEINES Task Force (VEnous INsufficiency Epidemiologic and Economic Study), set up in part to review the classification of chronic venous disorders of the leg, proposes a scoring system which also uses the CEAP clinical classification but weighs venous disease according to the probability of future leg ulceration.[27] The Task Force's suggested scoring system is shown in Table 4. Scores reflect the outcome values in individual patients, not the treatment efficacy, so that the maximum value is achieved if the problem is completely cured. The classification purposely mixes symptoms and signs as this is how patients present to their physicians, and does not require the use of investigations that may not be universally available. This system also has still to be assessed for its validity.

Table 3: Classification of venous disease presented by Darke and Ruckley.

Clinical presentation	
Grade 1	Asymptomatic
Grade 2	Cosmetic/trivial pain or swelling
Grade 3	Severe pain/swelling
Grade 4	Skin change (lipodermatosclerosis) without ulcer
Grade 5	Chronic ulceration
Morphology	
1	Primary:
	1.1 Superficial incompetence alone (long/short saphenous with or without perforator incompetence)
	1.2 Deep incompetence with or without superficial incompetence (without evidence of post-phlebitic damage)
2	Secondary (post-phlebitic/traumatic/obstruction)

Table 4: VEINES Task Force proposed scoring system for chronic venous disorder of the leg.

Class (based on CEAP clinical class)	Weight
Symptoms and/or telangiectases	1
Varicose veins	5
Oedema (venous)	10
Skin changes	20
Healed venous ulcer(s)	50
Active venous ulcer(s)	100

Source: Kurz et al.[27]

Sub-categories for the Health Care Needs Assessment

The sub-categories used in this chapter are displayed in Table 5 and are based on the above classifications and a similar classification proposed by Krijnen et al.[36] For ease of use by commissioners, we have grouped asymptomatic with cosmetic/mild discomfort or swelling, and severe pain/swelling with skin change

Table 5: Sub-categories of varicose veins and venous disease to be used in this chapter.

A	Mild discretionary	• Asymptomatic • Cosmetic/mild discomfort or swelling
B	Severe non-discretionary	• Severe pain/swelling • Skin change without ulcer
C	Venous ulcer	Chronic ulceration (healed and active)

without ulcer, based on the Darke and Ruckley scheme. However, our sub-categorisation is not perfect. A study in Edinburgh[64] has concluded that if decisions to operate on varicose veins are based simply on the nature, severity and chronicity of symptoms, or on the extent and severity of varicosities on clinical examination, they are likely to be unreliable.

4 Prevalence and incidence

This section presents information on the prevalence and incidence of venous disease of the leg gathered from a multitude of studies. It highlights the differing epidemiological terminology, populations studied, assessment methods and definitions used.

Meaningful interpretation of the epidemiological studies on varicose veins requires the following knowledge.

1   The method of measurement/assessment of varicose veins varies greatly. Some studies rely on simple questionnaires completed by the patient,[65,66] a method of data collection liable to error[67] and of little value in most epidemiological studies of varicose disease.[68] Others involve physical examination, photography and the use of continuous-wave Doppler measurement.[69] There can be a lack of precision when diagnosing varicose veins by examination alone, and observation criteria used by different research teams are unlikely to be strictly comparable. The more recent studies are probably easier to interpret as they have new assessment techniques available to them. However, studies in general seldom provide data on the validity of the method used.[70]

It has been reported that the use of self-assessment questionnaires leads to the lowest prevalence, interviewer-assisted questionnaires result in higher prevalence, while the use of physical examination leads to the highest values.[37]

2   The comparability of population studies estimating the prevalence and incidence of varicose veins is limited by the varying definitions of varicose veins used. As the previous section emphasises, there is a lack of consensus concerning which definition/classification system for venous disease and varicose veins should be used. There were 18 different definitions employed in the prevalence studies identified, ranging from no definition[65,71,72] to a definition using classification of type and severity.[73,74] An important variation is the specific inclusion or omission of hyphenwebs/telangiectasias and small subcutaneous (reticular) veins, both of which could lead to a marked variation in the overall prevalence of varicose veins reported. Even if the same definition is used, considerable variations in the interpretation of the observer/respondent can occur. This problem was highlighted in the 1960s by a WHO expert:

> *as long as the terminology varies between the different schools and languages, as long as generally acceptable criteria for the clinical diagnosis of primary and secondary varicose veins have not been developed, the data of national surveys as well as of other samples are not comparable.*[10]

3   Many of the epidemiological data relate to highly selected groups rather than a representative sample of the general population. Many studies consider patients or people who probably do not represent the general population in the UK – for example, residents of villages in New Guinea,[75] provincial towns in Tanzania[76] and residents of Cook Island.[77] The age and sex distribution of the populations examined also varied widely. In the majority of studies a minimum age of around 15 to 20 years was used, in others a maximum age was employed, and some studies only included specific age groups. The nature of many of the populations studied renders most of these studies of limited value in determining levels of service requirement in the UK.

Prevalence of varicose veins and other venous disorders of the leg

Callam[78] analysed all studies looking at the prevalence of varicose veins available in 1994 and estimated the prevalence of venous disease in the lower limb (*see* Table 6). This shows that venous disease in the general population is common and that women appear to be affected more than men. It also shows that at the more severe end of the scale only a small percentage of the population is affected.

Table 6: Prevalence of lower-limb venous disease in adults.

Severity	Prevalence (%)	
	Men	Women
Venous disease (all types)*	40–50	50–55
Visible varicose veins†	10–15	20–25
Chronic venous insufficiency‡	2–7	3–7
Chronic venous leg ulceration	0.5–1	1–1.5

Source: Callam.[78]
* Any evidence of venous disease including venectasia.
† Reticular and truncal varicosities.
‡ Hyperpigmentation, eczema and liposclerosis.

A review of the literature to October 2001 has revealed a number of studies published since this review. Some of these are probably more relevant to the UK population. The results of all studies identified by this literature review are tabulated in Appendix 3.

The prevalence studies that are more representative of the UK population are described below.

Prevalence studies: Europe and the USA

National studies

In early national health surveys recording a number of chronic disorders, the prevalence of varicose veins was found to be relatively low. An estimated national prevalence of around 2% was found in a number of surveys among random samples of the population (US National Survey 1961–63, UK Survey of Sickness 1950, the Sickness Survey of Denmark 1952 and the Canadian Sickness Survey of 1950–51).[80] However, the results from these surveys are questionable – the definition of varicose veins was often not stated and the surveys were by questionnaire alone and usually administered by untrained non-medical personnel.[81] This low prevalence is made more questionable by other population and regional surveys and Callam's study,[78] designed specifically to consider prevalence of varicose veins, which have shown higher rates of prevalence.

Regional studies

Ideally, a population study including either the whole population or a stratified random sample defined by age and sex is required to reveal the true prevalence of a disease such as varicose veins.[82] However, regional surveys that are limited to a specific neighbourhood or city have proved to be of great value in epidemiological research.[37] In addition, unlike the early national surveys, the majority of regional surveys identified are designed primarily for investigating venous disorders rather than a number of diseases.

Regional studies in Europe and the USA identified in a MEDLINE search to October 2001 are listed in Table 7. This information shows a wide variation in the prevalence of varicose veins with reported prevalences between 6% and 85%, depending on the type and severities of varicose vein included in the study and the methodology of the study. Several of the studies indicate that if all types of varicose veins are included, more than half of the adult population is affected,[83] as per Callam above.

Table 7: Regional population studies – Europe and the USA.

Study	Country	Year	Population/setting	Total number	Prevalence of varicose veins		
					Female	Male	Total
Preziosi et al.[84]	France	1994–98	Participants of the SUVIMAX cohort. Women 35–60; men 45–60 (representative of the French population for the age range under consideration)	3,065 (1,747 women, 1,318 men)	18.1% – medically diagnosed 12.4% – self-diagnosed	10.8% – medically diagnosed 7.4% – self-diagnosed	
Evans et al.[83] Bradbury et al.[64]	Scotland	1994–96	Men and women aged 18–64 resident in Edinburgh	1,566 (867 women, 699 men)	Trunk 1: 26% 2 or 3: 6% Hyphenweb 1: 84% 2 or 3: 10% Reticular 1. 85% 2 or 3: 6%	Trunk 1: 33% 2 or 3: 6% Hyphenweb 79% 2 or 3: 6% Reticular 82% 2 or 3: 4%	
Cesarane et al.[82]	Italy	1994	Residents of San Valentino, a village in Central Italy, aged 8–94 (mean age 46.3 ± 7)	746 (379 women, 367 males)			About 8% (venous diseases)
Canonico et al.[85]	Italy	1991–92	Males and females aged 66–96 (mean 74.2) (a random sample drawn by means of a stratified multi-stage sampling design using electoral rolls)	1,319 (560 men, 759 women)	35.2%	17.0%	362 (27.4%)
Franks et al.[65]	England	1989	Patients from general practices in West London aged 35–70	1,338	31.5%	17.5%	25%
Leipniz et al.[86]	Germany	1989	Randomly selected from population. Males and females aged 45–65	2,821	29%	14.5%	20.2%

Table 7: Continued.

Study	Country	Year	Population/setting	Total number	Prevalence of varicose veins		
					Female	Male	Total
Laurikka et al.[66]	Finland	1989	People born in 1929, 1939 and 1949, i.e. 40, 50 and 60-year-olds	5,568	42%	18%	
Rudofsky[87]	Germany	1988	Community sample. Males and females aged >15 years	14,000			15%
Henry and Corless[88]	Ireland	1986	Random sample of households	4,900			622 (12.7%)
Fischer[89]	Germany	1983	Random sample aged 17–70 (intracutaneous to trunk varices)	4,530			59%
Novo et al.[90]	Western Sicily, Italy	1977–79	A sample of the population of the village of Trabia, which mainly comprises farmers, fishermen and a few craftsmen and traders	1,122	46.2%	19.3%	35.2%
Weddell[67]	Wales	1966	Randomly selected from the electoral roll. Males and females aged 15+	289	53% (non-clinical: 36%; clinical: 17%)	37% (non-clinical: 31%; clinical: 6%)	
Coon et al.[91]	USA	1959–60 and 1962–65	Residents of Tecumseh, a city in SE Michigan, aged 10 years +	6,389	25.9% (moderate to severe 16.7%)	12.9% (moderate to severe 7.4%)	
Arnoldi[92]	Denmark	1958	Clinic attendees aged >25 years	1,981	38%	18.4%	28%
Lake et al.[71]	USA	1942	Males and females over 40 years representing four different types of occupational activity: sitting, standing, walking, climbing	536	73.2%	40.7%	57%

The Edinburgh vein study[39,64,83] is probably the most relevant study to the UK population and will be described in more detail. It looks at the prevalence of varicose veins and chronic venous insufficiency. It considers a wide age range, includes both sexes, defines the classification of chronic venous disease and uses clinical examination in addition to a questionnaire. It does not, however, have any data on non-Caucasians.

The Edinburgh vein study

The primary aim of the study was to conduct a detailed population survey of the prevalence of all grades of venous disease in a randomly selected age-stratified sample of the adult population. It was a cross-sectional survey of men and women aged 18–64 years old resident in Edinburgh. The sample was selected from computerised registers of 12 general practices with catchment areas geographically and socio-economically distributed throughout Edinburgh. There were 1566 participants out of 2912 people who were initially approached, giving a response rate of 53.8%. A follow-up of a sample of 194 non-respondents suggested that participants were more likely to have a history of diagnosed venous disease than the general population. Hence the prevalence figures may be overestimates. Participants were also more likely to be women ($n = 867$) than men ($n = 699$) and from the older age group range (mean age was 44.8 for women and 45.8 for men).

Subjects attended a research clinic or, if they were unable to do this, were visited at home. All participants completed a self-administered questionnaire which was subsequently checked by a member of the research team. The questionnaire asked about the presence of various symptoms often attributed to venous disease. It also recorded personal and occupational details, relevant medical and family history and possible risk factors for venous disease. After completion of the questionnaire both legs were examined. The method of classification of venous disease was adapted from Widmer (*see* Table 2). Trunks were defined as 'dilated, tortuous trunks of the long and short saphenous vein and their branches of the first or second order', reticulars as 'dilated, tortuous subcutaneous veins not belonging to the main trunk or its major branches' and hyphenwebs as 'intradermal varices'. Each of these three groups was subdivided into grades of severity 1–3. In practice, grade 1 trunks ranged from a small, discrete, visible or palpable length of dilated trunk vein to more obvious but not grossly dilated veins, grade 2 trunks were more extensive and/or more grossly dilated trunk varices, and grade 3 trunks were varices at the most severe end of the spectrum.[39] Patients were examined after they had been standing for at least two minutes and varices were graded 1 to 3 accordingly using standard reference photographs. Subjects were also examined for the presence of any pitting ankle oedema, and assessed for CVI. Grade 1 CVI corresponds to malleolar flare, grade 2 CVI corresponds to skin changes, and grade 3 CVI corresponds to healed or active ulceration.

Prevalence of leg symptoms

Women were more likely than men to have lower leg symptoms (*see* Table 8), despite fewer women having trunk varices than men (32% vs. 40% age-adjusted prevalence). The prevalence of symptoms increased with age in both men and women, and this links in with the increased prevalence of varicose veins (all severities) with age.

Table 8: Age-adjusted prevalence (%) of leg symptoms in men and women (Edinburgh vein study).

Leg symptoms	Men ($n = 699$)	Women ($n = 867$)	*p*-value
Heaviness or tension	16.0	28.6	$\leqslant 0.010$
Feeling of swelling	9.2	23.0	$\leqslant 0.010$
Aching	32.5	53.8	$\leqslant 0.010$
Restless legs	20.0	35.1	$\leqslant 0.010$
Cramps	34.0	42.0	$\leqslant 0.010$
Itching	19.0	25.3	$\leqslant 0.010$
Tingling	16.0	19.8	$\leqslant 0.084$

Source: Bradbury *et al.*[64]

Prevalence of venous disease

Hyphenweb and reticular varices were very common in both sexes (*see* Table 9), although the majority had these varices only to a mild degree. Trunk varices were more common in men than women, the age-adjusted prevalence of trunk varices being 39.7% in men and 32.2% in women. Again, the majority of affected subjects had mild lower limb varices. The figures for varicose veins are higher than Callam's figures, partly due to the detailed physical examination undertaken in the Edinburgh study. However, the prevalence of venous insufficiency is comparable to Callam's figures.

Table 9: Age-adjusted prevalence of grades of varices by sex (Edinburgh vein study).

	Grade	Males (*n* = 699)		Females (*n* = 867)		*p*-value
		%	*n*	%	*n*	
Hyphenweb varices	1	79.2	554	84.4	732	0.260
	2	5.9	44	9.2	76	0.030
	3	0	0	0.6	5	–
Trunk varices	1	33.3	238	26.2	223	0.009
	2	5.4	39	5.6	47	0.888
	3	1.0	7	0.5	4	0.241
Reticular varices	1	81.6	571	85.3	739	0.422
	2	4.0	29	6.4	54	0.042
	3	0	0	0	0	–
CVI	1	6.9	51	5.3	44	0.157
	2	1.3	10	1.1	9	0.607
	3	1.0	8	0.2	2	0.058

Source: Evans *et al.*[39]

Studies of selected populations

Many studies investigate limited age groups, samples of clinic populations or specific occupational groups (*see* Appendix 3). Studies of selected populations can be useful in identifying the risk factors for varicose veins but are limited in estimating the overall prevalence of varicose veins in a population.

Incidence

The incidence of varicose veins is the development of new cases over a period of time in a population. The Framingham study[93] followed up men and women who were living in Framingham, USA. Every 2 years from 1966 over a 16-year period, subjects were examined for varicose veins. Over the 16 years, 396 of 1720 men and 629 of 2102 women who were initially free from varicose veins developed varicose veins. The two-year incidence rate of varicose veins was on average 39.4 per 1000 for men and 51.9 per 1000 for women, i.e. 4–5%. The incidence rate beyond the age of 40 years did not increase with age, suggesting that the relationship between age and prevalence is due to a relatively constant development of new cases as people age.[27]

The 11-year Basel vein follow-up study[94] found that in a group of 660 adult subjects who were free of varicose veins at the initial examination, after 11 years 87% had developed non-relevant varicose veins and 5% relevant varicose veins. Amongst the 510 subjects with relevant varicose veins at entry, 27% developed deep vein thrombosis or superficial phlebitis and 10% developed venous leg ulcers. Among the subjects with non-relevant varicose veins at entry, these proportions were 8% and 0.8%, respectively.

Risk factors

Risk factors for varicose veins include fixed factors (female sex, age, pregnancy, ethnicity, geographic location, left iliac vein compression by the right iliac artery, family history) and potentially preventable factors (obesity, occupations requiring prolonged standing or sitting, lack of dietary fibre, use of constricting corsets, and sitting posture for defecation).[78] Table 11 summarises the available evidence on risk factors for varicose veins. The VEINES Task Force[27] found that apart from age and sex, evidence linking most factors to varicose vein development is limited, and concluded that the evidence was adequate only for pregnancy and obesity. The findings on the aetiology of primary varicose veins do not suggest that there is large scope for primary prevention.

Sex

It is generally believed that women are more commonly affected by varicose veins than men and most studies have shown a female predominance of varicose veins.[66,67,72,84,85,88,90,91,95–97] In the majority of studies the sex ratio decreases with increasing age. For example, a study in Israel found that in 20–34-year-olds the sex ratio was 6 females:1 male, but in people aged 65–74 this ratio fell to 1.5 females:1 male.[95]

There are a number of exceptions to this rule, notably the Edinburgh vein study (*see* Table 10), which found that there was a significantly higher prevalence of trunk varices in men compared with women,[39] a study in Switzerland[98] where there was no significant difference between the prevalence of varicose veins in men and women, and a study in New Zealand[74] where, although the prevalence of mild and moderate varicose veins was higher in women, gross varicose veins were equally prevalent in men. Higher rates in women might be related to greater self-reporting, especially of less severe varicose veins.

Table 10: Prevalence of trunk varices and CVI by age and sex (Edinburgh vein study).

	Age (years)										*p*-value
	18–24		25–34		35–44		45–54		55–64		
	%	*n*	%	*n*	%	*n*	%	*n*	%	*n*	
Trunk varices (all severities)											
Men	20.0	11	15.5	16	36.1	57	42.0	76	61.4	124	0.000
Women	5.3	4	13.9	22	22.6	42	41.9	95	50.5	111	0.000
Total	11.5	15	14.6	38	28.8	99	41.9	171	55.7	235	0.000
Chronic venous insufficiency (all severities)											
Men	–	0	–	0	2.5	4	7.7	14	25.3	51	
Women	1.3	2	1.3	2	3.8	7	7.9	18	12.3	27	

Source: Evans *et al.*[39]

Age

The association between age and prevalence of varicose veins is fairly conclusive. The majority of surveys listed in Table 11 (*see* overleaf) show a steady increase in prevalence of varicose veins with increasing age for all grades of varicosity. The increase, however, was not as significant in the older age groups or was not apparent at all in some studies.[76,97] In addition, the incidence rate flattens in the Framingham study, suggesting that age is a less important risk factor in older ages. The Edinburgh vein study (*see* Table 10) showed that the prevalence of trunk varices increased linearly with age in both sexes, and ranged from 11.5% in the 18–24-year-olds to 55.7% in the 55–64-year-olds when both sexes were combined ($p \leqslant 0.001$).[39] The same trend was found in the prevalence of reticular and hyphenweb varices ($p \leqslant 0.001$).

Varicose veins can be present before adulthood. In a longitudinal study (not presented in Table 11) a cohort of schoolchildren aged 10–12 years was examined. The presence of discrete reticular varices was found in only 10% of the pupils. Four years later this figure had risen to 30%, with a number of children developing stem and branch varices.[99]

The age-related patterns suggest that the prevalence of venous disease will increase as demographic change shifts to an older population.

Pregnancy

It is generally believed that pregnancy leads to varicose veins due to the pressure of the uterus obstructing venous return from the legs. However, this has been refuted, as the majority of varices appear during the initial 3 months when the uterus is not large enough.[100] A hormonal factor is thought to be responsible or the increased circulating volume of blood.

The majority of studies in Table 11 show an association between the onset of varicose veins and pregnancy.[67,71–74,76,77,90,96,101] Women with at least one pregnancy generally had a higher prevalence of all types of varicose veins than women who had no pregnancies.[69,74,84,90,95,97,102,103] Some studies found that parity was only a significant risk factor in younger women.[96,101] With increasing age, the influence of pregnancy on the prevalence of varicose veins is smaller.[69] A study in Switzerland[73] found that when the age factor was excluded no significant association remained between the prevalence of varicose veins and childbirth. In addition, the Tecumseh community health study[91] and a study in Tanzania[76] failed to show a rising prevalence with increasing number of pregnancies.

Ethnicity and Western lifestyle

A striking feature of the epidemiological studies of varicose veins is a marked geographical variation in prevalence rates, suggesting a possible association with ethnic group or with lifestyle factors. Several studies suggest that varicose veins are rare in Africa and other developing countries[75] compared with Western societies.[76,104] A study in Jerusalem[95] showed that men born in North Africa had significantly lower age-adjusted prevalence rates than immigrants from Europe, America and Israel. Other variations shown in different ethnic groups within a country include a higher prevalence in Southern Indian railway workers than in Northern Indian railway workers,[105] a higher prevalence of varicose veins in whites than non-whites in Brazil[97] and a lower prevalence in Southern Europeans than in other Europeans in a study of women in Switzerland.[73] A study comparing female cotton workers in England and Egypt found that the prevalence of varicose veins was significantly higher in English women than in Egyptian women.[101]

The key question is: do Indo-Asians and African Caribbeans in the UK have higher or lower rates of varicose veins than Caucasians? No studies were identified that answer this question, as it is difficult to assess the contributions of genetic predisposition and environmental (e.g. Western lifestyle) influences.

Table 11: A summary of the evidence on risk factors for varicose veins (continued opposite).

Study	Age	Sex	Race	Family	Occupation	Parity	Obesity	Height	Smoking	Other
Edinburgh[39]	Prevalence increases with age ($p=0.000$)	Mild trunk varices were more prevalent in males ($p=0.009$). Other varices more prevalent in females (NS)	–	–	–	–		–	–	Social class (NS)
Western Sicily[90]	Prevalence increases with age (SNR)	More prevalent in females (SNR)	–	–	–	Increased prevalence in women with one or more babies (SNR)	More prevalent in respondents with a higher relative body weight (SNR)	–		Patients suffering constipation showed a higher prevalence (SNR)
Tampere, Finland[66]	Increases with age (SNR)	More prevalent in females (SNR)	–	–	–	–	–	–		–
Tecumseh, USA[91]	Increases with age (SNR)	More prevalent in females (SNR)	–	–	–	No correlation	–	–		–
Campania, Southern Italy[85]	No correlation ($p=0.75$)	More prevalent in females ($p=<0.0001$)	–	–	No relationship between varicose veins and previous occupation	–	More prevalent in female subjects with a higher BMI ($p<0.0001$). Males – no correlation	–	No correlation	Alcohol consumption – no correlation (women $p=0.005$, NS in men). Constipation – no correlation
Cardiff, Wales[67]	Prevalence increases with age (SNR)	More prevalent in females	–	–	Varicose veins more prevalent in men and women whose work involved heavy lifting ($p<0.05$). No correlation with work involving long hours of standing	Increased prevalence with parity ($0.2<p<0.3$)	–	–	–	Constipation – no correlation

	Age	Sex	Geography/race	Family history	Occupation/standing	Pregnancy/parity	Obesity/body weight		Other
Ireland[88]	Prevalence increases with age	More prevalent in females	–	–	Increased prevalence in standing employment	Increased prevalence with number of pregnancies	–	–	–
New York[102] (female sample)	–	–	–	Family history ($p<0.0001$)	Increased prevalence with standing vocation (>6 hours/day) ($p<0.0001$)	Increased prevalence with pregnancy ($p<0.0001$)	Increased prevalence with obesity ($<20\%$ over ideal weight) ($p<0.0001$)	–	Oral contraceptive use – no correlation
France[84]	Prevalence increases with age (SNR)	More prevalent in females (SNR)	–	–	–	Increased prevalence with parity ($p=0.007$)	Increased prevalence with increasing BMI ($p=0.003$)	–	–
Turkey[103]	Prevalence increases with age	More prevalent in females than males but NS ($p>0.005$)	–	Positive family history ($p=0.001$)	–	Association with at least one pregnancy (S)	No association	No association	–
Czechoslovakia[69] (female sample)	Prevalence increases with age ($p<0.05$)	–	–	Positive family history ($p<0.01$)	Increased prevalence in women standing compared to sitting and changing position	Higher prevalence with at least one pregnancy ($p<0.001$)	Increased prevalence with rising body weight (S)	–	Physical activity – NS. Blood pressure – NS
Switzerland[73] (female sample)	Prevalence increases with age ($p<0.001$)	N/A	Prevalence lower in Southern Europeans than in Central Europeans (S)	–	Prevalence higher in women standing at work but no significant correlation ($p=0.11$ after removing age factor)	Prevalence increased with number of children born but NS when age factor was excluded	Increased prevalence with increasing body weight but NS when age factor was excluded	No significant association	Corsetry – NS
England and Egypt[101] (female sample)	Prevalence increases with age ($p<0.001$)	N/A	Prevalence higher in England than in Egypt ($p<0.001$)	Positive family history ($p<0.001$)	Higher prevalence in women standing (England: $p<0.001$, Egypt: NS)	Prevalence higher in women who had children (England: $p<0.05$, Egypt: $p<0.01$). Only in 15–34 age group	Increased prevalence with body weight (England: $p<0.001$, Egypt: NS)	–	Constipation – NS. Corsetry – England: $p<0.001$ or $p<0.01$ when standardised, Egypt: NS

Table 11: Continued.

Study	Age	Sex	Race	Family	Occupation	Parity	Obesity	Height	Smoking	Other
Basle, Switzerland[98]	Prevalence increases with age	NS	–	–	–	–	NS	NS	–	–
New York[71]		More prevalent in females (SNR)	–	–	Walkers have higher prevalence than sitters, but NS	–	–	–	–	–
Finland[72]	Prevalence increases with age	More prevalent in females	–	–	No association in occupational groups. Standing S in women (p<0.001)	More prevalent in women who have had children, increasing linearly up to 5 children (p<0.001)	Increased prevalence with increasing body weight and BMI (S)	In women, more prevalent in taller women (p<0.001)	In women, less prevalent in smokers (p<0.01)	–
Western Jerusalem[95]	Prevalence increases with age (p<0.001)	Prevalence higher among women	Prevalence lower in men born in North Africa (p<0.01)	–	Higher prevalence in workers who spend a lot of time standing (p<0.01)	More prevalent with at least one pregnancy (p=0.0011)	More prevalent in heavier groups (p<0.00001)	More prevalent in taller subjects (p=0.007)	No significant association	Corset – more prevalent (p<0.01). Stockings (p<0.01). Inguinal hernia in men (p=0.0006)
New Zealand[74]	Prevalence increases with age	Prevalence higher among women for mild and moderate varicose veins but equally prevalent for gross varicose veins	–	–	–	More prevalent with one or more pregnancies	No association	–		–
Japan[96] (female sample)	Prevalence increases with age	Prevalence higher in women	–	–	–	More prevalent with one or more pregnancies but only in younger age groups	No association	No association	No association	–

Tanzania[76]	No association	Prevalence higher in men but NS	–	–	–	No association	–
Brazil[97]	Prevalence increases with age (S) but not after 40 years of age in women	Prevalence higher in women (S)	Prevalence higher in white than non-white (S)	No association	No association	–	–
India[105] (male sample)	Increasing prevalence with increasing age	–	Prevalence higher in South Indian than North Indian ($p \leq 0.001$)	No association	–	No association	–
Amsterdam, The Netherlands[36]	Increasing prevalence with age ($p < 0.0005$)	–	–	Large number of years in a standing profession on severity ($p < 0.05$)	Increasing prevalence with increasing weight ($p < 0.005$)	Correlation between prevalence and number of pregnancies (S)	Posture adopted for defaecation – no association

S = significant.
NS = not significant.
SNR = significance not reported.
– = not investigated or reported.

Family history

A number of studies have found that the risk of varicose veins was higher in those with affected relatives,[69,101–103] perhaps suggesting a genetic element or shared environmental factors. However, it has been noted that these results should be regarded with caution. In most studies considering a family history, the relatives were not examined. In addition, family members are not good judges of the presence of varicose veins in the rest of the family,[67] and people with varicose veins are more likely to notice this condition in their relatives than individuals without varicose veins.[37]

Body weight and height

Several authors have found an association between weight and body mass and an increased risk of varicose veins. Of the studies in Table 11, a positive correlation with varicose veins was found in seven studies[69,72,84,90,95,101,102] and no correlation was found in three of the studies.[69,74,96] In a further study, the higher the body mass index, the more prevalent varicose veins were in women, but there was no association in the male participants.[85] In a female population in Switzerland, although there was an increased prevalence of varicose veins with increasing body weight, this was not significant when the age factor was excluded.[73] The rising prevalence of obesity in Western countries may lead to a greater burden of venous disease.

A number of studies reported an association between body height and varicose veins.[72,95] The mini-Finland study showed a smoothly graded increase in prevalence with increasing height.[72] However, more studies found no correlation between height and varicose veins.[73,96,98,103]

Occupation

A person's occupation has been put forward as a possible risk factor for varicose veins. A standing occupation has been indicated in some studies as a significant risk factor for varicose veins,[69,72,88,95,101,102] although this has been found to be insignificant in other studies[71,73] and refuted in yet others.[67,105] Work involving heavy lifting was significantly related to the presence of varicose veins in one study.[67] A number of studies show no correlation between occupation and the prevalence of varicose veins.[71,85,97] A review of venous insufficiency at work concluded that there are undoubted risk factors in the workplace but recommended further research in this area.[106]

Other risk factors

Smoking

A correlation between cigarette smoking and varicose veins was found among men in the Framingham study,[93] but other studies have shown no relationship between cigarette smoking and varicose veins.[85,95,96,103] In one study varicose veins were less prevalent in women who smoked.[72]

Constipation

A diet deficient in fibre has been implicated as a major factor in the causation of varicose veins.[107] It is thought that fibre-depleted diets lead to constipation, and the subsequent straining to produce a stool produces high intra-abdominal pressure which is transmitted to the leg veins and progressively dilates them.[76] A positive correlation was shown between constipation and the prevalence of varicose veins in one study[90] but not in others.[85,101]

Constricting undergarments

The role of corsets in the development of varicose veins was investigated in a number of studies[73,95,101] and was found to be significant in two of them.[95,101]

Social class

In the Edinburgh vein study there was no obvious relationship between social class (classified by occupation) and the age- and sex-adjusted prevalence of trunk varices.[39]

Post-thrombotic limb

Post-thrombotic limb is the term used to describe venous insufficiency when there is evidence of previous deep vein thrombosis (DVT). Studies have reported frequencies of the syndrome in between 5% and 100% of patients having an acute DVT, especially when the DVT extends proximal to the popliteal fossa. This can be reduced by using a compression stocking post-DVT.[32]

Prevalence of oedema and skin changes (chronic venous insufficiency)

The prevalence of venous-related oedema and skin changes is not well documented. In Tecumseh, USA,[91] 37% of women and 3.0% of men had skin changes. The prevalence increased markedly with age from 1.8% in women aged 30–39 years to 20.7% in women over 70 years of age. The marked gender difference was not demonstrated by the Edinburgh study,[39] which found that 1.1% of women and 1.3% of men had skin changes (hyper- or de-pigmented areas, with or without corona phlebectatica), but again the prevalence increased with age. Under the age of 35 years, CVI (all severities) was extremely rare in women and did not occur at all in men, but it increased to 12.3% in women and 25.2% in men in the oldest age group investigated (55–64 years).

CVI is more common if varicose veins are more severe – if both deep and superficial systems are involved, if both long and short saphenous veins are varicose and if there is below-knee involvement.

Prevalence of venous ulcers

There have been many studies on the prevalence of leg ulceration but, as with the studies on varicose veins, the variations between definitions and methodology employed in these studies make it difficult to give a definitive prevalence figure. A review by Callam[108] of the prevalence of chronic leg ulceration in Western countries concluded that active chronic leg ulceration has a point prevalence of 0.1–0.2% of the adult population and approximately 1% of the population will suffer from leg ulceration at some time in their lives. Studies by Nelzen agree with this figure, suggesting that the prevalence of healed ulcer is 2 to 4 times higher than that of active ulcers and that the prevalence of both together in the population is around 1%.[109–111]

The sex ratio (M:F) is generally thought to be 1:2 to 1:3 at all ages,[27] but the Edinburgh study[39] found that 1% of men and 0.2% of women had grade 3 CVI (i.e. healed or active ulceration). The prevalence of venous ulcers increases consistently with age,[109–114] with chronic leg ulceration being relatively uncommon below the age of 60,[112] unlike varicose veins. The annual incidence rate in the population over 45 years of age was estimated at 3.5 per 1000 in one retrospective study.[115]

Health service utilisation data

Primary care: morbidity statistics from general practice (1991–92)

The results from the Fourth National Study of Morbidity Statistics from General Practice[116] can be used to estimate the incidence and prevalence of varicose veins and venous ulcer as they present to general practitioners (GPs) in the community (*see* Table 12) and therefore the potential workload of a typical primary care trust (PCT). The study, carried out in 1991–92, presents data on the level and detail of morbidity seen in general practice and covers a 1% sample of the population of England and Wales (502 493 patients, 468 042 person-years at risk). These people were on the list of 60 practices volunteering to take part. The prevalence estimates include all severities of varicose veins covered by ICD-9 code 454 (*see* Appendix 1), and include venous ulcers.

The data from the study reflect the main trends and information gathered from the prevalence studies mentioned earlier, particularly the higher presentation rates in females. They also show the strong prevalence age gradient that continues up to the over-75s.

The data suggest that for a typical PCT ($n = 100 000$) there would be around 1770 people in the PCT with varicose veins (with or without venous ulcer), around 1250 cases presenting with varicose veins for the first time each year and around 2540 consultations with a doctor for varicose veins (with or without venous ulcer) each year. The prevalence suggested by these data does appear to be lower than in most of the prevalence studies. However, it should be recognised that the figures in the GP study are only based on people who present to their general practitioner and do not include those who do not see their GP for their complaint (i.e. they do not describe population rates). As mentioned earlier, a significant proportion of people with varicose veins do not present to primary care.

Table 12: Results from the Fourth National Study of Morbidity Statistics from General Practice.

Varicose veins of lower extremities (ICD 454*)		Age group (years) and sex								
		Total	0–4	5–15	16–24	25–44	45–64	65–74	75–84	85 and over
Patients consulting (rates [prevalence] per 10,000 person-years at risk)	Male	58	1	1	10	31	97	197	232	232
	Female	119	1	1	33	96	186	263	307	244
	Total	177	2	2	43	127	283	460	539	476
New and first ever episodes (rates per 10,000 person-years at risk)	Male	40	0	1	8	24	70	123	166	119
	Female	85	1	1	27	75	138	177	193	158
	Total	125	1	2	35	99	208	300	359	277
Consultations with doctor (rates per 10,000 person-years at risk)	Male	95	0	1	14	42	177	296	432	368
	Female	169	3	1	37	111	270	431	482	364
	Total	254	3	2	51	153	447	727	914	732

*This code includes varicose veins with ulcers and inflammation.

Summary

The best available data likely to be representative of the population in England and Wales appear to be those from the Edinburgh vein study (albeit a Scottish study, but recent and population based). Incorporating the results of this study into the sub-categories defined in the previous section, a prevalence of varicose veins and CVI has been estimated (see Table 13). This estimate is likely to be low if applied to the whole population, as the population in the Edinburgh study was limited to 18–64-year-olds. Other studies have indicated that there is a strong age gradient which continues up to the over-75s age group.

Table 13: Estimated prevalence of varicose veins and CVI (population aged 18–64 years).

		Estimated prevalence (%)	
		Male	**Female**
A	Mild discretionary*	40	31
B	Severe non-discretionary†	8	7
C	Venous ulcer‡	1	1

* Based on the prevalence of trunk varices (Grade 1) and CVI (Grade 1).
† Based on the prevalence of trunk varices (Grade 2–3) and CVI (Grade 2).
‡ Both healed and active ulceration (latter about 0.1–0.25%).

5 Services available and their costs

The services and treatment options available to a person in the general population who has varicose veins and related diseases will depend on:

- the nature of the patient's complaints and expectations. What is their perception of the severity of the condition? How important is the cosmetic appearance to them? Do they know what treatments are available to them, the side-effects of these treatments and the levels of recurrence? Are they willing to undergo these treatments?
- the clinical severity of the varicose veins and venous ulcer(s)
- the cause of the varicose veins/venous ulcer(s) and the site of incompetence (which guides treatment)
- the policies of local health providers
- waiting lists which reflect supply and demand
- diagnostic facilities and expertise.

Corbett[117] stated that in terms of providing services to a population there are two important considerations: the proportion of patients who are likely to require surgery for symptoms, and whether varicose vein surgery plays any part in preventing ulceration in old age. The latter is debatable, as indicated in Section 4.

Figure 2 summarises the various service options likely to be used by patients with chronic venous disease of the lower limb. At any point of the referral process, patients may decide to circumvent long NHS waiting times and seek private treatment.

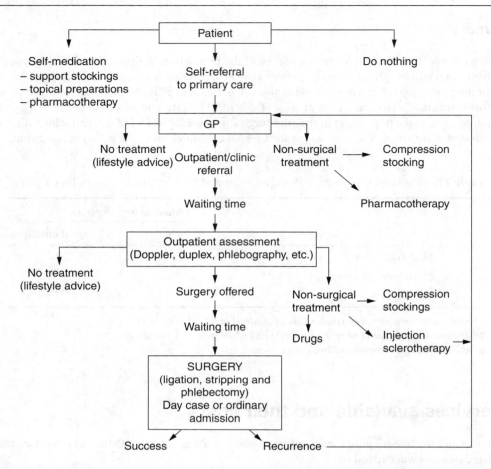

Figure 2: Flow chart illustrating points of decision making in the treatment of chronic venous disease.

Primary prevention

The VEINES Task Force concluded that the evidence on associated risk factors for varicose veins was only adequate for pregnancy and obesity.[27] There are also thought to be some risks with occupations involving much standing (*see* Section 4). Specific measures suggested to help prevent the development of varicose veins include weight control, reducing the amount of standing in certain jobs, and greater physical activity.[69] The use of a prophylaxis to prevent DVT in high-risk situations (e.g. hospitalised medical and surgical patients) and the use of compression stockings following definite DVT to prevent post-thrombotic limb are discussed elsewhere.

Initial contact with health care services

Many people with varicose veins will choose not to seek any medical advice. When they do, a significant proportion of patients seek an opinion because they are primarily concerned about the cosmetic appearance of their veins.[64] Concern about the future course of the varicose veins (fear of thrombosis, ulcers and concern about family history of vein problems) is an additional common underlying reason for presentation.[7] Many will also present with symptoms associated with varicose veins (this will be commoner at secondary care level). Aching, heaviness and swelling were the most frequent reasons for presentation among both men and women in a survey of 229 patients referred over a 10-month period to two vascular surgeons for management of varicose veins.[118] Cosmetic concerns accounted for a total of 26% of presentations to the vascular surgeons (33% of women and 8% of men).

Symptoms draw attention to varicose veins but it has been found that varicose veins may not be the cause of the symptom.[64] Sisto *et al.*[72] showed a statistically significant association between varicose veins and osteoarthritis of the knee, which commonly coexist.

Women are more likely to consult their GP with varicose veins than men.[116] In line with this a frequent finding of studies looking at the prevalence of treatment of varicose veins is that treatment for the latter is more prevalent in women than in men.[119] One study[72] reported that 53% of affected women had received surgical treatment compared to 29% of affected men.

Assessment

An initial diagnosis of varicose veins is usually made up of the signs observed by the general practitioner and the symptoms reported by the patient. Whether a diagnosis of varicose veins then becomes a referral for treatment and/or further assessment at an outpatient clinic depends upon the severity of the signs and symptoms, the likelihood of complications, patient preference and the local provision of treatment. Indications considered appropriate for further investigation by surgeons responding to a survey of members of the Vascular Surgical Society in 1999[120] were suspected deep venous disease (90%), recurrent varicose veins (83%), past history of deep venous thrombosis or fracture (81%), skin damage or ulceration (57%), suspected sapheno-popliteal reflux (63%) and all varicose veins (7%).

The continuous-wave Doppler ultrasound (hand-held Doppler) is rarely used at the time of the clinical examination to assist in this initial diagnosis. In fact no UK medical school expects final-year students to be skilled in the use of hand-held Doppler for assessment of varicose veins.[121]

The National Institute for Clinical Excellence has published a guide to appropriate referral from general practice to specialist services for varicose veins. The guide emphasises that most varicose veins require no treatment and says that the key role of primary care is to provide reassurance, explanation and education. Table 14 outlines the referral advice for referral to a specialist service in patients in whom varicosities are present or suspected.

There is no single test available to provide answers to the many questions that need to be asked to decide if and how to treat varicose veins and other venous disorders of the leg.[123] For this reason a number of specialised investigations have evolved over the years (*see* Table 15). These are used to objectively assess the presence and amount of venous outflow obstruction and the presence and amount of venous reflux in the superficial, communicating and deep venous system. The tests will help the assessor/surgeon answer the following questions.[124]

1 Are the symptoms of which the patient complains attributable to venous disease and, if not, what other pathological processes may be involved?
2 Is the patient's pattern of venous disease amenable to surgery and, if so, what operation should the patient have? For this the sites of incompetence and whether the deep system is involved need to be accurately identified, especially in the context of CVI or ulceration.

The selection of the appropriate tests will depend on the local facilities, the clinical presentation and the severity of the symptoms.[123] A survey of members of the Vascular Surgical Society[120] found that 65% of

Table 14: Referral advice for patients in whom varicosities are present or suspected.

Referral timings	Condition
Patient is seen immediately (within a day)	Patient is bleeding from a varicosity that has eroded the skin
Patient is seen urgently (max. 2-week wait recommended)	Patient has bled from a varicosity and is at risk of bleeding again
Patient is seen soon	Patient has an ulcer which is progressive and/or painful despite treatment
Patient has a routine appointment	Patient has an active or healed ulcer and/or progressive skin changes that may benefit from surgery
	Patient has recurrent superficial thrombophlebitis
	Patient has troublesome symptoms attributable to their varicose veins, and/or they and their GP feel that the extent, site and size of the varicosities are having a severe impact on quality of life

Source: National Institute for Clinical Excellence.[122]

Table 15: Methods of assessment for venous disease.

Non-invasive	Invasive
Continuous-wave Doppler ultrasound	Phlebography/varicography
Duplex scanning	Foot venous pressure measurements
Plethysmography (strain-gauge/air/photo)	Ambulatory venous pressure
Near-infra-red spectroscopy	

surgeons routinely use hand-held Doppler in the assessment of varicose veins. Duplex scanning was used as the first-line investigation by 83%, venography or varicography by 10% and plethysmography by 1%. Facilities for duplex scanning were available to 97% of respondents, venography to 94%, plethysmography to 32% and ambulatory venous pressure measurements to 16%. For most cases, duplex has become the investigation of choice, especially for recurrent disease or venous ulcer/CVI cases, though there are no cost-effectiveness data to support this.

The less invasive tests detect and quantify obstruction and reflux, and define the locality of the abnormality. They have lower risks associated with them, are well tolerated and are readily repeatable. The more invasive tests are not usually necessary for simple varicose veins. However, they may be needed when there is uncertainty over whether the varicose veins are primary or secondary to deep vein damage,[99] or if there is a history of calf perforator incompetence or surgery.

There are no perfect tests of venous physiological function.[80] Each technique of investigation has its own advantages and disadvantages, and out of the series of tests available in the vascular laboratory, several methods will measure the same thing. Whatever the method used, the interpretation is open to inter-observer variation and can be expensive and time-consuming.[125] Belcaro *et al.* stated that the optimum useful information can be obtained using only three instruments: the Doppler, duplex scanning (preferably with colour-flow imaging) and air plethysmography.[126] In the UK, it is unusual for a patient to undergo any test other than a duplex outside a research protocol.[127]

Description of assessment methods

Clinical examination

Traditionally, the requirement for surgery for varicose veins was based on a full history and clinical examination,[128] although this rarely happens. Inspection and palpation (which can include the cough/thrill test, the tap test and the tourniquet test) constitute the clinical examination.

Continuous-wave Doppler ultrasound

The accuracy of the clinical examination has been improved by the additional use of continuous-wave Doppler ultrasound (CWDU) examination,[51] commonly referred to as hand-held Doppler and sometimes pocket Doppler.[129] Its use has become routine in outpatient clinics for screening because it is quick, inexpensive and non-invasive.[123] CWDU emits a continuous beam of ultrasound waves that detect red blood cells moving within the targeted vein.[11] The principle behind Doppler ultrasonography is that the frequency of signals reflected from the moving red blood cells shifts in proportion to the velocity of the cells. The output from a CWDU is normally presented as an audible signal, so that a sound is heard whenever there is movement of blood in the vessel being examined.[130] CWDU is used for detecting reflux at the sapheno-femoral and sapheno-popliteal junction.[131,132] Its main function is to detect incompetence of valves between the deep venous system and the superficial veins. CWDU is particularly useful in the examination of obese legs where the results of a tourniquet test are more difficult to interpret.

Duplex scanning

Duplex scanning combines an image and a Doppler signal. Colour units indicate flow from the heart in red and toward the heart in blue.[11] Colour flow duplex scanning has become the 'gold standard' varicose vein assessment technique,[56,133] speeding up the assessment procedure and improving its accuracy.[123,134] This non-invasive technique allows the operator to locate and identify specific structures using real-time imaging and then obtain information on the presence, direction and velocity of blood flow from a specific location or vessel within the image.[135] The femoral, popliteal, deep calf and perforating veins can be specifically and individually tested as well as determining the involvement of the long and short saphenous veins and their tributaries.[123] It has also been suggested that colour duplex should be the investigation of choice for patients presenting with recurrent varicose veins.[136] Duplex scanning has been recommended for all patients with varicose veins,[6,137,138] but the feasibility of this has been questioned due to time and cost implications.[138,139] It has been suggested that duplex scanning be used selectively on primary varicose veins, reducing the workload of the vascular laboratory without compromising patient care.[140,141] There are few diagnostic evaluation studies on which to base practice.

Plethysmography (strain gauge/air/photo/foot volumetry)

The term plethysmography describes several techniques used to measure volume changes. A plethysmograph consists of a mechanism to sense displacement. Sensors include air-filled, water-filled, mechanical, light, capacitance and electrical impedance devices.[11] These techniques attempt to quantify the physiological significance of Doppler findings and are only very rarely required for clinical purposes.

Near-infra-red spectroscopy

Near-infra-red spectroscopy is a relatively new non-invasive technique that allows measurement of changes in deoxygenated haemoglobin and oxygenated haemoglobin in tissue.[142] It is currently mainly used as a research tool for the assessment of ambulatory venous function in the leg as a whole and the severity of CVI in patients with primary varicose veins. An advantage of the technique is that it can be used to assess venous insufficiency during exercise.

Phlebography/varicography

Phlebography is the term used to refer to X-ray contrast imaging, which used to be the only method available for examining the venous system. It used to play an important role in the management of patients with secondary or recurrent varicose veins.[2] Earlier contrast media were associated with frequent side-effects because of their hyperosmolarity, but the introduction of low-osmolarity contrast media has significantly improved patient comfort and safety, reducing the risk of contrast-induced thrombophlebitis. The technique should be tailored to the diagnostic problem, and the site of injection of contrast will depend on the clinical problem to be clarified.[135] Specific phlebographic techniques include:

- *ascending phlebography*, where the contrast medium is injected into a foot vein. This technique investigates the state of deep veins and detects incompetent communicating/perforating veins[2]
- *varicography*, where the superficial veins are directly injected with contrast medium and the channels it takes on its way to the deep system of veins in the legs or to the groin and perineum are screened.[135,143] This technique investigates the site, extent and connections of superficial and deep varices[2]
- *descending phlebography*,[144] where contrast medium is injected into the femoral vein and the amount of reflux towards the periphery is assessed and graded.[145] This technique is performed to show abnormal reflux in the deep or long saphenous vein.[2]

Phlebography is not necessary in the majority of cases but would be considered if the ultrasound examinations (CWDU or duplex) had not provided all the information required for a decision to be made. The disadvantages of phlebography are that it is invasive, costly and non-repeatable, it exposes the patient to radiation and there is potential for complications.

Ambulatory venous pressure examination

This test measures the net effect of all the abnormalities that affect venous haemodynamics. Venous pressure is measured by inserting a needle in a vein on the dorsum of the foot with the patient standing. Pressures are recorded during a ten tiptoe exercise test. The ambulatory venous pressure (AVP) is defined as the lowest pressure reached during the exercise.[126] Ambulatory venous pressure is a function of the calf muscle pump ejecting capacity, the magnitude of reflux and the outflow resistance. If venous reflux is present the AVP is high and the refill time is quick.

Arm–foot pressure differential technique

This technique, developed by Raju,[146] is considered to be an excellent method of quantifying outflow obstruction.[126] The technique consists of recording the venous pressure in the veins of the foot and hand simultaneously after venous cannulation.

Treatment

The general indications for treatment of varicose veins are to prevent complications related to venous disease (especially venous ulcer), to relieve symptoms, and to improve the appearance of the leg.[59]

However, there is no national consensus as to which varicose veins should be treated based on site of incompetence, severity, etc. and as to which types of treatment to be offered.

There is an uncertain relationship between the location(s) of venous incompetence and the severity of the signs and symptoms of varicose veins. Since the natural history of varicose veins is largely undocumented, it is not clear whether varicose veins involving only the superficial venous system, and not accompanied by skin changes or great discomfort, should be treated for reasons other than cosmetic considerations, i.e. whether surgery has a prophylactic role in preventing severe venous disease. There is an argument that prompt surgery of patients with asymptomatic or mild varicose veins is likely to result in the maintenance of healthy skin, since the capillaries are undamaged. Once skin changes have occurred, surgery will improve the macrocirculation but will have no effect on the already damaged microcirculation.[147] There is scant evidence showing how many patients with asymptomatic or mild varicose veins progress on to more severe forms of venous insufficiency, and so it is extremely difficult to either support or refute the argument of prophylactic surgery. Whilst research is needed, current evidence would suggest that operating on only mildly symptomatic or asymptomatic varicose veins would be largely for cosmetic reasons and hence might not be deemed a priority for the NHS.

Conversely, there is general agreement that skin changes (CVI) and ulceration represent an indication for treatment. Symptoms of discomfort reported by the patient are variably interpreted as indications for treatment. Moderate and severe (clearly symptomatic) varicose veins are generally thought to be worthy of surgical treatment, with an improvement in venous return likely to be achieved at least in the short term. In some cases surgery is not warranted,[148] and a thorough assessment is therefore needed prior to surgery to define whether surgery is likely to be effective and at what sites to intervene to maximise long-term outcome and reduce recurrence rates.

Unless there are severe complications such as haemorrhage, treatment for varicose veins remains elective. There is evidence that other disorders (e.g. inguinal hernia and benign prostatic hyperplasia) which are generally treated electively can reach a stage where surgery is urgently required and patients can be admitted on an emergency basis. For varicose veins this is unlikely to happen (only 154 out of 55 512 episodes in 1998–99 were emergency admissions [HES data]), and there is thus little prospect of circumventing the long waiting lists for specialist treatment.

Treatment options

Conservative management

Pharmacotherapy

A variety of medications have been suggested to be effective for the relief of various individual symptoms of venous disease, such as heaviness, discomfort, itching, cramps, pain and aching, and swelling[27] (*see* Table 16). These are principally represented by the venoactive drugs, which may improve venous tone and the lymphatic and microcirculatory disturbances that result from increased venous pressure.

Compression therapy

Upon self-referral to a general practitioner, conservative treatment in the form of compression therapy may be offered. This may also be the preferred form of treatment if surgical intervention is not sufficiently indicated, or if the patient is seen as unfit for general anaesthesia. In addition, when varicose veins are severely complicated by deep vein incompetence, the only form of treatment offered may be compression therapy. Compression therapy can also be used as a therapeutic test – if symptoms improve with stockings it is likely that they are due to varicose veins and so surgery may be of value.

Table 16: Medications suggested to be effective for relief of the symptoms of venous disease.

Symptoms	Suggested medication
Heaviness	Diosmin coumarine rutine
	Dihydroergocristine
	Calcium dobesilate
Swelling	Rutosides
	Combination of ruscus, favonoids and proteolytic enzymes
Global symptoms	Diosmin
	Ruscus asculeatus
	Calcium dobesilate
	Hydroxyrutosides
Venous tone	Diosmin
Oedema	Rutosides
	Diosmin
	Calcium dobesilate
	Coumarine rutine
	Horse-chestnut extract
Active ulceration	Oral micronized diosmin
	Pentoxifylline

Source: Kurz *et al.*[27]

Compression relieves the symptoms of varicose veins, helps to heal and prevent the recurrence of ulcers and helps to prevent the deterioration of skin changes. It is the mainstay of venous ulcer treatment, acting to reduce vein calibre, capillary filtration and venous reflux and improving venous pumping.[27,149] These effects increase venous return, improve lymphatic drainage and decrease oedema. Materials used for compression include elastic and inelastic bandages, and elastic stockings. There are many ways of applying compression, such as single layers of bandaging, multiple layers of bandaging, compression stockings or a combination of bandages and stockings which are usually used to treat the more severe end of the spectrum (*see* Table 17). Intermittent pneumatic compression, a mechanical method of delivering compression to swollen limbs, is an alternative method.

It is now recommended that the external compression be graduated, with the amount of external pressure being greatest at the ankle and lower at the knee. This has been shown to increase blood velocity within the deep venous system.[150] The recommended gradients are that the calf pressure should be not

Table 17: Combination compression systems used in the treatment of venous ulcers.

Type	System
Short stretch/inelastic	Orthopaedic wool plus 1–3 rolls of short stretch bandage
Inelastic paste system	Paste bandage plus support bandage
Unna's boot	Non-compliant paste bandage
Three-layer elastic multi-layer	Orthopaedic wool plus class 3c bandage plus shaped tubular bandage
Four-layer elastic multi-layer	Orthopaedic wool plus support bandage (crepe) plus class 3a bandage plus cohesive bandage

more than 75% of the pressure exerted at the ankle and the thigh pressure not more than 50%.[3] The most suitable amount of pressure to apply to the leg is still disputed,[151] but it is generally accepted that this will depend on the severity of the condition.[152] It is important to note that before undertaking compression therapy the ankle brachial pressure index (ABPI) should be assessed. This is because patients with peripheral arterial disease with poor arterial circulation can develop ischaemia if compression is too high. The precise ABPI below which compression is contraindicated is often quoted as 0.8.[153]

Stockings are divided into three classes according to the British Standard (BS7505: 1995). The support offered and indications for their use are presented in Table 18. Bandages are categorised as retention, support or compression. The latter are further subdivided according to the level of compression they apply to the limb (*see* Table 19).

Table 18: Classes of compression stockings according to the British Standard (BS7505: 1995).

Class	Compression	Indications
I	Light support, 14–17 mmHg at the ankle	Mild varicose veins, venous hypertension in pregnancy
II	Medium support, 18–24 mmHg at the ankle	Mild oedema, moderate to severe varicose veins, prevention of ulcer recurrence in small, light people
III	Strong support, 25–35 mmHg at the ankle	Treatment of severe varicose veins and prevention of venous ulcers, large heavy legs

Table 19: Bandages.

Class	Compression
1	Retention bandages (used to retain dressings)
2	Support bandages (used to support strains and sprains, and for mild to moderate compression when particular application techniques are used and the bandages are reapplied frequently
3a	Light compression, 14–17 mmHg at the ankle
3b	Moderate compression, 18–24 mmHg at the ankle
3c	High compression, 22–35 mmHg
3d	Extra high compression, up to 60 mmHg

Source: Cullum *et al.*[279]

A patient requiring compression hosiery will need a detailed assessment, measurement to ensure the hosiery fits properly and advice on application and care. Two to three pairs of compression hosiery are recommended per patient to allow for washing, and if worn continuously they should be replaced every six months as frequent washing and wearing cause a loss of elasticity. Where daily removal is not possible Class I hosiery is recommended as this can be worn continuously and changed once a week by a carer.[152] In the presence of ulceration, it is recommended that stockings should be worn continuously, as long as there is no concomitant arterial disease, in order to improve the hypertensive microangiopathy.[147]

Elastic stockings are more difficult to manage in the elderly, obese or arthritic who may have problems reaching their feet and pulling on a tight stocking.[125,154] For this reason, elastic or impregnated bandages might be preferred, although this generally needs the assistance of someone else. In addition, there are special aids to assist someone putting on compression stockings. They consist of slippery plastic; the aid is put inside the stocking and the foot 'walks' the stocking on by pushing against a special pad placed on the floor.[155] Patient compliance is essential but is generally problematic, particularly when compression therapy has been prescribed for long-term use.

Once healing has occurred, hosiery is recommended lifelong to prevent ulcer recurrence, especially when no surgery has been performed on superficial varicose veins. The cost of compression hosiery varies depending on class and design. Most compression hosiery and bandages are available as a prescription item. There are some products though where unless the patient is willing to pay, choice is limited by the restrictions imposed by the Drug Tariff (FP10).

Sclerotherapy

Sclerotherapy is the injection of an irritant solution into an empty vein, resulting in an endothelial reaction, fibrosis and complete venous destruction. The aim of sclerotherapy is to eliminate reflux in the superficial venous system and thereby eliminate visible varicose veins.[59] Injection sclerotherapy has a long history. In 1855 Chassaignac tried to obliterate veins by injecting a solution of ferric chloride.[156] Since then three names have been linked with the development of modern sclerotherapy techniques: Tournay (the French technique), Sigg (the Swiss technique) and Fegan (the Irish technique). The sclerotherapy process works such that a sclerosant causes damage to the endothelial and sub-endothelial layers, resulting in an inflammatory reaction of the venous wall which evolves to fibrosis over a period ranging from 6 months to several years. The aim of sclerotherapy is fibrotic obliteration and not thrombosis of the varicose vein.[59] Different sclerosants have been experimented with. Sodium tetradecyl sulphate is a popular choice, along with iodine, polidocanol and sodium salicylate.

A consensus statement on sclerotherapy of varicose veins[59] reached the following conclusions.

- Sclerotherapy can treat varicose veins but it cannot cure the underlying venous disease and will therefore not halt the formation of new varices.
- General indications for sclerotherapy are to prevent complications related to venous disease, to relieve symptoms and to improve the appearance of the leg.
- Sclerotherapy must be practised by a physician who is trained in phlebology and has specific experience in sclerotherapy.
- Sclerotherapy of secondary varicose veins, i.e. those with reflux and/or obstruction of the deep venous system, can be considered only after careful functional assessment.
- Sclerotherapy is the preferred treatment in patients presenting with telangiectases and reticular veins without reflux, i.e. cosmetic surgery.
- Sclerotherapy is an adequate treatment for large non-saphenous varicose veins:
  - there is no agreement as to whether sclerotherapy is suitable for treating large or small perforating veins, or whether thigh or calf perforators are amenable to sclerotherapy. The choice between surgery and sclerotherapy will depend on the experience of the clinician and the characteristics of the varicose vein.
- Sclerotherapy may be considered for the treatment of saphenous varicose veins:
  - there is no consensus regarding the role of sclerotherapy in the treatment of long saphenous veins but if it is used it should be performed by an experienced physician
  - short saphenous varicose veins may be treated by either surgery or sclerotherapy.
- Contraindications for sclerotherapy are:
  - a known allergy to the sclerosing agent
  - severe systemic disease

- recent DVT
- local or general infection
- inability to ambulate
- severe arterial disease, especially critical limb ischaemia.

- Sclerotherapy must be performed with caution in pregnant or breastfeeding women and when the following conditions are present:
  - allergic diathesis
  - hypercoagulability
  - recurrent DVT.

- Risks such as thromboembolism and intra-arterial injection, as well as cosmetic deterioration, must be weighed against the benefits of the treatment.

The evidence for the above statements is presented in Section 6.

Compression usually accompanies sclerotherapy, especially for larger varicose veins. Its importance in the sclerotherapy process, the strength of compression and the length of time it is applied vary and depend on the technique used. Compression is thought to aid the occlusion of the lumen by making opposing surfaces stick together without any intervening thrombus. The vein is theoretically converted into a thin fibrosed cord, not a vein full of red thrombus which can recanalise.[157] The effectiveness of sclerotherapy is open to debate and the amount and length of time of compression have been questioned.[158–161]

As a mode of treatment, sclerotherapy has been variably popular in Europe and the USA.[162–164] In France, sclerotherapy is used to obliterate even the sapheno-femoral junction, while in the UK this would more likely be treated by surgical ligation. Compression sclerotherapy is regarded as ideal for solitary varicose tributaries in the absence of main saphenous incompetence, and is used to varying extents for the treatment of incompetent lower leg communicating veins.[157] Sclerotherapy is advised for patients who are too old or unfit or who refuse operation, and constitutes the better mode of treatment for telangiectases.[163,165–167] Sclerotherapy can be combined with surgery either during or after operation.[59]

Complications of sclerotherapy include vasovagal attacks, allergic or anaphylactic reactions,[168] toxic reactions, skin necrosis and ulceration, recanalisation,[163] venous thrombosis,[169] pulmonary embolism (0.1%),[170] intra-arterial injection, injection of a nerve and skin discoloration.[171] This latter complication is a common side-effect of sclerotherapy. Brown pigmentation develops over the thrombosed vein and can (but not always) fade after one to two years.

In a survey of members of the Vascular Surgical Society,[120] 62% of respondents performed sclerotherapy for varicose veins privately, and 68% on the NHS. For thread veins the figures were 27% on the NHS and 49% privately. The main indicators for sclerotherapy were considered to be for missed varicose veins following surgery (60%), for isolated small varicose veins (73%) and for thread veins (50%). Only 18% of respondents ran a sclerotherapy clinic and injections were performed predominantly by consultants (65%) and surgical trainees (63%). An earlier survey of the Vascular Surgical Society of Great Britain and Ireland to determine the current practice and attitude towards venous sclerotherapy found that sclerotherapy is being used less frequently for varicose veins than in previous years and that most surgeons use it for residual varicose veins after operation and for those without proximal incompetence.[172]

In conclusion, sclerotherapy has a role to play in cosmetic surgery and in isolated varicose veins, especially those missed by surgery. It therefore has a small role in any NHS venous disease service as a complement to varicose vein surgery and compression. It should only be performed by trained surgeons.

Echosclerotherapy

Echosclerotherapy is a relatively new technique which involves injection of a sclerosing agent into a vein under ultrasound guidance. This allows accurate localisation of junctions. There are two main techniques, one using a catheter and the other using a needle connected to the syringe.[59]

Surgical management

Surgery is both the established treatment and the treatment of choice for sapheno-femoral vein incompetence and long saphenous vein varicosity.

The types of operation are listed below:

1   flush ligation of the sapheno-femoral junction, also called high saphenous ligation
2   stripping of the long saphenous vein[173]
3   sapheno-popliteal junction ligation, also called short saphenous ligation
4   stripping of the short saphenous vein (although avoided by most surgeons for fear of damaging the sural nerve)[127]
5   ligation of the medial lower leg communicating veins[174,175]
6   ligation of other communicating veins (i.e. gastrocnemius, lateral calf, Hunterian and miscellaneous veins)
7   phlebectomies (avulsions) of varicosities, ligation of tributaries and local excision of tributaries[176–180]
8   operations on recurrent varicose veins.[181]

There is growing interest in surgery for cases with isolated superficial vein incompetence and venous ulcer. If there is no deep vein incompetence, surgery may successfully hasten healing and reduce recurrence, though high-grade evidence is still lacking on this issue.

Post-operatively, compression is used to reduce the incidence of haematoma formation, and may reduce the incidence of deep vein thrombosis (heparin may be given during the admission for the same reason).[182] A survey in 1995 of members of the Vascular Surgical Society of Great Britain and Ireland ($n = 363$) found that surgeons use a variety of bandages and stockings after varicose vein operations, but crepe bandages were the most usual (52%) at the end of surgery and anti-embolism socks were the most common support recommended in the days that followed (55%).[183] As soon as anaesthesia wears off, patients are encouraged to mobilise as much as possible. Length of stay in hospital varies with the extent of the surgery, but day surgery is possible using both local and general anaesthesia.[184–187] This will depend on patient age and general fitness. Patients may be reviewed after three months when the wounds have healed and bruising disappeared (many patients who have had mild or moderate varicose veins do not get reviewed post-operatively). Residual varicose veins can be obliterated by injection sclerotherapy[188] or by local excision. The initial use of the long saphenous vein in coronary artery bypass grafting (CABG) encouraged a conservative approach to stripping,[186,189–192] but nowadays the long saphenous vein has been replaced by the internal mammary artery as the replacement graft of choice for CABG.

Contraindications to surgery include general ill-health affecting fitness for anaesthesia, arterial ischaemia of the lower limb, pregnancy, severe coexistent skin infection, lymphoedema and bleeding diatheses.[80] It is generally thought that there is an association between varicose veins and DVT, especially if there are other risk factors for DVT such as a past or family history,[193,194] although many surgeons with specialist interest in the venous system are sceptical of this association in patients with primary varicose veins.[183]

A survey of members of the Vascular Surgical Society found that the commonest indications for surgery were symptomatic (97%) and complicated (98%) varicose veins, although 55% of surgeons also performed surgery for cosmesis.[120] It also found that surgery is the preferred option for primary treatment of varicose veins associated with long or short saphenous reflux.

Surgical treatment, typically consisting of inpatient admission for high ligation, stripping and phlebectomy under general anaesthesia, is not in the main regarded with much enthusiasm by surgical staff for reasons of technical interest, operating position, and length of time of surgery (40–60 minutes for the completion of the three stages in one leg; double the time for the 50% of patients with bilateral veins).[18] This surgery has in the past often been performed by junior members of a surgical team,[5] but this may be associated with higher recurrence rates due to inadequate primary surgery.[195,196] There is an increasing recognition of the need for consultant-led supervision of juniors.

Types of surgery performed for different conditions

A survey of members of the Vascular Surgical Society asked respondents what method of surgery they used for a range of types of varicose veins.[120] The results were as follows.

- For the treatment of primary long saphenous varicose veins, 90% of surgeons performed sapheno-femoral disconnection, 82% stripped the long saphenous vein to the knee (20% stripped to the ankle), and 95% performed multiple phlebectomies, and 1% performed specific perforator ligation.
- For recurrent varicose veins associated with reflux in the groin, 94% performed groin re-exploration, 75% stripping of a residual long saphenous vein and 94% multiple avulsions.
- For recurrent varicose veins associated with reflux in the popliteal fossa, 91% performed re-exploration of the popliteal fossa, 27% stripping of a residual short saphenous vein and 90% multiple phlebectomies.

However, it is important to understand that the choice of method for recurrences depends on the investigation carried out beforehand on each patient.

Post-operative morbidity of varicose vein surgery

The morbidity after surgical treatment is poorly documented in the literature.[197,198] However, post-operative mortality is extremely low and post-operative complications are mainly associated with damage to the superficial nerves when veins are stripped to the ankle (range of 23–50% incidence of damage to the saphenous or sural nerve – because of this, most surgeons now strip veins to just below the knee),[199–202] deep vein damage, arterial damage, wound necrosis, haemorrhage, haematoma formation, lymphoedema and lymphocele, unsightly or keloid scars, persisting eczema,[203] recurrent ulceration and recurrence of varicose veins.[204] Operator experience has a significant effect on the outcome of surgery.[205,206]

In a study of 997 consecutive patients undergoing treatment in a district general hospital, complications occurred in 7 inpatients and a further 16 patients developed complications requiring readmission to hospital.[198] The complication rate appeared to be operator-dependent with an increased complication rate occurring after surgery by junior surgeons. Major complications included femoral vein injury, post-operative DVT, pulmonary embolism and groin lymphatic fistula requiring re-operation. In a retrospective review[197] of 599 patients (973 limbs) who had undergone varicose vein surgery between 1985 and 1993, wound complications occurred in 2.8% of limbs and minor neurological disturbance in 2.8%. Leakage of lymph from the groin occurred in 5 patients and major complications included three cases of DVT, one pulmonary embolism, one injury to the common femoral vein and one drop-foot. The overall incidence of major complications was 0.8% and minor complications occurred in 17% of patients.

Recurrent varicose veins

A major problem with varicose vein surgery is the high risk of recurrence, which is a common, complex and costly problem. The frequency of recurrent veins is stated to be between 20 and 80%,[48] depending on the definition, method of assessment, duration of follow-up, initial case-mix and quality of surgery. A consensus meeting on recurrent varicose veins in 1998 decided to adopt the definition 'the presence of varicose veins in a lower limb previously operated on for varices'.[48] Whilst some recurrence is inevitable due to the development of new varicose veins, some may be due to inadequate assessment and initial surgery. This is more likely if trainees operate, particularly when they are unsupervised.[195,196] Up to 20% of varicose vein surgery is for recurrence. One solution is much closer supervision and training of surgical trainees by consultants. Methods for the treatment of recurrent varicose veins include compression, drugs, sclerotherapy and redo surgery, although there is no general consensus in favour of sclerotherapy, surgery or both.[48]

New treatments for varicose veins

There are a number of new treatments for varicose veins[207,208] that claim advantages over conventional surgery by reducing operative trauma and bruising and speeding up post-operative recovery. The methods all close off the long saphenous vein under duplex ultrasound control. They are:

- radiofrequency ablation, where a radiofrequency probe obliterates the vein by controlled thermal energy[209,210]
- the use of a laser probe to obliterate the long saphenous vein[211,212]
- a novel application of sclerotherapy where a sclerosant is mixed forcibly with air to produce a foam that spreads rapidly and widely through the veins after injection.[213]

The procedures can be performed under local anaesthetic, but general anaesthetic is necessary if there are extensive varicosities. All the methods require a duplex ultrasound machine with a skilled operator.

Surgery in venous ulcer disease

The surgical management of venous ulcer can be considered once venous hypertension is established as the cause of the ulcer and the possible venous abnormalities have been demonstrated. In the 50% of venous ulcers that have superficial reflux as the main component, appropriate ligation can heal the ulcer. The role of perforator ligation is thought to be limited except in a group of patients with primary deep incompetence, in whom ulceration persists in spite of saphenous ligation.[214]

Skin grafts for venous ulcers

Skin grafts are used by some clinicians in order to stimulate healing of venous ulcers.[215] The skin grafts may be taken from the patient's own uninjured skin (e.g. thigh), grown from the patient's skin cells into a dressing (autografts), or applied as a sheet of bioengineered skin grown from donor cells (allograft). Preserved skin from other animals, e.g. pigs, has also been used and these are known as xenografts. They can provide immediate relief for patients with very painful ulcers, but they often fail after a period of time.

Other treatments

Laser treatment[216] has been investigated as a replacement for invasive sclerosing procedures for thread veins. Continuous-wave laser systems, such as carbon dioxide lasers and argon lasers, have been tested for their effects on leg veins but there were a number of adverse sequelae. Pulsed-dye lasers have also given poor results. There are six laser systems that are currently advocated for the treatment of leg veins. It is suggested that these show promise as alternative or complementary therapies for thread veins.[217] Whilst compression therapy is the main venous ulcer therapy, various other interventions, including electrical stimulation, laser therapy and ultrasound, have been used in addition to or in replacement of compression where the latter is contraindicated.[218]

Configuration of services

Day surgery

Day-case surgery for varicose veins has been shown to be economic, safe and effective and to reduce waiting time for surgery.[184,219–221] It is now accepted as the most appropriate way to treat many patients who need common surgical procedures, and there has been a national drive to increase the percentage of varicose veins dealt with as day cases.[222] Some reported advantages of day-case varicose vein surgery are listed in Box 2. Despite this, day-case surgery is disliked by a proportion of patients and in the private sector varicose vein surgery is almost never carried out as a day case.[127]

Levels of day surgery have risen significantly since the early 1990s (*see* Health Episode Statistics later). A survey of members of the Vascular Surgical Society found that the percentage of operations performed as day cases was 50% (range 0–96%), the most common conditions operated on as day cases being unilateral primary long saphenous varicose veins and unilateral primary short saphenous varicose veins.[120] The Royal College of Surgeons guidelines on day-case surgery state that patients for general anaesthesia should be under 70 years old, of physical status ASA group I or II and that the procedure duration must be less than 60 minutes.[223] Patients for whom day surgery may be unsuitable include those with extensive varicosities, those needing open calf perforator surgery (rare), those requiring post-operative bed rest for venous ulcers, and those with pre-existing medical conditions.

The decision to perform day-case surgery can also be related to the anticipated duration of the procedure. Varicose vein operations often take a long time to perform, especially when carried out by a single surgeon. Two or more surgeons reduce the time taken to operate and decrease the risk of a DVT.[183] This level of resources is therefore recommended for NHS varicose vein operations.[7]

Box 2: Reported advantages of day-case varicose vein surgery. *Source*: Lane and Bourantas.[224]

- Efficient organisation with planned patient care
- Minimal disruption to the patient's working or domestic life
- Less risk of cancelled operation
- More experienced surgeons and anaesthetists
- Lower infection rate than for inpatients
- No 'hotel' charges
- Staff recruitment for normal working hours is easy
- Reduced cost

Waiting lists/effects of delaying surgery

Increasing pressure on surgical resources in terms of inpatient beds and operating-theatre availability has led to increasing waiting lists for chronic low-risk disorders such as varicose veins.[225] In an attempt to rate waiting lists by the expected level of benefit to patients, varicose vein surgery ranked low when considering benefits per resource requirement (hours of operating time, benefits per day-bed occupied).[226] A number of waiting-list initiatives have demonstrated that varicose vein waiting lists can be significantly reduced by careful assessment, an efficient system to minimise hospital stay and maximise bed utilisation, and the increased provision of day-case facilities.[225,227] A study looking at the deterioration in the condition of lower limbs in a group of 36 patients considered to be at low risk of worsening of their varicosities who were waiting for a median of 20 months for varicose surgery concluded that there was a significant deterioration in the clinical condition of patients and considerable morbidity for the patients while they waited.[228]

Management of venous ulcers

There is wide variation in the management of venous leg ulcers, with types of care including hospital inpatient care, hospital outpatient clinics, primary care clinics and home visits. There is some debate about whether every patient with a venous ulcer needs to see a vascular surgeon for thorough assessment and overseeing of preventive strategies. The initial assessment is to exclude non-venous ulcers and decide whether any varicose vein surgery is indicated. This suggests a multi-disciplinary team led by a vascular surgeon to assess all ulcers.

The care of ulcers associated with varicose veins is a burden which is normally carried by the primary health team, in particular the community nursing service (87% of patients with ulcers are managed by the primary care team). Chronic ulceration can of course become a considerable problem, a source of anguish and pain to the patient, and a cost to the community of an estimated £1200 to £2500 per unhealed ulcer per year in dressings and medical time.

Community ulcer clinics

A community leg ulcer service allows structured patient assessment and appropriate research-based treatment as well as providing a focus for nurse training in leg ulcer management.[229] The service normally consists of a multi-disciplinary team led by a clinical nurse specialist, often with the support of the consultant vascular surgeon and senior medical physicist from the local hospital. Dermatologists have been involved in and have set up services for venous ulcers in many places.[7] The leg ulcer team functions alongside the district nursing service under the overall direction and supervision of the clinical nursing lead. There are a number of requirements for a community leg ulcer clinic, including:

1   *good location* – the clinic needs to allow easy access for the majority of patients
2   *accurate wound assessment* – a simple hand-held Doppler is essential and will determine which patients may benefit from referral for more detailed evaluation.

The introduction of community ulcer clinics has been shown to significantly improve leg ulcer healing and reduce costs by about £150 000 per 250 000 population per annum.[230]

Patient preference

A questionnaire-based study investigating the preferences of patients with varicose veins for injection treatment or surgery, based on a series of explicit facts about each method, found that 25% expressed an overall preference for injections and 63% preferred surgery.[231] The majority of patients with bilateral varicose veins preferred a single bilateral inpatient procedure compared to two unilateral day-case operations.

Current practice and service provision

The assessment and treatment of varicose veins by members of the Vascular Surgical Society of Great Britain and Ireland has been investigated by a postal questionnaire.[120] The study identified current practice of vascular surgeons in the treatment of varicose veins and provided an overview of what is considered by surgeons within this field to be the appropriate management of varicose veins.

Sixty-five per cent of those sent a questionnaire responded, of whom the majority (77%) were general surgeons with a vascular interest, 21% were vascular surgeons only and 2% were non-vascular surgeons. The results of this survey have been presented throughout this section, but general findings were as follows.

- Of the respondents, 73% saw varicose vein patients in a vascular and/or dedicated venous clinic.
- Approximately five new patients (range 0–78) with varicose veins were seen per surgeon per week in clinics.
- The median waiting time to be seen in a clinic was 12 weeks (range 1–150 weeks).
- A median of three varicose vein operations per surgeon per week was undertaken.
- In total, 10–15% of surgery was performed for recurrent disease.

Health services utilisation data

The following data on current service provision are based on hospital episode data from NHS hospitals in England (HES data) from 1990–91 to 2000–01.[45] The data have been analysed on the basis of admissions rather than finished consultant episodes (FCEs), and were extracted on the basis of procedure codes (OPCS Fourth Revision Operations Codes L83, L85, L86 and L87; *see* Appendix 1). The procedure rates and any trends in service provision in the NHS need to be considered in the light of private health care provision over the same time period (*see* below).

There are several problems in making use of routine NHS health services utilisation data.

- The operation codes and diagnostic codes for varicose veins of lower extremities (*see* Appendix 1) allow little discrimination between medically complicated and uncomplicated varicose veins, and do not provide information on the site of incompetence, the extent of the varices, whether they affect one or both limbs, and whether they are recurrent or whether they are performed primarily for cosmetic or symptomatic reasons.
- NHS routine data exclude activity in private-sector hospitals.
- HES data exclude outpatient activity. In the absence of data on outpatient procedures, it is impossible, for example, to derive rates of injection sclerotherapy in the population. Data relating to episodes of injection sclerotherapy performed during an inpatient admission are available but they are unrepresentative of the total level of activity. Data relating to the level of injection sclerotherapy carried out in general practice are also unavailable.
- There are no data on venous ulcer disease, as this is largely undertaken by district nurses in the community.

- There are problems related to the quality and comparability over time of these data.

Volume of surgery

There were 107 020 operations for varicose veins in NHS hospitals in England in 2000–01, with 45 216 of these being main operations. Around two-thirds of operations were performed on women. Considering main operation rates only, the rates of surgical treatment for varicose veins showed an increase from 96 per 100 000 in 1990–91 to 121 per 100 000 in 1995–96. Since then the rates have generally shown a downward trend; with the exception of an increase in 1998–99, the overall rate was 92 per 100 000 in 2000–01 (*see* Figure 3).

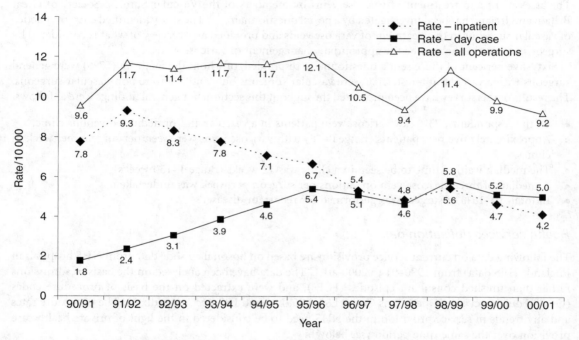

Figure 3: Rate of varicose vein operations (L83, L85, L86, L87) per 10 000, by admission type, England (1990–91 to 2000–01).

The type of operation most commonly performed is ligation (L85), followed by 'other operations on varicose veins of the leg', e.g. stripping of long and short saphenous veins and avulsion of varicose veins (L87). This is for both day surgery and patients who are admitted as inpatients. L85 is more likely to be performed on patients who are admitted as inpatients, whereas L86 (injection into varicose vein of the leg) is more likely to be performed as day surgery.

The rates for treatment for varicose veins are highest amongst females between 35 and 64 years of age (*see* Figure 4). In 1998–99, the highest rate of operations was for day-case admissions in females in the 35–44-year-old age group, with a rate of 17.1 per 10 000, whilst the highest rates in males were in the 55–64-year-old age group for ordinary admissions, with a rate of 10.3 per 10 000. When comparing the rates of operations that are performed on women compared to men, the difference is very apparent in the age groups up to 64 years. In particular, in the 35–44 years age group, women are almost three times

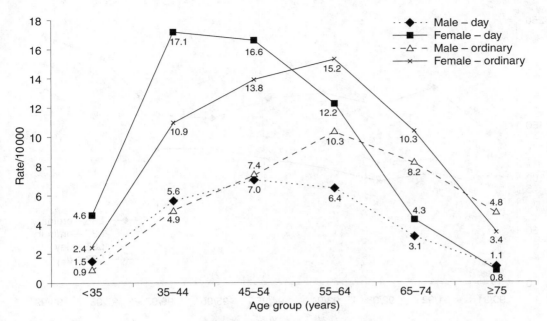

Figure 4: Rate of operations (L83, L85, L86, L87) per 10 000, by age, sex and admission type (1998–99, HES data).

more likely to have an operation than men. The median ages at start of episode for all admission types are 56 (L83), 48 (L85), 47 (L86) and 47 (L87) years.

The most notable trend over the eight years reviewed is that the proportion of operations for varicose veins carried out as day surgery has increased considerably, from 19% of operations in 1990–91 to 55% of operations in 2000–01 (*see* Figure 3). The age and sex profile of patients undergoing day surgery is such that there are more females than males admitted for day surgery (as is the case for all operations for varicose veins), but the ratio of females to males having day surgery is higher than the ratio of females to males who are admitted as inpatients (2.5:1 compared to 1.8:1). Females are more likely to be admitted for day surgery rather than as inpatients up to the age of 55; for males it is up to the age of 45. The age groups where the rate of day-case surgery is highest are 45–54 for males and 35–44 for females (*see* Figure 4). These data suggest there may be unmet need in older age groups who have higher rates of varicose veins. However, older people may be less concerned with the cosmetic appearance and, as they are less active, may have less limiting symptoms, although these hypotheses require testing.

Waiting times and length of stay

Other important trends are the increase in waiting times for varicose vein operations despite the growth of day surgery, and the noticeable decrease in length of stay for those patients admitted as inpatients. Trends over the years 1990–91 to 1998–9 show that the median waiting time for patients admitted for inpatient surgery has steadily increased, particularly for the most frequently carried out operations, since 1996–97 (*see* Figure 5). In 1998–99 the median waiting time for L85 was 237 days and for L87 was 238 days. This is compared to a median wait of 145 days and 122 days, respectively, in 1990–91. Median waiting times for patients admitted for day-case surgery have also increased but not as dramatically. Median waiting times for L85 and L87 operations in 1998–99 are 213 days and 185 days. This is compared to 107 and 94 days in 1990–91.

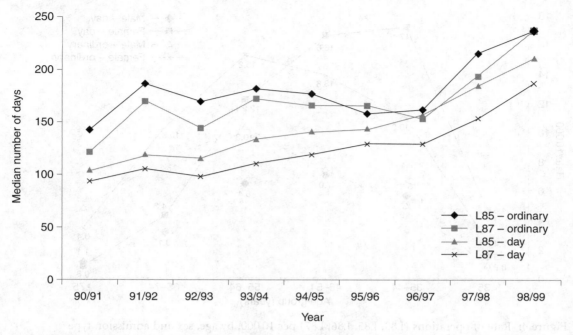

Figure 5: Median duration of wait for operation types L85 and L87 by admission type (1990–91 to 1998–99).

The increases in waiting times are despite a reduction in the median length of stay for surgery for all procedures. The median duration of stay for ordinary-admission operations coded as L85 and L87 has been one day since 1994–95, compared to two days previous to this year. The median length of stay for operations coded as L83 has decreased from 6 days to 2 days. The median length of stay for operations coded as L86 (injection into varicose vein of the leg) was 1 day in 1990–91 but since then has been 0 days (i.e. day cases).

Emergency surgery

There was a marked reduction in the percentage of patients undergoing varicose vein operations who were admitted as an emergency in 1989–90 compared to earlier years. This trend has continued. In 1989–90, 1% of patients having a varicose vein operation were admitted as an emergency, compared to only 0.4% in 2000–01. Some of these episodes may be miscoded HES data.

Rate of operations by health authority

The mean crude rate of operations for all health authorities (now PCTs) per 10 000 of the population was 10.8 in 1996–97, 9.7 in 1997–98 and 11.6 in 1998–99 (Department of Health, Hospital Episode Statistics, 1996–97 to 1998–99). However, there are variations in rates between health authorities, with the crude rate ranging from 2.6 per 10 000 to 38.7 per 10 000 in 1996–97, 1.8 per 10 000 to 31.6 per 10 000 in 1997–98, and 5.1 per 10 000 to 40 per 10 000 in 1998–99 (*see* Figure 6). Such variation is likely to be due to a combination of factors, including chance, age/gender population differences, the quality of local HES coding, and true differences in the prevalence of varicose veins and in the referral and treatment pathways and provision.

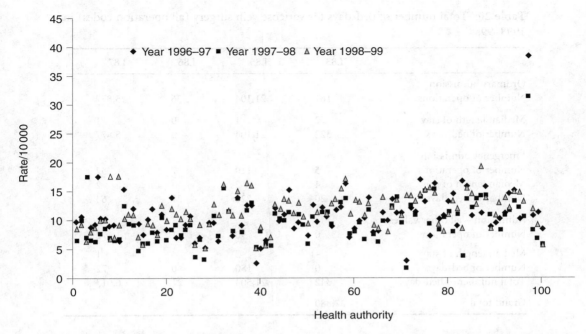

Figure 6: Rate of operations per 10 000 per year (1996–97 to 1998–99) for health authorities in England.

Number of bed-days required for varicose vein operations

Utilising the information on the median duration of stay and the number of operations performed in NHS hospitals it is possible to estimate the total number of bed-days required for elective varicose vein surgery in NHS hospitals in England. In 1998–99 this equated to an estimated 27 880 bed-days (*see* Table 20).

Independent-sector activity

There are no routinely collected data on elective hospital treatment carried out in England and Wales by the independent sector. Williams *et al.* found that in 1981 the proportion of elective treatments purchased privately in England and Wales was 13.2% and in 1986 it was 14.8%.[232] A similar survey comparing the volume and nature of elective hospital care funded publicly and privately was carried out in 1997–98.[5] This found that 14.5% of elective treatments were privately funded. More specifically, surgery performed in independent hospitals accounted for 24% of the ligation or stripping operations for varicose veins in England and Wales in 1997–98, and the number of operations privately funded accounted for 21%[5] (*see* Table 21).

Costs associated with the treatment of varicose veins

The National Schedule of Reference Costs, updated in January 2000 and based on costed activity for 1998–99, gives the average national reference costs for varicose vein procedures (HRG code Q11; *see* Appendix 1) as £747 for elective surgery, £921 for non-elective surgery and £495 for day-case surgery.[233]

Table 20: Total number of bed-days for varicose vein surgery (all operation codes) in 1998–99.

	L83	L85	L86	L87
Ordinary admission				
Number of operations	161	21,104	36	5,877
Median length of stay	2	1	0	1
Number of bed-days	322	21,104	0	5,877
Emergency admission				
Number of operations	5	110	7	32
Median length of stay	4	2	3	2
Number of bed-days	20	220	21	64
Admission – all other values				
Number of operations	0	90	1	72
Median length of stay	–	2	–	1
Number of bed-days	0	180	0	72
Total number of bed-days	342	21,504	21	6,013
Grand total	27,880			

Table 21: Number of operations for varicose veins (ligation or stripping) according to source of funding for residents of England and Wales, 1997–98.

Funding	Independent hospitals			NHS hospitals			Percentage privately funded
	Private	NHS	Total	Private	NHS	Total	
Ligation or stripping	12,782	733	21,186	505	48,340	48,845	20.8

Source: Williams *et al.*[5]

Table 22: Summary of services available.

Sub-category	Assessment methods	Treatment options
Mild discretionary	Clinical examination Continuous-wave Doppler ultrasound Duplex scanning	Do nothing Pharmacotherapy Compression therapy Sclerotherapy
Severe non-discretionary	Clinical examination Continuous-wave Doppler ultrasound Duplex scanning Other investigation, e.g. venography, phlethysmography	Pharmacotherapy Compression therapy Sclerotherapy Surgery
Venous ulcer	Clinical examination Continuous-wave Doppler ultrasound Duplex scanning Other investigation, e.g. venography, phlethysmography	Compression therapy Pharmacotherapy Surgery

6 Effectiveness

The effectiveness of the different forms of management for varicose veins can be assessed by the amount of reduction in the presenting symptoms and signs, and in the long term, by the volume of need for further treatment, particularly venous ulcer care. The goal of interventional procedures has been said to be to normalise venous physiology.[11]

Recurrence is frequently used as a measure of effectiveness, although it is extremely difficult to measure and classify, as there is always difference of opinion between observers on what constitutes a recurrence. Campbell *et al.*, on following up a small cohort for 10 years, have concluded that the rate of recurrence depends entirely on the question that is asked.[299] Almost every published long-term study lacks validity and credibility because of the large proportion of patients who cannot be followed up (partly due to the necessity of evaluating outcome after five and ten years),[234] and the absence of a clearly defined anatomical and physiological assessment by an independent observer.

When using recurrence as a measure of effectiveness it is important to distinguish between residual veins, recurrent veins and recanalised veins.[235,236] Residual veins are veins that were not treated at the original operation because they were not detected pre-operatively, were not found during the operation, were deliberately left untreated or were incompletely treated.[237] A failure to remove the full length of a tortuous vein is the most common cause of residual varicosities, but short saphenous vein incompetence may only become obvious when long saphenous vein incompetence has been treated, especially if it has not been carefully excluded before the first operation.

Recurrent varicose veins are veins which have become varicose after the original treatment, having been 'normal' at the time of that treatment. This often occurs when all the visible varicosities were treated but the underlying physiological abnormalities were not corrected; the remaining 'normal' veins therefore continue to be subjected to abnormal pressures and subsequently dilate. The role of incompetent thigh perforating veins has become recognised as a common cause of recurrence (39% of patients with recurrent varicose veins have incompetent thigh perforating veins demonstrated by venography),[238,239] as has failure to strip the LSV in the thigh and the involvement of the deep venous system.

The effectiveness of different types of treatment still remains unclear. A Task Force on Chronic Venous Disorders of the Leg was established in September 1993 with the purpose of comprehensively evaluating this area of medicine.[26] One of its mandates was to critically review existing scientific evidence on the diagnosis and treatment of the condition. A paper published in 1999 summarised their main findings. MEDLINE was searched from 1983 to 1996, the reference lists of review articles, theses and unpublished reports on the subject were screened, and a manual search was done of 30 scientific journals (including 15 not indexed by MEDLINE) for randomised controlled trials (RCTs) of drug treatment for venous disease. The titles and abstracts of articles located were then subjected to a number of tiers of screening by members of the Task Force. The main findings of the Task Force form the basis of this section on effectiveness. Where more current effectiveness data have been identified, this information has been included.

Effectiveness of assessment methods

In assessing data on the reliability and validity of diagnostic tests the Task Force only considered studies that had moderate to strong scientific evidence. Also, for assessment of validity, only studies providing quantitative information on specificity, sensitivity and/or predictive accuracy were considered.

Clinical examination

A study which assessed the validity of vein palpation by an experienced vascular surgeon for the prediction of long saphenous vein reflux, as verified by colour Doppler, reported a sensitivity of 0.43, and a very high specificity and positive predictive value of 1.0 each, and a negative predictive value of 0.58.[240] None of the studies retained by the Task Force allowed formal assessment of the validity of the Trendelburg test for diagnosing venous valvular incompetence, although there is some evidence to suggest it may help predict functional improvement after vein-stripping surgery.[241,242] Browse *et al.* consider that in conjunction with clinical examination, tourniquet tests provide sufficient understanding of the venous abnormality for management decisions in 80–90% of patients,[243] but other investigators dispute this.[125,141] Clinical examination may accurately diagnose valvular incompetence where there is gross long saphenous incompetence, but it will often miss short saphenous reflux and is poor for detecting reflux in the deep veins.[141]

Doppler

A hand-held Doppler provides clear answers regarding the presence or absence of reflux at the sapheno-femoral and/or sapheno-popliteal junctions in 90% of patients when used by an experienced practitioner.[126] A limitation of continuous-wave Doppler ultrasound is that it cannot detect the exact site of reflux.[244] It is also not accurate in localising incompetent perforating veins[245] and it is unreliable in the assessment of veins in the popliteal fossa.[141] The VEINES Task Force considered only validity data on the Doppler examination when Doppler was compared to duplex, phlebography or venous pressure measurements. Only two studies met the methodological criteria of the Task Force. Doppler had high sensitivity but low specificity for detecting incompetent sapheno-femoral junctions – this is confirmed by a study carried out in 1998.[56] The Task Force concluded that Doppler examination would be best used as a screening test rather than for diagnosis.

Duplex scanning

Studies assessing the validity of duplex scanning in detecting the site and severity of reflux compared to descending phlebography and venous pressure measurement found that sensitivity for deep vein reflux was 0.79–1.0, but specificity was only 0.63–0.88.[246–249] Popliteal incompetence as demonstrated by duplex was shown to be a good predictor of post-operative leg ulcer recurrence in patients undergoing perforator ligation for chronic ulceration (high sensitivity and specificity).[250]

Plethysmography

In the VEINES review, among the various phlethysmographic techniques, the Task Force found that photoplethysmography (PPG) was the only one for which validity data[240,251–254] were available once criteria for study selection were applied. PPG consistently demonstrated low sensitivity and specificity and poor predictive accuracy for the detection of venous reflux, and in some studies gave uninterpretable results in nearly a quarter of limbs.[252] Strain-gauge plethysmography, foot volumetry and air plethysmography may be useful for assessing venous function but their validity has not been formally tested.

Phlebography

Descending phlebography had high sensitivity but low specificity for the detection of deep reflux when compared to venous pressure measurement.[251]

Treatment of venous disease

In assessing the efficacy of treatment of varicose veins and venous disorders the outcomes evaluated by the VEINES Task Force were, where possible, treatment success, effect on symptoms, effect on signs, adverse effects, patient satisfaction and acceptability, patient compliance, effect on laboratory parameters and effect on quality of life (QoL).[24,26] The Task Force's results are summarised in Table 24 (*see* p. 60). More recent effectiveness evidence is discussed below.

Pharmacotherapy

- A placebo-controlled trial of 30 mg/day oral naftazone found that naftazone was more effective than placebo in providing clinical improvement in women with primary uncomplicated symptomatic varicose veins.[255] (Level of evidence: B I-2.)
- A systematic review assessing the evidence for or against horse-chestnut seed extract (HCSE) as a symptomatic treatment of venous insufficiency found that HCSE is superior to placebo and as effective as reference medications in alleviating the objective signs (lower leg volume and a reduction in leg circumference at the calf and ankle) and subjective symptoms (leg pain, fatigue, etc.) of CVI.[256] (Level of evidence: B I-1.)

Surgery

- A systematic review on the use of tourniquet in surgery for varicose veins is available on the Cochrane Library.[257] There were significant quality issues with available evidence, but the use of tourniquet would appear to reduce blood loss during surgery.
- A randomised controlled trial that investigated the possible long-term clinical advantages of stripping the long saphenous vein during routine primary varicose vein surgery vs. sapheno-femoral ligation alone found that stripping reduced the risk of re-operation by two-thirds after 5 years.[258] (Level of evidence: B I-2.)
- A prospective randomised trial has examined the efficacy of perforate invagination (PIN) stripping of the long saphenous vein in comparison to conventional stripping in the surgical management of primary varicose veins. There were no statistically significant differences between the two techniques in terms of time taken to strip the vein, percentage of vein stripped or the area of bruising at one week. However, the size of the exit site was significantly smaller with the PIN device, resulting in better cosmesis.[259] (Level of evidence: C I-2.)
- A prospective randomised trial comparing sequential avulsion with stripping of the long saphenous vein found that sequential avulsion is less painful, reduces bruising and avoids a significant scar below the knee.[260] (Level of evidence: B I-2.)
- A prospective, randomised controlled study with patients serving as their own controls compared the post-operative discomfort and long-term outcome following standard stripping and long saphenous vein-saving surgery. It concluded that the long-term results of long saphenous vein-saving surgery are as good as standard stripping provided the incompetent perforators are thoroughly mapped

pre-operatively and ligated at surgery. It also concluded that long saphenous vein-saving surgery causes less subjective post-operative discomfort than standard stripping.[261] (Level of evidence: C I-2.)

- A randomised study comparing the 5-year recurrence frequency and 3-year frequency of neural complications after partial and total stripping of the long saphenous vein showed that stripping the long saphenous vein below the knee increases the permanent nerve damage sixfold without reducing long-term recurrence.[262] (Level of evidence: E I-2.)
- A prospective study of 102 consecutive patients who underwent varicose vein surgery that included stripping of the LSV to the knee concluded that LSV surgery leads to a significant improvement in disease-specific health-related QoL for as much as two years.[263] (Level of evidence: B II-2.)
- Evidence for the newer treatments for varicose veins (radiofrequency ablation, endovenous laser treatment and sclerosing foam) is limited to case series and registry data, largely in private practice settings.[207] (Level of evidence: C III.)
- Sclerosant delivered into a vein as a microfoam preparation has shown promising results and is currently being compared with surgery in an RCT.[127]

Sclerotherapy

- A consensus statement on sclerotherapy published in 1997, considering literature classified in the *Index Medicus* from 1966 to 1994,[59] states that the published literature reports conflicting data on the efficacy of sclerotherapy and is greatly limited from a scientific and statistical point of view. This is compounded by doubts about the most appropriate outcome measures to use for assessing the results. Six randomised controlled studies comparing sclerotherapy with surgery were identified. The results of these are poor with regard to the rate of recurrence (*see* Table 23). However, the consensus participants were prevented from formulating a definitive statement regarding the results of sclerotherapy because of shortcomings in the studies. (Level of evidence: D I-1.)
- A systematic review on injection sclerotherapy for varicose veins is available on the Cochrane Library.[270] The main aims of the review were to determine whether injection sclerotherapy for treatment of varicose veins is effective in terms of symptomatic improvement and cosmetic appearance, to determine whether sclerotherapy has an acceptable complication rate and to define the rate of symptomatic or cosmetic recurrence following sclerotherapy. It compares the following:

1 sclerotherapy vs. other treatment options:
   - sclerotherapy vs. graduated compression stockings for varicose veins with superficial venous incompetence
   - sclerotherapy vs. graduated compression stockings or observation for varicose veins in the absence of superficial venous incompetence
   - sclerotherapy vs. laser treatment or no treatment (i.e. simple follow-up) in patients with thread veins
2 different sclerosants and sclerosant dose
3 injection techniques, bandaging and compression techniques and repeat treatment intervals.

The conclusions of the review are that evidence from RCTs suggests that type of sclerosant, local pressure dressing, degree and length of compression have no significant effect on the efficacy of schlerotherapy for varicose veins. This supports the place of sclerotherapy in modern clinical practice, which is usually limited to treatment of recurrent varicose veins following surgery and thread veins.

- In a study in the USA, the efficacy and adverse sequelae of two sclerosants were investigated. Both polidocanol and sodium tetradecyl sulphate were found to be safe and effective sclerosing agents for varicose and thread veins.[271]

Table 23: Randomised controlled trials comparing sclerotherapy with surgery.

Study	Chant et al.[264]	Beresford et al.[265]*	Hobbs[266]	Hobbs[267]†	Jacobsen[268]	Einarsson et al.[269]
Year	1972	1978	1974	1984	1979	1993
Number of patients	115	115	250	250	157	84
Sclerosing technique	Fegan	Fegan	Fegan	Fegan	Sigg	Fegan
Follow-up	3 years	5 years	6 years	10 years	3 years	1, 3, 5 years
Failure criteria	Patient did not come for treatment; retreatment	Patient did not come for treatment; retreatment	Objective evaluation of the limb	Objective evaluation of the limb	Subjective and objective evaluation	Subjective and objective evaluation
Rate of failure	22% at 3 years	40% at 5 years	66% at 6 years	90% at 10 years	Subjective: 30% at 3 years; objective: 64% at 3 years	Subjective: 50% at 5 years; objective: 74% at 5 years

* Beresford *et al.* report the 5-year follow-up of the same sample of patients as in the Chant *et al.* study.
† The second Hobbs study reports the 10-year follow-up of the same sample of patients as in the first Hobbs study.

Echosclerotherapy

The consensus statement on sclerotherapy reported that as echosclerotherapy is a recent technique only short-term studies are available.[59] The three studies identified reported failure rates of 18.7% at end of treatment, 13.3% at end of treatment and 21.5% at second session of echosclerotherapy (maximum of 18 months).[272,273] A study that retrospectively investigated major and minor complications associated with 1009 ultrasound-guided injections in two series of consecutive patients found that most complications were minor and localised and that the incidence of major complications was 0.1%.[274]

Venous ulcers

A review by Nelson *et al.*[275] conducted in 1999 came to the following conclusions on the effectiveness of treatments for venous ulcers.

- A systematic review of RCTS has found that compression heals venous leg ulcers more effectively than no compression (*see* 'Compression therapy' below). (Level of evidence: A I-1.)
- Limited evidence suggests that recurrence rates are lower with higher compression pressures but higher pressures are less well tolerated by patients. (Level of evidence: B II-1.)
- The effects of occlusive and non-occlusive compared with simple dressings such as gauze have not yet been adequately evaluated in RCTs.

- Limited evidence suggests that human skin equivalent or granulocyte–macrophage colony-stimulating factor may accelerate healing. (Level of evidence: C II-1.)
- Oral pentoxifylline increases the proportion of ulcers that heal completely. (Level of evidence: B.)
- Two RCTs suggest that flavonoids may accelerate healing, but there is no evidence that either stanozolol or rutoside decrease recurrence rates. (Level of evidence: C I-2.)
- There is no good evidence on the effects of intermittent pneumatic compression, ultrasound and vein surgery.

A review by Peters[276] on the factors influencing non-recurrence of venous leg ulcers concluded that there is some evidence that the use of compression hosiery is effective in reducing the incidence of venous leg ulcer recurrence. However, other strategies cited for ulcer prevention are not supported by documented evidence. (Level of evidence: C III.)

Pharmacotherapy

- A systematic review assessing the effects of pentoxifylline ('Trental 400') for treating venous ulcers, when compared with placebo or in comparison with other therapies, in the presence or absence of compression therapy, has been published on the Cochrane Library.[277] Nine trials involving 572 adults were included. Pentoxifylline appeared to be an effective adjunct to compression bandaging for treating venous ulcers. In the absence of compression it may be effective for treating venous ulcers, but the evidence should be interpreted cautiously. (Level of evidence: B I-1.)
- An RCT to assess the cost-effectiveness of using cadexomer–iodine vs. hydrocolloid dressing or paraffin gauze dressing in the treatment of patients with non-infected, venous leg ulcers concluded that cadexomer–iodine paste is an efficient, cost-effective and safe alternative.[278] (Level of evidence: B I-2.)

Compression therapy

- A Cochrane Review to assess the effectiveness and cost-effectiveness of compression bandaging and stockings in the treatment of venous ulcers concluded that compression (applied as bandages or stockings) increases ulcer healing rates compared with no compression.[279] It also concluded that multi-layered systems are more effective than single-layered systems and that high compression is more effective than low compression, but there are no clear differences in the effectiveness of different types of high compression. Rather than advocating one particular compression system, the authors concluded that it is more sensible to promote the increased use of any correctly applied compression therapy. (Level of evidence: A I-1.)

The Cochrane Review mentions two ongoing studies that will add to the current knowledge base. One is a study at St Thomas' Hospital in London comparing three- and four-layer compression bandaging. The other is the VenUS Bandage Trial, an RCT comparing short-stretch and four-layer bandaging, involving 400 patients, 4 clinical centres and the University of York. In addition, a randomised controlled trial involving 400 patients to compare the four-layer bandage and the short-stretch bandage systems has been commissioned by the HTA programme.

- A further Cochrane Review considered the effects of compression hosiery or bandages in preventing the recurrence of venous ulcers.[280] No trials were identified that compared compression with no compression for prevention of ulcer recurrence, but not wearing compression was associated with recurrence in two studies identified in the review. The authors concluded that recurrence rates may be

lower in high-compression hosiery than in medium-compression hosiery and therefore patients should be offered the strongest compression with which they can comply. (Level of evidence: B I-1.)
- A Cochrane Review to determine whether intermittent pneumatic compression (IPC) increases the healing of venous leg ulcers and the effects of IPC on health-related quality of life of patients identified four RCTs and concluded that further trials are required to determine whether IPC increases the healing of venous leg ulcers.[281] (Level of evidence: C I-1.)

Laser therapy

- A Cochrane Review to assess the effectiveness of low-level laser therapy in the treatment of venous leg ulcers concluded that there is no evidence of any benefit associated with this therapy on venous leg ulcer healing. One small study was identified which suggests that a combination of laser and infra-red light may promote the healing of venous ulcers but it was concluded that more research is needed.[282] (Level of evidence: D I-1.)

Electrical stimulation

- A systematic review assessing the effectiveness of electromagnetic therapy for treating venous leg ulcers has been published on the Cochrane Library.[283] A total of three eligible RCTs were identified and the reviewers concluded that there is currently no reliable evidence of benefit of electromagnetic therapy in the healing of venous leg ulcers. (Level of evidence: D I-1.)

Therapeutic ultrasound

- The potential role of ultrasound in the treatment of venous leg ulcers has been assessed in a Cochrane Review.[284] The authors identified seven eligible RCTs. None of the trials found a difference in healing rates between any of the therapies, but the direction of treatment effect was consistently in favour of ultrasound. (Level of evidence: D I-1.)

Skin grafting for venous ulcers

- A Cochrane Review assessing the effectiveness of skin grafts in the treatment of venous leg ulcers found that there is limited evidence that artificial skin used in conjunction with compression bandaging increases the chance of healing a venous ulcer compared to compression alone. Further research was recommended to assess whether other forms of skin grafts increase ulcer healing.[215] (Level of evidence: C I-1.)

Community leg ulcer clinics

- A randomised controlled trial study to establish the relative cost-effectiveness of community leg ulcer clinics that use four-layer compression bandaging vs. usual care provided by district nurses concluded that the former are more effective.[285] (Level of evidence: A I-2.)
- A study comparing two health authorities' approaches to care for leg ulcers found that the introduction of community clinics and four-layer compression bandaging in one health authority (Stockport) improved care and resulted in lower costs than the traditional approach employed by the other health authority (Trafford).[230] (Level of evidence: A II-1.)

There is debate about whether a venous ulcer service should include a vascular surgery-led clinic for the initial assessment to exclude arterial ulcer and to determine the role of surgery for superficial varicose veins in the absence of deep vein incompetence.

Table 24: Summary of the effectiveness of treatments based on an evidence-based report of the VEINES Task Force.

Sub-category	Pharmacotherapy	Compression therapy	Sclerotherapy	Surgery
Mild – discretionary	• Heaviness relieved by diosmin coumarine rutine, dihydroergocristine and calcium dobesilate • Swelling improved by rutosides and a combination of ruscus, flavonoids and proteolytic enzymes • Venous tone improved by diosmin • Reported adverse effects with drug therapies included nausea, headaches, gastric pain and insomnia • There is no scientific evidence for the efficacy of medications to treat telangiectases, spider veins or reticular veins	• Evidence for the use of compression in patients with symptoms alone is limited • There is no scientific evidence for the efficacy of compression to treat telangiectases, spider veins or reticular veins, but symptoms associated with these can be relieved by gradual compression stockings	• Properly controlled studies examining the efficacy, cost and long-term benefits of sclerotherapy for telangiectases, spider veins and reticular veins are lacking • Complication rates are thought to be related to the type and concentration of the sclerosing agent and to the operator's experience • 80% of patients in one study reported being satisfied or very satisfied with the outcome	• Telangiectases *per se* should not be treated by surgery
Severe – non-discretionary	• Rutosides, diosmin, calcium dobesilate, coumarine rutine and horse-chestnut extract improve objective indices of oedema • The available scientific evidence does not support the use of medications for skin changes	• Symptoms associated with varicose veins can be relieved by gradual compression stockings • Graduated compression stockings in excess of 35 mmHg and fixed or stretched bandages have been shown to be effective in improving objective indices of oedema • There is some evidence that graduated compression stockings in excess of 35 mmHg are effective for skin changes	• The reported treatment success when sclerotherapy is used to treat non-saphenous varicose veins (including residual and recurrent varicose veins after surgical treatment), and local varicose veins and varicose tributaries of the saphenous trunk without saphenous insufficiency, is approximately 70–80% at one year • Adverse effects include superficial phlebitis, subcutaneous clot retraction, pain, blistering, pruritis, swelling and pigmentation	• Randomised studies comparing sclerotherapy and surgery in the treatment of long saphenous varicose veins showed a significantly higher recurrence rate at long-term follow-up after sclerotherapy • There is no evidence to determine whether surgery or sclerotherapy is the best treatment for short saphenous varicose veins • In patients with symptoms caused by primary varicose veins who have evidence of sapheno-femoral

Sub-category	Pharmacotherapy	Compression therapy	Sclerotherapy	Surgery
			• Patient satisfaction is reported to be 80% at one year or less, dropping to 40% by 5 years • It is unlikely to improve skin changes secondary to venous insufficiency	junction or sapheno-popliteal junction reflux, there is clear evidence to support the use of surgical treatment • Surgery is indicated in patients without evidence of reflux in the large veins but with large tributaries feeding varicose veins[27] • Complications of surgery include saphenous vein and saphenous nerve injury in up to 39% of patients after total long saphenous vein stripping, a 2–15% risk of infection, up to 7% risk of haematoma and 3% risk of phlebitis • Reported patient satisfaction ranged from 75% to 90%
Venous ulcers	• No evidence available of the effectiveness of medications in preventing ulcer recurrence • Evidence of the efficacy of systemic medications, including antibiotics, and local topical therapies, including topical antibiotics, on venous ulcer healing is limited • A multi-centre clinical trial found that oral micronised diosmin in addition to compression might be more effective than compression alone in achieving complete ulcer healing for ulcers less than 10 cm in diameter	• There is some evidence that graduated compression stockings in excess of 35 mmHg are effective at preventing ulcer recurrence • Bandages, both fixed and stretched, have been shown to be effective in the treatment of venous ulcers. They must be properly applied to produce significant benefits. Compression stockings in excess of 35 mmHg may also be used • Patient acceptability and compliance with compression therapy have both been reported to be about 70%, with few adverse effects	• No evidence showing that sclerotherapy prevents venous ulcer recurrence • It is unlikely to be effective in patients with venous ulceration unless there is superficial venous insufficiency, in which case it may have a role which is as yet unproven	• Patients with active venous ulceration and sapheno-femoral or sapheno-popliteal junction incompetence benefit from surgical treatment

Source: Adapted from Kurz *et al.*[27]

Cost-effectiveness

To determine the cost-effectiveness of treatment for the various severities of venous disease, costs must be considered in association with outcomes. There are no studies on the relative cost-effectiveness of treatment for varicose veins compared with other elective surgical procedures. A randomised controlled trial study by Piachaud and Weddell in the UK in the early 1970s found that outpatient treatment by injection/compression sclerotherapy was less costly than routine surgical removal, but the data are based on price, volume and outcome information related to 1972.[286,287]

Costs and benefits are likely to differ depending on both the severity of the varicose veins and the characteristics of the patient. The data currently available are not helpful in distinguishing those patients for whom treatment for varicose veins is most cost-effective, nor are they able to give any indication of the ideal levels of treatment. In the present climate of the NHS, in which some PCTs have explicitly decided not to treat some or all patients presenting with varicose veins on the basis of cutting costs, it seems that there is an urgent need to obtain better cost-effectiveness data for this condition to establish those categories of patients that should be treated. Without such data there is no real indication where the treatment of varicose veins should be on the list of NHS priorities.

An assessment of the cost-effectiveness of the treatment of varicose veins is being carried out as part of the HTA programme and is due for publication in 2005. The project will assess the cost-effectiveness of the commonly used treatments for varicose veins by the Markov process decision model. The model will allow an assessment of the incremental cost-effectiveness of each treatment modality in subgroups of patients based upon their symptomatic, investigative and demographic features. The review will also assess patient and societal priorities for treatment using a 'willingness-to-pay' technique.

Venous ulcers

A multi-centre randomised controlled trial to assess the cost-effectiveness of using clinic-based weekly treatment of leg ulcers with 4-layer bandaging vs. the usual home-based care by district nurses for the treatment of venous leg ulcers[285] was carried out between September 1994 and May 1995. Using 1995 prices, community-based leg ulcer clinics with specially trained nurses and single 4-layer bandaging were more effective than traditional home-based treatment. The benefit was achieved at a small additional cost which could be reduced further if certain service configurations were used.

7 Models of care/recommendations

Determining population need

This is difficult because of the uncertainty about what types of venous disease would benefit from NHS intervention. Local need would be increased substantially if cosmetic and mild symptomatic varicose veins were thought to warrant NHS treatment. The need represented by more serious venous disease is smaller, but quantifying it is hindered by the lack of good population-based prevalence data, especially in the elderly – need will be driven by policy for the management of venous disease in the elderly. The best estimate from the Edinburgh study would be 1% venous ulcer and 7–8% considered for surgery for CVI or symptoms. The future need is likely to rise as the population ages and the epidemic of obesity continues unabated.

Who to treat?

For commissioners the key question is to which groups of patients they should offer varicose vein surgery. Consensus is that the NHS should provide venous ulcer care, with a key element being the use of compression bandages overseen by trained nurses in accessible community clinics. However, there is debate about whether there should be a specialist vascular clinic overseen by a vascular surgeon, which would undertake the initial assessment to exclude arterial ulcers and to decide whether surgery of any superficial varicose veins should be performed – this approach being dependent on evidence that such surgery will aid healing and prevent ulcer recurrence.

Minor varicose veins with cosmetic effect should not be treated on the NHS. There is a growing private market in the care of such patients which needs regulation.

The difficult question is the identification of patients with significant symptoms due to varicose veins who would benefit from surgery and also the group at high risk of progressing to venous ulcer who might benefit from prophylactic surgery. Clearly, operating on 30% of the adult population to prevent ulcers in 1% is not feasible.

Organisation of a venous disease service

Key features of a venous disease service appear to be as follows:

1 appropriate referral of patients in whom varicosities are presented or suspected (*see* NICE referral advice)[122]
2 availability of appropriate diagnostic assessment tests and staff trained in their use – this includes not only Doppler but also ideally duplex ultrasound
3 trained junior surgical staff and supervision of inexperienced surgical trainees by consultants
4 maximal use of day surgery – wherever possible varicose vein treatment should be provided in a day-care setting
5 consideration of the opening of elective treatment centres following the model established in South Wales evaluated by Harvey *et al.*[288] Such centres reduced waiting times and increased the volume of varicose vein surgery. Direct-access assessment, whereby GPs can refer direct to the surgeon for operation, bypassing outpatients, did not however lead to substantially increased referral, probably because of the strong onus on GPs to undertake detailed assessment[289]
6 community venous ulcer clinics with appropriately trained nurses and an optimal flow of patients.

Prevention

The scope for prevention of varicose veins seems limited. Population strategies to halt the rising tide of obesity have not been effective. DVT prophylaxis, e.g. in hospitalised medical and surgical patients, may help reduce the consequences of DVT in terms of subsequent chronic venous disease. Compression stockings post-acute DVT may prevent the post-thrombotic limb.

8 Outcomes measures and audit methods

The most commonly evaluated outcome of medical and surgical treatment is the rate of recurrence. However, the definition, timing and method of assessment as well as case-mix should be stated. Other outcomes that need to be evaluated should be related to the reasons for treatment (symptomatic or not, presence of ulceration, etc). These may include prevention of complications and an improvement in appearance and symptoms. Other outcomes may include patient satisfaction, side-effects and costs.

Objective outcome measures could include any of the assessment methods, although the less invasive and easiest/most cost-effective to use (continuous-wave Doppler) would be preferable.

Quality of life

The Aberdeen Varicose Vein Questionnaire is a disease-specific questionnaire that measures health-related quality of life for patients with varicose veins.[290] The questionnaire consists of 13 questions relating to all aspects of the problem of varicose veins. The questionnaire has been assessed for reliability, validity, responsiveness and practicality, and was deemed a valid measure of quality of life for patients with varicose veins.[41] The Short Form 36 (SF-36) Health Assessment Questionnaire has also been used to assess patient outcomes following varicose vein surgery.[291] The Nottingham Health Profile and the SF-36 are the most popular generic tools used in the study of leg ulceration.

9 Information and research

There has been an expansion of interest in venous disease research. There is a need for more information on the following:

- epidemiology of venous disease in the elderly and in ethnic minorities
- the link between varicose veins and venous ulcer and prediction of risk of venous ulceration
- surgical vs. medical therapy for CVI
- the efficacy of varicose vein surgery in improving ulcer healing rates and in preventing recurrence
- the relationship between the location of venous incompetence and the severity of venous insufficiency
- the relationship between DVT and varicose veins.

There are protocols for systematic reviews of RCTs of the use of phlebotonics for CVI, community clinics vs. home management for venous leg ulcer treatment, oral antibiotics for treating venous leg ulcers and dressings for venous leg ulcers registered on the Cochrane Library.

The Cochrane Review on sclerotherapy recommended a comparison of surgery vs. sclerotherapy.[270] A consensus statement on sclerotherapy concluded that there is a need for proper randomised controlled trials to assess the effectiveness of sclerotherapy, and listed the essential characteristics that any new study considering the effectiveness of sclerotherapy should have[59] (*see* Box 3). These characteristics can also be applied to any study of the effectiveness of surgery.

Box 3: The characteristics of an ideal study on sclerotherapy. *Source*: Baccaglini *et al.*[59]

---

1 The study should be prospective, randomised and controlled.
2 The patient sample should be as homogeneous as possible, particularly with respect to the type of varicose veins to be treated. For this reason a careful pre-treatment assessment would be necessary.
3 The sclerotherapy technique should be standardised and clearly described.
4 All complications and side-effects of the treatment should be recorded.
5 An independent assessor should evaluate the results, and objective criteria should be used in evaluating the symptoms, the appearance of the leg and the instrumental examinations.
6 Follow-up should last for at least 5 years and subsequent treatments should be recorded.

Better information is required on the reasons for varicose vein treatment rate variation, using HES data. For much of venous disease (e.g. outpatients, private sector), information is lacking which would be useful for commissioning services. Locally, one needs to be able to determine local treatment rates that can be compared with national results. The proportion of varicose veins having day-case surgery and the size of the known venous ulcer disease population would also be valuable local figures. Recurrence rates are more difficult to determine and interpret – in terms of definitions, assessment and duration of follow-up.

A conference on venous disease held in Edinburgh, Scotland in 1999 highlighted the many gaps in the research and information base for varicose veins and venous disease in general. A book summarising the conference proceedings has been drawn upon in the writing of this chapter.[298]

Appendix 1: Selection of codes for analysis

OPCS Operation Codes

Table A1: OPCS Operation Codes, Fourth Revision (April 1988 onwards).

Code	Operation
L83	Operations for venous insufficiency
L85	Ligation of varicose vein of leg
L86	Injection into varicose vein of leg
L87	Other operations on varicose vein of leg (stripping of long and short saphenous veins, and avulsion of varicose veins)

Diagnostic codes

Table A2: Relevant ICD-9 codes.

Code	Operation
	Varicose veins of lower extremities
454.0	With ulcer
454.1	With inflammation
454.2	With ulcer and inflammation
454.9	Without mention of ulcer and inflammation (includes phlebectasia, varicose veins and varix of any part of lower extremity or of unspecified site) (456 includes varicose veins of five other sites but when the site is not specified, code 454.9 is used, apart from retinal varices, which are 362.1)

Table A3: Relevant ICD-10 codes (introduced in 1995–96).

Code	Operation
	Varicose veins of lower extremities:
183.0	With ulcer (any condition in 183.9 with ulcer or specified as ulcerated). Varicose ulcer (lower extremity, any part)
183.1	With inflammation (any condition in 183.9 with inflammation or specified as inflamed. Statis dermatitis NOS)
183.2	With ulcer and inflammation (any condition in 183.9 with both ulcer and inflammation)
183.9	Without mention of ulcer and inflammation (includes phlebectasia, varicose veins and varix of any part of lower extremity or of unspecified site) (186 includes varicose veins of other sites – sublingual, scrotal, pelvic, vulval, gastric – and varicose ulcer of nasal septum, but when the site is not specified, code 183.9 is used, apart from retinal varices which are H35)

Health care resource groups (HRG codes)

Health care resource groups are used to identify groups of patients expected to consume similar amounts of health care resources. They were adapted to suit the requirements of the UK health system from diagnosis-related groups (DRGs), which were developed in the USA.

Following modification, version 3 has been in use since 1998. HRGs are now being used to compare clinical efficiency between different hospitals nationally. The version 3 HRG code for varicose veins is Q11.

Appendix 2: CEAP classifications

All limbs diagnosed as having chronic vascular disease are assessed for clinical signs, aetiological problems, anatomical distribution of the process and pathophysiological nature of the dysfunction.

Clinical classification

There are seven categories based on objective signs of CVD.

Table A4: Categories of clinical classification.

0	No visible or palpable signs of venous disease
1	Telangiectases or reticular veins
2	Varicose veins
3	Oedema
4	Skin changes ascribed to venous disease (e.g. pigmentation, venous eczema, lipodermatosclerosis)
5	Skin changes (as defined above) in conjunction with healed ulceration
6	Skin changes (as defined above) in conjunction with active ulceration

Each numbered category is further characterised by a subscript for the presence or absence of symptoms, such as pain, aching or heaviness:

- S: symptomatic
- A: asymptomatic.

Aetiological classification

The roles of congenital, primary and secondary causes in venous dysfunction are recognised in the aetiological classification.

Table A5: Categories of aetiological classification.

Congenital	E_c	Apparent at birth or recognised later, e.g. Klippel–Trenaunay syndrome
Primary	E_P	Undetermined cause
Secondary	E_s	Known cause – post-thrombotic, post-traumatic, other

Anatomical classification

This has been presented in a simplified and expanded form. In the simplified version, the vasculature involved is classified as superficial (A_s), deep (A_d) or perforating (A_P). When more detail is required, the site and extent of involvement of the superficial, deep and perforating veins may be categorised using the anatomical segments listed below.

Table A6: Categories of anatomical classification.

Segment	
	Superficial veins (A_s)
1	Telangiectases/reticular veins
2	Greater (long) saphenous veins, above the knee
3	Greater (long) saphenous veins, below the knee
4	Lesser (short) saphenous veins
5	Non-saphenous veins
	Deep veins (A_d)
6	Inferior vena cava
7	Iliac, common
8	Iliac, internal
9	Iliac, external
10	Pelvic, gonadal, broad ligament, other
11	Femoral, common
12	Femoral, deep
13	Femoral, superficial
14	Popliteal
15	Crural, anterior tibial, posterior tibial, peroneal (all paired)
16	Muscular, gastrocnemial, soleal, other
	Perforating veins (A_P)
17	Thigh
18	Calf

Pathophysiological classification

The physiological cause of venous dysfunction can be categorised as reflux (P_R) or obstruction (P_O), or both ($P_{R,O}$).

Appendix 3: A review of the published evidence concerning the population distribution of varicose veins

The diagnosis of varicose veins in the clinical setting obviously differs from the diagnosis of varicose veins that can be made in the field setting of a population study of prevalence. The use of criteria such as raised and elongated tortuous veins visible on the lower limbs is a subjective and crude ascertainment mechanism. For the examination of large numbers of individuals such a screen should be understood as a measure of the prevalence of palpable/visible varicosities, rather than a measure of the prevalence of venous abnormalities with varying potential for relief by surgical intervention. In this sense, estimates of the population prevalence of visible varicose veins in the population are of little relevance to the question of requirements for varicose vein treatment.

Studies which have attempted to estimate the prevalence of skin changes and different types of venous incompetence in series of clinic patients with varicose veins are limited in their comparability by selection bias, inclusion criteria and methods of investigation. The patient profiles revealed in these studies are unlikely to be representative of the general population of people with varicose veins. These studies do, however, point to a means of assessing the severity of the venous conditions which present in clinics, with an indication of the appropriateness of the different treatment options.

Table A7 lists the published studies of the prevalence of varicose veins in the UK, Europe and worldwide.

Table A7: Studies of the prevalence of varicose veins in different countries.

Study	Assessment methods/ design	Country	Year	Population/setting	Total number	Prevalence of varicose veins		
						Female	**Male**	**Total**
Preziosi et al. [84]	Yearly systematic clinical examination. Monthly follow-up by a telematic network and a non-specific questionnaire	France	1994–98	Participants of the SUVIMAX cohort. Women: 35–60; men: 45–60 (representative of the French population for the age range under consideration)	3,065 in total; 1,747 women; 1,318 men	18.1% medically diagnosed; 12.4% self-reported	10.8% medically diagnosed; 7.4% self-reported	
Bradbury et al. [64]	Cross-sectional population study. Self-administered questionnaire on the presence of lower limb symptoms and a physical examination to determine presence and severity of varicose veins	Scotland	1994–96	Men and women aged 18–64 resident in Edinburgh	867 women; 699 men	Trunk:174; 2 or 3. 30; Hyphenweb: 707; 2 or 3. 60	Trunk:191; 2 or 3. 32; Hyphenweb: 519; 2 or 3. 36	
Krijnen et al. [36]	Questionnaire about the presence of subjective complaints of the legs. Medical history followed by clinical examination. Doppler ultrasound investigation and light reflection rheography (LRR) of the lower legs performed and the volume of the lower legs measured twice daily	The Netherlands		Male European workers with a standing position at work (five companies in the meat industry, four shoe factories, two flower-packing departments, a foam-rubber industry, a small factory and a printing office)	387 men		58% (any size of varicosity); 38% (excluding intracutaneous veins	
Komsuoglu et al. [103]	Medical history and examination by a physician	Turkey	1994	Elderly people over 60 (mean age 73.3 ± 9) in a city in NE Turkey	850	38.3%; (saphenous type: 7.1%; segment type: 17.7%; reticular type: 3.7%; web type: 2.0%)	34.5% saphenous 6.4% 14.8% 6.1% 2.9%	36.7% 5.6% 16.5% 4.7% 2.3%

Table A7: Continued

Study	Assessment methods/ design	Country	Year	Population/setting	Total number	Prevalence of varicose veins		
						Female	Male	Total
Cesarone et al.[82]	Clinical history, clinical examination visually and duplex scanner used for ultrasound evaluation	Italy	1994	A sample of male and female residents of San Valentino, a village in Central Italy, aged 8 to 94 years (mean 46.3 ± 7)	746 in total; 379 women; 367 men			8%
Canonico et al.[85]	Interviews and a clinical assessment (always done in vertical posture where possible)	Italy	1991–92	Males and females aged 66–96 (mean 74.2). A random sample drawn by means of a stratified multi-stage sampling design using electoral rolls	1,319 in total; 560 men; 759 women	35.2%	17.0%	362 (27.4%)
Hirai et al.[96]*	Interview and examination by palpation of lower extremities and colour photographs	Japan	1990	Japanese women aged 15–90 (mean 43 ± 23). Patients without vascular disease, hospital staff and residents in homes for the elderly. Japanese men aged 19–90 (mean 45 ± 15)	646 in total; 541 women; 105 men	45% (saphenous type: 22%; segment type: 35%; reticular type: 28%; web type: 16%)	34%	
Franks et al.[65]*	Self-administered questionnaire. Randomly selected from age–sex register	England	1989	Patients from general practices in West London aged 35–70	1,338	31.5%	17.5%	25%
Leipnitz et al.[86]*	Interview. Physical examination	Germany	1989	Randomly selected from population. Male and female, aged 45–65	2,821	29%	14.5%	20.2%

Study	Method	Country	Year	Sample	N			
Stvrtinova et al.[69]	Examination of the lower limb and questionnaire. Continuous-wave Doppler measurement made to assess patency and valvular function of the lower limb venous system	Czechoslovakia	1987–89	Workers in a large department store in Bratislava. Data on women only analysed	696 women	60.5% (hyphenwebs: 30.7%; reticular: 15.4%; trunk: 14.4%)		
Rudofsky[87*]		Germany	1988	Community sample. Males and females over 15 years of age	14,000			15%
Henry and Corless[88]	Questionnaire (interview) attached to the quarterly Economic Consumer Survey in Ireland	Ireland	1986	Random sample of households	4,900			622 (12.7%)
Maffei et al.[97*]	A questionnaire completed by a social worker and data from a physical examination of the lower limbs carried out by a general physician	Brazil	1986	Patients attending a university health centre in a country town. Men and women over 15 years of age. Mostly farm workers, railway workers or housewives of low socio-economic class	1,755	50.9%	37.9%	47.6%; 21.2% (severe or moderate)
Fischer[89*]	Interview. Colour slide examination	Germany	1980	Random sample of males and females aged 17–70. City	4,530			59%
Sisto et al.[72]	Cross-sectional study with self-administered questionnaires and examination. Prevalence of varicose veins diagnosed by a physician	Finland	1978–81	Adults over 30 years of age. A national health examination survey	7,217	25%	7%	

Table A7: Continued

Study	Assessment methods/design	Country	Year	Population/setting	Total number	Prevalence of varicose veins		
						Female	Male	Total
Novo et al.[90]	Clinical examination	Western Sicily, Italy	1977–79	A sample of the population of the village of Trabia, which mainly comprises farmers and fishermen and a few craftsmen and traders	1,122	46.2%	19.3%	35.2%
Richardson and Dixon[76]*	Examination	Tanzania	1977	Tanzanians in a provincial town, aged 18 and over, attending outpatient clinics with various mild illnesses	1,000	5%	6.1%	5.5%
Beaglehole et al.[77]	Examination whilst standing	Cook Island (Pukapuka)	1975	Males and non-pregnant females aged 15–64	377	4.0	2.1	
Beaglehole et al.[77]	Examination whilst standing	Cook Island (Rarotonga)	1975	Males and non-pregnant females aged 15–64	417	14.9	15.6	
Beaglehole et al.[77]	Examination whilst standing	New Zealand (Maori)	1975	Males and non-pregnant females aged 15–64	721	43.7	33.4	
Beaglehole et al.[77]	Examination whilst standing	New Zealand Pakehas (European)	1975	Males and non-pregnant females aged 15–64	356	37.8	19.6	
Beaglehole et al.[77]	Examination whilst standing	New Zealand (Tokelau Island)	1975	Males and non-pregnant females aged 15–64	786	0.8	2.9	
Daynes & Beighton[104]	Examination	South Africa	1973	Rural community in South Africa. Women aged 18 and over	297	7.7%		
Stanhope[75]*	Examination whilst standing	New Guinea	1972	Residents of home villages or Madang town aged 20 years or over	1,457 in total; 729 females; 728 males	0.1%	5.1%	

Malhotra[105]*	Survey carried out by one observer	India (North)	1972	Railway sweepers working in Amjer. The work involves standing for long hours sweeping roads	354 males	6.8%
Malhotra[105]*	Visual inspection and palpation from the groin to the toes and survey carried out by one observer	India (South)	1972	Railway sweepers working in Madras. The work involves standing for long hours sweeping roads	323	25.1%
Widmer[292]*	Phlebologic examination consisting of an interview and an examination including inspection, palpation and documentation with colour photography	Switzerland, (Basle Study III)	1971–73	'Healthy' employees and workers of the Basle chemical companies	4,529	55% 56%
Prior et al.[74]*	Medical interview and examination	New Zealand (European)	1970	A cluster sample of European adults aged 20 and over from the North Island town of Carterton	432	42%; Mild: 29%; Moderate: 10%; Gross: 2.5% 25%; Mild: 16%; Moderate: 4%; Gross: 5%
Guberan et al.[73]*	Interviews and colour slides analysed by three observers	Switzerland	1970	Women working full-time in five department stores and in one department of a watch factory. Mean age 37.6 years	610	29.0%
Abramson et al.[95]*	An interview and examination by a physician using standardised questions, procedures and criteria	Western Jerusalem, Israel	1969 –71	Residents aged 15 and over in a Jewish neighbourhood of Western Jerusalem mainly populated by immigrants from central and eastern Europe, North Africa and Middle Eastern countries and their offspring	4,802	29% 10%

Table A7: Continued

Study	Assessment methods/ design	Country	Year	Population/setting	Total number	Prevalence of varicose veins		
						Female	Male	Total
Mekky et al.[101]*	Questionnaire and examination by one researcher	Egypt	1969	Women cotton workers from five mills in and around the Nile Delta. Aged 15–74	467	6%		
Mekky et al.[101]*	Questionnaire and examination by one researcher	England	1969	Women cotton workers from two mills, one in Rochdale and one in Carlisle. Aged 15–74	504	32%		
Weddell[67]*	Questionnaire and examination (standing up) carried out by one observer	Wales	1966	Randomly selected from the electoral roll. Males and females aged 15 and over	289	53%; Type 2: 36%; Type 3: 17%	37%; Type 2: 31%; Type 3: 6%	
Bobek et al.[293]*		Bohemia	1966	Community sample over 15 years of age	15,060	14.1%	6.6%	11%
Da Silva et al.[98]	Colour slides	Switzerland (Basle Study II)	1965–67	Employees and workers of the Basle chemical companies. Average age 47 ± 11 (men) and 43 ± 10 (women)	4,376	68%; (n = 778)	57%; (n = 3,598)	62%
Recoules-Arche[294]*		France	1965	Community sample aged 16–54	5,424			14%
Berge and Feldthusen[295]*		Sweden	1963	Community sample, aged 50 and aged 20	1,354			Aged 50: 50%; aged 20: 20%

	Description	Country	Year	Population	Number			
Coon et al.[91]*	A longitudinal study of a total community. Physical examination in the standing position	USA	1959–60 and 1962–65	Residents of Tecumseh, a city in SE Michigan, aged 10 years and over	6,389	25.9% (moderate to severe: 16.7%)	12.9% (moderate to severe: 7.4%)	28%
Arnoldi[92]*		Denmark	1958	Clinic attenders over 25 years old	1,981	38%	18.4%	
Lake et al.[71]*	Complete physical examination of the lower extremities	USA	1942	Males and females over 40 years of age representing four different types of occupational activity: sitting, standing, walking, climbing	536	73.2%	40.7%	

* Identified by Callam in his review on the epidemiology of varicose veins in 1994.[78]

References

1 Callam M. Leg ulcer and chronic venous insufficiency in the community. In: Ruckley CV, Fowkes FGR, Bradbury AW (eds). *Venous Disease: epidemiology, management and delivery of care.* London: Springer-Verlag, 1999, pp. 15–25.

2 Thomas M. Radiological assessment of varicose veins. *Br J Hosp Med* 1992; **48**: 157–62.

3 Hobbs J. Varicose veins. In: Wolfe J (ed.). *ABC of Vascular Diseases.* London: BMJ Publications, 1995, pp. 51–4.

4 Campbell W. Varicose veins: an increasing burden for the NHS. *BMJ* 1990; **300**: 763–4.

5 Williams B, Whatmough P, McGill J, Rushton L. Private funding of elective hospital treatment in England and Wales, 1997–8: national survey. *BMJ* 2000; **320**: 904–5.

6 Frankel S. The natural history of waiting lists – some wider explanations for an unnecessary problem. *Health Trends* 1989; **21**: 56–8.

7 Campbell WB. Personal communication, 2002.

8 Anonymous. *Oxford Concise Medical Dictionary.* Oxford: Oxford University Press, 1996.

9 Porter J, Rutherford R, Clagett G *et al.* Reporting standards in venous disease. *J Vasc Surg* 1988; **8**: 172–81.

10 Prerovsky I. *Diseases of the Veins.* Geneva: World Health Organization, 1990 (internal communication).

11 Mitchel P, Goldman M, Robert A, Weiss M, Bergan J. Diagnosis and treatment of varicose veins: a review. *J Am Acad Dermatol* 1994; **31**: 393–413.

12 Alguire P, Mathes B. Chronic venous insufficiency and venous ulceration. *J Gen Intern Med* 1997; **12**: 374–83.

13 Burnand K. What makes veins varicose? In: Ruckley C, Fowkes F, Bradbury A (eds). *Venous Disease: epidemiology, management and delivery of care.* London: Springer-Verlag, 1999, pp. 42–50.

14 Ludbrook J. Primary great saphenous varicose veins revisited. *World J Surg* 1986; **10**: 954–8.

15 Alexander C. The theoretical basis of varicose vein formation. *Med J Aust* 1972; **1**: 258–61.

16 Gjores J. The incidences of venous thrombosis and its sequellae in certain districts of Sweden. *Acta Chir Scand* 1956; **206** (Suppl.): 11.

17 Tibbs D. *Varicose Veins and Related Disorders.* Oxford: Butterworth–Heinemann Ltd, 1992.

18 Cotton L. Varicose veins: gross anatomy and development. *Br J Surg* 1961; **48**: 589–98.

19 King E. The genesis of varicose veins. *Aust N Z J Surg* 1950; **20**: 126.

20 Ackroyd J, Pattison M, Browse N. A study of the mechanical properties of fresh and preserved human femoral vein wall and valve cusps. *Br J Surg* 1985; **72** : 117–19.

21 Rose S, Ahmed A. Some thoughts on the aetiology of varicose veins. *J Cardiovasc Surg* 1986; **27**: 534–43.

22 Gandhi R, Irizarry E, Nackman G, Halpern V, Mulcare R, Tilson M. Analysis of the connective tissue matrix and proteolytic activity of primary varicose veins. *J Vasc Surg* 1993; **18**: 814–20.

23 Clarke G, Vasdekis S, Hobbs J, Nicolaides A. Venous wall function in the pathogenesis of varicose veins. *Surgery* 1992; **111**: 402–8.

24 Travers J, Brookes C, Evans J *et al.* Assessment of wall structure and composition of varicose veins with reference to collagen, elastin and smooth muscle content. *Eur J Vasc Endovasc Surg* 1996; **11**: 230–7.

25 Douglas W, Simpson N. Guidelines for the management of chronic venous leg ulceration. Report of a multidisciplinary workshop. *Br J Dermatol* 1995; **132**: 446–52.

26 Gilliland E, Wolfe J. Leg ulcers. *BMJ* 1991; **303**: 776–9.

27 Kurz X, Kahn S, Abenhaim L *et al.* Chronic venous disease of the leg: epidemiology, outcomes, diagnosis and management: summary of an evidence-based report of the VEINES task force. *Int Angiol* 1999; **18**: 83–102.

28 Nelzen O, Bergqvist D, Lindhagen A. Leg ulcer etiology – a cross-sectional population study. *J Vasc Surg* 1991; **14**: 557–64.

29 Dodd H, Crockett F. *The Pathology and Surgery of the Veins of the Lower Limb*. Edinburgh: Churchill Livingstone, 1976.

30 Hoare M, Nicolaides A, Miles C *et al.* The role of primary varicose veins in venous ulceration. *Surgery* 1982; **92**: 450–3.

31 Nicolaides A, Hussein MK, Szendra G, Christopoulos D, Vasdekis S, Clarke H. The relation of venous ulceration with ambulatory venous pressure measurement. *J Vasc Surg* 1993; **17**: 414–19.

32 Brandjes DPM, Buller HR, Heijboer H *et al.* Randomised trial of effect of compression stockings in patients with symptomatic proximal vein thrombosis. *Lancet* 1997; **349**: 759–62.

33 Browse N, Burnand K. The cause of venous ulceration. *Lancet* 1982; **ii**: 234–5.

34 Coleridge Smith P, Thomas P, Scurr J, Dormandy J. Causes of venous ulceration: a new hypothesis. *BMJ* 1988; **296**: 1726–7.

35 Herrick S, Sloan P, McGurk M *et al.* Sequential changes in histological pattern and extracellular matrix deposition during the healing of chronic venous ulcers. *Am J Pathol* 1992; **141**: 1085–95.

36 Krijnen R, de Boer E, Ader H, Bruynzeel D. Venous insufficiency in male workers with a standing profession. Part 1. Epidemiology. *Dermatology* 1997; **194**: 111–20.

37 Krijnen R, de Boer E, Bruynzeel D. Epidemiology of venous disorders in the general and occupational populations. *Epidemiol Rev* 1997; **19**: 294–309.

38 Laing W. *Chronic Venous Diseases of the Leg*. London: Office of Health Economics, 1992.

39 Evans CJ, Fowkes FGR, Ruckley CV, Lee AJ. Prevalence of varicose veins and chronic venous insufficiency in men and women in the general population: Edinburgh vein study. *J Epidemiol Community Health* 1999; **53**: 149–53.

40 Biland L, Widmer L. Varicose veins and chronic venous insufficiency: medical and socio-economic aspects. Basle study. *Acta Chir Scand* 1988; **544** (Suppl.): 9–11.

41 Smith J, Garratt A, Guest M, Greenhalgh R, Davies A. Evaluating and improving health-related quality of life in patients with varicose veins. *J Vasc Surg* 1999; **30**: 710–19.

42 Roe B, Cullum N, Hamer C. Patients' perceptions of chronic leg ulceration. In: Cullum N, Roe B (eds). *Leg Ulcers: nursing management*. Harrow: Scutari Press, 1995, pp. 125–34.

43 Franks P, Moffat C, Connolly M *et al.* Community leg ulcer clinics. *Phlebology* 1994; **9**: 83–6.

44 Bosanquet N, Franks P. Venous disease – the new international challenge. *Phlebology* 1996; **11**: 6–9.

45 Department of Health. *Hospital Episode Statistics, 2002*. London: Department of Health; www.doh. gov.uk/hes/index.html.

46 Bosanquet N. Costs of venous ulcers: from maintenance therapy to investment programmes. *Phlebology* 1992; **S1**: 44–6.

47 Charles H. The impact of leg ulcers on patients' quality of life. *Prof Nurse* 1995; **10**: 571–4.

48 Perrin M, Guex J, Ruckley C *et al.* Recurrent varices after surgery (REVAS): a consensus document. *Cardiovasc Surg* 2000; **8**: 233–45.

49 Juhan C, Haupert S, Miltgen G, Barthelemy P, Eklof B. Recurrent varicose veins. *Phlebology* 1990; **5**: 201–11.

50 Redwood N, Lambert D. Patterns of reflux in recurrent varicose veins assessed by duplex scanning. *Br J Surg* 1994; **81**: 1440–51.

51 Bradbury A, Stonebridge P, Ruckley C, Beggs I. Recurrent varicose veins: correlation between preoperative clinical and hand-held Doppler ultrasonographic examination, and anatomical findings at surgery. *Br J Surg* 1993; **80**: 849–51.

52 Jones L, Braithwaite B, Selwyn D, Cooke S, Earnshaw J. Neovascularisation is the principal cause of varicose vein recurrence: results of a randomised trial of stripping the long saphenous vein. *Eur J Vasc Endovasc Surg* 1996; **12**: 442–5.

53 Royle J. Recurrent varicose veins. *World J Surg* 1986; **10**: 944–53.

54 Negus D. Recurrent varicose veins: a national problem. *Br J Surg* 1993; **80**: 823–4.

55 Darke S. The morphology of recurrent varicose veins. *Eur J Vasc Surg* 1992; **6**: 512–17.

56 Mercer K, Scott D, Berridge D. Preoperative duplex imaging is required before all operations for primary varicose veins. *Br J Surg* 1998; **85**: 1495–7.

57 Baker S, Stacey M, Jopp-McKay A, Hoskin S, Thompson P. Epidemiology of chronic venous ulcers. *Br J Surg* 1991; **78**: 864–7.

58 Callam M, Harper D, Dale J, Ruckley C. Chronic ulcer of the leg: clinical history. *BMJ* 1987; **294**: 1389–91.

59 Baccaglini U, Spreafico G, Castoro C, Sorrentino P. Consensus conference on sclerotherapy or varicose veins of the lower limbs. *Phlebology* 1997; **12**: 2–16.

60 Widmer L. Classification of venous disease. In: Widmer L (ed.). *Peripheral Venous Disorders*. Bern: Hans Gruber, 1978, pp. 1–90.

61 Beebe H, Bergan J, Bergqvist D *et al.* Classification and grading of chronic venous disease in the lower limbs. A consensus statement. *Eur J Vasc Endovasc Surg* 1996; **12**: 487–92.

62 Darke S, Ruckley C. Classification and grading of chronic venous disease in the lower limbs. A consensus statement (commentary). *Eur J Vasc Endovasc Surg* 1996; **12**: 491–2.

63 London N, Nash R. ABC of arterial and venous disorders: varicose veins. *BMJ* 2000; **320**: 1391–4.

64 Bradbury A, Evans C, Allan P, Lee A, Ruckley C, Fowkes F. What are the symptoms of varicose veins? Edinburgh vein study cross-sectional population survey. *BMJ* 1999; **318**: 353–6.

65 Franks P, Wright D, Moffatt C, Stirling JFA, Bulpitt C, McCollum C. Prevalence of venous disease: a community study in West London. *Eur J Surg* 1992; **158**: 143–7.

66 Laurikka J, Sisto T, Auvinen O, Tarkka M, Laara E, Hakama M. Varicose veins in a Finnish population aged 40–60. *J Epidemiol Commununity Health* 1993; **47**: 355–7.

67 Weddell J. Varicose Veins Pilot Survey, 1966. *Br J Prev Soc Med* 1969; **23**: 179–86.

68 Evans C, Fowkes F. Measuring varicose veins in population surveys. *J Epidemiol Community Health* 1994; **48**: 212–13.

69 Stvrtinova V, Kolesar J, Wimmer G. Prevalence of varicose veins of the lower limbs in the women working at a department store. *Int Angiol* 1991; **10**: 2–5.

70 Laurikka J, Laara E, Sisto T, Tarkka M, Auvinen O, Hakama M. Misclassification in a questionnaire survey of varicose veins. *J Clin Epidemiol* 1995; **48**: 1175–8.

71 Lake M, Pratt G, Wright I. Atherosclerosis and varicose veins: occupational activities and other factors. *JAMA* 1942; **119**: 696–701.

72 Sisto T, Reunanen A, Laurikka J *et al.* Prevalence and risk factors of varicose veins in lower extremities: Mini-Finland health survey. *Eur J Surg* 1995; **161**: 405–14.

73 Guberan E, Widmer L, Glaus L *et al.* Causative factors of varicose veins: myths and facts. *Vasa* 1973; **2**: 115–20.

74 Prior I, Evans J, Morrison R, Rose B. The Carterton Study. 6. Patterns of vascular, respiratory, rheumatic and related abnormalities in a sample of New Zealand European adults. *N Z Med J* 1970; **72**: 169–77.

75 Stanhope J. Varicose veins in a population of lowland New Guinea. *Int J Epidemiol* 1975; **4**: 221–5.

76 Richardson J, Dixon M. Varicose veins in tropical Africa. *Lancet* 1977; **i**: 791–2.

77 Beaglehole R, Prior I, Salmond C, Davidson F. Varicose veins in the South Pacific. *Int J Epidemiol* 1975; **4**: 295–9.

78 Callam M. Epidemiology of varicose veins. *Br J Surg* 1994; **81**: 167–73.

79 MacKenzie R, Ludlam CA, Ruckley CV, Allan PL, Burns P, Bradbury A. The prevalence of thrombophilia in patients with chronic venous leg ulceration. *J Vasc Surg* 2002; **35**(4): 718–22.

80 Browse N, Burnand K, Thomas M. *Diseases of the Veins: pathology, diagnosis and treatment.* London: Edward Arnold, 1988.

81 Madar G, Widmer L, Zemp E, Maggs M. Varicose veins and chronic venous insufficiency: disorder or disease? A critical epidemiologic review. *Vasa* 1986; **15**: 126–34.

82 Cesarone M, Belcaro G, Nicolaides A *et al.* Epidemiology and costs of venous diseases in Central Italy. *Angiology* 1997; **48**: 583–93.

83 Evans C, Fowkes F, Ruckley C *et al.* Edinburgh vein study: methods and response in a survey of venous disease in the general population. *Phlebology* 1997; **12**: 127–35.

84 Preziosi P, Galan P, Aissa M, Hercberg S, Boccalon H. Prevalence of venous insufficiency in French adults of the SUVIMAX cohort. *Int Angiol* 1999; **18**: 171–5.

85 Canonico S, Gallo C, Paolisso G *et al.* Prevalence of varicose veins in an Italian elderly population. *Angiology* 1998; **49**: 129–35.

86 Leipnitz G, Kiesewetter P, Waldhausen F, Jung F, Witt R, Wenzel E. Prevalence of venous disease in the population: first results from a prospective study carried out in great Aachen. In: Davy A, Stemmer R (eds). *Phlebologie '89.* Paris: John Libbey Eurotext Ltd, 1989, pp. 169–71.

87 Rudofsky G. Epidemiology and pathophysiology of primary varicose veins. *Langenbecks Arch Chir* 1988; **Suppl. 2**: 139–44.

88 Henry M, Corless C. The incidence of varicose veins in Ireland. *Phlebology* 1989; **4**: 133–7.

89 Fischer H. Sozioepidemiologische studie über die Venenleiden bei einer erwachsenen Wohnbevölkerung in der Bundesrepublik Deutschland. *Phlebol Proktol* 1980; **9**: 147–52.

90 Novo S, Avellone G, Pinto A *et al.* Prevalence of primitive varicose veins of the lower limbs in a randomized population sample of western Sicily. *Int Angiol* 1988; **7**: 176–81.

91 Coon W, Willis P, Keller J. Venous thromboembolism and other venous disease in the Tecumseh Community Health Study. *Circulation* 1973; **XLVIII**: 839–45.

92 Arnoldi C. The heredity of venous insufficiency. *Dan Med Bull* 1958; **5**: 169.

93 Brand F, Dannenberg A, Abbott R, Kannel W. The epidemiology of varicose veins: the Framingham study. *Am J Prev Med* 1988; **4**: 96–101.

94 Holtz D, Erni D, Widmer M, Jager K. Epidemiology of varicose veins with special regard to socioeconomic status. *Acta Chir Austriaca* 1998; **30**: 68–70.

95 Abramson J, Hopp C, Epstein L. The epidemiology of varicose veins. A survey in Western Jerusalem. *J Epidemiol Community Health* 1981; **35**: 213–17.

96 Hirai M, Naiki K, Nakayama R. Prevalence and risk factors of varicose veins in Japanese women. *Angiology* 1990; **41**: 228–32.

97 Maffei F, Magaldi C, Pinho S *et al.* Varicose veins and chronic venous insufficiency in Brazil: prevalence among 1755 inhabitants of a country town. *Int J Epidemiol* 1986; **15**: 210–17.

98 da Silva A, Widmer L, Martin H, Mall T, Glaus L, Schneider M. Varicose veins and chronic venous insufficiency. *Vasa* 1974; **3**: 118–25.

99 Schultz-Ehrenburg U, Weindorf M, Von Uslar D, Hirche H. Prospective epidemiological investigations on early and preclinical stages of varicosis. In: Davy A, Stemmer R (eds). *Phlebologie '89.* Paris: John Libbey Eurotext Ltd, 1989, pp. 163–5.

100 Evans C, Fowkes F, Hajivassiliou C, Harper D, Ruckley C. Epidemiology of varicose veins. *Int Angiol* 1994; **13**: 263–70.

101 Mekky S, Schilling R, Walford J. Varicose veins in women cotton workers. An epidemiological study in England and Egypt. *BMJ* 1969; **2**: 595.

102 Sadick N. Predisposing factors of varicose and telangiectatic leg veins. *J Dermatol Surg Oncol* 1992; **18**: 883–6.

103 Komsuoglu B, Goldeli O, Kulan K, Cetinarslan B, Komsuoglu S. Prevalence and risk factors of varicose veins in an elderly population. *Gerontology* 1994; **40**: 25–31.

104 Daynes G, Beighton P. Prevalence of varicose veins in Africans. *BMJ* 1973; **3**: 354.

105 Malhotra S. An epidemiological study of varicose veins in Indian railroad workers from the south and north of India, with special reference to the causation and prevention of varicose veins. *Int J Epidemiol* 1972; **1**: 177–83.

106 Hobson J. Venous insufficiency at work. *Angiology* 1997; **48**: 577–82.

107 Burkitt D. Varicose veins, deep vein thrombosis, and haemorrhoids: epidemiology and suggested aetiology. *BMJ* 1972; **2**: 556–61.

108 Callam M. Prevalence of chronic leg ulceration and severe chronic venous disease in western countries. *Phlebology* 1992; **Suppl. 1**: 6–12.

109 Nelzen O, Bergqvist D, Lindhagen A, Hallbook T. Chronic leg ulcers: an underestimated problem in primary health care among elderly patients. *J Epidemiol Community Health* 1991; **45**: 184–7.

110 Nelzen O, Berqvist D, Fransson I, Lindhagen A. Prevalence and aetiology of leg ulcers in a defined population of industrial workers. *Phlebology* 1996; **11**: 50–4.

111 Nelzen O, Berqvist D, Fransson I, Lindhagen A. The prevalence of chronic lower-limb ulceration has been under-estimated: results of a validated population questionnaire. *Br J Surg* 1996; **83**: 255–8.

112 Cornwall JV, Doré C, Lewis J. Leg ulcers: epidemiology and aetiology. *Br J Surg* 1986; **73**: 693–6.

113 Dale J, Callam M, Ruckley C, Harper DR, Berrey P. Chronic ulcers of the leg: a study of prevalence in a Scottish community. *Health Bull (Edinb)* 1985; **1985: 41**: 310–14.

114 Henry M. Incidence of varicose ulcers in Ireland. *Ir Med J* 1986; **79**: 65–7.

115 Lees T, Lambert D. Prevalence of lower limb ulceration in an urban health district. *Br J Surg* 1992; **79**: 1032–4.

116 McCormick A, Fleming D, Charlton J. *Morbidity Statistics from General Practice: fourth national study 1991–1992*. London: HMSO, 1995.

117 Corbett C. Which patients should be selected for venous surgery? In: Ruckley C, Fowkes F, Bradbury A (eds). *Venous Disease: epidemiology, management and delivery of care*. London: Springer-Verlag, 1999, pp. 174–83.

118 O'Leary D, Jones S, Chester J. Management of varicose veins according to reason for presentation. *Ann R Coll Surg Engl* 1996; **78**: 214–16.

119 Evans C, Lee A, Ruckley C, Fowkes F. How common is venous disease in the population? In: Ruckley C, Fowkes F, Bradbury A (eds). *Venous Disease: epidemiology, management and delivery of care*. London: Springer-Verlag, 1999, pp. 3–14.

120 Lees T, Beard J, Ridler B, Szymanska T. A survey of the current management of varicose veins by members of the Vascular Surgical Society. *Ann R Coll Surg Engl* 1999; **81**: 407–17.

121 Campbell W, Aitken M, Tooke J. Expectations for the skills of final-year medical students in examining lower limb arteries and veins. *Eur J Endovasc Surg* 2002; **23**: 270–1.

122 National Institute for Clinical Excellence. *Referral Advice: a guide to appropriate referral from general practice to specialist services*. London: National Institute for Clinical Excellence, 2001.

123 Nicolaides A. How do we select the appropriate tests of venous function? In: Ruckley C, Fowkes F, Bradbury A (eds). *Venous Disease: epidemiology, management and delivery of care*. London: Springer-Verlag, 1999, pp. 80–8.

124 Bradbury A. Venous symptoms and signs and the results of duplex ultrasound: do they agree? In: Ruckley C, Fowkes F, Bradbury A (eds). *Venous Disease: epidemiology, management and delivery of care*. London: Springer-Verlag, 1999, pp. 98–114.

125 Scott H, McMullin G, Coleridge Smith P, Scurr J. Venous disease: investigation and treatment, fact or fiction? *Ann R Coll Surg Engl* 1990; **72**: 188–92.

126 Belcaro G, Labropoulos N, Christopoulos D *et al.* Noninvasive tests in venous insufficiency. *J Cardiovasc Surg* 1993; **34**: 3–11.

127 Bradbury A. Personal communication, 2002.

128 Rivlin S. The surgical cure of primary varicose veins. *Br J Surg* 1975; **62**: 913–17.

129 McIrvine A, Corbett C, Aston N, Sherriff E, Wiseman P, Jamieson C. The demonstration of saphenofemoral incompetence: Doppler ultrasound compared with standard clinical tests. *Br J Surg* 1984; **71**: 509–10.

130 Donnelly R, Hinwood D, London N. Non-invasive methods of arterial and venous assessment. *BMJ* 2000; **320**: 698–701.

131 Salaman R, Salaman J. Improving the preoperative assessment of varicose veins. *Br J Surg* 1997; **84**: 1747–52.

132 Berridge D, Scott D, Beard J, Hands L. Trials and tribulations of vascular surgical benchmarking. *Br J Surg* 1998; **85**: 508–10.

133 van der Heijden F, Bruyninckx C. Preoperative colour-coded duplex scanning in varicose veins of the lower extremity. *Eur J Surg* 1993; **159**: 329–33.

134 Belcaro G, Laurora G, Cesarone MR. Colour duplex scanning (angidynography). Evaluation of venous diseases using the slow flow systems. In: Davy A, Stemmer R (eds). *Phlebologie '89*. Paris: John Libbey Eurotext Ltd, 1989, pp. 357–9.

135 Allan P. Imaging of chronic venous disease. In: Ruckley C, Fowkes F, Bradbury A (eds). *Venous Disease: epidemiology, management and delivery of care*. London: Springer-Verlag, 1999, pp. 89–97.

136 Khaira H, Crowson M, Parnell A. Colour flow duplex in the assessment of recurrent varicose veins. *Ann R Coll Surg Engl* 1996; **78**: 139–41.

137 Georgiev M. The preoperative duplex examination. *Dermatol Surg* 1998; **24**: 433–40.

138 Campbell W, Ridler B, Halim A, Thompson J, Aertssen A, Niblett P. The place of duplex scanning for varicose veins and common venous problems. *Ann R Coll Surg Engl* 1996; **78**: 490–3.

139 Darke S, Vetrivel S, Foy D, Smith S, Baker S. A comparison of duplex scanning and continuous-wave Doppler in the assessment of primary and uncomplicated varicose veins. *Eur J Vasc Endovasc Surg* 1997; **14**: 457–61.

140 Kent P, Weston M. Duplex scanning may be used selectively in patients with primary varicose veins. *Ann R Coll Surg Engl* 1998; **80**: 388–93.

141 Campbell W, Niblett P, Ridler B, Peters A, Thompson J. Hand-held doppler as a screening test in primary varicose veins. *Br J Surg* 1997; **84**: 1541–3.

142 Hosoi Y, Yasuhara H, Shigematsu H, Aramoto H, Komiyama T, Muto T. A new method for the assessment of venous insufficiency in primary varicose veins using near-infrared spectroscopy. *J Vasc Surg* 1997; **26**: 53–60.

143 Keeling F, Lea Thomas M. Varicography in the management of primary varicose veins. *Br J Radiol* 1987; **60**: 235–240.

144 Lea Thomas M, Bowles J. Descending phlebography in the assessment of long saphenous vein incompetence. *Am J Roentgenol* 1985; **145**: 1254–7.

145 Ackroyd J, Lea Thomas M, Browse N. Deep vein reflux: an assessment by descending phlebography. *Br J Surg* 1986; **73**: 31–3.

146 Raju S. New approaches to the diagnosis and treatment of venous obstruction. *J Vasc Surg* 2000; **4**: 42.

147 Christopoulos D, Nicolaides A, Belcaro G, Kalodiki E. Venous hypertensive microangiopathy in relation to clinical severity and effect of elastic compression. *J Dermatol Surg Oncol* 1991; **17**: 809–13.

148 Hanrahan L, Kechejian G, Cordts P *et al.* Patterns of venous insufficiency in patients with varicose veins. *Arch Surg* 1991; **126**: 687–91.

149 Partsch H. Compression therapy: is it worthwhile? In: Ruckley C, Fowkes F, Bradbury A (eds). *Venous Disease: epidemiology, management and delivery of care*. London: Springer-Verlag, 1999, pp. 117–25.

150 Lawrence D, Kakker W. Graduated external compression of the lower limb. *Br J Surg* 1980; **67**: 119–21.

151 Alberta Heritage Foundation for Medical Research. *Graduated Compression Stockings to Prevent and Treat Venous Insufficiency*. Alberta: Alberta Heritage Foundation for Medical Research, 1997.

152 Armstrong S, Woollons S. Compression hosiery. *Prof Nurse* 1998; **14**: 49–59.

153 Nelson E, Cullum N, Jones J. Venous leg ulcers. *Clin Evid* 2002; **7**: 1806–17.

154 Gutman H, Zelikovski A, Haddad M, Reiss R. Clinical experience treating varicose veins in the aged. *Am Surg* 1989; **55**: 625–8.

155 Disabled Living Foundation; http://factsheets.disabledliving.org.uk/equipment-to-assist-with-dressing-and-putting-on-footwear/socks-and-stocking-aids.html. 2002.

156 Chassaignac E. *Nouvelle Methode pour la Traitement des Tumours Haemorhoidales*. Paris: Bailliere, 1885.

157 Raymond-Martimbeau P. Two different techniques for sclerosing the incompetent saphenofemoral junction: a comparative study. *J Dermatol Surg Oncol* 1990; **16**: 626–31.

158 Fraser I, Perry E, Hatton M, Watkin D. Prolonged bandaging is not required following sclerotherapy of varicose veins. *Br J Surg* 1985; **72**: 488–90.

159 Scurr J, Coleridge-Smith P, Cutting P. Varicose veins: optimum compression following sclerotherapy. *Ann R Coll Surg Engl* 1985; **67**: 109–11.

160 Shouler P, Runchman P. Varicose veins: optimum compression after surgery and sclerotherapy. *Ann R Coll Surg Engl* 1989; **71**: 402–4.

161 Goldman M. Compression in the treatment of leg telangiectasia: theoretical considerations. *J Dermatol Surg Oncol* 1989; **15**: 184–8.

162 Goldman M. Sclerotherapy treatment for varicose and telangiectatic veins in the United States: past, present and future. *J Dermatol Surg Oncol* 1990; **16**: 606–7.

163 Bodian E. Sclerotherapy: a personal appraisal. *J Dermatol Surg Oncol* 1989; **15**: 156–61.

164 de Groot W. Treatment of varicose veins: modern concepts and methods. *J Dermatol Surg Oncol* 1989; **15**: 191–8.

165 Puissegur Lupo M. Sclerotherapy: review of results and complications in 200 patients. *J Dermatol Surg Oncol* 1989; **15**: 214–19.

166 Goldman P. Polidocanol (aethoxyskerol) for sclerotherapy of superficial venules and telangiectasias. *J Dermatol Surg Oncol* 1989; **15**: 204–9.

167 Ouvry P. Telangiectasia and sclerotherapy. *J Dermatol Surg Oncol* 1989; **15**: 177–81.

168 Shmunes E. Allergic dermatitis to benzyl alcohol in an injectable solution. *Arch Dermatol* 1984; **120**: 1200–1.

169 Williams R, Wilson S. Sclerosant treatment of varicose veins and deep vein thrombosis. *Arch Surg* 1984; **119**: 1283–5.

170 Rhodes D, Hadfield G. The treatment of varicose veins by injection and compression. *Practitioner* 1972; **208**: 809–17.

171 Georgiev M. Post-sclerotherapy hyperpigmentations: a one-year follow-up. *J Dermatol Surg Oncol* 1990; **16**: 608–10.

172 Galland R, Magee T, Lewis M. A survey of current attitudes of British and Irish vascular surgeons to venous sclerotherapy. *Eur J Endovasc Surg* 1998; **16**: 43–6.

173 Fullarton G, Calvert M. Intraluminal long saphenous vein stripping: a technique minimising perivenous tissue trauma. *Br J Surg* 1987; **74**: 255.

174 Cheung P, Lim S. Evaluation of the posterior approach for subfascial ligation of perforating veins. *Aust N Z J Surg* 1985; **55**: 369–72.

175 Johnson W, O'Hara E, Corey C, Widrich W, Nasbeth D. Venous stasis ulceration: effectiveness of subfacial ligation. *Arch Surg* 1985; **120**: 797–800.

176 Chester J, Taylor R. Hookers and French strippers: techniques for varicose vein surgery. *Br J Surg* 1990; **77**: 560–61.

177 Perry E. Avulsion versus dissection and ligation of the varicose short saphenous trunk. *Aust N Z J Surg* 1985; **55**: 61–3.

178 Large J. A conflict in vascular surgery. *Aust N Z J Surg* 1985; **55**: 376.

179 Corbett C, Jayakumar K. Clean up varicose veins surgery – use a tourniquet. *Ann R Coll Surg Engl* 1989; **71**: 57–8.

180 Goren G, Yellin A. Ambulatory stab evulsion phlebectomy for truncal varicose veins. *Am J Surg* 1991; **162**: 166–74.

181 Greaney M, Makin G. Operation for recurrent saphenofemoral incompetence using a medial approach to the saphenofemoral junction. *Br J Surg* 1985; **72**: 910–11.

182 Scott H, Scurr J. Varicose veins: optimum compression after surgery and sclerotherapy. *Ann R Coll Surg Engl* 1990; **720**: 148.

183 Campbell W, Ridler B. Varicose vein surgery and deep vein thrombosis. *Br J Surg* 1995; **82**: 1494–7.

184 Bishop C, Jarrett P. Outpatient varicose vein surgery under local anaesthesia. *Br J Surg* 1985; **73**: 821–2.

185 Hubner K. The out-patient therapy of trunk varicosis of the greater saphenous vein by means of ligation and sclerotherapy. *J Dermatol Surg Oncol* 1991; **17**: 818–23.

186 Schobinger R. Conservative varicose vein surgery – a modern necessity. *Helv Chir Acta* 1985; **52**: 7–9.

187 Sutherland J, Horsfall G. Anaesthesia for the outpatient treatment of hervia and varicose veins. *Lancet* 1961; **13**: 1044–6.

188 Phornphibulaya P, Limwongse K. Surgical treatment of varicose veins: a study of 123 patients. *J Med Assoc Thai* 1987; **70**: 563–6.

189 Almgren B, Eriksson I. Valvular incompetence in superficial, deep and perforator veins of limbs with varicose veins. *Acta Chir Scand* 1990; **156**: 69–74.

190 MacFarlane R, Godwin R, Barabas A. Are varicose veins and coronary artery bypass surgery compatible? *Lancet* 1985; **19**: 859.

191 Schraubman IG. The case for not stripping the long saphenous vein. *Br J Hosp Med* 1987; **37**: 178.

192 Large J. Surgical treatment of saphenous varices, with preservation of the main great saphenous trunk. *J Vasc Surg* 1985; **2**: 886–891.

193 Thromboembolic Risk Factors (THRIFT) Consensus Group. Risk of and prophylaxis for venous thromboembolism in hospital patients. *BMJ* 1992; **305**: 567–74.

194 European Consensus Statement. *Prevention of Venous Thromboembolism*. London: Med-Orion, 1992.

195 Lees T, Singh S, Beard J, Spencer P, Rigby C. Prospective audit of surgery for varicose veins. *Br J Surg* 1997; **84**: 44–6.

196 Turton E, Berridge D, McKenzie S, Scott D, Weston M. Optimising a varicose vein service to reduce recurrence. *Ann R Coll Surg Engl* 1997; **79**: 454.

197 Critchley G, Handa A, Maw A, Harvey A, Harvey M, Corbett C. Complications of varicose vein surgery. *Ann R Coll Surg Engl* 1997; **79**: 105–110.

198 Miller G, Lewis W, Sainsbury J, Macdonald R. Morbidity of varicose vein surgery: auditing the benefit of changing clinical practice. *Ann R Coll Surg Engl* 1996; **78**: 345–9.

199 Holme J, Skajaa K, Holme K. Incidence of lesions of the saphenous nerve after partial or complete stripping of the long saphenous vein. *Acta Chir Scand* 1990; **156**: 145–8.

200 Koyano K, Sakaguchi S. Selective stripping operation based on Doppler ultrasonic findings for primary varicose veins of the lower extremities. *Surgery* 1988; **103**: 615–19.

201 Holme J, Holme K, Sorensen L. The anatomic relationship between the long saphenous vein and the saphenous nerve. *Acta Chir Scand* 1988; **154**: 631–3.

202 Ramasastry S, Dick GO, Futrell J. Anatomy of the saphenous nerve: relevance to saphenous vein stripping. *Am Surg* 1987; **53**: 274–7.

203 Wilkinson G, Maclaren I. Long-term review of procedures for venous perforator insufficiency. *Surg Gynecol Obstet* 1986; **163**: 117–20.

204 Brighouse D, McQuillan P. An unusual complication of varicose vein surgery. *Anasthesia* 1990; **450**: 68–9.

205 O'Shaughnessy M, Rahall E, Walsh T, Given HF. Surgery in the treatment of varicose veins. *Ir Med J* 1989; **82**: 54–5.

206 Abramowitz I. Peripheral venous disorders – changing patterns in management. *S Afr J Surg* 1984; **22**: 211–22.

207 Campbell B. New treatments for varicose veins. *BMJ* 2002; **324**: 690–1.

208 Myers K. Updates in medicine: vascular surgery. *Med J Aust* 2002; **176**: 43.

209 Fassiadis N, Kiarnifard B, Holdstock J, Whiteley M. No recurrences of reflux following radio-frequency ablation of the long saphenous vein (VNUS closure) at one year. *Br J Surg* 2001; **88**: 49–50.

210 Kabnick L, Merchant R. Twelve and twenty-four month follow-up after endovascular obliteration of saphenous reflux: a report from the multi-centre registry. *JP* 2001; **1**: 17–24.

211 Navvaro L, Min R, Bone C. Endovenous laser: a new minimally invasive method of treatment for varicose veins – preliminary observations using an 810-nm diode laser. *Dermatol Surg* 2001; **27**: 117–22.

212 Min R, Zimmet S, Issacs M, Forrestal M. Endovenous laser treatment of the incompetent greater saphenous vein. *J Vasc Interv Radiol* 2001; **12**: 1167–71.

213 Tessari L, Cavezzi A, Frullini A. Preliminary experience with a new sclerosing foam in the treatment of varicose veins. *Dermatol Surg* 2001; **27**: 58–60.

214 Darke S. Can we tailor surgery to the venous abnormality? In: Ruckley C, Fowkes F, Bradbury A (eds). *Venous Disease: epidemiology, management and delivery of care.* London: Springer-Verlag, 1999, pp. 139–49.

215 Jones J, Nelson E. Skin grafting for venous leg ulcers (Cochrane Review). In: *The Cochrane Library.* Oxford: Update Software, 2000.

216 Apfelberg D, Smith T, Maser M, Lash H, White D. Study of three laser systems for treatment of superficial varicosities of the lower extremity. *Laser Surg Med* 1987; **7**: 219–23.

217 Lee P, Lask G. Telangiectasias of the legs. In: Lask G, Lowe N (eds). *Lasers in Cutaneous and Cosmetic Surgery.* Philadelphia, PA: Churchill Livingstone, 2000, pp. 47–51.

218 Flemming K, Cullum N. Laser therapy for venous ulcers (Cochrane Review). In: *The Cochrane Library.* Oxford: Update Software, 2000.

219 Liew S, Hubber D, Jeffs C. Day-only admission for varicose vein surgery. *Aust N Z J Surg* 1994; **64**: 688–91.

220 Price A, Makin G. The cost of day-case surgery for varicose veins. *Phlebology* 1991; **6**: 223–5.

221 Ruckley C, Cuthbertson C, Fenwick N, Prescott R, Garraway W. Day care after operations for hernia or varicose veins: a controlled trial. *Br J Surg* 1978; **65**: 456–9.

222 Innes-Williams D. *Guidelines for Day Case Surgery: commission on the provision of surgical services.* London: Royal College of Surgeons of England, 1985.

223 Royal College of Surgeons of England. *Guidelines for Day Case Surgery.* London: Royal College of Surgeons, 1992.

224 Lane IF, Bourantas NE. What is the scope of day care for venous surgery. In: Ruckley C, Fowkes F, Bradbury A (eds). *Venous Disease: epidemiology, management and delivery of care.* London: Springer-Verlag, 1999, pp. 216–21.

225 Brewster S, Nicholson S, Farndon J. The varicose vein waiting list: results of a validation exercise. *Ann R Coll Surg Engl* 1991; **73**: 223–6.

226 Gudex C, Williams A, Jourdan M *et al.* Prioritising waiting lists. *Health Trends* 1990; **22**: 103–8.

227 Grouden M, Sheelan S, Colgan M, Moore D, Shanik G. Results and lessons to be learned from a waiting list initiative. *Ir Med J* 1998; **91**: 90–1.

228 Sarin S, Shields D, Farrah J, Scurr J, Coleridge Smith P. Does venous function deteriorate in patients waiting for varicose vein surgery? *J R Soc Med* 1993; **86**: 21–3.

229 Ellison D, McCollum C. Hospital or community: how should leg ulcer care be provided? In: Ruckley C, Fowkes F, Bradbury A (eds). *Venous Disease: epidemiology, management and delivery of care*. London: Springer-Verlag, 1999, pp. 222–9.

230 Simon D, Freak L, Kinsella A *et al.* Community leg ulcer clinics: a comparative study in two health authorities. *BMJ* 1996; **312**: 1648–51.

231 Campbell B, Dimson S, Bickerton D. Which treatments would patients prefer for their varicose veins? *Ann R Coll Surg Engl* 1998; **80**: 212–14.

232 Nicholl J, Beeby N, Williams B. The role of the private sector in elective surgery in England and Wales. *BMJ* 1986; **298**: 243–7.

233 NHS Information Authority. *The National Schedule of Reference Costs*. London: Department of Health, 2000.

234 Basain H. Treatment for primary varicose veins. *Can Med Assoc J* 1985; **133**: 731.

235 Royle J. Recurrent varicose veins. *World J Surg* 1986; **10**: 944–53.

236 Starnes H, Vallance R, Hamilton D. Recurrent varicose veins: a radiological approach to investigation. *Clin Radiol* 1984; **35**: 95–9.

237 de Groot W. Failure in surgery of the long and short saphenous vein. *Phlebologie* 1988; **41**: 746–9.

238 Savolainen H, Toivio I, Mokka R. Recurrent varicose veins – is there a role for varicography? *Ann Chir Gynaecol* 1988; **77**: 70–3.

239 Papadikis K, Christodoulou C, Christopoulos D *et al.* Number and anatomical distribution of incompetent thigh perforating veins. *Br J Surg* 1989; **76**: 581–4.

240 Iafrati M, O'Donnell T, Kunkemueller A, Belkin M, Mackey W. Clinical examination, duplex ultrasound and plethysmography for varicose veins. *Phlebology* 1994; **9**: 114–18.

241 Partsch H. Besserbase und nicht besserbase chronische venöse Insuffizienz. *Vasa* 1980; **9**: 165–7.

242 Partsch H, Gisel I. Funktionelle Indikation zur Krampfadernoperation. *Wien Klin Wochenschr* 1977; **89**: 627–32.

243 Coleridge Smith P, Scurr J. Modern treatment of varicose veins. *Br J Surg* 1988; **75**: 725.

244 Vasdekis S, Clarke G, Hobbs J, Nicolaides A. Evaluation of non-invasive methods in the assessment of short saphenous vein termination. *Br J Surg* 1989; **76**: 929–32.

245 O'Donnel J, Burnand K, Clemenson G *et al.* Doppler examination vs clinical and phlebographic detection of the location of incompetent perforating veins. *Arch Surg* 1977; **112**: 31.

246 Szendro G, Nicolaides A, Zukowski A *et al.* Duplex scanning in the assessment of deep venous incompetence. *J Vasc Surg* 1986; **4**: 237–42.

247 Rosfors S, Bygdeman S, Nordstrom E. Assessment of deep venous incompetence: a prospective study comparing duplex scanning with descending phlebography. *Angiology* 1990; **41**: 463–8.

248 Welch HJ, Faliakou EC, McLaughlin RL, Umphrey SE, Belkin M, O'Donnel T. Comparison of descending phlebography with quantitative photoplethysmography and duplex quantitative valve closure time in assessing deep venous reflux. *J Vasc Surg* 1992; **16**: 913–20.

249 Baker S, Burnand K, Sommerville KM, Lea Thomas M, Wilson NM, Browse N. Comparison of venous reflux assessed by duplex scanning and descending phlebography in chronic venous disease. *Lancet* 1993; **341**: 400–3.

250 Bradbury A, Ruckley C. Foot volumetry can predict recurrent ulceration after subfascial ligation of perforators and saphenous ligation. *J Vasc Surg* 1993; **18**: 789–95.

251 Raju S, Fredericks R. Evaluation of methods for detecting venous reflux – perspectives in venous insufficiency. *Arch Surg* 1990; **125**: 1463–7.

252 Rutgers PA, Kitslaar P, Ermers E. Photoplethysmography in the diagnosis of superficial venous valvular incompetence. *Br J Surg* 1993; **80**: 351–3.

253 van Bemmelen P, van Ramshorst B, Eikelboom B. Photoplethysmography re-examined: lack of correlation with duplex scanning. *Surgery* 1992; **112**: 544–8.

254 Sarin S, Scurr J, Coleridge-Smith P. What do venous photoplethysmography tests measure? *J Dermatol Surg Oncol* 1992; **18**: 144–5.

255 Vayssairat M, Aubin B, Badina B *et al*. Placebo-controlled trial of naftazone in women with primary uncomplicated symptomatic varicose veins. *Phlebology* 1997; **12**: 17–20.

256 Pittler M, Ernst E. Horse chestnut seed extract for chronic venous insufficiency. A criteria-based systematic review. *Arch Dermatol* 1998; **134**: 1356–60.

257 Rigby KA, Palfreyman SJ, Beverly C, Michaels JA. Surgery for varicose veins: use of tourniquet (Cochrane Review). In: *The Cochrane Library. Issue 3*. Oxford: Update Software, 2003.

258 Dwerryhouse S, Davies B, Harradine K, Earnshaw J. Stripping the long saphenous vein reduces the rate of reoperation for recurrent varicose veins: five-year results of a randomized trial. *J Vasc Surg* 1999; **29**: 589–92.

259 Durkin M, Turton E, Scott D, Berridge D. A prospective randomised trial of PIN versus conventional stripping in varicose vein surgery. *Ann R Coll Surg Engl* 1999; **81**: 171–4.

260 Khan B, Khan S, Greaney M, Blair S. Prospective randomised trial comparing sequential avulsion with stripping of the long saphenous vein. *Br J Surg* 1996; **83**: 1559–62.

261 Campanello M, Hammarsten J, Forsberg C, Bernland P, Henrikson O, Jensen J. Standard stripping versus long saphenous vein-saving surgery for primary varicose veins: a prospective randomized study with the patients as their own controls. *Phlebology* 1996; **11**: 45–9.

262 Holme K, Matzen M, Bomberg A, Outzen S, Holme J. Partial or total stripping of the great saphenous vein: 5-year recurrence frequency and 3-year frequency of neural complications after partial and total stripping of the great saphenous vein. *Ugeskr-Laeger* 1996; **158**: 405–8.

263 MacKenzie R, Paisley A, Allan P, Lee A, Ruckley C, Bradbury A. The effect of long saphenous vein stripping on quality of life. *J Vasc Surg* 2002; **35**: 1197–203.

264 Chant A, Jones H, Weddell J. Varicose veins: a comparison of surgery and injection compression sclerotherapy. *Lancet* 1972; **2**: 1188–91.

265 Beresford S, Chant A, Jones H, Pichaud D, Weddell J. Varicose veins: a comparison of surgery and injection sclerotherapy. *Lancet* 1978; **29**: 921–4.

266 Hobbs J. Surgery and sclerotherapy in the treatment of varicose veins. *Arch Surg* 1974; **190**: 793–6.

267 Hobbs J. Surgery or sclerotherapy for varicose veins: 10-year results of a random study. In: Tesi M, Dormandy J (eds). *Superficial and Deep Venous Diseases of the Lower Limbs*. Torino: Edizioni Minerva Medica, 1984, pp. 243–6.

268 Jacobsen BH. The value of different forms of treatment for varicose veins. *Br J Surg* 1979; **66**: 72–6.

269 Einarsson E, Ekloff B, Neglen P. Sclerotherapy of surgery as treatment for varicose veins: a prospective randomized study. *Phlebology* 1993; **8**: 22–6.

270 Tisi P, Beverly CA. Injection sclerotherapy for varicose veins (Cochrane Review). In: *The Cochrane Library. Issue 3*. Oxford: Update Software, 2003.

271 Goldman M. Treatment of varicose and telangiectatic leg veins: double-blind prospective comparative trial between aethoxyskerol and sotradecol. *Dermatol Surg* 2002; **28**: 52–5.

272 Grondin L, Soriano J. Echosclerotherapy: a Canadian study. In: Raymond-Martimbeau P, Prescott R, Zummo M (ed.). *Phlébologie, 1992*. Paris: John Libbey Eurotext Ltd, 1992, pp. 828–31.

273 Schadeck M. Echosclérose de la grande saphène. *Phlebologie* 1993; **4**: 665–70.

274 Hill DA. *Complications of Open-Catheter Echosclerotherapy*. Atlanta, GA: 14th Annual Congress of the American College of Phlebology, 16 November 2000.

275 Nelson E, Cullum N, Jones J. Venous leg ulcers. In: Godlee F, Donald A, Barton S *et al.* (eds). *Clinical Evidence*. London: BMJ Publishing Group, 1999, pp. 792–801.

276 Peters J. A review of the factors influencing nonrecurrence of venous leg ulcers. *J Clin Nurs* 1998; **7**: 3–9.

277 Jull A, Waters J, Arroll B. Pentoxifylline for treating venous leg ulcers (Cochrane Review). In: *The Cochrane Library*. Oxford: Update Software, 2001.

278 Hansson C. The effects of cadexomer iodine paste in the treatment of venous leg ulcers compared with hydrocolloid dressing and paraffin gauze dressing. *Int J Dermatol* 1998; **37**: 390–6.

279 Cullum N, Nelson E, Fletcher A, Sheldon T. Compression bandages and stockings for venous leg ulcers (Cochrane Review). In: *The Cochrane Library*. Oxford: Update Software, 2000.

280 Nelson EA, Bell-Syer SEM, Cullum N. Compression for preventing recurrence of venous ulcers (Cochrane Review). In: *The Cochrane Library. Issue 4*. Oxford: Update Software, 2001.

281 Mani R, Vowden K, Nelson EA. Intermittent pneumatic compression for treating venous leg ulcers (Cochrane Review). In: *The Cochrane Library. Issue 4*. Oxford: Update Software, 2001.

282 Flemming K, Cullum N. Laser therapy for venous ulcers (Cochrane Review). In: *The Cochrane Library*. Oxford: Update Software, 2000.

283 Flemming K, Cullum N. Electromagnetic therapy for treating venous leg ulcers (Cochrane Review). In: *The Cochrane Library. Issue 4*. Oxford: Update Software, 2001.

284 Flemming K, Cullum N. Therapeutic ultrasound for venous leg ulcers. In: *The Cochrane Library. Issue 4*. Oxford: Update Software, 2001.

285 Morrell C, Walters S, Dixon S *et al.* Cost-effectiveness of community leg ulcer clinics: randomised controlled trial. *BMJ* 1998; **316**: 1487–91.

286 Piachaud D, Weddell JM. The economics of treating varicose veins. *Int J Epidemiol* 1972; **1**: 287–94.

287 Piachaud D, Weddell JM. Cost of treating varicose veins. *Lancet* 1972; **2**: 1191–2.

288 Harvey I, Webb M, Dowse J. Can a surgical treatment centre reduce waiting lists? Results of a natural experiment. *J Epidemiol Community Health* 1993; **47**: 373–6.

289 Smith F, Gwynn B. Direct-access surgery. *Ann R Coll Surg Engl* 1995; **77**: 94–6.

290 Garratt A, Macdonald L, Ruta D, Russell I, Buckingham J, Krukowski Z. Towards measurement of outcome for patients with varicose veins. *Qual Health Care* 1993; **2**: 5–10.

291 Baker D, Turnbull N, Pearson J, Makin G. How successful is varicose vein surgery? A patient satisfaction study following varicose vein surgery using the SF-36 health assessment questionnaire. *Eur J Vasc Endovasc Surg* 1995; **9**: 299–304.

292 Widmer LE. *Peripheral Venous Disorders. Prevalence and socio-medical importance: observations in 4529 apparently healthy persons. Basle Study III*. Bern: Hans Huber, 1978.

293 Bobek K, Cajzl L, Cepelak V, Slaisova V, Opatzny K, Barcal R. Etude de la frequence des malaides phlebologiques et de l'influence de quelques facteurs etiologiques. *Phlebologie* 1966; **19**: 217–30.

294 Recoules-Arche J. Importance du sedentarisme debout dans l'evolution et les complications des varices. *Angiologie* 1965; **17**: 17–20.

295 Berge T, Feldthusen U. Varicer hos kvinnor. Faktorer av betydelse for deras oppkommst. *Nord Med* 1963; **69**: 744–9.

296 Bradbury AW, MacKenzie RK, Burns P, Fegan C. Thrombophilia and chronic venous ulceration. *Eur J Vasc Endovasc Surg* 2002 **24**: 97–104.

297 Hollinsworth H. Venous leg ulcers. Part 1. Aetiology. *Prof Nurse* 1998; **13**(8): 553–8.

298 Ruckley CV, Fowkes FGR, Bradbury AW (eds). *Venous Disease: epidemiology, management and delivery of care*. London: Springer-Verlag, 1999.

12 Benign Prostatic Hyperplasia

David E Neal, Rebecca R Neal and Jenny Donovan

1 Summary

Introduction and statement of problem

Symptoms of lower urinary tract dysfunction are very common in ageing men and women. They are found in 25 to 40% of men aged over 60 years and are not synonymous with benign prostatic enlargement (BPE), which is found in about 30% of men aged over 60. Histological evidence of benign prostatic hyperplasia (BPH) is found in more than 50% of men aged over 60.

Serious complications can occur as a consequence of BPE. Of men in England undergoing prostatectomy, no fewer than 25% presented with acute retention of urine, which carries a twofold risk of death and complications compared with prostatectomy for symptoms alone. Chronic urinary retention can lead to renal failure and is an indication for 15% of prostatectomies carried out in England and Wales. Other complications such as bladder stone, infection and haematuria can also occur. Nevertheless, the majority (c. 60%) of men undergoing prostatectomy do so electively because of the presence of symptoms.

However, men undergoing prostatectomy (42 000 per year in England and Wales) represent the minority of those presenting to the general practitioner with lower urinary tract symptoms (LUTS). LUTS are frequently caused by pathology other than BPE, including ageing-related changes in the bladder smooth muscle (detrusor muscle), idiopathic detrusor instability (phasic changes in bladder pressure found during filling, giving rise to symptoms of urgency and frequency) and prostate cancer. The GPs need to develop protocols for referral and assessment with the local urological team.

In the past, most men in the UK with LUTS were not actively treated by their GP. Men either did not complain or were managed conservatively. The advent of new drugs (mainly α-adrenergic blockers and 5-α-reductase inhibitors) is more likely to increase the total proportion of men treated in primary care rather than reduce the rate of operative treatment (because of the relatively low baseline rates of operative treatment in the UK, which is often performed for complicated BPE). Prescriptions for α-adrenergic blockers have increased from 812 400 per annum in 1995 to 1 207 300 per annum in 1997, whereas prescriptions for finasteride (a 5-α-reductase inhibitor) have been relatively constant (from 279 200 per annum in 1995 to 299 100 per annum in 1997).

Within hospitals, a number of new technologies have been introduced, mainly in efforts to decrease the need for inpatient beds. However, in most instances such new technology has not been compared in large randomised trials with conventional treatments. Many men treated with such capital expensive new technology may also subsequently need conventional treatment.

Patients needing operative treatment are usually classified under the following codes:

- ICD 10   general symptoms: N320a, N40a, N320b, R39, N40b
                         retention: R33a, R33b, R33c, R33d, R33e R33f
                         BPH: N40c, D291.
- Read codes: general symptoms: X30Nx, X30O0, K160, 1AA, X30Nz
                         retention: 1A32, X30O4, X30O5, X30O6, X30O7, X30O8
                         BPH: K20, B7C2.

Operative procedures on the prostate done for BPE include the following codes:

- OPCS4:   M619, M612, M613, M641, M704, M678b, M678e, M678d, M652a, Y118, M672, M671,
                        M662, M658a, M651b, M651a, M651c, M678a, M658b.
- Read codes: 7B360 (*Note*: this is radical prostatectomy, usually done for cancer), 7B361, 7B362,
                        7B372, 7B380, 7B3C4, X30FN, 7B3B5, 7B3B7, 7B3B8, 7B391, X30FP, 7B3B6 (qual),
                        7B360, 7B3A1, 7B393, 7B390, X30FK, Xa40r (qual), X30FM, X30FL.
- HRG codes: L29, L30, L31, L32.

Sub-categories of lower urinary tract symptoms (LUTS) and complications caused by benign prostatic enlargement (BPE)

Men presenting with LUTS can be classified according to the severity of symptoms and the degree of problems they experience (mild, moderate or severe). They can also be classified according to whether they have symptoms alone or complications which require more urgent treatment. The main subgroups are:

1   symptomatic categories based on severity and on degree of problems:
    - severe
    - moderate
    - mild
2   complicated BPE:
    - acute retention
    - chronic retention
    - chronic sepsis and bladder stones.

The prevalence of LUTS

Histological BPH is very common, being found histologically in more than 50% (500/1000) of men aged more than 60 years. Moderate to severe LUTS (roughly equivalent to those in men undergoing prostatectomy) are found in the community in 15 to 35% (*c.* 300/1000) of men aged more than 60 years. In general, many men in the UK have accepted such symptoms as being associated with ageing and have not consulted their GP. This is changing, however, because of publicity about men's health, worries about prostate cancer, and the advent of new drugs and new treatment methods (*see* Appendix 1), which are likely to increase the total proportion of men with symptoms who are treated.

Services and treatments available and cost

Costs are based on mid-1998 figures. Men with LUTS are assessed by their GP before referral to the urologist. Increasingly, assessment in primary care might include a more thorough assessment, which could involve measurement of urinary flow rates.

Non-operative treatment includes 'watchful waiting' or initial treatment with α-adrenergic blockers or finasteride.

Investigations in hospital include measurement of flow rates and, in some cases, bladder pressure tests (urodynamics) to determine whether symptoms are caused by prostatic enlargement. Such visits would cost a total of £250 to £300 (including tests and subsequent reattendance).

Increasingly, hospitals or GPs are setting up nurse-led prostate assessment clinics which can provide easy access to a full history, clinical examination, flow rates, prostate assessment and, subsequently, feedback to GPs. At first sight, these clinics would seem likely to be cost-effective, but they have not been fully assessed, nor have they been fully costed.

Conventional surgical treatment includes transurethral resection of the prostate (TURP), bladder neck incision (BNI) or open operation. These operations cost purchasers in the order of £1600–1800, though the real costs may well be higher.

Unfit men who require treatment for retention may be treated by permanent indwelling catheterisation, which carries disposable and nursing costs, which may be high, since the treatment may be continued for long periods.

New technologies include the use of indwelling urethral stents (for unfit men who might have been treated previously by indwelling urethral catheterisation), balloon dilatation, microwave energy, ultrasound therapy, laser treatments and other new devices.

Effectiveness and cost-effectiveness of services

Improvements are seen after treatment with placebo, but α-adrenergic blockers are more effective than placebo and currently cost about £23 per month (c. £275 per annum). Finasteride may take up to 6 months to produce maximum benefit and costs £25 per month (£300 per annum). Prescriptions for these agents amounted to 1.5 million per annum in 1997, costing the NHS about £37 000 000. Men who respond to drug treatment may require long-term treatment, which will not totally prevent the need for prostatectomy. Following drug treatment the rates of elective prostatectomy are 4.2% in men treated with finasteride compared with 6.5% in men treated with placebo, and the rates of urinary retention were 1.1% in men treated with finasteride compared with 2.7% in men treated with placebo. Compared with placebo, about 40% of men feel that symptoms improve, but the average degree of improvement is relatively small (symptom scores improve by about 2/35 points more than placebo [17/35 to 14/35] and flow rates improve by about 1.5 ml/s more than placebo [9 to 11 ml/s]). The evidence from drug trials is based on large randomised clinical trials (I-1 evidence), but tight inclusion criteria mean that many men presenting with symptoms would have been excluded from such trials. Drugs and placebo have measurable clinical effects.

Operative treatment by transurethral prostatectomy or open retropubic prostatectomy produces the best improvement, a good outcome being found in about 80% of men (a doubling of flow rates [9 to 18 ml/s] and a marked reduction in symptom scores [from 17/35 to 4/35]), but there are side-effects. One in 1000 men dies as a result of the operation and about 5–10% develop complications such as urinary infection. After eight years, 15% have undergone a repeat operation. The evidence about TURP is based largely on non-randomised trials (II-1), but in most cases has included all patients. The procedure has a moderate to strong beneficial effect (depending on the degree of problems or the presence of complications owing to BPE), but carries risks of complications.

So far as new technologies are concerned, most of these treatments have been assessed in open-phase I/II studies, which have shown a good safety profile and measurable to moderate effects on symptoms, but which have not as yet demonstrated long-term effectiveness. The need for large-scale, long-term randomised trials before such treatments are accepted into the NHS would seem to be obvious. The disposable costs for some of these treatments are up to £500 and the capital costs are also high, at up to £180 000. Some can be performed as a day-case procedure without general anaesthesia, but total NHS costs for many of these treatments have not been fully worked out. Such new technologies can be very capital expensive and indeed often carry recurrent costs for special catheters or probes. The degree of improvement observed is less than that found after TURP. In total, 60% of men report improvement, flow rates change from 9 to 14 ml/s and symptom scores decrease from 17/35 to 8/35. The duration of benefit and the likely reoperation rates are unknown.

Recommendations and models of care

Easy access to an informed GP for all men with LUTS seems to be the key. Initial assessment should be carried out by the GP. Nurse-led prostate assessment clinics staffed by specially trained nurses and overseen by a consultant or committed interested GP might in the future offer an intermediate form of assessment, which may make urology outpatient visits more effective. If GPs are going to manage men with LUTS in primary care by means of drug treatment, they should be confident in their own technique of rectal examination so that they can exclude locally advanced prostate cancer, which can also be a cause of symptoms. Access to a general urology clinic should also be available. Between 150 and 250 per 100 000 men aged over 60 have significant symptoms.

The evidence suggests that men with mild or moderate symptoms without evidence of complications or prostate cancer can be managed by 'watchful waiting'. The evidence also suggests that α-adrenergic blockers and finasteride are more effective than placebo treatments and that in some trials finasteride is less effective than α-blockers. Long-term data have shown that men who have responded to finasteride in the short term and who are kept on long-term treatment have fewer admissions with acute retention or for prostatectomy. However, the number of operations prevented is relatively low. Long-term drug treatment may be provided in primary care.

Men seen in outpatient clinics should undergo clinical history taking and examination; renal function should be assessed and urinary infection and diabetes should be excluded. There is no need for routine intravenous urography or upper tract imaging, but flow rates should be measured and urodynamic studies should be available for selected patients.

Men with acute retention require urgent catheterisation and either urgent admission or urgent assessment by the urologist. Men with chronic retention require urgent outpatient assessment; those with renal impairment need urgent admission. Men with severe symptoms or problems should be referred to the urologist.

Age-specific prostatectomy rates vary widely on a district, regional and international scale. The degree of uncertainty about indications and benefit makes it difficult to provide a recommendation of an optimum rate for prostatectomy. The rate is currently 100 per 100 000 total population (about 10% of the general population are men aged over 60 years).

Outcome measures, audit information and research needs

Treatment is provided for symptoms so the best outcome measures are provided in terms of symptom relief (often measured by specific scores). Objective measures that should be available easily include flow rates and residual urine volumes.

Conventional operative management that is of proven effectiveness includes TURP, BNI and open prostatectomy. New technologies should be used only if they have been or are being formally assessed in the context of a randomised clinical trial.

TURP has been shown to be an effective treatment for approximately 70–80% of men receiving it. The reasons for a poor outcome among the remaining 20–30% may well be due to the fact that not all men with LUTS have bladder outlet obstruction. TURP is likely to be less effective for problems such as detrusor instability or detrusor failure. The surgical treatment of LUTS and the complications of BPE must be viewed within the wider context of the urinary problems of the ageing male and the increasing availability of alternative new technologies.

Audit of TURP has been carried out nationally by the Royal College of Surgeons of England and the British Association of Urological Surgeons. These data have shown, in general, that outcomes have been good, comparable to those published by specialised centres. However, some areas of concern were noted. Some men were not investigated by flow rate assessment, and complications after discharge remain relatively frequent.

Future research needs include good comparative studies of new technologies vs. conventional operative treatments, new technologies vs. drug treatment, and research into the effectiveness and cost-effectiveness of management in primary care.

2 Introduction and statement of the problem

The broad questions that are addressed in this chapter include the following.

- How do men with lower urinary tract symptoms (LUTS) or the complications of benign prostatic enlargement (BPE) present and what is the prevalence of the problem?
- How should men be assessed and managed? What is the role of the general practitioner and what magnitude of service should be provided?
- What is the role of drug treatment?
- What is the role of conventional surgical treatment (prostatectomy) compared with new technology?
- What are the areas of future research needs?
- Is it possible to determine the magnitude of service provision from current data?

The management of men with LUTS comprises a significant proportion of the urologist's workload and the prevalence of benign prostatic hyperplasia (BPH) increases with advancing age.[1–11] However, there is a problem of definition. Recent classifications have emphasised the differences between the following:

- the presence of lower urinary tract symptoms, which may be caused by many problems other than the prostate
- the presence of histological evidence of BPH, which precedes enlargement of the prostate
- the presence of BPE
- urodynamic evidence of bladder outlet obstruction (BOO).

The aetiology of histological benign prostatic hyperplasia

The aetiology of BPH leading to BPE is unknown, but is likely to have an endocrine basis[12,13] in that dihydrotestosterone and oestrogen are essential to the formation of BPH – at least in the dog. Other factors that have been described (but not proven) as positively associated include the intake of dietary fat, sexual activity, alcohol, genetic factors,[2–14] age, a lower socio-economic group, Jewish ethnicity, current non-smoking,[11] daily meat and milk consumption,[15] age, low body mass index, urine pH > 5, and history of kidney X-ray and tuberculosis.[16]

The natural history of lower urinary tract symptoms

The natural history of LUTS is becoming somewhat clearer as some large-scale, long-term community epidemiological studies have now been performed, though in the past investigators have not distinguished clearly between LUTS (symptoms), prostatic enlargement (BPE) and outlet obstruction (BOO). Symptoms and prostatic enlargement both become more common with increasing age. The normal prostate is estimated to weigh 20 (± 6) g at 21–30 years and to remain that size unless BPH develops.[17] By the age of 40 years, histological evidence of BPH is found in 8% of men. This rises to about 90% over the age of 80 years (see Table 1, and Table 2 opposite). The early phase of the development of BPH seems to be the most rapid, with a doubling time of 4.5 years for weight between the ages of 31 and 50 years, compared with a doubling time of 10 years between 51 and 70 years of age.[17] The literature suggests that at present a 40-year-old man has about a 20–30% chance of undergoing an operation for LUTS in his lifetime (this has risen from the one in ten chance quoted in the 1970s because of an increase in the numbers of prostatectomies undertaken and the increase in life expectancy).[2,11,18] As indicated above, a 55-year-old man in England has a 25% chance of having a prostatectomy in his lifetime, assuming current NHS operation rates. Studies by Black and the Olmsted County research group have shown that about 25% of men in the community have moderate or severe symptoms, that these symptoms impact significantly on quality of life, and that men with more severe symptoms and problems are more likely to consult a urologist.[19–24]

Table 1: Age-specific prevalence rates (per 10 000) for autopsy evidence of BPH.

Study population	Age (years)					
	< 41	41–50	51–60	61–70	71–80	> 80
Lytton* (n = 1,075)	800	2,300	4,200	7,100	8,200	8,800
Isaacs and Coffey†						
Microscopic BPH	800	2,200	4,200	6,200	7,900	9,000
Barry‡	800	2,200	4,100	7,000	8,000	8,800
Isaacs and Coffey§ macroscopic BPH	200	800	2,100	3,500	4,400	5,300
Lytton¶ gross histology (n = 2,632)	–	–	2,360	3,730	3,910	–

* Lytton:[2] figures based on an average of five autopsy studies.
† Isaacs and Coffey:[3] figures based on an average of six studies in Europe, Asia, and approximated from a graph of composite averages.
‡ Barry:[4] figures taken from a graph of a meta-analysis of five autopsy studies of histologic BPH.
§ Isaacs and Coffey:[3] figures based on an average of three studies in England and the USA.
¶ Lytton:[5] based on a study of 2632 autopsies on males over 50 years, using the criteria of gross morphology and histology of sections.

Table 2: Age-specific prevalence rates (per 10 000) for clinical evidence of BPH.

Study population	Age (years)						
	⩽ 54	55–59	60–64	65–69	70–74	75–79	⩾ 80
Watanabe stage 1* (*n* = 180/1,121)	270	1,270	1,060	1,580	1,700	2,410	4,170
Watanabe stage 2 (*n* = 52/1,121)	0	70	380	490	610	620	1,250
Watanabe stages 1 + 2 (*n* = 232/1,121)	270	1,340	1,440	2,070	2,310	3,030	5,420
Gofin† (*n* = 217)	–	–	–	2,800	4,570	5,950‡	–
Lytton§ (*n* = 6,975)	800	2,000	–	3,500	–	4,290	–
Lytton¶ (*n* = 827)	260	1,050	–	3,910	–	3,670	1,110
Isaacs and Coffey**	20	1,800	–	830	–	1,900	2,500
Garraway *et al.*††	1,380	2,370	–	4,300	–	4,000	–

* Watanabe[6] used figures taken from a mass screening programme in Japan. BPH stage 1 is an indication for drug administration; stage 2 is an indication for surgery. The combination of stages 1 and 2 gives a prevalence of clinical BPH. Watanabe also cited overall prevalence rates of 18.6% for BPH stage 1, and 5.0% for BPH stage 2, with an average age of 65.2 years, out of a sample of 4,885 screened in 1975–85.

† Gofin[7] studied the health status of 217 elderly men living in Jerusalem. Probable prostatic hyperplasia was inferred from the presence of at least three of the following: frequency of micturition, nocturia, hesitancy, weak stream, terminal dribbling, self-reported prostatectomy.

‡ All over 75 years.

§ Lytton:[5] figures based on men with palpable prostatic enlargement per rectum, derived from 6,975 life insurance examinations.

¶ Lytton:[8] figures derived from records of patients treated in New Haven hospitals for benign prostatic obstruction between 1953 and 1961 (residual urine of more than 75 ml, 82%; acute retention or catheter indwelling, 15%).

** Isaacs and Coffey[3] used the adjusted figures of Lytton *et al.*[8]

†† Garraway *et al.*:[9] age groups specified were 40–49, 50–59, 60–69, 70–79 years. BPH was defined as enlargement of the prostate gland of equivalent weight > 20 g in the presence of symptoms of urinary dysfunction and/or urinary peak flow rate < 15 ml/s and without evidence of malignancy.

Though pathological changes in the prostate can begin as early as the third or fourth decade, symptoms do not usually occur until men are aged 50 years or more.[2] The growth of the prostate gland does not always result in symptomatic problems. Indeed, there is no strong relationship between the size of the gland and obstructive (voiding) symptoms.[6,25,26]

LUTS can be caused by outlet obstruction that is produced by BPE. However, they can also be caused by:

- ageing-related smooth muscle dysfunction
- idiopathic detrusor instability
- neurological disorders such as stroke, cerebrovascular insufficiency and previous transient ischaemic attacks, Parkinson's disease and dementias.

BOO may be caused by BPE or other problems, such as bladder neck dyssynergia. In BOO, there is an increase in outlet resistance, but for some time the bladder is able to increase detrusor contraction and maintain flow under higher pressures.[27] This has been termed 'silent prostatism' and can occur for considerable lengths of time[28,32] If the obstruction continues, detrusor function is affected and symptoms begin to develop. In some men, residual urine is retained, increasing the risk of chronic retention.[27] The cause of acute urinary retention is not known, and it is not possible to predict accurately who will develop acute urinary retention.[29] Men with worse symptoms, who have larger prostates (> 40 g) and who are older (> 70 years) are at increased risk.[30] Acute retention is associated with significantly increased morbidity following TURP.[31]

Studies evaluating drug therapies have reported high levels of spontaneous symptomatic improvement and marked placebo effects.[32–35] However, long-term studies of men who responded well in the short term to finasteride have found that men treated with placebo were significantly more likely to develop retention and severe symptoms requiring prostatectomy.

Symptoms (LUTS)

As mentioned above, symptoms may have a number of causes other than enlargement of the prostate and there are no symptoms that are specific for BPE or BOO.[35] In the past, such symptoms were known as 'prostatism' and were classified into obstructive (now known as voiding) and irritative (now known as storage).[14,36]

Voiding (obstructive) symptoms

These include the following.

- **Hesitancy:** This is a sensation of delay in the onset of micturition. It is the time taken from the initiation of micturition to the commencement of flow. It may last from a few seconds to several minutes. It is a reflection of the time required by the detrusor muscle to generate enough pressure to overcome bladder outlet resistance.[37] It can also be produced by a weak detrusor muscle.
- **Poor urinary stream and/or straining:** Obstruction caused by BPE may develop slowly and so flow changes may occur gradually or even go unnoticed. A measured flow rate of < 10 ml/s is highly suggestive of bladder outlet obstruction, but can also be produced by a weak detrusor muscle.[27,37,38]
- **Sensation of incomplete bladder emptying:** This usually signals the development of residual urine as the bladder is unable to produce enough pressure to overcome the outlet resistance. Similar symptoms, however, can be produced by detrusor instability because the patient's bladder is sensitive to small increases in bladder volume.
- **Terminal and post-micturition dribbling:** At the end of normal voiding, flow ends abruptly. In the obstructed male, the flow may continue at a low level for some time (terminal dribbling).[27] In post-micturition dribbling, the patient thinks voiding is over, only to experience a small leakage some seconds or minutes later, usually resulting in embarrassing staining of clothes. However, these symptoms are not significantly associated with bladder outlet obstruction and may be caused simply by ageing-related weakness in the bulbo-spongiosus muscle, which empties the urethra.
- **Prolonged voiding time:** As the force of the stream is reduced, it takes the obstructed patient longer to void. This may develop gradually or rapidly.
- **Urinary retention:** Some men develop urinary retention. The conventional view is that as obstruction increases and the detrusor becomes less able to compensate, urinary retention can occur. It takes two major forms:
  - *acute retention*: it is commonly held that acute retention requires immediate catheterisation and surgery, but some believe that initial catheterisation should be followed by observing the patient without a catheter, and then making the decision as to whether or not to operate.[39] Acute retention is the reason given for prostatectomy in 20% of men undergoing operation.[27,40]

- *chronic retention*: this can occur over a long period of time asymptomatically, where urine remains uninfected and under low pressure. Patients may have an unnoticed, painless, palpable bladder. Alternatively, they may present with recurrent urinary infections, irritative symptoms (*see* below) or overflow incontinence as the amount of residual urine finally equals bladder capacity, or with more serious symptoms of renal impairment such as nausea, malaise, vomiting and polyuria.[27,41]

Storage (irritative) symptoms

Irritative symptoms are caused when the detrusor becomes unstable and unable to cope with the increased workload caused by obstruction.[14,42] Men with urge incontinence may have increased risk of underlying detrusor instability, which may persist following operations in about 50% of cases.[43]

- **Frequency:** Normal daytime frequency is taken to be less than seven times per day, depending on fluid intake.[27] More frequent micturition can be caused by BPE and BOO producing a small-capacity, irritable bladder, sometimes with associated detrusor instability. In some cases, small volumes of urine have to be voided at frequent intervals, causing some social embarrassment.
- **Nocturia:** This is the sensation of being awoken during sleep by the desire to void. With ageing, nocturia becomes more likely, but in the obstructed male it can become common enough to seriously affect sleeping. As residual urine increases, the frequency of nocturia increases. The use of diuretics or an ageing-related reversal of the normal diurnal rhythm of urinary concentration can produce nocturia.
- **Urgency:** This is the urgent desire to void, usually accompanied by the fear of impending leakage. It is one of the classical symptoms of prostatism, particularly in association with frequency and nocturia. It is commonly associated with idiopathic detrusor instability.
- **Urge incontinence:** This is caused by severe instability, which may be produced by bladder outlet obstruction, but is more likely to be due to idiopathic detrusor instability.
- **Pain:** This is not a symptom of BPE, but may accompany urinary retention, bladder conditions such as bladder stone, and urinary tract infections, some of which may be associated with BPE.

Many of the symptoms associated with BPE are also associated simply with increasing age, and this further complicates the diagnosis of the condition. The evidence that has been collected suggests that large numbers of men may be prepared to accept symptoms of prostatism without seeking help, and that there may also be large numbers of men in the community with undisclosed symptoms.[44]

3 Sub-categories of lower urinary tract symptoms (LUTS) and complications caused by benign prostatic enlargement (BPE)

The clinically important groups or sub-categories of men with LUTS and complications of BPE are based on different use of resources, either because they require more investigation or because they have increased risks of complications and therefore increased lengths of stay.

- Men presenting with straightforward LUTS (60% of men presenting to the urological clinic).
- Men presenting with mixed symptoms (e.g. LUTS plus previous stroke or Parkinson's disease; 20% of men presenting to the clinic).
- Men presenting with retention (25–45% of men who have operations in the UK).
- Men aged over 75 years (30% of men presenting to the clinic).

Men presenting with acute or chronic retention are older and less fit than men presenting for elective prostatectomy. They have significantly longer stays in hospital and have increased rates of post-operative complications and of death.[40]

4 The prevalence of LUTS

Estimates of the prevalence of moderate or severe LUTS are immensely variable, ranging from 5% to 43% in the 65–69 years male age group, depending on the criteria chosen (*see* Table 2). As pointed out above, the term BPH has in the past been used to define benign enlargement of the prostate gland (BPE), the presence of symptoms (LUTS) or the need for drugs or surgery.

Autopsy evidence for histological BPH

Autopsy studies have looked at microscopic and macroscopic lesions in prostate glands.[3] Only a small proportion of men with microscopic lesions will have symptoms of urinary outlet obstruction. Over the age of 80 years, approximately 90% of men will have microscopic histological lesions in their prostates, compared with between 40% and 50% having gross, macroscopic changes (*see* Table 1).

Population survey data

Attempts have been made to measure the prevalence of LUTS (*see* Table 2), but each study employed different definitions, making comparisons difficult. These definitions range from the presence of at least three classic symptoms to a strong indication for surgery. A population survey published in 1991 has suggested that the prevalence of LUTS is higher than has been reported in clinical retrospective and necropsy studies.[9] Certainly the prevalence of LUTS is far higher than historical rates of surgery.[19–24]

The incidence of LUTS and complications of BPE

There is some confusion in the literature about incidence and prevalence.[5] Incidence rates suffer from similar problems of definition, but they are also often based on small samples. Incidence rates of LUTS vary between 5% and 7% per annum in the 65–69 years age group (*see* Table 3). Prostatectomy rates vary between 0.5% and 1.7% per annum (*see* Table 4). The presence of moderate or severe LUTS indicates that there is a huge pool of need not being satisfied. These issues have not been clearly addressed in the literature. Existing evidence about the prevalence and incidence of LUTS is thus fraught with uncertainty. Only those studies that reflect the number of new cases per annum of LUTS registered in a given population are considered here. As with prevalence rates, different authors employ different criteria for determining the presence of LUTS and complications of BPH, and their choices of criteria are not always clear. Rates of follow-up are not always specified. In both the studies cited in Table 3, the process of the 'clinical diagnosis' was not made explicit.

Table 3: Age-specific incidence rates of BPH per 10 000 per annum.

Study population	Age (years)								
	40–44	45–49	50–54	55–59	60–64	65–69	70–74	75–79	>79
Arrighi et al.*	95.3	66	158	228	529	523	750	1,080	1,590
Glynn et al.† (all men)	37	94	–	313	–	513	–	592	–
Jewish†	–	107	–	443	–	715	–	293	–
Not Jewish†	–	91	–	302	–	476	–	533	–

* Arrighi et al.:[10] figures taken from the Baltimore Longitudinal Study of Aging established in 1958. Based on 1057 men in the study who did not have a history of prostatectomy or prostate cancer upon entry to the study and who had at least one follow-up visit beyond the baseline data.

† Glynn et al.:[11] figures taken from the Normative Aging Study, based on 2037 men with no surgical treatment for BPH before entry to the study (between 1961 and 1970) to the last examination in 1982.

Table 4: Age-standardised prostatectomy rates, per 10 000 per annum.[45]

Country	Operation rate
England and Wales	9
Norway	9
USA	30
Australia	9

Prevalence and incidence of LUTS and complications of BPE in different population groups

Given the uncertainties mentioned above, it is not surprising that the evidence about prevalence and incidence of LUTS and complications of BPE among different population groups is difficult to interpret,[2,11,45] but on the whole, sample sizes have been small and many important factors such as age, place of birth, socio-economic factors and availability of health services have been ignored or glossed over. There are, however, two findings that have repeatedly emerged from these studies: first, that men of Caucasian origin have much higher incidence and treatment rates than men of Far Eastern/Southern Asian origin[1,2,5]; and secondly, that Jewish men tend to have much higher rates than Protestant or Catholic men[8,11] (see Tables 5 to 7 overleaf).

Table 5: Age-specific prostatectomy rates per 10 000 per annum.

Study population	Age (years)								
	40–44	45–49	50–54	55–59	60–64	65–69	70–74	75–79	⩾80
Surgery*	15.9	13.2	29.2	39.9	142.0	136.0	145.0	244.0	368.0
Surgery† (all men)	–	2.0	–	40.7	–	120.8	–	193.5	–
Jewish†	–	–	–	100.0	–	176.0	–	482.0	–
Not Jewish	–	3.0	–	34.0	–	117.0	–	172.0	–
Surgery‡	–	2.0	–	12.0	–	57.0	–	100.0	109.0

* Arrighi *et al.*:[10] figures taken from the Baltimore Longitudinal Study of Aging established in 1958. Based on 1057 men in the study who did not have a history of prostatectomy or prostate cancer upon entry to the study and who had at least one follow-up visit beyond the baseline data.
† Glynn *et al.*:[11] figures taken from the Normative Aging Study, based on 2037 men with no surgical treatment for BPH before entry to the study (between 1961 and 1970) to the last examination in 1982.
‡ Lytton *et al.*:[8] based on data for men undergoing prostatectomy in three New Haven hospitals between 1953 and 1961.

Table 6: Median age (interquartile range) of men undergoing prostatectomy.[8,10,11]

Operation	Method of admission			
	Elective		Emergency	
	n	Age (range) in years	n	Age (range) in years
TURP	20,692	70 (65–76)	6,773	74 (67–79)
Open	1,449	72 (67–77)	773	74 (68–79)

Table 7: Age of men undergoing elective prostatectomy.[8,10,11]

Age group (years)	TURP	Open prostatectomy
⩽ 54	702	20
55–64	4,204	207
65–74	8,632	626
75–84	5,660	497
⩾ 85	675	46

The analysis of treatment variations

There is variation in treatment rates.[45] Explanations for treatment variations are of five broad types: misleading data, differing distributions of disease, differing availability of resources, differing patterns of therapeutic choice, and differing patient perceptions.

Data deficiencies

Deficiencies in the data have been detailed. They include problems of ascertainment, comparability, consistency and comprehensiveness.

Differing distributions of disease

There is no current evidence that age-standardised rates of LUTS and complications of BPE and BOO are likely to differ markedly between differing district populations, e.g. according to ethnic composition. It may be that this simply reflects inadequate information for the UK. For instance, areas with higher Jewish populations may have increased rates, as may areas with more men of Afro-Caribbean origin.

Differing availability of resources

Supply factors are known to influence many treatment rates. Demand for hospital treatments is a complex matter which compounds disease levels, public expectations and referral patterns. One proxy for demand is the waiting list. There is no relationship between median waiting times and prostatectomy rates in district health authorities (now primary care trusts [PCTs]) according to 1989–90 HES data (correlation coefficient $= 0.03$, $p = 0.7$ for TURPs; correlation coefficient $= -0.04$, $p = 0.6$ for open operations).[46]

Differing therapeutic choice

The lack of consensus surrounding definitions of the significance of LUTS and the complications of BPE and its treatments suggests that a large proportion of the variation in surgical rates may be caused by the different therapeutic choices open to individual surgeons. The incomplete explanation of treatment variations under the first three headings supports the contention that differing therapeutic choice is a key factor. This view also emerges from an audit of urological practice[47] and a study of regional variations in Denmark.[48]

Differing patient perceptions

There have not been many studies examining the perceptions of individual men concerning their requirement for treatment of urinary symptoms. It has been shown in a population study published in 1991 that a large proportion of men in the community aged between 40 and 79 years experience urinary symptoms without the desire for treatment.[9] Variations in treatment rates are likely to occur as a result of the different levels of knowledge in the community about treatments for LUTS, and the resulting variability in numbers attending GPs about urinary problems. It is also likely that the differing referral patterns of GPs will contribute to treatment variations. Recent attention of the media to 'men's health' is likely to increase GP consultations and increase referral rates to a urologist.

Incidence of LUTS and complications of BPH according to sub-categories

These are effectively described in Tables 2, 5, 6 and 7. It can be noted for instance that the incidence of symptoms (LUTS) varies according to age. In general in the UK, 10% of the population are men aged between 50 and 65. About 1000/10 000 of this age group (10%) have significant symptoms compared with about 35% of men aged over 65. The incidence of urinary retention is strongly related to age, the size of the prostate and the severity of LUTS, older men (> 70 years) with large prostates (> 40 g) and severe LUTS being at greatest risk. Likewise the incidence of surgery is strongly related to age (*see* Tables 5 to 7). Emergency operations (mainly for retention) are carried out on 25% of men undergoing prostatectomy and occur mostly in older men.

5 Services and treatments available and costs

These include services provided by primary care, urologists in secondary care, drug costs, infrastructure costs and fixed costs in hospitals. The total spend for urological care is not freely available. Information available from informal sources suggests that there are around 100 urological finished consultant episodes (FCEs) per year per 10 000 population (1%). The actual cost of this would be of the order of £80 000 per 10 000 population. Drug costs for LUTS are outlined below. Hospital costs are outlined later, but would be of the order of £23 000 to £37 000 per 10 000 population. One question is whether changing rates of referral and increased management with drug treatment will alter these costs. These effects are modelled later, but the difficulty is the relatively low baseline provision of prostatectomy in the UK, which is heavily predicated on emergency admission with retention. It is therefore likely that increased management of men with LUTS in the community will tap the unmet need rather than markedly reduce the rates of referral and prostatectomy.

The first point of contact for men with symptoms is the GP. The GP will be supported by a range of nursing and professions allied to medicine. Until recently there were few active drugs available for GPs and most men presented late, requiring surgical treatment. In general, therefore, the GP had to decide whether the patient's symptoms and signs warranted reassurance or referral to the urologist at the local district hospital.

Now, however, diagnostic facilities such as ultrasound scanning and flow rate measurement may be available to the GP either locally in the practice or at an open-access clinic in the hospital. Moreover, a variety of drug treatments are now available, including α-adrenergic-blocking agents and 5-α-reductase inhibitors. The GP may wish to assess the patient locally, treat the patient and refer to a urologist only those patients whom they consider require an operation. Another option would be to refer all patients, but ask the urologist to refer back those patients requiring reassurance or drug treatment. Many GPs have not had urological training so may not feel confident about excluding prostate cancer or chronic retention or assessing LUTS and BPE.

Services available at the local hospital will be access to outpatient urological clinics, flow rate tests and other investigations. Increasingly 'hub-and-spoke' services are being set up between smaller local hospitals and larger specialist hospitals (there are models in Newcastle, Middlesbrough and Stockport), which will involve men being assessed locally, but which may involve them having their operation centrally.

None of these different models of assessing and managing men have been fully costed, nor have they been tested for cost-effectiveness of service provision.

The diagnosis of LUTS, BPE, BOO and complications

Diagnosis of BPE is based on clinical history, rectal palpation of the prostate, investigations to search for urinary infection and kidney damage, and some form of urinary flow measurement.[27,42,49] There is no specific symptom pattern that is indicative of BOO – the symptoms of bladder outlet obstruction are the same irrespective of cause[26] – and so the urologist has to eliminate possible malignancies, neurological problems, urethral strictures and calculi, and psychological disturbances before diagnosing bladder outlet obstruction caused by BP.[27]

A major problem in the diagnosis arises from the fact that there is little correlation between the size of the prostate gland and symptoms,[6,25,26] or between reported symptoms and other 'objective' measures, such as findings from urodynamics and scanning.[50] All authors advocate a thorough physical examination to aid diagnosis.

In all cases, a rectal examination of the prostate gland by an experienced examiner is considered essential.[40] The rectal examination allows an estimation of the size of the gland and exclusion of locally advanced prostate cancer (but not exclusion of early prostate cancer in which the gland feels benign). Although not important in terms of diagnosis in relation to symptoms, the size of the gland is crucial in determining the type of surgery to be offered.

Physical examination is required to exclude a palpable bladder (chronic retention) and to check the cardiovascular and respiratory tract, penis, urethra, perineum, anal sphincter tone, rectum, scrotum and testicles.[27]

The assessment of symptoms largely depends on the patient's reporting of them. Some urologists have tried to incorporate standardised questionnaires in their assessments, which focus on the perceived severity of obstructive and irritative symptoms.[10,36,40,49–51,53] Most conclude that these questionnaires need to be used in conjunction with other results because patients find them difficult and because the relationship between symptoms and other more objective findings is uncertain.[50] The most commonly reported LUTS are poor stream and nocturia.[45] Most clinicians rely on a combination of symptoms, an assessment of severity and measurement of flow rates.[26,36,38,50–55] Guidelines for the management of men with LUTS are available in the UK and point out that careful assessment of symptoms and examination is mandatory. Measurement of flow rates is strongly recommended, but urodynamic examination is optional for certain problematic patients because of the risk of producing harm (urinary infections).

Many European urology centres include urodynamic studies in their assessment before invasive treatment is carried out. The reason for this is that men with proven outlet obstruction do best after operation.[56–58,60,61] However, there is debate over how much better men with severe LUTS do compared with men with proven BOO, and in the UK, urodynamic investigations are not strongly recommended.

There is debate as to the usefulness of urodynamics in the management of LUTS. Indeed its use represents another area of controversy.[59] Most urologists now measure flow rates.[56,62] There is agreement that renal function should be assessed by measurement of serum creatinine. There is no indication for a routine intravenous urography (IVU), and many urologists do not image the upper urinary tract at all on the grounds that upper tract tumours and stones are not found more frequently in this group of men.

Prostate-specific antigen (PSA) testing and the exclusion of early prostate cancer

One major current debate is whether men presenting with LUTS should be investigated to diagnose early prostate cancer. There is no evidence that men with a clinically benign gland have an increased risk of prostate cancer. The controversy really is whether men in their fifties and sixties should be screened for early prostate cancer by means of serum prostate-specific antigen (PSA) measurement. This debate is complex.[63] However, current evidence suggests that the guidelines in Table 8 should be followed. Routine PSA screening is not recommended by a UK consensus panel. However, in practice many GPs will have carried out a PSA measurement before referral because of concerns over litigation if prostate cancer is subsequently diagnosed.

Table 8: Guidelines for PSA testing.

PSA testing (category B evidence)

- Is not recommended for routine clinical use
- Is not recommended in men with less than a 10-year life expectancy
- Should only be offered following full counselling of men about the implications

Implications of PSA testing that should be explained prior to testing (category B evidence)

- The test may detect early prostate cancer in approximately 5% of men aged 50 to 65 years
- The test will fail to detect some early tumours
- PSA testing and subsequent treatment of early prostate cancer may incur risk and may not improve life expectancy
- A transrectal ultrasound scan and biopsy, which carry some morbidity, may be needed
- The test may diagnose a tumour which we are uncertain how best to treat

Imaging of the prostate

The prostate can be evaluated by computerised tomography (CT), magnetic resonance imaging (MRI), cystoscopy and ultrasound examination. Experience with CT has proved disappointing for the diagnosis of LUTS, although it can be useful in the assessment of the weight of glands.[42] MRI scans have not proved capable of distinguishing BPE from other conditions.[44] Flexible cystoscopy can provide an easy assessment of the prostate, but its drawbacks are that it requires a local anaesthetic and so is difficult to use routinely, and it increases the risk of introducing infection. Ultrasound has proved extremely useful in the diagnosis of LUTS. The prostate can be scanned transabdominally, perurethrally and per-rectally, and ultrasound can also represent internal details of the prostate.[42] The most convenient method is through the per-rectal route, from which the weight of the gland can be estimated. There is no indication for imaging the prostate routinely in men with LUTS.

Summary of assessment of LUTS

The diagnosis of LUTS is a residual diagnosis, which is applied after other conditions such as malignancy, neurological disturbance, infection and so on have been excluded. The diagnosis can include a wide range of urinary symptoms and involve a wide range of tests, depending on an individual clinician's preferences and beliefs. It is important to note that the diagnosis of LUTS does not necessarily lead to a requirement for treatment because of the variable nature of the natural history, particularly the tendency for spontaneous remission and the wide-ranging levels of tolerance of symptoms by individual sufferers.

Treatments

Following assessment and diagnosis, the major types of non-operative treatment include:

- reassurance and discharge
- 'watchful waiting' and conservative treatment
- drug treatment, including α-adrenergic agents or 5-α-reductase inhibitors.

The major operative treatments include:

- open prostatectomy (retropubic prostatectomy; RPP)
- endoscopic or transurethral prostatectomy (TURP)
- transurethral incision of the prostate (TUIP; sometimes described as bladder neck incision or BNI)
- various new technologies.

Urologists treat LUTS rather than histological BPH or BPE[64,65] (i.e. a combination of symptoms and low urinary flow rates) because symptoms of obstruction are not related to the size or development of the prostate gland. It has been suggested that there may be three principal stages of treatment: drugs for early symptoms, prostatectomy for complications and advanced symptoms, and a catheter for men with severe comorbidity.[6] Currently, the most common treatment option is prostatectomy, with drug therapies typically being used before surgery. Permanent catheterisation is used primarily in patients considered unsuitable for surgery.

The aims of surgical treatment are to remove outlet obstruction, restore easy and comfortable micturition and prevent the progress of renal damage.[26] BPE can lead to irreversible renal insufficiency and thus death,[6] but this is very rare. Patients may be admitted for an emergency prostatectomy as a result of acute urinary retention. The literature suggests that approximately 25% of men undergoing TURP in the UK are admitted with acute retention.[25,65] A further 15% are admitted with chronic retention. The majority of patients are therefore treated electively for their urinary symptoms.

'Watchful waiting' and conservative treatment

'Watchful waiting' can essentially be defined as careful assessment and reassurance and then arranging to review the patient. A more active approach can be beneficial. This includes giving general advice about the timing of fluid intake and the adoption of postponement of mictutition with the aim of decreasing symptoms of frequency and urgency. The use of pelvic floor exercises can also be of help. There is little literature on this topic but this approach is cheap, can be effective and perhaps should be more widely used before resorting to drug treatment. A randomised prospective clinical trial performed by Wasson and his colleagues has confirmed that 'watchful waiting' is safe, and can be effective for some men with moderate symptoms, but that it has a higher failure rate than TURP.[66,67]

Drug therapies

There are two basic types of drug therapy in the treatment of LUTS, including α-adrenergic antagonists and inhibitors of 5-α-reductase. Other agents such as phytotherapeutic substances (e.g. saw palmetto extract) are more widely used in Europe, and in a meta-analysis[68] were shown to be effective.

Alpha-adrenergic antagonists or blockers

These drugs cause the relaxation of the smooth muscle of the prostate.[14,25] They thereby relieve temporarily the symptoms of outlet obstruction, but do not affect the size of the gland and so are not always effective for long periods of time.[25,69–71]

Hormonal therapies

The importance of hormones in the development of BPH and BPE is the subject of debate, but as it seems clear that intact testes and ageing are necessary for its development, the blocking of androgens has interested some authors. Castration has been shown to cause the regression of BPE after about three months, by shrinking the prostate gland.[34] The treatment has gone out of favour, however, because of its side-effects of loss of libido and potency.[14,30,35,71,72] Finasteride is an agent that blocks the conversion of testosterone to dihydrotestosterone.[13,35] This treatment is safe and is more effective than placebo.

Prostatectomy in the treatment of LUTS and complications of BPE

The aim of a prostatectomy is to remove the inner tissue of the prostate, leaving the outer caudal capsule.[65] There are two basic methods of prostatectomy: open and transurethral. Open surgery can be done by three routes: perineal, suprapubic and retropubic. Pioneered in 1909,[73] TURP increased in popularity from the 1960s with the development of the resectoscope. It is now the most common form of treatment, although in recent years there has been some controversy about its long-term safety and effectiveness (*see* below). Resection of an average 30 g gland is reported to take a specialist urologist about 15–20 minutes.[65]

Prostatectomies can be performed with general, spinal or local anaesthetics.[74,75] Spinal anaesthesia is preferred in patients with cardiovascular or respiratory problems, and reduces blood loss.[70] Prostatectomies are now carried out by specialist urologists. Open prostatectomy, the enucleation of the adenoma of the prostate gland for BPE, has been performed on a regular basis for over 100 years.[76] With the advent of the transurethral resection technique, open prostatectomies are now principally indicated for large glands that are difficult to resect or for patients with osteoarthrosis of the hips, which prevents their being positioned correctly for resection.[77]

The most common open approach is the retropubic route, which allows a clear view of the prostatic cavity and an easier convalescence for the patient.[26,77,78] The catheter is removed from retropubic patients after three or four days (six to seven for transvesical), and so the patient requires a 5- to 10-day stay after open surgery.[76]

Transurethral resection of the prostate is the hallmark of the specialist urologist.[77] Some 400 000 TURPs are carried out per annum in the USA.[78] In the UK, 42 000 were carried out in NHS hospitals in England in 1989–90. It is the most common operation performed by specialist urologists, with around 98% of their prostatectomies now TURPs.[26,77] NHS data show that in 1989–90, 93% of all prostatectomies were TURPs. TURP is the tenth most frequently performed operation in the USA, and the second most common reimbursed under Medicare.[78] Urologists in the UK carry out a mean of 67 TURPs per annum. It is known as the 'gold standard' for the treatment of BPE.[79] TURP is considered to be the best treatment for most patients, with a low mortality rate at around 0.4% for elective operations.[80] TURPs can be performed using general, spinal or local anaesthesia. Patients have to be catheterised after the operation for about 48 hours, so it is not possible to do TURPs on a day-case basis. More than 90% of prostatectomies are performed transurethrally. Estimating the population requirement for prostatectomy is very difficult because of the uncertainty surrounding the definition of the condition. In practice, however, around 40 000 operations per year are carried out in England and Wales, which means that about one man per 1000 of the population base (male and female) requires this operation per year. Increasingly, a number of men are being treated by new technologies.

Indications for prostatectomy or new technologies

Absolute contraindications for a prostatectomy are few and it is becoming rare for patients to be considered unfit for a prostatectomy.[78] As Miller stated in 1965, 'if a patient is requested to "get out of bed, walk round it, and get back again" and he can comprehend this and then do it, we can get him through a prostate operation'.[81] It is considered that gross mental disturbance and a life expectancy of less than six months are the clearest absolute contraindications.[26] Relative contraindications include renal failure, extreme age, diabetes, cardiovascular and cerebrovascular disease, and respiratory failure.[34,65,82,83] These relative contraindications can increase the risk of mortality by between 3 and 15 times.[34,84] Age alone is not considered to be a clear contraindication to surgery, but the reduced capacity for adaptation in the elderly, particularly in the cardiovascular system and altered pharmacokinetics have to be taken into account.[85] One study reported an 80% success rate with patients over the age of 80 years.[86] Very high-risk patients may be given long-term catheterisation as an alternative to surgery,[34] but this is very much a last resort. There have been steady reductions in overall morbidity and mortality rates following prostatectomies, but they have remained the same for high-risk patients.[87]

Although useful as a starting point, the classification shown in Table 9 and Table 10 (*see* overleaf) does not specify volumes or rates, nor does it explain what is meant by 'symptoms (severe > moderate)', which could thus be interpreted variably. Table 9 shows the American Urological Association clinical indications for TURP.[59] Table 10 shows Christensen and Bruskewitz's suggested three levels of confidence for indications for intervention in LUTS and complications caused by BPE.[29]

Table 9: American Urological Association clinical indications for TURP.[29]

A patient who is a reasonable surgical risk with one or more of the following:

1 urinary retention due to prostatic obstruction
2 intractable symptoms due to prostatic obstruction
3 recurrent or persistent urinary tract infection related to prostatic obstruction
4 a patient who is a reasonable surgical risk with two or more of the following:

    A documented post-voiding residual urine
    B pathophysiological changes of kidneys, ureters or bladder caused by prostatic obstruction
    C abnormally low urinary flow rate or a normal flow rate, but with an abnormally high voiding pressure
       secondary to outlet obstruction

Table 10: Indications for intervention in BPH.[29]

Strong
- azotaemia (with hydronephrosis)
- overflow incontinence
- high post-voiding urinary residual (volume not specified)
- urinary tract infection (recurrent, with increased residual)
- severe haematuria

Moderate
- acute retention (recurrent > single episode)
- symptoms (severe > moderate)
- increased post-voiding residual urine (volume not specified)
- reduced maximum urinary flow rate (rate not specified)

Weak
- cystoscopy findings (trabeculation > 'visual obstruction')
- prostate size

New technologies used in the treatment of LUTS and BPE (*see* appropriate tables)

Balloon dilatation

Balloon dilatation has been used as an alternative to prostatectomy. It is very similar to the operation of angioplasty done for coronary artery disease. A balloon is placed into the prostatic urethra by either visual or finger guidance and it is then inflated. This has the end result of tearing the prostate gland (usually anteriorly) and creating a wider channel. No prostate tissue is removed and the procedure does not work well for large prostates. It is not now recommended.

Prostatic stents

Stents are wire devices, shaped like small springs or coils, placed in the prostatic urethra. They are generally placed under local anaesthesia and require about 20 minutes to fit. Their use has in general been reserved for patients thought to be medically unfit, although some centres fitted them in men with severe symptoms while they were waiting for an operation. Given our present knowledge, this approach is difficult to support. Major problems with stents concern the irritation and debris that form on the stent, as well as a higher incidence of urinary tract infections. A number of types of stents have been used. Some (e.g. Memokath) are made of metal whose shape is thermostable so that they can be fitted while they are malleable, and then at body temperature their shape reverts to the original coil. Other stents (e.g. Urolume) become incorporated into the wall of the urethra over time, which makes them difficult to remove. Most authors would reserve the use of stents for the very unfit who would otherwise be fitted with a permanent catheter. The evidence that has been produced by a large number of small observational studies suggests that most types of stent can be successful in the treatment of men unsuitable for surgical treatment because of comorbidity and whose only alternative is seen to be an indwelling catheter. There are no data to support the notion that this treatment might be effective in treating a wider range of men with BPH, or that stents are a suitable treatment for men currently on the surgical waiting list.

The various type of stents include the following:

- temporary stents, including the Nissenkorn catheter, which is positioned under local anaesthesia. It can be removed through a lubricated urethra by a pull-cord. Other stents include the Prostakath, which is an intraprostatic spiral. It is gold-plated to minimise encrustation
- second-generation temporary stents, made of nickel–titanium alloys that are flexible and expand when heated, but are malleable when cool. The most common type is the Memokath
- permanent stents, which become covered with epithelium within the urethra. These include the Urolume, Wallstent and ASI titanium stent.

High-intensity focused ultrasound

High-intensity focused ultrasound (HIFU) is delivered to the prostate via a transrectal probe and causes prostatic lesions without damage to the rectal wall or other tissues. It is still at a developmental stage, but does have promise for future use.

Microwave therapy

Heating of cells using microwaves to 42–44°C destroys malignant tumour cells, but normal cells are destroyed only at temperatures in excess of 50°C. The rationale is that heat will destroy benign tissue, although this has not been proven. Three basic modalities of tissue destruction can probably be described: hyperthermia (40–45°C), thermotherapy (46–60°C) and thermal ablation (61–75°C).

Early treatments heated the prostate to about 42–46°C and were known as hyperthermia. The energy was applied per rectum or per urethra. Although there were some symptomatic improvements, no objective evidence of destruction of prostatic tissue could be confirmed.[88]

Later machines were fitted with more sophisticated methods of controlling rectal and urethral temperature and heated the prostate to >45°C. They may produce more tissue damage and greater effects on symptoms and flow rates. This is known as thermotherapy. The situation is even more complex because later machines provide even greater energy and the treatment is known as high-energy thermoablation.

Microwave hyperthermia

Transurethral microwave therapy involves an ultrasound generator and receiver which converts the energy into heat, which is focused on the centre of the prostate lobes. The amount of energy determines the degree of heating. Hyperthermia results in very little tissue damage as measured by changes in serum PSA. No prostate tissue is removed for pathological diagnosis.

Microwave thermotherapy

The new-generation microwave machines use a catheter that cools the lining of the prostatic urethra while the prostate tissue deep inside is heated.

Laser therapy

Laser therapy, using a neodymium:yttrium-aluminium-garnet (Nd:YAG) laser, was first used in the treatment of BPH using bare fibres, but with disappointing results. Later special probes were used, which resulted in discrete lesions being produced within the prostate. Another development is transurethral ultrasound-guided laser-induced prostatectomy (TULIP), which combines a standard Nd:YAG laser with a TULIP device, which fires the laser beam through a water-filled inflated plastic balloon at a 90° angle (side-firing) near the end of a probe.

With laser therapy, patients are typically catheterised for several days following treatment, while tissue sloughs. Improvement in symptoms and flow rates is reached after approximately six weeks. The laser is a source of high energy that has gained much attention as a unique surgical tool. In urology, the light energy is converted to heat on contact with tissue to produce its surgical effect. It is an energy modality utilised in breaking stones, treating bladder tumours and removing prostate tissue.

Several types of laser treatment have been used to treat men with BPH. Initially rather non-specialised probes were used to vaporise tissue, but the rate of tissue destruction was so slow as to limit their use to carrying out a bloodless bladder neck incision of TUIP. The next development was a contact laser probe, which resulted in tissue destruction but not vaporisation using an Nd:YAG laser. This is known as visual endoscopic laser ablation of the prostate (VLAP or ELAP). Recent developments include the use of hybrid lasers using Nd:YAG plus high-power potassium titanyl phosphate (KTP), which result in the destruction of larger volumes of prostate.

TULIP has also been used, as has interstitial laser therapy (ILP), but no large-scale trials have been reported. The next development is likely to be holmium laser treatment used to dissect out the prostatic adenoma, which is then pushed into the bladder where it can be morcellated transurethrally or by placement of a suprapubic tract. The advantage of this technique is that large amounts of adenoma are removed, which is likely to result in better long-term outcomes compared with other minimally invasive methods.

In general, laser treatments have resulted in improvements in symptoms and flow rates only a little inferior to conventional TURP. However, no long-term randomised studies have been done to allow us to determine whether these treatments should be introduced into routine clinical practice.

Transurethral incision of the prostate (TUIP)

TUIP is a long-standing, simplified alternative to TURP that simulates its results in both symptom relief and flow rate improvements. The procedure is performed by making a simple, deep cut or incision along the entire length of the prostate to split it open. This allows the circular muscle fibres running around the prostate to spring open and increase urinary flow by opening the prostatic urinary urethra. TUIP is ideally suited to smaller prostates and has a lower incidence of retrograde ejaculation. In appropriately selected patients with relatively small and anatomically appropriate prostates, the success rates for TUIP are similar to those for TURP, with the advantage that hospital stays and recovery are much shorter. Large-scale, long-term trials have not been done.

Transurethral electrovaporisation of the prostate (TVP)

A new modification of TURP is transurethral electrovaporisation of the prostate (TVP). Essentially, this technique uses a grooved roller-ball to apply electrical energy to vaporise the prostatic tissue. Compared to the standard TURP, the procedure results in less bleeding, shorter hospitalisation and catheter times, and a faster recovery period.

The procedure allows the grooved roller-ball electrode to rapidly heat the tissue to turn it into steam, leaving a space where the prostate tissue was previously present. The majority of heat is dispersed by a constant flow of water. The defect does not bleed because it is coagulated and sealed by the roller-ball electrode. However, large veins may still bleed and reports of late rebleeding following separation of slough have appeared. Technically, this is a new way to do a TURP, and TVP can also be utilised to perform a TUIP.

Transurethral needle ablation of the prostate (TUNA)

This technique involves the application of radio-frequency current through small needles placed bilaterally into the prostate gland via a transurethral approach, to induce tissue destruction by local heating. It can be performed with minimal anaesthesia and as an outpatient procedure. Preliminary data on a small series of patients suggest it has the potential to be a viable, minimally invasive surgical alternative for the treatment of BPH. The amount of tissue destruction is likely to be small and to limit the size of gland treated by this technique.

Conclusions about new technology

There are serious problems with many of the studies of new technologies. Initial phase I studies looking at safety are done well, as are the non-randomised studies showing safety, side-effects and effectiveness. However, randomised studies are in general small and short term, which has not allowed proper comparison with conventional treatment. Cost-effectiveness has not usually been calculated. Moreover, the generalisability of many of the trials is uncertain.

Costs

It is often assumed that a certain proportion of men currently treated by surgery could be managed by 'watchful waiting'. However, in many instances this approach has been practised for many years by the patient and GP. In addition, the advent of medical therapy will be likely to delay referral to the urologist. Data suggest that a small number of men will be saved prostatectomy by this approach.[85]

The cost of provision of treatment for BPH is considered here.

General practice

A visit is estimated to cost £15. The attendance rates per year to the GP in connection with BPH are not entirely clear, but would be of the order of 5% of men aged over 60 (who represent about 10% of the average practice). Therefore 0.5% of the total of the GP's patients will present each year. In a population of 10 000 people there will be 1000 men aged over 60 years. Fifty will go to see their GP each year, 20 will be reassured or treated by 'watchful waiting', 20 will be referred for assessment to hospital (10 of these will undergo operative treatment) and 10 will be managed by drug treatment.

Initially, the cost of providing the present average level of care is calculated. This is divided into costs falling on general practice, costs falling on the hospital sector of the NHS, and costs of private care (which will fall on both the general public and the insurance companies). These calculations are rather simplistic and it is likely that the true costs are much higher. For instance, the treatment of LUTS and BPE will cost around £40 000 per annum, most of the costs falling on the hospital. However, these costs are likely to be 'subsidised' by other, more minor procedures. Fixed overheads are significant. It is likely that costs would be double in these estimated costs.

Two alternative calculations are then made. First, it is assumed that 20% of those currenty treated by surgery will be subject to 'watchful waiting' rather than immediate treatment. 'Watchful waiting' is assumed to consist of the initial two visits to the outpatient department, plus a further two visits per year, making a total of four visits in the first year. When notice is taken only of the change in costs in the present year, it appears that resource use is much reduced. It is, however, apparent from a more detailed consideration that the cost of 'watchful waiting' will have costs in future years that will not be incurred where operation takes place in the current year.

Second, it is assumed that there is an increase of 25% in the number of patients receiving surgery. It appears that this course of action will lead to an increase in cost to the NHS. However, although not explicitly calculated, it is likely that some of this cost will be offset by a reduction in costs of emergency operations and further consultations for these same patients.

(i) Costs per 10 000 of the total population (per 1000 men aged over 60 years)

GP costs – 50 men

20 referred – NHS	1 visit	@ £15	£300
4 referred – privately	1 visit	@ £15	£60
26 not referred	3 visits	@ £15	£1,170

NHS hospitals – 20 referred

10 treated medically/untreated	2 outpatient visits	@ £100	£2,000
10 prostatectomies	3 outpatient visits	@ £100	£3,000
	Operation	@ £1,600	£16,000

Private hospitals – 4 referred

3 operated on:	2 outpatient visits	@ £120	£720
	Operation	@ £2,500	£7,500
1 not operated on	1 outpatient visit	@ £120	£120

Total expenditure on BPH

GP	£1,530
NHS hospital	£21,000
Private hospital	£8,340
Total	**£40,870**

(ii) Change in NHS cost based on the assumption that 20% of those currently treated by surgery will now be treated by 'watchful waiting'

NHS hospitals – 20 referred

6 treated medically/untreated	2 outpatient visits	@ £100	£1,200
4 treated by 'watchful waiting'	4 outpatient visits	@ £100	£1,600
8 prostatectomies:	3 outpatient visits	@ £100	£2,400
	Operation	@ £1,600	£12,800

Total NHS hospital expenditure   **£18,000**

It may be suggested that much of the 'watchful waiting' costs could be transferred to general practice. However, the situation is complex because many GPs are already practising 'watchful waiting' on men who are never referred. The referral takes place because of the other complexities, such as worse symptoms, or other conditions, such as strokes or Parkinson's disease. While such men may be referred back to the GP, it is likely that one or two further visits to the urologist will be indicated to ensure that this policy is correct. The above figures show an apparent saving of approximately £3000 for the NHS hospital resulting from the reduction in the number of prostate operations and the increase in 'watchful waiting'. This policy will, however, lead to an increase in costs in further years as the 20% of patients referred to the 'watchful waiting' (medically treated) group are observed regularly. If it is assumed that these patients are observed in outpatient departments every six months over a five-year period, this would lead to a cost of £200 per person per year. This is just the cost of 'watchful waiting', and does not include the costs of operating on any patients requiring a prostatectomy during the period of 'watchful waiting'. It also does not include the costs falling on patients who decide to opt for an operation in the private sector. The analysis is thus, in a sense, incomplete. It does, however, show the importance of considering all aspects in changes in policy.

(iii) Change in NHS cost based on the assumption that there is an increase of 20% in the number of patients receiving surgery

NHS hospitals – 20 referred

8 treated medically/untreated	2 outpatient visits	@ £100	£1,600
12 prostatectomies:	3 outpatient visits	@ £100	£3,600
	Operation	@ £1,600	£1,200
Total NHS hospital expenditure			**£24,400**

The figures in section (iii) show an apparent increase in costs of £3400 for the NHS hospital resulting from the increase in the number of prostate operations and the reduction in 'watchful waiting'. However, just as a reduction in the number of operations caused changes in future resource use, so the policy of increasing operations is likely to have future effects. In particular, it is likely that there will be a reduction in future resource use as patients no longer need to be observed at future consultations.

Again, it should be stressed that in this model no consideration is given to changes in the benefit received by the patient. It is not, therefore, possible to determine the most cost-effective option for districts to pursue. In addition, the considerable uncertainty surrounding many aspects of the model, and the poverty of the data used, mean that the model should not be used to draw sweeping conclusions.

6 Effectiveness and cost-effectiveness of services

The effectiveness of treatments for LUTS and BPE

The evidence is that in England and Wales, men wait for a number of years before visiting their GP. The advent of medical treatments has meant that a further period of treatment with these agents then takes place. Some men respond well to 'watchful waiting' or medical treatment and do not require referral to hospital. The increasing publicity about prostate diseases is likely to result in more men going to their GP earlier.

New technology has also meant that fewer men proceed straight away to prostatectomy, although there have been few direct comparisons by means of randomised controlled trials (RCTs).

Drug therapies and their effectiveness

Alpha-adrenergic antagonists or blockers

Clinical trials of phenoxybenzamine showed it to be effective, but to have unacceptable side-effects.[35] Other drugs are currently being tested, and it is hoped that multi-centre studies will clarify the precise role of α-adrenergic antagonists in the treatment of LUTS.[35] The role of drugs has been reviewed in a systematic review. Recent drugs include alfuzosin, terazosin and tamsulosin, which are more 'prostate selective'. These α-selective agents are more expensive and appear to have fewer side-effects than the older agents. In addition, some can be given as single-dose treatments. The side-effects include postural hypotension, dizziness, nasal stuffiness and headaches. Modern drugs are more selective for α-1 receptors and some can be given as single doses per day, which may offer improvement with compliance.

Hormonal therapies

Finasteride is safe and is better than placebo, but may be less effective in smaller glands (< 30–40 g).

Studies evaluating drug therapies have reported high levels of spontaneous symptomatic improvement and marked placebo effects.[33,34] One study suggested that 60% of patients may get better on a placebo drug, and another that more than one third of untreated men with symptoms of urinary obstruction caused by BPH experienced a spontaneous improvement based on subjective criteria and a 20% improvement according to objective findings.[69–71] It has been suggested that drugs have been administered in incorrect doses and over too short periods of time to show their true effectiveness but, on the whole, drug therapies have so far been limited to providing temporary relief for those who do not want surgery or are awaiting a prostatectomy. One paper suggested that finasteride was less effective than α-blockers, but this agent may be less effective in smaller glands (< 40 ml) and this trial did contain rather more patients with smaller glands than might usually have been expected.[71] Two years on, men taking active treatment had lower rates of prostatectomy (89 of 2113 [4.2%] vs. 138 of 2109 [6.5%]) and of retention (24 of 2113 [1.1%] vs. 57 of 2109 [2.7%]). However, 36% of men reporting retention (45/126) and 21% of men reporting surgical intervention (60/287) were excluded from this study. Though the trials were large and differences significant, the number of events prevented (49 prostatectomies and 33 episodes of retention) was small. The cost of drugs would have been over £1.6 million while the NHS cost of treating these 82 events surgically would have been no more than £200 000. While more men may benefit in the forthcoming years from drug treatment, so will the cost of drug treatment increase.

The effectiveness of prostatectomy

Information about the effectiveness of prostatectomy is hampered by lack of knowledge about the natural history of LUTS and the likelihood of spontaneous improvement. Prostatectomy has been the treatment of choice because it has been assumed to relieve the symptoms of urinary outlet obstruction. Studies have suggested that 75–90% of men improve after a TURP,[77–79] and that 79–90% are satisfied with the results.[89] It is thought that the most severely affected individuals experience the greatest levels of success; more than 90% of severely and nearly 80% of moderately symptomatic individuals can expect to improve after a prostatectomy.[90] There have also been studies that have examined the failure rate of prostatectomies. Failure rates range from 2% to 35% for TURP,[91–99] and were 0% in the only study to look at open procedures.

Prostatectomies are associated with some post-operative complications. Studies mentioning complications are presented in tabular form opposite so that they can be compared (*see* Tables 11 and 12).

Some complications occur following both TURPs and open prostatectomies. Both have relatively low operative mortality rates, ranging from 0 to 2.1%,[100–120] slightly higher for open procedures than TURPs. The most common cause of death after TURP is cardiovascular complications. One of the most common post-operative complications is a urinary tract infection, occurring in 4–63% of cases. Urethral strictures have been found in approximately 1–29% of cases.

Several complications are shown in the literature to occur only in men having TURPs. A syndrome has been documented (called TUR syndrome) that is characterised by a rise in blood pressure, bradycardia, mental confusion, nausea, vomiting and visual disturbance, thought to be caused by intoxication with the

Table 11: Complications (%) of open prostatectomies (quoting papers with population figures).

Reference number	93	98*	98†	25†
Number of operations	53	621	223	98
Complications (%)				
Urethral strictures	3.8	–	–	–
Urinary tract infections	51	19.3	4	38
Incontinence	0	–	–	–
Pulmonary infection	11.3	–	–	–
Operative mortality	0	2.1	0.9	–
90-day mortality	–	0.6	0.5	–

* Suprapubic route.
† Retropubic route.

Table 12: Complications (%) of TURPs (quoting papers without population figures).

Reference number	98	103	108	110	111	25	105	101
Complications (%)								
Urethral strictures	–	1–29	–	–	–	–	–	–
Urinary tract infections	–	–	–	–	–	–	–	5–63
TUR syndrome	–	–	–	–	–	–	2–7	–
Incontinence	–	–	3	–	–	1–3	–	–
Impotence	10	–	–	16–30	4–40	< 13	–	–
Retrograde ejaculation	50	–	–	–	–	–	–	–
Operative mortality	0.4	–	–	–	–	0.2	–	–

irrigating solution.[105] Incontinence has been reported in a small proportion of cases (3%) immediately post-operatively,[108] although the problem can rectify itself, and only 1% of these patients have to undergo further surgery to correct incontinence. Impotence has proved much more difficult to evaluate.[109] The TUR procedure results in the bladder no longer being shut off from the prostatic cavity, and this can lead to dry or retrograde ejaculation in many cases (between 11 and 100%). Figures for impotence also vary among studies (between 0 and 40%).[109–111] TURPs are generally associated with a deterioration in various aspects of sexual expression,[109] but this should not necessarily occur. Some of these post-operative problems are thought to be caused by involuntary erections during the resection procedure, which cause the surgeon to resect incorrectly.

Some men are more likely to have poorer outcomes than others. These tend to be men with the smallest prostates and low voiding pressures, weak detrusor function or bladder muscle instability and urge incontinence.[113,114] These men are more likely to have a TURP than an open prostatectomy, and perhaps to undergo more than one procedure.

Work in the late 1980s by Wennberg et al. reopened the debate about the outcomes and effectiveness of TURPs compared with open surgery.[115–117] Up to 1987 it was generally accepted that TURP was the most effective operative procedure for men with relatively small glands, and that TURPs could be used electively as a solution to embarrassing symptoms. TURPs had largely replaced open prostatectomies in most modern health systems. Roos and Ramsey analysed the outcomes for prostatectomy in Manitoba, Canada, over an 8-year period. They showed that post-operative mortality rates were similar to or higher for TURPs compared with open surgery, and that reoperation rates were much higher (16.8%) for TURPs than for open prostatectomies (7%).[98]

Wennberg's team followed this with a study comparing men undergoing TURP and open prostatectomy in Denmark, in Oxfordshire, UK, and in Manitoba, Canada over eight years.[115] This showed that the cumulative percentage of patients undergoing a second prostatectomy was substantially higher after TURP than open prostatectomy (12.0 vs. 4.5% in Denmark, 12.0 vs. 1.8% in the UK, and 15.5 vs. 4.2% in Canada). It also showed that long-term age-specific mortality rates were higher for TURP than open prostatectomy.[110] Other studies confirmed the finding of higher death rates and reoperation rates for patients having TURP.[111,112] A rate of 2.0–2.8% per annum for recurrences has been suggested. Another study in Denmark also found that the risk of dying within 10 years of a prostatectomy was significantly higher for TURPs than open procedures, with the most common cause of death being chronic bronchitis.[118] This debate is somewhat sterile because it has been shown that men undergoing TURP are less fit than men undergoing open operation and that men who undergo open operation have significantly increased life expectancies compared with control populations.[119]

The other major question of effectiveness concerns the rate of reoperation. After eight years, 12–18% of men who had had a TURP required a repeat procedure. This indicates an excess risk of three to five times that of open surgery.[98,115] It may be that many TURPs may not be complete, although this is usually denied by urologists. There is little evidence of major differences in the symptomatic and urodynamic outcomes of the two procedures, although peak urinary flow is reported to be higher in open prostatectomy, implying that it is more complete. It is suggested that it is more likely that a surgeon will operate on a borderline case using the transurethral procedure, and this may contribute to the increased numbers of reoperations.[103] It is not known, however, why men required repeat procedures – whether for more complete resection, persistent symptoms or because of more severe symptoms resulting from the iatrogenic effects of the first procedure. Further research is required to determine the reasons for the high revision rate, and in the UK, improvements need to be made to routine health service data so that issues such as late mortality and repeat procedures can be investigated.

Other therapies in the treatment of LUTS and BPE

Minimally invasive procedures

Balloon dilatation (*see* Tables 13 and 14[120–129])

Recent studies have demonstrated that most patients who undergo balloon dilatation have recurrence of their symptoms relatively soon afterwards and require repeat treatments within two years. With the availability of more efficacious minimally invasive treatments, balloons are less acceptable. No large-scale controlled trials have been reported. In some of the uncontrolled studies, men were stated to be unfit for prostatectomy and might otherwise have been treated by catheterisation. However, some studies recruited a large number of patients over a short time and the definition of lack of fitness was not explicit. This criticism also applies to many studies of prostatic stents. Other studies recruited men at the other end of the symptomatic spectrum, taking those with only mild symptoms (who now are most likely to be managed by 'watchful waiting' or with α-blockers).

Conclusions on balloon dilatation

Balloon dilatation has been shown to be safe, and results in some symptomatic improvement in some patients with LUTS, but whether it is better than placebo remains uncertain. The exact mechanism of this improvement is unknown. Morbidity following the procedure is low, particularly for epididymitis, urinary

Table 13: Results for non-controlled trials of balloon dilatation.

Trial	Number	Mean age (years)	Length of follow-up (months)	Symptom score (baseline)	Symptom score (after follow-up)	Improvement in symptom score (%)	PFR (before)	PFR (after)	Improvement in PFR (%)
Marks[126]	43	59.6	9.8	15.7		77%			73%
McLoughlin[127]	54	74	9			51%			
Moseley[128]	77	64.4	24	16 (approx.)	4	91%	8	15	
Renfer[129]	27	66	12	17.3	10	42%	11.5	14.3	24%

Table 14: Results for controlled trials of balloon dilatation vs. TURP, TUIP and observation.

Trial	Number	Mean age (years)	Length of follow-up (months)	Symptom score before	Symptom score after	Improvement in symptom score (%)	PFR (before)	PFR (after)	Improvement in PFR (%)
Chiou[121]									
Balloon	16			15 (Madsen)	3.4	77	8.3	12.8	54
TUIP	14			15.4	4.2	73	9	18.1	101
Donatucci[124]									
Balloon	20		18	14.1 (Madsen)	7.3	49	11.8	16.1	36
TURP	18			13.6	7.7	43	12.2	19.8	62
Klein[125]									
Balloon	5	60.2	24						
Observation	3	60.3							

tract infection and incontinence, but mortality rates are high (3.5%), probably due to the numbers of high-risk patients treated. Studies indicate poor long-term results from balloon dilatation – with a cumulative failure rate at five years of 32% (90% CI: 15–52), and with a high proportion of failures tending to occur in the first year (*see* Tables 13 and 14).

Prostatic stents (*see* Table 15[130–136])

The studies shown in Table 15 have been mostly carried out in patients with acute or chronic retention. In general, the short-term success rates have been about 60%, the other 40% requiring stent removal and catheterisation. The rates of complication (such as haematuria, encrustation, displacement and blockage) in men fitted with temporary stents are not clear because large-scale, long-term results have not been published, but many short-term series report that up to 25% require their stents to be replaced or resited. Similar problems apply to review of permanent stents, but certainly some cause encrustation and calcification and may require open surgical removal, which is technically difficult.

High-intensity focused ultrasound (HIFU) (*see* Table 17[137–140])

Early results indicated that this therapy was well tolerated. Most patients suffer from transient retention and haematospermia. Therapy resulted in an increase in maximum flow rate, and reduction in both residual urine and American Urological Association (AUA) symptom score. There have been no large-scale randomised trials of HIFU. The results of the non-controlled studies are shown in Table 16 (*see* opposite).

Microwave therapy (*see* Table 17 (p. 122) and Table 18 (p. 123)[141–161])

The results of these treatments need to be stratified according to the type of energy used. Early treatments heated the prostate to about 42–46°C and were known as hyperthermia. The energy was applied per rectum or per urethra. Though there were some symptomatic improvements no objective evidence of destruction of prostatic tissue could be confirmed.[82]

Microwave hyperthermia

Transurethral microwave thermotherapy (TUMT) involves an ultrasound generator and receiver which converts the energy into heat, which is focused in the centre of the prostate lobes. The amount of energy determines the degree of heating. Hyperthermia results in very little tissue damage as measured by changes in serum PSA. No prostate tissue is removed for pathological diagnosis.

Conclusions on thermotherapy

The majority of studies report that this treatment is well tolerated by patients, but some indicate that temporary retention occurs in 25% of men following TUMT. Symptomatic improvement is found in all studies. Most studies have also found increased maximum flow rates or reduced residual urine. There is concern about the long-term effectiveness of the therapy, with some authors finding increasing failure over time, but others reporting a stable 60% success rate at two years. Hyperthermia is going out of fashion because of poor results. We are still awaiting the results of large-scale randomised trials incorporating acceptability, costs and long-term follow-up (*see* Table 18).

Table 15: Results for non-controlled trials of stents.

Trial	Number	Mean age (years)	Length of follow-up (months)	Symptom score (baseline)	Symptom score (after follow-up)	Improvement in symptom score (%)	PFR (before)	PFR (after)	Improvement in PFR (%)
Guazzoni[130]									
I	91	69.3	12	14.1	6.4	55	9.3	15.7	69
II	44	73.1	12		4.5			13.1	
Kaplan[131]									
I	144	73.5	24	16.3	6.21	62	4.95	12.04	143
Milroy[132]									
I	54	75.7	6	17.9	5.2	71	9.9	19.41	96
II					8.3			16.61	
Oesterling[133]									
I	126	68	24	14.3	5.4	62	9.1	13.1	44
II					4.1			11.4	
Vincente[134]	22	80.3	12					66% in 6–4 ml/s 33% in < 6 ml/s	
Williams[135]									
I	96	(52–95)	12	17.94	3.36 (Madsen Iversen)	81	8	18.1	126
II					1.53		15		
Yachia[136]	65		16						

I = non-retention; II = retention.

Table 16: Results for non-controlled trials of high-intensity focused ultrasound (HIFU).

Trial	Number	Mean age (years)	Length of follow-up (months)	Symptom score (baseline)	Symptom score (after follow-up)	Improvement in symptom score (%)	PFR (before)	PFR (after)	Improvement in PFR (%)
Narayan[137]	42	68	6	24	7.8	68	8.8	20	127
Madersbacher[138]	50	67	12	24.5	10.8	56	8.9	13.1	47
Nakamura[139]	37	67.2	3	23.6	10.5	56	7.6	9.3	22
Uchida[140]	28	71.4	6	5.2 (IPSS)	2.8	46	8.8	10.8	28

Table 17: Results for trials of hyperthermia.

Trial	Number	Age (years)	Length of follow-up (months)	Symptom score	Post-treatment symptom score	Change in symptom score (%)	Flow rate (pre-operative)	Flow rate (post-operative)	Change in flow rate (%)
Abbou[141]									
Hyperthermia (TU)	66	65	12	10.9 (Madsen)		50	10.4		14
Sham	31	66		12.8		17	9.9		17
Hyperthermia (PR)	65	66		11.7		25	9.8		8
Sham	38	66		12.1		39	9		16
Kaplan[144]									
Hyperthermia	21	60.6	6.7	16.4	6.5	60	5.9	13.2	124
Montorsi[145]									
Hyperthermia <70 years (5 sessions)	158	61	24	18.2 (Boyarski)	13.8	24	9.2	10.4	13
Hyperthermia >70 years (0 sessions)	98	75	24				8.8	9.2	4.5
Retention	64	71	24		12		ng	12.1	
Bdesha[143]									
Hyperthermia	22	63.7	3	30 (WHO)	11.7	61	12.3	14.6	19
Sham	18	63.7	3	31	26	16	10.8	9.8	−9
Petrovich[146]									
Hyperthermia	63	66	12				8.3	11.91	43
Venn[142]									
TUMT	47	70.5	6	12.7		42			
Stawawtz[147]									
PR	22	63	19						
Sapozink[148]	21	67	12.5				11	15.9	
Richter[149]	37	70.5	11				3.4	9	

TU = transurethral; PR = per rectal.

Table 18: Results for trials of microwave thermotherapy.

Trial	Number	Mean age (years)	Length of follow-up (months)	Symptom score (baseline)	Symptom score (after follow-up)	Improvement in symptom score (%)	PFR (before)	PFR (after)	Improvement in PFR (%)
Blute[155]	150		12	13.7	5.4	61	8.5	11.3	33
de la Rosette[157]	75		6	14.15	5.31	62	8.75	12.32	41
de la Rosette[157] (high energy)	105	66.6	6	13.6	5.5	60	9.6	14.1	47
de la Rosette[158] (high energy)	120	67	6	13.9	5.3	62	9.4	14.1	50
Eliasson[159]	172	68	12	12.7	6.6	48	9.8	10.9	11
Höfner[160]	140	69	40	13 (Madsen)				11.5	
Porru[161]	44	69	12	11.61 (Boyarsky)	3.04	74	8.29	12.78	54
de la Rosette[88] TUMT	25	64.1	3	13.2 (Madsen)	5.9	55	9.6	14	46
Sham	25	62.7	3	21.1 (Madsen)	8.2	61	9.7	9.5	−2
de Wildt[152] TUMT	47	66.3	12	13.7 (Madsen)	8.2	64	9.2	13.4	46
Sham	46	63.9	12	12.9	4.2	67	9.6	10.5	9.4
de la Rosette[150] (2-year follow-up)	301			14.1 (Madsen)	5		9.7	13.8	42
d'Ancona[153] TUMT	31	69	12	13.3 (Madsen)	4.2	68	10	16.9	69
TURP	21	69	12	13.8	2.8	80	9.3	18.6	100

Laser therapy (*see* Tables 19 and 20 (opposite) and Table 21 (p. 126)[162–191])

Transurethral visual laser ablation of the prostate (VLAP) or endoscopic laser ablation of the prostate (ELAP)

With contact ablation, a lower laser energy is applied, which heats up the tissue enough to cause it to necrose and slough with time. Compared to standard transurethral resection or TURP, the advantages of laser procedures are no significant bleeding, shorter hospitalisation and reduced operating time. On the other hand, there is a large amount of swelling in the prostatic urethra for 3–10 days, which requires temporary catheter drainage. In addition, patients can experience a few weeks of urinary frequency and irritation while the prostatic channel is healing. Its significant advantages are no bleeding and a short hospital stay.

One concern is that no prostate tissue is removed. Therefore, one cannot be certain that cancer does not exist. However, PSA and ultrasound-guided biopsy carried out before VLAP can minimise the risk.

Interstitial laser coagulation of the prostate (ILC[171–172])

This is similar to transurethral needle ablation of the prostate. A thin laser fibre is inserted into the prostatic adenoma via a transurethral or transrectal route under ultrasound or visual guidance. Laser energy is then utilised to induce local tissue destruction by heating. Preliminary data on small series of patients suggest it has potential as a viable minimally invasive surgical alternative for the treatment of BPH.

There are no large-scale studies of ILC. In one study, 20 men were treated with the indigo machine.[172] Flow rates increased from 7.9 ml/s to 13 ml/s and symptom scores decreased from 22.6 to 14.3 at six months. Another study[174] assessed 28 men. Flow rates increased from 6.7 ml/s to 16.2 ml/s and symptom scores decreased (pre-operative range was 19–26; post-operative range was 10–16).

Holmium laser treatment[173–174]

There are no large-scale randomised trials against TURP, but this is the procedure that most closely resembles the standard operation because large amounts of tissue are removed. It can be a time-consuming procedure.

TULIP (transurethral ultrasound-guided laser-induced prostatectomy) (see *Tables 22 and 23 on p. 127*)

In general, laser treatments have been shown to be effective, but associated with fewer serious side-effects compared with TURP. However, they are not quite as effective as conventional treatments and the duration of effectiveness is open to doubt. Finally, in the short term after treatment men suffer quite severe side-effects of dysuria and frequency, which have not been well documented.

Transurethral incision of the prostate (TUIP) (*see* Table 24 (p. 127) and Table 25 (p. 128)[192–199])

Previous studies have shown that this operation is nearly as effective as TURP and may be associated with fewer side-effects, such as retrograde ejaculation. However, large-scale studies with long-term outcomes have not been done. In addition, the procedure is best suited to small glands, which means that it might apply to only about 30% of men undergoing treatment. At present it is perhaps an underutilised procedure, but systematic reviews have brought this out. However, the number of men included in the trials is relatively small and the procedure has not become more widely adopted.

Table 19: Results of non-controlled trials of laser prostatectomy.

Trial	Number	Mean age (years)	Length of follow-up (months)	Symptom score (baseline)	Symptom score (after follow-up)	Improvement in symptom scores (%)	PFR (before)	PFR (after)	Improvement in PFR (%)
Costello[175]	69	66.08	12		18.85	8	8.86	16.82	89
Cummings[176]	25		3		11.4	7	6.1	14.5	137
de Wildt[177]	40	63.8	6	21.7	6.3	71	8	17.1	114
Furuya[178]	66	72.6	12	18.5	4.8	74	6.4	10.4	63
Muschter[184*]	239	67.8	12	25.4	6.2	76	7.7	17.6	128
Narayan[179]	61	71.6	12	27.5	8	71	9.3	24.6	164
Narayan[179]									
(I)	41	70.4	6	23.2	8.6	63	8.5	18.4	116
(II)	39	73.9	6	24.9	7.2	71	9.1	16.6	82
(III)	20	67.9	6	23.2	7	70	8.6	17.8	107
Te Slaa[181]	105		6	21.3 (IPSS)	5.3	75	7.9	17	115
Te Slaa[182]	233	66.3	12	21.1 (IPSS)	3.6	83	7.5	16.3	117
Tubaro[183]	100		6	14.8 (Madsen)	5.45	63	8.59	11.6	35

*Also reported in de la Rosette et al.[88]
I = prostate volume < 40 ml; II = prostate volume 41–80 ml; III = prostate volume > 80 ml.

Table 20: Results of non-controlled trials of visual laser ablation of the prostate.

Trial	Number	Mean age (years)	Length of follow-up (months)	Symptom score (baseline)	Symptom score (after follow-up)	Improvement in symptom score (%)	PFR (before)	PFR (after)	Improvement in PFR (%)
Kablin[185]	227	70	24	20.3	8.6	58	7.3	18.3	151
Kablin[186]	50	68	12	20.8	8.4	60	7.6	18.7	146
Malek[187]	47	69.6	5	22	10	55	9.5	15.7	65

Table 21: Results for controlled trials of laser prostatectomy vs. TURP.

Trial	Number	Mean age (years)	Follow-up (months)	Symptom score (before)	Symptom score (after)	Improvement in symptom score (%)	PFR (before)	PFR (after)	Improvement in PFR (%)
Anson[162]									
ELAP	76	67.9	12	18.1	7.7	57	9.6	15.4	60
TURP	75	68.3		18.2	5.1	72	10	21.8	118
Costello[163]									
Laser	34	67.9	6		9.27			15.75	
TURP	37	68.2			4.43			19.1	
Cowles[165]									
VLAP	56	65.8	12	18.7	9.7	48	8.9	13.9	56
TURP	59	67		20.8	7.5	64	9.5	16.5	74
de la Rosette[188]									
Ultraline	44	65	12	32 (IPSS)	6.6	69	7.8	19.7	153
Urolase	49	64.6		21	1.7	92	7.9	12.7	61
Kabalin[168]									
Urolase	13	65	6	20.9	4.6	78	8.5	20.5	141
TURP	12	69		18.8	5.7	70	9	22.9	154
Kabalin[186]									
Urolase	13	67	12	20.9	4.3	79	8.5	21.6	154
EALP	12			18.8	6.3	66	9	21.6	140
Keoghane[167]									
Laser (contact)	76	69	3	19.9	9.6	52	11.8	21.3	81
TURP	72	70		19.4	6.5	66	11.4	21.8	91
Orihuela[189]									
Low-power laser	15	66	12	27.3	c. 4	66	5	c. 17	
High-power laser	14	59		26.1	c. 3		4.5	c. 20	
Uchida[166]									
VLAP (urolase)	50	71	12	22	7.6	65	9.1	16.4	80
TURP	50	66.7		21.1	3.5	83	8.5	21.6	154

Table 22: Results for non-controlled trials of transurethral ultrasound-guided laser-induced prostatectomy.

Trial	Number	Mean age (years)	Follow-up (months)	Symptom score (baseline)	Symptom score (after follow-up)	Improvement in symptom score (%)	PFR (before)	PFR (after)	Improvement in PFR (%)
Schulze[190]	89	67	12	17 (Boyarsky)	5		7	15	

Table 23: Results for non-controlled trials of transurethral ultrasound-guided laser-induced prostatectomy.

Trial	Number	Mean age (years)	Follow-up (months)	Symptom score (before)	Symptom score (after)	Improvement in symptom score (%)	PFR (before)	PFR (after)	Improvement in PFR (%)
Schulze[191]									
TULIP	20	64.5	12	19	c. 1		3.2	c. 15	
TURP	21	65.9		17.7	c. 3		2.4	c. 17	

Table 24: Results for non-controlled trials of transurethral incision of the prostate (TUIP).

Trial	Number	Mean age (years)	Follow-up (months)	Symptom score (baseline)	Symptom score (after follow-up)	Improvement in symptom score (%)	PFR (before)	PFR (after)	Improvement in PFR (%)
Sirls[193]	41	63.4	12	12.5	6.9		10.3	15.3	

Table 25: Results for controlled trials of transurethral incision of the prostate (TUIP) vs. TURP.

Trial	Number	Mean age (years)	Length of follow-up (months)	Symptom score (baseline)	Symptom score (after follow-up)	Improvement in symptom score (%)	PFR (before)	PFR (after)	Improvement in PFR (%)
Christensen[194]									
TUIP	35	63	36	16	8	50	7.8	10.9	40
TURP	38	62		16	4	75	9.7	14.6	51
Dorflinger[195]									
TUIP	17	67	3	15	2.5	83	10	15	50
TURP	21	71		17	1	94	9	19	111
Dorflinger[196]									
TUIP	22	69	3	14.5	2.5	83	10	8	−20
TURP	29	71		16	1	94	8	18.8	135
Larsen[197]									
TUIP	19	63	3	17	2	88	7.4	14.4	95
TURP	19	63	3	17	2	88	7.4	14.4	95
	18	61		17	2	88	8.6	16.3	90
Riehmann[198]									
TUIP	61	65	72	c. 15	c. 9		c. 11	c. 12	
TURP	56	64		c. 15	c. 10		c. 10	c. 19	
Soonawalla[199]									
TUIP	110	62.2	12			(96% satisfied)	3.82	11.21	
TURP	110	62.2	12			(90% satisfied)	3.99	10.91	
Sham	46	68		13		20			

Table 26: Results for non-controlled trials of electrovaporisation of the prostate.

Trial	Number	Mean age (years)	Length of follow-up (months)	Symptom score (baseline)	Symptom score (after follow-up)	Improvement in symptom score (%)	PFR (before)	PFR (after)	Improvement in PFR (%)
Issa[201]	LP								
Narayan[202]	42	68	6 months	24 (IPSS)	7.8	67.5%	8.8	20	135.2
Kaplan[203]	25	67.4	3 months	17.8	4.2		7.4	15.3	

Transurethral electrovaporisation of the prostate (TVP) (*see* Table 26 (p. 128) and Table 27 (p. 130)[200])

Compared to the standard TURP, this procedure results in less bleeding, shorter hospitalisation and catheter times, and faster recovery period.

The procedure allows the grooved roller-ball electrode to rapidly heat the tissue to turn it into steam, leaving a space where the prostate tissue was previously present. The majority of heat is dispersed by a constant flow of water. The defect does not bleed because it is coagulated and sealed by the roller-ball electrode. However, large veins may still bleed and reports of late rebleeding following separation of slough have appeared. Technically, this is a new way to do a TURP and it can also be utilised to perform a TUIP.

Long-term data on its efficacy are not yet available, but multi-centre trials are under way to compare it to other procedures such as standard TURP. The major potential advantages of TVP compared to the conventional TURP and laser-assisted prostatectomy are lower cost, fewer side-effects, more rapid convalescence time and short hospital stay (overnight), as well as the simplicity of the procedure. This makes TVP a useful, safe and versatile tool in the treatment of the enlarged prostate disease that causes urinary outflow obstruction or BPH. Potential side-effects include delayed bleeding caused by separation of slough and an increased rate of later reoperation. Considerable energy is absorbed by the prostate and we do not know the optimum size of the prostate that can be treated by this technique.

Transurethral needle ablation of the prostate (TUNA) (*see* Table 28 (p. 130)[200–206])

Preliminary data on small series of patients suggest that this has the potential to be a viable, minimally invasive surgical alternative for the treatment of BPH. The amount of tissue destruction is likely to be small and to limit the size of gland treated by this technique.

One large-scale randomised trial was found in abstract form.[153] Over 50 men were randomised to the two treatments and followed up for over a year. Flow rates and symptom scores improved in both groups, but were better following TURP. On the other hand, fewer men developed complications after TUNA.

Minimal TURP vs. standard TURP[207]

This procedure is effectively an incomplete TURP and is meant to be a lesser procedure than standard TURP with fewer side-effects. The rationale appears dubious, and it is not recommended without further evaluation.

Economic evaluation of LUTS and BPE

The aim of economic evaluation is to compare alternative uses of resources. This is done by relating the benefits which result from one particular activity to the associated costs in terms of real resource use. It is then possible to detect projects with the maximum net present value or greatest cost-effectiveness (depending on the type of evaluation).

Any economic evaluation of health care should involve the comparison of at least two alternatives. Cost studies that do not involve comparisons of competing alternatives are merely descriptions of the costs of a procedure rather than evaluations. These are sometimes called cost-of-illness studies. The simple description of costs cannot support policy recommendations, as no indication is given of the benefits of one project relative to another.

Research reports concerning prostatectomy often mention the costs associated with the procedure, at least briefly. A number of these studies are not particularly helpful in that they only make assertions, e.g. that the yearly cost of surgery and hospitalisation for LUTS and BPE in the USA is in excess of

Table 27: Results for controlled trials of electrovaporisation of the prostate vs. TURP.

Trial	Number	Mean age (years)	Length of follow-up (months)	Symptom score (baseline)	Symptom score (after follow-up)	Improvement in symptom score (%)	PFR (before)	PFR (after)	Improvement in PFR (%)
Patel[200]									
TURP	21			22.5	5.3	76	8.2	18.2	122
EVAP	17			22.4	4.1	82	7.3	18.9	159
Kaplan[203]									
EVAP	29		3	15.3	5.3	65	8.2	14.9	82
LAP	29			14.7	7.6	48	9.7	13.7	41

Table 28: Results of trials of transurethral needle ablation of the prostate (TUNA).

Trial	Number	Mean age (years)	Length of follow-up (months)	Symptom score (baseline)	Symptom score (after follow-up)	Improvement in symptom score (%)	PFR (before)	PFR (after)	Improvement in PFR (%)
Bruskewitz[205]									
TURP	56	66	12	24.1	7.9	67	8.9	21	136
TUNA	65			23.9	11.7	51	8.9	14.6	64
Issa[201]	12		6	25.6	9.8	62	7.8	13.5	72
Schulman[204]	20		3	21.9 (IPSS)	10.2	53	9.5	14.7	55
Schulman[206]	48		36	21.6	8.5	61	9.9	16.9	71

US$1 million,[12] or that prostatectomy costs more than US$1 billion per year in the USA, or that the cost of managing LUTS is large in the UK.[35] Such pronouncements do not generally assist the policy decisions that must be made regarding prostatectomy.

Cost-of-illness studies

While these studies are not forms of economic evaluation, it is helpful to consider the costs obtained by such work. One study considered the cost of prostatectomy given various rates of operation based on variations both within and between countries. It was found that the dollar expenditure in the USA on TURP could vary between US$366 million and US$1195 million, depending on whether there was a low or high rate of operation (1975 prices).

Cost analyses/cost-minimisation analyses/cost-effectiveness analyses

There are a number of types of economic evaluation that can be pursued. In a cost analysis it is assumed that the outcomes of alternative policies are identical in order that the costs of the alternatives can be compared. A cost-minimisation analysis (CMA) is similar, though it is a full economic evaluation as there is some evidence on which to believe that outcome differences of the alternatives are non-existent or unimportant.[208] A cost-effectiveness analysis (CEA) compares the cost of an intervention with its benefits in terms of one outcome measure, e.g. increase in life expectancy or increase in continence or reduction in sexual functioning. It is not possible to compare more than one outcome measure with costs and obtain an unambiguous answer unless all indicators move in one direction or unless the outcomes can be combined in index form, as in a cost-utility analysis (CUA).

A CMA by Meyhoff compares the costs of TURP and open prostatectomy,[214] having previously carried out a randomised trial which found few differences between the clinical outcomes of the two operations for those with medium-sized prostates (25–75 g). Clinical outcomes considered included symptom relief, sexual functioning and long-term results. The economic evaluation was from the societal viewpoint, and both direct and indirect costs were included. The estimated average cost for one patient undergoing TURP was US$4071, and for open prostatectomy was US$7534 (1983 prices). It was therefore concluded that TURP was more cost-effective than open prostatectomy for medium-sized BPE.

Other clinical trials[93] and observational studies[116] have concluded that TURP has a significantly shorter length of stay than open prostatectomy and that at least from the point of view of the hospital it is likely to be more cost-effective.

An economic evaluation was also carried out concerning the cost-effectiveness of uroflowmetry as a means of screening patients for prostate problems.[209] Instrumental measurements of peak flow conducted in the hospital were compared with a simple method of timed urine flow measurement performed at home by the patient. It was concluded that this was a valid method of revealing a weak stream, and therefore the possibility of prostate problems. A broad estimation of costs from the hospital viewpoint led to the conclusion that, as the home method was free, it was more cost-effective.

Cost-utility analyses

A particular form of the cost-effectiveness study is the cost-utility analysis (CUA). In the CUA, as in the CEA, there is only one measure of outcome. In a CUA this is usually the quality-adjusted life-year (QALY), a measure of utility in the form of life expectancy weighted for quality of life. The QALY is in its infancy as a practical outcome measure and still has many associated problems. Several studies have considered utility measures in conjunction with prostatectomy. However, none has combined patients' utility measures of outcome with equivalent costs.

In 1983 a paper was published by Woodward *et al.* that combines two indices regarding prostatic disease to form the Prostatic Health Status Index (PHSI).[210] Although the authors state that transformations should be based on utility functions, the authors' clinical evaluations are used to demonstrate the index. The PHSI is combined with data from the nine years of the project to form QALYs, and with cost data, although it is not made explicit where these cost data come from or what they represent. The index is then used to show the effects of discounting on whichever of the alternatives, open or TURP, is eventually chosen. As the QALY data are based on the authors' clinical evaluations and the cost data are unexplained, it is inappropriate to use the results to recommend particular policies. The authors show that, given different assumptions and with different discount rates, it is possible to present either policy as preferable.

Research has been furthered by the formation of quality-adjusted life-months (QALMs).[211] The authors combine data on patient preferences and Medicare claims data with the utilities estimated by Woodward *et al.* to compare immediate transurethral resection of the prostate with a do-nothing alternative, referred to as 'watchful waiting'. QALMs are compared for a number of alternatives, but for the base-case analysis of a 70-year-old, sexually active, continent man it was discovered that immediate surgery resulted in the loss of 1.01 months of life expectancy compared with 'watchful waiting', but taking quality of life into account, there was a gain of 2.94 QALMs.

The figures for QALMs are, of course, heavily dependent on the probabilities and utilities assigned to various outcomes. Operative mortality was found to be the single most influential probability affecting the QALMs, while some evidence was given that the baseline utility for men with moderate symptomatic prostatism was too low. Without accurate assessment of risks, and utilities based on societies' preferences, the QALM (or QALY) is unlikely to be helpful in making policy decisions. In addition, the utility data must be combined with cost data for a full economic evaluation. Despite this, the analysis is useful in that it compares many different alternatives, with the aim of identifying those particular patients for whom a TURP is most beneficial. It therefore goes some way towards answering fundamental questions regarding which diseases and what level of severity of disease should receive priority in treatment.

The time trade-off approach has been used to elicit utility values for surgical and non-surgical management from 20 men with LUTS.[212] The values obtained in this way were generally higher than those of Woodward *et al.* For example, the value obtained by time trade-off for a state of incontinence was 0.8, while that of Woodward *et al.* was only 0.5. Although the utility values in this study were not incorporated into QALY outcome measures and the sample size was very small, it was shown that such a methodology was a feasible means of eliciting patients' utility scores for prostatectomy and the effects of LUTS.

Cost–benefit analyses

An alternative to the CUA is the cost–benefit analysis (CBA), in which the benefits of an intervention are valued in monetary terms so that they can be directly compared with the costs. This is the only type of economic evaluation that can indicate whether it is intrinsically worthwhile carrying out an intervention, rather than just whether one intervention is relatively more beneficial than another for equal costs. The problems associated with the valuation of the essentially intangible benefits of interventions in the area of health care are inevitably large, and such evaluations often generate much criticism. Perhaps for this reason, no CBAs have been found concerning prostatectomy.

Conclusion

There has been only one study[213] performed which takes into consideration both the costs and outcomes of prostatic surgery. This concluded that for medium-sized prostates a TURP was more cost-effective than open prostatectomy. However, the formation of utility measures, if combined with cost data, could potentially be of great value in informing policy on elective surgery for LUTS and BPE.

Ideally, research should be implemented which considers both the relative costs and benefits of prostatectomy for varying severity of LUTS, and the relative costs and benefits of prostatectomy for BPE compared with the relative costs and benefits of other elective surgery. Only when this is done will it be possible to establish priorities in treatment.

7 Recommendations and models of care

In considering purchasing decisions, it is necessary to distinguish between those patients with acute and chronic urinary retention who require emergency catheterisation and prostatectomy, and those who elect for a prostatectomy because of bothersome urinary symptoms. Clearly, all patients with acute urinary retention will require emergency catheterisation, but there is some uncertainty over whether patients should progress immediately from catheterisation to a prostatectomy or to a 'trial of voiding' before deciding on the necessity for a prostatectomy. Currently, practice differs among urologists.[40]

In men who only have symptoms, the risk of progression to retention if they are not offered TURP has been shown in an overview of men entered into a trial of finasteride. Following drug treatment, the rates of elective prostatectomy were 4.2% in men treated with finasteride compared with 6.5% in men treated with placebo, and the rates of urinary retention were 1.1% in men treated with finasteride compared with 2.7% in men treated with placebo.[214] The number of men prevented from developing complications by medical treatment is, however, relatively small[215] and it would not be cost-effective to offer medical treatment to all men with symptoms solely on the grounds of preventing complications in the very few.

The largest group of patients receiving prostatectomy are those electing for the operation because of bothersome urinary symptoms (approximately 65%). The uncertainty and debate surrounding the diagnosis and treatment of LUTS, and the lack of consensus about who should have treatment and at what stage in the development of the disease means, however, that purchasers have very limited information on which to base their decisions. To place too much stress on a refined analysis of the status quo would be quite inappropriate in the face of accumulating research evidence that calls into question any certainties concerning appropriate criteria for treatment. That prostatectomy is an effective intervention in some cases is not in doubt. There is considerable doubt, however, concerning the circumstances in which it is effective, and which procedure is preferable in certain cases. It should also be noted that provision of prostatectomy in England and Wales is currently low by international standards.

Conventional model

In this current model, GPs see men with symptoms or complications of BPH as they present. A GP will expect to see 50 men per year per 1000 men aged over 60 (equivalent to 10 000 of the general population). Twenty will be referred on, 20 may be reassured, 10 will have operative treatment and 10 will be treated by drug therapy. The standard mode of operative management will be by means of TURP or TUIP. Total costs will be £40 000 per year for a group of 1000 men aged over 60 years, but as pointed out earlier, the true in-hospital costs of the provision of this service are likely to be much greater than this. Increased information about prostate diseases among men in the community is likely to increase the number of men presenting to GPs. Our recommendations are that men with mild to moderate symptoms and no evidence of prostate cancer or impaired bladder emptying can be safely managed by 'watchful waiting'. Men who do not respond to this management may be treated by drugs (α-adrenergic blockers or finasteride) or referred to a local urologist.

Increased local management

It may be that by the provision of easy-access prostate assessment clinics and the use of specially trained nurses provided with flow meters, more men might be managed locally, and only those with severe symptoms or complications would be referred on to hospitals. This may be more costly – particularly because more men would be likely to be managed with drug treatment, which costs in the order of £300 per year. A more ready policy of treatment of such men by means of drugs might at first sight be likely to result in decreased demand for surgery. However, there are likely to be more subtle changes. First, in the UK, men are offered treatment only when they have severe symptoms and side-effects and a reduced demand for surgery may not be seen. Second, the pool of treated men may well increase significantly, increasing global costs without decreasing the numbers referred for surgery. Another cost is the requirement to maintain and check up on the accuracy of flow meters and ultrasound scanners.

The numbers of men presenting to a GP per year may not justify the costs of specially trained nurses and it may be more cost-effective to arrange nurse-led clinics to be held and supervised by urologists in secondary care. The other option is for primary care trusts (PCTs) to set up prostate assessment clinics, but the comments about quality control are important.

New technology

More men are being managed by means of new techniques, such as stents, microwaves and lasers. While these treatments may be less prone to side-effects, they may turn out to be more costly and less cost-effective in the long term. It is our view that purchasers should be asking providers for details of when men are treated with new technology because we consider that, in general, such treatments should be provided only in the context of large randomised trials.

Conclusions

The current provision of TURP in England and Wales of about 40 000 to 45 000 operations per year is low compared to international standards. There are no data suggesting that this number is incorrect or unsafe. The proportion of men with chronic retention and acute retention compared to the whole is relatively large, suggesting that UK urologists are relatively conservative. Guidelines produced by the Royal College of Surgeons and British Association of Urological Surgeons are likely to iron out some of the differences among urologists for threshold for intervention in men with symptoms.

Men with LUTS and BPE are not more prone to develop prostate cancer compared with the rest of the population. However, prostate cancer can present with lower urinary tract symptoms, and exclusion of locally advanced prostate cancer is important.

There is no indication for setting up routine screening for early prostate cancer. Initial assessment should be carried out by the GP. Nurse-led prostate assessment clinics staffed by specially trained nurses and overseen by a consultant or committed, interested GP might in the future offer an intermediate form of assessment which might make urology outpatient visits more effective. If GPs are going to manage men with LUTS in primary care by means of drug treatment, they should be confident in their own technique of rectal examination so that they can exclude locally advanced prostate cancer, which can also be a cause of symptoms. Access to a general urology clinic should also be available. Between 150 and 250 per 100 000 men aged over 60 have significant symptoms in the community.

The evidence suggests that men with mild or moderate symptoms without evidence of complications or prostate cancer can be managed by 'watchful waiting'. The evidence also suggests that α-adrenergic blockers and finasteride are more effective than placebo treatments and that, in some trials, finasteride is less effective than α-adrenergic blockers. Long-term data have shown that men who have responded to finasteride in the short term and who are kept on long-term treatment have fewer admissions with acute retention or for prostatectomy. However, the number of operations prevented is relatively low. Long-term drug treatment may be provided in primary care.

Men seen in outpatient clinics should undergo clinical history taking and examination. Renal function should be assessed, and urinary infection and diabetes should be excluded. There is no need for routine IVU or upper tract imaging, but flow rates should be measured and urodynamic studies should be available for selected patients.

Men with acute retention require urgent catheterisation and either urgent admission or urgent assessment by the urologist. Men with chronic retention require urgent outpatient assessment; those with renal impairment need urgent admission. Men with severe symptoms or problems should be referred to a urologist.

8 Outcome measures, audit information and research needs

This chapter has drawn attention to the paucity of evidence that may support an informed judgement as to the health care requirements for treatment for LUTS and BPE.

In particular, it should be noted that there are no good data on:

- true costs of new treatments
- cost-effectiveness of new treatments and new technologies
- long-term outcome for new treatments.

Information

Hospital data can never permit an assessment of the natural history of LUTS and BPE, the requirement for treatment, or the outcome or effectiveness of treatments, because of the large number of men who are not referred.

Increasing management of men in primary care should be monitored, as should the use of potentially expensive medications.

Audit

Large-scale audits of TURP have now been carried out in England and have shown good levels of performance in keeping with international standards. The costs of such complex audits are considerable. It may be that PCTs will want urologists to demonstrate participation in audit programmes. Monitoring of complications and feedback of untoward incidents would be a good initial step, rather than insisting on more precise measurements which might carry considerable costs.

Possible measures of quality might include:

- management of acute retention – if men are discharged home with a catheter, how soon are they readmitted for elective surgery (excluding those who are waiting for intercurrent illness to improve)?
- return to theatre rates
- late reoperation rates
- proper treatment of intercurrent urinary infection.

Death rates are not a good measurement because they are so low, even in men with retention or prostate cancer.

In primary care, it may be that demonstration of appropriate 'watchful-waiting' periods before referral to secondary care might be a good measurement. Ensuring that men with severe symptoms or impaired bladder emptying are referred to secondary care might be another measurement.

Research

There are weak relationships among BPH, BPE, BOO, LUTS, clinical findings, autopsy evidence and objective measures of urinary function (e.g. urodynamic studies). Prostatectomy is the current standard treatment for BOO caused by BPE, but there is uncertainty about how to distinguish obstruction from other problems of the urinary tract. There is also debate about which type of prostatectomy is the most effective (open or transurethral), and whether or not alternative therapies (drug and new technology) might be more appropriate in some cases.

There is a need for population-based data to build up a greater understanding of the natural history of LUTS and BPE, to investigate patient perceptions of the disease and its treatments, and to assess the outcomes of patients choosing drug treatments and/or surgical procedures compared with those preferring more conservative treatments, including 'watchful waiting' and no treatment. There is also clearly a need for outcomes research, which draws on existing data (mortality and readmission rates, length of hospital stay, use of medication), and dedicated enquiries (measures of perceived health, including activities of daily living, patient satisfaction and well-being, perceived levels of change in life and state of health, as well as specific post-operative complications).

There is a need for research into the following areas:

- comparison of drug treatments and 'watchful waiting' in primary care
- comparison of drug treatment in primary care and the use of new technology as a single treatment
- long-term data on the randomised trials that have been funded by NHS R&D to compare new technologies with conventional treatment
- provision of care and assessment by GPs with a more conventional approach
- basic science studies of prostate growth
- basic science studies of the pathophysiology of the ageing prostate and bladder.

Appendix 1

New treatments used in the management of men with LUTS and BPE

Balloon dilatation

At the time of our review there were three major balloon designs: Optilume, Dowd-II and ASI Uroplasty. Balloon dilatation is a technique that has become part of urological practice without evaluation of its effectiveness and cost-effectiveness.

A number of small, observational studies have been undertaken.[120–121] These studies reported mixed results. A success rate, in terms of symptomatic and maximum flow rate improvement, was reported in 46–66% of patients, but in other studies the success rate was lower (one patient out of 28). Most studies reported that the procedure was best for small glands, and resulted in low levels of complications, including retrograde ejaculation. One study reported poor results using the technique in patients with acute urinary retention, with only three of 19 patients able to void following the treatment.

Lepor et al.[120]

Lepor et al.[120] randomised 31 symptomatic men to either balloon dilatation or cystoscopy. Both groups reported statistically significant improvement in symptoms, as measured on the Boyarsky schedule, but there was no statistical difference between the two groups. Changes in maximum flow rates were not significantly different from baseline in either group.

Chiou et al.[121]

This paper has been included for analysis because it has a treatment control group. However, it did not meet the required minimum number of patients and did not state whether baseline parameters for the two groups were similar. Balloon dilatation was compared to TUIP. Symptomatic assessment was measured by the Madsen–Iverson score and dilatation involved the use of the sized-to-fit Uroplasty balloon (Advanced Surgical Intervention, California, USA); TUIP was as described by Orandi.[123] Good responses were defined by an improvement in symptom scores of 50% or more.

The results demonstrated a mean increase in peak flow of 54% in the balloon dilatation group ($n = 16$) vs. an improvement of 101% in the TUIP group ($n = 14$). Side-effects were mild and short-lived for balloon dilatation. In the TUIP group one patient (7%) had delayed bleeding and clot retention, while three (21%) developed a urethral stricture, although these were mild and responded to treatment. Success rates in terms of symptom scores were 87% (dilatation) and 86% (TUIP). Marked improvements were seen in 56% and 71%, respectively. The method of randomisation was not reported. Moreover, after between 6 and 41 months of follow-up, 75% of the balloon dilatation patients had developed symptomatic recurrence compared to 20% of those treated by TUIP.

Donatucci et al.[124]

This was a randomised trial of balloon dilatation vs. TURP in 51 men. Balloon dilatation was performed using a 75-F double balloon dilatation system (Advanced Surgical Intervention, California, USA). Twenty-six patients were randomised to receive balloon dilatation and 25 to the TURP arm. The two groups had similar baseline measurements for all parameters. Symptom scores (using the Madsen scale) decreased from 14.1 to 7.3 over 18 months for balloon dilatation compared with a decrease from 13.6 to 7.7 for TURP. Uroflowometry showed an increase in peak flow (ml/s) from 11.8 to 16.1 for balloon dilatation compared with an increase of 12.2 to 19.8 for the TURP group. Complications reported for TURP included clot retention (8%), retrograde ejaculation (84%) and bladder neck contracture (4%). Only retrograde ejaculation was reported as a complication of balloon dilatation (7.7%).

Klein et al.[125]

This trial included only eight patients. However, it did include a control group and the patients were followed up for 24 months. Very little detail was reported. Of the five men undergoing dilatation, two had long-term improvements and at two years did not require any further intervention, although neither was voiding as well at this time as immediately post-operatively. Two patients had small improvements and sought surgical intervention for their continuing symptoms and one had no improvement. Of the three men in the observation group, two remained stable and one deteriorated. Only a single size balloon was used in this trial. Patients were randomly assigned either to receive treatment or for observation only.

Microwave treatments

Abbou et al.[141]

Two hundred male patients with LUTS were randomised to hyperthermia or placebo (i.e. a sham operation) in a single-centre trial. A second experimental group was randomised to receive hyperthermia via the transrectal route, and was also matched to a sham treatment group. Evaluation was carried out at 3, 6 and 12 months.

Both transurethral and transrectal hyperthermia treatment groups showed an improvement in peak flow rates (4% and 8%, respectively). However, the flow rates in the sham-treated men also improved and there was no significant improvement in objective response for hyperthermia treatment via the transrectal or transurethral routes in this trial. Symptom scores measured using the Madsen score improved by 50% and 25% for transurethral and transrectal routes, respectively. This was a statistically significant benefit for the transurethral route (17% improvement in the sham group), but not for the transrectal group (39% improvement in sham group).

Complications of both routes included urethral bleeding, pain and acute retention. These were found more frequently in men treated by the transrectal route, who also reported complications of rectal pain, faecal incontinence, chest pain, tachycardia and fainting. This route also resulted in more men withdrawing from treatment. No complications were reported for sham treatment.

Early complications of transurethral hyperthermia included urethral bleeding (27%), cystitis (18%), prostatitis and 6% unspecified other complications. Overall, 45% of patients who received treatment suffered from complications vs. 35% of the sham treatment group. In men treated via the transrectal route, 11% suffered from urethral bleeding vs. 13% in the sham group, 3% suffered from cystitis vs. 11% in the sham group, and 18% suffered from overall complications vs. 24% in the sham group. The study used three different devices for transrectal treatment (Prostathermer system, Biodan Medical Systems; Prostcare, Brucker Spectrospin; and Tecnomatix Medical, Belgium) and three devices for transurethral treatment (Theorem II, Technorex; Prostcare, Brucker Spectrospin; and BSD-50, Medical Corps, USA). The frequency of treatment was 1–3 hours and consisted of a single occasion for the transurethral route and six sessions over three weeks for the transrectal route.

Venn et al.[142]

In this controlled clinical trial, 96 patients were randomised to receive hyperthermia ($n = 48$) or sham treatment ($n = 48$). The method of randomisation was by selection of a sealed envelope. The baseline parameters of the two groups prior to operation were similar. Outcome was assessed subjectively, by AUA and Madsen symptom scores, AUA bothersome score and objectively by uroflowmetry.

The subjective evaluation demonstrated a decrease in symptom scores of around 40% in both groups. The only significant difference between the hyperthermia and sham treatment groups was the AUA bothersome score at 3 months, but this difference was not significant by 6 months. Objective parameters did not show any statistically significant difference between active and sham treatment.

Bdesha et al.[143]

This study did not fulfil the minimum requirement for trial size. However, it was carried out as a prospective randomised trial and included a control group. Residual urine volume decreased significantly in the control group vs. the group receiving sham treatment, but there was no difference in peak flow rates between the experimental and control groups. However, in terms of symptom score, taking into account frequency, nocturia, force of stream, hesitancy, terminal dribble, urgency, intermittency and incomplete voiding, there was a significant decrease in the active treatment arm vs. the control group ($p < 0.001$, $n = 22$ in treatment group and $n = 18$ in sham treatment group). The mean decrease in overall symptom scores was 63% in the thermotherapy group and 16% in the control group. No formal analysis of global outcome was reported. However, patients were asked for their opinion on the treatment they received. In the treatment group, 77% said they felt better, compared with 50% of the sham treatment group. Fifty per cent of those in the sham treatment group thought they had received active treatment, although the authors do not confirm whether these were the same patients who said they felt better; 86% of those receiving hyperthermia guessed correctly that they were in the treatment group. Complications of treatment were briefly reported, but did not include any severe mid- or post-treatment complications and all resolved within 48 hours of treatment.

The outcome was assessed at 3 months, and the trial was randomised by use of sealed envelopes. Patients had heat pads placed on their abdomens to minimise the suspicion of sham treatment. The treatment consisted of one single 90-minute session using a LEO (Laser Electro Optics) Microtherm with a variable power outlet and a maximum delivery of 20 W at 915 MHz.

Microwave thermotherapy

de la Rosette[88]

In this study patients were randomised to receive thermotherapy ($n = 25$) or a sham procedure ($n = 25$). The method of randomisation was not described. The delivery of the microwave therapy was carried out using the Prostatron device. However, no further details of the treatment were given in this article.

Parameters including average age and prostatic size were similar for the treatment and sham groups. Although both groups were followed up for one year, statistical analysis between the groups has only been made at 12 weeks as patients in both groups were offered active treatment after this time, minimising the usefulness of the study. There was a significant reduction in Madsen symptom scores in patients who received TUMT (13.2 to 5.9 at 12 weeks, falling further to 3.2 at 26 weeks). In the sham group, the reduction was markedly less, although symptom scores did record a drop from 12.1 to 8.2 at 12 weeks, rising to 9.1 after one year. At one year, 92% of those receiving TUMT and 38% of those in the sham operation group had a reduction in severity of symptoms of > 50%. Uroflowmetry showed a statistically significant improvement in those receiving TUMT, but not in the sham group. In patients who had been given sham treatment, repeat treatment with TUMT brought symptomatic and uroflowmetric improvement. However, in patients who had received TUMT and who had a second round of TUMT treatment, no further improvement was observed. Only four patients in the TUMT group, but more than half of those in the sham group, opted for a second treatment. There was no observed relationship between prostatic size and treatment effectiveness, by subjective or objective evaluation.

A study available in abstract form only[150] demonstrates that the benefits seen following TUMT appear to be persistent at 2–3 years, but start to decline at 4 years.

Roehrborn et al.[151]

This study, available in abstract form only, compared active and sham treatment with the Dornier machine in 205 men. AUA scores decreased in both groups (active, 23.7 to 12.1; sham, 23.8 to 17.5) and flow rates increased in both groups (active, 7.7 to 9.6 ml/s; sham, 8.1 to 9.1 ml/s), but active treatment was superior.

de Wildt et al.[152]

In this prospective, randomised controlled trial, 93 patients received TUMT ($n = 47$) or sham treatment ($n = 46$). The method of randomisation was not reported. There were no statistically significant differences between the baseline parameters of the two groups. Eighty-eight patients were available for assessment at 3 months and 63 patients at 1 year. Patients in the sham treatment group reported an early significant improvement in symptoms (Madsen scores decreased from 12.9 to 10.4), but peak flow rates did not improve in the sham group. Both active and sham treatments caused a sustained improvement in symptom scores and flow rates at 1 year. However, the improvement in patients who received TUMT was significantly better than in those receiving sham treatment. The only significant difference between the two groups after 1 year was in the post-void residual volume and the voided fraction, which favoured TUMT over sham treatment.

D'Ancona et al.[153]

This randomised study of TUMT vs. TURP was published in 1997. A total of 52 men were studied and outcomes were assessed at 12 months: 78% of men felt significantly improved after TURP compared with 68% after TUMT, and flow rates were improved by 100% and 69%, respectively. At 1 year, TURP provided slightly better results.

Dahlstrand and Pettersson[154]

A total of 71 men were randomised. Madsen scores decreased in both groups (TUMT, 12.1 to 3; TURP, 13.6 to 2) and flow rates increased (TUMT, 8.4 to 11.9 ml/s; TURP, 8.3 to 18.6 ml/s). Four men required TURP in the TUMT group. Five men required reoperation after TURP (three early operations for bleeding and two late ones for bladder neck stenosis). The results were maintained at 5 years, but flow rates were better after TURP.

Laser treatments

Anson et al.[162]

In this controlled trial, 151 patients were randomised to receive ELAP ($n = 76$) or TURP ($n = 75$). Patients were followed up for 1 year. The method of randomisation was by means of computer-generated randomised lists. The urolase right-angle laser fibre was the delivery system used to deliver 60 W energy from a Nd:YAG laser. Treatment was delivered at 2, 5, 7 and 10 o'clock positions and lasted 60 s at each point. The baseline characteristics of the two groups were similar. Of the initial patients enrolled to each group, nine withdrew from the ELAP group and five from the TURP group. Of the patients who had received ELAP, five had treatment failure resulting in further surgery (BNI or TURP). Of the remaining patients, 131 were available for follow-up at 1 year. Both groups reported statistically significant improvements in symptom scores (AUA) and peak flow rates. There were significant differences between the two groups with respect to symptom scores, which favoured TURP over ELAP. The scores for patients treated by TURP fell from pre-operative levels of 18.2 to 5.1, compared with patients treated by ELAP whose scores fell from an average of 18.1 to 7.7. TURP was also favoured over ELAP for objective outcomes such as flow rates, voided volumes and post-void residual urine volume.

The reported complications included dysuria in five patients who had received TURP (7%), and 25 patients following ELAP (33%). This decreased with time, but was still significantly higher in the ELAP group (15%) at 3 months than in the TURP group (1%).

One advantage of ELAP over TURP was the lack of haemorrhage requiring blood transfusion. None of the patients treated by ELAP required a transfusion, compared with 16% of patients treated by TURP.

Costello et al.[163]

In this randomised prospective trial, 34 patients were treated by laser prostatectomy and 37 were treated by TURP. The method of randomisation was by assigning alternate patients to different groups, which is not an ideal method. Both groups had similar baseline parameters for age and prostate volume. However, objective uroflowmetry and symptom scores for the groups prior to treatment are not reported. Fifty patients were followed up for evaluation at 6 months. The urolase right-angle laser fibre was the delivery system used to deliver 60 W energy from a Nd:YAG laser. Treatment was delivered at 2, 5, 7 and 10 o'clock positions and lasted 60 s at each point. No difference was found between the two groups when evaluated by maximum flow rates 6 months after treatment. However, evaluation by symptom scores demonstrated that they remained higher in patients who had been treated by laser prostatectomy (9.27) than in men treated by TURP (4.43). Mean flow rate for patients treated by laser was 16 ml/s, compared with 19.1 ml/s in men treated by TURP. More serious complications were reported in the TURP group (22%, including three patients who required blood transfusions) compared with the laser group. However, 41% of the patients treated by laser therapy required treatment for dysuria, although these symptoms eventually resolved. Sexual potency and urinary continence were maintained in all sexually active patients post-operatively. However, while 87.5% of sexually active patients treated by laser maintained antegrade ejaculation, this was only preserved in 27% of those treated by TURP. It is assumed, although not specified, that treatment was ultimately successful for all of those treated by TURP, as no reoperations were recorded. In the group treated by laser, three patients (9%) underwent TURP during the 6-month follow-up period because of failure to improve. One of these patients underwent a second TURP and was reported as suffering from detrusor failure, and the other two patients are reported as having received inadequate laser energy for the size of prostate.

The authors of this study report that with equivalent lengths of hospital stay for both groups, there is a slight economic advantage of TURP compared with laser. However, they also report that if laser treatment can be carried out on an outpatient basis, as reported by Leach et al.,[164] then there is a significant economic advantage of laser treatment over TURP.

Cowles et al.[165]

A total of 115 men with symptomatic BPH were treated by TURP ($n = 59$) or VLAP ($n = 56$). The method of randomisation was a computer-generated chart, and the baseline characteristics of the patients (age, prostate volume, peak flow rate [PFR] and post-void residual urine [PVR]) were similar for both groups, with the exception of the AUA symptom score, which differed between the groups, VLAP patients having a mean symptom score of 18.7 compared with 20.8 for those patients in the TURP group. There was also a difference in the percentage of patients who had received previous treatment for BPH, which was higher for those randomised to receive TURP (28.8%) than those randomised to receive VLAP (16.1%). The urolase fibre was employed for delivery of the Nd:YAG laser energy (Trimedyne, CA, USA). In total, 40 W of power was directed at segments of the prostate for 60 s at the 3 and 9 o'clock positions, and for 30 s at the 12 and 6 o'clock positions. Patients were followed up for 12 months and evaluated by AUA symptom score, peak urine flow, post-void residual volume and quality of life. After follow-up for 1 year the clinical results for VLAP demonstrated a mean decrease in symptom scores of 9, compared with a mean decrease for TURP of 13.3. The peak flow rate increased in patients treated by TURP by 7 ml/s, compared with an increase of only 5.3 ml/s for patients treated by VLAP. TURP had a significantly longer procedure time (45.2 minutes) than VLAP (23.4 minutes) and also required a longer hospital stay (3.1 days) than VLAP (1.8 days). A significantly greater proportion of the group treated by TURP reported that their quality of life was improved 1 year post-operatively (93%) compared with those treated by VLAP (78.2%). The authors categorised complications as serious (i.e. impotence, infection, stricture, blood transfusion) or non-serious (i.e. retention, dysuria, hesitancy, dribbling). By these definitions, a significantly lower number of serious complications was suffered by VLAP patients (10.7%) than by TURP patients (35.6%). Patients treated by VLAP, however, had a considerably higher frequency of non-serious complications (51.8%) than those treated by TURP (28.8%).

Uchida *et al.*[166]

One hundred patients were enrolled in this non-randomised trial and treated by TURP ($n = 50$) or VLAP ($n = 50$). The urolase right-angle laser fibre (CR Bard, Covington, KY, USA) was used as the delivery system for Nd:YAG laser energy. Laser energy was delivered at 2 or 10 spots, 60 W per application, each for 60 s and the patients were followed up for 12 months. The effectiveness of the treatments was assessed by IPSS symptom scores, peak flow rates, post-void residual volume and estimated prostate volume. The clinical response was judged as excellent, good, fair, poor or worse. The baseline characteristics of the two groups were similar, with the exception of mean age, which was lower in the TURP group (66.7 years) than the VLAP group (71 years). This was a statistically significant difference, but the authors do not report how the patients were selected to receive TURP or VLAP. Therefore it is not clear whether younger patients were specifically selected to receive TURP or not. This may have some bearing on the overall outcomes. VLAP was a significantly shorter procedure than TURP (18.2 minutes, compared with 46.5 minutes for TURP), and resulted in a shorter hospital stay (8.3 days, compared with 13 days for TURP). However, the catheterisation time for VLAP (8.1 days) was significantly higher than that for TURP (3.5 days). The overall effectiveness at 12 months was measured by improvements in symptom scores, peak flow rates and PVR. International Prostate Symptom Score (IPSS) decreased from 22 to 7.6 for patients treated by VLAP, and from 21.1 to 3.5 for patients treated by TURP. Peak flow rates increased from 9.1 to 16.4 ml/s for VLAP and from 8.5 to 21.6ml/s for TURP. At 12 months, the overall clinical response after VLAP ($n = 29$) was judged to be excellent, good or fair in 93.1% of patients, compared to 100% of those treated by TURP ($n = 16$).

Keoghane *et al.*[167]

A total of 148 patients were enrolled into a double-blinded randomised trial to assess the effectiveness of laser ablation of the prostate (LAP; $n = 76$) compared with TURP ($n = 72$). The outcome was evaluated using uroflowmetry and AUA symptom scores. Patients were followed up for 3 months only. They were selected for treatment by the use of random-number tables in a 1:1 ratio, and treatment options were determined by sealed envelopes kept in the operating theatre. Laser-energy delivery was achieved using an Nd:YAG system (Surgical Laser Technologies, USA). The baseline characteristics of the two groups were not reported. The mean operating times for the two procedures were similar. However, the median blood loss suffered by patients treated by TURP was 200 ml, compared with 39 ml for patients treated by LAP. The median catheterisation time for LAP patients was 1 day (range 0–9) compared with 2 days for TURP patients (range 1–20), and the median number of nights in hospital was also lower for patients treated by LAP (3) than TURP (4). Mean symptom scores for patients treated by LAP were not significantly different from those for patients treated by TURP at 3-month follow-up. However, the frequency of complications reported for laser was lower than for TURP.

Kabalin et al.[168]

Twenty-five patients were entered into this comparative study of laser prostatectomy vs. TURP. The effectiveness of treatment was evaluated by AUA symptom scores and uroflowmetry. Laser energy was delivered by the urolase right-angle firing fibre. A standard Nd:YAG laser was used at 40 W power setting and energy was applied for 60 s to each lateral lobe at the 3 o'clock and 9 o'clock positions, and for 30 s at 6 o'clock and 12 o'clock. The trial was randomised but the method of randomisation was not reported. Patients were followed up for 18 months, by which time peak flow rates for laser therapy had increased by 135%, and for TURP by 136%. Symptom scores for patients treated by laser decreased from 20.9 to 6, and they decreased from 18.8 to 6.4 for patients treated by TURP. Only one patient in the TURP group reported a long-term complication (urethral stricture), and this was successfully treated. The early results of this trial were previously published, and included baseline characteristics of the two groups which showed a significant difference in the estimated size of the prostate. Short-term complications were reported and were more frequent in the TURP group (42%) than in the laser prostatectomy group (15%). Antegrade ejaculation was preserved in 100% of the patients treated by laser at 3 months, although one patient (8%) subsequently developed retrograde ejaculation. In the TURP group, 90% developed retrograde ejaculation.

Carter et al.[169]

A total of 204 men were randomised. Most patients were improved, but better results were found after TURP compared with laser in terms of symptom scores and quality of life in the first 2 months.

Tuhkanen et al.[170]

This study assessed 34 men. Laser treatment caused less bleeding than TURP (71 vs. 310 ml) and took longer (71 vs. 46 minutes). Catheter time was greater following laser treatment. TURP resulted in greater flow rates (TURP, 7.1 ml/s to 16 ml/s; laser, 8.7 ml/s to 13.9 ml/s) and reductions in symptom scores (TURP, 23.9 to 7; laser, 18.6 to 7.1).

Gilling et al.[173]

This randomised study assessed 86 men. Average operating times were 65 minutes for laser treatment and 49 minutes for TURP. Blood loss was greater after TURP, and hospital stays were longer.

Kitagawa et al.[174]

This small randomised study of 20 men treated by TURP and laser is only available in abstract form. Similar results were found with respect to changes in symptom scores (19.6 to 3.6) and flow rates (6.1 ml/s to 21.5 ml/s) after laser compared with TURP (20.4 to 3.7 and 6.7 ml/s to 21.5 ml/s). Both studies have shown that holmium laser treatment takes 20 minutes longer on average than TURP, but results in shorter stays and less blood loss (*see* Tables 19 to 23).

Transurethal ultrasound-guided laser prostatectomy (TULIP)

Schulze et al.[190]

In a trial comparing TULIP with TURP, 41 patients were randomised and enrolled, though the method of randomisation is not reported. Baseline characteristics of the groups were similar. Laser treatment was a significantly shorter (by 20 minutes) procedure than TURP. The TULIP ultrasound transducer is coupled to an Nd:Yag laser (Intrasonics Inc., Burlington, MA, USA) and power is delivered at a setting of 30–40 W. With ultrasound visualisation, laser passes are initiated at a pull rate of 1 mm/s, with 8 to 10 laser passes being conducted per procedure. The patients were followed up for 1 year, and evaluated by symptom score, peak flow rate and post-void residual volume. The clinical results demonstrate substantial improvements in each of the parameters. However, those patients treated by TULIP lagged behind those treated by TURP in the length of time required to improve, and the improvements in TURP patients were slightly better. Owing to the small size of the trial, the lack of statistical significance is not reliable. There were slightly fewer complications in the TULIP group (10%), and one treatment failure (5%). Men treated by TURP had three complications (14%) and one treatment failure (5%). Sexual function was not assessed.

Transurethral incision of the prostate (TUIP)

Nielson et al.[192]

In this prospective randomised trial, 24 patients underwent TUIP and 25 patients were treated by TURP. The average age of patients receiving TURP was slightly greater than those treated by TUIP (73 vs. 69 years), but in other respects the two groups were similar. The TUIP group had three more patients with very large glands (> 50 g), while the TURP group had four more patients with very small glands (< 30 g). TUIP had a significantly shorter operation time than TURP, and also resulted in significantly less peri-operative bleeding and a smaller number of blood transfusions required. The catheterisation time and length of hospital stay were the same for both groups. The patients were followed for 12 months, after which time there were no significant differences between the two groups for peak flow rates. Complication rates were higher for TURP, and included incontinence (4%) and stricture (17%). Of those randomised to the TUIP group, 12.5% developed post-operative retention and were treated by TURP. Although the authors cite an 82% success rate for TUIP, their analysis of this group includes the three patients who underwent subsequent treatment by TURP (*see* Tables 24 and 25).

Christensen et al.[194]

In this randomised controlled trial of TUIP vs. TURP, 93 patients with prostates weighing less than 20 g were randomised to one of the two treatment arms. The method of randomisation is not stated. The patients were assessed by uroflowmetry and symptom scores and followed up for 2 years. At 3 months of follow-up the total symptom scores were the same for both TUIP ($n = 35$) and TURP ($n = 38$). This was an improvement from pre-operative scores of 16 for each group. Three years after intervention, however, total symptom scores for TURP remained at 4 whereas the scores for TUIP had risen to 8 ($p = 0.09$), although n for each group was lower at this stage (TUIP, $n = 9$; TURP, $n = 11$). In terms of individual-specific improvement, there was little difference between the groups 1 year post-operatively, with patients in both groups reporting around 75% improvements. However, by 2 years the symptomatic improvement in those treated by TUIP had fallen to 56%, whereas improvement in those treated by TURP remained higher at 76%. Due to the large range of variation in scores for both groups, however, this was not statistically significant.

There was a significant difference in peak flow rates between the groups, with those treated by TUIP demonstrating less improvement than those who were treated by TURP. However, when the flow rates were analysed in terms of individual-specific change, there was no statistically significant difference between the two groups.

There were significant differences between the TUIP and TURP groups for operating times, blood loss, catheter time and post-operative hospital stays, all in favour of TUIP. In this study the operating time for TUIP was less than half that for TURP, and blood loss was only 20% of that for TURP.

Dorflinger et al.[195]

Thirty-eight patients were included in this study comparing the effectiveness of TUIP with that of TURP. Eligibility criteria included a prostate weighing less than 20 g. Baseline parameters were broadly similar between the two groups. However, the group that underwent TURP had a slightly higher symptom score than those who underwent TUIP (17 vs. 15), although this was not significant. There was a significant difference in the pre-operative frequency of micturition between the TURP and TUIP groups (14% and 29%, respectively). There were statistically significant differences in the surgical parameters, including operation time, which for the TUIP process was half of the mean time for TURP. Bleeding during surgery was also less for TUIP, and no TUIP patients ($n = 17$) required blood transfusions, compared to 19% of TURP patients ($n = 21$).

Complications for patients treated by TUIP included urinary retention in 12%, which was resolved by TURP. One patient (5%) in the TURP group developed retention, but there were no differences in incidence of treatment failures between the two groups. Patients were only followed up for 3 months. However, at the end of this period total symptom scores and peak flow rates had improved significantly for patients treated by either procedure.

Dorflinger et al.[196]

Thirty-one patients were randomised to be treated by TURP and 29 by TUIP. Pre-operative parameters for the two groups were similar. However, there were statistically significant differences between the groups, including length of operation and blood loss, both of which were lower for patients undergoing TUIP. Thirteen per cent of patients in the TURP group required blood transfusions compared with none in the TUIP group. However, this was not statistically significant. Complications reported included one patient (3%) receiving TURP who developed a urethral stricture. This compared well with the TUIP group, which reported eight treatment failures within the first year after surgery. Despite this, at the 3- and 12-month follow-up assessments both TUIP and TURP groups reported significantly improved symptom scores and peak flow rates. Men treated by TURP demonstrated significantly better improvements in peak flow rates and voided volume compared with those treated by TUIP, and subjective evaluation of the procedures gave improvements of 92% and 95% for TURP and TUIP, respectively, at both 3- and 12-month follow-ups. Four men (17%) who underwent TURP felt that their potency had worsened as a result of the operation, compared with 5% of TUIP patients, but these results were not significantly different. The number of patients who suffered from retrograde ejaculation after TURP (50%) was significantly greater than the number that suffered from retrograde ejaculation as a result of TUIP (5%).

Larsen et al.[197]

Thirty-seven patients with BPH were randomised to undergo TURP ($n = 18$) or TUIP ($n = 19$). The method of randomisation was not reported. Patients were assessed by uroflowmetry and symptom scores (Madsen and Iversen), and were followed up for 12 months.

The baseline characteristics of both groups were similar. Results at 12 months showed a statistically significant decrease in symptom scores as a result of both TUIP and TURP. Peak flow rates significantly increased after treatment by TURP and TUIP. However, the increase was greater for TURP than for TUIP. Of the men undergoing TUIP, 28% developed retrograde ejaculation compared to 100% of those being treated by TURP. For TUIP, catheterisation time and hospital stay were significantly shorter, although no information about the length of operation or blood loss was given. One patient in the TUIP group was readmitted to hospital with haematuria, which resolved spontaneously.

Riehmann et al.[198]

In one of the largest studies included here, 120 patients were randomised to receive either TURP or TUIP. Patients were evaluated by uroflowmetry and symptom scores (Madsen) and were followed up for 6 years. The method of randomisation was not reported. Total symptom scores decreased significantly after both TUIP ($n = 61$) and TURP ($n = 56$). There were no significant differences between the two groups, although TURP resulted in significantly higher peak flow rates than TUIP. Despite the randomisation process, patients in the TURP group had significantly higher pre-operative as well as post-operative flow rates. Of the patients in the TUIP group, 23% received additional treatment for BOO. This compared with 16% of TURP patients who required treatment other than TURP for infra-vesical obstruction. There was, however, no significant difference between the two groups in the numbers of patients who required additional treatment. Other measurements favoured TUIP over TURP, with significant decreases in operating time, blood loss, catheter time and hospital stay compared with TURP. Of the patients who were treated by TURP, 68% reported retrograde ejaculation compared with 35% of patients who were treated by TUIP. This difference was statistically significant. One patient died 90 days after TURP.

Soonawalla et al.[199]

In this trial, 220 men were randomised in equal numbers to be treated by TURP or TUIP. The method of randomisation was not reported. The duration of the operation, number of patients requiring blood transfusion, and duration of catheterisation and hospitalisation were all lower for TUIP than for TURP. However, it was not clear whether these differences were significant. The duration of surgery for TUIP ranged from 10 to 40 minutes (mean = 20.4) and for TURP it ranged from 30 to 95 minutes (mean = 59.2). None of the patients treated by TUIP, but 38 patients (35%) who received TURP, required blood transfusions during the procedure. All patients were followed up for at least 3 months. About 70 men in each group were followed for 1 year and about 20 men were followed for 2 years. At 3 months, peak flow rates in both groups had increased substantially, and this rise was maintained in patients followed up for 2 years. Of the patients who were treated by TUIP, 95.5% were satisfied with the outcome compared with 90% of patients who were treated by TURP. Serious complications (TUR syndrome or haemorrhage) were found more frequently in patients who had received TURP than in those who received TUIP. However, more patients in the TUIP group (6%) than in the TURP group (4%) failed to void following surgery.

Ttransurethral electrovaporisation of the prostate (TUEVP)

Patel et al.[200]

In one small randomised trial, 38 men were studied. Marked improvements were shown after TURP and vaporisation. No significant differences in outcome were found, but catheter time (48 vs. 23 hours) and hospital stay (2.5 vs. 1.2 days) were shorter after vaporisation. Complications included secondary bleeding

(3/21 after TURP and 1/17 after TUEVAP), stress incontinence (1/17 after TUEVAP) and ejaculatory dysfunction (5 new cases after TURP and 2 new cases after TUEVAP).

Standard TURP and 'minimal' TURP

Aagard et al.[207]

Conventional TURP was compared with minimal transurethral resection of the prostate (M-TURP) in 167 patients with BPH. The patients were randomised to the two treatment groups, although the method of randomisation was not reported. Follow-up analysis of symptoms and uroflowmetry were carried out at 6 and 12 months. Of 83 patients who underwent TURP and 84 who received MTURP, 33 and 29 patients, respectively, were available for further examination at 10 years. Nineteen patients who had had repeat operations in the interim period were not included in this analysis. Ten-year follow up showed that obstructive and irritative symptom scores remained stable over the follow-up period with no significant differences between the two groups. However, there was an increased need for repeat surgery in those who were treated by M-TURP compared with the TURP group (23% vs. 7%), which was reflected in a decreased average weight of tissue resected by MTURP (8 g) and TURP (14 g). The incidence of urethral stricture was increased after TURP (14%) compared with MTURP.

References

1 Ekman P. BPH epidemiology and risk factors. *Prostate Suppl* 1989; **2**: 23–31.

2 Lytton B. Demographic factors in benign prostatic hyperplasia. In: Fitzpatrick JM, Krane RJ (eds). *The Prostate*. London: Churchill Livingstone, 1989, pp. 85–9.

3 Isaacs JT, Coffey DS. Etiology and disease process of benign prostatic hyperplasia. *Prostate Suppl* 1989; **2**: 33–50.

4 Barry MJ. Epidemiology and natural history of benign prostatic hyperplasia. *Urol Clin North Am* 1990; **17**(3): 495–507.

5 Lytton B. Interracial incidence of benign prostatic hypertrophy. In: Hinman F (ed.). *Benign Prostatic Hypertrophy*. New York: Springer-Verlag, 1983, pp. 22–6.

6 Watanabe H. Natural history of benign prostatic hypertrophy. *Ultrasound Med Biol* 1986; **12**(7): 567–71.

7 Gofin R. The health status of elderly men: a community study. *Public Health* 1982; **96**: 345–54.

8 Lytton B, Emery JM, Harvard BM. The incidence of benign prostatic obstruction. *J Urol* 1968; **99**: 639–45.

9 Garraway WM, Collins GN, Lee RJ. High prevalence of benign prostatic hypertrophy in the community. *Lancet* 1991; **338**: 469–71.

10 Arrighi HM, Guess HA, Metter EJ, Fozard JL. Symptoms and signs of prostatism as risk factors for prostatectomy. *Prostate* 1990; **16**: 253–61.

11 Glynn RJ, Campion EW, Bouchard GR, Silbert JE. The development of benign prostatic hyperplasia among volunteers in the normative aging study. *Am J Epidemiol* 1985; **121**(1): 78–90.

12 Geller J. Overview of benign prostatic hypertrophy. *Urology* 1989; **34**(4)(Suppl.).

13 Walsh PC. Human benign prostatic hyperplasia: etiological considerations. *Prog Clin Biol Res* 1984; **145**(1): 1–25.

14 Milroy E, Chapple C. The aetiology and treatment of benign prostatic obstruction. *Practitioner* 1988; **232**: 1141–5.

15 Araki H, Watanabe H, Mishina T, Nakao M. High-risk group for benign prostatic hypertrophy. *Prostate* 1983; **4**: 253–64.

16 Sidney S, Quesenberry C, Sadler MC, Lydick E, Guess H, Cattolica E. Risk factors for surgically treated benign prostatic hyperplasia in a prepaid health care plan. *Urology* 1991; **38**(1)(Suppl.): 13–19.

17 Berry SJ, Coffey DS, Walsh PC, Ewing LL. The development of human benign prostatic hyperplasia with age. *J Urol* 1984; **132**: 474–9.

18 Anon. Second-best prostatectomy? *BMJ* 1980; **280**(6214): 590.

19 Hunter DJW, McKee M, Black NA, Sanderson CFB. Health status and quality of life of British men with lower urinary-tract symptoms – results from the SF-36. *Urology* 1995; **45**(6): 962–71.

20 Hunter DJW, McKee M, Black NA, Sanderson CFB. Urinary symptoms – prevalence and severity in British men aged 55 and over. *J Epidemiol Community Health* 1994; **48**: 569–75.

21 Hunter DJW, McKee M, Black NA, Sanderson CFB. Health-care sought and received by men with urinary symptoms, and their views on prostatectomy. *Br J Gen Pract* 1995; **45**: 27–30.

22 Girman CJ, Jacobsen SJ, Rhodes T, Guess HA, Roberts RO, Lieber MM. Association of health-related quality of life and benign enlargement. *Eur Urol* 1999; **35**: 277–84.

23 Roberts RO, Jacobsen SJ, Rhodes T, Girman CJ, Guess HA, Lieber MM. Natural history of prostatism: impaired health states in men with lower urinary tract symptoms. *J Urol* 1997; **157**: 1711–17.

24 Jacobsen SJ, Girman CJ, Guess HA, Rhodes T, Oesterling JE, Lieber MM. Natural history of prostatism: longitudinal changes in voiding symptoms in community-dwelling men. *J Urol* 1996; **155**: 595–600.

25 Blandy JP. The history and current problems of prostatic obstruction in benign prostatic hypertrophy. In: Blandy JP, Lytton B (eds). *The Prostate*. London: Butterworths, 1986, pp. 12–22.

26 Walsh A. Indications for prostatic surgery and selection of operation. In: Fitzpatrick JM, Krane RJ (eds). *The Prostate*. London: Churchill Livingstone, 1989, pp. 137–42.

27 Shah PJR. Clinical presentation and differential diagnosis. In: Fitzpatrick JM, Krane RJ (eds). *The Prostate*. London: Churchill Livingstone, 1989, pp. 91–101.

28 Blaivas JG. Differential diagnosis. In: Hinman F (ed.). *Benign Prostatic Hypertrophy*. New York: Springer-Verlag, 1983, pp. 747–62.

29 Christensen MM, Bruskewitz RC. Clinical manifestations of benign prostatic hyperplasia and indications for therapeutic intervention. *Urol Clin North Am* 1990; **17**(3): 509–15.

30 Jacobsen SJ, Jacobson DJ, Girman CJ *et al*. Natural history of prostatism: risk factors for acute urinary retention. *J Urol* 1997; **158**: 481–7.

31 Pickard RS, Emberton M, Neal DE. The management of men with acute urinary retention. *Br J Urol* 1998: **81**; 712–20.

32 Castro JE. The effect of prostatectomy on the symptoms and signs of benign prostatic hypertrophy. *Br J Urol* 1973; **45**: 428–31.

33 Lepor H. Nonoperative management of benign prostatic hyperplasia. *J Urol* 1989; **141**: 1283–9.

34 de Klerk DP, Allen F. Medical therapy for benign prostatic hyperplasia. In: Fitzpatrick JM, Krane RJ (eds). *The Prostate*. London: Churchill Livingstone, 1989, pp. 119–27.

35 Chisholm GD. Benign prostatic hyperplasia: the best treatment. *BMJ* 1989; **299**: 215–16.

36 Beier-Holgersen R, Bruun J. Voiding pattern of men 60 to 70 years old: population study in an urban population. *J Urol* 1990; **143**: 531–2.

37 Smith RA, Wake R, Soloway MS. Benign prostatic hyperplasia. *Postgrad Med* 1988; **83**(6): 79–85.

38 McGuire EJ. Functional changes in prostatic obstruction. In: Blandy JP, Lytton B (eds). *The Prostate*. London: Butterworths, 1986, pp. 23–32.

39 Taube M, Gajraj H. Trial without catheter following acute retention of urine. *Br J Urol* 1989; **63**: 180–2.

40 Pickard RS, Emberton M, Neal DE. The management of men with acute urinary retention. *Br J Urol* 1998; **81**: 712–20.

41 Styles RA, Ramsden PD, Neal DE. The outcome of prostatectomy on chronic retention of urine. *J Urol* 1991; **146**: 1029–33.

42 Peeling WB. Diagnostic assessment of benign prostatic hyperplasia. *Prostate Suppl* 1989; **2**: 51–68.

43 Lynch TH, Waymount B, Beacock CJ, Dunn JA, Hughes MA, Wallace MA. Follow-up after transurethral resection of the prostate: who needs it? *BMJ* 1991; **302**: 27.

44 Steyn M. Just old age? A study of prostatism in general practice. *Fam Pract* 1988; **5**(3): 193–5.

45 McPherson K. Why do variations occur? In: Andersen TF, Mooney G (eds). *The Challenge of Medical Practice Variations*. London: Macmillan Press, 1990.

46 Esho JO, Ntia IO, Kuwong MP. Synchronous suprapubic prostatectomy and inguinal herniorraphy. *Eur Urol* 1988; **14**: 96–8.

47 Lloyd SN, Kirk D. Who should have a prostatectomy? A survey of the management of patients presenting with bladder outlet obstruction. *R Soc Med* 1991; **84**: 533–5.

48 Sejr T, Andersen TF, Madsen M *et al*. Prostatectomy in Denmark: regional variation and the diffusion of medical technology, 1977–85. *Scand J Urol Nephrol* 1991; **25**(2): 101–6.

49 Nielsen KT, Madsen PO. Pathogenesis, diagnosis, and management of benign prostatic hypertrophy. *Compr Ther* 1988; **14**(11): 21–6.

50 Barry MJ. Medical outcomes research and benign prostatic hyperplasia. *Prostate* 1990; **3**(Suppl.): 61–74.

51 Boyarsky S, Woodward RS. Prostatic health status index. In: Hinman F (ed.). *Benign Prostatic Hypertrophy.* New York: Springer-Verlag, 1983, pp. 766–70.

52 Boyarsky S, Jones G, Paulson DF, Prout GR. New look at bladder neck obstruction by the Food and Drug Administration regulators. *Am Assoc Genito-Urinary Surg* 1977; **68**: 29–32.

53 Herbison AE, Fraundorfer MR, Walton JK. Association between symptomatology and uroflowmetry in benign prostatic hypertrophy. *Br J Urol* 1988; **62**: 427–30.

54 Abrams PH, Feneley RCL. The significance of the symptoms associated with bladder outflow obstruction. *Urol Int* 1978; **33**: 171–4.

55 Epstein RS, Lydick E, deLabry L, Vokonas PS. Age-related differences in risk factors for prostatectomy for benign prostatic hyperplasia: the VA Normative Aging Study. *Urology* 1991; **38**(1)(Suppl.): 9–12.

56 Castro JE, Griffiths HJL, Shackman R. Significance of signs and symptoms in benign prostatic hypertrophy. *BMJ* 1969; **2**: 598–601.

57 Robertson AS, Griffiths C, Neal DE. Conventional urodynamics and ambulatory monitoring in the definition and management of bladder outflow obstruction. *J Urol* 1996; **155**: 506–11.

58 Neal DE, Ramsden PD, Sharples L *et al.* Outcome of elective prostatectomy. *BMJ* 1989; **299**: 762–7.

59 Graversen PH, Gasser TC, Wasson JH, Hinman F, Bruskewitz RC. Controversies about indications for transurethral resection of the prostate. *J Urol* 1989; **141**: 475–81.

60 Hald T. Urodynamics in benign prostatic hyperplasia: a survey. *Prostate Suppl* 1989; **2**: 69–77.

61 Jensen KM, Jorgensen JB, Mogensen P, Bille-Brahe NE. Some clinical aspects of uroflometry in elderly males. *Scand J Urol Nephrol* 1986; **20**: 93–9.

62 Neal DE, Ramsden PD, Powell PH. Authors' reply to letter from PH Abrams. *BMJ* 1989; **299**: 1030.

63 Selley S, Donovan JL, Faulkener A, Coast J, Gillatt D. Diagnosis, management and screening of early localised prostate cancer. *Health Technol Assess* 1997; **1**(2).

64 Schröder FH, Blom JH. Natural history of benign prostatic hyperplasia. *Prostate Suppl* 1989; **2**: 17–22.

65 Blandy J. Prostatic enlargement. *Practitioner* 1989; **233**: 512–17.

66 Wasson JH, Reda DJ, Bruskewitz RC, Elinson J, Keller AM, Henderson WG. A comparison of transurethral surgery with watchful waiting for symptoms of benign prostatic hyperplasia. *NEJM* 1995; **332**: 75–9.

67 Flanigan RC, Reda DJ, Wasson JH, Anderson RJ, Abdellatif M, Bruskewitz RC. Five-year outcome of surgical resection and watchful waiting for men with moderately symptomatic benign prostatic hyperplasia: a Department of Veterans Affairs co-operative study. *J Urol* 1998; **160**: 12–16.

68 Wilt TJ, Ishani A, Stark G, MacDonald R, Lau J, Mulrow C. Saw palmetto extracts for treatment of benign prostatic hyperplasia. *JAMA* 1998; **280**: 1604–9.

69 Chapple C. Medical treatment for benign prostatic hyperplasia. *Lancet* 1992; **304**: 1198–9.

70 Isaacs JT. Importance of the natural history of benign prostatic hyperplasia in the evaluation of pharmalogic intervention. *Prostate* 1990; **3**(Suppl.): 1–7.

71 Lepor H, Williford WO, Barry MJ *et al.* for the Veterans Affairs Cooperative Studies Benign Prostatic Hyperplasia Study Group. The efficacy of perazosin, finasteride, or both in benign prostatic hyperplasia. *NEJM* 1996; **335**: 533–9.

72 De Klerk D. Human trials of endocrine management. In: Hinman F (ed.). *Benign Prostatic Hypertrophy.* New York: Springer-Verlag, 1983, pp. 262–9.

73 Walsh TN, Kelly DG. Historical view of prostatectomy. In: Fitzpatrick JM, Krane RJ (eds). *The Prostate.* London: Churchill Livingstone, 1989, pp. 143–7.

74 Peters PC. Future of surgery for prostatic hypertrophy. In: Hinman F (ed.). *Benign Prostatic Hypertrophy.* New York: Springer-Verlag, 1983, pp. 1033–5.

75 Birch BR, Gelister JS, Parker CJ, Chave H, Miller RA. Transurethral resection of the prostate under sedation and local anaesthesia. *Urology* 1991; **38**(2): 113–18.

76 Smith JM. Open prostatectomy. In: Fitzpatrick JM, Krane RJ (eds). *The Prostate*. London: Churchill Livingstone, 1989, pp. 207–14.

77 Blandy JP. Transurethral prostatectomy. In: Blandy JP, Lytton B (eds). *The Prostate*. London: Butterworths, 1986, pp. 51–61.

78 Mebust WK. Transurethral prostatectomy. In: Fitzpatrick JM, Krane RJ (eds). *The Prostate*. London: Churchill Livingstone, 1989, pp. 149–55.

79 Lepor H, Rigaud G. The efficacy of transurethral resection of the prostate in men with moderate symptoms of prostatism. *J Urol* 1990; **143**: 533–7.

80 Moretti KL. Transurethral prostatic resection: a safe operation. *BMJ* 1989; **299**: 259.

81 Miller A. When is prostatectomy indicated? *Br J Surg* 1965; **52**(10): 744–5.

82 Persky L. Diseases complicating management of benign prostatic hypertrophy. In: Hinman F (ed.). *Benign Prostatic Hypertrophy*. New York: Springer-Verlag, 1983, pp. 714–19.

83 Woodhouse CRJ. Investigations and preoperative assessment. In: Fitzpatrick JM, Krane RJ (eds). *The Prostate*. London: Churchill Livingstone, 1989: pp. 129–35.

84 Pientka L, van Loghem J, Hahn E, Guess H, Keil U. Comorbidities and perioperative complications among patients with surgically treated benign prostatic hyperplasia. *Urology* 1991; **38**(1)(Suppl.): 43–8.

85 Adams AK. Perioperative problems in elderly patients. *Ann Acad Med* 1987; **16**(2): 267–70.

86 Wyatt MG, Stower MJ, Smith PJB, Roberts JBM. Prostatectomy in the over-80-year-old. *Br J Urol* 1989; **64**: 417–19.

87 Sach R, Marshall VR. Prostatectomy: its safety in an Australian teaching hospital. *Br J Surg* 1977; **64**: 210–14.

88 de la Rosette JJ, de Wildt MJ, Alivizatos G, Froeling FM, Debruyne FM. Transurethral microwave thermotherapy (TUMT) in benign prostatic hyperplasia: placebo versus TUMT. *Urology* 1994; **44**(1): 58–63.

89 Nielsen KT, Christiansen MM, Madsen PO, Bruskewitz RC. Symptom analysis and uroflowmetry 7 years after transurethral resection of the prostate. *J Urol* 1989; **142**: 1251–3.

90 Larsen EH, Dorflinger T, Gasser T, Graversen PH, Bruskevitz RC. Transurethral incision versus transurethral resection of the prostate for the treatment of benign prostatic hypertrophy. *Scand J Urol Nephrol* 1987; **104**(4): 83–6.

91 Styles RA, Ramsden PD, Neal DE. The outcome of prostatectomy on chronic retention of urine. *J Urol* 1991; **146**(4): 1029–33.

92 Mebust WK, Valk WL. Transurethral prostatectomy. In: Hinman F (ed.). *Benign Prostatic Hypertrophy*. New York: Springer-Verlag, 1983, pp. 829–46.

93 Chilton CP, Morgan RJ, England HR, Paris AM, Blandy JP. A critical evaluation of the results of transurethral resection of the prostate. *Br J Urol* 1978; **50**: 542–6.

94 Fowler FJ, Wennberg J, Timothy RP, Barry MJ, Mulley AG, Hanley D. Symptom status and quality of life following prostatectomy. *JAMA* 1988; **259**(20): 3018–22.

95 Malone PR, Cook A, Edmonson R, Gill MW, Shearer RJ. Prostatectomy: patients' perception and long-term follow-up. *Br J Urol* 1988; **61**: 234–8.

96 Jensen KM, Andersen JT. Urodynamic implications of benign prostatic hyperplasia. *Urologe A* 1990; **29**: 1–4.

97 Mayo ME. Evaluation and management of symptoms after prostatectomy. In: Hinman F (ed.). *Benign Prostatic Hypertrophy*. New York: Springer-Verlag, 1983, pp. 957–70.

98 Roos NP, Ramsey EW. A population-based study of prostatectomy. *J Urol* 1987; **137**: 1184–8.

99 Mebust WK. Transurethral prostatectomy. *Urol Clin North Am* 1990; **17**(3): 575–85.

100 Caine M. Late results and complications of prostatectomy. In: Hinman F (ed.). *Benign Prostatic Hypertrophy*. New York: Springer-Verlag, 1983, pp. 971–8.

101 Fitzpatrick JM. Urinary infection after prostatectomy. In: Fitzpatrick JM, Krane RJ (eds). *The Prostate*. London: Churchill Livingstone, 1989, pp. 167–71.

102 Boyarsky S. Results of surgery. In: Hinman F (ed.). *Benign Prostatic Hypertrophy*. New York: Springer-Verlag, 1983.

103 Webster GD. Urethral strictures after prostatectomy. In: Fitzpatrick JM, Krane RJ (eds). *The Prostate*. London: Churchill Livingstone, 1989, pp. 181–9.

104 Rous SN. Internal urethrotomy. In: Hinman F (ed.). *Benign Prostatic Hypertrophy*. New York: Springer-Verlag, 1983, pp. 847–50.

105 Krane RJ, Siroky MB. Transurethral resection syndrome. In: Fitzpatrick JM, Krane RJ (eds). *The Prostate*. London: Churchill Livingstone, 1989, pp. 173–80.

106 Ghanem AN, Ward JP. Osmotic and metabolic sequelae of volumetric overload in relation to the TUR syndrome. *Br J Urol* 1990; **66**: 71–8.

107 Hahn RG. Fluid and electrolyte dynamics during development of the TURP syndrome. *Br J Urol* 1990; **66**: 79–84.

108 Krane RJ, Fitzpatrick JM. Postprostatectomy incontinence. In: Fitzpatrick JM, Krane RJ (eds). *The Prostate*. London: Churchill Livingstone, 1989, pp. 191–5.

109 Boyarsky S, Boyarsky RE. Psychosexual counseling. In: Hinman F (ed.). *Benign Prostatic Hypertrophy*. New York: Springer-Verlag, 1983, pp. 939–47.

110 Libman E, Fichten CS, Creti L, Weinstein N, Amsel R, Brender W. Transurethral prostatectomy: differential effects of age category and presurgery sexual functioning on postprostatectomy sexual adjustment. *J Behav Med* 1989; **12**(5): 469–85.

111 Kaufman JJ, Casey WC. Effect of benign prostatic hypertrophy and consequent operations on potency. In: Hinman F (ed.). *Benign Prostatic Hypertrophy*. New York: Springer-Verlag, 1983, pp. 1023–8.

112 McNicholas A, Thomson K, Rogers HS, Blandy JP. Pharmacological management of erections during transurethral surgery. *Br J Urol* 1989; **64**: 435.

113 Neal DE. Prostatectomy: an open or closed case. *Br J Urol* 1990; **66**: 449–54.

114 George NJR, Feneley RCL, Roberts JBM. Identification of the poor-risk patient with prostatism and detrusor failure. *Br J Urol* 1986; **58**: 290–5.

115 Roos NP, Wennberg J, Malenka DJ *et al*. Mortality and reoperation after open and transurethral resection of the prostate for benign prostatic hyperplasia. *NEJM* 1989; **320**(17): 1120–4.

116 Malenka DJ, Roos NP, Fisher ES *et al*. Further study of the increased mortality following transurethral prostatectomy. *J Urol* 1990; **144**: 224–8.

117 Wennberg J, Roos NP, Loredo S, Schori A, Jaffe R. Use of claims data systems to evaluate health care outcomes. *JAMA* 1987; **257**(7): 933–6.

118 Andersen TF, Bronnum-Hansen H, Sejr T, Roepstorff C. Elevated mortality following transurethral resection of the prostate for benign hypertrophy – but why? *Med Care* 1990; **28**(10): 870–9.

119 Seagroatt V. Mortality after prostatectomy: selection and surgical approach. *Lancet* 1995; **346**: 1521–4.

120 Lepor H, Sypherd D, Machi G, Derus J. Randomized double-blind study comparing the effectiveness of balloon dilation of the prostate and cystoscopy for the treatment of symptomatic benign prostatic hyperplasia. *J Urol* 1992; **147**(3): 639–44

121 Chiou RK, Binard JE, Ebersole ME, Horan JJ, Chiou YK, Lynch B. Randomized comparison of balloon dilation and transurethral incision for treatment of symptomatic benign prostatic hyperplasia. *J Endourol* 1994; **8**(3): 221–4.

122 Kaplan SA, Merrill DC, Mosely WG *et al*. The titanium intraprostatic stent – the United-States experience. *J Urol* 1993; **150**: 1624–9.

123 Orandi A. Transurethral incision of the prostate. *J Urol* 1973; **110**(2): 229–31.

124 Donatucci CF, Berger N, Kreder KJ, Donohue RE., Raife MJ, Crawford ED. Randomized clinical trial comparing balloon dilatation to transurethral resection of prostate for benign prostatic hyperplasia. *Urology* 1993; **42**(1): 42–9.

125 Klein LA, Lemming B. Balloon dilatation for prostatic obstruction. Long-term follow-up. *Urology* 1989; **33**(3): 198–201.

126 Marks LS. Value of balloon dilation in treatment of youthful patients with prostatism. *Urology* 1992; **39**(1): 31–8.

127 McLoughlin J, Keane PF, Jager R, Gill KP, Machann L, Williams G. Dilatation of the prostatic urethra with 35 mm balloon. *Br J Urol* 1991; **67**(2): 177–81.

128 Moseley WG. Balloon dilatation of prostate: keys to sustained favorable results. *Urology* 1992; **39**: 314–18.

129 Renfer L, Thompson IM, Desmond PM, Zeidman EJ, Mueller EJ. Balloon dilation of the prostate: correlation with magnetic resonance imaging and transrectal ultrasound findings. *J Endourol* 1995; **9**(3): 283–6.

130 Guazzoni G, Bergamaschi F, Montorsi F *et al.* Prostatic urolume wallstent for benign prostatic hyperplasia patients at poor operative risk: clinical, uroflowmetric and ultrasonographic patterns. *J Urol* 1993; **150**: 1641–7.

131 Kaplan SA, Chiou RK, Morton WJ, Katz PG. Long-term experience utilizing a new balloon expandable prostatic endoprosthesis: the Titan stent. North American Titan Stent Study Group. *Urology* 1995; **45**(2): 234–40.

132 Milroy E, Chapple CR. The urolume stent in the management of benign prostatic hyperplasia. *J Urol* 1993; **150**: 1630–5.

133 Oesterling JE, Kaplan SA, Epstein HB, Defalco AJ, Reddy PK, Chancellor MB. The North American experience with the UroLume endoprosthesis as a treatment for benign prostatic hyperplasia: long-term results. The North American UroLume Study Group. *Urology* 1994: **44**(3): 353–62.

134 Vincente J, Salvador J, Chechile G. Spiral urethral prosthesis as an alternative to surgery in high-risk patients with benign prostatic hyperplasia: prospective study. *J Urol* 1989; **142**(6): 1504–6.

135 Williams G, Coulange C, Milroy EJG, Sarramon JP, Rubben H. The urolume, a permanently implanted prostatic stent for patients at high risk for surgery. Results from 5 collaborative centres. *Br J Urol* 1993; **72**: 335–40.

136 Yachia D, Beyar M, Aridogan IA. A new, large-calibre, self-expanding and self-retaining temporary intraprostatic stent (ProstaCoil) in the treatment of prostatic obstruction. *Br J Urol* 1994; **74**: 47–9.

137 Narayan P, Tewari A, Garzotto M *et al.* Transurethral vaportrode electrovaporization of the prostate: physical principles, technique, and results. *Urology* 1996; **47**: 505–10.

138 Madersbacher S, Kratzik C, Susani M, Marberger M. Tissue ablation in benign prostatic hyperplasia with high-intensity focused ultrasound. *J Urol* 1960; **152**(6): 1956–60.

139 Nakamura K, Baba S, Fukazawa R *et al.* Treatment of benign prostatic hyperplasia with high-intensity focused ultrasound: an initial clinical trial in Japan with magnetic resonance imaging of the treated area. *Int J Urol* 1995; **2**(3): 176–80.

140 Uchida T, Yokoyama E, Iwamura M *et al.* High-intensity focused ultrasound for benign prostatic hyperplasia. *Int J Urol* 1995; **2**(3): 181–5.

141 Abbou CC, Payan C, Viens-Bitker C *et al.* Transrectal and transurethral hyperthermia versus sham treatment in benign prostatic hyperplasia: a double-blind randomized multicentre clinical trial. The French BPH Hyperthermia. *Br J Urol* 1995; **76**(5): 619–24.

142 Venn SN, Montgomery BS, Sheppard SA *et al.* Microwave hyperthermia in benign prostatic hypertrophy: a controlled clinical trial. *Br J Urol* 1995; **76**(1): 73–6.

143 Bdesha AS, Bunce CJ, Kelleher JP, Snell ME, Vukusic J, Witherow RO. Transurethral microwave treatment for benign prostatic hypertrophy: a randomised controlled clinical trial. *BMJ* 1993; **306**(6888): 1293–6.

144 Kaplan SA, Shabsigh R, Soldo KA, Olsson CA. Prostatic and periprostatic interstitial temperature measurements in patients treated with transrectal thermal therapy (local intracavitary microwave hyperthermia). *J Urol* 1992; **147**(6): 1562–5.

145 Montorsi F, Guazzoni G, Rigatti P, Pizzini G, Miani A. Is there a role for transrectal microwave hyperthermia in the treatment of benign prostatic hyperplasia? A critical review of a six-year experience. *J Endourol* 1995; **9**(4): 333–7.

146 Petrovich Z, Ameye F, Pike M, Boyd S, Baert L. Relationship of response to transurethral hyperthermia and prostate volume in BPH patients. *Urology* 1992; **40**(4): 317–21.

147 Stawarz B, Szmigielski S, Ogrodnik J, Astrahan M, Petrovich Z. A comparison of transurethral and transrectal microwave hyperthermia in poor surgical risk benign prostatic hyperplasia patients. *J Urol* 1991; **146**(2): 353–7.

148 Sapozink MD, Boyd SD, Astrahan MA, Jozsef G, Petrovich Z. Transurethral hyperthermia for benign prostatic hyperplasia: preliminary clinical results. *J Urol* 1990; **143**(5): 944–9.

149 Richter S, Rotbard M, Nissenkorn I. Efficacy of transurethral hyperthermia in benign prostatic hyperplasia. *Urology* 1993; **41**(5): 412–16.

150 de la Rosette JJ, Francisca EA, Carter CS St *et al.* Long-term follow-up TUMT 2.0: a multicentre study. *Br J Urol* 1997; **80**(Suppl. 2): 188.

151 Roehrborn CG, Sech SM, Preminger GM *et al.* A randomized blinded study comparing microwave thermotherapy (Dornier Urowave) with a sham procedure in patients with clinical benign prostatic hyperplasia (BPH). *Br J Urol* 1997; **80**(Suppl. 2): 192.

152 de Wildt MJAM, Hubregtse M, Ogden C, Carter SC St, Debruyne FMJ, de la Rosette JJ. A 12-month study of the placebo effect in transurethral microwave thermotherapy. *Br J Urol* 1996; **77**: 221–7.

153 D'Ancona FCH, Francisca EAE, Witjes WPK, Welling L, Debruyne FMJ, de la Rosette JJ. High-energy thermotherapy versus transurethral resection in the treatment of benign prostatic hyperplasia: results of a randomized study with 1 year of follow-up. *J Urol* 1997; **158**: 120–5.

154 Dahlstrand C, Pettersson S. Prospective randomized study of TURP versus TUMT for benign prostatic hyperplasia with 5-year follow-up. *Br J Urol* 1997; **80**(Suppl. 2): 211.

155 Blute ML, Tomera KM, Hellerstein DK *et al.* Transurethral microwave thermotherapy for management of benign prostatic hyperplasia: results of the United States Prostatron Cooperative Study. *J Urol* 1993; **150**(5): 1591–6.

156 de la Rosette JJ, Tubaro A, Trucchi A, Carter SS, Hofner K. Changes in pressure-flow parameters in patients treated with transurethral microwave thermotherapy. *J Urol* 1995; **154**(4): 1382–5.

157 de la Rosette JJ, de Wildt MJ, Hofner K, Carter SS, Debruyne FM, Tubaro A. High-energy thermotherapy in the treatment of benign prostatic hyperplasia: results of the European Benign Prostatic Hyperplasia Study Group. *J Urol* 1996; **156**(1): 97–101.

158 de la Rosette JJ, de Wildt MJ, Hofner K, Carter SSC, Debruyne FMJ, Tubaro A. Pressure-flow study analyses in patients treated with high-energy thermotherapy. *J Urol* 1995; **156**: 1428–33.

159 Eliasson TU, Abramsson LB, Pettersson GT, Damber JE. Responders and non-responders to treatment of benign prostatic hyperplasia with transurethral microwave thermotherapy. *Scand J Urol Nephrol* 1995; **29**: 183–91.

160 Höfner K, Gonnermann O, Grünewald V, Oelke M, Jonas U. Long-term results of TUMT 2.0. *Br J Urol* 1997; **80**(Suppl. 2): 189.

161 Porru D, Scarpa RM, Delisa A, Usai E. Urodynamic changes in benign prostatic hyperplasia patients treated by transurethral microwave thermotherapy. *Eur Urol* 1994; **26**(4): 303–8.

162 Anson K, Nawrocki J, Buckley J et al. Multicenter, randomized, prospective study of endoscopic laser ablation versus transurethral resection of the prostate. *Urology* 1995; **46**(3): 305–10.

163 Costello AJ, Crowe HR, Jackson T, Street A. A randomised single institution study comparing laser prostatectomy and transurethral resection of the prostate. *Ann Acad Med Singapore* 1995; **24**(5): 700–4.

164 Leach GE, Sirls L, Ganabathi K, Roskamp D, Dmochowski R. Outpatient visual laser-assisted prostatectomy under local anesthesia. *Urology* 1994; **43**(2): 149–53.

165 Cowles RS III, Kabalin JN, Childs S et al. A prospective randomized comparison of transurethral resection to visual laser ablation of the prostate for the treatment of benign prostatic hyperplasia. *Urology* 1995; **46**(2): 155–60.

166 Uchida T, Egawa S, Iwamura M et al. A non-randomized comparative study of visual laser ablation and transurethral resection of the prostate in benign prostatic hyperplasia. *Int J Urol* 1996; **3**(2): 108–12.

167 Keoghane SR, Cranston DW, Lawrence KC, Doll HA, Fellows GJ, Smith JC. The Oxford Laser Prostate Trial. A double-blind randomized controlled trial of contact vaporization of the prostate against transurethral resection: preliminary results. *Br J Urol* 1996; **77**: 382–5.

168 Kabalin JN, Gill HS, Bite G, Wolfe V. Comparative study of laser versus electrocautery prostatic resection: 18-month follow-up with complex urodynamic assessment. *J Urol* 1995; **153**(1): 94–7.

169 Carter AC, Speakman MJ, O'Boyle PJ, MacDonagh RP. Quality-of-life changes following KTP/Nd:YAG laser treatment and TURP: results of a prospective controlled randomized trial. *Br J Urol* 1997; **80**(Suppl. 2): 210.

170 Tuhkanen K, Ala-Opas M, Heino A. Early results comparing contact laser prostatectomy to TURP in prostatic hyperplasia over 40 ml. *Br J Urol* 1997; **80**(Suppl. 2): 199.

171 Manlio S, Massimo D, Pasquale F, Marcello M, Andrea V, Michele G. Interstitial laser coagulation of the prostate: 12-months follow-up. *Br J Urol* 1997; **80**(Suppl. 2): 217.

172 Kogan MI, Kratsova TY, Skorikov II, Pavolv SV. Interstital laser coagulation of the prostate using an indigo 830 apparatus. *Br J Urol* 1997; **80**(Suppl. 2): 210.

173 Gilling P, Cresswell M, Frauendorfer M, Kabalin K. Holmium laser resection of the prostate (HoLRP) vs transurethral resection of the prostate (TURP). *Br J Urol* 1997; **80**(Suppl. 2): 196.

174 Kiagawa M, Furuse H, Fukuta K, Aso Y. A randomized study comparing holmium laser resection of the prostate to transurethral resection of the prostate. *Br J Urol* 1997; **80**(Suppl. 2): 209.

175 Costello AJ, Lusaya DG, Crowe HR. Noncontact sidefire laser ablation of the prostate. *J Endourol* 1995; **9**(2): 107–11.

176 Cummings JM, Parra RO, Boullier JA. Laser prostatectomy: initial experience and urodynamic follow-up. *Urology* 1995; **45**(3): 414–18.

177 De Wildt MJAM, te Slaa E, Rosier PFWM, Wijkstra H, Debruyne FMJ, de la Rosette JJMCH. Urodynamic results of laser treatment in patients with benign prostatic hyperplasia. Can outlet obstruction be relieved? *J Urol* 1995; **154**: 174–80.

178 Furuya S, Tsukamoto T, Kumamoto Y, Daikuzono N, Liong ML. Transurethral balloon laser thermotherapy for symptomatic benign prostatic hyperplasia: preliminary clinical results. *J Endourol* 1995; **9**(2): 145–9.

179 Narayan P, Fournier G, Indudhara R, Leidich R, Shinohara K, Ingerman A. Transurethral evaporation of prostate (TUEP) with Nd:YAG laser using a contact free beam technique: results in 61 patients with benign prostatic hyperplasia. *Urology* 1994; **43**(6): 813–20.

180 Narayan P, Tewari A, Fournier G, Toke A. Impact of prostate size on the outcome of transurethral laser evaporation of the prostate for benign prostatic hyperplasia. *Urology* 1995; **45**(5): 776–82.

181 te Slaa E, de Wildt MJ, Rosier PF, Wijkstra H, Debruyne FMJ, de la Rosette JJ. Urodynamic assessment in the laser treatment of benign prostatic enlargement. *Br J Urol* 1995; **76**: 604–10.

182 te Slaa E, Mooibroek J, de Reijke T *et al.* Laser treatment of the prostate using the Urolase fiber: the Dutch experience. *J Urol* 1996; **156**(2): 420–4.

183 Tubaro A, St Clair Carter S, de la Rosette JJ *et al.* The prediction of clinical outcome from transurethral microwave thermotherapy by pressure-flow analysis: a European multicenter study. *J Urol* 1995; **153**: 1526–30.

184 Muschter R, Hofstetter A. Technique and results of interstitial laser coagulation. *World J Urol* 1995; **13**(2): 109–14.

185 Kabalin JN, Bite G, Doll S. Neodymium:YAG laser coagulation prostatectomy: 3 years of experience with 227 patients. *J Urol* 1996; **155**(1): 181–5.

186 Kabalin JN, Gill HS, Bite G. Laser prostatectomy performed with a right-angle firing neodymium:YAG laser fiber at 60 watts power setting. *J Urol* 1995; **153**(5): 1502–5.

187 Malek RS, Barrett DM, Dilworth JP. Visual laser ablation of the prostate: a preliminary report. *Mayo Clin Proc* 1995; **70**(1): 28–32.

188 de la Rosette JJ, te Slaa E, de Wildt MJ, Debruyne FM. Experience with the Ultraline and Urolase laser fibers: is there any difference? *World J Urol* 1995; **13**(2): 98–103.

189 Orihuela E, Motamedi M, Pow-Sang M *et al.* Randomized clinical trial comparing low power–slow heating versus high power–rapid heating noncontact neodymium:yttrium-aluminum-garnet laser regimens for the treatment of benign prostatic hyperplasia. *Urology* 1995; **45**(5): 783–9.

190 Schulze H, Martin W, Hoch P, Finke W, Senge T. TULIP (transurethral ultrasound-controlled laser-induced prostatectomy) – experiences with over 80 patients. *Urologe A* 1995; **34**(2): 84–9.

191 Schulze H. TULIP: transurethral ultrasound-guided laser-induced prostatectomy. A review. *World J Urol* 1995; **13**(2): 94–7.

192 Nielsen HO. Transurethral prostatotomy versus transurethral prostatectomy in benign prostatic hypertrophy. A prospective randomised study. *Br J Urol* 1988; **61**(5): 435–8.

193 Sirls LT, Ganabathi K, Zimmern PE, Roskamp DA, WoldeTsadik G, Leach GE. Transurethral incision of the prostate: an objective and subjective evaluation of long-term efficacy. *J Urol* 1993; **150**: 1615–21.

194 Christensen MM, Aagaard J, Madsen PO. Transurethral resection versus transurethral incision of the prostate. A prospective randomized study. *Urol Clin North Am* 1990; **17**(3): 621–30.

195 Dorflinger T, Oster M, Larsen JF, Walter S, Krarup T. Transurethral prostatectomy or incision of the prostate in the treatment of prostatism caused by small benign prostates. *Scand J Urol Nephrol* 1994; **104**: 77–81.

196 Dorflinger T, Jensen FS, Krarup T, Walter S. Transurethral prostatectomy compared with incision of the prostate in the treatment of prostatism caused by small benign prostate glands. *Scand J Urol Nephrol* 1992; **26**(4): 333–8.

197 Larsen EH, Dorflinger T, Gasser TC, Graversen PH, Bruskewitz RC. Transurethral incision versus transurethral resection of the prostate for the treatment of benign prostatic hypertrophy: a preliminary report. *Scand J Urol Nephrol* 1994; **104**: 83–6.

198 Riehmann M, Knes JM, Heisey D, Madsen PO, Bruskewitz RC. Transurethral resection versus incision of the prostate: a randomized, prospective study. *Urology* 1995; **45**(5): 768–75.

199 Soonawalla PF, Pardanani DS. Transurethral incision versus transurethral resection of the prostate. A subjective and objective analysis. *Br J Urol* 1992; **70**(2): 174–7.

200 Patel A, Fuchs G. A prospective randomized double-blind study of transurethral resection (TURP) vs electro-vaporization (TUEVAP) of the prostate. *Br J Urol* 1997; **80**(Suppl. 2): 190.

201 Issa M. Transurethral needle ablation of the prostate: report of initial United States clinical trial. *J Urol* 1996; **156**(2): 413–19.

202 Narayan P, Tewari A, Garzotto M *et al.* Transurethral vaportrode electrovaporization of the prostate: physical principles, technique, and results. *Urology* 1996; **47**: 505–10.

203 Kaplan SA, Te AE. Transurethral electrovaporization of the prostate: a novel method for treating men with benign prostatic hyperplasia. *Urology* 1995; **45**(4): 566–72.

204 Schulman CC, Zlotta AR. Transurethral needle ablation of the prostate for treatment of benign prostatic hyperplasia: early clinical experience. *Urology* 1995; **45**(1): 28–33.

205 Bruskewitz R, Oesterling JE, Issa MM *et al.* Long-term results of a prospective randomized clinical trial comparing TUNA to TURP for the treatment of symptomatic BPH. *Br J Urol* 1997; **80**(Suppl. 2): 228.

206 Schulman CC, Zlotta AR. Transurethral needle ablation (TUNA) of the prostate: clinical experience with three years follow-up in patients with benign prostatic hyperplasia (BPH). *Br J Urol* 1997; **80** (Suppl. 2): 201.

207 Aagaard J, Jonler M, Fuglsig S, Christensen LL, Jorgensen HS, Norgaard JP. Total transurethral resection versus minimal transurethral resection of the prostate – a 10-year follow-up study of urinary symptoms, uroflowmetry and residual volume. *Br J Urol* 1994; **74**(3): 333–6.

208 Drummond MF, Stoddart GL, Torrance GW. *Methods for the Economic Evaluation of Health Care Programmes.* Oxford: Oxford University Press, 1987.

209 Bloom DA, Foster WD, McLeod DG, Mittemeyer BT, Stutzman RE. Cost-effective uroflowmetry in men. *J Urol* 1985; **133**: 421–4.

210 Woodward R, Boyarsky S, Barnett H. Discounting surgical benefits: enucleation versus resection of the prostate. *J Med Syst* 1983; **7**(6): 481–93.

211 Barry MJ, Mulley AG, Fowler FJ, Wennberg J. Watchful waiting vs immediate transurethral resection for symptomatic prostatism. *JAMA* 1988; **259**(20): 3010–17.

212 Krumins PE, Fihn SD, Kent DL. Symptom severity and patients' values in the decision to perform a transurethral resection of the prostate. *Med Decis Making* 1988; **8**: 1–8.

213 Meyhoff HH, Nordling J, Hald T. Economy in transurethral prostatectomy. *Scand J Urol Nephrol* 1985; **19**: 17–20.

214 Albertsen P, Roehrborn CG, Walsh P *et al.* The effect of finasteride on the risk of acute urinary retention and the need for surgical treatment among men with benign prostatic hyperplasia. *NEJM* 1998; **338**(9): 557–63.

215 Neal DE. Watchful waiting or drug therapy for benign prostatic hyperplasia (leading article). *Lancet* 1997; **49**(6): 305–6.

13   Severe Mental Illness

John K Wing

1 Summary

Defining 'severe mental illness' (SMI)

The term 'severe mental illness' (SMI) brings together two complex concepts. The first is defined in terms of five groups of disorders from the *International Classification of Diseases* (ICD):

- schizophrenic and delusional disorders
- mood (affective) disorders, including depressive, manic and bipolar forms
- neuroses, including phobic, panic and obsessive–compulsive disorders
- behavioural disorders, including eating, sleep and stress disorders
- personality disorders of eight different kinds.

Five other groups of *ICD* mental disorders, not in SMI, can be comorbid. They are:

- F0, dementias
- F1, drug misuse
- F7/8, learning disability and developmental problems, e.g. autism
- F9, disorders starting in childhood.

Each of these, plus forensic issues and primary mental health care, has a separate chapter in the health care needs assessment series.

   The second component of SMI places the *ICD* symptoms and disorders within the context of a judgement of behaviour, course and potential vulnerability. For example:

- active self-injury, food refusal, suicidal behaviour
- threatening or injurious behaviours, drug abuse, severe personality disorder
- embarrassing, overactive or bizarre behaviours
- long-term 'negative' symptoms, such as slowness, self-neglect, social withdrawal
- physical disability, learning disabilities, social disadvantage.

Although the concept of SMI is fuzzy, it has gained substantial official and professional acceptance because it is relevant to the reality of the case-mix decisions that have to be made, in particular those that involve crossing the invisible boundaries between primary and secondary services. The decisions usually turn on a judgement as to whether a patient's needs can or cannot be fully met by treatment within the practice. There is as yet little research focused on making such judgements reliable.

Incidence and prevalence of mental illness (F2–F6)

A large-scale national study of prevalence carried out in 1993–94 provided an epidemiological snapshot of symptoms that are below the threshold for diagnosing a disorder according to *ICD* criteria. The four most prevalent single items were fatigue (the commonest, at 27% of the sample), sleep problems, irritability and worry. Two-thirds of the sample had scores on very few or none of these symptoms.

The one-week prevalence for an 'official' *ICD* diagnosis of one or more above threshold neurotic disorder was 6.9% for men and 9.6% for women (8.3% overall). All except panic and alcohol dependence were more common in women than men. Higher rates overall were associated with divorce, lone parents, living alone, unemployment, other economic inactivity and domicile in urban areas. The numbers in non-white ethnic groups were small, but other studies have found higher rates than for whites.

The prevalence of 'psychoses' (including schizophrenic, manic, bipolar and severe depressive disorders) is much lower. There is some suggestion that the incidence and prevalence of schizophrenia are falling, but the evidence is not substantial. A steady prevalence of about 4–5 per 1000 is assumed for present purposes. The risk factors are similar to those for neurosis (*see* above), with the addition of geographical drift towards more deprived and isolated areas. Comorbidity and excess mortality (e.g. physical illness, self-harm, suicide and other premature death) are common.

Services available and their costs

Two themes underlie consideration of services now available compared with those likely to be required in future. The first is a gradual acceptance of the high prevalence of milder forms of mental symptomatology reflected in self-referral to primary care. The consequent need for assessment and care within the practice, and for a decision as to when to call in specialist advice or help, raises issues for primary care trusts (PCTs). Current NHS plans require that they should commission services, foster collaboration between practices, link with the local community and social services, consider problems arising from uneven quality of care, promote good practice and encourage public participation in decisions. The use of guidelines in primary care has not yet achieved common standards for diagnosis and management, which are the key factors in deciding issues of referral.

The relative severities of mental health problems presented at primary, secondary and forensic service levels present an insight into questions of cost. Districts with the highest morbidity have about twice the prevalence of minor 'disorders' in primary care compared with those with the lowest morbidity. At the secondary level, where clinically more severe mental disorders are concentrated, the calculated range is about 2.5:1 (actual range up to 5:1). For the forensic sector the range is over 20:1.

The second theme concerns the extent to which the development of more effective treatments and changes (if any) in public attitudes compensate for the loss of the former system of large mental hospitals by substantially improving upon it.

Plans for secondary care

A Government document, *Modernising Mental Health Services* (December 1998), provided a list of coming reforms and promised an extra budget of £700 million over the years 1999–2003. The document said that care in the community had failed 'because it left some people vulnerable, others a threat to themselves and a nuisance to others, with a small minority a danger to the public'. Other observations concerned the burden placed on families, underfunding, variable standards, low morale, failure to use the potential of the new medications, problems with the Mental Health Act and inability to provide continuity of care.

Broader issues involved poor co-ordination between services, mismatches between health and local authorities, problems of staff recruitment and shortages of several other kinds. User, carer and professional groups agreed.

In the event, the Modernisation Fund allocation for mental health services for 1999–2000 was an extra £19 million for 24-hour staffed units, outreach and expensive atypical drugs, with £21 million biddable for more secure beds, risk management and family intervention. Two out of 100 health authorities received more than £1 million extra, while 53 received less than £50 000. A single acute bed costs £50–70 000 per anum.

Delivering secondary care

The Care Programme Approach (CPA) and supervision register policies in England (now amalgamated) have been intended to ensure priority for patients with SMI needing to receive specialist help. The basic features include assessment of need for health and social care, to be met by a written care plan periodically updated and a key worker responsible for its implementation. Patients and carers should be closely involved. About 1% of the total population of England were subject to the CPA at any one time, of whom about 1% were included in local supervision registers. Community teamworking can be efficient: hospital time can be somewhat reduced (with some saving of cost) and patients prefer it. But symptom severity and social functioning change little and carers carry more of the burden. A survey of all English NHS trusts found the main administrative elements in place but little harmonisation and very variable involvement by users and carers. Quality of care was not assessed.

Key changes in this system are intended to integrate CPA with care management in all areas, under a new name 'care co-ordination'. There would be a standard and an enhanced level, the latter for very vulnerable users, including prisoners. All parties should be able to request a review at any time and annual audits would be introduced to ensure quality.

Acute wards

Acute admission to hospital is still required, not only in the big cities. The latest in a succession of studies of 12 inner London trusts, including ten of the most deprived areas in the country, found in mid-January 1999 half the patients detained under the Mental Health Act, over a third resident for more than 3 months, 64 recent incidents of first-degree violence and a bed occupancy of 121% (counting patients displaced in order to house yet more urgent cases).

Longer-stay wards

Some patients still accumulate in hospital accommodation for periods from 6 months to 3 years (the 'new long-stay'). Data on 905 such patients from 59 UK services, aged 18–64 at admission, gave an overall point prevalence of 6.1 per 100 000 population. A third of the English patients were unsuitably placed on acute wards, although assessors thought that half of them would have been better placed in a community-based residential home if such had been available. Insufficient sheltered housing is a block to discharge from new long-stay wards, which in turn creates a log jam in the acute wards. There are virtually no adequately large and technically robust comparative studies of daytime activities for patients in these wards.

A comparison of districts

There have been few comparisons of district services. One, commissioned by the Clinical Standards Advisory Group, assessed 11 NHS districts against a protocol of 156 questions based on current 'best practice'. Visiting teams found widely varying achievement of the standards. Four districts approached an overall profile of 'good', five approached 'average' and two were 'poor'. There was no provision for follow-up to discuss findings with district personnel and agree changes as necessary, or for reassessment a year or so later to complete the audit cycle.

Effectiveness of treatments and services

Several of the new medications for schizophrenia (e.g. risperidone and olanzapine) have raised expectations, although recent systematic reviews suggest that it is too soon to make a solid judgement on efficacy, side-effects or longer-term progress. The cash price is high, but success would bring it down. Much the same is true of other disorders within the spectrum of SMI, such as severe depression, where two types of medication – serotonin reuptake inhibitors and tricyclic antidepressants – are in competition. The latter are, for the moment, cheaper. The proliferation of 'new' medications, often minor variants of drugs already in use and often poorly researched, poses a problem that the National Institute for Clinical Excellence (NICE) will investigate. A clear success is skilled cognitive behavioural therapy, alone or together with medication.

Quantified models of care

Two studies of residential services provided for people with SMI provide useful information about current numbers and costs. One project surveyed a range of districts in England and Wales (including London) in 1995; the other examined services in the inner (poorer) and outer (richer) boroughs of London in the same year. Data for inner and outer London illustrate the expected substantial differences in service use and needs. More general indices suggest that other large cities are similar to outer London in many respects, although with better resources, while 'all other districts' across the country have the fewest problems.

- England and Wales: 147 per 100 000, of which 20% are in hospital.
- London: 153 per 100 000 (outer 120, inner 185), of which 30% are in hospital.
- Weekly cost in London, 1995: £5.2 million per 100 000.

The proportions of patients in hospital vs. other residential facilities differed as expected according to the respective epidemiology.

Peak numbers in the large hospitals: where are the successor patients now?

At their peak in 1954, the large psychiatric hospitals housed 345 people per 100 000 population. There is no evidence that disorders requiring substantial support have decreased in prevalence or severity since then. The two 1995 studies (*see* above) suggest numbers of current residents that amount to about half the complement at the former peak, represented today by a wide range of residential facilities, including acute wards, hostels, group homes in variety and other forms of housing with a degree of shelter. Most residents also need day care and occupation, preferably off the ward if in hospital, and off the premises if in other settings. This raises a question about the other half of the 1954 complement. It is likely that some, perhaps a quarter or more of the original total, would be regarded as better placed in other specialist accommodation, e.g. for dementia, physical illnesses or learning disability. The rest, also a quarter, would need at least some form of supervision, day care and/or sheltered activity within the psychiatric and social services.

Estimating need for residential care

Judgement is inevitably required when putting together figures from the studies summarised so far, in order to give an overall estimate of the number of residential places needed, as opposed to currently available. The specific types of residential care used in the two 1995 studies vary substantially from each other, although the overall numbers are very similar. They provide snapshots of usage, not of need. Both are very close to the independent estimate given in the first edition of this chapter. The tentative solution provided here is based on these figures, plus an item for extra housing at the lower end of the England and Wales range (*see* Table 30).

The estimate for England is 175 (range 87–261) residential places per 100 000 on average, costing £93 731 a week or about £5 million (range £2.5–7.5 million) a year per 100 000 overall population at 1995 prices. These numbers are intended to be used with local health and demographic data and local authority welfare information, particularly taking into account the Mental Illness Needs Index (MINI) level for the area. The three-to-one ratio allows a fair degree of tolerance within which to adjust for local history, practice and epidemiology, although there will be districts with configurations beyond these limits. Clearly, all such estimates must come with a clear 'health warning'.

Needs of users for occupation and subsidy: carers also have needs

In the absence of sound data (the literature is very scarce), the clinical assumption for computing day-care need is that half of those in formally supported residences (other than intensive and acute care wards) would also benefit from day care, mostly away from the housing. This criterion suggests that 68 per 100 000 would be candidates for realistic day care outside the setting. Some would already be attending such units. This still leaves the modern equivalent of the less severely disabled group in the 1950s hospitals (another 175/100 000). About half of these (87/100 000) are likely to need long-term non-residential help from mental health services. They should be listed on a community mental health or local authority team, with a care plan that includes meaningful day activities, paid sheltered work for those who can cope and subsidy for those whose income is insufficient. Altogether this brings to 155/100 000 the estimated numbers of people with SMI now in probable need of daytime facilities (*see* Table 31).

Finally, these calculations do not take into account the numbers of people attending psychiatric outpatient clinics, or those who went unrecognised in the primary services of the mid-1950s and in consequence were not referred or treated. It would be wise to bear in mind that all estimates are likely to be on the low side. However, even as they stand, the suggested numbers needing some form of day care and occupational help are almost certainly well above what is actually available in most districts.

Audit, outcome, information and research requirements

Government policy decisions involving primary, secondary and forensic systems have emphasised the dearth of studies intended to monitor how far specific plans for improvement are feasible and, if so, are put into practice. Standards (some of which have already been tested, with others adumbrated and many others still to be created) will be used routinely to monitor progress. From a clinical point of view five areas in particular need to be covered:

- clinicians' performance with patients
- assessment and delivery of standards of care
- organisation and management of care
- training and supervision of staff
- population needs assessment, resource allocation and joint planning.

Some of the measuring techniques needed, such as a minimum data set with continually updated information on patients' progress and service use, including a brief clinical appraisal contributed by clinicians (HoNOS), are already under realistic test. A Department of Health (DoH) working party has proposed a set of outcome indicators. Care standards for purchaser and provider have been laid down and tested.

The CPA provides an opportunity for core training and supervision in such methods. The NHS Information Authority is intended to deliver seamless care for patients and shared information between trusts, PCTs and social services. Methods of appraising and comparing the performance of trusts have been tried out with some success. A further development that would greatly advance the relevance and accuracy of such comparisons would be to feed back information to each participating trust, so that each could decide on a knowledge-based plan to improve specified areas of practice in anticipation of a subsequent further appraisal, thus continuing and enriching the audit cycle.

In the same spirit, it is important to provide good, easily accessible communication between primary, secondary and social care services. Without such knowledge, clinical governance and evidence-based practice cannot be achieved. The Commission for Health Improvement (CHI) reviews the work of trusts and PCTs, including their implementation of the Mental Health Framework. This has required the creation of much tougher and more specific target standards, and really rigorous standards of appraisal.

Even more basic is the aim of NICE to identify new treatments and other measurable methods of care likely to impact on the health and welfare of patients, consider their clinical and cost-effectiveness, and accept or reject them. More generally, it appraises evidence on health technologies, co-ordinates guideline development, promotes clinical audit and undertakes confidential enquiries. An objective for NICE, therefore, is to apply high and comparable standards of inspection to trials of treatments, including sampling, design and methodology, standardised disclosure of side-effects and drop-outs, and detailed evidence for claims of sizeable improvement over other methods of care. The extra costs of atypical drugs that have proved useful so far (though not yet with a long-term record) are already nearly enough to account for much of the £700 million over three years announced in *Modernising Mental Health Services*.[1,2] Enquiries into the efficacy of treatment for mental illnesses have formed a welcome part of the first NICE studies. Together with CHI, which has also looked at mental health services, there is the potential to provide truly knowledge-based health recommendations with a fair chance of their being carried into action.

2 Statement of the problem: severe mental illness (SMI)

The approach

Severe mental illness is an amalgam of two key concepts. The first is derived from five disorders described in chapter F (mental illness) of the tenth revision of the *International Classification of Diseases* (*ICD-10*),[3] named as follows:

- F2, schizophrenic and delusional disorders
- F3, mood (affective) disorders, including severe depressive, manic and bipolar forms, and a range of severe, moderate and mild depressive disorders
- F4, neuroses, including phobic, panic and obsessive–compulsive disorders
- F5, behavioural disorders, including eating, sleep and stress disorders
- F6, personality disorders of eight different kinds.

Various other chapters of the *Health Care Needs Assessment* series deal with the remaining five *ICD*-F groups:

- F0, dementias
- F1, drug misuse
- F7, learning disability
- F8, psychological development
- F9, children and adolescents.

Two other chapters are highly relevant, namely 'forensic issues' and 'primary mental health care'. *ICD-10* F disorders are defined in terms of patterns of symptoms for general use, and also in more specific detail for research purposes. Severity is assessed at the time of diagnosis and appraised throughout the course of the disorder.

The other key concept is 'severe mental illness' (SMI), which places the current *ICD* diagnosis within the context of a much wider range of problems, including severity, persistence and potential vulnerability. For example:

- active self-injury, food refusal, possibility of suicide
- threatening or injurious behaviours towards others
- embarrassing, overactive or bizarre behaviours
- active delusions, depression, phobias, obsessions
- long-term 'negative' symptoms, such as slowness, self-neglect, social withdrawal
- substance misuse
- physical disabilities
- learning disabilities
- social disadvantage and disablement
- likelihood of relapse.

Thus the concept of SMI is basically descriptive.[4-6] It has gained substantial official and professional acceptance because it is relevant to the reality of 'case-mix' decisions, particularly those that involve crossing the boundaries between primary and secondary services, which involve a judgement as to whether a patient's problems require treatment outside the practice.

Components of SMI

The chief factors taken into account when assessing whether a patient's problems are severe enough to warrant the designation of SMI are the type and intensity of symptoms and signs of disorder, the degree of comorbidity and the severity of social disablement.

Diagnosis and clinical severity

The clinical severity of the disorders under review can be measured by:

- the intensity of subjective experiences, such as hallucinations, depression, elated mood, obsessions, anxiety, worry, etc. Intensity involves involuntary intrusion of such experiences into more general mental and social functioning, thus affecting motivation, behaviour and social interaction as well
- the manifestation of signs in behaviour, such as talking aloud to 'voices', acting on delusions, self-harm, over- or under-eating, bizarre or aggressive behaviour, incoherence or poverty of speech, poor self-care, occupational problems, slowness or overactivity
- the course and outcome.

In addition, any of the five main *ICD* diagnostic groups considered in this chapter can present with any degree of symptomatic or social severity. For present purposes it is assumed that SMI includes all the mental health problems in scope that require specialist skills and/or interventions that are not available in primary care.

Comorbidity

The diagnostic and clinical issues discussed above are further broadened by the fact that any of the disorders specified may overlap with one or more of the others. Symptoms that are least prevalent in the populations studied tend to be most severe, and also tend to be associated with many less severe but more common symptoms. Thus symptoms of schizophrenia are frequently accompanied by symptoms of mania, depression, anxiety, etc., as well. Higher-level symptoms are also associated with higher social disability scores. Moreover, severe schizophrenic and affective disorders are themselves stressful. It is not surprising, for example, if people who experience terrifying hallucinations have symptoms of depression, panic and anxiety as well, and may even show the typical symptoms of post-traumatic stress disorder (PTSD).

Social disablement

This clinical complexity is further complicated by interaction between symptoms and any social problems the patient might have. The disadvantages that ensue from a background of deprivation, few social or working skills, and lack of social support can be hugely augmented when a mental disorder is added. The stigma that attaches to some varieties of mental illness further exacerbates the difficulties. Self-esteem, and motivation to find a solution, which may already be low, can be lost altogether. The interactions between clinical and social problems tend to make the allocation of specific causation more difficult. Overall social disablement is thus associated with an amalgam of causal factors and it is this pattern, severity and duration that principally determine needs for care and services.

Key issues and themes raised in Sections 4 to 9

Section 4

Key problems raised in this section involve the high community prevalence of neurosis, in terms both of individual 'symptoms' such as fatigue and sleeplessness, and of disorders such as *ICD-10* depression and anxiety. Is there any evidence that the incidence or prevalence of severe psychiatric disorders is increasing?

Section 5

Can boundaries between primary, secondary and forensic care be specified? What is the structure of 'care in the community'? What does the CPA mean and how will it change? What are the reasons for 'staff burn-out' and can it be prevented? Do users and carers get a look-in?

Section 6

What are the benefits and the disadvantages of the new treatments for mental illness? Are the new medications and the 'talking therapies' cost-effective? Can 'community care' be applied in emergency situations? What is known about the quality of care as appraised by users and carers?

Section 7

Do current and forecast provisions fully replace and improve on the former large psychiatric hospitals? What should a comprehensive secondary psychiatric and social service look like? How can total funding of mental illnesses be distributed equitably across primary, secondary and forensic services? Will the National Service Framework (NSF) work? In particular, will it provide for the social and occupational needs of users and carers, as well as their medical needs?

Sections 8 and 9

What are the implications of NICE, CHI, *Modernising Mental Health Services*, the minimum data set and other Government innovations, and the new research they will encourage, for audit and the improvement of services?

Overlap with other chapters in this series

The remit for this chapter is restricted to SMI, but the concept requires consideration of a broad range of issues that are dealt with in detail in other chapters. The most relevant of these include the following: F0, dementias; F2, drug and alcohol misuse; F7, learning disability; F8, developmental disorders; F9, disorders that originate in childhood and adolescence; mental health in primary care and mentally disordered offenders.

3 Sub-categories of SMI

Mental illness in *ICD-10* F

This chapter is concerned with the five major categories of *ICD-10* (F2–F6) that are likely to contain 'severe mental disorders'. All of the categories have subdivisions, making some 60 disorders in all, each with its own clinical provenance and each often interacting in various ways with one or more of the others. In spite of the complexity of the system, it does for the first time make it feasible to collect reasonably comparable diagnostic and symptomatic data for public health and clinical research purposes. The term 'disorder' is used throughout *ICD-10* F instead of 'disease' to emphasise that, while there are plenty of promising leads, none of the diagnostic groups has yet been definitively described in terms of underlying brain or other somatic dysfunctions or pathologies. The categories are simply the current standards for reference and comparison. At the rate that scientific knowledge is growing, they will be very different in the 11th and 12th editions of the *ICD*. The term 'symptom' is used in two distinct ways. One applies only to a dysfunction, usually rare (e.g. 'hallucination'), that is defined as part of a specific disorder. The other is applied to isolated subjective complaints, such as 'worrying' or 'panic', that appear in isolation or in groups that do not conform to World Health Organization (WHO) definitions of disorder.

Substantial progress has been made towards providing a system of collecting and classifying clinical information that can be used reliably by trained interviewers. The process started with the ninth revision of the *ICD* (*ICD-9*),[7] which gave lists of symptoms for each of the main diagnoses. The ninth edition of a standard clinical interviewing system (Present State Examination, PSE-9) was modified to provide ratings of *ICD-9* symptoms based on a glossary of differential definitions. The authors also provided an algorithm and software for making a standard *ICD-9* diagnosis.[8]

The subsequent tenth edition of the *ICD* has two forms. The 'Blue Book'[9] contains brief instructions for general use, while the 'Green Book'[10] provides detailed algorithms defining the most important categories. The PSE interview, glossary and software were modified to include standardised symptom profiles for *ICD-10* diagnoses and renamed 'schedules for clinical assessment in neuropsychiatry' (SCAN). The PSE-10.2 is its main component. *ICD-10* has not yet become fully incorporated into official systems and some statistics are still provided in terms of *ICD-9*. Further information about SCAN, its history and its current status is given later in this section.

The five diagnostic *ICD-10* F groups under consideration are briefly described below, together with some of the commoner sub-categories. A full list is given in Appendix I. A note about the course of each of the main disorders is also provided.

As emphasised in the previous section, each of the following *ICD* categories can occur in conjunction with any of the others. For example, affective and neurotic disorders are commonly comorbid with schizophrenia, as is drug and alcohol misuse.

F20–25, schizophrenia, schizotypal and delusional disorders

The term 'psychotic' is commonly used to describe the abnormal subjective experiences and accompanying behaviours listed below. Diagnosis depends largely on the patient's account of mental experiences, such as the first four in the list, which can be extremely severe in their initial impact. The three 'negative' items are very common in schizophrenia, but rarely sufficient for a diagnosis in themselves because they can occur in other disorders.

The key 'positive' symptoms of schizophrenia are:

- thoughts experienced as echoed, inserted, withdrawn or broadcast
- delusions of control, influence or passivity
- other delusions with bizarre and culturally inappropriate content
- hallucinatory voices, e.g. commenting on the subject's thoughts.

The key 'negative' symptoms of schizophrenia (overt organic disease absent) are:

- incoherence or poverty of speech
- catatonic behaviours
- apathy, slowness, lack of initiative, social withdrawal.

Recognised subgroups of schizophrenia include paranoid (20.0), hebephrenic (20.1) and catatonic (20.2) disorders. Separate groups include the following: F21, schizotypal; F22, persistent delusional; F23, acute and transient psychotic; F24, induced delusional (including 'folie a deux'); F25, schizoaffective disorders. Virtually any of the symptoms of F3 or F4 disorders can, and often do, accompany the diagnostic symptoms.

Course

After a first episode, about one quarter of patients make a good recovery within five years, two-thirds will have multiple episodes with a variable degree of disability between them, and 10–15% will develop severe continuous disability from negative symptoms.

F30–34, mood (affective) disorders

The affective disorders include the following: F30, manic episode; F31, bipolar affective disorder; F32, depressive episode; F33, recurrent depressive disorder; F34, persistent mood disorder, including cyclothymia and dysthymia.

The basic disturbance in all categories is a change in mood to depression or apathy (with anxiety very common) and/or to elation. The two moods can occur together or alternately, and overall activity is affected accordingly. At their most severe, depression, mania and the mixed 'bipolar' disorders are manifested in ideas (sometimes with delusional force, though usually with content congruent to mood) that may be expressed in self-harm or grandiosely dissocial behaviour. The term 'psychotic' is often used to describe the most severe phenomena, such as delusions, hallucinations, retardation, stupor, flight of ideas or loss of insight. 'Neurotic' (see F4, below) ideation and behaviour are common adjuncts. Severity is graded as mild, moderate or severe. A less severe hypomania is also recognised. The following lists illustrate the relationship between the two major kinds of mood disorder.

Common symptoms of depressive episode	**Common symptoms of mania**
Depressed mood	Elated mood
Loss of interest and enjoyment	Loss of social inhibitions
Reduced energy, activity, concentration	Overactivity, poor concentration
Low self-esteem, guilt, pessimism	Inflated self-esteem, grandiosity
Ideas or acts of self-harm or suicide	Inadvertent harm to self/others
Diminished sleep and appetite	Decreased need for sleep
Delusions, e.g. of sin, poverty, sickness	Grandiose, religious delusions
Mood-congruent hallucinations	Mood-congruent hallucinations
Severe psychomotor retardation or stupor	Flight of ideas, pressure of speech

Subgrouping is chiefly in terms of severity and pattern of recurrence. Nearly all episodes of depression that pass the threshold for diagnosis are mild to moderate in intensity. Cyclothymia (34.0) is a persistent instability of mood, involving numerous periods of depression and mild elation. Dysthymia (34.1) is a chronic depression of mood that does not meet the criteria for F32 or F33.

Course

The course of depression can vary from a brief episode (particularly if in response to stress that resolves rapidly) to a long and severe 'melancholia'. Bipolar disorders tend to be intermittent, but the pattern can recur over a lifetime.

F40–48, neurotic, stress-related and somatoform disorders

The term 'neurosis', like 'psychosis', is retained in *ICD-10* because of its common use rather than for its specific content. Phobias, general anxiety disorders and obsessive–compulsive disorder, together with mild to moderate depression (in *ICD-9* called 'neurotic depression'), are the commonest conditions presenting in general practice.

F40, phobic anxiety disorders
- Agoraphobia: fear of open spaces, crowds, trains, planes, leaving home, etc.
- Social phobias: fear of scrutiny by other people.
- Specific (isolated) phobias: fear of specific situations such as particular animals, heights, thunder, darkness, dentistry, etc.

F41, other anxiety disorders
- Panic attacks, rising rapidly to a climax and then gradually decreasing in severity.
- Generalised anxiety disorder.

F42, obsessive–compulsive disorder (OCD)

- Obsessional thoughts, ruminations and actions, despite conscious resistance.

F43–48, include stress, conversion, dissociative and somatoform disorders.

Course

Anxiety disorders tend to follow the pattern of any stress that provokes them, but can occur *sui generis* and be intermittent or long-lasting. Concomitant depression is common. OCD is also often long-lasting.

F50–55, behavioural syndromes associated with physiological disturbance

This sub-chapter covers the eating disorders anorexia and bulimia, sleep disorders (non-organic), sexual dysfunctions and disorders associated with the puerperium.

F50.0–50.8, anorexia nervosa and bulimia

- Over-valued dread of fatness, leading to body weight deliberately maintained at least 15% below normal, with consequent widespread endocrine disorder. Associated with overeating and attempts to mitigate this by extreme purging, vomiting, etc.

F51–53, sleep and sexual disorders.

Course

Prolonged anorexia leads to under-nutrition resulting in endocrine and metabolic changes, particularly with onset before puberty and in older women up to the menopause. Bulimia often, but not always, follows an earlier episode of anorexia.

F60–68, disorders of adult personality and behaviour

The grouping adopted by the WHO has the advantage of definitions that can be used in conjunction with a system of interviewing, the International Personality Disorder Examination,[11] to ensure a degree of comparability in the data collected and thus also in the categories derived from the *ICD-10* F rules. Eight personality types are listed in Appendix I.

Course

The abnormal behaviour pattern tends to appear in late childhood and then to persist. Several areas of functioning are involved. Problems are not limited to periods of mental illness.

Publications on the *ICD-10* F disorders

The WHO 'Blue Book' provides a prose paragraph and diagnostic guidelines for each major rubric. The more detailed 'Green Book' has specific algorithms (diagnostic criteria for research, DCR) for each disorder. The American Psychiatric Association (APA) has very similar, though not identical, lists of operational criteria, namely the *Diagnostic and Statistical Manual*, 4th revision (*DSM-IV*).[12]

A standardised interview and software for *ICD-10*, the most recent versions of the tenth edition of the Present State Examination (SCAN/PSE-10.2), based on a glossary of differential definitions of symptoms and signs, including all those in the five categories under review here, and CAPSE-2 software has been published by the WHO. Accounts of the PSE and SCAN developments are also available.[13,14] Updated information concerning SCAN and its components, including the PSE-10.2 interview manual, item group check list, clinical history schedule, glossary, training manual and software applications, is available on the WHO website for SCAN (www.who.ch\msa\scan). Alternatively, contact Dr TB Ustun, Division of Mental Health and Prevention of Substance Abuse, Room L3.19, WHO, CH-1211 Geneva 27, Switzerland.

Another system in common use is the *Diagnostic and Statistical Manual* of the American Psychiatric Association.[12] The three most recent editions are *DSM-III*, *DSM-IIIR* and *DSM-IV*. The Composite International Diagnostic Interview (CIDI)[15] is for use by non-clinical interviewers and tends to provide higher morbidity rates than SCAN.

4 Incidence and prevalence

Reliability and applicability of methods

The incidence and prevalence of the five major categories described in Section 3 provide the main basis for consideration in this chapter, but the epidemiology of sub-categories and individual symptoms also has to be considered. For example, affective disorders (F3) are divided for some purposes into 'psychotic' (manic, bipolar, severe depressive), 'other depressive', 'cyclothymic', 'dysthymic' and 'symptomatic'. F4 (neuroses) contains two particularly important subgroups, 'anxiety' and 'obsessional states', each with further divisions. Similarly, 'anorexia' (F50) and 'bulimia' (F52) can occur separately, together or in sequence. Multiplex concepts such as SMI, which are particularly useful when discussing important practical issues, such as the disposition and use of services, are for obvious reasons too fuzzy to be of much use when measuring rates of inception or prevalence of specific *ICD-10* disorders.

The prevalence of 'neurosis'

The National Psychiatric Morbidity Surveys (NPMS)[16,17] were intended to provide an estimate of the prevalence, in 1993–94, of psychiatric morbidity, disability and use of services among adults living in private households in the UK (excluding the Highlands and Islands) who were aged 16–64. A follow-up, Psychiatric Morbidity Among Adults Living in Private Households, was published in 2000.

The sample in 1993–94 consisted of 13 000 adults, of whom 10 108 were interviewed at home using a screening instrument, the CIS-R (Clinical Interview Schedule – Revised), designed for lay interviewers. This gave a prevalence profile for 14 individual neurotic symptoms, such as sleep problems, irritability and worry occurring during the previous week, each scored for severity. A score was also derived, with a cut-off at and beyond which algorithms could be applied to provide approximate rates for some *ICD-10* 'neurotic' diagnoses.

Of the 14 individual CIS-R items, all were commoner in women than men. In keeping with the hierarchy of severity discussed in Sections 2 and 3, the four most common symptoms were non-specific for diagnosis: fatigue (the most common at 270 per 1000), sleep problems, irritability and worry. Two-thirds had scores on few symptoms, while 16% of the sample were on or above the cut-off score for 'neurosis'.

The one-week prevalence of all disorders meeting *ICD-10* criteria was 6.9% for men and 9.6% for women (8.3% overall; *see* Table 1). All except panic disorder and alcohol dependence were more common in women than men. The *ICD* rates fall roughly within the scope of other recent surveys. The category of 'non-specific neurosis' added a further 5.4% for men, 9.9% for women and 7.7% overall, almost doubling the *ICD* rates.

Table 1: Prevalence per 1000 (95% CI) of psychiatric disorders, hierarchical (NPMS).

Diagnosis	Women	Men	All
One-week prevalence			
Non-specific neurotic disorder	99 (89–109)	54 (46–62)	77 (71–83)
General anxiety disorder	34 (28–40)	28 (24–32)	31 (27–35)
Depressive episode	25 (21–29)	17 (13–21)	21 (19–23)
All phobias	14 (10–18)	7 (5–9)	11 (9–13)
Obsessive–compulsive disorder	15 (11–19)	9 (5–13)	12 (10–14)
Panic disorder	9 (7–11)	8 (4–12)	8 (6–10)
Any neurotic disorder	195 (181–209)	123 (113–133)	160 (150–170)
One-year prevalence			
Functional psychosis	4 (2–6)	4 (2–6)	4 (2–6)
Alcohol dependence	21 (17–25)	75 (65–85)	47 (41–53)
Drug dependence	15 (11–19)	29 (23–35)	22 (18–26)

Tables 2 to 6 show the overall prevalence rates for *ICD* neuroses, by personal, socio-economic, ethnic and geographic variables. These generally confirm the picture found in earlier studies. In summary, after appropriate adjustment for confounders, there are higher rates in women, in the divorced, separated or widowed, in lone parents and those living alone, in the unemployed and economically inactive, and in those domiciled in urban areas. There were no differences between regions. Ethnicity was not a significant factor after age, class and family type were allowed for, but the numbers in the Asian/Oriental and Afro-Caribbean samples were very small. Rates of individual disorders per 1000 in the general adult population sampled are summarised in Table 6. Alcohol dependence was much more prevalent in men than in women (7.5% vs. 2.1%), as was drug dependence (2.9% vs. 1.5%).

Table 2: One-week prevalence of neurotic disorder by gender and age (NPMS).

	Sample size	Prevalence, cases per 1000 (95% CI)	Adjusted* odds ratios
Gender			
Male	4,859	123 (113–133)	1.00†
Female	4,933	195 (181–209)	1.72 (1.53–1.93)
Age (years)			
16–24	1,871	150 (132–168)	1.00†
25–39	496	166 (152–180)	1.07 (0.88–1.28)
40–54	2,878	170 (156–184)	1.09 (0.91–1.33)
55–64	1,547	137 (111–163)	0.67 (0.54–0.84)

* Adjusted for age or sex and social class and household size.
† Baseline.

Table 3: One-week prevalence of neurotic disorder by marital status and family type (NPMS).

	Sample size	Prevalence, cases per 1000 (95% CI)	Adjusted* odds ratios
Marital status			
Never married	2,357	157 (142–172)	1.00†
Married/cohabiting	6,484	147 (138–156)	0.89 (0.76–1.05)
Divorced/separated	692	261 (228–294)	1.77 (1.45–2.16)
Widowed	213	254 (202–306)	1.51 (1.10–2.07)
Family type			
Couple, no children	2,586	134 (118–150)	1.00†
Couple with children	3,925	155 (141–169)	1.01 (0.88–1.28)
Lone parent	562	281 (249–313)	1.74 (0.91–1.33)
One person	1,323	209 (189–229)	1.64 (1.39–1.93)
In parental home	1,397	124 (104–144)	0.71 (0.53–0.95)

* Adjusted for age, sex, social class, employment status, and urban/rural residence.
† Baseline.

Table 4: One-week prevalence of neurotic disorder by social class and employment status (NPMS).

	Sample size	Prevalence, cases per 1000 (95% CI)	Adjusted* odds ratios
Social class			
I	649	102 (78–126)	1.00†
II	2,554	145 (129–161)	1.33 (0.76–1.05)
III non-manual	1,484	182 (160–284)	1.41 (1.45–2.16)
III manual	2,778	158 (142–174)	1.46 (1.10–2.07)
IV	1,482	182 (158–206)	1.49 (1.11–2.00)
V	512	185 (149–221)	1.42 (1.00–2.01)
Employment			
Full-time	5,034	118 (106–130)	1.00†
Part-time	1,666	160 (140–180)	1.20 (1.01–1.44)
Unemployed	847	259 (225–293)	2.39 (1.98–2.89)
Economically inactive	2,238	212 (192–232)	1.87 (1.60–2.18)

* Adjusted for social class or employment status and age, sex, urban/rural residence and family type.
† Baseline.

Table 5: One-week prevalence of neurotic disorder by urban/rural residence and geographical area (NPMS).

	Sample size	Prevalence, cases per 1000 (95% CI)	Adjusted* odds ratios
Residence			
Rural	1,010	113 (83–143)	1.00†
Mixed	2,331	137 (123–151)	1.16 (0.91–1.48)
Urban	6,450	175 (163–187)	1.41 (1.14–1.76)
Geographical area			
Southern England	4,478	156 (144–168)	1.00†
Northern England	4,136	164 (152–176)	1.03 (0.92–1.17)
Wales	499	169 (133–205)	1.19 (0.92–1.56)
Scotland	678	153 (119–187)	1.05 (0.84–1.32)

* Adjusted for social class or employment status and age, sex, urban/rural residence and family type.
† Baseline.

Table 6: One-week prevalence of neurotic disorder by ethnic group (NPMS).

	Sample size	Prevalence, cases per 1000 (95% CI)	Adjusted* odds ratios
Ethnic group			
White	9,179	159 (149–169)	1.00†
Asian/Oriental	299	182 (118–246)	1.14 (0.79–1.65)
Afro-Caribbean	148	173 (119–227)	1.02 (0.68–1.52)

* Adjusted for age, sex, social class, urban/rural residence, family type and employment status.
† Baseline.

Other studies on depression and anxiety

Table 7 summarises data on rates of treated depression and anxiety known to general practitioners (Key Health Statistics from General Practice, Office for National Statistics, 1994). The rates (4% for males and 9.8% for females) are quite close to those in the NPMS studies.

By way of contrast, Table 8 provides estimates of prevalence in Australia. The criteria used for 'serious mental disorder' are equivalent to the US definition of SMI. 'Chronic disorders' are present throughout a one-year period and are associated with disability. 'Mild' and transient disorders are non-handicapping and/or remit without treatment within a year.

Bebbington et al.[18] measured the prevalence and need for services in a two-stage sample of the population of a deprived area in south-east London, comprising parts of Camberwell and East Lambeth. The overall weighted one-month prevalence of PSE-10 cases was 9.8%, and that for the year was 12.3% (see Table 9). The data support the observations of enhancement through comorbidity demonstrated in the NPMS. Although the NPMS rate for one-week prevalence was substantially higher at 16%, the rate omitting 'non-specific neurosis' is comparable at 8.3%.

Table 7: GP-treated depression and anxiety, and treated schizophrenia, per 1000 in 1994.

	Treated depression/anxiety			Treated schizophrenia	
	Male	Female		Male	Female
England and Wales	40.3	98.2		2.2	2.2
Highest regions					
North Western	50.1	121.0	Yorkshire	2.8	–
Northern	47.4	114.0	Northern	3.1	2.6
			North Western	2.9	–
Lowest regions					
Oxford	31.5	83.3	Oxford	1.2	–
NW Thames	28.7	69.8	SW Thames	2.0	1.0
			Wessex	2.0	–
			Trent	–	1.7

Table 8: One-year prevalence of mental disorders in Australia, by severity.

Disorder	Serious mental disorder	Chronic mental disorder	Mild and transient disorder	Twelve-month total
Schizophrenia	0.5	0	0	0.5
Any affective disorder	2.1	2.2	5.2	9.5
Any anxiety disorder	1.2	2.2	9.2	12.6
Any substance use	1.0	2.2	6.3	9.5
Total (%)	2.9	5.0	18.8	26.8

Table 9: Prevalence of *ICD-10* disorders (hierarchical) in a south-east London sample.

Diagnosis	One month			One year		
	n	Weighted %	SE	n	Weighted %	SE
Bipolar disorder	1	0.14	0.14	1	0.14	0.14
Severe depression	2	0.24	0.17	5	0.59	0.26
Moderate depression	5	0.74	0.34	8	1.32	0.50
Panic disorder	2	0.24	0.17	3	0.35	0.20
Mild depression	13	2.14	0.64	20	3.34	0.80
Agoraphobia	4	0.71	0.37	4	0.71	0.37
Social phobia	1	0.14	0.14	1	0.14	0.14
Specific phobia	7	1.40	0.56	6	1.27	0.55
General anxiety disorder	1	0.14	0.14	1	0.14	0.14
Depersonalisation	1	0.28	0.28	1	0.28	0.28
Sleep disorder	9	2.43	0.96	9	2.43	0.91
Alcohol dependency*	–			5	0.78	0.37
Drug dependency*	–			2	0.26	0.19
Anorexia*	–			2	0.33	0.24

*These can overlap with the other disorders: prevalence for the previous year only.

Course of depression

A substantial Danish case register study included all 20 350 hospital-first-admitted patients who were discharged with a diagnosis of primary affective disorder during 1971–93.[19] The authors found that the rate of recurrence increased with the number of previous episodes. Although the early course was different for the unipolar and bipolar forms, the rate of recurrence was similar later in the course. The authors conclude from their study of this unique database that 'the course of severe unipolar and bipolar disorder seems to be progressive despite the effect of treatment'.

Relationship to physical health and age

The literature on the physical health consequences of depression is discussed by Dinan,[20] who concludes that there is an increased risk of coronary artery disease and reduced bone density.

Scott Henderson and colleagues quote Cicero, who described the common view of old age. It is wretched because it withdraws us from active life, weakens the powers of the mind and body, robs one of sensual pleasures and is overshadowed by dread of approaching death. He went on to refute all four suggestions (De Senectute). The authors measured the prevalence of depression and anxiety in a cross-section of people aged 18–79 (*n* = 2725) and found that the risk of depression and, to some extent, of anxiety, decreased with age. Other studies have not been so thorough but tend to the same conclusion. The NPMS shows a lower odds ratio for neurotic disorders in those aged 55–64 than in the younger groups. Seneca himself came to a sticky end but he lived and died by his principles and perhaps there is some compatibility between second-century Rome and modern Canberra.

Epidemiology of particular F4, F5 and F6 disorders

F40, phobic anxiety disorders

ICD-10 distinguishes three main groups of phobias: agoraphobia, social phobia and specific (isolated) phobia. Most are commoner in women. Anxiety is evoked primarily by well-defined situations or objects that are not currently dangerous but are feared, avoided or endured only with great discomfort. The symptoms are autonomic, e.g. palpitations, chest pain, choking, dizziness, with secondary fears of going mad, losing control or dying. Comorbid depression is common.

In a probability sample of 8098 community respondents, the most prevalent of 19 specific phobic items were fear of animals among women and fear of heights among men.[21,22] However, most respondents had multiple fears. The number of fears powerfully predicted impairment, comorbidity, the course of illness and parental history, independently of sub-diagnosis.

A questionnaire survey of 2000 randomly selected adults in Sweden found 188 respondents (15.6% point prevalence) beyond the set cut-off point for social phobia (95% CI: 13.5–17.6). Prevalence rates ranged from 1.9% to 20.4% across the spectrum of severity and impairment. Public speaking was the most common social fear.[23]

F41, panic disorder and general anxiety disorder

In contrast to the phobic variety, anxiety in panic disorder is unpredictable. There is a characteristic course in which the symptoms (otherwise identical to those in the other anxiety disorders) rise to a climax and then fade over a few minutes. The symptoms often cause great distress and fear of dying. A strict diagnosis requires three or more such attacks within a period of three weeks. The lifetime prevalence of this acute form is about 3%, while a sporadic form that does not meet the strict criteria has a prevalence about twice as high. Women are twice as likely to suffer as men. A positive family history is found in about 45% and impairment of work and social activities is very common. Those with panic attacks have a high risk of comorbidity with major depression (overlap 37.2, OR 2.1) or bipolar disorder (25.6, OR 3.0). General anxiety disorder (F41.1) is a more diffuse concept, diagnosed on the basis of 6 months of prominent tension, worry and apprehension about matters of daily living, as well as symptoms of autonomic arousal.

Eight well-selected studies of the course of anxiety and depressive disorder followed up for 2 years or more were analysed by Emmanuel and colleagues in 1998.[24] Depression had a somewhat better outcome than anxiety, but both disorders singly had a much better outcome than either with comorbidity.

F42, obsessive–compulsive disorders

The *ICD-10* definition specifies that obsessions or compulsions must be described as originating in the mind and be repetitive, unpleasant, experienced as forced against conscious resistance, and distressing or disabling. A London survey of a sample of 800 people[25] gave a prevalence for checking and repeating of 12% for females and 6% for males. The equivalent figures for cleanliness rituals were 3% for females and none for males, and for obsessional ideas and ruminations, 0.3% for females and 1.6% for males. Overall, about 15% of women and 7% of men were diagnosed. A more detailed analysis suggested that about half of those identified had relatively minor symptoms. Many of the others had comorbid problems, such as depression, which had a greater priority for treatment. The NPMS study (*see* Table 1) found a prevalence of 15 and 9 per 1000 in women and men, respectively. A group of studies using a different instrument, the Diagnostic Interview Schedule (DIS), and definitions from *DSM-IV* found an overall 6-month prevalence between 0.7% and 2.1%. The lifetime prevalence was 3.1–1.9%, with generally higher rates in women. The age at onset was found in one study to be relatively young, starting at 10 years in some people, with an average of 19 years in both men and women.

F48.0, chronic fatigue syndrome

An account of the prevalence, epidemiology, aetiology, treatment and prognosis of chronic fatigue syndrome is provided by Reid and colleagues.[26] The prevalence is estimated as 0.2–2.6%, according to the criteria used. Socio-economic status and ethnicity do not affect rates. Female sex is the only risk factor (RR 1.3–1.7). Despite the burden of morbidity, there is no evidence of increased mortality.

F43, reaction to severe stress

ICD-10 provides for several categories of stress and adjustment disorders, of which post traumatic stress disorder (PTSD) (F43.1) is the most familiar. It requires an exceptionally threatening or catastrophic event or situation, followed by 'flashbacks' and avoidance of circumstances reminiscent of the stressor. It can co-occur with virtually any other disorder in *ICD-10* F. In the National Comorbidity Survey it was found that PTSD was associated with 50% of rape cases, 39% of combat-related events and 21% of women faced with criminal assault.[27] The probability of PTSD among those exposed to a trauma is approximately twice as high in females due to their greater risk following assaults.[28] A follow-up study of 469 men after extreme exposure to a bush fire found that neuroticism score and a past history of treatment were better predictors of post-traumatic morbidity than degree of exposure to the fire and its aftermath.

F5, eating disorders

A comprehensive review of the epidemiology of eating disorders has been provided by Hans Hoek.[29] The incidence was estimated at 8.1 per 100 000 per year for anorexia and 11.4 per 100 000 per year for bulimia.

A study screening the General Practice Research Database for GPs' detection of cases in 1993[30] produced rates of 4.2 and 12.2, respectively. A threefold increase in the recording of bulimia was found from 1988 to 1993, but it is difficult to disentangle increased incidence from increased recognition. Most patients (80% and 60%, respectively) were referred on to secondary care. Osteoporosis, infertility, psychiatric and behaviour disorders and major social disruption are complications. Eating disorders, once established, can be very severe, with outcomes including death from malnutrition, suicide or electrolyte imbalance.

A study of the onset of new eating disorders (*DSM-IV* criteria) in a large adolescent school cohort in Australia over a period of 3 years suggested that the prevalence of partial (two or more criteria) syndromes at the start of the study was 3.3% for females and 0.3% for males.[31] The rate of onset of new disorders per 1000 person-years of observation was 21.8 in females and 6.0 in males. Dieting at a severe level was 18 times, and at a moderate level five times, more likely to lead to an eating disorder than less severe dieting. Subjects initially in the highest category for psychiatric morbidity had an almost sevenfold increase in risk of developing an eating disorder. The authors conclude that dieting is the major contributor to risk. Controlling weight by exercise is less risky.

F6, severe personality disorders

Given the uncertainty of diagnosis, even when using WHO or *DSM* criteria, it is no surprise that substantial problems are encountered in assigning an *ICD-10* category for personality disorder. Co-morbidity is very common and associated problems, such as drug and alcohol misuse, self-harm, cognitive disorders, physical illness and social pressures, generally take precedence for purposes of treatment. Much of the literature focuses on F60.2, dissocial (in the USA, antisocial) personality disorder. A recent review of the epidemiology[32] suggested a prevalence of 2–3% in community surveys, rising to 60% among male prisoners. Coid[33] provides data on risk factors for personality disorders based on 260 people in maximum-security hospitals and prisons.

The incidence and prevalence of psychoses

Risk factors

The psychoses accounted for more than 27 million disability-adjusted life-years worldwide in 1990 and were among the 30 leading causes of disability. Twin studies show that genetic factors are probably important in all of these disorders but 'up to half of monozygotic twins do not develop them'.[34] Hultman and colleagues[35] studied prenatal and perinatal risk factors for schizophrenia, affective and reactive psychosis in a Sweden-wide cohort of all children born during 1973–79, by linking the Swedish birth register to the inpatient register. Schizophrenia was associated with multiparity (odds ratio, OR: 2.0), maternal bleeding during pregnancy (OR: 3.5) and birth in late winter (OR: 1.4). The associations with affective psychosis were uterine atony (OR: 2.1) and late winter birth (OR: 1.5). Reactive psychosis was associated only with multiparity (OR: 2.1). A higher risk for schizophrenia was also found in boys who were small for their gestational age at birth (OR: 3.2), who were number four or more in birth order (OR: 3.6) and/or whose mothers had bleeding during late pregnancy (OR: 4.0). Small size for gestational age in boys and bleeding during pregnancy could reflect placental insufficiency.

Premorbid characteristics associated with an increased incidence of schizophrenia include never having been married or had a partner, movement down the occupational scale, perinatal abnormalities, increased incidence in blood relatives, migration between countries, and internal movement to socially isolated city areas. Males have equal incidence but earlier onset. There is a higher risk among second-generation people from the Caribbean region, but no clear explanation for this. Odegard's hypothesis in 1932[36] that people at genetic risk are over-represented in migrant populations still stands.

Incidence and first-admission rates

Jablensky and colleagues[37] calculated a mean incidence from epidemiological studies of 0.11 per 1000 (range 0.07–0.17 per 1000) using a strict definition and 0.24 per 1000 (range 0.07–0.52 per 1000) for a wider one. Table 10 gives age-standardised first-admission rates for specified *ICD-9* disorders in Scotland in 1969 and 1988. Full data for the intervening years are provided by Geddes and colleagues.[38] There was a steady decline in the incidence of schizophrenia. Many theories have been put forward, notably that there is a 'seasonal etiological agent'. Procopio and Marriott[39] provide evidence, based on first diagnoses in England and Wales between April 1993 and March 1994, against this hypothesis. The disappearance of a non-seasonal factor might be responsible. A lower use of hospital beds, a change in diagnostic habits or simply a decline in morbidity are other possibilities. An incidence within a relatively restricted band (7–14 per 100 000) was observed in an international population study of schizophrenia, narrowly defined using standard techniques.

Scottish age-specific first-admission rates by gender for schizophrenia in 1993–94 show (as do most other calculations) that females have a lower incidence than males at age 15–24 (60 vs. 210 per 100 000). Both sexes peak at 25–34 (175 vs. 440 per 100 000), after which both decline. Male rates decline more rapidly; by age 55–64 they equal those of females (125 per 100 000), and by 85+ both sexes are about 50 per 100 000.

The first-admission rates for affective disorders (*ICD-9*, 296) are also shown in Table 10. They include bipolar disorders and psychotic and neurotic depression. Rates for mania are much lower than for the other disorders (only 3.1 and 4.0 per 100 000 for males and females, respectively, in 1988). The first-admission rate for depressive disorders not classified as affective psychoses was 21 per 100 000.

Table 10: Age-standardised first-admission rates per 100 000 in Scotland, 1969 and 1988.

ICD-9 diagnosis	1969	1988
Schizophrenia 295		
Male	14.7	8.4
Female	11.2	4.8
Affective psychoses 296		
Male	15.5	12.6
Female	34.0	22.9
Mania 296.1–3		
Male	2.4	3.1
Female	3.1	4.0
Neurosis 300.4		
Male	15.5	10.3
Female	25.5	18.9

Source: Geddes *et al.*[38]

Prevalence

The size of the prevalence rate for schizophrenia depends largely on the proportion of patients who develop the negative syndrome. Table 7 gives a 'diagnosed' rate for schizophrenia in general practice of 3.8 per 1000 for males and 3.4 per 1000 for females. The NPMS gave an estimate of 4 per 1000 for 'psychosis' in the two sexes combined. The Australian figure for schizophrenia (*see* Table 8) was 5 per 1000. The lifetime prevalence of both schizophrenia and bipolar disorder is about 1%.

Sociodemographic factors associated with higher rates of mental morbidity

The data obtained in the NPMS surveys provide recent confirmation of risk factors for mental illness that have been studied for half a century. Further confirmation is provided in Chapter 3 of the King's Fund Report on Mental Health in London.[40] Inner London is particularly disadvantaged in comparison with inner-city environments elsewhere, and even more markedly compared with outer London and other urban areas. The key sociodemographic ingredients harmful to mental health listed above for schizophrenia are also risk factors for depression and suicide, and act to increase comorbidity more generally. The implications for need are considered in Section 5.

Commander and colleagues[41] provide a cross-section of the services in west Birmingham (*see* Table 11). The estimated prevalence (28.6%) is higher than the estimate given by the NPMS (16%, *see* Table 1), due partly to the multi-cultural nature of the area but also to the use of different instruments. Confirmation that poverty and unemployment increase the duration of episodes of common mental disorders (though not the likelihood of their onset) comes from a prospective cohort study of 7726 adults in the UK (OR: 1.86; 95% CI: 1.18–2.94). Initial financial strain was independently associated with both onset (OR: 1.57; CI: 1.19–2.07) and maintenance (OR: 1.86; CI: 1.36–2.53) after adjusting for standard of living.

Table 11: Pathways to care in west Birmingham.

Level	Method	Rates per 1,000	Ratio
6 Mental Health Act*	Case register	0.4	
			2.8
5 Inpatient care*	Case register	1.1	
			12.9
4 Psychiatric service use*	Case register	14.2	
			5.8
3 Primary care: conspicuous morbidity†	GP rating	82.8	
			2.2
2 Primary care: total morbidity†	GHQ-301	81.7	
			1.6
1 Community‡	GHQ-30	286.4	

* Specialist services survey.
† Primary care survey.
‡ General population survey.

There is a large literature on the incidence, prevalence and outcomes of mental illness in relation to ethnicity. High rates of schizophrenia in the UK's African-Caribbean population are well documented but the allocation of cause between nature, nurture and unfavourable quality of life has not been resolved.

Deliberate self-harm, suicide and homicide

The *Health of the Nation* initiative highlighted priority problems and set targets for amelioration, e.g. a strategy for reducing suicide rates by the year 2000. Together with the target to improve mental health, these intentions were worthy but unattainable.[42] They have subsequently been modified within an 'evidence-based framework on mental health', to be audited by NICE (*see* Section 8). The *Report of the National Confidential Inquiry into Suicide and Homicide*[43] has 51 key findings on suicide and 27 on homicide, with a further 31 recommendations covering both kinds of problem.

Durkheim[44,45] first demonstrated the relative stability of suicide within particular communities, with high rates in males, the single or separated, Protestants rather than Catholics, urban rather than rural and socially isolated rather than integrated communities. A recent replication of parts of his work shows mortality from suicide increasing with social fragmentation score.

A meta-analysis of studies of suicide by Harris and Barraclough[46] provides an estimate of suicide risk and death from natural causes. Tables 12 and 13 summarise the results. Affective disorders have very high standardised mortality rates, followed by schizophrenia and personality disorders. Some increase occurs in all disorders under review.

Baxter and Appleby[47] used the Salford Register to identify 7921 deaths from suicide or undetermined cause during a follow-up period up to 18 years. The risk was more than tenfold higher, with rates of 11.4 for males and 13.7 for females. Risk was highest in young people, and in people with schizophrenia, affective and personality disorders, and substance dependence.

Table 12: Meta-analysis of suicide rates, by *DSM-III-R* diagnosis.

CD-9 equivalent	Number of studies	Observed	Expected	SMR (95% CI)
Schizophrenia	16	886	98.4	900 (842–962)
Bipolar disorder	4	12	1.0	1,173 (608–2,055)
Major depression	8	142	6.7	2,124 (1,789–2,504)
Dysthymia	3	1,405	117.7	1,194 (1,132–1,258)
Mood disorder NOS	6	192	9.7	1,984 (1,714–2,286)
Eating disorders	5	14	0.4	3,333 (1,822–5,593)

All comparisons significant at 5% level.

Table 13: Mortality from schizophrenia.

ICD-9 category	Male			Female		
	Observed	Expected	SMR (95% CI)	Observed	Expected	SMR (95% CI)
All natural causes	2,836	2,203	129 (124–134)	2,755	2,139	129 (124–134)
All unnatural causes	905	188	480 (450–513)	407	108	378 (342–417)
Suicide	607	162	979 (903–1,060)	200	25	802 (695–921)

All comparisons significant at 5% level.

Crawford and Wessely[48] collected data over a period of 18 months from 16 general practices in Southwark and from local A&E departments, during which 324 patients presented in 415 episodes. Only 15 presented (mostly with self-injury rather than overdose) to their GP. Appleby and colleagues[49] investigated the circumstances of a sample of 2370 people in England and Wales who had committed suicide after having been in contact with services during the previous year. 'Better suicide prevention is likely to need measures to improve the safety of mental health services as a whole rather than specific measures for people known to be at high risk'.[49]

Powell and colleagues,[50] using a case–control design, compared 112 people who committed suicide while inpatients with 112 randomly selected controls. Although several factors were identified that were strongly associated with suicide, their clinical utility is limited by low sensitivity and specificity, combined with the rarity of suicide, even in this high-risk group.

Kennedy and colleagues[51] used Coroners' statistics for homicide and suicide in the 32 London boroughs, and police-reported homicide and violence rates, in relation to population density, UPA (under-privileged area) score and the MINI. The variables were strongly inter-correlated. Rates were highest in boroughs with high population density and deprivation.

Taylor and Gunn[52] provide data from Home Office statistics for England and Wales from 1957 to 1995. There was little fluctuation in the numbers of people with a mental illness committing criminal homicide over the 38 years (mean 36 per year.) The authors conclude that the annual risk that any individual in the UK will be killed by someone with a mental illness (mostly someone close to the assailant, not a stranger) is very small.

Munro and Rumgay[53] analysed the findings of public enquiries into homicide by people with mental illness (1988–97). About a quarter were judged to have been predictable, 65% preventable and 60% had a long-term history of violence or relevant risk factors for violence. The authors conclude that improved risk assessment has only a limited role in reducing homicides. Better all-round mental health care would be more effective.

5 Services available and their costs

Introduction

Two major themes influence discussion of the quality of services currently available for the diagnosis and care of people with SMI. The first involves the balance of factors influencing thresholds at which recognition of a mental health problem occurs, e.g. in primary care, and whether referral for a specialist opinion or treatment is required (the concept of SMI). A separate chapter on primary care in this series is specifically relevant. The second theme concerns the extent to which the development of more effective interventions, community services and changes in public attitudes substantially improve on the services of the 1960s and 1970s. The two themes are clearly linked but the main emphasis here is placed on the secondary sector. A third, forensic tier is also relevant. Effectiveness is considered in Section 6.

Mental health needs in the primary, secondary and forensic sectors, by district

Approximately 11% of all health care resources are spent on mental health. Glover and colleagues[54] have studied the numbers at primary, secondary and forensic levels, in each case approximating a range of need across the English health authorities (now primary care trusts [PCTs]).

The magnitude of primary sector need was computed using data from the NPMS study (*see* Section 3) for caseness and the prevalence of depression (score of 2+), as a percentage of the population aged 15–64 in each health district. At the secondary level, population data were used to calculate likely need, using the York index and the Community Psychiatric Needs Index, together with the MINI (*see* Appendix II) and average daily numbers of occupied beds per 100 000 population. No modelled data were available for the forensic level and two sources of real data were used, namely occupied bed-days for medium and other secure units (1995–96), and special hospital use (1995), classified by health authority of residence of the patients.

Table 14 shows the overall maximum and minimum, and two percentile ratios (75th/25th and maximum/5th), for each of these indicators. Districts with the most morbidity had about twice as much mental illness in primary care compared with those with the least. At the secondary level, with more severe disorders, the predicted range between highest and lowest districts was about 2.5:1, although the actual data showed roughly double that. For forensic services the range was over 20-fold.

When the eight indices were calculated, the rank orders for individual health districts were reasonably consistent with each other, although some districts (notably Birmingham) had to be omitted because of boundary changes. Although the three broad types of care and the scales used to measure them were very different from each other, one 'clear conclusion is that forensic mental health care is much more tightly concentrated' than that estimated at general psychiatric and primary levels.[54] The concentration of forensic need, and the huge disparity when compared with the pattern of general mental health care 'is so great as to require a completely different type and scale of organisation'.[54] The authors calculate that the top 5% of districts are spending about 20% of their mental health resources (2–2.5% of the entire district budget) on forensic services. The median figure is 7.5% of mental health spend. The implications for apportioning an overall mental health budget are considered in Section 7.

Table 14: Indicators of need in forensic, secondary and primary sectors, 1995–96.

Type of care	Minimum	Maximum	Ratio 75th/25th percentile	Ratio maximum/ 5th percentile
Primary care				
CIS-R 12+ cases	10.8%	21.0%	1.3	1.9
Percentage population 15–64				
Depression scores	6.6%	13.6%	1.4	2.0
2+ cases 15–64				
Secondary psychiatric care				
Admission need index	24.2	67.4	1.4	2.5
Community need index	70.5	180.6	1.3	2.3
MINI predicted admission per 100,000	160.6	454.6	1.4	2.5
Average MI beds per 100,000 population	3.8	151.9	1.6	4.8
Mentally disordered offenders				
Special hospital residents per 100,000 population	0.0	14.8	2.0	23.1
Average secure beds per 100,000 population	0.3	20.1	2.2	26.9

Source: Glover *et al.*, unpublished data.

In a separate study, Glover[55] calculated the sums allocated to and the actual spend on hospital and community health services for mental illness and learning disability. Figures for spending in deprived inner-city authorities ranged from 17.7% to 19.3% of the total budget (mean 18.6%), while the actual allocation was 14.1–14.7% (mean 14.4%). In mixed-status areas, the figures were 12.1–17.7% (mean 15.4%) against an allocation of 12.1–13.0% (mean 12.5%). In high-status authorities, the equivalents were 9.0–18.0% (mean 12.8%) with an allocation range of 10.2–11.6% (mean 11.0%). A group of inner-city deprived areas outside London resembled the London pattern, with a spending range of 9.9–20.7% (mean 13.7%), and allocation range of 11.2–12.7% (mean 12.0%). The author suggests that if an identifiable group is spending substantially above its allocation, others must be spending below theirs. If so, the allocation formula, in spite of attempts to be as fair as possible, is failing to reflect significant elements in the national distribution of need. The DoH could present the results of the service elements explicitly, enabling a more informed public debate.

There is growing evidence that the relationship between social deprivation and need is curvilinear. At lower MINI scores (< 100) there is no clear relationship. At higher scores the relationship increases exponentially.

Primary care referral for specialist advice and/or care

A new system came into operation in April 1999 with the formation of primary care groups (PCGs) and unified cash-limited budgets. These groups, now replaced by primary care trusts (PCTs), commission services, foster collaboration between practices, link with the local community and social services, consider problems arising from uneven quality of care, promote good practice and encourage public participation in decisions. About 75% of the PCT budget is likely to be used for hospital and community services. It is too early to assess the impact on specialist services, but it is clear that opportunities will arise for both co-operation and conflict as the boundaries between the sectors become more blurred.[56]

Consensus has not yet been achieved on common thresholds or procedures in general practice for obtaining care from specialists such as community psychiatric nurses, psychologists and psychiatrists. The alternatives are to recruit specialists into the primary care team, refer to a specialist community mental health team (CMHT) or use the local outpatient department (OPD). There are further variants on each of these options.[57,58] National, regional and local data for monitoring rates of referral across the range of primary–secondary contacts and for assessing their cost-effectiveness are not yet available. Issues associated with the efficacy of guidelines to help recognition and adequate treatment of depression and other disorders by general practitioners are considered in Section 6.

The background of specialist hospital and community care for SMI

Official statistics

Peak bed occupancy in the large psychiatric hospitals was 345 per 100 000 in 1954, since when there has been a more or less continuous decline. There are somewhat similar trends in France, Italy, Spain and Sweden. By 1985, when the current system of data collection was under way, the average daily number of available beds (as distinct from bed occupancy) was down to 76 per 100 000, and in 1995–96 to 39 per 100 000.

DoH statistics provide a general sketch of residential and other service provision, but there is wide variation between districts in quality and completeness of data. A study of seven English districts in 1994 was used to compare comprehensive information about residential accommodation for people with mental illness. Altogether, 236 facilities with 1208 beds were found. DoH returns did not identify 130 (51%) of these. Official data were not detailed enough, nor sufficiently anchored in local provision, to allow an appraisal of how far need was met (Audini *et al.*, submitted).

Table 15 provides an overview of DoH data concerning changes in available residential services in England between 1991–92 and 1996–97. The number of hospital beds in secure units more or less doubled, while the number of beds in short- and long-stay units more or less halved. Beds in private nursing homes, staffed residential homes and small registered homes showed relatively small increases from a low base.

Table 15: Hospital beds, and places in residential and nursing homes, available for people with mental illness, between 1991–92 and 1996–97 (children and elderly not included), in England.

	Numbers					
	1991–92	1992–93	1993–94	1994–95	1995–96	1996–97
Average daily available NHS beds						
Secure units	880	930	1,030	1,080	1,370	1,580
Short stay	15,720	15,300	14,680	15,210	15,080	14,500
Long stay	12,430	11,000	8,870	7,830	6,730	5,410
	29,030	27,230	24,580	24,120	23,180	21,490
Places in staffed residential homes	11,540	12,300	12,740	12,960	13,370	14,930
Places in local authority unstaffed (group) homes		1,840	1,700	1,680	1,660	1,840
Beds in private nursing homes	3,710	4,550	4,750	4,860	5,300	6,590
Places in small registered residential homes (mostly private)	–	–	1,130	1,610	1,920	2,690

Figures for bed occupancy during the final 10 years of the preceding data collection system (the Mental Health Enquiry) provide an approximate baseline for comparison of changes in bed use. In 1977, the rates per 100 000 for patients in hospital for less than a year, for 1–5 years and for more than 5 years were 57, 40 and 79 per 100 000, respectively. In 1986, the equivalent rates were 55, 32 and 42 per 100 000. There was little change in short-term care; the rate remained close to the then DHSS-recommended figure of 50 per 100 000. The medium-term rate (the 'new long-stay') declined slowly. The long-stay rate was already on a sharp downward trend. The medium- plus long-term rate (74 per 100 000 in 1986) can roughly be compared with the rate for available 'long-stay' beds (43 per 100 000 in 1996–97) shown in Table 15.

Table 16 shows hospital and community occupied bed-days purchased from 1991–92 to 1996–97. Hospital bed-days decreased by 2.8 million from 14.6 million, and community bed-days increased by 1.4 million from 2.3 million. Table 17 (*see* overleaf) shows the numbers, starting from a low base, in specified non-residential community services during the period 1991–97.

Table 16: Hospital- and community-occupied bed-days purchased for people with mental illness in England.

	Millions					
	1991–92	1992–93	1993–94	1994–95	1995–96	1996–97
Hospital-occupied bed-days	4.6	13.9	12.6	12.4	12.1	11.8
Community-occupied bed-days	2.3	2.4	2.8	3.2	3.5	3.7

Table 17: Other NHS activity (mental illness) for the period 1991–92 to 1996–97 in England.

	Thousands						
	1990–91	1991–92	1992–93	1993–94	1994–95	1995–96	1996–97
Outpatient first attendance	–	218	238	245	257	271	285
Ward attenders	–	15	14	11	17	16	15
First contacts with services:							
Community psychology	169	175	191	202	221	227	–
Community nursing	370	372	406	475	493	532	–
First contact at day care	60	55	60	66	63	66	63
Places at day centres (nearest 1,000)	–	–	40	45	51	5	58

Variations in the use of specialist care (FCEs) across the UK

Finished consultant episodes (FCEs) for 1994–95 allow a more detailed all-England comparison between four groups of local authorities: inner London, outer London, other large cities and all other local authorities (*see* Table 18). The differences shown (for people aged 16–64) are substantial, by area and by sex. Inner London had 22% more FCEs than other large cities, 83% more than outer London, and 72% more than the rest of the country. FCEs for men in inner London were 94% above those for outer London, 33% above those for other large cities and 99% above all other local authorities. Equivalent figures for 1989–90 show a marked increase in the number of FCEs for men in all areas during the intervening 5 years (most obvious in inner London). There was no such increase for women. Indicators with a similar rank order include detention under the Mental Health Act, proportion of single, divorced or widowed people, and diagnosis of schizophrenia.

Table 18: FCEs per 100 000 in four groups of English local authorities.

Groups of local authorities	Males	Females	Total
Inner London	872	619	744
Other inner city	656	559	608
Rest of the country	439	426	433
Outer London	450	364	407

Source: London's Mental Health, p. 173.

The CPA and care co-ordination

The CPA has been the policy framework within which specialist mental health services in the UK are or should be provided.[59,60] The intention is that priority should be allocated according to need and those most at risk are identified through supervision registers. The effectiveness of the policy is considered in Section 6. Within this general framework the aims of 'case management', first developed in the USA, are generally agreed. They are to maintain contact, reduce hospital admissions and improve social functioning and quality of life. The method requires systematic assessment of client need, development of a care plan, specification and provision of the resources needed, monitoring of progress by an identified key worker or small team, and regular recording and updating of the procedure. Assertive community treatment (ACT) is a variant emphasising multi-disciplinary teams with low staff–client ratios (10–15) practising 'assertive outreach', medication compliance and 24-hour emergency cover. Effective functioning of such systems requires support at all levels of governance.

Responsibility for the CPA was given to NHS provider units in co-ordination with the social services.[61] Since then, there has been much discussion of the policy's value. An unopposed motion carried at the AGM of the Royal College of Psychiatrists in 1996 stated that the policy of care in the community was in a deep state of crisis. It was intended that patients and their relatives should be closely involved and that health and social services should harmonise procedures to ensure needs were met. Schneider and colleagues[62] surveyed all 83 relevant English NHS trusts in 1997–98, with a response rate of 79%. The main elements of the CPA were found to be in place but the survey did not include a quality criterion. Harmonisation was not widespread, and involvement by users and carers 'was far from universal'.

Later Government plans acknowledged that standards have been patchy. It was therefore proposed that the NHS input should be fully integrated with that of local social services, responsible for all service users, including those in residential settings such as prison, hospitals, hostels, group homes and supported housing. Two levels were recommended – standard and enhanced. At each review, the date of the next review must be set and recorded. Audit should focus on the quality of implementation, including risk assessment, care plans, treatment goals, inter-agency working, sensitivity to ethnic, gender and sexuality needs, and support for family and other carers. The new service is referred to as care co-ordination.

Liaison of psychiatry with general medical and surgical services

Four areas of general hospital care involve patient problems that require psychiatric consultation: prevention of suicide, comorbidity between physical and mental illness, care and rehabilitation (particularly of patients with somatoform disorders), and training. Services are patchy in the UK compared with Germany and the USA. They are often based in separate specialist trusts so that an extra budget is needed for referrals from general hospitals with no prior earmarked resources. A report from the Royal Colleges of Physicians and Psychiatrists recommended that, as a minimum, one psychiatrist (half- or full-time according to the size of hospital), working with a multi-disciplinary team of psychologist, nurses and social workers, should be available. A survey of 52 London hospitals found that a quarter of them had such resources and 14% had none at all. The current concentration of care funds on severely mentally ill people has resulted in relative neglect of psychiatric services for people with cancer, myocardial infarction, deliberate self-harm or chronic fatigue syndrome. Comorbidity and suicide risks in primary care are other areas that require liaison.[63,64]

Acute psychiatric care

The amount and quality of acute (often emergency) care depends to a substantial extent on the amount and quality of more routine services. This is illustrated by a succession of seven *Milmis Surveys* of acute wards in 12 inner-London trusts, including ten of the most deprived areas in the country.[65,66] The problems are evident to a lesser extent in outer-London boroughs and other large cities. On 14 January 1999 or during the previous week there were:

- 53% patients detained under the Mental Health Act

- 39% remaining for 3–12 months
- 64 incidents of first-degree violence
- 25 incidents resulting in minor physical injuries and 38 incidents of sexual harassment
- a true bed-occupancy (taking account of people who should be in the ward but whose place had been taken for yet more urgent cases) of 121%.

A report by the Mental Health Act Commission covering the period April 1997 to March 1999, while acknowledging that many facilities were more than adequate, described a significant number as not meeting basic standards. Threatening language and behaviour, and racial and sexual harassment were growing problems. Drug and alcohol use were common comorbid factors. The problems faced by clinical staff and managers are described by Williams and Cohen.[67] The results of a survey of 173 trusts confirmed high over-occupancy and problems with bed availability, particularly in southern England.[68]

Longer-term hospital care of patients with SMI

A national audit of patients newly accumulating beyond a limit of 3 months was conducted in 1992.[69,70] The concept assumed that most patients admitted for acute crises should be discharged within this time, given adequate follow-on care. Some patients would need longer hospital treatment, but would improve sufficiently during a stay of up to 3 years to be able then to cope with a lesser level of shelter. This 'new long-stay' group[71] should not be expected to live on acute wards. They also have different accommodation needs from those likely to need staffed residential care for longer or indefinite periods of time.

The national audit included 59 UK mental health services. Data were returned on 905 patients, aged 18–64 on admission, who had been in hospital for between 6 months and 3 years. Two particular subgroups were prominent. One was composed of younger patients (aged 18–34), predominantly single men with schizophrenia, 43% of whom had a history of dangerous behaviour or admission to a special hospital, and more than a third of whom had been formally detained. The second group was mostly composed of older women (55–64), married or widowed, with poor personal and social functioning. The average point-prevalence was 6.1 per 100 000 population. A third of the English patients were housed on acute wards, half of whom would have been better placed in a community-based residential setting if the option had been available.

A description of a well-functioning rehabilitation hostel in Gloucester, mainly for patients admitted from acute wards, is provided by Macpherson and Butler.[72]

Nursing and residential care homes and other supported housing

Since 1993, new residents in long-term care are assessed by local authorities for their ability to contribute towards the cost. There were about 5000 mentally ill people aged under 60 years, 6000 under 80 and 2000 over 80. These figures include dementia. The numbers discharged from mental hospitals under the former dowry system are decreasing, as are income-support claimants with reserved rights. Of residents in residential care or nursing homes, 1000 aged under 60 years, 2000 under 80 and 1000 over 80 had a mental illness. There is uncertainty as to future administration. Changes in housing benefit rules make it necessary to find other sources of cash for this kind of supported housing.[73] The TAPS (Team for the Assessment of Psychiatric Services) reprovision project (*see* Section 7) has similar problems.

Rehabilitation, day activities and shelter

There is no official register of day settings. In 1997, the Personal Social Services Research Unit conducted a postal survey of day-activity settings for adults in the South Thames NHS Region.[74] Of the 261 valid addresses contacted, 155 predominantly urban settings completed a postal questionnaire. About half employed social care staff on-site (65 nurses, 35 occupational staff and 19 other therapists). Only 11 had support from a psychiatrist or psychologist. Revenue costs per user session were between £0.88 and £68.26, around a low mean value of £11.65. Most settings opened only during working hours, with an average of 20 people per session. Regular users attended between two and six times weekly.

Estimates of the numbers attending day hospitals, day centres and work schemes, and their costs, were included in the London studies (Chisholm, personal communication). Table 19 includes costs per generic daytime community mental health team (CMHT) worker, and also out-of-hours time.

Table 19: Numbers and costs of non-residential NHS services.

Service component	Unit cost range £ pa 1995–96		Range of provision per 100,000 population	Total cost £000 pa 1995–96 per 100,000 population	
	Inner London	Outer London		Inner London	Outer London
CMHTs					
Daytime worker	38,010–43,575	35,024–40,151	2,537	950–1,612	875–1,485
Out of hours	20,000–40,000	20,000–40,000	–	20–40	20–40
Day hospital	11,539	10,586	50–100	577–1,154	529–1,059
Day centre	9,918	9,163	40–80	397–793	367–733
Work schemes	2,500–6,500*	2,500–6,500*	50–70	125–455	125–455

Source: Chisholm *et al.*, 1996.
*Net expenditure per place, based on seven schemes, including ITU, vocational rehabilitation and clubhouse settings.

A range of care settings, providing graded degrees of supervision and protection, is available in experimental or one-off examples, virtually all administered by social service departments or the voluntary and private sectors[75] (evidence of effectiveness not provided). Table 20 shows the results of an analysis of needs for care in the south-east London survey described in Section 4.[18] The overall weighted rate percentage of all potentially meetable needs for treatment in the month before interview was 10.8% (14.3% for the year). Of these, less than half had been met.

Table 20: Needs for care in the south-east London survey.

Need status	Past month		Past year		Total	
	*n**	(%)	*n**	(%)	*n**	(%)
Met need	19	(4.0)	10	(2.1)	29	(6.1)
Unmet need	41	(6.8)	8	(1.4)	49	(8.2)
No meetable need	9	(1.5)	4	(0.8)	13	(2.3)

*Unweighted numbers (weighted %).

Chapter 5 of a report on schizophrenia by the Clinical Standards Advisory Group,[76] while not based on a large sample, does clearly describe substantial agreement between users and carers on the problems they had experienced with services in the 11 districts surveyed. None of those interviewed seemed to know what the CPA was. There were long waiting lists for residential and rehabilitative care. Five-minute outpatient visits allowed no time for queries to be dealt with properly. There were few or no facilities for sheltered work or for out-of-hours occupation and little collaboration between health and social services.

Five extended community support services, run by charities receiving some or all of their funding from statutory sources, are described in a Sainsbury Centre booklet, which provides practical information on how to set up and run them.[77] The staff costs per care hour were as follows: community mental health worker, £62; community psychiatric nurse, £47; auxiliary nurse, £21; social worker (generic caseload), £12; local authority home care worker, £8. More such non-researched examples are described in the National Service Framework (NSF) for mental health.[75]

Users' and carers' interests

Three major charities, the National Schizophrenia Fellowship (NSF), SANE and MIND, provide much-valued services to people with mental illnesses. NSF and SANE are particularly focused on SMI and both have effective telephone helplines. NSF and MIND also provide services such as local membership groups, newsletters and more detailed materials on relevant topics (e.g. caring, coping, and medication and its side-effects). Both run local day centres.

Users' issues

Lawson and colleagues[78] assessed the degree of user involvement (recommended in the original guidelines) in 50 CPA meetings. They found it to be poor, partly because of limited resources. Users would have liked a copy of their care plan and updated information about medication, diagnosis and services. These points are taken up in the National Service Framework[75] (see Section 7).

Brown and Birtwhistle[79] followed up a sample of 179 people with schizophrenia who were living with their families in 1981–82 and found that 39 had died and six were not traceable. Of the rest, 74 were still with their families, 31 were in hospital or alternative care, 26 lived alone and three were homeless. Overall, there was little change in the level of clinical or social morbidity or carer distress. The authors calculated that about a quarter of the surviving patients would need residential care during the next 15 years, some of them in intensive settings.

Carers' issues

Kuipers has pointed out that carers are not usually offered much of a choice when someone they live with has an SMI. Many studies have been made of the specifics of such care.[80–84] A study of the 'burden of care', stress and satisfaction with services of relatives of patients first referred to a community-based service ($n = 24$) or to a district hospital ($n = 17$) in Newcastle suggested that the initial severity of the disorder was the chief factor associated with burden in both locations. At follow-up, there were few differences between the two groups. Levels of burden had decreased in both, but levels of 'caseness' (general health questionnaire) remained high. Relatives were generally tolerant and caring, and accepted a duty to offer and, if necessary, provide for the patient.

Malcolm and colleagues[85] interviewed 91 carers who had, on average, 21 years' experience and 53 hours a week contact. Of these, 73 would have liked their relative to have respite care so long as this did not mean loss of their own status as carers. Hostels, staffed group homes and flats/bedsits were acceptable alternatives. Day care was a particular need.

A large literature has accumulated around the concept of 'expressed emotion' (EE). In the first paper,[86] this term was used to describe features noted in samples of speech. It was neutral as to cause but was misinterpreted by some later therapists in a way that seemed to attribute blame to relatives for precipitating or exacerbating onset or relapse. Used according to the original intention, there is limited support from a meta-analysis of controlled trials.[87,88] Scazufca and Kuipers[89] found EE, as expected, to be related to burden of care. EE can be found in staff as well.[90]

The substantial burden from bipolar disorder experienced by the majority of caregivers is described in detail by Perlick and colleagues.[91]

Staffing issues

Tables 21 and 22 show the official numbers of medical, nursing and local authority staff employed in caring for mentally ill people within the scope of this chapter. According to the College Annual Census, the number of consultants in 'general adult psychiatry' in post in 1994 was 1232, with another 140 posts vacant. In 1997, the numbers were 1321 and 222. Thus both posts occupied and posts vacant have increased.

Table 21: Summary of trends in numbers of hospital medical staff caring for the mentally ill, by grade, 1987–96.

Sub-specialty	Consultants		Senior registrars		Registrars	
	1987	1996	1987	1996	1987	1996
Mental illness, specialist	1,465	1,935	379	668	714	606
Mental illness, general	1,044	1,180	257	344	670	516
Forensic	59	91	15	53		
Psychotherapy	65	82	23	30		

Table 22: Summary of trends in numbers of nursing and local authority staff caring for the mentally ill, by grade (whole-time equivalents), 1988–97.

Nurses			Local authority staff		
	1988	1996		1993	1997
Qualified	33,390	35,440	Residential	1,874	1,824
Unqualified	17,740	17,140	Day centre	1,757	1,848
Private RMN	1,197	5,111	Mixed group*	2,300	2,483

*Mixed groups: elderly, learning disability, mental health.

A series of papers has been published describing an unsatisfactory state of clinical staffing, in terms of training, conditions of work and stress. The term 'burnout' has been applied to a perceived loss of morale in personnel working with severely ill people, particularly in acute wards and in community teams. The problems are greater in inner-city areas but are found throughout the mental health services.[92–95]

So far as medical staff are concerned, the clearest evidence of a problem comes from an inquiry by a working party set up by the College and the Department of Health. A questionnaire was sent in March 1997 to all consultants thought to have resigned during 1995 or 1996, before their 65th birthday. There were 142 replies to 173 enquiries (82%). The reasons given indicated disillusion with earlier NHS reforms, which were regarded as increasing bureaucracy, paperwork, undue bed closures, staff shortages and interference by managers in clinical matters.[96] 'Urgent action is required to overcome the medical staffing problems in mental health, which will otherwise destabilise the existing services'.[97]

Studies made of mental health staff more generally suggest that work in the community, at least in inner London, may be more stressful than inpatient care, but not that levels of stress are rising. Most staff believed that their jobs could be improved by further training. For mental health staff, the main training gap was in development of skills in clinical intervention, while ward staff identified a need for further skills in diffusing potentially aggressive situations.[98,99]

Clinical psychologists

In their written evidence to the Commons Health Committee considering NHS staff requirements on 31 July 1998, the British Psychological Society (BPS) made several points germane to the role of psychologists in the mental health services. In particular, in spite of growing demand, the long-standing shortage of trained psychological therapists has not diminished. The total number employed in the NHS is about 3250. The shortage is due in large part to the lack of training places, and full training takes 6 years. Decisions concerning recruitment need to take this timescale into account.

Occupational therapists

In principle, occupational therapists (OTs) with training and experience in mental health problems should be deeply involved in all psychiatric services. However, a ratio of OT to nurse of 1:13 is not uncommon in the community services and OTs are often expected to work across several medical disciplines.

Support staff

A group of 25 professionals, users and senior managers was invited by the Sainsbury Trust to consider the role, training and specific activities of support staff. It was agreed that the help provided was complementary to that of professionals, although there might be a problem in defining boundaries. There should be close supervision. If tasks involving benefits, housing or side-effects of treatment were required, appropriate training would be essential. 'The notion that effective care can be delivered by less expensive care has obvious attraction . . . but the debate must be about the correct balance between professional and non-professional skills'.[100]

The costs of care in London

The problems of providing care for severely mentally ill people in inner London, summarised earlier, are far more serious than in any other location in the UK. The rest of London is less skewed but still has higher input prices for staffing and land, more case-mix complexity and more deprivation, poverty and social isolation. The economic component of the London survey[101] incorporated a study of costs of current provision and of unmet local needs. Units of baseline measurement were used to price seven types of residential care (from regional secure units [RSUs] to unstaffed group homes), together with three other types (supportive housing, day hospitals and day centres). Each had an identified source of information.

Nine staff categories, from consultant to support worker, were specified and a method for costing CMHTs laid down. Assumptions of many kinds were made by the authors, who have listed them and entered appropriate caveats.

A simplified version of the authors' table of places and costs for residential accommodation (omitting the ranges except for the totals) is presented in Table 23. 'Inner London boroughs contribute 43% towards the London-wide number of places and costs, although the population of these boroughs (2.3 million) is only 35% of the total population. The mean number of inpatient hospital beds and residential care places is 190 per 100 000 population for inner boroughs (range 69–412) and 124 for outer boroughs (66–216), costing £6.4m (range 3.3–12.7) and £4m (2.3–6.8) respectively.'

Estimates for the non-residential costs (CMHTs, day hospitals, day centres, supported housing and employment schemes) were made separately. For example, the estimate for the annual cost of providing

Table 23: Hospital and other residential provision in London: places and costs (£000) per 100 000 population.

Service component	Inner London Mean	Outer London Mean	Total Mean (range)	
Local secure ward				
Places	7	3	5	(0–16)
Cost	500	221	360	(0–1,175)
Acute ward				
Places	46	29	37	(19–66)
Cost	2,454	1,437	1,946	(934–3,551)
Hostel wards				
Places	14	24	19	(0–65)
Cost	670	1,028	849	(0–3,012)
24-hour staffed hostel				
Places	79	38	59	(12–266)
Costs	1,723	779	1,251	(240–5,794)
Day-staffed hostel				
Places	20	7	14	(0–54)
Costs	220	75	148	(0–564)
Unstaffed hostel/GrpH				
Places	19	19	19	(0–83)
Cost	170	158	164	(0–706)
Other residential*				
Places	*	*	*	
Cost				
Total residential				
Places	185*	120*	153*	(66–412)
Cost	6,370	4,052	5,211	(2,315–12,668)
Places/cost (%)	43%	57%		

Source: Edited from Chisholm *et al.*, 1997, p. 319.

*In a separate table, the authors provide for an estimated 10–20 per 100 000 places for supported housing/flats. To compare with other data in Section 7, an average of 15 is added to all three totals for the calculations. The costs of these are estimated by the authors as follows: inner London, 10–20 places, £77–158; outer London, 10–20 places, £73–146.

comprehensive CMHT support to a population of 100 000 'is between £950 000 and £1.5m in inner London boroughs, and between £875 000 and £1.5m in outer London boroughs'. Costs for eight different combinations of these elements are provided. The authors end by pointing out some of the calculations that planners can make (with appropriate caution) using these data. For example, if all inpatient units (RSU, local secure and acute) were reduced by 10% (291 beds across London), costs would be reduced by an estimated £16.7 milliom, equivalent to the creation of 744 other kinds of residential places if this were deemed appropriate on clinical and public health grounds. Several other options are listed.

Sources of information concerning the costs of implementing such decisions were not available, but the amount to be added would presumably be very substantial. The issues involved are now (as they were in the 1960s when the large hospitals were beginning to close) central to rational planning of health services. They are taken up in Section 7. A calculation of theoretical interest would also show the number of places for the severely ill (not necessarily in hospital) that could accrue by reducing the services available to people with the least severe mental health problems.

Costs of residential facilities: mentally ill people over 65 in England and Wales

A study of residential facilities in eight areas of England and Wales was carried out by the Research Unit of the Royal College of Psychiatrists and the Centre for the Economics of Mental Health. Local researchers identified 368 facilities for mentally ill people under 65 years of age, providing accommodation for more than 3000 people, of whom just under 2000 met the study criteria.[102]

Table 24 summarises the results for seven types of accommodation. Staffing levels varied as expected with the extent of day and night cover. Half to two-thirds of staff in hospital wards were qualified; in other settings most staff were unqualified. There was substantial variation between sites in the number of places with 24-hour cover (79–218 per 100 000 local population) and in the total number of residential places available per unit population (36–136 per 100 000). These differences were not closely related to the levels of need expected from local deprivation indices. Most residents had severe, long-term psychiatric illnesses, manifested in positive and/or negative symptoms. More than a quarter had moderate to severe

Table 24: Residential services in eight areas of England and Wales: MHRC project.

Services	Extent of cover		Staffing		Weekly cost per client (£)		Places/ 100,000
	Night	Day	Bed ratio	Qualified (%)	Accommodation	Other	
Forensic	Waking	Constant	1.33	62	1,501	41	N/A
Acute ward	Waking	Constant	1.27	68	844	349	33.6
Long-stay ward	Waking	Constant	0.95	51	665	42	18.4
High-staffed hostel	Waking	Constant	0.67	18	285	53	36.7
Mid-staffed hostel	Sleep-in	Constant	0.39	20	238	93	23.7
Low-staffed hostel	Call/none	Regular	0.19	25	173	99	12.2
Group home*	Call/none	Visited	0.16	39	140	122	14.1
Staffed care home*	Sleep-in	Constant	1.01	11	369	94	n7.9

Source: Chisholm *et al.*, 1997; Lelliott *et al.*, 1996.[102]

Bed ratio = number of staff per resident; staff qualification = in nursing or social work.

*Number of residents ⩾ 7 except for the two starred, which are 6 or fewer.

physical disabilities or ill health. About one-third were judged to pose a moderate or severe risk of acting violently if discharged, and an overlapping two-thirds to be at risk from self-neglect. The most disabled were in settings with 24-hour cover.

An important finding was the great variation in how local workers defined hostel types. The authors recommend a classification that includes size and extent of day and night cover, so that like can be compared with like.

A further observation was that high-staffed hostels housed fewer people with a history of violence than long-stay wards, probably because the latter had higher levels of qualified staff. The implication is that the new 24-hour staffed hostels supported by the modernisation fund must have sufficient adequately trained registered male nurses permanently on site.

Costs varied as expected with the intensity of care. However, staffed care homes (small, privately managed units) were more expensive per resident than larger hostels. Care package costs were highest in NHS-managed facilities, mostly hospital wards. Costs were higher for inner-city districts. In all districts, costs for units run by local authorities were significantly higher than for voluntary or private sector facilities.[103,104]

Mental illness specialty costs

Table 25 (*see* overleaf) shows the gross expenditure on inpatient and outpatient mental health services. Services for dementia are included, but not those for the learning disabled. The decline in NHS bed-days is apparent and might be linked both to the decline in inpatient expenditure and to the increase in outpatient attendances. The total sum calculated for 1996–97 is £1.6 billion. Inpatient care accounted for about two-thirds (cost per patient-day £132, cost per GP episode £8140). Inpatient psychotherapy is relatively expensive.

Secure provision

The equivalent figures for forensic patients, not including the special hospitals shown in Table 26 (*see* p. 197), were £3.5 million for inpatients, £247 per patient-day and £66 000 per GP episode; patient-days and expenditure more or less doubled during the five years.

Detailed studies have been made of admissions under Part II of the Mental Health Act, covering admissions on section in 20 local authorities and six NHS trusts, which represent 18% of the population of England and Wales, and of admissions under Section 136 (Metropolitan Police, 1996–97). Between 1991 and 1997 the annual rate of use of Part II increased by 32%. Significant predictors of the rate of Part II admissions were as follows: MINI score; the total number of mental health beds; the number of community psychiatric nurses, approved social workers and consultants; suicide rates; and the number of undetermined deaths. The rate depends strongly on age, and peaks at 25–29. Three minority groups, black (26%), Asian and 'other' (14%), also had high rates of admission under Section 136. The authors suggest that the increase under Part II might reflect pressures on acute-admission beds in an increasingly 'risk-averse' culture. Comorbidity with drug misuse is another likely factor.[105]

A separate study of NHS medium-secure provision in England and Wales was mounted because of failure to meet demand, particularly in London, and the consequential growth of provision by the independent sector. Information was collected about all patients occupying a bed in an inner-London medium-secure unit on a census day in August 1997. Of the 183 patients (25 per 100 000), 90 (49%) were in independent-sector facilities. They were similar to those in NHS units but more likely to have been referred from general psychiatric services (48% vs. 19%) and less likely to have been referred from the

Table 25: Mental illness specialty costs in England, 1991–92 to 1996–97 (includes elderly with psychiatric disorders but does not include mental handicap, forensic).

	Patient-days	GP episodes	Expenditure (£)	Cost/patient-day (£)	Cost/GP episode (£)
Mental illness: inpatients					
1992–93	8,591,348	164,435	1,158,181,535	123	7,043
1993–94	8,157,880	105,794	901,452,269	47	8,521
1994–95	8,021,234	163,288	996,007,086	124	8,101
1995–96	7,858,207	161,039	1,110,267 315	141	8,894
1996–97	7,638,523	164,455	1,009,755,854	132	8,140

	First attendances	Total attendances	Expenditure (£)	Cost/attendance (£)
Mental illness: outpatients				
1992–93	164,285	1,354,436	94,102,169	69
1993–94	92,285	1,484,858	102,381,868	70
1994–95	170,865	1,577,784	118,553,487	75
1995–96	175,870	1,703,382	128,364,884	75
1996–97	190,746	1,710,289	134,435,246	78

	Patient-days	GP episodes	Expenditure (£)	Cost/patient-day (£)	Cost/GP episode (£)
Psychotherapy: inpatients					
1992–93	28,018	151	3,389,536	121	22,447
1993–94	17,287	1,014	6,641,177	317	8,522
1994–95	40,381	532	5,209,926	156	11,623
1995–96	19,237	235	3,793,915	197	16,144
1996–97	21,760	307	3,487,544	161	11,390

	First attendances	Total attendances	Expenditure (£)	Cost/attendance (£)
Psychotherapy: outpatients				
1992–93	9,296	139,116	10,285,522	74
1993–94	10,729	150,876	16,550,147	110
1994–95	10,822	129,465	12,698,208	98
1995–96	10,386	147,595	15,988,120	108
1996–97	12,325	159,109	16,610,140	104

Community mental illness expenditure (also includes child guidance, psychology assessment, psychosexual services, substance use)

1992–93	251,014,983
1993–94	275,186,270
1994–95	314,404,372
1995–96	385,556,469
1996–97	423,609,095

Source: NHS Trusts Manual for Accounts, TFR2.

Table 26: Forensic psychiatry specialty costs in England, 1991–92 to 1996–97.

	Patient-days	GP episodes	Expenditure (£)	Cost/patient-day (£)	Cost/GP episode (£)
Forensic psychiatry: inpatients					
1992–93	270,161	1,557	54,639,912	202	35,093
1993–94	312,608	1,933	63,573,398	203	32,888
1994–95	377,408	2,376	79,251,884	210	33,355
1995–96	412,303	1,839	100,255,371	243	54,516
1996–97	485,903	1,819	119,994,590	247	65,967

	First attendances	Total attendances	Expenditure (£)	Cost/attendance (£)
Forensic psychiatry: outpatients				
1992–93	3,325	18,821	2,227,261	118
1993–94	5,469	19,434	3,158,278	163
1994–95	5,863	24,032	3,004,558	125
1995–96	6,026	31,953	4,443,134	139
1996–97	4,548	30,238	4,796,097	159

Source: *NHS Trusts Manual for Accounts, TFR2.*

criminal justice system or a special hospital. There were few differences between black and white patients. It is concluded that the NHS does not meet the need for medium-secure care of patients in the general psychiatric services.[106]

Proposed changes to the Mental Health Act

A postal survey of the views of general and forensic psychiatrists concerning the adequacy of Part III of the current Mental Health Act, 1983, has suggested that there is little demand for change.[107] The Government has published a 'root and branch' review of the Act for consultation. Much attention revolves round the concept of pathological personality, and its relationship on the one hand with serious personal and/or sexual violence and, on the other, with what sounds like an *ICD* disorder. Dissocial personality disorder F60.2 is the only *ICD* diagnosis to mention 'a low threshold for discharge of aggression, including violence'. The proposals are controversial,[108,109] insofar as they imply a role for doctors that goes beyond the provision of a responsible opinion on mental state and medical treatment. A Draft Mental Health Bill was published for consultation in 2002.

The costs of SMIs

The most recent and comprehensive estimate of the costs, at 1996–97 prices, of all mental illnesses in England is summarised by Patel and Knapp.[110] The total at 1996–97 prices is given as £32 billion, including £11.8 billion for 'lost employment', £7.6 billion for DSS payments, £4.1 billion for NHS services, £2.8 billion for 'informal care', £2.5 billion for lost productivity due to suicide and £1.7 billion for social services. Non-NHS costs came to almost seven times those of the NHS.

Separate details for three specific kinds of care – schizophrenia (*ICD-9*: 295), other psychoses (*ICD-9*: 296–298) and neuroses (*ICD-9*: 300) – are given in Table 27 (*see* overleaf), amounting to £3358 million in all. The cost for schizophrenia and other psychoses comes to £1131 million, not including £7.6 billion

Table 27: Costs of SMI in England, 1992–93.

Diagnosis*	Inpatient (£m)	Outpatient (£m)	Primary care (£m)	Medication (£m)	Community health (£m)	Social services (£m)
Schizophrenia	652	1	2	32	26	96
Other psychoses	294	12	16	–	–	–
Neuroses	75	49	39	96	139	150
Total	1,021	62	57	128	165	246

Source: Summarised from Table 1; Patel and Knapp.[110]
*ICD-9 diagnoses are as follows. Schizophrenia: 295.0 simple, 295.1 hebephrenic, 295.2 catatonic, 195.3 paranoid, 295.4 acute, 295.5 latent, 295.6 residual, 295.7 schizoaffective. Other psychoses: affective 296, paranoid states 297, reactive psychosis 298. Neuroses: 300.0 anxiety, 300.1 hysterical, 300.2 phobic, 300.3 obsessional–compulsive, 300.4 depressive, 300.5 neurasthenia, 300.6 depersonalisation, 300.7 hypochondriasis.

for social security benefits or £146.5 million for homeless mentally ill people. The costs are substantially higher (largely because of inpatient costs) than for diseases such as hypertension, diabetes or breast cancer.

McCreadie and Kelly[111] have calculated that 'with a prevalence of psychosis at 4 per 1000 aged 16–64, there are probably at least 200 000 people with schizophrenia in the UK. If 60% smoke on average 26 cigarettes a day, the contribution to the treasury is £139m per year. If direct treatment costs are estimated at between £397m and £714m per annum they are contributing substantially to the cost of their own care'.

Counselling, helplines and newspapers

Counselling should be distinguished from cognitive behavioural therapies (CBT) in which therapy may be offered weekly for up to 60 minutes over 20 sessions. Techniques are highly structured and entail working with clients to identify negative thoughts and feelings linked to specific situations, and to problems such as symptoms, in order to understand and eventually control them. CBT methods have been fruitfully applied to many F2-6 disorders and are discussed in the context of specific disorders in Section 6. Friedli and King[112] provide an overview of the methods and efficacy.

Counsellors

Data collected during May and June 1993 on the employment of counsellors and mental health professionals in 210 out of 300 responding fundholding practices showed that a third employed counsellors only, 12% employed specialist clinicians only and 10% employed both types. Practices that had formed links with a psychiatrist, psychologist or community psychiatric nurse (CPN) were more likely to employ a counsellor. The proportion of practices employing counsellors (49%) was substantially higher than the 17% found in 1992, and is presumably now higher still. The authors were worried, with reason, by the fact that half the GPs entered 'not known' in answer to a question on the qualifications of the counsellors employed.[113]

The question of how far counsellors employed in general practice contribute substantially either to patient satisfaction or to reduction of disability is still difficult to answer. At best there must be some doubt.[114–117]

Helplines

Telephone helplines deserve attention. Three charities provide them and Government proposals envisage a network run from psychiatric emergency clinics (*see* Section 7). Fakhoury[118] analysed data from one of the best known (SANELINE), concluding that the clientele was largely female and concerned with depression (55%) or psychosis (31%).

Newspaper coverage

A survey of relevant headlines in nine daily newspapers was carried out for a month to judge whether the content was positive, neutral or negative. During this time, 213 article headlines on general health-related topics were identified, of which 99 (46%) were critical, with a tendency to criticise doctors. Of the 47 equivalent headlines on psychiatry, 30 (64%) were critical, with a tendency to blame patients. Tabloids and broadsheets did not differ in their rates of negative coverage (OR: 4.42; 95% CI: 1.64–11.94). The author adds that negative statements tend to be made about physical medical practitioners, while psychiatric patients are more likely to get the blame.[119]

6 Effectiveness of services and interventions

Introduction

This section provides information on the effectiveness of the methods of care described in Section 5. Sampling issues are particularly difficult when designing research to provide guidance on the effectiveness of community care or personal treatment. Patients who are unco-operative, violent or addicted, and those with a long history of disablement, tend to be excluded or drop out. The small number entering and even fewer completing many of the trials, and the possibly transitory effects of innovative and motivated researchers on outcomes, are other confounders. Inconsistency in reporting the costs or unwanted side-effects of care or treatment also limits the value of comparisons (*see* Section 8).

Sources of information on effectiveness

The documents used have been edited from four main sources:

- *Evidence-Based Mental Health* (Volumes 1 and 2) (marked * in the text)
- *Cochrane Reviews* (Schizophrenia, Depression, Anxiety and Neurosis) (marked ** in the text)
- relevant psychiatric and epidemiological journals and publications
- suggestions from colleagues and reviewers.

Community services for people with severe mental disorders

Uptake of the CPA

The CPA and the supervision register (now amalgamated with CPA) policies in England are intended to ensure priority for patients needing to receive specialist mental health care. Bindman and colleagues[120] describe their application by provider trusts and address the hypothesis that the numbers prioritised match population-based estimates of local need. CPA co-ordinators in English trusts completed a postal questionnaire. NHS quarterly data from the CPA and supervision registers provided the total number of patients under the care of psychiatric services. The MINI (*see* Appendix II) provided a composite score estimating need in single or combined electoral wards. The study showed that almost all trusts are implementing the CPA, using a tiered system. About 1% of the total population of England is subject to the CPA at any one time, of which about 1% are included in local supervision registers. Substantial variations were found between trusts. Local application of the policies is variable, priority is not closely based on need and inequitable use of resources may result. The authors acknowledge that the numbers are a proxy for the true provision and that the MINI, or any other such system, may not closely represent population needs. It can be argued further that variation is often beneficial and that top-down rules may act to stifle local initiative. In principle, however, an epidemiological and experimental approach should unite both parties.

Hospital vs. CMHTs

Several randomised controlled trials (RCTs) of community teamworking compared with hospital care for severely mentally ill patients in the UK have been published. The designs used, although by no means identical, are sufficiently similar to allow a judgement of the quality of evidence.[121–127]

In summary:

- whatever the interventions are called, a fairly consistent effect is that teamworking helps reduce time spent in hospital; four English studies found some decrease in costs
- there is little or no difference in terms of symptom severity
- social relationships, role functioning and occupations do not improve much
- on the whole, patients prefer a community regimen
- carers experience an increase in burden, but tend to understand the patient's preferences
- acute hospital facilities remain an essential part of comprehensive community care.

Varieties of case management

Marshall and colleagues[128**] made a systematic review of the effectiveness of specific case management compared with 'standard care', finding that the former increased the numbers remaining in contact with services (OR: 0.70; 99% CI: 0.50–0.98; $n = 1210$). However, the numbers admitted to hospital nearly doubled (OR: 1.84; 99% CI: 1.33–2.57; $n = 1300$). There was no difference in clinical or social outcome, or in costs.

Merson and colleagues[129] allocated 100 patients presenting to an A&E clinic at random to a community-based or hospital-based service. Information was collected retrospectively for 3 months, and for a 3-month prospective period. The use of non-psychiatric services was similar for each group, but hospital patients (£130 000) made more use of inpatient beds, while the community group (£56 000) used more home-based interventions. There was no difference in clinical outcome.

Tyrer and colleagues[130]** evaluated the effectiveness of CMHT management compared with non-team standard care for people with both SMI and disordered personality, using randomised or quasi-randomised controlled trials. They concluded that CMHTs might be associated with fewer deaths by suicide or in suspicious circumstances (OR: 0.32; CI: 0.09–1.12). Fewer people were dissatisfied with their care (OR: 0.34; CI: 0.2–0.56) or left the studies early (OR: 0.61; CI: 0.45–0.83). Admission rates, overall clinical outcomes and duration of inpatient treatment did not differ between the groups.

A review of RCTs of assertive community treatment (ACT) for people with SMI, compared with standard community care, hospital-based rehabilitation or case management, is provided by Marshall and Lockwood.[131]** Against standard care, the ACT group were more likely to remain in contact (OR: 0.51; 99% CI: 0.37–0.70), less likely to be admitted (OR: 0.59; 99% CI: 0.41–0.85) and spent less time in hospital. There were advantages in accommodation, activities and patient satisfaction, but not in mental state or social functioning. Compared with hospital rehabilitation services, time in contact was much the same, but ACT patients were less likely to be admitted and more likely to be living independently. Compared with case management, ACT patients spent fewer days in hospital. The reviewers suggest that ACT can reduce costs while improving outcome and satisfaction.

Burns and colleagues[122]* compared two randomised groups of patients with SMI in four inner-city services – one allocated to intensive case management (10–15 per manager, $n = 353$) and the the other to standard care (30–35 per manager, $n = 355$). Over a 2-year period, hospital use did not differ between the groups. There were no differences between African-Caribbean patients and others, or between severely socially disabled patients and others.

A controlled but unblinded trial of rehabilitation was made of 152 unemployed people with SMI who were attending an agency in Washington, DC and receiving intensive case management*. Half were allocated to individual placement and support and half to enhanced vocational rehabilitation. After 18 months, more of the first group were in competitive jobs and fewer in sheltered employment. Quality of life, self-esteem and client satisfaction were also enhanced.[132]

Two demographically similar sectors of Camberwell, a deprived area in south-east London with a long history of community research, were compared in order to assess the value of their different models of inner-city community care.[133] One adopted standard community management, while the other provided more admissions to fewer beds, more non-hospital residential places, a wider range of interventions, more community involvement, and more staff but higher turnover and costs. At follow-up after 2 years, both models produced some improved outcomes, but symptom and disability levels changed little. Occupation in day centres and sheltered work fell off in the intensive sector while remaining steady (day centres) or improving (sheltered work) in the standard sector. Gains were much less pronounced than in experimental studies, and might have been even lower without the stimulation of a research project.

Standards for acute wards

A large-scale literature search was carried out as part of the Clinical Guidelines Programme of the Royal College of Psychiatrists to construct a set of guidelines for the management of imminent violence in acute wards. The only controlled trials found were related to the use of medication and, of these, the designs of most left much to be desired. However, there were sufficient papers, reviews and consensus statements by respected organisations to allow the work and steering groups to develop a set of guidelines for good practice. Recommendations are provided for three overlapping areas – ward design and organisation, anticipating, preventing and dealing with violence, and medication. A fourth area, prediction, could not be rated because of lack of good material.[134]

Costs and effectiveness of pharmacological and psychological treatments

F2, schizophrenia, delusional disorder, 'acute psychosis', unspecified SMI

Medications

The first medications shown to have an unequivocally useful effect (not simply due to sedation) in the treatment of schizophrenia were chlorpromazine and reserpine, both introduced during the 1950s. Haloperidol is probably the commonest of the 'typical' or 'conventional' neuroleptics now in use. Medications are used principally for the positive symptoms described in Section 3, but are much less or not at all effective in ameliorating the negative symptoms. All typicals have unwanted side-effects, some of which can be serious, such as extrapyramidal symptoms (parkinsonism and dystonia) and tardive dyskinesia. Others, such as sedation, dry mouth, constipation, dizziness and impotence, can lead to understandable non-compliance.

Among the more recent 'typicals', clozapine has the longest track record, but it can cause a lowering of the white cell content of the blood, which necessitates a cautionary period under observation when it is first prescribed. More recently there have been reports of cardiomyositis and cardiomyopathy. For these reasons it is only considered for use when others have failed. The cost is an important factor, e.g. £979–1957 per patient-year (maintenance dose 150–300 mg) compared with (at the other end of the scale) £9–29 per patient-year (75–300 mg) for chlorpromazine and £45–790 (5–100 mg) for haloperidol. A further disadvantage is that many atypicals cannot be administered by injection in an emergency or as a 'depot' for longer-term effect.

The atypicals most commonly used are risperidone (£940–1424 per annum for a daily dose of 4–6 mg) and olanzapine (£687–2750 per annum for 5–20 mg daily). Other atypicals under test include quetiapine, ziprazidone and zotapine. None is entirely free from side-effects and all need to establish a long-term track record in properly conducted trials. A useful source of up-to-date information is provided in the report discussed in the next paragraph.

A report from the Centre for Reviews and Dissemination[135]** provides a synopsis of systematic reviews of treatments for schizophrenia. It emphasises that trials are difficult to interpret for everyday use and have such loss to follow-up that the reader is left to speculate on the meaning of the data. Attention is drawn to the fact that trials are generally 'small, short in duration, include participants that are not typical of everyday practice, randomise care regimens that are difficult to generalise, have high attrition rates, and report outcomes that are of dubious clinical value. Most relevant trials are undertaken by those with clear pecuniary interest in the results' (*see also* Section 8). It is not certain that the higher costs of the new drugs can be offset by a decrease in hospital time or indirect costs. Lists are provided of the characteristics of the chief typical, less typical and atypical antipsychotics. Chlorpromazine has clinically valuable antipsychotic properties, evident for a year or more, but can cause irreversible movement disorders.

The National Schizophrenia Guideline Group[136] is also undertaking a comprehensive evaluation of the literature on atypical medication for schizophrenia and allied disorders, focusing on amisulpride, clozapine, olanzapine, quetiapine and risperidone.

A study from the Canadian Co-ordinating Office for Health Technology Assessment (CCOHTA)[137]* computed the cost-effectiveness of treatment with risperidone and clozapine for resistant schizophrenia compared with that of haloperidol and chlorpromazine. Clozapine proved more cost-effective than chlorpromazine or haloperidol. Risperidone was more cost-effective than haloperidol, haloperidol decanoate or fluphenazine decanoate. The evidence-based mental health (EBMH) reviewer, Steven Lawrie, pointed out that the main way to decrease costs is to close beds. Since bed numbers are insufficient in England, the alternative is to spend more on treatment and care for schizophrenia.

In June 2002, NICE published guidance on atypical antipsychotics (amisulpride, olanzapine, quetiapine, risperidone and zotepine) recommending that they are considered in the choice of first-line treatments for individuals with newly diagnosed schizophrenia.

Cognitive behavioural therapy (CBT) for schizoprenia

A series of controlled studies of CBT, mostly in conjunction with medication, has demonstrated an additional value in the combination. The benefits are found in earlier resolution of the positive and negative symptoms and are also evident in the chronic state.[124,126,138] The paper by Tarrier and colleagues[139*] is summarised as an example. Patients on stable medication for schizophrenia ($n = 87$) were stratified by severity and sex to intensive CBT (20 hours in 10 weeks) plus routine care ($n = 33$), supportive counselling plus routine care ($n = 26$), or routine care alone ($n = 28$). The number of symptoms decreased in the CBT group (1.6, 95% CI: 0.7–2.5; mean decrease in number 7.8, CI: 3.8–12.0). The decrease was less in the supportive counselling group, and slightly increased in the routine care group.

Jones and colleagues[140**] reviewed the effects of CBT for schizophrenia compared with standard care, specific medication and non-intervention. Four small trials were identified. The results favoured CBT plus standard care over standard care alone for reducing relapse rates (short-term OR: 0.31; CI: 0.1–0.98; medium-term OR: 0.38; CI: 0.17–0.83; long-term OR: 0.46; CI: 0.26–0.83, number needed to treat [NNT] = 6, CI: 3–30). CBT did not keep people in care longer than a standard approach. There were no data on compliance with medication.

There is limited support from a meta-analysis of controlled trials[87,88] for methods of helping patients and families to understand the basic symptoms and problems that accompany the experience of schizophrenia. Assessing cost-effectiveness requires a more solid measure of consumer judgement.

F30–31, bipolar disorder and mania

Two recent papers contain reviews of the literature on the efficacy of treatment with lithium for manic and bipolar disorders. They come to opposite conclusions. The review by Moncrieff[141] found that most controlled trials had compared lithium with chlorpromazine and also that they were methodologically flawed. Antipsychotics are now most frequently and usefully prescribed for mania, and clinicians are more familiar with their advantages and deficiencies than they are with lithium, which has risks from toxicity and of mania provoked by withdrawal. She concluded that the time may have come to abandon it. The second paper[142] presents the literature as generally more supportive of lithium. Useful information on monitoring, side-effects and toxicity is provided in the *Drug and Therapeutics Bulletin*,[143] which lists six RCTs. Johnston and Eagles[144] provide prevalence data for hypothyroidism (10.4%; women 14%, men 4.5%) and other risk factors, which are highest (at 20%) for women starting lithium when aged 40–59 years.

If lithium is prescribed, patients need to learn how to use it. Thirty attendees at a lithium clinic were given a video-tape lecture and handout, compared with another 30 controls who were given the demonstration later. There was a substantial and significant improvement in knowledge and patients' attitudes became more favourable. Efficacy was not addressed.[145,146]

In 2003, NICE issued guidance on the use of olanzapine and valproate semisodium for the treatment of the acute symptoms of mania associated with bipolar I disorder.

F32–33.4, depressive disorders

Electroconvulsive therapy (ECT)

This method is used rarely, and almost exclusively, for severe depression resistant to other treatments. Convulsions are induced by electrical stimulation of the brain. Three audits of its use have resulted in clear guidelines for administration. All emphasise the need for training. In spite of the provision of official courses, the most recent survey found that only one-third of the clinics met College guidelines.[147] A survey of use in Wales[148] showed that the number of patients treated had fallen by 44% between 1990 and 1996, and a survey published by the DoH in 1999[149] also showed a reduction in usage. A new system of recording came into operation from January 1999. The College has introduced a new system of accreditation for ECT clinics.

In April 2003, NICE issued guidance on the use of ECT in severe depressive illness, catatonia and prolonged or severe manic episodes.

Medications

The history of antidepressive medications has features similar to those described for neuroleptics, and similar caveats should be observed. Imipramine was the first to be shown to have useful antidepressant effects. The more recent drugs fall into two main groups. The tricyclic antidepressants (TCAs) have to be started at a low dose, which is slowly increased to around 150 mg daily. They can cause dry mouth, constipation, hypotension and sedation. They are cheaper than the selective serotonin reuptake inhibitors (SSRIs). CBT is used, with and without medication, in both primary and secondary care.

A substantial review by the Canadian Co-ordinating Office for Health Technology Assessment (CCOHTA)[150*] provides a clinical and cost comparison between SSRIs and TCAs. Data analysed from 162 RCTs showed that the two methods were equally effective. Patients on SSRIs had a greater number of side-effects and reported nausea and anxiety. Those on TCAs had constipation and dry mouth. Drop-out rates differed little, suggesting similar toleration. The reviewer regarded tricyclics as the most cost-effective first-line treatment for depression but pointed out that SSRIs have advantages and, as prices fell, might become first-line treatment.

Hotopf and colleagues[151] examined 122 RCTs to discover why there was no consensus as to whether SSRIs or tricyclic/heterocyclic antidepressants should be used as the first line of treatment. Design shortcomings were found under five headings: randomisation, outcomes, dosage, generalisation and statistics.

Cornelius and colleagues[152*] studied the effectiveness of fluoxetine (an SSRI) in reducing depression associated with comorbid major depression and alcohol dependence (RCT, 12-week follow-up). They concluded that the drug reduced both symptoms and dependence.

Blackburn and Moore[153] report an RCT of 75 outpatients with recurrent major depression, comparing antidepressants and cognitive therapy during 16 weeks of acute and 2 years of maintenance therapy. During the treatment phase all patients improved, with no difference between groups. The same was true in the maintenance phase. CBT was consistently superior to medication.

Ray and Hodnet[154*] found two RCTs (142 patients, 111 completed the study) concerned with post-partum depression. One ($n = 61$) compared fluoxetine plus CBT with placebo plus counselling. The other ($n = 50$) compared weekly non-directive counselling with routine postpartum care. Women who received extra support were significantly improved ($p = 0.002$; relative risk reduction 47%; 95% CI: 18–66; NNT = 4; CI: 3–10). Gavin Young, the commentator, points out that an earlier study[155] also compared fluoxetine with placebo and showed the drug to be as effective as extra counselling sessions, so that women have a choice.

Hawton and colleagues[156**] reviewed 23 RCTs of psychosocial and/or pharmacological treatment vs. standard or less intensive types of aftercare for deliberate self-harm. They conclude that uncertainty remains as to which forms of psychosocial and physical treatment are most effective. Evans and colleagues[157] studied 827 people admitted to medical wards for deliberate self-harm and followed for 6 months after the index event. Half of them at random were offered a 24-hour crisis telephone consultation service with an on-call psychiatrist and given a card with instructions. There was no overall effect from this intervention (OR: 1.20; 95% CI: 0.82–0.75).

Termon and colleagues[158*] conclude that bright morning light and negative air ionisation alleviate depressive symptoms in patients with seasonal affective disorder. Lee and Chan[159*] conclude from a meta-analysis that there is a dose–response relationship between intensity of light and reduction in typical depressive symptoms (effect size for strong light 2.9; 95% CI: 2.3–3.6).

Upton and colleagues[160] assessed the extent to which guidelines for diagnosing and managing mental disorders in primary care improved recognition, accuracy of diagnosis and treatment standards. Their paper deals chiefly with depression. Bristol GPs already routinely recording morbidity data were invited to participate and 17 GPs were selected. They attended a study day and were given a reference book with diagnostic and management guidelines. Data were collected for 11 weeks before and after the training. Ten per cent of the patients were also interviewed before and after this period, and completed relevant scales. In the event, 'the guidelines had no effect on the detection of mental disorders or on patient satisfaction'.

A large RCT of an educational approach using a clinical practice guideline did not produce improvement in the recognition or successful management of depression by practitioners.[161] The chapter on mental health in primary care to be published in the *Health Care Needs Assessment* (third series) is devoted to these issues, and a substantial CSAG Report[162] is also available.

F34.1, dysthymia (persistent mood disorder)

Dysthymia (F4.1) has survived as a chronic low-grade depression mixed with other symptoms such as insomnia, tearfulness and inadequacy. Two papers by protagonists have come to no firm conclusion about its value as an independent category.[163]

Lima and colleagues[164]** reported on 15 RCTs of medication vs. placebo for dysthymia. The results were similar for all groups of drugs (TCA, SSRI, MAOI, etc.). The Cochrane reviewers concluded that 'in general, drugs are effective in the treatment of dysthymia with no difference between and within class of drugs. Tricyclic antidepressants are more likely to cause adverse events and dropouts'.

F40–42, phobias

After stratification by sub-type, Heimberg and colleagues[165]* compared cognitive behavioural group therapy (CBGT, $n = 36$) for social phobia, using phenelzine, increasing as necessary to 90 mg per day after 5 weeks ($n = 31$), matching placebo ($n = 33$) and supportive group therapy ($n = 33$), during a 12-week RCT. CBGT consisted of 12 sessions of 2.5 hours with between five and seven patients in each group. The relative benefit increase for CBGT vs. placebo was 114% (95% CI: 19–307, NNT = 4, 2–14); that for phenelzine vs. placebo was 94% (95% CI: 15–243, NNT = 4, 2–16). The two sites had the same results, i.e. both CBGT and phenelzine were effective.

F40–41, 42, panic and general anxiety disorders

It is particularly difficult to separate the psychological and pharmacological effects of treatments for these disorders. Lader and Bond[166] provide an overview of controlled trials. They conclude that benzodiazepines are useful for severe general anxiety disorders in the initial stages because they produce rapid symptomatic improvement; psychological treatments can then take over after 2–4 weeks. TCAs, benzodiazepines and, most recently, SSRIs such as paroxetine have been found helpful for panic disorder. Loerch and colleagues[167] assigned 55 patients with panic disorder and agoraphobia at random to treatment with moclobemide plus CBT, moclobemide plus clinical management, placebo plus CBT, or placebo plus clinical management, over an 8-week period. CBT was effective and remained so during a 6-month follow-up period. Moclobemide with clinical management was not superior to placebo.

F42, obsessive–compulsive disorder

Piccinelli and colleagues[168] provide a meta-analysis of data on the efficacy of drug treatments for OCD, using work published from 1975 to 1994. Clomipramine was superior to placebo for both obsessions and compulsions, but SSRIs were less so.

Abramowitz[169]* also evaluated RCTs of OCD, including a total of 37 treatment comparisons. The results support exposure with response prevention (ERP) and CBT vs. placebo. SSRIs were more effective than placebo (effect size 0.71 for self-ratings, $p < 0.05$). Non-SSRIs were no better than placebo. Clomipramine had no more effect than other SSRIs (effect size 0.15).

F43, post-traumatic stress disorder

Consecutive patients aged 16–65 ($n = 133$) admitted to the Welsh Regional Burns Unit agreed to enter at random a trial of psychological debriefing (PD). Of these, 32 were excluded for major physical or psychiatric disorder, residence outside Wales or failure to complete the questionnaire. An interviewer blind to PD status followed up 3 and 13 months later, 23 patients being lost at one or both stages. The outcome was that 16 (26%) of those counselled and four (9%) of the controls still had PTSD after 13 weeks. 'This study seriously questions the wisdom of one-off interventions post-trauma'.[170]

Wessely and colleagues[171]** found eight RCTs of short debriefing for distress after trauma (PTSD). Single sessions did not reduce distress, prevent later onset or reduce depression or anxiety.

Marks and colleagues[172]* selected 87 patients with PTSD (*DSM-III-R* criteria) who were allocated at random to exposure therapy ($n = 23$), cognitive restructuring ($n = 19$), exposure plus cognitive restructuring ($n = 24$) or relaxation ($n = 21$). By the end of the treatment, percentage improvement was 60%, 50% and 58% for the exposure, cognitive and combined therapy groups, respectively, compared with 20% in the relaxation group.

F45, chronic fatigue syndrome (CFS)

Price and Couper[173]** found three usable trials of CBT for chronic fatigue syndrome (CFS). There were significant benefits in physical functioning in adult outpatients compared with orthodox management or relaxation. Patients liked it.

Deale and colleagues[174]* randomised 60 patients with CFS to CBT or relaxation. At 6 months, function and fatigue improved (e.g. 70% and 63% CBT vs. 19% and 15%, respectively).

Clark and colleagues,[175] following an earlier controlled study suggesting that CBT was useful for patients with hypochondriasis, carried out a further trial to amplify the results. Patients referred by GPs and specialists in Oxfordshire who met *DSM-III-R* criteria were randomised to cognitive therapy (CT, $n = 16$), behaviour stress management (BM, $n = 17$) or waiting list (WL, $n = 15$). Both treatments were effective compared with placebo, e.g. the time spent seriously worried at the beginning and end of treatment (on a scale of 0–100) was 56 and 13 (CT), 51 and 23 (BM) and 58 and 35 (WL). A year after treatment all patients were significantly better than before.

Reid and colleagues[26] provide a comprehensive description of CFS and its treatment. RCTs do not provide sufficient evidence to support treatment with antidepressants or corticosteroids. Graded exercise can produce improvement in fatigue and physical functioning. No evidence was found for prolonged rest, which might be harmful. CBT by skilled therapists in specialist centres is effective.

F50, anorexia and bulimia

Eisler and colleagues[176]* compared RCTs of individual supportive therapy vs. family therapy for 80 people who had been in hospital for anorexia or bulimia. After discharge (i.e. when patients had been 'nutritionally rehabilitated') they were divided into four groups: early onset and short history of anorexia; early onset and long history (> 3 years); late onset of anorexia; bulimia. Ninety-one per cent were followed up. In each group people were allocated to individual or family therapy. In conclusion, patients with early onset and short history of anorexia had a good outcome in terms of body weight and regular menstrual cycles after family therapy, compared with those who received individual therapy.

Whittal and colleagues[177*] selected nine RCTs of medication (870 patients) and 26 RCTs of CBT (460 patients) for analysis. Both methods were effective for all outcomes (binge and purge frequency, depression and eating attitudes). For each outcome the effect sizes for CBT were higher than those for medication.

Carter and Fairburn[178*] compared a CBT self-help book about binge eating with six to eight sessions on the book with a facilitator. Women with weekly bulimic episodes were allocated to one of the two groups or to a waiting list. Both methods were successful compared with none, but guided self-help led to a greater reduction in binge eating.

Palmer and Treasure[179] surveyed the arrangements whereby regions commission specialist services and also discuss possible models for care. A specialised treatment service is described by Millar.[180]

F51, non-organic sleep disorders

Nowell and colleagues[181*] provide a meta-analysis of literature on the efficacy of benzodiazepines and zolpidem tartrate for chronic insomnia. There were 22 studies involving 1894 mostly middle-aged patients (60% women) who met the inclusion criteria. The authors conclude that both drugs are effective in reducing sleep-onset latency, increasing total sleep time, reducing the number of awakenings and improving sleep quality. The reviewer points out that diagnoses were not uniform, daytime functioning was not measured and the period of treatment was only 5 weeks. An earlier meta-analysis showed that behavioural treatments were effective and durable[182] but no study has yet been published comparing the two kinds of treatment.

F6, personality disorders

The point is made in Section 3 that, given the uncertainty of definition, it is no surprise that substantial problems are encountered when assigning a diagnosis of one of the eight types of disorder included in the *ICD-10* diagnostic criteria (F60). Apart from interventions aimed at helping the comorbid problems that are often the cause of referral, admission to hospital is not generally regarded as appropriate. People involved with forensic services and those in prison have often been involved with general services before and after any period of special accommodation.

The Office for National Statistics (ONS) for the DoH found that 63% of men on remand, 49% of sentenced men and 31% of women in each group had a 'personality disorder'. Psychosis during the previous year was diagnosed in 7% of sentenced men, 10% of men on remand and 14% of women in both categories – all higher than the national yearly prevalence. Substance use was common. Twenty-five per cent of women had attempted suicide at least once during the previous year and 2% of men and women within the previous week.

Milton[183] did a postal survey of 50 inpatient forensic health care and prison services concerning the use of routine assessment instruments, which elicited 35 responses. A total of 54 different instruments were routinely employed, of which two-thirds dealt with personality assessment; the others included diagnosis, symptom severity, neuropsychology and behaviour. It is concluded that more uniformity, based on an instrument such as the International Personality Disorder Examination (IPDE),[11] should be encouraged throughout the system.

The College guidelines on the management of imminent violence on acute wards provide a list of risk factors and detailed methods of coping, but found insufficient evidence to formulate a recommendation on how to predict violence.[134]

Dissocial personality disorder (F60.2) is the only *ICD* diagnosis to mention 'a low threshold for discharge of aggression, including violence'. A Home Office consultation paper identifies a group of 'dangerous severely personality disordered' people who need to be detained. Two sets of options are considered, both intended to ensure risk reduction. The proposals are controversial[108,109] insofar as they imply a role for doctors that goes beyond a responsibility to provide an expert opinion on mental state and medical treatment.

Size of effect and quality of evidence

The report from the Centre for Reviews and Dissemination, used in Section 6 as part of the evidence for or against the efficacy of medications for schizophrenia, emphasises that trials are difficult to interpret. Attention is drawn to the fact that trials are generally 'small, short in duration, include participants who are not typical of everyday practice, randomise care regimens that are difficult to generalise, have high attrition rates, and report outcomes that are of dubious clinical value. Most relevant trials are undertaken by those with clear pecuniary interest in the results'. The initial sampling is particularly crucial. A further point to bear in mind is that the new generation of drugs has not been tested for long enough to provide adequate information on the course of the disorder or to ensure that all important side-effects have been revealed. Finally, it is not yet certain that the higher costs of the new drugs can be offset by a decrease in hospital time or in indirect costs. The strictures also apply to new medications for the other *ICD-10* disorders and, in a different context, to procedures such as CBT. No selection from the recent technical literature can have been entirely successful in avoiding these problems.

Can standards based on general medicine be applied more widely?

Methods of assessing community services, such as the CPA, hospital and ward functioning, sheltered housing and occupational rehabilitation, are also open to question about their adequacy, but nevertheless should be included in evaluations of the present kind. The ratings on scales of 'size of effect' and 'quality of evidence', in particular, must be interpreted in terms of the content and context of the procedures, as briefly summarised in Section 5 and earlier in this section.

In addition to the caveats expressed above, it should be understood that the summaries are not sufficient in themselves to provide a basis for ratings. Recourse should be had to the original documents.

Two scales for rating treatments and services

Size of effect

A The procedure/service has a strong beneficial effect.
B The procedure/service has a moderate beneficial effect.
C The procedure/service has a measurable beneficial effect.
D The procedure/service has no measurable beneficial effect.
E The harm of the procedure/service outweighs its benefits.

Quality of evidence

I-1   Evidence from several consistent or one large randomised controlled trial.
I-2   Evidence from at least one properly designed randomised controlled trial.
II-1 Evidence from well-designed controlled trials without randomisation, or from well-designed cohort or case–control analytic studies.
II-2 Evidence from multiple time-series with or without the intervention; dramatic results in uncontrolled experiments.

III   Opinions of respected authorities: based on clinical experience, descriptive studies, or reports of expert committees.

IV   Evidence inadequate and conflicting.

Community services for people with severe mental disorders

There are substantial variations in quality of service, but overall the more active and skilled the regimen the greater the benefits: A, I-1
- satisfaction of user
- independence of user
- increased contact with staff.

There is some impact in the longer term on: C, I-1
- social functioning
- occupation
- burden on family.

There are some useful examples of sheltered activities and work,   A, III
but insufficient provision and little research.

There is some action to support carers,   B, I-2
but insufficient provision and little research.

Use of residential accommodation

Acute wards in vulnerable inner-city areas are unsatisfactory due to   C, III
overcrowding and staff shortages.

Guidelines for containing violence on acute wards   A, III
Detailed protocols are provided in four key areas:
- a safe ward environment, calming features and activities
- risk assessment and action to de-escalate violence
- use of and training for restraint
- use of and training for medication and care in the context of violence.

24-hour nurse-staffed hostels in these areas can provide satisfactory   A, III
care for some, thus relieving the pressure on acute wards.

There is a shortage of accommodation for people who need   A, III
longer-term non-hospital residential care.

Treatments

All ratings assume that a specified regimen is followed.

Medication for schizophrenia   A, I-1
Adjunctive CBT for schizophrenia   B, I-1
Antipsychotics for bipolar disorder and mania   A, I-1
Lithium for bipolar disorder and mania   C, III
when severe and resistant to antipsychotics
Medication for major depression and bipolar disorder   A, I-1
Medication and/or CBT* for phobias, anxiety and panic disorder   A, I-1
Medication and/or CBT* for OCD   A, I-1
Debriefing for distress after trauma   D, I-2
CBT for somatoform disorder   B, I-1

Medication and/or CBT* for bulimia   A, I-2

Therapy in family context also helpful

*CBT tends to be somewhat more effective than medication.

7 Quantified models of care

Introduction

Authors in this series are allowed discretion in Section 7 to outline what they think future services should look like. It begins with brief reminders of the near-best and near-worst of the previous system, as the large psychiatric hospitals began to run down during the mid-1950s. Both offer important lessons. It goes on to list the seven official standards proposed in the National Service Framework for Mental Health (NSF), then deals briefly with responsibilities in primary care. The roles of secondary psychiatric and social care are discussed in the context of the material in the earlier parts of this section and the ideas in the NSF. The final part of the section provides a tentative table of needs and costs. Key technical issues vital for the design of future health and social services are discussed in Section 8.

Hospital-based to community-based services

Three hospitals chosen for study in the late 1950s provided very different social environments for their patients and also differed in the nature and degree of their contacts with local communities. One (Netherne) provided a wide range of facilities, including paid work and other occupations on-site for every patient who could benefit from them, together with sheltered housing and work outside the hospital. The second hospital (Mapperly) was adequate but not outstanding. The third (Severalls), part of which in 1961 still typified those with coercive and deadening regimens, was turned round by the appointment of a new and innovative psychiatrist. At the final 8-year follow-up its standards were close to those of Netherne. Two factors were common, although in different degrees, to all three hospitals. First, the longer patients had been resident the more likely they were to want to stay ('institutionalism'). Second, the negative symptoms of schizophrenia were augmented by a poor social environment, although this effect was reversible. The authors warned that either factor could be found in any setting, including 'in the community', that allowed long-term neglect of people with cognitive problems like those in schizophrenia.[184]

    The second study involved the same three hospitals, in their role as providers of acute and follow-up care to patients, during the 5 years after first admission in 1956. The most innovative practice was the early discharge and subsequent vigorous follow-up policy initiated at Mapperley. The hypothesis for test was that this would bring rewards in the shape of fewer symptoms, greater autonomy and more satisfied families, compared with patients discharged from the other two hospitals. In fact, the clinical and care profiles at follow-up were not found to be better than those for Netherne patients. In particular, the most disabled patients were not given priority in follow-up care.[185]

Substituting for long-term hospital care: the TAPS project

An opportunity to appraise the results of deliberate reprovision in the community was later offered when two hospitals (Friern and Claybury) were earmarked for closure. The experiences of long-stay patients have been measured, first in hospital and then in new community accommodation, from 1985 to 1993 ($n = 670$). Of 523 patients (80% with schizophrenia) who survived a 5-year follow-up period, 90% were living in the community, 59% in their original housing. One-third had been readmitted at least once, but there was little crime or vagrancy. Residents valued their independence.[186,187] Residential homes had tended to increase in size to restrict costs. Most staff were untrained. Judged by restrictions, activities and social networks, the private and larger homes were least successful. Housing and staff support accounted for 90% of the care costs. Costs at Friern in 1985–86, at 1994–95 prices, were £595 per patient, compared with £665 in the community. Purchasers and providers are now concerned about the mismatch between service demand and supply, poorly defined responsibilities and cost-shifting between agencies entailed by changes to housing benefit rules.[73,188]

A National Service Framework* for mental health

The Government document adumbrating changes to be made, beginning in spring 1999, stated that care in the community had failed 'because it left some people vulnerable, others a threat to themselves or a nuisance to others, with a small minority a danger to the public'. Other observations included the undue burden placed on families, underfunding, variable standards, low staff morale, failure to exploit the potential of the new medications, problems with the Mental Health Act and failure to provide continuity of care after discharge from hospital. Broader issues involved poor co-ordination between services, and between primary and secondary care, mismatches between health and local authorities, problems of recruitment, and shortages of many kinds. The NSF is intended to try to put these problems right.

The NSF is part of 'a package of measures to drive up the quality of services to service users and to reduce unacceptable variations'. Standards are set by the Framework and NICE, delivered by clinical governance and monitored by CHI (*see* Section 8). The Framework is to be implemented according to seven standards.

- Health and social services should promote mental health and combat discrimination.
- Primary care teams should identify mental health needs, offer effective treatment and refer to specialist services as necessary.
- Patients should have access to services at all times.
- There should be a written care plan on action to be taken by users, carers and care co-ordinators, 'round the clock', when in crisis.
- Users who need it should have access to a bed, under the least restriction possible and as close to home as possible, consonant with their and the public's protection.
- Carers' needs should be assessed and a written care plan provided.
- Health and social services should prevent suicides by implementing the above six standards. They should also help to reduce prison suicides and develop local suicide audit.

The Framework has not been without its critics. Tyrer[189] commented that the solid base of evidence needed for these standards 'have all the firmness of blancmange. . . . A few oases of excellence shine out . . . but no explanation is given why they remain local'. He also pointed out that a specific suggestion in the Framework, to provide a new telephone helpline (NHS Direct*)*, was not backed by evidence and seemed unlikely to work. A further point could have been added to this criticism – that the much valued and used

---

* The National Service Framework (NSF) should not be confused with the National Schizophrenia Fellowship (NSF), which has a 27-year prior claim on the acronym.

phone lines already provided by voluntary organisations such as NSF, SANE and MIND were not mentioned.

Allocation of funds

A key passage in the Framework stated that the Government had 'already committed an extra £700m over 3 years to help local health and social care communities reshape mental health services. . .'. The future speed of implementation will be shaped by evidence of increased cost-effectiveness in delivering mental health services, available resources, and rigorous performance management.

Such statements will be tested in due course. Meanwhile the amounts specified in the *Modernising Mental Health Services* circulars (HSC 1999/038; LAC 99/8) show a total of £40 million extra to be invested in general mental health services for those of working age during 1999–2000. Of this, £19 million was allocated to health authorities (now PCTs) for 24-hour staffed beds, outreach teams and atypical drugs. 'The net result is that only two of the 100 health authorities received more than £1m additional money for new developments; 71 received less than £100 000 and 53 less than £50 000.' By contrast, a placement in a private secure hospital costs about £100 000 per annum, an acute psychiatric bed £50 000–70 000 per annum, and an independent homicide enquiry £500 000–£1 million.[2]

There is £22 million earmarked mainly for social care services, and the remaining £84 million is for selected local authorities in the Mental Health Social Care Partnership Fund. Another £21 million, mainly for extra secure beds and support for the Framework, was 'biddable'.

Interaction between primary and secondary services

The second Framework standard specifies the duties of primary care teams. Goldberg and Huxley[190] described the pathways to care for mental illness in terms of five levels of prevalence:

1 in the community
2 in primary care (including those unrecognised by the GP)
3 identified in primary care
4 in contact with secondary services
5 in hospital.

At each level the prevalence becomes smaller but the disorders become more severe and costly (*see* Table 28).

Table 28: Pathways to psychiatric care.

Level 1: Prevalence in the community; 260–315 per 1000 population at risk per year
Level 2: Prevalence in primary care; 230 per 1000 at risk per year
Level 3: Identification in primary care; 101.5 per 1000 at risk per year
Level 4: Contact with mental illness services; 23.5 per 1000 at risk per year
Level 5: Hospital care; 5.7 per 1000 at risk per year

Source: Goldberg and Huxley.[190]

Depression and/or anxiety are the commonest problems and comprehensive guidelines have been published for the care required.[162] Skilled CBT, which is helpful for many of the common mental disorders and liked by patients, is not available to meet the actual let alone the potential demand from patients or GPs. The extent to which secondary services are unavailable to meet the needs of emergency and out-of-hours services is a further problem, slow to be rectified. Other difficulties identified by CSAG-1999[162] include a failure of information management, insufficient priority given to a strategy for primary mental health care, lack of information about psychotic disorders and their management, insufficient education and training programmes, and uncertainty about guidelines for prescribing. Requirements based on the conclusions of CSAG-1999[162] are generalised below for the broader range of mental health problems encountered in primary care:

- clear definition of responsibilities of PHCTs, CMHTs and specialist services
- access to appropriate psychological therapies
- practical information to support the primary care of mental disorders
- PCT strategies to prioritise disorders and identify a lead GP for planning and commissioning; DoH to ensure recording of morbidity and prescribing
- training, supervision, clinical audit and monitoring according to guidelines, including risk assessment for suicide, as part of clinical governance.

Kendrick[117] points to three problems with many guidelines on severe depression, often based mainly on an earlier joint consensus statement. The diagnosis is difficult to make in primary care, social factors are difficult to take into account and patients are often unwilling to accept drugs.

Two further observations should also be noted. Churchill and McGuire[191] found that of 1990 controlled trials of pharmacotherapies for mental disorders, based solely in primary care, 1872 were assessing medications, mostly funded by pharmaceutical firms. Mann and Tylee,[192] discussing confounders relevant to prescribing, pointed out that 'At any one time in the UK there are at least a thousand drug company representatives seeing GPs about prescribing for depression alone'. The task of evaluating the clinical value and efficacy of medications is now entrusted to NICE (*see* Section 8).

Teamwork with severely mentally ill people: morale and efficiency

Multi-disciplinary visiting panels taking part in the assessment of 11 district services (based on detailed standards created for the purpose) noted the comments of local GPs, clinical specialists and social service representatives to the effect that lines of mutual communication and consultation were often few and ineffective. The users and carers who were interviewed would have liked to be involved but their role as useful participants in the quality-control process had not been recognised. A central conclusion from the audit was that the district services providing the best care were those where personal relationships and communications between staff and management were open (*see* Table 29). High scores for morale were associated with satisfaction for patients, staff and management, and with good clinical practice throughout the organisation. Many of the recruitment and turnover problems mentioned in Section 5 are due to poor morale in wards and teams.[76,193]

The Health Advisory Service (HAS-2000) has since published an updated set of standards for adult mental health care against which services can be tested. The set covers more detail than the Framework. The role of HAS will be reviewed in relation to that of CHI, but there is no doubt that its functions must be continued.

Residential care

Official returns: a health statistics warning

A study of the coverage and accuracy of DoH central returns on the provision of mental health care in 1994 found wide discrepancies between the degree of completion in seven English districts compared with data

Table 29: Mean scores on presence and quality of district services.

District	Purchaser	Provider	Total
District A	18	37	55
District B	21	32	53
District C	16	34	50
District D	18	31	49
District E	18	23	41
District F	13	27	40
District G	11	23	34
District H	10	23	33
District I	13	19	31
District J	7	12	19
District K	8	10	18
Total	153	271	424
Mean per point	21.9	20.9	21.2

Source: CSAG-1995. There were 7 purchaser and 13 provider key points.
Correlation between purchaser and provider scores = 0.70.

specially gathered locally using defined criteria. About half the facilities were not recorded, with a range of accuracy from 30% to 78% across districts. The authors conclude that a new classification is needed, using stricter definitions (Audini *et al.*, in preparation). The sparse official data available and the need to use a large variety of sometimes incompatible sources mean that all interpretations and conclusions must be regarded as tentative.

Meeting the accommodation needs of the most acutely ill

In a descriptive study of an acute psychiatric ward in London, all violent incidents were recorded during a 15-month period. The proportion of permanent staff halved during this time, and that of agency nurses and other temporary staff doubled. Other factors changed little. The frequency of violence on the ward more than doubled. Two-thirds of the relevant variance was associated with changes in staffing patterns.[92]

The data on inner-London acute wards provided in Section 5 reinforce these observations. It is evident that many, particularly in vulnerable areas, do not meet high standards. To adopt a word that was commonly used (sometimes unfairly) in the 1950s and 1960s, at worst they can be 'dustbins'. Over-crowding is also due to a lack of 24-hour accommodation in high-staffed, community-based hostels, particularly in inner-city areas. The intention to commission extra hostel accommodation, with fully trained staff on call throughout the 24 hours (not just sleeping in), is welcome, but substantial dedicated funding is essential. Acute wards are needed, particularly in vulnerable areas, to cope with emergencies.

Protocols set out the essential parameters[134] as follows:

- provision of a calming physical and social environment with plenty of space
- access to single-sex accommodation
- separate rooms for private interactions between patients, visitors and staff
- separate provision for indoor activities and exercise, and for smokers
- adequate and safe outside space and equipment

- training of ward teams in the de-escalation, prevention and restraint of violence
- equivalent training, part multi-disciplinary, for the staff of community teams
- effective team management with high morale
- collaboration with users and carers.

Dangerousness – and the real problems

Dangerousness is a familiar topic for political and media preoccupation, one that further echoes the pressure put on the large hospitals during the late 1950s and 1960s. That pressure would have been more effective in the long run if it had focused attention on specific problems, such as undue isolation in 'disturbed wards', the poor training of administrators, the need to build up decent residential and day-care services in the community and, above all, identification of adequate supporting funds in advance of attempting closure. The major problem today is not danger of homicide by patients, which is very rare and seldom involves an unknown member of the public. The really serious problems are suicide and suicide attempts, self-harm, self-neglect, poor accommodation, penury, loss of self-respect and burden on families.

Longer-term residential care and the concept of 'institutionalism'

The term 'institutionalism', in the context of residential care, was originally used to describe a process whereby long-stay patients in psychiatric hospitals could gradually adopt, over a period of years, an attitude of indifference about leaving or of positively wishing to stay. A similar phenomenon has been observed in other types of institution, such as the tuberculosis sanatorium in Thomas Mann's novel, *The Magic Mountain*. Particularly at risk were people vulnerable because of a lack of drive and blunting of affect. These problems are risk factors in some forms of schizophrenia, learning disability, dependent personality or physical debility. Such extra disability is often preventable or reversible, as was shown by pioneering hospital staff in the 1950s.[184,194]

Rehabilitation and the new CPA

Equivalents to institutionalism can equally occur 'in the community', where negative symptoms allied with destitution, comorbidity with drugs and disease, lack of physical and social care, and general isolation can have the same effect.[195] Twenty years on, the basic principles of care are still the same, although the large hospitals have mostly gone. Everyone at risk needs a range of available options:

- a secure, non-stigmatising home with a domestic regimen
- private, peaceful, outdoor space that does not intrude on neighbours
- daytime occupation and leisure-time activities
- graduated steps towards independence that allow for the possibility of relapse
- supervision and care by a comprehensive district and social psychiatric service.

Models of services for people with longer-term mental illness who need a degree of shelter lack specification. There is a range of options from normal but adapted and specially sited (housing) to 'core and cluster', centred round a well-staffed hostel ward or local hospital. The TAPS scheme went some way towards achieving similar objectives. Although the needs are clear, there is very little hard data on the numbers, types and costs of the provision required. This is also true of the details and numbers of long-term day centres, workshops and industrial (e.g. Remploy) enterprises required. The Framework gives only two examples, both with the worthy aim of achieving open employment, but no specification of the numbers and needs of the totality of handicapped people. There are no targets and no costings.

Slade and colleagues[196] made a similar point about disincentives that reduce the uptake of benefit entitlements by patients. Mental ill health is already associated with poverty in general. Negative symptoms plus apathy born of helplessness add a form of institutionalism without an institution. The areas of everyday living that should be considered in every district and authority when assessing the numbers, needs and quality of life of people with SMI are summarised in Figure 1.

WORKING HOURS	HOME	LEISURE
No occupational problem	Copes well domestically	Plenty of interests
Sheltered paid work	Supervised flat or lodging	Users' club
Industrial therapy day unit	Visited group home	Reserved hours recreation
Occupational therapy unit	Staffed hostel or haven	OT at home or centre
High-dependency day unit	Ward or secure day unit	Special facilities

Figure 1: Need levels of people at risk from mental illness. People can be in need in any one area and in any combination of areas.

The figure contains a set of three areas of everyday living, each with five levels of disability. A particular individual with SMI could be at different levels of competence in each area: for example, living in a staffed hostel, attending an industrial therapy day unit and belonging to a users' club. A successful project that provides a challenging work environment for people with a mental illness (most with SMI) is provided by the First Step Trust, which provides services for over 300 people in six UK centres. The work available is sufficiently flexible to provide appropriate occupation in any setting, including longer-term hospital (contact: First Step Trust, 32 Hare Street, London SE18 6LZ, www.fst.org.uk).

The costs of teams, day hospitals, day centres and workshops, estimated in the context of the survey of London's Mental Health (*see* Section 5), are shown in Table 19. There are virtually no well-designed comparisons of occupational schemes in specified districts, and only sparse data on size, costs and efficacy. The techniques needed to collect such information and place it in the context of a routinely collected data system are considered in Section 8. Meaningful occupation is the next priority after providing adequate housing. The third element in Figure 1, covering leisure activities appropriate to the needs of all disabled people, including the most handicapped, constitutes perhaps the most challenging task.

An outline model for non-residential care

According to these priorities, a numerical estimate of need should be based on a first assumption that all those in hospital or other protected housing should be offered a choice of formal or informal day activity, either within the setting or (ideally) outside it, with the expectation that at least half of such options would be taken up. Workshops with a financial incentive should be available for those who can work to a standard and keep set hours. The same range of specialist day-care opportunities should be available for all those who, whether or not in protected housing, are on the list of a CMHT, with an average of four to five half-days weekly. At least half of those with long-term disability should be attending some form of day setting. Any travel costs should be subsidised.

Allocation formulae for primary care trusts

Attention needs to be given to ensuring a fair distribution of funds to and by districts. The socio-demographic differences involved are well understood, but checks are required to ensure that poorer areas receive their full (weighted) compensation. Local implementation of the CPA is variable, prioritisation is not always based closely on need and inequitable use of resources may result. The technical problems of designing good research are undoubtedly formidable, but a start could be made by providing accurate, explicit and usable data on the service elements of the allocation formula for primary care trusts.

The dominance of forensic problems in some districts is a specific example of the problem. A suggestion for regional funding of the forensic element draws on the Government commitment in *Modernising Mental Health Care* to centralise the relevant services. The prospect of regional commissioners allocating such monies from the PCT budget has wider and interesting implications.

Quantifying the need for services of people with SMI

The peak occupation in the large hospitals was 345 per 100 000 in 1954 (*see* Section 5). None of the evidence quoted in earlier sections suggests that the incidence of SMI or the longer-term prognosis or prevalence have improved much since the mid-1960s. On the plus side, treatments are slowly getting better, and acute episodes tend to be shorter. However, the long-term course is not, so far, much improved. The official data provided in Section 5 are not of sufficient quality to allow comparison between the 1950s and the 1990s, although the minimum data set (*see* Section 8) will in time provide really useful information. Meanwhile all estimates come with a further substantial 'health warning'.

Estimated needs for sheltered residential and day occupation

The lack of a quantifiable definition for SMI is a handicap when using the numbers in hospital during the late 1950s and early 1960s to estimate the numbers of people now in need of services. The estimate derived from the London survey (*see* Table 23) suggests that a mean of about 168 people per 100 000 population of London are now using a wide range of forms of residential accommodation. The estimate for England and Wales was 147 (*see* Table 24). The estimate that was provided in the first edition of this chapter was 166. These closely similar figures were derived independently of each other. They amount to about half the complement of hospital beds that were occupied in the mid-1950s, i.e. half of 345, or 173 per 100 000. A threefold range around this figure (87–261 per 100 000) allows room for adjustment for local epidemiology and other local clinical and administrative characteristics (Table 30, *see* overleaf). Districts with unusual outliers would need further correction.

Excluding patients in intensive and acute wards, i.e. 40 (20–60 per 100 000), who should have their own comprehensive on-site facilities, at least half of those in residential care (about 68 per 100 000) would need day occupation away from the housing.

The calculation in Table 30 raises the a question of whether the present-day counterparts of the less severe users of the mid-1950s bed complement (about half, i.e. another 173 per 100 000) are also represented in, and should be candidates for, present-day services. It would be sensible to assume that some of the former residents, who had little or no need of medical or nursing facilities, simply lacked

Table 30: Estimated need for residential care: numbers and costs per 100 000 population.

Services	Places/100 000 (range)	Weekly cost (£ per client)			Total weekly cost (£ all clients)
		Housing	Other†	Total	
Intensive-care ward and acute wards	40 (20–60)	844	349	1,193	47,720
Rehabilitation and hostel wards	20 (10–30)	665	42	707	14,140
Hostels, staff awake at night	40 (20–60)	285	53	338	13,520
Hostels, staff sleep-in	24 (12–36)	238	93	331	7,994
Day-staffed or visited group homes	12 (6–18)	173	99	272	3,264
Group homes on call	14 (7–21)	140	122	262	3,668
Supported housing*	25 (12–36)	118	19	137	3,425
Total	175 (87–261)				93,731

* Includes supported bedsits, licensed landladies, etc. Costs estimated from LA sheltered housing for elderly.
† Other costs include residents' living expenses and use of non-residential services apart from staff.
The total estimate is for £93,731 per week = £4,874,012 per year.
London equivalents: inner = £6,370,000; outer = £4,052,000; total = £5,211,000.

housing alternatives. Others, like those with learning disability, dementia or other handicap, would need more specialist accommodation. The rest, perhaps about a quarter of the 1950s complement (87 per 100 000), would at least need formal day provision of the kind outlined above, under rehabilitation and the CPA.

These calculations do not take into account the numbers of people attending psychiatric outpatient clinics, nor those who went unrecognised in the primary care services of the 1950s and consequently were not referred or treated. It would be wise to assume that the estimates are on the low side. However, even as they stand, the suggested numbers needing some form of day care are likely to be substantially higher than is actually available in many if not most districts. Proper data are lacking.

Tables 30 and 31 assume that all those with an SMI who need sheltered residential and/or supported daytime and leisure-time activities should at least be offered a range of alternatives. As far as possible, opportunities should be available for gradual rehabilitation through a sequence of stages, choosing from a wide range on offer, as they were in the best hospitals like Netherne, though not in the community aftercare

Table 31: Estimated numbers of patients needing residential and/or day care per 100 000 population.

Residential setting (number/100,000)		Formal day activities (number/100,000 and range)
Intensive and acute wards	40	(20 inpatient, but off-ward day activities not included in total)
Other formal residential	135	68 (34–102) day centre/workshop, etc.
'Own accommodation'		87 (44–132)
Total	175	155 (78–234)

The term 'formal' indicates that patients' care has been formally agreed and funded.

of those early days. Figure 1, together with the two estimates of numbers and costs (*see* Tables 30 and 31), is put forward as a conservative basis for quantifying the likely needs for care in the year 2000. The total residential need is assessed at 87–261 places/100 000 population, with 78–234 places/100 000 for day care. The uncertainties in this exercise provide a reminder of the urgent need to improve the national, regional and local data on which the future of the mental health and social services should be intelligently planned. Section 8 is highly relevant.

8 Audit, outcome, information and research

Monitoring progress towards a better mental health service

The paragraph that opens 'A National Service Framework for mental health' in Section 7 lists Government intentions to bring about radical changes in the mental health services. To judge progress, and thus anticipate problems before they become insolvable, a proper monitoring system should be put in place. This requires a system of new and demanding standards, the achievement of which could be regularly monitored. In particular, relevant information of a high standard should be routinely collected and made available to all relevant health and social agencies.

Options, guidelines and standards

Geddes and Wessely[197] suggest three levels of clinical policy statement.

- 'Options' are systematically derived, up-to-date statements, providing summaries of evidence on given topics.
- 'Guidelines' are similar, but are aimed at helping individual patients and clinicians to make decisions. They should be supported by evidence.
- 'Standards' need to be applied rigidly. The authors point to the CPA as an example of a standard that should have been a guideline, since the overall outcomes from case management are actually unclear (*see* Section 6). Another example is compulsory debriefing after trauma, now regarded as being unnecessary and perhaps even harmful.

A systematic review of the evidence is required at all three levels, but it is dangerous to call something a standard unless the outcomes are truly known. The distinctions are clear, but top-down adjudication on terminology (e.g. from CHI) is required.

Standards and the wider quality agenda

Lelliott[198] suggests five levels at which 'standards' (the term here covers guidelines as well) can usefully be applied. Each is contingent on the others:

- desired clinical practice, e.g. performance of a practitioner with a patient
- service delivery standards, e.g. assessment, care planning
- organisation of care, e.g. responsibilities and activities of managers
- intra-organisational, e.g. training and supervision, staff levels and skills mix
- population needs assessment, resource allocation and joint planning.

Implementing clinical standards

Claire Palmer[199] points out that getting standards used in routine clinical practice is even more complicated than creating them. The health service has not been very successful in these crucial areas, and helpful advice is provided.

The audit cycle provides an effective basis for clinical information systems

- Assessment of a person's needs.
- Formulation of actions required to meet those needs (e.g. staff, treatments, settings).
- Follow-up to review outcome and, if necessary, reassess needs for another cycle.
- Although every patient's profile is unique, a core of such information (a clinical data set) can be recorded that makes clinical comparisons possible.

The uses of a minimum data set (MDS)

A data set for general psychiatry has been tested and revised.[200] The MDS aggregates data required for existing statistical returns and for the new CPA information systems.

- The MDS does not make large demands on busy clinicians.
- It provides a profile of clinical symptoms and their severity (HoNOS) within a setting of clinical and administrative information that is already collected.
- Training, supervision and confidentiality are required to ensure reasonable comparability and security when HoNOS is used as part of an MDS.

When aggregated and anonymised across a specified clientele, supervised for quality and protected against misuse, such profiles can provide a basis not only for clinical needs, but also for sector, district and regional information systems.[201] Currently, trusts have a complex array of information systems, but a data set could be implemented nationally over a 4-year period.[202]

Outcome indicators

A working group convened by the DoH has undertaken a comprehensive review of outcome indicators for SMI and suggested 18 items to be implemented by periodic survey, with a further six items to be developed. Pilot trials are needed to establish feasibility and usefulness in practice.[203]

Care co-ordination research base

Care co-ordination (*see* Sections 5 and 6) when fully implemented, together with the minimum data set, could provide a useful profile of bottom-up information for comparison across as well as within districts. Rapid progress also needs to be made towards providing compatible information about local authority activities, since many patients use both medical and social care, whether simultaneously or at different times.

Standards for auditing hospital care

A method for auditing and comparing the hospital services provided in 11 districts has been tested in a pilot project, the design of which could be adapted for more extensive comparative studies of standards of care.[76,193]

- Create clinical and administrative standards relevant for the purpose.
- Compare against performance in the chosen facilities.
- Report results to each facility and agree any action needed.
- Repeat the procedure after an agreed period to continue the audit cycle.
- Compare across facilities to extract maximum value from the data.

The information gathered in the CSAG study addressed issues (such as organisational culture and staff morale) that are vital for efficiency but difficult to measure routinely.[204] It also demonstrated the need for tight collaboration between health and social systems. Such studies should be of interest to the CHI (*see* below).

Collecting, using and protecting routine information

A study of the coverage and accuracy of DoH central returns on the provision of mental health care in 1994 found wide discrepancies between the degree of completion in seven English districts compared with data specially gathered locally using defined criteria. About half the facilities were not recorded, with a range of accuracy from 30% to 78% across districts. The authors conclude that a new classification is needed using stricter definitions. The sparse official data available, and the need to use a large variety of other, sometimes incompatible sources, means that all interpretations and conclusions must be regarded as tentative. Collecting the information needed at these levels in order to provide a solid base for the care of people with the full range of mental disorders raises precisely the same problems. The Health Advisory Service-2000 has provided standards for adult mental health services (May 1999). The NHS Information Authority (April 1999) is intended to deliver lifelong electronic health records, 24-hour access, seamless care for patients and fast public access to information. A key issue raised by electronic patient records is the necessity for ensuring privacy.[48,205]

Communication between the bodies responsible for community care requires compatible information on services and needs in common-core data sets. Without such knowledge, clinical governance and evidence-based practice cannot be achieved. CHI has developed clinical governance using reviews of trusts, health authorities and PCGs, and more recently PCTs, e.g. reviewing implementation of the Mental Health Framework (*see* Section 7). The incorporation of social data will become essential.

A fair distribution of funds for mental health services

The York resource allocation formula is intended to provide an equitable distribution of funds for mental health services to each English health authority (now PCTs). The amount actually spent on services is decided by the commissioning agency. A comparison of expenditure and allocation amongst health authorities showed wide variability, with relative underspending in deprived areas other than the four inner-London boroughs. PCTs (particularly in deprived areas outside London) should be informed of the implications of any formulae so that shortfalls in expenditure relative to allocation are avoided.

The National Institute for Clinical Excellence (NICE)

A central aim of NICE is to identify new treatments likely to impact on the NHS, consider their clinical and cost-effectiveness, and accept or reject them. More generally, it is to appraise evidence on health technologies, co-ordinate or take over guideline development, promote clinical audit and undertake confidential enquiries, thus covering many of the tasks outlined above. There will be no lack of work. Two of the first NICE enquiries were concerned with mental health treatments. An early objective for NICE was to apply high and comparable standards of inspection to drug trials, including sampling, design and methodology, standardised disclosure of side-effects and drop-outs, and evidence for claims of improvement over other drugs. This concern with stringent methodology is fully compatible with the concern expressed by Ellis and Adams[206] about the 'cult of the double-blind placebo-controlled trial', which is not the be-all and end-all of methodology. The extra costs of the 'atypical medications' that have proved useful so far could almost account for the £700 million over 3 years announced in *Modernising Mental Health Services*. The old question 'Who pays for community care?' still needs to be answered.[207]

Appendix I: List of *ICD-10* categories, F2–F6

[F0: Dementia, including symptomatic mental disorders]
[F1: Mental and behavioural disorders due to psychoactive substance abuse]

F2: Schizophrenia, schizotypal and delusional disorders

F20.0	Paranoid schizophrenia
F20.1	Hebephrenic schizophrenia
F20.2	Catatonic schizophrenia
F20.3	Undifferentiated schizophrenia
F20.4	Post-schizophrenic depression
F20.5	Residual schizophrenia
F20.6	Simple schizophrenia
F21	Schizotypal disorder
F22.0	Delusional disorder
F23.0	Acute polymorphic psychotic disorder
F23.1	With symptoms of schizophrenia
F23.2	Acute schizophrenia-like psychotic disorder
F23.3	Other acute delusional psychotic disorder
F24	Induced delusional disorder
F25.0	Schizoaffective disorder, manic type
F25.1	Schizoaffective disorder, depressive type
F25.2	Schizoaffective disorder, mixed type

F3: Mood (affective) disorders

F30.0	Hypomania
F30.1	Mania without psychotic symptoms
F30.2	Mania with psychotic symptoms
F31.0	Current episode, hypomanic
F31.1	Manic without psychotic symptoms
F31.2	Manic with psychotic symptoms
F31.3	Moderate or mild depression
F31.4	Severe depression without psychotic symptoms
F31.5	Severe depression with psychotic symptoms
F31.6	Current episode, mixed
F31.7	Currently in remission
F32.0	Depressive episode, mild severity
F32.1	Moderate severity
F32.2	Severe depressive episode without psychotic symptoms
F32.3	With psychotic symptoms
F33.0	Recurrent depressive disorder, current episode mild severity
F33.1	Moderate severity
F33.2	Severe without psychotic symptoms
F33.3	With psychotic symptoms
F33.4	Currently in remission
F34.0	Cyclothymia
F34.1	Dysthymia
F38.0	Other single affective disorders
F38.1	Other recurrent affective disorders

F4: Neurotic, stress-related and somatoform disorders

F40.0	Agoraphobia
F40.1	Social phobias
F40.2	Specific (isolated) phobias
F41.0	Panic disorder (episodic paroxysmal anxiety)
F41.1	Generalised anxiety disorder
F42	Obsessive–compulsive disorder
F43.0	Acute stress reaction
F43.1	Post-traumatic stress disorder
F43.2	Adjustment disorders
F44.0	Dissociative amnesia
F44.1	Dissociative fugue
F44.2	Dissociative stupor
F44.3	Trance and possession disorders
F44.4	Dissociative motor disorders
F44.5	Dissociative convulsions
F44.6	Dissociative anaesthesia and sensory loss
F44.7	Mixed dissociative (conversion) disorders
F44.8	Other dissociative (conversion) disorders
F45.0	Somatisation disorder
F45.1	Undifferentiated somatoform disorder
F45.2	Hypochondriachal disorder
F45.3	Somatoform autonomic dysfunction
F45.4	Persistent somatoform pain disorder
F48.0	Neurasthenia (fatigue syndrome)
F48.1	Depersonalisation–derealisation syndrome

F5: Behavioural syndromes associated with physiological disturbances and physical factors

F50	Eating disorders
F51	Non-organic sleep disorders
F52	Sexual dysfunction
F53	Mental and behavioural disorders associated with the puerperium
F54	Psychological disorders associated with disorders classified elsewhere
F55	Abuse of non-dependence-producing substances

F6: Disorders of adult personality and behaviour

F60.0	Paranoid personality disorder
F60.1	Schizoid personality disorder
F60.2	Dissocial personality disorder
F60.3	Emotionally unstable personality disorder
F60.4	Histrionic personality disorder
F60.5	Anankastic personality disorder
F60.6	Anxious (avoidant) personality disorder
F60.7	Dependent personality disorder
[F7:	Mental retardation]
[F8:	Disorders of psychological development]
[F9:	Behavioural and emotional disorders with onset in childhood and adolescence]

Appendix II: Mental Illness Needs Index (MINI): one-year predicted period prevalence per 100 000 population

This index is intended to meet three requirements:

- grounded conceptually on evidence that the factors used are associated with mental illness
- empirically quantified
- based on statistical indicators available for the relevant geographical areas.

The MINI was commissioned by the DoH as part of the Mental Illness Research and Development Programme. The empirical work was undertaken in the former North East Thames Region, concentrating chiefly on a set of 558 electoral wards. There was a sharp gradient of bed use and admission prevalence, the highest values being in the inner city.

The predictor variables used were as follows:

- permanently sick
- unemployed
- moved in last year
- Black Caribbean
- Indian subcontinent
- proportion single, widowed or divorced
- proportion living in hostels or common lodging houses
- proportion living in a house with no access to a car.

The numbers were calibrated from 1991 data using ONS clusters. They are likely to be a little higher now but there is no reason to suppose that they will have changed relative to each other. Details of the analyses are given by Glover and colleagues (1998), who also provide caveats as to the strengths and weaknesses of the model. 'The MINI seems to predict the substantial variation in mental health care as well as the York index and seems to perform better than Jarman's UPA. . . . A computer program calculating the index for any sector definable in terms of electoral wards in England and Wales and relating this to published ranges of required service provision is available from the authors.'

Reference

Glover GR, Robin E, Emami J, Arabscheibani GR. A needs index for mental health care. *Soc Psychiatry Psychiatr Epidemiol* 1998; **33**: 89–96.

Health authority	MINI predicted prevalence	ONS cluster*
Northern and Yorkshire		
Bradford	292.0	4 Urban
Calderdale and Kirklees	264.3	4 Urban
County Durham	304.0	5 Mining and industrial
East Riding	270.8	4 Urban
Gateshead and South Tyneside	347.3	5 Mining and industrial
Leeds	293.8	4 Urban
Newcastle and North Tyneside	343.6	5 Mining and industrial
North Cumbria	243.1	1 Rural
North Yorkshire	220.1	1 Rural
Northumberland	249.6	4 Urban

Reference (continued)

Health authority	MINI predicted prevalence	ONS cluster*
Sunderland	357.4	5 Mining and industrial
Tees	316.9	5 Mining and industrial
Wakefield	274.5	5 Mining and industrial
Trent		
Barnsley	311.3	5 Mining and industrial
Doncaster	299.4	5 Mining and industrial
Leicestershire	213.7	1 Rural
Lincolnshire	210.0	1 Rural
North Derbyshire	231.2	1 Rural
North Nottinghamshire	244.1	1 Rural
Nottingham	270.8	4 Urban
Rotherham	274.5	5 Mining and industrial
Sheffield	306.7	5 Mining and industrial
South Derbyshire	227.5	1 Rural
South Humberside	244.1	5 Mining and industrial
Anglia and Oxford		
Bedfordshire	201.7	2 Prospering
Berkshire	184.2	2 Prospering
Buckinghamshire	163.0	2 Prospering
Cambridge and Huntingdon	177.7	2 Prospering
East Norfolk	209.1	3 Maturing
North West Anglia	203.5	1 Rural
Northamptonshire	200.8	1 Rural
Oxfordshire	191.5	2 Prospering
Suffolk	187.9	1 Rural
North Thames		
Barking and Havering	231.2	4 Urban
Barnet	254.2	3 Maturing
Brent and Harrow	298.4	3 Maturing
Camden and Islington	455.1	6 Inner London
Ealing, Hammersmith and Hounslow	333.5	3 Maturing
East and North Hertfordshire	175.0	2 Prospering
East London and the City	419.2	6 Inner London
Enfield and Haringay	324.2	2 Prospering
Hillingdon	201.7	2 Prospering
Kensington, Chelsea and Westminster	437.6	6 Inner London
North Essex	184.2	2 Prospering
Redbridge and Waltham Forest	285.5	3 Maturing
South Essex	207.2	4 Urban
West Hertfordshire	182.3	2 Prospering
South Thames		
Bexley and Greenwich	256.1	3 Maturing
Bromley	209.1	2 Prospering
Croydon	257.0	3 Maturing
East Kent	249.6	3 Maturing
East Surrey	170.4	2 Prospering
East Sussex, Brighton and Hove	270.8	3 Maturing

Kingston and Richmond	238.5	2	Prospering
Lambeth, Southwark and Lewisham	408.1	6	Inner London
Merton, Sutton and Wandsworth	304.9	3	Maturing
West Kent	193.4	2	Prospering
West Surrey	164.8	2	Prospering
West Sussex	195.2	2	Prospering
South and West			
Avon	234.9	2	Prospering
Cornwall and Isles of Scilly	222.9	1	Rural
Dorset	215.5	3	Maturing
Gloucestershire	198.9	2	Prospering
Isle of Wight	244.1	3	Maturing
North and East Devon	218.3	1	Rural
North and Mid Hampshire	160.2	2	Prospering
Portsmouth and South East Hampshire	233.9	4	Urban
Somerset	190.6	1	Rural
South and West Devon	254.2	3	Maturing
Southampton and South West Hampshire	219.2	4	Urban
Wiltshire	182.3	2	Prospering
West Midlands			
Birmingham	322.4	4	Urban
Coventry	289.2	4	Urban
Dudley	218.3	1	Rural
Herefordshire	202.6	1	Rural
North Staffordshire	265.3	5	Mining and industrial
Sandwell	290.1	4	Urban
Shropshire	206.3	1	Rural
Solihull	185.1	2	Prospering
South Staffordshire	189.7	1	Rural
Walsall	265.3	4	Urban
Warwickshire	201.7	1	Rural
Wolverhampton	294.8	4	Urban
Worcestershire	192.5	1	Rural
North and West			
Bury and Rochdale	279.1	4	Urban
East Lancashire	287.4	4	Urban
Liverpool	422.8	5	Mining and industrial
Manchester	425.6	5	Mining and industrial
Morecambe Bay	264.3	3	Maturing
North Cheshire	263.4	5	Mining and industrial
North West Lancashire	306.7	3	Maturing
Salford and Trafford	308.6	4	Urban
Sefton	313.2	3	Maturing
South Cheshire	210.0	1	Rural
South Lancashire	212.7	1	Rural
St Helen's and Knowsley	335.3	5	Mining and industrial
Stockport	223.8	2	Prospering
West Pennine	288.3	4	Urban
Wigan and Bolton	289.2	5	Mining and industrial
Wirral	300.3	3	Maturing

* Column 3 refers to the ONS area classification.

Government and other official documents

Department of Health. *Caring for People: the Care Programme Approach for people with a mental illness referred to the specialist psychiatric services.* London: HC(90)23/LASSL(90)11. London: Department of Health, 1990.

Department of Health. *Care Management and Assessment: practice guidance: managers' guide.* London: Department of Health, 1992

Department of Health. *Mental Illness. Health of the Nation key area handbook.* London: Department of Health, 1993.

Department of Health. *Introduction of Supervision Registers for Mentally Ill People.* HSG(94)5. London: Department of Health, 1994.

Department of Health. *Building Bridges. Interagency working for the care and protection of severely mentally ill people.* London: HMSO, 1995.

Department of Health. *A First Class Service: quality in the new NHS.* London: Department of Health, 1998.

Department of Health. *A National Service Framework for Mental Health.* HSC99/223:LAC 99/34. London: Department of Health, 1999.

Department of Health. *Clinical Governance. Quality in the new NHS.* HSC 1999/065. London: Department of Health, 1999.

Department of Health. *Drug Misuse and Dependence: guidelines on clinical management.* London: The Stationery Office, 1999.

Department of Health. *Health Outcomes. Report of a working group.* London: Department of Health, 1999.

Department of Health, Home Office. *Managing Dangerous People with Severe Personality Disorder.* London: Home Office.

Department of Health and Social Services Inspectorate. *Care Management and Assessment: summary of practice guidance.* London: HMSO, 1991.

Health Advisory Service. *Standards for Adult Mental Health Services.* London: Health Advisory Service, 2000.

House of Commons Committee of Public Accounts. *Health of the Nation: a progress report.* London: The Stationery Office, 1998.

HM Government. *Caring about Carers: a national strategy for carers.* London: The Stationery Office, 1999.

Modernising Mental Health Services. HSC(99)38:LAC(99)8.

National Health Service Executive. *Burden of Disease.* Leeds: NHSE, 1996.

National Health Service Executive. *The New NHS: a national framework for assessing performance.* Leeds: NHSE, 1998.

Social Exclusion Unit. *Rough Sleeping.* London: The Stationery Office, 1998.

Social Services Inspectorate. *A Matter of Chance for Carers. Inspection of local authority support for carers.* London: Department of Health, 1998.

Social Services Inspectorate. *Still Building Bridges: report of a national inspection of arrangements for the integration of the Care Programme Approach with Care Management.* London, Department of Health, 1999.

References

1 Gilbody S. Potential and problems for psychiatry in the new NHS. *Psychiatr Bull* 1999; **23**: 513–16.

2 Lelliott P. Money to modernise adult mental health services is insufficient. *BMJ* 1999; **319**: 992.

3 World Health Organization. *International Classification of Diseases, Tenth Revision (ICD-10)*. Geneva: World Health Organization, 1992.

4 National Institute of Mental Health. *Towards a Model for a Comprehensive Community-Based Mental Health System*. Bethesda: National Institute of Mental Health, 1992.

5 Shinnar A, Rothbard A, Kanter R *et al.* An empirical literature review of definitions of severe and persistent mental illness. *Am J Psychiatry* 1990; **147**: 1602–8.

6 Tyrer P. Comorbidity or consanguinity. *Br J Psychiatry* 1996; **168**: 669–71.

7 World Health Organization. *Glossary of Mental Disorders and Guide to Their Publication (ICD-9)*. Geneva: World Health Organization, 1974.

8 Wing J, Cooper J, Sartorius N. *Description and Classification of Psychiatric Symptoms*. Cambridge: Cambridge University Press, 1974.

9 World Health Organization. *Classification of Mental and Behavioural Disorders. Clinical descriptions and diagnostic guidelines*. Geneva: World Health Organization, 1992.

10 World Health Organization. *Classification of Mental and Behavioural Disorders. Diagnostic criteria for research*. Geneva: World Health Organization, 1993.

11 Loranger A, Sartorius N, Andrioli A. The International Personality Disorder Examination. *Arch Gen Psychiatry* 1994; **51**: 215–24.

12 American Psychiatric Association. *Diagnostic and Statistical Manual*, 4th edn (*DSM-IV*). Washington, DC: American Psychiatric Association, 1994.

13 Wing J, Sartorius N, Ustun T. *Diagnosis and Clinical Measurement in Psychiatry. A reference manual for SCAN*. Cambridge: Cambridge University Press, 1998.

14 Wing J, Brugha T. The schedules for clinical assessment in neuropsychiatry and the tradition of the PSE. In: Thornicroft G (ed.). *Mental Health Outcome Measures*. London: Gaskell, 2000.

15 Robins L, Wing J, Wittchen H *et al.* The composite international diagnostic interview. *Arch Gen Psychiatry* 1988; **45**: 1069–77.

16 Jenkins R, Beddington P, Brugha T *et al.* The national psychiatric morbidity surveys of Great Britain. Strategy and methods. *Psychol Med* 1997; **27**: 765–74.

17 Jenkins R, Lewis G, Bebbington P *et al.* The national psychiatric morbidity surveys of Great Britain. Initial findings from the household survey. *Psychol Med* 1997; **27**: 775–90.

18 Bebbington P, Marsden L, Brewin C. The need for psychiatric treatment in the general population. The Camberwell needs for service survey. *Psychol Med* 1997; **27**: 821–34.

19 Kessing L, Anderson P, Mortensen P *et al.* Recurrence in affective disorder. I. Case register study. *Br J Psychiatry* 1998; **172**: 23–8.

20 Dinan T. The physical consequences of depressive illness. *BMJ* 1999; **318**: 826.

21 Curtis G, Magee W, Eaton W *et al.* Specific fears and phobias. Epidemiology and classification. *Br J Psychiatry* 1998; **173**: 212–17.

22 Kessler R, McGonagle K, Zhao S *et al.* Lifetime and 12-month prevalence of *DSM-III-R* psychiatric disorders in the United States. Results from the national comorbidity survey. *Arch Gen Psychiatry* 1994; **51**: 8–19.

23 Furmark T, Tillfors M, Everz I *et al.* Social phobia in the general population. *Soc Psychiatry Psychiatr Epidemiol* 1999; **34**: 416–24.

24 Emmanuel J, Simmonds S, Tyrer P. Systematic review of the outcome of anxiety and depressive disorders. *Br J Psychiatry* 1998; **173**: 35–41.

25 Bebbington P. Epidemiology of obsessive-compulsive disorder. *Br J Psychiatry* 1998; **173**: 2–6.

26 Reid S, Chalder T, Cleare A. Chronic fatigue syndrome. *BMJ* 2000; **320**: 292–6.

27 Kessler R, Sonnega A, Bromet E *et al.* Post-traumatic stress disorder in the national comorbidity survey. *Arch Gen Psychiatry* 1995; **52**: 1048–60.

28 Breslau N, Chilcoat H, Kessler R *et al.* Vulnerability to assaultive violence. *Psychol Med* 1999; **29**: 813–23.

29 Hoek W. Review of the epidemiological studies of eating disorders. *Int Rev Psychiatry* 1993; **5**: 61–74.

30 Turnbull S, Ward A, Treasure J *et al.* The demand for eating disorder care. *Br J Psychiatry* 1996; **169**: 702–5.

31 Wade T, Martin M, Neale M *et al.* The structural and environmental factors for three measures of disordered eating. *Psychol Med* 1999; **29**: 925–34.

32 Moran P. The epidemiology of antisocial personality disorder. *Soc Psychiatry Psychiatr Epidemiol* 1999; **34**: 231–42.

33 Coid J. Aetiological risk factors for personality disorders. *Br J Psychiatry* 1999; **174**: 532–8.

34 Geddes J. Prenatal and perinatal risk factors for early onset of schizophrenia, affective psychosis and reactive psychosis. *BMJ* 1999; **318**: 426.

35 Hultman C, Sparen P, Takei N *et al.* Prenatal and perinatal risk factors for schizophrenia, affective psychosis and reactive psychosis of early onset. *BMJ* 1999; **318**: 421–6.

36 Odegard O. Emigration and insanity. A study of mental disease among the Norwegian-born population in Minnesota. *Acta Psychiatr Neurol Scand* 1932; **Suppl. 4**.

37 Jablensky A, Sartorius N, Ernberg G *et al.* Schizophrenia: manifestations, incidence and course in different cultures. *Psychol Med* 1992; **20** (Suppl.): 1–97.

38 Geddes J, Black R, Whalley L *et al.* Persistence of the decline in the diagnosis of schizophrenia among first admissions to Scottish mental hospitals from 1969 to 1988. *Br J Psychiatry* 1993; **163**: 620–6.

39 Procopio M, Marriott P. Is the decline in diagnoses of schizophrenia caused by the disappearance of a seasonal aetiological agent? An epidemiological study in England and Wales. *Psychol Med* 1998; **28**: 367–73.

40 Johnson S, Ramsay R, Thornicroft G. *London's Mental Health. The report to the King's Fund London Commission.* London: King's Fund Publishing, 1997.

41 Commander M, Dharan S, Odell S *et al.* Access to mental health care in an inner-city district. *Br J Psychiatry* 1997; **170**: 312, 317.

42 Cheung P, Pali A, Hungin S *et al.* Are the Health of the Nation targets attainable? Postal survey of general practitioners' views. *BMJ* 1997; **314**: 55–61.

43 Appleby L, Shaw J, Amos T *et al. Safer Services. Report of the national confidential inquiry into suicide and homicide by people with a mental illness.* London: Department of Health, 1999.

44 Durkheim E. *Suicide. A study in sociology.* London: Routledge, 1970.

45 Lukes S. *Emile Durkheim. His life and work.* London: Allen Lane, 1973.

46 Harris E, Barraclough B. Excess mortality of mental disorder. *Br J Psychiatry* 1998; **173**: 11–53.

47 Baxter D, Appleby L. Case register study of suicide risk in mental disorders. *Br J Psychiatry* 1999; **175**: 322–6.

48 Denley I, Smith S. Privacy in clinical information systems in secondary care. *BMJ* 1999; **318**: 1328–30.

49 Appleby L, Shaw J, Amos T *et al.* Suicide within 12 months of contact with mental health services. *BMJ* 1999; **318**: 1235–43.

50 Powell J, Geddes J, Deeks M *et al.* Suicide in psychiatric hospital in-patients. Risk factors and their predictive power. *Br J Psychiatry* 2000; **176**: 266–72.

51 Kennedy H, Iveson R, Hill H. Violence, homicide and suicide: strong correlation and wide variation across districts. *Br J Psychiatry* 1999; **175**: 462–6.

52 Taylor J, Gunn J. Homicides by people with mental illness: myth and reality. *Br J Psychiatry* 1999; **174**: 9–14.

53 Munro E, Rumgay J. Role of risk assessment in reducing homicides by people with mental illness. *Br J Psychiatry* 2000; **176**: 116–20.

54 Glover G, Leese M, McCrone P. More severe mental illness is more concentrated in deprived areas. *Br J Psychiatry* 1999; **175**: 544–8.

55 Glover G. How much English health authorities are allocated for mental health care. *Br J Psychiatry* 1999; **175**: 402–6.

56 Majeed A, Malcolm L. Unified budgets for primary care groups. *BMJ* 1999; **318**: 772–6.

57 Kendrick T, Sibbald B, Addington-Hall J *et al.* Distribution of mental health professionals working on site within English and Welsh general practices. *BMJ* 1993; **307**: 544–6.

58 Thomas R, Corney R. The role of the practice nurse in mental health: a survey. *J Ment Health* 1993; **2**: 65–72.

59 Department of Health. *Caring For People: the Care Programme Approach for people with a mental illness referred to the specialist psychiatric services.* London: HMSO, 1990.

60 Department of Health. *Building Bridges. Inter-agency working for the care and protection of severely mentally ill people.* London: HMSO, 1995.

61 Department of Health and Social Security Inspectorate. *Care Management Assessment.* London: Department of Health and Social Security Inspectorate, 1991.

62 Schneider J, Carpenter J, Brandon T *et al.* Operation and organisation of services for people with SMI in the UK. A survey of the Care Programme Approach. *Br J Psychiatry* 1999; **175**: 422–5.

63 Lucas B, Doyle H. Thirty years of in-patient consultation-liaison psychiatry at Guy's. *Psychiatr Bull* 1995; **19**: 631–4.

64 Prothero D, House A. In-patient liaison psychiatry. *Psychiatr Bull* 1999; **23**: 525–7.

65 Audini B, Duffet R, Lelliott A *et al.* Over-occupancy in London's acute psychiatric units – fact or fiction? *Psychiatr Bull* 1999; **23**: 590–3.

66 Sainsbury Centre. *Acute Problems. A survey of the quality of care in acute wards.* London: Sainsbury Centre, 1998.

67 Williams R, Cohen J. Substance use and misuse in psychiatric wards. *Psychiatr Bull* 2000; **24**: 43–6.

68 Greengross P, Hollander D, Stanton R. Pressure on adult acute psychiatric beds. *Psychiatr Bull* 2000; **24**: 43–6.

69 Lelliott P, Wing J, Clifford P. A national audit of new long-stay psychiatric patients. 1. Method and description of the cohort. *Br J Psychiatry* 1994; **165**: 160–9.

70 Lelliott P, Wing J. A national audit of new long-stay psychiatric patients. 2. Impact on services. *Br J Psychiatry* 1994; **165**: 170–8.

71 Wing J. How many psychiatric beds? *Psychol Med* 1971; **1**: 188–90.

72 Macpherson R, Butler J. Effect of treatment in an active rehabilitation hostel on the need for hospital treatment. *Psychiatr Bull* 1999; **23**: 594–7.

73 Hallam A. Identifying the problems of financing long-term residential care. *Ment Health Res Rev* 1998; **5**: 17–22.

74 Beecham J, Schneider J, Knapp M. *Survey of Day Activity Settings for People with Mental Health Problems.* Canterbury: Personal Social Sciences Research Unit, 1998.

75 Department of Health. *National Service Framework for Mental Health.* London: The Stationery Office, 1999.

76 Clinical Standards Advisory Group. *Schizophrenia* (1). London: HMSO, 1995.

77 Warner L, Ford R, Bagnall S, Morgan S. *Down Your Street*. London: The Sainsbury Centre, 1998.

78 Lawson M, Strickland C, Wolfson P. The Care Programme Approach from the users' perspective. *Psychiatr Bull* 1999; **23**: 539–41.

79 Brown S, Birtwistle J. People with schizophrenia and their families. *Br J Psychiatry* 1998; **173**: 139–44.

80 Creer C, Wing J. *Schizophrenia at Home. The impact of schizophrenia on family life and how relatives cope*. London: National Schizophrenia Fellowship, 1988.

81 Creer C, Sturt E, Wykes T. The role of relatives. In: Wing J (ed.). *Long-Term Community Care. Experience in a London borough*. Cambridge: Cambridge University Press, 1982.

82 MacCarthy B, Lesage A, Brewin C *et al*. Needs for care among the relatives of long-term users of day care. *Psychol Med* 1988; **19**: 725–32.

83 MacCarthy B, Kuipers L, Hurry J *et al*. Counselling the relatives of the long-term mentally ill. *Br J Psychiatry* 1989; **154**: 768–75.

84 Merinder L, Viuff A, Laugesen H *et al*. Parent and relative education in community psychiatry. A randomised trial regarding its effectiveness. *Soc Psychiatry Psychiatr Epidemiol* 1999; **34**: 287–94.

85 Malcom K, Rowlands P, Inch H. Assessment of respite needs for carers of persons with severe mental illness. *Psychiatr Bull* 1998; **22**: 354–5.

86 Brown G, Birley J, Wing J. Influence of family life on the course of schizophrenic disorders: a replication. *Br J Psychiatry* 1972; **121**: 241–58.

87 Mari J, Streiner T. An overview of family interventions and relapse in schizophrenia. Meta-analysis of research findings. *Psychol Med* 1994; **21**: 423–42.

88 Pharoah FM, Mari JJ, Streiner D. Family intervention for schizophrenia (Cochrane Review). In: *The Cochrane Library*. Oxford: Update Software, 1999.

89 Scazufca M, Kuipers E. Links between expressed emotion and burden of care in relatives of patients with schizophrenia. *Br J Psychiatry* 1996; **168**: 580–7.

90 Tattan T, Tarrier N. The expressed emotion of case managers of the seriously mentally ill. *Psychol Med* 2000; **30**: 195–204.

91 Perlick D, Clarkin J, Sirey J *et al*. Burden experienced by care-givers of persons with bipolar affective disorder. *Br J Psychiatry* 1999; **175**: 56–62.

92 James D, Fineberg N, Shah A *et al*. An increase in violence on an acute psychiatric ward. A study of associated factors. *Br J Psychiatry* 1990; **156**: 846–52.

93 Prosser D, Johnson S, Kuipers E *et al*. Mental health 'burnout' and job satisfaction among hospital and community-based mental health staff. *Br J Psychiatry* 1996; **169**: 334–7.

94 Prosser D, Johnson S, Kuipers E *et al*. Mental health, burnout and job satisfaction in a longitudinal study of mental health staff. *Soc Psychiatry Psychiatr Epidemiol* 1999; **34**: 295–315.

95 Wing J, Rix S, Curtis R *et al*. Protocol for assessing services for people with severe mental illness. *Br J Psychiatry* 1998; **172**: 121–9.

96 Kendell R, Pearce A. Consultant psychiatrists who retire prematurely in 1995 and 1996. *Psychiatr Bull* 1997; **21**: 741–5.

97 Jenkins R, Scott J. Medical staffing crisis in psychiatry. *Psychiatr Bull* 1998; **22**: 239–41.

98 Reid Y, Johnson S, Morant N *et al*. Explanations for stress and satisfaction in mental health professionals. *Soc Psychiatry Psychiatr Epidemiol* 1999; **34**: 301–8.

99 Reid S, Johnson S, Morant N *et al*. Improving support for mental health staff. *Soc Psychiatry Psychiatr Epidemiol* 1999; **34**: 309–15.

100 Murray A, Shepherd G, Onyett S *et al*. *The Role of Support Workers in Community Mental Health Services*. London: Sainsbury Centre for Mental Health, 1997.

101 Chisholm D, Lowin A, Knapp M. Mental health services in London: costs. In: Johnson S *et al*. (eds). *London's Mental Health*. London: King's Fund, 1997.

102 Lelliott P, Audini B, Knapp M *et al.* The mental health residential care study. Classification of facilities and description of residents. *Br J Psychiatry* 1996; **169**: 139–47.

103 Chisholm D, Knapp M, Astin J *et al.* The mental health residential care study. III. The costs of provision. *Br J Psychiatry* 1997; **170**: 37–42.

104 Knapp M, Chisholm D, Astin J *et al.* The cost consequences of changing the hospital–community balance: the mental residential care study. *Psychol Med* 1997; **27**: 681–92.

105 Audini B, Lelliott P. *An Analysis of the Use of Part II of the Mental Health Act and of Section 136.* London: Royal College of Psychiatrists Research Unit, 2000.

106 Lelliott P, Audini B, Duffett R. Survey of patients from an inner-London health authority in medium-secure psychiatric care. *Br J Psychiatry* 2001; **178**: 62–6.

107 Buchanan A, Gunn J. What psychiatrists think about Part III of the Mental Health Act 1983. *Psychiatr Bull* 1999; **23**: 721–5.

108 Mullen P. Dangerous people with severe personality disorder. *BMJ* 1999; **319**: 1146–7.

109 Maden T. Treating offenders with personality disorder. *Psychiatr Bull* 1999; **23**: 707–10.

110 Patel A, Knapp M. Costs of mental illness in England. *Ment Health Res Rev* 1998; **5**: 4–10.

111 McCreadie RG, Kelly C. Patients with schizophrenia who smoke. *Br J Psychiatry* 2000; **176**: 109.

112 Friedli K, King M. Psychological treatments and their evaluation. *Int Rev Psychiatry* 1998; **10**: 123–6.

113 Mutale T. Employment of counsellors and mental health professionals by fundholding general practices. *Psychiatr Bull* 1995; **19**: 627–30.

114 Cape J, Parham A. Relationship between practice counselling and referral to out-patient psychiatry and clinical psychology. *Br J Gen Pract* 1998; **48**: 1477–80.

115 Catalan J, Gath D, Edmonds G *et al.* The effects of non-prescribing of anxiolytics in general practice. *Br J Psychiatry* 1984; **144**: 693–702.

116 Friedli K, King M, Lloyd M *et al.* Randomised controlled assessment of non-directive psychotherapy versus routine general practitioner care. *Lancet* 1997; **350**: 1662–5.

117 Kendrick T. Why can't GPs follow guidelines on depression? *BMJ* 2000; **320**: 200–1.

118 Fakhoury W. Suicide: a call sheet audit. Data from SANELINE. *Psychiatr Bull* 2000; **24**: 98–100.

119 Lawrie S. Newspaper coverage of psychiatric and physical illness. *Psychiatr Bull* 2000; **24**: 102–8.

120 Bindman T, Beck A, Glover G *et al.* Evaluating mental health policy in England. Care Programme Approach and Supervision Registers. *Br J Psychiatry* 1999; **175**: 327–30.

121 Burns T, Beadsmoore A, Bhat A *et al.* A controlled trial of home-based acute psychiatric services. I. Clinical and social outcome. *Br J Psychiatry* 1993; **163**: 55–61.

122 Burns T, Creed F, Fahy F *et al.* Intensive versus standard case management for severe psychotic illness. *Lancet* 1999; **353**: 2185–9.

123 Creed F, Mbaya P, Lancashire S *et al.* Cost-effectiveness of day and in-patient treatment: results of an RCT. *BMJ* 1997; **314**: 1381–5.

124 Drury V, Birchwood M, Cochrane R *et al.* Cognitive therapy and recovery from acute psychosis: a controlled trial. II. Impact on recovery time. *Br J Psychiatry* 1996; **169**: 602–7.

125 Holloway F, Carson J. Intensive case management for the severely mentally ill. Controlled trial. *Br J Psychiatry* 1998; **172**: 19–22.

126 Kuipers E, Fowler D, Garety P *et al.* London–East Anglia randomised controlled trial of cognitive-behavioural therapy for psychosis. III. Follow-up and economic evaluation at 18 months. *Br J Psychiatry* 1998; **173**: 61–8.

127 Simpson C, Seager C, Robertson J. Home-based care and standard hospital care for patients with severe mental illness: a randomised control trial. *Br J Psychiatry* 1993; **162**: 239–43.

128 Marshall M, Gray A, Lockwood A *et al.* Case management for people with severe mental disorders (Cochrane Review). In: *The Cochrane Library.* Oxford: Update Software, 1998.

129 Merson S, Tyrer D, Carlen D *et al.* The cost of treatment of psychiatric emergencies: a comparison of hospital and community services. *Psychol Med* 1999; **26**: 727–34.

130 Tyrer P, Coid J, Simmonds S *et al.* CMHT management for those with severe mental illnesses and disordered personality increases satisfaction with care (Cochrane Review). In: *The Cochrane Library.* Oxford: Update Software, 1998.

131 Marshall M, Lockwood A. Assertive community treatment for people with severe mental disorders (Cochrane Review). In: *The Cochrane Library.* Oxford: Update Software, 1998.

132 Drake R, McHugo G, Bebout R *et al.* A randomised clinical trial of supported employment for inner-city patients with severe mental disorders. *Arch Gen Psychiatry* 1999; **56**: 627–33.

133 Thornicroft G, Wykes T, Holloway F *et al.* From efficacy to effectiveness in community mental health services. *Br J Psychiatry* 1998; **173**: 423–7.

134 Royal College of Psychiatrists. *Management of Imminent Violence. Clinical practice guidelines to support mental health services.* London: Royal College of Psychiatrists, 1998.

135 Centre for Reviews and Dissemination. Drug treatments for schizophrenia. *Effect Health Care* 1999; **5**: 1–12.

136 National Schizophrenia Guideline Group. *The Management of Schizophrenia. Part 1. Pharmacological treatments.* London: Royal College of Psychiatrists Research Group, 2000.

137 Glennie J. *Pharmacoeconomic Evaluations of Cozapine in Treatment-Resistant Schizophrenia and Risperidone in Chronic Schizophrenia.* Ottawa: Canadian Co-ordinating Office for Health Technology Assessment, 1997.

138 Mojtabai R, Nicholson R, Carpenter B. Role of psychosocial treatments in the management of schizophrenia: a meta-analytic review of controlled outcome studies. *Schizophr Bull* 1998; **24**: 569–87.

139 Tarrier N, Yusapoff L, Kinney C *et al.* Randomised controlled trial of intensive cognitive behaviour therapy for patients with chronic schizophrenia. *BMJ* 1998; **317**: 303–7.

140 Jones C, Cormac I, Mota J *et al.* Cognitive behaviour therapy for schizophrenia (Cochrane Review). In: *The Cochrane Library.* Oxford: Update Software, 1998.

141 Moncrieff J. Lithium: evidence reconsidered. *Br J Psychiatry* 1997; **171**: 113–19.

142 Cookson J. Lithium: balancing risks and benefits. *Br J Psychiatry* 1997; **171**: 120–4.

143 Anon. Toxicity of lithium. *Drug Ther Bull* 1999; **37**: 22–4.

144 Johnston A, Eagles J. Lithium-associated clinical hypothyroidism. Prevalence and risk factors. *Br J Psychiatry* 1999; **175**: 336–9.

145 Peet M, Harvey N. Lithium maintenance. *Br J Psychiatry* 1991; **158**: 191–7.

146 Harvey N, Peet M. Lithium maintenance. *Br J Psychiatry* 1991; **158**: 198–200.

147 Duffett R, Lelliott P. Auditing electroconvulsive therapy. *Br J Psychiatry* 1998; **172**: 401–5.

148 Duffet R, Siegert D, Lelliott P. Electroconvulsive therapy in Wales. *Psychiatr Bull* 1999; **23**: 597–601.

149 Government Statistical Service. *Electroconvulsive Therapy: survey covering the period from January 1999 to March 1999, England.* London: Department of Health, 1999.

150 Trindade E, Menon D. *SSRIs for Major Depression. Part 1. Evaluation of the clinical literature.* Ottawa: Canadian Co-ordinating Office for Health Technology Assessment, 1997.

151 Hotopf M, Hardy R, Lewis G. Discontinuation rates of SSRI and tricyclic antidepressants: a meta-analysis and investigation of heterogeneity. *Br J Psychiatry* 1997; **170**: 120–7.

152 Cornelius J, Salloum I, Ehler J. Fluoxetine reduced depressive symptoms and alcohol consumption in patients with comorbid depression and alcohol dependence. *Arch Gen Psychiatry* 1997; **54**: 700–5.

153 Blackburn I, Moore R. Controlled acute and follow-up trial of cognitive therapy and pharmacotherapy in outpatients with recurrent depression. *Br J Psychiatry* 1997; **171**: 328–34.

154 Ray KL, Hodnet ED. Caregiver support for post-partum depression (Cochrane Review). In: *The Cochrane Library. Issue 1*. Oxford: Update Software, 1998.

155 Appleby L, Warner R, Whitton A *et al*. Comparison of six counselling sessions with a psychologist over 11 weeks with a single 1 hour session. *BMJ* 1997; **314**: 932–6.

156 Hawton K, Townsend E, Arensman E *et al*. Deliberate self-harm: the efficacy of psychosocial and pharmacological interventions (Cochrane Review). In: *The Cochrane Library*. Oxford: Update Software, 1999.

157 Evans M, Morgan A, Hayward A. Crisis telephone for deliberate self-harm patients: effects on repetition. *Br J Psychiatry* 1997; **175**: 23–7.

158 Terman M, Terman JS, Ross DC. A controlled trial of timed bright light and negative air ionization for treatment of winter depression. *Arch Gen Psychiatry* 1998; **55**: 875–82.

159 Lee T, Chan C. Dose-response relationship of phototherapy for seasonal affective disorder: a meta-analysis. *Acta Psychiatr Scand* 1999; **99**: 315–23.

160 Upton M, Evans M, Goldberg D *et al*. Evaluation of ICD-10 PHC mental health guidelines in detecting and managing depression within primary care. *Br J Psychiatry* 1999; **175**: 476–82.

161 Thompson C, Stevens L, Ostler K *et al*. The Hampshire Depression Project. *Int J Methods Psychiatr Res* 1996; **Suppl.**: 27–31.

162 Clinical Standards Advisory Group. *Depression*. London: The Stationery Office, 2000.

163 Waintraub L, Guelfi J. Nosological validity of dysthymia. *Eur Psychiatry* 1998; **13**: 173–87.

164 Lima MS, Moncrieff J. Drugs versus placebo for the treatment of dysthymia (Cochrane Review). In: *The Cochrane Library*. Oxford: Update Software, 1998.

165 Heimberg R, Liebowitz M, Hope D *et al*. Cognitive-behavioural therapy and phenelzine were both effective in social phobia. *Arch Gen Psychiatry* 1998; **55**: 1133–41.

166 Lader M, Bond A. Interaction of pharmacological and psychological treatments of anxiety. *J Psychiatry* 1998; **173**: 165–8.

167 Loerch B, Graf-Morgenstern M, Hautzinger S *et al*. Randomised placebo-controlled trial of moclodemide, cognitive-behavioural therapy and their combination in panic disorder with agoraphobia. *Br J Psychiatry* 1999; **174**: 205–12.

168 Piccinelli M, Pini S, Bellantuono C *et al*. Efficacy of drug treatment in obsessive-compulsive disorder. *Br J Psychiatry* 1995; **166**: 421–3.

169 Abramowitz J. Effectiveness of psychological and pharmacological treatments for obsessive-compulsive disorder. *J Consult Clin Psychol* 1997; **65**: 44–52.

170 Bisson J, Jenkins P, Alexander J *et al*. Randomised controlled trial of psychological debriefing for acute burn trauma. *Br J Psychiatry* 1997; **171**: 78–81.

171 Wessely S, Rose S, Bisson JI. A systematic review of brief psychological interventions (debriefing) for the treatment of immediate trauma-related symptoms and the prevention of post-traumatic stress disorder (Cochrane Review). In: *The Cochrane Library*. Oxford: Update Software, 1998.

172 Marks I, Lovell K, Noshirvani H *et al*. Treatment of PTSD by exposure and/or cognitive restructuring. A controlled study. *Arch Gen Psychiatry* 1998; **55**: 317–25.

173 Price JR, Couper J. Cognitive behaviour therapy for chronic fatigue syndrome in adults (Cochrane Review). In: *The Cochrane Library. Issue 3*. Oxford: Update Software, 1999.

174 Deale A, Chalder T, Marks I *et al*. Cognitive behaviour therapy for chronic fatigue syndrome. *Am J Psychiatry* 1997; **154**: 408–14.

175 Clark D, Salkovskis P, Hackmann A *et al*. Two psychological treatments for hypochondriasis. A randomised controlled trial. *Br J Psychiatry* 1998; **173**: 218–25.

176 Eisler I, Dare C, Russell G *et al*. Family and individual therapy in anorexia nervosa. A five-year follow-up. *Arch Gen Psychiatry* 1997; **54**: 1025–30.

177 Whittal M, Agras W, Gould R. Bulimia nervosa: a meta-analysis of psychosocial and pharmacological trials. *Behav Ther* 1999; **30**: 117–35.

178 Carter J, Fairburn G. Cognitive-behavioural self-help for binge-eating disorder: a controlled effectiveness study. *J Consult Clin Psychol* 1998; **66**: 616–23.

179 Palmer R, Treasure J. Providing specialised services for anorexia nervosa. *Br J Psychiatry* 1999; **175**: 306–9.

180 Millar H. New eating disorder service. *Psychiatr Bull* 1998; **22**: 751–4.

181 Nowell P, Mazumder S, Buysse D *et al*. Benzodiazepines and zolpidem for chronic insomnia. A meta-analysis of treatment efficacy. *JAMA* 1997; **278**: 2170–7.

182 Morin C, Culbert J, Schwartz S. Nonpharmacological interventions for insomnia. *Am J Psychiatry* 1994; **151**: 1172–80.

183 Milton J. A postal survey of the assessment procedure for personality disorder in forensic settings. *Psychiatr Bull* 2000; **24**: 254–7.

184 Wing J, Brown G. *Institutionalism and Schizophrenia*. Cambridge: Cambridge University Press, 1970.

185 Brown G, Bone M, Dalison B, Wing J. *Schizophrenia and Social Care*. London: Oxford University Press, 1966.

186 Leff JE. *Care in the Community. Illusion or reality?* Chichester: John Wiley & Sons, 1997.

187 Leff J, Trieman N. Long-stay patients discharged from psychiatric hospitals. *Br J Psychiatry* 2000; **176**: 217–23.

188 Beecham J, Hallam A, Knapp M *et al*. Costing care in hospital and in the community. In: Leff J (ed.). *Care in the Community. Illusion or reality?* Chichester: John Wiley & Sons, 1997.

189 Tyrer P. The National Service Framework: a scaffold for mental health. *BMJ* 1999; **319**: 1018–19.

190 Goldberg DP, Huxley P. *The Detection of Psychiatric Illness by Questionnaire*. Monograph No. 21. London: Oxford University Press, 1972.

191 Churchill R, McGuire H. Developments in the evidence base in primary care psychiatry. *Int Rev Psychiatry* 1998; **10**: 143–7.

192 Mann A, Tylee A. Evaluation of change in primary care practice. *Int Rev Psychiatry* 1988; **10**: 148–53.

193 Wing J, Beevor A, Curtis R *et al*. Health of the Nation Outcome Scales (HoNOS). Research and development. *Br J Psychiatry* 1998; **172**: 11–18.

194 Wing J. Institutionalism and institutionalisation. *J Forensic Psychiatry* 2000; **11**: 7–10.

195 Leach J, Wing J. *Helping Destitute Men*. London: Tavistock, 1980.

196 Slade M, McCrone P, Thornicroft G. Uptake of welfare benefits by psychiatric patients. *Psychiatr Bull* 1995; **19**: 411–13.

197 Geddes J, Wessely S. Clinical standards in psychiatry. *Psychiatr Bull* 2000; **24**: 83–4.

198 Lelliott P. Clinical standards and the wider quality agenda. *Psychiatr Bull* 2000; **24**: 85–9.

199 Palmer C, Lelliott P. Encouraging the implementation of clinical standards into practice. *Psychiatr Bull* 2000; **24**: 90–3.

200 Glover G, Knight S, Melzer D *et al*. The development of a new minimum data set for specialist mental health care. *Health Trends* 1998; **29**: 48–51.

201 Slade M, Thornicroft G, Glover G. The feasibility of routine outcome measures in mental health. *Soc Psychiatry Psychiatr Epidemiol* 1999; **34**: 231–43.

202 Glover G, Robin E, Emami J *et al*. A needs index for mental health. *Soc Psychiatry Psychiatr Epidemiol* 1998; **33**: 89–96.

203 Charlwood P, Mason A, Goldacre M *et al*. *Health Outcomes. Report of a working group to the Department of Health*. Oxford: National Centre for Health Outcomes Development, 1999.

204 MacKee M, Rafferty A, Aikin L. Measuring hospital performance. *J R Soc Med* 1997; **90**: 187–91.

205 Caldicott Committee. *Report on the Review of Patient-Identifiable Information.* London: Department of Health, 1997.

206 Ellis S, Adams R. The cult of the double-blind placebo-controlled trial. *Br J Clin Pract* 1997; **51**: 36–9.

207 Lelliott P, Sims A, Wing J. Who pays for community care? The same old question. *BMJ* 1993; **307**: 991–4.

Acknowledgements

Thanks are due to the many people who have patiently commented on successive drafts of this chapter, in particular Paul Lelliott, Sian Rees, Gyles Glover, Claire Palmer and Daniel Chisholme.

14   Alzheimer's Disease and Other Dementias*

David Melzer, Katherine Pearce, Brian Cooper and Carol Brayne

1 Summary

Statement of the problem

Upwards of one in 20 of the population aged 65 and over in England and Wales suffer from a significant degree of dementia, and rates for dementia and cognitive impairment of up to 80% have been reported from institutional care settings for the elderly. Numbers of people in need of care over the coming decades are due to increase at a faster pace than the overall elderly population increases, due to the disproportionate rise in the number of people aged 85 and over.

Alzheimer's disease and the other dementias are characterised by progressive decline in memory and other cognitive functions, although the course of these conditions is highly variable. Severity varies from mild impairment with little impact on everyday life through to the severe, in which patients need help with activities such as dressing, washing, eating and toileting. In addition, supervision may be needed to guard against wandering or dangers, such as leaving gas taps on. Aggressive or 'challenging' behaviour can be a feature, with verbal abuse, shouting and hitting. Informal carers, who provide the mainstay of support, experience high rates of stress and depression.

Subgroups

Dementia can be subdivided into specific diagnostic entities (*see* pp. 245–6) by age of onset (early or late) or by place of care receipt (institutionalised, living alone, etc.). For organising supportive services, classification into mild, moderate and severe stages on the basis of dependency in daily living is probably the most helpful approach. At the clinical level, diagnostic classification is becoming important, with, for example, new drugs requiring identification of mild to moderate Alzheimer's disease, and dementia with Lewy bodies requiring avoidance of major tranquillisers.

---

* This chapter was prepared in 1999 with some updates in 2000. Since then there have been many new research findings in the field of dementia, which are not incorporated here. The reader is advised to use this chapter as an initial reference source, but to check for more recent information where appropriate.

Prevalence and incidence

The prevalence of dementia rises rapidly with age, and as the population aged 85 and over is projected to increase fastest, the total number of people in need of care could rise dramatically over the coming decades.

Table 1: Prevalence of dementia by age and sex (%) (pooled results from five centres of the Medical Research Council Cognitive Function and Ageing Study).

Age group (years)	Men (%)	Women (%)
65–69	1.4	1.5
70–74	3.1	2.2
75–79	5.6	7.1
80–84	10.2	14.1
85+	19.6	27.5

Services available

Table 2 lists the principal services currently available to people with dementia.

Table 2: Principal services currently available to people with dementia.

Service provider	Service functions
Primary health care	Early recognition, assessment and treatment of coexisting illness, rationalising prescribed medication, specialist referral, monitoring, arranging support services, medical supervision in long-stay institutional settings, terminal care and bereavement counselling
Local authority social services departments	Social care assessment, including assessment of caregivers' needs, social care plan, appointment of a care manager. Care offered may involve carer support and practical assistance with caring tasks, including home help, meals on wheels, day and respite care, funding for residential or nursing home care depending on needs and financial entitlement
Old age psychiatry services	Specialist psychiatric service offering investigation and diagnosis, symptomatic treatment including management of behaviour problems, treatment of coexisting psychiatric illness, specialist day care and carer support/education
Geriatric medicine and other hospital specialties	Acute and follow-up care for physical illness in hospital and community settings

Residential and nursing homes provide the bulk of formal practical care to people with dementia, and rates of cognitive impairment in these institutions are very high. Voluntary organisations provide a great deal of information and support, as well as some direct services.

Enid Levin lists ten key requirements for good dementia care (*see* p. 259):

- early identification of dementia
- integrated medico-social assessment
- active medical treatment (of concurrent physical illness, serious behavioural disturbance, etc.)
- timely referral (for diagnostic or treatment problems, or for practical advice and help)
- information, advice and counselling
- continuing back-up and review
- regular help with household and personal care tasks
- regular breaks from caring
- regular financial support
- permanent residential care.

This list reflects many of the current problems in the care system. Late recognition of dementia is not uncommon. Polypharmacy and drug interactions can contribute to confusion, and inappropriate use of psychotropic drugs is a problem, especially in institutional care. Insufficient practical support and information often result in unmet needs and contribute to high rates of emotional distress and depression in carers. Those with behavioural problems can find it particularly difficult to get access to respite, day and other care. Lack of community services can lead to unnecessary use of acute hospital beds and accelerate entry into long-stay institutional care. Specific skills are needed to cope with the many people with dementia who are admitted to acute hospitals, where some remain longer than they need to for lack of suitable alternatives. Residential and nursing care homes are of variable quality, and skills training and quality improvement programmes could improve the lives of many residents.

Evidence of effectiveness

The available evidence at the time of writing (2000) and implications for service provision are summarised below in relation to the stages of illness. Much of the experimental evidence is fragmentary and drawn from efficacy trials, mostly from the USA. Interventions can have consequences not only for the patient, but also for carers and the public purse.

Before clinical onset:

- no measures are proven to be effective for primary prevention of dementia, although steps to reduce the incidence of cerebrovascular disease and head trauma may be important and are justified in their own right (*see* p. 264)
- genetic testing is currently only indicated for families where several members have developed early dementia (*see* p. 264)
- general population screening for dementia is not indicated (*see* p. 265)
- clinical recognition of established dementia should be improved, in order to rationalise medication, allow family and patient to make financial and other arrangements, prepare advance directives and avoid inappropriate care.

In mild to moderate dementia:

- much of the diagnostic assessment and management can be carried out by the primary health care team, either alone or in collaboration with specialist services (*see* pp. 253–5). There is a consensus that the diagnosis is essentially a clinical one, with laboratory investigations being employed to identify the uncommon treatable forms and comorbid conditions
- currently licensed anticholinesterase symptomatic drug treatments for Alzheimer's disease offer between two- and four-point improvements on the 70-point ADAS-cog cognitive function scale in

six-month trials on selected patients with mild to moderate impairments. A large number of new drugs are currently under development and updated sources, especially the Cochrane Reviews and NICE, should be consulted for evidence of their efficacy

- available trials of neuroleptics show significant but small effects in the control of agitation, unco-operative behaviour and hallucinations in dementia. Side-effects and drug interactions are a significant problem, especially in the elderly. There is at present much inappropriate prescribing of psychoactive medication for this patient group, especially in long-term care homes (*see* p. 269)

- a number of psychosocial and behavioural therapies have shown promise in improving behaviour and patient comfort (*see* pp. 270–3). Unfortunately, good trials are scarce due to technical difficulties and lack of funding. Although these need more rigorous development, several may prove useful if they can be incorporated into quality-of-care programmes using existing staff. Reality orientation, behaviour modification, validation therapy and activity groups have all shown promise in at least one study in improving important outcomes. Environmental approaches in long-stay settings, e.g. providing circular walkways in homes, can also contribute

- organisational approaches (*see* pp. 273–4) to improving care co-ordination, such as case management, have reduced carer burdens and delayed institutionalisation. Studies of a multi-disciplinary community team in London suggest that non-medical team members can diagnose and plan care with good agreement with the research psychiatrists

- respite care programmes (*see* pp. 274–5) are much praised, especially by the carers using them, but trials have shown little impact on carer stress or time to institutional placement

- two methodologically sound randomised trials have shown that support groups can reduce or delay institutional admission of patients with dementia by a mean of 11 months or more (*see* pp. 278–9). These trials included provision of information, counselling and support on an individual or group basis, and some element of ongoing support over time.

In moderate to severe dementia:

- supportive and practical care needs predominate
- social care 'case management' with flexible budget holding and small case loads can be effective in supporting disabled old people, including many with dementia. Multi-disciplinary community teams with joint health and social care elements can provide a 'one-stop shop' for specialist support and management
- the quality of care in institutional settings (*see* pp. 280–1) needs improvement, through meeting physical care needs, rationalising medication, improving recognition and treatment of depression, and bridging gaps to community care. Also provision of hospice-style care in the terminal stages of dementia should be explored. A number of new forms of supported provision have emerged along the spectrum from own home to nursing home, but their effects and relevance to the UK are as yet unclear
- standards of care for older people with dementia and milder cognitive impairment admitted to acute hospitals are in great need of improvement.

Models of care

There is insufficient evidence on which to base a quantified model of resources and care for dementia. This is partly due to the many possible substitutions in role (between primary and secondary care, between informal, community and institutional care, etc.), and partly due to the lack of adequate evaluation of many of the elements in the care system. Nevertheless, there are a number of key elements that are needed to address the current problems.

These key elements include:

- a central role for primary care professionals in diagnosis, provision of information, management of medication and coexisting illness, referral and monitoring
- meeting informal caregivers' needs for information and practical support
- integrated secondary health and social care provision, preferably in multi-disciplinary teams, providing a 'one-stop shop' for specialist help
- specialist psychiatry of old age services, providing a hub for the network of required services, and special provision for those with complex problems, including challenging behaviour
- improved care of people with dementia in acute hospital settings, with geriatric medicine and psychiatry of old age departments able to play a crucial part in raising clinical standards, including better recognition of dementia, delirium and confusional states and establishing better discharge and aftercare planning
- active programmes to improve care in institutional settings, monitoring psychoactive drug use, actively managing coexisting illness and introducing behavioural, environmental and other approaches to improving quality of life
- adequate continuing-care provision within the NHS for dementia associated with severe behavioural disorder and/or physical illness, combined with an equitable system of cost coverage for both community support services and long-term residential care deemed to be outside the responsibility of the NHS.

Conclusion

Dementia poses one of the great care challenges of ageing societies. Its gradual progression results in a spectrum of care needs from early mild impairments in functionally independent people through to complete dependence in daily living in those with severe impairments. Coexisting illness and challenging behaviour pose special problems in care and supervision, with most of the burden of care falling on informal caregivers and residential and nursing homes.

Current provision, mostly targeted at moderate and severe dementia, has many shortcomings, but the evaluative literature points to a number of important interventions that could be made widely available and which could improve quality of life for patients, reduce behaviour disturbance, reduce stress for carers and avoid premature entry into long-term care. Well-coordinated community provision is probably also essential to avoid inappropriate and wasteful acute hospitalisation.

Research in dementia is a rapidly changing field in which substantial advances in knowledge can be anticipated for the next decade. Thus far, new drugs have targeted mild and moderate Alzheimer's disease, adding a new range of service needs rather than replacing the established ones. The advent of new, more effective therapies may call for programmes of diagnosis and treatment in the early stages of disease, before irreversible brain atrophy has occurred. It is, however, imperative that any resulting change in health service priorities should not be at the expense of supportive and long-term care for the moderately and severely demented elderly, whose numbers are bound to continue to increase in the years ahead.

2 Introduction and statement of the problem

Alzheimer's disease (AD) and the other dementias are characterised by progressive decline in memory and other cognitive functions. The spectrum of cognitive decline is broad, ranging from mild forgetfulness, which many would regard as 'normal', through to severe impairment and dependence on others. Just as the manifestations are variable, so are the requirements for care.

Those organising and funding health services need to view the care of people with dementia as part of their larger responsibility for the elderly dependent and mentally ill. As informal care, social support, practical assistance, and residential and nursing home care are major elements in the management of these conditions, care must be provided in partnership with local authority social services departments, voluntary organisations and the neighbours, friends and particularly the relatives of sufferers. Within the health service, people with dementia will be seen in a variety of settings, including acute hospitals and surgical wards. However, psychiatry of old age is the specialty with the most specific interest in the management of the majority of people with dementia. Around 40–50% of the case load of the specialty is made up of people with dementia,[1,2] with some targeting of the subgroup of patients with behavioural or psychiatric problems.

Since the last edition of this book, there have been a number of new developments in the care of people with AD and other dementias. These have included the appearance of symptomatic treatments for mild to moderate AD and the identification of genetic markers of risk, which are of particular importance in early-onset dementia. At the service level, the phasing out of much NHS long-term care, with the transfer of funds to social services, has effectively moved most direct responsibility for the medical care of institutionalised patients into the hands of general practitioners. At the same time, evidence has accumulated on the benefits of specific types of supportive interventions, especially structured carer education and support.

Since substantial increases in the numbers of very old people are projected over the coming decades and the highest rates of dementia are in old age, the public health importance of the dementias is likely to increase substantially.[3] Indeed, as individuals, we are likely to experience the impact of these conditions in a number of ways – as professional or 'informal' carers of those affected, as decision makers, through the challenges they pose for health and social care organisation and funding, and in many cases directly through their effects on our own mental and social functioning in the future.

Nature of needs and impact on caregivers

As outlined below, dementias generally progress from mild disturbances of recent memory and abstract thinking through to a late stage of loss of personal identity and of unintelligible speech, incontinence and gross impairment of mobility.[4] In moderate and severe dementia the sufferer becomes increasingly dependent on daily care and supervision. Care needs include support with daily activities, such as dressing, washing, eating and toileting. In addition, supervision might be needed to guard against wandering or dangers, such as leaving gas taps on. Aggressive or 'challenging' behaviour can be a feature, with verbal abuse, shouting and hitting.

Much of the burden of care falls to informal carers, frequently spouses or children.[5] Caregiving can result in social isolation and psychological stress, and high rates of depression have been detected.[6,7] The caregiver's psychological well-being is a key factor in admission into nursing or residential care.[8] There is evidence that carers' needs for support and help often go unmet.[9]

Concern with the problem of elder abuse by relatives and other informal caregivers has grown in recent years, but information on this subject is still fragmentary. According to Fisk,[10] findings of interview surveys in the USA and Canada suggest a prevalence of abuse of around 4% in the population over 65. Extrapolations of this estimate to the UK are uncertain as the concept is poorly defined and there may be important inter-country differences. Systematic research in this area is urgently needed in the UK.

Course and outcome

Institution-based studies using informant histories to define the point of onset of overt mental decline indicate that the mean duration of survival is currently of the order of seven to eight years,[11,12] though with a wide range of variation. Remaining life expectancy is lower for men than for women, and for people with an early disease onset than for those with a later onset, after correcting for age. A number of other possible factors have been noted in individual studies, including concomitant physical illness, severity of cognitive and behavioural disorder, and presence of neurological signs such as apraxia. Medical therapy for intercurrent infection or other physical illness probably increases survival, but the effect on survival of therapy for the dementing process itself is so far unclear.

AD and related dementias are associated with an increase in age-specific mortality which becomes less pronounced with advancing age. A UK study[13] of AD patients found that they were 3.5 times more likely to die than those not demented, with a decline from 5.0 times more likely for those aged 65–74 years to 2.8 times more likely for those aged over 85 years.

3 Sub-categories of dementia

The diverse population suffering from AD and other dementias can be subdivided into more homogenous subgroups in a number of ways, to suit different purposes. These include the following:

- specific diagnostic entities (including delirium which can be mistaken for dementia)
- age of onset – early or later
- global severity – mild, moderate or severe
- type of living situation and quality of social support (e.g. living in the community alone, with a carer or in an institutional setting).

Diagnostic classifications are based on underlying neuropathology, and in the context of needs assessment are most useful when discussing specific drug treatments or palliation. In practice, much of the care needed depends on the severity and degree of dependence, rather than the precise diagnosis.[14] Factors influencing the level of care required include severity of cognitive decline, nature of associated behavioural disturbance, presence or absence of other physical or sensory impairment, and the availability of informal caregivers.

Diagnostic definitions of the dementias

Dementia is defined in the *International Classification of Diseases* (10th revision)[15] as 'a syndrome due to disease of the brain, usually of a chronic and progressive nature, in which there is impairment of multiple higher cortical functions'. These cognitive impairments (of memory, thinking, orientation, learning, etc.) are commonly accompanied by deterioration in emotional control, social behaviour and motivation. The ICD-10 classification of dementias and relevant codes are set out in Appendix I. The medical features of the principal disorders are summarised below, but it is important to remember that mixed forms are frequent, and thus there is considerable overlapping of these stereotypes.

Alzheimer's disease

AD is a primary degenerative cerebral disease of unknown aetiology, with characteristic neuropathological and neurochemical features.

Clinical features include:

- insidious onset, usually in late life with gradual development over a period of years
- brain pathology with progressive loss of neurons leading to cerebral atrophy
- progression apparent as increasing impairment of memory storage and retrieval, going on to global disorder of cognition, orientation, linguistic ability and judgement
- clinical course accompanied by growing disability and dependency on care
- widely variable rate of progression.

Vascular dementia (VaD)

VaD (formerly referred to as arteriosclerotic or multi-infarct dementia) is distinguished from AD by its clinical features and course. Typically there is:

- a history of transient ischaemic attacks with brief impairment of consciousness, fleeting pareses or visual loss
- dementia following on a succession of acute cerebrovascular accidents or, less commonly, a single major stroke
- either abrupt onset, following a single major cerebral insult, or a more gradual, stepwise progression
- mental deterioration resulting from infarction of the brain due to cerebrovascular disease, the individual lesions usually being small but cumulative in their effect.

Mixed forms of vascular and Alzheimer-type dementia occur frequently, especially at older ages, and separation of the two is problematic and difficult in practice.

Dementia with Lewy bodies

This form of dementia is not listed in ICD-10, but on the grounds of its symptomatology and specific neuropathological changes has since gained wide recognition, although it overlaps on the one hand with AD and on the other hand with Parkinson's disease.[16]

The condition is characterised by five clinical features:

- fluctuation in the level of cognitive impairment
- visual and auditory hallucinations
- paranoid delusions
- depressive symptoms
- falls or unexplained episodes of loss of consciousness.

Here again the aetiology is unknown and onset is usually in late life.

Other dementias

A number of other dementing disorders are clinically important but, because they are infrequent in the elderly population, contribute less to the public health problem of dementia as a whole. Among these are fronto-temporal degeneration (including Pick's disease), Huntington's disease, Creutzfeldt–Jakob disease and dementia associated with acquired immunodeficiency syndrome (AIDS).

Health resource groups

The National Casemix Office has developed broad classifications covering dementia. In the health resource groupings (version 3), dementia is divided simply into T01 ('senile dementia') and T08 ('presenile dementia'). This classification appears to include many conditions that are not normally included under the diagnosis of dementia, especially under the T08 grouping.

Delirium

Delirium, while distinct from dementia, is commonly associated with it. It is a state characterised by:

- fluctuating mental confusion, with reduced alertness and attention
- disorders of perception, misinterpretation of one's surroundings and, in many cases, fearfulness and agitation
- accompanying tremor, sweating and tachycardia
- lapse into coma in severe cases.

Provoking causes include infections (e.g. pneumonia), cardiac failure and rapid withdrawal of alcohol or drugs, but an underlying predisposition in terms of old age and cognitive decline is common. Although most episodes of acute or subacute delirium are responsive to medical treatment, the presence of an underlying dementing process, even in its early stages, spells a continuing vulnerability to further episodes of delirium.

Early-onset dementia

Dementias affecting those under the age of 65 are known as 'early onset'. While AD does account for some of these, a number of rare genetic conditions are also important. People with Down's syndrome are at greatly increased risk for AD. A survey of the Cambridge Health District[17] estimated prevalence rates rising from 3.4% at 30–39 years to 40% at 50–59 years, suggesting a prevalence curve similar to that for the general population but brought forward 30 to 40 years. The present chapter cannot provide detailed guidance on needs assessment for early-onset dementia. Recent guides to this area include *Young Onset Dementia*[18] and *Mental Health Services: heading for better care – commissioning and providing mental health services for people with Huntington's disease, acquired brain injury and early-onset dementia.*[19]

Severity and relation to normal ageing

Mild, moderate and severe degrees of dementia can be distinguished, though the dividing lines between these are not clearly defined. A fourth group, on the borderline between mild dementia and normal ageing, is now sometimes differentiated in research projects, and has been variously designated 'ageing-associated cognitive decline', 'benign senescent forgetfulness', 'mild cognitive disorder', 'minimal dementia', 'cognitive impairment, no dementia (CIND)' or simply 'query dementia'.

Following the CAMDEX guidelines[20] the four categories can be briefly characterised as follows.

- Minimal dementia: difficulty in recalling recent events and in unfamiliar situations; a tendency to mislay and lose things; increasing errors in activities of daily living (ADL), but without loss of ability for self-care.

- Mild dementia: manifest impairment of attention and memory; forgetting of recent information; occasional confusion or disorientation; some help or guidance needed with any activities outside the daily routine.
- Moderate dementia: amnesia for recent events; some disorientation for time and place; severe impairment of reasoning and ability to understand events, resulting in dependency on others in personal care and routine daily tasks.
- Severe dementia: incoherent speech; disorientation for time, place and person; failure to recognise close relatives; incontinence of urine and faeces; complete dependence on others for basic personal care.

These categories correspond roughly to those provided by the 'interval of need for care' classification,[21] which divides old people into the following groups:

- independent of care
- long interval – care needed at least once a week
- short interval – care needed at least once daily
- critical interval – care or supervision needed continually or at brief irregular intervals each day.

Sub-categories for planning: a pragmatic approach

Of the systems of classification outlined above, the system based on severity provides the most useful guidance for planners and providers of care, since it is essentially in the stages of moderate and severe dementia that individuals are dependent on continuing care and supervision on a daily (and nightly) basis, whether provided by family or other informal caregivers or by professional staff. Indeed the presence of dementia-related disability for self-care and routine daily activities to an extent requiring help or care within each 24-hour period is a practical indication that the stage of moderate severity has been reached, and the probability of admission to long-stay residential care will increase steeply once this threshold is crossed.

Severity grade alone is, however, only a crude indicator of need because:

- it represents a stage in the disease progression, not a permanent state
- care requirements at each stage are strongly influenced by (a) type of residence and (b) availability of family and social support
- they may also be influenced by particular features of the dementing process, e.g. wandering or aggression.

Thus assessment of care needs in a defined population area calls for an estimate of the current numbers of moderate and severe cases according to the above criteria, broken down by type of residence and, for those in private households, presence or absence of informal caregivers.

4 Incidence and prevalence of dementia

Dementia is a complex syndrome and its definition includes three major dimensions: cognition, behaviour and function. Studies of dementia in populations have used a variety of approaches to identify the condition, from simple measurement of cognitive function to detailed examination including observational and clinical techniques. Different methods inevitably lead to different estimates. Needs assessment requires identifying modifiable factors and needs for care or formal services, yet few epidemiological studies have addressed these issues directly.

Epidemiological measures include prevalence (the frequency of dementia in a population at a set point in time), incidence (the rate of occurrence of new cases in a population over a specific time period) and survival (the remaining life expectancy from time of onset). Although decline in cognitive function is the central criterion for the diagnosis of dementia, some decline is observed in most old people. Abnormally steep decline combined with behavioural changes is particularly important in establishing the diagnosis.

Sources of information

Death certification is a poor indicator of the prevalence of dementia since its presence is recorded in only a small proportion of cases.[22] It is becoming more acceptable to record AD in Part II of the death certificate, but reliance on such reporting is unlikely to provide reliable or complete figures for comparison between places or over time. Routine hospital statistics only identify the selected subset of patients referred during the recording time period, and many community services provide care for patients who have had no formal hospital diagnosis. Even at the primary care level dementia is not always recognised or recorded. A complete picture can thus only emerge from systematic population surveys.

Prevalence studies

The most satisfactory compilation of prevalence data for dementia comes from the work of EURODEM (European Commission Concerted Action on the Epidemiology and Prevention of Dementia). Hofman et al.[23] have published age- and sex-specific prevalence estimates for dementia (defined as DSM-III[24] or equivalent) derived from 12 European population-based studies conducted or published since 1980 (see Table 3). These studies all had sample sizes sufficiently large to enable stable age- and sex-specific estimates of prevalence to be calculated (at least 300 subjects aged 65 years or over). They all employed an individual examination of subjects and included both institutionalised and non-institutionalised cases.

Table 3: Prevalence (%) of dementia by age and sex (pooled results from 12 European studies).

Age group (years)	Prevalence of dementia (%)	
	Men	Women
60–64	1.6	0.5
65–69	2.2	1.1
70–74	4.6	3.9
75–79	5.0	6.7
80–84	12.1	13.5
85–89	18.5	22.8
90+	31.8	34.1

Source: Hofman et al.[23]
The 12 studies included by Hofman et al. were carried out in Germany, Finland, Italy, The Netherlands (two studies), Norway, Spain, Sweden and the UK (four studies).

The most recent relevant source of UK data from population samples is the Medical Research Council's Cognitive Function and Ageing Study (MRC CFAS).[25] This study involved a longitudinal examination of population samples of people aged 65 and over in six sites across England and Wales. Table 4 summarises the prevalence estimates for dementia (indicated by '03' and above on the Geriatric Mental State computerised algorithm for organicity) in five of the six sites. The overall estimate at age 65 and over, weighted to the 1991 population, is 6.6% (95% CI: 5.7–7.3).

Table 4: Prevalence (%) of dementia by age and sex (pooled results from five centres of CFAS study).

Age group (years)	Men (%)	Women (%)
65–69	1.4	1.5
70–74	3.1	2.2
75–79	5.6	7.1
80–84	10.2	14.1
85+	19.6	27.5

The overall estimates from the MRC study vary slightly but not consistently from the estimates in Table 3, but the overall pattern is similar. No significant differences in prevalence were found between sites in the MRC CFAS study.

Harvey et al.[18] report the following prevalence rates for early-onset dementia, based on a study of all cases aged up to 65 in two London boroughs ($n = 185$). Estimated prevalence was 67.2 cases per 100 000 at risk in the 30–64 age group. The prevalence rates for specific dementias included AD (21.7/100 000 [15.6–29.3]) , VaD (10.9/100 000 [6.7–16.5]) and fronto-temporal dementia (9.3/100 000 [5.5–14.7]). It is notable that AD accounted for fewer than half of the cases of dementia. Non-cognitive and behavioural symptoms were common in the patients, 53% experiencing delusions and 44% hallucinations.

Incidence studies

Launer et al.[26] have provided pooled estimates of the incidence of all dementia and AD derived from four European studies. They give the incidence rate for dementia as 2.5 per 1000 person-years (95% CI: 1.6–4.1) at age 65, rising to 85.6 (95% CI: 70.4–104) at age 90. These rates are inclusive of mild dementia, however, and may not reflect the numbers of new cases needing care.

Numbers potentially in need of care

Of more relevance to primary care trusts than the predicted numbers of individuals with dementia are the numbers likely to require formal supporting services. For any given individual, dependency will vary with time and be influenced by a variety of factors. These include the degree of intellectual decline but also, perhaps more importantly, the degree of behaviour disturbance, the presence of coexisting physical illness or disability, and the presence or absence of willing carers (see p. 244 and pp. 259–60).

Systematic information on the nature and extent of different forms of need is still sparse, but evidence is now available which enables the broad outlines of the problem to be discerned.

Epidemiological estimates of numbers by setting and severity

The MRC CFAS study provides data covering impairments and informal support for all respondents, and service data were collected from records for those classified as frail. Set out below are estimates derived from the four sites covered by the service data collection.

Subjects were classified as having 'dementia' if they scored 3 or above on the organicity scale of the Automated Geriatric Examination Computer Assisted Taxonomy (AGECAT) and physically disabled if they scored 11 or more on the modified Townsend disability scale.[27] The population surveyed included 10 377 people aged 65 or over. Service data were collected for 1391 of the 1446 people classified as having dementia or disability. All estimates have been weighted to reflect the population structure of England and Wales in 1996.

Table 5 provides estimates of the numbers of people with dementia and physical disability per 10 000 population in each age group. Estimates here are lower than those in Table 4 because people with Mini-Mental State scores above 23 (indicating minimal impairment) have been excluded from this table.

Table 5: Numbers of people with mild to severe dementia or physical disability per 10 000 population in each age group, by type of residence.

	Community		Institutions		All*	
	65–84	85+	65–84	85+	65–84	85+
Dementia†						
Mild (MMSE‡ 18–23)	116	397	7	92	124	486
Moderate (MMSE 10–17)	98	601	43	360	142	967
Severe (MMSE 9)	36	168	45	540	82	739
Physical disability only	633	2,027	93	804	726	2,839
Total	883	3,193	189	1,797	1,074	5,031

* The numbers in the 'All' columns do not equal the sum of the numbers in the Community and Institutions columns because 0.2% of the original CFAS sample who had missing information on accommodation have been included. Those mentally frail people with missing MMSE scores (1.5%) were distributed in the same proportions as those with these scores.
† Based on screen, not full AGECAT diagnosis.
‡ Mini Mental State Examination.[100]

An alternative way of subdividing the group with dementia is on the basis of the frequency with which care or supervision is needed – the so-called 'Interval of need for care'.[21] Of those with mild to severe dementia, 6% were classified as independent (not needing care), 11% as long interval (care needed some time during the week), 48% as short interval (care needed at some time daily) and 34% as critical interval (constant care or supervision needed daily).

The MRC CFAS study also provided mortality data, the percentage dying during the two-year follow-up being 10% of all elderly compared to 25% of mild, 35% of moderate and 54% of severe cases of dementia.

Specific needs in groups with moderate or severe cognitive impairment

A re-analysis of data collected in the OPCS National Survey of Disability, 1985–86, found evidence of 'cognitive disability' (a rough approximation to moderate and severe dementia) in 5.5% of people aged 65 or over.[28,29] Thirty-four per cent of those affected were in institutional care and, as Table 6 demonstrates, members of this group were, on average, more severely handicapped than the remaining 66% still living in private households. Nonetheless, the profile of disabilities among affected elderly community residents points to a considerable burden of care on their families. Of this group (of whom 27% were living alone), daily assistance was required with toileting by 50%, basic self-care generally by 61%, mobility by 61%, and control of disturbed behaviour (aggression, wandering, shouting, etc.) by 17%.

Table 6: Associated disabilities and impairments in people with cognitive disability, based on OPCS national disability survey, 1985–86.*

Medium or high level of disability/impairment†	Community residents (%)	In institutional care (%)
Basic self-care	61 [40]	95 [32]
Continence	50 [33]	64 [22]
Unassisted mobility	61 [40]	92 [31]
Aggressive behaviour	17 [11]	29 [10]
Vision	28 [18]	23 [8]
Hearing	26 [17]	5 [2]

Source: Ely et al.[28]
* Figures in brackets = proportions of total sample (community + institutional).
† Medium or high level of disability defined as follows: self-care – unable to wash, dress, feed, toilet or get up from chair or bed unassisted; continence – bladder incontinence at least daily and/or bowel incontinence at least weekly; unassisted mobility – bedfast, chairbound, or restricted to within house or establishment; aggressive behaviour – injures self, hits other people, breaks things and/or has frequent temper outbursts; vision – unable to recognise friend close up, or to read large print or headlines; hearing – unable to recognise friend's voice close up, or to hear doorbell or telephone.

Assessing numbers in contact with services

In a study of people in contact with services in an area of central Scotland with 40 000 elderly inhabitants, Gordon et al. [30,31] identified around 2000 people suffering from dementia and assessed the total number of those affected at 2700, of whom 45% were in some form of institutional care and 55% were resident in the community. Estimates of the need for care are summarised in Table 7. Here again, while the levels of

Table 7: Proportions of elderly people with dementia in contact with services and needing different forms of help and supervision on a daily basis: Forth Valley survey.

Help required at least once daily with	Community residents (%)	In institutional care (%)
Basic self-care	63.7	93.8
During the night	28.6	82.2
Mobility	22.6	68.8
Domestic tasks	73.6	83.6
Control of behavioural disorder	47.3	73.5
During the night	29.7	72.4
Estimated number of cases	893	1,217

Source: Adapted from Gordon et al.[32]

need were generally higher among institutional cases, those in private households (of whom 38% were living alone) also represented a heavy burden. Daily help was judged necessary with basic self-care for 64%, with mobility for 23%, with domestic tasks for 74% and with control of disturbed behaviour for 47%.

There are, however, some quite large disparities in estimated frequencies between the various surveys, which are unlikely to reflect true population differences, and hence serve to underline the importance of having a clear-cut operational definition of each type of disability and a valid, reliable method for assessing it. Over the past few years a number of techniques of this kind have been developed and tested, including the Care Needs Assessment Pack for Dementia (CARENAP)[33] and an old-age version of the Camberwell Assessment of Need (CAN),[34] developed at the Institute of Psychiatry and UCL Medical School Department of Psychiatry, London. These are in addition to a number of more general standardised medico-social assessment schedules for use with the elderly.[35] These various research tools offer the prospect of more accurate needs assessment and greater comparability between area survey findings in the future. But in the mean time much valuable information can be gathered by local service audits and formative evaluation studies, making use of very simple descriptive data, as the recent Scottish surveys have demonstrated.

5 Services and resources currently available

This section reviews services for dementia available in the UK at the time of writing (2000). Although for convenience these are summarised in terms of the different service agencies concerned, it should be stressed that for most people with dementia, a package of care with contributions from a number of services will be necessary. Many patients have coexisting medical or surgical conditions and require a wide range of provision. An older person with dementia and a fractured neck of femur, for example, may need orthopaedic surgery, geriatric assessment, liaison psychiatry, rehabilitation services, and eventually residential placement and long-term care. Effective co-ordination of specialist medical, general medical, community nursing and social welfare services is therefore a basic prerequisite. This point is emphasised by Table 8, which sets out the principal forms of care provision called for during the course of a dementing illness, according to the different service providers, service functions and professional groups involved.

The following subsections are set out according to the different service needs and functions, rather than according to the individual agencies which, singly or in combination, supply these.

The primary health care services

Most old people in the community depend for their medical care on GP teams and this applies in large measure to dementia sufferers.[36] Together with health visitor and district nursing services (many of which have attachments in general practice) and social service fieldworkers, these constitute the front-line services by whom the onset of dementing illness must be detected and much of its care be provided. In the Forth Valley survey, 235 (29%) of the ascertained cases in private households were notified by GPs, while the primary care team as a whole, including attached district nurses and health visitors, notified 437 community cases (55%).[31]

Population ageing has made GPs and their co-workers increasingly aware of the importance of old-age mental disorders, though their skills in diagnosis and management in this field still vary widely,[37,38] and there is some evidence that as a body they remain sceptical about the value of early diagnosis and specialist

Table 8: List of principal services currently available to people with dementia.

Service provider	Service functions
Primary health care agencies	Screening, early recognition, assessment and treatment of coexisting illness, rationalising prescribed medication, arranging support services, specialist referral, monitoring, medical supervision in long-stay institutional settings, terminal care and bereavement counselling
	Staff include GPs and practice nurses, health visitors, district nurses and nurses with specific roles, such as incontinence advisers
Local authority social services departments	Social care assessment, including assessment of caregivers' needs, social care plan, appointment of a care manager. Care offered may involve carer support and practical assistance with caring tasks, including home help, meals on wheels, day and respite care, residential or nursing home care, depending on needs and financial entitlement
	Staff include social workers, home-care assistants, day-care workers
Old-age psychiatry services	Specialist psychiatric service offering investigation and diagnosis, symptomatic treatment, including management of behaviour problems, and monitoring
	Usually work in a multi-disciplinary team. Staff include psychiatrist and community psychiatric nurses. May have access to specialists, including psychologists, physiotherapists and occupational therapists. May have joint team with social services
Geriatric medicine and other hospital specialties	Acute and follow-up care for physical illness in hospital and community settings
Voluntary agencies	Advice, carer support, provision of services
Private care agencies	Provide nursing and home help in people's own homes
Long-term institutional care	Local authority, voluntary and private residential care, private and voluntary nursing homes, and NHS continuing inpatient care
Social security	Financial assistance, including attendance allowance

referral for dementia.[39] Nevertheless, there is a strong case for early diagnosis of established dementia, and this could be best achieved in primary care.

The GP, as leader of the primary health care team, is responsible for co-ordinating and directing long-term management.[40] GP knowledge of the availability and limitations of local community services is important. In the care of those with dementia, this role would be shared with community psychiatric nurses (CPNs), particularly where the latter are linked to individual practices. Involvement of the district nurse from the outset, whether the patient lives alone or with carers, can promote a joint approach in identifying needs for care. As yet, however, neither district nurses nor health visitors have realised their potential in case detection or management of dementia – district nurses because they have been trained and accustomed to focus exclusively on physical illness and disability, and health visitors because of their overwhelming commitment to families with young children. Designation of specialist health visitors for the elderly could be an important step in redressing the balance,[41,42] but has thus far been on an experimental scale only.

The health of family caregivers is crucial for successful maintenance of community care. Since patient and carer are often registered with the same practice, the GP may assume a pivotal role in support for the latter By gauging the family's capacities, knowing which of its members can contribute and giving them the information they need about services and benefits,[43] the practice team can play a decisive part. Regular home visits provide the best means of reviewing each case, encouraging caregivers and monitoring the need for further action. The GP also acts as gatekeeper to specialist medical services, a function that has gained importance in recent years as restructuring of the NHS has brought a shift of resources from hospital to community. In parallel with this trend there has been a growth in general practice of psychiatric consultation and liaison schemes,[44,45] which are now extending to old-age psychiatry.

Social and community support services

These services extend from information and counselling to 'substitution' services (e.g. home help, bathing and dressing, meals on wheels, transport), to respite care, which itself ranges from sitter services in people's own homes to day care and intermittent short stays in residential or nursing homes.

A number of objectives stated in the 1990 Community Care Act were intended to improve the quality and delivery of such support:

- assessment of need and appropriate care management
- definition of agency responsibilities and accountability
- development of domiciliary, day care and respite care
- practical help for family and professional caregivers.[46]

While this strengthening of the legislative infrastructure has been welcomed, progress on the ground has generally proved disappointing. Because local authorities have not been given adequate resources to maintain and develop the services for which they are responsible under the Act, for many families the perceived effect has been a worsening of their situation.[47]

Moreover, support services are provided by local authority departments independently of the NHS, and standards of liaison and co-operation between the two administrations vary widely. Assessment of a dementing old person's needs must pay regard not only to his or her current capacity for self-care, but to the presence of emotional or behavioural disturbance, the likely progress of the condition, and the co-existence of physical or sensory impairments. Care managers and 'approved social workers' under the 1983 Mental Health Act are trained in this work, but in practice much individual casework has to be dealt with by less well-trained and experienced personnel.

Specialist old-age psychiatry

Old-age psychiatry as a service-based discipline has its UK origins within the NHS, where the number of clinicians specialising in this field increased from a handful in 1969 to over 400 in 1996.[48] In order to meet the needs of the elderly, service teams are population based and accept responsibility for defined geographic areas. The average over-65-year-old population served by a team appears to have fallen from 36 000 in 1981 to around 22 000 in 1996.[48]

The team normally includes a consultant and one or more psychiatrists in training, trained nursing staff, a clinical psychologist and an occupational therapist, and should have ready access to physiotherapy and other remedial services, as well as a close liaison with social services. Though teams are usually based on hospital units, much of their work is located in the surrounding community. Their tasks and activities are summarised in Table 9.

Table 9: What does an old-age psychiatry service do?

- Home visits and community 'outreach'
- Hospital assessment, diagnosis, treatment and rehabilitation
- Outpatient and day care
- Consultation/liaison in relation to other hospital clinical departments and primary health care services
- Liaison with statutory social services, voluntary agencies and other care professionals
- Supervision of continuing and respite care; consultation in long-term residential care
- Information, counselling (including legal and financial advice) and support for informal caregivers
- Participation in training and further education courses
- Participation in health education and public relations
- Research activities and service auditing

Source: Adapted from Jolley & Arie.[49]

Hospital units for psychiatry of old age

Acute inpatient units are now often located in general hospitals, where they are linked with outpatient and often also day hospital facilities. Here mentally ill old people are treated in the same setting as the physically ill, with the resources of modern medical technology to hand. Some modification of the acute hospital regime is, however, required for patients who, because of confusion and disorientation, cannot adapt to new and strange surroundings, and an effective placement service must be provided to ensure that those who require long-stay care do not block urgently needed acute beds. Day hospital facilities can help both to relieve the pressure on beds and to act as a link between hospital and community. The special requirements of dementia patients are most readily met where day care is located, together with the corresponding inpatient and respite care facilities in combined units, permitting easy transfer of patients as the need arises.

No distinctive model of hospital-based outpatient care for dementia patients has yet emerged, though home-based assessment by psychiatrists or other members of the team plays a crucial part. Innovative schemes tried out in different regions include consultation in the general practice setting,[45] 'memory clinics',[50] open hospital referral[51] and mobile units.[52] Further evaluative research is required to assess the respective importance of these different approaches.

Memory clinics deserve special mention because of their possible significance for early case detection. The first such units were set up in the USA in the 1970s, and aimed to identify people in the early stages of the disorder, before it would present to the ordinary medical agencies. Since 1983 there has been a similar development in the UK. Wright and Lindesay[50] identified 20 memory clinics in the British Isles (14 in England, two in Wales, three in Scotland and one in Eire), 12 of which had started up within the preceding three years. Most patients were referred by physicians (GPs, psychiatrists or geriatricians), but some clinics accepted family or self-referrals, and nearly all took patients from outside their own areas. All provided a multi-disciplinary assessment (psychiatric, psychological and geriatric) and most shared a common core of tests and investigations (physical examination; Mini Mental State Examination [MMSE]; full blood count; urea and electrolytes; thyroid and liver function tests; vitamin B_{12} and folate levels; serum glucose). The proportion of patients found to be suffering from dementia varied from under 20% to nearly 100%, indicating major differences in patient selection and clinic function.

The conclusions of this study were that memory clinics were still at an exploratory stage of development and had not yet been integrated into a population-based system of provision, but that maintenance of a national network would be valuable both for research purposes and for the testing and evaluation of innovative approaches to early case detection and diagnosis – a need likely to increase with the advent of new pharmacological or other modes of therapy.

Psychogeriatric care in the community

The consultant domiciliary visit, widely employed in cases where the patient is unable or unwilling to attend as an outpatient, has strong advantages for initial assessment of the elderly patient.[53] In addition to history-taking and brief clinical examination, it provides an opportunity to assess the patient's home environment and capacity for self-care, and to observe family interaction and quality of caregiving, all in a highly practical and economic way. Beyond that it can be used to plan care management and establish an understanding with regard to hospital or long-stay care. The tradition of domiciliary visiting and home assessment of the elderly represents a largely undocumented success of the British NHS.

Tasks involved in care management include co-ordination of medical treatment with the patient's GP, explanation to caregivers concerning the patient's medication and other matters, eliciting of caregivers' emotional problems and avoidance as far as possible of family crises. Admission to hospital or long-stay residential care may have to be arranged. Help and guidance may also be needed if, for example, a driving licence must be withdrawn or an enduring power of attorney arranged.

CPNs specialising in care of the elderly have become key members of the old-age psychiatry team. It has been reported that around 60% of all CPNs are engaged in this field of activity,[54] and that a large part of their work deals with dementing old people and their informal caregivers.[55] The standard of provision of two CPNs for an area population of 10 000 elderly, recommended by the Royal College of Psychiatrists (*see* Table 11), is probably attainable as a national average, but there appears to be wide variation in current levels, even within single districts.[56] It has long been argued that, while national provision of CPNs is the result of a basically haphazard development, there is now a need for systematic auditing and controlled evaluative studies in order to establish firmer guidelines as a basis for future provision.[57] This general point applies with particular force to the field of dementia care, where the match between the needs of patients and informal caregivers on the one hand, and the functions of the specialist CPN on the other, remains ill-defined.

Other hospital specialist care

Rates of cognitive impairment are raised among elderly patients admitted to acute hospital beds compared with the background elderly population. A high case-frequency has been found in geriatric units in particular,[58] but extends to medical inpatients more generally,[59,60] and applies to some extent to all general hospital wards.[61]

Cognitively impaired patients are prone to be admitted with delirium, or to become delirious while in hospital. They have, on average, a significantly longer hospital stay than other patients of the same age[61] and also a less favourable prognosis in terms of illness outcome, admission to long-stay care and mortality.[62] Despite the high prevalence of cognitive disorder, medical and nursing staff on the wards often appear unaware of the problem, unless the patient's behaviour is disturbed.[58]

It is important that the condition should be recognised and correctly diagnosed, because of its implications for future treatment and care.[63] The routine use of standardised dementia screening tests could, however, lead to harmful consequences because of the high proportions of false positives they yield and the consequent unnecessary 'labelling' of elderly patients that might ensue. More pressing, therefore, is the need for better training of hospital doctors and nurses in awareness and recognition of confusion and memory disorders.

Long-stay care and sheltered housing

Rates of admission to long-stay residential care increase steeply with severity, but vary between populations, according to their age structures, the proportions of old people living alone and the availability of long-stay beds, as well as according to the prevalence of dementing illness. Findings of dementia case registers and cohort studies in urban societies suggest that about half the cases known to services will be in residential care within two to two and a half years of referral and up to three-quarters before death, and that the mean duration of such care – as a rule terminating only with death – is from two to three years.[64–66]

Long-stay residential care for the elderly includes old people's homes, for those who are still relatively independent, and geriatric nursing homes and designated NHS 'continuing-care' units, both intended for those in need of long-term nursing care and supervision. While numbers in local authority old people's homes have declined, there has been a steep increase in numbers in independent (mostly privately owned) nursing and residential homes catering for the growing numbers of old people who can no longer benefit from intensive medical investigation or treatment but who, because of chronic disablement, cannot lead independent lives.[67]

An underlying problem is the division between NHS care, free at the point of consumption, and social care provision outside the NHS (whether by local authorities, independent charities or the private sector), for which charges apply, often with means tests. Formerly this was resolved by the availability of long-stay hospital beds (geriatric and psychiatric), and guidelines on care requirements were used to limit the pressure of demand upon them. In the mid-1980s old-age psychiatry services had on average 3.4 long-stay beds per 1000 population aged over 65.[68] A change in national policy at that time resulted over the following decade in a halving of this level of provision to an average of 1.7 per 1000, and a large-scale shift to nursing and residential homes.

Only 8% of nursing homes cater explicitly for the elderly mentally ill. However, the prevalence of dementia in both residential and nursing homes is high. Darton[69] reported that 67% of admissions have significant cognitive impairment (on the 'US-MDS CPS' score), although only 39% had been diagnosed as having dementia. Thirty-four per cent of all admissions displayed behaviour problems.

Wattis and Fairbairn,[70] reporting on an expert group consensus, concluded that NHS continuing care units, medically supervised by a specialist consultant, are an essential part of the service. Characteristics of patients who need to be cared for in such units are:

- sustained or frequently recurrent difficult behaviour arising from dementia or other major mental disorder
- associated physical illness and sensory impairments, if the patient's needs cannot be better met elsewhere
- dementia or other major mental illness, with failure to cope or more rapid deterioration in other care settings.

Equitable and transparent (non-financial) criteria are necessary to decide who needs NHS continuing care and who can be adequately served by social care and support alone. In view of continued population ageing, the previously recognised guideline for NHS continuing-care beds of three per 1000 people aged over 65 is unlikely to be an overestimate of true need.

Surveys of geriatric homes in the UK continue to report wide variation in the quality of care.[71,72] Criticism of the less satisfactory units has focused on structural inadequacies and reliance on untrained caregivers (both of which may result in overuse of sedatives and tranquillisers), the lack of properly structured activity programmes for residents, the inadequacy of residents' documentation (medical and personal) and the absence of bridges to the surrounding communities. Efforts are being made to improve standards in the homes. A code of practice, with guidelines for home managers and inspectors, has been circulated,[73] and the Department of Health (DoH) has set up a number of projects to promote staff training, encourage self-assessment and performance review, strengthen links between homes and their local communities, ensure better information and choice for 'consumers', and facilitate complaints procedures. It remains to be seen what impact this action will have. Implementation will depend on the resources local authorities can devote to the required tasks.

Mounting professional disquiet regarding the haphazard arrangements that currently characterise long-term residential care led to the setting up of a joint working party of the Royal College of Physicians, the Royal College of Nursing and the British Geriatrics Society. Their report[22] sets out a number of specific recommendations, including:

- adoption of an agreed comprehensive assessment tool
- a population-based approach to the planning and provision of residential services
- development of specialist nurses as the lead practitioners in care homes
- re-engagement of geriatric medicine and old-age psychiatry in the field of long-term residential care
- introduction of a special pharmacy service for care-home residents.

Although these recommendations are not focused explicitly on the problems of dementia, they have implications for the severely cognitively impaired elderly who now make up a high proportion of the care-home population.

Sheltered housing, which has undergone a large expansion in the past 15 years, offers for many old people a pleasant alternative to residential home admission[74,75] but is less suitable for those who require any degree of nursing care. Warden supervision is more useful for alerting support agencies when necessary than as a direct care resource. In practice, most personal care must still be provided by families or by community support agencies based outside the housing development. In general, therefore, it is inadvisable for people with serious mental health problems – and especially with dementia – to be moved into sheltered housing unless sufficient support is available from other sources.[47] Schemes for 'very sheltered' or 'extra-care' housing offered by some local authorities and housing associations are more suitable for old people with progressive disabilities, including dementia.[74]

Meeting the needs of informal caregivers

There is growing awareness of the need to give help and support to the informal caregivers – usually, though not always, family relatives – who carry out most of the nursing and supervision of people with dementia in the community.[76] Providing support is not the sole responsibility of any one professional agency, but should be seen rather as an integral part of the package of care for each individual sufferer, to which a number of services may contribute. The voluntary sector, including the Alzheimer's Disease Society, provides a range of direct services, including much practical information.

A list of ten key requirements set out by Levin[77] serves as a useful framework, both for identifying the current contributions of the various agencies and for locating weak points in the existing provision.

1 *Early identification of dementia*: health screening of patients over 75 years of age in general practice should include simple testing of cognitive function.
2 *Integrated medico-social assessment*: recognising the presence of cognitive impairment and decline needs to be combined with an informant account and an overall appraisal of the domestic situation.
3 *Active medical treatment*: medical and home nursing care may be required for concurrent physical illness, as well as for serious behavioural disturbance. District nurses must often deal with cognitive disorder in old people they visit, and need both additional training and reduced case loads to be able to cope adequately with the resulting problems.
4 *Timely referral*: whether indicated because of diagnostic or treatment problems, or for practical advice and help in management.
5 *Information, advice and counselling*: a survey undertaken by the Alzheimer's Disease Society (1995) found that 50% of respondents were dissatisfied with their GPs on this score, though the Alzheimer's

Disease Society membership is not necessarily representative of carers in general. In many areas these functions are now shared either by local branches of national voluntary bodies (Alzheimer's Disease Society, Age Concern, etc.) or by small neighbourhood and mutual-help groups. A proportion of family caregivers, however, require professional mental health counselling because of the psychological distress they suffer.[7,78]

6   *Continuing back-up and review*: because episodes of NHS specialist care tend to be fairly brief, responsibility here often devolves to primary care professionals, together with CPNs working in the community mental health teams.

7   *Regular help with household and personal care tasks*: under the Chronically Sick and Disabled Persons Act, local authorities have a duty to assess disabilities and to provide aids and adaptations for the physically disabled, as well as (at a charge) support services such as meals on wheels and incontinence laundry. At the same time, they often lack the resources to provide regular home help for the growing numbers of very elderly people who suffer from combined physical and mental impairment.

8   *Regular breaks from caring*: this broad category extends from 'sitting' services, through day-care attendance (as a rule involving daily transport) to spells of 'respite care', in which the affected old person is admitted to continuing care for a week or so because the main caregiver is ill, or so that he or she can take a holiday. Responsibility may therefore be shared between the specialist team and the local authority, and calls for a co-ordinated approach.

9   *Regular financial support*: attendance allowance is a benefit for people aged over 65 who have needed help with personal care for six months, a higher rate being payable where help is required both day and night. Invalid care allowance (ICA) is a benefit intended for carers who cannot work full time because they are looking after someone who needs a great deal of care. To be eligible, the affected old person must be receiving attendance allowance, and the caregiver must initially be under 65 years and providing care for at least 35 hours a week.

10 *Permanent residential care*: families confronted by the prospect of long-term care for an old person may need support and guidance for a number of reasons – to reach their decision that the time has come, to help them come to terms with this and deal with any emotional conflicts, to know how to gauge the quality of care on offer and find a place in a well-run home, to avoid unwise actions, such as buying unsuitable sheltered accommodation, and to take full advantage of any financial provisions made by the state.

Norms, averages and recommended levels for service provision

A high proportion of people with dementia are in contact with formal health and social services. Table 10 summarises the numbers of disabled older people living outside institutions and using various services, as measured in the MRC's CFAS study (*see* p. 251).

In a study sample of 700 people aged 65 or over in a district of London, the 5.6% of people with dementia consumed 15.6% of community care.[79]

At a local level there is considerable variation in provision of health and social services, in terms of both type and level. However, routine data accurately identifying this patient group are scarce. The available data in social services performance indicators cover either the elderly as a group or all those with mental illness, and are not specific to people with dementia. Even hospital diagnostic or health care resource group data should be treated with caution, as many people with dementia will be admitted with coexisting illness and the presence of dementia may not be recorded.

Recommended levels of provision of old-age psychiatry services

Quantitative guidelines for the provision of old-age psychiatry services appear in the Royal College of Psychiatrists model job descriptions for consultants[1] and are summarised in Table 11 (*see* p. 262).

In addition, 8 to 18 beds and 8 to 16 day places are recommended as needed for younger people with dementia per 1 000 000 population.

In the 1998 report of a joint working party[80] these target figures are extrapolated to a service planning population of 250 000, with 37 500 people aged over 65, the recommended levels of provision remaining basically the same.

Table 10: Percentage (estimated number in England and Wales) of disability groups aged 65 or over (living outside institutions) using hospital and community services during a two-year follow-up period.*

	Physical† impairment only		Dementia‡					
			Mild (MMSE 18–23)		Moderate (MMSE 10–17)		Severe (MMSE ⩽ 9)	
	%	Thousand	%	Thousand	%	Thousand	%	Thousand
Any hospital contact (short-term)	71	392.4	61	64.6	63	70.2	60	18.3
Acute inpatient	49	269.6	39	42.1	48	53.1	51	15.6
Outpatient	58	319.8	41	43.5	38	42.5	29	9.0
Day hospital	8	44.4	15	16.0	10	10.8	12	3.6
Community nursing services§	57	312.3	41	43.5	52	58.2	54	16.6
Social worker	10	53.8	13	13.5	15	16.4	26	7.9
Specialist community services¶	60	327.1	39	41.1	52	57.6	45	13.9
Day centre	13	70.1	16	16.6	19	21.6	27	8.2
Home care services**	55	303.4	32	33.7	51	56.9	45	13.8
Meals on wheels	22	122.6	10	11.2	25	28.0	13	3.9
Home help	47	258.6	28	30.0	41	45.9	32	9.8
Any of the above community services	87	475.7	63	67.5	77	85.8	82	25.1
Total people (thousand)		549.6		106.8		111.8		30.7

* Sample data weighted to 1996 England and Wales population by age and sex.
† Includes sensory impairment.
‡ Diagnosis based on screen positive caseness, not full AGECAT.
§ GP and community nurses, including psychiatric and Marie Curie nurses, health visitors and continence advisers.
¶ Chiropodists, physiotherapists, audiologists and occupational therapists.
** Meals on wheels, laundry, home help, private domestic help and incontinence service.

These recommended targets are substantially higher than average existing provision. For example, in 1996 there were 328 whole-time equivalent (wte) consultant posts (across 418 posts) in England, corresponding to a rate of 0.42 wte posts per 10 000 population aged 65 plus,[81] less than half the target figure.

Costs of dementia care

The dementias are responsible for large amounts of care spending, but cost estimates are hampered by difficulties in obtaining representative and accurate service data and in the costing of informal care.

Gray and Fenn,[82,83] using mainly routine service data, estimated the total cost of AD alone for England as £1.04 billion at 1990–91 prices, excluding the costs of informal care. Sixty-six per cent of these costs were in residential and nursing homes and 17% in mental hospitals. However, the mental hospital estimate will have changed with the rundown of NHS long-stay facilities.

Table 11: Recommended Royal College of Psychiatrists minimum service levels: resources per 10 000 people aged 65 and over.

Resource	Numbers	Comment
Consultant in psychiatry of old age	1 wte	
Community psychiatric nurse	2 wte	
Occupational therapist	At least 1 wte	
Physiotherapist	0.5 wte	
Clinical psychologist	0.5 wte	
Secretary	1 wte	
Acute beds	15–20	Lower numbers if day hospital places available
Day hospital places	20–30	Two-thirds of places for people with dementia
Long-stay and respite beds	up to 30 beds	Lower numbers possible, depending on NHS eligibility criteria

wte = whole-time equivalent.

Kavanagh et al.,[84] applying a 'bottom-up' approach based on the total number of people with moderate and severe cognitive disabilities estimated from the Office for Population Censuses and Surveys (OPCS) disability survey, arrived at total costs of £5.1 billion at 1992–93 prices, mostly falling to social security and social services. NHS annual expenditure was estimated at £1.26 billion, or just under a quarter of the total. Estimated annual costs per person varied from around £11 000 per annum for those living alone at home (generally mild cases) through £17 000 per annum for those in private or voluntary residential homes, to £40 000 per annum in long-stay hospital wards, at 1992–93 prices. More recently Knapp et al.,[85] using data for 1992–93 from the NHS Executive, estimated the direct health and social services costs for dementia in England to be £850 million, or 3.2% of all public service expenditure on health and social services.

The large discrepancies between these basically comparable studies demonstrate the fragility of health-economic computations in a field where so many assumptions have to be made, especially when they deal with service structures undergoing transition. Some of the differences can be explained simply by the fact that Gray and Fenn restricted their analysis to AD, whereas Kavanagh et al. considered dementia as a whole. In addition, however, there were disparities in the estimation of numbers and expenditure for dementia sufferers in nursing home care and even more for those in private households. Kavanagh et al. emphasise that for a realistic costing, a monetary value must be placed on the opportunity costs of relatives and friends who give up their time and energy to act as informal caregivers. According to their calculations, these and other 'invisible costs' of dementia amount to around £1.8 billion annually.

Patients and their families are liable for only a small fraction of hospital care costs, but for much larger proportions of those for long-stay care and – partly for the reasons given above – for the total costs of community support. By 1991, so much of dementia care was already located outside the NHS that, as Table 12 demonstrates, half the total costs were borne either by patients and families or by social security funds. Since then the balance has continued to change.

Official policy from around 1980 onwards has led to a steep reduction in both NHS and local authority provision for long-stay care, while at the same time promoting a boom in the private care sector. Over a period of some 11 years (1982–83 to 1993–94), geriatric hospital bed numbers fell by 33%[86] and local

Table 12: Summary of average weekly care package costs, at 1992–93 prices.

Type of residence	Proportion of costs payable by:				
	DHA	FHSA	SSD	Patients/ DSS	Total costs
	(%)	(%)	(%)	(%)	
Hospital (long-stay)	95.7	0.0	2.8	1.5	773.1
Local authority residential home	2.3	2.3	92.0	3.4	354.5
Private or voluntary residential home	2.2	2.2	27.3	68.3	240.5
Private or voluntary nursing home	2.3	2.3	42.5	52.9	337.7
Private household, living alone	8.2	1.4	12.9	77.5	212.1
Private household, living with others	13.6	1.3	8.3	76.8	243.5

DHA = district health authority; FHSA = family health service authority; SSD = local authority social services department; DSS = Department of Social Security (government).
Source: Adapted from Kavanagh *et al.*[84]

authority home places by 41%, whereas 'independent' (chiefly private) nursing homes increased their capacity by over 700%.[87]

Although cost estimates for the same period, provided by the above studies, amount to very different totals, the ratio of NHS expenditure to direct social costs is similar in each, with a proportion of around 25% contributed by the NHS. Gray and Fenn[82] emphasise that this relative contribution to dementia treatment and care is disproportionately low when compared to the expenditures for other chronic disabling conditions, such as stroke, coronary artery disease, arthritis, diabetes, epilepsy or multiple sclerosis, due to the much higher proportion of long-term residential care associated with dementia. This is a point to be borne in mind when considering models of care and the development of local strategies (*see* pp. 287–8).

The Royal Commission on Long-Term Care Report (1999)[88] recommended that the costs of care for those individuals who need it should be split between living costs, housing costs and personal care. Personal care should be available after an assessment, according to need, and paid for from general taxation; the rest should be subject to co-payment according to means.

The Commission considered that the cost of this proposal to public health and social expenditure would be £800 million to £1.6 billion in the base year, rising (at 1995 prices) to £1.7 billion in the year 2010, £2.4 billion in 2021, £3.4 billion in 2031 and £6.0 billion in 2051. They pointed out that these sums would amount to around only a quarter of private expenditure on long-term care, under the existing system.

From the definition of personal care supplied in the report, it seems clear that people with severe or moderately severe dementia should normally be assessed as eligible, and hence that this proposal, had it been accepted, would have a large impact on the financing of dementia care in the UK. However, in the Government's response to the Royal Commission, now published as an addendum to the NHS Plan,[222] this recommendation is rejected on cost grounds, with the justification that making personal care universally free is not the best use of available resources. The task of differentiating NHS nursing care from personal care for dementing elderly residents is likely to prove a difficult one.

6 Effectiveness of treatments and services

The following section reviews evidence available at the time of writing (2000) of the effectiveness of specific treatments and care services for dementia. Each subsection summarises the evidence and conclusions. In some instances, good systematic reviews of evidence already exist, in which case their findings are cited. Where there is no evidence for or against a particular intervention, this has been stated. (A description of the search methods used to identify studies is contained in Appendix II.)

In each subsection we have reviewed the evidence in the light of favourable outcomes which may be expected from an intervention. Broadly these fall into three groups:

- effects for the patient
- effects for the carer
- effects for the service provider or funder, the NHS or the State.

Favourable outcomes for the patient include improvement in functional performance (particularly in the activities of everyday living) and cognitive function, and reduction in behavioural disturbance, dependency and risk of death. In addition, the safety or side-effects of interventions or treatments are important. Other central criteria such as reduction in distress and maintenance of quality of life are less well studied, perhaps because of difficulties in measurement.

Favourable outcomes for caregivers include improvement in both physical and mental health, reduction of burden (objective and subjective) and gains in social support. Outcomes for health services and the State tend to be considered primarily in terms of resource expenditure. From this perspective, avoidance of admission to hospital or to an institution has been seen by some authors as a desirable outcome in itself. However, for a true perspective these factors must also be seen in the context of patient and family functioning.

The importance of each type of outcome may vary in individual cases, but together they provide a framework within which to consider the evidence of effectiveness of services.

In addition to the measurement of outcomes, there are a number of other problems in assessing the available evidence. One important consideration is that while it is assumed that results of drug trials can be generalised across countries with different health and social care systems, this assumption is clearly less defensible when examining service and organisational studies.

Primary prevention

So far, there is no firm evidence that any form of intervention can prevent dementia, or that the tempo of cognitive decline in old age can be reduced. The clearest potential for primary prevention is to be found in those areas where there is high vascular risk, e.g. prevention of stroke and transient ischaemic attacks, prevention of type 2 diabetes and of vascular complications in those who have type 2 diabetes, and smoking reduction.[89] More general health measures, such as nutritional programmes, may prove important if they are shown to prevent certain diseases earlier in life and thus reduce the risk for dementia in old age. There is also growing inferential evidence that reduction in the risk of brain trauma in earlier life (e.g. by imposing speed limits, drink and drive legislation, seat belts and crash helmets) may help to prevent dementia in later life.[90]

Specific interventions, such as hormone replacement therapy in older women or sustained use of non-steroidal anti-inflammatory medication, must await the results of ongoing trials. The Cochrane Collaboration is preparing reports on these topics.

Genetics and prevention

A number of specific genetic mutations have been shown to be associated with AD in families where several members develop early-onset disease, and the pedigree indicates an autosomal dominant transmission. Such families are rare, and their individual members require services and counselling akin to those available for Huntington's disease (HD). Genetic testing in these families follows guidelines established for HD and is provided by genetics departments.[91]

The only genetic finding so far which is relevant to the common forms of dementia is that the allelic variations of the apolipoprotein E (ApoE) gene are associated with varying risk of dementia.[92] While research has been focused mainly on AD, the mutations may also be associated with other forms of dementia. The mechanism of effect is not yet understood, and more data are required from longitudinal population studies before any valid assessment of risk conferred by such genetic factors can be made. Genetic testing at the ApoE locus is not recommended at present, but may play a future role in aiding diagnosis. Testing of unaffected individuals, however, is unlikely to have a role in the foreseeable future.[93]

Population screening

As dementia is a serious and relatively common condition in which early symptoms are often overlooked, the issue of screening segments of the population, perhaps in certain age bands, has been considered. In a review of the literature undertaken by an independent panel of experts set up by the US Agency for Health Care Policy and Research[94] in 1992, conclusions were that:

- none of the available screening tests has a high sensitivity for early or mild dementia
- no evidence supports the efficacy of general screening for AD or related dementias, given the lack of unequivocally effective treatment and the difficulties of recognising early dementia.

In addition, genetic markers of increased risk of dementia, such as ApoE, are too unspecific to be recommended for use in screening.

Simple cognitive screening can already achieve some success in predicting the onset of clinical dementia within two to three years, but also generates a high proportion of 'false positives'.[95,96] The numbers of reversible cases are likely to prove small. Clarfield,[97] in a review of published studies, found an average of 13%, mostly related to faulty medication, metabolic disorders and depression, but stressed that the corresponding figure for an unselected case series might well be much lower than this. So far any potential gains from early detection probably have less to do with specific therapy than with more general measures of care management and family support, but this could change in future as new treatments emerge.

Clinical diagnosis and assessment

Quality of evidence: III C

Accurate diagnosis can reduce anxiety for patients and caregivers, identify treatable coexisting conditions and steer patients towards appropriate services. High sensitivity and specificity mark out superior diagnostic tests, together with evidence of improved management. For the NHS, cost-effectiveness of the test or investigation is an important criterion.

Important questions include the following.

1 Which tests should be used?
2 Is the accuracy of diagnosis or assessment influenced by who administers it?
3 Does accurate and timely diagnosis affect management?

Controlled trials are scarce, but much of the available evidence bearing on these questions is reviewed in two professional Consensus Statements – one from the Royal College of Psychiatrists in the UK[98] and one jointly from the American Association for Geriatric Psychiatry, the Alzheimer's Association and the American Geriatrics Society.[99] A citation search did not reveal any favourable or critical comments on either of these documents.

The Royal College of Psychiatrists in October 1995 published a Consensus Statement on the assessment and investigation of elderly people with suspected cognitive impairment. Consensus was apparently achieved by 'extensive and lengthy discussion within and without the RCPsych Specialist Section for Psychiatry of Old Age, and after a large nation-wide exercise'. The document was not clearly referenced.

The Consensus stated that to facilitate the referral process there should be collaboration between primary and secondary care, with information for GPs on the referral process, and an agreed timescale for responsiveness. Assessment should include assessment at home (usually) and medical assessment under the supervision of a consultant. A history should be obtained from the carer. Assessment of mental state should be made using, for example, the MMSE, the Abbreviated Mental Test Score or the Clifton Assessment Procedure for the Elderly. Physical examination should be performed to detect indications of aetiology or of aggravating factors. Regarding laboratory investigations, the paper concludes that there is insufficient firm evidence to allow authoritative recommendation of a definitive list of tests. Tests may include full blood count, ESR, vitamin B_{12} and folate levels, blood glucose, liver and thyroid function tests, and syphilis serology. Computerised tomography (CT) scanning should be performed 'if practicable' unless the illness has a duration of more than a year and the picture is typical. In summary, the diagnosis is mainly clinical; further tests should aim to exclude coexisting or aggravating comorbid pathology.

The US joint Consensus Statement published in October 1997 was based on a conference at which presenters summarised and presented data from the world literature to a panel of experts. The resulting statement emphasises that the most important diagnostic tools are the informant interview and a clinical assessment. Physicians should conduct a comprehensive physical examination, including a brief neurological and mental state examination. The MMSE,[100] as a quantitative measure of cognitive function, and laboratory tests including full blood count, blood chemistry, liver function, serological test for syphilis, thyroid function and vitamin B_{12} level were recommended. Other investigations as suggested by the history or physical examination should be undertaken. Though brain imaging was considered optional, the value of functional imaging, by means of positron emission tomography (PET) or the more economic photon emission tomography (SPECT), in resolving diagnostic difficulties was stressed. Consensus was also reached that the diagnosis of dementia is usually a clinical one, and laboratory or other specific investigations are performed to identify uncommon treatable causes and comorbid conditions.

In summary, the two consensus documents are in agreement that the diagnosis of dementia is essentially a clinical one, laboratory and other investigations being employed in differential diagnosis. Diagnosis and assessment should include an informant interview and attention to both cognitive performance and abilities in everyday activity. Much of the assessment can be undertaken in the community or the primary care setting, though diagnostic uncertainty may necessitate hospital admission.

Pharmacological treatment of dementia

Therapeutic drugs are used for a variety of purposes in people with dementia, including:

- targeting the disease itself (although these are still experimental)
- providing symptomatic improvement in cognitive function
- controlling psychotic symptoms or treating coexisting depression
- managing aggressive and challenging behaviour, and sleep disorder
- treating coexisting physical conditions.

In this section we review the evidence related to the principal agents. As a large number of drugs are under development, it is likely that new agents will appear over the next decade. In theory, if new drugs are effective in reversing, arresting or slowing the disease process, benefits could include amelioration of all the symptoms of dementia. Patients might therefore be expected to show improved cognitive and functional performance, and caregivers would experience a reduction in the adverse consequences of caring. Ultimately, if effective, drugs could potentially reduce the resource requirement for dementia care, with a reduction in inpatient and residential admissions. However, no such consequences have been reliably documented so far.

Acetylcholinesterase inhibitors*

Quality of evidence: I-1 C

At post-mortem, the brain tissue from patients with AD shows a loss of cholinergic neurons and a deficiency of the neurotransmitter acetylcholine. This has led to the hypothesis that the cholinergic system is involved in the pathophysiology of AD. Possible therapeutic options therefore include cholinesterase inhibitors and cholinergic agonists.

Thus far, two of these drugs have been the subject of most study: tetrahydroaminoacridine (Tacrine) and donepezil (Aricept), the latter being licensed for the symptomatic treatment of AD in the UK.

Although cumulative evidence from randomised trials has confirmed that there are at least short-term benefits to cognitive performance from the anticholinesterase inhibitors, so far there are few data on their long-term efficacy, effects on patients' quality of life, or the cost-effectiveness of treatment. More information on these questions will be forthcoming from research now under way, including a large 'real-life' trial of donepezil now being undertaken by the University of Birmingham/West Midlands Consortium AD2000 Trial Group. Meanwhile, however, we remain at a watershed in the use of these forms of treatment.[223]

Tetrahydroaminoacridine (Tacrine)

Quality of evidence: I (one meta-analysis and several randomised controlled trials)

The Cochrane Collaboration has published a review of 18 published trials of the efficacy of Tacrine in AD,[101] which met inclusion criteria. From a meta-analysis of five comparable included randomised controlled trials (RCTs),[102–106] they conclude that there is no significant difference between Tacrine and placebo in the effect on overall clinical status, behaviour disturbance or cognitive function as assessed by the MMSE. However, barely significant improvements in cognitive function were evident on a more sensitive cognitive function measure, the Alzheimer's Disease Assessment Scale, cognitive subscale (ADAS-cog).[107] Formal comparison of adverse events was difficult, but changes in liver function tests were a major reason for withdrawal from trials, followed by gastrointestinal side-effects.

In the USA it has been claimed that systematic prescribing of Tacrine for AD could result in a significant reduction of total care costs, mainly by reducing the mean duration of nursing home care for those affected.[108] This conclusion, however, was based on a non-blind, non-randomised follow-up of a six-month double-blind RCT, and must therefore be regarded with great caution.

In summary, a Cochrane Collaboration review of trials of Tacrine concluded that there is no convincing evidence currently that Tacrine is useful in AD.

Donepezil (Aricept)

Quality of evidence: I

The Development and Evaluation Committee in Wessex published a review in June 1997 of the likely benefits and financial implications of donepezil use.[109] The *Drug and Therapeutics Bulletin* in October 1997 likewise published a commentary on donepezil.[110]

---

* Since this chapter was prepared, NICE has produced guidance on the use of donepezil, rivastigmine and galantamine for the treatment of mild and moderate Alzheimer's disease.

The first published RCT of donepezil[111] studied the effect of 1, 3 or 5 mg donepezil daily in 161 patients aged 55–85 years with mild to moderately severe AD. A more recent large-scale trial, published in January 1998,[112] examined the effect of donepezil on 473 patients aged over 50 with uncomplicated mild to moderate AD. Excluded from the trial were patients with insulin-dependent diabetes, other endocrine disease, asthma or obstructive pulmonary disease, or major gastrointestinal, hepatic or cardiovascular disease, or if taking anticholinergics, anticonvulsants, antidepressants or antipsychotics. A double-blind RCT of 24 weeks' treatment, followed by a six-week single-blind washout period, compared the effects of 5 mg or 10 mg donepezil daily with those of placebo. The principal outcome measures used were ADAS-cog and the Clinical Interview Based Impression of Change (CIBIC)[113] scores. At 24 weeks, the mean placebo–drug differences in the 70-point ADAS-cog score were −2.49 (5 mg) and −2.88 (10 mg), indicating a small benefit in the treated groups compared with the placebo group. The CIBIC ratings also indicated a beneficial effect in the treated groups. After the six-week washout period, neither the ADAS-cog nor the CIBIC scores showed a significant difference between treatment groups compared with placebo. No evidence was reported of adverse effects due to abrupt cessation of the drug.

These findings have since been substantially replicated in a large-scale multi-national clinical trial, likewise industry-supported, which employed the same research design and instruments.[114] A total of 818 patients, with a mean age of 72 years, were recruited at treatment sites in nine countries, and over three-quarters of these completed the trial. Donepezil vs. placebo differences in mean change from baseline ADAS-cog scores were −1.5 and −2.9 points for the 5 mg and 10 mg daily donepezil groups, respectively.

In a 12-week study of similar design, reported in the American prescribing information sheet, similar results emerged, indicating the effect of the drug as positive improvement on baseline function. Examination of the details of the CIBIC scores shows, however, that fewer than 8% of patients were rated by trial clinicians as either avoiding non-minimal worsening or achieving more than minimal improvement in global clinical assessments.[115]

In addition, an open-label, long-term cohort has been compared to an historical cohort and purports to show that gains on cognitive tests are maintained over longer periods.[116] Unfortunately, the estimate for the normal rate of cognitive decline is far larger than was reported for the control groups in the donepezil trials – linear extrapolations of the latter would suggest that the effects of donepezil disappear with time, but given the large numbers leaving treatment over the two years, only a good trial can settle the question.

In summary, short-term trial results show that donepezil has limited positive effects on cognitive function in selected patients with mild or moderate AD. The clinical significance of this effect is probably quite small although, given the numbers randomised, it was statistically significant. Both trials excluded patients with many coexisting diseases, which are common in the elderly population with AD. Longer-term effects are less clear and the NHS Research and Development programme is currently setting up a further trial of donepezil in the UK.

Rivastigmine (Exelon)

Quality of evidence: I

In a large-scale, multi-centre, randomised controlled trial,[117] the acetylcholinesterase drug rivastigmine at a dosage of 6–12 mg daily was reported to yield small but significant improvements over both the same drug at a low dosage (1–4 mg daily) and a placebo. Patients were aged 45–95 years (mean age 72 years) and had a diagnosis of mild to moderate dementia (MMSE scores 10–26). Outcome of the 26-week trial was measured using the ADAS-cog subtest, CIBIC ratings and the Progressive and Global Deterioration Scales. About a quarter of the high-dosage treatment group showed an improvement of four or more points on the ADAS-cog scale, compared with one-sixth of the placebo group. Relative improvement in ADL was indicated by the Progressive Deterioration Scale scores, but not further substantiated. As with other drugs of this type, it appears that a small subgroup of patients obtains at least temporary benefit, but the composition of this group cannot be predicted beforehand.

The Standing Medical Advisory Committee recommends at present that treatment with either donepezil or rivastigmine should be initiated and supervised only by a specialist in the management of dementia. Benefit should be assessed at 12 weeks, and treatment then continued only for those patients who show evidence of benefit.

Other pharmacological therapies

Quality of evidence: I-2 C

There are a number of trials in the literature of other drug therapies. A trial of selegiline and α-tocopherol (vitamin E) (both antioxidants) found a significant effect on survival.[118] A trial of ginkgo biloba (a plant extract) showed a small treatment:placebo benefit on the ADAS-cog scale similar in magnitude to the benefit seen with donepezil.[119] A meta-analysis of four trials meeting stated inclusion criteria[120] found a small but significant effect of three- to six-month treatment with 120–240 mg of ginkgo biloba extract, amounting to a 3% difference between treated and placebo groups on the ADAS-cog subtest. A review of 47 trials of the effects of Hydergine (a cerebral vasodilator) concluded that a modest consistent treatment effect was seen, especially in vascular dementia.[121]

The Cochrane Collaboration is shortly to publish reviews of the effectiveness of ginkgo biloba, selegiline, was vitamin E, Hydergine and naftidrofuryl (cerebral vasodilators), lecithin (a choline which may enhance acetylcholine synthesis), metrifonate (an antihelminthic which is a cholinesterase inhibitor), thiamine (vitamin B_1), thioridazine (an antipsychotic), donepezil and other drugs. A review of the treatment of depression in patients with dementia is also planned.

Many other drugs are under development, some of which will appear on the market over the next few years. Until such time as the results of evaluative trials are published, there is little point in speculating about the place of these substances in the treatment of patients with dementia.

Symptomatic treatment of psychotic and behavioural problems

Quality of evidence: I-1 C

For many years, psychotropic drugs have been administered to patients with dementia to control behavioural problems, particularly aggression and wandering. Studies of elderly nursing home patients in a number of countries show that high proportions of them are maintained on prolonged neuroleptic medication, although variations in prescribing bear little relation to the frequency of behavioural disorders. As the use of these drugs has become widespread, it is now logistically difficult to conduct new trials of their effects.

Schneider *et al.*[122] identified seven double-blind placebo-controlled trials of neuroleptics in inpatients with (mostly severe) primary dementia, in a meta-analysis published in 1990. Neuroleptics were significantly more effective overall than placebo, but the effect size was small, 18% of dementia patients deriving benefit from neuroleptics beyond that which would be derived from placebo. They also found that neither dose nor duration of treatment was correlated with effect size. Agitation, unco-operative behaviour and evidence of hallucinations were all reduced to some extent. In a separate analysis comparing different neuroleptics,[122] no evidence was found of greater improvement with any single drug.

A review by the same group of the effects of non-neuroleptic drug treatment on agitation in dementia[123] looked at a variety of drugs, including lithium, β-blockers, carbamazepine and antidepressants, and concluded that the available studies were few and small and that there was little evidence of effectiveness.

A Swedish health technology assessment report[124] concluded that the scientific literature does not support the use of neuroleptic therapy in elderly people, except for those with psychotic symptoms. Current evidence suggests a restrictive approach towards neuroleptics in elderly patients, mainly because they are more susceptible to side-effects from neuroleptics, but also because the effects of neuroleptics are enhanced by interactions with other drugs, and because drugs remain active longer in elderly people. Moreover, there is some evidence that continued use of neuroleptics may accelerate the pace of cognitive decline.[125] Guidelines to good practice in the prescribing of neuroleptics for home residents have been published by Age Concern.[126]

Psychosocial and behavioural therapies for dementia

Quality of evidence: I-2/II-2 C-D

There are a number of interrelated psychosocial therapies and strategies which aim to improve symptoms or enhance comfort and quality of life in patients with dementia. Strategies which have been used to try to manage the behavioural disturbances associated with the condition include:

- memory training
- psychotherapy and counselling
- reality orientation
- behaviour modification
- reminiscence therapy
- validation therapy
- activity groups
- remotivation and resocialisation therapies
- psychomotor therapy
- snoezelen
- modification of environment and living arrangements in long-stay facilities.

Published studies of most such approaches have shortcomings, including lack of clarity in defining therapies, the inclusion of small numbers of patients, the use of a variety of instruments to evaluate effectiveness and relatively brief follow-up periods.[127] Much of the available research does not focus on patients with dementia specifically, but rather studies broad groups of elderly mentally ill patients, and most of the work has been undertaken in long-stay institutions.

Dröes reviewed a number of these strategies in *Care Giving in Dementia*, published in 1997.[128] Although she does not make explicit her search or critique methods, 163 references are quoted. Dröes concluded that although in the past 20 years there has been an increase in the interest accorded to the experiences of the demented elderly, there have been few experimentally designed studies of effect of therapies, and little focus on specific diagnostic groups. The evidence from this review, and the evaluative studies cited in it, can be summarised as follows.

Memory training

The scope for techniques of memory training, or memory management, is still unclear. Psychologists in clinical practice employ mnemonic and other coping strategies to improve individual patients' ability to recall simple, important information, such as names of friends and neighbours,[129] but there have been few evaluative studies. Experimental research suggests that ability to benefit from memory training diminishes with increasing clinical severity.[130] As yet, however, the gains at any stage appear to be small and may not generalise to daily living. Brodaty and Gresham,[131] in a controlled trial based on already established cases of dementia, found that a combination of memory training for patients and instructions for family caregivers showed clear benefits when compared with memory training alone, and that the advantages were maintained over a follow-up period of 30 months. Zarit found that cognitively impaired patients who participated in memory training had improved cognitive functioning (recall), although they also had deterioration on a depression scale.[128]

Psychotherapy and counselling

Although formal psychotherapy is not indicated for dementia, psychotherapeutic skills can be of value in coping with problems of management. First, they can help in dealing with the early stages of a dementing process, when the patient's perception of his or her growing mental impairment may lead to distress and affective disturbance. Second, they may be called upon in informing the patient's partner and other family members, in helping them to come to terms with the situation and in gauging their likely responses and needs in confronting what lies ahead.

Reality orientation

Reality orientation is designed to make the demented person's physical and social orientation easier to comprehend and to cope with, by supplying three basic needs:

- constant explanation, encouragement and verbal re-enforcement by caregivers
- a simple, regular daily routine, making it as easy as possible for the patient to know what to expect
- simple auditory and visual cues to help his or her orientation for place and time: this extends, for example, to having clocks and calendars clearly visible, doors clearly labelled and, for patients still living at home, important telephone numbers and other reminders displayed.

These techniques have been used extensively, and the general findings are that they do improve cognitive functioning.[128] However, the extent of the effect and the groups for whom it is most beneficial have not been adequately defined.

Behaviour modification

Behaviour modification is based on rewards for appropriate behaviour, and a randomised trial of 72 patient/caregiver pairs in which the patient suffered from dementia and depression found an improvement in mood in both patients and caregivers among the treated group.[132] The approach has also been used to help reduce incontinence.[128]

Reminiscence therapy

Reminiscence therapy aims to improve intrapersonal and interpersonal functioning by means of reliving, structuring, integrating and exchanging memories. Basically, patients are encouraged with the help of photographs and other aides-mémoires to reminisce about their earlier lives and experiences. In practice, this approach can be helpful for patients who have not adjusted to group living in a home, by enhancing their perception of their own value and interest for others. A review published in 1987 cast doubt on its usefulness more generally, but it is not clear how studies were selected for inclusion in the review.[133] Baines et al. have shown that reminiscence therapy may be more useful if preceded in the confused or cognitively impaired by reality orientation.[134] Subsequently, a small study found that reminiscence therapy was helpful in improving communication between patients with dementia and staff, but it was only effective in an environment that had lacked psychological aspects to care.[135]

Validation therapy

Validation therapy is aimed at helping patients who have withdrawn into the past, by exploring their experiences in a group situation, and helping them to feel understood and accepted. Toseland, in a small RCT ($n = 66$), compared validation therapy with social contact or usual care.[136] The study found that validation therapy reduced physically and verbally aggressive behaviour, but had no effect on other behavioural disturbance or on the use of medication or physical restraints.

Activity groups

Activity groups focus on art and music therapies, and other activities designed to stimulate the senses. A systematic review of 30 studies of music therapy in AD concluded that this therapy could increase participation in group members over time, improve mood, and reduce behavioural problems, particularly agitation.[137] There was no evidence, however, that it had an effect on cognitive function.

Remotivation and resocialisation therapies

Remotivation and resocialisation therapies are aimed at getting patients who have withdrawn into themselves to become interested in their environment and surroundings again. One study showed that patients with dementia had more interest in group activities after a period of remotivation therapy and their verbal communication increased.[128]

Psychomotor therapy

Psychomotor therapy makes use of body movements and actions to sharpen awareness. For people with dementia, whose ability to participate becomes severely restricted, simple actions such as throwing and catching a soft ball or moving around a ring may be suitable. Some success with cognitively impaired people has been reported.[128]

Snoezelen

Snoezelen was created in the 1970s, as an approach combining relaxation and sensory stimulation for mentally disabled people.[138] It is an individually oriented approach that employs active sensory stimulation, using light and sound, and materials for touching, smelling and tasting, to share the experience of the demented person, in an attempt to increase their well-being. It is mainly used for severely demented patients. In *Care Giving in Dementia*, Achterberg *et al.* describe its use in dementia, including an observation period, a snoezelen plan and use in daily care.[138] In this chapter, Achterberg *et al.* report a number of benefits for patient and caregiver, including improving the relationship between patient and caregiver, improving communication, increasing empathy and reducing feelings of power-lessness for the carer. However, they conclude that very few research studies have been undertaken looking at the effectiveness of snoezelen in dementia. A search found an abstract of a Dutch paper[139] reporting a randomised cross-over trial looking at the effect of snoezelen in 16 severely demented people in a nursing home. During the experimental observation, a relatively low level of behavioural problems was observed. The authors conclude that more research is needed.

Environmental strategies

Such strategies aim to make the environment in long-stay settings more homely, to minimise disruption and enable patients to keep functioning as independently as possible for as long as possible. They can include normal tea, coffee and meal provision, adjusting the furnishings or furniture arrangement, or allowing pets. In general, studies of these techniques in the institutionalised elderly have shown improvements in activity, happiness and sense of control. However, cognitive changes or ADL functioning have not improved.[128]

In summary, a number of the above-outlined approaches are relevant to psychogeriatric care. Some have been assessed specifically for patients with dementia, although most studies have been based on small numbers ($n < 30$) and few have been rigorous or controlled. One difficulty is that good trials of such measures are harder to conduct, and less popular candidates for funding than trials of pharmacological agents. The conclusions from the existing evidence are that some of these techniques may prove of value insofar as they can be incorporated into long-term care programmes, as part of a more general endeavour to improve quality of care and also the morale of nurses and other caregivers. So far there is no information on their cost-effectiveness. Whether any of them should be recognised as a distinct form of therapy is also an open question.

The Cochrane Collaboration is planning to publish reviews of some of these techniques, which may aid future decision making. As one editorial put it, 'neuropathology may set limits on performance, but psychological approaches could assist the person with dementia in functioning closer to these limits'.[127]

Supportive services in the community

Organisation and delivery of community care

Community care is here taken to mean treatment and management of dementia in people residing at home, and the support from health and social services that they and their families receive. Certain of its components (respite care, day care, support for informal carers) are dealt with separately because of the large body of published research.

The following questions are considered.

- How effective is the care of such patients by community teams?
- What is the evidence regarding 'case management' in dementia?
- What is the role of day hospitals and outpatient clinics?

Community mental health teams for the elderly

Several studies have looked at the case load and activities of multi-disciplinary teams, and the characteristics of patients cared for by them. Approximately half of a sample of new referrals to four community teams in Cambridgeshire were cases of dementia.[140] At six-month follow-up, such patients were more likely than those with functional mental illness to have social workers as their key workers. Brown et al.,[141] comparing a one-in-three sample of open cases on the case loads of two community teams with a cross-section of newly referred patients, found that the former group had relatively more diagnoses of affective disorder and fewer of dementia. The dementia patients also had shorter episodes of care by the teams than did those with affective disorders. The authors concluded that this could be due to the kinds of problem for which dementing patients were referred (e.g. behavioural difficulties) being amenable to swift resolution, and because such patients are more often disposed of to other services.

Can non-medical members of multi-disciplinary old-age teams diagnose and manage patients effectively? A multi-disciplinary approach need not be associated with greater risks of misdiagnosis.[142] Assessment and management plans formulated by multi-disciplinary teams for patients with a variety of conditions, including dementia, have been found to agree well with those assigned by research psychiatrists, though there was less agreement between the groups as to which patients should receive psychological treatment.[143] It should be noted, however, that the studies in question were focused on process measures rather than outcomes.

Case management

Case management can be defined most simply as a strategy for organising and co-ordinating care services for the individual patient or client, and the term has been applied both to health and social care. It can be put into effect most successfully where the different agencies are co-operating, not competing, and where service structures and cost-bearing modalities are flexible enough to permit effective continuity of care over the course of the illness. A series of geographically extensive UK studies of case management in the social care of the elderly has been reported,[144–146] in each of which a case manager was responsible for assessing and arranging services to meet the needs of individual patients within a budget. Service delivery appeared to be more flexible and responsive to patients' needs than the traditional social work approach. An application of this model to patients with clinical dementia living at home was undertaken as an RCT in the London Borough of Lewisham.[147] Case loads were kept low to allow individual packages of care to be developed. Outcome after two years was better for the experimental group, as gauged by proportions in institutional care, levels of carer stress and burden, and measures of patients' self-care and degree of stimulation. Estimated costs of care management were higher in the experimental than in the control group.

Hospital day-patient and outpatient services

Day hospitals for the elderly are intended to provide treatment, promote rehabilitation and help to avoid relapse, but hard evidence regarding their effectiveness is still scarce.[148,149] They have been criticised for encouraging chronicity and dependence, and being costly and inflexible in operation.[150] A report on these facilities by the Audit Commission noted that review and monitoring of patients' progress were often patchy.[151]

While outpatient assessment and management programmes have been found effective in geriatric medicine,[152,153] there are no corresponding studies for demented patients specifically. Hence the role of outpatient clinics in the management of dementia is still unclear. The rapid increase in demand for acetylcholinesterase inhibitors and other 'anti-dementia' drugs must, however, bring an increasing pressure on those services in the years ahead, so that the need for evaluative studies can be predicted to grow.

Routine inpatient admission for diagnostic assessment is wasteful and may distress elderly patients, yet special investigations calling for hospital resources are often required. Under these circumstances there are strong arguments for a flexible system of assessment based partly on domiciliary visits and partly on diagnostic evaluation in specialist departments, whether on a one-day or brief (24–48-hour) admission basis.

In summary, it appears that multi-disciplinary teams can work well, and that non-medical staff in them can contribute to diagnosis and appropriate management. Within the team, patients with dementia may be under the direct care of a social worker or CPN, but through this 'key worker' they should have access to the skills and services of other team members as the need arises. Social case management (with budget holding) has been shown to be effective for many elderly people in the community, and may be applicable in dementia.

Respite care

Respite care aims to provide informal caregivers with periodic or occasional breaks from the caring tasks, to reduce the physical and psychological burdens of care, and to provide an opportunity for other tasks and activities to be carried out (e.g. shopping, family and social contacts, holidays). The term is used here to include all spells of care in a clinical or residential facility for a (usually prearranged) period, ranging from a few days to two or three weeks.

The following questions are considered.

- Is there evidence that respite has a beneficial, or at least non-detrimental, effect on the patient?
- Does it in practice reduce carer burden?
- Are informal caregivers satisfied with respite care?
- Does it appear to reduce or delay admission to long-term care?

Flint,[154] who conducted a systematic review of the effects of respite care on patients with dementia and their carers, found four studies that met his inclusion criteria.[155–158] Our own more recent search identified four additional studies of varying size and rigour. All eight are summarised in Table 13 (see overleaf). They are comprised of two large RCTs,[158,159] together with several smaller RCTs and other studies.

The studies varied in methodology, and compared different forms of respite for different time periods, but their findings are fairly consistent. Of those listed in the table, Burdz et al.[155] reported that patients in a respite-care group manifested no change in cognitive performance, but improved in behaviour. Adler et al.,[161] in an observational study, found no deterioration in behaviour after two weeks' respite care, and although there was a slight deterioration in ADL capacity in the Alzheimer patients, they ascribed this to normal disease progression over the six-week study period. No difference in mean duration of patient survival has been observed between respite care and control groups.[158] Another study, not included in the table,[163] suggested that there may be hazards associated with respite care, and there is some anecdotal evidence that the upheaval of respite can lead to a worsening in the patient's condition.

All the studies in Table 13 assessed carer burden and stress, and in general found little or no difference resulting from respite care. One trial[159] did show a decrease in carer burden in the support groups, but the interventions in question included measures other than respite care. On the whole, carers seem to appreciate this facility. A survey by the National Institute of Social Work of 267 carers[8] concluded that respite care is valued by carers, and once commenced, rarely given up. Often, however, there is an initial reluctance to make use of it, partly because of guilt about sharing care tasks, and partly from uncertainty about the effects it will have on the patients, and partly because of practical difficulties in preparing them for the move.

Four of the studies looked at effects on institutional admission. Lawton et al.[158] estimated that respite-care group members remained in the community for a mean of 22 days longer than did controls during one year – a significant difference. Montgomery and Borgatta[159] found no overall difference in nursing home admissions with or without respite care. In their study, nursing home placement was delayed for patients cared for by younger adults, whereas when the carer was a spouse, placement actually occurred earlier in the respite care group. They concluded that respite care may make spouse caregivers more aware of their own need for help, as well as of the ability of others to care for their dependants, in some cases leading to longer-term admission. In contrast, younger adult carers can derive benefit from the rest afforded by respite and be enabled to carry on longer. The two smaller studies[156,157] found no difference in admission rates between experimental and control groups.

In summary, despite strong clinical impressions that respite care is helpful to many family caregivers and helps bridge the gap between community and residential care, the results of controlled trials have been generally inconclusive, failing to provide clear confirmation of its effectiveness in terms of direct benefit to patients, relief of carer burden, or delay in institutional admission. Brodaty and Gresham,[164] reviewing the evidence, concluded that attempts at formal evaluation had been hampered on the one hand by a lack of clear guidelines for respite care, and on the other by methodological weaknesses. They argued for matched control studies to be applied to well-defined respite care programmes with clear objectives.

Table 13: Studies of effectiveness of respite care.

First author	Publication year	Type of study (number of participants)	Intervention studied	Outcomes studied	Effect of respite
Burdz[155]	1988	Controlled trial (*n* = 74)	Institutional respite: mean 15.3 days	Patient behaviour; carer burden and perception of respite	Patient's behaviour improved; no difference in carer burden; attitude to patient worse post-respite
Conlin[156]	1992	Controlled trial (*n* = 15)	Respite over 10 weeks; day care or in home	Carer stress and mood; institutional admissions	No difference in carer stress or mood, or in admission rates
Mohide[157]	1990	RCT (*n* = 60)	In-home respite and support	Patient time in community; carer burden and depression	No difference in any outcome measure
Lawton[158]	1989	Randomised by support group (*n* = 632)	Respite care: institutional or day care	Patient survival (days) and time in community; carer burden and satisfaction	No difference in survival; respite group remained longer in community; carer satisfaction higher
Kosloski[160]	1993	Controlled trial (*n* = 116)	Day care or in-home respite, or both	Carer burden and morale	Carers' morale improved; decreased subjective burden, but no increase in time for themselves
Montgomery[159]	1989	RCT (*n* = 541)	Five groups with different combinations of respite and support, plus control group	Carer burden; nursing home placement	Decreased carer burden; delayed nursing home placement with adult carers, but earlier nursing home placement with spouse carers
Adler[161]	1993	Observational (*n* = 37)	Inpatient respite on geriatric medical ward	Patient behaviour; carer burden and depression	Patient's behaviour no different; carer burden decreased during respite, but no different two weeks post-respite
Larkin[162]	1993	Non-controlled observational (*n* = 23)	Inpatient respite	Patient's ADL; carer stress and satisfaction	ADL decreased (not quantified), high proportion admitted for long-term care; carer stress showed no change pre/post-respite, but 95% satisfied

Day care and other relief care

Similar questions have been posed in trying to evaluate other forms of relief care. Day care (as distinct from day-hospital treatment in a clinical setting) is normally provided in local centres, on a basis of up to five days weekly, and can be flexible within the constraints of available transport. Other relief facilities include night-sitting or day-sitting services, in which somebody – usually from a voluntary or charitable organisation – attends to sit with the patient for a few hours so that the carer can have a break.

Most control studies of day care have detected only limited effects. A number of them[165–168] have found no or only small benefit to patients. However, in one small inquiry,[169] day-centre staff noted improvement in over 50% of patients receiving day care. Wells et al.[166] reported a small reduction in carer stress after three months of day care, but a significantly greater improvement in this respect among others whose dependants had been admitted to long-term care.

Two Scandinavian studies have looked at the effects on institutional admission. Wimo et al.[165] found that at one year, 24% of a day-care sample had been admitted, compared with 44% of a control group. In a randomised trial by Engedal[168] there was no overall difference in frequency of long-term admission after 12 months, but the control group had more admissions to acute hospitals during the year (1171 days for the 38 day-care patients compared with 2078 days for the 39 control-group patients). In view of this difference, day care was considered to be cost-effective. Wimo et al.[169] estimated that the cost of day care each 'well year' (i.e. year spent in the community) was the equivalent of £4293, while the corresponding cost of care by relatives was £3922. This again suggests that day care is cost-effective, though one cannot assume that proportionate costs would be the same in the UK.

No trials of sitting services in dementia have been identified. A general survey of informal carers by the National Institute of Social Work[8] found that only one-third had received any sitting service, and that nearly all the sitters came from voluntary organisations. Those carers who had received sitting services valued them, but raised issues regarding the amount and timing of sitting, and the relationship with the sitter (in particular, whether there was any choice of person). For dementia patients especially, there appeared to be a lack of available provision.

Carer groups and counselling

Approaches to supporting informal carers, other than respite care, include support groups, information and education programmes, and individual counselling. Support groups are defined as any setting in which a number of carers come together to meet in a planned way, usually for one to two hours at a time, with a professional or lay person as leader. They may be run on either a time-limited or an ongoing basis. The intention is that participants should learn together and gain mutually by sharing their experiences. In educational sessions, information is shared by means of talks and discussions, as well as by provision of written material. Information and education of carers are aimed at enhancing their knowledge about the illness and their ability to cope with associated behaviour disorders and other symptoms.

Questions to be considered are as follows.

- What is the effect of support groups on carers?
- Do they affect the probability of institutional admission?
- Are peer-led or professionally led groups more effective?
- Do information and teaching enhance carers' understanding of the problems and, if so, what effect does this have on their ability to cope?
- How do support groups compare with individual counselling?
- Are any of these interventions best suited to particular groups of carers?

Toseland and Rossiter,[170] reviewing publications up to 1987, found nearly 30 studies that met their inclusion criteria. Knight et al.[171] conducted a meta-analysis of studies from 1980 to 1990 dealing with psychosocial interventions and respite care. In addition, our own search identified a number of more recent papers on this subject. Table 14, however, is restricted to reports of systematic controlled trials. Of these, two were relatively large RCTs, two were small RCTs, and one had alternate group allocation.

The two larger RCTs found that carer depression was reduced in the treated groups, whereas the smaller studies looking at subjective burden felt by carers found no difference. Carers in the small studies by Hebert et al.[177,178] and Sutcliffe and Larner[179] improved in knowledge about dementia. As regards institutional admission, the two larger studies both found a delay in the treated groups (by nearly 11 months in one[174] and by 20 months in the other[176]). None of these studies looked specifically at whether the groups enhanced carers' support networks.

The question of who is best placed to lead the groups has been studied in the field of carer support generally, though not specifically with respect to dementia patients' carers. Toseland et al.[181] found no difference between peer- or professionally led groups in terms of effects on carer burden, psychological symptoms or social support. Different types of group appeared equally effective in improving social support and coping, although there was no significant change in degree of burden or psychological symptoms.

Because most support groups provide information, it is hard to identify any specific effects of this component. In one study comparing an information-giving and an emotional support group,[179] participants in both showed gains in knowledge, but only those in the latter experienced a reduction in stress.

With respect to carer support, a comparison of group and individual support for carers of elderly people more generally found that improvement in psychological symptoms, coping and satisfaction were the same with both, but that social support networks were enhanced more by the group approach.[182] In this study, individual counselling by professionals was associated with improvement in subjective well-being and reduction in psychological symptoms, whereas mutual support by peers produced a reduction in symptoms only. Knight et al.[171] concluded from their meta-analysis that individual counselling was more effective than group interventions in reducing subjective burden and emotional dysphoria. Here again the effect sizes varied widely between individual studies, so that any conclusions drawn by combining them must be guarded.

Some authors have concluded that support group or individual interventions may be differentially beneficial for carers with different needs. Toseland and Rossiter[170] concluded that an individual approach may be better for carers with psychological symptoms or particular problems in their caring role, whereas group participation provides more social support. Studies to further identify which interventions work best with which kinds of caregiver could help to elucidate the value of carer support groups more precisely.[171]

To summarise, many studies have examined the effects of group or individual interventions to support carers. While early studies were largely descriptive and non-experimental, in the late 1980s and early 1990s there have been a number of controlled trials. Because of variation in the types of care offered, the outcomes measured and the instruments used, it is difficult to draw firm conclusions. However, in overview:

- two methodologically sound, randomised trials have shown that support groups can reduce or delay institutional admission of patients with dementia (by a mean of 11 months or more)
- in general, carers express satisfaction with support groups
- carers' depression and psychological symptoms are reduced, although there is little evidence that subjective burden of care is diminished
- it is unclear whether, or to what extent, participation in support groups is helpful in building up carers' social networks in the longer term
- individual counselling has been shown to improve well-being and reduce psychological symptoms among informal carers generally, though not specifically for carers of demented patients.

Table 14: Controlled trials of carer support and educational programmes.

First author	Publication year	Type of study (number in trial)	Intervention studied	Outcomes studied	Effects of support
Mittelman[172]	1993	RCT (n = 206)	Individual and family counselling, then support group attendance; control	Nursing home placement	Placements reduced (OR = 0.4)
Mittelman[173]	1995	..	..	Carer depression	Depression reduced
Mittelman[174]	1996	..	..	Nursing home placement at follow-up	Mean delay of 47 weeks in placement
Brodaty[131]	1989	RCT (n = 96)	Carer training programme; waiting list for respite (control)	Nursing home placement; carer depression	Mean delay of 5 months in placement; reduced carer depression
Brodaty[175]	1993	..	..	Nursing home placement; patient mortality	Reduced nursing home admissions; non-significantly reduced mortality
Brodaty[176]	1997	..	..	Nursing home admissions and survival at eight-year follow-up	Mean delay of 20 months in admission; non-significant increase in survival
Hebert[177]	1994	RCT (n = 45)	Support group; control	Carer burden, mood and knowledge	Non-significant change in burden or psychological symptoms; improved knowledge
Hebert[178]	1995	..	..	Admissions over two years	No significant difference in rates of admission
Sutcliffe[179]	1988	RCT (n = 15)	'Emotional' and 'information' support groups, plus control group	Carer depression, burden, knowledge and contact with services	'Emotional' support reduced depression and increased knowledge; information improved knowledge, but stress unchanged
Dellasega[180]	1990	Alternate group allocation (n = 75)	Stress management programme vs. 'normal' support group	Carer burden and coping	Stress management programme improved coping but no change in burden

Long-term care settings

This subsection is concerned with long-stay facilities caring for patients with dementia who can no longer be maintained in the community. In the UK, the well-established forms of institutional care consist of nursing and residential homes, together with NHS continuing care units and the remaining long-stay hospital wards (psychogeriatric and geriatric). Cognitive impairment is among the dominant medical conditions in these long-term care settings. A UK study[69] indicated that 67% of people admitted to residential and nursing homes have cognitive impairment. Prominent among the factors determining admission to long-term care are a number directly associated with dementia, namely behavioural disturbance, incontinence, wandering and aggression, lack of an informal carer, and carers' reluctance or inability to continue. The care of patients with dementia in long-term settings is therefore a major issue for providers and commissioners of care.

Various new forms of care are developing, including:

- special care units – generally nursing homes or parts of homes specialising in dementia only
- adult foster care – perhaps broadly equivalent to small residential homes
- 'assisted-living' arrangements – with congregate housing and care facilities, including what in the UK are called residential homes, and also, for example, individual living units with control over personal space, furnishings and appointments, and specific support services brought in where needed
- group living facilities.

Two main questions are considered here.

1 What is the evidence on quality of care in long-term settings?
2 What is the relative effectiveness of care in different types of setting?

Quality of care in long-term care settings

A number of aspects of quality of long-term care, whether on hospital wards[183] or in geriatric nursing and residential homes,[184] have aroused concern. Prominent among these is the use and misuse of psychoactive medication.[185] A UK study of residential care[186] found that 19% of residents were on major tranquillisers, and that variation between homes in the use of both major tranquillisers (5–28%) and hypnotics (0–18%) could not be explained by differences in residents' health status. Nearly a quarter of old people with dementia were being prescribed major tranquillisers. The authors commented that prescribing sedative drugs for people with dementia appears to be used as a substitute for more labour-intensive psychosocial approaches.

Similar problems have been uncovered in surveys of long-term care in the USA and elsewhere,[187] and a number of innovative approaches have been used to try to overcome them. A randomised trial of withdrawal of neuroleptic medication[188] in demented nursing-home patients revealed no significant difference in behaviour problems between the comparison groups. Subsequently, over half the patients in the 'withdrawal' group stayed off their medication for an extended period. This trial, however, examined effects of withdrawal from relatively low-dosage neuroleptics, so the findings cannot be generalised to all settings. In a controlled trial of an education programme for nursing home staff,[189] antipsychotic medication was reduced in the experimental homes over a period of four months, with no corresponding increase in problem behaviours. A Swedish study[190] demonstrated that multi-disciplinary team meetings and enhanced teamwork could result in reduced prescribing of psychotropics. Furthermore, physical restraints on patients in long-term care can be discarded without any increase in psychotropic medication.[191]

In summary, there is widespread reporting of inappropriate and excessive reliance on tranquillising drugs in long-term care settings, despite all the evidence that these substances are of modest therapeutic benefit in dementia and have serious adverse effects. Overprescribing and inappropriate use of drugs provide important indications of an unsatisfactory quality of care. A systematic reduction in their use would be beneficial to elderly patients and residents, including many with dementia, and is most likely to be achieved where there are adequate trained staffing ratios and adequate opportunities for staff training and teamwork.

Effectiveness of different settings of care

In the 1980s, dissatisfaction with conditions on long-stay hospital wards led to the setting up and testing of new types of care unit within the NHS. Bond et al.[192] conducted an evaluation of a new nursing home scheme, randomly allocating 464 patients either to the experimental units or to long-stay hospital wards, and examining survival, well-being and other outcome measures after one year. They found no significant difference between the two types of setting on any of the measures apart from stated preferences, which favoured nursing home care. An observational study showed, however, that patients in the nursing homes had more activity and contacts, and were more stimulated by that environment. Bowling et al.,[193] in an RCT comparing a long-stay geriatric ward with two NHS nursing homes, randomly allocated 122 patients and studied functional and mental ability, depression, satisfaction and death after one year. They found a greater decline in functional and mental ability among the nursing home patients, but in a related observational study[194] concluded that these showed greater flexibility of response and had a better quality of life. A third project set out to evaluate the 'Domus' style of residential care, which is based on four postulates:

1   that the Domus is the residents' home for life
2   that staff needs are as important as residents' needs
3   that the Domus should aim to correct avoidable consequences of dementia and accommodate those that are unavoidable
4   that residents' psychological and emotional needs may take precedence over their physical care.

The study compared care on a Domus unit with traditional psychogeriatric ward care, and found significantly higher levels of residents' activity and staff–resident interactions with the former.[195] However, costs were substantial – over £900 per week at 1992–93 prices.[196]

As a result of central Government policy effectively placing most long-term care for the elderly outside the NHS[197] and the ongoing closure of most long-stay hospital wards, these evaluative studies have lost much of their immediate relevance. In theory, their findings are to some extent applicable to the contemporary nursing and residential home scene, but here interest in scientific evaluation is so far very limited, and tends to be focused narrowly on cost–benefit issues. Hence progress in this field of health service research has become increasingly dependent on projects in North America and elsewhere.

Considerable attention in the USA has been focused on the so-called special care units (SCUs) for dementia.[198–200] A review of evaluative research undertaken by the Office of Technology Assessment (OTA)[201] found little evidence in their favour, but concluded that more research was needed. Since then, a cohort study of 77 000 elderly residents in the USA, including some 1200 in 48 SCUs, has shown no significant difference over one year between SCU residents and those in other types of facility, in terms of decline in locomotion, toileting, eating, dressing, urinary and bowel continence, ADL or body weight.[202] One difficulty is defining what is 'special' about SCUs. Maslow,[203] in reporting the OTA review, emphasised the underlying philosophy and principles, which constituted the core of what this is or should be. But as in the case of Domus units and other types of residential setting, in practice it is likely to be the day-to-day quality of care provision that influences measurable outcomes.

Issues of alternative care provision

For the reasons given above, evaluative research focused on comparisons between NHS hospital ward and nursing home environments has been overtaken by central policy changes and in consequence has declined in importance. By the same token, other issues have gained in topicality, in particular:

- the relative contribution that should be made by NHS continuing care units (a subject of heated debate within old-age psychiatry)
- the extent to which local authorities should continue to be involved in direct management of homes
- the scope for reduction (or at least containment) of demand for residential care, by dint of improved community support.

Systematic evaluation – including cost-effectiveness studies – is necessary to resolve these issues, but care providers must be induced to co-operate, and problems of patient allocation to the different facilities tackled to ensure that the comparisons are meaningful. The research findings outlined above indicate that geriatric home placement can be significantly delayed by improving community support. Research in the USA suggests that monetary saving from reduction in nursing home placements is unlikely to balance the additional costs of high-quality community care, but that such a shift could improve the quality of life of many affected old people, and the morale of their families.[204]

Overview of effectiveness and economic evaluation

There are a small number of reviews that have aimed to collate research results or report professional consensus on the operation of the whole care system for dementia or major sectors of it. Johnston and Reifler,[205] for example, come to essentially the same conclusions as are set out above, although they highlight studies of greater concern for American policy makers. These include the ability of day centres to pay for themselves in demonstration projects, and the development of social health maintenance organisations, providing integrated care to older people at risk in the community.

In the UK, the North of England Evidence-Based Guidelines Group has published a guideline for the primary care management of dementia.[206] This considered all aspects of primary care management, ranging from the prevalence and identification of people with dementia, to non-drug and drug therapies, and support for carers. The guideline is broadly in agreement with the conclusions presented in this review but there are areas in which their conclusions differ from our own.

Areas of disagreement relate mainly to the value of respite and day care, and of carer education groups. The guideline concludes that respite care may delay institutionalisation of patients. Our search did not support this conclusion, as three of the four studies we found examining institutionalisation reported no significant differences. The group's conclusion that respite care has not yet been demonstrated to improve carers' well-being is in agreement with our own. For day care, the only RCT we found likewise showed no significant difference in institutionalisation of patients. On the other hand, we concluded that groups providing support, training and information to carers, taken together (as many groups offer elements of all three), are of proven benefit in this respect. The two large, well-conducted studies we identified both gave evidence of reduced depression in carers and significant delays in institutionalisation of patients whose carers attended.

In terms of health economics of dementia, Wimo *et al.*[207] have provided a detailed multi-author review. Unfortunately, patterns of care and costs vary greatly between countries and the editors argue that economic studies from one country cannot be generalised: 'economic evaluation of dementia care is country specific'. They also argue that the subject is still in its infancy. Methodological difficulties, the use of different approaches to costing and the critical impact of assumptions in some economic models limit the usefulness of the current literature for the UK. Critical appraisal skills will be needed by policy makers in this area, as commercially funded studies accompany the licensing of the many new drugs under development.

In the next section, we attempt to integrate the studies we have reviewed above into a set of recommendations for an evidence-based system of care for dementia.

7 Models of care – towards rationally based services for dementia

In this section, we draw together the conclusions outlined above to delineate an integrated model of care for AD and other dementias.* For this purpose, the main components of such a model are discussed in a rough order of progression from specialised to generalist care, and from hospital and residential to community-based agencies. It must be stressed that this is simply a convenient schema, and no more represents a hierarchy of importance than do the hub, spokes and rim of a bicycle wheel.

Specialist mental health services must deal with the most difficult problems of diagnosis and treatment, but also have consultative functions. Because dementia so often occurs with major physical comorbidity, acute hospital departments are deeply involved in the medical care of patients with dementia. Given the large numbers of affected people in the elderly population, the primary health care team must be seen as a focal point, both for early detection and for case management. Because health and social needs are intertwined, joint provision with social service departments, perhaps even in a 'one-stop shop', may be a desirable goal, but needs to be more firmly tested. Patients' families carry most of the burden of care in the community and must be given help and support if this balance is to be maintained. Severe, late-stage dementia is a terminal condition, and new care modalities emphasising the comfort and quality of life at this stage need to be developed. At successive stages of dementia, different priorities will apply. As new pharmacological or other treatments become available, new service responses will be called for to test them in practice and to deliver those that are effective to the patients most likely to benefit.

Role and functions of specialist health services

Central to all the issues of specialist care is the requirement for integrated old-age psychiatry services with inpatient, day-care, outpatient and consultative functions, based on defined elderly populations and accepting responsibility for the mental health problems that arise within them. Attempts to define the general form of psychiatric services for older people across widely differing populations have been made at international level by the World Health Organization (WHO)[208] and at UK national level by the DoH[76] and the Royal Colleges of Psychiatrists and Physicians.[80] These suggest that services should be characterised by the following features:

- a strong primary and community care focus
- acceptance of referrals from a range of professionals
- a multi-disciplinary approach to assessing needs
- integral membership of a consultant in old-age psychiatry
- multi-agency liaison as an integral part of its working practices
- initial assessment in patients' own homes, followed by further assessment and case management in hospital or in the community as required

---

* Since this chapter was prepared the National Service Framework (NSF) for Older People has been published. Standard seven in the NSF refers to mental health in older people.

- a systematic care-programme approach, with assignment of key workers to individual cases
- a close working liaison with specialist medical services for older people
- support for family carers, which is effective without subjecting them to attention from a variety of different agencies
- provision of continuing health care, based on accepted eligibility criteria.

In addition, local services should provide carer support, respite care and crisis intervention, as well as consultative services to long-term care homes.

The UK NHS model of old-age psychiatry has, on the whole, proved a success. It is being emulated in other countries, and should remain the central focus of specialist care for dementia. In many parts of the UK, however, stronger links to primary health care teams will be required as the role of the latter gains in importance. Moreover, old-age psychiatry has been increasingly restricted in scope by the withdrawal of NHS responsibility for long-term care, and its functions in this major area of care now need to be urgently revitalised. Philpot and Banerjee,[147] in their review of priorities for London, recommended development of multi-disciplinary teams along the lines of the Guy's model,[142] wider application of case management principles, and deployment of trained carers, appointed within the NHS, to assist in day-to-day care of mentally ill elderly people at home.

There is no firm consensus with regard to the logistics of specialist care. Even if the 'minimum' target of one consultant team for 10 000 people aged over 65, recommended by the Royal College of Psychiatrists (see Table 11), could be achieved, it would hardly be feasible to provide a full range of inpatient, continuing care, ambulatory and consultative services for each such population unit, quite apart from the fact that this would bear little if any relationship to local authority or other administrative boundaries. A more realistic basis for planning and provision may therefore be an area population served by two or three consultant teams working in co-ordination and with sharing of resources.

Care for dementia on acute hospital wards

The high rates of both clinical dementia and milder cognitive impairment found among elderly patients on acute medical and surgical wards call for recognition and action by hospital trusts. Old people admitted from long-term care homes are in particular need of skilful diagnosis and patient understanding care. Departments of geriatric medicine (clinical gerontology, health care of the elderly) can play a crucial part in raising clinical standards, including better recognition of delirium and confusional states.

Acute beds are often 'blocked' by care-dependent elderly patients awaiting nursing home placement. For resolution of this problem, medical and social care planning must be co-ordinated for defined area populations, and greater emphasis must be placed on provision of long-term care within the area boundaries.

In the terminal stages of dementia, the patient's family may understandably not wish to let him or her be subjected to any further acute hospital treatment, and in this situation hospice-style care aimed at relieving pain, reducing distress and improving the quality of remaining life may represent a better alternative. The location, staffing and funding of such units is a policy issue of growing importance.

Improving the quality of long-term residential care

A large majority of old people in nursing and residential homes today suffer from dementia, and the quality of care they receive can be improved substantially, often without extra cost. The Social Services

Inspectorate[73] has a list of features to be considered when inspecting for quality, and others can be added on the basis of existing knowledge.

- Psychoactive drugs should be prescribed only on clear clinical indications, for limited periods subject to regular review, and given by staff trained to detect adverse effects.
- All homes classed as suitable for dementia care should maintain a basic documentation and nursing record system, including information on previous medical history.
- Daily programmes of simple communal activities should be introduced and residents encouraged to help with any tasks of which they are still capable.
- Caregiving staff should be instructed in recognising depression, and encouraged in training and practice, under supervision, of simple psychosocial and behavioural techniques (*see* pp. 270–3).
- Visual cues should be used to assist residents' orientation for place and time (e.g. wall clocks, calendars, labelling and colours of doors).

Over and above such improvements within individual homes, national policies should be formulated to meet the growing challenge of dementia care in the decades ahead. The general principles of good care practice itemised by Murphy[209] should be adapted to the special problems of dementia.

- The design and location of new, purpose-built homes should meet specified criteria of suitability for dementia care, e.g. single-storey, open-plan layout with promenade, easy access to garden – as well as stringent safety regulations.
- Segregation of old people in long-term care needs to be broken down (a) by planning for such care to be located within or close to the local communities from which they are drawn, and (b) by establishing bridges between homes and communities (including respite and day care).
- The present imbalance in Government incentives, as between local authorities and independent providers, should be corrected.
- Eligibility criteria for continuing care within the NHS must be made compatible with the medical realities, and applied uniformly across the country.
- NHS continuing care units should be located within the area communities they serve, to facilitate visiting, and should provide respite as well as long-term care.[80]

The role of the primary health care team

Given the high and growing prevalence of dementing disorders in the general population, the contribution of primary health care teams must be seen as a major component of care provision. Most old people are registered with GPs and known to members of the practice team. Improvement in the services offered to affected patients and carers is likely to be reflected in changing public perceptions as well as in the overall standards of diagnosis and case management. The impact of the newly created primary care trusts on mental health care for the elderly will require careful monitoring.

While prescriptive screening programmes for dementia are not indicated, earlier recognition and diagnosis of the developing condition can bring real gains in avoiding misguided treatment and advice, giving patients and families time to prepare, and identifying those likely to benefit from the newly available medication. Regular over-75 health checks provide a useful framework for early case detection, particularly among infrequent attenders. In general, diagnosis depends predominantly on accurate history taking and simple investigations, most of which can be undertaken in primary care. Evidence of benefit from more precise differential diagnosis in late-onset cases is not strong, and the indications for special diagnostic investigations should be more clearly defined.

Firm guidelines will also be required for the prescribing of new acetylcholinesterase inhibitors and other anti-dementia drugs as these become available in the UK.* Auditing of the use of newly licensed substances seems desirable, both on cost grounds and to monitor their effects on relatively unselected patient populations.

Many GPs provide medical services to geriatric nursing and residential homes, where a number of specific measures are needed to improve quality of care (see pp. 280–1 and 284–5).

The contribution of social service departments

Social service departments are the lead agency for community care, residential placement and financial subvention for the disabled and dependent, codified in legislation.[210] In latter years, however, they have been handicapped by inadequate resources and the political downgrading of local government. Levels of care and practical help, e.g. home help, are now generally low, and evidence of unmet needs is everywhere apparent. Development of day care and respite care facilities (see pp. 274–7) is equally hindered. In addition, the massive shift of long-term care from NHS hospitals to nursing and residential homes has confronted social services with huge new problems. As Murphy[211] has stressed, money is supposed to follow the patient, but in this context often fails to do so. If standards of care are to be maintained – let alone improved – transfer of responsibility must be accompanied by transfer of resources.

Social service departments for their part should recognise that dementia and cognitive impairment are the dominant causes of old-age dependency, ensure that staff are alert to these conditions and equipped with the necessary skills, and strive for a closer co-operation with community mental health teams. There is scope too for the development, in collaboration with housing departments, of affordable, sheltered housing for the disabled and frail elderly, which for many could provide a suitable alternative to geriatric home placement. For progressive dementia, however, careful appraisal of the scope for 'very sheltered' housing will be required, since conventional warden-supervised accommodation can soon become inadequate.

There is evidence supporting the use of budget-holding care managers, with small case loads, helping to organise flexible packages of care for disabled old people, including those with dementia (see pp. 273–4). This should preferably be provided conjointly with health care, in multi-disciplinary teams. While budget holding has now, in principle, been accepted in community care, the degree to which the evaluated methods have been implemented in practice is so far unclear.

The statutory services should accord higher priority to development of liaison and co-operation with a number of voluntary bodies concerned with old-age disability and dependency. Prominent among these are area branches of national associations such as Age Concern and the Alzheimer's Disease Society, but local community and self-help groups should also be involved where possible, including in many areas those which support ethnic minorities.

Supporting informal carers

As emphasised above, it is informal caregivers – chiefly family members – who carry most of the burden in the community, especially for people suffering from mild to moderate dementia, and any serious breach of this line of defence would soon produce an acute crisis. Hence improving information, support and practical help for the carers must be accepted as a vital priority. Evaluative research into the effects of supportive care – respite and day care, support groups and counselling – has on the whole confirmed the value of these facilities, while at the same time underlining the need for clearer objectives and better auditing (see pp. 274–9). Skilled individual counselling is often necessary because the carer's ability to cope

---

* NICE has produced guidance on the use of donepezil, rivastigmine and galantamine.

is so heavily influenced by the quality of his or her earlier relationship with the affected old person, and by family dynamics more generally.

Measures of practical help, in contrast, have seldom been included in evaluative research. Yet studies focused on family caregivers have repeatedly confirmed that the physical demands of personal care and household tasks – dressing and undressing, washing and bathing, toileting, cleaning, shopping, etc. – rank high as causes of burden and stress, and that help with these tasks is often a critical factor.[212] A reliable, well co-ordinated and affordable home-help service must therefore be seen as an integral component of supportive care.

Family care for dementia involves financial expenses and, in many instances, loss of income from paid employment. A diagnosis of moderate to severe dementia implies a need for caregiving at frequent intervals, day and night, and should be recognised as an adequate justification for both high-rate attendance allowance (for the affected person) and invalid care allowance (for the caregiver). Systematic auditing is required to ensure a high uptake, i.e. that family carers are informed about their entitlements, and that the diagnosis is regularly notified to, and accepted by, social security officers.

Services in need of closer scrutiny

Services which in recent years have been subjected to a good deal of criticism include, in particular, memory clinics, day hospitals for the elderly and respite care. Memory clinics established in teaching centres may serve useful functions in development and research (e.g. in recruitment to controlled clinical trials), and merit continuing support on these grounds. More generally, however, any memory clinics that are located outside teaching centres and not integrated into their area service networks stand in need of careful assessment.

Day hospitals for the elderly within the NHS also require some reappraisal, not because the basic need for this type of facility is in doubt, but rather to determine how it can most effectively be supplied, e.g. within inpatient and continuing care units or separately, jointly for demented and other EMI patients or with segregation, linked to non-clinical day-care centres or independently of them. Simple auditing methods, as against formal, controlled evaluative studies, might well provide answers to most of these questions.

Respite care differs in that it does not require separate buildings or staff, but is simply one facility offered as an adjunct to existing inpatient and long-term care, in the same units. As such, it should remain on offer, but the largely disappointing findings of research to date suggest a requirement for better-defined objectives and a careful assessment of the way respite care is working in practice.

It must be emphasised that those aspects of care provision which have been subjected to repeated critical appraisal are not necessarily the ones whose reform is most important or urgent. Indeed, the quality and effectiveness of care for dementing old people in acute general hospitals and geriatric nursing homes have been subjected to far fewer evaluative studies than have aspects of community care, although – as our review suggests – they are equally in need of scrutiny.

Allocating resources and developing local strategies

While quantification of such an integrated model of care in terms of skilled manpower and resources might be deemed ideal, it is hardly feasible at present to supply a blueprint for use by service managers. Levels of provision still vary widely across the country, and the existing service authorities (primary care trusts) administer widely varying budgets for populations of differing size. Moreover, there are major disparities in the available estimates of national care costs for dementia (summarised on pp. 261–3), and all such estimates tend to become outdated rapidly because of population ageing and cost inflation. Lastly, there is still no consensus as to what proportion of total costs should be borne by the NHS, as opposed to local authority social services, the Department of Social Security and the affected families themselves.

For all these reasons, the most that can be done here is to provide a rough orientation based on a notional 'average' health district (now a large PCT) with a population of about 250 000, and to give some indication as to how individual health authorities (now PCTs) might arrive at more accurate figures for their own areas. Kavanagh et al.,[84] on the basis of a careful, detailed analysis, estimated a total NHS expenditure of £1.26 billion annually at 1992–93 prices, corresponding to some £6.4 million (around £8 million at 2002 prices) for such an average health district (PCT).

The relative costs of different providers would, however, be affected by changes in the overall model of care. Kavanagh et al.[84] went on to list eight distinct policy options giving different priorities to NHS continuing care, community support systems and long-term nursing home placement. Of these alternatives, the one most immediately relevant is that combining a reduction of 50% in long-stay hospital beds (which in fact has since happened) with improved quality of both community and nursing home care. This option, according to the authors, would mean an increase in total expenditure of 7.6% over baseline, but while district health authority (now PCT) costs would rise by only 5.3% (because of the compensatory fall in long-stay beds), local authority social service departments would require an additional 27.4%. It is unrealistic, in short, to consider the burden of dementia on the NHS without setting this in the broader perspective of health and social costs as a whole. The inseparable nature of medical and social care for dementia makes joint service planning and provision essential.

The *Handbook on the Mental Health of Older People*[76] provides detailed advice on developing a local strategy for services, with a strong emphasis on formative evaluation and project planning. A central element in strategy development is the assessment of local needs. A picture of both the needs and the existing provision must be built up to inform policy for funding. Demographic structures will influence the numbers of cases to be expected in the area population.[75,213] While crude estimates can be made on the basis of published epidemiological findings and projections, service monitoring can reveal more specific local priorities. Gordon et al.[31] have shown that a census of agency users can locate a high proportion of the expected case numbers at fairly low cost. Deficiencies in care provision can be highlighted by relatively simple monitoring and assessment of unmet needs, based in part on interviewing of informal caregivers.[140] The views of caregiver groups and voluntary bodies should be taken into account in developing local care strategies.

8 Health information systems

A clear distinction must be drawn between management information, necessary to operate a service effectively and measure its 'outputs', and research aimed at comparing different care systems and testing innovations – bearing in mind, however, the need for an ongoing exchange between the two.[214] Recent attention to mental health information systems in the UK has been focused on efforts to standardise data collection and recording required for management, chiefly under three headings:

- minimum data sets (MDS) – basic data collected by service providers
- Health of the Nation outcome scales (HoNOS)[75] – standardised ratings intended to enable progress towards stated targets to be monitored; these are currently due to become part of the national MDS project

- health care resource groups (HRGs) – clinically meaningful groupings of different types of treatment/ care episode which appear to make similar demands on resources (essentially a way of simplifying and summarising disparate information for budgeting and related purposes).

To what extent these different systems will prove useful in relation to dementia care is so far unclear. Outcome scales for the elderly (HoNOS 65+) currently being tested would seem to meet the criteria proposed in Section 2 above, in that they include simple rating scales for severity of cognitive impairment, physical/sensory disability and behavioural disturbance, and are reported to be reliable.[215] They thus offer a potential framework within which defined targets could be set and progress monitored by individual primary care trusts. Their practical utility in this context, however, has yet to be demonstrated.

HRGs appear to be less useful in psychiatry as a whole than in some other clinical specialties because they are, in practice, poor predictors of duration of episode, which tends to be influenced by factors other than diagnosis.[216] This is likely to be the case with respect to dementia in particular, because of the chronic, progressive nature of the condition, and the fact that demand for supportive (including residential) care is determined largely by the patient's family situation.

More generally, meaningful targets can be set in this field only if it becomes possible to collect and collate relevant data over periods extending well beyond the single episodes of NHS specialist care, each of which typically provides only a small window on the course and outcome of the illness. For this purpose, communication and transfer of information becomes vital – between specialist and generalist health services, between each of these and local authority social service departments, and between all three and the providers of long-term residential care (now increasingly in the independent sector). A number of major obstacles will have to be overcome before systematic exchange of data can be achieved at this level, and the most urgent requirement at the present stage is for the mounting of pilot schemes in selected areas where conditions are particularly favourable.

9 Research and development (R&D)

The review of studies of service effectiveness (*see* Section 6) has highlighted the many gaps in present knowledge. The fast-moving nature of biomedical and drug development in dementia research makes it difficult to identify priorities for NHS R&D. However, a review of this field identified few currently funded projects dealing with models of service provision, and most of the research was based in specialist settings rather than in the community or long-term care facilities.[217]

Two main policy objectives, with corresponding research strategies, must be distinguished:

- in the longer term, through scientific advances to find ways of reducing the incidence of dementing conditions (primary prevention) and treating more effectively those that occur (secondary prevention)
- in the shorter term, to ameliorate distress and handicap among existing dementia sufferers, and to relieve the social and economic burdens which the illness imposes on their families and on society at large.

While the former objective is pursued internationally, the latter calls for research adapted to the populations and health service structures of individual countries, and hence is in large measure a responsibility of national Government. Given the massive and increasing costs of dementia care (*see* pp. 261–3), a large-scale Government-supported R&D programme for this field is now indicated. Aside from the input into biomedical research through the MRC, this should be concentrated in three areas:

- development of standardised medico-social assessment and outcome measures (*see* below)

- epidemiological studies to extend knowledge about the incidence, prevalence and distribution of dementing illness to cover:
  - presence of physical comorbidity
  - assessment of specific impairments and disabilities
  - family, social and caregiving situations
- controlled evaluation of local innovative developments, centred on:
  - early detection and diagnostic assessment
  - community care and support services
  - sheltered housing schemes
  - contributions of voluntary bodies.

Medico-social assessment and outcome measures

The importance of having standardised needs and outcome measures in dementia research is now widely recognised. Clancy and Cooper,[218] in a review of this field, point out that treatment-related physiological changes, even if robust in nature, have little meaning in the practical context of disablement and caregiving. Existing generic functional measures are better from this standpoint, but much confounded by the presence of physical and sensory impairments. Needs assessment scales of the kind currently being developed (*see* p. 253) come closer to the everyday realities of caregiving, but do not yet take sufficient account of housing and transport problems, financial burden, availability of services and other determinants of unmet needs. Dementia treatment studies rarely measure the strain on the household of patients' aggressiveness or the stress of inappropriate sexual behaviour. These authors argue that efforts to evaluate new treatments should take due account of family and social perspectives.

Ramsay *et al.*,[219] reviewing the literature on community support for dementia, enumerated the following measures of individual outcome.

For patients:

- cognitive performance, orientation and memory
- physical health, including mobility, sight and associated physical symptoms
- psychological well-being – evidence of depression, anxiety or other psychiatric symptoms
- personal self-care – getting in and out of bed, dressing and undressing, bathing and toileting, shopping, household chores and other activities of daily life
- behaviour patterns – aggression, wandering, sleep rhythm, confusion
- social functioning – quality of communication and social contacts
- treatment compliance, satisfaction with services and places of care.

For informal caregivers:

- physical symptoms resulting directly from caring activities
- psychological symptoms, including depression, guilt and anxiety
- social resources, including 'time to oneself'
- satisfaction with services received
- knowledge about and understanding of the condition.

The authors identified a large number of specific scales, developed mainly in research projects, some of which may prove useful in local service settings, either for case assessment or in formative evaluation.

In addition, measures are required to assess the standards and quality of available services, co-ordination between services and communication with informal caregivers. HAS2000 (the former Health Advisory Service) is developing a district and service level audit tool for old-age psychiatry services.

10 Future directions

Dementia research is a rapidly developing field, with a stream of new findings in biomedical research that offer promise of real advances in our understanding of the underlying processes, and perhaps of effective new interventions. The rapid pace of development of genetic and other markers, as well as of new pharmacological treatments, may well result in changes of priority in health care. Over the next generation, however, this group of conditions will inevitably continue to pose major public health, social and political challenges. Three requirements are likely to remain dominant:

- careful testing and appraisal of new research findings and emerging technologies
- improvement in the quality and provision of existing services for those with a clinical degree of dementia
- the need to develop methods of earlier detection, diagnosis and treatment so as to combat the underlying disease process at an early stage and prevent or delay its progression.

Striking the right balance between these requirements is likely to present the central challenge to a national health policy over the coming decades.

UK mental health policy for the elderly is part of the National Service Framework for Older People. A Government circular[220] required health and local authorities to work together, with special reference to joint investment planning for continuing and community care, multi-disciplinary assessment of old people and development of rehabilitation services. An audit of mental health services for older people is to be undertaken by the Audit Commission and DoH jointly (published in 2002), and an 'evaluation instrument' is being developed by HAS2000.

Opportunities to organise dementia research jointly with professional bodies, such as the Royal Colleges of Psychiatrists, General Practice and Nursing, will increase as these become increasingly aware of the challenge, and deserve to be pursued vigorously. Collaboration should also be promoted between the NHS and university centres with the necessary research capacity. The tendency, conspicuous in some countries, for central government to rely on health survey research commissioned from market research and similar commercial firms in general has been uneconomic and inimical to good-quality R&D, and should be avoided.

The tempo of change in the dementia field will call for a system of continuous monitoring by working groups, concentrating on:

- assessment of clinical trial results, and their implications for practice, in an international perspective
- implications of new scientific progress and also the emergence of new risk factors (e.g. AIDS, designer drugs).

Appendix I: Classification of dementia

The International Classification of Diseases, tenth revision (ICD-10),[15] provides the following classification of dementia.

Table 15: Classification of the dementias in ICD-10.

F00	Dementia in Alzheimer's disease (AD):
F00.0	Dementia in AD, with early onset
F00.1	Dementia in AD, with late onset
F00.2	Dementia in AD, atypical or mixed type
F00.9	Dementia in AD, unspecified
F01	Vascular dementia (VaD):
F01.0	VaD of acute onset
F01.1	Multi-infarct (predominantly cortical) dementia
F01.2	Subcortical VaD
F01.3	Mixed cortical and subcortical VaD
F01.8	VaD, other
F01.9	VaD, unspecified
F02	Dementia in diseases classified elsewhere:
F02.0	Dementia in Pick's disease
F02.1	Dementia in Creutzfeldt–Jakob disease
F02.2	Dementia in Huntington's disease
F02.3	Dementia in Parkinson's disease
F02.4	Dementia in human immunodeficiency virus (HIV) disease
F02.8	Dementia in other diseases classified elsewhere
F03	Unspecified dementia.

Appendix II: Search strategies and terms

The previous edition of this chapter was based on searches of the literature published up to the early 1990s. For this update the following databases have been searched:

- MEDLINE and Embase databases for the years 1987–97 for English-language papers
- the Cochrane database of trials, with related databases (Dare, ACP)
- NHS R&D database
- HSTAT (National Library of Medicine, Health Services/Technology Assessment Text)
- other guidelines – identified through TRIP and other sources.

For the MEDLINE and Embase searches, the terms 'dementia' and 'Alzheimer's disease' were used. For specific topic areas, the additional search terms used are stated. Searches were carried out looking for RCTs, controlled trials and review literature. Citation searches were conducted on key papers so discovered, and within each topic area, citation searches were also carried out on the names of key authors. The bibliographies of retrieved papers were searched and any additional references obtained. The Cochrane database of systematic reviews was searched for relevant reviews.

Internet sites relating to dementia or care of the elderly identified through the TRIP site were searched for additional relevant material. These included the National Institute on Aging, the US Agency for Health Care Policy and Research, Age Concern, the Alzheimer's Disease Society, the Royal College of Psychiatrists and the Department of Health. Lastly, experts in the field were consulted for their knowledge of additional work.

For all searches, the terms dementia and Alzheimer's disease were used. Additional search terms for specific therapies were as follows:

- diagnosis and assessment: diagnosis, assessment, recognition
- cholinesterase inhibitors: drug therapy, cholinesterase inhibitors, anticholinesterase, donepezil, Tacrine, meta-analysis, randomised controlled trials
- non-drug treatments for behavioural problems in dementia: therapy, behaviour therapy, cognitive therapy, reality orientation, reminiscence therapy, validation therapy, music therapy, psychotherapy, randomised controlled trial
- respite care and day care: respite care, day care, relief, controlled trial
- support groups, information and education, and individual counselling: support group, psychosocial intervention, information, education, counselling, therapy
- management of patients with dementia in the community: community team, community mental health team, community mental health services, community resource team, case management
- long-term settings: long-term care, nursing homes, residential homes, special care units.

References

1 Royal College of Psychiatrists. *Model Consultant Job Descriptions (OP39)*. London: Royal College of Psychiatrists, 1997.

2 Glover G, Knight B, Pearce L, Melzer D. The development of a new minimum data set for specialist mental health care. *Health Trends* 1998; **29**: 48–51.

3 Melzer D, Ely M, Brayne C. Cognitive impairment in elderly people: population-based estimates of the future in England, Scotland and Wales. *BMJ* 1997; **315**: 462.

4 Cohen-Mansfield J, Reisberg B, Bonnema J *et al*. Staging methods for the assessment of dementia: perspectives. *J Clin Psychiatry* 1996; **57**: 190–8.

5 Twigg J. *Carers: research and practice*. London: HMSO, 1992.

6 O'Connor DW, Pollitt PA, Roth M, Brook CPB, Reiss BB. Problems reported by relatives in a community study of dementia. *Br J Psychiatry* 1990; **156**: 835–41.

7 Buck D, Gregson B, Bamford C, McNamee P, Farrow GBJ, Wright K. Psychological distress among informal supporters of frail elderly people at home and in institutions. *Int J Geriatr Psychiatry* 1997; **12**: 737–44.

8 Levin E, Moriarty J, Gorbach P. *Better for the Break* (National Institute of Social Work Research Unit). London: HMSO, 1994.

9 Philp I, McKee KJ, Meldrum P *et al*. Community care for demented and nondemented elderly people – a comparison study of financial burden, service use, and unmet needs in family supporters. *BMJ* 1995; **310**: 1503–6.

10 Fisk J. Abuse of the elderly. In: Jacoby R, Oppenheimer C (eds). *Psychiatry in the Elderly*. Oxford: Oxford University Press, 1998, pp. 736–48.

11 Barclay L, Zemcov A, Blass J, Sansone J. Survival in Alzheimer's disease and vascular dementia. *Neurology* 1985; **35**: 834–40.

12 Diesfeldt H, van Houte L, Moerkens R. Duration of survival in senile dementia. *Acta Psychiatr Scand* 1986; **73**: 366–71.

13 Burns A, Lewis G, Jacoby R, Levy R. Factors affecting survival in Alzheimer's disease. *Psychol Med* 1991; **21**: 363–70.

14 Kay DWK. The diagnosis and grading of dementia in population surveys – measuring disability. *Dementia* 1994; **5**: 289–94.

15 World Health Organization. *The ICD-10 Classification of Mental and Behavioural Disorders: clinical description and diagnostic guidelines*. Geneva: World Health Organization, 1992.

16 McKeith I, Perry R, Jabeen S *et al*. Operational criteria for senile dementia of Lewy body type (SDLT). *Psychol Med* 1992; **22**: 911–22.

17 Holland A, Hon J, Huppert F *et al*. Population-based study of the prevalence and presentation of dementia in adults with Down's syndrome. *Br J Psychiatry* 1998; **172**: 493–8.

18 Harvey R, Rossor M, Skelton-Robinson M, Garralda E. *Young-Onset Dementia: epidemiology, clinical symptoms, family burden, support and outcome*. London: Dementia Research Group, Imperial College School of Medicine, 1998.

19 NHS Health Advisory Service. *Mental Health Services: heading for better care – commissioning and providing mental health services for people with Huntington's disease, acquired brain injury and early-onset dementia*. London: HMSO, 1996.

20 Roth M, Huppert FA, Tym E, Mountjoy CQ. *CAMDEX: the Cambridge Examination for Mental Disorders of the Elderly*. Cambridge: Cambridge University Press, 1988.

21 Isaacs B, Neville Y. *The Measurement of Need in Old People*. Edinburgh: Scottish Home and Health Department, 1975.

22 Burns A, Jacoby R, Luthert P, Levy R. Cause of death in Alzheimer's disease. *Age Ageing* 1998; **19**: 341–4.

23 Hofman A, Rocca WA, Brayne C *et al.* The prevalence of dementia in Europe: a collaborative study of 1980–1990 findings. *Int J Epidemiol* 1991; **20**: 736–48.

24 American Psychiatric Association. *Diagnostic and Statistical Manual of Mental Disorders.* Washington, DC: American Psychiatric Association, 1994.

25 Medical Research Council Cognitive Function and Ageing Study (MRC CFAS). Cognitive function and dementia in six areas of England and Wales. *Psychol Med* 1998; **28**: 319–35.

26 Launer L, Andersen K, Dewey M *et al.* Rates and risk factors for incident dementia and Alzheimer's disease: results from EURODEM pooled analyses. *Neurology* 1999; **52**: 78–84.

27 Bond J, Carstairs V. *Services for the Elderly: a survey of the characteristics and needs of a population of 5,000,000 old people.* Scottish Home and Health Studies No 42. Edinburgh: Scottish Home and Health Department, 1982.

28 Ely M, Melzer D, Brayne C, Opit L. *The Cognitively Frail Elderly: estimating characteristics and needs for service in populations of people with cognitive disability, including dementia.* Report to the NHS Mental Health R&D programme. NHS Executive (Northern and Yorkshire Office), 1995 (unpublished).

29 Ely M, Melzer D, Opit L, Brayne C. Estimating the numbers and characteristics of elderly people with cognitive disability in local populations. *Res Policy Plan* 1997; **12**: 883–7.

30 Gordon D, Carter H, Scott S. Profiling the care needs of the population with dementia: a survey in central Scotland. *Int J Geriatr Psychiatry* 1997; **12**: 753–9.

31 Gordon D, Spiker P, Ballinger B, Gillies B, McWilliam N. A population needs assessment profile for dementia. *Int J Geriatr Psychiatry* 1997; **12**: 642–7.

32 Gordon D, Carter C, Scott S. *The Needs of Elderly People with Problems of Memory/Confusion: survey report.* Stirling: Department of Public Health Medicine, Forth Valley Health Board, 1995 (unpublished).

33 McWalter G, Toner H, McWalter A. A community needs assessment: the base needs assessment pack for dementia (CarenapD) – its development, reliability and validity. *Int J Geriatr Psychiatry* 1998; **13**: 16–22.

34 Phelan M, Slade M, Thornicroft G. The Camberwell Assessment of Need: validity and reliability of an instrument to assess the needs of people with severe mental illness. *Br J Psychiatry* 1995; **167**: 589–95.

35 Philp I. Can a medical and social assessment be combined? *J R Soc Med* 1997; **90**(Suppl. 32): 11–13.

36 Downs M. The role of general practice and the primary care team in dementia diagnosis and management. *Int J Geriatr Psychiatry* 1996; **11**: 937–42.

37 Philp I, Young J. Audit of support given to lay carers of the demented elderly by a primary care team. *J R Coll Gen Pract* 1988; **38**: 153–5.

38 O'Connor D, Pollitt P, Hyde J *et al.* Do general practitioners miss dementia in elderly patients? *BMJ* 1988; **297**: 1107–10.

39 Wolff LE, Woods JP, Reid J. Do general practitioners and old-age psychiatrists differ in their attitudes to dementia? *Int J Geriatr Psychiatry* 1995; **10**: 63–9.

40 Graham H. General practice and the elderly mentally ill. In: Jacoby R, Oppenheimer C (eds). *Psychiatry in the Elderly* (2e). Oxford: Oxford University Press, 1997, pp. 318–35.

41 Norman A. *Severe Dementia: the provision of long-stay care.* London: Centre for Policy on Ageing, 1987.

42 Vetter N, Jones D, Victor C. Effects of health visitors working with elderly patients in general practice: a randomised controlled trial. *BMJ* 1984; **288**: 369–72.

43 British Medical Association. *Taking Care of the Carers.* London: British Medical Association, 1998.

44 Strathdee G, Williams P. A survey of psychiatrists in primary care: the silent growth of a new service. *J R Coll Gen Pract* 1984; **34**: 615–18.

45 Royal College of General Practitioners. *Shared Care of Patients with Mental Health Problems.* Occasional Paper 60. London: Royal College of General Practitioners, 1993.

46 Department of Health. *Caring for People. Community care into the next decade and beyond.* London: HMSO, 1989.

47 Bradshaw M. Social work with older persons. In: Jacoby R, Oppenheimer C (eds). *Psychiatry in the Elderly* (2e). Oxford: Oxford University Press, 1997, pp. 217–31.

48 Wattis J. The state of the nation: the 1996 survey of old age psychiatry. *Old Age Psychiatrist* 1998; **11**: 1.

49 Jolley D, Arie T. Developments in psychogeriatric services. In: Arie T (ed.). *Recent Advances in Psychogeriatrics.* London: Churchill Livingstone, 1992.

50 Wright N, Lindesay J. A survey of memory clinics in the British Isles. *Int J Geriatr Psychiatry* 1995; **10**: 379–85.

51 Herzberg J. Can multidisciplinary teams carry out competent and safe psychogeriatric assessments in the community? *Int J Geriatr Psychiatry* 1995; **10**: 173–7.

52 Hettiarachy P. UK travelling day hospital. *Ageing Int* 1985; **12**: 10–11.

53 Dening T. Community psychiatry of old age – a UK perspective. *Int J Geriatr Psychiatry* 1992; **7**: 757–66.

54 Adams T. A descriptive study of the work of community psychiatric nurses with elderly demented people. *J Adv Nurs* 1996; **23**: 1177–84.

55 Hughes C, Summerfield L. Community psychiatric nursing for elderly people in the Derbyshire Dales: a census of case-loads. *J Clin Nurs* 1998; **2**: 149–52.

56 Junaid O, Bruce JM. Providing a community psychogeriatric service: models of community psychiatric nursing provision in a single health district. *Int J Geriatr Psychiatry* 1994; **9**: 715–20.

57 Mangen S, Griffith J. Community psychiatric nursing services in Britain: the need for policy and planning. *Int J Nurs Stud* 1982; **19**: 166.

58 Bowler C, Boyle A, Bramford M. Detection of psychiatric disorder in elderly medical inpatients. *Age Ageing* 1994; **23**: 307–11.

59 Cooper B. Psychiatric disorders among elderly patients admitted to hospital medical wards. *J R Soc Med* 1997; **80**: 13–16.

60 Feldman E, Mayou R, Hawton K. Psychiatric disorder in medical in-patients. *Q J Med* 1987; **214**: 405–12.

61 Johnston M, Wakeling A, Graham N, Stokes F. Cognitive impairment, emotional disorder and length of stay of elderly patients in a district general hospital. *J Med Psychol* 1987; **60**: 33–9.

62 Cooper B, Bickel H, Wincata J. Psychiatric disorders among elderly general hospital patients: frequency and long-term outcome (English summary). *Nervenarzt* 1993; **64**: 53–61.

63 Lindesay J. Recognition of cognitive impairment in elderly medical in-patients. *J R Soc Med* 1995; **88**: 183.

64 Holmes C, Cooper B, Levy R. Dementia known to mental health services: first findings of a case register for a defined elderly population. *Int J Geriatr Psychiatry* 1995; **10**: 875–81.

65 Severson M, Smith G, Tangalos E *et al.* Patterns and predictors of institutionalization in community-based dementia patients. *J Am Geriatr Soc* 1994; **42**: 181–5.

66 Welch H, Walsh J, Larson E. The cost of institutional care in Alzheimer's disease: nursing home and hospital use in a prospective cohort. *J Am Geriatr Soc* 1992; **40**: 221–4.

67 Harrington C, Pollock A. Decentralisation and privatisation of long-term care in the UK and USA. *Lancet* 1998; **351**: 805–8.

68 Wattis J. Geographical variations in the provision of psychiatric services for old people. *Age Ageing* 1998; **17**: 171–80.

69 Darton R. PSSRU survey of residential and nursing home care. In: Knapp M (ed.). *Mental Health Research Review*. Canterbury: Personal Social Services Research Unit, University of Kent, 1998, pp. 26–30.

70 Wattis JP, Fairbairn A. Towards a consensus on continuing care for older adults with psychiatric disorder – report of a meeting on 27 March 1995 at the Royal College of Psychiatrists. *Int J Geriatr Psychiatry* 1996; **11**: 163–8.

71 Booth T. *Home Truths: old people's homes and the outcome of care*. Aldershot: Gower, 1998.

72 Counsel and Care. *No Such Private Places*. London: Counsel and Care, 1991.

73 Social Services Inspectorate and Department of Health. *Inspecting for Quality: standards for the residential care of elderly people with mental disorders*. London: HMSO, 1993.

74 Tinker A. Housing for frail elderly people. *Public Health* 1992; **106**: 301–5.

75 Wing J, Beevor A, Curtis R *et al*. Health of the Nation outcome scales (HoNOS). Research and development. *Br J Psychiatry* 1998; **172**: 11–18.

76 Department of Health. *A Handbook on the Mental Health of Older People*. London: Department of Health, 1997.

77 Levin E. *Carers: problems, strains, and services*. Oxford: Oxford University Press, 1997, pp. 392–402.

78 Coope B, Ballard C, Saad K *et al*. The prevalence of depression in the carers of dementia sufferers. *Int J Geriatr Psychiatry* 1995; **10**: 237–42.

79 Livingston G, Manela M, Katona C. Cost of community care for older people. *Br J Psychiatry* 1997; **171**: 57–69.

80 Royal College of Psychiatrists and Royal College of Physicians. *The Care of Older People with Mental Illness: specialist services and medical training*. London: Royal College of Psychiatrists and Royal College of Physicians, 1998.

81 Royal College of Psychiatrists. *Annual Census of Psychiatric Staffing 1996*. Occasional Paper 38. London: Royal College of Psychiatrists, 1996.

82 Gray A, Fenn P. Alzheimer's disease: the burden of the illness in England. *Health Trends* 1993; **25**: 31–7.

83 Gray A. The economic impact of Alzheimer's disease. *Rev Contemp Pharmacother* 1995; **6**: 327–34.

84 Kavanagh S, Schneider J, Knapp M, Beecham J, Netten A. Elderly people with dementia: costs, effectiveness and balance of care. In: Knapp M (ed.). *The Economic Evaluation of Mental Health Care*. Aldershot: Arena, 1996, pp. 125–56.

85 Knapp M, Wilkinson D, Wigglesworth R. The economic consequence of Alzheimer's disease in the context of new drug developments. *Int J Geriatr Psychiatry* 1998; **13**: 531–43.

86 Department of Health. *NHS Responsibilities for Meeting Continuing Care Needs*. London: Department of Health, Health Committee Minutes of Evidence. 1995, p. 18.

87 Laing and Buisson. *Care of Elderly People-Market Survey* (8e). London, 1995.

88 Royal Commission on Long-Term Care. *With Respect to Old Age: long-term care – rights and responsibilities*. London: The Stationery Office, 1999.

89 Hachinski V. Preventable senility: a call for action against the vascular dementias. *Lancet* 1992; **340**: 645–8.

90 Gentleman S, Graham D, Roberts G. Molecular pathology of head trauma: altered beta-APP metabolism and the aetiology of Alzheimer's disease. *Prog Brain Res* 1993; **96**: 237–46.

91 Lovestone S. Genetics consortiums can offer views facilitating best practice in Alzheimer's disease. *BMJ* 1998; **317**: 471.

92 Saunders AM, Hulette C, Welsh-Bohmer K *et al*. Specificity, sensitivity, and predictive value of apolipoprotein E genotyping for sporadic Alzheimer's disease. *Lancet* 1996; **348**: 90–3.

93 American College of Medical Genetics/American Society of Human Genetics Working Group. Statement on use of apolipoprotein E and Alzheimer's disease. *JAMA* 1998; **274**: 1627–9.

94 Agency for Health Care Policy and Research. *Early Alzheimer's Disease: recognition and assessment.* Guideline Overview No. 19. Silver Spring, MD: Agency for Health Care Policy and Research, 1992.

95 O'Connor D, Pollitt P, Hyde J *et al.* The progression of mild idiopathic dementia in a community population. *J Am Geriatr Soc* 1991; **39**: 246–51.

96 Cooper B, Bickel H, Schaufele M. Early development and progression of dementing illness in the elderly: a general practice-based study. *Psychol Med* 1996; **26**: 411–19.

97 Clarfield A. The reversible dementias: do they reverse? *Ann Intern Med* 1988; **109**: 476–86.

98 Royal College of Psychiatrists. *Consensus Statement on the Assessment and Investigation of an Elderly Person with Suspected Cognitive Impairment by a Specialist Old-Age Psychiatry Service* (Council Report CR 49). London: Royal College of Psychiatrists, 1995.

99 Small GW *et al.* Diagnosis and treatment of Alzheimer disease and related disorders – consensus statement of the American Association for Geriatric Psychiatry, the Alzheimer's Association and the American Geriatrics Society. *JAMA* 1997; **278**: 1363–71.

100 Folstein MF *et al.* 'Mini Mental State': a practical method for grading the cognitive state of patients for the clinician. *J Psychiatr Res* 1975; **12**: 189–98.

101 Qizilbash N, Birks J *et al.* for the Cochrane Collaboration Dementia and Cognitive Impairment Group. *The Efficacy of Tacrine in Alzheimer's Disease.* Oxford: The Cochrane Collaboration, 1997, pp. 1–18.

102 Davis KL *et al.* A double-blind, placebo-controlled multicentre study of Tacrine for Alzheimer's disease. *NEJM* 1992; **327**: 1253–9.

103 Forette F *et al.* A double-blind, placebo-controlled, enriched population study of Tacrine in patients with Alzheimer's disease. *Eur J Neurol* 1995; **2**: 229–38.

104 Foster NL *et al.* An enriched population double-blind, placebo-controlled, cross-over study of Tacrine and lecithin in Alzheimer's disease. *Dementia* 1996; **7**: 260–6.

105 Knapp MJ *et al.* A 30-week randomized controlled trial of high-dose Tacrine in patients with Alzheimer's disease. *JAMA* 1994; **271**: 985–91.

106 Wood PC, Castleden M. A double-blind, placebo-controlled, multicentre study of Tacrine for Alzheimer's disease. *Int J Geriatr Psychiatry* 1994; **9**: 649–54.

107 Rosen WG, Mohs RC, Davis KL. A new rating scale for Alzheimer's disease. *Am J Psychiatry* 1984; **141**: 1356–64.

108 Henke C, Burchmore M. The economic impact of Tacrine in the treatment of Alzheimer's disease. *Clin Ther* 1997; **19**: 330–45.

109 Development and Evaluation Committee. *Donepezil in the Treatment of Mild to Moderate Senile Dementia of the Alzheimer Type (SDAT).* Southampton: Wessex Institute of Public Health, 1997, pp. 1–30.

110 Donepezil for Alzheimer's disease? *Drug Ther Bull* 1997; **35**: 75–6.

111 Rogers SL *et al.* for the Donepezil Study Group. The efficacy and safety of donepezil in patients with Alzheimer's disease: results of a US multicentre, randomized, double-blind, placebo-controlled trial. *Dementia* 1996; **7**: 293–303.

112 Rogers SL *et al.* for the Donepezil Study Group. A 24-week, double-blind, placebo-controlled trial of donepezil in patients with Alzheimer's disease. *Neurology* 1998; **50**: 136–45.

113 Guy W. *ECDEU Assessment Manual for Psychopharmacology.* Rockville, MD: National Institute of Mental Health, 1976.

114 Burns A, Rossor M, Hecker J *et al.* for the International Donepezil Study Group. The effects of donepezil in Alzheimer's disease – results from a multi-national trial. *Dementia Geriatr Cogn Disord* 1999; **10**: 237–44.

115 Melzer D. The launch of a new drug for Alzheimer's disease: lessons for health care policy. *BMJ* 1998; **316**: 762–4.

116 Rogers S, Friedhoff L. Long-term efficacy and safety of donepezil in the treatment of Alzheimer's disease. *Eur Neuropsychopharmacol* 1998; **8**: 67–75.

117 Rösler M, Anand R, Cicin-Sain A *et al*. Efficacy and safety of rivastigmine in patients with Alzheimer's disease: international randomized controlled trial. *BMJ* 1999; **318**: 633–40.

118 Sano M *et al*. A controlled trial of selegiline, alpha-tocopherol, or both as treatment for Alzheimer's disease. *NEJM* 1997; **336**: 1216–22.

119 Le Bars PL *et al*. A placebo-controlled, double-blind, randomized trial of an extract of ginkgo biloba for dementia. *JAMA* 1997; **278**: 1327–32.

120 Oken BS, Storzbach DM, Kaye JA. The efficacy of ginkgo biloba on cognitive function in Alzheimer's disease. *Arch Neurol* 1998; **55**: 1409–15.

121 Schneider LS, Olin JT. Overview of clinical trials of Hydergine in dementia. *Arch Neurol* 1994; **51**: 787–98.

122 Schneider LS, Pollock VE, Lyness SA. A meta-analysis of controlled trials of neuroleptic treatment in dementia. *J Am Geriatr Soc* 1990; **38**: 553–63.

123 Schneider LS, Sobin PB. Non-neuroleptic medications in the management of agitation in Alzheimer's disease and other dementia: a selective review. *Int J Geriatr Psychiatry* 1991; **6**: 691–708.

124 Wiesel FA, Agenäs I, Allgulander C *et al*. *The Use of Neuroleptics (summary)*. Stockholm: Swedish Council on Technology Assessment in Health Care, 1997.

125 McShane R *et al*. Do neuroleptic drugs hasten cognitive decline in dementia? Prospective study with necropsy follow-up. *BMJ* 1997; **314**: 266–70.

126 Levenson R. *Drugs and Dementia*. London: Age Concern England, 1998.

127 Orrell M, Woods B. Tacrine and psychological therapies in dementia – no contest? *Int J Geriatr Psychiatry* 1996; **11**: 189–92.

128 Dröes RM. Psychosocial treatment for demented patients: overview of methods and effects. In: Miesen BML, Jones GMM (eds). *Care Giving in Dementia: research and applications*. London: Routledge, 1997, pp. 127–48.

129 Wilson B, Moffat N. *Clinical Management of Memory Problems*. London: Chapman and Hall, 1992.

130 Backman L. Memory training and memory improvements in Alzheimer's disease: rules and exceptions. *Acta Psychiatr Scand* 1992; **139**(Suppl.): 84–9.

131 Brodaty H, Gresham M. The effect of a training programme to reduce stress in carers of patients with dementia. *BMJ* 1989; **299**: 1375–9.

132 Teri L *et al*. Behavioural treatment of depression in dementia patients: a controlled clinical trial. *J Gerontol B Psychol Sci Soc Sci* 1997; **52B**: 159–66.

133 Thornton S, Brotchie J. Reminiscence: a critical review of the empirical literature. *Br J Clin Psychol* 1987; **26**: 93–111.

134 Baines S, Saxby P, Ehlert K. Reality orientation and reminiscence therapy: a controlled cross-over study of elderly confused people. *Br J Psychiatry* 1987; **151**: 222–31.

135 Head D, Portnoy S, Woods R. The impact of reminiscence groups in two different settings. *Int J Geriatr Psychiatry* 1990; **5**: 295–302.

136 Toseland RW *et al*. The impact of validation group therapy on nursing home residents with dementia. *J Appl Gerontol* 1997; **16**: 31–50.

137 Brotons M, Koger S, Pickett-Cooper P. Music and dementias: a review of literature. *J Music Ther* 1997; **34**: 204–45.

138 Achterberg I, Kok W, Salentijn C. 'Snoezelen': a new way of communicating with the severely demented elderly. In: Miesen BML, Jones GMM (eds). *Care Giving in Dementia: research and applications. Volume 2*. London: Routledge, 1999, pp. 119–26.

139 Holtkamp CC *et al*. Effect of snoezelen on the behaviour of the demented elderly. *Tijdschr Gerontol Geriatr* 1997; **28**: 124–8.

140 Bedford S, Melzer D *et al.* What becomes of people with dementia referred to community psychogeriatric teams? *Int J Geriatr Psychiatry* 1996; **11**: 1051–6.

141 Brown P, Challis D, Von Abendorff R. The work of a community mental health team for the elderly: referrals, caseloads, contact history and outcomes. *Int J Geriatr Psychiatry* 1996; **11**: 29–39.

142 Collington G, Macdonald A, Herzberg J *et al.* An evaluation of the multidisciplinary approach to psychiatric diagnosis in elderly people. *BMJ* 1993; **306**: 821–4.

143 Lindesay J, Herzberg J, Collinghan G, Macdonald A, Philpot M. Treatment decisions following assessment by multidisciplinary psychogeriatric teams. *Psychiatr Bull* 1996; **20**: 78–81.

144 Challis D *et al. Case Management in Social and Health Care.* Canterbury: Personal Social Services Research Unit, University of Kent, 1990.

145 Challis D *et al.* An evaluation of an alternative to long-stay hospital care for frail elderly patients: costs and effectiveness. *Age Ageing* 1991; **20**: 245–54.

146 Challis D *et al.* An evaluation of an alternative to long-stay hospital care for frail elderly patients: the model of care. *Age Ageing* 1991; **20**: 236–44.

147 Philpot M, Banerjee S. Mental health services for older people in London. In: Johnson S, Ramsay R, Thornicroft G *et al.* (eds). *London's Mental Health: the report for the King's Fund London Commission.* London: King's Fund, 1997, pp. 46–62.

148 Howard R. Day hospitals – the case in favour. *Int J Geriatr Psychiatry* 1994; **9**: 525–9.

149 Howard R. The place of day hospitals in old age psychiatry. *Curr Opin Psychiatry* 1995; **8**: 240–1.

150 Fasey C. The day hospital in old-age psychiatry – the case against. *Int J Geriatr Psychiatry* 1994; **9**: 519–23.

151 National Audit Office. *Health Service Day Hospital for Elderly People in England.* London: HMSO, 1994.

152 Boult C *et al.* A controlled trial of outpatient geriatric evaluation and management. *J Am Geriatr Soc* 1994; **42**: 465–70.

153 Toseland RW *et al.* Outpatient geriatric evaluation and management: results of a randomized trial. *Med Care* 1996; **34**: 624–40.

154 Flint AJ. Effects of respite care on patients with dementia and their caregivers. *Int Psychogeriatr* 1995; **7**: 505–17.

155 Burdz MP, Eaton WO, Bond JB. Effect of respite care on dementia and non-dementia patients and their caregivers. *Psychol Aging* 1988; **3**: 38–42.

156 Conlin MM *et al.* Reduction of caregiver stress by respite care: a pilot study. *South Med J* 1992; **85**: 1096–100.

157 Mohide EA *et al.* A randomized trial of family caregiver support in the home management of dementia. *J Am Geriatr Soc* 1990; **38**: 446–54.

158 Lawton MP, Brody EM, Saperstein AR. A controlled study of respite service for caregivers of Alzheimer's patients. *Gerontologist* 1989; **29**: 8–16.

159 Montgomery RJV, Borgatta EF. The effects of alternative support strategies on family caregiving. *Gerontologist* 1989; **29**: 457–64.

160 Kosloski K, Montgomery RJV. The effects of respite on caregivers of Alzheimer's patients: one-year evaluation of the Michigan Model Respite Programs. *J Appl Gerontol* 1993; **12**: 4–17.

161 Adler G *et al.* Institutional respite care: benefits and risks for dementia patients and caregivers. *Int Psychogeriatr* 1993; **5**: 67–77.

162 Larkin JP, Hopcroft BM. In-hospital respite as a moderator of caregiver stress. *Health Soc Work* 1993; **18**: 132–8.

163 Rai GS *et al.* Hazards for elderly people admitted for respite ('holiday admissions') and social care ('social admissions'). *BMJ* 1986; **292**: 240.

164 Brodaty H, Gresham M. Prescribing residential respite care for dementia – effects, side-effects, indications and dosage. *Int J Geriatr Psychiatry* 1992; **7**: 357–62.

165 Wimo A *et al.* Dementia day care and its effects on symptoms and institutionalisation – a controlled Swedish study. *Scand J Prim Health Care* 1993; **11**: 117–23.

166 Wells YD *et al.* Effects on care-givers of special day care programmes for dementia sufferers. *Aust N Z J Psychiatry* 1990; **24**: 82–90.

167 Gilleard CJ, Gilleard E, Whittick JE. Impact of psychogeriatric day hospital care on the patient's family. *Br J Psychiatry* 1994; **145**: 487–92.

168 Engedal K. Day care for demented patients in general nursing homes: effects on admissions to institutions and mental capacity. *Scand J Prim Health Care* 1989; **7**: 161–6.

169 Wimo A *et al.* Impact of day care on dementia patients – costs, well-being and relatives' views. *Fam Pract* 1990; **7**: 279–87.

170 Toseland RW, Rossiter CM. Group interventions to support family caregivers: a review and analysis. *Gerontologist* 1989; **29**: 438–48.

171 Knight BG, Lutzky SM, Macofskyurban F. A meta-analytic review of interventions for caregiver distress – recommendations for future research. *Gerontologist* 1993; **33**: 240–8.

172 Mittelman MS, Ferris SH *et al.* An intervention that delays institutionalization of Alzheimer's disease patients: treatment of spouse-caregivers. *Gerontologist* 1993; **33**: 730–40.

173 Mittelman MS, Ferris SH *et al.* A comprehensive support program: effect on depression in spouse-caregivers of AD patients. *Gerontologist* 1995; **35**: 792–802.

174 Mittelman MS, Ferris SH *et al.* A family intervention to delay nursing home placement of patients with Alzheimer's disease: a randomized controlled trial. *JAMA* 1996; **276**: 1725–31.

175 Brodaty H, McGilchrist C *et al.* Time until institutionalization and death in patients with dementia: role of caregiver training and risk factors. *Arch Neurol* 1993; **50**: 643–50.

176 Brodaty H, Gresham M, Luscombe G. The Prince Henry Hospital dementia caregivers' training programme. *Int J Geriatr Psychiatry* 1997; **12**: 183–92.

177 Hebert R, Leclerc G, Bravo G, Girouard D, Lefrancois R. Efficacy of a support group program for caregivers of demented patients in the community – a randomized controlled trial. *Arch Gerontol Geriatr* 1994; **18**: 1–14.

178 Hebert R *et al.* The impact of a support group programme for care-givers on the institutionalization of demented patients. *Arch Gerontol Geriatr* 1995; **20**: 129–34.

179 Sutcliffe C, Larner S. Counselling carers of the elderly at home: a preliminary study. *Br J Clin Psychol* 1988; **27**: 177–8.

180 Dellasega C. Coping with caregiving: stress management for caregivers of the elderly. *J Psychol Nurs* 1990; **28**: 15–22.

181 Toseland RW, Rossiter CM, Labrecque MS. The effectiveness of peer-led and professionally-led groups to support family caregivers. *Gerontologist* 1989; **29**: 465–71.

182 Toseland RW, Rossiter CM *et al.* Comparative effectiveness of individual and group interventions to support family caregivers. *Soc Work* 1990; **May**: 209–17.

183 Mountain G, Bowie P. The quality of long-term care for dementia: a survey of ward environments. *Int J Geriatr Psychiatry* 1995; **10**: 1029–35.

184 Booth T. *Home Truths: old people's homes and the outcome of care.* Aldershot: Gower, 1985.

185 Furniss L, Lloyd S, Burns A. Medication use in nursing homes for elderly people. *Int J Geriatr Psychiatry* 1998; **13**: 433–9.

186 Schneider J, Mann A, Netten A. *Residential Care for Elderly People: an exploratory study of quality measurement.* Mental Health Research Review No 4. Canterbury: Personal Social Services Research Unit, University of Kent, 1997.

187 Harrington C, Tompkins C, Curtis M, Grant L. Psychotropic drug use in long-term care facilities – a review of the literature. *Gerontologist* 1992; **32**: 822–33.

188 Bridges-Parlet S, Knopman D, Steffes S. Withdrawal of neuroleptic medications from institutionalised dementia patients: results of a double-blind, baseline treatment controlled pilot study. *J Geriatr Psychiatry Neurol* 1997; **10**: 119–26.

189 Ray WA, Taylor JA, Meador KG *et al.* Reducing antipsychotic drug use in nursing homes – a controlled trial of provider education. *Arch Intern Med* 1993; **153**: 713–21.

190 Schmidt I *et al.* The impact of regular multi-disciplinary team interventions in psychotropic prescribing in Swedish nursing homes. *J Am Geriatr Soc* 1998; **46**: 77–82.

191 Werner P *et al.* Effects of removal of physical restraints on psychotropic medication in the nursing home. *J Geriatr Drug Ther* 1994; **8**: 59–71.

192 Bond J, Gregson BA, Atkinson A. Measurement of outcomes within a multicentred randomised controlled trial in the evaluation of the experimental NHS nursing homes. *Age Ageing* 1989; **18**: 292–302.

193 Bowling A *et al.* A randomized controlled trial of nursing home and long-stay geriatric ward care for elderly people. *Age Ageing* 1991; **20**: 316–24.

194 Clark P, Bowling A. Quality of everyday life in long-stay institutions for the elderly: observational study of long-stay hospital and nursing home care. *Soc Sci Med* 1990; **30**: 1201–10.

195 Lindesay J *et al.* The Domus philosophy: a comparative evaluation of a new approach to residential care for the demented elderly. *Int J Geriatr Psychiatry* 1991; **6**: 727–36.

196 Beecham J, Cambridge P, Hallam A, Knapp M. The costs of Domus care. *Int J Geriatr Psychiatry* 1993; **8**: 827–31.

197 Department of Health. *NHS Responsibilities for Meeting Continuing Health Care Needs.* London: HMSO, 1995.

198 Volicer L, Collard A, Hurley A, Bishop C, Kern D, Karon S. Impact of special care unit for patients with advanced Alzheimer's disease on patients' discomfort and costs. *J Am Geriatr Soc* 1994; **42**: 597–603.

199 Maslow K. Current knowledge about special care units – findings of a study by the US Office of Technology Assessment. *Alzheimer Dis Assoc Disord* 1994; **8**: S14–40.

200 Maslow K. Special care units for persons with dementia – expected and observed effects on behavioral symptoms. *Alzheimer Dis Assoc Disord* 1994; **8**: 122–37.

201 Office of Technology Assessment. *Confused Minds, Burdened Families: finding help for people with Alzheimer's and other dementias.* Washington, DC: US Government Printing Office, 1990.

202 Phillips CD *et al.* Effects of residence in Alzheimer's disease special care units on functional outcomes. *JAMA* 1997; **278**: 1340–4.

203 Maslow K. Special care units for persons with dementia: expected and observed effects on behavioural symptoms. *Alzheimer Dis Assoc Disord* 1994; **8**: 122–37.

204 Kemper P. The evaluation of the long-term care demonstration. 10. Overview of findings. *Health Serv Res* 1988; **23**: 161–74.

205 Johnston D, Reifler B. Comprehensive care of older people with Alzheimer's disease. In: Calkins E, Boult C, Wagner E, Pacala J (eds). *New Ways to Care for Older People: building systems based on evidence.* New York: Springer, 1998, pp. 158–67.

206 Eccles M, Clarke J, Livingstone M, Freemantle N, Mason J. North of England Guidelines evidence-based guidelines development project: guideline for the primary care management of dementia. *BMJ* 1998; **317**: 802–9.

207 Wimo A, Jonsson B, Karlsson G, Winblad B. *Health Economics of Dementia.* Chichester: John Wiley & Sons, 1998.

208 Division of Mental Health and Prevention of Substance Abuse. *Psychiatry of the Elderly: a consensus statement*. Geneva: World Health Organization, 1996.

209 Murphy E. A more ambitious vision for residential long-term care. *Int J Geriatr Psychiatry* 1992; **7**: 851–2.

210 *The National Health Service and Community Care Act*. London: HMSO, 1990.

211 Murphy E. A clinical role in service development: what should geriatric psychiatrists do? *Int J Geriatr Psychiatry* 1994; **9**: 947–55.

212 Levin E, Sinclair I, Gorbach P. *Families, Services and Confusion in Old Age*. Aldershot: Gower, 1989.

213 Melzer D, Ely M, Brayne C. Local populations and service needs of people with moderate and severe cognitive impairment. *Int J Geriatr Psychiatry* 1997; **12**: 883–7.

214 Knight S, Hughes J, Challis D *et al*. Developments in mental health information systems. *PSSRU Ment Health Res Rev* 1998; **5**: 41–3.

215 Burns A, Beevor A, Lelliott P *et al*. Health of the Nation outcome scales for the elderly (HoNOS 65+). *Br J Psychiatry* 1999; **174**: 424–7.

216 Sanderson H, Anthony P, Mountney L. Health care resource groups – version 2. *Public Health Med* 1995; **17**: 349–54.

217 Bedford S, Melzer D. *NHS Research in Old Age Psychiatry*. Unpublished presentation to Section of Old Age Psychiatry April Conference, Royal College of Psychiatrists, 1997.

218 Clancy C, Cooper J. Outcomes and effectiveness research in Alzheimer's disease. *Alzheimer Dis Assoc Disord* 1997; **11**: 7–11.

219 Ramsay M, Winget C, Higginson I. Review – measures to determine the outcome of community services for people with dementia. *Age Ageing* 1995; **24**: 73–83.

220 Department of Health. *Better Services for Vulnerable People*. London: Department of Health, 1997.

221 Royal College of Physicians, Royal College of Nursing and British Geriatrics Society. *The Health and Care of Older People in Care Homes: a comprehensive interdisciplinary approach. Report of a Joint Working Party*. London: Royal College of Physicians, 2000.

222 Department of Health. *The National Plan for the New NHS. The Government's response to the Royal Commission on Long-Term Care*. London: The Stationery Office, 2000.

223 Harvey RJ. Health economic aspects of dementia drugs. *Dementia Bull* 2000; **February**: 1–4.

Acknowledgements

We thank the Medical Research Council Cognitive Function and Ageing Study management committee, as well as the respondents, RIS project team and fieldworkers for access to the data from that study. We also thank Dr Tom Dening for comments on earlier drafts and Brenda McWilliams for her careful work on the manuscript.

15 Alcohol Misuse

Christopher CH Cook

1 Summary

This chapter focuses on alcohol misuse, defined as the use of alcohol such as to damage or threaten to damage the health or social adjustment of the user, or those people directly affected by his or her drinking.

The main arguments presented are that:

- services should be planned with a maximum of integration between different agencies, and between different levels of care, preferably with a community alcohol team or substance misuse integration team playing a key integrative and facilitatory role
- service improvement should seek to improve the use, and training, of staff in existing service settings rather than invent new ad hoc arrangements
- primary care and generalist care should be the main settings for treatment, with specialist care skill necessary on occasions, but deployed selectively.

Statement of the problem

Alcohol misuse is a pervasive problem impinging on all sectors of health and social care. The planning context is described and mapped.

Sub-categories of alcohol misuse

For the purposes of this chapter a three-point classification will be used:

- Category I: excessive drinking without problems or dependence
- Category II: excessive drinking with problems but without dependence
- Category III: excessive drinking with the occurrence of both problems and dependence.

Additional and cross-cutting groups can be defined in relation to gender, ethnicity, age, handicaps, homelessness and 'significant others'.

Prevalence and incidence

Surveys suggest that:

- 30% of men and 15% of women may be classified as fulfilling criteria for Category I alcohol misuse
- during the course of 12 months, about 20% of men and 5% of women in the UK fulfil criteria for Category II alcohol misuse

- during the course of 12 months, about 8% of men and 2% of women in the UK fulfil criteria for Category III alcohol misuse.

Services available

The pervasiveness and the varied types and intensities of alcohol misuse have provoked an extraordinary array of service responses, including prevention, treatment and social services, with wide variations by area. This section maps the field and offers a framework for reviewing the baseline of provision at a district level.

Components focused on prevention include:

- health education in schools, workplace or targeted at general or special populations
- community local action on prevention, including intersectoral mechanisms.

Treatment interventions include counselling/psychotherapy, '12-step' programmes, detoxification and pharmacological treatments, as well as treatment or other help to address the problems arising from alcohol misuse. These may be provided in a variety of settings:

- statutory social services deal with many aspects of alcohol misuse in passing, notably in relation to child care and protection
- non-statutory general social services often deal with alcohol misuse as a complicating factor
- general practitioners (GPs) and primary health services constitute a highly important front line of engagement with alcohol misuse, but there are currently deficiencies in terms of the support and training offered to GPs to enable them to engage effectively in this work
- NHS general (non-psychiatric) hospital services
- NHS general district psychiatric services. Working in liaison with specialist alcohol services, these general services carry responsibility for up to 75% of the district case load generated by Category III misuse
- NHS inpatient alcoholism treatment services are an increasingly scarce component of local alcohol misuse service provision
- NHS community alcohol services (community alcoholism teams or substance misuse integration teams) have been developed as a vehicle for providing specialist support and shared care and training in relation to GP, generalist, NHS and voluntary sector provisions, and social work agencies
- specialist non-statutory agencies provide outreach, day-centre and hostel facilities for homeless drinkers, and have also developed counselling and information centres
- private hospitals are developing a capacity to offer relevant packages of district-level care
- alcohol misuse and the criminal justice system. Counselling and treatment liaison activities are being developed, mostly by the voluntary sector.

Effectiveness of services

Prevention

The most effective prevention is likely to come from central policies directed at pricing and control. Education may offer benefits in the long term as it influences the ground swell of public opinion. Local community initiatives, while commendable in terms of common sense, have been little tested.

Treatment of Category I alcohol misuse

Simple intervention in primary care and in general hospital settings is highly effective.

Treatment of Category II and III alcohol misuse

More does not always mean better, and research suggests that for many subjects less intensive, outpatient and shared-care responses may be as effective as intensive, inpatient and exclusively specialist care. Patients should, however, be matched individually to treatment, and for the more severely affected a more prolonged and intensive approach may be indicated.

Cost-effectiveness

Cost-effectiveness of prevention strategies

Evidence confirms the cost-effectiveness of central fiscal and control strategies. Failure to utilise these provisions in the public health interest will have a profound effect on district costs. There is a clear relationship between affordability and alcohol consumption. Health education is cheap but only moderately cost-effective, at least in the shorter term, while community action is cost-effective if it can be implemented successfully.

Interventions directed at Category I misuse

Simple advice provided by the GP or on hospital wards is highly cost-effective.

Interventions directed at Category II and III misuse

Failure to provide appropriate help constitutes an extremely costly policy; untreated alcoholics incur twice the health care costs of treated alcoholics. Relatively simple interventions are thought to be the first choice even for these categories of misuse in terms of cost-effectiveness, but that does not preclude the likelihood that for a troubled minority more intensive methods may be cost-effective. GP and outpatient approaches are more to be recommended than inpatient or residential voluntary agency approaches.

Models of care

Strategic options include:

- integration with drugs services or separate purchasing of alcohol services
- enhancement of effectiveness of existing services
- high-volume/low-intensity service provision
- low-volume/high-intensity service provision
- a comprehensive approach.

Building a planned, integrated and prioritised response requires at least three priorities to be addressed:

- a strategic review of existing services and needs
- establishment of a community alcohol service
- inter-agency integration and liaison.

Outcome measures

Separate outcome measures are required for different types of substance use. While multiple measures should be employed, reduction in drinking provides a good pointer to overall improvement. Local monitoring of alcohol-related deaths (liver cirrhosis, accidents) can provide useful pointers.

Targets

Targets are suggested in relation to overall reduction in alcohol misuse, enhancement of primary care and the effectiveness of generalist services and services for Category III patients.

Information and research priorities

The importance of creating a 'research culture' is stressed. Suggested priorities for research include evaluation of the effectiveness of:

- liaison teams
- service needs for the severely dependent alcohol misuser
- the respective and complementary roles of different providers
- the cost-effectiveness of the various approaches.

2 Introduction and statement of the problem

Alcohol misuse can be defined as the personal use of alcohol such as to threaten or damage the health or social adjustment of the user or those other persons directly affected by his or her drinking. This pragmatic and over-arching definition equally invites awareness of drinking over safe limits, alcohol-related problems and alcohol dependence.

Context

The context for understanding and responding to alcohol misuse in the UK is that of a society within which alcohol is freely available and acceptable, and in which only a minority of people choose not to drink alcohol at all (*see* Section 4). It is known that the degree of morbidity (social, physical and psychological) and mortality associated with alcohol use in a given population is correlated with the amount of alcohol consumed by that population. At an individual level, also, the risk of alcohol-related harm rises in direct proportion to the amount of alcohol consumed. Thus prevention (*see* Sections 5 and 6) has to address the per capita amount of alcohol consumed, as well as matters of individual variation in vulnerability to harm.

The problems arising from alcohol misuse are many and varied (*see* Figure 2 and Section 3). Social problems impact upon the family, workplace and wider society. They have implications for safety on the roads, law and order, and the economy. Health problems involve almost every aspect of medical practice and include the behavioural and traumatic consequences of intoxication, as well as acute alcoholic poisoning and the behavioural and medical consequences of chronic heavy drinking. Alcohol misuse is also commonly associated with other psychiatric disorders and with other forms of substance misuse.

A particular alcohol-related problem with especial significance for treatment and prognosis is that of alcohol dependence (*see* Section 3). Individuals who have become alcohol dependent will experience a physical withdrawal syndrome if they stop drinking. This withdrawal syndrome is associated with potentially serious medical complications, and thus requires appropriate medical management (*see* Sections 5 and 6). When dependence is severe, a different approach to treatment and rehabilitation is indicated (*see* Sections 5 and 6).

Alcohol misusers are not a discrete category of people different to, or separate from, 'normal' drinkers. Alcohol misuse and dependence represent the extreme end of a continuum of drinking behaviour, which may be contrasted strikingly with the behaviour and experiences of light social drinkers who are at the opposite end of the spectrum.

It is also important to note that alcohol consumption may have beneficial consequences as well as being associated with harm. In particular, there is now reason to believe that moderate alcohol consumption may be associated with a reduced incidence of coronary heart disease in men over the age of 40 years and in postmenopausal women.[1]

Prevention

It is quite obviously preferable to prevent alcohol misuse and thus minimise the need for treatment services. Furthermore, there is extensive research to underpin the value and effectiveness of preventative measures at a whole population level.[2] However, despite this, prevention is often neglected and health care resources are directed primarily towards treatment. This occurs for a variety of reasons.

First, as described above, the per capita quantity of alcohol consumed within the population is a fundamental consideration in respect of reducing alcohol misuse. Many of the controls that are effective in influencing per capita consumption are only available to national government. Thus, for example, we know that increased taxation is an effective preventative measure, but this is not available to NHS commissioners or providers.

Secondly, there is a great need for a co-ordinated national alcohol strategy to guide and inform local and national preventative measures, but at present such a strategy is still awaited.

Thirdly, as with treatment provision, there is a need to bring together a wide range of services in order to effectively prevent alcohol misuse. The criminal justice system, social services, local government, education and a range of non-statutory agencies, as well as health services, all have an important part to play. With no co-ordinating body to address prevention of alcohol misuse in many parts of the country it is easy for each organisation to imagine that prevention is the responsibility of the others.

Preventive interventions have also encountered controversy surrounding the 'sensible drinking' message. The Royal College of Physicians, the Royal College of Psychiatrists, the Royal College of General Practitioners and the British Medical Association (BMA) have all recommended that men should drink fewer than 21 units of alcohol per week and women fewer than 14 units per week.[1,3] Both women and men are also advised that it is probably sensible to ensure that they have 'drink-free days'. There has been some debate about the most appropriate drinking limits, with advice from the Department of Health (DoH) referring to increased morbidity and mortality associated with drinking 'more than 3 to 4 units a day' for men and 'more than 2 to 3 units a day' for women.[4] The weight of medical and scientific argument, which relates largely to the longer-term effects of drinking on morbidity and mortality, would appear to support the recommendations of the Royal Colleges and the BMA. However, there is undoubtedly also a need to promote sensible daily limits which seek to avoid the dangerous effects of acute heavy drinking sessions.

An integrated response

In view of the multi-disciplinary nature of the problem, a degree of integration in health and social service responses is increasingly necessary. The appropriate vision should be of an integrated, interactive, multi-level and sustained response system targeted at multiple types and degrees of problem. Figure 1 offers a diagrammatic representation of the 'response contexts', while Figure 2 gives a representation of the 'problem contexts'.

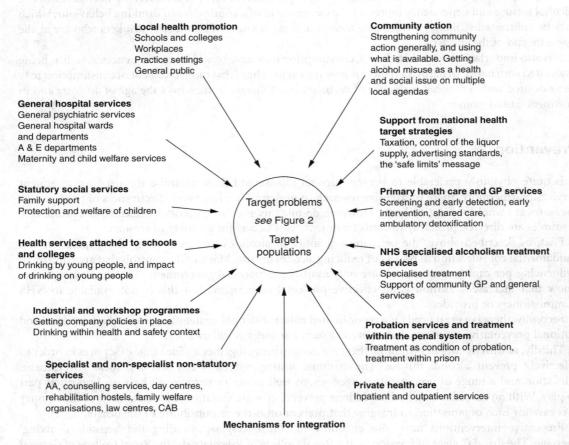

Local health promotion
Schools and colleges
Workplaces
Practice settings
General public

Community action
Strengthening community
action generally, and using
what is available. Getting
alcohol misuse as a health
and social issue on multiple
local agendas

General hospital services
General psychiatric services
General hospital wards
and departments
A & E departments
Maternity and child welfare services

**Support from national health
target strategies**
Taxation, control of the liquor
supply, advertising standards,
the 'safe limits' message

Statutory social services
Family support
Protection and welfare of children

Primary health care and GP services
Screening and early detection, early
intervention, shared care,
ambulatory detoxification

**Health services attached to schools
and colleges**
Drinking by young people, and impact
of drinking on young people

**NHS specialised alcoholism treatment
services**
Specialised treatment
Support of community GP and general
services

Industrial and workshop programmes
Getting company policies in place
Drinking within health and safety context

**Probation services and treatment
within the penal system**
Treatment as condition of probation,
treatment within prison

**Specialist and non-specialist non-statutory
services**
AA, counselling services, day centres,
rehabilitation hostels, family welfare
organisations, law centres, CAB

Private health care
Inpatient and outpatient services

Target problems
see Figure 2
Target
populations

Mechanisms for integration

Figure 1: Alcohol misuse: the response system context.

The definition of the central issue as alcohol misuse implies the integration and totality of primary care and generalist and specialist services. Such an integrated service would meet the needs of the different categories of patients.

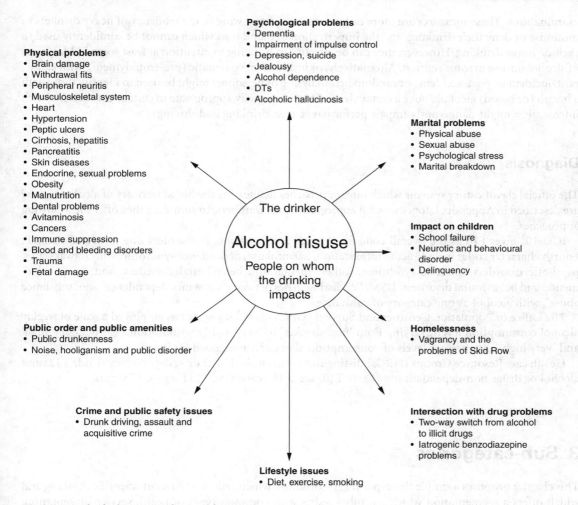

Psychological problems
- Dementia
- Impairment of impulse control
- Depression, suicide
- Jealousy
- Alcohol dependence
- DTs
- Alcoholic hallucinosis

Physical problems
- Brain damage
- Withdrawal fits
- Peripheral neuritis
- Musculoskeletal system
- Heart
- Hypertension
- Peptic ulcers
- Cirrhosis, hepatitis
- Pancreatitis
- Skin diseases
- Endocrine, sexual problems
- Obesity
- Malnutrition
- Dental problems
- Avitaminosis
- Cancers
- Immune suppression
- Blood and bleeding disorders
- Trauma
- Fetal damage

Marital problems
- Physical abuse
- Sexual abuse
- Psychological stress
- Marital breakdown

The drinker

Alcohol misuse

People on whom the drinking impacts

Impact on children
- School failure
- Neurotic and behavioural disorder
- Delinquency

Public order and public amenities
- Public drunkenness
- Noise, hooliganism and public disorder

Homelessness
- Vagrancy and the problems of Skid Row

Crime and public safety issues
- Drunk driving, assault and acquisitive crime

Intersection with drug problems
- Two-way switch from alcohol to illicit drugs
- Iatrogenic benzodiazepine problems

Lifestyle issues
- Diet, exercise, smoking

Figure 2: Alcohol misuse: the problem context.

Screening and identification

Identification of people with alcohol misuse occurs in all of the services shown in Figure 1, as well as in a range of other health and social services, and in wider society. Problems of alcohol misuse are frequently detected in the workplace and in the criminal justice system. However, the underlying 'diagnosis' of alcohol misuse is often missed, and individual problems may be addressed without identifying or responding to the underlying cause. There is thus a need for social workers, workers in primary health care settings, managers, police and others to be better trained and supported in identifying clients and patients who have an underlying alcohol problem.

In some contexts, systematic attempts to screen a population for individuals who are heavy drinkers or who are misusing alcohol may be justified. Thus in safety-sensitive industries (e.g. transportation, operation of dangerous equipment, armed forces, etc.) it may be helpful to include questions about drinking, and possibly blood tests, to identify heavy drinkers within the process of regular medical examinations. These measures are more or less unsatisfactory owing to the tendency of heavy drinkers to minimise or deny their drinking, and the imperfection of blood tests which cannot be confidently used to exclude heavy drinking. However, they can be effective in bringing to attention at least some hidden cases of alcohol misuse in some settings. Alternatively, or in addition, systematic (pre-employment, 'with cause', post-incident or post-accident) or random breathalysing of personnel might be used to identify those with a breath (or blood) alcohol above a certain level. This is especially appropriate in certain contexts in which intoxication might dangerously impair performance (e.g. drinking and driving).

Diagnosis

The official classificatory systems which offer approaches delineating the broad territory of alcohol misuse are described in Appendix I, together with appropriate code numbers. In summary they offer the following approaches.

ICD-10[5] gives F10 as the overall code for 'Mental and behavioural disorders due to use of alcohol'. Fourth character codes include acute intoxication, harmful use, dependence syndrome, withdrawal states, psychotic disorders, amnesic syndrome, 'other' mental and behavioural disorders, and 'unspecified' mental and behavioural disorders. DSM-IV[6] distinguishes between 'substance dependence' and 'substance abuse', with alcohol as one category of substance.

The Office of Population Censuses and Surveys (OPCS) in survey work has employed a scale of weekly alcohol consumption levels, varying from 'non-drinker' to 'very high' consumption. 'Fairly high', 'high' and 'very high' all represent levels of consumption above recommended limits.

Health care Resource Groups (HRGs) distinguish between alcohol or drug dependency (Code T12) and alcohol or drugs non-dependent use (Code T10, age > 16 years; Code T11, age < 17 years).

3 Sub-categories

This chapter proposes a simple three-point categorisation which reflects the recent scientific thinking and which offers a segmentation which usefully meshes with common types of health service presentation. Other categorisations will also be considered briefly.

Scientific consensus has moved towards a formulation which sees consumption, 'problems' and 'dependence' as three conceptually distinct dimensions of alcohol misuse. Each of these dimensions may vary in magnitude (consumption) or severity (problems/dependence). As indicated above (*see* Section 2) they are not independent of each other, but are strongly inter-correlated. Bearing in mind these relationships, the following categorisation is suggested as being helpful for the process of planning and delivering services.

Category I

Excessive drinking

Category I comprises anyone drinking over recommended limits (21 units/week for men or 14 units/week for women).[1,3] Strictly, for purposes of considering need for service provision, this should be limited to anyone who has not incurred problems or developed dependence. In practice, surveys of alcohol consumption often do not exclude those individuals with such problems. Typically, this kind of misuse falls within the province of primary health care as a target for health education and advice. It should also be picked up in many general hospital settings.

Category II

Excessive drinking with occurrence of problems

The problems may be acute (e.g. an alcohol-related accident, pancreatitis resulting from a Saturday-night binge, the Mallory–Weiss syndrome) or chronic (e.g. hypertension, cirrhosis, non-specific alcohol-induced brain damage). These problems will have to be dealt with partly by the primary care team, but they also contribute to the case load of the general hospital.

Category III

Excessive drinking with problems and dependence

Although problems and dependence are conceptually distinct, in clinical reality patients who have developed dependence usually also have alcohol-related problems. Patients with dependence typically present to psychiatric services or specialised non-statutory services for help with the dependence itself or because of a cluster of associated health, interpersonal and social problems. The physical complications which such patients sustain imply that they will also present to general hospitals. Furthermore, severely dependent patients may on withdrawal suffer from a range of complications, which at the extreme can include delirium tremens and alcohol withdrawal fits; these patients require medical detoxification.

Other classifications

For most planning purposes this three-point system meshes conveniently with the required developments at different levels of health promotion and health service response. On occasion, however, it may also be useful to think in terms of certain additional and cross-cutting categories.

Dual diagnosis

Considerable concern has been generated recently in relation to patients with comorbid psychiatric and substance use disorders. Given the special service requirements of this group, separate consideration may need to be given to alcohol misusers with and without other psychiatric disorders.

It has been suggested that alcohol misuse can be separated into 'primary' and 'secondary' categories, depending upon whether it is merely a secondary consequence of another psychiatric disorder. In practice, this distinction is often difficult, if not impossible, to make. It is unlikely to be a helpful categorisation as a basis of service delivery, although a judgement as to the 'primary' disorder, in a general sense of severity and need for treatment, may often determine whether a patient is primarily under the care of a general psychiatric team or a specialist alcohol service.

Misuse of multiple substances

The combination of alcohol and other substance misuse can pose particular therapeutic challenges. As with dual diagnosis, separate purchasing and/or provision of services to these two groups may require that special consideration be given to their needs as distinct from those of people who misuse alcohol alone.

Gender

As women and men with drinking problems can have different service needs, the needs of women should not be overlooked.

Ethnicity

Service provision for ethnic minorities may require special attention, especially when the cultural and religious background stigmatises (or indeed tolerates) drinking.

Age

The occurrence of drinking problems in old age should not be ignored, nor should the fact that drinking can be a problem among children of school age.

Disability

Blind people and the deaf can develop drinking problems, as can the mentally handicapped or people who have suffered brain damage.

Homelessness

In many inner-city areas a special category of problem arises in relation to the interacting difficulties caused by drinking, homelessness, public drunkenness and petty crime.

Significant others

Service users might be classified into those seeking help for their own drinking problem and those seeking help because of the drinking of a spouse, relative or friend.

Type I/II

A popular classification in academic and scientific work distinguishes between alcohol misusers with early onset, a family history of drinking problems and greater severity, who are usually male, contrasted with those of later onset, no family history and lesser severity, who may be male or female.[7] This classification is currently of little relevance to issues of service provision.

4 Prevalence and incidence

Category I alcohol misuse

General Household Survey data

The General Household Survey (GHS) has been conducted annually by the OPCS since 1971. The 1996 survey[8] shows that 27% of men and 14% of women aged 16 years and over are drinking more than the recommended weekly limits (*see* Table 1). GHS findings over the preceding decade show little overall change in the proportion of men drinking more than 21 units/week. However, the proportion of women drinking more than 14 units/week has risen from 10% to 14%.

Health Survey for England

The Health Survey for England (HSE) has been commissioned annually by the DoH since 1991. The 1996 survey[9] showed that 30% of men and 15% of women aged 16 years and over drank more than the recommended limits (*see* Table 1). HSE surveys from 1993 to 1996 show that there has been little change in the amount of alcohol consumed by men. The proportion of women drinking more than 14 units/week has risen slightly since 1993, from 13.3% to 15.3%.

Table 1: Alcohol consumption by sex, in the General Household Survey, 1996, and the Health Survey for England, 1996.

Alcohol consumption	Males (%)		Females (%)	
	GHS	HSE	GHS	HSE
Non-drinker	7	7	13	11
Very low	8	8	20	20
Low	35	33	37	37
Moderate	23	22	16	17
Fairly high	15	15	9	8
High	7	8	2	5
Very high	6	7	2	2

Base 100, rounding errors. GHS, General Household Survey 1996 (adults aged 18 years and over); HSE, Health Survey for England 1996 (adults aged 16 years and over).

Age and social class

Alcohol consumption in both sexes tends to decrease in later life, with a marked decline evident in those aged 65 years or more in both the GHS 1996 and HSE 1996. In both surveys, consumption is seen to be heaviest among young adults under the age of 25 years.

In the HSE 1996, women showed higher consumption in higher social classes, especially classes I and II. For men, consumption was higher in classes II and V, with no consistent overall pattern. A similar trend for women, and a similar lack of consistent pattern for men, was evident in the GHS 1996.

Geographical variation

There is wide variation in drinking patterns around the country (*see* Table 2). In North Thames, only 25% of men were drinking more than the recommended limits according to HSE 1996, but in the North West this figure rises to 35%.

Category II alcohol misuse

In the UK a number of surveys have reported on problem rates, but the results of such research are dependent on the geographical area and the year of sampling. Furthermore, different surveys have used different definitions. Prevalence will be highly dependent on whether one is measuring point prevalence or 12-month prevalence, the types of problem which the survey instrument includes in its 'problem' schedule, and the cut-off point for scale scoring.

In the National Psychiatric Morbidity Survey, conducted in the UK in 1993–94,[10] it was found that 12% of all adults had experienced an alcohol-related problem during a 12-month period. Alcohol problems become increasingly frequent with higher levels of alcohol consumption (*see* Table 3, p. 318).

Geographical variation and cirrhosis death rates

Cirrhosis deaths provide a useful indirect indicator of alcohol problem prevalence. Table 2 gives data on death by 'chronic liver disease and cirrhosis' by health region, for the year 1990. The evidence points to considerable geographical variation in problem prevalence, with areas containing conurbations likely to have higher prevalence rates than predominantly rural areas.

Geographical variation and drink-driving

Drink-driving provides another indicator of alcohol-related problems. As with alcohol-related liver disease, there is considerable geographical variation (*see* Table 4, p. 319).

Hospital Episode Statistics 1995–96

Tables 5, 6 and 7 (pp. 320–24) show data from the Hospital Episode Statistics for 1995–96. It is not possible to determine from these data whether a particular episode was associated with alcohol dependence, and hence we may assume that many of these admissions will in fact belong appropriately to Category III alcohol misuse, rather than Category II.

A primary diagnosis of alcohol misuse (F10) is given in respect of over 30 000 NHS admissions per year (Table 5, p. 320). A further 9000 admissions relate to alcoholic liver disease. Over 17 000 NHS admissions are to psychiatric beds and over 22 000 admissions are to medical beds (Table 6, p. 321). On average, general medical admissions for alcohol-related diagnoses are three times longer than for other general medical admissions. When the statistics are viewed according to HRGs (Table 7, pp. 322–24), we may see that almost 9000 admissions are specifically for non-dependent use of alcohol and almost 6000 relate to chronic liver disorders.

Table 2: Alcohol consumption, deaths by chronic liver disease and cirrhosis, and alcohol dependence, by health region.

| | Health region | Proportion drinking over recommended weekly limits | | Deaths due to all chronic liver disease and cirrhosis (ICD 571)* | Deaths due to alcohol-related liver disease (ICD 571.0–571.3)* | Alcohol dependence† |
		HSE (%)	GHS (%)	Rate/100,000	Rate/100,000	Rate/1,000
Males	North and Yorkshire	34	32	10.5	7.3	75
	Trent	31	27	8.7	5.3	55
	Anglia and Oxon	27	25	6.4	3.7	51
	North Thames	25	23	9.5	3.4	79
	South Thames	27	27	9.7	5.5	68
	South and West	28	26	7.8	4.7	76
	West Midlands	31	28	9.5	6.9	67
	North West	35	31	13.2	8.3	105
	England	30	27	–	–	72
	Wales	–	25	9.7	5.5	99
	Scotland	–	25	–	–	87
Females	North and Yorkshire	17	15	6.4	1.3	24
	Trent	15	12	5.8	3.0	11
	Anglia and Oxon	12	15	5.1	2.6	18
	North Thames	14	11	5.7	2.4	24
	South Thames	18	14	5.9	2.5	19
	South and West	14	13	5.3	2.8	19
	West Midlands	14	12	6.2	3.6	32
	North West	19	18	8.2	4.1	18
	England	15	14	–	–	21
	Wales	–	16	6.8	2.9	21
	Scotland	–	11	–	–	20

GHS, General Household Survey 1996; HSE, Health Survey for England 1996.
* 1997 statistics supplied by ONS Mortality Statistics Section (personal communication, 1998).
† National Psychiatric Morbidity Survey 1993–94. In this survey, figures were quoted for smaller regions (e.g. the figures for Northern and Yorkshire were given separately). The figures given here are for the average of the smaller groups.

Table 3: Alcohol problems (%) in the UK, 1993–94,* according to consumption level.†

Alcohol problem	Light	Moderate	Fairly heavy	Heavy	Very heavy	All
Belligerence	1	10	21	29	43	8
Health problems	0	2	6	14	26	3
Problems with friends	0	3	7	10	19	3
Problems with spouse	0	2	6	11	16	2
Problems with relatives	0	1	3	5	17	2
Police problems	0	2	3	5	12	2
Accidents	0	1	2	3	8	1
Job problems	–	0	2	2	0	0
Any alcohol problem	2	13	29	43	63	12

* National Psychiatric Morbidity Survey.
† These categories are broadly similar to those used by the OPCS (*see* Appendix I).

Alcohol misuse and other substance use

Some but not all of the regional drug misuse databases collect information on alcohol as well as illicit drugs. Data for 1996–97 are summarised in Table 8 (p. 325). It is apparent from these data that the prevalence of alcohol misuse among illicit drug users on the database ranges from about 4% to 18%. However, the information collected is variable in definition, so that for some databases the quoted prevalence might represent a closer approximation to Category I alcohol misuse, and in other cases the prevalence of Category II alcohol misuse might have been underestimated. Despite this, it is probably fair to suggest that the prevalence of alcohol misuse is generally high in this group.

Category III alcohol misuse

The 12-month prevalence for alcohol dependence in the UK, as measured in the National Psychiatric Morbidity Survey in 1993–94,[10] was 47 per 1000. Prevalence was higher in urban (54 per 1000) than in rural (34 per 1000) areas.[11] Geographical variation by health region is shown in Table 2.

Hospital Episode Statistics show that there were almost 22 000 admissions for alcohol dependence in 1995–96 (*see* Table 7). However, this (misleadingly named) HRG actually includes ICD-10 diagnoses which related to non-dependent use, and thus includes Category II as well as Category III alcohol misuse.

Local needs assessment prevalence studies

Detailed local information about the prevalence of alcohol misuse can be obtained by conducting a needs assessment study. Further information on when and how to conduct such a study is provided in Section 7.

Table 4: Positive alcohol breath tests of drivers by police force area, 1995–96.

Police force area	1995		1996	
	Positive/refused per 100,000 pop.	Positive/refused (%)	Positive/refused per 100,000 pop.	Positive/refused (%)
Avon and Somerset	89	19	205	20
Bedfordshire	147	14	202	17
Cambridgeshire	187	8	187	8
Cheshire	225	15	225	11
Cleveland	197	4	179	4
Cumbria	184	11	184	9
Derbyshire	146	7	188	6
Devon and Cornwall	123	29	130	22
Dorset	177	20	192	17
Durham	197	27	214	31
Essex	146	8	133	6
Gloucestershire	145	16	271	22
Greater Manchester	299	7	291	7
Hampshire	207	21	184	18
Hertfordshire	198	26	198	28
Humberside	169	17	124	14
Kent	103	17	97	18
Lancashire	182	16	224	12
Leicestershire	217	17	228	20
Lincolnshire	180	7	163	6
London, City of	–	16	–	16
Merseyside	175	16	182	17
Metropolitan	211	13	204	12
Norfolk	104	20	117	16
Northamptonshire	167	20	200	17
Northumbria	202	51	222	38
North Yorkshire	233	35	233	22
Nottinghamshire	233	43	262	29
South Yorkshire	153	18	161	16
Staffordshire	123	20	133	15
Suffolk	167	14	167	14
Surrey	193	16	206	15
Sussex	157	15	178	11
Thames Valley	274	12	274	14
Warwickshire	221	13	221	12
West Mercia	171	9	171	11
West Midlands	102	29	137	18
West Yorkshire	133	17	152	7
Wiltshire	254	15	220	21
Dyfed-Powys	148	15	169	14
Gwent	133	12	199	10
North Wales	258	12	258	12
South Wales	158	17	180	16
Total	182	13	194	13

Table 5: NHS Hospital Episode Statistics, 1995–96, for diagnostic categories including alcohol-related diagnoses.*

ICD code	Diagnosis	Admissions with primary diagnosis			Admissions with secondary diagnosis		
		Finished consultant episodes	Average length of stay†	Number of cases with length of stay > 100 days	Finished consultant episodes	Average length of stay	Number of cases with length of stay > 100 days
F10	Mental and behavioural disorders due to use of alcohol	30,427	9.2	263	40,574	5.9	183
G31	Other degenerative diseases of nervous system not elsewhere classified	189	12.8	2	258	14.4	3
G62	Other polyneuropathies	91	15	2	117	14.1	2
G72	Other myopathies	29	11.5	0	39	10.4	0
K29	Gastritis and duodenitis	869	2.4	0	257	5.2	372.2
K70	Alcoholic liver disease	8,933	9.2	14	7,944	7.9	11
K86	Other diseases of pancreas	1,098	6	4	355	7.5	1
T51	Toxic effect of alcohol	1,256	1.2	1	9,270	1.2	1
Y90	Evidence of alcohol involvement determined by blood alcohol level	0			196	2	0
Y91	Evidence of alcohol involvement determined by level of intoxication	0			657	2.2	1
Z50	Care involving use of rehabilitation procedures	1,125	10.7	1	1,223	13.4	10
Z71	Persons encountering health services for other counselling and medical advice not elsewhere classified	32	4.3	2	77	5	0
Z72	Problems related to lifestyle	69	6	0	3,497	5.3	5

* *See* Appendix I for a list of alcohol-related ICD diagnoses.
† For calculation of means, lengths of stay > 100 days were all 'trimmed' to 100 days' length. Day cases were counted as 0 days.

Table 6: NHS Hospital Episode Statistics, 1995–96, for admissions for alcohol-related diagnoses* by medical speciality.

Specialty	Finished consultant episodes for alcohol-related diagnosis (n)	Average length of stay† (days)	Number of cases with length of stay > 100 days (n)	Total finished consultant episodes (n)	Average length of stay (days)	Alcohol-related finished consultant episodes as proportion of total (%)	Ratio of average length of stay (alcohol related: total) ratio
Mental illness	16,534	13.8	933	33,776	14.7	49	0.9
Old age psychiatry	526	23.6	852	15,810	18.2	3.3	1.3
Other psychiatric specialties	15	31.2	9	66	23.4	22.7	1.3
General medicine	16,119	6.5	348	478,154	2.3	3.4	2.8
Gastroenterology	1,126	8.5	9	100,758	0.5	1.1	17
Geriatric medicine	1,325	10	1,304	86,796	13.3	1.5	0.8
Other medical specialties	3,465	2.3	182	105,049	3.3	3.3	0.7
Trauma and orthopaedics	199	1.4	169	90,899	12.5	0.2	0.1
Accident and Emergency	2,559	0.6	1	25,969	0.5	9.9	1.2
General surgery	1,623	5.4	343	507,484	2.8	0.3	1.9
Other surgical specialties	63	4.4	32	551,832	0.7	0	6.3
Other secondary care	134	6.8	44	303,534	2.1	0	3.2
Primary care	435	6.2	88	19,627	12.8	2.2	0.5

* *See* Appendix I for a list of alcohol-related ICD diagnoses.
† For calculation of means, lengths of stay > 100 days were all 'trimmed' to 100 days' length. Day cases were counted as 0 days.

5 Services available

The pervasiveness of alcohol misuse as a health and social problem has stimulated multiple and diverse health promotion, health service and social service responses at a district level. Much of the work is handled in passing by general services, but there are also elements of specialism. Non-statutory as well as statutory services are involved. Inter-sectoral issues arise in relation to the relevance to prevention of, say, police activity or liquor licensing. As already indicated in the descriptions of context given in Figures 1 and 2, a mapping of the total field of responses at the district level is likely to constitute a task of unusual complexity with uncertain boundaries. The account given in this section describes the general principles of prevention and treatment, and the main organisational elements in this web of activities.

Table 7: NHS Hospital Episode Statistics, 1995–96, for admissions for alcohol-related diagnoses,* by Health care Resource Group.†

HRG code	Health care Resource Group	Finished consultant episodes (alcohol-related)	Average length of stay‡	Number of episodes trimmed for length of stay >100 days	Total finished consultant episodes	Total average length of stay	Alcohol-related finished consultant episodes as proportion of total	Ratio of average length of stay (alcohol-related: total) ratio
		(n)	(days)	(n)	(n)	(days)	(%)	
A09	Peripheral nerve disorders, age >69 years or with complications	25	11.1	24	2,168	11.9	1.2	0.9
A10	Peripheral nerve disorders, age <70 years without complications	58	17.1	17	3,946	6.5	1.5	2.6
A11	Neuromuscular disorders	25	12.1	12	1,697	8.1	1.5	1.5
A16	Cerebral degenerations, age >69 years or with complications	54	16.9	738	14,564	19.1	0.4	0.9
A17	Cerebral degenerations, age <70 years without complications	124	10.8	110	5,366	8.8	2.3	1.2
C54	Mouth/throat procedures – Cat 6	16	23.5	57	3,276	22.1	0.5	1.1
F04	Oesophagus – therapeutic endoscopy/internal procedures with complications	84	8.3	13	2,789	7.8	3	1.1
F05	Oesophagus – therapeutic endoscopy/internal procedures without complications	210	2.9	5	14,243	1.7	1.5	1.7
F06	Oesophagus – diagnostic procedures	435	0.2	0	217,414	0.01	0.2	20
F13	Stomach/duodenum – major procedures, age >49 years or with complications	12	12	12	5,849	11.3	0.2	1.1
F15	Stomach/duodenum – therapeutic endoscopy/internal procedures	18	0.1	0	3,200	0.1	0.6	1
F16	Stomach/duodenum – diagnostic procedures	129	0.3	0	133,584	0.01	0.1	30
F17	Stomach/duodenum disorders, age >69 years or with complications	123	4.7	41	27,502	7.3	0.4	0.6

Continued opposite

Table 7: Continued.

HRG code	Health care Resource Group	Finished consultant episodes (alcohol-related) (n)	Average length of stay‡ (days)	Number of episodes trimmed for length of stay > 100 days (n)	Total finished consultant episodes (n)	Total average length of stay (days)	Alcohol-related finished consultant episodes as proportion of total (%)	Ratio of average length of stay (alcohol-related: total) ratio
F18	Stomach/duodenum disorders, age < 70 years without complications	613	2.3	6	19,389	3.4	3.2	0.7
F35	Large intestine – endoscopy/internal procedures	14	0.2	0	129,510	0.1	0	2
F43	General abdominal – endoscopy/internal procedures, age > 69 years or with complications	43	8.6	3	5,661	6.9	0.8	1.2
F44	General abdominal – endoscopy/internal procedures, age < 70 years without complications	88	5.3	1	8,549	3	1	1.8
F45	General abdominal – diagnostic procedures	16	16.3	4	2,322	9.3	0.7	1.8
F61	Gastrointestinal bleed – very major procedures	40	11.2	4	2,100	12.3	1.9	0.9
F62	Gastrointestinal bleed – major/therapeutic endoscopic procedures	327	5	1	4,097	4	8	1.3
G01	Liver transplant	59	19.5	4	440	22.7	13.4	0.9
G03	Liver – very major procedures	124	13.6	1	1,298	8.2	9.6	1.7
G04	Liver – major procedures, age > 69 years or with complications	180	9.5	4	3,559	9.3	5.1	1
G05	Liver – major procedures, age < 70 years without complications	616	4.8	2	7,536	3	8.2	1.6
G07	Chronic liver disorders, age > 69 years or with complications	2,312	10.5	21	7,513	10	30.8	1.1
G08	Chronic liver disorders, age < 70 years without complications	3,284	8.8	4	6,906	7.1	47.6	1.2
G15	Therapeutic pancreatic/biliary procedures	28	12.4	4	14,021	5.7	0.2	2.2
G21	Pancreas – complex procedures	24	22.1	10	737	23	3.3	1

Continued overleaf

Table 7: Continued.

HRG code	Health care Resource Group	Finished consultant episodes (alcohol-related)	Average length of stay‡	Number of episodes trimmed for length of stay > 100 days	Total finished consultant episodes	Total average length of stay	Alcohol-related finished consultant episodes as proportion of total	Ratio of average length of stay (alcohol-related: total) ratio
		(n)	(days)	(n)	(n)	(days)	(%)	
G24	Chronic pancreatic disorders, age > 69 years	117	7.3	6	3,251	9.3	3.6	0.8
G25	Chronic pancreatic disorders, age < 70 years	774	5.1	0	3,714	5.7	20.8	0.9
G99	Complex elderly with a hepato-biliary/ pancreatic system procedure	14	10.2	2	400	13.2	3.5	0.8
J12	Soft tissue procedures	889	15.7	7	4,119	13.4	21.6	1.2
J37	Minor skin procedures – Cat 1 without complications	37	0.02	4	88,191	0.3	0	0.1
L20	Bladder minor endoscopic procedure with complications	13	15.7	65	20,043	3.7	0.1	4.2
L21	Bladder minor endoscopic procedure without complications	10	13.2	19	173,735	0.4	0	33
P14	Ingestion poison/ allergies	611	0.7	0	20,391	1.1	3	0.6
Q07	Miscellaneous internal/minor vascular procedures	22	14.7	16	7,520	5.7	0.3	2.6
S16	Poison toxic effects/ overdoses	599	1.6	28	79,038	1.7	0.8	0.9
S22	Planned procedures not carried out	72	2.4	8	57,435	0.9	0.1	2.7
S24	Holiday relief care	38	8.7	276	44,788	12.8	0.1	0.7
S25	Other admissions	83	5.5	536	62,959	6.9	0.1	0.8
T08	Presenile dementia	298	26.3	221	1,940	22	15.4	1.2
T11	Alcohol/drugs non-dependent use, age < 17 years	8,683	3.3	18	9,664	4	89.8	0.8
T12	Alcohol/drugs dependency	21,616	11.5	296	28,676	12	75.4	1
U01	Invalid primary diagnosis	251	13.1	102	2,124	15.2	11.8	0.9
U02	Invalid dominant procedure	649	7.5	449	83,721	6	0.8	1.3
U04	Age outside range 0–130 years	50	8.2	179	3,114	17.7	1.6	0.5
U08	Poorly coded dominant procedure	39	14.8	18	6,194	9.2	0.6	1.6

* *See* Appendix I for a list of alcohol-related ICD diagnoses.

† Only HRGs with 10 or more alcohol-related admissions for the year in question have been included in this table.

‡ For calculation of means, lengths of stay > 100 days were all 'trimmed' to 100 days' length. Day cases were counted as 0 days.

Table 8: Prevalence of alcohol misuse among drug users listed on regional drug misuse databases in the UK, 1996–97.

Database	Database includes secondary* alcohol (mis)use	Database includes primary† alcohol (mis)use	Prevalence of alcohol (mis)use (%)	Total drug users on database (n)	Prevalence of alcohol misuse amongst new drug users on the database (%)	Total new drug users on database (n)
Anglia and Oxford	Yes	No	12	4,285	–	–
Mersey	Yes	No	3.7	2,899	–	–
North West	Yes	No	6	7,897	–	–
Northern and Yorkshire	Yes	Yes	3.2 (secondary) 31.4 (primary)	14,623	–	–
North Thames	Yes	No	18	7,451	18.1	4,697
South Thames (West)	Yes	Yes	15.6 (secondary) 43.7 (primary)	5,930		
South Thames (East)	Yes	No	11.5	5,012	12.6	3,384
Trent	No	No	–	–	–	–
West Midlands	Yes	No	8.3	4,625	–	–
South West	Yes	Yes	7.7 (secondary) 2.4 (primary)	9,771	–	–
Welsh	Yes‡	Yes	29.5 (primary and secondary)	2,752	21.8 (primary)	1,808
Scottish	Yes	No	–	–	11.7	7,507

* Secondary alcohol (mis)use refers to use/misuse of alcohol among those subjects entered in the database primarily by virtue of their illicit drug misuse.
† Primary alcohol (mis)use refers to subjects for whom alcohol misuse is considered to be the primary problem and for whom secondary illicit drug misuse may or may not be a problem.
‡ It is not possible to discriminate between primary and secondary alcohol misuse, however, for the database as a whole. The overall prevalence is therefore for primary and secondary alcohol (mis)use.

In addition to the 'provider' services themselves, there are important sources of advice and information available to purchasers and providers of services. In particular, purchasers of services for alcohol misuse should be aware of the following.

Alcohol Concern (32–36 Loman Street, London SE1 0EE; Tel 020 7928 7377; Fax 020 7928 4644; www.alcoholconcern.org.uk) is the national agency on alcohol misuse in England and Wales. It works to reduce the costs of alcohol misuse and to develop the range and quality of helping services available to problem drinkers and their families. Since it began work in 1984 it has built up expertise on a wide range of alcohol-related issues. It uses this expertise to influence and support health and social policies both nationally and locally. Its services are available to purchasers, providers and others.

The Alcohol Harm Reduction Strategy for England was published by the Prime Minister's Strategy Unit in March 2004 (www.strategy.gov.uk/files/pdf/a104su.pdf). It sets out the Government's strategy for tackling the harms and costs of alcohol misuse in England. It will become a key feature of the public health policy.

Prevention

Alcohol policy and prevention of alcohol misuse

A broad range of policy issues is relevant to the prevention of alcohol misuse. In particular, taxation, licensing laws, minimum legal drinking age, drink-driving laws, workplace alcohol policy, by-laws governing drinking in public places and advertising all have an important part to play. Social and cultural attitudes towards drinking and drunkenness are also highly influential, although less readily open to manipulation by means of policy. The remainder of this section will focus on those preventative interventions which are most relevant to local community action.

Health education

Health education on drinking and alcohol misuse is likely to be provided through a number of different outlets.

Schools

The National Curriculum[12] specifies that children should be taught about alcohol, in the context of drug education, in school. The content of teaching includes:

- Key Stage 1 (5–7 years): the role of drugs as medicines
- Key Stage 2 (7–11 years): that tobacco, alcohol and other drugs can have harmful effects
- Key Stage 3 (11–14 years): that the abuse of alcohol, solvents, tobacco and other drugs affects health
- Key Stage 4 (14–16 years): the effects of solvents, tobacco, alcohol and other drugs on body functions.

The requirements of the National Curriculum may be supplemented by input from outside speakers (e.g. local health promotion officer, community police officer, etc.), but this should not detract from the responsibility of teachers to provide drugs education themselves. The objectives of such input should be considered carefully and the suitability of the outside speaker should be assessed carefully.

Health Promotion Unit

These departments function in supporting various types of community-directed educational work through, for example, schools, GP services and workplace programmes. They may provide information and resources, training and consultancy/advice for other agencies. They also support local focused projects and programmes, which can usefully include alcohol-related matters. There is a great need for more work of this type to continue over a longer period. In some areas they may have more of a role in influencing commissioning than in direct service provision.

Local Community Health Council (CHC)

With their direct access to the community, such councils played a role in the provision of educational pamphlets and in pointing individual callers or families toward help. CHCs have recently been abolished.

Health Education Materials

Background support and materials for local educational activities used to be available from the Health Education Authority (HEA). Relevant HEA leaflets intended for the public include 'Drinking for two', 'Say when . . . How much is too much?' and 'Think about drink'. The HEA was replaced by the Health Development Agency (HDA) in April 2000. The HDA have produced a review of interventions for tackling alcohol misuse. Other resources can be found on HealthPromis, the national public health database for England (http://healthpromis.hda-online.org.uk). Alcohol Concern also produce materials for health professionals, educators and others.

As well as aiming at primary prevention, health education may also be targeted at encouraging alcohol misusers earlier into treatment by self-referral. A media campaign in the North-East demonstrated that such an initiative could (at least in the short term) increase self-referral rates. Before launching a campaign of this type it would indeed be wise to ensure that the relevant services had the capacity to deal with the increased case load that may be stimulated.

Community action on prevention

Many opportunities exist for local action at a community (non-NHS) level, directed at the prevention or amelioration of alcohol misuse or specific types of alcohol-related problem.[13] Examples include:

- the use of existing licensing provisions for public houses in the health interest rather than letting decisions be directed entirely by trade interests
- mobilisation of police activity in preventing under-age drinking
- alerting housing departments to the fact that non-payment of rent can be indicative of a drinking problem
- enhancing opportunities for using personal health insurance examinations as a stimulus toward help with drinking
- local inter-agency community safety groups which bring together council, police, probation, social services, education, health, church, commerce and other agencies to address a broad range of safety issues, within which alcohol-related crime is likely to be one of the priority concerns
- police encouragement to put into effect law on not serving drunk clients.

The ability of any district, in an imaginative and purposive fashion, to 'make use of what is there' does, however, depend on leadership and on mechanisms for integration which, at present, are too seldom in place.

Treatment of Category I alcohol misuse

Category I alcohol misuse is treated in the community (*see* below) by means of brief counselling and health education. Given that Category I drinking is, by definition, not yet associated with problems or dependence, it is also the focus of the preventative interventions described above.

Treatment of Category II and III alcohol misuse

Category II and III alcohol misuse is currently managed by a range of interventions, from brief counselling through to extended residential rehabilitation. In particular, the following approaches are commonly utilised (for more details, *see* Edwards *et al.*[73]).

Counselling or psychotherapy

These may take a variety of forms. Currently, cognitive-behavioural forms of psychotherapy are particularly popular, with motivational interviewing and relapse prevention being widely employed. Counselling and psychotherapy may be offered on an individual basis or in a group setting, and in some facilities there may be provision for family or marital therapy.

12-Step groups and programmes

Alcoholics Anonymous or 'AA' (for 'alcoholics') and 'Al-Anon' (for families of 'alcoholics') operate a self-help programme based upon a philosophy enshrined in their '12 steps'. Many non-statutory treatment centres (and a few NHS units) now operate a programme based upon the 12 steps, which strongly encourage involvement in AA and working of the 'steps'.[14] Psychotherapeutic techniques used within these programmes tend to be eclectic, and are also offered on an individual or group basis, often with attention also being given to the needs of families.

Detoxification

Prescription of a benzodiazepine tranquilliser may be necessary to reduce the discomfort and complications of alcohol withdrawal. In more severe cases, injections of vitamin supplements and other medications may be necessary to reduce or prevent serious morbidity and mortality.

Pharmacological treatments

Two drugs are currently licensed in the UK to assist in the maintenance of abstinence from alcohol. Disulfiram is a deterrent drug which produces an unpleasant interaction with alcohol, thus discouraging a patient from further drinking. Acamprosate also acts to support abstinence from alcohol, by means of its action on brain neurotransmitters, possibly by effecting a reduction in 'craving' for alcohol. Acamprosate is only licensed for use in conjunction with psychological treatments.

Treatment providers and settings

There is a substantial overlap in treatment provision, with certain agencies tending to focus more on Category I or Category II/III alcohol misuse, but with an inevitable mixture of categories being addressed in any particular agency. Similarly, many agencies now operate in a variety of treatment settings. For example, an NHS community team may offer 'satellite' clinics in primary care and also provide a liaison service to medical and surgical teams in a district general hospital, as well as operating clinics from its own premises. However, it is useful to consider here the main agencies/settings in which treatment is offered.

A detailed and comprehensive national quantification of alcohol services in the UK is not centrally available. However, Alcohol Concern publish an *Alcohol Services Directory*[15] biannually, and they regularly invite service providers (on a voluntary basis) to update the information that they hold. A summary of this information is shown according to type of service provider and type of service in Table 9. The information is summarised according to geographical region in Table 10.

On 4 December 1996, the first national census of UK alcohol treatment agencies was conducted.[16] On that day, 302 alcohol agencies (41% of the total) completed census forms on every person to whom they provided a service relating to problem alcohol use. Data were provided for 3990 people, based upon which it has been estimated that, across the UK, 10 000 people per day are receiving help with a drinking problem. Of these, 7% are seeking help concerning a relative or a friend with a drinking problem. Based upon the

Table 9: UK alcohol services in 1997 by type of service and provider.

	Advice and counselling services	Community alcohol teams	Residential services	Others	Total (%)
Non-profit/charity/voluntary	197	3	137	5	342 (63)
Statutory	62	50	28	4	144 (27)
Private	3	0	44	5	49 (9)
Partnership	5	2	2		9 (2)
Total (%)	267 (49)	55 (10)	211 (39)	14 (3)	544 (100)

Table 10: UK alcohol services in 1997 by region.

Region	Non-residential services (*n*)	Number/million of population	Residential services
North	32	10.5	12
Yorkshire and Humberside	29	5.7	13
North West	38	5.9	18
East Midlands	16	3.9	13
West Midlands	26	4.9	6
East Anglia	11	5.1	3
Greater London	77	10.9	48
South East (excl. London)	56	5.1	48
South West	23	4.7	32
Wales	30	10.3	10

Table 11: Main type of service received by users of UK alcohol services.

Main service received	Users (%)
Individual counselling/therapy	39
Residential rehabilitation	15
Group work	13
Detoxification	7
Assessment	6
Telephone counselling	6
Day care	5
Initial referral	5
Day programme	4

Figures taken from *First National Census of UK Alcohol Treatment Agencies.*[16]

census data, it has been possible to calculate the extent to which the main types of service were being offered by alcohol agencies on census day (*see* Table 11). Over half the clients/patients were receiving counselling/therapy on an individual or group basis in the community. A further 15% were in residential rehabilitation.

Statutory social services

A report by the Social Services Inspectorate discussed the role of social workers in dealing with drinking problems.[17] Current types of provision can be summarised as follows.

- Social services often deal with drinking problems only in passing, and as a complication affecting the main focus of the case.
- Authorities are aware of the potential importance of parental drinking in relation to child protection, and drinking is also seen as an issue which can complicate the problems and needs of the elderly.
- A minority of social work departments have appointed a specialist worker.
- Most departments do not see referral to them of a single person with a drinking problem as appropriate.

Social work training in this area is not well developed, and there are many other demands on time and resources. Dealing with drinking problems is, however, an inevitable if insufficiently recognised part of the social work job.

Under community care legislation, local authorities also have a duty to provide assessment for suitability for residential rehabilitation for alcohol misuse (*see* below).

Social services are now also often working closely with primary care trusts in the commissioning of services, and joint finance is often used to fund services with a joint health and social service relevance.

Non-statutory general social services

These organisations also encounter the problems set by alcohol misuse. While the problem drinker will no doubt often be dealt with wisely on the basis of much experience, and with appropriate referral to other agencies if needed, adequate training is rare. Some of the facilities particularly likely to encounter alcohol misuse include:

- those dealing with homeless people (including homeless young people)
- youth organisations in general
- legal advice centres
- organisations offering family and marital counselling
- ex-service welfare organisations.

GP and primary health care services

Primary health care services provide a highly important front line for dealing with alcohol misuse, as recognised by the Royal College of General Practitioners.[18] These services hold the major responsibility for screening, diagnosis and early intervention directed at excessive drinking and early problems. They also carry shared-care responsibilities for dealing with alcohol-related problems and alcohol dependence, the continuing care of the chronic case and for dealing with family problems. The GP contract requires that enquiry into drinking should be made of all new patients, and there are also opportunities for alcohol-related health promotion within the primary care setting. Many practices now have access to counselling services, which may include specialist addiction counsellors with a role in prevention as well as early intervention for alcohol misuse.

Category III drinkers may receive detoxification, management of medical complications and prescribing of medication in primary care. However, they are also the group which is most often referred by GPs to specialist services.[19]

Previous research evidence generally suggests that the gap between the ideal and reality of GP involvement has been wide. Although most patients over the course of a year contact their GP at least once, and although GPs see primary care as the proper setting for the detection of alcohol misuse, such problems are identified infrequently in practice. There is evidence that GPs see patients with alcohol misuse as a difficult group to work with, that they do not see themselves as adequately trained for this work, and that they lack both the confidence and adequate support which are necessary for such work.[20]

Where a specific service has responsibility for alcohol misuse, such as a community alcohol team (CAT) or substance misuse integration team (SMIT), it might play an important role in supporting and facilitating improved links with GPs. There is also evidence of a need for guidelines to assist GPs with the management of all categories of alcohol misuse,[19] and at least one such set of guidelines has now been published.[21]

NHS general (non-psychiatric) hospital services

Hospital-wide responses to alcohol misuse

The majority of general hospitals lack systems to integrate relevant action on a hospital-wide base. A lead has, however, sometimes been taken by an interested department (public health medicine, for instance, or general practice) or by a specially committed consultant.

Joint clinics

Some joint medical/psychiatric clinics have been situated within a general hospital setting, which concentrate on liaison work and take referrals from all departments within the hospital.[22]

Screening and intervention on general hospital wards

A specially trained nurse can identify and counsel the many patients on general hospital wards who have been directly or indirectly hospitalised because of their alcohol misuse.[23]

Obstetric services

Despite evidence of significant levels of alcohol misuse among pregnant women, with possible risk to the health of the fetus, no programmes appear to have been developed in the UK specifically to target this population.

Accident and Emergency departments

As with maternity services, the prevalence of alcohol misuse among attenders at Accident and Emergency departments outruns treatment developments. The pressure on Accident and Emergency staff is such that any immediately presenting alcohol-related problems are likely to be dealt with (the intoxication, for example, or the broken bone), but the need to offer/arrange treatment for the underlying alcohol problem is ignored.

NHS general district psychiatric services

Even where specialist alcohol services have been established, it is unlikely that they will carry more than 25% of the overall case load of patients with alcohol dependence who are referred to psychiatric services.[24] Psychiatric admissions for alcohol dependency were 25 per 100 000 in 1986.[25] Alcohol misuse can exacerbate psychiatric problems in a variety of ways. It may destabilise community care plans for a chronic schizophrenic, it may render the depressed patient unresponsive to antidepressant medication or increase the risks of suicide, it may be a cause of dementia, and it can exacerbate anxiety and phobia. Care delivered to drinkers by the NHS general psychiatric services will usually be according to the care programme approach (CPA).[26] Alcohol misuse also intersects with the work of drug misuse clinics.

NHS inpatient alcohol services

In the mid to late 1980s, there were about 30 specialised alcoholism treatment centres in England and Wales,[27,28] with 520 beds and 34 consultants, i.e. about two consultants per region, or 0.2 per health district. Most units provide an eclectic and varied range of services, and emphasise liaison with other statutory and non-statutory services.

Principal service elements include:

- inpatient detoxification
- inpatient treatment, often employing behavioural and relapse prevention methods, within a therapeutic milieu
- liaison with community services.

The overall tendency among UK specialists in recent years has been to move towards outpatient rather than inpatient care,[29] not least on grounds of cost-effectiveness. Most of these units have developed liaison teams to work with GPs and generalists, which are discussed below.

NHS community alcohol services

Very few of those suffering from alcohol misuse are in contact with appropriate services. One study showed that as few as 10–20% were in contact with appropriate help over a 12-month period.[30] The then existing pattern for service provision was failing to make contact with the majority of patients in need. The Maudsley Alcoholism Pilot Project[31] developed the concept of the community alcohol team (CAT). The adoption of the CAT formula was subsequently commended in an official report on 'Patterns and Range of Services'[32] as a key strategy for strengthening service provision and facilitating the work of GP and generalist services. Stockwell and Clement[33] reviewed experiences with implementation of this initiative. More recent developments have extended the CAT concept beyond a single-substance team toward a SMIT which integrates liaison work across substances (alcohol, tobacco, illicit drugs, benzodiazepines).

Principal service elements include:

- outpatient/community detoxification
- outpatient treatment, often employing behavioural and relapse prevention methods
- provision of day-patient treatment within a therapeutic milieu
- introduction to Alcoholics Anonymous
- liaison with other community services
- referral where appropriate to hostels or 'dry houses' for longer-term rehabilitation.

Specialised non-statutory services

The non-statutory sector makes an important contribution to service provision for alcohol misuse. The organisations involved include:

- Alcoholics Anonymous, which offers 2900 meetings in England and Wales each week (an average of 190 per region and 15 per district)

- alcohol counselling services, which are usually run by local Councils on Alcoholism (no national data are available)
- organisations such as Turning Point and the Alcohol Recovery Project, which provide half-way house, therapeutic community, lodging, day centre, detoxification and shelter facilities, often concentrating on the needs of the homeless drinker or the drunkenness offender.

A report[34] published in 1992 showed around 100 registered voluntary sector establishments offering residential care for alcohol and drug users, and 300 counselling, information and educational agencies. A breakdown in terms of those working exclusively with alcohol or drugs or jointly across substances is not available. This same document provided guidance on the implications for these agencies of the 1990 NHS and Community Care Act. The type of patient or client who is being dealt with by such agencies will predominantly be in Category III (alcohol dependence), but alcohol counselling services may also deal with less advanced problems.

Under community care legislation, local authorities have a statutory responsibility to provide assessment for suitability for residential rehabilitation for alcohol misuse. By way of example, Kent County Council Social Services (which now excludes the Medway Towns) placed 37 people from West Kent Health Authority area (population approximately 725 000) and 32 people from East Kent Health Authority area (population approximately 575 000) in such facilities during a 12-month period in 1997–98.

Private health care organisations

Private health care companies are developing more comprehensive packages of district-level specialist services for alcohol misuse. Although often purchased to provide social rehabilitation under community care funding, they are also used by PCTs, often for extra-contractual referrals (ECRs).

Alcohol misuse and the criminal justice system

Alcohol misuse frequently leads to court appearances. The alcohol-relatedness of the offence is most obvious with public drunkenness or drunk-driving, but alcohol is often involved in many other offences. Non-statutory organisations have worked closely with the courts and probation service in an attempt to divert the repeated-drunkenness offender from prison towards rehabilitation. Partnership between specialist statutory alcohol agencies and the probation service has also been used as a means to promote sensible drinking among offenders.[35] Some experiments have been set up to provide treatment for the group of drunk-drivers who have an underlying drinking problem.

Under the Criminal Justice Act 1991, where a court is satisfied that an offender is dependent on alcohol, that his or her dependency caused or contributed to the offence in question, and that his or her dependency requires and may be susceptible to treatment, a probation order may be made to include a requirement that the offender shall submit to treatment for alcohol dependence. This should be 'under the direction of a person having the necessary qualifications or experience', and may be residential or non-residential.

Professional training

Basic training in most professions fails to impart the competence or confidence that staff require to deal effectively with alcohol misuse. University courses are available (e.g. at the University of London and University of Kent), mostly on a multi-disciplinary basis, at certificate, diploma and Masters level for the training of staff in the necessary skills for working as a specialist in this field. Most of these courses are offered on a part-time or block-teaching basis, so as to allow admission of students who are currently working in the field. Some also offer a full-time option. Many short courses and day courses are also available.

A number of other agencies are available to provide help and advice. Alcohol Concern provides information on many aspects of relevant training. The Royal College of Nursing has fostered certain initiatives, social worker training has been reviewed, and for medical practitioners the key responsibilities are handled through the usual postgraduate training mechanisms. Finally, the Medical Council on Alcoholism can provide advice.

Establishing what services are currently provided

Table 12 provides a summary check-list of district-level organisations and activities as they commonly exist today. Not all these entries operate in the same way or to the same extent in all districts, but the list and the attached questions provide a framework at a local level for reviewing and auditing the baseline of relevant provision.

The service commissioner is in a key position to assess the needs of the population, the current service provision and the most appropriate strategy for future service provision. However, this position will only be exploited fully where there is close liaison with social services, with those working in education and the criminal justice system and with service providers. The Drug and Alcohol Action Team or primary care trust with commissioning responsibility can usefully provide a key co-ordinating function in the overall process of planning and delivering alcohol services.

6 Effectiveness and cost-effectiveness of services

Effectiveness

The literature review of different types of prevention and treatment response to alcohol misuse is summarised briefly here and in Table 13 (*see* p. 336). Treatment of drinking problems and assessment of service delivery systems have been the subject of extensive research and critical review. The overriding conclusion to be drawn from this literature is that different drinking problems and different patients require different types of help. The diversity of patients who present with alcohol misuse prompts complex questions. In appraising the effectiveness of services, it is important not to lose sight of the need to match the treatment to the patient, and to allow the patient to choose.

Prevention

Alcohol policy and prevention of alcohol misuse

Any strategy which prevented alcohol misuse would of course be preferable to treating the casualties. The most uncontroversial evidence on preventative efficacy relates not to any locally available option, but to national policies to control the liquor supply through pricing. Per capita alcohol consumption is related directly to indices of alcohol misuse, while consumption shows an inverse relationship to price. The affordability of alcohol is therefore an important public health issue.

Table 12: Establishing current service provision.

Prevention	
Health promotion	What role is being taken by the local Health Promotion Unit or equivalent?
Local action on prevention	Where does responsibility reside for the multiple aspects of community action?
Generic social services	
Statutory social services	Is there a specialist social worker?
	What mechanisms exist for training, and for monitoring the level of case work that involves alcohol misuse?
Non-statutory social services	What contribution may particular organisations be making to dealing with alcohol misuse?
	Are their support or training needs being met?
GP and primary health care	
GP and primary health care	Are the implications of the GP contract in relation to alcohol misuse being met?
	Is there liaison team (CAT or SMIT) support for the GP?
	What relevant training is being provided in screening, early detection and simple interventions?
NHS non-specialist hospital services	
General (non-psychiatric) hospital services	Is there an integrated policy or identifiable leadership on alcohol misuse?
	Has a joint clinic been established?
	At the level of individual wards or departments, have mechanisms for screening for alcohol misuse been introduced?
General district psychiatric services	Is there an articulated policy on the interlocking responsibilities of general and specialist psychiatric responses to alcohol misuse?
	What role are general psychiatric services able to play here?
	Are multi-disciplinary training needs being met?
Specialist services for alcohol misuse	
NHS Inpatient Alcohol Service	Has the commissioning body established such a service and defined its specific and liaison functions?
	Is the specialist service satisfactorily integrated with general psychiatric services?
NHS Community Alcohol Service	Has a liaison team been established within the CAT or SMIT model, and is it able to provide district-wide support to all relevant statutory (GP, hospital, social services) and non-statutory agencies?
Private and non-statutory alcohol services	Is a private health care organisation or other non-statutory service contributing to district provisions for alcohol misuse?
Alcohol misuse and the criminal justice system	
	What mechanisms have been established to support work with the drunkenness offender, the drunk driver and other types of offender where alcohol misuse may often be implicated?
Three over-arching questions	
	Within the locality, what mechanisms currently exist to determine adequacy of multi-disciplinary, multi-sectoral training in alcohol misuse?
	What mechanisms for integration exist?
	Has a local plan on alcohol misuse been formulated? Is it being implemented and updated?

Table 13: Effectiveness of different types of prevention and treatment response to alcohol misuse.

	Extent and nature of evidence on efficacy	Size of effect	Quality of evidence
1 Prevention (i) National strategies to control real price of alcohol and thus per capita consumption	Substantial international studies involving epidemiological analysis both across time and between countries, and often using cirrhosis as an indirect indicator, show that controlling the liquor supply is an effective way of reducing alcohol misuse.	A	II-2
(ii) Health education directed at general or school-age populations	It is difficult to determine impact on long-term behavioural changes in a multi-variable field where many other and longer-term influences may be at work. A considerable international research literature for the most part offers equivocal conclusions.	C	I-1
(iii) Local community action	Research has so far usefully mapped the multiple feasibilities but there is as yet little work to test objectively the efficacy of these strategies.	C	II-2
2 Treatment of Category I (misuse without problems or dependence)	Substantial evidence from controlled studies conducted in the UK and elsewhere indicates that advice given by the GP or other primary health care worker can reduce prevalence of alcohol misuse.	A	I-1
3 Treatment of Category II (problems) and Category III (dependence) (i) Advice	Advice, often of a fairly minimal intensity, if given by a credible professional informant can be effective in the treatment of Category II patients.	A	I-1
(ii) Intensive treatment	There is no evidence that the generality of Category II and Category III patients benefit more from intensive treatment than from less intensive interventions. There is evidence to suggest that the more severely dependent patients respond preferentially to sustained and intensive help.	A	I-1 for across-the-board approach II-2 for heavily dependent patients
(iii) Outpatient care	For the generality of patients in Categories II and III, outpatient care will be as effective as inpatient care.	A	I-2
(iv) Inpatient care	Inpatient care offers no general advantage over outpatient care, but clinical experience indicates the need for inpatient resources to deal with the complicated case and life-threatening situations.	A	I-1 (as routine) II-2 (as clinically determined)
(v) Detoxification	Clinical discrimination is needed, and by no means all such patients require drug treatment in withdrawal. In some circumstances (e.g. DTs), full medical cover is needed and can be life-saving.	A	I-1
(vi) Rehabilitation hostels and related day programmes	Uncontrolled descriptive outcome studies have reported on hostel rehabilitation for homeless drinkers and the drunkenness offender. Despite the lack of controlled experiment it is likely that hostels can confer benefit, and without such help there is often no way out of the cycle of drinking and homelessness.	B	III
(vii) Alcoholics Anonymous and Al-Anon	AA is not susceptible to controlled evaluation, but subjects who affiliate to AA fare substantially better than those who do not. AA is most effective with the severely dependent drinker. Al-Anon is an effective support for families of such patients, in terms of anxiety relief and aid to coping.	B	II-2

Health education

Although public and school-based education on alcohol misuse can be expected to influence the ground swell of public awareness in the long term, there is little research evidence to support the effectiveness of school-based educational programmes in reducing alcohol use, or in changing attitudes to alcohol use, although they may increase knowledge about the subject.

The limitations of widespread campaigns based on the 'sensible drinking' message must also be recognised. While recommended drinking limits may offer useful guidance to inform a doctor–patient consultation, there is no evidence that such guidance on a wider scale is an effective means of primary prevention of alcohol misuse.[36] Public education can, however, be effective in stimulating earlier self-referral and help-seeking.

Community action on prevention

Although improved 'use of what is there' has seldom been assessed through formal research designs, it has much to recommend it in terms of common sense. One may initially suspect that the potential effectiveness should be rated quite favourably.

Treatment of Category I alcohol misuse

The conclusions from a substantial research literature are unequivocal. Advice given in the primary care setting significantly reduces individual levels of alcohol misuse and thus the prevalence of misuse. Wallace et al.[37] showed for instance that at 1-year follow-up, 47% of alcohol misusers who received advice from their GP had reduced their drinking, as opposed to 25% of those who received no such advice.

Treatment of Category II and III alcohol misuse

It is necessary to remember that different patients will have different treatment needs in terms of setting, type, intensity and duration of help. Even when major drinking problems have been incurred, or significant dependence has been established, minimal intervention in terms of advice can often be as effective as more intensive treatments in improving drinking outcomes.[38,39] In general, about 50–60% of alcohol-dependent patients show a significant improvement over a 12-month period following treatment contact, whatever the intensity of the treatment offered.

Counselling or psychotherapy

Chick et al.[23] demonstrated the efficacy, in terms of reduced alcohol consumption 12 months later, of counselling given by a nurse on a general hospital ward to patients with drinking problems. A large multi-centre study of the treatment of alcohol misuse in the USA showed that motivational interviewing, cognitive-behavioural psychotherapy (incorporating relapse prevention) and '12-step facilitation' were all equally effective in improving drinking outcomes 12 months after treatment.[40] There is now an extensive research base to support the efficacy of motivational interviewing and cognitive-behavioural psychother-apy in the treatment of alcohol misuse.[41]

12-Step groups and programmes

If professional staff encourage attendance at these self-help groups, more patients attend. Encouragement can enhance attendance from perhaps 10% to 40% in the short term. Subjects who attend AA regularly do better than those who do not, with 40–50% of the former achieving several years of abstinence and 60–68%

showing at least some improvement.[42] Thus although there are no satisfactory controlled trials on AA's effectiveness, there are reasons to believe that treatment policies which encourage AA attendance are likely to confer benefit. In terms of drinking outcomes, 12-step therapy (in an outpatient setting) is at least as effective as motivational interviewing or cognitive-behavioural therapy, and 3 years after treatment appears to be more effective than motivational enhancement for patients with social networks that strongly support their drinking.[40,43] Residential 12-step programmes are probably also of at least equal efficacy, in terms of drinking outcomes at 1 year, to alternative inpatient treatments.[44]

Detoxification

In previous decades the mortality associated with delirium tremens was about 10%, and alcohol withdrawal fits and status epilepticus could also be life-threatening. The decline in the mortality associated with withdrawal status to zero (in competent hands) represents a therapeutic advance which deserves greater attention. Withdrawal at moderate levels of dependence can be handled safely and effectively by a GP or a CAT. Withdrawal in a sheltered environment with minimal medical care can also be effective in some circumstances. However, to deny medical care to the severely dependent patient is to put their life at risk, and inpatient detoxification remains the only safe option for a minority of cases. Benzodiazepines are recommended as the pharmacological agent of choice for almost all cases in which medication is necessary, but the dosage regime must be tailored to the individual case.[45]

Pharmacological treatments

Disulfiram, when accompanied by psychological support, is effective in reducing the number of drinking days, and the amount drunk, in compliant patients. For some it assists in maintaining abstinence, but interpretation of the research evidence is complex, and it clearly does not benefit all patients.[46] It is probably of most help to those patients who would in any case have the best prognosis. In 10 of 11 randomised controlled trials, acamprosate has been shown to double the locally achieved abstinence rates following treatment. The effect was achieved not only during the 12 months of administration, but also for a year or more afterwards.[47]

Treatment providers and settings

Statutory social services

Psychological support provided by trained social workers would be as effective as that provided by other suitable trained personnel (*see* above). Effectiveness of the performance of statutory duties, for example under the Community Care Act, as a means of enhancing outcomes has not yet been the subject of research attention.

Non-statutory general social services

There has been remarkably little research on the efficacy of non-statutory services, but the general comments (*see* above) regarding counselling, psychotherapy and 12-step programmes would all apply.

GP and primary health care services

There is one study which showed that management of alcohol misuse in primary care, when supported by specialist services, can be just as effective (in reducing alcohol consumption and alcohol-related problems at 6 months) as with specialist outpatient care.[48] However, this research would not be expected to apply in circumstances in which primary care staff were reluctant or unwilling to engage in such work, or specialist support and liaison were not available.[49]

NHS general (non-psychiatric) hospital services

The effectiveness of such services in the management of alcohol-related morbidity (e.g. alcohol-related liver disease, pancreatitis, trauma due to alcohol-related accidents, etc.) is beyond the scope of this review. However, there is considerable research evidence to support the effectiveness of most of the treatments in question. There is also research evidence to support the efficacy in such settings of counselling by a nurse, directed at reducing the underlying alcohol consumption (*see* above).

NHS general district psychiatric services

Similar comments apply here to those made above for non-psychiatric hospital services.

NHS inpatient alcohol services

In general, inpatient and outpatient treatment have been shown to be equally effective in their impact on drinking outcomes.[29] However, some studies have shown that outcomes after inpatient treatment may be superior to other treatment options, in terms of both drinking[50] and mortality,[51] and a review of the research literature in this area suggests that traditional conclusions regarding the equivalence of outcomes for inpatient and community treatment should be reviewed.[52]

NHS community alcohol services

The work of the community alcohol service involves counselling, psychotherapy, use of detoxification and pharmacological treatments, and liaison with primary care, etc., all of which have been discussed above. For most patients, detoxification can be conducted as safely and effectively in the community as in hospital.[53] However, a significant minority cannot be detoxified safely in the community, and successful completion of detoxification (but not enhanced outcome 6 months later) may be somewhat more likely with hospital than community detoxification.[54]

Specialised non-statutory services

Rehabilitation hostels and associated day programmes are largely targeted at a disadvantaged group who are experiencing many social problems. While controlled studies on efficacy are few and unconvincing, these hostels may provide help of a type not available elsewhere, and succeed in ameliorating the drinking of perhaps 30–40% of their clients and help towards a good long-term adjustment of 20% who would otherwise circulate expensively around many other facilities.[55]

Private health care organisations

These services generally use similar techniques to those described above, although they may (in the UK) employ a 12-step programme more frequently than NHS services. Relevant comments made above would all therefore be applicable here.

Alcohol misuse and the criminal justice system

There is some evidence to suggest that drinking outcomes, and the proportion of patients reporting improvements in social functioning, 12 months after treatment are as good following court referral as they are following voluntary referral.[56] Rehabilitation programmes for drink-drivers are, however, apparently not effective in reducing recidivism.[57]

Cost-effectiveness

As data on cost-effectiveness are not available for many of the interventions described, and as there is no central source of information on costs of alcohol services in the UK, East Kent will be used here as an example of what the costs of alcohol services might be (based on actual 1997–98 costs). Consideration of these figures alongside the information provided on effectiveness (*see* above) will allow some impression of cost-effectiveness to be formed. East Kent has a population of about 600 000.

Prevention

Alcohol policy and prevention of alcohol misuse

The economic implications of national policies on alcohol pricing and liquor control are beyond the scope of this chapter. However, any national policy which allowed the progressive cheapening of alcohol would eventually have a follow-through in terms of district health and social service costs, while tighter tax policies would have positive consequences on reducing local health costs.

As alcohol consumption has doubled in the post-war period, with consequences for alcohol-related morbidity and mortality as well as health service spending, service commissioners might want to monitor the affordability of alcohol and the mortality associated with it (liver cirrhosis and alcohol-related accidents).

Health education

Other than large-scale media campaigns, public education at a local level represents a relatively low-cost activity. Even if short-term effectiveness is uncertain, such local initiatives seem likely to offer at least moderate long-term value for money. In the late 1990s, East Kent Health Authority spent approximately £10 000 per annum on health promotion.

Community action on prevention

This type of strategy can make little or no call on health or social service budgets, but could put increased pressure on other agencies. For example, increased police action to curb under-age drinking or drink-driving implies costs on their budget. Estimates of cost-effectiveness that take account of such broad definitions of cost are difficult. In general, however, a favourable cost-effectiveness might be expected from measures which use available mechanisms to benefit the public health.

Treatment of Category I alcohol misuse

Brief interventions aimed at the patient/person drinking over safe limits take only a few minutes to deliver and are effective. As the costs of detection and provision of advice are low, in the region of between £15 and £47, the cost-effectiveness of such interventions is likely to be high.[58]

Treatment of Category II and III misuse

The relevant literature bearing on cost offset, cost–benefit and cost-effectiveness has been reviewed by Godfrey,[59,60] with the following conclusions.

- Failure to provide appropriate treatment for these types and degrees of alcohol misuse constitutes a policy of cost-ineffectiveness. Untreated or inappropriately treated patients make heavy and repeated demands on treatment services in an ad hoc, unplanned and often entirely unproductive fashion. One US study has suggested that the untreated alcoholic, on average, incurs 200% of the general health care costs of a non-alcoholic, with a sustained reduction in this excess after treatment.[61]
- Relatively simple advice directed at these types of patient will often confer benefit. Inpatient counselling and outpatient care are also likely to constitute highly cost-effective strategies.
- While, in general, a primarily inpatient approach to treatment is not cost-effective, inpatient care will be cost-effective for the complicated case.

A study of patients treated in the Edinburgh Alcohol Problems Clinic, which had been utilising both inpatient and outpatient treatment, revealed an average cost of £1134 over a 6-month period.[62] Costs correlated with a measure of alcohol-related problems, but not with the number of days of abstinence.[63]

Counselling or psychotherapy

Brief interventions are likely to be highly cost-effective in Category II misuse (although not Category III – for which they have not been evaluated), given the low cost of the intervention, the high cost of untreated alcohol misuse and the evidence of efficacy.[58] Where cognitive-behavioural therapy (or other psychotherapy) is provided by a clinical psychologist, the costs are likely to be much higher.

12-Step groups and programmes

AA, being a self-supporting organisation and a freely available service to all who wish to attend, must be a uniquely cost-effective resource, even given the little research evidence concerning its efficacy.

Detoxification

It is not clinically necessary to treat mild dependence on an inpatient basis. In one study, costs of inpatient detoxification for mild/moderate dependence were 9–20 times greater, with no difference in outcomes at 6 months after treatment.[54] However, for selected cases inpatient detoxification is essential in order to prevent serious morbidity and mortality, and in such cases cost-effectiveness (if evaluated) would undoubtedly be high.

Pharmacological treatments

Little is known about the cost-effectiveness of disulfiram or acamprosate. Acamprosate is a relatively expensive treatment (c. £650 for a year's course of treatment for one patient), but if used appropriately, given the evidence of efficacy, it is still likely to be highly cost-effective. Unfortunately, it is not clear from currently published literature that we know how to define 'appropriate' use in terms of health economic benefits. However, an evaluation conducted in Germany, and based upon the costs in their health care system, has estimated a benefit of 2600 DM per additional abstinent patient.[64] A year's course of disulfiram costs about £130 at standard dosage.

Treatment providers and settings

Statutory social services

If we assume that services will only be cost-effective when used for appropriate clients, the role of statutory social services in making assessments for community care funding must place them in a highly significant position in this regard. However, the actual cost-effectiveness of community care assessments will presumably depend upon the selection criteria employed for assessing clients as suitable for residential rehabilitation or other forms of community care. Given that these are not consistent around the country, and given the lack of research, we do not know how cost-effective this process is.

Non-statutory general social services

Little is known about the cost-effectiveness of such services, but the general comments made above concerning counselling and psychotherapy, etc., are probably applicable.

GP and primary health care services

It would be expected that interventions offered in primary care will be at least as cost-effective, and possibly more so, as similar interventions offered in secondary care.

NHS general (non-psychiatric) hospital services

Cost-effectiveness of such services, in terms of medical and surgical outcomes, is beyond the scope of this review, and is difficult to cost accurately. However, in the late 1990s, East Kent Health Authority estimated that it spent approximately £260 000 per annum on such services. Brief alcohol counselling by a nurse in this setting is highly effective, relatively cheap and probably also therefore highly cost-effective.

NHS general district psychiatric services

The cost-effectiveness of such services, in terms of general psychiatric outcomes, is beyond the scope of this review. However, liaison with specialist alcohol services would be expected to produce a mutual benefit in terms of both drinking and psychiatric prognosis. The cost-effectiveness of such liaison is therefore potentially good.

NHS inpatient alcohol services

Evidence of greater costs of inpatient treatment, and equal efficacy of inpatient and outpatient treatment, have generally been taken to indicate the greater cost-effectiveness of the latter. However, in selected cases (e.g. following the failure of outpatient treatment) inpatient treatment may still be more cost-effective.

NHS community alcohol services

A CAT is not a low-cost resource. For example, in the late 1990s, East Kent Health Authority spent approximately £430 000 per annum on its NHS community alcohol service. However, to the degree that it mobilises relatively cost-effective activity in primary and generalist settings, as well as delivering education and facilitation skills, it could be highly cost-effective.

Specialised non-statutory services

Specialised alcohol rehabilitation hostels are more cost-effective than the alternatives of placing such drinkers for long periods in psychiatric hospitals or hostels (psychiatric or non-specialist), where their behaviour may be uncontrolled and disruptive. The cost-effectiveness of non-residential services is subject to the considerations outlined above (e.g. for counselling). In the late 1990s, East Kent Health Authority spent approximately £10 000 per annum on such services.

Private health care organisations

Private providers, who cater largely for fee-paying patients, have been criticised for their emphasis on inpatient treatment with its attendant costs, which it has been suggested was driven by the profits associated with institutional rather than outpatient care.[65] ECRs for services available within the NHS are clearly not cost-efficient. However, the costs and efficacy of the treatments provided by different organisations are likely to vary, and therefore cost-effectiveness is also likely to be variable, and will usually be unknown. In 1997–98, East Kent Health Authority spent £25 000 on detoxification in private facilities, but its expenditure on such treatments in these settings was in continuing decline.

Alcohol misuse and the criminal justice system

Given the significant human, social and financial costs of alcohol-related crime, we might expect that services for offenders would be potentially highly cost-effective.

7 Models of care

The general requirements of any model to be developed are that it should emphasise the role of the primary care sector, while acknowledging local variation in its capacity or willingness to respond, and at the same time acknowledging a continuing supportive role for specialist services. In many districts, development of responses to alcohol misuse is likely to start from a relatively low baseline of activity and commitment. The problem will not be how to fund and hold in place a comprehensive, integrated and effective district response, but rather how to remedy extensive gaps in provision. It is therefore necessary to begin with an assessment of the nature and extent of present needs and services, before moving on to a consideration of the strategic options that are available.

Local needs assessment prevalence studies

In any given locality, a full needs assessment for alcohol misuse would ideally be conducted in order to provide an accurate guide to the type and volume of services required. In practice, this may not be possible due to lack of resources, time or expertise. It may also be perceived that such an exercise is unnecessary when good-quality services are available and seen to be meeting the need, or when there is a dearth of good services and the need is 'obvious'. There may be some truth in any or all of these reasons, in any particular locality. Equally, however, they may all be bad reasons for failing to conduct such a study. Investment of relatively few resources in such an exercise could avert an expensive waste of resources devoted to a service which is inappropriate or unnecessary. Apparently good service provision can mask unmet needs, and 'obvious' needs are not necessarily high priorities in relation to hidden ones.

A full health needs assessment should include an attempt to measure incidence/prevalence, existing service provision and effectiveness/cost-effectiveness of potential/actual services.[66] Only the first of these components will be considered here, the others having already been referred to above. However, it must be remembered that incidence and prevalence alone do not necessarily provide a good indicator of need. Also, information on all of these components will be available from national or regional sources, without the need for any specific or new research. Many such statistics are provided in this publication. However, routinely collected statistics can be inaccurate or misleading, and nationally collected data do not necessarily provide evidence of local variation.

If a decision is made to proceed with a local epidemiological study of alcohol misuse, then it will probably be appropriate to invite tenders from local organisations with the necessary expertise. This may result in the submission of proposals from very different groups. A 'market-research' survey by a firm of consultants is likely to provide very different data to an academic study by a university research group. Each may have its merits, but it will be important to clarify whether applicants have familiarity with working in this field (clinically as well as in survey or research work), what the limits of their methodology may be, and what definitions of target problems will be employed. Support from an independent research adviser with experience in this field will be valuable for purchasers who do not have the necessary 'in-house' expertise to assess the merits and demerits of competing submissions.

Given the prevalence of alcohol misuse in most parts of the UK, it will be necessary to sample a reasonably large population in order to gauge accurately the incidence and prevalence in various sub-samples (e.g. by age, sex, geography of residence, etc.). A decision will also need to be taken about the choice of general population sampling compared with sampling of 'at-risk' populations, which might require particular services, such as hospital or primary care patients, drink-drivers, offenders in the criminal justice system, etc. Numbers of clients/patients receiving help for alcohol misuse in specialist alcohol agencies, or in other services, can be useful but do not indicate unmet need. Certain alcohol-related problems may provide a proxy indicator of the overall level of alcohol misuse. For example, cirrhosis mortality, drink-driving convictions, drunkenness convictions or hospital admissions for alcohol-related diagnoses might all be useful for this purpose, and also provide information about specific services that might be required.

Ideally, information should be collected on quantity and frequency of consumption, as well as a range of social, psychological and medical alcohol-related problems, and alcohol dependence. This will allow a comprehensive picture of need to be built up, including an approximate allocation to Categories I, II and III, described above. A wide range of existing questionnaires and survey instruments of known reliability and validity is available for use in such an exercise. Personal interviews by trained staff will always provide superior estimates to self-report questionnaires, but will inevitably be more time-consuming and expensive, and may suffer from a lower response rate.

Strategic options

Having assessed the present needs of a community, and given the high prevalence of alcohol misuse, the high social and financial costs and the serious morbidity and mortality, it is assumed that no Drug and Alcohol Action Team or primary care trust will consider 'no response' as being an acceptable option.

Integration with drugs services or separate purchasing of alcohol services

A decision must be made as to whether alcohol and drugs services will be purchased separately or as a seamless whole. Clinical and scientific principles of treatment are very similar, and in many cases identical, for both alcohol and other drug misuse. Many patients/clients have problems with a range of drugs/

substances and it is somewhat artificial to separate out alcohol for separate attention. For these and other reasons, many substance misuse teams offer services to those with problems concerning alcohol misuse, other drug misuse, and both types of problem.

However, the similarities between different drugs often tend to highlight their differences. Quite apart from the pharmacological differences between alcohol and many other drugs, there are significant social and political differences. Alcohol is a socially and legally acceptable drug. The size of the alcohol problem in this country is correspondingly far greater than that of the illicit drug problem, so that there are much larger numbers of people requiring and requesting help with alcohol problems (85% of people attending alcohol agencies have not used illegal drugs).[16] Furthermore, although stigmatised themselves, alcohol misusers often do not consider themselves to be 'drug' users and prefer to receive help away from 'drug' services. Perhaps more importantly, alcohol services have often received far fewer resources, and bodies such as drug and alcohol reference groups can easily find their time, money and political concerns being primarily directed to other drugs. For these and other reasons it can therefore be beneficial to keep funding and delivery of alcohol services separate from other drugs services. However, neither option is lacking in advantages or disadvantages, and views of local service users and providers should play a significant part in any decisions on this matter.

Enhancing the effectiveness of existing services

A low cost and undemanding option in prevention and care is to maximise the effectiveness of existing mechanisms (e.g. licensing or policy) or resources (e.g. GPs and general hospitals). Effective treatment of alcohol misuse implies the ability to make better use of what is already to hand. This option may fail to address gaps in existing services, and will probably fail to match services to the needs of the population. However, although it is generally discouraged here, its success will depend to a large extent upon the appropriateness of existing service provision.

Responses to alcohol misuse are often fragmented, due to the diversity of medical and social needs of the affected population, and the haphazard growth of existing services spread between many agencies (NHS, statutory social services, private hospitals, voluntary sector). Fragmentation must be avoided by an integrated response to alcohol misuse and by co-ordination between these strategies and wider district health and social planning. A fragmented response to alcohol misuse is likely to waste money. Co-ordination of service provision, and enhanced liaison between services may therefore be a key to enhancing the effectiveness of existing services without increasing expenditure.

This approach might be extended to include the relatively unco-ordinated purchasing of additional services. This strategy adds to the fragmentation. Examples include:

- the funding of a counselling centre rather than enhancing the screening and intervention skills of GPs or hospital ward staff
- the setting up of a free-standing detoxification centre rather than strengthening the capacity of GP or outpatient services to meet detoxification withdrawal needs.

High-volume/low-intensity interventions

If a more strategic response is sought, the evidence of efficacy of brief interventions, the low cost of such interventions and the known high prevalence of Category I, and that proportion of Category II cases who are less severely affected, might be taken as a good basis for concentrating resources on providing brief interventions to a community on a large scale. This would almost certainly be very cost-effective and, especially if combined with other preventive measures (education and community action programmes, etc.), might effect a longer-term reduction in more serious alcohol misuse.

However, this approach leaves no provision for a smaller number of the more severely affected individuals in Categories II and III. These individuals are likely to inflict considerable ongoing costs upon health and social services and, moreover, will inappropriately consume the resources intended for individuals with a less serious problem. Overall, this strategy will therefore completely fail to meet the needs of the most seriously affected alcohol misuser, and this will in turn impose significant costs upon health and social services, families, employers and the criminal justice system.

Low-volume/high-intensity interventions

An alternative strategic response would be to prioritise only the more severe cases of Category II and III alcohol misuse. Service provision would therefore focus on more intensive and expensive longer-term or residential interventions, and on services for those who continue to drink heavily despite all efforts to help them. The rationale might be that if resources are limited, the more severe problems should be prioritised.

This option suffers from the reverse of the problems described for high-volume/low-intensity interventions. Although the most serious cases might be addressed effectively (and in fact this strategy may well be relatively ineffective and expensive), the bulk of alcohol-related problems in a community are contributed by the relatively more 'moderate' drinkers, because of their larger numbers. A considerable cost to the community would therefore continue to accrue as a result of this unaddressed large-scale albeit less severe alcohol misuse. If a low priority were also given to other preventative interventions, the problem might even escalate with time.

A comprehensive approach

The only strategy which can be recommended here is the creation of a planned and integrated response to alcohol misuse. Preferably this should be informed by a prior needs assessment study to identify and quantify the local prevalence of alcohol misuse and existing service provision. This approach requires both a sense of priority and a willingness to move in logical steps. It also implies integrated planning between service commissioners, primary care trusts and local authorities.

An integrated district response to alcohol misuse

This developmental model is summarised with approximate indications of staffing and costs in Table 14.

Table 15 (*see* p. 348) indicates the likely divisions of responsibility. Figure 3 (*see* p. 349) shows how different cases should present and flow through the system.

Planning of the integrated response, and provision of clinical services within it, should attempt to provide the optimum balance of low- and high-intensity interventions. Less intensive treatment should therefore more often be the initial treatment of choice. Such minimal intervention can be seen as a carefully observed 'therapeutic experiment'. This should not be misread as implying that there is no place for intensive treatment. The clinical indications for more intensive deployment of resources include:

- more heavily dependent patients
- the homeless and unsupported
- those with severe concomitant psychological or physical illness or drug misuse
- patients who present a suicide risk or who are a danger to other people.

Table 14: Building an integrated and prioritised community response to alcohol misuse.*

Item	Functions	Staffing	Cost pa (× £1,000)
1 CAT or SMIT liaison team	Functions multiple, flexible, exploratory and entrepreneurial, but likely to include: (i) first wave of generalist services collaborations including GPs, general hospitals, district psychiatric and social services (ii) liaison with voluntary sector alcohol agencies including AA and Al-Anon (iii) immediate specialised service delivery and shared care through outpatient and liaison clinics (iv) direct/indirect assistance with detoxification (v) pharmacological treatments (disulfiram and acamprosate) (vi) professional training (vii) overseeing and stimulating prevention (viii) special responsibility to liaise with district drug dependence services.	Full-time consultant, half-time specialist registrar, full-time SHO, 8-person team with variable skills mix drawn from CPN, SRN, social worker, occupational therapist, psychologist, counsellor, with in and out attachments from voluntary agencies, and secretarial support.	400–500
2 Access to 8–10 hospital beds in psychiatric setting (or larger facility shared by two districts)	Dealing with psychiatric comorbidity; detoxification of severely dependent patients who cannot be managed in outpatient departments.	Medical cover from liaison team. Full nursing cover, occupational therapist, psychology support, investigation facilities.	300–400
3 Services for the homeless drinker	Outreach shop-front, day centre and hostel facilities.	Likely to be provided by non-statutory agency.	Determined by very variable extent of district need.
4 Counselling and information centre	Ready access to confidential advice and information in community setting; development of initiatives for special population groups; training of volunteers.	Two to three trained counsellors, volunteers, secretarial support.	80–100
5 Ensuring that prevention receives adequate attention	Education through schools and workplace; local community action; the GP component.	Liaison team to stimulate and support these activities.	Option 1: 10–20 for material and resources. Option 2: (additional) appoint staff person, 25
6 Additional resources for liaison team	Functions include: (i) holding in place established collaborations (ii) expansion of multi-disciplinary training (iii) second wave of collaboration, e.g. courts, workplace programmes (iv) development of family support system.	Add one or more extra staff to mixed skills team, possibly on basis of attachment or training attachment from other statutory or voluntary services.	25–50

* Figures assume a population of *c.* 500 000.

Table 15: Level of different types of service involvement with three categories of substance misuse.

Category of alcohol misuse	Service involvement*				
	Generalist		Specialist		
	Primary care	General hospital	General psychiatric	Specialist psychiatric	Specialist voluntary sector
Excessive drinking without problems	•••	•			
Excessive drinking with problems	••	•••	•	•	•
Alcohol dependence	••	•	••	•••	•••

* •, Slight; ••, considerable; •••, very considerable.

Key priorities

The first priority should be for a strategic review of what services are already available and what services would be provided ideally. This should preferably be accompanied by an assessment of the local prevalence of alcohol misuse.

The second priority is to establish a community alcohol service with responsibilities for liaison and the support of other providers, as well as a role in service provision to the more severely affected Category II and III drinkers.

The third and ongoing priority is for the community alcohol service to take a lead in developing ongoing liaison and collaboration between all service providers. This is strategically important for service planning, and some or all of this aspect of the work could be delegated to a multi-agency alcohol service providers group, convened by the Drug and Alcohol Action Team or primary care trust. In some areas, this function might be undertaken by a drug and alcohol reference group, although the size of the drugs agenda is likely to be such that there is a danger of alcohol-related matters being given insufficient committee time.

It is also important that there is a separate forum for liaison concerning clinical matters so that, giving due regard to issues of confidentiality, the most appropriate form of care is offered to each individual client/patient, with cross-referrals and joint working taking place on a regular basis, governed by clinical need.[67] Where patients are already receiving care from general psychiatric services, the CPA will already be in place and the involvement of alcohol workers should be encouraged as a part of it. Where general psychiatric services are not involved, the general principles of CPA (assessment of health and social needs, a named key worker, identifiable care plans and setting of care review dates) would seem to be very relevant to this client/patient group, whether they are being seen by a statutory or non-statutory agency. However, it is unlikely that formal CPA meetings will be necessary, feasible or desirable for all Category II and III drinkers, and an inter-agency clinical liaison meeting will ensure that multi-agency involvement of patients not involved in the formal CPA process is nonetheless regularly reviewed.

Prevention

The liaison team might be charged with monitoring preventive initiatives, and a small support and development budget will be needed. Alternatively, a specialised member of staff might be provided to give focus to this work. Multi-agency collaboration will again be vital, and should also be addressed by the multi-agency alcohol services provider group described above.

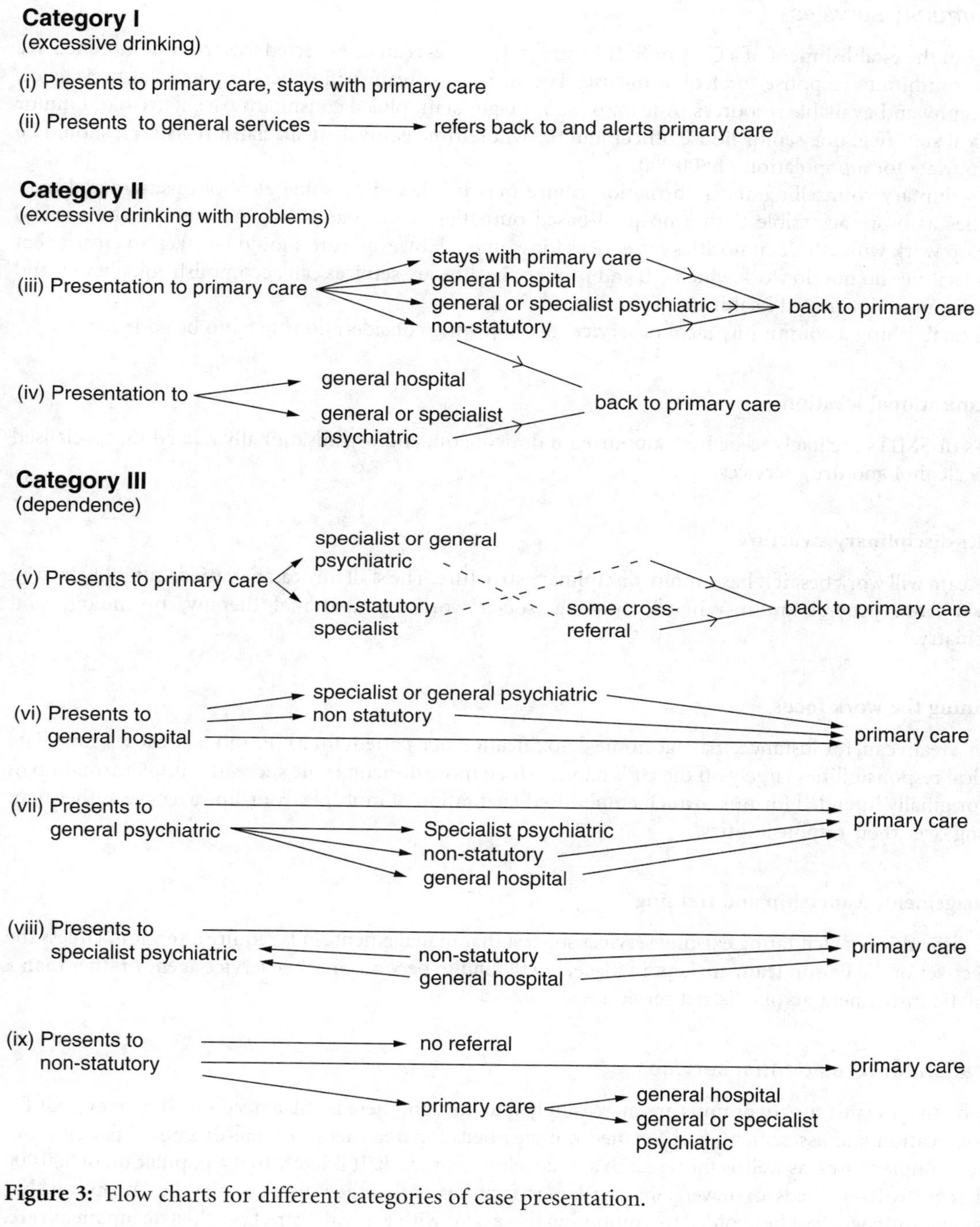

Category I
(excessive drinking)

(i) Presents to primary care, stays with primary care

(ii) Presents to general services ⟶ refers back to and alerts primary care

Category II
(excessive drinking with problems)

(iii) Presentation to primary care ⟶ stays with primary care
⟶ general hospital
⟶ general or specialist psychiatric ⟶ back to primary care
⟶ non-statutory

(iv) Presentation to ⟶ general hospital
⟶ general or specialist psychiatric ⟶ back to primary care

Category III
(dependence)

(v) Presents to primary care ⟨ specialist or general psychiatric
non-statutory specialist ⟶ some cross-referral ⟶ back to primary care

(vi) Presents to general hospital ⟶ specialist or general psychiatric ⟶ primary care
⟶ non statutory ⟶ primary care

(vii) Presents to general psychiatric ⟶ Specialist psychiatric ⟶ primary care
⟶ non-statutory
⟶ general hospital

(viii) Presents to specialist psychiatric ⟶ non-statutory ⟶ primary care
⟶ general hospital

(ix) Presents to non-statutory ⟶ no referral
⟶ primary care
⟶ primary care ⟨ general hospital
general or specialist psychiatric

Figure 3: Flow charts for different categories of case presentation.

Community services

Without the establishment of a CAT or SMIT team, no progress can be expected towards a comprehensive local community response to alcohol misuse. The size of the team will depend upon local prevalence, geography and available resources. A team of about eight staff, plus a consultant psychiatrist and junior medical staff (e.g. one senior house officer and 0.5 whole-time equivalent specialist registrar), should be appropriate for a population of 500 000.

A voluntary counselling and information centre may be viewed by some alcohol misusers and their families as more accessible than a hospital-based outpatient centre and can, for example, be used to develop work with ethnic minorities or services for women. However, care should be taken to ensure that such facilities do not do work which GP and primary health care services can accomplish equally well and within a more integrated health care formula.

In establishing a community alcohol service, the following considerations need to be addressed.

Organisational location

CATs or SMITs are likely to be best supported if drawing on, and organisationally related to, specialised NHS alcohol and drug services.

Multi-disciplinary structure

The team will work best if it has a multi-disciplinary structure. The skill mix can be varied, but is likely to be drawn from general and psychiatric nursing, social work, occupational therapy, psychology and psychiatry.

Defining the work focus

Such a team can, for instance, manage home detoxification of a patient for a GP, and take those immediate clinical responsibilities largely off the GP's hands. Much more difficult is the successful implementation of the originally intended formula, which emphasised facilitation of multiple front-line agencies rather than taking over their responsibilities.

Management, leadership and training

The difficulties of facilitating existing services suggest that management skills require attention. Unless the objectives of the liaison team are kept in place, it will tend to become another service agency rather than a catalytic instrument across district services.

Inpatient and residential services

Although specialist inpatient units are increasingly uncommon, there is still a need for short-stay beds for detoxification and assessment, and for medium-stay beds for treatment of 'dual-diagnosis' patients and other complex cases, as well as for research and development work. It is likely that a population of 500 000 will require 10–12 beds or fewer. Sharing larger facilities with other districts may be an option, but fragmentation will best be avoided by combining these beds with general district psychiatric inpatient care.

Services for the homeless drinker

Provision of help to homeless drinkers may consume disproportionate NHS resources. The most likely provider will be a non-statutory organisation and advice will be obtainable from Alcohol Concern or Turning Point. Shopfront day centres, court liaison and residential facilities may be required. Good liaison between these services and the CAT or SMIT is likely to be helpful in enhancing entry into treatment and ensuring the most efficient use of resources. The community reinforcement approach to treatment (employing social, recreational, vocational and other reinforcers to modify drinking behaviour) has been found to be particularly successful with homeless drinkers in the USA.[68] There is a need to develop and evaluate this and other approaches to helping the homeless drinker in the UK.

(Non-specialist) secondary care within an integrated response

The overall conclusion to be drawn in relation to general hospitals' engagement with alcohol misuse must be that there are large opportunities waiting to be taken up. Those few innovations which have been implemented, such as joint clinics and ward counselling, point to feasible and promising new directions. In psychiatric and general hospital services, all professional disciplines require competence in dealing with drinking problems, and the complementary roles of generalists and specialists need to be defined and agreed. Since alcohol misuse may coexist and complicate every type of general psychiatric presentation,[69] a policy based only on specialism runs against the clinical realities.

Primary care within an integrated response

The role of primary care within a comprehensive service provision for alcohol misuse is crucial. However, it must be recognised that not all GPs are able or willing to manage specialist problems of alcohol misuse themselves. The CAT will therefore need to make liaison with primary care a priority, and should advise and support GPs according to their level of interest, training and expertise in this field. Where possible, patients can and should be managed within the primary care setting. Where this is not possible, many GPs will be happy to work in liaison with the CAT. If neither of these options is feasible, CATs should be ready to assist in the process of referral to their own or other services.

Gaining further GP involvement in screening, early detection and early interventions directed at alcohol misuse constitutes a potentially fruitful priority. We may hope that increased influence of GPs in the purchasing of health services through primary care trusts will improve this situation. Close liaison between service commissioners and local medical committees is also vital.

Training

A backlog of training deficit may be met in the short term by day courses, or by short courses or training secondments directed at individual professions. However, a longer-term and more definitive view will require that key members of staff are encouraged and allowed to pursue specialist training in the field.

8 Outcome measures

A process of monitoring service delivery in partnership with purchasing authorities, and of routine clinical audit and outcome evaluation, should normally be set in place. This should include monitoring of such considerations as numbers of patients seen, clinics offered, educational interventions offered, liaison and support offered to other services, detoxifications completed, etc. The quality of the service should also be considered and patient satisfaction, record keeping, delay between referral and appointment offered, etc., should be monitored. Alcohol Concern has published a guide to such considerations. However, clinical outcomes will be of most interest to purchasers, providers and patients, and these will be the most difficult to measure. Good outcome monitoring requires an investment of staff time and resources to set adequate procedures in place. Advice can be obtained from Alcohol Concern and elsewhere.

Category I

Outcome here can be measured individually in terms of reduction of alcohol intake to safe limits at, say, 6 or 12 months, or in population terms of average percentage reduction, or percentage of patients reducing to safe limits. In practice, such patients would not normally be routinely followed up and so outcome monitoring would either become a research question or the subject of additional funding to support the process of tracing patients and identifying outcomes. As ample research has demonstrated the benefits of such interventions, it may be more cost-effective simply to monitor the quality of the intervention and to ensure adequate training of the staff who deliver it.

Category II

Here outcome may be measured in terms of both reduction in alcohol intake (as above) and amelioration of stated problems or overall problem score (Alcohol Problems Questionnaire, APQ). In general, there is a high correlation between amelioration in drinking and decrease in problem experience. Simple measures are available to rate time spent in different drinking-level bands over a 12-month period.[70] Health economists favour a 'quality-of-life' type of measure.[59] In one health economic study, quality of life was found to correlate inversely with a measure of alcohol-related problems, and the latter also correlated with an estimate of resource costs.[63] Alcohol-related problems, or at least the measure of them used in this study, may therefore act as a proxy measure for quality of life and resource use.

Category III

Outcome measurement with dependent patients sets similar problems to Category II. Outcome measures should be multiple and be able to discriminate graded levels of improvement in drinking, health and social adjustment, rather than dealing with the issue only in categorical terms such as 'drinking vs. sober'.

9 Targets

Overall reduction in alcohol misuse

The *Health of the Nation* strategy proposed an overall reduction of alcohol misuse from 28% of men and 11% of women drinking more than recommended limits in 1990, to 18% and 7%, respectively, by 2005.[71]

Our Healthier Nation[72] also recognises the impact of alcohol on health, and refers to the Government's intention to introduce a national alcohol strategy. Alcohol Concern has produced proposals for such a strategy which include, for example, a target to reduce the level of alcohol misuse by 5% over a 5-year period.

Concerted district-level initiatives to support primary care will help to meet these targets, but such patient-directed efforts will achieve little without increased taxation of alcohol.

Targets for enhancement of primary care and generalist involvement and effectiveness

At a district level, an appropriate and achievable initial target would be to ensure that effective ongoing contact has been established between the liaison team and every general practice and relevant service of the district general hospitals, and also with statutory and relevant non-statutory social services. Co-ordination with local medical committees, primary care trusts and Drug and Alcohol Action Teams is necessary.

Service provisions for Category III patients

A reasonable target would be the establishment of a case register at district level and evidence that provision was in place to ensure shared and ongoing care with effective liaison between medical and social services. For all patients receiving care from general psychiatric services, implementation of the CPA would seem to be a helpful target. Similar principles of care should be expected for all Category III patients not receiving general psychiatric treatment.

10 Information and research priorities

Creation of a 'research culture'

Research is often seen as a luxury or, worse still, as an unnecessary inconvenience. Quite apart from the general importance of research for advancing medical knowledge and informing purchasing or delivery of effective health care, a 'research culture' has benefits for the recruitment, continuing professional development and commitment of high-quality staff. Clinical audit is also likely to be facilitated in such an environment. Drug and Alcohol Action Teams, primary care trusts and NHS trusts should therefore encourage research activity and, where possible, foster links with academic institutions.

As a part of the creation of a research culture, routine data collection within clinical services should be reviewed and enhanced. This does not necessarily mean that more data should be collected, but that the reasons for data collection and the process of data collection need careful consideration. Thought should be given to research and audit requirements, as well as the practicalities of data collection and analysis, in order to ensure that adequate and complete data are available to support relevant and realistic research and audit requirements. Purchasers of health services are also in a good position to ensure that there is comparability of data collection across different service providers.

The effectiveness of the liaison team

Given the potential importance of the primary care and generalist sectors in responding to alcohol misuse, research on the effectiveness and cost-effectiveness of CAT or SMIT in enhancing competence at these levels is a priority. Only before-and-after controlled designs can provide the necessary answers.

Service needs and the severely dependent alcohol misuser

Up to now, the conventional research approach in relation to this problem has been the controlled study which determines the relative efficacy of different treatments at, say, 12 months. Such research ignores the fact that many of these patients will be setting service needs far beyond the closure of that study. Research is needed on long-term needs and costs of different methods for long-term handling and community care. Poorly handled, a small proportion of severely dependent patients may be disproportionate consumers of resources.

Prevalence studies

Prevalence studies should be conducted and repeated in different settings such as primary care, Accident and Emergency departments, general hospital wards and maternity services. Rather than describing drinking levels and enumerating problems, surveys should be service- and need-oriented. Thus they should examine issues such as alcohol misuse within health belief contexts, the need for and relevance of information or help, and the ability of family members, employer or onlooker to respond to an individual's alcohol misuse.

The complementary contributions of different providers

Patterns of response to alcohol misuse have grown by chance and local circumstances. The respective NHS, private and voluntary sections need to be charted, tested and more rationally defined. The principles used by community care assessors in their allocation of scarce resources to particular patients need to be studied scientifically.

Research in the area of health economics

Better information is needed on the costs of alcohol misuse, and the cost-effectiveness and cost–benefits of different prevention and treatment strategies.

Appendix I: Classificatory systems

ICD-10[5]

F10, Mental and behavioural disorders due to use of alcohol: 4th- and 5th-character codes for specifying the clinical condition

.0   Acute intoxication
    .00   Uncomplicated
    .01   With trauma or other bodily injury
    .02   With other medical complication
    .03   With delirium
    .04   With perceptual distortions
    .05   With coma
    .06   With convulsions
    .07   Pathological intoxication

.1   Harmful use

.2   Dependence syndrome
    .20   Currently abstinent
    .21   Currently abstinent, but in a protected environment
    .22   Currently on a clinically supervised maintenance or replacement regime (controlled dependence)
    .23   Currently abstinent, but receiving treatment with aversive or blocking drugs
    .24   Currently using substance (active dependence)
    .25   Continuous use
    .26   Episodic use (dipsomania)

.3   Withdrawal state
    .30   Uncomplicated
    .31   With convulsions

.4   Withdrawal state with delirium
    .40   Without convulsions
    .41   With convulsions

.5   Psychotic state
    .50   Schizophrenia-like
    .51   Predominantly delusional
    .52   Predominantly hallucinatory
    .53   Predominantly polymorphic
    .54   Predominantly depressive symptoms
    .55   Predominantly manic symptoms
    .56   Mixed

.6   Amnesic syndrome

.7   Drug- or alcohol-induced residual state
    .70   Flashbacks
    .71   Personality or behaviour disorder
    .72   Residual affective disorder
    .73   Dementia

.74   Other persisting cognitive impairment
.75   Late-onset psychotic disorder

.8   Other mental and behavioural disorders

.9   Unspecified mental and behavioural disorder

These diagnoses are defined according to general criteria applicable to all groups of substances. The criteria for F1x.1 *Harmful Use* and F1x.2 *Dependence Syndrome* will be given here. The reader is referred to the ICD-10 manual for further information regarding other diagnoses.

F1x.1 Harmful use

A pattern of psychoactive substance use that is causing damage to health. The damage may be physical, as in cases of hepatitis from the self-administration of injected drugs, or mental, for example, episodes of depressive disorder secondary to heavy consumption of alcohol.

Diagnostic guidelines

The diagnosis requires that actual damage should have been caused to the mental or physical health of the user.

Harmful patterns of use are often criticised by others and frequently associated with adverse social consequences of various kinds. The fact that a pattern of use or a particular substance is disapproved of by another person or by the culture, or may have led to socially negative consequences, such as arrest or marital arguments, is not in itself evidence of harmful use.

Acute intoxication (*see* F1x.0) or 'hangover' is not in itself sufficient evidence of the damage to health required for coding harmful use.

Harmful use should not be diagnosed if dependence syndrome (F1x.2), a psychotic disorder (F1x.5) or another specific form of drug- or alcohol-related disorder is present.

F1x.2 Dependence syndrome

A cluster of physiological, behavioural and cognitive phenomena in which the use of a substance or a class of substances takes on a much higher priority for a given individual than other behaviours that once had greater value. A central descriptive characteristic of the dependence syndrome is the desire (often strong, sometimes overpowering) to take psychoactive drugs (which may or may not have been medically prescribed), alcohol or tobacco. There may be evidence that return to substance use after a period of abstinence leads to a more rapid reappearance of other features of the syndrome than occurs with non-dependent individuals.

Diagnostic guidelines

A definite diagnosis of dependence should usually be made only if three or more of the following have been experienced or exhibited at some time during the previous year:

- a strong desire or sense of compulsion to take the substance
- difficulties in controlling substance-taking behaviour in terms of its onset, termination or levels of use
- a physiological withdrawal state (*see* F1x.3 and F1x.4) when substance use has ceased or been reduced, as evidenced by the characteristic withdrawal syndrome for the substance or use of the same (or a closely related) substance with the intention of relieving or avoiding withdrawal symptoms

- evidence of tolerance, such that increased doses of the psychoactive substance are required in order to achieve effects originally produced by lower doses (clear examples of this are found in alcohol- and opiate-dependent individuals who may take daily doses sufficient to incapacitate or kill non-tolerant users)
- progressive neglect of alternative pleasures or interests because of psychoactive substance use; increased amount of time necessary to obtain or take the substance or to recover from its effects
- persisting with substance use despite clear evidence of overtly harmful consequences, such as harm to the liver through excessive drinking, depressive mood states consequent to periods of heavy substance use, or drug-related impairment of cognitive functioning; efforts should be made to determine that the user was actually, or could be expected to be, aware of the nature and extent of the harm.

Narrowing of the personal repertoire of patterns of psychoactive substance use has also been described as a characteristic feature (e.g. a tendency to drink alcoholic drinks in the same way on weekdays and at weekends, regardless of social constraints that determine appropriate drinking behaviour).

It is an essential characteristic of the dependence syndrome that either psychoactive substance taking or a desire to take a particular substance should be present; the subjective awareness of compulsion to use drugs is most commonly seen during attempts to stop or control substance use. This diagnostic requirement would exclude, for instance, surgical patients given opioid drugs for the relief of pain, who may show signs of an opioid withdrawal state when drugs are not given but who have no desire to continue taking drugs.

The dependence syndrome may be present for a specific substance (e.g. tobacco or diazepam), for a class of substances (e.g. opioid drugs) or for a wider range of different substances (as for those individuals who feel a sense of compulsion regularly to use whatever drugs are available and who show distress, agitation and/or physical signs of a withdrawal state upon abstinence).

It includes:

- chronic alcoholism
- dipsomania
- drug addiction.

Physical diagnoses attributable to alcohol misuse

In addition to the above F10 codes, the following diagnoses related to alcohol use/misuse are included elsewhere in ICD-10:

G31	G312	Degeneration of nervous system due to alcohol
G62	G621	Alcoholic polyneuropathy
G72	G721	Alcoholic myopathy
	G721	Alcoholic myopathy
K29	K292	Alcoholic gastritis
K70	K700	Alcoholic fatty liver
	K701	Alcoholic hepatitis
	K702	Alcoholic fibrosis and sclerosis of liver
	K703	Alcoholic cirrhosis of liver
	K704	Alcoholic hepatic failure
	K709	Alcoholic liver disease, unspecified
K86	K860	Alcohol-induced chronic pancreatitis
T51	T501	Toxic effects of ethanol
Y90	Y900	Blood alcohol level of less than 20 mg/100 ml
	Y901	Blood alcohol level of 20–39 mg/100 ml
	Y902	Blood alcohol level of 40–59 mg/100 ml

Y903	Blood alcohol level of 60–79 mg/100 ml
Y904	Blood alcohol level of 80–99 mg/100 ml
Y905	Blood alcohol level of 100–119 mg/100 ml
Y906	Blood alcohol level of 120–199 mg/100 ml
Y907	Blood alcohol level of 200–239 mg/100 ml
Y908	Blood alcohol level of 240 mg/100 ml or more
Y909	Presence of alcohol in blood, level not specified

Y91

Y910	Mild alcohol intoxication
Y911	Moderate alcohol intoxication
Y912	Severe alcohol intoxication
Y913	Very severe alcohol intoxication
Y919	Alcohol involvement, not otherwise specified

Z50 Z502 Alcohol rehabilitation
Z71 Z714 Alcohol abuse counselling and surveillance
Z72 Z721 Alcohol use

DSM-IV[6]

Alcohol use disorders

303.90   Alcohol dependence
305.00   Alcohol abuse

These diagnoses are defined according to the general criteria for substance dependence and substance abuse (*see* below).

Alcohol-induced disorders

303.00   Alcohol intoxication
291.8   Alcohol withdrawal
291.0   Alcohol intoxication delirium
291.0   Alcohol withdrawal delirium
291.2   Alcohol-induced persisting dementia
291.1   Alcohol-induced persisting amnestic disorder
291.5   Alcohol-induced psychotic disorder, with delusions
          Specify if: with onset during intoxication/with onset during withdrawal
291.3   Alcohol-induced psychotic disorder, with hallucinations
          Specify if: with onset during intoxication/with onset during withdrawal
291.8   Alcohol-induced mood disorder
          Specify if: with onset during intoxication/with onset during withdrawal
291.8   Alcohol-induced anxiety disorder
          Specify if: with onset during intoxication/with onset during withdrawal
291.8   Alcohol-induced sexual dysfunction
          Specify if: with onset during intoxication
291.8   Alcohol-induced sleep disorder
          Specify if: with onset during intoxication/with onset during withdrawal
291.9   Alcohol-related disorder not otherwise specified

Criteria for substance dependence

A maladaptive pattern of substance use, leading to clinically significant impairment or distress, as manifested by three (or more) of the following, occurring at any time in the same 12-month period:
1 tolerance, as defined by either of the following:
   (a) a need for markedly increased amounts of the substance to achieve intoxication or desired effect
   (b) markedly diminished effect with continued use of the same amount of the substance
2 withdrawal, as manifested by either of the following:
   (a) the characteristic withdrawal syndrome for the substance (refer to Criteria A and B of the criteria sets for withdrawal from the specific substances)
   (b) the same (or a closely related) substance is taken to relieve or avoid withdrawal symptoms
3 the substance is often taken in larger amounts or over a longer period than was intended
4 there is a persistent desire or unsuccessful efforts to cut down or control substance use
5 a great deal of time is spent in activities necessary to obtain the substance (e.g. visiting multiple doctors or driving long distances), use the substance (e.g. chain-smoking) or recover from its effects
6 important social, occupational or recreational activities are given up or reduced because of substance use
7 substance use is continued despite knowledge of having a persistent or recurrent physical or psychological problem that is likely to have been caused or exacerbated by the substance (e.g. current cocaine use despite recognition of cocaine-induced depression, or continued drinking despite recognition that an ulcer was made worse by alcohol consumption).

Specify if:

* with physiological dependence: evidence of tolerance or withdrawal (i.e. either Item 1 or 2 is present)
* without physiological dependence: no evidence of tolerance or withdrawal (i.e. neither Item 1 nor 2 is present).

Course specifiers (see DSM-IV for definitions):

* early full remission
* early partial remission
* sustained full remission
* sustained partial remission
* on agonist therapy
* in a controlled environment.

Criteria for substance abuse

A. A maladaptive pattern of substance use leading to clinically significant impairment or distress, as manifested by one (or more) of the following, occurring within a 12-month period:
1 recurrent substance use resulting in a failure to fulfil major role obligations at work, school or home (e.g. repeated absences or poor work performance related to substance use; substance-related absences, suspensions or expulsions from school; neglect of children or household)
2 recurrent substance use in situations in which it is physically hazardous (e.g. driving an automobile or operating a machine when impaired by substance use)
3 recurrent substance-related legal problems (e.g. arrests for substance-related disorderly conduct)
4 continued substance use despite having persistent or recurrent social or interpersonal problems caused or exacerbated by the effects of the substance (e.g. arguments with spouse about consequences of intoxication, physical fights).
B. The symptoms have never met the criteria for substance dependence for this class of substance.

OPCS drinking categories

OPCS drinking categories are shown in Table A1.

Table A1: OPCS drinking categories.

Alcohol consumption level	Units per week	
	Male	Female
Non-drinker	No alcohol in the last year	No alcohol in the last year
Very low	< 1	< 1
Low	1–10	1–7
Moderate	11–21	8–14
Fairly high	22–35	15–25
High	36–50	26–35
Very high	51+	36+

Health care Resource Groups

The main HRGs specifically relating to alcohol misuse are shown, with corresponding ICD-10 diagnoses, in Table A2. HRGs relating to specific complications of alcohol misuse are shown, with corresponding ICD-10 diagnoses, in Table A3.

Table A2: Health care Resource Groups relating to alcohol misuse and corresponding ICD-10 diagnoses.

Health care Resource Group	ICD-10 diagnoses
T10 Alcohol or drugs, non-dependent use, age > 16 years	F10.0 Mental and behavioural disorders due to use of alcohol: acute intoxication
T11 Alcohol or drugs, non-dependent use, age < 17 years	F19.0 Mental and behavioural disorders due to use of multiple/psychoactive drugs: acute intoxication
	R780 Finding of alcohol in blood
	Z502 Alcohol rehabilitation
T12 Alcohol or drugs, dependency	F10.1 Mental and behavioural disorders due to use of alcohol: harmful use
	F10.2 Mental and behavioural disorders due to use of alcohol: dependence syndrome
	F10.3 Mental and behavioural disorders due to use of alcohol: withdrawal state
	F10.4 Mental and behavioural disorders due to use of alcohol: withdrawal state with delirium
	F10.5 Mental and behavioural disorders due to use of alcohol: psychotic disorder
	F10.7 Mental and behavioural disorders due to use of alcohol: residual and late-onset psychotic disorders
	F10.8 Mental and behavioural disorders due to use of alcohol: other mental and behavioural disorders
	F10.9 Mental and behavioural disorders due to use of alcohol: unspecified mental and behavioural disorders

Table A3: Health care Resource Groups relating to specific complications of alcohol misuse and corresponding ICD-10 diagnoses.

Health care Resource Group		ICD-10 diagnoses	
A09	Peripheral nerve disorders, age > 69 years or with complications	G621	Alcoholic polyneuropathy
A10	Peripheral nerve disorders, age < 70 years without complications		
A11	Neuromuscular disorders	G721	Alcoholic myopathy
A16	Cerebral degenerations, age > 69 years or with complications	G312	Degeneration of nervous system due to alcohol
A17	Cerebral degenerations, age < 70 years without complications		
G07	Chronic liver disorders, age > 69 years or with complications		
G08	Chronic liver disorders, age < 70 years without complications	K700	Alcoholic fatty liver
		K701	Alcoholic hepatitis
		K702	Alcoholic fibrosis and sclerosis of liver
		K703	Alcoholic cirrhosis of liver
		K704	Alcoholic hepatic failure
		K709	Alcoholic liver disease, unspecified
G24	Chronic pancreatic disease, age > 69 years	K860	Alcohol-induced chronic pancreatitis
G25	Chronic pancreatic disease, age < 70 years		
K05	Other endocrine disorders, age > 69 years or with complications	E244	Alcohol-induced pseudo-Cushing's syndrome
K06	Other endocrine disorders, age < 70 years without complications		
N01	Neonates – died < 2 days old	P043	Fetus and newborn affected by maternal use of alcohol
		Q860	Fetal alcohol syndrome (dysmorphic)
N02	Neonates with multiple minor diagnoses	P043	Fetus and newborn affected by maternal use of alcohol
N03	Neonates with one minor diagnosis	Q860	Fetal alcohol syndrome (dysmorphic)
N04	Neonates with multiple major diagnoses	P043	Fetus and newborn affected by maternal use of alcohol
N05	Neonates with one major diagnosis	Q860	Fetal alcohol syndrome (dysmorphic)
N12	Other maternity events	O354	Maternal care for (suspected) damage to fetus from alcohol
		P043	Fetus and newborn affected by maternal use of alcohol
P14	Ingestion poisoning or allergies	T510	Toxic effects – ethanol
S16	Poisoning, toxic effects or overdoses	T510	Toxic effects – ethanol
S25	Other admissions	Z040	Blood-alcohol and blood-drug test
		Z714	Alcohol abuse counselling and surveillance
		Z721	Alcohol use
		Z811	Family history of alcohol abuse
T08	Presenile dementia	F106	Mental and behavioural disorders due to use of alcohol: amnesic syndrome

References

1 Royal College of Physicians, Royal College of Psychiatrists and Royal College of General Practitioners. *Alcohol and the Heart in Perspective: sensible limits reaffirmed.* London: Royal Colleges of Physicians, Psychiatrists and General Practitioners, 1995.

2 Edwards G, Anderson P, Babor TF *et al. Alcohol Policy and the Public Good.* Oxford: Oxford University Press, 1994.

3 British Medical Association. *Alcohol: guidelines on sensible drinking.* London: British Medical Association, 1995.

4 Department of Health. *Sensible Drinking: the report of an inter-departmental working group.* London: Department of Health, 1995.

5 World Health Organization. *The ICD-10 Classification of Mental and Behavioural Disorders.* Geneva: World Health Organization, 1992.

6 American Psychiatric Association. *Diagnostic and Statistical Manual of Mental Disorders* (4e). Washington, DC: American Psychiatric Press, 1994.

7 Cloninger CR. Neurogenetic adaptive mechanisms in alcoholism. *Science* 1987; **236**: 410–16.

8 Thomas M, Walker A, Bennett N. *Results from the 1996 General Household Survey.* London: The Stationery Office, 1998.

9 Prescott-Clarke P, Primatesta P (eds). *Health Survey for England 1996.* London: The Stationery Office, 1998.

10 Meltzer H, Gill B, Petticrew M, Hinds K. *The Prevalence of Psychiatric Morbidity Among Adults Living in Private Households.* OPCS Surveys of Psychiatric Morbidity Among Adults Living in Private Households. Report 1. London: HMSO, 1995.

11 Meltzer H, Gill B, Petticrew M, Hinds K. *Economic Activity and Social Functioning of Adults with Psychiatric Disorders.* OPCS Surveys of Psychiatric Morbidity in Great Britain. Report 3. London: HMSO, 1995.

12 Lankester T. *Drug Prevention and Schools.* London: Department for Education, 1995.

13 Tether P, Robinson D. *Preventing Alcohol Problems.* London: Tavistock, 1986.

14 Cook CCH. The Minnesota model in the management of drug and alcohol dependency: miracle method or myth? Part I. The philosophy and the programme. *Br J Addict* 1988; **83**: 625–34.

15 Alcohol Concern. *Alcohol Services Directory.* Godalming: Dolomite Publishing, 1997.

16 Alcohol Concern. *First National Census of UK Alcohol Treatment Agencies.* London: Alcohol Concern, 1997.

17 Thornton L, Holding A. *Alcohol Misuse: a study of social work practice.* London: Department of Health, Social Services Inspectorate, 1990.

18 Royal College of General Practitioners. *Alcohol: a balanced view.* London: Royal College of General Practitioners, 1986.

19 Deehan A, Templeton L, Taylor C *et al.* How do general practitioners manage alcohol-misusing patients? Results from a national survey of GPs in England and Wales. *Drug Alcohol Rev* 1998; **17**: 259–66.

20 Deehan A, Templeton L, Taylor C *et al.* Low detection rates, negative attitudes and the failure to meet the 'Health of the Nation' alcohol targets: findings from a national survey of GPs in England and Wales. *Drug Alcohol Rev* 1998; **17**: 249–58.

21 UK Alcohol Forum. *Guidelines for the Management of Alcohol Problems in Primary Care and General Psychiatry.* London: UK Alcohol Forum, 1998.

22 Glass-Crome IB, Jones P, Peters TJ. A joint problem drinking clinic: the King's College and Maudsley hospitals initiative. *Alcohol Alcohol* 1994; **29**: 549–54.

23 Chick J, Lloyd G, Crombie E. Counselling problem drinkers in medical wards: a controlled study. *BMJ* 1985; **290**: 965–7.

24 Glass IB, Jackson P. Maudsley hospital survey: prevalence of alcohol problems and other psychiatric disorders in a hospital population. *Br J Addict* 1988; **83**: 1105–9.

25 Department of Health and Social Security. Mental illness hospitals and units in England. Report 12. In: *Mental Health Statistics for England*. London: Department of Health and Social Security, 1986.

26 Kingdon D. Making care programming work. *Adv Psychiatr Treat* 1994; **1**: 41–6.

27 Ettorre EM. A study of alcoholism treatment: some findings on units and staff. *Alcohol Alcohol* 1985; **20**: 371–8.

28 Ettorre EM. A follow-up study of alcoholism treatment units: exploring consolidation and change. *Br J Addict* 1988; **83**: 57–65.

29 Edwards G, Guthrie S. A controlled trial of inpatient and outpatient treatment of alcohol dependency. *Lancet* 1967; **1**: 555–9.

30 Edwards G, Hawker A, Hensman C *et al*. Alcoholics known or unknown to agencies: epidemiological studies in a London suburb. *Br J Psychiatry* 1973; **123**: 169–83.

31 Shaw S, Cartwright A, Spratley T, Harwin J. *Responding to the Problem Drinker*. London: Croom Helm, 1978.

32 Advisory Committee on Alcoholism. *The Pattern and Range of Services for Problem Drinkers*. London: HMSO, DHSS and Welsh Office, 1977.

33 Stockwell T, Clement S. *Community Alcohol Teams: a review of studies evaluating their effectiveness with special reference to the experience of other community teams – final report*. London: Department of Health, 1988.

34 Department of Health. *A Future for Alcohol and Drug Misuse Services*. London: HMSO, 1992.

35 Massey P, Roberts P. *Promoting Sensible Drinking with Offenders: a two-year partnership evaluation April 1994–March 1996*. Stafford: Staffordshire Probation Service, 1997.

36 Edwards G, Anderson P, Babor TF *et al*. *Alcohol Policy and the Public Good*. Oxford: Oxford University Press, 1994, p. 209.

37 Wallace P, Cutler S, Haines A. Randomised controlled trial of general practitioner intervention in patients with excessive alcohol consumption. *BMJ* 1988; **297**: 663–8.

38 Chick J, Ritson B, Connaughton J *et al*. Advice versus extended treatment for alcoholism: a controlled study. *Br J Addict* 1988; **83**: 159–70.

39 Edwards G, Orford J, Egert S *et al*. Alcoholism: a controlled trial of 'treatment' and 'advice'. *J Stud Alcohol* 1977; **38**: 1004–31.

40 Project MATCH Research Group. Matching alcoholism treatments to client heterogeneity: project MATCH post-treatment drinking outcomes. *J Stud Alcohol* 1997; **58**: 7–29.

41 Miller WR, Brown JM, Simpson TL *et al*. What works? A methodological analysis of the alcohol treatment outcome literature. In: Hester RK, Miller WR (eds). *Handbook of Alcoholism Treatment Approaches* (2e). Boston, MA: Allyn and Bacon, 1995, pp. 12–44.

42 Emrick CD. Alcoholics Anonymous: affiliation processes and effectiveness as treatment. *Alcohol Clin Exp Res* 1987; **11**: 416–23.

43 Longabaugh R, Wirtz PW, Zweben A, Stout RL. Network support for drinking, Alcoholics Anonymous and long-term matching effects. *Addiction* 1998; **93**: 1313–33.

44 Cook CCH. The Minnesota model in the management of drug and alcohol dependency: miracle method or myth? Part II. Evidence and conclusions. *Br J Addict* 1988; **83**: 735–48.

45 Mayo-Smith MF. Pharmacological management of alcohol withdrawal. *JAMA* 1997; **278**: 144–51.

46 Hughes J, Cook CCH. Disulfiram in the management of alcohol misuse – a review. *Addiction* 1997; **92**: 381–95.

47 Anonymous. Acamprosate for alcohol dependence? *Drug Ther Bull* 1997; **35**: 70–2.

48 Drummond DC, Thom B, Brown C *et al.* Specialist versus general practitioner treatment of problem drinkers. *Lancet* 1990; **336**: 915–18.

49 Deehan A, Marshall EJ, Strang J. Tackling alcohol misuse: opportunities and obstacles in primary care. *Br J Gen Pract* 1998; **48**: 1779–82.

50 Walsh DC, Hingson RW, Merrigan DM *et al.* A randomized trial of treatment options for alcohol-abusing workers. *NEJM* 1991; **325**: 775–82.

51 Bunn JY, Booth BM, Cook CA, Blow FC, Fortney JC. The relationship between mortality and intensity of inpatient alcoholism treatment. *Am J Public Health* 1994; **84**: 211–14.

52 Finney JW, Hahn AC, Moos RH. The effectiveness of inpatient and outpatient treatment for alcohol abuse: the need to focus on mediators and moderators of treatment settings. *Addiction* 1996; **91**: 1773–96.

53 Stockwell T, Bolt L, Milner I *et al.* Home detoxification from alcohol: its safety and efficacy in comparison with inpatient care. *Alcohol Alcohol* 1991; **26**: 645–50.

54 Hayashida M, Alterman AI, McLellan AT *et al.* Comparative effectiveness and costs of inpatient and outpatient detoxification of patients with mild-to-moderate alcohol withdrawal syndrome. *NEJM* 1989; **320**: 358–65.

55 Otto S, Orford J. *'Not Quite Like Home': small hostels for alcoholics and others.* Chichester: John Wiley & Sons, 1978.

56 Laundergan JC, Spicer JW, Kammeier ML. *Are Court Referrals Effective? Judicial commitment for chemical dependency in Washington County, Minnesota.* Center City, MN: Hazelden, 1979.

57 Peacock C. International policies on alcohol-impaired driving: a review. *Int J Addict* 1992; **27**: 187–208.

58 Freemantle N, Gill P, Godfrey C *et al.* Brief interventions and alcohol use. *Effective Health Care.* Number 7. Leeds: University of Leeds, 1993.

59 Godfrey C. *The Cost–Benefit Analysis of Treatment of Alcoholism.* York: Centre for Health Economics, 1989.

60 Godfrey C. *The Cost-Effectiveness of Alcohol Services: lessons for contracting?* YARTIC Occasional Paper 2. York: Centre for Health Economics, University of York, 1992.

61 Holder HD. Alcoholism treatment: potential health care costs saving. *Med Care* 1987; **25**: 52–71.

62 McKenna M, Chick J, Buxton M *et al.* The Seccat survey. I. The costs and consequences of alcoholism. *Alcohol Alcohol* 1996; **31**: 565–76.

63 Patience D, Buxton M, Chick J *et al.* The Seccat survey. II. The alcohol-related problems questionnaire as a proxy for resource costs and quality of life in alcoholism treatment. *Alcohol Alcohol* 1997; **32**: 79–84.

64 Schädlich PK, Brecht JG. The cost-effectiveness of acamprosate in the treatment of alcoholism in Germany. *Pharmacoeconomics* 1998; **13**: 719–30.

65 Curson DA. Private treatment of alcohol and drug problems in Britain. *Br J Addict* 1991; **297**: 663–8.

66 Williams R, Wright J. Epidemiological issues in health needs assessment. *BMJ* 1998; **316**: 1379–82.

67 Rake MO, Spratley TA. Alcohol liaison in action. *J R Coll Physicians Lond* 1995; **29**: 275–9.

68 Smith JE, Meyers RJ, Delaney HD. The community reinforcement approach with homeless alcohol-dependent individuals. *J Consult Clin Psychol* 1998; **66**: 541–8.

69 Edwards G, Marshall EJ, Cook CCH. *The Treatment of Drinking Problems* (4e). Cambridge: Cambridge University Press, 2003, pp. 94–132.

70 Drummond DC. The relationship between alcohol dependence and alcohol-related problems in a clinical population. *Br J Addict* 1990; **85**: 357–66.

71 Department of Health. *The Health of the Nation: a summary of the Strategy for Health in England.* London: HMSO, 1992.

72 Department of Health. *Our Healthier Nation.* London: The Stationery Office, 1998.

73 Edwards G, Marshall EJ, Cook CCH. *The Treatment of Drinking Problems* (4e). Cambridge: Cambridge University Press, 2003, pp. 369–89.

Acknowledgements

I am particularly grateful to Professor Griffith Edwards and Dr Sujata Unnithan for allowing me to use as a basis for this chapter the previous version, which they wrote for the first series of *Health Care Needs Assessment* reviews. I would also like to thank Louise Hope and Michelle Povey, who assisted in obtaining and collating much of the statistical information incorporated in the review. Thanks are due to all the following individuals and organisations for the data and other information that they provided. Dr Sanderson, at the National Casemix Office of the NHS Executive, provided the data on Hospital Episode Statistics. Brian Rainsley, at East Kent Health Authority, provided the information on expenditure on alcohol services in Kent. Paul Fisher, at Kent County Council Social Services, provided the information on placements into residential rehabilitation in Kent. The Office for National Statistics supplied the data on cirrhosis by health region (Table 2). The various regional drug misuse database managers supplied the data in Table 8. Fran Walker and Caroline Bradley at Alcohol Concern kindly provided the data in Tables 9 and 10 and other information.

16 Drug Misuse*

John Marsden and John Strang
with Don Lavoie, Dima Abdulrahim, Matthew Hickman
and Simon Scott

1 Summary

This chapter reviews the treatment needs of people with drug misuse problems in the UK, with a focus on England and Wales. The chapter is intended primarily for treatment commissioners from primary care trusts (PCTs) and for Drug Action Team members who wish to employ population needs assessment methods to guide their strategies for tackling drug misuse. Our specific objectives are:

- to estimate the size and nature of the drug-misusing population
- to conceptualise treatment need by describing particular groups
- to describe the array of treatment services that should be provided or made accessible in a region or locality
- to consider the access routes, coverage, capacity, strengths and weaknesses of current services for the treatment of drug misuse
- to outline methods for assessing needs and to identify information priorities.

A central principle of our review is that no single commissioning agency or provider can meet the health and social care needs of the drug-misusing population. An effective response requires the combined efforts of all Government departments to greater or lesser degrees. The key ingredients for a successful national response are balanced joint service commissioning, appropriate joint purchasing between the health, social welfare and criminal justice agencies, and shared working between specialist and generic providers.

Statement of the problem

In England and Wales, around half of the population aged 16–29 years have used an illicit drug, the majority using cannabis. Approximately 1.2 million people aged 16–24 report that they have consumed an illicit psychoactive drug in the previous month. The ten-year Government strategy to tackle drug misuse covers all illicit drugs but gives priority to the reduction of use of and harm by opioids, cocaine, amphetamine and amphetamine-type stimulants, sedative/hypnotics, hallucinogens and volatile substances (solvents and inhalants).

---

* Several changes to the national drugs strategy have occurred since the preparation of this chapter. The interested reader should consult the following for information: www.drugs.gov.uk and www.nta.nhs.uk

Most people who present to primary care and specialist treatment facilities have problems with opiates, mainly illicit heroin. The use of multiple substances (polydrug use) is the norm rather than the exception, and many people with health care needs have multiple problems relating to the use of several types of drugs, spanning the opiates, psychostimulants, benzodiazepines and alcohol.

There is a well-established range of treatment services (with primary and secondary prevention aims) across statutory and non-statutory sectors to help affected individuals and to provide support to family members and others. Primary prevention in the form of drug education in schools is less developed, and there is currently a general lack of reliable research evidence for its effectiveness. Since 1998, a national drug misuse control strategy has been established. This emphasises the central importance of primary, secondary and tertiary prevention and seeks to integrate efforts across central Government departments.

A thorough appraisal of the risks and harmful consequences of drug use and drug dependence involves consideration of a range of personal, health, social, economic and legal risks and harm, which can be experienced at the individual, familial and community levels. For most people, initiation into illicit drug use does not lead to regular and problematic use, and use substantially declines with age. Vulnerability to drug use is highest amongst young people, with most problem drug users initiating use before the age of 20. For a sizable minority of people (notably for heroin users), problem drug use is a chronic, relapsing condition during which an individual develops a 'career' of both drug use and treatment.

Subgroups

Drug misusers form a highly heterogeneous population. Their treatment needs are influenced to varying degrees by personal demographic characteristics, types of drugs used, the extent of impairment and complications, and the nature of their living situation and social environmental supports and stressors. At the population level, seven non-independent subgroups can be identified:

- drug misuser (non-dependent)
- injecting drug misuser
- dependent user
- acutely intoxicated drug misuser
- drug misuser with comorbidity
- drug misuser in withdrawal
- drug misuser in recovery.

Complex cases for treatment will usually (but not always) be characterised by drug-related impairment, dependence, regular injecting, high tolerance levels and comorbid problems across physical, psychological, and personal and social functioning domains. In addition to complex priority cases, there are three groups that have specific treatment needs: young people under 25 years (particularly the under-18s), people with comorbid substance misuse and psychiatric problems, and people who are homeless or not in regular accommodation.

Prevalence and incidence

Prevalence estimates suggest that there are around 1 220 000 (95% CI: 1 045 000–1 400 000) current users of illicit drugs (mainly cannabis) among the 16–24-year-old population in England and Wales. Cocaine has been used on at least one occasion by around 6% of the 16–29 age group and by 9% of the 20–24 subgroup, and is most prevalent in London and the South, and Merseyside. The 1998 British Crime Survey (BCS), conducted with 10 000 participants aged 16–59 in England and Wales,[7] reported the following previous 12-month prevalence rates: cannabis, 9%; amphetamines, 3%; cocaine, 1%. Corresponding rates for 20–24-year-olds were 26%, 10% and 5%, respectively.

The main available measure of the incidence of drug misuse comes from the reports of those drug misusers (almost all of whom are dependent on a psychoactive substance) who have commenced a treatment episode. During the six-month period up to 30 September 1999, the Department of Health Drug Misuse Database recorded some 30 545 people in England who commenced a treatment episode for drug misuse. This corresponds to about 62 cases per 100 000 population (derived from population estimates for mid-1998 based on the 1991 Census). Most drug users presenting for treatment reported opiate problems, with 59% citing heroin as their main problem drug. The overall ratio of males to females was 3:1, and half (52%) of those in treatment were in their twenties.

Services available

Activities aimed at reducing the demand for drugs and drug misuse span primary, secondary and tertiary levels. Drug education in UK schools varies in approach, content and duration, but collectively aims to delay the onset of drug use, reduce the frequency and intensity of use, and reduce risk factors and minimise harm. The seven subgroups described earlier in the chapter may come into contact (through self- or family-referral or referral by a professional agency) with a wide range of agencies and service providers who are either predominantly drug misuse specialists or generic. Four tiers of services can be identified:

- Tier I: open-access services
- Tier II: community treatment, counselling and support services
- Tier III: specialist community treatment services
- Tier IV: specialist residential and rehabilitative services.

Table 1 summarises the general function of the services provided across these four tiers.

Table 1: Services provided in the four tiers of services for drug misusers.

Tier	Core function	Severity of client problem at contact
I (open access)	Advice, information; syringe exchange/distribution; education; primary medical services	Mild to severe
II (community treatment, counselling and support)	Assessment, education, advice, counselling; GP-led substitute prescribing; counselling, prescribing and assistance for psychiatric comorbidity; aftercare and support	Mostly moderate
III (specialist community treatment)	Specialist (supervised) prescribing; structured counselling/day programmes; treatment of complex cases; pregnancy; comorbidity; community detoxification; counselling; referral; training and development	Mostly moderate to severe
IV (specialist residential and rehabilitative)	Specialist detoxification in controlled environments with counselling to prevent relapse; rehabilitation	Mostly severe

There is well-established international research evidence for the beneficial impact of the main modalities of treatment for drug misuse problems. The body of evidence for UK services is growing, with most outcome evaluation studies based on work in England. Table 2 summarises the specialist structured treatment services and their effectiveness.

Table 2: Specialist structured treatment services and their effectiveness.

Treatment service	Approx. no. of services	Effectiveness rating	Comment
Syringe-exchange schemes	300	II-2 (B)*	Evidence is positive in UK, but somewhat mixed in USA
Specialist community prescribing[a]	163	I-1 (B)**	
Shared-care prescribing	40 per district	II-1 (B)***	
Counselling	112+	I-1 (B)****	CBT from international studies[b]
Hospital inpatient units	16	II-1 (B)	
Residential programmes	70	II-1 (B)	

[a] Using oral methadone with dependent opiate misusers.
[b] Cognitive-behavioural therapy (international research evidence).
* Evidence obtained from well-designed cohort or case–control analytical studies (service has a measurable beneficial effect).
** Evidence obtained from several consistent randomised controlled trials (service has a moderate beneficial effect).
*** Evidence obtained from well-designed cohort or case–control analytical studies (service has a moderate beneficial effect).
**** Evidence from at least one properly designed randomised controlled trial (service has a moderate beneficial effect).

Models of care – towards integrated services

Given the broad range of health, social and economic harm associated with drug misuse, an integrated approach based on partnership is needed to underpin the commissioning and delivery of support services. Partnership arrangements are vital between agencies spanning specialist drug treatment services, general medical services and general practice, and across primary care trusts, social services, non-statutory agencies and criminal justice services. A fully integrated treatment system contains an array of mainly generic, predominantly drugs-specialist providers, together with referring agencies and services whose personnel come into contact with drug users during the course of their work. These staff can be a valuable source of brief advice and referral into the treatment system as appropriate – for instance, to voluntary agencies and telephone helplines.

Based on the four tiers outlined above, Figure 1 summarises the shape of a fully integrated treatment system for substance misuse.

In this tier system, each agency has a role to play as part of a co-ordinated response. A person in need of treatment for drug misuse may present to any one of the predominantly identification and referral services shown in the bottom row of Figure 1. The processes for referral and assessment decision making are complex. The assessment and appropriate placement of a client are crucial and will be influenced not only by needs at presentation but also by those evolving over the course of a treatment episode and aftercare. We see the Substance Misuse Team (SMT) as occupying a critical role at the hub of the treatment system. The

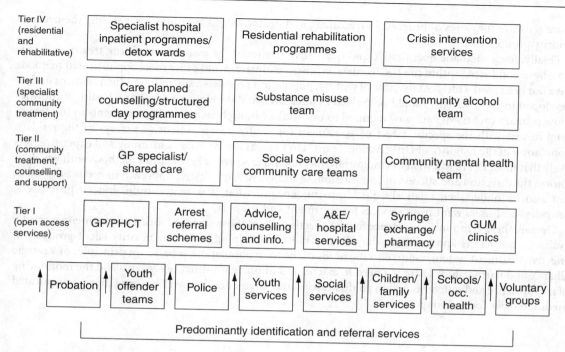

Figure 1: A fully integrated treatment system for substance misuse.

SMT should serve important functions across client assessment, direct treatment provision, onward referral and community liaison, and should promote users' groups, professional and volunteer training and service development areas.

Information and research requirements

The field of drug misuse treatment is undergoing rapid change, especially because of new funds coming into the criminal justice system and because of the development of new interventions in this sector. Periodic monitoring of existing services and new treatment programmes is required to inform commissioners of their capacity. Waiting lists and times, staff recruitment issues and organisational responses to changes in demands will all be critical indicators of the health of the treatment system for drug misuse over the next five years. In several places we have stressed the importance of staff training to ensure that services can adapt to meet the needs of priority care groups. There remains an urgent need for more research into the prevalence of hepatitis C (HCV) and its course amongst intravenous drug users (IDUs) and other drug users who are infected.

Regional Drug Misuse Databases (DMDs) have made good progress towards meeting national and regional information needs, but little is known about how such data are used in practice by commissioners and treatment providers. Greater use also needs to be made of the DMDs to inform the commissioning process and in particular to develop purchasing intentions, service agreements and specifications. There has also been some progress in the development of treatment outcome measures for drug misusers. The principle behind existing measures is to gauge treatment benefit in terms of a reduction of important problems. As a complement to these core measures, two areas need to be developed, namely improved and more sensitive measures of progress in treatment, and protocols and measures for assessing the needs of priority groups.

Finally, few systematic quantitative and qualitative studies of the assessment of drug treatment needs have been conducted within the UK. To date, synthetic estimation and other more sophisticated methods have not been used widely. At the time of writing, population needs assessment in this field remains under-developed in the UK. This should be tackled as a research and development priority. Health authorities (now primary care trusts) are now required to undertake comprehensive needs assessments in the area of drug misuse with the specific target of assessment for young people. Intensive surveys of the resident population in the majority of Drug Action Team (DAT) areas will be time-consuming and expensive. It is likely that most DATs will wish to employ alternative (and less precise) estimation methods with which to inform the direction and success of commissioning strategies. A qualitative approach to needs assessment can also be undertaken relatively quickly to understand what it is that commissioners, purchasers, providers and users want from services for treatment and support.

Overall, there is mounting evidence for the effectiveness of those standard forms of treatment currently available, but less is known about the effective means of helping particular priority client groups. An effective treatment system, tailored to the needs of the local population, is based on principles of strategic alliance and partnership. There is a need to extend and improve information systems and the monitoring of performance and outcome, and to guide strategic and service development by using more sophisticated methodologies for assessing need.

2 Introduction and statement of the problem

This chapter presents an epidemiologically based review of the treatment needs of people with harmful or dependent use of psychoactive substances* in the UK, with a focus on England and Wales. The target audiences for the chapter are Drug Action Teams (DATs)†, their associated Drug Reference Groups (DRGs) and the commissioners, purchasers and providers of treatment and care services across the health and social care arenas and in the criminal justice system.

There are three broad sections to the chapter. We first introduce the main features of drug misuse in the UK, the prevalence of drug use and the characteristics of several specific population and priority sub-groups. We then describe the main types of treatments and treatment programmes in the UK, summarising the current national and international research evidence for their impact. Next, we describe the access and referral routes into UK treatment services and the elements of the current treatment system. In this section, we promote an integrated approach to organising services and providing treatment. Finally, we describe the direction of the treatment system for tackling drug misuse and discuss several important issues, including methods for assessing needs and the monitoring of performance and outcome from treatment programmes. In focusing on the need for health and social care, we emphasise treatments and treatment services that are aimed at the secondary and tertiary prevention of drug misuse. Although primary prevention is at the root of any effective strategic response to tackling the problem, a detailed consideration of primary prevention activities falls outside the scope of the present discussion.

---

* The World Health Organization uses the term 'Psychoactive Substance Use Disorder (PSUD)' to denote harmful drug use or dependence. For convenience, we use the terms 'problematic drug use' and 'drug misuse' as shorthand terminology.

† For convenience, we further use the acronym 'DAT' to refer to a combined Drug and Alcohol Team (D[A]AT).

A central principle of our review is that one single commissioning agency or provider cannot meet the entire range of health and social care needs of the drug-misusing population. An effective response requires the combined efforts of all Government departments to greater or lesser degrees. Balanced, joint service commissioning, appropriate joint purchasing between the health, social welfare and criminal justice agencies together with shared working between specialist and generic providers are all essential ingredients for a successful national response.

The chapter should be read in conjunction with the review of needs assessment for alcohol in this volume.[1] This is especially important, since the division between alcohol misuse and the misuse of other psychoactive substances is generally more apparent than real. As we shall describe, it is the norm for people with illicit drug misuse to use several different kinds of mood-altering substance including alcohol, either independently, in combination or as substitutes. There are also perennial debates about the wisdom of providing separate treatment services for the alcohol- and drug-misusing populations. We do not attempt to resolve these issues here, but note that around 50% of DATs in England include alcohol misuse as part of their strategies and that this proportion may well increase in coming years. Thus it is quite common in practice to undertake a common strategic plan for both drugs and alcohol, and not uncommon for drug users to have concurrent alcohol-related problems and treatment needs.

The objectives of the review are:

- to estimate the size and nature of the drug-misusing population
- to conceptualise the need for treatment by describing particular groups
- to describe the array of treatment services that should be provided or made accessible in a region or locality
- to consider the access routes, coverage, capacity, strengths and weaknesses of current services for the treatment of drug misuse
- to outline methods for assessing needs and to identify information priorities.

The material presented is explicitly intended to be a resource document for commissioners to consult when they are planning prevention and treatment services to meet the objectives of the national drugs strategy. This strategy, published as the Government White Paper *Tackling Drugs to Build a Better Britain*, is designed to link Government departments together through shared working, and is overseen at Cabinet Office level by the UK Anti-Drugs Co-ordinator and Deputy.[2] The chapter is designed to serve as a companion document to the discussion of commissioning standards developed by the Substance Misuse Advisory Service[3] and the Quality in Alcohol and Drugs Services (QuADS) initiative developed by Alcohol Concern and DrugScope (formerly the Standing Conference on Drug Abuse).[4]

It is important to note the limitations of a review of this kind. In particular, the chapter is a framework document and is not a practical guide on how to undertake a needs assessment.

The problem

There is considerable concern about the misuse of illicit psychoactive substances worldwide and an international commitment to reduce demand and supply. The global annual population prevalence rate for illicit drug use is estimated at 3–4%. Global population totals for the use of heroin and cocaine alone are estimated at 8 and 13.3 million adults, respectively.[5,6] In England and Wales, population survey data suggest that around 50% of people aged 16–29 have used an illicit drug on at least one occasion (with the majority having used cannabis) and approximately 1.2 million people aged 16–24 have consumed an illicit drug in the past month.[7]

Strategic context

Recent policy and consultation documents aimed at improving health and social services have had an important influence on the national response. In the NHS, policies published in the late 1990s have encouraged treatment services to strive to deliver higher-quality and more effective services that are closely informed by research evidence and guided by performance monitoring.[8,9] The ten-year national strategy on drug misuse, launched in 1998, is now well under way. Cross-Government commitment to tackling drug misuse is based on a recognition of the value of well-implemented treatment and a stated desire to invest in the further development of treatment and prevention services. The strategy clearly identifies treatment services as the main means of helping people who misuse drugs to 'reduce and overcome their problems and live healthy and crime-free lives'.[2] New investment funds have been provided to develop resources for treatment. The extent to which these investments prove to be a balanced, efficient and effective allocation of funds to tackle drug misuse remains to be assessed.

The national drugs strategy sets a timetable for the attainment of key performance targets, with important achievement milestones during 2005 and 2008. As well as attempting to plan for the health and social care needs of drug users, the strategy emphasises a primary prevention aim 'to help young people resist drug misuse in order to achieve their full potential in society'. The Home Office Drugs Prevention Initiative and its successor, the Drug Prevention Advisory Service (DPAS), function to develop expertise on primary prevention research and development and to disseminate this evidence across the country.* DPAS has also recently expanded its remit to provide support and guidance on treatment service provision.

Local co-ordination

The national drugs misuse strategy is implemented at three population levels through the following planning structures:

- local authority and probation service (approximately 0.5 million people)
- DAT area (usually 0.5 million)†
- primary care trust (PCT) (usually 0.1–0.2 million).

The health, social services and criminal justice system commissioners are expected to be the driving force behind both the assessment of need at the DAT level and the co-ordination of a strategic response to meet it within the DAT boundary. Currently it is unclear how the newly formed primary care trusts will operate in relation to drug misuse within the overall DAT structure. Until recently, health authorities (HAs) have had primary responsibility for the funding of treatment services for people with drug misuse. Local authorities (LAs) are primarily responsible for the physical and social care of their resident populations and are currently the key funding agencies for residential care. Unsurprisingly, the range of health and social care problems that can be caused by drug misuse means that an effective treatment system is one in which

---

* The interested reader is encouraged to obtain publications from the Home Office Drugs Prevention Initiative (DPI) and to understand the work of the Drug Prevention Advisory Service (DPAS) in this regard (www.homeoffice.gov.uk/dpas).

† Population needs assessment planning is complicated by the geographical boundaries of the statutory authorities, which may not be coterminous. A DAT may contain several PCTs.

health care commissioners and LAs work closely together and have shared as well as unique responsibilities for care management. Joint commissioning brings senior officers from the health setting, the LAs and the police and probation services to the DAT to co-ordinate efforts across the three commissioning sectors. Many DATs also have a representative from the Prison Service. This is particularly but not exclusively the case when the DAT contains a prison within its boundaries.

The organisation and financial investment in the DAT structure by its membership varies quite widely across the country. Many DATs have commissioned focused assessments for needs, particularly relating to young people. In many areas, however, DAT strategies have not been guided explicitly by the systematic gathering of data on the prevalence and incidence of drug misuse problems and a systematic assessment of need in the target population. We hope that the material presented in this chapter will encourage more DATs to commission needs assessments.

Drugs of misuse

The UK drugs misuse strategy covers all illicit drugs, but gives priority to the reduction of use and harm across the following classes: opioids, cocaine, amphetamines and amphetamine-type stimulants, sedative/hypnotics, hallucinogens and volatile substances (solvents and inhalants). Alcohol is implicitly included in the strategy, and a dedicated national Government alcohol harm reduction strategy was published in March 2004.

Although a range of drug types are tackled across the country, the majority of treatment services are oriented towards the health and social care needs of people with primary opioid dependence, usually on illicit heroin. However, many such people have histories that include problematic use of cocaine, sedative/hypnotics (mainly the benzodiazepines) and alcohol. In the past decade, the treatment needs of some users of cocaine have received increased attention.[10,11] The use of volatile solvents (including glues and gases) to achieve psychoactive effects is mainly restricted to a small segment of young people of school age whose use is usually intermittent and brief.[12] Available data suggest a lifetime prevalence rate of volatile solvent use of 3% across people aged 16–59 (and 6% across ages 16–24).[7] Two per cent of young people aged 16–19 report using solvents in the previous year and 1% in the previous month. Cannabis, the synthetic hallucinogenic amphetamines and alcohol require special consideration.

Cannabis

In spite of the relatively high prevalence of cannabis use in the UK, studies of the health effects of chronic cannabis use are only beginning to emerge. International studies have shown that prolonged cannabis use can lead to respiratory, psychological and interpersonal problems.[13,14] Research shows that a cluster of affective and behavioural symptoms may follow the cessation of chronic cannabis use.[15,16] The majority of participants sampled by chronic cannabis use studies appear to meet the standard clinical criteria for dependence (*see* p. 381). Individuals seeking help with treatment for cannabis problems appear to be quite likely to experience withdrawal symptoms at intake and to report a history of withdrawal symptoms during previous periods of abstinence.[17] There is a need for further epidemiological and longitudinal studies on the health problems associated with long-term cannabis use and on the development of specific treatment interventions.[18,19]

Hallucinogenic amphetamines

Little specific attention has been given to the health care and treatment needs of users of synthetic hallucinogenic amphetamines. In the UK, the most prevalent substance in this broad group at present is

3,4-methylamphetamine (MDMA, 'Ecstasy'). Although there is widespread 'recreational' use of Ecstasy, few people present to specialist drug misuse treatment services with Ecstasy-related problems. For example, treatment incidence data for 1 April to 30 September 1999 indicate that just 238 people began treatment and reported Ecstasy to be their main drug (1% of the total).[20] It is likely that they had quite sustained histories of Ecstasy use and had problems with the use of other substances at treatment admission. This is not to overlook the substantial public health concerns about Ecstasy use. Public attention has focused largely, but not exclusively, on problems associated with acute toxicity effects on users who consume the drug in recreational settings. The rare but problematic toxic reactions to Ecstasy pose aetiological and medical management challenges for hospital Accident and Emergency services. Although Ecstasy use itself can produce dehydration, unlimited consumption of water during prolonged dancing in club/dance events that have high ambient temperatures can lead to acute cerebral oedema due to inappropriate levels of antidiuretic hormone secretion.[21]

On rare occasions, use of amphetamines and cocaine can lead to intracerebral and subarachnoid haemorrhage. This has also been reported for Ecstasy users.[22,23] McEvoy and colleagues reported treatment of 13 patients (with an average age of 31) who had sustained intracerebral haemorrhage after using Ecstasy, cocaine or amphetamines. In nine of these cases the haemorrhage appeared to be related to an underlying vascular malformation. Several studies have also reported that long-term neurodegeneration may result from Ecstasy administration both in animals and in humans.[24,25] Other studies have suggested that regular use of Ecstasy can lead to the user experiencing withdrawal problems, with short-term mood and concentration difficulties.[26]

Turning to psychosocial needs, the Stimulant Needs Assessment Project, commissioned by the Department of Health, interviewed 541 cocaine and amphetamine users (90% not in contact with treatment services) of whom 33% had used Ecstasy in the previous month.[27] Polydrug use was the norm amongst the sample (with cannabis, LSD and heroin use also reported in the previous month). Twenty per cent of the sample considered that they needed help in managing and controlling their stimulant use, and wanted help with other stimulant-related problems. Perceived treatment needs were greatest amongst users of crack cocaine (the alkaloid, base form of the drug). The study team also compared the needs of 50 amphetamine, cocaine and Ecstasy users currently in treatment vs. those of a non-treatment group. The in-treatment group were older, reported higher levels of stimulant consumption and had higher levels of problems with drug misuse. There was no difference in the length of time that they had been using stimulants, suggesting that the development of problems is more associated with patterns of use than with length of use *per se*. The treatment group presented to drug misuse services with difficulties in controlling the amount they used, with emotional and relationship problems, and in some cases with severe physical health problems. Respondents considered that counselling and information services providing harm-reduction advice would be appropriate to meet their needs. Residential services and support and advice from family members were also considered important.

Alcohol

Up to 50% of people with illicit drug misuse problems in specialist treatment programmes are heavy alcohol users and have alcohol-related problems.[28–32] Excessive alcohol use and tobacco smoking are also established aspects of the lifestyles of some clients in methadone maintenance treatment (MMT).[33] Underscoring the profile of multiple-drug use in this population, research has also shown that MMT clients who meet alcohol dependence criteria are more likely to have psychological problems and family and relationship difficulties at intake to treatment.[34] Studies in the USA suggest that alcohol-dependent clients in drug misuse treatment stay in treatment longer but may be concurrently dependent on cocaine.[35] Lehman and colleagues followed up 298 ex-heroin users 12 years after they entered methadone treatment in the USA and found that approximately a quarter were classified as heavy drinkers, and that half reported using alcohol as a substitute for heroin.[36] There is also evidence that to engage and treat American outpatient MMT clients who present with combined opiate, cocaine and alcohol problems is more challenging than to work with clients who have lower opiate polydrug use.[37]

In terms of the impact of treatment on heavy alcohol use, intake and one-year follow-up data have been reported for 753 drug users enrolled in the National Treatment Outcome Research Study (NTORS) in the UK.*,[38] At intake, 70% of clients entering residential services and 65% of clients entering methadone services reported drinking during the 90 days before intake, and across both groups one-third were consuming alcohol over the recommended limits. The amount of alcohol drunk on a typical drinking day was 17.8 units (1 unit = 8 g ethanol) for the residential clients and 10.6 units for the methadone clients. At one-year follow-up, the percentage of clients in the residential setting drinking over the recommended limits reduced from 33% to 19%, and reductions were observed in the frequency and intensity of consumption amongst those who were drinking at intake. For the community treatments, there was no overall change in the percentage of clients drinking over the recommended limits, and a modest reduction in consumption amongst those drinking at intake. Overall, there continued to be heavy drinking by many of the NTORS cohort who were heavy drinkers at intake. These results suggest that drug misuse treatment programmes should make a more concerted effort to assess and respond to heavy drinking and alcohol-related problems amongst their clients.

Drug-related risks and harm

This section builds on issues discussed above and further considers the health risks, social risks and harm related to drug use. It is important to recognise that the population of drug misusers is heterogeneous and that the profile of risks and harm experienced by individuals can vary substantially from mild to severe, and across the different drugs used and over time. Understanding the risks and harmful consequences of drug misuse requires consideration of personal, health, social, economic and legal aspects of the problem, and harmful consequences can be experienced at the individual, familial and community levels. Specific harm experienced by users ranges from minor adverse physical or psychological morbidities induced by an illicit substance, through acute problems such as overdose to chronic health disorders. The following paragraphs consider mortality, physical and psychiatric comorbidity, health risk behaviour, personal and social functioning and criminal behaviour.

Mortality

Public health considerations of drug-related mortality centre on opiate use. Compared with users of other drugs and with the general population, heroin users have an elevated risk of mortality and drug-related death. For example, one long-term follow-up study of dependent heroin users estimated that this population has a 12-fold increased risk of mortality compared with the general population.[39] Across the past two decades in England and Wales there has been a ninefold increase in mortality recorded as 'self-poisoning with opiates'.[40] Accidental deaths recorded as due to drug poisoning for young people aged 15–19 years also showed a marked increase between 1985 and 1995.[41]

---

* NTORS is the first major prospective observational study of treatment outcome for drug misusers to be conducted in the UK. Methodological descriptions of the study and summaries of research products can be found at www.ntors.org.uk.

Physical and psychiatric comorbidity

Comorbidity refers to the co-occurrence of any additional health functioning disorder in an individual with a particular primary or index health condition (such as psychoactive substance use disorder). It is important to note that drug misuse populations may be multiply comorbid. Individuals may experience physical health symptoms and medical complications that relate to the action of the drug(s) taken, to the route(s) of their administration and to general issues of poor nutrition and health care.[42,43]

The likelihood of substance use disorders covarying with other psychiatric disorders (sometimes labelled somewhat misleadingly as 'dual diagnosis') has received a lot of attention. Improvement in psychological well-being and functioning is an important treatment goal for people with substance dependence, but the nature and course of their psychiatric symptoms and disorders remain under-researched. It is worth noting that it may be difficult to determine the nature of the relationship between the comorbid psychiatric disorders, and particularly to determine which disorder preceded the other and which is the more severe. For people with primary substance-use problems, particularly those who are dependent on one or more drug types, a history of concurrent problems with mood disorders (anxiety and affective conditions) is common.[44–46] Clinical studies suggest that half of opioid- or cocaine-dependent individuals have a lifetime depressive episode, while a third have depressed mood at intake to addiction treatment.[47] Amongst the 1075 clients recruited to the NTORS, some 29% reported having had suicidal thoughts during the three months before intake to treatment, and female clients had more severe symptoms than did males for all psychological symptoms measured.[48,49]

In the UK, psychotic disorders and drug-induced psychosis are currently rarely encountered by specialist drug treatment services attending individuals with primary substance-use disorders. In contrast, community mental health services and other psychiatric service providers typically encounter clients with severe mental illness, with bipolar and psychotic disorders being relatively prevalent. Amongst this severely mentally ill population, use of certain types of drugs – particularly alcohol and cannabis – appears to be quite common. Worrying findings from the University of Manchester survey of 10 040 suicide cases in England and Wales (April 1996–March 1998) indicated that the sample had substantial social problems and health care needs before their deaths.[50] The most frequently reported psychiatric disorders recorded were depression, schizophrenia, personality disorder and alcohol-related problems. Combined alcohol and drug misuse was reported in 17% of cases. The assessment of substance-related problems amongst populations with primary severe mental health disabilities is now a priority research area.

Health risk behaviour

Injecting drug users (IDUs) may be exposed to bloodborne infections through the sharing of infected needles/syringes, and through the sharing of other injecting paraphernalia. Since many substance users are sexually active, several sexual behaviours including penetration without condom use also increase the risk of viral exposure.[51,52] Injecting drug use is a major risk factor for the acquisition and transmission of human immunodeficiency virus (HIV), hepatitis B (HBV) and hepatitis C (HCV). HCV represents a major global clinical and public health challenge. It is estimated that 3% of the world population is infected with the virus, amounting to 170 million chronic carriers.[6] Infection with HCV and HBV is highly prevalent for IDUs.[53–56] A recent study has reported an HCV prevalence rate for IDUs in East Anglia of 59%, with 22% of IDUs being HBV-positive. A study in a London NHS clinic found that 86% of IDUs were HCV-seropositive, with 55% being HBV-positive.[56,57] In many places, the high prevalence and incidence rates of HCV infection amongst IDUs are in sharp contrast to trends in HIV infection in the last decade.[58,59] A test for the antibody to HCV became available in the early 1990s, but many who have been exposed to risk of HCV infection have yet to be tested.

Social functioning

Drug misuse is linked with social functioning problems of varying intensity and duration. Many drug users report conflict in their personal relationships with family and friends and this has been shown to be a negative predictor of treatment outcome.[60] Many users also have enduring problems with obtaining and keeping paid employment. Involvement in work has been found to be a predictor of retention in treatment and of good outcome.[61] Although the ability of a treatment programme to secure a job for a client may be limited, community services will usually seek to support a client in order to improve his or her employment opportunities, and securing or maintaining a job is recognised as being an important goal.[62]

Criminal behaviour

Concern about drug use and criminal behaviour has been a major factor in the orientation of the national drugs strategy, the resources secured to implement it and the action priorities established. Police surveillance estimates suggest that half of all recorded crimes are drug related, with associated costs to the criminal justice system reaching some £1 billion per annum.[2] There is a longstanding awareness of links between drug use and social and economic deprivation and the fact that some individuals (particularly those dependent on opiates) become involved in crime to support their dependence.[63,64] The link between crime and drug use may also be related to lifestyle. People who engage in criminal behaviour are perhaps more likely to come into contact with others who use and/or sell/distribute drugs, and this exposure may be a risk factor for using drugs.[65] Drug use and criminal involvement may be a cultural fact of life in areas of economic and social deprivation.[66] It is also important to acknowledge that the involvement of individuals in drug distribution can pose serious risks to personal and community safety.

Course of drug misuse problems

For most people, initiation into illicit drug use does not lead inexorably to regular and problematic use.[67] Although approximately one-third of the population have used an illicit drug, the proportion of people reporting use in the previous year is much lower (at around 1 in 10), and drug use declines substantially with age.[68] Vulnerability to drug use is highest among young people, with most problem drug users initiating use before the age of 20. Epidemiological studies conducted in the USA since 1971[69] suggest that very few people begin using any illegal drug after the age of 29 and that the major risk periods for initiation into alcohol, tobacco and cannabis peak by age 20. However, in a significant segment of the drug-using population (and notably for users of heroin), problem drug use represents a chronic, relapsing condition. For example, in one long-term outcome study that conducted a 24-year follow-up of 581 male opioid users, some 29% were currently abstinent, but 28% had died, 23% had positive urine tests for opiates and 18% were in prison.[70]

For many people, the relapsing nature of drug misuse means that they will also have extensive treatment histories. In fact, treatment for people with established substance-use problems is rarely a discrete, single event. Rather, several episodes of treatment may be provided over several years. Certain groups such as ethnic minorities are under-represented in treatment populations, and some members of these groups may develop a long-term drug-using career with minimal or no treatment contact. Nevertheless, some users of dependent substances can make dramatic changes in their drug use without recourse to formal treatment. Studies of the natural history of drug use have increased our understanding of how drug problems develop, are maintained and eventually end. In addition to those who require substantial treatment input, some individuals stop using drugs because of a perceived need to change their lifestyles or because of external pressures and responsibilities.[70]

Diagnostic definitions of psychoactive substance use disorder

Official international diagnostic classifications of drug misuse are based on the consideration of drug use (intoxication), harmful use and dependence. Dependence is an important and central concept in diagnosis. In pioneering work on alcohol, Edwards and colleagues suggested that alcohol dependence is not absolute, but exists in degrees with an intensity that may be measured across a range of behaviours and experiences.[71] The two most prominent international systems are the World Health Organization's *International Classification of Diseases* (ICD-10) and the American Psychiatric Association's *Diagnostic and Statistical Manual of Mental Disorders* (DSM-IV).[72,73] Although there is substantial overlap between the two, they represent distinct diagnostic frameworks, with DSM being the more detailed and specific. ICD-10 distinguishes between harmful use of a psychoactive substance, which is damaging to health, and a dependence syndrome. ICD broadly defines 'harmful use' as discernible psychological and/or physical health damage to an individual. ICD-10 provides diagnostic guidelines designed to help distinguish a range of disorders varying along the dimensions of severity of intoxication, harmful use and dependence. These are denoted for specific substances, together with the likely extent of withdrawal symptoms encountered following abrupt cessation of use. DSM defines the characteristic and essential features of substance dependence as:

> *A cluster of cognitive, behavioural, and physiological symptoms indicating that the individual continues use of the substance despite significant substance-related problems . . . there is a pattern of repeated self-administration that usually results in tolerance, withdrawal, and compulsive drug-taking behaviour.*[73] [p. 176].

The ICD-10 and DSM-IV diagnostic criteria and relevant codes are set out in Appendices I and II.

Table 3 shows the format of a short screening questionnaire that we have adapted from DSM and ICD, and which can establish diagnoses of hazardous use/abuse and dependence for psychoactive drugs, together with a rating of the severity of dependence. Items a–d are the criteria for substance abuse and items e–k are those for substance dependence.

If an individual endorses one or more of items a–d, they are considered to have harmful use or substance abuse, and to be drug dependent if they score at least 1 on three or more of items i–l. The use of a severity scaling for items j–l reflects the conceptualisation of dependence as having degrees of severity, and may be a useful clinical research measure. The precise wording of each question may be altered for each substance (e.g. providing examples of substance-specific withdrawal phenomena, such as sweating, shakes/tremor or anxiety). There are several other standardised instruments that assess various aspects of dependence and which may usefully be applied.[74,75]

Diagnostic specifiers

Under the DSM classification, a 'specifier' (in this case, evidence of tolerance or withdrawal) is also used for each substance to indicate whether physiological dependence is present. In the absence of this specifier, dependence is characterised by compulsive use. In addition, six course-specifiers describe the treatment and recovery course of the disorder for an individual. These are:

- early full remission (no signs of dependence or misuse for a period of between a month and a year)
- early partial remission (one or more criteria of dependence or abuse not seen for a period of between a month and a year)
- sustained full remission (no criteria seen for a year or more)
- sustained partial remission (full criteria for dependence not met for a year or more, but one or more criteria are seen)
- on agonist therapy (e.g. MMT)
- in a controlled environment (e.g. a residential rehabilitation facility or a hospital unit).

Table 3: Screening questions for drug abuse and dependence, compatible with DSM-IV/ICD-10.

In the past 12 months:

a   Have you found that using [named drug, e.g. heroin] has led you to neglect things OR cause problems socially or at home, or at work?

b   Have you used heroin in a risky or dangerous situation (e.g. driving a car when under the effects)?

c   Have you had problems with the law resulting from your heroin use?

d   Have you continued to use heroin despite having problems with it in your social life or with relationships?

e   Have you found that you needed to use more heroin to get the desired effect OR that the same amount had less of an effect?

f   Have you reduced or given up work, recreational or social activities as a result of your heroin use?

g   Have you had problems cutting down, controlling how often OR how much heroin you have used?

h   Have you continued to use heroin despite having physical or psychological problems with it?

i   How often have you felt sick or unwell when the effects of heroin have worn off OR have you taken more heroin or a similar drug to relieve or avoid feeling unwell?

j   How often would you say that you have had a persistent or strong desire to take heroin?

k   How often have you used heroin in larger amounts OR for a longer period of time than you intended?

l   How often have you taken large amounts of time obtaining OR using OR recovering from the effects of heroin?

Responses to items a–h are scored as No = 0; Yes = 1.
Responses to items i–l are scored as No = 0; once or twice = 1; 3–5 times = 2; once every 2 months = 3; monthly = 4; 2–3 times a month = 5; once a week = 6; 2–3 times a week = 7; 4–6 times a week = 8; every day or almost every day = 9.

The four remission-specifiers can be applied only after none of the criteria for dependence or misuse has been seen for at least a month. A summary of the clinical features of all drugs of misuse is beyond the scope of the present chapter. As examples, the clinical features of opioid and cocaine intoxication, dependence and withdrawal are listed in Appendix III.

3 Sub-categories of drug misuse

The heterogeneous population of drug users in the UK can be divided into different groups for the purposes of needs assessment planning. At the highest level, the population may be grouped by gender and age, and in this review we describe gender-specific issues for needs assessment in several areas. In terms of the individual drug misuser, the following general factors are important in considering the nature of each case encountered:

- age, gender, race and culture
- pregnancy
- familial pattern
- type of drug(s) used, including quantity and frequency of administration

- acute intoxication (overdose liability)
- extent of impairment and complications
- route of administration (oral, inhalation, intramuscular, intravenous)
- nature of living situation and social environmental supports and stressors.

Complex cases will usually, but not always, be characterised by drug-related impairment, dependence, regular injecting, high tolerance levels and comorbid problems across physical, psychological and personal/social functioning domains.

Population subgroups

Putting aside complexities from the number of different drugs that may be used and their combinations, for the purposes of needs assessment we can identify six non-independent (overlapping) population subgroups (*see* Table 4). These all have specific ramifications for the assessment of health care needs and for the commissioning and purchasing of treatment services.

Table 4: Population subgroups for drug misuse.

Subgroup	Nature
A	Non-dependent drug user
B	Injecting drug user (IDU)
C	Dependent drug user
D	Acutely intoxicated drug user
E	Drug user with comorbidity
F	Drug user in withdrawal
G	Drug user in recovery

Subgroup A

This group comprises people experiencing drug-related problems who do not meet the criteria for dependence. It may include many younger users who have begun to use drugs relatively recently. Because members of this group (particularly young people) are at risk of advancing their drug involvement to more serious levels, they may be ideal clients for early intervention services.

Subgroup B

This group comprises people injecting drugs who may be at risk of acquiring and transmitting blood-borne diseases. People who inject drugs are much more likely to be dependent and to experience drug-related harm. They constitute a priority group to be attracted to appropriate programmes for harm reduction and structured treatment, and to be retained in treatment as appropriate.

Subgroup C

This group comprises people with drug-related problems who meet ICD/DSM dependence criteria. The majority of people presenting to specialist drug misuse services are in this group. They may require intensive community and residential treatment and aftercare support, together with social inclusion services to help resolve problems with housing, employment and training.

Subgroup D

We highlight the specific needs of this subgroup because of the morbidity and mortality risks to health from adverse reactions and drug overdose. This subgroup may overlap with subgroup B (IDUs). There is evidence that some two-thirds of heroin users have experienced an overdose.[76,77] The risk of overdose is increased for users of opiates who have also consumed other central nervous system depressants – commonly other opiates, alcohol and benzodiazepines.[78–81]

Preventing drug overdose and overdose mortality is a specific priority area. A review of drug-related deaths and prevention options has recently been published by the Advisory Council on the Misuse of Drugs (ACMD).[82] Acute intoxication is a discrete event, although a person's needs may increase to those associated with dependence, comorbidity and withdrawal management and support. Most services provided to the intoxicated drug user will be found outside specialist drug or mental health services (e.g. in Accident and Emergency departments or in police custody). All services that have contact with opiate users should have prompt access to naloxone, an injectable opiate antagonist which may be administered intravenously, intramuscularly or subcutaneously and can be life-saving in the event of an opiate overdose.[83,84] Further guidance on needs assessment for this subgroup will be provided through the ACMD.

Subgroup E

This group consists of people who have concurrent substance-related problems and other psychiatric disorders. Substance use disorders covary with other psychiatric problems, particularly affective and anti-social and other personality disorders. This group is discussed further in the 'Priority groups' section below.

Subgroup F

This group comprises people who are undergoing neuro-adaptive reversal (withdrawal) following cessation of use of one or more classes of drug. For example, cessation of opiate use produces a withdrawal syndrome characterised by observable physiological and subjective effects, including somatic flu-like symptoms of varying severity, together with sleep disturbance and anxiety. For heroin, the onset of withdrawal symptoms is typically within 8–12 hours from the last dose, reaching peak intensity between 48–72 hours and then diminishing over a period from 5–7 days. This group overlaps with subgroup D. Clinical management and treatment approaches to assist this group are discussed in Section 6.

Subgroup G

This subgroup consists of people who have achieved a state of abstinence from their main problem drug (or from all drugs), usually through successful completion of a health care treatment episode. This group may require residential rehabilitation services or community-based aftercare programmes and other support.

Ramifications

Within each of the seven subgroups, people are not all the same and must be considered on the basis of the individual severity of their problems and the extent of any complications. It is important to note that these subgroups are not mutually exclusive. Indeed, it is likely that an individual patient will occupy more than one category at any particular time (e.g. the injecting dependent heroin user with comorbidity of HBV infection). A person may also belong to different categories at different times. In addition to these seven primary subgroups, there is a further category, which can be labelled 'at risk'. There is particular concern about segments of the younger population (*see* below) thought to be at risk, and prevention initiatives and general educational programmes are required.

We should also stress that the subgroups are not meant to convey a hierarchy of problem severity *per se*. Appropriate interventions should be based on a comprehensive assessment of need, a functional analysis of the level of drug involvement and a programme of brief counselling and support. These may then trigger the identification of other health and social care needs.

Priority groups

In addition to prioritising complex cases, special consideration should be given to three priority groups with specific treatment needs. The current Drug Misuse Special Allocation within the NHS Modernisation Fund is intended to provide impetus for the development of new treatment services for drug misusers based on primary care, a substantial widening of the HBV immunisation programme for high-risk individuals (subgroup B) and the development of appropriate services for young people.

Young people

The national drugs strategy places special emphasis on preventing drug misuse among young people and on providing appropriate services for those who have drug-related problems or are at risk of developing them.[2] The national strategy defines three groups: children (aged 12 or less), young people (aged 13–17 years) and young adults (aged 18–24 years). At the general population level the following groups have been identified:

- those who have been excluded from school or who are poor attenders
- young people who are socially excluded
- young people who are looked after by local authorities
- the young homeless
- young people living in environments with high levels of drug misuse
- young people involved in prostitution
- young people who have a parent with a drug misuse problem
- young people with a psychiatric disorder
- young offenders.

Guidance material published by DrugScope gives further information on the characteristics of these groups.[85] The expansion of appropriate treatment and prevention services for young people – particularly for the under-18s – is now a key priority. In taking this work forward, one must recognise that there are substantial challenges for the appropriate assessment of multiple risks and problems that may be experienced by young people.[86–88] Further work is required to develop assessment instruments and procedures for young substance users that build confidence and the motivation to engage with treatment and support services.[89,90] There are also real challenges in designing appropriately matched treatments and support for young people, and little experience of service delivery. Unsurprisingly, there is scant literature on the outcome of services for young people. In one short-term follow-up study of 48 young heroin users who were prescribed methadone, 38% had reduced or had been withdrawn from methadone and were judged to have made specific and wide-ranging improvements in their personal and social functioning.[91] However, a fifth of the sample was considered to have had a poor outcome (they had not engaged in treatment or had dropped out). A typical member of this poor-outcome group was characterised by a disturbed childhood, a psychiatric history, involvement with crime and poor school attendance and performance.

Pregnancy and childcare issues

Pregnant drug users should be specially targeted by services at an early stage. Levels of support for pregnant users vary quite widely between specialist services. This situation, coupled with a reluctance to disclose drug misuse, may deter many pregnant users from presenting to maternity and treatment services at an early stage, and this may increase the risk of obstetric and neonatal complications.[92] Since some pregnant users present to treatment services precisely because of their pregnancy, this should be seen as an important opportunity to offer treatment and support.[93] The importance of meeting the needs of young people also extends to issues of childcare. For example, crèche and nursery scheme facilities for drug users attending treatment services may not be commonly available.[94]

People with comorbidity

There is widespread concern about improving services and outcomes for people who have comorbid psychiatric and substance-use disorders.[95] There is currently no base of research or clinical evidence for the effective management and care of patients in psychiatric inpatient units with psychoactive substance misuse comorbidity, and this is an important development area. There is some evidence that people with substance-use problems and comorbid psychiatric disorders appear to have a relatively high contact with medical services and may require more intensive treatment.[96,97] However, it would appear that substance-use disorders among people admitted for psychiatric treatment are of a less severe nature than those for people entering treatment primarily for problems of substance use.[97] It is also important to consider and plan for the possibility that people who are misusing drugs and have severe mental illness will not respond well or comply with traditional care plans and arrangements.

Homeless people

There is also widespread concern about drug and mental health problems among homeless populations. Further, there is some evidence that drug misuse is a risk factor for accommodation instability.[98] Homeless people encompass those who use night shelters, temporary hostels and the accommodation of friends and acquaintances, as well as those sleeping rough on the streets. The most common health-related problems cited by people who sleep rough concern psychological issues, alcohol consumption and illicit drug use.[99,100]

Although there are signs that fewer people are sleeping rough, there is widespread recognition by local authority homelessness outreach teams and specialist service providers that there is still a substantial segment of this population whose needs for drug-misuse treatment and related support have not been met.[101] It is important to recognise that some homeless people also have psychiatric and substance-use disorder comorbidity and may have complex treatment and support needs.

Minority ethnic groups

Overall, the UK population is ethnically very mixed, particularly in London and the major cities. Variations in attitudes and beliefs concerning psychoactive drugs across ethnic minority populations are important influences on drug consumption.

Commissioners and service providers must be sensitive to issues of race, culture and religion, and ensure that service agreements/contracts and specifications reflect the particular needs of ethnic groups. Survey data suggest that drug use is distributed across different ethnic groups, with white respondents reporting the highest levels of cannabis and amphetamine use, followed by African–Caribbean respondents, Indian respondents and people from the Bangladeshi and Pakistani ethnic groups.[102] Results from several studies have consistently shown that people from Asian communities are less likely to report drug use than are white people or people of African–Caribbean descent.[103] There is a perception that many drug users from ethnic minority populations are reluctant to approach substance-misuse treatment services and that they are harder to reach than other priority groups.[104] It is vital that treatment commissioners, purchasers and providers do not regard non-white drug misusers as a homogenous cultural group.[105] Equally, it is important to recognise that risk and protective factors may be quite different across cultural and minority groups.[106]

4 Prevalence and incidence of drug misuse

Epidemiological measures focus on estimating the frequency of drug misuse in a given population at a set point or period (prevalence), and the rate of new cases in a population during a specific period (incidence). There are major challenges for the reliable estimation of the prevalence and incidence of drug use and drug-related problems. This section describes procedures and results using direct and indirect methods to estimate prevalence. A combination of direct and indirect prevalence estimation is probably the only viable strategy for estimating the prevalence of drug use and related problems.

Prevalence data

Direct prevalence estimation is mainly undertaken through population surveys. However, directly estimating the number of illicit users – particularly users of heroin – is notoriously difficult, given the stigmatised nature of drug use and the marginalised position in society that many drug users occupy. Problem drug users are often described as a hidden population, meaning that a large proportion of the target population are not in contact with services or included in routine sources of data on drug users. This makes contact and accurate reporting problematic if only household survey methods are used. Nevertheless, several major surveys have provided valuable data, and information concerning some of the priority groups is becoming more widely available for use when constructing assessment strategies.

Direct estimation of prevalence

Direct population surveys reveal a high prevalence of some types of drug use in the UK. For example, a classroom survey of 7700 children aged 15–16, conducted by Miller and Plant, found that over 40% had used an illicit drug.[107] The 1998 British Crime Survey (BCS), conducted with 10 000 participants aged 16–59 in England and Wales,[7] suggests that around one-third of the population have used an illicit drug at some point in their lives. Table 5 shows the prevalence rates for users of any drug, by lifetime, during the previous 12 months, during the previous 30 days and by age group.

Table 5: Users of any drug by age group in England and Wales ($n = 9988$).

Age group (years)	Lifetime	Previous 12 months	Previous 30 days
16–19 ($n = 502$)	246 (49%)	155 (31%)	110 (22%)
20–24 ($n = 794$)	437 (55%)	222 (28%)	135 (17%)
25–29 ($n = 1,244$)	597 (45%)	236 (19%)	137 (11%)
30 and over ($n = 7,448$)	1,862 (25%)	372 (5%)	223 (3%)
All ages ($n = 9,988$)	3,142 (32%)	985 (10%)	605 (6%)

Source: Ramsay and Partridge.[7]

Turning to drug use in the previous 12 months, Table 6 shows that cannabis is the most widely used drug (used by over a quarter of people aged 20–24). Cocaine was used on at least one occasion by 6% of the 16–29 age group and by 9% of the 20–24 subgroup. Use of cocaine was most prevalent in London and the South of England and Merseyside.

Table 6: Users of various drugs in the previous 12 months ($n = 9988$).

Substance*	All ages ($n = 9,988$)	Under 20 ($n = 502$)	20–24 ($n = 794$)	25–29 ($n = 1,244$)	30 and over ($n = 7,448$)
Cannabis	899 (9%)	140 (28%)	206 (26%)	199 (16%)	372 (5%)
Amphetamines	299 (3%)	45 (9%)	79 (10%)	62 (5%)	74 (1%)
Cocaine	100 (1%)	5 (1%)	40 (5%)	37 (3%)	37 (0.5%)

* Heroin usage is less than 0.5% for all ages.
Source: Ramsay and Partridge.[7]

Overall, the prevalence of recent use is highest for people in their teens to mid-twenties, and around half of all users who enter treatment are in their mid- to late twenties. Only one in seven people in treatment are under 20 years of age. Using mid-year population estimates for 1997 from the Office for National Statistics, the BCS researchers focused on the 16–24-year-old group ($n = 6\ 430\ 000$) and estimated the total number of recent drug users, together with numbers of recent cannabis users, cocaine users and a broad category comprising users of opiates and other 'hard drugs' (*see* Table 7 overleaf).

These estimates suggest that some 29% of people aged 16–24 are recent users of an illicit drug, with cannabis accounting for 93% of this figure. Population estimates for heroin in the BCS are available only for lifetime-prevalence use, because of the small figures involved. The best estimate for the number of heroin users in the 16–29 age range is 105 000 (CI: 55 000–155 000). Valuable data have also been gathered for the UK Psychiatric Morbidity Survey, conducted in 1998 by the Office for National Statistics (ONS).[108] Table 8 (*see* overleaf) summarises the prevalence of drug use found by the household survey of the main general population (aged 16–64 years) and the aggregate rates of use for people surveyed in psychiatric treatment and homeless-service settings.

Data on the prevalence of drug use amongst homeless people are a particularly useful feature of the Psychiatric Morbidity Survey. Estimates indicate that approximately one-quarter of homeless respondents have used cannabis recently, and one in ten have used stimulants. The ONS data suggest that around one in

Table 7: Estimated prevalence of drug use for people aged 16–24 (years) ($n = 6\,430\,000$), 1998.

Substance use	Population estimate	95% Confidence interval (CI)
Any drug		
Using in the previous year	1,865,000 (29%)	1,660,000 (26%)–2,070,000 (32%)
Using in the previous month	1,220,000 (19%)	1,045,000 (16%)–1,400,000 (21%)
Cannabis		
Using in the previous year	1,735,000 (27%)	1,535,000 (24%)–1,935,000 (30%)
Using in the previous month	1,095,000 (17%)	925,000 (14%)–1,265,000 (20%)
Cocaine		
Using in the previous year	195,000 (3%)	120,000 (2%)–270,000 (4%)
Using in the previous month	65,000 (1%)	25,000 (0.4%)–105,000 (2%)
Heroin, methadone, cocaine and crack		
Using in the previous year	195,000 (3%)	120,000 (2%)–265,000 (4%)
Using in the previous month	65,000 (1%)	25,000 (0.4%)–105,000 (2%)

$n = 9988$ (weighted data).
The number of people aged 16–24 years in England and Wales is 6 430 000.
Source: Ramsay and Partridge.[7]

Table 8: Users of drugs from surveys of households, treatment services and homelessness services, 1998.

Sample	Cannabis	Stimulants	Hallucinogens (inc. Ecstasy)	Hypnotics	Opiates	Any drug
Household survey ($n = 9,741$)	487 (5%)	97 (1%)	97 (1%)	97 (1%)	–	487 (5%)
Institutions survey* ($n = 755$)	45 (6%)	6 (1%)	6 (1%)	30 (4%)	–	76 (10%)
Homelessness survey† ($n = 1,061$)	265 (25%)	106 (10%)	95 (9%)	64 (6%)	64 (6%)	297 (28%)

* Sample composed of residents with schizophrenia or delusional disorders ($n = 588$), those with affective psychoses ($n = 68$) and those with neurotic disorders ($n = 99$).
† Sample composed of homeless people in contact with hostels ($n = 470$), night shelters ($n = 176$) and private-sector accommodation ($n = 234$), and those sleeping rough but using day centres ($n = 181$).
Figures less than 1% have been omitted.
Source: Farrell *et al*.[108]

20 people being treated for a psychiatric disorder have used cannabis recently. Estimates for drug dependence have also been calculated from the 1998 Psychiatric Morbidity Survey and are shown in Table 9.

In the general population sample, neurotic disorders were twice as common among adults who used drugs (31%) as among those who did not (15%). Having a neurotic disorder was also found to be independently associated with increased odds of using drugs (odds ratio [OR]: 2.66) and in addition greatly increased the likelihood of being drug dependent (OR: 3.41). Local studies have also shed some light on the prevalence of drug use amongst psychiatric patients. In one study conducted in South London, 16% of a sample of 121 psychotic patients had experienced drug misuse problems within the previous 12 months. Patients with substance misuse problems reported spending twice as many days in hospital in the previous two years as those with no drug misuse issues.[109]

Table 9: Number of people with drug dependence*, from the Psychiatric Morbidity Survey, 1998.

Sample	Any drug including cannabis	Any drug excluding cannabis
General population survey ($n = 9,741$)	195 (2%)	–
Homeless using shelters ($n = 176$)	19 (11%)	5 (3%)
Homeless using private-sector accommodation ($n = 234$)	16 (7%)	2 (1%)
Homeless using night shelters ($n = 176$)	51 (29%)	19 (11%)
Homeless sleeping rough, but using day centres ($n = 181$)	43 (24%)	11 (6%)

* The criterion for dependence was a positive response to one of five questions reflecting dependence criteria, which may have produced a marginally elevated estimate.
Source: Farrell *et al.*[108]

Research has further shown that primary drug misusers are also users of psychiatric treatment services. Of the 1075 clients recruited to the NTORS, 215 (20%) had received treatment for a psychiatric disorder (other than drug or alcohol dependence) in the two years before intake to the current treatment episode.[48] Ten per cent ($n = 112$) had received inpatient psychiatric hospital treatment within this period, and 14% ($n = 151$) had received outpatient hospital treatment for a mental health problem from a community mental health team or general practitioner. The 1997 ONS survey on psychiatric morbidity amongst prisoners in England and Wales estimated the prevalence of drug use for people receiving custodial sentences. Around 1704 prisoners participated in the survey, and Table 10 summarises the prevalence of drug use during the 12 months before admission to prison.

Table 10: Drug use among prisoners during the year prior to admissions, 1999.

Drug type	Number using drug during the year prior to prison
Cannabis	835 (49.0%)
Heroin	400 (23.5%)
Non-prescribed methadone	196 (11.5%)
Amphetamines	366 (21.5%)
Crack	324 (19.0%)
Cocaine (powder)	264 (15.5%)

$n = 1704$.
Source: Singleton *et al.*[109]

A Home Office study of people under arrest, using interviews and voluntary drug testing, has also suggested that the prevalence of recent use is remarkably high.[110] In a sample of 622 subjects, the rate of drug-positive urine tests was 61%. Cannabis was the most commonly identified drug (46%), followed by opiates (18%), benzodiazepines (12%), amphetamines (11%), cocaine (10%) and methadone (8%). Almost half of those arrested under suspicion of shoplifting tested positive for opiates, and one-third tested positive for cocaine. One in five reported that they had received some kind of treatment for drug dependence in the past, and about the same proportion said that they would like to receive treatment at the time of interview.

Indirect estimation of prevalence

Indirect methods for estimating the number of drug users are based on ratios. The most common are multiplier and nomination methods. An example of the use of a multiplier is taking the annual number of people dying in a locality, applying a multiplier for drug-related mortality and assuming that these deaths represent a fraction of the drug-using population.[111] In the most basic form of the nomination method, a benchmark (e.g. the total number of drug users recorded in treatment in a particular year) is combined with a multiplier (e.g. a survey estimate of the proportion of the drug-using population who were in treatment in the same year) to produce a total estimate of the size of the population.[112]

Synthetic estimation methods

Synthetic estimation methods are valuable in the UK context, given the general absence of direct prevalence or incidence measures. They involve employing calibration data from existing prevalence data for a specified segment of the population (e.g. prevalence data on drug use in a metropolitan area) and using them for estimation in a target area where these prevalence data are lacking but information is available about general population characteristics.[113] Essentially, the number of individuals in the population who are estimated from the large-scale population study to be at risk of drug misuse is then multiplied by the number of people in the target area. The reliability of these estimates hinges on the accuracy of the large-scale population data sets and the comparability of the calibration and target areas. There may also be opportunities to perform synthetic estimations using social indicator data (e.g. deprivation indices) that may be assumed to correlate with drug use.[114]

Capture–recapture studies

Because some of the population is hidden or not in contact with services at any one point or period of time, the capture–recapture method (CRM) is becoming one of the most accepted methods of estimation in drug-use epidemiology.[115] CRM uses the overlap between two or more (ideally independent) samples to estimate the number of the target population *not* in either of the samples, and hence to derive an estimate of the total population.[116] It operates on the assumption that there is an equivalence between the probability of the observed subjects being in two (or more) samples and the probability of the unknown target population being captured by the study samples. However, CRM cannot be employed to estimate national prevalence and is more appropriate for use in cities or regions.[117] Equally, rural areas and small populations are unlikely to generate sufficient numbers of cases to allow CRM to be used.

For drug-use populations, estimate studies have been conducted in Glasgow, Dundee, Liverpool, London, Cheshire and Wales. Table 11 summarises the estimates made by studies conducted between 1990 and 1995.

Conclusions from capture–recapture studies should be drawn cautiously in the light of a number of general methodological and study-specific problems that cannot be addressed in detail in the present discussion.[125] Essentially, CRM is used to estimate the number of problem drug users who might enter or have been in treatment and/or might be engaged in drug-related crime, and not just the number of unreported cases. This means that a complete list or sampling frame of problem drug users would not exist even if record keeping and reporting from multiple sources were complete. Because of this, there may be a greater risk of obtaining biased and unreliable estimates than if other prevalence methods such as ratio estimation or nomination were used. Overall, since no one method of gauging prevalence is capable of generating reliable estimates, it is better to use several methods for triangulation.

Table 11: Summary of UK capture–recapture prevalence estimation studies, 1990–95.

Study	Year	Subjects	Age range	Population	Study sample	Total estimate	95% CI
South London[118]	1992	Problem drug users	15–49	458,000	1,832	14,300	11,500–18,000
North London[119]	1993–94	Problem drug users	15–49	232,000	1,321	8,400	6,300–11,300
East London[119]	1995	Problem drug users	15–49	135,000	543	4,400	2,600–7,700
Wales[120]	1994	Serious drug users	15–55	1,565,000	2,610	8,360	5,300–11,400
Glasgow[121]	1991	Drug injectors	15–55	628,000	2,866	8,500	8,000–9,700
Cheshire[122]	1993	Problem opiate users	Total	440,000	518	1,094	682–4,153
Liverpool[123]	1991	Problem drug users	Total	453,000	1,427	2,344	1,972–2,716
Dundee[124]	1990–94	Opiates and benzodiazepines	15–55	888,000	855	2,557	1,974–3,458

Incidence data

Information on the incidence of drug misuse is available from several sources, including national and regional surveys, criminal justice agencies and specialist drug services. Following the demise of the Home Office's Addicts Index of individuals presenting to general or specialist medical practitioners, the Department of Health's (DoH) Regional Drug Misuse Databases (DMDs) are now a key data source. The DMDs provide information, including data on age, gender and drugs misused, that can be used for the monitoring of the Key Performance Indicator on treatment in the national drug misuse strategy. (This indicator is aimed at increasing the participation of problem drug misusers, including prisoners in drug treatment programmes.) DMDs have grown in importance in the light of an increasing body of evidence showing that a range of secondary and tertiary prevention services are effective in reducing the harm associated with drug use. Trends in reports to DMDs cannot simply be taken as a measure of incidence in the population. However, new work that estimates and adjusts for the lag between the onset of drug use and presentation for treatment may transform the utility of DMD data, at least for estimating the incidence of heroin use.[126]

DMDs do not collect relevant data about the consequences of problem drug use, though they began to use process measures from April 2001. There is interest in developing outcome-monitoring initiatives alongside DMDs, which will be able to report on treatment outcomes by administering a core instrument at fixed intervals during treatment (*see* the section on outcome measures). Returns to the DMDs enable the profile of treatment to be summarised for England. Table 12 (*see* overleaf) shows the main drug by age group for users starting a new treatment, as reported by the DMDs for the six-month period ending 30 September 1999.

Most drug users presenting for treatment report opiate problems, with 59% citing heroin as their main problem drug. The overall ratio of males to females is 3:1, and half (52%) of those in treatment are in their twenties. For the six-month period ending September 1999, 11 510 people who had injected in the previous

Table 12: Number of users starting agency episodes, by age (years) and category of main drug of misuse, 1 April 1999 to 30 September 1999.

Main drug	All ages		16–19		20–24		25–29		30 and over	
Heroin	17,936	(59.7%)	2,481	(53.5%)	5,384	(65.9%)	4,779	(63.1%)	5,292	(52.0%)
Methadone	2,893	(9.5%)	118	(2.5%)	541	(6.6%)	760	(10.0%)	1,474	(14.5%)
Other opiates	591	(1.9%)	36	(0.8%)	92	(1.1%)	144	(1.9%)	319	(3.1%)
Benzodiazepines	618	(2.0%)	42	(0.9%)	113	(1.4%)	132	(1.7%)	331	(3.3%)
Amphetamines	2,334	(7.6%)	328	(7.1%)	551	(6.7%)	573	(7.6%)	882	(8.7%)
Cocaine	2,075	(6.8%)	207	(4.5%)	431	(5.3%)	510	(6.7%)	927	(9.1%)
Cannabis	3,342	(10.9%)	1,202	(25.9%)	888	(10.9%)	532	(7.0%)	720	(7.1%)
Ecstasy	238	(0.8%)	79	(1.7%)	84	(1.0%)	50	(0.7%)	25	(0.2%)
Other drugs	518	(1.7%)	141	(3.0%)	83	(1.0%)	91	(1.2%)	203	(2.0%)
Total	30,545	(100%)	4,634	(100%)	8,167	(100%)	7,571	(100%)	10,173	(100%)

Source: Department of Health.[20]

four weeks began a treatment episode. This amounted to 39% of the total number of cases recorded during that period where injecting status was recorded. For the same period, the overall estimated number of cases entering treatment in England was 62 per 100 000 population (estimated on 1991 Census-based population estimates for mid-year 1998). The rates by age band were as follows: under 20 years, 37 per 100 000; 20–24 years, 280 per 100 000; 25–29 years, 205 per 100 000; 30 years and over, 33 per 100 000. In interpreting and reporting the DMD data, it is important to note that they are not an accurate indicator of treatment utilisation. The current system records only those people who are undertaking new treatment episodes (or who have not entered treatment for six months or more) and does not include people retained in ongoing treatments such as opioid substitution. Under-reporting to the databases is associated with agencies that do not record a client's full date of birth or initials (attributers). For many years, a minority of community-based programmes services have voiced concerns about the confidentiality of the database information and do not participate, or do so rather sporadically. In consequence, if there are fewer reports to DMDs, it is not immediately possible to distinguish between poorer reporting rates, an increase in the proportion of clients retained in ongoing treatment and a decrease in the number of drug users in treatment. This has serious implications for the commissioning of drug services, given that DMDs are often the only source of data for strategic planning. Adjustment factors can be derived for under-reporting and differences in retention, but it is less satisfactory to adjust for two biases, which may operate in different directions. Future developments in the operation of DMDs will tackle these issues, once annual follow-up of reports has been introduced in order to monitor new attendances as well as the prevalence of continuing contact with treatment agencies.

The example of DMD returns for London can be used to explore the issue of under-reporting to the databases. During the year October 1998–September 1999, just over 10 000 new episodes of drug treatment were reported to the database. This corresponded to data from just under 10 000 individuals, 5677 of whom were classified as 'new users'. These figures do not take into account the number of people who are continuously in treatment (and do not therefore generate a second episode), nor can it be assumed that all agencies reported all their client contacts to the DMD. To estimate the total number of people in treatment, DMD figures should be increased by 15% to reflect the number of cases where there is no information about postcode, and then multiplied by 1.67 to reflect the number of people who are continuously in treatment across two reporting periods and for the number of agencies who do not send database returns.[122] Given these weights, it can be estimated that there are over 19 000 individuals in treatment for drug misuse in London over the course of a year.

Normative models

In addition to having a basic monitoring function for reporting the demand for treatment, treatment utilisation data can be used for forecasting. Normative models provide forecasts of treatment demand for populations in a defined geographical area. Using this method, a composite risk index of treatment need is calculated from (usually national) prevalence data (e.g. homelessness, arrest data, mortality estimates, etc.) and applied to the target area to obtain an estimate of the relative size of risk for that population. Data are then obtained on the number of people treated and the capacity of treatment services provided or purchased across standard categories (e.g. structured counselling, methadone prescribing, inpatient detoxification and residential rehabilitation). These data are then combined according to the size of the population and its estimated risk for treatment. The critical indicator is the size of the discrepancy between the expected treatment capacity (as estimated from the model) and the current actual treatment capacity of the area.

Other characteristics of drug misusers seeking treatment

Additional information about treatment-seeking drug users has been gathered by the client-intake assessments used by the NTORS. The cohort of 1075 dependent-substance users recruited to the study provided a representative profile of people entering community methadone prescribing and residential programmes in 1995.[48] Whilst 90% ($n = 966$) of the cohort had used heroin or had illicitly obtained methadone in the three months prior to intake, polydrug use was the norm within the cohort. The mean duration of heroin use was 9 years, with 25% of the cohort having used heroin for 13 years or more. Regular use (defined as weekly or more frequent use) of other drugs was as follows: illicit methadone, 29%; benzodiazepines, 38%; stimulants, 31%. Regular use of specific stimulants included cocaine powder (6%), crack cocaine (17%) and amphetamines (11%). Fifty-five per cent were regular users of two or more drugs and 62% had injected a drug in the three months before treatment entry. Almost a quarter of the IDUs reported sharing needles and syringes. It is crucially important for treatment commissioners to recognise that the NTORS data reveal that drug misusers seeking treatment constitute a polydrug-using population. The assessment and management of multiple drug use pose challenges to treatment providers. Patterns of change across different substance types, including alcohol, may be complex, and ongoing assessment of polydrug use is important.

5 Services available

This section reviews the primary, secondary and tertiary prevention interventions for drug misuse that are currently available in the UK. Primary prevention in the form of drug education is outlined first, followed by a more detailed description of treatment services.

Drug education

Drug education in schools varies considerably in approach, content and duration. Six approaches have been identified:[127]

- resistance education (aiming to help pupils resist pressure from peers and others to use drugs)
- affective approaches (using fear arousal and scare tactics to discourage experimentation with drugs)

- information dissemination (providing accurate information about drugs and their effects and consequences)
- harm minimisation (aiming to raise awareness and knowledge of drug misuse to reduce risks)
- cultural approach (a teaching approach that acknowledges cultural values and fosters effective information processing, decision making and self-esteem)
- life skills (an integrated approach that combines information giving, health decision making, conflict resolution and interpersonal skills).

Collectively, these approaches have a variety of aims, including a delay of onset of drug use, reduction in frequency and intensity of use, reduction of risk factors and the minimisation of harm. Drug education can be defined as planned educational provision within a curriculum, which has clear aims and objectives and learning outcomes. From September 2000 in England and Wales, the National Curriculum Order for Science required the following.

- At key stage 1 (age 4–7)
  - pupils should be taught about the role of drugs as medicines.
- At key stage 2 (age 7–11)
  - pupils should be taught about the effects of tobacco, alcohol and other drugs, and how these relate to their personal health.
- At key stage 3 (age 11–14)
  - pupils should be taught that the abuse of alcohol, solvents and other drugs affects health, how the growth and reproduction of bacteria and viruses can affect health, and how the body's natural defences may be enhanced by immunisation and medicines.
- At key stage 4 (age 14–17):
  - pupils should be taught about the effects of solvents, alcohol, tobacco and other drugs on body functions.

Contact points for the treatment system

Before we describe treatment services, it is important to restate the fact that treatment for drug misuse may be discrete or can involve a process of several stages, with provision by different providers and in community/outpatient or residential settings. The seven population needs subgroups described earlier may come into contact (through self- or family referral or referral by a professional agency) with a wide range of agencies and service providers who are either predominantly drug specialists or predominantly generic.[128] This matrix of predominantly generic services and contact routes is shown in Table 13.

Table 13: Contact by drug misusers with predominantly generic services

Contact usually by self-referral	Contact usually by referral
General practice	Hospital services
Retail pharmacies	Community mental health teams
Social Service departments	Maternity services
Children and family services	Genito-urinary medicine clinics
Housing department	Social Services residential care (child care)
Counselling and advice agencies	Probation service (including youth offender teams)
Accident and Emergency	Prisons
Police	

The probation service is an important point of referral into community treatment, and provision of treatment within prisons is growing. There may be additional contact and screening points that can be identified, including schools/colleges and employment settings. Effective co-ordination and joint working between primary health care, specialist treatment agencies and social support agencies are considered essential to manage the needs of most people with established drug misuse problems. As with other health problems, services are summarised in terms of the different agencies concerned, but it is stressed that many individuals require treatment and support from several different types of provider, and over a protracted period. The local authority Social Services department has an essential role in the assessment of the community care needs of drug users. The assessment teams occupy an important position for assessing the need for residential rehabilitation treatment, and can assess need for complex cases, namely those with drug-using parents, pregnant drug users, and children and young people.

Treatment services for drug misuse

Succinct categorisations of treatments for substance misuse are surprisingly difficult to develop. Treatment of drug misusers ranges from brief interventions delivered by primary health care teams (PHCTs) through to intensive services delivered in a controlled residential environment. Consideration of the range of treatments requires the following elements: the method or modality of treatment, the setting in which the treatment is delivered (i.e. community/outpatient or inpatient/residential) and the nature of the provider delivering it (i.e. public sector [statutory or voluntary] or independent/private). It is important to note that a 'treatment agency' or 'treatment programme' may contain several different types of treatment modality and setting. In general, services and treatment interventions for drug misuse can be categorised as follows.

- 'Open access':
  - advice, information and referral services
  - needle/syringe exchange/distribution services.
- 'Structured treatments':
  - prescribing interventions (inpatient and outpatient/community settings) delivering agonist/antagonist/symptomatic treatments
  - care-planned counselling and day programmes
  - residential rehabilitation.

Many individuals may require the provision of several different types of treatment service over time (i.e. a continuum of care). It is quite common for an individual receiving treatment from one provider to receive additional welfare support and other social inclusion services from other agencies (e.g. housing support or legal advice). Such support is an important part of an effective package of care services that can evolve over the course of an individual's treatment. In order to describe how referral to treatment services operates, and to structure this discussion efficiently, we identify four tiers of services for the treatment of drug misuse:

- Tier I: open-access services
- Tier II: community counselling
- Tier III: specialist prescribing and counselling services (community)
- Tier IV: specialist prescribing (hospital inpatient) and residential rehabilitation.

Table 14 (*see* overleaf) shows these tiers, to help service commissioners, purchasers and providers to plan the required range of services and access routes to them. The table briefly summarises the function of each tier and indicates the overall severity of drug misuse problems that it tackles. The four tiers of care are intended to be comparable to those levels of service described for adolescent services by the Health Advisory Service[129] in the Patient Placement Criteria developed by the American Society of Addiction Medicine, which readers are encouraged to consult.[130]

Table 14: Tier-based structure of specialist treatment and open-access services.

Tier	Core function	Severity of client problem at contact
I (open access)	Primary health care medical services; advice, information; syringe exchange/distribution; education; social and welfare services; specialist housing support	Mild to severe
II (community treatments)	Assessment, education, advice, general counselling; GP-led substitute prescribing; assistance for comorbidity; aftercare	Mild to moderate
III (community specialist treatments)	Specialist (supervised) prescribing; structured counselling/day programmes; treatment of complex cases (e.g. pregnancy or comorbidity); community detoxification; counselling; referral; training and development	Mostly moderate to severe
IV (specialist residential)	Specialist detoxification in controlled environments; relapse-prevention counselling; onward referral to rehabilitation programmes and aftercare	Mostly severe

Tier I

Tier I contains the broad array of generic services that may come into contact with large numbers of people with drug misuse problems and with a full range of problem severity. Self-help groups (e.g. Narcotics Anonymous) are also part of this first tier of service provision.

Tier II

The second tier contains specialist agencies (often provided by the voluntary sector) that target drug misusers and that have traditionally been labelled as 'low-threshold' services.

Tier III

This tier contains specialist (usually multi-disciplinary) services that are resourced to offer specialist treatment and referral. Many agencies in this tier are called Community Drug Teams, but this is by no means the only term used. Our impression is that there is now a diversity of team structures and labels used to describe them. Here we use the term Substance Misuse Teams (SMTs) as a generic label to denote these multi-disciplinary teams.

Tier IV

Tier IV comprises specialist services offering intensive and structured programmes delivered in residential, hospital inpatient or other controlled environments. Some crisis intervention services in this tier may have open access, while others require formal referral via a health or social care agency.

Together, these four tiers are meant to imply a continuum of care. Generic service providers and State agencies can refer an individual both up and down the tiers to access appropriate treatment or support services. Specialist providers may adopt a stepped-care approach to co-ordinate a programme of different treatments over time for any given patient. A thorough assessment of a drug-use disorder spans personal demographic features, health status, health symptoms and social functioning, together with an appraisal of the specific psychological and social functions that drug use is perceived to supply for the user.

An important principle is that services in Tier IV, which have higher unit costs than treatments in Tiers I to III, should be reserved for cases of significant treatment need that cannot be managed safely or effectively in a day-care setting. Other health and social care services that provide services to drug misusers will span sexual health and allied services, maternity and dentistry. Table 15 (*see* overleaf) summarises the treatment providers and services available.

The field of treatment for drug misuse is characterised by considerable diversity in the structure and operation of treatment services, their interventions and the nature of priority needs groups that they serve. We next describe the various specific interventions currently funded by the public health and social care system.

Syringe-exchange and distribution services

Access to sterile injection equipment is a central component of bloodborne virus prevention amongst the IDU population. In 1996 it was reported that there were over 300 dedicated syringe-exchange schemes in England.[128] Since the mid-1980s there has been sustained concern about the health problems experienced by the IDU subgroup and the risk of bloodborne viral infection. There is long-standing recognition of the importance of encouraging IDUs (including those not motivated to alter their current drug-taking behaviour) to inject more safely and to use clean injecting equipment. Harm-minimisation policies have been instituted to help users reduce the risk of acquiring and transmitting bloodborne viruses (HIV, HBV, HCV and sexually transmitted diseases). Specialist agencies and community pharmacists constitute important services, which aim to reduce the extent of harm accrued from injecting by promoting improved hygiene during intravenous drug use and encouraging the use of new needles and syringes and the safe disposal of used equipment. These services exist in two basic forms: providers of needles and syringes (who give out or sell new equipment, but do not provide facilities for the return of used equipment) and needle and syringe exchange schemes (offering facilities for the regular return of needles and syringes and their safe disposal). Some services also provide additional sterile injection equipment for users, including swabs, filters and water ampoules.

General practitioners

Nationally, GPs have a substantial overall level of treatment involvement with drug misusers. GPs issue 40% of methadone prescriptions to the dependent heroin use subgroup, and these are dispensed by retail pharmacists.[132] Between September 1997 and September 1998, a total of 3052 patient episodes were reported to the DMDs by general practice workers (some 5.7% of the total number recorded by returning

Table 15: Drug misuse services and treatment providers.

Provider	Potential service functions
PHCT/general medical and social care services (Tier I)*	Open access: advice, information and education; brief counselling and other interventions; illness screening; vaccination; health care information; pharmacy needle exchange; Accident and Emergency services; referral to specialist services, stand-alone or shared-care providers
Specialist and community syringe-exchange schemes (Tier II)	Open access: syringe and injecting equipment distribution; harm minimisation information; health checks (where feasible); referral advice and information
Community-based advice and information (Tier II)	Open access: drop-in facilities, assessment, education, referral, advocacy, outreach, advice and counselling, relapse prevention counselling and support; telephone helplines; individual support; specialist counselling; shared-care prescribing with local GPs
Structured individual/group counselling/programmes (Tier II)	Usually referral: comprehensive needs assessment, individualised counselling and/or psychotherapy; referral to other specialist providers; aftercare support; active work with relapsing clients; job skills and work experience
Non-statutory community-based drugs services (Tier II)	Usually open access: assessment and referral; shared-care prescribing with local GPs; counselling and support
Substance misuse teams (SMT) (Tier III)†	Usually open access: specialist assessment; vaccination; health care information; agonist prescribing (maintenance and reduction/detoxification regimes); management of complex cases; prescribing for psychological and physical comorbidity; education; general support; onward referral
Specialist day-care providers (Tier III)	Often referral based: structured individual and/or group counselling services
Specialist hospital inpatient units (Tier IV)†	Referral based: medically supervised drug withdrawal management; screening for illnesses; vaccination and provision of health care information; education; general health care; relapse prevention counselling; onward referral
Crisis intervention and detoxification units (Tier IV)†	Usually open access: rapid access for users in crisis; medically supervised withdrawal via agonist prescribing; primary health care; onward referral
Residential rehabilitation programmes (Tier IV)	Referral based: comprehensive assessment; medically supervised withdrawal management (in some units); group and individual counselling and support; training; aftercare

* Medical practitioners in Tier I correspond to general practitioners in drug misuse treatment teams (Level I: generalist) and specialised general practitioners (Level 2: specialist generalist) who have a special interest in treating drug misusers (*see Drug Misuse and Dependence: guidelines on clinical management*[131]).
† Specialist medical practitioners in this tier are usually those who provide expertise, training and competence in drug misuse treatment as their main clinical activity. Most specialists (Level 3: specialist) are consultant psychiatrists.

agencies).* PCTs are expected to continue to develop so-called shared-care arrangements for the treatment of drug misusers at the primary care level. Shared care is defined as follows:

> The joint participation of GPs and specialists (and other agencies as appropriate) in the planned delivery of care for patients with a drug misuse problem, informed by an enhanced information exchange beyond routine discharge and referral letters. It may involve the day-to-day management by the general practitioner of a patient's medical needs in relation to his or her drug misuse. Such arrangements would make explicit which clinician was responsible for different aspects of the patient's treatment and care. They may include prescribing substitute drugs in appropriate circumstances. (DH; EL (95)114).

In the case of methadone prescribing to a dependent heroin user, a specialist agency and GP usually agree who has overall clinical responsibility for the client. In some instances the agency will undertake the initial client assessment, and institute methadone induction and stabilisation. After this phase of treatment is completed, the client may then be transferred to the GP at an appropriate point.[133] In 1996, some 53% of all HAs reported specified arrangements for shared care, of which one-third met the criteria set out by the DH. Returns in 1996 from 24 HAs indicated that an average of 40 GPs per district were participating in shared-care arrangements. However, the level of participation varied widely from 1% to over 50% of all GPs in an area.[134]

Local studies have suggested that some GPs are not enthusiastic about overseeing long-term MMT with heroin users.[135] In a study in London, Groves and colleagues found that although many GPs reported having had recent contact with a drug-misusing patient, the majority of clients were seen by a small number of doctors.[136] Other studies have concluded that most GPs are only minimally involved with drug users and generally do not wish to develop this aspect of their practice.[137] Overall, current involvement of GPs in the treatment of drug misusers could be described as patchy. Nevertheless, there are signs that the GP specialists provide treatment that is not dissimilar to that provided by the specialist community teams and that the outcomes are similar.[138]

The guidelines on clinical management of drug users have promoted three levels of expertise to represent the types of treatment undertaken with drug users and the competencies required.

- Level 1: the generalist – a medical practitioner who engages in assessment and substitute prescribing (as appropriate) for a number of drug users, usually on a shared-care basis.
- Level 2: the specialist generalist – a medical practitioner with a special interest and skills in treating drug users, even though this does not constitute the practitioner's main work. The specialist generalist is equipped to assess and treat drug users with complex health care needs.
- Level 3: the specialist – a medical practitioner who 'provides expertise, training and competence in drug misuse treatment as their main clinical activity'.[131] The guidelines recommend that most specialists would normally be consultant psychiatrists holding a Certificate of Completion of Specialist Training in Psychiatry.

Specialist community prescribing services

A 1994 census of treatment programmes identified a total of 163 specialist community drug teams and other specialist prescribing services.[139] To date, new treatment episodes reported by SMTs account for just under 50% of the total reported cases for each reporting period. These services aim to reach drug users who are usually dependent on heroin and are usually current users of several other illicit substances. Specialist prescribing services provide opioid substitution treatment, usually with oral methadone hydrochloride in

---

* This figure is likely to be an underestimate because of confusion about the reporting arrangements of drug misusers following the demise of the Addicts' Index.

either a reducing or a maintenance regimen.[140,141] Two broad types of substitution programme are delivered, each with distinct goals and with more than 25 000 people receiving methadone at any one time.[142] In abstinence-oriented methadone reduction treatment, community-treated clients are first stabilised on methadone and then gradually withdrawn over a period ranging from several weeks to many months. There is also limited use of other pharmacological agents to manage withdrawal, notably the α_2-adrenergic agonist lofexidine (prescribed either singly or in combination with methadone).

In opioid maintenance treatment, where the retention of the client in treatment is a priority, the substitute (usually oral methadone) is administered at a stable level for a period of several months or sometimes years. There is also interest in using buprenorphine (Temgesic), a partial opioid agonist, for substitution treatment.[143] Despite substantial international interest in heroin prescribing, it is rarely prescribed to UK addicts (currently to an estimated 300 patients) and there are only a few reports of its effectiveness.[144–147] In contrast, ampoules of injectable methadone accounted for approximately 10% of the 30 000 methadone prescriptions dispensed at the time of a 1995 national survey, with this proportion ranging from 4% in some regions to a maximum of 23% in one health region.[148,149] Studies of staff supervision of injectable diamorphine maintenance treatment in Switzerland have recently been described.[150] Adoption of supervised injectable treatment has been recommended as a substantially safer means of delivering this treatment in the UK.[134] There are currently no plans to expand diamorphine prescribing in the UK.

In addition to dealing with heroin use, specialist community prescribing services must also deal with dependent use of other drugs by their clients. An increase in cocaine distribution and prevalence in the UK since the late 1980s has been accompanied by a growing concern to ensure that services can respond to the treatment needs of dependent cocaine users. A survey of 318 treatment services in England in 1995 revealed that 53% had received referrals from primary cocaine hydrochloride or crack users in the previous six months and that the majority had provided some form of planned treatment for these clients.[151] Consumption of another common illicit stimulant, amphetamine, is also rising in the UK and internationally. There is evidence that the prescribing of dexamphetamine sulphate may be quite widely undertaken by physicians providing treatment for dependent users.[152] Contemporary treatment approaches combine counselling, health care for physical and psychological symptoms and substitution prescribing. There is currently only a limited base of research evidence for treatments for dependent amphetamine users.[153] In one preliminary study, 63 injecting amphetamine users were prescribed dexamphetamine and compared with 25 clients who had attended the service before dexamphetamine prescribing began. The prescribed group reported statistically significant reductions in the frequency of illicit amphetamine use, benzodiazepine use, money spent on drugs and injecting needle sharing.[154] Further evaluation studies are now warranted.

Psychosocial counselling programmes

The provision of psychosocial treatments (counselling and support) for drug misusers, dependent users and users in recovery is quite widespread but remains under-researched in the UK. Almost all treatment programmes contain some form of counselling, which tends to be aimed at enhancing personal motivation for change and to be orientated towards problem solving and providing ongoing support to clients. These services aim to serve non-dependent drug misusers (especially younger users) and those at risk of drug use problems (e.g. children of drug-using parents, young people excluded from school and those in care), as well as dependent drug users and users in recovery. In the 1994 agency survey, 112 drug misuse advice and counselling centres were recorded.[139]

The importance of the therapist–client relationship appears to be a critical determinant of success in counselling. Relapse prevention is another important cognitive-behavioural treatment approach that employs skills-training techniques to teach drug users how to identify, anticipate and cope with the pressures and problems that may lead to a return to problematic drug use.[155] Specific prevention techniques include self-monitoring of high-risk situations, structured problem solving and rehearsal/role-play.

Since the 1994 agency survey, there has been growing interest in commissioning high-quality individual structured day programmes.[156] These services are designed to provide an intensive programme of counselling, tailored to the needs of the individual. Counselling is of a finite duration and is intended to be subject to high-quality monitoring of progress against objectives. To date, there has been no national audit of the number and operation of these services and there is no published study of their effectiveness.

Hospital inpatient programmes

Specialist inpatient units constitute a numerically small but important element of treatment provision in the UK. These programmes serve the user in withdrawal, and offer a medically supervised detoxification service in a controlled environment and a programme of counselling and education oriented towards preventing relapse. For some people, detoxification can be a gateway into drug-free counselling. Achieving a drug-free state is necessary for entry into many residential rehabilitation programmes or (for opiate users) to receive relapse-prevention treatments using the opiate antagonist naltrexone.

Withdrawal-management issues are most clearly required for dependent users of opiates and benzo-diazepines (and potentially cocaine), where cessation of use may be followed by a distinct withdrawal syndrome. The nature of the withdrawal syndrome will be determined by the substance class, while the time-course of the syndrome will be determined by the specific drug used. Several drugs and detoxification techniques may be used singly or in combination in these inpatient units to manage withdrawal symptoms. For opiate management, the most commonly used method is to transfer the client to oral methadone and then gradually reduce the dose. This is by no means the only withdrawal management strategy, and partial-agonist medications such as buprenorphine[157] may also be available, as may rapid detoxification procedures based on administration of antagonist medications.[158,159]

There has been no significant increase in the number of specialist inpatient detoxification beds in the UK since the 1960s, although several crisis intervention programmes have been developed in inner-city areas. In England in 1994 there were some 16 specialist units providing about 100 beds.[139] There are also a small number of crisis intervention facilities in several cities across the UK which can be rapidly accessed and which provide a withdrawal management and support service. Following a strategy for UK prisons, which endorsed the provision of maintenance treatment where appropriate, there is now limited availability of this treatment in the prison system.[160] Typically, inpatient programmes provide the following services:

- stabilisation of illicit drug use with suitable agonist medication and subsequent pharmacotherapy to manage withdrawal
- medical care for concurrent and consequential physical and psychological symptoms and conditions
- screening for illnesses, vaccination, and provision of health care information
- crisis support, harm-reduction information about patterns of drug and alcohol consumption, and education and short-term psychosocial support
- intensive programmes to prevent relapse
- planned discharge arrangements to facilitate continuing community support services or drug-free residential rehabilitation.

It is important to stress that detoxification should not be considered in itself a treatment for drug dependence, and in isolation it is seldom effective in leading to long-term abstinence. There has been some concern expressed about the need for improved links between the units and rehabilitation and continuing care.[134]

Residential rehabilitation programmes

Residential rehabilitation programmes focus on the health and social care needs of the user in recovery (subgroup G). These are largely services funded by community care that the voluntary sector has pioneered and sustained. Most residential rehabilitation programmes require their clients to be drug-free on entry, although some have dedicated detoxification facilities. There are about 70 programmes operating in England, with some 1200 beds available.[161] Residential rehabilitation programmes provide a structured programme of treatment that has the following basic features:

- maintenance of abstinence from illicit drugs in a controlled or semi-controlled therapeutic environment
- communal living with other drug users in recovery
- emphasis on shared responsibility by peers and group counselling
- counselling and support oriented towards preventing relapse
- individual support and promotion of education, training and vocational experience
- improved skills for the activities of daily living
- housing advocacy and resettlement work
- aftercare and support.

The treatment philosophy and structure of residential rehabilitation services vary quite widely in the UK. There are three broad types of rehabilitation provision:

- therapeutic communities
- 12-step programmes based on the US Minnesota model of addiction-recovery treatment
- general and Christian houses promoting a less structured programme, which favour a more individually tailored package of care for each client.

About half of all residential rehabilitation programmes provide medically supervised withdrawal to facilitate abstinence (*see* section on inpatient units). Many are based in rural or semi-rural locations and receive clients from a wide catchment area, particularly those from urban locations who need to receive treatment away from their usual drug-oriented environment.

People entering rehabilitation units often have fairly lengthy histories of treatment for drug misuse, and many have quite severe drug misuse problems at referral. Although opioid dependence is the most common problem, such clients may have higher rates of drug injecting and of sharing injecting equipment than clients attending specialist community prescribing services. Residential rehabilitation clients are also more likely to use stimulants (amphetamine and cocaine), to be drinking alcohol at risky levels and to be involved in criminal behaviour.[48] A somewhat patchy network of aftercare houses also exists in the UK. These provide a bridging rehabilitation programme for the drug user in recovery. Programmes usually start immediately after the completion of detoxification and last for a period of 3–15 months (the average length is 6 months). The care is often phased in intensity, so the resident may be in a minimum-supervision halfway house during the later stages of this care.

Levels of specialist treatment provision and staffing

The provision of specialist treatment for drug misuse is usually undertaken by multi-disciplinary teams encompassing psychiatry, nursing, psychology and social work. Numerically, community psychiatric nurses are the predominant workers in specialist treatment services. To date there has been no specific national audit of staffing levels in programmes for treating drug misuse. Staff levels vary widely both within treatment modalities (e.g. specialist community prescribing) and across geographic regions. Funding shortfalls mean that a proportion of treatment providers have unfilled posts on their staff establishment.

There is no nationally agreed schedule or framework for required staffing levels for levels of service provision for treatment in local areas. Based on our experience, Table 16 offers a crude estimate of the typical levels of provision for three types of treatment, namely specialist community prescribing services, hospital inpatient units and residential rehabilitation programmes. The table should not be used for planning and commissioning purposes and is offered for illustrative purposes only.

Table 16: Estimated resource levels for specialist treatment services per 0.5 million population.

Resource	Substance misuse team	Hospital inpatient unit	Residential rehabilitation programme
Consultant psychiatrist*	1 wte	0.5 wte	Sessional
Specialist registrar/other medical	0.5 wte	0.5 wte	2–5 sessions
Staff grade/GP	0.5 wte	0.5 wte	2 sessions
Co-ordinator/manager	1 wte	1 wte	1 wte
Community psychiatric nurse	4–6 wte	6–12 wte	0–0.5 wte
State-registered nurse/other nurse	1–5 wte	2–4 wte	1–3 wte
Clinical psychologist/counsellor	0–1 wte	0–0.25 wte	0–3 wte
Social worker	1–2 wte	0.25–0.5 wte	2–4 wte
Drug worker/care worker	1–3 wte	Usually 0	2–4 wte
Administrator/secretary	1–2 wte	1–2 wte	1–2 wte
Coverage	Around 150–200 places/500,000 pop. for maintenance and reduction	10–20 beds/500,000 pop.+	12–40 beds/500,000 pop.+

wte = whole-time equivalent.
* Reflecting the Royal College of Psychiatrists guidelines on the number of consultants needed at a local level in 1992.

Essentially, staffing levels for these services are based around an eight-person clinical team in a 'standard' SMT inpatient programme and medium-sized residential rehabilitation programme (say, 15 beds). The extent of medical staffing in the residential programmes is largely determined by the provision of medically supervised withdrawal. Abstinence houses do not usually have formalised medical staff.

Given the expansion in funding resources flowing into the probation service and the prison system, there are concerns that drug treatment services may be understaffed and may not have sufficient capacity to manage the increased demand envisaged. This shift in resource allocation comes at a time when the lower levels of new funding investment to the HAs (now PCTs) and LAs are being prioritised towards primary care (NHS Modernisation Fund), the much-needed HBV vaccination programme and services for young people.

Social costs of drug misuse and specialist drug treatment

Many drug misusers are frequent consumers of health and social care services. Data on the total burden on the general health and social care systems and specialist treatment providers are scarce. Around 48%

($n = 519$) of the NTORS cohort ($n = 1075$) had received medical treatment from an Accident and Emergency department in the two years before intake to their index treatment, a quarter had had a general hospital admission,[48] and 70% of clients ($n = 748$) reported visiting a GP at least once during this period. Costs to the health and social care system for the cohort during the year before admission to treatment were estimated at £744 000 and were composed of the elements listed in Table 17.

Table 17: Estimated health care costs* over the year before admission to treatment for the cohort of patients recruited to the National Treatment Outcome Study ($n = 1075$).

Service type	Total (£)	Mean (median) cost per patient	Standard deviation	Percentage of total
General medical inpatient	352,000	327 (0)	1,432	47
Psychiatric inpatient	161,000	150 (0)	748	22
Accident and Emergency	44,000	50 (27)	125	6
General practitioner visits	63,000	59 (16)	132	9
Community mental health/outpatient	124,000	115 (0)	605	17
Total	744,000	701 (93)	1,948	100

* Costs are in 1995–96 prices after inflation, using the Department of Health's index for hospital and community health services.
Source: Healey *et al.*[162]

As can be seen, some 69% of the total estimated health care costs arose through admissions to general medical and psychiatric inpatient services. Contact by the sample with community mental health and outpatient teams (where treatment was primarily for non-substance-related psychiatric disorder) accounted for 17% of the total estimated costs. During the two years before treatment entry, 80% of the cohort had received at least one episode of specialist treatment for drug misuse. Three-quarters had been prescribed an opiate substitute drug and more than a quarter had been in residential treatment during this time. Nineteen per cent had also been treated at inpatient agencies. Table 18 shows the estimated costs of this treatment for the year before admission.

Table 18: Estimated costs* of drug misuse treatment over the year before admission, for the cohort of patients recruited to the National Treatment Outcome Study ($n = 1075$).

Service type (during or before admission)	Total (£)	Mean (median) cost per patient	Standard deviation	Percentage of total
Drug dependency inpatient treatment	378,000	351 (0)	1,177	19
Residential rehabilitation	538,000	500 (0)	1,891	27
Methadone treatment (hospital based)	249,000	232 (27)	655	13
Methadone treatment (specialist community teams)	383,000	356 (16)	793	19
Methadone treatment (general practitioners)	209,000	195 (0)	353	11
Alcoholics Anonymous and Narcotics Anonymous	32,000	30 (0)	153	2
Street agency (advice, counselling and information)	184,000	172 (7.7)	566	9
Total	1,973,000	1,836	2,725	100

* Costs are at 1995–96 prices.
Source: Healey *et al.*[163]

It important to note that the costs of service provision (staffing and building costs) vary across the country and are, for example, around 22% higher in inner London than elsewhere.[164]

6 Effectiveness of primary, secondary and tertiary prevention services

This section presents a review of the research evidence for the effectiveness of primary, secondary and tertiary interventions for drug misuse.* The material presented draws largely on available evidence from the UK and Europe and from the substantial literature from the USA. There are relatively few statistical reviews of treatment effects in the drug misuse field and reviews are generally thematic†. It should be noted that a focused section of this kind cannot hope to review the research evidence for all types of treatment, and the reader is encouraged to consult the 1994 Task Force report, which assessed the available research evidence for the impact of treatment services. The present section focuses on information published later than the Task Force review. Before the NTORS was implemented in England, there was somewhat scant evidence for the effectiveness of the main modalities of treatment as delivered in the UK. Nevertheless, substantial information gaps about the impact of treatment remain in several areas. The lack of current research evidence for a specific treatment is noted in each relevant section. There is also a need to gather information on the impact of contemporary services as they are delivered on a day-to-day basis. Most evaluation studies have focused on the main effects of treatment for a group or cohort of clients. Increasingly, treatment strategists and the research community are looking for answers to more specific questions concerning the outcomes for priority groups. These include the main groups identified in this chapter: young people, people with comorbidity, the homeless and people from ethnic communities. A matrix of clients, treatments and referral and treatment management issues now exists and guides the formation of research questions.

Drug education

Very few studies in the UK have examined the effectiveness of drug education in schools. In one study, Coggans and colleagues examined the impact of drug education in Scottish schools through a cross-sectional survey of 1197 pupils aged 13–16.[165] No links between education and pupil attitudes and behaviour were found and there was only a modest increase in drug-related knowledge. Project DARE (Drug Abuse Resistance Education) from the USA has been evaluated in the UK with poor results.[166]

The general conclusion from international reviews is that outcomes from information-giving and affective approaches are either very weak or zero. In contrast, a number of studies from the USA have shown social-influence approaches to have positive effects on nicotine, alcohol and cannabis use. A meta-analysis of 91 drug prevention and education programmes by Tobler and Stratton[167] calculated that the average effect sizes (ES) on various outcome measures were as follows:

- knowledge (ES = 0.52)

---

* The literature search was performed using MEDLINE, PsychInfo and BIDS databases and by consulting *Addiction Abstracts* (1996–99).
† Statistical reviews (or meta-analyses) are undertaken by pooling the effect sizes reported by multiple studies of a particular treatment intervention. An effect size is usually the difference between two groups (e.g. the experimental and control groups) on a response measure, divided by the pooled standard deviation across the groups.

- behaviour (ES = 0.27)
- skills (ES = 0.26)
- drug use (ES = 0.24)
- attitudes (ES = 0.18).

When the programmes were analysed by type of approach, effect sizes were as follows:

- peer programmes (ES = 0.42)*
- knowledge only (ES = 0.07)
- affective only (ES = 0.05)
- knowledge plus affective (ES = 0.07).

In contrast to the information-dissemination and affective approaches, drug education based on a life-skills orientation is increasingly popular. This approach is most clearly expressed in the Life-Skills Training programmes developed by Botvin and colleagues in the USA, which have been subjected to quite rigorous experimental study with generally positive outcomes.[168–171]

Drug misuse services and treatment programmes

Summarising the effectiveness of drug misuse interventions is complicated by the fact that most people in need of treatment have multiple personal and social problems. In general, positive outcomes from treatment include a reduction in drug-use involvement, health-risk behaviour and physical and psychological health symptoms, together with positive outcomes in the social functioning domains (e.g. employment, relationship problems, accommodation and criminal behaviour).[172] Whilst the primary outcome measures from treatment tend to be related to substance involvement, a set of indicators for health, relationship functioning, employment and criminal behaviour are usually measured by comprehensive evaluation studies of outcomes.

In the following sections, we review the main services and treatment interventions across Tiers I to IV. The notation for indicating the quality and strength of the available evidence is that used in the *Health Care Needs Assessment* series.

Syringe-exchange schemes

Quality of evidence and size of effect: II-2 (B)

The main outcome measure for evaluating the impact of specialist and community syringe-exchange programmes is the frequency of needle- and syringe-sharing incidents during the month before interview. Research on the impact of the initial wave of syringe-exchange programmes in the UK was originally conducted by Stimson.[173] In the UK, there is evidence from observational studies that, on average, participation in exchanges is linked to a decrease in HIV-related risks for drug injectors and that contact with these services is associated with a reduction in injection-risk behaviour. In London, HIV prevalence amongst IDUs declined from 12.8% in 1990 to 9.8% in 1991, 7.0% in 1992 and 6.9% in 1993. The low and stable HIV prevalence rates across most UK cities have been attributed in part to the early introduction of harm-reduction interventions and syringe-exchange schemes.[174] Table 19 summarises the national surveillance data from the UK and the results of evaluation studies of syringe-exchange schemes in the USA.

---

* The peer programmes category included programmes focusing on refusal skills as well as programmes focusing on social and life skills.

Table 19: Summary of studies on syringe-exchange programmes, 1995–99.

First author	Publication year	Study	Sample (country)	Primary outcome measures	Key findings
Durante[173]	1995	National surveillance	1,876 IDUs in 1992 and 2,138 IDUs in 1993 (UK)	Sharing in previous month and proportion of sharers receiving previously used needles	Reduction of 1.3% in sharing rate (95% CI: −3.7, 1.1%); proportion of sharers receiving used needles fell by 18% (95% CI: 11%, 26%); syringe-exchange clients less likely to share than clients of other types of agencies (adjusted OR: 0.69; 95% CI: 0.51, 0.93)
Hahn[175]	1997	Syringe-exchange programme	1,093 IDUs recruited in MMT outpatient detoxification programmes in 1,988 (USA)	Risk behaviour and pre-needle exchange HIV-seroconversion rate	The number of sharing partners did not change among IDUs who attended, and seroconversion increased
Bluthenthal[176]	1998	Illegal syringe-exchange programme	1,304 IDUs interviewed; 684 (53%) returned for more than one interview (USA)	Participation in programme and sharing	Programme use increased, and syringe sharing declined from 1992 to 1995
Hagan[177]	1999	Syringe-exchange programme	Cohort study with 647 IDUs (USA)	Incidence of HBV and HCV	No protective effect found for HBV or HCV

Collectively, syringe-exchange and distribution services are also likely to have contributed to public health efforts to achieve a declining prevalence of markers of exposure to HBV. Current estimates for IDUs in London are around 20–30%.[169–178] Studies in England show lower rates of HBV exposure for people with shorter injecting careers,[179,180] with those starting to inject after the introduction of harm-reduction interventions having considerably lower rates of HBV exposure than those injecting before these initiatives were put in place. Overall, in spite of the mixed results from some recent US studies, the evidence base for these services is positive.

Specialist prescribing programmes

Quality of the evidence: I-1 (B)

Agonist prescribing with methadone is one of the most widely evaluated treatments for opioid dependence worldwide. Internationally, there is a well-established body of research and clinical evidence for substitution treatment with oral methadone.[181,182] On average, MMT is associated with lower rates of heroin consumption, reduced levels of crime and improved social functioning. A lower risk of premature mortality for maintained clients has been reported, and substitution programmes have also helped to prevent the spread of HIV infection, by discouraging risk-taking practices during injection. In the UK, results from the NTORS suggest that, on average, post-treatment outcomes from opioid substitution programmes are positive across a broad range of measures, including substance use, injecting and needle/syringe-sharing behaviours, health symptoms and crime measures.[183] Changes in drug use are summarised in Table 20.

Table 20: Drug use at 1-year follow-up* (methadone clients in NTORS).

Drug use measure	Intake	One-year follow-up
Abstinence from illicit opioids	5%	22%
Abstinence from stimulants	47%	64%
Injecting illegal drugs	62%	45%
Sharing injecting equipment	13%	5%

* Data based on follow-up with 478 clients ($n = 667$).
Source: Gossop *et al.*[182]

Marsch has reported the results of a statistical meta-analysis of 11 MMT outcome studies and 11 and 24 studies investigating the effect of MMT on HIV risk behaviours and criminal activities, respectively.[184] The results (*see* Table 21) showed a consistent, statistically significant relationship between maintenance treatment and the reduction of illicit opiate use, HIV risk behaviours and drug and property crimes.

Table 21: Unweighted effect sizes from meta-analysis of methadone maintenance studies.

Outcome domain	Effect size
Illicit opiate use	0.35
HIV-risk behaviours	0.22
Drug-related crime	0.70
Drug and property crime	0.23
Drug and non-property crime	0.17

Source: Marsch.[184]

The effectiveness of maintenance treatment appears to be greatest in reducing drug-related criminal behaviour. This treatment has a moderate effect in reducing illicit opiate use and drug- and property-related criminal behaviour, and a small to moderate effect in reducing HIV-risk behaviour.

Injectable methadone maintenance treatment

Methadone maintenance can also be instituted in an injectable form, and in fact the prescribing of ampoules of injectable methadone accounted for approximately 10% of the 30 000 methadone prescriptions dispensed at the time of the 1995 national survey.[132] The most obvious rationale for making injectable medication available to IDUs seeking treatment is to retain in treatment those people with entrenched injecting behaviours who have had previous unsuccessful treatment with oral substitution treatment or who would not be attracted to conventional oral methadone. An observational study of injectable heroin and methadone prescribing in the UK has been described,[185] together with encouraging reports from clinical audits of this practice.[186,187] Results from a randomised clinical trial in London have shown positive, equivalent six-month outcomes for IDUs assigned to oral or injectable MMT.[188] However, there is currently little practical guidance available to clinicians and commissioners as to which patients should be considered suitable to receive injectable methadone and how progress in treatment should be monitored and evaluated. The current research evidence for injectable MMT treatment is therefore I-1 (B).

Psychosocial counselling

Quality of evidence: I-1 (B) [Structured Counselling only]

There is widespread belief in the importance and value of counselling for drug misusers in the UK and internationally. However, the research evidence for the effectiveness of counselling in the UK is sparse. Looking at the international literature, outpatient drug-free counselling provision in the USA has been evaluated as part of the national series of field evaluation studies. The results suggest that abstinence-oriented counselling is associated with reductions in drug use and crime involvement and improvements in health and well-being.[189] There are positive reports of the value of this treatment with heroin users in helping to prevent relapse.[190] Drug-use outcomes for outpatient drug-free programmes that contain a counselling element were reported by the Drug Abuse Treatment Outcome Study (DATOS) in 1997 and are summarised in Table 22.

Table 22: Drug-use outcomes for outpatient drug-free programmes in the Drug Abuse Treatment Outcome Study (DATOS), 1997.

Drug use	Outpatient drug-free	
	Pre-admission year ($n = 2000$) (%)	Follow-up year ($n = 64$) (%)
Heroin	5.9	3.3
Cocaine	41.7	18.3
Cannabis	25.4	8.5
Alcohol	31.0	15.1

Substance use is presented as 'weekly or frequent' during the 1-year period.
Source: Hubbard *et al.*[191]

A number of mediators of treatment outcome have been identified. Individual psychotherapy has been found to enhance treatment outcomes when integrated with standard addiction counselling, and has a particular impact on clients with higher levels of psychopathology.[192] Client engagement in programme counselling has been reported to be a significant predictor of favourable outcome.[193,194] Increasing opportunities for participation by the client have been associated with greater treatment benefits.[195] Providing intensive, individually based counselling to targeted individuals with extensive treatment histories appears to be an effective clinical strategy for improving outcome in outpatient treatment for drug misuse.[196]

Of all the psychosocial counselling approaches, cognitive-behavioural therapies (CBT) oriented towards preventing relapse have received the most frequent evaluation in other countries.[197] Cognitive-behavioural approaches to building coping skills have been used successfully with heroin users to help prevent relapse.[198] Several psychological treatments that incorporate behavioural elements have also produced encouraging results, notably contingency reinforcement therapy.[199] Some 24 randomised controlled trials of CBT have been conducted with adult users of tobacco, alcohol, cocaine, marijuana, opiates and other substances.[200] In her review, Carroll concludes that there is good evidence for the effectiveness of CBT compared with no-treatment controls.

The most rigorous tests of CBT therapies are contrasts with existing treatments. Here findings have been more varied. These comparisons have led to somewhat mixed results in studies conducted in the USA. CBT has shown encouraging results in the treatment of cocaine misusers. In one study, 42 clients who met DSM criteria for cocaine dependence were randomised to receive a 12-week programme of individual CBT sessions or interpersonal psychotherapy.[201] The trial results showed that the CBT subjects were more likely to complete treatment (67% vs. 38%), achieve three or more continuous weeks of abstinence (57% vs. 33%) and be continuously abstinent for four or more weeks when they left treatment (43% vs. 19%). Treatment gains were most evident in a group of heavy cocaine users, who were more likely to achieve abstinence if assigned to receive CBT. Other studies have shown that CBT is effective in retaining depressed clients.[202]

Residential programmes

Quality of evidence: I-1 (B)

A relatively small number of studies have evaluated the impact of hospital inpatient units and residential rehabilitation programmes. One early English follow-up study of patients treated by a specialist inpatient unit found that 51% were drug-free at a six-month follow-up.[203] The only controlled study of inpatient and outpatient treatment of opiate withdrawal in the UK found inpatient withdrawal to be four times more effective in terms of the proportion of patients who completed the withdrawal regime.[204]

For residential rehabilitation programmes, US and UK studies have shown positive psychosocial benefits after treatment.[205–208] In the USA, outcome from longer-term residential rehabilitation programmes is related to total time spent in treatment, with episodes of at least three months associated with positive outcome. The majority of evaluations have been of therapeutic community (TC) programmes. Programme length varies from short-term with aftercare to long-term programmes of more than a year. The evidence points to the considerable success of these services for the recovering user subgroup. US studies show that, on average, clients receiving TC treatment show enduring post-discharge reductions in illicit drug use.[209–211]

In 1989, the Treatment Outcome Prospective Study (TOPS) found that regular use of illicit drugs (weekly or more frequent consumption) was reported by 31% of clients in the year before admission to residential programmes.[31] For those clients who had received at least 23 months of treatment, this rate reduced to zero during the first 90 days of treatment. It then stabilised across three further intervals: the first 3 months after treatment (11%), the year after treatment (11%) and the period 3–5 years after treatment (12%). Drug-use outcomes for the long-term residential and short-term inpatient treatment modalities studied by the DATOS in 1997 are summarised in Table 23.

Table 23: Drug-use outcomes from the Drug Abuse Treatment Outcome Study (DATOS).

Drug use	Long-term residential treatment		Short-term inpatient treatment	
	Pre-admission year ($n = 2293$) (%)	Follow-up year ($n = 676$) (%)	Pre-admission year ($n = 2613$) (%)	Follow-up year ($n = 799$) (%)
Heroin	17.2	5.8	7.0	2.2
Cocaine	66.4	22.1	66.8	20.8
Cannabis	28.3	12.7	30.3	10.5
Alcohol	40.2	18.8	48.1	19.7

Substance use is presented as 'weekly or frequent' during the 1-year period.
Source: Hubbard *et al.*[191]

In the UK, NTORS has examined outcomes after discharge from 8 inpatient units and 16 residential rehabilitation programmes. Table 24 shows the one-year follow-up results.

Table 24: Outcomes at one-year follow-up (residential clients in NTORS).

Drug use measure	Intake	One-year follow-up
Heroin	74.5%	49.5%
Other opiates	78.2%	50.5%
Crack cocaine	36.7%	18.2%
Other stimulants	70.5%	32.4%
Benzodiazepines	56.7%	28.4%
Alcohol*	33.1%	18.9%
Injecting	60.7%	32.7%
Sharing injecting equipment	18.9%	6.9%

Data based on follow-up with 275 clients. Measures are rates in the 90 days before interview.
* Refers to drinking above the recommended weekly limits.
Source: Gossop *et al.*[210]

Cost-effectiveness of treatment for drug misuse

Quality of evidence: II-2 (C)

Economic evaluations examine the resources required to provide treatment and assess the resulting benefits. A central question posed by many economic evaluations is whether the treatment or treatment system studied is an efficient use of resources.[212] Outcomes relevant to health economics in the field of drug misuse are usually conceptualised as a change in desired, positive behaviour.[213] Several cost-effectiveness studies, mostly in the USA, have looked at the outcomes of treatment achieved for specific costs. It is important to differentiate two other kinds of economic study: cost–benefit and cost offset. The former yields measures of benefit in units of monetary return. The latter usually involves the estimation of whether the costs of a drug misuser's treatment are offset by reductions in expenditure in other health care services or in reduced victim costs because of lower involvement with crime.[214]

Almost all studies that have examined changes in crime (largely acquisitive or property oriented) during and after an index treatment episode have shown a reduction in victim costs to individuals, retailers and insurers.[215] For example, the US TOPS study included two summary cost measures (costs to victims and cost to society) and found that in most instances the ratio of benefits to costs was quite substantial (*see* Table 25).

Table 25: Ratio of benefits to costs of treatment (TOPS).

Impact category	Outpatient methadone	Residential	Outpatient drug-free
Costs to victims*	4.04	3.84	1.28
Costs to society†	0.92	2.1	4.28

* Comprises a total estimate of costs to victims of crime and costs borne by the criminal justice system.
† Includes estimates of costs of crime career and productivity (legitimate earnings).
Source: Hubbard *et al.*[31]

Also as part of DATOS, Flynn and colleagues have reported on the costs and reduced crime-related benefits of long-term residential rehabilitation and outpatient drug-free treatments for cocaine dependence.[216] Follow-up interviews with 300 residential clients and 202 outpatient drug-free clients a year after departure indicated that the combined during-treatment and after-treatment benefit-to-cost ratios ranged from 1.68 to 2.73 for residential treatment, and from 1.33 to 3.26 for outpatient drug-free treatment (according to the degree of conservatism used for the benefit estimates employed).

In the UK, basic economic analyses from NTORS have focused on the overall costs of providing treatment in relation to the costs due to crime within the cohort. Around £1.4 million was spent in the year before intake on those clients who were followed up at one year. During this time the cost of providing drug treatments for these clients was approximately £3 million.[139] Reductions in criminal behaviour at one year represented cost savings of around £5.2 million to victims and the criminal justice system, leading to the conclusion that for every extra £1 spent on treatment there is a return of more than £3 in terms of costs savings to victims and the criminal justice system. It is worth considering that, for drug misusers who also have multiple social and mental health problems, comprehensive (and higher-cost) interventions are likely to be more effective than more basic lower-cost interventions.[217]

Critical issues in treatment effectiveness

Research has identified several general mediating and moderating influences on the impact of treatment. An issue current in both the USA and the UK concerns the importance of retention in treatment and completion of programmes that have a predetermined duration. In TOPS and DATOS, clients who stay in outpatient drug-free treatment and residential programmes for at least six months have better post-departure outcomes than do those clients who stay below this threshold.[218,219] Also, clients who stay for one year or more in outpatient methadone treatment have substantially better outcomes than clients who leave before this point. In NTORS, the planned duration of the residential services studied varied considerably, but three general categories of programmes were identified: hospital inpatient programmes (2–5 weeks), shorter-term rehabilitation programmes (6–12 weeks) and longer-term rehabilitation programmes (13–52 weeks).[218] The median number of days spent in treatment in these programmes by the clients in the study was 15 (inpatient), 42 (short-term rehabilitation) and 70 (longer-term rehabilitation). Critical times in treatment, which were associated with the highest levels of abstinence for opiate use at one-year follow-up, were 28 days for inpatient and shorter-stay and 90 days for longer-term programmes. The percentages of clients staying for these critical times were as follows: 20% in inpatient programmes, 64% in shorter-term rehabilitation programmes and 40% in longer-term rehabilitation programmes.

Important advances have also been made in understanding what happens during a client's stay in a treatment programme for drug misuse. Assessing the extent to which clients are ready and motivated to make changes in their substance-use behaviours is another important issue. For example, analyses from the DATOS data sets have shown that treatment readiness is related to retention and early therapeutic engagement for clients entering long-term residential treatment or outpatient methadone and drug-free treatments.[218] Other work has combined several factors, including the client's degree of engagement in the programme and the extent of positive therapeutic working relationships established with programme staff.[220,221] For example, Joe and colleagues have shown that therapeutic involvement (measured by rapport between client and counsellor, and clients' ratings of their commitment to treatment and its perceived effectiveness) together with counselling-session attributes (measured by the number of sessions attended and the number of health and other topics discussed) have a direct positive effect on retention in outpatient drug-free, long-term residential and outpatient methadone treatments.[222,223] These findings are supported by several other valuable studies suggesting that those programme counsellors who possess strong interpersonal skills are also organised in their work, see their clients more frequently, refer clients to ancillary services as needed and generally establish a practical and therapeutic relationship with the client.[224,225]

In terms of client attributes, the presence of psychiatric comorbidity in drug users entering treatment has been linked to poorer outcomes. Pretreatment psychiatric severity has been found to be predictive of outcome and this should be taken into account when selecting appropriate treatments.[226] The importance of providing social inclusion and reintegration services, particularly in the first three months of treatment, has been advocated for community-based treatment services.[220] However, the intensity or comprehensiveness of services *per se* is not consistently associated with improved outcome. The matrix of client attributes and treatment factors and processes has important implications for referral, assessment and client treatment–placement activities.

7 Quantified models of care

Following our discussion of the research evidence for effective treatment, we turn to quantifying the models of care for treating drug misuse. Given the broad range of health, social and economic harm associated with drug misuse, we advocate an integrated approach based on partnership with which to underpin the commissioning and delivery of services. We also see partnership arrangements as vital between agencies that span specialist drug-treatment services, general medical services, general practice, primary care trusts, social services, non-statutory agencies and criminal justice services. Most treatment services for drug misuse are funded through PCTs. The local authority Social Services departments make an important contribution through their funding of appropriate community care, residential treatment and aftercare support. However, there are generally few specialist professionals within the commissioning and purchasing authorities.

It is important for service planners to strive to ensure the availability of the full range of drug-related interventions, drug education, prevention and treatments (open-access services, counselling, prescribing, detoxification, rehabilitation and aftercare). Meeting the needs of certain groups (e.g. young drug misusers or drug-misusing rough sleepers) may be undertaken efficiently through the sharing of existing resources across several local areas. Problems may arise if the four tiers are only partially covered in a local area – for example, if advice and information services are commissioned without access to specialist treatment services.

Contact and referral through the treatment tiers

In Figure 2 we present the elements of what we consider is a fully integrated treatment system. This system contains an array of mainly generic and predominantly specialist providers, together with agencies and services that may come into contact with drug users during the course of their work (e.g. voluntary agencies and telephone helplines). The latter services are important, since they can provide brief advice and referral for individuals into the treatment system as appropriate.

In the near future, the probation and police services are likely to make direct referrals and specific placements for drug misusers at an appropriate point in the tiered system. Generic and specialist providers are likely to make referrals to higher tiers as well as to lower ones according to the presenting or current needs of their case loads. To an extent, the unit costs of treatment services increase from Tier I up through Tier IV as access to each service moves from an open to a referral basis.

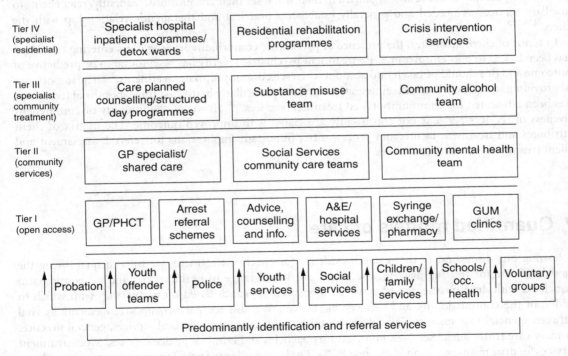

Figure 2: Tiered-care delivery system for treatment of drug misuse.

In this tiered system, all agencies have a role to play in staging a co-ordinated response. A person in need of treatment for drug misuse may present to any one of the predominantly identification and referral services shown at the bottom of the tiers. Assessment and appropriate placement of a client within the system are crucial and will be influenced both by immediate need and by needs that emerge over time. We see the SMT as occupying a critical role at the hub of the treatment system. The SMT should serve important functions across client assessment, direct treatment provision, onward referral and community liaison, and should promote users' groups, professional and volunteer training and service development areas. The kinds of professional linkages for specific client needs initiated by an SMT in a locality are as follows:

- shared care management with the Community Alcohol Team in cases of significant alcohol-related problems
- referral to general hospitals in cases of significant physical illness
- liaison and referral to general psychiatric services in cases of drug misuse and psychiatric comorbidity
- liaison with other community service providers in the voluntary sector
- active participation in performance monitoring (in concert with the DAT)
- liaison with local criminal justice services (police, probation, courts and prisons).

The commissioning and organisation arrangements for services in the tiered system vary widely across and sometimes within the treatment systems in many countries. Additionally, special initiatives are required alongside targeted prevention and treatment interventions aimed at priority client groups. There is great variability in the scope and effectiveness of commissioning and purchasing arrangements for drug misuse services across the UK. There are no nationally agreed standards for single or joint commissioning and purchasing. Nor are there any universally agreed specifications for drug misuse treatment, although valuable work has been undertaken in recent years on guidelines from the DoH, together with clinical management, quality standards and audit guidelines.

Extent of contact for subgroups across treatment tiers

In this section, we apply the seven population-level subgroups identified earlier in the chapter to the four tiers of treatment. These can be combined into a matrix. Table 26 indicates the likely extent of required contact of each subgroup at each level of the tiered treatment system.

Table 26: Likely required level of contact with the treatment system by subgroups of drug misusers.

Subgroup	Treatment system tier			
	I	II	III	IV
A (drug misuser)	***	**	**	*
B (IDU)	***	***	***	**
C (dependent user)	*	**	***	***
D (intoxicated user)	***	*	**	*
E (user with comorbidity)	*	***	***	***
F (user in withdrawal)	*	*	***	***
G (user in recovery)	*	***	*	***

Likely extent of contact: * low; ** medium; *** high.

In this scheme, the non-dependent drug misuser (subgroup A) is likely to be helped effectively in the first instance by community treatment services within Tier I and as required by services in Tiers II and III. Residential treatment provision for this group should not be needed in most cases. The provision of risk and harm reduction services to the subgroup of injecting drug users is a priority for non-residential services across Tiers I to III. We have noted previously that most members of this group will also be drug dependent. The immediate health care needs of the intoxicated user are appropriately delivered by emergency services in Tier I, with expertise in overdose management likely to be available by agencies in Tier III. The subgroup of users with comorbidity is unlikely to be managed effectively by Tier I provision, at least initially. The user in withdrawal will require planned contact with specialists provided in Tiers III and IV who can support medically supervised withdrawal in either a community or a residential setting. Finally, support and treatment aftercare for the subgroup of users in recovery falls to residential providers in Tier IV and to community support and counselling services in Tier II.

Expansion of intervention models in the criminal justice system

The Government intends criminal justice referral and treatment systems to be developed as partnership arrangements, with the DAT serving a crucial role in co-ordinating the assessment of local need, the development of commissioning arrangements and the monitoring of treatment service delivery. To date, the specific subgroups of drug misusers who are eligible for treatment services via the criminal justice system have not been clearly described, but it is likely that in the first instance the primary subgroups will be adult dependent users and non-dependent misusers (particularly young offenders). There are multiple contact points in the system that are now intended to trigger both referral to assessment for drug misuse treatment and specific forms of intervention (*see* Table 27).

Table 27: Development of criminal justice referral systems and interventions.

Contact point/ stage	Intervention	Function
Arrest	Arrest Referral Schemes (ARS)	Police-commissioned proactive assessment and referral from arrest referral workers who are based at police-station custody suites or are on call to attend the station as required
Caution	Informal mechanism	Information based, concerning local services
Pre-sentence	Police, probation, court-initiated referrals (may be bail/probation conditions)	Designed to gather assessment information and prevent further offending prior to sentencing
Community sentence	Drug Treatment and Testing Orders (DTTOs) and other probation orders with a linked treatment condition	Designed to provide treatment according to need (prescribing, detoxification, counselling or support); degree of structure will vary
Custodial and post-sentence	Counselling Assessment Referral and Throughcare (CARAT)	The basic treatment framework to improve the assessment, advice, throughcare and support of drug-misusing prisoners; community aftercare via probation

The ARS have received £20 million in Challenge Fund support to assist their expansion, and are intended to target all arrested people regardless of offence. There is a major commitment by the police services in many areas to commission local ARS. Positive results have been obtained from local studies of ARS.[227] These schemes are not uniform in their operation, ranging from information-only approaches to more contemporary, proactive models in which dedicated arrest referral workers act in close co-operation with the police, usually with direct access to detainees in custody suites.[228] A major development in the structure of the treatment system is the Counselling Assessment Referral Advice and Throughcare (CARAT) initiatives within prison service areas. These have been funded by some £76 million of Government money and are intended to be a comprehensive approach to tackling the subgroups of users in withdrawal and users in recovery. Medically supervised detoxification is to be provided on an outpatient or inpatient basis within the prison setting, and there is a planned expansion of prison-based therapeutic communities for appropriate institutions and for suitable offenders.

The Government has also set about establishing Youth Offending Teams (YOTs) to work with young offenders throughout all stages of the youth justice process. The multi-disciplinary YOTs include representatives from education, social services, the police, probation service and health services. In addition to working with identified young offenders, these teams are designed to work with young people identified as being at risk of becoming involved in crime, including those who are regular truants. YOTs are tasked with reducing re-offending by young people aged 10–17 years and, through proactive primary prevention strategies, reducing the number of young people starting to offend. These objectives are to be fulfilled through the YOTs' direct work with young people and their co-ordination of the local crime reduction strategy. The multi-agency nature of YOTs is meant to ensure that a young offender gains access to the appropriate mix of welfare, educational and health services, and that strategic responses are fully co-ordinated.

The Crime and Disorder Act 1998 and the Youth Justice and Criminal Evidence Act 1999 introduced new powers to tackle social disorder and youth offending. In relation to substance use, the most relevant orders are the final warning scheme, the action plan order and the referral order. All these are designed to compel young offenders to take part in interventions designed by the YOT to address issues such as substance misuse. Offenders can be ordered to attend a substance misuse programme and their involvement in it will be monitored for compliance and completion. The new orders have been piloted in selected areas, with the final warning scheme and action plan orders expected to be fully implemented by 2001 and referral orders in 2002–03.

There is a YOT in every local authority in England and Wales. Some are still finalising staff recruitment, and have yet to establish protocols for working with clients and local support agencies. After much revision, the YOT assessment tool ASSET has been finalised and contains a section on substance use. Some YOTs recruit a dedicated drugs worker to the team, but the majority do not. In some cases, the health post on a YOT is split between a health specialist and a drugs worker. YOTs should become key agencies in screening for and responding to needs related to substance use amongst young offenders. However, a number of crucial factors could compromise the effectiveness of YOTs in reducing substance misuse in their clients.

- If a client reports illegal drug use, YOT workers may be required to report this to the police as they would any other criminal offence.
- While a YOT is required to have a health specialist, the person recruited does not necessarily have to have experience of working with young people in relation to substance use, or of assessing needs related to substance use.
- When a YOT does identify a need related to substance misuse, in many areas there will not be adequate and appropriate service provision available locally to respond to this.[229]

Meeting the needs of priority groups

In this section, we offer recommendations for strategies that aim to meet the needs for treatment of drug misuse in the three priority groups described earlier in the chapter: young people, people with co-morbidity and homeless people. We also summarise guidance on the treatment needs of drug misusers from minority ethnic groups.

Young people

There has been no systematic national audit of the needs for treatment of drug misuse in young people. Nevertheless, substantial advances have been made in conceptualising the efficient and appropriate delivery of services for young people, and there are a small number of dedicated specialist services.[230] Based on recommendations from the Substance Misuse Advisory Service (SMAS)[3] and quality standards developed by Alcohol Concern and the Standing Conference on Drug Abuse (SCODA),[4] and with additional guidance from SCODA and the Children's Legal Centre,[231] commissioners should, through the DAT, develop a child-centred commissioning strategy in consultation with relevant departments (e.g. education, children's services and housing). This should ensure that:

- there is a balance between education, prevention, care and treatment services for this group
- appropriate treatment services are integrated with other services rather than being provided opportunistically
- appropriate assessment procedures are developed and adhered to
- there are clear service agreements for child-centred services
- access can be provided to specialist services, including child-centred specialist addiction services, certain components of child and adolescent mental health services and other specialist youth services and youth offender teams
- access can be arranged for children and adolescents to specialised clinics, secure facilities and aftercare and rehabilitation services for young people who have serious difficulties.

The Health Advisory Service[232] has described a tier-based structure designed to clarify arrangements and services for young people, ranging from education through to intensive treatment for acute cases. This is shown in Appendix IV. The Health Advisory Service recommends that services for young people with drug and alcohol problems should be (i) comprehensive (in order to meet a wide range of needs), (ii) competent (requiring a multi-disciplinary team structure) and (iii) child-specific (involving provision that is separate from adult services).[233]

People with drug misuse and psychiatric comorbidity

There is a growing recognition of the importance of understanding the links between substance-use behaviours and psychiatric disorders, and the implications for treatment services.[234] SMAS recommends that there should be:

- clear arrangements for giving specialist care to people with both drug misuse and psychiatric comorbidity
- specialist services to screen and provide brief interventions for anxiety and mood disorder in drug-misuse clients
- efficient referral arrangements in place to manage severe cases of comorbidity
- a comprehensive risk assessment, including a full and comprehensive history of drug and alcohol use and its relationship to episodes of violence

- provision for people with severe mental illness and drug misuse to be treated under the Care Programme Approach (CPA) with a named key worker. Those with complex needs should be managed under a high-intensity CPA regime, with regular meetings of involved professionals, patients and carers.

It may also be valuable to conduct as thorough a psychiatric assessment as is practicable in the context of routine clinical practice. Such an assessment should attempt to trace the histories of substance-use disorders and psychiatric disorders and gauge their interaction and dynamics.[235] Overall, there is currently no accepted model of service provision for people with drug misuse and psychiatric comorbidity, but work is accelerating on its development. Informal linkages are being established in some areas between community mental health teams (CMHTs) and SMTs, but little is known about the extent to which these arrangements are efficient or sustainable. In terms of more formalised arrangements, at least three non-independent service models can be identified:

- the creation of a specialist dual-diagnosis community team
- specific training input on drug misuse to members of CMHTs
- the appointment of special link or liaison staff to work in both SMTs and CMHTs/PHCTs.

There are no concrete examples to indicate whether one model has clear advantages over the others, but information from DoH-funded pilot services and reviews in this area should provide guidance.

Homeless people

The Rough Sleepers Unit's strategy on rough sleeping advocates a social inclusion approach that targets work in areas with the highest concentration of the problem (e.g. central London). It calls for specific outreach work by Contact and Assessment Teams to assess the needs of people sleeping rough and then to facilitate referral to housing, support and specialist substance-misuse services as required.[236] Specific work will include:

- support to accommodation providers by specialist agencies on care management
- development of specific needs assessment protocols for this group
- development of care management arrangements
- referral and shared-care arrangements between housing agencies and providers of community treatment
- training for homelessness outreach teams on the assessment of drug misuse
- referral of rough sleepers to stable accommodation, and the provision of treatment and support as required.

People from minority ethnic groups

A critical issue is that of attracting drug misusers from minority ethnic groups into culturally appropriate services. Mainstream services must be supported to ensure that provision is appropriate to clients' needs and is culturally and racially appropriate. Services should strive to avoid simplistic views of minority ethnic communities and should develop ways of addressing their needs. Commissioners are strongly encouraged to promote racial equality and to try to counter the perception of some minority ethnic drug misusers that existing drug misuse services largely serve white people.[237] The importance of individual assessment for determining treatment needs remains a central concern. SMAS notes that commissioners should ensure that:

- all treatment and care takes into account the very real diversity of the general population

- minority ethnic drug misusers have equitable access to treatment and care
- there are race-specific services where appropriate.

In London, the City University's Race and Drugs Project offers the following recommendations to service providers:[238]

- develop anti-discriminatory policies, action plans and evaluation systems for anti-discriminatory monitoring
- increase the number of employees from minority ethnic groups
- improve community outreach, liaison and networking
- ensure that individual assessment processes are in accordance with an anti-discriminatory policy and are culturally sensitive.

8 Outcome measures

This section addresses important issues about measuring performance, outcome and quality across treatment systems and individual programmes. The establishment of a monitoring culture for service performance is an explicit goal of the national drug misuse strategy. The Government has set the following medium- and long-term targets for the nation:

> *To increase the participation of problem drug misusers, including prisoners in drug treatment programmes which have a positive impact on health and crime, by 100% by 2008, and by 66% by 2005.*

There is now an increasing expectation, and a requirement from the Government, that commissioners, DATs and treatment services should be subject to monitoring against national objectives. The short-term targets for commissioners and DATs in the areas of criminal justice, young people, professional issues, treatment services and drug-related deaths are shown in Table 28.

Table 28: National performance targets for tackling drug misuse.

Area	Targets to be met by the end of 2002
Criminal justice	30 new prison-based treatment services (with a throughput of 5,000 cases per year) To ensure that the CARAT annual case load reaches 20,000
Young people	To strongly encourage all schools to adopt DofEE guidance on drug education and to deliver integrated education programmes on drug issues
Professional issues	To have in place National Occupational Standards for specialist drug and alcohol workers
Treatment	To ensure that all treatment programmes accord with nationally accepted quality standards
Drug-related deaths	To establish a baseline of drug-related deaths (by the end of 2001) To have prepared a plan of action to reduce drug-related deaths from the baseline

Performance and outcome monitoring

Commissioners and purchasers are increasingly motivated to direct resources to treatment services that have research evidence for their effectiveness.[239,240] There is a growing expectation that services will participate in data-collection initiatives to assess the impact of their services or will implement their own evaluations. In the USA, the value of monitoring treatment outcomes has been promoted and several major initiatives have been developed.[241–243] Although there is recognition of the importance of assessing the progress of individual client outcomes in the UK, work in this area has been relatively modest. In its comprehensive review of the research evidence for drug misuse treatment, the DoH established a framework of key treatment outcomes (*see* Appendix V).

Assessing outcome

The most logical and practical means of assessing treatment outcome is to gather a set of measures from a client at intake to a programme (baseline) and then collect the same measures again at one or more points during and ideally following treatment. In this way, outcome monitoring is conceptualised as reassessment and can be incorporated into routine clinical practice. We regard it as essential that outcome assessments must involve an active appraisal of the client through a face-to-face or telephone interview or by the client completing a self-assessment questionnaire. Other methods, such as estimating outcome from case notes, are unlikely to be valid and are not recommended.

Most of the variables suitable for repeated assessment will be continuous or scale measures, which are sensitive to assessing change over time. A satisfactory assessment of outcome requires status measures to be recorded at intake, at treatment completion and at follow-up. Choice of a suitable outcome questionnaire should be guided by the following principles.

- It should be relevant to the target population and treatment programme.
- It should be relevant to the drugs strategy and capable of direct reporting against national targets and priorities.
- It should be suitable for face-to-face interviewing with a client or for self-completion by the client.
- The instrument must have established psychometric properties (validity and reliability).
- The measures must be sensitive to change over time.
- Ideally, the administration time should be brief.
- The client and other non-professional audiences should be able to understand scores and reports immediately.

Measures designed to assess a broad range of outcomes have been developed in the USA (e.g. the Addiction Severity Index or ASI[244]) and Australia (the Opiate Treatment Index or OTI[245]). A brief, validated research instrument for multi-dimensional treatment outcome, the Maudsley Addiction Profile (MAP), has been developed in the UK[172] and validated in three countries in continental Europe.[246] The MAP requires less than 15 minutes to complete. Its structure is summarised in Table 29.

The MAP has now been taken up and adapted for outcome-monitoring purposes in several DAT areas, following development work in East Sussex and Kent. Core MAP items have also been included in the CARAT assessment form and in Arrest Referral monitoring forms in London.

Table 29: Structure of the Maudsley Addiction Profile (MAP).

Domain	Outcome measure (previous 30 days)
Operational information	Programme setting; client demographics; case identifiers; referral information
Substance use	Number of days used opioids, cocaine, amphetamines, illicit benzodiazepines, alcohol Typical amount consumed on a using day Main route(s) of administration
Health-risk behaviour	Days injected Typical times injected per day Times sharing needles or syringes Number of partners (non-condom sex) Times had sex without using condoms
Health symptoms	Frequency of physical symptoms Frequency of psychological symptoms
Personal/social functioning	Days of contact/conflict with partner, relative, friends Days had paid job Days missed (sickness/unauthorised) Days unemployed Days committed illegal activities Times committed crime (on a typical crime day)

Commissioning standards and quality

The Substance Misuse Advisory Service[3] recommends that commissioners ensure that:

- there is a clear definition of the characteristics of the client groups of drug misusers served across the region and that new groups are defined as encountered
- a set of output and outcome measures is used to monitor the service
- the service will complete and return the DMD forms
- output and outcome monitoring reports will be provided to the managing body and service commissioners as specified within the contract
- output and outcome monitoring information is used to inform strategic/business planning processes and the policies and practices of the region.

For service providers, the Quality in Alcohol and Drugs Services (QuADS) initiative supports these recommendations and also promotes the following service quality standards:[4]

- well-publicised service users' rights, confidentiality and complaints statements and procedures, which are subject to periodic monitoring and review
- a written policy on equal opportunities and anti-discrimination practices, spanning staff, volunteers and service users.

QuADS also encourages the routine gathering of information about clients' satisfaction with treatment services, as a valuable adjunct to the collection of primary outcome measures described above. Several instruments have been developed for measuring treatment satisfaction in the general mental health service arena. The most notable is the Client Satisfaction Questionnaire (CSQ), which has been developed in several forms and is widely used in health services research.[247,248] In contrast to the situation in the general mental health field, there is a rather sparse literature on client-treatment satisfaction issues within the arena of substance-use treatment. Outcome research from the USA, which has administered the CSQ and other instruments, has reported high levels of service satisfaction by clients in methadone maintenance, therapeutic community and outpatient drug-free programmes.[249] However, the usefulness of traditional satisfaction ratings derived from drug-misuse treatment populations is not clear. For example, Chan and colleagues observed that pre-treatment problem severity and duration of the index treatment assessed were positively correlated with treatment satisfaction.[250] Only modest associations were observed between satisfaction, length of treatment and favourable outcome in a methadone maintenance outcome study.[251] In the UK, many treatment providers have undertaken satisfaction surveys of their clients as part of audit and quality assurance initiatives. Table 30 summarises the structure of the Treatment Perceptions Questionnaire (TPQ), a treatment satisfaction instrument recently developed in the UK with the drug misuse treatment population in mind.[252]

Table 30: Structure of the Treatment Perceptions Questionnaire (TPQ).

Please indicate the extent to which you agree or disagree with the following statements*

The staff have not always understood the kind of help I want.
The staff and I have had different ideas about my treatment objectives.
There has always been a member of staff available when I have wanted to talk.
The staff have helped to motivate me to sort out my problems.
I think the staff have been good at their jobs.
I have been well informed about decisions made about my treatment.
I have received the help that I was looking for.
I have not liked all of the counselling sessions I have attended.
I have not had enough time to sort out my problems.
I have not liked some of the treatment rules or regulations.

---

* Responses are invited using a five-point scale from strongly agree to strongly disagree.
Source: Marsden et al.[253]

The 1994 Task Force recommended a framework for monitoring treatment outputs and key outcomes for service contract monitoring by commissioners. This appears in Appendix VI.

9 Information and research requirements

In this section, we outline our perception of the current information needs and research and development priorities in the field of drug-misuse treatment. In spite of advances in knowledge about the effectiveness of existing services in the UK, there are gaps in knowledge in many important areas.

HBV and HCV

There is an urgent need for more research on the prevalence of HCV and its course amongst IDUs and other drug users who are infected. To date, many studies of HCV have recruited older cohorts of injectors who began injecting before or during the introduction of harm-reduction measures in their respective countries. Studies of incidence have also been hampered by small sample sizes, or by large proportions of older injectors already being infected at baseline.

Capacity and human resource issues

The field of drug-misuse treatment is undergoing rapid change, particularly because of the size of new funding streams into criminal justice for the development of ARS, DTTOs and CARAT initiatives. Periodic monitoring of existing services and new treatment programmes is required to inform commissioners of their capacity. Waiting lists and times, staff recruitment issues and organisational responses to changes in demand will all be critical indicators of the health of the treatment system for drug misuse over the next five years. In several places in this chapter we have stressed the importance of staff training to ensure that services can adapt to meet the needs of priority care groups. Commissioners should ensure that all services are able to maintain reasonable training budgets within their contract specification, and shared training initiatives and resources should be developed and sustained.

Information systems

DMDs have made good progress towards meeting national and regional information needs, but there is little knowledge about how such data are used in practice by commissioners and treatment providers. Commissioners should be able to look at the nature of the clients referred to a particular agency, as well as at the number and characteristics of cases across the PCT and/or DAT area. It should also be possible for the PCT to compare the characteristics and numbers of drug takers in contact with services in their area with data available from adjacent PCTs or from the region as a whole. The current review of the system will see the DMDs incorporate an annual re-reporting component that will enable both the incidence and prevalence of clients treated for problem drug use to be known. It will then be possible to produce estimates of the number of people seeking or receiving treatment at any one time.

Greater use also needs to be made of the DMD databases to inform the commissioning process, and in particular to develop purchasing intentions, service agreements and specifications. The strategic review of the DMD by the Department of Health has recognised the importance of outcome monitoring and is committed to facilitate the expansion of efforts to monitor outcomes. The further development of the DMD and outcome monitoring must be done in complementary ways to ensure that the reporting requirements are not compromised and that the reporting burden on service providers and their clients is kept to a minimum.

Measures of effectiveness

There has been some progress in developing measures of treatment outcome for the population of drug misusers. The principle behind existing measures is to gauge treatment benefit in terms of a reduction of key problems. As a complement to these core measures, the following areas need to be developed:

- improved and more sensitive measures of progress in treatment
- protocols and measures to assess needs for priority groups.

Researchers into treatment outcome are increasingly encouraged to incorporate economic assessments into evaluations of drug misuse services. Standard measures of economic effectiveness (e.g. adjusted life-years gained) have not been devised with the drug-misusing population in mind, and there is a pressing need for health economists and specialists in drug-misuse evaluation to develop suitable indicators.

New interventions

Some public health interventions (e.g. HBV vaccination) are relatively simple procedures that can be undertaken on a large scale. However, health commissioners require increasingly specialised and focused interventions for priority health resource groups. There is a real danger that political imperatives to reach new client groups (e.g. the homeless and young people) are not being followed up by research and development activities to define precisely the needs of these groups and the treatments from which they are likely to benefit. For young people, research has identified stimulant use as a key problem, and research and intervention studies are now required to assess ways of tackling this emerging need.[254] Systematic individual-level research on treatment needs should be commissioned to inform the development of new interventions. These interventions should be developed as treatment manuals that describe the nature, intensity and duration of treatment for the priority group, the content of treatment sessions and their measurable goals.

Evaluation studies

Good-quality research on treatment and treatment outcomes is critical in order to inform the orientation and operation of treatment services. There is almost universal admiration in the NHS for the use of the randomised controlled trial (RCT) design for the evaluation of health care treatments. Particularly in the case of new treatments, where a controlled research design is usually feasible, and assuming the trial is well conducted, the results obtained have high internal reliability and great authority. However, an RCT may have poor external validity when used to evaluate existing treatments where there is no compelling evidence one way or the other that they are unsatisfactory. Nevertheless, the RCT should be considered as the design of first choice for new treatments or for treatments for specific groups. Where experimental studies of the standard vs. an enhanced or new treatment are conducted, the potential for subgroup responses (client, treatment interactions) must be considered thoroughly before the trial begins. We also consider it is essential that the implications for clinical practice be considered in advance. Further, observational studies are required to examine the operation of the treatment system itself. For example, we know very little about how rehabilitation and aftercare processes operate after a period of health care treatment has been completed. The evolving treatment and support needs of drug misusers should be studied systematically and this information needs to be used to cement inter-agency partnerships.

Developing methodologies for assessing needs

DATs and commissioners are actively encouraged to undertake comprehensive needs assessments in the area of drug misuse with a specific target of assessing the needs of young people. However, there have been few systematic quantitative and qualitative studies conducted in the drug misuse field in the UK. In fact, most studies in the mental health service field have been mainly or exclusively qualitative, relying on discussion material from focus groups.[255] To date, synthetic estimation and normative models (and other more sophisticated methods) have not been widely used. There is great variability in the extent of the population needs assessment work that has been conducted to date, but it is fair to say that, in general, service commissioning has not followed detailed data-based needs assessment. Assessment in the drug misuse field in the UK remains under-developed and should be tackled as a research and development priority. Concern has also been expressed that the provision of residential rehabilitation treatment has often been determined largely on the basis of available resources rather than of identified client needs.[256]

Service commissioners should follow a sequence of steps to inform the needs assessment for their population. The overarching goal is to produce a strategic commissioning framework that can be agreed across the five funding agencies: PCT, LA and the three criminal justice partners (police, probation and prison services). We must stress that this is an evolving area and that there are currently no examples of thorough needs assessment studies to guide current practice. For a focused review of the steps that can be followed when conducting a needs assessment for drug misuse, *see* Rawaf and Marshall.[257]

The usual steps when conducting a needs assessment are as follows:

- the allocation of resources and establishment of an agreed plan and set of methods
- a prevalence estimation of the target population, and identification and profiling of subgroups
- the mapping of treatment services provided in the locality, and an audit of treatment purchasing from services located outside the geographical boundary of the DAT (e.g. Social Services purchasing of residential rehabilitation) to determine the extent to which demand is being met elsewhere
- an audit of the demand profile of treatment services (capacity, number of episodes and estimated number in need)
- personal interviews with key informants across commissioning, provision and advocacy sectors
- focus group discussions with key stakeholders (commissioners, clinicians, DRG members, treatment providers and service users) to explore what they want from services
- a 'gaps' analysis of the current and desired profiles of service provision (often a qualitative exercise involving the estimation of the desired range of services to increase coverage for specific special groups)
- recommendations for increasing treatment coverage, purchasing efficiency and service effectiveness based on available evidence
- an assessment of reactions to recommendations from strategists, commissioners, purchasers, service providers and service users
- the development of an implementation plan based on the identification of activities, resources and timetables.

Appraisal of the health care needs of the target populations and commissioning of strategic service responses should be flexible and should adapt to changing circumstances in each locality. These may include:

- variations and new trends in drug use and consumption patterns
- the geographical distribution and concentration of drug use
- variations in demand for services
- the changing relationship between drug use and other conditions (notably HIV infection and blood-borne viral hepatitis)
- changing policy in response to drug strategy
- changes in organisation of health services
- monitoring the evidence base for current and new treatment services.

Needs-assessment activities are potentially costly. Intensive surveys of the resident population in most DAT areas will be time-consuming and expensive. It is quite likely that most DATs will wish to employ alternative (and less precise) estimation methods with which to inform the direction and success of commissioning strategies. A qualitative approach to needs assessment can be undertaken relatively quickly and can answer important questions about what commissioners, purchasers, service providers and service users want from treatment services and supports.

Service-user satisfaction surveys may be a useful means of gathering information about the extent to which a programme is perceived to have met an individual's treatment wants and needs. A range of issues has been examined, including the accessibility, adequacy, content and impact of services received. In addition to serving a simple monitoring function for treatment-service providers and their funders, treatment satisfaction is argued to be a valuable indicator of treatment experience. Treatment satisfaction can act as a moderator of treatment outcome, since it is reasonable to assume that less satisfied clients may leave treatment prematurely or have different responses to interventions.[258] As a method of gaining rapid intelligence about a particular local problem, action research approaches called Rapid Assessment and Response (RAR) methods have also been promoted as an efficient and economic methodology for assessing need.[259] In terms of quantitative methods for such assessment, two realistic methodologies are available (but *see* Dewitt and Rush[260] for a general description and discussion of the strengths and weaknesses of various procedures).

10 Conclusions

This chapter has used an epidemiological framework to address the treatment needs of people with psychoactive substance use problems. Diverse material has been used to encourage and help DAT personnel and other relevant agencies to consider the coverage and effectiveness of local treatment strategies, to identify unmet needs for treatment and to develop more efficient and effective health and social care responses. The key point is that the population of drug misusers in the UK is heterogeneous with respect to the types of drugs used, the risks and harm experienced and the types of treatment services required. Drug misuse is associated with a wide range of personal, social and economic problems. A ten-year Government strategy has been established to co-ordinate and integrate the work of Government departments where this impinges on drugs issues. There continues to be a strong emphasis on local determination of the precise focus and structure of plans in different areas under the direction of Drug Action Teams. There is growing evidence for the effectiveness of standard forms of treatment currently available, but less is known about the effective means of helping particular priority client groups. An effective treatment system tailored to the needs of the local population is based on principles of strategic alliance and partnership. Further work is required to extend and improve information, performance and outcome monitoring systems, and to use more sophisticated methodologies for assessing needs in order to guide strategic and service development.

Appendix I: Classification of substance-related disorders

The *International Classification of Diseases*, Tenth Revision (ICD-10), (World Health Organization, 1992, 1993) provides the following classification of substance-related disorders.

Table A1: Classification of drug misuse in ICD-10.

F10	Alcohol
F11	Opioids
F12	Cannabinoids
F13	Sedatives or hypnotics
F14	Cocaine
F15	Other stimulants, including caffeine
F16	Hallucinogens
F17	Tobacco
F18	Volatile solvents
F19	Multiple drug use and use of other psychoactive substances

The following four- and five-character codes are used to specify specific clinical conditions:

F1x.0	Acute intoxication
	.00 Uncomplicated
	.01 With trauma or other bodily injury
	.02 With other medical complications
	.03 With delirium
	.04 With perceptual distortions
	.05 With coma
	.06 With convulsions
	.07 Pathological intoxication
F1x.1	Harmful use
F1x.2	Dependence syndrome
	.20 Currently abstinent
	.21 Currently abstinent, but in a protected environment
	.22 Currently on a clinically supervised maintenance or replacement regime [controlled dependence]
	.23 Currently abstinent, but receiving treatment with aversive or blocking drugs
	.24 Currently using the substance [active dependence]
	.25 Continuous use
	.26 Episodic use [dipsomania]
F1x.3	Withdrawal state
	.30 Uncomplicated
	.31 With convulsions
F1x.4	Withdrawal state with delirium
	.40 Without convulsions
	.41 With convulsions
F1x.5	Psychotic disorder
	.50 Schizophrenia-like
	.51 Predominantly delusional
	.52 Predominantly hallucinatory
	.53 Predominantly polymorphic
	.54 Predominantly depressive symptoms
	.55 Predominantly manic symptoms
	.56 Mixed

F1x.6	Amnesic syndrome
F1x.7	Residual and late-onset psychotic disorder
	.70 Flashbacks
	.71 Personality or behaviour disorder
	.72 Residual or affective disorder
	.73 Dementia
	.74 Other persisting cognitive impairment
	.75 Late-onset psychotic disorder
F1x.8	Other mental and behavioural disorders
F1x.9	Unspecified mental and behavioural disorder

Appendix II: ICD-10 and DSM-IV dependence criteria

Under ICD, dependence for a specific substance is diagnosed if three or more of the following criteria have been seen (e.g. in the previous 12 months):

Table A2: Psychoactive dependence criteria in ICD-10.

1		A strong desire or compulsion to use
2		Difficulty in controlling use
3	(a)	Experience of a physiological withdrawal state; or
	(b)	Use of same or similar substance to relieve or avoid withdrawal symptoms; or consumption of increased doses to achieve desired effects
5	(a)	Progressive neglect of alternative pleasures or interests; or
	(b)	Increased amounts of time taken to obtain, use or recover from substance effects
6		Continued use despite evidence of harmful consequences

Source: Adapted from World Health Organization.[72]

DSM-IV uses the following criteria for diagnosing abuse and dependence for recent patterns of use (e.g. previous 12 months) for each screened substance:

Table A3: Psychoactive dependence criteria in DSM-IV.

Abuse (defined by scoring 1 or more on items 1–4)		
1		Use leading to neglect of personal, social or occupational roles
2		Use in an unsafe or dangerous situation
3		Use leading to repeated problems with the law
4		Continued use despite relationship, domestic, occupation or educational problems
Dependence (defined as scoring 3 or more on items 5–10)		
5	(a)	Need to use increased amount to achieve desired effect; or
	(b)	Experience of lowered effect from continued use
6	(a)	Feeling sick or unwell when drug effects have worn off; or
	(b)	Use of substance or similar to relieve or avoid withdrawal symptoms
7		Use in larger amounts or for a longer time than intended
8		A persistent desire to use or problems trying to control or cut down use
9		Large amounts of time spent either getting or using or recovering from effects
10		Use leading to quitting, reducing or having problems in domestic, occupational, educational or social roles

Source: Adapted from American Psychiatric Association.[73]

Appendix III: Clinical features of opioid and cocaine disorders

Opioid disorders

The opioid substances include both natural products (e.g. morphine) derived from the poppy (*Papaver somniferum*), semi-synthetic substances (e.g. diamorphine) and synthetic products (e.g. methadone and dihydrocodeine). Illicit heroin is the most commonly used. Heroin is a powerful, relatively short-acting analgesic, and heroin powder is prepared for consumption either through inhalation or insufflation (sniffing into the nose), or by intravenous or intramuscular injection routes. The clinical features of opioid intoxication (which are largely determined by dose levels, route of administration and tolerance) may include:

- initial euphoria
- increased well-being and diminished anxiety
- drowsiness and dysphoric mood
- pupillary constriction
- in acute intoxication (overdose), pupillary dilation due to anoxia
- slurred speech and impairment in attention.

Opioid dependence (ICD-10 code, F11.2; DSM-IV code, 304.00) is defined under DSM in the following manner. Most individuals with opioid dependence have significant levels of tolerance and will experience withdrawal on abrupt discontinuation of opioid substances. Opioid dependence includes signs and symptoms that reflect compulsive, prolonged self-administration of opioid substances. Clinical features may include:

- a subjective awareness of compulsion to use
- a diminished capacity to control use
- salience of drug-seeking behaviour.

People who misuse opioids, but are not dependent, are likely to represent a small segment of the opioid-using population and will tend to use heroin infrequently. The usual clinical features of opioid withdrawal that follow abrupt cessation of use in someone who has used the drug on a heavy and prolonged basis (or are precipitated by the administration of an opioid antagonist such as naloxone) are as follows:

- dysphoric mood and distress
- yawning
- nausea and vomiting
- diarrhoea
- muscle aches
- insomnia.

The speed of onset of these symptoms is usually between 6–12 hours for heroin, reaching peak intensity between 48–72 hours and then diminishing over a period from 5–7 days. The time-course for methadone is considered to be more protracted, with a slower onset but longer duration of the withdrawal syndrome.

Cocaine disorders

Cocaine is a psychostimulant (benzoylmethylecgonine) extracted from the leaves of the plant *Erythroxlon coca*. In the UK, two illicit cocaine products are available: cocaine hydrochloride (a white crystalline salt usually containing other local anaesthetics and/or other bulk additives) and a whitish crystalline free-base form known as 'crack' or 'rock'. The effects of cocaine include elevated mood, increased alertness, and suppression of appetite and fatigue. It also has local anaesthetic and vasoconstrictive properties. The clinical features of cocaine intoxication (determined largely by dose, route of administration and tolerance) are quite complex and include:

- euphoria and increased confidence
- becoming talkative and mentally alert
- reduced appetite
- restlessness
- social withdrawal (with chronic administration).

The short-term physiological effects of cocaine include constricted blood vessels, dilated pupils, and increased temperature, heart rate and blood pressure. Large amounts (several hundred milligrams or more) may lead to bizarre, erratic and violent behaviour. Relatively short periods of problematic use may be encountered by non-dependent users (characterised by interpersonal conflicts, financial problems, tiredness and irritability) but usually ameliorate following cessation of cocaine use. On the other hand, cocaine dependence (ICD-10 code, F14.2; DSM-IV code, 304.20) is characterised by the following features:

- substantial impairment of the ability to control the amounts used
- high-dose, usually episodic consumption pattern
- increased anxiety and depression
- paranoid-type ideation (in some users)
- weight loss.

The existence of a defined withdrawal syndrome following termination of heavy and prolonged cocaine use has been somewhat controversial. No coherent syndrome is usually seen, and there are marked intra- and inter-individual variations in the type and severity of problems experienced. Some studies have reported no or few signs of cocaine withdrawal amongst clients receiving inpatient treatment, while other research has suggested a transient cluster of symptoms, including dysphoric mood, general depression and sleep disturbance. Diagnostic criteria for cocaine withdrawal include:

- dysphoric mood
- fatigue
- unpleasant dreams
- insomnia or hypersomnia
- increased appetite
- psychomotor retardation or agitation.

Appendix IV: Infrastructure of drug misuse services for young people

Table A4: Drug misuse services for young people.

Tier	Function	Relevant professionals/agencies
I	Education, information, screening/ identification, referral	General youth workers, teachers, school nurses, social workers, health visitors and general practitioners
II	All Tier I functions, plus drug-related education, advice and counselling services	Youth workers, youth justice workers, educational psychologists, Accident and Emergency
III	Specialist drugs and health care services with complex need requiring multi-disciplinary team-based work	SMTs, local authority residential unit staff, child and adolescent health teams, youth offender teams
IV	Specialist and intensive treatment and support for young people with complex care needs	Specialist child and adolescent workers, forensic psychiatry and psychology services

Source: Health Advisory Service.[129]

Appendix V: Domains and measures for treatment outcome

The original impetus toward establishing a minimal data set for outcomes was the framework used by the Department of Health's Task Force. This established a set of measures against which the outcomes of different services could be assessed across three key domains: drug use, physical and psychological health, and social context and life functioning.

Table A5: Domains and measures for treatment outcome.

Outcome domain	Measure
Drug use	1 Abstinence from drugs
	2 Near abstinence from drugs
	3 Reduction in the quantity of drugs consumed
	4 Abstinence from street drugs
	5 Reduced use of street drugs
	6 Change from injecting to oral route of administration
	7 Reduction in the frequency of injecting
Physical and psychological health	1 Improvement in physical health
	2 No deterioration in physical health
	3 Improvement in psychological health
	4 No deterioration in psychological health
	5 Reduction in sharing injecting equipment
	6 Reduction in sexual-risk behaviour
Social functioning and life context	1 Reduction in criminal activity
	2 Improvement in employment status
	3 Fewer working/school days missed
	4 Improved family relationships
	5 Improved personal relationships
	6 Domiciliary stability/improvement

Appendix VI: Performance indicators for drug misuse treatment

Guidance on a framework for determining performance measurement for drug misuse services has been suggested by the Department of Health's Task Force to Review Services for Drug Misusers (pp. 140–6). This framework is adapted below.

The performance indicators marked with an asterisk are considered by the Task Force to be the most appropriate measures for initial consideration.

Table A6: Performance indicators for drug misuse treatment.

1 Outreach services
  (a) Number of new clients contacted in a 4-week period (i.e. not seen by any other service during the previous 3 months)
  (b) Number of clients remaining in contact with a worker for longer than 3 months
  (c) Number of clients referred per month to other services for help with drug misuse problems
  (d) Cost per new client contacted*

2 General practitioners
  (a) Percentage of specialist service clientele registered with a GP
  (b) Percentage of participating GPs with clear guidelines for shared care, including well-defined liaison arrangements
  (c) Percentage of GPs prepared to take and/or undertaking a shared-care responsibility*
  (d) Percentage of specialist drug service clients cared for in general practice*
  (e) Costs per GP-managed client

3 Community retail pharmacies
  (a) Percentage of pharmacies participating in:
      (i) needle exchange
      (ii) supervised consumption
      (iii) offering advice
  (b) Number of exchange packs given out per month
  (c) Number of needles/syringes sold per month
  (d) Number of individuals using the service (by gender)
  (e) Number of pharmacies prepared to provide facilities for the return of used injecting equipment*
  (f) Return rates of used equipment*
  (g) Cost per pack distributed*

4 Arrest referral
  (a) Number of clients who enter treatment following arrest
  (b) Percentage of drug misusers cautioned for drug offences, and percentage arrested for drug offences following caution (for consideration by DATs)

5 Hepatitis B
  (a) Percentage of clients offered vaccination
  (b) Percentage of clients reporting completed vaccination

Table A6: Continued.

6 Syringe-exchange schemes
   (a) Percentage of clients reporting having shared injecting equipment in the previous 4 weeks*
   (b) Number of new attenders (those not having used a scheme in the previous 3 months) per month
   (c) Number of exchange packs given out per month per client
   (d) Number of individuals using the service (by gender)
   (e) Return rates of used equipment*
   (f) Numbers moving on to engage in treatment
   (g) Percentage of staff trained in giving basic health checks
   (h) Cost per registered client-month*

7 Counselling
   (a) Percentage of people working in drug services with accredited counselling qualifications or equivalent professional qualifications
   (b) Percentage of clients receiving counselling who report improvements in one of more of the three domains defined by the Task Force
   (c) Cost per completed counselling course

9 Methadone reduction
   (a) Number of clients entering reduction programmes
   (b) Percentage who become drug-free by:
       (i) 3 months
       (ii) 6 months
       (iii) 1 year*
   (c) Percentage of clients in treatment who report improvements in one or more of the other broader outcome domains
   (d) Number using other support after treatment completion, e.g. Narcotics Anonymous or other self-help group
   (e) Cost of methadone reduction per client completing*

10 Methadone maintenance
   (a) (i) Number of clients in a maintenance programme
       (ii) Number of clients retained at 1 year
       (iii) Average duration of retention*
   (b) Percentage of clients who report improvements in one or more of the other broader outcome domains
   (c) Percentage of clients whose urine tests positive for other opiates
   (d) Cost per client per year*

11 Non-specialist detoxification services
   (a) Number of clients entering detoxification programmes
   (b) Percentage of clients (by main drug of use) who complete detoxification*
   (c) Percentage of clients who attend follow-up treatment
   (d) Costs of detoxification per client completing detoxification*

12 Inpatient detoxification
   (a) Number of clients entering for treatment
   (b) Percentage successfully completing inpatient detoxification (per main drug of use)*
   (c) Percentage successfully completing programme (by programme length)
   (d) Percentage of clients who report improvements in one or more of the other broader outcome domains
   (e) Percentage of completers who remain drug-free after:
       (i) 3 months
       (ii) 6 months
       (iii) 1 year
   (f) Cost of inpatient detoxification (per main drug of use)*

13 Residential rehabilitation
   (a) Percentage assessed within a defined period
   (b) Percentage gaining admission within a defined period
   (c) Percentage remaining in treatment after 4 weeks (by main drug of choice)*
   (d) Percentage successfully completing programme (by type of programme and length)
   (e) Percentage of clients who report improvements in one or more of the other broader outcome domains*
   (f) Percentage of completers who remain drug-free after:
       (i) 3 months
       (ii) 6 months
       (iii) 1 year
   (g) Cost per completed programme*

References

1 Cook C. Alcohol misuse. In: Stevens A, Raftery J, Mant J, Simpson S (eds). *Health Care Needs Assessment: the epidemiologically based needs assessment reviews.* First Series Update. Oxford: Radcliffe Medical Press, 2004.

2 United Kingdom Anti-Drugs Coordinating Unit. *Tackling Drugs to Build a Better Britain: the Government's 10-year strategy for tackling drug misuse.* London: The Stationery Office, 1998.

3 Abdulrahim D, Lavoie D, Hasan S. *Commissioning Standards. Drug and alcohol treatment and care: helping commissioning in tackling drugs to build a better Britain.* London: Substance Misuse Advisory Service, 1999.

4 Alcohol Concern and Standing Conference on Drug Abuse. *QuADS: Quality in Alcohol and Drug Services. Draft quality standards manual for alcohol and drug treatment services.* London: Alcohol Concern and Standing Conference on Drug Abuse, 1999.

5 Office of the National Drug Control Policy, *United States Office of National Drug Control Strategy.* Washington, DC: Office of the National Drug Control Policy, 1999.

6 United Nations International Drug Control Programme. *World Drug Report.* New York: Oxford University Press, 1997.

7 Ramsay M, Partridge S. *Drug Misuse Declared in 1998: results from the British Crime Survey.* Home Office Research Study 197. London: Home Office, 1999.

8 Department of Health. *The New NHS: modern, dependable.* London: The Stationery Office, 1997.

9 Department of Health. *Saving Lives: our healthier nation.* London: The Stationery Office, 1999.

10 Strang J, Johns A, Caan W. Cocaine in the UK – 1991. *Br J Psychiatry* 1993; **162**: 1–13.

11 Marsden J, Griffiths P, Farrell M, Gossop M, Strang J. Cocaine in Britain: prevalence, problems and treatment responses. *J Drug Issues* 1998; **28**: 225–42.

12 Advisory Council on the Misuse of Drugs. *Volatile Substance Abuse.* London: HMSO, 1997.

13 Stephens RS, Roffman RA. Adult marijuana dependence. In: Baer JS (ed.). *Addictive Behaviors Across the Lifespan: prevention, treatment and policy issues.* Newbury Park, CA: Sage Publications, 1993.

14 Channabasavanna SM, Paes M, Hall W. Mental and behavioural disorders due to cannabis use. In: Kalant H, Corrigall WA, Hall W, Smart RA (eds). *The Health Effects of Cannabis.* Toronto: Centre for Addiction and Mental Health, 1999.

15 Weisbeck GA, Schuckit MA, Kalmijn JA, Tipp JE, Bucholz KK, Smith TL. An evaluation of the history of a marijuana withdrawal syndrome in a large population. *Addiction* 1996; **91**: 1469–78.

16 Crowley TJ, Macdonald MJ, Whitmore EA, Mikulich SK. Cannabis dependence, withdrawal, and reinforcing effects among adolescents with conduct disorder symptoms and substance use disorders. *Drug Alcohol Depend* 1998; **50**: 27–37.

17 Budney AJ, Novy PL, Hughes JR. Marijuana withdrawal among adults seeking treatment for marijuana dependence. *Addiction* 1999; **94**: 1311–21.

18 World Health Organization. *Cannabis: a health perspective and research agenda.* Geneva: Division of Mental Health and Prevention of Substance Abuse, World Health Organization, 1997.

19 Hall W, Babor T. Cannabis use and public health: assessing the burden. *Addiction* 2000; **95**: 485–90.

20 Department of Health. *Drug Misuse Statistics.* London: Department of Health, 1999.

21 Matthai SM, Sills JA, Davidson DC, Alexandrou D. Cerebral oedema after ingestion of MDMA ('ecstasy') and unrestricted intake of water [letter]. *BMJ* 1996; **312**: 1359.

22 Gledhill JA, Moore DF, Bell D, Henry JA. Subarachnoid haemorrhage associated with MDMA abuse [letter]. *J Neurol Neurosur Psychiatry* 1993; **56**: 1036–7.

23 McEvoy A, Kitchen ND, Thomas DGT. Intracerebral haemorrhage in young adults: the emerging importance of drug misuse. *BMJ* 2000; **320**: 1322–4.

24 Green AR, Cross AJ, Goodwin GM. Review of the pharmacology and clinical pharmacology of 3,4-methylenedioxymethamphetamine (MDMA or 'Ecstasy'). *Psychopharmacology* 1999; **119**: 247–60.

25 McCann UD, Ridenour A, Shaham Y, Ricaurte GA. Serotonergic neurotoxicity after (+/-) 3,4-methylenedioxymethamphetamine (MDMA; 'Ecstasy'): a controlled study in humans. *Neuropsychopharmacology* 1994; **10**: 129–38.

26 Krystal JH, Price LH. Chronic 3,4-methylenedioxymethamphetamine (MDMA) use: effects on mood and neurophysiological function. *Am J Drug Alcohol Abuse* 1992; **18**: 331–41.

27 Farrell M, Howes S, Griffiths P, Williamson S, Taylor C. *Stimulant Needs Assessment Project*. London: Department of Health, 1998.

28 Maddux JF, Elliot B. Problem drinkers among patients on methadone. *Am J Drug Alcohol Abuse* 1975; **2**: 245–54.

29 Simpson DD, Lloyd MR. *Alcohol and Illicit Drug Use: national follow-up study of admissions to drug abuse treatments in the DARP during 1969–1971*. Services Research Report. Rockville, MD: National Institute on Drug Abuse, 1977.

30 Joseph H, Appel P. Alcoholism and methadone treatment: consequences for the patient and programme. *Am J Drug Alcohol Abuse* 1985; **11(1/2)**: 37–53.

31 Hubbard RL, Marsden ME, Rachal JV, Harwood HJ, Cavanaugh ER, Ginzberg HM. *Drug Abuse Treatment: a national study of effectiveness*. Chapel Hill, NC: University of North Carolina Press, 1989.

32 Best D, Noble A, Gossop M *et al*. Identifying alcohol problems among methadone patients. *J Maint Addictions* (in press).

33 Best D, Lehmann P, Gossop M, Harris J, Noble A, Strang J. Eating too little, smoking and drinking too much: wider lifestyle problems among methadone maintenance patients. *Addiction Res* 2000; **6**: 489–98.

34 Chatham LR, Rowan-Szal GA, Joe GW, Brown BS, Simpson DD. Heavy drinking in a population of methadone-maintained clients. *J Stud Alcohol* 1995; **56**: 417–22.

35 Chatham LR, Rowan-Szal GA, Joe GW, Simpson DD. Heavy drinking, alcohol-dependent vs. nondependent methadone-maintenance clients: a follow-up study. *Addict Behav* 1997; **22**: 69–80.

36 Lehman WEK, Barrett ME, Simpson DD. Alcohol use by heroin addicts 12 years after drug abuse treatment. *J Stud Alcohol* 1990; **51**: 233–44.

37 Rowan-Szal GA, Chatham LR, Simpson DD. Importance of identifying cocaine and alcohol dependent methadone clients. *Am J Addictions* 2000; **9**: 38–50.

38 Gossop M, Marsden J, Stewart D, Rolfe A. Patterns of drinking and drinking outcomes among drug misusers: 1-year follow-up results. *J Subst Abuse Treat* 2000; **19**: 45–50.

39 Oppenheimer E, Tobbutt C, Taylor C, Andrew T. Death and survival in a cohort of heroin addicts from London clinics. *Addiction* 1994; **89**: 1299–1308.

40 Neeleman J, Farrell M. Fatal methadone and heroin overdoses: time trends in England and Wales. *J Epidemiol Community Health* 1997; **51**: 435–7.

41 Roberts I, Barker M, Li L. Analysis of trends in deaths from accidental drug poisoning in teenagers 1985–1995. *BMJ* 1997; **315**: 289.

42 Wartenberg AA. Management of common medical problems. In: Miller NS, Gold MS, Smith DE (eds). *Manual of Therapeutics for Addictions*. New York: Wiley-Liss, 1997.

43 Rubin JM, Benzer DG. Treatment of comorbid medical complications. In: Miller NS, Gold MS, Smith DE (eds). *Manual of Therapeutics for Addictions*. New York: Wiley-Liss, 1997.

44 Kessler RC, McGonagle KA, Zhao S *et al*. Lifetime and 12-month prevalence of DSM-III-R psychiatric disorders in the United States: results from the National Comorbidity Survey. *Arch Gen Psychiatry* 1994; **51**: 8–19.

45 Farrell M, Howes S, Taylor C *et al.* Substance misuse and psychiatric comorbidity: an overview of the OPCS National Psychiatric Morbidity Survey. *Addict Behav* 1998; **23**: 909–18.

46 Rounsaville BJ, Weissman MM, Kleber HK, Wilber C. Heterogeneity of psychiatric diagnosis in treated opiate addicts. *Arch Gen Psychiatry* 1982; **39**: 161–6.

47 Kleinman PH, Miller AB, Millman RB *et al.* Psychopathology among cocaine abusers entering treatment. *J Nerv Ment Dis* 1990; **178**: 442–7.

48 Gossop M, Marsden J, Stewart D *et al.* Substance use, health and social problems of clients at 54 drug treatment agencies: intake data from the National Treatment Outcome Research Study (NTORS). *Br J Psychiatry* 1998; **173**: 166–71.

49 Marsden J, Gossop M, Stewart D, Rolfe A, Farrell M. Psychiatric symptoms amongst clients seeking treatment for drug dependence: intake data from the National Treatment Outcome Research Study. *Br J Psychiatry* 2000; **176**: 285–9.

50 Appleby L, Shaw J, Amos T *et al.* Suicide within 12 months of contact with mental health services: national clinical survey. *Br Med Survey* 1999; **318**: 1235–9.

51 Magura S, Shapiro JL, Siddiqi Q, Douglas DS. Variables influencing condom use among intravenous drug users. *Am J Public Health* 1990; **80**: 82–4.

52 Donoghoe MC. Sex, HIV and the injecting drug user. *Br J Addiction* 1992; **87**: 405–16.

53 Crofts N, Nigro L, Oman K, Stevenson E, Sherman J. Methadone maintenance and hepatitis C virus infection among injecting drug users. *Addiction* 1997; **92**: 999–1005.

54 Majid A, Holmes R, Desselberger U, Simmonds P, McKee TA. Molecular epidemiology of hepatitis C virus infection among intravenous drug users in rural communities. *J Med Virol* 1995; **46**: 48–51.

55 Serfaty MA, Lawrie A, Smith B *et al.* Risk factors and medical follow-up of drug users tested for hepatitis C – can the risk of transmission be reduced? *Drug Alcohol Rev* 1997; **16**: 339–47.

56 Rhodes T, Hunter GM, Stimson GV *et al.* Relevance of markers for hepatitis B virus and HIV-1 among drug injectors in London: injecting careers, positivity and risk behaviour. *Addiction* 1996; **91**: 1457–67.

57 Best D, Noble A, Finch E, Gossop M, Sidwell C, Strang J. Accuracy of perceptions of hepatitis B and C status: a cross-sectional investigation of opiate addicts in treatment. *BMJ* 1999; **319**: 290–1.

58 Bloor M, Frischer M, Taylor A *et al.* Tideline and turn: possible reasons for the continuing low HIV prevalence among Glasgow's injecting drug users. *Sociol Rev* 1994; **42**: 738–57.

59 van Beek I, Dwyer R, Dore GJ, Luo K, Kaldor JM. Infection with HIV and hepatitis C virus among injecting drug users in a prevention setting: retrospective cohort study. *BMJ* 1998; **317**: 433–7.

60 Moos RH, Fenn C, Billings A. Life stressors and social resources: an integrated assessment approach. *Soc Sci Med* 1988; **27**: 999–1002.

61 Simpson DD, Joe GW, Lehman WEK. *Addiction Careers: summary of studies based on the DARP 12-year follow-up.* NIDA Treatment Research Report. Rockville, MD: National Institute of Drug Abuse, 1986.

62 French MT, Dennis M, McDougal GL, Karuntzos GT, Hubbard RL. Training and employment programs in methadone treatment: client needs and desires. *J Subst Abuse Treat* 1992; **9**: 293–303.

63 Hammersley R, Forsyth A, Morrison V, Davies J. The relationship between crime and opioid use. *Br J Addiction* 1989; **84**: 1029–43.

64 Maden A, Swinton M, Gunn J. A survey of pre-arrest drug use in sentenced prisoners. *Br J Addiction* 1992; **87**: 27–33.

65 Nurco DN, Shaffer JW, Cisin IH. An ecological analysis of the interrelationships among drug abuse and other indices of social pathology. *Int J Addictions* 1984; **19**: 441–51.

66 Pearson G, Gillman M. Local and regional variations in drug misuse: the British heroin epidemic of the 1980s. In: Strang J, Gossop M (eds). *Heroin Addiction and Drug Policy: the British system.* Oxford: Oxford University Press, 1994.

67 Chen K, Kandel D. The natural history of drug use from adolescence to mid-thirties in a general population sample. *Am J Public Health* 1995; **85**: 41–7.

68 Joe GW, Chastain RL, Simpson DD. Length of careers. In: Simpson DD, Sells SB (eds). *Opioid Addiction and Treatment: a 12-year follow-up.* Malabar, FL: Keiger, 1990.

69 Johnston LD, O'Malley PM, Bachman JG. *National Survey Results on Drug Use from the Monitoring the Future Study, 1975–1994.* Washington, DC: US Government Printing Office, 1995.

70 Hser Y, Anglin MD, Powers K. A 24-year follow-up of California narcotic addicts. *Arch Gen Psychiatry* 1993; **50**: 577–84.

71 Edwards G, Arif A, Hodgson R. Nomenclature and classification of drug and alcohol related problems: a shortened version of the WHO memorandum. *Br J Addiction* 1981; **77**: 287–306.

72 World Health Organization. *International Statistical Classification of Diseases and Related Health Problems* (10e). Geneva: World Health Organization, 1992.

73 American Psychiatric Association. *Diagnostic and Statistical Manual of Mental Disorders* (4e). Washington, DC: American Psychiatric Association, 1994.

74 Gossop M, Darke S, Griffiths P, Powis B, Hall W, Strang J. The Severity of Dependence Scale (SDS) in English and Australian samples of heroin, cocaine and amphetamine users. *Addiction* 1995; **90**: 607–14.

75 Raistrick D, Bradshaw J, Tober G, Winer J, Allison J, Healey C. Development of the Leeds Dependence Questionnaire (LDQ): a questionnaire to measure alcohol and opiate dependence in the context of a treatment evaluation package. *Addiction* 1994; **89**: 563–72.

76 Darke S, Zador D. Fatal heroin 'overdose': a review. *Addiction* 1996; **91**: 1765–72.

77 Darke S, Ross J, Hall W. Overdose among heroin users in Sydney, Australia. II. Responses to overdose. *Addiction* 1996; **91**: 413–17.

78 Gossop M, Griffiths P, Powis B, Williamson S, Strang J. Frequency of non-fatal heroin overdose: survey of heroin users recruited in non-clinical settings. *BMJ* 1996; **313**: 402.

79 Darke S, Ross J, Hall W. Overdose amongst heroin users in Sydney. I. Prevalence and correlates of non-fatal overdose. *Addiction* 1996; **91**: 405–11.

80 Powis B, Strang J, Griffiths P, Taylor C. Self-reported overdose among injecting drug users in London: extent and nature of the problem. *Addiction* 1999; **94**: 471–8.

81 Strang J, Griffiths P, Powis B, Fountain J, Williamson S, Gossop M. Which drugs cause overdose among opiate misusers? Study of personal and witnessed overdoses. *Drug Alcohol Rev* 1999; **18**: 253–61.

82 Advisory Council on the Misuse of Drugs. *Reducing Drug-Related Deaths.* London: The Stationery Office, 2000.

83 Strang J. Take-home naloxone: the next steps [letter]. *Addiction* 1999; **94**: 207.

84 Strang J, Darke S, Hall W, Farrell M, Ali R. Heroin overdose: the case for take-home naloxone [editorial]. *BMJ* 1996; **312**: 1435.

85 Evans K, Britton J, Farrant F, Dale-Perera A. *Assessing Local Need: drug interventions for vulnerable young people.* London: DrugScope (formerly Standing Conference on Drug Abuse), The Good Practice Unit for Young People and Drug Misuse, 1999.

86 Newcombe MD. Identifying high-risk youth: prevalence and patterns of adolescent drug abuse. In: Rahdert E, Czechowicz D (eds). *Adolescent Drug Abuse: clinical assessment and therapeutic interventions.* NIDA Monograph No. 156. Rockville, MD: National Institute on Drug Abuse, 1995.

87 Smart RG, Stoduto G. Treatment experiences and the need for treatment among students with serious alcohol and drug problems. *J Child Adoles Subst* 1997; **7**: 63–72.

88 Boys A, Fountain J, Marsden J, Griffiths P, Stillwell G, Strang J. *Drug Decisions: a qualitative study of young people.* London: Health Education Authority, 2000.

89 Myers K, Hagan TA, Zanis D *et al.* Critical issues in adolescent substance use assessment. *Drug Alcohol Depend* 1999; **55**: 235–46.

90 Gowers S, Harrington RC, Whitton A. *Health of the Nation Outcome Scales for Children and Adolescents (HoNOSCA).* London: Department of Health, 1996.

91 Crome IB, Christian J, Green C. Tip of the national iceberg? Profile of adolescent patients prescribed methadone in an innovative community drug service. *Drugs Educ Prev Policy* 1998; **5**: 195–7.

92 Visscher WA, Bray RM, Kroutil LA. Drug use and pregnancy. In: Bray RM, Marsden ME (eds). *Drug Use in Metropolitan America.* Thousand Oaks, CA: Sage, 1999.

93 Chavkin W, Breibart V. Substance abuse and maternity: the United States as a case study. *Addiction* 1997; **92**: 1201–5.

94 Drugs and Alcohol Women's Network (DAWN). *When a Crèche is Not Enough. A study of drug and alcohol services for women.* London: DAWN, 1994.

95 Johns A. Substance misuse: a primary risk and a major problem of comorbidity. *Int Rev Psychiatry* 1997; **9**: 233–41.

96 Alterman AI, McLellan T, Shifman RB. Do substance patients with more psychopathology receive more treatment? *J Nerv Ment Dis* 1993; **181**: 576–82.

97 Lehman AF, Myers CP, Corty E. Severity of substance use disorders among psychiatric inpatients. *J Nerv Ment Dis* 1994; **182**: 164–7.

98 Dennis ML, Bray RM, Iachan R, Thornberry J. Drug use and homelessness. In: Bray RM, Marsden ME (eds). *Drug Use in Metropolitan America.* Thousand Oaks, CA: Sage, 1999.

99 Klee H, Reid P. Drugs and youth homelessness. *Drugs Educ Prev Policy* 1998; **5**: 269–80.

100 Randall G, Brown S. *From Street to Home: an evaluation of Phase 2 of the Rough Sleepers Report No. 60.* London: Department of the Environment, Transport and the Regions, 1996.

101 Department of the Environment, Transport and the Regions. *Coming in From the Cold.* London: Department of the Environment, Transport and the Regions, 1999.

102 Ramsay M, Percy A. *Drug Misuse Declared: results of the 1994 British Crime Survey.* Home Office Research Study 151. London: Home Office, 1996.

103 Parker H, Measham F, Aldridge J. *Drug Futures: changing patterns of drug use amongst English youth.* ISDD Research Monograph 7. London: Institute for the Study of Drug Dependence, 1995.

104 Abdulrahim D. Power, culture and the 'hard to reach': the marginalisation of minority ethnic populations from HIV prevention and harm minimization. In: Barbour R, Huby G (eds). *The Social Construction of Post-AIDS Knowledge.* London: Routledge, 1998.

105 Khan K. Plaster over the cracks: anti-racism policies are just skin deep. *Druglink* 1999; **14**: 10–12.

106 Epstein JA, Botvin G, Baker E, Diaz T. Impact of social influences and problem behaviour on alcohol use among inner-city Hispanic and Black adolescents. *J Stud Alcohol* 1999; **60**: 595–604.

107 Miller P, Plant M. Drinking, smoking, and illicit drug use among 15 and 16 year olds in the United Kingdom. *BMJ* 1996; **313**: 394–7.

108 Farrell M, Howes S, Taylor C *et al.* Substance misuse and psychiatric comorbidity: an overview of the OPCS National Psychiatric Morbidity Survey. *Addict Behav* 1998; **23**: 909–18.

109 Singleton N, Farrell M, Meltzer H. *Substance Use Among Prisoners in England and Wales.* London: Office for National Statistics, 1999.

110 Bennett T. *Drugs and Crime: the results of research on drug testing and interviewing arresters.* Home Office Study No. 183. London: Home Office, 1998.

111 Frischer M. Estimating the prevalence of drug abuse using the mortality method: an overview. In: Stimson G, Hickman M *et al.* (eds). *Estimating the Prevalence of Problem Drug Use in Europe.* European Monitoring Centre for Drugs and Drug Addiction (EMCDDA) Scientific Monograph Series No. 1. Lisbon: EMCDDA, 1997.

112 Taylor C. Estimating the prevalence of drug use using nomination techniques: an overview. In: Stimson G, Hickman M *et al.* (eds). *Estimating the Prevalence of Problem Drug Use in Europe.* European Monitoring Centre for Drugs and Drug Addiction (EMCDDA) Scientific Monograph Series No. 1. Lisbon: EMCDDA, 1997.

113 Wickens TD. Quantitative methods for estimating the size of a drug-using population. *J Drug Issues* 1993; **23**: 185–216.

114 Sherman RE, Gillespie S, Diaz JA. Use of social indicators in assessment of local community alcohol and other drug dependence needs within Chicago. *Subst Use Misuse* 1996; **31**: 691–728.

115 Hser Y, Anglin MD, Wickens TD, Brecht M-L, Homer J. *Techniques for the Estimation of Illicit Drug User Prevalence: an overview of relevant issues.* New York: National Institute of Justice, 1992.

116 Brecht ML, Wickens TD. Application of multiple capture methods for estimating drug use prevalence. *J Drug Issues* 1993; **23**: 229–50.

117 Hook EB, Regal RR. Capture–recapture methods in epidemiology: methods and limitations. *Epidemiol Rev* 1995; **17**: 243–64.

118 Howe S, Farrell M, Taylor C, Griffiths P, Lewis G. *Estimating Local Prevalence of Drug Use: a feasibility study of the complementary roles of capture–recapture and household survey techniques.* London: National Addiction Centre, 1994.

119 Cox S, Shipley M, Lester M. The ten-year growth of drug misuse in two inner-city London boroughs. *Health Trends* 1999; **30**: 90–3.

120 Bloor M, Wood F, Palmer S. *Estimating the Prevalence of Injecting Drug Use and Serious Drug Use in Wales.* Cardiff: University of Wales, School of Social and Administrative Studies, 1997.

121 Frischer M. Estimated prevalence of injecting drug use in Glasgow. *Br J Addiction* 1992; **87**: 235–43.

122 Brugha R, Swan AV, Hayhurst GK, Fallon MP. A drug misuser prevalence study in a rural English district. *Eur J Public Health* 1998; **8**: 34–6.

123 Squires NF, Beeching NJ, Schlect JM, Ruben SM. An estimate of the prevalence of drug misuse in Liverpool and a spatial analysis of known addiction. *J Public Health Med* 1995; **17**: 103–9.

124 Hay G, McKegany N. Estimating the prevalence of drug misuse in Dundee, Scotland: an application of capture–recapture methods. *J Epidemiol Community Health* 1996; **50**: 469–72.

125 Hickman M, Cox S, Harvey J *et al.* Estimating the prevalence of problem drug use in inner London: a discussion of three capture–recapture studies. *Addiction* 1999; **94**: 1653–62.

126 Hickman M, Seaman S, De Angelis D. Estimating the relative incidence of heroin use: application of a method to adjust observed reports of presentations at specialist treatment agencies. *Am J Epidemiol* 2001; **153**: 632–41.

127 Standing Conference on Drug Abuse. *The Right Choice.* London: Standing Conference on Drug Abuse, 1998.

128 Task Force to Review Services for Drug Misusers. *Report of an Independent Review of Drug Treatment Services in England.* London: Department of Health, 1996.

129 Health Advisory Service. *The Substance of Young Needs: services for children and adolescents who misuse substances.* London: HMSO, 1996.

130 American Society of Addiction Medicine. *Patient Placement Criteria for the Treatment of Substance-Related Disorders* (2e). Chevy Chase, MD: American Society of Addiction Medicine, 1996.

131 Department of Health, The Scottish Office, Department of Health, Welsh Office and Department of Health and Social Security in Northern Ireland. *Drug Misuse and Dependence: guidelines on clinical management.* London: The Stationery Office, 1999.

132 Strang J, Sheridan J, Barber N. Prescribing injectable and oral methadone to opiate addicts: results from the 1995 national postal survey of community pharmacists in England and Wales. *BMJ* 1996; **313**: 270–4.

133 Waller T. A GP's role: past, present and future. In: Beaumont B (ed.). *Care of Drug Users in General Practice: a harm minimisation approach.* Oxford: Radcliffe Medical Press, 1997.

134 Department of Health. *Purchasing Effective Treatment and Care for Drug Misusers: guidance for health and social services departments.* London: The Stationery Office, 1997.

135 McKegany N, Boddy FA. General practitioners and opiate-abusing patients. *J R Coll Gen Pract* 1998; **38**: 73–5.

136 Groves P, Heuston J, Durand A. The identification and management of substance misuse problems by general practitioners. *J Ment Health* 1996; **5**: 183–93.

137 Deehan A, Taylor C, Strang J. The general practitioner, the drug misuser, and the alcohol misuser: major differences in general practitioner activity, therapeutic commitment, and shared care proposals. *Br J Gen Pract* 1997; **47**: 705–9.

138 Gossop M, Marsden J, Stewart D, Lehmann P, Strang J. Treatment outcome among opiate addicts receiving methadone treatment in drug clinics and general practice settings. *Br J Gen Pract* 1999; **49**: 31–4.

139 MacGregor S, Smith LE, Flory P. *The Drugs Treatment System in England.* Middlesex University: School of Sociology and Social Policy, 1994.

140 Farrell M, Ward J, Mattick R *et al.* Methadone maintenance treatment in opiate dependence: a review. *BMJ* 1994; **309**: 997–1001.

141 Marsden J, Gossop G, Farrell M, Strang J. Opioid substitution: critical issues and future directions. *J Drug Issues* 1998; **28**: 231–48.

142 Sheridan J, Strang J, Barber N, Glanz A. Role of community pharmacists in relation to HIV prevention and drug misuse: findings from the 1995 national survey in England and Wales. *BMJ* 1996; **313**: 272–4.

143 Johnson RE, Eissenberg T, Stitzer ML, Strain EC, Liebson LA, Bigelow GE. A placebo-controlled clinical trial of buprenorphine as a treatment for opioid dependence. *Drug Alcohol Depend* 1995; **40**: 17–25.

144 Bammer G, Dobler-Mikola A, Fleming P, Strang J, Uchtenhagen A. The heroin-prescribing debate: integrating science and politics. *Science* 1999; **284**: 1277–8.

145 Sell L, Farrell M, Robson P. Prescription of diamorphine, dipipanone and cocaine in England and Wales. *Drug Alcohol Rev* 1997; **16**: 221–6.

146 McCusker C, Davies M. Prescribing drug of choice to illicit heroin users: the experience of a UK community drug team. *J Subst Abuse Treat* 1996; **13**: 521–31.

147 Strang J, Ruben S, Farrell M, Gossop M. Prescribing heroin and other injectable drugs. In: Strang J, Gossop M (eds). *Heroin Addiction and Drug Policy: the British system.* London: Oxford University Press, 1994, pp. 192–206.

148 Strang J, Sheridan J, Barber N. Prescribing injectable and oral methadone to opiate addicts: results from the 1995 national postal survey of community pharmacists in England and Wales. *BMJ* 1996; **313**: 270–2.

149 Strang J, Sheridan J. National and regional characteristics of methadone prescribing in England and Wales: local analysis of data from the 1995 national survey of community pharmacies. *J Subst Abuse* 1998; **3**: 240–6.

150 Perneger TV, Giner F, del Rio M, Mino A. Randomised trial of heroin maintenance programme for addicts who fail in conventional drug treatments. *BMJ* 1998; **317**: 13–18.

151 Donmall M, Seivewright N, Douglas J, Traycott T, Millar T. *National Cocaine Treatment Study: the effectiveness of treatments offered to cocaine/crack users.* A report prepared for the Department of Health's Task Force to Review Services for Drug Misusers. London: Department of Health, 1995.

152 Strang J, Sheridan J. Prescribing amphetamines to drug misusers: data from the 1995 national survey of community pharmacists. *Addiction* 1997; **92**: 833–8.

153 Fleming PM, Roberts D. Is the prescription of amphetamine justified as a harm reduction measure? *J R Soc Health* 1994; **114**: 127–31.

154 McBride AJ, Sullivan G, Blewett AE, Morgan S. Amphetamine prescribing as a harm reduction measure: a preliminary study. *Addict Res* 1997; **5**: 95–112.

155 Marlatt GA, Gordon JR (eds). *Relapse Prevention: maintenance strategies in the treatment of addictive behavior.* New York: Guilford Press, 1985.

156 Standing Conference on Drug Abuse. *Structured Day Programmes: new options in community care for drug users.* London: Standing Conference on Drug Abuse, 1996.

157 Bickel WR, Stizer ML, Bigelow GE, Liebson IA, Jasinski DE, Johnson RE. A clinical trial of buprenorphine comparison with methadone in the detoxification of heroin addicts. *Clin Pharm Rev* 1988; **43**: 72–8.

158 Brewer C. Ultra-rapid, antagonist-precipitated opiate withdrawal under general anaesthesia or sedation. *Addict Biol* 1997; **2**: 291–302.

159 Bearn J, Gossop M, Strang J. Rapid opiate detoxification treatments. *Drug Alcohol Rev* 1999; **18**: 75–81.

160 HM Prison Service. *Drug Misuse in Prisons: policy and strategy.* London: HM Prison Service, 1996.

161 Cook C. *Residential Rehabilitation.* A report prepared for the Department of Health's Task Force to Review Services for Drug Misusers. London: Department of Health, 1995.

162 Healey A, Knapp M, Astin J *et al.* The economic burden of drug addiction: social costs incurred by clients at intake to NTORS. *Br J Psychiatry* 1998; **173**: 160–5.

163 Healey A, Knapp M, Astin J *et al. op. cit.*

164 Akehurst R, Hutton J, Dixon R. *Review of the Higher Costs of Health Care Provision in Inner London and a Consideration of Implications for Competitiveness.* York: York Health Economics Consortium, University of York, 1991.

165 Coggans N, Shewan D, Henderson M, Davies JB. The impact of school-based drug education. *Br J Addiction* 1991; **86**: 1099–109.

166 Whelan S, Moody M. *An Evaluation of a Drug Prevention Programme for Children Attending a Middle School in Mansfield, Notts.* Nottingham: North Nottinghamshire Health Promotion, 1994.

167 Tobler NS, Stratton HH. Effectiveness of school-based drug prevention programmes: a meta-analysis of the research. *J Prim Prevention* 1997; **18**: 71–128.

168 Botvin GJ, Dusenbury L, Baker E. A skills training approach to smoking prevention among Hispanic youth. *J Behav Med* 1989; **12**: 279–96.

169 Botvin GJ, Baker E, Filazzola AD, Botvin EM. A cognitive-behavioral approach to substance abuse prevention: one-year follow-up. *Addict Behav* 1990; **15**: 47–63.

170 Botvin GT, Baker E *et al.* Long-term follow-up results of a randomized drug abuse prevention trial in a white middle-class population. *JAMA* 1995; **273**: 1106–12.

171 Botvin GJ. Substance abuse prevention through life skills training. In: Peters RD, McMahon RJ *et al.* (eds). *Preventing Childhood Disorders, Substance Abuse and Delinquency.* Banff International Behavioural Science Series. Volume 3. Thousand Oaks, CA: Sage Publications, 1996, pp. 215–40.

172 Marsden J, Gossop M, Stewart D *et al.* The Maudsley Addiction Profile (MAP): a brief instrument for assessing treatment outcome. *Addiction* 1998; **93**: 1857–68.

173 Stimson GV. Has the United Kingdom averted an epidemic of HIV-1 infection among drug injectors? *Addiction* 1996; **91**: 1085–8.

174 Durante AJ, Hart GJ, Brady AR, Madden PB, Noone A. The Health of the Nation target on syringe sharing: a role for routine surveillance in assessing progress and targeting interventions. *Addiction* 1995; **90:** 1389–96.

175 Hahn JA, Vranizan KM, Moss AR. Who uses needle exchange? A study of injection drug users in treatment in San Francisco, 1989–1990. *J Acquir Immune Defic Syndr Hum Retrovirol* 1997; **15**: 157–64.

176 Bluthenthal RN, Kral AH, Erringer EA, Edlin BR. Use of an illegal syringe exchange and injection-related risk behaviors among street-recruited injection drug users in Oakland, California, 1992 to 1995. *J Acquir Immune Defic Syndr Hum Retrovirol* 1998; **18**: 505–11.

177 Hagan H, McGough JP, Thiede H, Weiss NS, Hopkins S. Syringe exchange and risk of infection with hepatitis B and C viruses. *Am J Epidemiol* 1999; **149**: 214–16.

178 Unlinked Anonymous Surveys Steering Group. *Prevalence of HIV in England and Wales in 1996. Annual Report of the Unlinked Anonymous Prevalence Monitoring Programme.* London: Department of Health, 1997.

179 Rhodes T, Hunter GM, Stimson GV *et al.* Prevalence of markers for hepatitis B virus and HIV-1 among drug injectors in London: injecting careers, positivity and risk behaviour. *Addiction* 1996; **91**: 1457–67.

180 Hunter G, Stimson GV, Jones S, Judd A, Hickman M. *Survey of Prevalence of Sharing by Injecting Drug Users Not in Contact With Services: an independent study carried out on behalf of the Department of Health.* London: Centre for Research on Drugs and Health Behaviour, 1998.

181 Ward J, Mattick RP, Hall W. *Key Issues in Methadone Maintenance Treatment.* Sydney: New South Wales University Press, 1992.

182 Ward J, Mattick RP, Hall W (eds). *Methadone Maintenance Treatment and Other Opioid Replacement Therapies.* Amsterdam: Harwood Academic Publishers, 1998.

183 Gossop M, Marsden J, Stewart D. *National Treatment Outcome Research Study: NTORS at one year.* London: Department of Health, 1998.

184 Marsch LA. The efficacy of methadone maintenance interventions in reducing illicit opiate use, HIV risk behavior and criminality: a meta-analysis. *Addiction* 1998; **93**: 515–32.

185 Metrebian N, Shanahan W, Wells B, Stimson GV. Feasibility of prescribing injectable heroin and methadone to opiate-dependent drug users: associated health gains and harm reductions. *Med J Aust* 1998; **168**: 596–600.

186 Ford C, Ryrie I. Prescribing injectable methadone in general practice. *Int J Drug Policy* 1999; **10**: 39–45.

187 Matin E, Canavan A, Butler R. A decade of caring for drug users entirely within general practice. *Br J Gen Pract* 1998; **48**: 1679–82.

188 Strang J, Marsden J, Cummins M *et al.* Randomised trial of supervised injectable versus oral methadone maintenance: report on feasibility and six-month outcome. *Addiction* 2000; **95**: 1631–45.

189 Simpson DD, Sells SB (eds). *Opioid Addiction and Treatment: a 12-year follow-up.* Malabar, FL: Keiger, 1990.

190 Platt JJ, Metzger DS. Cognitive interpersonal problem-solving skills and the maintenance of treatment success in heroin addicts. *Psychol Addict Behav* 1987; **1**: 5–13.

191 Hubbard RL, Craddock SG, Flynn P, Anderson J, Etheridge RM. Overview of 1-year outcomes in the Drug Abuse Treatment Outcome Study (DATOS). *Psychol Addict Behav* 1997; **11**: 261–78.

192 Woody GE, Luborsky L, McLellan AT *et al.* Psychotherapy for opiate addicts: does it help? *Arch Gen Psychiatry* 1983; **40**: 639–45.

193 Ball J, Ross A. *The Effectiveness of Methadone Maintenance Treatment.* New York: Springer, 1991.

194 Fiorentine R, Anglin D. Does increasing the opportunity for counselling increase the effectiveness of outpatient drug treatment? *J Subst Abuse Treat* 1997; **23**: 369–82.

195 Hser Y, Grella CE, Hsieh S, Anglin MD, Brown BS. Prior treatment experience related to process and outcomes in DATOS. *Drug Alcohol Depend* 1999; **57**: 137–50.

196 Joe GW, Simpson DD, Hubbard RL. Treatment predictors of tenure in methadone maintenance. *J Subst Abuse* 1991; **3**: 73–84.

197 General Accounting Office. *Cocaine Treatment: early results from various approaches.* Washington, DC: General Accounting Office, 1996.

198 Saunders B, Wilkinson C, Phillips M. The impact of a brief motivational intervention with opiate users attending a methadone programme. *Addiction* 1995; **90**: 415–24.

199 Higgins ST, Budney AJ, Bickel WK, Badger GJ, Foerg FE, Ogden D. Outpatient behavioural treatment for cocaine dependence. *Exp Clin Psychopharmacol* 1995; **3**: 205–12.

200 Carroll KM. Relapse prevention as a psychosocial treatment approach: a review of controlled clinical trials. *Exp Clin Psychopharmacol* 1996; **4**: 46–54.

201 Carroll KM, Rounsaville BJ, Gawin FH. A comparative trial of psychotherapies for ambulatory cocaine abusers: relapse prevention and interpersonal psychotherapy. *Am J Drug Alcohol Abuse* 1991; **17**: 229–47.

202 Carroll KM, Nich C, Rounsaville BJ. Differential symptom reduction in depressed cocaine abusers treated with psychotherapy and pharmacotherapy. *J Nerv Ment Dis* 1995; **183**: 251–9.

203 Gossop M, Green L, Phillips G, Bradley B. Lapse, relapse and survival among opiate addicts after treatment. *Br J Psychiatry* 1989; **154**: 348–53.

204 Gossop M, Johns A, Green L. Opiate withdrawal: inpatient versus outpatient programmes and preferred versus random assignment to treatment. *BMJ* 1986; **293**: 697–9.

205 Georgakis A. *Clouds House: an evaluation of a residential alcohol and drug dependency treatment centre.* Salisbury: The Life-Anew Trust Ltd, 1995.

206 DeLeon G, Jainchill N. Male and female drug abusers: social and psychological status two years after treatment in a therapeutic community. *Am J Drug Alcohol Abuse* 1982; **8**: 465–97.

207 Bennett G, Rigby K. Psychological change during residence in a rehabilitation centre for female drug misusers. Part I. Drug misusers. *Drug Alcohol Depend* 1990; **27**: 149–57.

208 Simpson DD. Effectiveness of drug abuse treatment: a review of research from field settings. In: Egertson J, Fox D, Leshner A (eds). *Treating Drug Abusers Effectively.* Oxford: Blackwell, 1997.

209 DeLeon G, Andrews M, Wexler H, Jaffe J, Rosenthal M. Therapeutic community dropouts: criminal behaviour five years after treatment. *Am J Drug Alcohol Abuse* 1979; **6**: 253–71.

210 Gossop M, Marsden J, Stewart D, Rolfe A. Treatment retention and 1-year outcomes for residential programmes in England. *Drug Alcohol Depend* 1999; **57**: 89–98.

211 Simpson D, Lloyd MR. Client evaluation of drug abuse treatment in relation to follow-up outcomes. *Am J Drug Alcohol Abuse* 1979; **6**: 397–411.

212 Drummond MF, Stoddart GL, Torrance GW. *Methods for the Economic Evaluation of Health Care Programmes.* Oxford: Oxford University Press, 1987.

213 Hser Y-I, Anglin D. Cost-effectiveness of drug abuse treatment: relevant issues and alternative longitudinal modelling approaches. In: Cartwright W, Kaple J (eds). *Economic Costs, Cost-Effectiveness, Financing, and Community-Based Drug Treatment.* National Institute on Drug Abuse Research Monograph 113. Washington, DC: US Government Printing Office, 1991.

214 Plotnick R. Applying benefit–cost analysis to substance abuse prevention programs. *Int J Addictions* 1994; **29**: 339–59.

215 Gerstein DR, Johnson RA, Harwood HJ, Suter N, Malloy K. *Evaluating Recovery Services: the California Drug and Alcohol Treatment Assessment (CALDATA).* Sacramento, CA: California Department of Alcohol and Drug Programs, 1994.

216 Flynn P, Kristiansen PL, Porto JV, Hubbard RL. Costs and benefits of treatment for cocaine addiction in DATOS. *Drug Alcohol Depend* 1999; **57**: 167–74.

217 McLellan AT, Hagan TA, Levine M *et al.* Supplemental social services improve outcomes in public addiction treatment. *Addiction* 1998; **93**: 1489–99.

218 Hubbard RL, Craddock SG, Flynn P, Anderson J, Etheridge RM. Overview of 1-year outcomes in the Drug Abuse Treatment Outcome Study (DATOS). *Psychol Addict Behav* 1997; **11**: 261–78.

219 Simpson DD, Joe GW, Brown BS. Treatment retention and follow-up outcomes in the Drug Abuse Treatment Outcome Study (DATOS). *Psychol Addict Behav* 1997; **11**: 239–60.

220 Lovejoy M, Rosenblum A, Magura S, Foote J, Handelsman L, Stimmel B. Patients' perspectives on the process of change in substance abuse treatment. *J Subst Abuse Treat* 1995; **12**: 269–82.

221 Simpson DD, Joe GW, Rowan-Szal G, Greener J. Client engagement and change during drug abuse treatment. *J Subst Abuse* 1995; **7**: 117–34.

222 Joe GW, Simpson DD, Broome KM. Retention and patient engagement models for different treatment modalities in DATOS. *Drug Alcohol Depend* 1999; **57**: 113–25.

223 Fiorentine R, Anglin D. More is better: counselling participation and the effectiveness of outpatient drug treatment. *J Subst Abuse Treat* 1996; **13**: 241–8.

224 Horvath AO, Symonds BD. Relation between alliance and outcome in psychotherapy: a meta-analysis. *J Counsel Psychol* 1991; **38**: 139–49.

225 Hser YL. Drug treatment counselor practices and effectiveness: an examination of the literature and relevant issues in a multilevel framework. *Eval Rev* 1995; **19**: 389–408.

226 McLellan AT, Wisner C. Achieving the public health potential of substance abuse treatment: implications for patient referral, treatment 'matching' and outcome evaluation. In: Bickel W, DeGrandpre R (eds). *Drug Policy and Human Nature*. Philadelphia, PA: Wilkins & Wilkins, 1996.

227 Edmunds M *et al*. *Arrest Referral: emerging lessons from research*. Home Office Drugs Prevention Initiative Paper No. 23. London: Home Office, 1998.

228 Edmunds M, Hough M, Turnbull PJ. *Doing Justice to Treatment: referring offenders to drug treatment services*. Drugs Prevention Initiative Paper No. 2. London: Home Office, 1999.

229 Newburn T, Elliot J. *Risks and Responses: drug prevention and youth justice*. Drug Prevention Advisory Service. DPAS Paper No. 3. London: Home Office, 1999.

230 Crome IB, Christian J, Green C. A unique dedicated community service for adolescents: policy, prevention and education implications. *Drugs Educ Prev Policy* 1999; **7**: 87–108.

231 Standing Conference on Drug Abuse and the Children's Legal Centre. *Young People and Drugs: policy guidance for drug interventions*. London: Standing Conference on Drug Abuse, 1999.

232 Health Advisory Service. *The Substance of Young Needs: services for children and adolescents who misuse substances*. London: HMSO, 1996.

233 Health Advisory Service. op. cit.

234 Johnson S. Dual diagnosis of severe mental illness and substance misuse: a case for specialist services. *Br J Psychiatry* 1997; **171**: 205–8.

235 Scott J, Gilvarry E, Farrell M. Managing anxiety and depression in alcohol and drug dependence. *Addict Behav* 1998; **23**: 919–31.

236 Department of the Environment, Transport and the Regions. *Coming In From the Cold*. London: Department of the Environment, Transport and the Regions, 1999.

237 Dale-Perera A, Farrant F. At home with diversity: race, rehab and drugs. *Druglink* 1999; **14**: 15–17.

238 Khan K. *Drug Prevention, Care and Treatment in the Greater London Area, Focusing on Race*. Middlesex University: Race and Drugs Project, 1999.

239 Mason P, Marsden J. The state of the market: revisited. *Druglink* 1994; **9**: 8–16.

240 Hayward J. Purchasing clinically effective health care. *BMJ* 1994; **309**: 823–4.

241 Institute of Medicine. *Broadening the Base of Treatment for Alcohol Problems*. Washington, DC: National Academy Press, 1990.

242 Center for Substance Abuse Treatment. *Developing Outcomes Monitoring Systems for Alcohol and Other Drug Treatment Services*. Treatment Improvement Protocol Series 14. Rockville, MD: US Department of Health and Human Services, 1995.

243 Harrison PA, Beebe TJ, Fulkerson JA, Torgerud CR. The development of patient profiles from Minnesota's treatment outcomes monitoring system. *Addiction* 1996; **91**: 687–99.

244 McLellan AT, Kushner H, Metzger D *et al.* The fifth edition of the Addiction Severity Index. *J Subst Abuse Treat* 1992; **9**: 199–213.

245 Darke S, Hall W, Wodak A, Heather N, Ward J. Development and validation of a multi-dimensional instrument for assessing outcome of treatment among opiate users: the Opiate Treatment Index. *Br J Addiction* 1992; **87**: 733–42.

246 Marsden J, Nizzoli U, Corbelli C *et al.* New European instruments for treatment outcome research: reliability of the Maudsley Addiction Profile and Treatment Perceptions Questionnaire in Italy, Spain and Portugal. *Eur Addiction Res* 2000; **6**: 115–22.

247 Larsen DL, Attkisson CC, Hargreaves WA, Nguyen T. Assessment of client/patient satisfaction: development of a general scale. *Eval Progr Plan* 1979; **2**: 197–207.

248 Greenfield TK, Attkisson CC. Steps toward a multifactorial satisfaction scale for primary health care and mental health services. *Eval Progr Plan* 1989; **12**: 271–8.

249 Simpson D, Lloyd MR. Client evaluation of drug abuse treatment in relation to follow-up outcomes. *Am J Drug Alcohol Abuse* 1979; **6**: 397–411.

250 Chan M, Sorensen JL, Guydish J, Rajima B, Acampora A. Client satisfaction with drug abuse day treatment versus residential treatment. *J Drug Issues* 1997; **27**: 367–77.

251 Joe GW, Friend HJ. Treatment process factors and satisfaction with drug abuse treatment. *Psychol Addict Behav* 1989; **3**: 53–64.

252 Marsden J, Stewart D, Gossop G *et al.* Assessing client satisfaction with treatment for substance use problems: development of the Treatment Perceptions Questionnaire (TPQ). *Addict Res* 2000; **8**: 455–70.

253 Marsden J, Stewart D, Gossop G *et al.* op. cit.

254 Boys A, Marsden J, Griffiths P. Reading between the lines. *Druglink* 1999; **14**: 20–3.

255 Hostick T. Research design and methodology for a local mental health needs assessment. *J Psychiatr Ment Health Nurs* 1995; **2**: 295–9.

256 Social Services Inspectorate. *Inspection of Social Services for People who Misuse Alcohol and Drugs.* London: Department of Health, 1995.

257 Rawaf S, Marshall F. Drug misuse: the ten steps for needs assessment. *Public Health Med* 1999; **1**: 21–6.

258 Pascoe G. Patient satisfaction in primary health care: a literature review and analysis. *Eval Progr Plan* 1983; **6**: 185–210.

259 Rhodes T, Stimson GV, Fitch C, Ball A, Renton A. Rapid assessment, injecting drug use, and public health. *Lancet* 1999; **354**: 65–8.

260 Dewit DJ, Rush B. Assessing the need for substance abuse services: a critical review of needs assessment models. *Eval Progr Plan* 1996; **19**: 41–64.

Acknowledgements

The authors would like to express their thanks to Mrs Rosemary Jenkins (Department of Health) and to three anonymous reviewers for helpful comments on an earlier draft of the chapter. The guidance and support of the series editors during preparation of the chapter are also gratefully acknowledged. The authors extend their thanks to Ms Annabel Boys and Dr Michael Farrell of the Institute of Psychiatry and Mr Peter Child, Director of the Consultancy Partnership, for their help during preparation of the material.

Disclaimer

The views expressed in this chapter are those of the authors and do not necessarily reflect the views of their respective organisations.

17 Learning Disabilities

Siân Rees, Chris Cullen, Shane Kavanagh and Paul Lelliott

1 Summary

Statement of problem

People with learning disabilities have a wide range of social and heath care needs. They may also have coexisting conditions that can contribute to need, including physical or developmental disabilities, mental and physical ill-health and a range of behavioural problems. It is often the presence of these conditions that defines need for services.

The following are basic understandings that should underpin the commissioning and delivery of services.

- People with learning disabilities should be recognised as individuals who have the same citizenship rights as the rest of the population.
- Care is increasingly in the community, and family members often provide the majority of care.
- Most individuals will predominantly need social care services. However, health services play a significant role to ensure that all needs are met.
- Disability may lead to the need for additional and/or specialist support/benefits and services. However, generic services should always be accessible to people with learning disabilities.
- Service planning must be based on partnership working, including health, social care, education, housing, users and their carers. This is particularly important at transition points in people's lives, such as leaving full-time education.
- Service planning and commissioning must include the needs of carers, particularly given the increased life expectancy of many people with learning disabilities and the inevitable ageing of their carers.
- Collaboration between commissioners will be required, as some conditions affect relatively small numbers of individuals within each primary care trust (PCT) population.

Policy context

Central themes in national health care policy include increasing the extent of community-based care and ensuring equivalence of service receipt between subgroups of the population. In order to promote joint working there is a requirement for health and local authorities, with partner agencies, to produce a joint investment plan (JIP) for learning disabilities. Local authorities lead this process. The objective of the JIP should be to 'promote independence and social inclusion'. In 2001, a national strategy for learning disabilities, *Valuing People*,[296] was published by the Department of Health, giving further guidance on the organisation and development of services. It emphasised four key principles – rights, independence, choice and inclusion – that should underpin the way forward.

Analysis of health and social care provision suggests that there is still a significant amount of work needed to ensure that people with learning disabilities have access to high-quality, comprehensive health and social care. Collaboration between commissioners will be essential.

Definitions and classification

The term 'learning disability' commonly refers to a group of individuals with a history of developmental delay, a delay in or failure to acquire a level of adaptive behaviour and/or social functioning expected for their age, and in whom there is evidence of significant intellectual impairment. Many terms are used with little consensus. Classification and terminology are important, both with respect to acceptability to those with learning disability, and also in order to allow accurate communication between those who plan, provide and evaluate services. Lack of standardisation of terms hampers progress. Comparison of research data is difficult, and the translation of research findings to local services, where case-mix may be significantly different, is hard to achieve.

Classification needs to be multi-axial in order to describe the complexity of need. Classification systems generally combine a measure of intellectual functioning (usually intelligence quotient [IQ]) with measures of social and behavioural functioning. The main systems are ICD-10, DSM-IV and the American Association on Mental Retardation Manual of Definitions.

In all, low IQ must be present during the developmental period of life. Other conditions in which IQ is lowered are excluded, e.g. acquired head injuries, schizophrenia and dementia.

The abbreviation 'PWLD' is used here to refer to people with learning disabilities or difficulties.

The use of categories

There is no simple way of categorising PWLD into groups that need a particular service; individual need should dictate the level and type of service input. An individual's social, behavioural and learning abilities must be assessed, in conjunction with measures of intellectual capability. Intellectual impairment refers to a loss of intellectual function. Severe intellectual impairment refers to those with an IQ of < 50 and mild intellectual impairment covers IQs of 50–69 (*see* Section 3 for discussion of the relationship between intellectual impairment and learning disabilities).

Categories used in this chapter include:

- conditions that are often, or always, associated with intellectual impairment, e.g. Down's syndrome and fragile X syndrome
- impairments/disabilities that occur more frequently in PWLD, e.g. epilepsy and cerebral palsy; developmental disorders, e.g. autistic spectrum disorders (ASD) and mental illness
- losses of function, e.g. hearing and mobility problems
- restriction of participation, e.g. social difficulties with housing or relationships and the impact on carers and families, such as inability to maintain paid employment or to sustain family relationships.

Aetiology

The aetiology of learning disabilities can be subdivided into those conditions that arise at conception (whose prevention lies before conception) and those that arise during pregnancy, labour and after birth. Aetiological agents fall into three main categories: genetic, infective and environmental.

No aetiological cause is found in approximately 30% of cases of severe learning disabilities. The same is true for the majority of cases of mild learning disabilities. Iodine deficiency disease is the commonest cause of severe learning disabilities worldwide. In the UK, the majority of cases are due to genetic factors, non-inherited Down's syndrome and X-linked disorders, such as fragile X, being the most common. Maternal alcohol consumption appears to play a significant role in the development of learning disabilities. It is considered the greatest cause of learning disabilities in the USA, although European research suggests lower figures. Neural-tube defects are also associated with learning disabilities.

Prevalence and incidence of learning disabilities and associated conditions

Some degree of intellectual impairment is relatively common in the general population. A minority of these individuals have severe intellectual impairment. Coexisting medical, psychiatric or other conditions are also common. There has been a steady increase in the prevalence of severe learning disabilities over the past 20 years. This is likely to continue into the next decade. The number who have multiple and complex disabilities will also increase. These trends need to be taken into consideration in service planning.

There are a number of difficulties in arriving at an exact prevalence figure for learning disabilities.

Most population figures for the UK have been determined from service contact, often derived from case registers. This will tend to underestimate overall prevalence. Another consequence is that more is known about those with severe impairment or milder impairment and coexisting conditions (i.e. those in touch with services) than about the much larger group of people with relatively uncomplicated mild or borderline intellectual impairment.

The prevalence of mild intellectual impairment (IQ 50–69) reflects the statistical distribution of IQ in a population and will therefore be in the region of 2.27% of the population. This does not equate with the prevalence of mild learning disabilities. It is likely that those with mild intellectual impairment and additional problems such as challenging behaviours or mental illness will come into contact with services and therefore be identified as having mild learning disabilities. Many individuals with mild intellectual impairment without such problems will not be labelled learning disabled. The population prevalence for mild learning disabilities is estimated to be 1–2% of the population.

Prevalence estimates for severe intellectual impairment (IQ < 50) range from 300–400/100 000 of the general population. All those with an IQ of < 50 will be identified as having severe learning disabilities.

Factors that affect incidence and prevalence

Time trends

In the UK, successive birth cohorts are of different size. The largest cohort comprises those in their mid-thirties. Analysis of UK case registers suggests that, for adults with IQs of < 50, there has been an increasing prevalence of 1% per year, mainly owing to increases in survival. Projections predict a further increase in the population prevalence of severe learning disabilities of 11% between 1998 and 2008.

Geography

There are clear international differences in incidence and prevalence rates, particularly between the developed and developing worlds. It is often assumed that geographic factors have no impact in the UK. However, some authors suggest that there may be regional differences in prevalence, if not in incidence.

Socio-economic factors

Some causes of severe learning disabilities are socially determined or influenced. There is, however, little evidence for an effect of social class on the incidence of severe intellectual impairment, though social deprivation is associated with cognitive development. There is some evidence to suggest that there is an increased prevalence of severe learning disabilities in the British Asian population.

Specific conditions associated with learning disabilities

Down's syndrome

The frequency of occurrence of Down's syndrome is clearly linked to maternal age. The risk of having an affected child at varying maternal ages is approximately 0.5/1000 when aged 20 years, 10/1000 when aged 40 and 150/1000 when aged 50. The majority of individuals with Down's syndrome have IQs in the range 35–55 and have a higher incidence of medical problems than the general population.

Fragile X syndrome

Fragile X syndrome is the most commonly occurring X-linked disorder. Birth frequencies often quoted are 0.8/1000 for males and 0.32/1000 for females, although recent estimates suggest considerably lower figures (0.25/1000 and 0.125/1000, respectively).

Phenylketonuria

Phenylketonuria (PKU) is the most common metabolic disorder linked with learning disabilities, with reported birth frequencies of 0.05–0.07/1000 live births.

Congenital hypothyroidism

Congenital hypothyroidism is the most common hormonal disorder associated with learning disabilities, with a birth frequency of 0.25–0.3/1000 live births. It is much more common in individuals with Down's syndrome. In the UK, screening and early treatment should ensure that very few cases of PKU or hypothyroidism resulting in severe learning disabilities occur in the UK.

Epilepsy

People with learning disabilities have a higher risk of having epilepsy than the rest of the population. This risk increases with severity of impairment, as does the severity of the epilepsy.

Cerebral palsy

Cerebral palsy develops in 2–3/1000 live births. Estimates suggest that up to half of those with cerebral palsy will have some difficulties with intellectual functioning, and 23–34% will have an IQ of < 50.

Mental disorder

Many risk factors known to contribute to the development of mental illness occur more frequently in PWLD. These include sensory impairments, communication difficulties, low self-esteem, stigma, low levels of social support, poor coping skills and chronic ill-health. There is an increased prevalence of psychiatric disorder and behavioural disturbance over that found in the general population. There is considerable difficulty in determining exact figures due to poor detection, misdiagnosis and methodological difficulties.

The occurrence of mental ill-health in children increases with intellectual impairment; 30–42% of 9–11-year-olds with IQs of < 70 were found to require treatment for mental health problems, compared with 6–7% of those with higher IQs.

Estimates of coexisting mental illness and/or behavioural disorder in adults with learning disabilities vary from 14.3–67.3% depending on the methodology and study group. If challenging behaviours are excluded then the rates found fall dramatically. All types of mental disorder are found. Rates of substance misuse and affective disorders found are lower than those in the general population.

Older people with learning disabilities have been shown to have a higher prevalence of mental illness than either the general population or younger age groups of PWLD. This is mainly accounted for by the increase in early dementia, particularly in people with Down's syndrome.

Challenging behaviours

This term encompasses a diverse group of behaviours, the prevalence of which increases with the severity of intellectual impairment, but differs between groups of PWLD. There is a high prevalence of challenging behaviours in those with ASD, whilst people with Down's syndrome are less likely to demonstrate challenging behaviours.

About 40% of children with an IQ of < 70 display challenging behaviours. Approximately 20 adults with learning disabilities per 100 000 of the total population display behaviours that present a *significant* challenge. Using a broader definition of challenging behaviours, 25% of adults were shown to have behavioural problems that posed a major challenge to the achievement of an ordinary life (approximately 100/100 000). This figure may more accurately reflect the group that will require input from specialist health and social services.

People with learning disabilities seem to be over-represented at all levels of the criminal justice system. Offending behaviours are more likely in those with mild and borderline learning disabilities than in those with the most severe impairment.

Autistic spectrum disorders

This term refers to developmental disability affecting social and communication skills. Prevalence rates vary according to the diagnostic criteria used. For the whole spectrum, approximately 900/100 000 of the population may be affected. If only those with the most severe disorder are included, then rates are of the order of 40–50/100 000. Autistic spectrum disorders are, overall, about four times more common in boys than in girls. This is most marked in those of higher ability. There is a very strong association with learning disabilities; approximately half of those with severe learning disabilities have some type of autistic spectrum disorder. Autistic spectrum disorders are also strongly associated with challenging behaviours.

Losses of function

Losses of function leading to restriction of activity are common. Sensory impairment, mobility and communication difficulties all occur.

Other associated conditions

Some medical conditions are found more commonly in PWLD, e.g. problems with continence, congenital heart conditions, obesity and some infective conditions, such as hepatitis B. Poor oral health is also common. Improvements in medical care have led to the survival into adulthood and old age of a new cohort of very severely disabled individuals with complex medical needs.

Restriction of participation: social consequences

PWLD often have limited capacity to exercise choice and control over many areas of their lives. This includes where to live, with whom and how to occupy their time. It also applies to choices about service provision. For the majority of PWLD in the community and in residential care, relationships outside immediate family/carers are usually with service providers.

PWLD experience high levels of sexual, physical and emotional abuse. This applies both to those living in their own homes and to those in residential care. Many people with severe learning disabilities have difficulties with activities of daily living.

Families and carers

Caring for a person with learning disabilities can place considerable strain on carers and families, having an impact on emotional well-being, financial resources and relationships.

Services available

A range of health, social and educational services are available – generic services, such as primary care, and specialist learning disabilities services. Services are provided by the statutory and increasingly the voluntary and private sectors. The types of services and service providers vary greatly across the UK. There are gaps in service development across the spectrum of health and social care. It is unlikely that differences in need can explain the pattern of provision that exists.

A key issue in the provision of services is their accessibility. This covers a range of issues, including physical access, information in appropriate formats (e.g. Braille), transport provision, the knowledge and attitudes of staff, and the provision of training and support to generic staff, users and their carers.

Primary care

Primary care services are central to the organisation of adequate health surveillance for PWLD, who have ordinary needs for primary care and special needs relating to the increased rates of certain conditions. There is, however, significant under-detection of both physical and mental ill-health and low uptake of screening and immunisation programmes. Chiropody, continence, dietetics, pharmacy and dentistry services are all needed. Primary care also provides for the needs of families and other carers.

Specialist learning disability services

The majority of PWLD will not need the input of specialist health services. However, those with mild intellectual impairment and coexisting conditions such as mental ill-health and those with severe impairment are likely to need specialist input. The organisation of services varies significantly across the country.

Community learning disability teams (CLDTs) are one of the commonest means of co-ordinating specialist community services for adults with learning disabilities. Most CLDTs in the UK will see people with an IQ of up to 70. There may be gaps in provision for those with higher IQs and associated conditions. There is a need for hospital beds for the assessment and treatment of a small number of PWLD, such as those with mental illness, sensory impairments or challenging behaviour.

Children's services may include input from dedicated teams and paediatric and child and adolescent mental health services. The provision of health services that support transition for disabled people with complex health and support needs has been described as 'very patchy'. The organisation of services for people over 65 with learning disabilities also varies considerably across the country.

Audiology and ophthalmology services with interest and expertise in screening and the fitting of aids for PWLD are needed, as there are high levels of unrecognised morbidity.

Accommodation

Considerable change has occurred in the provision of accommodation – the closure of large institutions, the increasing role of the independent sector, and the acceptance that PWLD should have the opportunity for ordinary life experiences and should be supported to live independently in the community whenever possible. There is significant variation in the type, quality and quantity of residential accommodation across the country. Despite the encouragement of supported living in the community, there are still relatively few PWLD in their own homes or in supported lodgings. The ageing of carers and increasing life expectancy for PWLD will increase future need for a range of accommodation options.

Daytime activity

The capacity to engage in meaningful activity during the day is a key measure of quality of life. This may include paid work, leisure activities and structured day-care programmes. It should be dictated by the needs and desires of the individual. The majority of organised daytime activities are provided by day-care facilities. This is increasingly organised in small community units. Day-care programmes may include centre-based activities, adult education and training and community leisure activities.

Employment

PWLD may be in ordinary employment or a variety of sheltered or supported work schemes. Supported employment schemes have significantly increased in number over the past 10 years. There is, however, uneven distribution across the country and mismatch between supply and demand.

Education

The emergence of education as a key service for both children and, increasingly, adults with learning disabilities has been a marked feature of provision since the 1981 Education Act.

Portage is probably the most common pre-school scheme. Mainstream education increasingly includes children with disabilities, including those with learning disabilities. There is, however, significant variation between LEAs in the rate at which this is being achieved.

The provision of further education seems to have increased for some people with learning disabilities, although those with more severe disabilities may have suffered.

Services for mental disorder

There is a perceived gap in many services in the provision of mental health services for PWLD. This is particularly true for individuals with mild or borderline impairment, for children and the elderly. Most services for adults with learning disabilities and mental illness are associated with specialist learning disability services, with specialist learning disability mental health teams in some areas.

Services for challenging behaviours and offending

A range of specialist day care, inpatient and outpatient services may be provided. Alternatively, general learning disabilities teams cover this group.

There has been a decrease in the number of high-secure hospital beds for PWLD and an increase in medium-secure and other alternative provision. High-secure learning disability services are now centred at Rampton Hospital.

Services for autistic spectrum disorders

A wide range of services is required to meet the diversity of need displayed by both children and adults with ASD. Individuals with ASD require highly structured environments, and services should be organised to provide the familiarity and predictability needed. Children with ASD may attend mainstream education (with or without specialist support), generic special schools, designated units for ASD or receive home-based tuition. Most PWLD and ASD will eventually need some form of residential care. It is often the case that neither adult psychiatric services nor specialist learning disabilities services are set up to provide adequately for those with ASD and higher IQs.

Restriction of participation: social consequences

PWLD may require help to access and understand services and to take an active part in the way in which their care is organised. The development of advocacy services, alongside the provision of interpreters and training for front-line staff in issues relevant to dealing with PWLD, are essential components of adequate service organisation. The development of parenting programmes can also aid independent living.

Families and carers

Families and carers need information, advice, training and support from a range of services. Respite care is a key component in care packages to support carers. It can provide a break for carers, particularly if the client has multiple problems, severe challenging behaviours, or terminal or severe physical illness, and can cover carer illness or other emergencies. Most local authorities have some respite facility, but there is considerable variability in its availability. Family-based rather than residential care is increasingly common.

The cost of services

In 1996, 5% of health and 13% of national social services expenditure was spent on PWLD.

These figures underestimate the total cost, as significant expenditure is not identifiable as being spent on specific care groups. Estimates of total spend are in the region of £3 billion per year.

Effectiveness of services

The determination of effectiveness is challenging for a number of reasons, including differences in research methodologies, the multi-agency and multi-intervention nature of care provided, difficulties in ascertaining the views of PWLD, and the trade-off that may exist between positive outcomes for carers and those that they care for. The literature on the effectiveness of treatments, interventions and service models for PWLD is mainly limited to descriptive and uncontrolled research studies. By far the largest body of work is in the field of accommodation and behavioural interventions.

- Prevention programmes such as genetic counselling for fragile X syndrome, folate supplementation pre and post conception, antenatal screening for Down's syndrome, immunisation and postnatal testing for phenylketonuria and congenital hypothyroidism can all contribute to reducing the incidence and/or severity of learning disabilities.
- An overall measure of the effectiveness of primary and specialist services is the extent to which PWLD have unmet needs for which there are effective interventions. Analysis of the needs of PWLD in the Avon area suggests that many needs are unmet.
- Accommodation – the conclusion often drawn from the available literature is that community-based provision is preferable to hospital care, albeit at a higher cost. However, debate continues about the appropriate mix of alternative provision in terms of scale, the organisation of facilities and the sector of management. Community placements have been associated with improved self-reported outcomes for those individuals who were able to express a view. Longer-term research has demonstrated little change in social functioning and symptomatology one and five years after discharge, although generally at greater cost. Specialist accommodation for individuals with challenging behaviours seems to have better outcomes than hospital-based care.
- Day-centre care is of unknown effectiveness. Evaluation of supported employment schemes has shown positive benefits.
- Psychological interventions, particularly behavioural approaches, can produce changes in behaviours, although long-term sustainability is open to question.
- Antipsychotic medication is commonly used to treat emotional and behavioural disorders in PWLD. Systematic review of randomised controlled trials has provided no evidence as to whether such medication does or does not help adults with learning disabilities and challenging behaviours, or with schizophrenia. Internationally agreed guidelines on the use of psychotropic medication cover issues such as reducing polypharmacy and monitoring.
- In autism there is some evidence from some studies to suggest that the early educational intervention may have benefits.
- Advocacy services are viewed positively by clients. Their overall impact on quality of life or the provision of services is not known.
- Respite care is valued by carers.
- Alternative therapies are also valued by carers and clients and they can contribute to a sense of well-being. There is little evidence to prove or disprove their overall effectiveness or their specific benefits in PWLD.

Models of care

There is no one model of care that can be recommended, given the diversity of the group and the relative lack of effectiveness information. A systems approach to service provision is necessary if comprehensive, integrated and inclusive services are to be provided. Processes of care, such as the nature of inter-agency working, as well as structural elements will determine the adequacy of local service provision. It is likely that the technical ability of staff will be a greater determinant of local service capacity than the availability of specific settings. It is therefore not possible to examine one element of a service in isolation. It is possible to outline both structural and process components of services that should form the basis for local planning discussions. Local providers and commissioners may then determine the most appropriate local configuration of structure and process needed to achieve a comprehensive service. Local discussion between commissioners and providers will need to cover:

- population need for services
- planning and inter-agency working
- service provision covering health promotion, primary care and specialist learning disability services, daytime activity, accommodation, information and support.

This necessitates partnership working at all levels and between all the relevant agencies. Commissioners of services for PWLD need to recognise the range and complexity of the condition and consequently the inevitable complexity and variability of the system that will be needed to meet their needs. The level at which commissioning is carried out may well be different for discrete aspects of the condition. Individualised packages and joint funding will be needed for those with the most complex needs. Challenging behaviour and sensory impairment services, for example, may well need to be purchased at population levels larger than the average PCT in order to ensure service integrity and expertise. Prevention services and primary care can more easily be provided and commissioned for smaller population groups. The capacity for flexible, local approaches is likely to produce the most comprehensive commissioning and development of services.

Target setting

The precise nature of local targets will be determined by the current nature of provision and local data collection capabilities. Overall aims should be improvement in quality of life and reduction in social exclusion. Targets can be set with respect to the range of activities and services:

- health promotion: primary and secondary prevention, tertiary prevention – the physical and mental health of PWLD
- accommodation
- daytime activities
- information and support
- specialist services
- commissioning.

For a further discussion of target setting, *see* the All Wales Health Gain Protocol.[2]

Information and research requirements

Data sources

Routine data sources are limited in their usefulness. The extent to which data can be disaggregated to client group or severity is very variable. Information on a large number of services necessary for comprehensive provision is unavailable, e.g. employment or leisure services. Where local registers have been developed and well maintained, they have been found to be helpful in planning services.

Research

There are significant gaps in research evidence. An extensive research programme is required covering aetiology, epidemiology and effectiveness of service interventions.

2 Statement of problem

Introduction

People with learning disabilities have a wide range of social and heath care needs. This reflects the spectrum of severity for learning disabilities and the different conditions that may coexist. People with learning disabilities also have needs generated by social exclusion, such as poverty, lack of housing and unemployment. Those with mild learning disabilities may need specialist support in mainstream education while they are children. Subsequently, they may need the same support/benefits as others in socially excluded groups, rather than specialist services. At higher levels of disability, however, many individuals will have lifelong needs for health and social care.

The coexisting conditions that may contribute to need include:

- physical disabilities, e.g. sensory impairments and mobility difficulties
- mental ill-health across all diagnostic categories
- developmental disabilities, e.g. autistic spectrum disorders (ASD)
- medical conditions, e.g. epilepsy
- a wide range of behavioural problems, from self-injury to inappropriate social behaviours.

This range and diversity of need represent a significant challenge to carers, families and service providers. Planning services is complex, as health, social care, education and housing must all be involved. As learning disability is lifelong, partnership working and the quality of the interfaces between services are crucial. This is particularly true at transition points in people's lives, such as leaving full-time education. The necessity for partnership and collaboration between agencies is emphasised by the knowledge that mental and physical ill-health is often undetected or under-treated (*see* Sections 4 and 5).

People with learning disabilities must be recognised as individuals and treated as having the same citizenship rights as the rest of the population. This means that:

- people with learning disabilities have the same right of access to NHS and other services as the rest of the population
- although disabilities may lead to the need for additional and/or specialist support/benefits and services, generic services should be accessible to everyone
- people with learning disabilities may need help to access services

- individuals should be seen as having health *and* social care needs, not health *or* social care needs (for further discussion of this distinction, *see* Appendix I).

Parents and/or other family members provide the majority of care for people with learning disabilities. Precise figures are not available, but estimates from the old North West Thames Region suggested that the vast majority of individuals between 15 and 24 who were in contact with services (on registers) were cared for by their families. Even up to age 35 a substantial proportion were living in the family home.[1] Many more of those with mild learning disabilities live in their own homes. Service planning and commissioning must therefore include the needs of carers. This is of particular importance given the increased life expectancy of many people with learning disabilities and the inevitable ageing of their carers.

Policy context

Central themes in national health care policy include increasing the extent of community-based care and ensuring equivalence of service receipt between subgroups of the population. The process of deinstitutionalisation of service provision began in the 1950s. This has led to increasing numbers of people with learning disabilities being cared for in their own homes or non-hospital residential care. The NHS and Community Care Act reinforced the social care emphasis by giving social services the lead for service planning. There remains, however, a significant role for health services, which should meet health needs in all settings. There is considerable scope for both health promotion and health gain.[2]

Policy guidance was released in 1992 as circulars to health and local authorities.[3,4] The Department of Health guidance on continuing care further reinforced the need for agreements between health and social care on their relative responsibilities.[5] In order to promote joint working there is now a requirement for health (now PCTs) and local authorities, with partner agencies, to produce a joint investment plan (JIP) for learning disabilities. Local authorities lead this process. The objective of the JIP should be to 'promote independence and social inclusion' through the promotion of activities such as supported employment, short-term breaks, health screening, and access to education, leisure and other resources available to the general public. In August 2001, a national strategy for learning disabilities, *Valuing People*, was published by the Department of Health, giving further guidance on the organisation and development of services. It emphasises four key principles – rights, independence, choice and inclusion – that should underpin the way forward.

Commissioning

The very varied rate of resettlement, adequacy of inter-agency working and consequent service development across the country has led to considerable differences in the nature and extent of health provision and funding at local levels. Inter-agency planning must therefore make clear the delineation of responsibilities for all aspects of service provision, so that artificial boundaries between health and social care are diminished.[6,7] Analysis of health and social care provision across 24 authorities suggested that trends in care, such as increased numbers of people living in their own homes, improved levels of day and respite care, and better carer support are occurring or are planned. There is, however, still a significant amount of work needed to ensure that people with learning disabilities have access to high-quality, comprehensive health and social care provision.[8] This is particularly true in relation to primary care and specialist services for those with complex physical and mental health needs.

The effect of the recent changes in the commissioning of health services and the development of primary care trusts (PCTs) is as yet unclear. Some analysis of the impact of GP fundholding suggested little impact on specialist learning disability services.[9] In any given PCT there will be relatively small numbers of individuals who will require specialist learning disability services. Collaboration between commissioners will therefore be essential.

The Department of Health publications *Signposts for Success* and *Once a Day* give clear advice on the commissioning of health services and the organisation of primary care.[10,11]

Definitions and classification

The term 'learning disability' commonly refers to a group of individuals with a history of developmental delay, a delay in or failure to acquire a level of adaptive behaviour and/or social functioning expected for their age, and in whom there is evidence of significant intellectual impairment.

There are many terms used to classify, categorise and describe the problems and abilities of people with learning disabilities. This is problematic because there is:

> *little professional consensus on terminology which has led to transient, culture-specific lay terms being used without discrimination or clear definition.*[12]

In this document, the abbreviation 'PWLD' will be used to describe the whole population under consideration. This acknowledges that, in the UK, both 'people with learning disabilities' and 'people with learning difficulties' are acceptable and commonly used terms, replacing mental handicap and mental retardation.

Classification systems

Systems used to classify PWLD generally combine a measure of intellectual functioning (usually intelligence quotient, IQ) with measures of social and behavioural functioning.

The main systems are as follows.

- **ICD-10:**[13] F7 – Mental Retardation. This is a bi-axial classification based on IQ (F70 – mild, IQ 50–69; F71 – moderate, IQ 35–49; F72 – severe, IQ 20–34; F73 – profound, IQ < 20) and impairment of behaviour (not further defined). In theory, classification is based on the use of IQ test results to allocate a code. In practice, it is often based on the subjective opinion of the interviewing clinician. This may lead to coding unreliability.

   F84 – Pervasive Developmental Disorders are also relevant. F84 is within Disorders of Psychological Development, F80–89. There are a number of sub-categories, including autism. These conditions deserve specific mention as, unlike other disorders within F80–89, autistic spectrum disorders (ASD) are often inherently associated with major behavioural disorders and, in adults, psychiatric disorder (*see* 'Autistic spectrum disorders' in Section 4 below).
- **DSM-IV:**[14] A multi-axial approach is taken which includes significantly sub-average intellectual functioning (IQ of approximately 70 or less), concurrent deficits or impairments in adaptive functioning, and onset before age 18. Sub-classification is based on severity, reflecting levels of intellectual impairment (IQ scores).
- **American Association on Mental Retardation Manual of Definitions:**[15] Three criteria must be met, namely significantly below average intelligence, deficits in adaptive behaviour (e.g. communication and self-care), and that these should be evident in the developmental period. A sub-classification approach looking at the intensity and provision of support (intermittent, limited, extensive and pervasive) is recommended. The lack of appropriate and precise measuring instruments may hamper use in quantitative research.

In all classification systems, low IQ must be present during the developmental period of life. Other conditions in which IQ is lowered are excluded, e.g. acquired head injuries, schizophrenia and dementia.

The use of terms

Classification should use internationally agreed terms. The International Classification of Impairments, Disabilities and Handicaps (ICIDH) is, however, not routinely used. ICIDH emphasises the importance of the interaction between the individual and their environment, and makes clear distinctions between impairment, disability and handicap.

- **Impairment:** The loss of, or abnormality of, psychological, physiological or anatomical structure or function.
- **Disability:** The restriction of (as the result of impairment), or lack of ability to perform, an activity considered to be within the normal range of human capacity.
- **Handicap:** The disadvantage resulting from impairment or disability that limits or prevents the fulfilment of a role that would be considered normal for that individual.

This classification is currently being revised, moving away from a medical model of disability to a more socially orientated one. The new definitions of the three dimensions are, in the context of a health condition, impairment, activity and participation.

- **Impairment:** The loss or abnormality of body structure or of a physiological function.
- **Activity:** The nature and extent of functioning at the level of the person. Activities may be limited in nature, duration and quality.
- **Participation:** The nature and extent of a person's involvement in life situations in relation to impairment, activities, health conditions and contextual factors (elements of the environment, e.g. buildings, services and community attitudes).

Individuals who have an impairment of intellectual functioning may have a wide range of restriction of both activity and participation and hence a wide range of needs. This makes a multi-axial approach to classification essential. It is not possible to determine need for services from a simple measure of intellectual functioning. An individual's social, behavioural and learning abilities must be assessed, in conjunction with measures of intellectual capability.

Legal terms

In England and Wales the Mental Health Act 1983 included the terms 'mental disorder' (which includes arrested or incomplete development of the mind), 'mental impairment' and 'severe mental impairment'. These are specific legal terms and as such are not synonymous with mental illness, learning disabilities or intellectual impairment (*see* 'Global categories' in Section 3). Within the Act, severe mental impairment is described as 'a state of arrested or incomplete development of the mind, which includes severe impairment of intelligence and social functioning and is associated with abnormally aggressive or seriously irresponsible conduct on the part of the person concerned'. Mental impairment is described as 'a state of arrested or incomplete development of the mind (not amounting to severe mental impairment), which includes etc.'. In the proposed reform of the Act a broader definition of mental disorder is proposed: 'any disability or disorder of mind or brain, whether permanent or temporary, which results in impairment or disturbance of mental functioning'.

Reformed legislation proposes provisions to protect the rights of people with long-term 'mental incapacity' who need care and treatment for serious mental disorder, but who cannot consent to it. There will be an obligation for a second opinion on the individual's care plan if care and treatment continue for longer than 28 days.[16]

Conclusions

Planning of services for PWLD requires an understanding of the complexities of need generated by the diversity of the condition and acceptance that social inclusion is a key objective.

Classification needs to be multi-axial in order to describe this complexity of need.

The way in which classification and terminology are used is important, both with respect to acceptability to those with learning disability, and in order to allow accurate communication between those who plan, provide and evaluate services (*see* 'The distribution of intellectual impairment and its relationship to learning disabilities' in Section 4).

3 The use of categories

This section describes an approach to categorisation that will be used in this chapter. There is no simple way of categorising PWLD into groups that need a particular service; individual need should dictate levels and type of service input. The aim is to describe groups that need consideration when planning services, rather than to describe service categories.

The global categories describe the difference between intellectual impairment, learning disability and dependency. The partial categories describe groups of health/social impairments/restrictions associated with intellectual impairment which are useful to consider when planning services. The last section describes aetiological groups. These are not generally helpful as a basis for service planning, but form important background understanding.

Global categories

Fryers describes the following global categories that relate to ICIDH.[12]

- **Intellectual impairment:** The loss of function experienced is in relation to the intellect. This is usually expressed by IQ which, although criticised, is widely used. 'Severe intellectual impairment' refers to those with an IQ of less than 50, whilst 'mild intellectual impairment' covers IQs of 50–69. In this chapter, when the term 'severe learning disabilities' is used it refers to those with an IQ of less than 50, 'mild learning disabilities' refers to those with IQs of 50–70 and 'borderline learning disabilities' to those with IQs of up to 80. This is consistent with the common usage of these terms. (For further discussion of the distinction between intellectual impairment and learning disability, *see* 'The distribution of intellectual impairment and its relationship to learning disabilities' in Section 4.)
- **Generalised learning disability:** Strictly speaking, this term should refer to difficulties in learning resulting from intellectual impairment. This is difficult to measure and covers a wide range of disabilities, not all related to IQ. In the UK, the term 'learning difficulty' is often used within the education system to refer to a wide range of learning disabilities. Specific difficulties, such as dyslexia, are included with more generalised learning disability. In educational practice, the term 'learning disabilities' is usually used to refer to those with an IQ of less than 70.

- **Generalised dependency:** Intellectual impairment may produce a range of handicaps which lead to dependency. The range of handicaps is determined by the severity of impairment and other factors, such as coexisting conditions and societal attitudes. If society gives high regard to the ability to read, for example, the inability to do so will be a significant handicap.

Partial categories

Fryers also describes 'partial categories'. They are described as partial because they are not simply sub-categories of the more general categories described above. There is overlap between intelligence and learning categories. For example, individuals with ASD, who are not intellectually impaired, may still have some degree of learning disability. These partial categories have been adapted slightly and are described below.

Physical impairments: aetiological and pathological groups

There are a large number of identifiable conditions, mainly secondary to chromosomal abnormalities, that are often or always associated with learning disabilities, such as Down's syndrome and fragile X syndrome. Some organic impairments are part of syndromes that include intellectual impairment, e.g. fetal alcohol syndrome. Many of these conditions are rare, and only the most common are discussed further.

Syndromes of impairments and/or disabilities

This covers impairments and disabilities, such as epilepsy and cerebral palsy, mental illness and developmental disorders, e.g. ASD. Challenging behaviours are also included here, although they are less well defined. These conditions all occur more frequently in PWLD. They may be found together with any underlying aetiology, although some associations are more common than others, e.g. fragile X syndrome and ASD.

Specific restriction of activities: losses of function

PWLD have higher frequencies of specific motor and sensory disabilities, such as hearing and mobility problems.

Restriction of participation: social consequences

This refers to the social difficulties PWLD may experience, such as lack of housing and employment or limited relationships and social support networks.

Restriction of participation: carers and families

Families and carers of PWLD may experience significant restriction of participation because they are unable to maintain paid employment or to sustain family relationships, for example.

Aetiology

The aetiology of learning disabilities can be subdivided into conditions that arise at conception (whose prevention lies before conception) and those that arise during pregnancy, labour and after birth (*see* Table 1).[17] Aetiological agents fall into three main categories: genetic, infective and environmental.

No aetiological cause is found in approximately 30% of cases of severe learning disabilities. The same is true for the majority of cases of mild learning disabilities. There is still considerable scope for preventative work, despite incomplete understanding of aetiology (*see* 'Health promotion' in Section 6).

Table 1: Major aetiological factors that cause learning disabilities.

Aetiological factor	Timing of injury/exposure		
Genetic	**Antenatal**		
	Chromosome aberrations		**Secondary neurological damage**

	• Trisomies:
	  – 21: Down's syndrome
	  – 18: Edwards' syndrome
	  – 13: Patou syndrome
	• Sex-linked, e.g. fragile X syndrome
			• Disorders of:
			  – protein metabolism, e.g. phenylketonuria
			  – lipid metabolism, e.g. Tay-Sachs
			  – carbohydrate metabolism
			  – mucopolysaccaride metabolism, e.g. Hurler's syndrome
			  – hormone system, e.g. congenital hypothyroidism

	Antenatal	**Perinatal**	**Postnatal**
Infective	• Rubella – damage more severe, the earlier in pregnancy contracted • HIV • Toxoplasma • Cytomegalovirus	• Herpes simplex	• Meningitis • Encephalitis • Encephalopathies, e.g. measles • Whooping cough – secondary to brain injury

Environmental	• Nutritional deficiencies, e.g. iodine
	• Rhesus incompatibility
	• Drugs/alcohol
	• Irradiation
		• Birth injury:
		  – trauma
		  – hypoxia
		  – hypoglycaemia
			• Trauma: accidents and non-accidental injury resulting in head injury
			• Lead
			• Nutrition

Genetic factors

Iodine deficiency disease is the commonest cause of severe learning disabilities worldwide. In the UK, the majority of cases are due to genetic factors. Non-inherited Down's syndrome causes approximately 30% of cases at birth. The second most common known cause is X-linked disorder, most commonly fragile X syndrome. Other single-gene disorders, of which more than 2000 have been identified, account for 12% of cases. Known genetic disorders cause only 5–10% of cases of mild learning disabilities, although more are being recognised.[18,19]

Non-genetic factors

Ante- and postnatal factors such as infection, non-accidental injury and accidents cause approximately 25% of severe learning disabilities. Obstetric complications and birth injury cause about another 10%. This accounts for some of the observed association between learning disabilities, epilepsy and cerebral palsy, low birth weight also being an important factor.[20]

Infective causes are uncommon and outcome is very variable. Rubella infection in early pregnancy severely affects the development of those who survive; later infection tends to be less damaging. Toxoplasma and cytomegalovirus infections can also cause impairment. Antenatal HIV infection may cause delay in cognitive development that requires educational support in mainstream schools in about a quarter of children.[21]

Maternal alcohol consumption is considered to be the leading cause of learning disabilities in the USA. European research gives lower figures.[22,23]

Neural-tube defects (NTDs) and other central nervous system malformations, such as microcephaly, are associated with learning disabilities. Dietary folate deficiency is associated with an increased risk of NTDs. A small number of cases have a genetic basis.

Conclusions

The recognition of intellectual impairment and the diagnosis of identifiable causes and associated physical and other impairments/disabilities are fundamental issues necessary for both the planning and evaluation of services. Appropriate classification and terminology should underpin these processes. The lack of standardisation of terms hampers progress across research, service planning and provision. Comparison of research data is difficult and the translation of research findings to local services, where case-mix may be significantly different, is hard to achieve. It is often the case that IQ is the only measure available with which to compare research findings.

In this chapter, learning disabilities as an overall group are discussed and, where appropriate, partial categories. There is also discussion of specific age groups (children, adults and older people) as necessary.

4 Prevalence and incidence of learning disabilities and associated conditions

This section describes what is known about the prevalence and incidence of learning disability and some of the conditions with which it commonly coexists.

There are a number of difficulties in arriving at an exact prevalence figure for learning disabilities. This is for the following reasons.

- The social construction of underlying concepts has varied over time.
- There is a wide spectrum of disorder.
- Definitions are not standardised (*see* 'Definitions and classification' in Section 2).
- Incidence and prevalence have changed over time.
- Service utilisation research methodologies are common and limit the population studied to those in touch with services.

The distribution of intellectual impairment and its relationship to learning disabilities

Most population figures for the UK have been determined from service contact, often derived from case registers. For the following reasons, these underestimate the true prevalence of learning disabilities and coexisting conditions.

- Delay in diagnosis skews case finding so that prevalence appears higher in 15–19-year-olds than in young children; case ascertainment is more complete with increasing age, as milder degrees of impairment are more likely to be identified later.
- Those with severe impairment, or with significant other disabilities/coexisting conditions, are more likely to use services and so be registered as a service contact.
- Many coexisting conditions remain unrecognised/undiagnosed.
- Data accuracy and completeness depend on the adequacy of local inter-agency working and the development of local information systems.

As a consequence, more is known about people with either severe impairment or mild impairment and co-existing conditions (i.e. those in touch with services) than about the much larger group of people with relatively uncomplicated mild or borderline intellectual impairment.

Mild intellectual impairment (IQ 50–69)

The number of individuals with mild intellectual impairment reflects the statistical distribution of IQs in a population around an arithmetic mean. IQ tests were standardised around a mean of 100. If this is taken to be the mean for a population, then 2.27% will have an IQ of less than 70, with a slight increase over the statistical distribution for IQs of less than 50, where specific pathologies come into play.

The terms 'mild intellectual impairment' and 'mild learning disabilities' are not equivalent. There is large variation in how the latter group is selected, i.e. it will vary between researchers, services, carers, etc. Societal and professional attitudes, service structures and legislation will determine selection and therefore prevalence figures. This results in wide variation in prevalence figures for mild learning disabilities. It is more likely that individuals with mild intellectual impairment and challenging behaviours or mental illness will come into contact with services and therefore be identified as having mild learning disabilities. There will, however, be many individuals with this level of intellectual functioning who are not in contact with services and who will not be labelled learning disabled. Estimates for prevalence of mild learning disabilities, i.e. those identified as having needs or problems, as opposed to all those with mild intellectual impairment, i.e. with an IQ of less than 70, will vary depending on definition. The population prevalence for mild learning disabilities is estimated at 1–2% (10–20/1000) of the population, whilst mild intellectual impairment will affect 2–3% (20–30/1000).[24,25]

Severe intellectual impairment (IQ of less than 50)

The commonly quoted prevalence for severe impairment is 3–4/1000 of the general population. There is a slight preponderance of males over females. All those with an IQ of less than 50 will be identified as having severe learning disabilities. Analysis of the Leicestershire case register gives a prevalence for severe intellectual impairment of 3.44/1000 and for severe learning disabilities of 3.95/1000. The latter group was defined as those in need of learning disability services, i.e. notified to the register. This definition of severe learning disabilities therefore includes those with severe intellectual impairment (IQ of less than 50) and those with mild/borderline impairment (IQ greater than 50) who have other conditions, such as mental illness, ASD or challenging behaviours, who need services.[26]

Table 2 shows the estimated age-specific prevalence for severe impairment.

Table 2: Estimates of age-specific prevalence for severe intellectual impairment in the UK.

Age (years)	Prevalence/1,000 population		
	1990	1995	1998
0–4	?2.50	?2.00	?1.75
5–9	3.00	2.25	2.00
10–14	4.00	2.75	2.25
15–19	4.50	3.50	3.00
20–24	5.00	4.00	3.75
25–29	4.50	4.50	4.25
30–34	4.00	4.00	4.50
35–39	3.50	3.75	4.00
40–44	3.00	3.25	3.50
45–54	2.50	2.75	3.00
55–64	2.00	2.25	2.50
65–74	1.00	1.25	2.00
75+	Very few	?1.0	?1.25

These estimates refer to a nominally distributed population in a stable district with no local factors which would significantly affect the prevalence of severe intellectual impairment. Therefore local relevant population variables should be taken into consideration before applying these figures.
Source: Fryers.[17]

Factors that affect incidence and prevalence

Time trends

It is suggested that, in the developed world, the incidence and prevalence of severe learning disabilities increased up until the mid-1960s, with decreases into the 1980s, albeit to a level that was still twice that in the 1960s.[17,26] This is thought to be the result of a complex series of changes, some of which increase incidence and prevalence, while others decrease them. These changes include:

- an overall decrease in the numbers of young children since the late 1960s
- the impact of oral contraception on conceptions in older women, i.e. those associated with the greatest risk of chromosomal abnormality
- antenatal screening for Down's syndrome, amniocentesis for older women and selective termination
- availability of neonatal care and consequent decreases in early mortality, particularly of low and very low birth weight babies
- new technologies, e.g. new anticonvulsants and advances in cardiac and gastrointestinal surgery, alongside improvements in general medical care leading to increased long-term survival

- immunisation programmes which decreased encephalitis, encephalopathies and rubella-associated prenatal damage.

As a result, in the UK, successive birth cohorts are of differing size, which in turn means that as each cohort ages, the age-specific prevalence varies accordingly (*see* Table 2). Currently, individuals in the largest cohort are aged in their mid-thirties.

Analysis of UK case registers suggests that, for adults with IQs of less than 50, there has been an increase in prevalence of 35% over the period 1960–95 (approximately 1% per year).[26] Projections based on the Leicestershire case register predict a further increase in the population prevalence of severe learning disabilities of 11% between 1998 and 2008. This is largely as a result of improved survival, especially into old age.

Mortality

PWLD have an increased risk of early death. The risk of dying before the age of 50 has been found to be 58 times greater than in the general population.[27] Life expectancy diminishes with severity of impairment. For those with mild impairment, rates differ little from the general population. Other predictors of early mortality include inability to walk, cerebral palsy, incontinence, residence in hospital and other coexisting medical problems, such as epilepsy.[28–30] The leading cause of death recorded in a London-based study was respiratory disease (52%, compared with 15% in the general population).[27] This finding, if not a recording bias, may indicate suboptimal treatment, in conjunction with a greater incidence of underlying pathology. A healthy survivor effect seems to exist; for the severely impaired aged over 50 years mortality approaches the mean.[27]

Socio-economic factors

Some causes of severe learning disabilities are socially determined or influenced (*see* 'Aetiology' in Section 3). There is, however, little evidence for an effect of socio-economic background on the incidence of severe intellectual impairment. Long-term cohort studies have nevertheless found a consistent effect of social class on cognitive development.[31] The incidence of cerebral palsy is also associated with socio-economic deprivation. Possible explanations for this include poor nutrition and low uptake of screening programmes and antenatal care.

Ethnicity

There is some evidence to suggest that there is an increased prevalence of severe learning disabilities in the British Asian population.[32]

Geography

There are clear international differences in incidence and prevalence rates, particularly between the developed and developing worlds. It is often assumed that geographic factors have no impact in the UK. However, some authors suggest that there may be regional differences in prevalence, if not incidence.[33,34] This may reflect socio-demographic factors and/or local service issues, such as the closure of large institutions and the availability of independent-sector provision.

Physical impairments: aetiological and pathological groups

Down's syndrome (trisomy 21)

The frequency of occurrence of Down's syndrome is clearly linked to maternal age. The risk of having an affected child at varying maternal ages is approximately 0.5/1000 when aged 20 years, 10/1000 when aged 40 and 150/1000 when aged 50.[35] The expected birth prevalence of Down's syndrome per 1000 live births increased from 1.67 in 1996 to 1.84 in 1998. The observed birth prevalence was 0.91/1000 live births in 1996 and 1.04/1000 live births in 1998.[36] The prevalence will be determined by rates of conception in differing maternal age groups and the impact of screening programmes (*see* 'Secondary prevention' in Section 6).

The majority of individuals with Down's syndrome have IQs in the range 35–55; 10% have an IQ of less than 20. People with Down's syndrome have a higher incidence of medical problems than the general population; 30–45% have congenital heart disease, 6% have gastrointestinal anomalies, 1% develop childhood leukaemia, there is an increased incidence of hypothyroidism, the majority of individuals develop early-onset dementia, 70% have hearing problems, 50% have sight difficulties and many have increased levels of severe periodontal disease.[37,38] The prevalence of behavioural problems is less than that seen in other groups with severe learning disabilities, although greater than in the general population.[39]

There is differential mortality between people with Down's syndrome and other groups with intellectual impairment. Rates are similar up to the early thirties, but over 35 years, rates are significantly higher for Down's syndrome. This may be the result of the increased incidence of early dementia, cardiac conditions and cancer in people with Down's syndrome. Approximately half of those with Down's syndrome live until the age of 60.

Antenatal screening for Down's syndrome is routine practice in the UK (*see* 'Secondary prevention' in Section 6).

Other trisomies

Trisomies 13 and 18 also occur (Patou syndrome and Edwards' syndrome). The birth frequencies are of the order of 0.25 and 0.3/1000, respectively, increasing with maternal age.

X-linked disorders

Fragile X syndrome is the most common X-linked disorder. There is continued debate over birth frequencies. Figures often quoted are 0.8/1000 for males and 0.32/1000 for females, though they may actually be considerably lower at 0.25/1000 and 0.125/1000, respectively.[40,41] About 6% of those with learning disabilities tested in institutions have the condition.[42]

Most affected males have IQs of less than 50, although there is a wide range in recorded IQs. Many will therefore need extra help at school and protected employment later. Only 30% of women with fragile X have the condition; the rest are carriers. Affected females usually have borderline or normal IQs, but most have some learning difficulties. Fragile X is associated with an increased risk of other conditions such as ASD and congenital cardiac abnormalities. The relationship between ASD and fragile X is not clear; there is a higher frequency of autistic traits in fragile X than in other groups with learning disabilities.[43]

There is no direct evidence of any great benefit from early diagnosis. Screening for the disorder is possible, but there is no national programme (*see* 'Primary prevention' in Section 6).

Other X-linked disorders, e.g. triple X and XXY (Klinefelter's syndrome), each occur in approximately 1/1000 of all live births. Individuals show a range of IQs, usually low normal or mildly impaired, and many will have learning difficulties.[44]

Metabolic disorders

Disorders of protein, lipid, carbohydrate or mucopolysaccharide production all occur. They are all rare. Phenylketonuria (PKU) is the most common disorder, with a birth frequency of 0.05–0.07/1000 live births. It is a single-gene recessive disorder, which usually results in severe impairment if untreated by dietary restriction. The current screening programme should ensure that virtually no new cases with learning disabilities occur in the UK (*see* 'Secondary prevention' in Section 6).

Hormonal disorders

Congenital hypothyroidism is the most common hormonal disorder linked with learning disabilities, with a birth frequency of 0.25–0.3/1000 live births. It is much more common in individuals with Down's syndrome. Intellectual functioning varies, but is severely impaired unless treatment is started early. As with PKU, screening should ensure that very few new cases with learning disabilities occur in the UK (*see* 'Secondary prevention' in Section 6).

Syndromes of impairments and/or disabilities

Epilepsy, cerebral palsy and neural-tube defects are discussed in this subsection. As there are a number of mental disorders they are discussed separately in the subsections on 'Mental disorders', 'Challenging behaviours', 'Offending behaviours' and 'Autistic spectrum disorders' below.

Epilepsy

People with learning disabilities have a higher risk of having epilepsy than the rest of the population. This risk increases with severity of impairment, as does the severity of the epilepsy. The risk of active epilepsy in the general population is 0.5%. For those with an IQ of 50–70 it is approximately 4%, for those with IQ of 20–50 it is 30%, and 50% of those with an IQ of less than 20 have had at least one seizure.[45] Epilepsy is more likely in cases of intellectual impairment associated with peri/postnatal brain injury.

There is debate as to whether the coexistence of learning disabilities and epilepsy leads to an increased risk of mental disorder. Some research suggests that this is not the case, if IQ and other factors are controlled for.[46]

Seizures are a significant cause of excess mortality in PWLD.

Cerebral palsy

Cerebral palsy develops in approximately 2–3/1000 live births.[47] Estimates suggest that up to half of those with cerebral palsy will have some difficulties with intellectual functioning and between 23% and 34% will have an IQ of less than 50.[18,48] In the UK, approximately 92–136/100 000 of the population have severe learning disabilities and cerebral palsy. This proportion is likely to increase with advances in neonatal medicine. The risk of cerebral palsy and severe learning disabilities increases with prematurity and low birth weight.

Physical disabilities are commonly associated with cerebral palsy. Half of those with cerebral palsy and severe learning disabilities also have epilepsy, 65% are immobile, 60% have severely limited manual dexterity and 60% have impaired vision.

Neural-tube defects (NTDs)

In the mid-1990s the incidence of anencephaly was estimated at approximately 0.3/1000 births (this includes all affected infants, whether live or still births, and pregnancy termination for NTDs) and 0.38/1000 for spina bifida.[49] Intellectual impairment is associated with NTDs. Screening is routine practice in the UK (*see* 'Secondary prevention' in Section 6).

Mental disorders

The prevalence of psychiatric disorder and behavioural disturbance is higher in all age groups of PWLD than in the general population. There is considerable difficulty in determining exact figures for the reasons listed below.

- **Poor detection:** This may arise from communication difficulties, because of lack of speech or appropriate vocabulary. Carers and relatives may not understand the signs of mental distress/illness, e.g. behavioural changes. Similarly, professionals may ascribe abnormal behaviours to the underlying intellectual impairment rather than make a diagnosis of mental illness.
- **Misdiagnosis:** This may also result from the above factors, e.g. depression may be mistaken for dementia or schizophrenia for autism. Concurrent physical ill-health may make diagnosis more difficult.
- **Medication:** The effects of medication may confuse the clinical presentation of mental illness.
- **Methodological issues:** Comparison between studies, and extrapolation of results, may be difficult because of differences in definition, case-mix and diagnosis, e.g. the inclusion or not of challenging behaviours. There is also uncertainty about the applicability of established systems of psychiatric diagnosis to those with severe intellectual impairment.[50]

The aetiology of mental illness in PWLD is, as in the general population, usually multi-factorial. Social, environmental and biological factors all have a potential impact on the development of disorder. Many risk factors known to contribute to the development of mental illness occur more frequently in PWLD. These include sensory impairments, communication difficulties, low self-esteem, stigma, low levels of social support, poor coping skills and chronic ill-health. Some causes of intellectual impairment are risk factors in their own right, e.g. Down's syndrome for dementia and fragile X syndrome for ASD.

Mental ill-health in children with learning disabilities

The frequency of mental ill-health in children increases with severity of intellectual impairment. In the Isle of Wight studies, 30–42% of 9–11-year-olds with IQs of less than 70 required treatment for mental health problems, compared to 6–7% of those with higher IQs.[51] A Swedish study of 13–17-year-olds showed 57% of children with IQs of 50–70 and 64% of those with IQs of less than 50 had diagnosable mental disorder, compared to 5% of controls.[52] In South East London, 47% of children under 16 with an IQ of less than 50 had a psychiatric disorder.[53]

The prevalence of anxiety and phobic states, depressive syndromes, conduct disorder and eating disorders seems to increase as IQ increases. This may result partly from difficulties in case ascertainment if communication skills are limited and/or disability prevents the expression of certain behaviours, e.g. overactivity will be restricted if mobility is limited.

Mental ill-health in adults with learning disabilities

Estimates of coexisting mental illness and/or behavioural disorder in adults with learning disabilities vary from 14.3% to 67.3%.[54] If challenging behaviours are excluded then the rates found fall dramatically.[55] The pattern of ill-health is somewhat different to that found in the general population. Higher rates of substance misuse and affective disorders are found in the general population.[56]

- **Affective and anxiety disorders:** Some studies suggest that the rates of affective disorders are lower in adults with learning disabilities than in the general population. Poor detection and misdiagnosis may account for some of this observed difference.[57,58] There may also be differences between those with Down's syndrome and other PWLD.[59]
- **Schizophrenia:** Studies suggest that the prevalence of schizophrenia in those with learning disabilities may be 3–4 times higher than in the general population. Accurate diagnosis, however, is difficult in those with severe impairment, particularly if communication is limited.[60]
- **Dementia:** The prevalence of dementia is higher in people with severe learning disabilities (*see* 'Mental ill-health in older people with learning disabilities' below).
- **Adjustment reactions:** PWLD may be more vulnerable to adverse life events and consequently suffer adjustment disorder more commonly than the general population. The significance of life events such as bereavement, for PWLD is often not recognised.[61]
- **Post-traumatic stress disorder:** PWLD suffer high levels of abuse and are therefore at greater risk of post-traumatic stress disorder.

Mental ill-health in older people with learning disabilities

Older people with learning disabilities have a higher prevalence of mental illness than either the general population or younger PWLD.[62] This is mainly the result of a small increase in anxiety and depression and a significant increase in dementia, particularly in people with Down's syndrome. A London study showed that 70% of people with Down's syndrome over the age of 50 had clinical signs of dementia.[63] In people with moderate to severe learning disabilities of mixed aetiology, 11.4% of those over 50 years had dementia.[64]

Challenging behaviours

There are a variety of definitions of challenging behaviours. The following is a broad definition that encompasses diverse behaviours, such as self-injury and stereotypy in people with severe intellectual impairment, and offending in those less severely affected:

> *culturally abnormal behaviour/s of such intensity, frequency or duration that the physical safety of the person or others is likely to be put in some serious jeopardy, or behaviour that is likely to seriously limit the use of, or result in the person being denied access to ordinary community facilities (this excludes behaviours which are caused by psychiatric disorder).*[65]

Other terms, such as 'interactional challenge', have been coined in an attempt to reduce stigma. This concept emphasises the primacy of the interaction between the environment and the individual.[66]

Challenging behaviours are not spread evenly through the population of PWLD. There is a high prevalence of challenging behaviours in people with ASD, whilst people with Down's syndrome are less likely to demonstrate challenging behaviours.[39] Some genetic conditions are associated with specific abnormal behaviours, e.g. Lesch-Nyhan's syndrome with self-injury, particularly of oral tissues, hypercalcaemia with hyperactivity and Prader-Willi's syndrome with overeating.[67] Alternatively, associated conditions, such as sensory impairment, pain or communication difficulties, may lead to changes in or challenging behaviour. This can create diagnostic difficulties. For example, visual impairment may lead to depression or challenging behaviours and be misdiagnosed as dementia or schizophrenia.

Challenging behaviours in children with learning disabilities

Challenging behaviours increase with the severity of intellectual impairment.[68,69] Estimates suggest that about 40% of children with an IQ of less than 70 display challenging behaviours, including overactivity, severe tantrums and self-injury.

Challenging behaviours in adults with learning disabilities

About 20 adults with learning disabilities per 100 000 of the whole population display behaviours that present a significant challenge.[70] As in children, the prevalence of challenging behaviours increases with the severity of impairment; 60% of people with severe impairment show some stereotypic behaviour. Analysis of the Leicestershire Learning Disabilities Register, using a broader definition of challenging behaviours (including significant risk from accidents and stress to carers, for example), suggested a higher figure. A quarter of adults on the register had behavioural problems that posed a major challenge to the achievement of an ordinary life (approximately 100/100 000).[26] This figure may more accurately reflect the group that need specialist health and social service provision. Self-injurious behaviour was also found to be common; 17% of adults on the Register self-injured.[71]

Reported variation in local prevalence may be at least partly accounted for by the differences between settings. Prevalence is generally highest in hospital residents.[72]

PWLD and challenging behaviours often have additional health and social problems. In one study, 24% had restricted mobility, 38% were not fully continent and 70% required assistance with washing.[73]

Offending behaviours

Risk factors for offending include mild/borderline learning disabilities, youth, low socio-economic status, poor parenting experience and early institutionalisation.[74]

Overall, it is suggested that there are:

- high numbers of offenders with mild and borderline learning disabilities[75]
- increased levels of offending amongst those with mild and borderline learning disabilities
- lower levels of offending amongst people with severe and profound learning disabilities
- differences in the quality of offending between people with mild learning disabilities and those with more severe learning disabilities; the former are more likely to commit violent crimes that require planning or complex skills[76]
- high levels of mental illness and/or substance misuse in offenders with learning disabilities
- probable increased rates of arson and sexual offences amongst offenders with learning disabilities, although bias in court referral to hospital may skew this picture[77]
- higher levels of recidivism amongst offenders with borderline learning disabilities.

Offending behaviour in PWLD is sometimes treated as a form of challenging behaviour and may consequently be decriminalised. Despite this, people with learning disabilities seem to be over-represented at all levels of the criminal justice system. This may be partly explained by a higher risk of detection. UK studies suggest that between 5% and 9% of people taken to police stations for questioning had used learning disabilities services in the past.[78,79]

Autistic spectrum disorders

This term refers to developmental disability that affects social and communication skills. All types of ASD share the following behavioural criteria, regardless of diagnostic sub-type or level of ability:[80,81]

- qualitative impairment in reciprocal social interaction
- qualitative impairment in verbal and non-verbal communication
- markedly restricted repertoire of activities and interests.

Reported prevalence rates vary according to the diagnostic criteria used. The earliest studies used Kanner's narrow criteria of elaborate repetitive routines, aloofness and indifference to others.* This gave rates of 20–50/100 000, depending on how strictly criteria were applied. Rates are significantly higher if the whole autistic spectrum is considered.† This includes individuals with the triad of behavioural criteria cited above, however they are manifested. Children who make positive but socially inappropriate approaches to others are included, as well as those who are aloof and indifferent. Some of those in the spectrum fit the syndrome described by Asperger in 1944 or that described by Wolf in 1995, 'schizoid personality disorder of childhood'.‡ It is now considered that there is overlap between these syndromes, which represent the most able end of the autistic spectrum. The only studies covering the whole spectrum are those by Wing and Gould, in which almost all of the subjects had IQs of less than 70, and Ehlers and Gilberg, who studied children in mainstream education with IQs of 70 or above.[82,83] The total prevalence combining these two studies is 910/100 000. The numbers in these studies were small and therefore caution should be attached to this estimate. Further research is required, particularly as some reports suggest that the number of cases is increasing, and there is controversy about reported links to MMR vaccination.

Autistic spectrum disorders are overall about four times more common in boys than in girls. This difference is most marked in those of higher ability, being much less marked in individuals with severe or profound learning disabilities.

The proportion of people with ASD and learning disabilities also depends on the diagnostic criteria used. The early studies of Kanner's syndrome suggested that one third had severe learning disabilities, one third had mild learning disabilities and one third were in the average or high range for IQ. The proportion is, however, higher if the whole spectrum of ASD is considered. Whatever criteria are used, it is clear that there is a very strong association with learning disabilities. Approximately half of those with severe learning disabilities have some type of autistic spectrum disorder.[84]

Autistic spectrum disorders are also strongly associated with challenging behaviours. Most individuals with severe learning disabilities and challenging behaviours also have ASD. Small proportions of more able

---

* The original description of Kanner's syndrome in 1943 consisted of the following features: a profound lack of affective contact with people, an anxious obsessive desire for the preservation of the sameness in the child's routine and environment, a fascination for objects, which are handled with skill in fine motor movements, mutism or a kind of language that does not seem intended for interpersonal communication, feats of memory or skills on performance tests and onset from birth or before 33 months. These were later modified so that two criteria were thought to be essential, namely profound lack of affective contact and repetitive, ritualistic behaviour, which must be of an elaborate kind.

† There is no really clear distinction between classical autism and the rest of the spectrum. Hence a dimensional rather than categorical approach is most appropriate. Generally, classical autism is most like that described by Kanner, only rather wider.

‡ Asperger's syndrome was first described in 1944, based on the case histories of a group of children with unusual patterns of behaviour, which included being socially odd, naive and emotionally detached, lacking common sense and good speech – which was often used for monologues rather than reciprocal conversation, and having borderline, normal or superior IQs, and circumscribed interests in specific subjects.

people with ASD commit crimes. This may be due to the pursuit of unusual special interests, e.g. fire setting, guns or other weapons, lack of understanding of social rules, e.g. making social advances to someone in the street, or continuing anger because of past teasing or bullying. A recent study suggested that around 2% of people in high-secure hospitals have ASD.[85]

The spectrum is also associated with epilepsy. Between one quarter and one third of those with typical autism will have at least one fit by the time they reach adulthood. This risk is increased for those with severe learning disabilities.

Specific restriction of activities: losses of function

Mobility

Of all those with severe learning disabilities, 15% have difficulty walking and 10% are unable to walk.[86]

Sensory impairments

Sensory impairments are common.

- **Sight:** Up to 30% of PWLD may have significant impairment of sight, whilst 10% are blind or partially sighted.[87] Three quarters of people with learning disabilities have refractive errors. There are particularly high levels of visual problems in those with Down's syndrome and fragile X syndrome. Up to 60% of people with Down's syndrome have acquired cataracts.
- **Hearing:** The reported prevalence of hearing impairment is in the range 22–68%, depending on the population studied. About 7% are deaf or partially deaf.[88] There are a number of different causes, e.g. congenital problems, recurrent infections or impacted earwax. Hearing deteriorates at a faster rate in people with Down's syndrome than in the general population or in other people with learning disabilities.

Communication

Many PWLD will have impairment of communication or social ability. Population estimates for the extent of such difficulties are not available. In the UK OPCS Disability Survey conducted during the 1980s, at least 50% of adults identified as having learning disabilities (in both communal establishments and private households) found it difficult to either understand or be understood by strangers.[89] The survey covered people with more severe learning disabilities, owing to the way cases were identified.

Multiple disabilities

Improvements in medical care have led to the survival into adulthood and old age of a new cohort of very severely disabled individuals with complex needs. The numbers of individuals in any one PCT may be small, but their support needs are significant. They often require complex support packages, which include technologies such as gastrostomy feeding, suction or nebulisers.

Specific medical conditions

Some medical conditions are found more commonly in PWLD, e.g. problems with continence, and some are associated with specific conditions (*see* 'Physical impairments: aetiological and pathological groups' and 'Syndromes of impairments and/or disabilities' above).

Cardiovascular disease (CVD)

PWLD have high levels of some CVD risk factors. Obesity is more common than in the general population; 19% and 35% of learning disabled men and women, respectively, are obese compared to 6% and 8% of the general population.[90] PWLD are also more likely to lead sedentary lifestyles.[91] There is, however, no evidence for higher levels of hypertension.

Congenital heart disease and its sequelae are common in some groups of PWLD.

Infections

Hepatitis B is reported to have increased prevalence in institutions for PWLD.[92]

Dental health

PWLD often have poor dental health and oral hygiene. Surveys of both children and adults show more extractions, less restorative care and high levels of treatment needed.[93,94] This may reflect low uptake of services and/or specific factors that may increase the need for intervention, such as dento-facial abnormalities, gastro-oesophageal reflux or the effects of regular medication.

Restriction of participation: social consequences

Choice

PWLD often have limited capacity to exercise choice and control over many areas of their lives. This includes where to live, with whom, and how to occupy their time. It also applies to choices about service provision. Studies of young adults with learning disabilities suggest significant lack of choice over future service provision at the transition from children's to adult services.[95,96]

Clearly, the issue of choice is linked to the capacity for consent. Studies suggest that consent and decision making are areas that are poorly understood and addressed by services.[97,98] A person's capacity to consent is a matter for clinical judgement. No one else can consent to or refuse treatment on behalf of another adult who lacks the capacity to consent. The views of carers/families may, of course, be solicited and taken into account.

The Bournewood Ruling and subsequent House of Lords decision clarified the issue of consent with respect to the use of the 1983 Mental Health Act. This made it clear that compliant, incapacitated patients could continue to be admitted and treated, in their best interests, under section 131 of the Mental Health Act, without the need for them to be formally detained under section 2 or section 3 of that Act.[99]

Relationships

The capacity to create and sustain relationships is fundamental to quality of life for most individuals. For the majority of PWLD in the community and in residential care, relationships outside immediate family/carers are usually with service providers.

It is estimated that there may be 250 000 parents with learning disabilities in the UK.[100] Most will have mild or borderline intellectual impairment and at least 60% will have children who have higher intellectual functioning than them. Many of these parents will need specialist help to acquire parenting skills and to live independently in the community. Without such help their children may be 'at risk' for developmental delay and abuse, probably arising from unintentional neglect. It is difficult to disentangle the role of learning disabilities in these outcomes, as opposed to the impact of socio-economic factors. The children are likely to be over-represented in childcare services.[101]

PWLD may have limited knowledge/access to information about family planning and safer sex.[102,103]

Abuse

PWLD suffer high levels of sexual, physical and emotional abuse. This applies to those living in their own homes and to those in residential care.[104] It has been estimated that 1400 adults with learning disabilities, both men and women, are reported as victims of sexual abuse in the UK each year. In a significant number of cases, abuse is perpetrated by other PWLD, predominantly a small number of men, who may offend on more than one occasion.[105]

Crime

PWLD are often the victims of minor crimes. The criminal justice system may not be involved, the situation being dealt with by service providers. This also applies in cases of sexual abuse.[105] Despite this, PWLD are often thought of as perpetrators rather than victims.[106]

Activities of daily living

Many individuals with severe learning disabilities will require help with the activities of daily living. Analysis of the OPCS Disability Survey suggested that the majority of adults identified as having learning disabilities and resident in private households needed help with meals/cleaning; 23% were unable to feed or use the toilet themselves and 11% needed help every night (Table 3 outlines the regularity of care needed by those identified in this survey).[89] Similarly, high need for care (based on carers' perception of the need for supervision to remain safe) has been described for individuals on the Leicestershire case register.[26]

Table 3: People with learning disabilities in the UK subdivided by age and category of care needs (based on OPCS Disability Survey).

Age group (years)	Care category			
	No care needs (%)	Long-interval self-care needs (%)	No self-care help required, but needs someone present (%)	Short and critical self-care needs (%)
5–15	19	11	15	55
16–34	41	7	23	29
35–49	44	12	26	19
50+	38	21	17	25

These figures are likely to represent people with more severe learning disabilities, as identification in the OPCS Survey was by door-to-door interviews.
Source: Kavanagh and Opit.[89]

Restriction of participation: carers and families

In the 1998 Welsh Health Survey, 7.5% of adults reported that they were carers and one in ten of those cared for had a learning disability.[107] Parents may find it difficult to make the emotional adjustment to having a learning-disabled child. Adjustment may be influenced by a number of factors, including whether or not they received a false-negative result on prenatal screening.[108,109]

Caring for a person with learning disabilities can place considerable strain on carers and families, having an impact on emotional well-being, financial resources and relationships. The average annual cost of bringing up a child with a severe disability has been estimated at £7355 (at least three times the cost of bringing up a child without a disability).[110] The majority of PWLD and many of their families are poor. Many families are unable to increase their income through paid work because of the demands of caring and/or the lack of suitable childcare.

Carers of adults with learning disabilities report 40% more health-limiting problems than the general population.[26] This is of particular importance as the number of elderly carers increases. A significant minority of PWLD who live in the family home have carers over the age of 70.

Conclusions

Some degree of intellectual impairment is relatively common in the general population. A minority of these individuals have severe intellectual impairment. There has been a steady increase in the prevalence of severe learning disabilities over the past 20 years. This is likely to continue into the next decade. The number who have multiple and complex disabilities will also increase. These trends need to be taken into consideration in service planning.

Service need is not, however, determined by level of intellectual functioning, although those with the most severe impairment will require services. An individual's need for services is often determined by co-existing conditions, such as those described in the partial categories (see 'Partial categories' in Section 3), and by the extent of their social support networks.

5 Services available

Introduction

A range of health, social and educational services is available, comprising both generic services, such as primary care, and specialist learning disabilities services. Services are provided by the statutory and, increasingly, the voluntary and private sectors. The types of services and service providers vary greatly across the country. A key issue in the provision of services is their accessibility. This covers a range of issues: physical access, information in appropriate formats (e.g. Braille), transport provision, the knowledge and attitudes of staff and the provision of training and support to generic staff, users and their carers.

Routine statistics are readily available for only a small proportion of relevant services; notable exclusions are the provision of education, employment and recreational services. In this section, routine statistics are included where they are available. Information on other types of service, such as respite care, is taken from the research literature. Some of the limitations of service provision are discussed in this section. Further information is found in Section 6 on effectiveness of services.

Health promotion, primary care and specialist learning disability services are described in the first part of this section. This is followed by a description of more specialised services for specific conditions, or that address specific needs, such as those described in the partial categories.

Health promotion

A number of population measures aimed at reducing the incidence or severity of specific conditions may also have an impact on the prevalence of intellectual impairment in the general population (primary and secondary prevention). These include immunisation, genetic counselling, general obstetric services and associated screening programmes (*see* Section 6 for further discussion of this).

Health promotion for people with learning disabilities

The Health of the Nation: a Strategy for People with Learning Disability outlines health promotion for PWLD.[111] It emphasises that they should be treated in the same way as the rest of the population and that health gain can be achieved by promoting health surveillance, health promotion and health care. This requires the co-ordinated activity of primary care services, including dentistry, continence, chiropody, etc., and secondary health care, both generic services and specialist learning disabilities services.

Screening programmes

- **Cervical and breast cancer:** Cervical and breast screening both have low levels of uptake in PWLD.[112] Theoretically, women with learning disabilities have a low risk of cervical cancer as they have low levels of sexual activity. High levels of sexual abuse may, however, have an impact. Some studies suggest low levels of breast cancer, despite the low birth rate in this group.
- **Hypertension:** PWLD have increased risk of cardiovascular disease and therefore blood pressure monitoring should form part of regular health checks, as should advice about diet and healthy living to help combat obesity.
- **Mental ill-health:** Routine screening does not occur. The low levels of detection and diagnosis suggest that increased awareness is needed amongst families, carers and professionals. The screening tool (PAS-ADD Checklist) may help to raise awareness and improve diagnosis.[113]
- **Thyroid function:** Screening is important given the high incidence of hypothyroidism in those with Down's syndrome.

Immunisation

Influenza, hepatitis B and tetanus vaccinations are important.

Primary care

Primary care services are central to the organisation of adequate health surveillance for PWLD, who have ordinary needs for primary care and special needs relating to their increased rates of certain conditions. Primary care will also need to provide for the needs of families/carers of PWLD.

General practice

The average practice list of 2000 might expect to have 40 patients with learning disabilities, including children, and approximately eight with severe learning disabilities.[8] In practices which provide services to community residential homes these figures are likely to be higher.

People with learning disabilities have greater physical and mental health needs than the general population (*see* Section 4).[114-116] Problems may only be identified if a screening tool is used, since they may have been missed by professionals, the patient and their carers. The reasons for this include learning disabilities masking symptoms, misinterpretation of symptoms and signs, communication difficulties, and negative or ill-informed attitudes of health care staff. In one survey, many GPs accepted that they were responsible for providing medical care for PWLD, and a third had positive views on health promotion. The majority, however, did not support organised health promotion for PWLD.[117] This could reflect uncertainty about how to meet needs once identified or worries about a perceived unremunerated increase in workload.[118] Estimates of the workload associated with caring for PWLD in primary care vary. Some studies suggest that there is no difference in consultation rates in comparison to control groups.[119,120] Consultation rates may be higher amongst those resettled from institutional care. A rate of eight consultations per year was found in one study, twice the average national rate for 16–44-year-olds and also higher than that for the over-74 group, who average seven consultations per year.[121] The consultation rate, however, says nothing about the assessment/interventions provided, an area much less researched.

Chiropody, continence, dietetics, pharmacy and dentistry services

People with learning disabilities need these services more frequently than those in the general population. Training and support to generic practitioners are required in order that services are easily accessible. In some areas, specialist approaches, such as mobile and domiciliary services, have developed. There are tensions between the development of specialist services for PWLD and encouraging/supporting access to generic services.

Community dental services are the primary provider for those with severe learning disabilities and some adults with mild disabilities, and have an active part to play in oral health promotion.

Specialist learning disability services

Most individuals with uncomplicated mild and borderline intellectual impairment will be able to live relatively independent lives without specific service provision. They may never come into contact with specialist health services, although many will have contact with educational services for assessments of educational need. The following service descriptions are consequently more relevant to the severely disabled group, most of whom will be in contact with services at some point. It is important to remember, however, that although the majority of people with mild or borderline impairment do not require specialist services, those that do include people with offending and challenging behaviours and other conditions such as mental illness. Many of these individuals may not be formally catered for by either specialist learning disability services or general mental health services (*see* 'Mental disorders' below).[122] Specialist learning disabilities services also have a role in helping those without additional problems to access generic services and primary care.

Recorded activity in learning disability services has increased in recent years. In England between 1987–88 and 1997–98 there was an increase in first attendances to consultant outpatients from 4000 to 6000. Subsequent attendance also increased. First contacts with community learning disability nurses increased by 40% between 1993 and 1998.[123]

Specialist services for children with learning disabilities

The organisation of services for children and adolescents with learning disabilities differs across the UK. Services may be provided by specialist learning disabilities teams, child and adolescent mental health services, local paediatric services or child development centres. In many areas, local authority multi-disciplinary disabilities teams provide the point of access to other services and provide community support. A survey of NHS trusts with responsibilities for PWLD found that 72% had services for children, including community services, respite and treatment beds.[124]

Services cover varying age ranges. In a few areas, there are specialist transition teams or social workers to ensure that continuity of care occurs at the vulnerable time of transfer from children's to adult services. The provision of health services that support transition for disabled people with complex health and support needs has been described as 'very patchy'.[125]

Specialist services for adults with learning disabilities

Community learning disability teams (CLDTs) have become one of the most common means of co-ordinating specialist community services for adults with learning disabilities. Most CLDTs in the UK will see people with an IQ of up to 70. Their distribution across the UK is not uniform.[126] Teams provide assessment, treatment interventions and continuing care, and organise support for carers and families. Their role has shifted since the introduction of care management and the transfer of services to the independent sector. This has led to a modest shift from providing specialist services to providing specialist help in accessing ordinary opportunities for housing, leisure and employment, including service brokerage and direct payments.

The breadth of services provided by CLDTs is variable. In some parts of the country they cater for all PWLD, including those with mental health and behavioural problems, whilst in other areas there is specialist provision for these groups.

It is difficult to describe an average team. A survey in London found a fivefold variation in the size of teams from 2.2–10.5 WTEs/100 000. Teams are usually multi-disciplinary, although the composition may vary considerably. Nursing, psychiatry, psychology, speech and language therapy were nearly always part of the team.[127] There is some evidence, however, that teams are increasingly not multi-agency in their organisation.[128]

Teams may include the following disciplines:

- **community nurses/careworkers:** their roles vary depending on the nature of the rest of the team and their background skills and training
- **social workers:** they are organised in different ways depending on the local authority; the role they play also varies
- **consultant psychiatrist:** their role includes assessment, diagnosis and treatment of coexisting conditions, as well as management of aspects of the underlying learning disabilities
- **psychologist(s):** they can provide assessment, functional analysis, a range of psychotherapeutic interventions and consultation/liaison work with other teams/organisations
- **occupational therapist(s):** they work with clients in a number of domains, including work-related activity, activities of daily living, functional assessment, house adaptation and creative therapy. There has been a shift from hospital-based practice to increasing work in the community, and OTs work largely in people's homes rather than in day services
- **speech and language therapist(s):** early intervention is the usual aim. This is more likely to be achieved in disorders that tend to be identified early, such as Down's syndrome. Functional communication is also important, i.e. increasing the range of uses for communication skills, e.g. to express choice
- **physiotherapist(s):** they provide direct interventions using specific therapeutic modalities. These can help to fulfil mobility potential. They may also help to train care and support workers
- **creative therapist(s):** they include art, music and drama therapists.

The organisation of the latter five professional groups is often variable. They might be an integral part of the CLDT, be attached to learning disability services without having a geographical focus, or be part of generic uni-disciplinary teams.

Specialist services for older people with learning disabilities

The organisation of services for people over 65 with learning disabilities varies considerably across the country. The results of small-scale interviews in some parts of the country suggested that there was confusion over responsibility for older people with learning disabilities.[129]

Inpatient provision

Inpatient beds are needed for a small number of PWLD to provide assessment and in some cases treatment for those with the most severe disabilities, physical, sensory or psychological problems. Inpatient facilities are usually provided within specialist learning disability services, but in some areas generic mental health beds are used. Specialist inpatient services for those with mental illness or challenging behaviours are described in 'Mental disorders' and 'Challenging and offending behaviours' below.

Other specialist services

In some areas there is specialist provision for other aspects of care, e.g. palliative care.

Alternative therapies

A wide range of alternative therapies exists, including aromatherapy, cranial osteopathy and massage. Some learning disabilities services have organised access to alternative therapies.

Accommodation

Background

There has been a profound change in the nature of accommodation provided over the past 20 years (*see* Figure 1 overleaf). This is a consequence of:

- the closure of long-stay institutions
- the impact of the NHS and Community Care Act, which encouraged pluralism of care and resulted in shifts from long-stay NHS and local authority residential accommodation into private and voluntary provision
- the acceptance that PWLD should have the opportunity for ordinary life experiences and hence that supported independent living in the community should be the aim wherever possible.

In England, the largest changes in NHS long-stay provision occurred between 1987–88 and 1996–97 when the number of hospital beds for PWLD fell from 31 320 to 7440. Changes in local authority provision were slower (*see* Tables 4 and 5, p. 487), the rate of change differing across the country. In England, local authority residential care places dropped by 10% between 1986 and 1996, more places being provided in

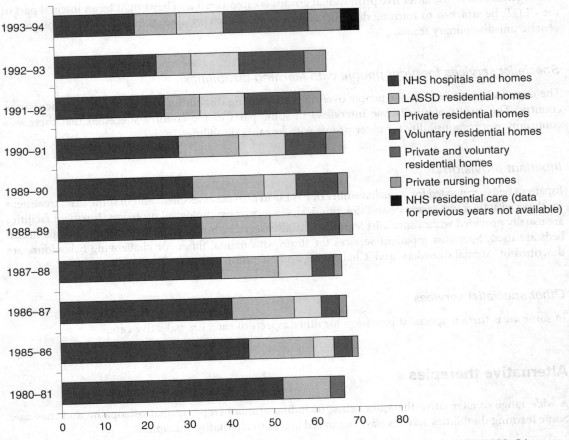

Figure 1: Changes in the residential care of people with learning disabilities in the UK, 1980–94.

smaller units. In Wales, over the same period, there was a 50% drop in the number of local authority places, with a significant rise in private-sector provision.

Types of accommodation

Most children and many adults with learning disabilities live with their families.

A wide spectrum of other types of accommodation/homes exists:

- remaining NHS long-stay beds
- nursing home provision
- village communities, catering for up to 300 residents
- staffed and unstaffed group homes
- adult placement schemes
- residential children's homes/schools
- semi-independent living, e.g. supported lodgings
- independent living.

Table 4: Residential and hospital provision for adults with learning disabilities in England, 1988–89 to 1998–99.

Type of establishment		1988–89		1998–99
Beds in private nursing homes, hospitals and clinics*		1,260		3,740
Staffed residential homes*†				
Local authority		12,620		7,380
Voluntary		6,530		17,220
Private		7,420		18,010
Places in small (< 4 beds) registered homes*				
Voluntary	(1994–95)	890		8,840
Private	(1994–95)	3,870		
Places in local authority unstaffed group homes*		2840	(1996–97)	2,990
Hospital beds – average daily available				
Short-stay		1,210		1,420
Long-stay		28,400		5,280
Secure	(1994–95)	330		420
NHS residential facilities‡ average daily available beds	(1996–97)	3,430		4,040

* Data relate to 31 March.
† Excludes nursing care places in dual registered homes.
‡ NHS residential facilities were recorded for the first time in 1996–97. Some of these beds may previously have been recorded under other headings.
Source: Government Statistical Service.

Table 5: Residential and hospital provision for children with learning disabilities in England and Wales, 1987–88 to 1997–98.

Type of establishment	1987–88		1997–98	
	England	Wales	England	Wales
Beds in private nursing homes, hospitals and clinics*	130	9	70	–
Places in staffed residential homes*†				
Local authority	2,120	60	1,070	66
Voluntary	370	61	290	145
Private	170		350	
NHS hospital beds – average daily available				
Short-stay	200	26	280	0
Long-stay	510		100	

* Data relate to 31 March.
† Excludes nursing care places in dual registered homes.
Source: Government Statistical Office and Welsh Office direct communication.

There is significant variation in the type, quality and quantity of residential accommodation across the country. Analysis of the 1991 Census showed that, in England, the number of residential places/100 000 general population varied from 9.2 in the old North East Thames Regional Health Authority to 18 in the South Western Region.[130] In Scotland, the average figure was 11.9, compared with 10.4 and 12.4 for Wales and England, respectively. This analysis excluded people living in their own homes, adult placement schemes and supported lodgings. These provide a relatively small proportion of all accommodation and their exclusion is unlikely to explain the differences reported. The fact that only designated places for PWLD were included may have had some effect.

Over the past 10 years there has been an increasing emphasis on providing supported living in the community (creating the opportunity for PWLD to live in their own homes through the provision of flexible, individualised support). The actual increase in supported living arrangements has, however, been slow. A survey of 10 local authorities in 1996 showed that 5% of adults with learning disabilities were in adult placement schemes and only 8% were in their own homes/tenancies.[131] Similar results were found in a more recent study.[132] In London in 1999, however, it was found that 27% of accommodation provided was some form of supported living.[127]

Planning for future provision will need to take into account decreasing NHS places, the increasing average age of carers and improving survival to old age, particularly amongst those with complex needs.[133,134]

Daytime activity

The capacity to engage in meaningful activity during the day is a key measure of quality of life. Activities may include paid work, education, day care, training and leisure activities, and should be dictated by the needs and desires of the individual. The majority of organised daytime activities are provided by day-care facilities.

Day care

There is up to 10-fold variation in the number of standardised day-care places across local authorities. Approximately 50% of all local authority day-care places are for PWLD, and 60% of all local authority-purchased places for the under-65s are for this group. Table 6 shows the purchasing of local authority and NHS day-care places. Equally variable is the nature of day-care programmes provided. They may include centre-based activities, adult education, training or community leisure activities.

Table 6: Day-care places for adults with learning disabilities in England, 1992–93 to 1996–97.

Purchaser/provider	1992–93	1996–97
Local authority		
Local authority	233,000	268,900
Voluntary	3,000	11,300
Private	200	6,700
NHS		
Total attendances	970,205	1,291,980
First attendances	4,145	8,980
On register 31 March 1999	8,469	

Sources: Government Statistical Service. *NHS Day Care Facilities England 1998/9*. London: Department of Health, 1999.
Government Statistical Service. *Community Care Statistics. Day and domiciliary personal social services for adults. Detailed statistics for England*. London: Department of Health, 1998.

Day care for PWLD may be provided by a variety of facilities.[135] Over the past decade there has been considerable change in the way in which day-care services are provided. The trend has been to move from the large segregated centres to supporting people in more ordinary everyday settings.[136] Key principles in this shift are integrated provision, person-centred planning and community inclusion. Despite this trend, the majority of local authority spend for day care is on day-centre places that tend to focus on large group activities.

Broad descriptions of models are listed below, although the model and way of working may not be fixed.

- **Adult training centres:** These were typically built for 100–120 people and are often located in light industrial estates. They are usually based on an industrial/work-training model. Special units for 10–20 people with special needs may be attached. Typical staffing ratios are 1:7–1:10 in training centres and 1:3–1:4 in special needs centres. In 1991 there were 662 local authority training centres and associated special care units in England.
- **Large day centres:** These accommodate up to 50–100 people. The centres were originally developed with a more educational focus than adult training centres.
- **Small day centres:** The limitations of large facilities led to smaller developments, typically for around 50 people, with staffing ratios of 1:5–1:7.
- **Community day centres:** These are typically built to accommodate up to 20 people. The growth of these centres has been encouraged by the increasing emphasis on community-based care and life skills training, alongside community integration. Staff ratios are typically 1:3–1:4, with an emphasis on 1:1 activity.
- **Day hospitals:** A small number of PWLD attend health care assessment and treatment units on a daily basis.

Employment

PWLD may be in ordinary employment or a variety of sheltered or supported work schemes. Over the past decade the trend has been to provide placements in supported work environments, with significant growth in supported employment schemes. The basic principles of supported employment are integrated settings, real work for real wages, ongoing support and training in the workplace. The term 'supported employment' is, however, sometimes used more generically to refer to all assisted employment.

The number of supported employment schemes for people with disabilities, including those with learning disabilities, has increased significantly since the early 1980s, although there has been some evidence of a slowing in growth.[137,138] In 1992, there were 1600 people in supported employment in the UK, with 79 agencies providing support. By 1995 this had increased to 200 agencies supporting 5000 individuals; the largest group were people with learning disabilities.[138]

Studies suggest that though many people in schemes earn less than £50/week, benefit cuts become an issue on higher incomes. Some people, particularly those with severe learning disabilities, are not paid at all. The majority of people work part-time.[139,140]

The provision of supported employment is unevenly distributed. There are relatively more schemes in Wales, the North West, the South East and London than in other parts of the country. Demand for placements always seems to outstrip supply. It has been estimated, for supported employment places in general, that at best there are only half the number of places needed and at worst up to 180 000 people are in need, with only 22 000 places.[141]

Schemes are usually funded through health and social services, some with contributions from the Department of Education and Employment. They are run by various agencies, including the voluntary sector and local authorities.

Education

The emergence of education as a key service for both children and, increasingly, adults with learning disabilities has been a marked feature of provision since the 1981 Education Act. The Special Educational Needs and Disabilities Rights in Education Bill 2000 clarifies the responsibilities set out in the 1996 Education Act for pupils with special educational needs.

Children

- **Pre-school provision:** A number of different schemes are available. Portage is probably the most commonly available for children with all types of special needs. This approach is designed to improve or ameliorate developmental delay. Portage teachers visit parents and their children at home. They work with parents to help develop skills and achieve specific targets. In 1992, there were 300 schemes in the UK.

  All local authorities must establish Early Years Development and Child Care Partnerships. Their annual plan should include provision for all young children, including those with disabilities and special educational needs. From 2001, all early years provision has been covered either by part 11 of the Disability Discrimination Act or by the Special Educational Needs and Disabilities Rights in Education Act. All early-years providers will be expected to make reasonable adjustments to increase access and inclusion for disabled children. Sure Start sites should also play a part in early identification of children with disabilities.

- **Schools:** The 1996 Education Act and Code of Practice sets out the framework for assessment and provision for children with special educational needs.[142] For those children with complex needs, including those with learning disabilities, the assessment process draws advice from the child's school, local education authority (LEA) and health and social services to determine the child's needs and how best to meet them. If this process concludes that the pupil needs provision over and above that which the local school could be reasonably expected to provide, then a statement of special educational needs will be made. This will specify the provision and set targets that will be reviewed annually.

  At the 14-plus review the LEA should create a transition plan. The Learning and Skills Act introduces a Connexions service which will provide a personal adviser from age 14 onwards. In the case of those with learning disabilities this service will continue until age 25.

  Estimates, although not precise, suggest that up to 28% of the school population may have special educational needs at some point during their childhood; only 2–4% will receive statements.[143]

  There is growing inclusion of children with disabilities, including those with learning disabilities, into mainstream education. There is, however, significant variation between LEAs in the rate at which this is being achieved. Children with learning disabilities are consequently educated in a variety of settings – specialist provision in boarding and day special schools, in special units attached to ordinary schools, and supported in mainstream classrooms. Clearly the level of disability will greatly dictate their placement, as will local provision. The proportion of children educated in special schools varies from 0.5–2%, depending on the LEA. Nationally, the special school population covers about 1% of the total school population (approximately 98 000 children).[143]

Adults

- **Further education:** The Learning and Skills Act 2000 replaces the Further and Higher Education Act and in effect gives new rights in education for all disabled people. The Further Education Funding Council has been replaced by the Learning and Skills Council with local Learning and Skills Councils being responsible for managing further education and training in their area. A person with learning disabilities will be entitled to ongoing assessment and review up to age 25.

The provision of further education seems to have increased for people with moderate learning disabilities. In one survey, 60% of colleges reported increased numbers since Further Education Funding Councils were given the responsibility for 'having regard for' the needs of PWLD. However, one in ten institutions had faced cuts, particularly for those with severe or profound disabilities. It was also found that the elderly might be marginalised.[144]

- **Adult education:** Provision of adult education is an important part of many day-care programmes, although the extent of provision is variable.

Leisure

Leisure activities may be organised by local authorities as part of day-centre programmes or as part of borough Gateway Clubs. Some projects are specifically for those with disabilities, whilst others aim to support people in accessing everyday activities, such as becoming members of local sports clubs. Self-advocacy groups also organise social and leisure activities.

Local authorities vary as to whether they provide grants for holidays.

Syndromes of impairment and/or disabilities

Mental disorders are dealt with separately under 'Mental disorders' and 'Challenging and offending behaviours' below.

Epilepsy services

A significant proportion of people with epilepsy who are in touch with specialist epilepsy services have learning disabilities.[145] Epilepsy management is often provided by consultants in learning disability, many of whom have developed specific expertise. In other areas, neurologists and paediatricians provide a service. Few neurologists have a special interest in epilepsy.[146] GPs have little specialist knowledge of epilepsy management and tend to rely on specialist services. An integrated approach to management should cover neurological, psychological and social care. There are national specialist centres for the treatment of refractory epilepsy.

Mental disorders

There is a perceived gap in many services in the provision of mental health services for PWLD. This is particularly true for individuals with mild or borderline impairment, for children and for the elderly.[147]

Services for children with learning disabilities and mental ill-health

It has been estimated that up to 50% of children with a learning disability are likely to need special services for emotional/mental health problems at some time during their childhood.[148] The provision of local services is highly variable. It may be any combination of paediatric, child development, specialist learning disability and child and adolescent mental health services.

Services for adults with learning disabilities and mental ill-health

Most services for adults with learning disabilities and mental illness are associated with specialist learning disability services, with specialist learning disability mental health teams in some areas. These teams usually provide interventions over the short to medium term. Few learning disability mental health services are part of generic mental health services. Occasionally a specialist learning disability team is integrated into generic services. In many areas, the specialist learning disability team also covers challenging behaviours.

There is some evidence to suggest that, in recent years, there has been a rise in demand for mental illness learning disability services. This may reflect changing criteria applied by social services to providing care for PWLD or increased detection of learning disabilities and mental illness by the criminal justice system and generic mental health services.

In most parts of the country there are specialist wards or community units, with a small number of areas relying on generic mental health service provision for inpatient care. There are relatively few joint inpatient schemes, where adult mental health beds are supported by learning disabilities teams.[149] Local service history and geography often dictate the model found. If there is no local service, inappropriately distant placements may occur.

Specialist day services are provided in some areas.

Challenging and offending behaviours

Challenging behaviours, especially aggression and self-injury, are amongst the most common reasons for referrals to psychiatrists and psychologists. A variety of specialist services exists, including outpatients, day care, supported accommodation, and open and secure inpatient units. In some areas, specialist challenging behaviours teams have been established.

The provision of secure services has changed significantly in recent years. The three high-secure hospitals provide beds for a small number of individuals, and high-secure learning disability services are now centred at Rampton Hospital. Admissions have decreased, acknowledging the inappropriateness of this setting for all but a few PWLD. Alternative services have developed, including a rise in the number of medium-secure beds. The number of places available in England increased from 300 in 1992–93 to 420 in 1998–99. Despite this increase there is still a perception that there is under-provision of the lower levels of secure care.

Autistic spectrum disorders

A wide range of provision is required to meet the diversity of need displayed by both children and adults with ASD.

Children with ASD

- **Education:** Children with ASD may attend mainstream education (with or without specialist support), generic special schools or designated units for ASD, or receive home-based tuition. It is often the level of intellectual impairment that dictates the type of placement. As IQ diminishes, specialist placement is more likely. There are, however, some children within the spectrum with good intellectual skills, whose needs may best be met by specialist provision if, for example, they find it too hard to cope with the social pressure of peers in mainstream education.

In 1997, there were 12 schools in England and one in Scotland solely for children with ASD, run by either the National Autistic Society ($n=5$) or local education authorities ($n=7$). There was one independent school for children with Asperger's syndrome, although most will be in mainstream education. A small number of independent schools offer places for ASD. There is enormous variation between LEAs as to the nature of local provision, and most schools use a variety of approaches to educational support.[150]

- **Speech and language therapists:** These professionals are often involved with services, as language delay and communication difficulties are key concerns for parents, and are predictors of prognosis.

Adults with ASD

Individuals with ASD require highly structured environments. Services should be organised to provide the familiarity and predictability needed. It is often the case that neither adult psychiatric services nor specialist learning disabilities services are set up to provide adequately for those with Asperger's syndrome.

Most PWLD and ASD will eventually need some form of residential care. Much of this is provided by the voluntary and independent sector.

Specific restriction of activities: losses of function

Sensory impairment

In some parts of the UK specialist provision exists, including hospital-based accommodation and specialist-staffed housing with structured programmes.

Audiology and ophthalmology services with interest and expertise in screening and the fitting of aids for PWLD are needed, given the high levels of unrecognised morbidity.

Multiple disabilities

- **Children with multiple disabilities:** The majority of children with complex and multiple disabilities are cared for by specialist teams, which include paediatricians, physiotherapists, speech and language therapists, occupational therapists and specialist nursing staff.

  Increasingly, packages of care allow treatment and care in a home setting, although regular respite care is needed. It may be necessary to provide this in a hospital setting for the most severely affected.

  Transition to adulthood is a vulnerable time, especially as some of the co-ordination of care may be lost with the shift to adult services.[97]

- **Adults with multiple disabilities:** Many people with the most complex disabilities are, since the closure of long-stay institutions, cared for in home environments or in residential/nursing homes. Only a few of the most disabled are looked after in hospitals. In some areas, high levels of community-based health care have been organised to allow individuals to live in ordinary home settings. This requires good collaboration between physical rehabilitation, learning disability and paramedical staff.

Restriction of participation: social consequences

PWLD often require help to access and understand services and to take an active part in the way in which their care is organised. Advocacy services, interpreters and training front-line staff to understand and deal with PWLD will help to achieve this.

Advocacy

There are a variety of approaches to advocacy, from the involvement of health and social care professionals in helping their clients to access services, to specific services for self- and citizen advocacy. Advocacy may provide a range of functions, including befriending, advice and direct representation.

There was a significant rise in advocacy services during the 1980s, particularly in self-advocacy groups. Nationally, between 1980 and 1987, there was an increase from 87 to 231 self-advocacy groups.[151] In Wales there was an increase from two groups in 1985 to 58 groups in 1995.[152]

Relationships

- **Parenting programmes:** Most parenting programmes in the UK are aimed at the general population, with no specific provision for parents with special needs. There are some specific services for parents with learning disabilities, such as the special parenting service in Cornwall.[153]

Restriction in participation: carers and families

Families and carers require information, advice, training and support from a range of services. Respite care is a key component in providing carer support.

Respite care

Respite care provides a break for carers, particularly if the client has multiple problems, severe challenging behaviours, or terminal or severe physical illness, and it covers carer illness or other emergencies. Most local authorities have some respite facility, but there is considerable variability in its availability.

Respite care may be provided in a variety of settings, including hospital wards, residential or nursing homes, specialist services such as outdoor-pursuit centres, and family settings. The current emphasis is on providing short respite breaks within a family setting rather than within residential units. This has been implemented to a varying degree across the UK.

- **Family-based respite:** At the end of the 1990s there were at least 400 family-based respite schemes in operation across England, Wales and Northern Ireland,[154] an increase of 26% in children's schemes and 4% in adult schemes since the previous survey at the beginning of the 1990s.[155] The majority of these services made provision for learning disabilities, and 85% of children's and nearly half of adult schemes accepted users with physical disabilities. The majority of schemes accepted people with sensory impairments. A significant proportion of the users had behaviour that was considered challenging. This finding is important, as the previous survey had found that there were difficulties in finding placements for those with physical dependency or challenging behaviours.[156]

  There has been some diversification in the types of services provided. Many schemes provide sitting services and others provide befriending or escorts to holiday placements.

  Adult and children's schemes usually had significant waiting lists, owing to a shortage of carers and/ or funding. A third of users waited over a year for the service. Schemes are funded from a variety of sources, the majority from social services budgets.

The cost of services

The costing of services for PWLD is complex. In 1996, total hospital and community health service expenditure on 'learning disabilities' was £1376 million (or 5% of the total for England). Personal social services expenditure for 'learning disabilities' was £1080 million (13% of the total).[157] These estimates exclude significant service utilisation, as data are not easily separated for particular diagnostic or client groups. Kavanagh and Opit's more comprehensive cost estimate (using the same baseline figures) includes social services, primary care and education, and suggests an annual figure in excess of £3 billion for the UK.[89] Funding mechanisms have diversified, as the balance of care has altered over time. Direct payment for services is now also an option for PWLD, although it is still relatively little used (*see* 'Choice' in Section 6).

Some commentators suggest that significant further investment is needed. The Mental Health Foundation estimated that a further £53 million was needed up to year 2001.[158]

Resource allocation

The original York formula used to allocate funds to health authorities (now PCTs) contained no weighting for learning disability services. It has been argued that this is inappropriate, as socio-economic indicators may predict need, not because they necessarily predict prevalence, but because need for services may be greater for those on low income.[159]

Health benefit groups (HBGs)

The development of HBGs for community care services presents considerable difficulties. This is particularly true for PWLD, as the main need is often for social rather than health care. Initial work on iso-resource groups suggests that approximately 30–40% of variation in costs can be accounted for using a bi-axial model that includes severity of intellectual impairment and presence or absence of severe challenging behaviours. This classification only accounts for a negligible reduction in variations in costs if NHS costs are considered in isolation (this may reflect either case-mix issues or methodological problems).[160] Further work on cost data is being undertaken.

Service costs

The Personal Social Services Research Unit (PSSRU) at the University of Kent at Canterbury produces annual costing schema for a variety of services and professional groups, based on the best available evidence. Table 7 (*see* overleaf) outlines the costs for individual practitioners.

The costs for specific aspects of learning disability services are hard to generalise, given that case-mix and service characteristics are so variable. Table 8 (*see* overleaf) shows a summary of the costs of different aspects of care.

Conclusions

Across the UK the organisation of services for PWLD differs significantly in both structure and level of provision. There are gaps in service development across the spectrum of health and social care. It is unlikely that differences in need can explain the pattern of provision that exists. Further investment is likely to be required if these disparities are to be addressed. Similarly, investment will need to take into consideration the potential increase in numbers of individuals with severe learning disabilities, the ageing of the existing population and the needs of carers, particularly as they also age.

Table 7: Costs of professional groups working with people with learning disability.

Professional group	Costs in 1997 (£)			
	Wages	On costs	Unit cost/hour	Cost/hour client contact
Occupational therapist – community	18,538	2,167	17	29
Speech and language therapist – community	20,753	2,415	19	31
Physiotherapist	20,753	2,415	19	31
Clinical psychologist	27,863	3,321	25	56
Community psychiatric nurse (G-grade)	20,774	2,417	19	52
Auxiliary nurse – B-grade community	10,300	921	9	15
Social worker	19,556	2,378	17	23/hour client-related work; 83/hour patient contact
Psychiatrist				
Consultant	56,407	7,375	50	68/hour client-related work; 207/hour patient contact
Senior registrar	36,144	4,096		17/hour on duty; 25/hour worked Costs based on average wages in 1997, excluding London weighting

Source: Netten et al.[295]

Table 8: Average cost per person with learning disability in different care settings (£/week, 1994–95 prices).

Care setting	NHS (£)	LASSD (£)	FHSA (£)	Family/DSS (£)	Education (£)	Total cost (£)
Adult fostering schemes*						658
Adults in sheltered housing*						560
Adults in ordinary households†	13.02	100.79	1.50	140.65	0.00	256
Children in ordinary households†	21.18	13.18	2.03	114.68	179.51	331

Other: Local authority residential care‡ – £659, £702 for care package including services provided by other agencies and personal living expenses.
Voluntary-sector activity-based respite care‡ – £53 per session per client.
Local authority social education and daycare centres[3] – £39 per place per day.
* Knapp et al.[219]
† Kavanagh and Opit.[89]
‡ Netten et al.[295]

6 Effectiveness of services

The determination of the effectiveness of services and interventions for PWLD is complex. This is for the reasons listed below.

- Definitional problems (*see* 'Definitions and classification' in Section 2) and the varied case-mix within services. The comparison and generalisation of research findings is thus difficult. In addition, what works in well-controlled research conditions may not work in the average service (the tension between known efficacy and actual effectiveness).
- The complexity of client problems and multi-agency/multi-intervention approaches to their management.
- The potential inappropriateness of extrapolating knowledge about effectiveness from non-learning disabled populations to PWLD.
- The determination of client satisfaction may be hampered by communication difficulties, reliance on the views of third parties and the fact that, historically, PWLD have not been encouraged to state their views.
- Different parties may place different values on the outcome of service provision, e.g. in relation to respite care there may be a trade-off between the benefit to the carer and the potential for dis-benefit to the person with learning disabilities.

Approaches to the determination of effectiveness

There are a variety of approaches to the determination of desirable outcomes. Overall, effectiveness should be gauged by improvements in the quality of life for individuals. The difficulties in defining quality of life, in addition to the methodological issues outlined, mean that this ideal is often not realised. Evaluation of service quality is more likely to measure the structure and process of provision that is thought to be associated with desirable outcomes, such as:[161]

- inputs, e.g. medication, physical characteristics of the care setting, staffing ratios and training
- processes, e.g. movement between settings and community presence
- technical processes, e.g. care planning
- interpersonal processes, e.g. staff/client interaction or the social environment of a facility.

Despite this, attempts should be made to measure well-being and subjective as well as objective outcomes.

Outcomes for the general population

The effectiveness of population measures for the prevention of disease, such as immunisation rates and coverage of screening programmes, will have an impact on the incidence and severity of learning disabilities and associated conditions. These interventions are discussed under 'Primary prevention' and 'Secondary prevention' below.

Outcomes for individuals

In learning disability services, the impact of aspirations to attain an ordinary life have probably had more of an impact than in other community care services. These aspirations are often underpinned by the five accomplishments defined by O'Brien, arising from work on the concept of normalisation.[162]

Normalisation principles are commonly used to define services and individual objectives and can therefore also be used to judge the quality of service provision.[163]

The five accomplishments are listed below.

- **Community presence:** The sharing of ordinary places that define community life.
- **Choice:** The experience of autonomy in small everyday matters and in large life-defining matters.
- **Competence:** The opportunity to perform functional and meaningful activities with whatever level or type of assistance that is required.
- **Respect:** Having a valued place among a network of people and valued roles in community life.
- **Community participation:** The experience of being part of a growing network of personal relationships, including close friends.

Given the vulnerability of many PWLD, safety and the protection from abuse could reasonably be added to these principles.[164]

Goal attainment in person-centred care planning may be used to measure effectiveness. This might include improvements in specific symptomatology/behaviours, improvement in specific skills, extension of social networks, social integration or meaningful occupation, expressed satisfaction (facilitated by staff, client and carer training or by advocates) or improvements in physical environments.[164] These can give outcomes of success at the individual level and, in theory, be aggregated to look at overall service outcomes. There are difficulties, however, in measuring change across the whole range of ability, including health and social care outcomes. Goal attainment scaling has been used in some learning disability services, but methodological and statistical difficulties limit its widespread usage.[165] Alternative approaches include care pathways or variance analysis of the attainment of care plan objectives.

A number of tools to assist the collection and collation of information about individuals have been developed:

- **HoNOS-LD:** a Health of the Nation outcome scale for PWLD[166]
- **CANDID:** the Camberwell Assessment of Need for adults with Developmental and Intellectual Disabilities.[167]

Outcomes for carers

The determination of carer satisfaction with service provision is also important, although the potential for conflict between desirable carer and client outcomes must be borne in mind. Outcomes relating to carer well-being should also be considered. This is a relatively poorly researched area.

Health promotion

This section does not discuss the ethics of preventing people from being born without impairment/disability, but rather it describes the programmes that exist which may contribute to it.

Population measures to reduce the incidence of a disorder can be divided into the following categories.

- **Primary prevention:** The prevention of occurrence of new cases of intellectual impairment through the removal of the causal agent(s), e.g. pre-conception genetic counselling (see 'Primary prevention' below).
- **Secondary prevention:** The early identification of intellectual impairment and its subsequent prevention, e.g. the identification of affected pregnancies and selective termination (see 'Secondary prevention' below).

- **Tertiary prevention:** The prevention of the development of disabilities associated with intellectual impairment, achieved through the provision of effective services for affected individuals (*see* from 'Primary care' on p. 500 to and including 'Restriction of participation: social consequences' on p. 512).

Primary prevention

The primary prevention activity that relates directly to intellectual impairment is the provision of genetic counselling. Other (indirect) measures aim to prevent pathology associated with learning disabilities, e.g. neural-tube defects or head injuries.

- **Genetic counselling:** High-risk families and individuals can be identified, counselled and offered genetic screening (cascade screening). This can increase choice and thus hopefully maximise quality of life, for example in relation to fragile X. In New South Wales, Australia, active case finding, screening and selective termination have been operating for 10 years. This has resulted in an estimated reduction in the prevalence of fragile X from 0.25/1000 males to 0.1/1000.[168] UK genetic testing centres offer testing to relatives of affected individuals, but case finding is not systematic. Further research is likely to be needed before active screening programmes could be implemented in the NHS.
- **Antenatal care:** General dietary advice is likely to be helpful in increasing pregnant women's energy and protein intake, although the maternal, fetal or infant health benefits are not clear.[169] Advice on limiting alcohol intake in pregnancy should also be of benefit.

  Randomised trials have shown that neural-tube defects can be reduced if folate supplements are taken before conception and in early pregnancy.[170] The incidence of neural-tube defects has reduced significantly over the past 30 years. Much of this occurred before the 1992 advice that all women trying to conceive should take daily folic acid supplements. This has led to recommendations that food should be fortified to ensure adequate population coverage.[171] General antenatal care measures, such as those aimed at reducing low birth weight, may be effective. Rhesus immunisation of rhesus-negative mothers has significantly reduced the birth of babies affected by rhesus incompatibility, many of whom would otherwise suffer brain damage.
- **Immunisation:** Programmes to reduce rubella, measles, mumps, haemophilus influenzae and whooping cough may all contribute to the reduction of brain damage associated with childhood infections. The routine use of rubella vaccination to increase the general population's level of immunity may also reduce the incidence of intrauterine infections.
- **Environmental strategies:**
  - **head injuries:** a reduction in the incidence of head injury caused by accidental and non-accidental injury (NAI) will have an effect on the incidence of intellectual impairment. Safety features in playground design and support measures for families with children at risk of NAI will theoretically therefore have an impact
  - **lead:** the Australian Port Pirie Cohort Study suggests an association between blood lead levels and IQ.[172] The impact on IQ is small and its importance is debated. At a population level, however, even small shifts in IQ may be significant. Exposure reduction, e.g. through removal of lead from paint, judicious siting of children's play areas and the use of unleaded petrol, may therefore be of benefit. There is some evidence to suggest that these measures may have an impact, as blood lead levels across all age groups in the UK are reported to be significantly lower than they were in the 1980s.[173]

Secondary prevention

Secondary prevention relies on screening programmes either to detect affected pregnancies and offer termination, or to identify affected babies and institute early treatment.

- **Antenatal screening:** Antenatal ultrasound screening at 16–18 weeks can detect a variety of major structural anomalies/disorders that are associated with learning disabilities. Antenatal detection of infections such as rubella, syphilis and HIV can also contribute to reductions in affected babies. Cost–benefit analysis has suggested that, even in areas where prevalence of syphilis is low (East Anglia), antenatal screening remains worthwhile.[174] Neural-tube defects can be detected antenatally by measuring maternal blood alphafetoprotein levels (routine antenatal practice in England and Wales). Some defects are detected at routine ultrasound scanning.

  The screening of pregnancies to detect a high risk of Down's syndrome is routine practice in England and Wales. Screening tests vary and may include blood tests (assays for two, three or four serum markers – double, triple or quadruple testing), ultrasound screening, including nuchal translucency measurement, and estimates of risk based on maternal age. Estimates suggest that, in 1998, serum screening was offered to about 70% of pregnant women in the UK.[175] Once high risk is identified, chromosome analysis (by amniocentesis or chorionic villous sampling) and selective termination can be offered. Chromosomal testing is also usually offered to women in known high-risk groups, defined by age and by having previously affected children. Current screening policy and practice vary considerably across the country, with some women being screened more than once at different stages of their pregnancy. There is a role for improved staff training and communication of information to patients.[176]

  Research evidence indicates that using the triple test with age is more effective, safe and cost-effective than the double test.[177] Depending on the combination of markers used, between 36% and 76% of affected fetuses can be detected in clinical practice.[178] However, the overall cost-effectiveness of the serum screening programme has been questioned, given the possibility of higher than predicted prenatal diagnosis based on maternal age and mid-trimester ultrasound alone.[179] There is continued debate about the relative effectiveness of nuchal translucency vs. serum screening.

  The usefulness of screening for cytomegalovirus and toxoplasma is less clear-cut, and it is not routinely used in the UK.

- **Postnatal screening:** The screening of all neonates to detect phenylketonuria and congenital hypo-thyroidism (Guthrie test at age 10 days) is routine practice in the UK. Early treatment can prevent significant intellectual impairment in both of these disorders. Cost–benefit analysis suggests that screening for PKU alone justifies the continuation of such neonatal screening, There is insufficient evidence to assess the economic value of screening for other inborn errors of metabolism.[180,181]

Primary care

The high levels of unrecognised morbidity and low uptake of health promotion suggest that the current provision of primary care to PWLD is not particularly effective. Primary health care teams have little expertise in the recognition and treatment of the complex physical or mental health problems that are associated with learning disabilities. Good collaboration between specialist and primary health care teams is therefore essential. This is particularly true with respect to prescribing and drug monitoring.[11]

A number of models have been developed to try to improve the delivery of primary health care to PWLD.[182] In a randomised, controlled trial, full health screening in general practice increased the amount of morbidity recognised and increased the uptake of tetanus immunisation. There is some evidence to suggest that a primary care facilitator, working with practice nurses and GPs, can increase screening and the detection of health problems.[183] A community learning disability nurse working with the primary health care team can also have a positive impact on the detection of medical conditions.[182–184]

The effectiveness of specific programmes, such as screening for breast and cervical cancer, is not established for women with learning disabilities.

Dental services

Although not specific to learning disabilities, there is some evidence to suggest that established good practice with respect to oral and dental care is not always put into practice.[185] In some cases, practice may include procedures that are detrimental to good oral health. Good practice guidelines are published by the British Society for Disability and Oral Health.[186]

Specialist learning disability services

As with primary care, an overall measure of the effectiveness of specialist services is the extent to which PWLD have unmet needs for which there are effective interventions. Analysis of the needs of PWLD in the Avon area suggests that many needs are unmet.[187] This was the case whether professionals, carers or clients were asked to assess the extent of unmet need (*see* Figures 2 and 3). Unmet need for daytime activity and respite care was particularly high.

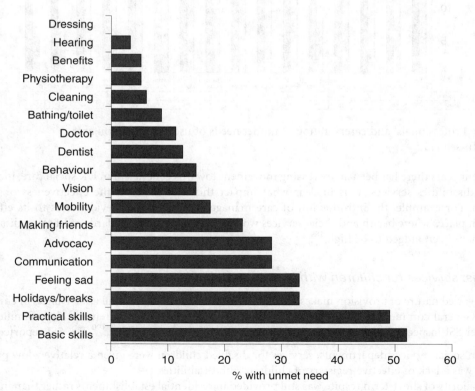

Figure 2: Users' perceptions of unmet needs in the Avon area. *Source*: Russell *et al.*[187]

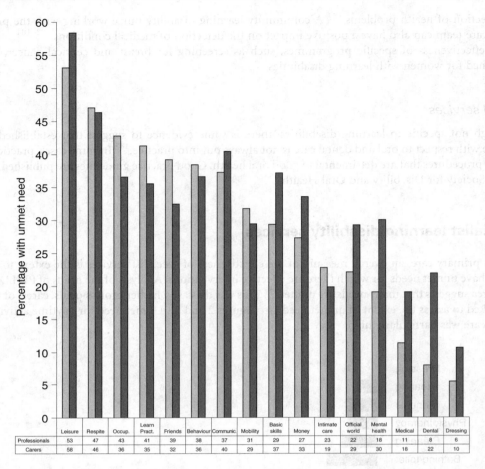

	Leisure	Respite	Occup.	Learn Pract.	Friends	Behaviour	Communic.	Mobility	Basic skills	Money	Intimate care	Official world	Mental health	Medical	Dental	Dressing
Professionals	53	47	43	41	39	38	37	31	29	27	23	22	18	11	8	6
Carers	58	46	36	35	32	36	40	29	37	33	19	29	30	18	22	10

Figure 3: Professionals' and carers' rating of unmet needs of users in the Avon area. *Source*: Russell *et al.*[187]

Over recent years there has been an increasing movement towards genericism in UK social care, including learning disabilities services. It is unclear what impact this may have on the effectiveness of service provision. For example, the introduction of care management has limited evidence as to its effectiveness.[188] In places where health and social services work well together the standards of learning disabilities services have been judged to be high.[189]

Specialist services for children with learning disabilities

The very varied nature of provision makes it difficult to comment on the overall effectiveness of children's services. General comments on the provision of services to all disabled children and their families were made after SSI inspection visits after the implementation of the Children Act.[190] The SSI reported that:

- within social services departments, services for disabled children were given a relatively low priority
- there was a lack of effective registers of children with disabilities
- the majority of short-term respite was still provided in residential establishments rather than in family settings

- there had been some improvement in consultation procedures with children and an increase in working with parents.

Particular concern has been raised about the effectiveness of transition planning. Highlighted concerns include loss of information, lack of information about services and lack of co-ordination and support.[191] Similar concerns, including lack of collaboration with adult services, were expressed after analysis of local Management Action Plans.[192]

Early intervention programmes

There is a considerable body of evidence for the effectiveness of early intervention, particularly from the USA, but there is relatively little for children identified as having learning disabilities.[193] It is likely that any effective early intervention will be family based, and positive outcomes may be family satisfaction and coping skills rather than lasting impact on cognitive ability of the child. Further research is needed.

Specialist services for adults with learning disabilities

The effectiveness of CLDTs is relatively under-researched, with the exception of specialist provision for challenging behaviours (*see* 'Challenging behaviours' below). Some suggest that CLDTs do, however, provide an example of co-operation between health and social care and have helped link service planning and delivery.[126] It has been suggested that their changing role, particularly with respect to the shift in philosophy around PWLD accessing generic rather than specialist services, has led to 'organisational confusion'. In addition, there may have been a trend towards the underuse of specialist expertise.[128] It is likely that PWLD will benefit most from a mixed approach using both specialist and generic staff.

Specialist services for older people with learning disabilities

There is little specific research. The results of small-scale interviews suggest that there is a lack of opportunity for developing networks with other people of similar ages.[129]

Pharmacological interventions

Only the prescribing of psychotropic drugs is reviewed. These drugs, particularly antipsychotics, are commonly used to treat emotional and behavioural disorders in PWLD.[194] Their use is controversial, in some settings may be widespread, and is often not associated with a formal diagnosis of mental illness.[195,196] The body of research on which to base prescribing policy is relatively poor.[197] Internationally agreed guidelines on the use of psychotropic medication have been published and cover issues such as reducing polypharmacy and close monitoring[197] (*see* also 'Mental disorders' and 'Challenging behaviours' below).

Psychological interventions

There is a significant body of research for some types of psychological therapies, particularly behavioural interventions. There is, however, relatively less published outcome research on cognitive or psychoanalytic therapies. Generally, psychological therapies are not widely used for PWLD, their learning disabilities being used as an exclusion criterion.[198]

- **Behavioural interventions:** There is an extensive published literature, particularly as applied to challenging behaviours (*see* 'Challenging behaviours' below), language and communication difficulties and the training of caregivers.[199] Research showing the benefits of intervention includes a few small RCTs, many uncontrolled studies and case reports.[200]

- **Cognitive therapy:** Positive results have been reported in the treatment of anxiety, depression and sexual problems and in anger management in people with less severe intellectual impairment. These studies were uncontrolled, with small numbers of subjects.[201]
- **Gentle teaching:** This approach aims to improve the nature of interactions between clients and their carers. There is controversy as to its effectiveness. Research results vary from showing that it has a positive impact to demonstrating that it has a detrimental effect.[202] As an approach, gentle teaching may be a useful adjunct to other more structured approaches.[203]

Occupational therapy interventions

The research base is small. A review by the College of Occupational Therapists suggests that the shift to community working that occurred in the 10 years prior to 1997 led to an increase in direct referrals and a change in their nature. Community referrals are more likely to be for specific interventions to improve skills and independence, rather than for the social and recreational activities.[204]

There is little published evidence for the effectiveness of specific occupational therapy interventions. Small case studies suggest that interventions can have a positive effect on skills and empowerment.[205]

Physiotherapy interventions

The research specific to PWLD is limited. Early intervention is considered important, although there is considerable scope for work with adults in improving functionality, independence and quality of life. Physiotherapists are also increasingly working in the community.

Speech and language therapy interventions

- **Children:** The effectiveness literature is based on small-scale 'before-and-after' research. Overall it suggests that intervention may have an impact on general communication and comprehension.[206,207] An impact on verbal expression has also been shown. Children with learning disabilities were randomised to either a communication training programme or an environmental approach with some structured teaching.[208] The results suggested that the more developmentally delayed children benefited most from the environment approach and the more able ones from the training programme.

  The results of research into signing are equivocal, some studies showing no advantage of sign and speech over speech alone.
- **Adults:** There is less evidence for the effectiveness of speech therapy for adults with learning disabilities. There are case studies to suggest that, in well-motivated clients and carers, communication can be improved. It may, however, be more appropriate for group work to be attempted in conjunction with staff training.
- **Carers:** There is some evidence in small-scale studies to suggest that parents' behaviour, in terms of their verbal communication with their children, can be altered. It is unclear what effect this may have on the child.[209]
- **Facilitated communication:** During this process the client is physically supported by a facilitator to help them communicate. There continues to be significant controversy over the usefulness of facilitated communication. There is currently no good evidence to show that it is effective. There is a growing body of evidence to suggest that facilitators may actually influence communication.[210,211]

- **Staff training:** There is some evidence to suggest that health and social services staff may be willing to teach language skills if they have the appropriate training and support.[212] Therefore, given the shortage of speech and language therapists, it may be appropriate for them to act as facilitators and consultants.

Alternative therapies

Carers and clients value alternative therapies, but there is little evidence to prove or disprove their overall effectiveness or their specific benefits in PWLD.

Accommodation

The majority of evaluations of services for people with learning disability have focused on evaluating residential care options. Early research compared various 'community' placements with long-stay hospital care. It is only recently that the emphasis has shifted to comparing different types of community accommodation.

The available research literature suffers from a number of methodological problems.

- There are no randomised controlled trials.
- Quasi-experimental and descriptive studies have often used poorly matched or unmatched comparison groups and small sample sizes.
- Costing methodologies vary. Not all studies include costs for capital and external services, such as primary care. External costs range from 15–25%. Placement cost estimates are often based on average costs for all residents in a facility, obscuring differences between individuals. Costs are inevitably associated with the level of disability and the presence of coexisting conditions, e.g. challenging behaviours and sensory impairments.[213–216]
- The generalisability of studies is undermined because evaluations are often based on particular schemes or areas where services and other conditions are atypical. Clear differences in the degree and type of disability between different sectors and types of provision have been shown. For example, adults in NHS provision show higher levels of both challenging behaviours and physical disabilities, whilst people in local authority provision are the most able.[217,218]

Despite these difficulties, a number of generalisations may be made concerning hospital and community residential care.

- Community placements have been associated with improved self-reported outcomes for those individuals who were able to express a view.[219] However, on average, resettlement into the community results in little if any improvement in social functioning and symptomatology, and resettlement may actually be associated with small deleterious changes with respect to some behavioural problems.[219] Where small gains in welfare have been reported, they were generally limited to the first few months after resettlement.[220]
- Longer-term research has demonstrated little change in social functioning and symptomatology one and five years after discharge.[221,222]
- Community residential care placements tend to be more costly than hospital care for former long-stay patients.[219,223] Although longer-term costs may alter for particular individuals, there was little change in the average costs of care between one and five years post-discharge.[222]

- A variety of cross-sectional studies also suggest that the costs of community residential placements were higher than for hospital care. The Northern Ireland Care in the Community Study is one of the few studies to show lower community costs over hospital residential care.[224]

The conclusion often drawn from the available literature is that community-based provision is preferable to hospital care, albeit at a higher cost. Debate continues, however, about the appropriate mix of provision in terms of scale, organisation of facilities and the sector of management. For example, an overview of the literature in 1996 found that, on average, smaller-scale dispersed housing schemes were associated with better quality and more positive outcomes for users than larger hostels. It was also noted, however, that significant variations in quality existed within each service type. For a significant minority of people in community residential accommodation schemes, including smaller dispersed housing schemes, quality of care was little better, and perhaps worse, than that experienced in hospital settings.[225] Personal relationships for PWLD in residential care have been reported as being limited in number and quality.[226]

Costs in different accommodation settings vary widely (*see* Table 8). Comparisons of costs are difficult, as residents' characteristics are heterogeneous both within and between different forms of residential care. Costs have been shown to be associated with disability, coexisting conditions and age – older and younger age groups being associated with higher costs.[213] There are also differences in costs between facilities managed by the private, voluntary and public sectors. In general, independent-sector facilities (private and voluntary) are less costly than statutory-sector provision. The lower costs associated with placement in private (for-profit) facilities may, in part, be due to lower utilisation of community services provided externally to the establishment, such as day care.[214,224] Generally speaking, the higher levels of quality reported for smaller staffed group homes compared to larger facilities, such as residential homes or hostels, seem to be achieved at somewhat higher costs.

Advocates for separate village communities for PWLD have suggested that existing community facilities were associated with isolation and an increased risk of misadventure, and incurred higher costs compared with 'village communities' (the definition of a village community appears to include both groups of houses based on a hospital site and clusters of houses in community settings).[227] A number of early studies suggested that clustered community-based accommodation might have lower costs than staffed group homes.[228,223] The extent to which costs were associated with differences in disability between the settings is, however, unclear. A preliminary study by the Department of Health and the PSSRU suggested that the revenue cost estimates which had been suggested were not realisable for people with more severe disabilities, but the results were inconclusive.[229] Consequently, the Department of Health commissioned a large research study.

This suggested that that for residents in community-based village communities the costs of care were £39 796 (1999–2000 prices), compared with costs of £45 532 for a matched sample of people living in dispersed housing schemes.[230] The difference in costs was not statistically significant. Analyses of a range of process measures of quality showed that on some measures the village community provided better quality of care, while on other measures dispersed housing scored better. For example, people in village communities were less likely to have been the victim of crime or verbal abuse, whilst people living in the dispersed housing schemes were more likely to have broader-based social networks. Similarly, people in village communities were more likely to receive preventive health care, while people in dispersed housing were more likely to engage in recreational activities.

The cost of dispersed housing was significantly higher (£57 359) in comparison to residential (NHS) campuses on a variety of hospital and green-field sites (£50 749) (comparisons were again based on two matched samples). Analyses of process measures suggested that dispersed housing provided less institutional and more individually oriented care.

Wide differences in residents' disability existed between the three settings. It was not possible to match a group of people from NHS residential campuses (generally more disabled) with people in community-based village communities (less disabled). Comparisons of costs adjusted for case-mix suggested that costs were highest in dispersed housing schemes (£52 791), with NHS residential campuses (£45 820) and village communities (£44 030) having broadly similar costs.

Supported living

There is relatively little research on supported living. Some schemes have been established that help PWLD to access and maintain tenancies in mainstream housing, e.g. Keyring in London. Interviews with tenants/ key professionals in touch with this scheme suggested that it had been successful in achieving this at a relatively low cost.[231]

Hospital-based care

There are no data on the relative effectiveness of the various models of inpatient care. Evidence (*see* above) seems to suggest that hospital-based bungalows are more costly than more traditional hospital-based care.

Accommodation for children with learning disabilities

There appears to be a gap between current practice and the information available in the research literature. The small research base may, in part, reflect the small amount of full-time residential provision that now exists for children with a learning disability. Most studies were conducted in the 1980s. At that time, the few studies that exist suggested that community care in small-scale units was feasible.[232] Evaluation of an intensive support unit for children suggested that it was an expensive option in comparison to an NHS community unit, once external costs were included, and that foster care was the least costly placement option.[233] Each study was made up of small numbers.

Daytime activity

Day care

The effectiveness of day-centre care is unknown. There seems to be a lack of consensus over its role and purpose, and debate as to whether it does provide a service that creates a meaningful day for people.[234] The people that use day-care centres are not always positive about the activities that they provide, although work and attending college are viewed positively.[235]

Employment

Only a small minority of PWLD are in paid employment (it will not be a realistic option for all). Small-scale interviews with PWLD in supported employment suggest the following:

- they prefer work to traditional day-care options, particularly adult training centres
- having any job is not necessarily preferable to having no job
- they need help to interact with non-disabled colleagues
- it is possible to support severely disabled people in employment.

The costs of supported employment for those with severe disabilities are likely to be higher than ordinary day care, but less for those with lesser disability.[236,138,234] A US review of the cost-effectiveness of schemes suggested that, overall, supported employment is more cost-efficient than sheltered work placements, although some studies showed advantage for sheltered work for those with severe disability.[237]

Leisure

This again is an area where there is little research on the effectiveness of various models, but carers and PWLD highlight unmet need.[127]

Syndromes of impairments and/or disabilities

Epilepsy services

A significant indicator of the quality of service provision is the level of seizure control achieved. Control may not be total, but can be measured against a baseline. There is some evidence to suggest that good seizure control can have a beneficial effect on activities of daily living.[238]

Mental disorders

The relative effectiveness of different models of service provision for PWLD and mental illness is unknown. Descriptions of the components of services required have been published, but there is no research that compares, for instance, the effectiveness of specialist mental health learning disabilities teams and more generic provision.[239] There is some evidence from a randomised trial to suggest that outreach treatment may be an effective alternative to hospital admission.[240] There is also some evidence to suggest that psychotic patients with borderline intellectual impairment may have better outcomes (less days in hospital and less overall admissions) with intensive case management in the community compared with standard case management.[241] The absence of specialised input may result in distant placements.[242]

There are also no comparisons between mental health units in learning disability hospitals and specialist community units. Similarly, there is no systematic evaluation of learning disability mental illness beds in generic wards with support from specialist learning disability teams. There is some anecdotal evidence that this may be a useful model for those with less severe impairment, but not for severe impairment.[243] A small number of studies have noted that admission facilities are developing a new long-stay population, particularly of people with severe psychiatric or behavioural problems.[244] This emphasises the importance of the development of appropriate community placements.

Pharmacological interventions

Medication may be prescribed for the range of psychiatric disorders, but systematic, specific research for PWLD is limited. A systematic review of relevant randomised controlled trials found no trial evidence to guide the use of antipsychotic medication for those with learning disabilities and schizophrenia. This is an area in need of further research.[245]

Challenging behaviours

As with other service provision, there is some evidence to suggest that many people with challenging behaviours receive relatively little support from services. In 1995, less than 30% of the HARC Challenging

Behaviour Project Group were receiving any contact from community learning disability nursing, psychology, speech therapy, specialist social work or occupational therapy services. This is despite the fact that many were living with their families and had other health and social problems. This study also suggested that there continued to be an under-utilisation of effective behavioural techniques and an over-reliance on psychoactive medication.[73]

Services for children with challenging behaviours

Early intervention is thought to be important, as there is evidence to suggest that children do not 'grow out of' behaviours.[246] A number of controlled intervention trials show positive outcomes for parent training. Some are designed to help deal with general issues, while others address specific problems/challenging behaviours (for a review *see* Chadwick *et al.*[247]).

Most studies suggest that parental knowledge about behavioural modification can be improved by training. This has been confirmed by videotaping that shows improved teaching expertise. The consequent impact on children's behaviours, however, is less certain. Some studies suggest an improvement in children's self-help skills. The literature is unclear as to whether improved self-help necessarily improves problem behaviours. This is because it is not certain whether the lack of basic skills, such as communication, is necessarily causal in the generation of the challenging behaviours.

Evaluation of interventions is further hampered by relatively low uptake of offers of help and some suggestion that those who accept help may have the capacity for better outcomes, thus biasing the results favourably. It has been suggested that individual rather than group interventions improve the uptake, acceptability and impact on behaviours. Flexibility in the nature of the package offered is likely to be important, particularly with respect to the number of sessions.[247]

Services for adults with challenging behaviours

- **Challenging behaviour teams:** Evidence suggests that staff with specialist skills working with PWLD and challenging behaviours are more effective than teams with more generic skills. The effectiveness of specialist teams is, however, very variable.[248] A number of factors have been suggested to explain this, such as staff training, staff turnover and the extent of teamworking.[249]
- **Day services:** US studies suggest that the availability of day placements is associated with successful community placement for people with challenging behaviours.[250]
- **Psychological interventions:** Small group studies show that the frequency and severity of challenging behaviours can be reduced in the short term using techniques such as functional communication training or behavioural treatments based on functional analysis of behaviours.[251–253] Longer-term effects are less certain; behaviour change is not always maintained by carers/parents after the initial intervention.[254]

  Behavioural interventions may not be as widely used as they could be. In one study, less than 40% of people with self-injurious behaviour received appropriate behavioural input.[255] A review of the available guidelines for the psychological management of challenging behaviours suggested that less than 15% were supported by RCT, systematic review or meta-analysis evidence.[256]
- **Pharmacological interventions:** There are case reports for the successful management of behavioural problems with medication, but a lack of long-term trials. Systematic review of randomised controlled trials has provided no evidence as to whether antipsychotic medication does or does not help adults with learning disabilities and challenging behaviours.[257] Furthermore, there is some evidence to suggest that up to 30% of PWLD with behavioural problems, in whom mental illness has been excluded, may have antipsychotics safely discontinued. A further group could be prescribed lower doses without detrimental effect.[258] Drug reduction was associated with a significantly higher

engagement in activities, and weight loss in some. The International Consensus Conference Guidelines highlight the over-prescribing of neuroleptics for behavioural management.[197]

There is some evidence, although the studies have small numbers, that opiate antagonists such as naloxone and naltrexone may improve self-injurious behaviour in a proportion of PWLD.[259]

- **Control of aggression:** There is no robust research basis for the effectiveness of interventions aimed at the control of aggression. The 1998 Royal College of Psychiatrists review, based on expert opinion, suggested that the following may be of use in mental health services:[260]
  - generation of calm environments
  - training of staff in de-escalation techniques and in restraint procedures
  - policies on the use of seclusion, especially as there is some evidence, from high-secure settings, that seclusion is used more frequently for those with learning disabilities[261]
  - policies and training in the use of sedation and emergency tranquillisation.

It is reasonable to suggest that these measures also represent good practice in learning disability services. A policy framework for the use of physical interventions in learning disabilities has also been published.[262]

- **Accommodation:** The review of general accommodation for people with learning disability (*see* 'Accommodation' above) includes a number of studies that included people with challenging behaviour as part of a general study population. Overall, research suggests that specialist staffed houses have better outcomes than hospital-based provision.

The costs for a sample of people with challenging behaviour in Wales have been reported. Care in staffed group homes was the most costly, followed by hostels. Hospital care was the least costly.[263,264] There was little difference in behaviour problems between settings, despite the fact that hospital and hostel residents were more disabled in their adaptive behaviour than staffed group home residents. Process measures of quality, such as staff attention, assistance and individual orientation, were higher in staffed group homes. Preliminary results for people with learning disabilities and challenging behaviours in the former North West Regional Health Authority suggested a different cost pattern.[265] Costs were greatest in hospital, followed by residential care, and care in family or foster homes was the least costly.

Evaluation of specialist challenging behaviour inpatient units suggests that the frequency and severity of challenging behaviours can be reduced and the number of individuals in community placements increased.[266] The longer-term impact of such units is less clear, as improvements in behaviours may not be maintained on discharge. Units may become 'silted up' with long-stay clients.[267] An alternative to inpatient provision is to increase the competence in mainstream services using specialist intensive home support teams.[70] There is no evidence for the relative effectiveness of these models.

Offending behaviours

There is relatively little evidence for the effectiveness of specific interventions for PWLD who offend.[268] Often offenders with intellectual impairment are mentioned as part of larger cohorts of offenders. Specific studies usually have small sample sizes.

Case studies have shown positive outcomes for inpatient treatment for individuals with mild impairment and violent, fire-setting or sexual-offending behaviours. Arsonists were over-represented in those with poorer outcome.[266]

There is some evidence to suggest that, for sexual offenders, individual goals can be improved through group therapy. As in non-learning disabled populations, recidivism is however high. It is suggested that treatment packages should be holistic, i.e. address environmental issues and displacement of offending with other behaviours, rather than using simple elimination/punitive behavioural approaches.[269]

Autistic spectrum disorders

Early intervention programmes

Reviews of the literature conclude that:[270,150]

- programme evaluation is very variable and often methodologically flawed
- for most approaches, there is some evidence of effectiveness
- effective programmes often share key characteristics, such as emphasis on increasing an individual's attention to their environment, imitation and the involvement of parents
- approaches that rely on integration between children with and without ASD have shown positive outcomes for both children with ASD and their normally developing peers
- further research, which controls for confounding variables such as the degree of parental involvement and the intensity of intervention, is needed.

Overall, the evidence suggests that some form of early intervention should be incorporated into service provision, but it is difficult to recommend one model over another.

Auditory integration training (AIT)

AIT involves the person with ASD listening to sessions of electronically altered music. Two randomised placebo-controlled trials from the USA and a number of case reports have suggested that AIT can significantly improve the behaviour of children and adults with autism.[271] This finding has not been replicated in UK controlled trials. Further studies are needed.[272]

Specific restriction of activities: losses of function

Sensory impairments

- **Structured teaching programmes:** There is limited case-report evidence to suggest that programmes which help the individual to deal with their disabilities (including the provision of aids) improve quality of life and may have a beneficial impact on challenging behaviours, e.g. self-injury.[273]
- **Multi-sensory stimulation:** The use of multi-sensory environments (MSE or Snoezelen rooms) has been advocated for PWLD, particularly for those with challenging behaviours maintained by sensory impairments. The evidence for their effectiveness is equivocal. A double cross-over study showed no effects beyond those that could be ascribed to the social interaction between participant and enabler.[274]
- **Accommodation:** There is some evidence to suggest that measures of quality of life are improved in small, specialist, supported housing in comparison to specialist hospital accommodation, although costs may be greater.[275] The costs of specialist accommodation in this study were considerably higher than those reported for more standard accommodation for PWLD in other studies.

Restriction of participation: social consequences

Choice

The opportunity to decide on which services to use is an important aspect of choice. The Community Care Act (direct payments) 1996 created new possibilities for individuals to have some control over the services provided for them. There is some evidence, however, to suggest that development in this field has been slow, particularly for PWLD, who may not have been included in local authority policies.[276,277]

Advocacy

The provision of advocacy services is viewed positively by clients. The overall impact of advocacy on quality of life or the provision of services is not known.[278] Despite the significant increase in advocacy services, many PWLD still do not have contact with an advocate.[73,279]

Relationships

There is currently little evidence to suggest that services for PWLD have been particularly effective at creating relationships for people, although as a group they may be less excluded than previously.[161,280]

- **Parenting:** Research on interventions to improve parenting skills is sparse and methodologically flawed. Training primary health professionals to recognise vulnerable or actual parents with learning disabilities may be of benefit. Adaptation of school-based parenting education and portage can also help PWLD to learn parenting skills.[281] Families are likely to need help at least until their children reach adulthood.

Abuse

Despite the existence of good-practice guidance on how to deal with the sexual abuse of PWLD it has been suggested that many cases remain unrecognised, unreported or inadequately dealt with. In one study of sexual abuse, the police were only involved in 42% of sexual abuse cases which were eventually proven or highly suspected.[105]

Restriction in participation: carers and families

Long-term support for carers/families has been recognised as important for coping and the maintenance of informal caring.[282] In one study, 60% of carers identified the need for such support, but the level of unmet need was high.[26] Support may involve a number of components, including information, counselling at the time of detection or training in behavioural techniques. There is some research to suggest that support may have a positive impact on family relationships.[283]

Respite care

Reports suggest that respite care is considered important by parents as a part of their coping strategies.[284] However, although respite care has received increased attention, there is little information about the cost-effectiveness of different arrangements. In one study the cost per night of placement was higher in residential care (particularly in NHS facilities) compared to foster care.[285] Although most parents expressed satisfaction with services, this study highlighted the trade-off between the welfare of parents and that of the children. A number of more recently developed respite care schemes providing activities, special clubs and outdoor pursuits have been described.[286] Most schemes focused on short-term relief, although some offered night cover. Cost-effectiveness cannot be determined, as the impact on utilisation of other services or on family costs was not calculated.

Conclusions

The literature on the effectiveness of treatments, interventions and service models for PWLD is mainly limited to descriptive and uncontrolled research studies. By far the largest body of work is in the field of accommodation and behavioural interventions. Despite this there remains significant uncertainty. Which model of accommodation or behavioural intervention is best for any particular individual? Further research to allow better tailoring of interventions for individuals is needed. Table 9 outlines key areas of knowledge on effectiveness.

Table 9: The effectiveness of services/interventions for people with learning disabilities.

Service/intervention	Comment
Accommodation	
Small dispersed housing vs. other provision	Measurable benefit from descriptive and well-designed uncontrolled studies
Non-hospital village communities vs. other provision	As above
Residential care for children	Inadequate and conflicting, but with some expert opinion in favour
Respite care for children	Inadequate and conflicting, but with some expert opinion in favour
Daytime activities	
Supported employment	Measurable benefit: III
Antipsychotic medication	
Schizophrenia	Measurable benefit for some: III
Challenging behaviours	Measurable benefit for some: IV
Psychotherapeutic interventions	
Behavioural approaches	Measurable benefit: II-1
Other	Measurable benefit: II-1
Challenging behaviour and behavioural approaches	Measurable benefit: II-1

For a description of allocated quality of evidence, *see* Introduction to this series.

7 Models of care

Components of a comprehensive learning disability service

A systems approach to service provision is necessary if comprehensive, integrated and inclusive services are to be provided. Processes of care, such as the nature of inter-agency working, as well as structural elements will determine the adequacy of local service provision. It is likely that the technical ability of staff will be a greater determinant of local service capacity than the availability of specific settings. It is therefore not possible to examine one element of a service in isolation. For example, the need for hospital beds will be determined by the capacity of community services to prevent admissions and expedite discharge as well as the number of PWLD in the population. For these reasons, and the dearth of relative effectiveness data for different models of provision, it is not possible to make recommendations to define a model service. It is possible, however, to outline both structural and process components of services that should form the basis for local planning discussions. Local providers and commissioners may then determine the most appropriate local configuration of structure and process needed to achieve a comprehensive service. This necessitates partnership working at all levels and between all of the relevant agencies.

It is possible to separate out issues at population and client levels, although clearly there is overlap.[287] Population need for services is discussed first, followed by client need for services. The various subsections consider elements of structure, process and outcome and should be considered in conjunction with Sections 5, 6 and 8.

Population need for services

At a population level the elements of a comprehensive service may be thought of in the following categories:

- planning, including needs assessment and service development
- inter-agency working, including consultation and liaison across services
- service provision, covering health promotion, primary, secondary and tertiary health care, social care, housing services, self-help, etc.
- organisations that are fit for purpose.

Planning and inter-agency working

Structures

Inter-agency planning forums with responsibility for the full population age range (i.e. child and adolescent, adult and elderly) should be in place. All relevant stakeholders should contribute to the work of these forums. In addition to specialist learning disabilities services, there should be representation from or defined ways of consulting with the following groups: clients, carers, independent sector, criminal justice system, housing, education, employment services, primary care services, mental health services, acute medical and community health services, e.g. physical disability teams and neurology services.

A number of mechanisms for consultation exist:

- direct representation on committees/groups
- cross-representation between groups/committees
- formal consultation processes, e.g. rolling search conferences/focus groups
- individuals with designated responsibility to consult with/advocate for particular stakeholders.

Guidance on the involvement of PWLD in the commissioning of services has been published.[288]

Table 10: Predicted numbers of people with learning disabilities and other conditions in a population of 100 000.

Condition	Predicted numbers per 100,000
Mild intellectual impairment	
IQ < 70, prevalence of 2.75%	2,700
Mild learning disabilities	
Prevalence 1–2%, depending on definition	1,000–2,000
Severe intellectual impairment	
IQ < 50 and others with coexisting conditions, prevalence 0.3–0.4%	300–400, of whom 75–100 will be < 16 years and 225–300 will be adults
Down's syndrome	
Prevalence 30% of severe learning disability	90–120
10% given up at birth	
10% full-time or part-time care required in childhood	
Challenging behaviours	
Point prevalence of significant challenge	20
Challenging behaviours	
Point prevalence of all those that may present difficulties to carers or risk to themselves	100
Autistic spectrum disorder	
Whole spectrum	910
Autistic spectrum disorder, IQ < 70:	
Classical (Kanner's) autism	50
Other spectrum disorders	150
Autistic spectrum disorder, IQ > 70:	
Asperger's syndrome	360
Other spectrum disorders	350
Epilepsy	
Severe learning disabilities and epilepsy	54–72
Epilepsy	
Profound learning disabilities and epilepsy	22–30
Cerebral palsy and severe learning disabilities	92–136

Processes

- **Macro needs assessment (commissioner led):** This should include the following areas.
  - Baseline description of population demography and delineation of local high-risk groups.
  - Baseline epidemiological prediction of numbers of PWLD in the population, using projections of national data or local research (*see* Table 10). Local sociodemographic and service factors that should be considered are the birth rate, uptake of screening and selective termination, ethnic minority groups, the rate of resettlement of the long-stay population, the numbers of PWLD in high-secure hospitals, the adequacy of local case finding and local migration over the past 50 years.
  - Profiling the age and needs of individuals coming up to transition from child to adult services.
  - Making predication from the age structure of local PWLD on the likely future numbers of dementia sufferers.
  - Profiling local PWLD according to categories of need, e.g. accommodation, leisure, employment, physical and mental health (i.e. using information from person-centred planning).
  - Profiling the age and needs of carers to help inform service planning for carers and transition planning as they age.[289]

- Baseline understanding of all sectors' current resources, including staff numbers and skills, and the identification of current spend within statutory agencies, including housing.
- Identification of gaps in funding/service provision.

- **Micro needs assessment (provider led):** This should include:
  - analysis of case loads/service demands across teams/services
  - analysis of skill-mix across teams
  - analysis of assessments of carer needs
  - collation of information from person-centred care planning to generate profiles of need
  - application of population needs assessment work to the determination of local service configuration.
- **Partnerships:** Specific work is needed to ensure that, at a population level, there are no gaps in service provision and that consultation and liaison about individual clients can occur with relative ease. A number of approaches may facilitate this:
  - agreed processes for referral
  - agreed standards for referral
  - named responsibility at both clinical and managerial levels for ensuring development and review of consultation and liaison structures and processes
  - development of inter-agency registers of PWLD, shared with primary care
  - development of information systems shared across agencies.

Formal agreements between specialist learning disability service providers and other providers/agencies may be of benefit.

- **Social/health care:** Agreement on the relative roles of health and social care providers in the management of the spectrum of learning disabilities and other coexisting conditions.
- **Primary/secondary care providers:** Agreement on shared care issues, e.g. prescribing costs, drug monitoring, physical health screening and monitoring, family planning. Agreements on how to improve access to generic services.
- **Other services (e.g. residential homes, educational establishments and day-care facilities):** Agreements on the level of support provided to them by specialised services, e.g. training.
- **Mental health services:** Defined responsibilities are particularly important at the boundaries of services. The following groups of PWLD merit specific local discussion between specialist mental health and learning disability services if they are to receive adequate service provision: mild and borderline learning disabilities, ASD (including Asperger's syndrome), the transition years (adolescence and the elderly), early-onset dementia, brain injury, challenging behaviours, mental illness and physical disabilities.
- **Generic medical and surgical specialities:** The organisation of support and information so that they are accessible to PWLD should be agreed.
- **Paediatrics/child development and child and adolescent mental health services:** Their relative roles and contributions should be defined.

Outcomes

Needs-based, person-centred planning and effective inter-agency working should help to develop local strategic and operational thinking leading to the following.

- Joint strategies with targets for service development/spend. The over-arching learning disability strategy will need subsections, or separate inter-linking strategies, to cover specific services/populations, e.g. offenders/primary care/housing.
- Staff and other resources within services can be deployed according to local need.

Health service provision: general population health promotion and disease prevention

Structures

- Genetic counselling.
- Screening programmes: local policies should ensure that screening protocols are appropriate, understood by staff and do not include unnecessary duplication of tests.
- Immunisation programmes.
- Accident prevention strategies.

Processes

- Folate and alcohol advice in antenatal and primary care settings.
- Appropriate information and counselling of parents undergoing prenatal testing.
- Sensitive disclosure policies covering all relevant services, e.g. children's services.

Outcomes

Reduction in the incidence of intellectual impairment, in the severity of disabilities and their associated disadvantage.

Health service provision: primary care

Structures

- Practice registers of PWLD and their needs.
- Screening programmes: hypertension, mental ill-health, thyroid function, etc.
- Primary care services, e.g. continence, chiropody, dentistry, pharmacy and dietetics, that have experience in dealing with PWLD.

Processes

- Annual physical, dental and mental health reviews.
- Support to carers/families, e.g. access to counselling services.

Outcomes

- Reduction in the amount of unrecognised physical and mental ill-health in PWLD.
- Improvements in the well-being of carers/families.

Health service provision: specialist learning disability services

Specialist services, provided by whichever sector is most appropriate, will need to make provision for:

- assessment, detection and diagnosis
- treatment and continuing care
- consultation and liaison.

Assessment

Structures

- **Multi-disciplinary/inter-agency locality-based teams:** Local circumstances will dictate the precise organisation.
- **Crisis intervention services:** These should be available during and outside office hours and should include arrangements with the criminal justice system, such as the provision of appropriate adults.

Processes

- Multi-disciplinary assessment based on comprehensive functional analysis.
- Person-centred care planning.
- Crisis intervention.
- Support for individuals to help them access generic services.
- Carer information and support.

Outcomes

- Appropriate and timely assessments.

Treatment and continuing care

Structures

- **Community follow-up:** Follow-up settings should be those most appropriate for the client.
- **Day care:** The distinction in use between health-based and day-centre care is important. Health-based day care should be provided when a clinical component is required and not simply daytime activity. This will only be needed for a very small number of PWLD.
- **Inpatient facilities:** A range of health care beds is required covering assessment, treatment and continuing care for a small number of individuals with complex disabilities, such as those with challenging behaviours who need a secure setting. Facilities should provide the least restrictive and most safe, homely and local environment for the client.

Processes

- **Case management:** The principles of key working, care planning and review should apply. This should include liaison over out-of-district placements.
- **Crisis intervention:** Identification of triggers to challenging behaviours or crisis and the development of crisis plans.
- **Psychological interventions:** At least the following types of interventions are needed, underpinned by functional analysis: group and individual therapies, cognitive/behavioural therapies, family interventions and counselling, e.g. for bereavement, families, in cases of abuse.
- **Speech and language therapy interventions.**
- **Occupational therapy interventions.**
- **Physiotherapy interventions.**
- **Pharmacological treatments.**

Outcomes

- Individualised care plans.
- Improvements and/or prevention of deterioration in symptomatology and social functioning.
- Prevention of abuse.

Consultation and liaison

Processes

- Support to primary care and other community services.
- Teaching to a spectrum of care providers.

Outcomes

- Improved access to and uptake of generic services.
- Improved understanding of the issues relating to learning disabilities in non-specialist providers.

Organisational competence

An in-depth discussion of this issue is outside the remit of this chapter. Key issues that should be considered include the following:

- the generation of a joint value base and of operational policies that are shared across agencies, e.g. on dealing with abuse
- structures and processes that encourage partnership and joint working between staff in different agencies
- teambuilding
- training, e.g. the availability of specialist skills nursing – RNLD enhanced by ENB accreditation in challenging behaviours or mental health
- the determination of clinical outcomes of care.

Client need for services

All clients will have some basic shared needs, irrespective of disability. Some of these will be met by specialist services, some by carers/families and some by other service providers. The level of disability, coexisting conditions and family circumstances are likely to dictate in which cases service provision is required in order that needs are met. A client's need for services may be for any or all of the following:

- daytime activity
- a home/accommodation
- information and support, including an income
- health and social care (*see* 'Health service provision' above).

Other needs, such as the need for relationship or respect, as outlined by O'Brien's five accomplishments, should inform all aspects of service provision.

Daytime activity

Guidance on the development of daytime activity has been published.[136]

Structures

- Day centres.
- Drop-ins.
- Employment schemes, including open employment, various types of supported employment and sheltered work schemes.
- Education ranging from pre-school programmes through formal mainstream schooling to specialist provision to adult and further education.
- Leisure activities.
- Befriending schemes.

Processes

- Social network development.
- Social skills development.
- Training and personal development.
- Meaningful/gainful employment.

Outcome

- Improvements in individuals' quality of life.

Accommodation

Whenever possible, supported independent living in ordinary homes should be the goal. Specialist accommodation and support may be needed for those with challenging behaviours, physical and sensory impairments, mental illness and ASD.

Structures

A range of accommodation is needed, including:

- day-staffed accommodation
- group homes with staff visiting daily
- group homes with staff on call
- supervised private lodgings
- own tenancies
- respite care
- specialist health care provision.

Processes

- In-home support, ranging from help with assessment and budgeting and help in carrying out activities of daily living to engaging in leisure activities.
- Home alterations for those with physical/sensory disabilities.
- Specific programmes of interventions for those with specialist needs.

Outcomes

- Individuals live in environments that are as close to ordinary homes as possible.

Information and support

These services are as important for carers and families as they are for clients.

Structures

- Advocacy services.
- Benefits advice services.
- Parenting education and support services for prospective and actual parents with learning disabilities.

Processes

- Information given in appropriate formats.

Outcomes

- Empowerment of individuals.
- Reduction in the stress of caring.
- Reduction in the levels of abuse, neglect and developmental delay in children of parents with learning disabilities.

Levels of provision

Background

Planning targets for learning disability services were set nationally in 1971.[290] The nature of service provision has changed to such an extent since this time that these norms are no longer applicable. A number of local needs assessment exercises have attempted to redefine appropriate levels of provision (*see* Table 11).[187,291]

Table 11: Estimates for local provision for adults with learning disabilities, aged > 20 years (excluding provision for mental illness, offending and challenging behaviours).

	NHS	Non-NHS
Residential care places	47/100,000	103/100,000
Day-care options, including employment		224/100,000
Respite care placements		36/100,000

Source: McGrother *et al.*[291]

Accommodation

It is important to recognise the changing need for accommodation over time both for the whole population of PWLD and for any one individual. A model that attempts to capture some of this complexity has been developed.[131] This model suggests that, over a five-year period, the following proportions of a local population of adults with learning disabilities (excluding those in hospital provision) will need new accommodation.

- **PWLD living with elderly carers:** 10% owing to carer stress/ill-health or other crisis and 10% planned move to avert crisis.
- **PWLD with younger carers:** 10% owing to carer stress or other crisis and 10% to accommodate the need for independent living.
- **PWLD in social services-run hostels:** 29%.
- **PWLD in other hostels:** 30%.
- **PWLD in nursing/residential care:** 10%.
- **PWLD living in their own tenancy:** 10%.

The relevance of the model is in thinking coherently about planning housing options. The actual percentages in the different groups may well vary in different populations.

Professional groups

A number of professional organisations have made suggestions for appropriate levels of input to local services.

- **Psychiatry:** One WTE consultant/100 000 for general learning disability services. Additional consultant input will be required for forensic and children's services.[292]
- **Psychology:** Four WTEs/250 000 are recommended for general adult learning disability services, with a B-grade consultant clinical psychologist heading the service.[293] Additional input of at least 1 WTE/ 75 000 general population will be required to work with 0–19-year-olds and their families. Similarly, a B-grade consultant child psychologist should head the service.[294]
- **Nursing:** There are no recommended levels of provision.
- **Occupational therapy/speech therapy/physiotherapy:** There are no recommended levels of provision. The perception is that many services do not have sufficient input and posts are often difficult to fill with appropriately trained staff.

Conclusions

Commissioners of services for PWLD need to recognise the range and complexity of the condition and consequently the inevitable complexity and variability of the system that will be needed to meet these needs. The level at which commissioning is carried out may well be different for discrete aspects of the condition. Individualised packages and joint funding will be needed for those with the most complex needs. Challenging behaviour and sensory impairment services may well need to be purchased at population levels larger than the average PCT in order to ensure service integrity and expertise. Prevention services and primary care can more easily be provided and commissioned for smaller population groups. The capacity for flexible, local approaches is likely to produce the most comprehensive commissioning and development of services.

8 Target setting

Introduction

The precise nature of local targets will be determined by the current nature of provision and local data collection capabilities. They should, however, be aimed at attempting to improve quality of life and reduce social exclusion. Targets should be reflected in local strategies. The targets may be set with respect to the structure, process and outcome variables discussed in Section 7.

The process of target setting may be helped by:

- local discussions between commissioning and provider managers and clinicians
- an understanding of local epidemiological data
- development of local policies and implementation plans, which include relevant time-scales and training
- review of the implementation of policies
- including local service and policy development in audit programmes.

The following subsections list areas in which local targets may be set covering the incidence of learning disabilities, the health of PWLD and the services that are provided for them.

Health promotion

Primary and secondary prevention

- Targeting of genetic counselling programmes.
- Coverage of screening programme for Down's syndrome and the rate of detection against incidence.
- Coverage of PKU and congenital hypothyroidism screening (Guthrie test).
- Birth frequency of low and very low birth weight babies, corrected for gestation.
- Reduction in the incidence of NTDs and of cerebral palsy.
- Reduction in the incidence of severe head injuries.

Physical and mental health of PWLD and their carers

- Rate of uptake of health promotion services, e.g. CVD, breast and cervical screening.
- Improvements in screening for mental ill-health.
- Reduction in levels of obesity.
- Reduction in levels of untreated hypothyroidism in people with Down's syndrome.
- Prevalence of and uptake of screening for hepatitis B and C.
- Improved rate of detection of sensory impairments.
- Reduction in mortality/morbidity associated with seizures.
- Reduction in prevalence of challenging behaviours.
- Reduction in levels of abuse.
- Reduction in the levels of prescribing of antipsychotic medication.
- Increased identification of parents with learning disabilities.
- Reduction in the levels of neglect, abuse and developmental delay in children of parents with learning disabilities.
- Increased use of facilities available to the general public, such as education, leisure and recreation.
- Reduction in the ill-health of carers.

Accommodation

- Increases in the numbers of PWLD who are in supported independent living.
- Reduction in the numbers of PWLD accommodated in long-stay hospital beds.
- Reduction in the numbers of PWLD accommodated in out-of-area placements.

Daytime activities

- Reduction in the numbers of PWLD who do not have organised daytime activities, whether employment/training/education or leisure.
- Reductions in school exclusions for children with learning disabilities.

Information and support

- Development of local information in appropriate formats.
- Increases in users' and carers' satisfaction with services provided.
- Increases in social networks.
- Improvements in the availability of respite care.
- Improved access to advocacy services.

Specialist services

- Development of expertise/specialist services for mental illness, challenging behaviours, ASD and complex disabilities, including sensory impairments.
- Staff training – increases in the proportion of staff with appropriate specific training in the management of mental ill-health and challenging behaviours in PWLD, e.g. training in de-escalation and restraint procedures and in behavioural interventions.

Commissioning

- Development of joint strategies with education, housing, specialist services, primary care and relevant acute services.
- Development of joint budgets.
- Development of direct payment schemes.
- Development and maintenance of local inter-agency registers of PWLD.
- Development of standards and the systematic collection of information with which to monitor services.
- Increased involvement of users and carers in the planning and evaluation of services.

For further discussion on target setting, *see* the All Wales Health Gain Protocol.[2]

9 Information and research requirements

Data sources

Routine data sources are limited in their usefulness. The extent to which data can be disaggregated to client group or further to severity is very variable. Furthermore, information on a large number of services necessary for rounded provision is unavailable, e.g. employment or leisure services.

This section indicates routine sources which may be helpful.

Health service

Development of a learning disabilities minimum data set is ongoing.

National data sets

- Bed numbers: no categorisation other than long/short-stay and secure.
- Completed consultant episodes: of limited use, as there are shifts away from inpatient care and lengths of stay are very variable.
- Community nurse contacts.

Local data

Some information may be available from primary care and nursing homes registers.

Social services

National

- Residential and nursing home places where they are designated for PWLD.
- Day-care places.
- Home help/home care usage.

Local

- **Registers:** About 60 local authorities hold registers. They are very variable in quality, with no standardised format, and only count those in contact with services. Their accuracy is dependent on notification, which is often incomplete. Where they are well kept they provide extremely helpful information. There is no central collation of information from registers.

The OPCS Disability Survey

This provides some useful information on activities of daily living and services. There are, however, criticisms of the criteria used to determine type and level of disability. The last survey was carried out in the mid-1980s. This also limits its usefulness, given the significant shifts in provision since that time.

Education

National

The Education Act 1981 abolished existing specific categories of handicap in favour of emphasis upon special educational need, which therefore covers learning disabilities, sensory impairments and emotional and behavioural problems. As a result, national data may not be very helpful, as learning disabilities cannot be identified as a separate group.

Local

- Numbers of children with statements of special educational need.
- School exclusion data.
- Placements in special schools.
- Home tuition numbers.
- Pre-school programmes.
- 14+ transition plans.

Research

This chapter highlights the paucity of research into many aspects of learning disabilities. An extensive research programme is required, ranging from the aetiology of learning disabilities to the effectiveness of service interventions. Some broad categories of research are outlined here.

Aetiology

- Exploration of the links between prenatal damage and birth trauma.
- Causation of mild learning disabilities.

Primary care

- Increased knowledge about health promotion activities in general, including evaluation of models to increase uptake.
- Appropriateness and effectiveness of screening programmes, e.g. cervical and cardiovascular screening.

Accommodation

- Effectiveness of home-based care packages.
- Cost–benefits of residential care options, including village communities.

Daytime activities

- Cost–benefits of the provision of various options from leisure to education and employment.
- Evaluation of techniques to maintain employment for PWLD.

Information and support

- Evaluation of different types of respite, their costs and their impact on carer and client well-being.
- Further development of specific, user-friendly quality-of-life measures.

- Use of the general population as a comparator in quality-of-life/satisfaction studies.
- Evaluation of methodologies to include user/carer views in service planning and evaluation.
- Evaluation of policies to increase community participation/social inclusion.

Service models and interventions

- Improved knowledge of the relative cost-effectiveness of different service models.
- Improved knowledge of the effectiveness of early interventions.
- Improved knowledge of the relative benefits of models of provision, such as specialist services for sensory impairment and challenging behaviours, including forensic care.
- Long-term outcomes for behavioural treatments for challenging behaviours.
- Impact of other psychotherapeutic interventions.
- Effectiveness of interventions, particularly early intervention, and of care environments for people with ASD.
- Effectiveness of the therapies (occupational, physiotherapy and speech and language therapies) in the learning-disabled population.
- A greater understanding of the usefulness of/indications for antipsychotic medication.

Appendix I: Health and social care for PWLD

It is generally agreed that health and social care needs cannot be easily separated. At a pragmatic level it may be possible to describe an individual's needs in three ways:

- universal
- additional
- special.

For PWLD these categories can be further described as follows:

- universal, e.g. a place to live, financial security, friendships, the opportunity to have a meaningful day
- additional needs arising from learning disability, e.g. help with mobility, help to access services, help to understand information, help with communication
- special needs, e.g. support in crisis situations, treatment to improve mental health or to help to reduce challenging behaviours.

For any one of these needs, the level of support required may vary. An individual may need limited, intermittent or extensive support.

- **Limited support:** This may be of high or low intensity and complexity. It is time-limited or limited by some other resource constraint and is typically applied at transitional periods.
- **Intermittent support:** This may be of high or low intensity and complexity. It is characterised by its ongoing nature and is applied for a specific purpose or to provide general support for an individual on an as-needed basis. It may also be required to support someone in a specific setting.
- **Extensive support:** This is characterised by its intensity, complexity and consistency across different settings.

A matrix can be devised from these categories. This can help to delineate where responsibilities may lie for carrying out health and social care functions rather than indicating whether these functions should take place in a health or social care setting.

Type of support	Type of need		
	Universal	Additional	Special
Limited	Social care	Social/health care	Social/health care
Intermittent	Social care	Social/health care	Health care
Extensive	Social/health care	Social/health care	Health care

Source: Adapted from Turnbull J and Cullen C. *A Report for Bromley Health Authority* 1998.

It is therefore the case that either health or social care agencies, or both, may meet many of the needs of PWLD.

References

1 Farmer R, Rhode J, Sacks B. *Dimensions of Mental Handicap: a study of people with mental handicaps in the North West Thames Region.* London: Charing Cross and Westminster Medical School, 1991.

2 Welsh Health Planning Forum. *Protocol for Investment in Health Gain: mental handicap (learning disabilities).* Cardiff: Welsh Office, 1992.

3 Department of Health. *Services for People with Learning Disabilities.* London: Department of Health, 1992.

4 Department of Health. *Social Care for Adults with Learning Disabilities.* London: Department of Health, 1992.

5 Department of Health. *NHS Responsibility for Meeting Continuing Health Care.* London: Department of Health, 1995.

6 Nocoon A. *Collaboration in Community Care in the 1990s.* Sunderland: Business Education Publishers, 1994.

7 Turnbull J. Learning disability nursing: a position paper. *J Learn Disabil Nurs Health Soc Care* 1997; **4**: 186–90.

8 Department of Health. *Facing the Facts. Services for people with learning disabilities: a policy impact study of health and social care services.* London: Department of Health, 1999.

9 Macadam M, Rodgers J. *Accounting for Care? The impact of GP fundholding on specialist secondary health care for adults with learning disability.* Bristol: Norah Fry Research Centre, University of Bristol, 1997.

10 Lindsey M. *Signposts for Success in Commissioning and Providing Health Services for People with Learning Disabilities.* London: NHS Executive, 1998.

11 Lindsey M, Russell O. *Once a Day.* London: NHS Executive, 1999.

12 Fryers T. Impairment, disability and handicap categories and classifications. In: Russell O (ed.). *Seminars in the Psychiatry of Learning Disabilities.* London: Gaskell, 1997.

13 World Health Organization. *The ICD-10 Classification of Mental and Behavioural Disorders. Clinical descriptions and diagnostic guidelines.* Geneva: World Health Organization, 1992.

14 American Psychiatric Association. *Diagnostic and Statistical Manual of Psychiatric Disorder* (4e). (DSM-IV). Washington, DC: American Psychiatric Association, 1994.

15 American Association on Mental Retardation. *Mental Retardation: definition, classification and systems of support.* Washington, DC: American Association on Mental Retardation, 1992.

16 Department of Health. *Reforming the Mental Health Act Part 1. The new legal framework.* London: The Stationery Office, 2000.

17 Fryers T. Public health approaches to mental retardation: handicap related to intellectual impairment. In: Holland WW, Detels R, Knox G (eds). *Oxford Textbook of Public Health Medicine.* Oxford: Oxford Medical Publications, 1997.

18 Alberman E, Nicholson A, Wald K. *Severe Learning Disability in Young Children: likely future trends.* London: Wolfson Institute of Preventative Medicine, 1992.

19 Muir W. Genetic advances and learning disabilities *Br J Psychiatry* 2000; **176**: 12–19.

20 MacLennan A for the International Cerebral Palsy Task Force. A template for defining a causal relation between acute intra-partum events and cerebral palsy: international consensus statement. *BMJ* 1999; **319**: 1054–9.

21 Melvin D. *Developmental Outcomes for Children with Vertically Acquired HIV.* Oxford: British HIV Association Meeting, 1998 (poster).

22 Albeman E (ed.). EUROMAC: maternal alcohol consumption and its relation to the outcome of pregnancy and child development at eighteen months. *Int J Epidemiol* 1992; **21**(Suppl. 1): 1–87.

23 Forest F, Florey C du V. The relationship between maternal alcohol consumption and child development: the epidemiological evidence. *J Public Health Med* 1992: **13**; 247–55.

24 Hatton C. Intellectual disability: epidemiology and causes. In: Emerson E, Hatton C, Bromley J, Carnie A (eds). *Clinical Psychology and People with Intellectual Disability*. Chichester: John Wiley & Sons, 1998.

25 Roeleveld N, Zielhuis GA, Gabreels F. The prevalence of mental retardation: a critical review of recent literature. *Dev Med Child Neurol* 1997; **39**(2): 125–32.

26 McGrother C, Thorp C, Taub N, Machado O. Prevalence, disability and need in adults with severe learning disabilities. *Tizard Learn Disabil Rev* 2001; **6**: 4–13.

27 Hollins S, Attard MT, von Fraunhofer N. Mortality in learning disability: risks, causes, and death certification findings in London. *Dev Med Child Neurol* 1998; **40**: 50–6.

28 Molsai PK. Survival in mental retardation. *Ment Handicap Res* 1994; **7**: 338–45.

29 Evans PM, Alberman E. Certified causes of death in children and young adults with cerebral palsy. *Arch Dis Child* 1990; **65**: 325–9.

30 Eyman RK, Batmick Duffy SA, Call TL, White JF. Prediction of mortality in community and institutional settings. *J Ment Defic Res* 1987; **32**: 203–13.

31 Jeffris BJMH, Power C, Hertzman C. Birth weight, childhood socio-economic environment, and cognitive development in the 1958 British birth cohort study. *BMJ* 2002; **325**: 305–8.

32 Emerson E, Azmi S, Hatton C *et al.* Is there an increased prevalence of severe learning disability amongst British Asians? *Ethnic Health* 1997; **2**(4): 317–21.

33 Russell O, Stanley M. *A Literature Review of Local Variation in the Needs of People with Learning Disabilities for Health Service Input*. Bristol: Norah Fry Research Centre, University of Bristol, 1996.

34 Morgan C, Ahmed Z, Kerr MP. Health care provision for people with a learning disability. *Br J Psychiatry* 2000; **176**: 37–41.

35 Nicholson A, Albeman E. Prediction of the number of Down's syndrome infants to be born in England and Wales up to the year 2000 and their likely survival rates. *J Intellect Disabil Res* 1992; **36**: 505–17.

36 Huang T, Watt HC, Wald NJ *et al.* Birth prevalence of Down's syndrome in England and Wales 1990 to 1997. *J Med Screen* 1998; **5**: 213–14.

37 Turner S, Moss C. The health needs of adults with learning disabilities and the Health of the Nation strategy. *J Intellect Disabil Res* 1996; **40**: 438–50.

38 Griffiths J, Boyle S. People with learning disabilities. In: *Colour Guide to Holistic Oral Care: a practical approach*. Aylesbury: Mosby, 1993.

39 Colacott R, Cooper S, Branford D, McGrother C. Behaviour phenotype for Down's syndrome. *Br J Psychiatry* 1998; **172**: 85–9.

40 Turner G, Webb D, Wake S, Robinson H. Prevalence of the fragile X syndrome. *Am J Med Genet* 1996; **64**: 196–7.

41 Murray A, Young SS, Dennis N *et al.* Population screening at the FRAXA and FRAXE loci: molecular analysis of boys with learning disabilities and their mothers. *Hum Mol Genet* 1996; **5**: 727–35.

42 Murray J, Cuckle H, Taylor G, Hewison J. Screening for fragile X syndrome. *Health Technol Assess* 1997; **1**(4): 1–71.

43 Sherman S. Epidemiology. In: Hagerman RJ, Cronister MS (eds). *Fragile X Syndrome: diagnosis, treatment and research*. Baltimore, MD: Johns Hopkins University Press, 1996.

44 Plomin R, Defries JC, McClearn GE, Rutter M. Cognitive disabilities. In: *Behavioural Genetics* (3e). Basingstoke: WH Freeman and Company, 1997.

45 Bird J. Epilepsy and learning disabilities. In: Russell O (ed.). *Seminars in the Psychiatry of Learning Disabilities*. London: Gaskell, 1993.

46 Deb S. Mental disorder in adults with mental retardation and epilepsy. *Compr Psychiatry* 1997; **38**: 179–84.

47 Bakketeig LS. Only a minor part of cerebral palsy cases begin in labour (editorial). *BMJ* 1999; **319**: 1017.

48 Pharoah PO, Cooke T, Johnson MA, King R, Mutch L. Epidemiology of cerebral palsy in England and Scotland, 1984–9. *Arch Dis Child Fetal Neonatal Ed* 1998; **78**: 21–5.

49 Kadir RA, Sabin C, Whitlow B, Brockbank E, Economidies D. Neural tube defects and periconceptual folic acid in England and Wales: a retrospective study. *BMJ* 1999; **319**: 92–3.

50 Einfeld SL, Aman M. Issues in the taxonomy of psychopathology in mental retardation. *J Autism Dev Disord* 1995; **18**: 99–117.

51 Rutter M, Tizarel J, Whitmore K. *Education, Health and Behaviour*. London: Longman, 1970.

52 Gilberg C, Persson E, Grufman M. Psychiatric disorders in mildly and severely retarded urban children and adolescents: epidemiological aspects. *Br J Psychiatry* 1986; **149**: 68–74.

53 Corbett JA. Mental retardation: psychiatric aspects. In: Rutter M, Hersov L (eds). *Child and Adolescent Psychiatry* (2e). Oxford: Blackwell, 1985.

54 Campbell MB, Malone RP. Mental retardation and psychiatric disorders. *Hosp Community Psychiatry* 1991; **42**: 374–9.

55 Lund J. The prevalence of psychiatric morbidity in mentally retarded adults. *Acta Psychiatr Scand* 1985; **72**: 563–70.

56 Moss S, Emerson E, Bouras N, Holland A. Mental disorders and problematic behaviours in people with intellectual disability: future directions for research. *J Intellect Disabil Res* 1997; **41**(6): 440–7.

57 Harper DC, Wadsworth J. Depression and dementia in elders with mental retardation. *Res Dev Disord* 1990; **11**: 177–98.

58 Day KA. Psychiatric disease in middle-aged and elderly mentally handicapped. *Br J Psychiatry* 1985; **147**: 660–70.

59 Collacott RA, Cooper SA, McGrother C. Differential rates of psychiatric disorder in adults with Down's syndrome compared to other mentally handicapped adults. *Br J Psychiatry* 1992; **161**: 671–4.

60 Reid AH. Psychiatry and learning disabilities. *Br J Psychiatry* 1994; **164**: 613–18.

61 Hollins S, Esterhuyzen A. Bereavement and grief in adults with learning disabilities. *Br J Psychiatry* 1997; **170**: 497–501.

62 Cooper SA. Epidemiology of psychiatric disorder in elderly compared to younger adults with learning disabilities. *Br J Psychiatry* 1997; **170**: 375–80.

63 Oliver C. Four-year prospective study of age-related cognitive changes in adults with Down's syndrome. *Psychol Med* 1998; **28**: 1365–77.

64 Patel P, Goldberg DP, Moss SC. Psychiatric morbidity in older people with moderate and severe learning disability (mental retardation). Part 11. The prevalence study. *Br J Psychiatry* 1993; **163**: 481–91.

65 Emerson E. Introduction. In: *Challenging Behaviour. Analysis in people with learning disability*. Cambridge: Cambridge University Press, 1995.

66 Cullen C, Brown F, Combes H, Hendy S. Working with people who have intellectual impairments. In: Marzillier J, Hall J (eds). *What is Clinical Psychology?* (3e). Oxford: Oxford University Press, 1999.

67 Berney TP. Born to . . . genetics and behaviour. *Br J Learn Disabil* 1998; **26**: 4–8.

68 Saxby H, Morgan H. Behavioural problems in children with learning disability: to what extent do they exist and are they a problem? *Child Care Health Dev* 1993; **19**: 149–57.

69 Einfeld SL, Tonge BJ. Population prevalence of psychopathology in children and adolescents with intellectual disability. II. Epidemiological findings. *J Intellect Disabil Res* 1996; **40**: 99–109.

70 Mansel JL. *Services for People with Learning Disability and Challenging Behaviour or Mental Health Needs: report of a project group*. London: HMSO, 1993.

71 Collacott RA, Cooper SA, Branford D, McGrother C. Epidemiology of self-injurious behaviour in adults with learning disabilities. *Br J Psychiatry* 1998; **173**: 428–32.

72 Quereshi H, Alborz A. The epidemiology of challenging behaviour. *Ment Handicap Res* 1992; **5**: 130–45.

73 Emerson E, Kiernan C, Alborz A *et al. The HARC Challenging Behaviour Project: summary report.* Manchester: Hester Adrian Research Centre, Manchester University, 1998.

74 Lund J. Mentally disordered criminal offenders in Denmark. *Br J Psychiatry* 1990; **156**: 726–31.

75 Singleton N, Meltzer H, Gatwood R. *Psychiatric Morbidity Among Prisoners.* London: HMSO/Office of National Statistics, 1998.

76 Holland T, Murphy G. Behavioural and psychiatric disorder in adults with mild learning difficulties. *Int Rev Psychiatry* 1990; **2**: 117–36.

77 Bernal J, Hollins S. Psychiatric illness and learning disability: a dual diagnosis. *Adv Psychiatr Treat* 1995; **1**: 138–45.

78 Lyall I, Holland T, Collins S, Styles P. Incidence of persons with a learning disability and detained in police custody: a needs assessment service development. *Med Sci Law* 1995; **38**: 61–71.

79 Gudjonsson GH, Clare ICH, Rutter S, Pearce J. *Persons at Risk During Interviews in Police Custody: the identification of vulnerabilities.* Royal Commission on Criminal Justice, Research Study No 12. London: HMSO, 1993.

80 Wing L. *The Autistic Spectrum.* London: Constable, 1996.

81 Wing L. *Aspects of Autism: biological research.* London: Gaskell/National Autistic Society, 1988.

82 Wing L, Gould J. Severe impairments of social interaction and associated abnormalities in children: epidemiology and classification. *J Autism Childhood Schizophr* 1979; **9**: 11–29.

83 Ehlers S, Gilberg C. The epidemiology of Asperger's syndrome. A total population study. *J Child Psychol Psychiatry* 1993; **34**: 1327–50.

84 Wing L. The definition and prevalence of autism; a review. *Eur Child Adolesc Psychiatry* 1993; **2**: 61–74.

85 Hare JL. *A Preliminary Study of People with Autistic Conditions in three Special Hospitals in England.* London: National Autistic Society, 1998.

86 Royal College of General Practitioners. *Primary Care for People with a Mental Handicap* (OP47). London: Royal College of General Practitioners, 1990.

87 Warburg M. Visual impairment among people with developmental delay. *J Intellect Disabil Res* 1994; **38**: 423–32.

88 Yates S. Have they got hearing loss? *Ment Handicap* 1992; **20**: 126–33.

89 Kavanagh S, Opit L. *The Cost of Caring: the economics of providing for the intellectually disabled.* London: Politeia, 1998.

90 Bell A, Bhate M. Prevalence of overweight and obesity in Down's syndrome and other mentally handicapped adults living in the community. *J Intellect Disabil Res* 1992; **36**: 359–64.

91 Beange H, McEldutt A, Baker W. Medical disorders of adults with mental retardation: a population study. *Aust J Ment Retard* 1995; **99**: 595–604.

92 Devuyst O, Maesen-Collard Y. Hepatitis B in a Belgian institution for mentally retarded patients: an epidemiological study. *Acta Gastroenterol* 1991; **54**: 12–18.

93 Nunn JH. The dental health of mentally and physically handicapped children: a review of the literature. *Community Dent Health* 1987; **4**: 157–68.

94 Gabre P, Gahnberg L. Inter-relationship among degree of mental retardation, living arrangement and dental health in adults with mental retardation. *Special Dent Care* 1997; **17**(1): 7–12.

95 Thomson GO, Ward KM. The transition to adulthood for children with Down's syndrome. *Disabil Society* 1995; **10**(3): 325–40.

96 Ryan T. *Making Our Own Way? Transition from school to adulthood in the lives of people who have learning disabilities.* London: Values into Action, 1992.

97 Hart SL. Meaningful choices: consent to treatment in general health care settings for people with learning disabilities. *J Learn Dis Nurs Health Soc Care* 1999; **3**(1): 20–6.

98 Turner NJ, Brown AR, Baxter KF. Consent to treatment and the mentally incapacitated adult. *J R Soc Med* 1999; **92**(6): 290–2.

99 Department of Health. *L v Bournewood Community and Mental Health NHS Trust: decision by the House of Lords HSC 1998/122.* London: Department of Health, 1998.

100 McGaw S. Practical support for parents with learning disabilities. In: O'Hara J, Sperlinger A (eds). *Adults with Learning Disabilities.* Chichester: John Wiley & Sons Ltd, 1997.

101 Levy SR, Perhats C, Nash-Johnson M, Welter JF. Reducing the risks in pregnant teens and those with mild mental retardation. *Ment Retard* 1992; **30**(4): 195–203.

102 Taylor G, Pearson J, Cook H. Family planning for women with learning disability. *Nurs Times* 1998; **94**: 60–1.

103 Ager J, Littler J. Sexual health for people with learning disabilities. *Nurs Standard* 1998; **13**(2): 34–9.

104 Sobsey D, Gray S, Wells D. *Disability and Abuse: an annotated bibliography.* Baltimore, MD: Paul H Brookes, 1991.

105 Brown H, Stein J, Turk V. The sexual abuse of adults with learning disabilities: report of a second two-year incidence survey. *Ment Handicap Res* 1995; **8**(No 1).

106 Williams C. *Invisible Victims: crime and abuse about people with learning disability.* London: Jessica Kingsley Publishers, 1996.

107 Health Evidence Bulletins – Wales. *Learning Disabilities: carers and caring.* National Electronic Library for Health: learning disabilities, 2000.

108 Hall S, Bobrow M, Martineau TM. Psychological consequences for parents of false-negative results on prenatal screening for Down's syndrome: retrospective interview study. *BMJ* 2000; **320**: 407–12.

109 Parsons L, Richards J, Garlick R. Screening for Down's syndrome. *BMJ* 1992; **305**: 1228.

110 Dobson B, Middleton S. *Paying to Care: the cost of childhood disability.* York: Joseph Rowntree Foundation/YPS, 1998.

111 Department of Health. *The Health of the Nation: a strategy for people with learning disability.* Wetherby: Department of Health, 1995.

112 Piachaud J, Rhodes J. Screening for breast cancer is necessary in patients with learning disability (letter). *BMJ* 1998; **316**: 1979–80.

113 Costello H, Moss SC, Prosser H, Hatton C. Reliability of the ICD-10 version of the Psychiatric Assessment Schedule for Adults with Developmental Disability (PAS-ADD). *Soc Psychiatry Psychiatr Epidemiol* 1997; **32**: 339–43.

114 Howells G. Are the needs of mentally handicapped adults being met? *J R Coll Gen Pract* 1986; **36**: 449–53.

115 Wilson DN, Haire A. Health screening for people with mental handicap living in the community. *BMJ* 1990; **301**: 1379–81.

116 Langan J, Russell O, Whitfield M. *Community Care and the GP: primary health care for people with learning disability.* Bristol: Norah Fry Research Centre, University of Bristol, 1993.

117 Kerr M, Dustan F, Thaper A. Attitudes of general practitioners to caring for people with learning disability. *Br J Gen Pract* 1996; **46**: 92–4.

118 Flynn M, Howard J, Pursey H. *GP Fundholding and Health Care of People with Learning Disability.* Manchester: National Development Team, 1996.

119 Langan J, Russell O. Assessing GP care of patients with learning disability: case-control study. *Qual Health Care* 1996; **5**: 31–5.

120 Kerr MP, Richards D, Glover G. Primary care for people with a learning disability – a group practice survey. *J Appl Res Intellect Disabil* 1996; **9**(4): 347–52.

121 Chambers R, Milsom G, Evans N, Lucking A, Campbell I. The primary care workload and prescribing costs associated with patients with learning disability discharged from long-stay care into the community. *Br J Learn Dis* 1998; **26**: 9–12.

122 Hassiotis A, Ukoumunne O, Tyrer P *et al*. Prevalence and characteristics of patients with severe mental illness and borderline intellectual function. *Br J Psychiatry* 1999; **175**: 135–40.

123 Government Statistical Service. *Health and Personal Social Services Statistics for England*. London: The Stationery Office, 1999.

124 Bailey NM, Cooper SA. The current provision of specialist health services to people with learning disabilities in England and Wales. *J Intellect Disabil Res* 1997; **41**: 152–9.

125 Harris J. *Hurtling into the Void: transition to adulthood for young disabled people with complex health and support needs*. Brighton: Pavilion Publishing/Joseph Rowntree Foundation, 1999.

126 Brown S, Flynn M, Wister G. *Back to the Future. Joint work for people with learning disabilities*. Manchester: National Development Team/Nuffield Institute for Health Service Development, 1992.

127 London Regional Office, NHSE/SSI. *London Learning Disabilities Strategic Framework: initial findings*. London: NHS Executive/SSI, 1999.

128 Grieg R, Peck E. Is there a future for the community learning disabilities team? *Tizard Learn Disabil Rev* 1998; **3**(1).

129 Fitzgerald J. *Time for Freedom? Services for older people with learning difficulties*. London: Values into Action/Centre for Policy Ageing, 1997.

130 Emerson E, Hatton C. *Residential Provision for People with Learning Disabilities: an analysis of the 1991 Census*. Manchester: Hester Adrian Research Centre, University of Manchester, 1998.

131 Watson L. *Housing Need and Community Care: the Housing Pathways Programme*. London: National Federation of Housing Associations and Chartered Institute of Housing, 1996.

132 Joseph Rowntree Foundation. *Housing Support Needs for People with Learning Disabilities: a local authority development programme*. York: Joseph Rowntree Foundation, 1999.

133 Farmer R, Rhode J, Sacks B. *Changing Services for People with Learning Disabilities*. London: Chapman and Hall, 1993.

134 Mental Health Foundation. *Learning Disabilities: the fundamental facts*. London: Mental Health Foundation, 1993.

135 NHS Estates. *Design Guide: day service for people with severe learning disability*. London: HMSO, 1993.

136 McIntosh B, Whittaker A (eds). *Days of Change: a practical guide to developing better day opportunities for people with learning difficulties*. London: King's Fund/National Development Team, 1998.

137 Beyers S, Goodener L, Kilsby M. *The Costs and Benefits of Supported Employment Agencies*. London: HMSO, 1997.

138 Beyers S, Kilsby M. Supported employment in Britain. *Tizard Learn Disabil Rev* 1997; **2**: 6–14.

139 Lister T, Ellis L. *Survey of Supported Employment Services in England, Wales and Scotland*. Manchester: National Development Team, 1992.

140 Pozner A, Hammond J. *An Evaluation of Supported Employment Initiatives for Disabled People*. Sheffield: Employment Department Research Services Series No 1, 1993.

141 Honey S, Williams M. *Supply and Demand for Supported Employment. Research Report 70*. London: Department for Education and Employment, 1998.

142 Department for Education/Welsh Office. *Code of Practice on the Identification and Assessment of Special Educational Needs*. London: HMSO, 1994.

143 Department for Education and Employment. *Excellence For All Children: meeting special educational needs*. London: The Stationery Office, 1997.

144 Macadam M, Sutcliffe J. *Still a Chance to Learn.* Leicester: National Institute of Adult Continuing Education, 1996.

145 Shorvon SD. Medical services. In: Laidlaw J, Richens A, Oxley J (eds). *A Textbook of Epilepsy.* Edinburgh: Churchill Livingstone, 1998.

146 Pinn S. Share care to manage epilepsy. *Med Interface* 1996; 29–30.

147 Hassiotis A, Barron P, O'Hara J. Mental health services for people with learning disabilities (editorial). *BMJ* 2000; **321**: 583–4.

148 Royal College of Psychiatrists. *Psychiatric Services for Children and Adolescents with a Learning Disability.* London: Royal College of Psychiatrists, 1999.

149 Singh I, Khalid MI, Dickinson MJ. Psychiatric advice services for people with learning disabilities. *Psychiatr Bull* 1994; **18**: 151–2.

150 Jordan R, Jones G, Murray D. *Educational Interventions for Children with Autism: a literature review of recent and current research. Research Report 77.* London: Department for Education and Employment/University of Birmingham, 1998.

151 Crawley B. *The Growing Voice: a survey of self-advocacy groups in adult training centres and hospitals in Britain.* London: Values into Action, 1988.

152 Whittell B, Rancharan P. The All Wales strategy, self-advocacy and participation. *Br J Learn Disord* 1998; **26**: 23–6.

153 McGaw S. Services for parents with intellectual disabilities. *Tizard Intellect Disabil Rev* 1996; **1**(1): 21–31.

154 Prewitt B. *Short-Term Break, Long-Term Benefit. Using family-based short-term breaks for disabled children and adults.* York: Joseph Rowntree Foundation, 1999.

155 Beckford V, Robinson C. *Consolidation or Change? A second survey of family-based respite care services in the UK.* Bristol: Norah Fry Research Centre, University of Bristol, 1993.

156 Orlk C, Robinson C, Russell O. *A Survey of Family-Based Respite Schemes in the UK.* Bristol: Norah Fry Research Centre, University of Bristol, 1991.

157 House of Commons. *Public Expenditure on Health and Personal Social Services.* London: House of Commons Health Committee, 1997.

158 Mental Health Foundation. *Building Expectations: opportunities and services for people with a learning disability.* London: Mental Health Foundation, 1996.

159 Peacock S, Smith P. *The Resource Allocation Consequences of the New NHS Needs Formula.* York: Centre for Health Economics, University of York, 1995.

160 Pendaries C. *The Maidstone Pilot Study on the Development of Learning Disability Health Benefit Groups.* Leeds: NHS Executive/National Casemix Office, 1997.

161 Hatton C, Emerson E. *Residential Provision for People with Learning Disabilities: a research review.* Manchester: Hester Adrian Research Centre, University of Manchester, 1996.

162 O'Brien J. A guide to lifestyles planning: using the activities catalogue to integrate services and natural support systems. In: Wilcox BW, Bellamy GT (eds). *The Activities Catalogue: alternative curriculum for youths and adults with severe disabilities.* Baltimore, MD: Brooks, 1987.

163 King's Fund. *An Ordinary Life. Project Paper 24.* London: King's Fund Centre, 1980.

164 Nocoon A, Quereshi H. *Outcomes of Community Care for Users and Carers: a social services perspective.* Buckingham, PA: Oxford University Press, 1996.

165 Mackay G, Somerville W, Lundie J. Reflections on GAS: cautionary notes and proposals for development. *Educ Res* 1996; **38**: 161–72.

166 HoNOS-LD. Enquiries: Dr Helen Matthews, Pembrokeshire and Derwen NHS Trust, Learning Disabilities Services, St David's Hospital, Carmarthen, SA31 3HB. Tel: 01267 237 481.

167 Xenitidis K. CANDID. *Br J Psychiatry* 2000; **176**: 473–8.

168 Turner G, Robinson H, Wake S *et al*. Case finding for the fragile X syndrome and its consequences. *BMJ* 1997; **315**: 1223–6.

169 Kramer MS. Nutritional advice in pregnancy (Cochrane Review). In: *The Cochrane Library. Issue 1.* Oxford: Update Software, 2000.

170 Lumley J, Watson L, Watson M, Bower C. Periconceptual supplementation with folate and/or multivitamins for preventing neural-tube defects (Cochrane Review). In: *The Cochrane Library. Issue 1.* Oxford: Update Software, 2000.

171 Alberman E, Noble JM. Commentary: food should be fortified with folic acid. *BMJ* 1999; **319**: 93.

172 Tong S, Baghurst P, McMichael A. Life-time exposure to environmental lead and children's intelligence at 11–13: the Port Pirie cohort study. *BMJ* 1996; **312**: 1569–75.

173 Gottlieb S. Sustained fall in blood lead levels reported. *BMJ* 1998; **317**: 99.

174 Welch J. Antenatal screening for syphilis (editorial). *BMJ* 1998; **317**: 1605–6.

175 Wald NJ, Huttly WJ, Hennessey CF. Down's syndrome screening in the UK in 1998. *Lancet* 1999; **354**: 1264.

176 Harris R, Lane B, Harris H *et al*. National confidential enquiry into counselling for genetic disorders by non-geneticists: general recommendations and specific standards for improving care. *Br J Obstet Gynaecol* 1999; **106**: 658–63.

177 Wald N, Kennard A, Hacksaw A, McGuire A. Antenatal screening for Down's syndrome. *Health Technol Assess* 1998; **2**.

178 Wald NJ, Kennard A, Hackshaw A, McGuire A. Antenatal screening for Down's syndrome. *J Med Screen* 1997; **4**: 181–246.

179 Howe DT, Girnall R, Wellesley D *et al*. Six-year survey of screening for Down's syndrome by maternal age and mid-trimester ultrasound scans. *BMJ* 2000; **320**: 606–10.

180 Pollitt RJ, Green A, McCabe CJ *et al*. Neonatal screening for inborn errors of metabolism: cost, yield and outcome. *Health Technol Assess* 1997; **1**(7): 1–202.

181 Seymour CA, Thomason MJ, Chalmers RA *et al*. Neonatal screening for inborn errors of metabolism: a systematic review. *Health Technol Assess* 1997; **1**(11): 1–95.

182 Martin DM. A comparative review of primary health care models for people with learning disabilities: towards the provision of seamless health care. *Br J Learn Disord* 1999; **27**: 58–63.

183 Martin DM, Roy A, Wells MB. Health gain through health checks: improving access to primary health care for people with learning disability. *J Intellect Disabil Res* 1997; **41**(5): 401–8.

184 Cook H. Primary health care for people with learning disabilities. *Nurs Times* 1998; **94**(30): 54–5.

185 Bowsher J, Boyle S, Griffiths J. *A Review of the Research Evidence for Oral Care Procedures Utilised by Nurses.* Cardiff: University Dental Hospital, 1999.

186 Fiske J, Griffiths J, Jamieson R, Manger D. *Guidelines for Oral Health Care for Long-Stay Patients and Residents.* London: British Society for Disability and Oral Health, 2000.

187 Russell O, Simons K, Laurol J, Foster K. *Quantifying the Needs and Looking Towards the Future: a survey of health and social care needs of people with learning disability living in Bristol and District.* Bristol: Norah Fry Research Centre, University of Bristol, 1996.

188 Cambridge P. Building care management competence in services for people with learning disabilities. *Br J Soc Work* 1999; **29**: 403–15.

189 Department of Health/SSI. *Moving into the Mainstream. The report of the National Inspection of Services for People with Learning Disabilities.* London: Department of Health, 1998.

190 SSI/Department of Health. *Services to Disabled Children and their Families.* London: HMSO, 1994.

191 Band R. *The NHS: health for all?* London: MENCAP, 1998.

192 Council for Disabled Children. *Quality Protects: first analysis of management action plans with reference to disabled children and their families.* London: Department of Health, 1999.

193 Guarlnick M (ed.). *The Effectiveness of Early Intervention.* Baltimore, MD: Brooks, 1997.

194 Clarke D. Towards the rational prescribing of psychotropic drugs for people with learning disability. *Br J Learn Disord* 1997; **25**(2): 46–52.

195 Linaker OM. Frequency and determinants for psychotropic drug use in an institution for the mentally retarded. *Br J Psychiatry* 1990; **156**: 525–30.

196 Kiernan C, Reeves D, Alborz A. The use of anti-psychotic drugs with adults with learning disabilities and challenging behaviour. *J Intellect Disabil Res* 1995; **39**: 263–74.

197 Riess S, Aman MG. *Psychotropic Medication and Developmental Disabilities: the International Consensus Handbook.* Columbus, OH: Ohio State University, 1998.

198 Hollins S, Sinason V. Psychotherapy, learning disabilities and trauma: new perspectives. *Br J Psychiatry* 2000; **176**: 32–6.

199 Remington B. Applied behaviour analysis and intellectual disability: a long-term relationship? *J Intellect Dev Disord* 1998; **23**(2): 121–35.

200 Lindsey WR, Walker B. *Curr Opin Psychiatry* 1999; **12**: 561–5.

201 Lindsay WR. Cognitive therapy. *Psychologist* 1999; **12**(5): 238–41.

202 McCaughey RE, Jones RSP. The effectiveness of gentle teaching. *Ment Handicap* 1992; **20**: 7–14.

203 Cullen C, Mappin R. An examination of gentle teaching of people with complex learning disability and challenging behaviour. *Br J Clin Psychol* 1998; **37**: 199–212.

204 Mountain G. *Occupational Therapy for People with Learning Disabilities Living in the Community: a review of the literature.* London: Royal College of Occupational Therapists, 1997.

205 Melton J. How do clients with learning disabilities evaluate their experience of cooking with the occupational therapist? *Br J Occup Ther* 1998; **61**: 106–9.

206 Watson J, Knight C. An evaluation of intensive interactive teaching with pupils with very severe learning disabilities. *Child Language Teach Ther* 1991; **7**: 310–25.

207 Ezell HK, Goldstein H. Observational learning of comprehension monitoring skills in children who exhibit mental retardation. *J Speech Hear Res* 1991; **34**: 141–54.

208 Yoder PJ, Kaiser AP, Alpert C. An exploratory study of the interaction between language teaching methods and child characteristics. *J Speech Hear Res* 1991; **34**: 155–67.

209 Tannock R, Girolametto L, Siegal L. Are the social-communicative and linguistic skills of developmentally delayed children enhanced by a conversational model of language intervention? In: Oswald LB, Thompson CK, Warren SF, Mingetti NG (eds). *Treatment Efficacy Research in Communication Disorders.* Rockville, MD: American Speech and Language Foundation, 1990.

210 Szempruch J, Jacobson JW. Evaluating facilitated communications of people with developmental disabilities. *Res Dev Dis* 1993; **14**: 253–64.

211 Moore S, Donovan B, Hudson A. Brief report: facilitator-suggested conversational evaluation of facilitated communication. *J Autism Dev Disord* 1993; **23**: 541–52.

212 Jones J, Turner J, Heard A. Making communication a priority. *CSLT Bull* 1992; **478**: 6–7.

213 Sheill A, Pettifer C, Raynes N, Wright K. The costs of community residential facilities for adults with a mental handicap in England. *Ment Handicap Res* 1993; **5**: 115–29.

214 Raynes N, Wright K, Sheill A, Pettifer C. *The Costs and Quality of Community Residential Care: an evaluation of the services for adults with learning disabilities.* London: David Fulton Publishers, 1994.

215 Felce D. The quality of support for ordinary living: resident interactions and resident activity. In: *Deinstitutionalisation and Community Living: intellectual disability services in Britain, Scandinavia and the USA.* London: Chapman and Hall, 1996.

216 Mansel J. Issues in community services in Britain. In: *Deinstitutionalisation and Community Living: intellectual disability services in Britain, Scandinavia and the USA.* London: Chapman and Hall, 1996.

217 Nesbitt S, Collins G. What is special about NHS residences for people with learning disability? An audit of residential need. *Br J Dev Disord* 1998; **4**: 86–93.

218 Farmer R, Holroyd J, Rhodes J. Differences in disability between people with mental handicap resettled in the community and those who remained in hospital. *BMJ* 1990; **301**: 640–8.

219 Knapp M, Cambridge P, Thomason C. *Care in the Community: challenge and demonstration.* Aldershot: Ashgate, 1992.

220 Cullen C. The effects of deinstitutionalization on adults with learning disability. *J Intellect Disabil Res* 1995; **39**: 484–94.

221 Wing L. *Hospital Closure and Resettlement of Patients.* Aldershot: Avebury, 1989.

222 Cambridge P, Hayes R, Knapp M. *Care in the Community: five years on.* Aldershot: Arena, 1994.

223 Korman N, Glennerster H. *Hospital Closure.* Milton Keynes: Open University Press, 1990.

224 Donnelly M, McGilloway S, Mays N *et al. Opening New Doors: an evaluation of community care for people discharged from psychiatric and mental handicap hospitals.* London: HMSO, 1994.

225 Hatton C, Emerson E. *Residential Provision for People with Learning Disabilities: a research review.* Manchester: Hester Adrian Research Centre, University of Manchester, 1996.

226 Newton J, Solson D, Horner R. Factors contributing to the stability of social relationships between individuals with mental retardation and other community members. *Ment Retard* 1995; **33**: 383–93.

227 Cox C, Pearson M. *Made to Care.* Brighton: Pavilion Publishing, 1996.

228 Davies L. Community care – the cost and quality. *Health Serv Manag Res* 1988; **1**(3): 145–55.

229 Cronshaw P. *Residential Provision for People with Learning Disabilities.* London: Department of Health/Personal Social Services Research Unit, University of Kent, 1996.

230 Emerson E, Robertson J, Gregory N *et al. Quality and Costs of Residential Supports for People with Learning Disabilities: summary and implications.* Manchester: Hester Adrian Research Centre, University of Manchester, 1999.

231 Simons K, Ward L. *A Foot in the Door: the early years of supported living in the UK.* Manchester: National Development Team, 1997.

232 Leonard A. *Homes of Their Own: a community care initiative for children with learning disability.* Aldershot: Avebury, 1991.

233 Sheill A, Wright K. *Assessing the Economic Cost of a Community Unit and the Case of Dr Barnardo's Intensive Support Unit.* York: Centre for Health Economics, 1987.

234 Simons K, Watson D. *New Directions? Day services for people with learning disabilities in the 1990s.* Bristol: Norah Fry Research Centre, University of Bristol, 1999.

235 Scottish Executive Central Research Unit. *If You Don't Ask You Don't Get. Review of services for people with learning disabilities: the views of people who use services and their carers.* Edinburgh: Scottish Executive, 1999.

236 Bass M, Drewett R. *Real Work: supported employment for people with learning disability.* York: University of Sheffield/Joseph Rowntree Foundation, 1998.

237 Cimera RE, Rusch FR. The cost-efficiency of supported employment programmes: a review of the literature. In: Master Glidden L (ed.). *International Review of Mental Retardation. Vol. 22.* San Diego, CA: Academic Press, 1999.

238 Litzinger M, Duvall B, Little P. Movement of individuals with complex epilepsy from an institution into the community: seizure control and functional outcomes. *Am J Ment Retard* 1996; **98**(Suppl.): 52–7.

239 Royal College of Psychiatrists. *Meeting the Mental Health Needs of People with Learning Disabilities.* London: Royal College of Psychiatrists, 1997.

240 van Minnen A, Hoogduin CAL, Broeken TG. Hospital v outreach treatment of patients with mental retardation and psychiatric disorders: a controlled study. *Acta Psychiatr Scand* 1997; **95**: 515–22.

241 Tyrer P, Hassiotis A, Ukoumunne O, Piachaud J and Harvey K for the UK 700 Group. Intensive case management for psychotic patients with borderline intelligence. *Lancet* 1999; **354**: 999–1000.

242 Simpson N. Developing mental health services for people with learning disabilities in England. *Tizard Learn Disabil Rev* 1997; **2**(2): 35–42.

243 Bouras N. Mental health and learning disabilities: planning and service development. *Learn Disabil Rev* 1999; **4**: 3–5.

244 Cumella S, Roy A. Bed blockage in an acute admission service for people with a learning disability. *Br J Learn Disord* 1998; **26**: 118–22.

245 Duggan L, Brylewski J. Effectiveness of antipsychotic medication in people with intellectual disability and schizophrenia: a systematic review. *J Intellect Disabil Res* 1999; **43**(2): 94–104.

246 Robertson J. Residential special education for children with severely challenging behaviours: the views of parents. *Br J Special Educ* 1990; **23**: 80–8.

247 Chadwick O, Taylor E, Benhard S. *The Prevention of Behaviour Disorders in Children with Severe Learning Disability*. London: Institute of Psychiatry, 1998.

248 Emerson E, Forrest J, Cambridge P, Mansell J. Community support teams for people with learning disability and challenging behaviour: results of national survey. *J Ment Health* 1996; **5**: 395–406.

249 Lowe K, Felce D, Blackman D. Challenging behaviour: the effectiveness of specialist support teams. *J Learn Disord Res* 1996; **46**: 336–47.

250 Einfeld SL, Tonge BJ. Population prevalence of psychopathology in children and adolescents with intellectual disability. II. Epidemiological findings. *J Intellect Disabil Res* 1996; **40**: 99–109.

251 Emerson E. Challenging behaviour and severe learning disability: recent developments in behavioural analysis treatment. *Behav Cogn Psychol Ther* 1993; **21**: 171–98.

252 Carr E, Durand VM. Reducing behaviour problems through functional communication training. *J Appl Behav Anal* 1995; **18**: 111–26.

253 Carr EG, Horner RH, Turnbull A *et al*. *A Positive Support for People with Developmental Disabilities: research synthesis*. Washington, DC: American Association on Mental Retardation, 1999.

254 Ager A. Effecting sustainable change in client behaviour: the role of the behavioural analysis of service environments. In: Remington B (ed.). *The Challenge of Severe Mental Handicap: a behaviour analytic approach*. Chichester: John Wiley & Sons, 1991.

255 Emerson E. *Leading the Edge*. Conference Paper, 1996.

256 Ball T, Bush A. *Clinical Practice Guidelines: psychological interventions for severely challenging behaviours in people with learning disabilities*. Leicester: British Psychological Society, 1998.

257 Brylewski J, Duggan L. Antipsychotic medication for challenging behaviour in people with learning disability: a systematic review of randomised controlled trials. *J Intellect Disabil Res* 1999; **43**(5): 360–71.

258 Ahmed Z, Fraser W, Kerr MP *et al*. Reducing antipsychotic medication in people with a learning disability. *Br J Psychiatry* 2000; **176**: 42–6.

259 Clarke D. Psychopharmacology of severe self-injury associated with learning disabilities. *Br J Psychiatry* 1998; **172**: 389–94.

260 Wing J, Marriott S, Palmer C, Thomas V. *Management of Imminent Violence: clinical practice guidelines to support mental health services (OP41)*. London: Royal College of Psychiatrists, 1998.

261 Mason T. Seclusion and learning disabilities: research and education. *Br J Dev Disord* 1996; **XLII**: 149–59.

262 Harris JC, Allen D, Crock M *et al*. *Physical Interventions: a policy framework*. Kidderminster: BILD Publications, 1996.

263 Felce D, Lowe K, Perry J *et al*. Service support to people in Wales with severe intellectual disability and the most severe challenging behaviours: processes, outcomes and costs. *J Intellect Disabil Res* 1998; **42**(5): 390–408.

264 Hallam A, Beecham J. *Service Packages for People with Severe Challenging Behaviour. Discussion Paper 1302/3*. Canterbury: Personal Social Services Research Unit, University of Kent, 1998.

265 Mannion R, Smith K, Ferguson B *et al.* The costs of packages of care for people with learning disabilities and challenging behaviour. In: Netten A, Dennett J (eds). *Unit Costs of Health and Social Care.* Canterbury: Personal Social Services Research Unit, University of Kent, 1997.

266 Xenitidis KI, Henry J, Russell AJ, Ward A, Murphy DG. An inpatient treatment model for adults with mild intellectual disability and challenging behaviour. *J Intellect Disabil Res* 1999; **43**(2): 128–34.

267 Newman I, Emerson E. Specialised treatment units for people with challenging behaviours. *Ment Handicap* 1991; **19**: 113–19.

268 Johnson SJ, Halstead S. Forensic issues in intellectual disability. *Curr Opin Psychiatry* 2000; **13**: 475–80.

269 Cullen C. The treatment of people with learning disabilities who offend. In: Hollin CR, Howells K (eds). *Clinical Approaches to the Mentally Disordered Offender.* New York: John Wiley & Sons, 1993.

270 Dawson G, Osterling J. Early intervention in autism. In: Guralnick M (ed.). *The Effectiveness of Early Intervention.* Baltimore, MD: Brookes, 1997.

271 Rimland B, Edelson SMA. Pilot study of auditory integration training in autism. *J Autism Dev Disord* 1995; **25**: 61–70.

272 Wessex Institute for Health Research and Development. *Auditory Training in Autism.* Development and Evaluation Committee Report No 66. Bristol: NHS Executive South and West, 1997.

273 Myrbakk E. The treatment of self-stimulation of a severely mentally retarded deaf-blind client by brief physical interruption: a case report. *Scand J Behav Ther* 1991; **20**: 41–9.

274 Martin NT, Gaffan EA, Williams T. Behavioural effects of long-term multi-sensory stimulation. *Br J Clin Psychol* 1998; **37**(1): 69–82.

275 Hatton C, Emerson E. Services for adults with learning disabilities and sensory impairments. *Br J Learn Disord* 1994; **23**: 11–17.

276 Joseph Rowntree Foundation. *Implementing Direct Payments for PWLD.* York: Joseph Rowntree Foundation, 1999.

277 Joseph Rowntree Foundation. *PWLD and Their Access to Direct Payment Schemes.* York: Joseph Rowntree Foundation, 1999.

278 Ward L (ed.). *Innovations in Advocacy and Empowerment for People with Intellectual Disability.* Chorley: Lisieux Hall Publications, 1998.

279 Joseph Rowntree Foundation. *Disparities in Service Provision for People with Learning Difficulties Living in the Community. Social Care Research Findings 75.* York: Joseph Rowntree Foundation, 1995.

280 Felce D, Grant G, Todd S *et al. Towards a Full Life.* Oxford: Butterworth-Heinemann, 1998.

281 McGaw S. *What Works for Parents with Learning Disabilities?* Cornwall: Special Parenting Service, 1998.

282 Beresford BA. Resources and strategies: how parents cope with the care of a disabled child. *J Clin Psychol Psychiatry Allied Discipl* 1994; **35**(1): 171–209.

283 Quine L. Working with parents: the management of sleep disturbance in children with learning disabilities. In: *Research into Practice? Implications of the challenging behavioural people with learning disability.* Clevedon: BILD Publications, 1993.

284 National Development Team. *Respite Services and Natural Breaks for Children with Learning Disability.* Manchester: National Development Team, 1995.

285 Gerard K. Economic evaluation of respite care for children with mental handicap: a preliminary analysis of problems. *Ment Handicap* 1990; **18**: 155–6.

286 Hayes L, Flynn M, Cotterill L, Sloper T. *Respite Services for Adult Citizens with Learning Disability. Report submitted to the Joseph Rowntree Foundation.* Manchester: Hester Adrian Research Centre, 1995.

287 Brotchie J, Rees S. *A Mental Health Framework for North Thames.* Report to the North Thames Mental Health Chief Executives Group, 1998.

288 Simon K. *A Place at the Table? Involving people with learning disabilities in purchasing and commissioning services*. Kidderminster: BILD Publications, 1999.

289 Joseph Rowntree Foundation. *People with Learning Disabilities and Their Ageing Family Carers*. York: Joseph Rowntree Foundation, 1998.

290 Department of Health and Social Services. *Better Services for the Mentally Handicapped*. London: HMSO, 1971.

291 McGrother CW, Hauck A, Burton PR. More and better services for people with learning disabilities. *J Pub Health Med* 1993; **15**: 263–71.

292 Royal College of Psychiatrists. *Mental Health of the Nation: the contribution of psychiatry. Council Report 16*. London: Royal College of Psychiatrists, 1992.

293 British Psychological Society. *Purchasing Clinical Psychology Services: services for people with learning disabilities and their carers. Briefing Paper Number 3*. Leicester: British Psychological Society, 1994.

294 British Psychological Society. *Purchasing Clinical Psychology Services: services for children, young people and their families. Briefing Paper Number 1*. Leicester: British Psychological Society, 1994.

295 Netten A, Dennett J, Knight J (eds). *Unit Costs of Health and Social Care*. Canterbury: Personal Social Services Research Unit, University of Kent, 1998.

296 Department of Health. *Valuing People: a new strategy for learning disability for the 21st century*. London: Department of Health, 2001.

18 Community Child Health Services*

David Hall, Sarah Stewart-Brown, Alison Salt and Peter Hill

1 Summary

Statement of the problem

Community child health services (CCHS) incorporate a range of disparate and evolving services provided by paediatricians, community nurses, mental health professionals and physiotherapists, speech and occupational therapists, in close liaison with public health and information management staff. The staff involved in provision of these services may be managed separately from one another. The aims of the CCHS are the prevention of disease and disability and the promotion of health. Over the last decade the balance of activity between disease prevention and health promotion has changed in favour of the latter, with a greater emphasis on public health approaches. The disparate nature of these services, their divided management, their separation from other paediatric services and their low academic profile have resulted in a lack of data about performance and effectiveness which has resulted in great variation in quality of and access to care for children according to where they live.

Sub-categories: the core business

The tasks carried out within the CCHS include aspects of both primary and secondary care as well as health promotion. They include management of and advice regarding child protection, adoption and fostering, and 'children looked after' (CLA), school health services, provision of child health surveillance (CHS) (provided in most areas by primary health care teams but by CCHS where GPs are unable or unwilling to offer this), planning and monitoring of CHS, health promotion programmes, child public health, services for disabled children and those with hearing impairment (paediatric audiology), and child and adolescent mental health services (CAMHS). This chapter addresses those services, designated tiers 1 and 2, which deal with the more common, less severe problems and with health promotion and disease prevention. These services may not be a formal part of the specialist child and adolescent psychiatry services.

---

* Several changes in community child health services have occurred since the preparation of this chapter during 2000–2001, and many new materials have been published. The reader is referred to the addendum on p. 630.

Prevalence and incidence

The number of children on the Child Protection Register varies from 100 to 740 per 100 000 total population. There are around 5000 adoptions per year and 53 000 children are 'looked after'. Between 1% and 3% of children have a Statement of Special Educational Need, which needs CCHS input. Up to 20% of children have educational difficulties at some time, and some but not all of these will need paediatric assessment. All children have a right to a basic programme of CHS, health promotion and school health.

There are 189 000 severely disabled children in the UK and 1.8% attend special schools. They make up 28% of children looked after.

The point prevalence of problematic psychological conditions in childhood and adolescence is around 20%, of whom half may need specialist assessment and half may benefit from professional help of lesser intensity.

Services available and their costs

The following duties of CCHS are statutory or set out in Department of Health (DoH) guidance: provision of designated doctor and nurse for child protection with input to the Area Child Protection Committee (ACPC); provision of medical advice for adoption panels; medical examinations of children taken into care (though these may be done by primary care staff in some areas); school health service including liaison regarding Special Educational Need procedures; role of immunisation co-ordinator; support for social services with regard to children in need; monitoring of PKU and hypothyroidism screening. A clear definition of medical duties regarding CLA is awaited.

CCHS provide medical, nursing and often other professional staff to manage the services set out above. A national programme of screening in child health has been put forward. Care of disabled children is usually based in a Child Development Centre or focused on a Child Development Team; this may be in a hospital or in a community setting.

Health promotion programmes in the pre-school period centre around support and advice for parents with the aim of improving the level of parenting in the population. For school-age children the most popular approach is now the health-promoting school. The role paediatricians and community nurses play in child health advocacy at local and national level varies greatly from one place to another.

CAMHS are organised in four tiers. Tier 1 is primary care, tier 2 is solo professional practice, tier 3 is specialist teams of child psychiatrists, mental health nurses, psychologists, etc., and tier 4 is highly specialised provision such as inpatient care or management of rare problems.

Costs are difficult to establish because of the wide and unacceptable variability between districts, in all aspects of CCHS and CAMHS.

Effectiveness

Many aspects of modern CCHS have a robust evidence base and others are a response to intolerable situations such as child abuse, or support legislative requirements. Many screening procedures have been discarded in recent years. Those that remain largely fulfil classic screening criteria. Immunisation and co-ordination of the service are highly effective. Health visitors and school health services are changing their practice in the light of accumulating evidence about what consumers want and what works. For disabled children, the aims are based on consumer views and quality-of-life issues rather than expectation of cure or dramatic neurological recovery. There is good evidence that high-quality services are linked with parent satisfaction. In the field of child mental health there is evidence of effectiveness of focused approaches to specific issues and of programmes aimed at parents to prevent or intervene with behavioural problems or parent depression, and to promote mental health.

Quantified models of care

There are insufficient data on the level of CCHS or CAMHS tiers 1 and 2 staffing needed. There are wide variations in the workload regarding child protection, CLA and school health work, due to socio-economic and policy differences, but variations in current staffing levels cannot be explained by these factors. Estimates have been made of time needed to discharge the duties set out in statute but not for the delivery of a quality service. For disabled children, staffing levels have been established on the basis of what is available in a sample of quality services.

Outcomes

For many CCHS activities, especially those required by statute, long-term outcome measures are of academic but not practical value, and process measures must be used as a proxy. Social, emotional and educational outcomes might in many cases offer better measures of the success of both disease prevention and health promotion programmes than measures of physical health. For disabled children, data on the process of early identification and support and parental satisfaction may be the best available measures. For CAMHS, measures for individual cases are available though not yet optimal, but population-wide measures are more elusive and depend in part on the declared stated aims for CAMHS tiers 1 and 2 of the local community and the State.

Targets

These are best defined at present in terms of coverage for all population-wide activities, and quality-of-service proxy measures for child protection, educational support, CLA, disability and CAMHS tiers 1 and 2.

Information

There is an urgent need for better information systems. A core public health data set has been devised but has yet to be included in Government policy or funded. Definition of impairments and disorders is difficult both in disability and in mental health problems, especially at the tiers 1 and 2 end of the spectrum of severity. Existing systems are outdated but could form the basis for a revised IT protocol.

Research

Research is needed on service delivery issues such as optimal staffing levels and configuration, on the impact and value of various ways of preventing and managing suspected or actual child abuse, on the benefits to be expected from better paediatric care for CLA, on new screening opportunities (especially in biochemical screening), on measures of process and outcome for disabled children and those with mental health problems, and on optimum methods of health promotion both with parents and in schools.

2 Statement of the problem

Scope

This chapter will consider community child health services (CCHS) that address the general health care needs of all children (aged 0–18 years), the health care needs of children who are vulnerable by reason of neglect, abuse or disability, and those of children who have mild or moderate psychological disorders.* Psychiatric disorders affecting young people (children and adolescents) are dealt with elsewhere in this series.[1]

Although any severe illness can be disabling, in terms of service provision the term disability will refer to conditions of the nervous system, special senses and locomotor system. Mild and moderate psychological disorders will refer to psychological problems which are less severe than psychiatric disorders but nevertheless are a source of considerable misery to children and their families.[2] Mild and moderate psychological disorders are indicated by persisting behaviour problems, distressed emotions, relationship difficulties and selective maturational delays which are, in type, common or normal in children at some stage of development. They become abnormal by virtue of their frequency, severity or inappropriateness for a particular child's age and situation compared to the majority of ordinary children. They are therefore more than the annoying behaviours displayed by most children at some time. Examples include persistent aggression towards peers, sleep problems, major tantrums, provocative behaviour towards parents, unhappy clinging or enuresis.

Child health

The general physical health of children has improved greatly over the last 100 years. However, social inequalities continue to play a major role in children's health and are related to emotional, behavioural and social problems, together with child abuse and neglect, which are now the most important causes of ill-health in childhood.[3] Worryingly, these are thought to be an important precursor to unhealthy lifestyles,[4] mental illness[5–7] and perhaps physical ill-health in adulthood.[8,9] Mild and moderate psychological problems are also a significant and widespread community child health problem. The emotional, behavioural, developmental and relationship problems included under this heading are a common source of family distress, clinically significant and represent a health care need.

Community child health services

The Children Act 1989, the Education Acts of 1981, 1987 and 1997, and the White Papers *Saving Lives* and *Making a Difference* (1999) define some of the aims and tasks carried out by the CCHS. The traditional core business of the CCHS includes primary, secondary and tertiary prevention of disease, disability and death in childhood, and the promotion of health.[10] Clinical services include the assessment and ongoing care of children with a range of disabilities (mainly but not exclusively affecting the nervous system), investigation and management of suspected child abuse, and responding to a range of other clinical concerns in clinics, schools and childcare facilities. Over the last decade the balance of activity between disease prevention and

---

* Also *see* Royal College of Paediatrics and Child Health (RCPCH). *The Next Ten Years*. London: RCPCH, 2002 and Royal College of Paediatrics and Child Health. *Strengthening the Care of Children in the Community*. London: RCPCH, 2002.

health promotion has changed in favour of the latter. The aims of the CCHS may vary from one district to another due to variations in provision by other agencies and the level of social deprivation within that district.

Professions involved in CCHS

The CCHS had their origins in health visiting, infant welfare clinics and school health services (SHS) and were originally staffed by doctors and nurses employed by local authorities. When these services were absorbed into the NHS in the reorganisation of 1974, Specialists in Community Medicine (child health) in the Area Health Authorities ran them. Following further NHS reorganisations in the 1980s, CCHS are now managed by consultant community paediatricians and nurse managers, with a variable input from public health consultants. Service provision is primarily by paediatricians, community nurses, mental health professionals and physiotherapists, speech and occupational therapists.

Over the past decade, child health screening, surveillance and immunisation, which were previously delivered by CCHS, have become subsumed into primary care. Health visitors, school nurses and dedicated health promotion staff usually provide clinical health promotion programmes. There is a rapidly changing balance between the disease prevention and health promotion roles of the CCHS. Some responsibility for an overview and for the non-clinical components ('child public health') remains with public health departments, although arrangements do vary.

This chapter does not attempt to review the rapidly changing relationship between the CCHS and 'acute' or 'general' paediatric care. The boundary between acute and community paediatrics is increasingly irrelevant and management arrangements are in a state of flux. Services such as day-assessment units,[11] short-stay observation wards and 'ambulatory' care are emerging as alternatives to hospital admission.[12] There are compelling arguments for a more integrated approach to paediatrics and child health. Children with disabilities or who have been abused often need hospital care. Specialist outreach nurses and community paediatric nurses support children with complex problems, such as cystic fibrosis, at home and in school. However, the services offered by CCHS staff are often less well understood than mainstream medical and surgical paediatrics, and this is the justification for the current overview.

CCHS and children with disabilities

Although both quality of care and availability of expertise for children with disabilities have improved substantially over the past 20 years, this is still to some extent a Cinderella service. There are wide variations in provision, in the level of training, knowledge and skill among staff, and in professional attitudes to families with disabled children.[13,14] There are often tensions between health service providers, education and social services and voluntary groups in assigning responsibility for aspects of care, exacerbated by poor communication between them. Commissioning and management of services for disabled children are often weak and information is scanty. The lack of progress in implementation of the 1989 Children Act requirements in respect of children with disabilities is cause for concern.

The CCHS and children with mild and moderate psychological pathology

The category of mild and moderate psychological pathology replaces the term 'mild psychological pathology' used in the first edition of this chapter. It is not the same as psychiatric disorder and is often dealt with by staff who are not specialist mental health professionals. It affects approximately 10% of the child and adolescent population and its manifestations are characteristically polymorphous and persistent. Establishing local mental health needs in this area would ordinarily be a priority, but is difficult because there is no consensus about method, although various strategies exist. There is quite good general epidemiological information about rates of mild and moderate psychological disorders in children. However, poor co-ordination between service providers and agencies is a major problem. The tiered-service approach is endorsed as a means of tackling this. Most mild and moderate psychological pathology will be dealt with by tiers 1 and 2. There is growing experience of the new concept of child mental health worker but no randomised evaluation of their effectiveness. Both general and focused interventions are available, though there is little information on effectiveness. Most interventions are psychological rather than physical, and it is worth considering health visiting and parent training as the basis for general interventions.[15]

CCHS and health promotion

The importance of promoting mental and emotional health relative to disease prevention is increasing,[16] but the resources devoted to this depend on the model adopted. Disease prevention follows a medical model of health in which services are delivered to individuals who have or are at risk of certain diseases. Health promotion follows a holistic model, encompassing mental and social as well as physical well-being. This stresses adverse environmental and psychosocial conditions and targets policy makers, parents, teachers, pre-school teachers and others who control the environment in which children grow up.[17] Over the last decade the balance of activity between disease prevention and health promotion has changed in favour of the latter.

The evidence base for CCHS

Evidence-based practice is important in CCHS, but the disparate nature of these services, their divided management and low academic profile have resulted in a lack of data on performance and effectiveness. Some services are provided because health authorities (now primary care trusts) are charged with legal duties; these in turn reflect political pressures and expert consensus, usually enshrined in legislation.

The functions of CCHS are intertwined with those of education and social services departments and the voluntary sector (*see* Appendix 1), and it may be impossible to disentangle the effectiveness of the CCHS from that of their partners.

Current difficulties in evaluating the effectiveness of CCHS include:

- recent wide-ranging changes in their role and function
- the changing interface between CCHS, public health medicine and primary care
- an increasing emphasis on health promotion, and particularly mental health promotion, in collaboration with other agencies
- recognition of the exceptional methodological difficulties in measuring effectiveness.

The lack of data on effectiveness and performance has resulted in great variation in quality of and access to care for children according to where they live.

3 Sub-categories

Sub-categorising CCHS

Community child health services are not neatly sub-categorised. The tasks carried out within the CCHS include aspects of both primary and secondary care as well as health promotion. In the following list of sub-categories, sub-categories (a) and (b) are core business defined in part by national legislation and central guidance. Sub-categories (f) and (g) are both major clinical services provided by the CCHS and can themselves be further sub-categorised. Sub-categories (c) to (e) are less well defined, and in the framework adopted below the somewhat artificial nature of the exercise needs to be recognised.

(a) Children who have been abused, or are to be adopted or 'looked after', are the primary responsibility of the social services departments of local authorities, but need health services input from the CCHS for assessment, management and service planning.

(b) All school-age children are entitled to a school health service and there is a requirement for the CCHS to provide support and advice to Local Education Authorities.

(c) All children are included in neonatal and pre-school childhood screening, immunisation and health education programmes. The provision of this service is now mainly through primary health care teams, but much of the organisation and training are currently provided by CCHS.

(d) All children should be included in health promotion programmes and preventive services provided by the CCHS which, by working with parents and teachers, aim to change the micro-environment in which children are raised.

(e) All children benefit from activities best described as child public health – CCHS activities which influence the macro-environment in which children are raised.

(f) Services for children with a disability.

(g) Services for children with a clinically defined mild or moderate psychological problem.

Sub-categorising services provided for children with a disability

Historically this category has evolved because children with disabilities relating to the nervous system, special senses and locomotor system have a number of service needs in common. Services for children with a disability can be further sub-categorised:

(a) by medical/diagnostic category
(b) by a conceptual framework set out by the World Health Organization (WHO)
(c) by prevalence – uncommon and severe conditions vs. common, less severe conditions and problems.

In this chapter the third approach will be used.

Medical/diagnostic category

Disability in childhood is often regarded as synonymous with neurodisability, i.e. disability related to disorders of the nervous system, including the special senses (these are listed in Tables 1 and 2). Many other chronic disorders cause disability and give rise to often unmet service needs, e.g. osteogenesis imperfecta, Morquio's disease, Marfan's syndrome, neurofibromatosis and chronic juvenile arthritis. The needs of children with chronic, common, non-neurological conditions such as diabetes, cystic fibrosis or asthma are generally catered for effectively by the appropriate specialist services.

Table 1: High-severity, low-prevalence conditions.

Condition	Incidence	Comments
Cerebral palsies	2.5/1,000	Many different types and aetiologies
Spina bifida + hydrocephalus; hydrocephalus alone	0.5–2.0/1,000	Incidence varies with geographic area, socio-economic conditions and screening policy
Muscular dystrophy	1/3,000 boys	The commonest muscle disease
Severe learning difficulties or disabilities (mental handicap)	3.7/1,000	Previously called 'mental retardation' or 'educationally subnormal – severe'. Many causes – Down's syndrome, other chromosomal defects, brain injury, dysmorphic syndromes, fetal insults (alcohol, rubella, etc.). Little social class gradient with severe learning disabilities (contrast mild/moderate, *see* below)
Sensorineural hearing impairment	1.3/1,000	Multiple causes: 1.1/1,000 are congenital – genetic, congenital infections, syndrome-related; remainder acquired, commonly post-meningitis
Severe vision defects (blind or partially sighted)	1–1.5/1,000	Includes many children who are multiply handicapped. Those for whom impaired vision is the only or main problem amount to perhaps one-half or one-third
Autism and autism spectrum disorders (ASD)	0.4–2.5/1,000	The higher figure includes children with mild autistic features and those in whom autistic behaviour is part of a pattern of severe learning difficulties; the lower figure refers to 'classic' autism. Asperger's syndrome is not included – 5/1,000
Other communication disorders (dysphasia, dysarthria, dyspraxia, severe language impairments – cause unknown)	Not well established: 2–5/1,000	Difficulty in definition, therefore incidence is not certain
Epilepsy	6–12/1,000	The epilepsy is inactive at any one time in about half. It is disabling or intractable in a small minority
Miscellaneous disabling conditions		Includes osteogenesis imperfecta (brittle bone disease), achondroplasia and other dwarfing conditions, limb defects, effects of trauma (head injury, anoxic brain injury, spinal cord injury), many others

Table 2: Low-severity, high-prevalence conditions.

Condition	Incidence	Comments
Delayed language development	3–10%	Figure depends on definition and on socio-economic status
General delay: mild or moderate learning disabilities	3–10%	Same applies. Previously called 'educationally subnormal – mild'
'Clumsiness' – developmental co-ordination disorder, developmental dyspraxia	3–7%	Same applies. Link with socio-economic status is less direct but clumsiness is more common in children of lower IQ
Glue ear (secretory otitis media [SOM], otitis with effusion)	8–11%: 2–4% have severe or persistent SOM	At least half of all children have at least one episode of SOM, but severe persistent SOM is potentially disabling and impairs language development. Possible links with lower socio-economic status, passive smoking, day care and other predisposing factors, e.g. Down's syndrome
Eye defects: squint, refractive error, amblyopia	5–10%	Prevalence of squint is 4–7%. Higher figure depends on complete ascertainment of subtle cases. Incidence of short sight (myopia) rises throughout childhood and adolescence. Little social class gradient except in use of services
School failure	20%	Up to 20% of children will have problems with education at some point. The differential diagnosis includes general learning disability (low IQ), specific learning disability (e.g. dyslexia), psychological disturbances, psychiatric illness, attention deficit hyperactivity disorder, abuse, bullying, bad teaching, home problems

Conceptual frameworks for classifying disability

There is no completely satisfactory classification of disabilities in childhood for the following reasons.

- Classification must not only describe what the child can and cannot do, but also relate this to the age of the child.
- Multiple disabilities interact, e.g. a minor hearing loss may cause major problems when combined with a mild learning disability.
- The attitude of the child, parents and teachers affects the perceived extent of handicap.

In 1980, the World Health Organization proposed a classification as part of the *International Classification of Diseases* (*see* Box 1). The new version is shown in Box 2.[18] The OPCS developed a system for a national survey,[19] and the British Association for Community Child Health classification is useful for special needs.[20] Several other methods have been used.[21] Other systems such as Read codes do not currently offer a satisfactory solution to the problem.

Box 1: Definitions of terms previously used in disability research.

Impairment	An abnormality of anatomical structure or physiological or psychological function.
Disability	The function effect or deficit caused by the impairment.
Handicap	The impact of the impairment or disability on the fulfilment of the person's desired or expected social role in society. Often caused by factors external to the person, e.g. access to buildings being unsuitable for wheelchairs, but in common usage is interpreted as a negative characteristic of the individual.
Disadvantage	Has a similar meaning to handicap but is less pejorative and emphasises how disability interacts with environmental factors and societal attitudes.

Box 2: Definitions of terms: new terminology proposed in ICIDH-2.

- The concept of impairment remains. **Impairment** is a loss or abnormality of body structure or of a physiological or psychological function.
- The concept of disability has been replaced by measures of activities. An **activity** is the nature and extent of functioning at the level of the person. Activities may be limited in nature, duration and quality.
- The concept of handicap has been replaced by measures of participation. **Participation** is the nature and extent of the person's involvement in life situations in relation to impairments, activities, health conditions and contextual factors. Participation may be restricted in nature, duration and quality.
- The term 'disability' has been dropped, while the term 'disablement' has been adopted as an umbrella over the concepts above.

Prevalence and incidence

It is convenient, though somewhat artificial, to divide disabling conditions of childhood into the following categories.

1 **High-severity, low-prevalence conditions:** Examples of these include sensorineural hearing loss, partial sight and blindness, cerebral palsy, spina bifida and Down's syndrome (*see* Table 1). These are:
   - individually uncommon
   - usually associated with identified or assumed pathology
   - likely to lead to disability
   - unlikely to resolve spontaneously or with treatment
   - often managed in a special centre by a multi-disciplinary team
   - likely to need services for the whole of the child's life.
2 **Low-severity, high-prevalence conditions:** Examples include speech and language impairments, mild learning disabilities and 'clumsiness'. Mild hearing loss (usually conductive in nature and caused by otitis media with effusion) and minor vision defects such as squint or amblyopia could also be included (*see* Table 2). Impaired learning and behaviour associated with attention deficit hyperactivity disorder (ADHD) may also be included in this list. ADHD is often managed within paediatric services rather than by mental health teams, either because of the potential volume of cases or because some child psychiatry services have been reluctant to take on this area of work. Low-severity, high-prevalence conditions:
   - are common

- are often either developmental (i.e. they improve with maturation, with or without intervention) or reversible by treatment
- sometimes represent the extremes of a distribution of a particular skill rather than a pathological deficiency
- are usually managed in a community setting by one or two individuals
- are unlikely to need services for the whole of the child's life.

Although high-severity, low-prevalence conditions are usually associated with substantial disability, this is not invariable. For example, some children with mild cerebral palsy walk well. Conversely, some children with low-severity, high-prevalence conditions may be quite disabled. For example, although the disability associated with the 'clumsy child syndrome' is for most children a minor inconvenience, for a minority it can cause considerable disability and unhappiness.

The two categories of disabling condition set out above are usually associated with different service needs. Guiding principles are listed in Appendix 3. Those with high-severity, low-prevalence conditions often have multiple and complex problems, and their treatment programme may involve many medical, therapy and educational specialties, often in a special school or in a unit of a mainstream school. Their families have well-defined needs[22] which were confirmed in a parent survey and summarised in the form of a 'Charter' (*see* Appendix 2).

Those with low-severity, high-prevalence conditions are more likely to be assessed in a community setting. Some, but not all, need a paediatric assessment (e.g. many children with delayed language development are seen only by a speech therapist and an audiologist), and they are likely to attend mainstream school.

Mild and moderate psychological disorders

When planning services for children with mild or moderate psychological disorders, it is appropriate to sub-categorise further by age and by number of problems in any particular child or adolescent, because these will influence the type of service delivery.

Age

It is relevant to differentiate between three main age groups, since the way in which children and teenagers come to the attention of services differs between them:

- pre-school children, who will be presented to health services by their parents
- school children, who may be presented either by their parents or by education staff
- older adolescents, who may present themselves.

Number of problems

This needs to be considered because of the type of clinic which is best placed to cope.

- Single problems, such as sleep difficulties or enuresis, may be addressed by special clinics or services.
- Several coexisting behaviour, mood or relationship problems in any one child or teenager will need a more flexible approach, tailored to the individual child and family, and to the priorities within a range of problems, so that a general clinic or service is therefore more relevant.

4 Prevalence and incidence

Children who are the primary responsibility of social services departments

Data are published each year on the numbers of children on Child Protection Registers, the categories of registration, the numbers of children put forward for adoption, and the numbers of children looked after by local authorities, including those in residential care and those looked after by foster parents.

Child abuse is not a well-defined clinical entity, and the level of abuse meriting intervention varies depending on prevailing social attitudes. An increasing number of health problems, including emotional and behaviour problems in childhood,[23] health-related lifestyles,[24] and physical and mental health in adulthood[25] appear to be attributable in part to common 'parenting styles' which are unhelpful to children's health and well-being but are not defined as abusive. The number of children on the Child Protection Register in the year ending March 1997 ranged from 100 to 740 per 100 000 total population. This wide range reflects real differences in the incidence of child abuse, differences in levels of ascertainment, variation in the services which facilitate the management of at-risk children without the need for registration, and the differing policies and attitudes of local authorities.

The number of adoptions reached a peak in the early 1970s and has since declined to a current level of around 5000 per year, but many adoptions are now of children with disabilities or complex emotional needs. The number of 'looked after' children is estimated to be around 53 000, but at local level varies by a factor of ten across the country.

School-age children: support and advice to the Local Education Authority

All school-age children are entitled to a school health service. The CCHS also provides support and advice to Local Education Authorities (LEAs). One such area is in the issuing of Statements of Special Educational Need (SSENs) (*see* Box 3 and Appendix 4). The number of children with SSENs varies widely between education authorities, from under 1% to over 3%. There is some correlation with deprivation levels and the proportion of children with SSENs, but the variation also reflects differing policies and interpretations of official guidance. Up to 20% of pupils may have special educational needs at some time, but only a minority of these progresses to stage 5 of the assessment process, which results in the issuing of a Statement of Special Educational Need. Most authorities are trying to reduce the number of children with Statements of Special Educational Need and deal with problems at levels 2 and 3 of the assessment process.

Box 3: Statements of Special Educational Need.

- A Statement of Special Educational Need is a legal document prepared by the Local Education Authority under the Education Acts of 1981, 1993 and 1996, and the Education Reform Act of 1988. It defines the child's needs and the provision to be made in order to meet those needs.
- The Code of Practice 1994 set out the details of how the process works; it has recently been revised.
- Preliminary steps are set out whereby efforts are made to resolve the child's difficulties without a formal Statement of Special Educational Need procedure.
- The health authority (now PCTs) is required to provide the necessary medical evidence regarding the child's needs.
- There must be a doctor designated to take responsibility for ensuring that the procedures and time limits are complied with.

All schools operate some process of identification of children with possible health problems or special needs at school entry, and identified children are usually referred for a medical assessment ('selective school entry medicals') (*see* 'School medical inspections' in Section 5). In published studies the number of children selected varies from 17% to 73% of the population.[26] Some of these may be seen more than once. The number of vision, hearing and growth problems identified at school entry is reviewed under disabilities.

Organisation of screening, immunisation and health education programmes

The aim of these programmes is to reach all children. The performance of screening programmes and the potential contribution of health education are discussed in *Health For All Children.*[27]

Organisation and provision of health promotion services and preventive services which focus on the micro-environment and child public health: services which influence the macro-environment

The main health problems which these programmes aim to prevent are summarised in Table 3. Important issues which will in general be aimed at parents, with the child being the benefactor, in the pre-school period include injuries[28] (accidental and non-accidental), sudden unexpected death in infancy, speech and language delay, emotional and behavioural problems, passive smoking and lack of breastfeeding. The latter

Table 3: Common health problems which the CCHS aims to prevent.

Deaths per annum	
Sudden unexpected death (0–1 years)	1.0/1,000
Unintentional injury (0–19 years)[30]	8.6/100,000
Suicide (15–19 years)	3.5/100,000
Child abuse (0–1 year)	1.4/100,000
Incidence of common health problems per annum	
Injury requiring attention at A&E (0–15 years)	200/1,000
Disabling injury (16–23 years)[31]	4.0/1,000
Pregnancy (16-year-old girls)[32]	20/1,000
Prevalence of common health problems and unhealthy lifestyles	
Emotional and behavioural problems (5–10 years)	5–20%
Speech and language delay	5–10%
Depressive symptoms (adolescent girls)	20%
Major depressive disorder (adolescent girls)	10%
Exposed to passive smoke at home (0–16 years)	50%
Not breastfed at six weeks	61%
Not breastfed at six months	79%
Sexually active at 16 years[33]	50%
Regular smoker before leaving school	25%
Drinking alcohol above limit (16–17 years)	5%

two, together with sound weaning practices, are important with respect to respiratory and gastrointestinal infection, glue ear and dental disease, which are common causes of consultation with doctors and dentists, and of hospital admission in the pre-school age group.

In the school years the focus of these programmes is on the children themselves and concentrates on promotion of mental health and healthy lifestyles, and the prevention of injuries, substance misuse, teenage pregnancy, sexually transmitted diseases and mental health problems in adult life.[29] Most common child health problems, particularly injuries, demonstrate social inequalities. A range of intertwined psychosocial and environmental factors, including poverty, unemployment, teenage parenting, single parenting, poor housing, inner-city neighbourhoods and parental criminality, increase the risk of all these problems.

Children with disabilities

There are 360 000 disabled children in the UK (32 per 1000 or 3% of the child population). Of these, 189 000 have severe disabilities, and of *these*, 5500 live in residential care and 16 000 attend residential schools. In total, 1.8% of all children attend special schools.[19] Disabled children are eight times more likely than non-disabled to be looked after by the local authority, and constitute 28% of all children looked after.[34] There are increasing numbers of children with disability who attend mainstream schools, and many need considerable support. There are many more children, estimated at 20% of the school population, who have special needs during their school career, and some though not all of these need paediatric services. Secondary problems are common among all such children, e.g. behavioural and emotional difficulties, family stress and disturbances, concomitant medical problems, bullying and loneliness. Tables 1 and 2 above summarise prevalence and incidence data for the more important disabling disorders.

Mild and moderate psychological disorders

Raw data from a number of epidemiological studies in childhood yield a point prevalence rate of approximately 20% for problematic psychological conditions in childhood and adolescence.[35] About half of these would be regarded as sufficiently severe for specialist assessment by a psychiatric service. The criterion for inclusion within this group is the presence of 'considerable distress and substantial interference with personal function' as well as the fact that the condition can be classified within the *International Classification of Diseases* (10th edition). (*Note*: These are the criteria used in the Office for National Statistics Survey to delineate 'mental disorder'[36] which is equivalent to the term 'psychiatric disorder'.) The remaining 10% are less impaired or not readily diagnosable in ICD-10 terms. This group normally has emotional, behavioural, relationship or psychological abnormalities which are clinically significant (by virtue of mild/moderate distress or impairment), and which are able to benefit from health care, but which are not sufficiently severe, pervasive, distressing or handicapping to be regarded as psychiatric disorders. This is the field of mild and moderate psychopathology. It includes subjective mental distress (e.g. obsessional symptoms unaccompanied by compulsions) which is complained of by the child or adolescent but which is mild/moderate because it does not intrude into the child's observed demeanour, does not affect their personal functioning and goes unnoticed by parents or teachers.

Risk factors can be identified for mild/moderate psychological pathology, and resemble those found in psychiatric disorder (*see* Box 4).

Box 4: Risk factors for mild and moderate psychopathology.

- Poor parenting practice.
- Inner cities.
- Socially disadvantaged or poor families.
- 'Looked after' children in public care.
- Being male rather than female.
- Having general and specific learning difficulties and, in young children, delayed language development.
- Having physical problems of health or development.
- Adolescence rather than earlier childhood.

If a population in which risk factors are common is sampled, figures for the prevalence of psychological problems are likely to be substantially higher since such factors tend not simply to sum, but usually multiply the impact of each other. For instance, work in inner South-East London[37] found that 68.6% of pre-school children in a random survey were judged by interviewers to have at least one psychological problem and 29.1% to have three or more problems.

Associated family relationship problems are common though not universal. They are most evident in association with multiple problems. In general terms they parallel findings for psychiatric disorder in childhood, so that there are higher rates of:

- marital discord/altercations/divorce
- mental health problems in other family members
- parental coldness or irritability towards the child
- low degree of parental supervision of the child.

For planning purposes, a number of proxies for child and adolescent mental health need have been used (*see* Box 5), and can logically be extended to suggest health need related to mild and moderate psychopathology in childhood. For most services, history has been the major factor in determining the volume of services for children with psychological pathology. Across the UK there is an extremely poor relationship between the volume of local relevant services and local need as suggested by such proxy indicators.[38]

Box 5: Proxies of need for estimating local child and adolescent mental health need.

- Perinatal mortality rate.
- Infant mortality rate.
- Under-16 pregnancy rate.
- Proportion of lone-parent families.
- Number of children in temporary housing.
- Number of children on the Child Protection Register.
- Number of children looked after by the local authority.
- Number of children with a Statement of Special Educational Need.
- Number of children on the disability register.
- Number of children accommodated with private fostering agencies.
- Number of children absent from school without authority.
- Number of children excluded from school.
- Number of young carers.
- Number of refugee children.
- Number of young people involved with the police.[7]

Rates for particular problems

Various epidemiological studies (predominantly UK-based) have yielded relatively precise point prevalence figures for some single problems, abnormal in terms of frequency, severity or age expectation. For the sake of illustration, some of these can be selected and collapsed to yield crude overall percentage figures for the general population in three age groups.[1,2,39–41]

In pre-school children (under 5 years of age)

- Waking and crying at night: 15%.
- Over-activity: 13%.
- Difficulty settling at night: 12%.
- Refusing food: 12%.

For polymorphous pre-school behavioural problems involving a combination of high activity levels, disobedience, tantrums and aggressive outbursts, associated with tearfulness and clinging, a point prevalence figure of about 10% can be estimated among 3-year-olds.

In middle childhood (age 6–12 years)

- Persistent tearful, unhappy mood: 12%.
- Bedtime behavioural rituals: 8%.
- Night terrors/other disturbances of sleep: 6%.
- Bedwetting: 5%.
- Inattentive over-activity: 5%.
- Faecal soiling: 1%.

A general rate of significant psychological problems in middle childhood is generally understood as being 12–25% (according to whether the domicile is semi-rural or urban, respectively), from which need to be subtracted those children with overt, handicapping psychiatric disorder (7–14%), yielding a prevalence rate for 'mild' emotional and behavioural abnormality of 5–11%. Much of this will be of a mixed, polymorphous type with various combinations of anxious unhappiness, difficult or antisocial behaviour, and poor relationships with other children.

In adolescence (age 13–18 years)

- Appreciable misery: 45%.
- Social sensitivity: 30%.
- Evident anxiety: 25%.
- Suicidal ideas: 7%.

On the basis of epidemiological data it has been estimated that about 10% of the general adolescent population suffer from more complex depressive moods ('marked internal feelings of misery and self-depreciation').[42] This is in addition to those diagnosed as having psychiatric disorder (including major depression, which appears to have a point prevalence rate of 2–3%).

Prevalence or incidence?

Current evidence strongly suggests that mild or moderate psychological problems are relatively persistent, particularly when linked with continuing abnormalities in family relationships. This is true even for young children. In two large studies, at least half of 3-year-olds rated as having behaviour problems were still rated as displaying problems several years later.[2,43] Studies on psychiatric disorder (interpreted widely) in adolescent populations imply a similar degree of continuity. For instance, nearly half the psychiatric disorder in 14–15-year-olds is constituted by conditions which have persisted since childhood.[9] Although some studies have used a follow-up design from which it might be possible to obtain an inception rate, the use of different instruments for different age groups and a lack of stratification of severity from one sampling period to the other makes this impossible. There is therefore no hard information on incidence within a total childhood population as far as mild and moderate psychological pathology is concerned. Sometimes a moderate disorder shows a tendency to develop into a psychiatric disorder. This is the case with the American concept of dysthymic disorder which, in clinic populations at least, shows a marked tendency to develop into major depression over a few years.[44] There are insufficient studies to establish how frequent this phenomenon is when applied to all mild and moderate psychopathology in childhood.

5 Services available

This section describes the range of services available in each of the sub-categories, most of which are provided by the same group of staff. Only a few sub-categories, e.g. school health services, are provided by dedicated staff, e.g. school nurses.

Costs of community paediatrician services are difficult to interpret because the division of labour between hospital and community trusts varies so widely. Clinical practice also varies.[45] There have been a few attempts to cost the sub-categories of the NHS independently of one another[46,47] (*see* Box 6). These are discussed throughout this section.

Box 6: Examples of attempts to cost CCHS.

The costs of 'core' CCHS have been assessed in four recent studies:[31,45,47]
- a detailed study on child protection and school health conducted in four districts
- a postal and telephone survey gathering data on school nursing and health visiting from 62 districts
- a resource allocation study on health-visiting activity in one city
- a questionnaire and observational study of child health surveillance.

In the first two studies, costs were referred to a notional primary care group (PCG) (now superseded by primary care trusts (PCTs)) population of 100 000, with 20 000 pre-school and school-age children. Figures were based on 1996 pay scales and were estimated or likely costs rather than actual costs as many community child health staff remain in post for a long time and are at or near the top of the salary scale. Employers' costs were added, but no overheads or capital costs. Costs were rounded to the nearest £1000, or to the nearest £10 000 where larger sums were concerned (*see* Figure 1). The term 'district' is used for convenience and a population of 1 million, or 10 PCGs, is assumed. 'Health visitors' (HVs) or 'school nurses' (SNs) are shorthand for any staff paid from these budgets.

The costs of disability care have not been studied in detail.

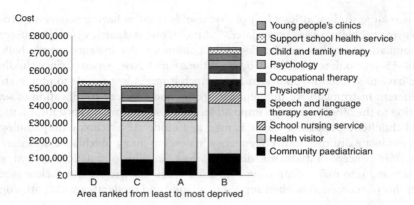

Figure 1: Comparative cost of core CCHS per 10 000 children aged 0–14 years, based on a detailed study in four districts.

Health service support for children who are the primary responsibility of social services departments

Key components include the early identification, prevention and management of child abuse,[48] adoption and fostering, and 'looked after' children (*see* 'Children who have been abused or are at risk of abuse', 'Adoption' and '"Looked after" children' below, respectively). There is a statutory obligation for CCHS to provide medical support to the social services departments of local authorities. Section 27 of the Children Act 1989 required health authorities (now PCTs) 'to comply with requests for help from local authorities in respect of children in need, provided the request is compatible with their statutory duties and does not unduly prejudice the discharge of any of their functions' (*see* Appendix 5). Social services may seek medical support for children whether they are at home, at school or in hospital. The statutory duties are undertaken by designated professionals[49,50] who are 'a nurse with health visiting experience' and 'a doctor with wide experience of child protection', plus supporting staff. The doctor is usually a consultant, but this is not specified in the guidelines (*see* Appendix 4, Appendix 5 and Appendix 6). The designated doctor role includes a substantial teaching and training element.

Children who have been abused or are at risk of abuse

There are four categories:

* physical abuse
* sexual abuse
* neglect (including failure to thrive)
* emotional abuse.

Children may present with overt injuries, failure to thrive or neglect, or because of parental distress. They may be identified at home or at school, or they may disclose sexual abuse to a trusted adult or a helpline; they may also be the victim of assault by a stranger. Much abuse goes unreported and occasionally the abuse is only recognised after death. NHS staff provide expert advice to social services, who have the lead responsibility to determine whether abuse has occurred, to decide whether children's names should be placed on the Child Protection Register and to construct a child protection plan. Prevention of child abuse is one of the aims of the general health promotion programmes (*see* below).

Costs

In calculations that assume a primary care group (PCG) (now PCT) has a population of 100 000 and a district has a population of 1 million, the mean clinical child protection costs for four districts studied in detail were £52 000 (range £35 000 to £75 000). The mean contribution to the annual cost of the nursing and support component was £20 000 per PCG, but the investment would be higher than this in areas with high deprivation scores. The health service input to support and help abused children and their families was a mean of £8000 (range £4000 to £12 000). This shows that more effort is invested in identification and investigation of abuse than in prevention or treatment.[51] Provision of counselling for children who have been abused is limited by inadequate resources. Formal therapy is rarely available and treatment for the perpetrator is the exception.

Adoption

Each health authority (now PCT) CCHS is required to provide a Medical Adviser (MA) for the local authority's adoption panel (*see* Appendix 6). This task ideally requires experience in paediatrics, adult medicine, genetics and psychiatry. In recent years, there has been a decline in the number of healthy babies offered for adoption and a steady increase in the number and proportion of children offered for adoption who are either disabled, or emotionally damaged due to abuse, neglect or multiple foster placements. Parental substance abuse has become an important reason for adoption. The prospective adoptive parents may themselves have a range of health problems or unusual lifestyles.[52] Adoptive parents need the same information and advice as would be given to natural parents. At present there is little investment in post-adoption services, but psychological support and guidance would be helpful for many adopted children and their birth and adoptive parents.

'Looked after' children

Organising and monitoring medical examinations for 'looked after' children is time consuming, but the legal responsibility for arranging these assessments lies with the social services departments. The MA of the health authority (now PCT) has a major role in ensuring appropriate medical care for 'looked after' children.[53] The requirements for medical examinations address the needs of children who are looked after in foster care or in a residential unit. It is important to respond to educational, emotional and mental health needs as well as physical illness or abnormality, and to offer opportunities for giving advice to foster or adoptive parents or other caregivers. Pre-school children and those known to have special needs coming into care for the first time may have unresolved health issues, and their first health assessment is likely to require the skills of a paediatrician. The needs of older children are generally for psychological support and health education, and above all they need continuity of care. This can be provided by a paediatrician, but a primary care team with an interest in the mental health of young people might be more appropriate. There is no statutory medical responsibility for meeting the needs of children fostered privately, but these children have similar needs.[34] (Part IX of the Children Act 1989 places duties on foster and natural parents and the local council in respect of private fostering, though these regulations are often ignored.)

The approach to the needs of 'looked after' children has been updated in the programme 'Quality Protects', which aims to tackle the very poor long-term outcomes, in terms of educational achievement and adjustment to adult life, observed in a high proportion of 'looked after' young people. A more flexible approach will be introduced involving paediatricians, nurses and other professionals, as needed.

Multi-agency working

The Children Act 1989 and the 1986 Disabled Persons Act specify the importance of and the requirement for collaboration between agencies. CCHS make a major contribution on behalf of the NHS to this work, and recent Government initiatives, e.g. in respect of 'looked after' children, underline its importance.

Support and advice to the Local Education Authority: the school health service

CCHS have statutory duties with regard to education (*see* Appendix 4),[54] but the existing legislation leaves the precise nature, volume and quality of input to local interpretation, and there is a resultant wide variation between districts. The term 'health needs of school-age children' is generally preferred to 'school health service' (SHS),[55] but the term SHS is convenient and will be used in this section. The main tasks undertaken by the SHS are shown in Box 7, though some of the tasks listed are no longer considered to be an appropriate or optimal use of professional time, in particular tasks 19 and 25. It is suggested that every school should have a named school nurse, although each nurse may provide services for more than one school.

Box 7: Tasks which may be carried out by the school health service.

1. Medical examination of all school entrants (age group 4–5 years)
2. Developmental examination of all school entrants
3. Assessment of all school entrants in person by school nurse
4. Assessment of school entrants by school nurse, using questionnaire to parents to select those who should be seen in person
5. Vision test at school entry
6. Hearing test at school entry
7. Screening for scoliosis
8. Height and weight at school entry
9. Vision, hearing and height in subsequent years
10. Immunisation
11. Medical examination required in connection with the 'Statementing' procedure specified in the 1981 Education Act
12. Child protection: examination, advice, support, liaison
13. Handover of children with special needs to adult services: required by Education Code of Practice 1994, but important even if the child has no Statement of Special Educational Need
14. Medical, psychological and social evaluation of children referred by teachers or parents because of problems in school
15. Preparation and support of care plan for special needs children in collaboration with Special Needs Co-ordinator (SENCO)
16. Information for and about special needs children, particularly when placed in mainstream schools, and relating to children with health problems
17. Counselling and consultation service, particularly in secondary schools
18. Support to educational social work service; working with parents for children out of school, etc.
19. Dealing with head lice
20. Environmental health issues
21. Sharing policy development for, and taking part in, health promotion and education programmes
22. Advice to school headteachers regarding the health of children travelling on school journeys or participating in unusual sports
23. Providing an informal support and advice network for teachers
24. Hands-on nursing care, e.g. gastrostomies, tracheotomies, tube feeding, medications
25. First aid

School medical inspections

When the school health service was developed at the beginning of the twentieth century, its main function was to undertake periodic medical inspections. Few CCHS now undertake routine medical examinations on all children at any age, but most offer a school entry health check by the school nurse, which might result in referral to the school doctor (selective school entry medical). These checks aim to identify health issues of relevance to the school, and unmet health needs such as lack of immunisation or unrecognised asthma. Most CCHS screen children's vision, height and hearing on school entry. Children who have problems or suspected problems may be seen again for further assessment. Substantial nursing resources are devoted to these routine health assessments, which are often also used for health education of parents.[46]

Immunisation programmes

Most districts offer schoolchildren both the BCG (bacille Calmette-Guèrin) vaccine and a booster dose of polio, tetanus and diphtheria in secondary school. Many schools still offer rubella immunisation to girls at 13 years. Mass immunisation campaigns, such as that conducted for the meningococcal C vaccine programme, and intensive short-term projects to deal with outbreaks of infectious disease in schools or nurseries, often enlist the help of CCHS. This is very disruptive to routine work.

Special needs children

The revised Code of Practice 2001 sets out guidance for the assessment and care of children with special needs.[56] Most of the CCHS activity related to the identification of children with special needs is undertaken in the pre-school period (see 'Organisation of neonatal and pre-school childhood screening, immunisation and health education programmes' below). The SHS may identify a small number of children with acquired rather than congenital problems at school entry (see 'School medical inspections' above). Integration of disabled children in local mainstream schools is rightly the aim where possible. However, children with complex disorders and needs require additional health service input and support. This is more difficult to provide for a few children scattered around a large number of mainstream schools than when these children are concentrated in a few special schools. The role of the SHS with regard to special needs children is to undertake medical examination and report on children who may have special educational needs and to ensure that they have access to the appropriate health services. The SHS may help teachers to manage these children, facilitating full integration into mainstream school. The school nurse interprets medical information for the school, though this may be difficult if the condition is obscure or the documentation unclear. Children may need specialised hands-on nursing care in school to enable them to continue in mainstream schooling. This may be provided by a school nurse, usually supported by a specialist nurse, or by a community-based or hospital outreach nursing team.

Other school nurse roles

School nurses have a supportive and advisory role for children with health problems and are involved in the assessment and follow-up of children for whom there are child protection concerns. Teachers value the advice of school health staff when dealing with other sensitive issues, such as teenage pregnancy, or use of medication, such as inhalers for asthma. Some school nurses identify and work with the educational welfare officer (educational social worker) to help children who are no longer in school because of exclusion (usually because of repeated or serious breaches of school behaviour policy), truancy, chronic fatigue syndrome, illness, school phobia, pregnancy, etc. (see Exclusions from School [DfE Circular 10/94] and Education by LEAs of Children Otherwise Than at School [DfE Circular 11/94]).

Profiles

Another task in some SHS is to compile a profile of health needs using the knowledge of health and education staff. This would include the number of children with Statements of Special Educational Need, health problems and teenage pregnancies, and the profile from each general practice of children with health needs attending those schools.

Health promotion

The SHS may support school-based health education initiatives to prevent substance misuse, injuries, teenage pregnancy and sexually transmitted diseases, or to promote healthy lifestyles and mental health in schools. School nurses and occasionally doctors may take part in classroom health education sessions, particularly those involving sex education, usually working with a teacher. Many school nurses want more involvement in school health promotion programmes (*see* 'Child public health: services which aim to influence the macro-environment' below) and some have been involved in the development of health-promoting schools and school policies on smoking, bullying or sex education.

Multi-agency working

The Education Act 1993 and its accompanying Code of Practice 1994 specify the importance of and requirement for collaboration between agencies.

Organisation of neonatal and pre-school childhood screening, immunisation and health education programmes

Responsibility for both the clinical and (in some practices) organisational aspects of the programme, originally called Child Health Surveillance and now re-defined as Child Health Promotion (identification and prevention of health and developmental problems) and immunisation, has now been largely taken over by the primary care teams. A few general practitioners have opted not to provide this service and it is offered by CCHS instead. The content of the programme was agreed by a national consensus, and is published as *Health for all Children*.[27] Formal screening programmes (*see* Table 4) are kept under review by the Children's Sub-Group of the National Screening Committee, which was established in 1998 to advise on screening policy for children. The recommended immunisation schedule is published and updated by a national committee organised by the Department of Health. The Child Health Promotion programme also ensures that parents have access to important health information, such as the dangers of passive smoking, recommended sleeping position, the advantages of breastfeeding and advice on weaning, diet and injury prevention.

Community paediatricians provide consultant advice for children with suspected developmental or learning disabilities, referred as a result of the screening programmes arising from parental or professional concern, to establish whether they do or do not have developmental problems and might in future have special educational needs. As the threshold for referral is necessarily low, the number of children seen is high relative to the number of problems identified, and the workload in community paediatric clinics may be substantial.

CCHS also co-ordinate provision of the above services, ensure that they evolve to meet changing health needs, monitor performance (uptake, false-positive rates and number of cases identified) and provide continuing medical education for GPs and in-service training for nursing and other staff. The introduction of new screening programmes and disinvestment in out-of-date programmes involve negotiation and

Table 4: Inventory of child health screening programmes.

Screening programme	Targets – aims	Evidence status*	Comments
Neonatal examination as an entity	Identify range of congenital anomalies	2	Under evaluation by working group of Colleges
Examination (clinical) for congenital dislocation of the hips (CDH)	Identify CDH	3	MRC research programme
Examination for CDH with ultrasound	Identify CDH; reduce false positives; facilitate management	4	MRC research programme
Check for heart disease in neonate	Identify congenital heart defects, especially those presenting early	2	Unresolved
Undescended testes in neonate	Identify undescended testes	2	Systematic review requested
Eyes: inspection	Identify anomalies, blindness	2	Evidence to be reviewed by CSG†
Eyes: ophthalmoscope	Identify cataracts	2	Evidence to be reviewed by CSG
Hearing screening in newborn – all babies	Identify permanent congenital hearing impairment	5	20-site pilot programme announced by Minister
Hearing screening in newborn – selected at-risk babies	Identify permanent congenital hearing impairment	1	20-site pilot programme announced by Minister
Biochemical screening; phenylketonuria/congenital hypothyroidism	Identify PKU and CHT; prevent intellectual impairment and brain injury	1	Established, but quality management mechanism under review
Biochemical screening: cystic fibrosis	Early detection; treatment; genetic advice	5	Minister announced intention to introduce nationwide screening
Biochemical screening; Duchenne muscular dystrophy	Early detection; genetic advice	4	Research project continuing in Wales
Biochemical screening; tandem mass spectrometry	Early detection of range of conditions: medium-chain acyl CoA dehydrogenase deficiency, glutaric aciduria type 1, others	5	HTA reports have been considered; new research to be commissioned
Biotinidase screening	Detection and treatment of rare disorder causing brain damage	5	Not regarded as priority
Biochemical screening for congenital adrenal hyperplasia	Early detection and treatment	5	Not regarded as priority
Biochemical screening for neuroblastoma	Detection and treatment	6	
Screening for coeliac disease	Detection of occult cases	6	

Continued overleaf

Table 4: Continued

Screening programme	Targets – aims	Evidence status*	Comments
Screening for haemoglobinopathy	Antenatal/pre-conceptional screening to offer reproductive choice; detect sickle-cell disease in neonate and prevent infection/crisis	2/5	Screening programme for sickle-cell disease announced; implementation study under way
Screening for neonatal liver disease	Detection of biliary atresia and related disorders	4	Research to be reviewed by CSG
6–8-week examination of infant	Identify range of anomalies, management problems, feeding problems	2	
Screening for postnatal depression	Treat mother; prevent adverse effects on baby	3	Evidence under review
6–8-week check for CDH	Identify CDH missed previously	3	MRC research programme in progress
Check for undescended testes (UDTs)	Identify UDT missed at birth; reduce referrals (fewer UDTs at 8 weeks)	2	Systematic review to be commissioned
Monitor weight gain	Identify failure to thrive	3	'Coventry consensus' meeting on growth monitoring – recommendations published
Observational check on CDH at 5–8 months	Identify missed cases	2	MRC research programme
Hearing test at 6–8 months	Identify permanent and transient hearing loss	3	Will be phased out when newborn screen established
General review of health and progress: 8 months	Identify range of developmental problems	2	
Check for iron deficiency at 1–2 years	Identify and treat anaemia and iron deficiency; improve diet	4	Primary prevention more likely to be effective
Review walking at 1–2 years	Identify missed CDH	2	MRC research programme
General review: 2 years	Identify developmental and speech problems, behaviour disorders	2	Evidence supports more parent involvement and primary prevention
General review: 3½ years	Ditto, plus health check	3	To be reviewed by CSG
Check heart and pulses at 3½ years	Identify heart defects and coarctation	2	To be reviewed by CSG
Check for UDTs at 3½ years	Identify missed cases and ascending testes	2	Systematic review to be commissioned
Height monitoring from 2 years of age to puberty	Detect conditions affecting growth; provide public health data	5	'Coventry consensus' meeting on growth monitoring – recommendations published
Weight monitoring: body mass index	Detect obesity and under-nutrition; intervene where needed; public health data	5	'Coventry consensus' meeting on growth monitoring – recommendations published

Vision screening: pre-school	Identify squint, impaired vision, amblyopia	3	Systematic review published in 1997
Vision screening: school entry	Identify squint, impaired vision, amblyopia	3	Recommendation to provide orthoptic screening between 4 and 5 years
Hearing test: school entry	Identify missed permanent hearing impairment, conductive hearing loss	3	Results of research in progress awaited
School entry examination by doctor	Identify anomalies and disease	3	Systematic review completed; *see website*‡
School entry review by nurse	Identify disease; health promotion	3	*See website*
Vision screening at ages 7, 9, 11 and 14	Identify acquired vision problems, myopia	3	*See website*
Colour vision screening at age 5, 7 or 11	Identify colour vision defects; educational advice, careers planning	3	*See website*
Blood pressure screening	Identify hypertension (secondary, essential)	6	
Dental care	Reduce decayed, missing, filled rates; reduce periodontal disease	3	Evidence to be reviewed by CSG
Haemoglobinopathy: screening of teenagers pre-conception	Detect carriers	4	Little evidence as yet
Cardiomyopathy (HOCM)	Detect at early stage; avoid sudden death risk	4	Probably not justified
Autism	Detect at or before age 2; possible early intervention	4	Not recommended
Specific developmental motor co-ordination disorder (dyspraxia)	Identify 'clumsy' children; therapy programme to improve educational outcome	4	Not recommended
Specific reading disorder (dyslexia)	Identify children at risk; investment in pre-literacy skills and remedial reading	4	Initiatives in both health and education sectors
Hyperlipidaemia	Identify in order to reduce risk of ischaemic heart disease	4	Primary prevention more important except possibly for those with significant family history

* 1 = established, accepted, good evidence; 2 = established but evidence base not secure; 3 = established and accepted but being actively reassessed/challenged; 4 = not established – small-scale implementations, pilot or research studies in progress; 5 = active evaluation of new proposal; 6 = proposals not currently being evaluated or implemented.

† CSG = Children's Sub-Group of the National Screening Committee.

‡ Websites refer to: www.health-for-all-children.org for updates on the progress and contents of *Health for All Children* (4e) and the website of the Children's Sub-Group of the National Screening Committee for information about screening: www.nsc.nhs.uk/ch_screen/child_ind.htm

liaison in addition to the teaching required for the staff. These substantial tasks are undertaken by or shared between a community paediatrician in CCHS, a hospital-based general paediatrician, a consultant in public health medicine and/or a senior manager.

In some districts, CCHS administer the scheduling of immunisations and health checks on behalf of primary care teams. CCHS carry out this function for all school health programmes. The management and administration of the community child health information system, including updating, quality control, downloads and analysis, feedback and audit, are also covered by CCHS. These computer systems support the monitoring of screening programmes and health needs assessment, but their full potential has not been exploited. The role of the immunisation co-ordinator is discussed below.

Three pre-school screening programmes in which the CCHS currently have a role in most districts are commissioned and provided outside primary care. These are the neonatal biochemical programme (which aims to identify phenylketonuria, hypothyroidism and, in some districts, cystic fibrosis and haemo-globinopathies), the pre-school vision screening programme and the neonatal hearing screening pro-gramme. The first of these involves midwives and regional laboratories, but the responsibility for service quality must be defined and may rest with a member of CCHS.

Many districts provide orthoptic pre-school vision screening programmes. These are usually managed by ophthalmic services, but the call and recall function and change management may be the responsibility of CCHS. In other districts, health visitors or GPs undertake some vision screening as part of the general preventive programmes.

Many districts now provide selective or high-risk neonatal hearing screening, using oto-acoustic omissions and brainstem-evoked response audiometry. These services are organised in various ways, but generally involve a department of audiology and/or an audiological scientist. Over 40 areas of England are currently carrying out neonatal screening (*see* www.nhsp.info for details of the newborn hearing screening programme).

There are some antenatal and neonatal screening programmes in which CCHS currently play little part, such as screening for haemoglobinopathies, HIV and hepatitis B, but the need for a more co-ordinated approach may mean a greater role for CCHS in the near future.

Organisation and provision of health promotion programmes and preventive services which influence the micro-environment

This role is undergoing rapid development in response to changing health needs. Resources are beginning to be devoted to the provision of emotional and social support to parents, and the development of parental self-awareness, self-esteem and parenting skills. These holistic programmes aim to reduce child abuse, neglect, postnatal depression and behaviour problems, and increase school readiness. The NHS may provide them alone or in collaboration with other agencies, on joint finance, by way of central government grants, or on charitable donations. Health-promoting programmes are not the sole preserve of health professionals[57] and may be undertaken, for example, by social workers, community workers, trained lay visitors, as in the 'community mothers' programme', or non-government (voluntary or charitable) organisations such as Home Start.[58] All those working with 'difficult' families need an effective support and management network.

Pre-school parent support programmes

The Child Health Promotion Programme includes a basic service in the home and in clinics for all families. All parents are visited at home at least once, and open-access clinics are provided by health visitors in general practice and community clinics. Parents who face specific difficulties (psychosocial, economic, environmental or health-related) are offered intensive health visitor support at home.[59,60] This targeting or high-risk approach enables health visitors to spend time with parents in greatest need and is widely supported as a good way of using scarce resources. The extent of and criteria for targeting vary widely. Targeting may be formal (selection on defined criteria) or informal (selection on the basis of professionally defined 'need', e.g. incipient postnatal depression). Resources may be targeted so that there are more health visitors in socio-economically deprived areas. Within each case load, health visitors may spend more time on clients with priority needs. Within each family, health visitors seek to ensure that the problems addressed are those which are most important for that individual.

An alternative to one-to-one work is to provide services to parents in groups, either on a drop-in basis or in structured programmes. Structured parenting programmes[61,62] are a recent development and, although provision is expanding rapidly, it is still patchy. These programmes[63,64] aim to increase parents' awareness of children's emotional needs, to develop parents' skills in meeting those needs, to promote parental well-being and prevent or reverse the development of emotional and behavioural problems in childhood. The commonest model is for groups to meet for two hours a week for 10 to 12 weeks. Although programmes may be run by health visitors or social workers, many are provided by non-government organisations, supported on grants from health or local authorities, central government or charitable donations. Other non-structured groups may be provided to support parents of children with specific problems (e.g. disability or chronic disease, or parents whose child has died), often combining support with fundraising activities. Drop-in centres providing social support and access to information and training, either as part of a more extensive parent support programme or on their own, may be provided by non-government organisations (NGOs) and sometimes by social services in high-risk areas.

Structured programmes have a variety of purposes. The earliest programmes were provided by mental health professionals to parents whose children had established behaviour problems, with a view to reversing or ameliorating the problems (secondary or tertiary prevention). Primary preventive initiatives may be targeted at parents living in areas where there is a high risk of behaviour problems. Programmes may also be provided, usually by NGOs, on an open-access basis in community centres, churches and schools, addressing the more ambitious population-wide health promotion goal of actively promoting emotional well-being in parents and children.

Costs

Prevention is implicit in all the work done by health visitors, and it is almost impossible to cost their various tasks separately. The overall mean cost of health visiting per PCG (now PCT) in four study districts was £510 000 (range £229 000 to £298 000), and there was a weak correlation with deprivation scores.

School programmes

In school-aged children, most successful health promotion programmes are multi-faceted, aiming to reach out to parents and the wider community as well as to children, and in addition changing the school environment.[65] Specific topics such as smoking prevention, healthy eating or sexual health can be tackled, but the most popular approach, namely the health-promoting school, is holistic (*see* Appendix 7).

School health promotion programmes may generate demand for and be complemented by appropriate individual health care. Some teenagers are happy to visit their GP for sexual and mental health advice, but many feel anxious about privacy and confidentiality in general practice premises. These considerations have prompted the creation of adolescent drop-in clinics in schools, primary care settings or other community venues.[66] Collaboration with primary care and family planning services is important.

Costs

The current SHS costs from £250 000 to £350 000 per PCG (now PCT) in the four survey districts, Of this, roughly half is spent on school nursing and half on doctors, administrative staff and others.

Child public health: services which aim to influence the macro-environment

Child public health is defined as health improvement for children achieved through the organised efforts of society. This is a shared role between public health and CCHS. The amount of time devoted to child public health varies widely from one district to another. In the context of CCHS it involves the following:

- The immunisation co-ordinator role: The tasks are summarised in Appendix 8.
- Child health advocacy: This is making the case for changes in services or social policy which would enhance health. Child health advocacy, and professional and public education on child health concerns, can help bring about improvements in the macro-environmental determinants of children's health. The level of involvement of CCHS in these activities varies widely between individuals and districts.
- Contribution to the development of multi-faceted, multi-agency health programmes: This involves working with local authorities, community groups, schools and non-government organisations (sometimes seeking financial support for the latter) to develop health-promoting policies.
- Management of CCHS staff and budget: In most districts this falls to CCHS even though some of the staff work in primary care teams. One person may have overall responsibility for staff, provision and long-term planning.

Disability services

The services available for children with a disability are considered under three headings: primary prevention, secondary prevention and tertiary prevention. The last of these is the main focus of discussion.

Primary prevention

Although better obstetrics, genetic expertise and better health care all play a part, the majority of severely disabling conditions (cerebral palsy, mental handicap, congenital deafness, etc.) are not yet preventable. Birth asphyxia is not the only or the main cause of disability, but is important both because of litigation and because it may to some extent be preventable.

Secondary prevention

The role of community services and primary care in early diagnosis and referral has been discussed earlier in this chapter. There is ample evidence that parents value an early diagnosis of disabling conditions in their child, even if this does not lead to an improved outcome.

Tertiary prevention: care of children with disabilities and developmental problems

The public health overview of services for disabled children

Service provision for disabled children encompasses a number of activities designed to meet the needs of a wide range of ages and problems. These include early identification, a child development team, an audiology programme, links to schools and the Child and Adolescent Mental Health Service (CAMHS), use of tertiary and specialist services, and a range of other community services. A public health overview of needs, referral pathways and information, and a management structure, may be part of the service. The Children Act 1989 calls for multi-agency planning, particularly with regard to shared responsibilities such as early diagnosis and intervention, respite care, expensive residential placements and equipment. The term 'Child Development, Disability and Rehabilitation Service (CDDRS)' has been recommended recently by several professionals in the field, since it can encompass all aspects and models of care.

District Handicap Team

The term 'District Handicap Team (DHT)' was introduced by Court.[67] The DHT may provide the planning and the overview referred to above, though in many districts it focuses only on children attending a child development centre (*see* 'Child Development Teams' below).

Child Development Teams

In the majority of districts, pre-school children with high-severity, low-prevalence conditions are assessed and often treated in a special centre where parents can access all the services they need and professionals can share information and skills. The original title, Child Assessment Centre, has been changed to Child Development Centre (CDC) to emphasise the treatment role. The term 'Child Development Team (CDT)' is now often preferred, first because not all teams operate from a Centre and in rural areas a peripatetic model is often more appropriate than centre-based care (although a team needs a base to meet, store and repair equipment, etc.), and secondly, because school-age children often receive their medical and therapy care from the same staff but at school or at home rather than in a CDC.

Variability in the Child Development, Disability and Rehabilitation Service

The CDDRS usually includes a consultant community paediatrician and one or more of each therapy discipline. Other specialists are recruited to deal with specific problems (*see* Appendix 9). There are startling variations in activity, in the composition of the core team and the availability of specialist inputs, and often there is a lack of any coherent pattern in philosophy or operational policy.[14,68–73] CDTs vary widely in the route(s) of access and referral, the services offered, and the diagnoses, disabilities and age range of the children seen. Some teams care for all forms of disability, whereas others focus on those with severely disabling conditions and exclude (either explicitly in policy statements or, more often, by default) children with acquired lesions, such as traumatic brain or spinal cord injury, and those with non-neurological disorders. Some provide only for the under-fives, whereas others offer support and advice until transfer to adult services. Furthermore, the alternative provision for those children not served by the team is often ill-defined or non-existent. Management arrangements for deciding, for example, how children with high-prevalence, low-severity conditions should be assessed, and for planning the service as a whole, are often weak. The value placed on teamwork, the extent to which parents are involved in case reviews and the readiness to share reports with parents all vary widely.[69,71,74]

Audiology services

Appendix 10 sets out an overview of audiology services. The staffing and economic implications of universal neonatal screening (UNS) are currently being reviewed following publication of a systematic review.[75] (*See* www.nhsp.info for information on the newborn hearing screening programme.)

Community-based services

Children with high-severity, low-prevalence conditions receive therapy and medical support within school. This is easy in special schools or units but more difficult for disabled children scattered among many mainstream schools, and has considerable resource implications for health care provision by nurses, therapists, etc.

Children with low-severity, high-prevalence conditions are often managed entirely in a community setting (health centres, clinics, day nurseries, nursery schools or at home) by therapists, clinical psychologists and community-based paediatricians.

Services shared with other agencies

Health professionals work with social services and education to provide other services. Respite care is an important service for many families and takes several forms, but varies widely in quantity and quality. Parents and children differ in their needs and want a choice of the following:

- hostel/home run by social services with health support or advice
- placement with a family in the child's home district for one or several nights (e.g. 'Share-a-Family' scheme)
- visiting carer looks after the child at home
- specialised facility if the child's needs are very complex; may also provide palliative or terminal care along hospice lines
- hospital ward, alongside sick children or in a specially designated unit or room; only appropriate for severe problems which limit use of other facilities.

The provision of appropriate education

This is the responsibility of the local authority. Health services play an important supporting role (*see* 'Support and advice to the Local Education Authority: the school health service' above). The 1994 Code of Practice (revised in 2001) and the Children Act require that agencies should co-operate to provide the best care for children with special needs. Pre-school programmes such as 'Portage' (a home-teaching package) are usually provided through the education authority,[76] although some are jointly funded or share resources between agencies. Therapists support Portage programmes for children with complex problems. The PCT may make a contribution to the cost of residential care and education of children with complex problems. The health service is responsible for providing medical evidence and for monitoring of children requiring assessment under the Education Act ('Statementing', *see* 'School-age children: support and advice to the Local Education Authority' above), and contributes to the transition process when the child reaches the age of 14 years.

Child protection

The Child Protection Service deals with abuse and neglect affecting disabled as well as able-bodied children. However, children with disability are at increased risk of abuse. North American data suggest a 50% higher risk compared to non-disabled children. Those with more severe disability and with communication problems are particularly at risk. Peer abuse in residential care can be a significant problem.[34] Disabled children who are looked after require statutory assessments.

Costs

There are no detailed data on the costs of the service as a whole. A cost analysis is a difficult undertaking and a cost–benefit analysis even more so, for several reasons.

- There are a great many disabling conditions, of varying severity.
- Multiple agencies are involved (the NHS, social services, education and the voluntary sector).
- Within the NHS, many disciplines are involved.
- It is difficult to measure the volume and effectiveness of interventions offered or needed.
- Reduced family stress, improved coping mechanisms and raised quality of life are as important as changing the child's physical health status.

In 1991, 78% of districts had some form of CDC, and of these, half also functioned as District Handicap Teams. The staffing and activity levels varied widely. Paediatrician sessions ranged from full-time to one session per month. One-fifth of CDCs would only see children under the age of five. Fifty-nine per cent of CDCs had no adult service to which they could refer their patients when they became adults. By 1998, most districts had some form of CDT. Less than a third offered a comprehensive service throughout childhood, while 70% mainly served under-fives with some other team providing for school-aged children. Over 50% of teams included a paediatrician, speech and language therapist, physiotherapist, occupational therapist, social worker and health visitor. One-third of teams included staff from social services and education. There was also wide variation in the number of specialist services provided within the team. For example, one-fifth offered a head injury service, and one-sixth offered a dyslexia clinic. There was similarly considerable disparity in frequency of team meetings, management arrangements, and the degree of parent involvement in service planning. Staff account for by far the largest part of the total cost of a disability service. Table 5 outlines the case load and Table 6 summarises the data on staffing. Taken together, the data suggest[70] that current per capita expenditure on services for children with disability must vary substantially between districts, perhaps by a factor of three or even more.

There are some data on equipment costs for children with high-severity, low-prevalence disorders. The estimated cost is £1070 per 1000 children (total population) aged 0–19 years. Of this, £341 is for communication aids and £729 for physical disability equipment (1997 figures).[77] There are no comparable data for shared educational or respite care placements.

Table 5: Estimates of case load.

Condition	Available incidence/ prevalence data	New cases per year in district with 1 million population	Case load in district with 1 million population
Cerebral palsy	2.5 per 1,000 births	25	500
Neural-tube defects and hydrocephalus	Varies from 0.4–2 per 1,000 births	4–20	80–400
Duchenne muscular dystrophy	1 per 3,000 male births	2	40
Severe learning difficulties	3.7 per 1,000 children	37	740
Moderate learning difficulties, developmental delay, etc.	2–3% of all children	200	4,000
Specific reading disorder (e.g. dyslexia*)	Said to affect at least 2% of population; mainly present between ages 5 and 10 years	200	1,000 active cases, i.e. aged 5–10 years
ADHD	1% of child population – boys > girls	100	500 active cases, i.e. aged 5–10 years
Epilepsy	6–12 per 1,000 children	60–120	1,200–2,400 cases in district; half active, half in remission
Permanent hearing impairment	Per 1,000 births; 1.3 per 1,000 children aged 5 years (includes acquired hearing loss)	13	260
Autism	1 in 2–3,000 births	4	80
Autism spectrum disorder	2–4 per 1,000 births	20–40	400–800; variable improvements over time
Long-term or permanent speech, language and communication disorders, excluding autism	2–5 per 1,000 children aged 5 years	20–50	At least 100–250 active cases but rate and extent of resolution vary widely
Blind and partially sighted (excluding multiple disability; 'cortical visual impairment')	0.7 per 1,000 children	7	140
Traumatic brain injury	160 per 100,000 children per year: 29 with permanent disability	58 with permanent disability – varying degrees	No data available

* Dyslexia or specific reading disorder is an example of the conditions known collectively as specific learning disabilities. Prevalence figures vary depending on definitions. Other examples include specific developmental motor co-ordination disorder.

Assumptions: 1 million people; one-fifth (200 000) in the age group cared for by paediatricians.

These figures are approximate, as data are scarce and data on *active* case numbers are very few.

Most disabling conditions are recognised within a year or two of birth and are present throughout childhood.

Exceptions: Traumatic brain injury is more common in older children. Mild learning disability, dyslexia, language impairment and ADHD are unlikely to present in the first two years, sometimes improve over time and may need little NHS input during the teens. Case-load estimates are correspondingly less reliable.

Death rates in the paediatric age group are too low to affect these estimates.

Table 6: Estimates of workforce requirements.

Post	Minimum	Mean or median	Upper end of range	Notes
Consultant paediatricians with interest in neurodisability	4	7	12	I
Non-consultant career-grade paediatricians	10	15	20	I
Physiotherapists	10	20	30	II
Occupational therapists	6	13	20	III
Speech and language therapists	30	50	90	IV
Clinical psychologists		13		V

The wide range of figures shown here is partly explained by the extent to which hospital-based paediatricians, paediatric neurologists and tertiary centres (neurology, rehabilitation, acquired brain injury, etc.) contribute to the care of the various patient groups listed above, by differences in the contribution of primary care, and by varying levels of input from other staff such as community paediatric nurses, liaison health visitors, personal assistants, etc.

Sources:

Establishment in WTEs (corrected to a population of 1 million people) as observed in unpublished surveys, supported by various documents[78] and reports as follows:

- The British Association for Community Child Health[20] recommended a total of 16 WTE career-grade staff per 1 million population for disability services (i.e. excluding other aspects of CCHS as set out in Section 1).
- The Association of Chartered Physiotherapists recommendations are based on case-load management. Extrapolation suggests that this approximates to the upper end of the range in the table.[78] However, some therapists also provide a service for hospital patients (intensive care, orthopaedics, etc.), so direct comparisons are difficult.
- The National Association of Paediatric Occupational Therapists makes no formal recommendations for staffing levels.
- Ideal speech and language therapy provision was suggested as 6 per 100 000 population by Quirk in 1972 and as 26 per 100 000 (all ages and service needs) by Enderby and Davies in 1989. The current figure is closer to 6. The Royal College of Speech and Language Therapists recently reviewed these figures but no longer makes any specific recommendation.[79]
- In the absence of other data, this figure is based on the guidance of the British Psychological Society that there should be at least one clinical psychologist working with children and families per 75 000 population, but this does not include more specialised input for particular services, e.g. disability.[78]

References

- Lloyd-Evans A. *Child Development and Disability Group. Standards for child development services.* London: British Association for Community Child Health/Royal College of Paediatrics and Child Health, 2000.
- British Association for Community Child Health Working Group. *Community Paediatric Workforce Requirements to Meet the Needs of Children in the 21st Century.* London: British Association for Community Child Health, 2000.
- van der Gaag A. *Communicating Quality. 2. Professional standards for speech and language therapists* (2e). London: Royal College of Speech and Language Therapists, 1996, p. 273.

Mild and moderate psychological disorders

Health services for young people with mild and moderate mental health problems are commonly provided by more than one provider unit in any one district. There may be contributions from primary care, community and hospital paediatrics, child mental health workers, clinical psychology, child and adolescent psychiatry, learning disability psychiatrists and, for older adolescents, adult mental health services. Moreover, services relevant to child and adolescent mental health are provided by several agencies: health, education and social services as well as the voluntary sector. Historically there has been poor co-ordination between all of these, and a tendency to duplicate each other's work.

The specialist Child and Adolescent Mental Health Services (CAMHS) are thought to see 10–20% of children with mental health problems and within those children seen in CAMHS, 25% will have their clinical problem rated as less than severe.[38] This suggests that most children with mild or moderate psychopathology are likely to be seen by other agencies, if at all. The ONS survey[36] indicated that for the more severe category of mental disorder, those agencies included primary health care teams, community paediatricians and, within education, educational psychologists, and it seems likely that the same would be true for in seeing children and adolescents with mild and moderate psychological pathology. The development of tier 2 services within CAMHS, which one might expect to be relevant, is still at an early stage.

6 Effectiveness

Assessing the effectiveness of CCHS activities is difficult, and much of the evidence is of indifferent quality (*see* Box 8).

Box 8: Problems in assessing the effectiveness of CCHS.

1 CCHS is a network of activities involving several different disciplines. 2 CCHS activities overlap with those of acute trusts and of many other agencies. 3 The important outcomes need to be measured many years into the future. 4 The need for preventive services is assessed by professional opinion, not demand, as public awareness is limited. 5 The effectiveness of any CCHS action (at individual or community level) may depend on other actions (synergy) that are not under the control of the CCHS. 6 Randomised controlled trials are difficult to apply to complex interventions such as those offered in the CCHS. 7 Collection of information to monitor the CCHS is complicated by the many sites where the services are delivered.

Economic analysis of preventive services with far-reaching aims, such as the majority of CCHS services, is complex. What might be achieved is as likely to be constrained by what society is prepared to invest as by potential effectiveness or impact. Consideration of cost-effectiveness has however been severely hampered in these services by lack of information on costs as well as on effectiveness (as in earlier sections, a PCG [now PCT] is assumed to have a population of 100 000).

Children who are the primary responsibility of social services departments

Much of the work done in support of social services is required by legislation and official guidance. It is a response to situations that society considers to be intolerable. There is only limited evidence about the long-term impact of these services. Legislation and official guidance may have inhibited experimentation and research.

The assessment of abused children can itself become abusive. This is less likely to occur if it is done by those with appropriate skills and training. Little is known about the value or diagnostic accuracy of examinations for abuse other than sexual abuse. Reliability is generally assumed to be high where physical abuse is concerned, but may be less so for emotional abuse or neglect.

Good practice in assessment and follow-up of sexually abused children includes provision of reassurance, exclusion of sexually transmitted diseases where appropriate, and provision of emergency contraception if indicated. Clinical experience in psychotherapeutic practice suggests that abused children would benefit from prolonged therapy to prevent future mental health problems,[80] but in view of the potential cost of such services and the possibility that they might have no benefit (or could even be harmful), they merit further research. Appropriate training and better co-ordination between existing agencies, notably child psychiatry and psychology and social services, might be a more effective way to provide such services than the creation of completely new teams.

The outcomes for children who suffer chronic abuse, or are looked after, are poor in terms of mental health and adjustment to adult life. Adoption outcomes are also often disappointing.[34] The potential benefits to be obtained from effective intervention are correspondingly large, but little information is available on the value of intervention at its current levels (*see* 'Organisation and provision of health promotion and preventive services which influence the micro-environment' below for effectiveness of preventive services).

- Size of effects: unknown. Quality of evidence: III.

Support and advice for Local Education Authorities: the school health service

Table 7 (*see* overleaf) summarises the effectiveness of the many activities included in school health services.

The routine examination by a doctor of all school entrants at age five is of doubtful value. Most of those who have carried out studies of this programme appear to have taken for granted that the detection of 'defects' is beneficial, and have focused their investigations on whether defects can be detected, but for many of the commonly identified conditions the need for and effectiveness of intervention are far from certain. None of the studies identified in a recent review were able to address the question 'Do school-entry medicals improve health?' Data from school-entry medicals have been used in the past by public health practitioners to identify health needs, but are no longer an efficient way to establish such needs.

Routine examination of all school entrants might be justified in areas where delivery of pre-school primary health care is poor. It could be useful to identify, perhaps by questionnaire, those children who have long-term health problems of importance for their schooling and those who have had little or no health care before starting school, e.g. recent immigrants and children from travelling families. Even in these circumstances, this function might be provided more effectively through the development of primary care rather than through the school medical service.

In most districts the school-entry medical examination has been replaced, on pragmatic grounds, by a school-nurse health assessment and interview. The aims have not been articulated any more clearly than

Table 7: Services provided for children of school age.

Task	Justification and aim	Evidence
Medical examination of all school entrants (age group 4–5 years).	Identification of previously missed defects, e.g., congenital heart disease, undescended testes.	Number and significance of defects found uncertain, but probably not cost-effective.
Developmental examination of all school entrants.	Identification of previously missed or ignored learning, motor or behavioural deficits.	Assessment by experienced person identifies defects, but no evidence that this is more effective than detection by teacher or that it improves outcome.
Assessment of all school entrants in person by school nurse.	Identification of symptoms of ill-health for onward referral. May be combined with health promotion interview and with vision/hearing tests. Opportunity for child and parents to meet nurse.	No evidence of benefit; no UK studies available to assess current practice, but no reason to expect as good a yield as examination by doctor. School nurse not well known to family in one study.
Assessment of school entrants by school nurse using questionnaire to parents to select those who should be seen in person.	As above; also to identify children with no previous medical care and those not registered with a primary care team.	No hard evidence, but a low-cost activity which is a necessary prelude to provision of primary and preventive care.
Vision test at school entry.	Detection of refractive error, squint and amblyopia by visual acuity test with each eye separately.	Adequately trained staff can produce acceptable results; benefits modest, but school entry is first time 100% of children can be reliably tested for vision defects.
Hearing test at school entry.	Detection of missed, late-onset, mild or unilateral sensorineural hearing loss; detection of persistent middle ear disease.	Number of cases of sensorineural loss very small; natural history and impact of middle ear disease variable and still uncertain.
Screening for scoliosis.	Detection of scoliosis in young teenagers.	Evaluations of programme not favourable.
Height and weight at school entry.	Detection of growth disorders; valuable public health function (trends in height and differences between social groups are a good marker of children's health – included in proposed core data set).	Yield of growth disorders very small, but acceptable false-positive rate.
Vision, hearing and height in subsequent years.	Detection of new-onset disorders.	Yield very low. Older children with refractive error can access optometrist on request. Height monitoring not useful.
Immunisation.	Prevention of TB; rubella and other immunisations when indicated; new programmes; school-leaving booster. Check on children who have missed programme.	Little data on role of school vs. primary care team. In deprived areas, probably more cost-effective when provided through school. PHCT may give better uptake in less deprived areas. BCG should be done in school – inexperienced operators get poor results.

Table 7: Continued.

Task	Justification and aim	Evidence
Medical examination required in connection with the 'Statementing' procedure specified in the 1981 Education Act.	Statutory requirement.	Necessary and useful for children with disabling conditions. Value for children with learning or behavioural problems less certain, but occasional finding of vision, hearing or other medical problem.
Child protection: examination, advice, support, liaison.	Statutory duty within local child protection and ACPC guidelines.	Benefits unknown, but essential role and support for suspected or actual cases is expected by education staff.
Identify and participate in handover of children with special needs to adult services: required by Education Code of Practice 1994, but important even if child has no Statement of Special Educational Need.	Ensure smooth transition into the most appropriate adult service at the right time, with full information to new specialist team and primary care staff.	Good evidence of current defects in system; upsetting to parents; examples of good practice involving community nursing as facilitator of handover.
Medical, psychological and social evaluation of children referred by teachers or parents because of problems in school.	Learning problems can be caused by biological or social factors; detailed diagnostic assessment desired by parents but not always available from psychologist.	Medical role in assessing school problems is ill-defined; logical that accurate diagnosis should improve remedial work; extensive anecdotal evidence but little rigorous data. Exception is attention deficit disorder – good evidence of benefit from accurate diagnosis and correct management.
Prepare and support care plan for special needs children in collaboration with Special Needs Co-ordinator (SENCO).	Children with disabilities need health care support in school. This can be provided by the education authority, but the SHS should offer information, support and training.	Need for this service is stressed by teachers and headteachers.
Provision and interpretation of information relating to special needs children, particularly when placed in mainstream schools, and to children with health problems.	Ensure that teachers understand implications of and care for health problems of children in school.	Teachers expect and value such advice from the school health service but complain it is often not available. No evidence as to quality or availability of advice given.
Counselling and consultation service, particularly in secondary schools.	Provision of advice and support for range of problems, mainly for older children and teenagers.	A service wanted by young people, separate from that provided by GPs. Measurable benefits in prevention of teenage pregnancy.
Support to educational social work service; working with parents of children out of school, etc.	Identification of children failing in school and children out of school for any reason. Follow-up to establish reason and assist re-entry to school or other educational intervention. Involves close liaison with educational welfare officer.	Examples of good practice support concept; obvious need for service – potential benefits considerable.

Continued overleaf

Table 7: Continued.

Task	Justification and aim	Evidence
Responding to concerns about head lice.	Advise parents and schools on management and prevention of head lice infestations.	No support for routine inspections; school nurses well placed to advise on treatment by insecticides or mechanical means ('wet combing, with conditioner', 'bug-busting').
Environmental health issues.	Avoidance of cross-infection by poor hygiene in toilets, responding to school concerns about infections, such as HIV, and epidemic diseases, such as outbreaks of meningitis; advice on individual children with infectious diseases such as chickenpox, skin diseases, etc.	Most interventions based on good evidence.
Share policy development for and take part in health promotion and education programmes.	Assist in preparing and teaching lessons on health topics; support staff in healthy school initiatives. Liaise with health promotion specialists to identify topics and resources.	Important role for health staff – initiate, support and contribute to health promotion schemes in schools. Can create opportunities through health promotion for pupils to use consulting/counselling service.
Advice to headteachers regarding the health of children travelling on school journeys or participating in unusual sports.	Reassurance of teachers, avoidance of medical problems away from home.	Uncertain value; serious medical problems need advice from child's specialist.
Provide an informal support and advice network for teachers.	Teachers have many problems of their own for which they might value advice.	No evidence available other than anecdotal reports.
Hands-on nursing care, e.g. gastrostomies, tracheotomies, tube feeding, medications.	May be provided in special schools; task shared with other carers and/or community paediatric nurses.	Valued by education staff, though few data on volume or training needs.
First aid.	School nurses do *not* normally consider it part of their role to provide a first-aid service in schools.	Little evidence, but teachers do value first-aid support and training; may play a part in health education.

those of medical examinations by doctors. A review[81] in 1998 did not identify any studies which could provide evidence of effectiveness, but one study showed that this approach might cost more than routine medical examination of all children. Although the evidence base is incomplete, school-entrant vision and hearing testing, and measuring height and weight, probably constitute the best-buy school-entrant screening at present. The benefits of these programmes depend in part on what pre-school programmes are in place. There is little evidence to support any further screening procedures of all children after the age of five. Repeated measuring of short children is not useful.

- Size of effect: probably D. Quality of evidence: IV.

The effectiveness of school immunisation programmes is kept under review by the Department of Health. Most programmes are universal but there is debate about BCG. Although a few districts with low prevalence rates have dropped the programme, most retain it. Although the incidence of TB was falling, it rose in the 1990s and is now causing considerable concern, especially in urban areas. This rise is related to a number of factors, including poverty/homelessness, increases in refugees/asylum seekers and incomplete treatment. Co-infection with HIV and TB is also a problem. Multi-drug-resistant organisms are a growing concern.[82]

- Size of effect: C. Quality of evidence: III.

Whilst there are no experimental studies of the effectiveness of the school nurse's role in safeguarding the health of children with specific problems, it is well described, thought to be important by school nurses and valued by teachers.[83,84]

- Size of effect: C. Quality of evidence: III.

The added value derived from the medical contribution to 'Statementing' of children has not been systematically assessed. Experimentation may have been inhibited by national guidance and legislation.

- Size of effect: unknown. Quality of evidence: III.

School nurses' involvement in school health promotion raises two issues: (a) the effectiveness of health promotion in schools and (b) the effectiveness of the school nurse's role in this process. These are dealt with in 'Organisation and provision of health promotion and preventive services which influence the micro-environment' below.

- Size of effect for (a): C. Quality of evidence: III.

Neonatal and pre-school child health screening, immunisation and health education programmes

There are two effectiveness issues here, namely the effectiveness of the screening, immunisation and health education programmes and the effectiveness of the CCHS role in that process. The key screening procedures have been reviewed extensively (*see* Table 4). The present programme is pragmatic, based on a best-buy concept that seeks to integrate the limited evidence from experimental research with consumer wishes and professional opinion. There is, for example, still doubt about screening for congenital dislocation of the hips and congenital heart disease, but these programmes will continue until further research is available. Three programmes are discussed in more detail below.

Neonatal hearing screening

For the past 40 years the hearing of infants at 7 to 8 months of age has been tested using the infant distraction test (IDT) as part of the programme delivered in primary care. Despite this, hearing-impaired children are still identified too late for optimal outcomes. Screening of all neonates is now possible and this programme is more cost-effective than the IDT.[75] The delivery and maintenance of an effective neonatal screening programme presents many challenges, and an implementation plan has been developed (*see* www.nhsp.info). The first step will be to ensure that excellent and timely care is available for babies identified in the programme.

- Size of effect: B. Quality of evidence: I-1.

Vision screening

Although screening by orthoptists has been demonstrated to be substantially more reliable and cost-effective (in terms of sensitivity and specificity) in pre-school children than screening by any other professional, there is still controversy about the extent of disability caused by minor visual defects (amblyopia, squint and refractive error), the effectiveness of treatment[85] and the extent of the additional benefit from screening at age three or four as opposed to age five. Trials of treatment for amblyopia are currently in progress. The interim solution proposed pending further evidence is screening by orthoptists for children between the ages of four and five.[27]

- Size of effect for treatment: unknown.

Biochemical and other laboratory-based screening

The neonatal screening programmes for phenylketonuria (PKU) and hypothyroidism (HT) are well established and are cost-effective. However, there are still weaknesses in the system, one of which is the lack of an identified individual to be accountable for the programme. The effectiveness of screening for cystic fibrosis is currently under review. New screening methods have been developed to detect medium-chain acyl CoA dehydrogenase deficiency (MCAD) and glutaric aciduria type 1, but these are not yet provided on a routine basis and studies of effectiveness are incomplete.[86] It is possible to provide reproductive choice for parents at risk of having children with haemoglobin disorders and to reduce the number of births affected by thalassaemia.[87] Effective programmes will include antenatal and neonatal components, review of the care of people with these disorders, and community education programmes which aim to encourage young people to determine their carrier status before conception.

- Size of effect: A for PKU and CHT; C for other potential programmes. Quality of evidence: II-2 for PKU; II-1 for CHT; III for others.

Organisation and provision of health promotion and preventive services which influence the micro-environment

Systematic reviews of holistic home-visiting programmes for new parents, offering general support and skill development, suggest that such programmes can be effective in high-risk groups, reducing the incidence of injuries and the antecedents of abuse and neglect, improving the mental health of parents and children and impacting beneficially on a variety of other outcomes.[28,88,89] Evaluation of their impact on child abuse has been confounded by the increase in identification and reporting which usually accompanies intensive intervention. Evaluated programmes have varied greatly in their target group, their length and intensity, and in the professional background of the visitors. Success is not uniform; it depends in part on programme intensity and length and presumably on many other factors, of which the interpersonal skills of the home visitor may be the most important. Most of the experimental studies of these programmes have been carried out in the USA, where home visiting is not routine practice as it is in the UK.

In the UK, a parent adviser service using home visiting by trained health visitors and clinical medical officers has been shown to reduce behaviour problems and improve parental mental health.[37] The author stresses the vital importance of respectful professional–parent relationships. There is conflicting evidence for the success of the First Parent Visiting Programme on a range of child health outcomes, including nutrition.[90,91] This programme, which involved training and development of health visitors to work in a more empowering and supportive way, together with a structured home-visiting programme covering nutrition, child development and health, was widely implemented in the UK. Whilst the structured programme may no longer be used in its entirety, the training programme has influenced how health visitors work with parents. Health visitors practising this programme observed that it was effective in improving parents' self-esteem.

Non-professional home visiting by community mothers has some benefits.[92] Several lay home visiting support services in the USA[93] and one in the UK have been subjected to an extensive qualitative appraisal and their benefits and limitations clearly described. Lay services support and build on, rather than substitute for, professional skills. More research is needed on these themes, but results are promising. In the UK, home-visiting programmes specific to one issue, e.g. postnatal depression or accident prevention, have been shown to have benefits.[71] Programmes offering advice and support to parents on language acquisition and pre-literacy skills seem effective and are likely to have wider educational benefits.[73]

Structured parent training or education programmes based on behaviour modification using role play, role modelling and feedback can improve established emotional and behavioural problems and prevent their development in high-risk groups.[15] Group-based programmes are not only more cost-effective but also more effective than one-to-one schemes. Programmes based on Adlerian, Rogerian or psycho-dynamic principles which aim to develop parental self-awareness and self-esteem, together with empathy and respect for their children, look promising.[37] Most currently available programmes are eclectic, combining elements of both approaches. Non-government organisations are the leading providers. Some NGOs offer training to health visitors and midwives. Many of these programmes have been evaluated using qualitative methods, which demonstrate that they are appreciated by parents and that they can improve family well-being in all social groups. The effectiveness of these programmes probably depends crucially on the interpersonal skills of the group leader.

- Size of effect: A/B. Quality of evidence: I1/I2.

There are strong theoretical grounds[94] to suggest that a population approach, offering programmes to all parents, is likely to be the most effective way to prevent problems such as postnatal depression, behaviour problems and child abuse. Whilst universal provision has been the accepted model for child health surveillance for many years, it is not yet accepted as an appropriate model for parent support and training. Current opinion favours a basic programme of professional home visiting for all children, together with a more intensive programme targeted at high-risk groups. Targeting of resources by geographic location can be based on one of several formulae, but these presuppose that objectives have been agreed. Targeting of individuals as high risk, without their knowledge and consent, either on the basis of socio-economic indicators or because of observed characteristics of the family, is no longer acceptable. Secretive targeting can interfere with the effectiveness of these programmes and introduces stigma and patronage to provision.

Mutual respect, professional judgement and negotiation are the best way of assessing which families need and will use professional help, who might benefit from support from the voluntary sector either on a one-to-one basis or in groups, and who can contact professional help when needed. Providing additional support to parents who request it, and offering additional resources to selected high-risk neighbourhoods, are both likely to be good investments.

Some NGOs delivering programmes to parents with widely differing health needs favour universal provision, but do not have the resources to sustain this. If universal parenting programmes were to be offered, uptake would be likely to start at around 10% of parents and increase gradually if those who attended found them helpful. In view of the potential for promoting health, studies of the longer-term effectiveness, population impact and methods of providing these programmes are urgently needed.

Table 7 summarises the evidence of effectiveness for school health services. There are several systematic reviews of health-promotion interventions in schools. Whilst universal programmes are the norm, targeted programmes have also been developed for obese children, pregnant teenagers, and children of divorce. Programmes which enable children to develop new skills – both interpersonal (e.g. self-awareness, communication, conflict resolution) and specific skills (e.g. road crossing, food choices) – can improve a wide range of health outcomes (mental health, emotional well-being, dietary intake, fitness, cholesterol levels, injury occurrence, obesity and, more rarely, substance use and sexual health), but cannot be relied upon to do so in every project. Mode of delivery may be critical. Programmes that gain the commitment and support of all the staff and are delivered to pupils in a respectful, empowering manner are more likely to be successful. Programmes delivered by or in conjunction with trained pupils (peer-led programmes) appear to be more effective in improving knowledge and changing attitudes. Children are sensitive to the discrepancy between the health messages they are taught and the environment and culture of the school. Thus programmes that address the school ethos and environment and include outreach to parents and community are more likely to be successful. Promoting the emotional well-being of children seems to be central to success, together with improving the health and well-being of teachers.[95,96] This is the philosophy of the 'health-promoting school'[97] (*see* Appendix 7).

- Size of effect: B. Quality of evidence: I-1-I-2.

There have been no experimental studies of the school-nurse role in the development of school health promotion programmes or policies, or in classroom teaching, though their input is especially valued by teachers who feel uncomfortable with the subject matter. Health promotion is a role for which few nurses are trained, but many have adopted and developed it. Time constraints limit involvement as there is at most one school nurse for one secondary school and often the ratio is lower. School nurses who are not known to staff and pupils and are unaware of the health promotion programmes running in the schools are unlikely to be able to fulfil this role effectively.

The aim of adolescent health services is that adolescents should be better able to look after their own health. This includes greater self-awareness, and greater knowledge of the significance and management of minor physical health problems, and of preventive health care. Little is known about why individuals do or do not make use of such services. Consumer satisfaction can be assessed directly by the extent to which the service is used. In one survey,[98] teenagers rated the following as important in primary health care facilities, in priority order: absolute confidentiality; access to advice over the telephone, if necessary without giving one's name; written information from the health centre; friendly and welcoming approach; notices and magazines suitable for young people. A drop-in type of clinic service which is friendly, practical, non-judgemental and above all confidential is likely to be well used – but such a reputation can take a year or more to develop. Good working relationships with primary care teams and other specialist services are essential. Primary care teams need to create a climate in which young people know that they can see a GP with complete confidentiality.

The best evidence of effectiveness in adolescent health care is in prevention of unwanted pregnancy.[99] Although teachers are required to undertake some sex education, they are not permitted to offer advice on sex or contraception to individual pupils. Government policy is that health and education professionals should be 'involved in the development of the school sex education policy' and that 'Teachers should take account of . . . the contribution which . . . health professionals can make'. A teacher approached by an individual pupil for specific advice on contraception or other aspects of sexual behaviour should 'encourage the pupil to seek advice from his or her parents and, if appropriate, from the relevant health service professional (for example, the pupil's GP, or the school doctor or nurse)' (Circular No. 5/94. *Sex Education in Schools*).

CCHS can provide special adolescent clinics either in schools, in primary care or in specialist community clinics (*see* Appendix 11). Both schools and individual pupils value access to a school nurse with counselling skills, though opinions differ as to whether this is best provided within the school campus or outside – probably there is a place for both. Little is known of any longer-term outcomes, but logic suggests that provision of what teenagers want would be the first step to an effective service.

Several of the health promotion interventions described in this section might have a delayed beneficial effect on health, but most of the studies reported here are based on short-term outcomes. The long-term follow-up studies of one US, high-risk, home-visiting programme have shown important benefits to mental and social well-being (criminality, employment, psychiatric diagnosis) which are very likely to be associated with improvements in adult health.[29]

Child public health: services which influence the macro-environment

Practical experience and experimental studies of public health interventions have demonstrated that effectiveness depends on multi-faceted multi-agency approaches. Individual interventions suitable for evaluation in trials may prove ineffective on their own, yet can be an essential part of a public health programme. Because public health interventions are so complex and experimental studies so expensive, the evidence base for public health is often to be found in observational studies of epidemiological trends and social analyses rather than in experimental studies.

Advocacy on behalf of children – making the case for change at societal level, like the banning of tobacco advertising – can overcome even powerful commercial vested interests, but this may take many years. National and local road safety services have delivered a remarkable reduction in car injuries in spite of a dramatic increase in traffic. They have been less successful in reducing childhood pedestrian injuries, where much of the downward trend may be the consequence of a more constrained and sedentary lifestyle among children.[30]

The school health services and the maternal and child health services were both public health interventions introduced at the beginning of the twentieth century. Collectively they have contributed to a dramatic improvement in the physical health of children and subsequently that of adults. It is, however, impossible and probably inappropriate to attempt to measure effect size or tease out the relative contribution of the different components.

The development of the immunisation co-ordinator role has played a part in raising childhood immunisation rates to their current high level, though other changes such as paying general practitioners based on their immunisation uptake rates have also contributed.

- Size of effect: A/B. Quality of evidence: II-2/III.

Effectiveness of services for children with disabilities

Children with high-severity, low-prevalence disabilities

Few disabilities can be 'cured'. Even major surgery is only an incident in the life of the disabled child. Very small gains can take a long time. Nevertheless, parents of disabled children have well-defined expectations of the health service. Measurements of the effectiveness of disability services can be undertaken in several ways:

- the impact of one particular intervention
- overall assessments of quality of the child's life or family functioning, parental satisfaction, adjustment and coping
- measuring processes of care – as a proxy for quality of life and patient satisfaction outcomes.

All three methods have been used in an attempt to evaluate the effectiveness of the care provided for severely disabled children.

Individual interventions

For children with severe disabling conditions, such as cerebral palsy, therapy aims to prevent deterioration and deformity (which otherwise are inevitable), to enable the child to make optimal use of residual skills, to assist the family to understand the child's problems and handle him in the best possible way, and to encourage the family and other carers to focus on quality of life and participation, rather than become obsessed with individual goals that are often unimportant and unachievable. No treatment has been shown to cure cerebral palsy or dramatically improve outcome, but some controlled studies have demonstrated modest functional gains over relatively short time-scales, and there is consensus that physiotherapy prevents or slows progressive deterioration and deformity.

The best known systems are the Bobath method (a method of physiotherapy and handling which requires skilled support from a trained therapist) and the Peto method of conductive education (which involves a holistic approach to education, therapy and daily living). No advantage of either system over the other has been demonstrated and there is little evidence as to the optimum frequency or intensity of therapy. The Peto approach is attractive to parents and many therapists because it involves a day-long routine, thus to some extent avoiding the issue of how much hands-on therapy is optimal. In addition there are several non-orthodox packages which are not offered through statutory agencies. Parents often feel that they must explore these. One such system has been investigated with the co-operation of the staff.[100] In the absence of any evidence that such systems are superior, and the low level of biological plausibility of some of them, there seems little reason to prefer them to the more conventional approaches available within the NHS and the education services.

Speech and language therapists guide the development of communication skills, and where necessary introduce augmented methods such as sign or symbol systems, or electronic equipment. Randomised trials of such methods have rarely been attempted, but observational measures of communicative function show that considerable gains in communicative capacity can be made. Children with cleft lip and palate do better if managed by a specialist team.

In children with communication impairment due to primary language disorders ('childhood aphasias'), therapy, augmented communication and special education, together with anticonvulsant medication in certain rare conditions, improve communicative skills and adaptation though they rarely produce complete resolution of the disorder.

Autism has been the subject of innumerable interventions and trials, both orthodox and alternative. Behavioural management and appropriate education improve quality of life for the child and their family, though dramatic changes in outcome are rarely achieved.

Intervention in children with moderate, severe or profound hearing impairment consists of amplification (by hearing aid or cochlear implant), education and parent support. This is a highly effective programme with substantial differences between the language skills of those receiving early intensive management and those not so fortunate.[75]

In children with visual impairment, low vision aids, education and parent guidance support greatly improve function. In addition, early intervention may prevent the autistic-like deterioration of behaviour and personality (so-called developmental setback) sometimes observed in these children (Salt A, unpublished data).

Areas of uncertainty include:

- for disabled children, how to measure changes in quality of life resulting from therapy and other interventions
- the optimal level of hands-on input by physiotherapists, speech therapists and occupational therapists, and the extent to which parents can and wish to acquire these skills
- the indications for and benefits of surgery for threatened hip dislocation and for scoliosis in children with cerebral palsy and other disabling conditions

- the benefits of investigation in a gait analysis laboratory, in children with cerebral palsy, prior to multi-level surgery in children with diplegia
- the optimum use of new treatments, e.g. botulinum toxin and intrathecal baclofen infusion for spasticity, neuropharmacological interventions for a range of developmental disorders
- the value of intensive rehabilitation services for children with acquired severe brain injury.

Overall measures of parent satisfaction

In the past, parents have commonly been very critical of the services available for their disabled children, and their views helped to formulate the Charter[22] set out in Appendix 2. Rosenbaum found that parents' top priorities were true parental involvement in assessing information, providing care and decision making, education and information about the condition and the services, treatment and evaluation of progress, care co-ordination between agencies, continuity of care, and a family-centred approach. The quality of 'news-breaking' could be improved and this resulted in greater parent satisfaction.[101] Key factors are the empathy of the professional and the clarity of explanation. Parental assessments of these aspects of the first consultation correlate with long-term parental satisfaction and mental health.

Processes of care

Effectiveness of services can be described in terms of overall parent satisfaction,[97,102,103] but as parental satisfaction is related to processes of care, these can be measured as a proxy. Qualitative studies involving interview data and checklists based on standards of care derived from research and professional consensus (*see* Appendix 2) enable quality of service to be assessed. In such studies, the same themes recur – clarity and adequacy of information when the parents want it, sharing in the planning for the child's present and future needs, being treated with respect, and wanting professionals in different agencies to work together.

Several strands of evidence indicate that access to and use of services are an important issue for parents. For most disabled children, the first important contacts are made with the health service rather than with education or social services, but under the Children Act 1989, the social services are expected to 'provide services for children with disabilities which are designed to minimise the effects of the children's disabilities and to give them the opportunity to lead lives that are as normal as possible . . . every effort should be made to work collaboratively in teams and multi-agency structures in order to avoid the creation of separate and segregated services'.

Each family needs an individual package of care. In the USA this is called an 'Individual Family Service Plan'. Someone has to organise and manage this. The concepts of 'case manager', 'care manager', 'care co-ordinator' and 'key worker' are still evolving alongside the changing role of the social services and, more recently, the notion of partnership with schools. Models differ in the extent to which they are obliged objectively to balance advocacy for the individual child with the needs of other children and the resources available. Parents value the key worker system, particularly with home visiting, and they prefer workers to be proactive in contacting them, rather than leaving it to the parents to initiate each visit.

Low-severity, high-prevalence conditions

Treatments or interventions for children with delayed language development, mild or moderate learning disabilities, clumsiness, etc. are high-volume services which explicitly set out to 'treat' the disorder rather than improve quality of life, as is the case with severe disability. They must therefore be judged accordingly – parent satisfaction is not a sufficient yardstick of success.

A systematic review of speech and language therapy[73] suggested that therapy is effective for children with language delay. For language content, the effect size is greater for protocols that involve carers than for those that rely on professional input alone. Primary prevention by identifying children likely to experience language problems in the first year of life has been adopted in some districts. There are insufficient data to justify a wholesale adoption of such methods at present, but what is now known about language and child development can be incorporated into primary prevention such as the Sure Start programmes, under the guidance of therapists and psychologists.

There is one systematic review (unpublished) of occupational therapy for children with clumsiness or learning problems. Many studies claim benefit, but there are insufficient data to draw generalisable conclusions. Neither the cost-effectiveness nor the coverage of children potentially able to benefit has been adequately investigated. Occupational therapy services often have difficulty meeting those needs where their skills are most essential, such as in seating and daily living assistance for severely disabled children.

Care of children with attention deficit disorder and with a range of emotional and behavioural problems is often shared between paediatric and child psychiatry services (*see* below).

Effectiveness of services for children with mild and moderate psychological disorders

Evidence for the effectiveness of services taken as a whole in this area is sparse. There are two broad approaches to treatment interventions:

- a focused problem-solving approach that targets a specified symptom
- a general, supportive, psycho-educational approach that aims to increase the general competence of parents (of younger children) or personal adjustment (for adolescents).

There is evidence for the effectiveness of both in particular areas. Sleeping and feeding problems in young children respond best to focused work using a behavioural approach.[104] Aggressive behaviour in the same age group can respond to enhancement of parenting.[105] Findings vary according to whether there is specific or polymorphous presentation of problems. In addition, the success of focused approaches is sometimes lost on follow-up because of the overwhelming impact of continuing psychosocial adversity.[106] Both approaches require little equipment but considerable staff time, though providing written information for parents can reduce this.[107] The general approach of focused interventions is psychological, though interventions using apparatus (e.g. enuresis alarms, video-training) are part of the evidence-based treatment repertoire and require an equipment budget.

There is relatively little evidence that has been derived from randomised controlled trials for the effectiveness of medication in this area of mental health. What little there is indicates short-term benefit only, so is not considered in depth here. For instance, small controlled trials support the short-term effectiveness of sedative antihistamines for sleep problems in young children,[108] and desmopressin for short-term relief of enuresis,[109] but in each case there is little or no long-term benefit. There is general support for the logical use of laxatives in constipation with overflow.[110] Prescribing clonidine for oppositional behaviour is quite popular in North America but lacks evidence from controlled trials. In general, medication is less likely to be used in mild and moderate psychological pathology than in psychiatric disorder, but a small drug budget for any service seeing children and adolescents with such difficulties may be required.

There appears to be a tendency to consider 'counselling' an appropriate approach to mild and moderate psychological problems in childhood and adolescence. There is no evidence to support this. The scientific literature on psychotherapeutic approaches to children is sparse and biased towards behavioural treatments, with more studies being devoted to this modality and being carried out by researchers sympathetic to it. Studies of psychodynamic psychotherapy carried out by dynamic psychotherapists which might show a positive treatment effect suggest that subjects in such studies are quite likely to be severely affected and not necessarily mild or moderate in their psychopathology.[111] Work in North America has failed to show an effect for 'traditional' psychodynamic psychotherapy carried out by humanistic–dynamic therapists in a population of children (mean age 10 years) identified by school and peers (rather than parents and health professionals) and probably best considered as having moderate psychopathology.[112]

The psycho-educational approach relies mainly upon general support and guidance for parents in responding to a range of childhood behaviours or emotions. It appears to be a widespread practice, but there has been virtually no attempt to gather outcome data to support its use. In general it seems less effective than short-term focused work.[113]

In view of the sparseness of evidence for particular interventions, it may be as relevant and profitable to focus on the evidence for particular ways of approaching service delivery.

Three issues that merit specific consideration are:

- health visiting
- parenting programmes
- prevention.

Health visiting

Health visitors are well placed to implement a number of interventions relevant to child and adolescent mental health, yet the difficulty in measuring their effectiveness in general has led to some scepticism about their value. There is good evidence for the following practices.

- Prevention of (some) postnatal depression using social support, education and discussion about forthcoming parenthood,[114] and promotion through home visiting during pregnancy of better obstetric outcomes.[115]
- Screening women for postnatal depression using the Edinburgh Postnatal Depression Scale.[116] Training is required to prevent this becoming a mechanical exercise and to find ways round the problem of women who protest their mental health because of a range of fears about what may happen to their baby if they admit to feeling depressed. Postnatal depression has been shown to be associated with minor but potentially significant psychological deficits affecting cognition, attachment and behaviour in the developing child.[117] Some of these are risk factors for child psychiatric disorders, and there is theoretically preventative potential here.
- Treating women with postnatal depression by counselling.[118] Antidepressant medication was not found to be superior to psychological treatment in a controlled study (though both were effective), and it appeared to be less acceptable to mothers.[119]

The role of health visitors in preventing and treating mental health problems of young children directly had been addressed by several studies during the 1980s, with somewhat mixed results. Particular problems arose because teaching skills using a narrow focus on behavioural approaches did not seem to yield expected results,[120] and demonstrable short-term improvements tended to be lost in the face of social adversity over the longer term.[106] Nevertheless, considerable enthusiasm has led to two substantial projects. The approach taken in the Bristol Child Development Programme[121] emphasises education of parents and promotion of joint activities for mothers and children. While this has been subsequently adopted by a number of centres and appeared to confer benefit, the evaluation has been less than rigorous and therefore criticised.[120] More recently, in South London the Parent Adviser Service, a counselling intervention for parents and pre-school children carried out by specially trained health visitors and community medical officers, has been described. A preliminary controlled (non-randomised) evaluation indicates a positive effect and is particularly important because it is claimed that a number of families were seen who would not otherwise have received professional support.[37] Nevertheless, the authors point out that just over a quarter of referred families did not take up the service when it was offered, and that it is therefore not likely to be suitable for all.

Current knowledge suggests that direct intervention by health visitors to ameliorate young children's mental health problems may be helpful, but replicated evidence has yet to be provided. Not all health visitors want to focus on children's mental health issues, but clearly some do. The distance-learning packs for health visitors on postnatal depression published by the Marcé Society[122] and on child mental health prepared at St George's Hospital Medical School[123] are in considerable demand. Stevenson[120] suggested that health visitors could function with various degrees of specialisation in child mental health. In one model the health visitor functions effectively as a child primary mental health worker, but this loses the principal advantage of health visitors – their statutory visiting role for all young children. In other words, some health visitors in a locality receive training and take primary care team referrals, yet continue with a reduced case load of routine family contacts.

Parent training

Given that poor parenting practice is one of the principal risk factors associated with mild to moderate psychological pathology, especially in young children, it would be logical to help parents develop their parenting skills. A number of packages to assist parents in recognising and correcting problematic behaviours in their children are available, and are nearly always based on social learning skills. In many approaches parents are seen in groups. Earlier seminar-style training was disappointing in terms of drop-out rates, but more recently a more democratic approach using videotape-based discussion groups has been shown to be effective in reducing problematic externalising behaviours in young children. The so-called Webster-Stratton model,[124] using her videotapes, has become the best-known method. The original tapes are American and feature young children. Similar packages are being developed in various centres and the original tapes have also been re-dubbed with English accents. Replication of American findings is under way by Dr Stephen Scott's group at the Institute of Psychiatry. The effect is greater if social problem-solving classes for the children themselves are provided in parallel.[125]

Parent training is at the heart of several large-scale prevention programmes in North America, and will be part of many Sure-Start programmes in the UK. In view of the way in which evidence for effectiveness depends upon how it is delivered, implementation should be evaluated and lessons learned over the last three decades heeded[125] (*see* Box 9).

It is also necessary to point out that, contrary to lay assumption, conventional family therapy alters patterns of roles and relationships and does not aim to teach parenting skills, nor is it a method for inserting parenting resources into families that lack them.

Box 9: Lessons from experience in offering parent training as a component of child and adolescent mental health prevention programmes.

- Clarity about what to evaluate: parent skills or child behaviour?
- In prevention, targeting socially disadvantaged families will have little overall impact on population rates because of their relatively low prevalence.
- Consideration of childcare arrangements to allow parents to attend.
- Discussion based, preferably with videotapes, more effective than didactic approach.
- Duration and persistence (e.g. 50 hours total) and follow-up improve maintenance of effect.
- Younger rather than older children.

Prevention

The previous edition of this chapter identified prevention as a research priority, stating that primary prevention efforts had not been very successful. Quite apart from the issue of parent training above, a general understanding of what is involved in child mental health promotion has advanced very considerably,[126] and the importance of the following has been established:

- early intervention concepts rather than prevention as such
- relating prevention and treatment interventions for much mild and moderate psychological pathology
- careful thought about choosing between universal, targeted and selective strategies
- active participant involvement
- younger rather than older children, and the need to relate to psychological development
- adequate volume and persistence of interventions
- nutritional rather than inoculation analogies.

It can be argued that the goal of prevention is the promotion of child mental health through the reduction of symptoms, facilitation of development and reduction of known risk factors. Child psychological pathology is an adverse risk factor for adult mental health problems, both in the affected child and in the child's parents at the time. It seems unlikely that there will ever be a sufficient resource for treatment of all child and adolescent psychological pathology. Therefore the consideration of prevention is sensible. One non-randomised study has shown a reduction in later emotional disorder as a result of an early home-visiting programme.[127] Other studies have found no effect, though these have mainly concentrated on antisocial behaviour.[126] Overall, no study has replicated any finding that a particular prevention programme has been unequivocally shown to stop the later emergence of psychiatric disorder. Long-term funding might well be needed to demonstrate this.

7 Models of care

The 1998 White Paper proposals offered an opportunity to change the structure and relationships of primary care and CCHS. Most health authorities anticipated that health visitors would be allocated to a primary care trust. Primary health care for children, both reactive and preventive, would then be largely provided in the setting of the primary care team and PCT, but with a place for reactive as well as preventive health care for adolescents within or close to schools.

The use of primary school premises for parent support and education in collaborations between health and education services has many attractions. Good practice recommendations suggest that each school should have a named school nurse to provide health advice and support for the education staff, and to contribute to school health promotion services. Individual screening tests might be done by dedicated staff. Liaison between individual school nurses and individual primary care teams is vital, though the relationships are difficult because, unlike primary care teams, schools have geographical catchment populations and school nurses often cover all schools in a pyramid from primary to sixth form. The optimum configuration of management arrangements for the SHS is also not clear, but the aim is for a closer relationship between schools, primary health care teams and PCTs. Purchasing and management of the SHS by the schools themselves is possible, but the resources involved are modest compared to school budgets, and it would be necessary to place firm controls on the use of these funds to ensure that statutory obligations were met, so the apparent increased freedom of choice for schools would therefore be largely illusory.

The New NHS did not alter the statutory responsibilities for child protection services and school health. In addition, an enhanced programme of care for 'looked after' children has been developed within the Department of Health. In view of the complexity of the problems faced by many 'looked after' children and young people, specialist support may be needed. PCTs could contract for provision of these services with a CCHS based in a community trust or (preferably) with a combined paediatric service, or even in the future employ a community paediatrician directly. The contract might include management of the common problems which arise in general practice, but for which a GP may not always have the time or the skills. The need for public health support to PCTs is well recognised, but the optimum model is not yet decided. Some community paediatricians already provide this expertise. Alternatively, child public health issues could be covered as part of this brief if the training of public health practitioners covered child public health. Immunisation and child health surveillance co-ordinators should be well known to the PCT members.

The variable and complex relationships between acute and community paediatric services are beyond the scope of this review. However, there is a strong belief amongst paediatricians that management arrangements which divide children's specialist services between two or more trusts are detrimental to provision of the best and most cost-effective care.

Costs

Cost analyses cannot directly answer questions about effectiveness, but they do raise the issue of equity, which is an important issue in the NHS. There are two principles. Populations with equal health needs should receive the same access to health care (horizontal equity). Populations with greater health needs should receive higher levels of access (vertical equity). The same applies to individuals.

The data collected in the four studies described previously (*see* Section 5) offer a basis on which an equitable allocation of health visiting and school nursing resources could be made within and between districts, though they do not provide direct evidence on the issue of value for money.

Support and advice to social services departments

A PCT may be too small a unit to efficiently provide a full CCHS covering continuing professional development and cross-cover. A district-based central child protection service is probably the best solution. The cost of the designated doctor service is difficult to assess, as it is usually combined with clinical child protection work and second opinions on child protection problems. The size of the district, the policies of the local ACPC, the level of deprivation and the existing infrastructure for training all affect the workload. It had been calculated that the basic minimum 'designated-doctor' duties defined by Department of Health guidance could be undertaken in 0.1 whole-time equivalent (WTE) per PCG. Effective proactive work in planning, prevention, training and monitoring (as envisaged in successive departmental guidance documents) needs substantially more than this, though not necessarily directly related to the size of the district, as there may be economies of scale in planning training and attending liaison meetings.

The variability in costs of child protection services described previously is partly related to deprivation levels, but is also strongly influenced by service patterns. For example, a regular daytime clinic slot for children who are not thriving or are suspected of being abused or neglected greatly reduces 'emergency' out-of-hours work in this field and, by reducing the sense of urgency and panic, benefits children and social services staff as well as the doctors concerned. The observed discrepancy between costs of detection and treatment suggests an unacceptable imbalance between investment in detection and diagnosis, and investment in intervention or treatment.

The adoption panel support requirement had been calculated at 0.1 WTE per PCG (usually a community paediatrician), but it varied between districts according to the local adoption rate. The division of the task between community child health doctors and GPs also varied. A range of 0.1–0.2 WTE per PCG was suggested as a baseline figure (a greater WTE may be required per PCT to reflect the larger size of the population covered by a PCT). These figures do not include those for service development, counselling children who have been abused, and meeting the health needs of 'looked after' children or those fostered privately.

Support and advice for Local Education Authorities

In four districts in the studies described previously, routine health assessment accounted for between 56% and 85% of nursing time. Figure 2 illustrates the correlation between deprivation and the investment in school nursing, and from this it is possible to calculate a level of investment which would be equitable.

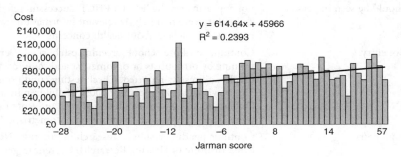

Figure 2: Relationship between cost and deprivation (school nurses).

The cost of fulfilling the statutory duties under the Code of Practice accounts for only a small part of the total SHS expenditure. The minimum health input implied by the 1977 NHS Act has not been defined. In fulfilment of Department of Health guidance, the resources currently attached to school nursing could be used effectively in a number of ways as set out in Table 8.

The commitment of the purchasing authorities to SHS varies widely, as do the expectations of parents and teaching staff. The entire service has been under threat in some districts, but the White Paper *Making a Difference* envisages an important role for this service, and seven elements are needed to secure its immediate future:

- a description of what the service can and cannot provide
- guidance to PCTs about the statutory duties, aims and research base for the SHS
- a commitment from school heads to support the introduction of a modern SHS (including provision of basic facilities such as a private place for children to consult health staff)
- a willingness on the part of the school nurses and doctors to re-examine their roles and, if necessary, produce new job descriptions and training plans
- a long-term commitment to encourage staff development and policy innovation
- a commitment to audit, monitoring and evaluation
- an SHS team leader with management skills and a familiarity with the emerging research evidence.

Some areas of work should be expanded in the SHS, and some might be reduced or discontinued (*see* Table 8 overleaf).

Table 8: Recommendations for school health services.

Task	Recommendation
Medical examination of all school entrants (age group 4–5 years).	No justification to continue except possibly in groups with no documented previous medical care, e.g. newly arrived immigrants or refugees, 'homeless' or traveller families, and possibly parents unable to access standard written information.
Developmental examination of all school entrants.	No justification to continue.
Assessment of all school entrants in person by school nurse.	Of doubtful value.
Assessment of school entrants by school nurse using questionnaire to parents or information from primary care team, to select those who should be seen in person.	Continue, but target the groups with no documented previous medical care as specified above and not those who return completed questionnaires. Targets: identification of all children not appearing on the list of a PHCT; successful referral of such children to care of a PHCT; relevant information transfer (with consent) to teachers about health concerns.
Vision test at school entry.	Continue until pre-school screening established;[27] ensure thorough training by orthoptists or optometrist and monitor quality by spot checks and results reported. Check testing conditions in school. Target: visual acuity record of 100% of children by age 5½. Outcomes: no child to be identified with unrecognised amblyopia thereafter. Reporting mechanism: via optometrists.
Hearing test at school entry.	Continue pending results of research in progress (Nottingham MRC Institute of Hearing Research). Current target: audiogram on 100% of children by age 5½.
Screening for scoliosis.	This is not recommended.
Height and weight at school entry.	Continue. Thorough training essential (inaccurate measurement worse than useless); better data collection and analysis/feedback to ensure quality; clear referral and investigation guideline needed (delays in diagnosis common at secondary-care level). Target: height and weight measures on all children by age 5½. Weight used to calculate BMI for public health use only. All screeners to receive annual feedback on quality and yield. Annual report on district profile of height and BMI by postcode/deprivation index. Seventy-five per cent of predicted numbers of children with growth hormone deficiency and Turner's syndrome to be identified by this age.
Vision, hearing and height in subsequent years.	No justification for hearing and height on present evidence – discontinue. Vision – evidence equivocal and under review – benefits modest but equity an issue. Test at 11 may be justified. Identification of problems depends on patient presenting with symptoms or signs. Inform parents and pupils about free access to optometrist services.
Immunisation.	Continue unless there is clear evidence that primary care team can deliver as high an uptake as the school health service. Target: 100% uptake for at-risk groups.
Medical examination required in connection with the 'Statementing' procedure specified in the 1981 Education Act.	Legal duty – continue. Target: fulfil Code of Practice requirements on turnaround time.
Child protection: examination, advice, support, liaison.	Continue; ensure regular training. Target: all staff to have appropriate training at intervals specified by ACPC.

Table 8: Continued.

Task	Recommendation
Identify and participate in handover of children with special needs to adult services: required by Education Code of Practice 1994 but important even if child has no Statement of Special Educational Need.	A service which can be developed within existing framework – a service to be developed and monitored. Targets: fulfilment of Code of Practice; all special needs children leaving school to have health care plan for their future PHCT and specialist support.
Medical, psychological and social evaluation of children referred by teachers or parents because of problems in school.	Benefits need research; meanwhile, best policy at local level depends on medical skills and other resources available (educational psychologist, child psychiatry service, remedial teaching).
Prepare and support care plan for special needs children in collaboration with Special Needs Co-ordinator (SENCO).	An important health service role which is perceived as being neglected by education staff.
Provision and interpretation of information relating to special needs children, particularly when placed in mainstream schools, and to children with health problems.	Important function, but paediatricians should convey information to schools about medical problems. School health staff might help by interpreting it, but if clear enough this should not be needed. Better training in communication with schools needed for paediatricians. Staff who advise teachers must be up to date with current guidelines.
Counselling and consultation service, particularly in secondary schools.	Current service fragmented and inadequate in many places – a service to be developed and monitored. Targets: all teenagers to have access to a choice of services. Steady year-on-year rise in use of the services. SHS staff to be aware of reasons for all children not in school for more than a specified period. Outcomes: teenage pregnancy rate; mental health referrals; suicide rates; school dropout rates; qualifications.
Support to educational social work service; working with parents for children out of school, etc.	A service to be developed and monitored.
Responding to concerns about head lice.	Ideal solution is public education so that head lice do not cause widespread panic, but school nurses best placed to reassure and educate. Target: steady fall in demands to school for head inspections; fall in use of insecticides.
Environmental health issues.	Although these are the responsibility of the environmental health officer and/or the consultant in communicable disease control, school doctor may advise in such situations.
Share policy development for and take part in health promotion and education programmes.	Vital role is in one-to-one support and advice for pupils. Target: depends on schools – aim should be introduction of health-promoting school philosophy in all schools. Use of health promotion services and resources good measure of effectiveness. Measures of smoking, etc. might be useful if they involve the pupils themselves.
Advice to school headteachers regarding the health of children travelling on school journeys or participating in unusual sports.	Minor issue occupying little time; probably of little value, but valued by teachers.
Provide an informal support and advice network for teachers.	School nurses may offer informal support to teachers with problems but should not be drawn into providing an unofficial occupational health service unless further training is provided and appropriate service agreements set up.
Hands-on nursing care, e.g. gastrostomies, tracheotomies, tube feeding, medications.	An essential service for a small number of children.
First aid.	This is not a school health service function.

In summary, the following suggestions are made.

- Investment should be reduced in routine screening, assessment and health-promoting interviews for those starting school, and school medical examinations. Involvement of parents in school health promotion is better carried out in conjunction with classroom teaching and whole-school initiatives.
- Those screening procedures that remain, the gathering of routine health data about children starting school and the identification of children with problems or with previously inadequate health care should be carried out by staff on a lower grade than current school nurses, with regular retraining and quality checks.
- Responsibility for communication with schools about children with health care needs should rest with GPs, consultant paediatricians or specialist outreach community nurses, although school nurses may help to ensure that the information is understood and acted upon.
- There is no evidence to support any further routine screening of all children after the first year in school (with the possible exception of a further vision screen).
- School nurses' major roles are providing advice and support for teachers regarding pupils with problems and special needs, working with teachers and the educational social work service to help pupils not in school for any reason, and providing an advice, consultation and counselling service for older children and teenagers, both in school and on separate premises.
- Current investment is too small for nurses to take a major role in initiating and planning the implementation of a health-promoting school programme, or in classroom teaching, but they should be members of the planning team and may contribute to classroom work.

Adolescent health services take time to develop and the need and demand are difficult to assess. Given the fact that teenagers make up half the school population, together with the evidence that they want such a service, it might be reasonable to devote at least half the SHS resources to work with older children and teenagers. A planning group that involves GPs, family planning or sexual health staff, health promotion workers, education representatives and spokespeople for the young people themselves is necessary to establish such a service at local level.

Organisation of neonatal and pre-school child health screening, immunisation and health education programmes and organisation and provision of health promotion and preventive programmes which aim to change the micro-environment

These two sub-categories are taken together since the main costs in both services are health-visiting services. The cost of the Child Health Promotion Programme is made up of six elements:

1   payments to doctors, usually GPs qualified to provide CHS (currently part of the 1990 Contract and set (as of 1997) at £11.75 per child under five)
2   the cost of the health-visiting service, since this is mainly (> 90% in many places) devoted to children and young families
3   the cost of the referrals generated – which is very difficult to estimate
4   the costs of continuing professional development, in-service training and advice to PHCTs
5   the costs of collecting and using data for managing the service
6   additional services, in particular the health promotion team, and various multi-agency schemes funded in various ways, and services provided by NGOs.

Some GPs like to offer most of the surveillance work themselves, but many limit their role to any physical examinations required, provision of facilities for children to be seen and for records to be kept, and management of problems presented as a result of surveillance. In many PHCTs, health visitors carry out most routine reviews and health education and some are learning to do physical examinations. There are a few deprived areas of the country where the perceived standard of general practice is poor and community medical officers offer an alternative. However, the number of such places is declining.

Assessing the current costs of health visiting is straightforward, but the optimum level of investment is not known because there is no uniform model of service provision. The cost of the health-visiting service varies widely between districts, apparently mainly for historical reasons rather than due to deprivation (*see* Figure 3). Within any one district there is variation in practice and workload, but equity of workload can be improved by formulae that adjust for deprivation and case-load size.[56] In a district with wide variations between the lowest and highest deprivation scores, the minimum differential in resource allocation needed to balance workload was a ratio of 5:4. Thus the case load could be 333 under-fives in the least deprived PHCT and 267 in the most deprived. This figure was an underestimate of the re-allocation needed, because it was based on what health visitors currently do, which is constrained by the need to prioritise and control their work. An alternative approach is to consider what health visitors might usefully do. For example, further rationalisation of the child health surveillance programme could allow a ratio of 3:2.

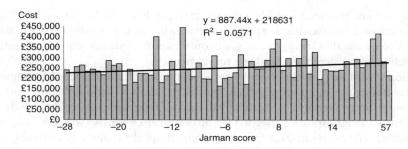

Figure 3: Relationship between cost and deprivation (health visitors).

In a district that has established targeting policies, around 20–25% of health visitor time is allocated to routine work such as the CHS programme. A further 20–25% is devoted to client-led requests for help originating from clients who had been offered the basic programme of CHS only. The other half of the health visitor's time is allocated to clients with identified needs receiving programmes of care. The amount of resource devoted to high-risk support depends on the level of risk at which intensive home-visiting support is offered. Other grades or types of staff can make an important contribution, but it requires considerable experience to identify problems which are unrecognised or concealed by parents. Lay workers are in general best regarded as an extension of rather than a replacement for professionals.

Resources invested in routine health-visiting work could be reduced further by redefining what the CHS minimum service should include. Parents with healthy children and uncomplicated life situations want easy access to their health visitor when they have a problem. They object to difficulties in making contact, failure to reply to messages and failure to provide clinics at times accessible to working mothers.[79] Efficiency might be increased by developing groups for parents to develop emotional awareness and parenting skills, at the same time as offering information about child development and common health problems. No costings have been developed as yet for universal provision of parenting programmes. However, it has been estimated that universal provision of parenting programmes in support of pre-school education, which have considerable overlap with the programmes discussed in this chapter, could be achieved for between £300 and £1800 per child.[78] Given the interest in these programmes from health, education and social services, joint funding of universal provision is potentially feasible.

Changes in health visitor distribution at the level of general practice may cause much disruption for little gain, since many case loads would gain or lose fractions of a WTE. Re-allocation to groups of GPs or PCTs is more feasible and more flexible at that level. An alternative could be a division of duties for some health visitors between case-load work and a role that covers several PHCTs or a whole PCT. For example, some health visitors might wish to retrain in mental health and parent support, and act as tutors and support workers to their colleagues. Others could facilitate the introduction and development of new screening programmes (e.g. neonatal hearing screening and haemoglobinopathy screening) and improve existing but low-quality schemes. Some health visitor time could be used for public health profiling, peer training, development work such as establishing or supporting new parent groups and voluntary schemes and TB control. More research is also needed on the optimum number of outreach nurses and the workload of 'hands-on' home care children's nursing.

Both the Green Paper *Supporting Families*[128] and the Sure-Start programme[129] launched in 1999 suggest that the Government envisages greater involvement of health visitors in supporting at-risk parents. The Sure-Start programme draws on North American research indicating long-term benefits from intensive early intervention with a strong educational focus and the sum of money to be invested in each community is substantial.

Screening programmes provided outside primary care are likely to be directed at national level, organised at 'district' level, but monitored at regional level, with quality-control measures set up and run centrally. A switch to neonatal hearing screening, discontinuation of routine distraction testing and a re-appraisal of the school entry sweep test has been recommended.

Pre-school vision screening is under review. Easy access to a community-based orthoptic service for poor families increases equity and minimises false-positive referrals to the ophthalmic outpatient clinic. Where primary population screening is not attempted, this can be regarded as secondary screening, where the primary screen is identification of parental or professional concerns (whether by question or by screening examination), or as an outreach from the specialist ophthalmology department.

Biochemical screening might be extended to include detection of MCADD and glutaric aciduria by TMS, and possibly other disorders in the future. The role of screening for cystic fibrosis is being reassessed. A good case can be made for screening of at-risk neonates for sickle-cell disorder.

Child public health: services which focus on the macro-environment

A survey of immunisation co-ordinators suggests that for a district of 1 million the role requires 0.4 WTEs. More time is needed whenever there is a 'scare' in the press or a new vaccine programme. For example, an enhanced programme of screening for hepatitis B in pregnancy will require greater efforts to ensure that all babies receive the full course of vaccine.

The input required to deliver the management, advocacy and planning roles is more difficult to quantify. Effective proactive planning as opposed to merely responding to proposals and crises requires a strong commitment of time and energy. Greater investment in this aspect of CCHS might have an important effect on child health and this hypothesis needs to be tested. At least one paediatrician with a public health orientation is likely to be needed per district if there is no other public health doctor committed to children's needs. There is currently a shortage of paediatricians trained in public health and of public health doctors with sufficient paediatric experience to make reliable decisions related to children's health.

Quality management

The effectiveness of the CCHS in the organisation of CCHS screening programmes has not been evaluated experimentally. Many child health screening activities with unacceptable sensitivities and specificities, offering little health gain, were continued longer than was justified due to lack of monitoring and evaluation by the CCHS or public health departments. This will be required in future as part of current Government strategy to improve screening programmes. Monitoring of coverage, timeliness and the quality of the experience for parents (informed consent, access to information, prompt referral for positive screening tests, etc.) should be the responsibility of one named person in each district. This will require improvements to child health IT systems, and there are good arguments in favour of implementing a national database. In spite of the efforts of a national co-ordinating group, each district seems at present to be developing its own ideas, resulting in duplication of cost and effort. The implications of the Data Protection Act in relation to confidentiality have yet to be fully absorbed into practice.

Quality management of health promotion services is complex. The views of the recipients have always been considered important in these services. The parent adviser service is developing some quality measures based on questions such as 'Did you feel respected/patronised by the parent adviser?' Further measures along these lines are likely to be developed over the next decade.

Children with disabilities

There are sufficient disabled children in each district to justify the existence of a CDDRS (for volume and workload estimates, see Tables 5 and 6). Most disabling conditions presenting in childhood are lifelong, and support and advice throughout childhood and the teens are needed. The principles underlying disability service provision have been defined in a European forum (see Appendix 3).

The optimal levels of staffing should ideally be based on demonstrations of benefit per unit cost but few robust data exist. Service specification and estimates of the volume of service provision are therefore based on a combination of the research reviewed above, quality standards proposed by the relevant professional bodies, calculations of the input needed by children with a range of conditions at different stages of evolution, and observed staffing levels in districts regarded by peers and parents as offering a 'good' service. Table 5 shows the predicted case load of children with disability in a 'typical' city population of 1 million. Table 6 summarises the data on staffing.

The findings from a range of studies suggest that the ideal service has the following characteristics.

- It offers a comprehensive plan for the management of children from birth to 18 or 19 years, with disabling conditions of any kind, whether mild or severe.
- It defines goals for intervention that can maximise the potential for growth and development, increase participation in a range of social situations (rather than achieve specific developmental milestones) and increase the likelihood that the individual with a disability will lead a useful and happy life.[11,130,131]
- It has a consumer/empowerment philosophy of care (see Appendix 12) that helps the parents and carers to cope rather than 'de-skilling' them, and considers the needs of the whole family rather than just those of the child. This implies no standard package of assessment or care, but options presented fairly to each family.
- It undertakes regular self-appraisal and strives to meet the standards set out in the Charter (see Appendix 2).
- It co-operates with other agencies to ensure liaison over the needs of individual children.
- It has a base from which services are organised and delivered.

- It provides facilities for prolonged assessments when the diagnosis and intervention needs are unclear – ideally, funded jointly with departments of education and social services.
- It provides an effective public health and management group (district handicap team or similar) with participants of sufficient seniority to make and implement decisions for the whole district.[132]
- It includes as core staff a paediatrician, psychologist (clinical and/or educational), social worker, member of each therapy discipline, links with teaching, health visitors and paediatric community nurses, and links with voluntary sector, but develops a team individualised for each family.
- It offers referral to tertiary and specialty services for complex and uncommon problems and a combined clinic setting when multi-disciplinary decisions have to be made.[133] Children who need such services include those with, for example, swallowing and feeding problems, cleft lip and palate, the dual impairment of deafness and blindness, arthrogryphosis, and neural-tube defects (spina bifida).
- It has a secretary/administrator as an easy point of contact for parents, providing a 'single front door', i.e. access to all the services needed without a complex bureaucracy.
- It offers families a key worker or case manager. The key worker can be provided by any of the statutory agencies.
- It ensures a well-planned transition from school to adult life and arranges for adult-oriented services to take over care.
- It undertakes teamwork with child and adolescent psychiatrists and child psychologists to prevent and deal with behavioural and emotional difficulties, particularly in those with severe learning disabilities.
- It provides mainstream services for children with learning disabilities (mental handicap) by the paediatric team and uses a community learning disabilities team as an expert resource (CMHT).[134]
- It keeps a register of disabled children or collaborates with social services register staff and has arrangements to share data between agencies wherever possible, remembering the requirements of the Data Protection Act 1998 (parents' permission for registration must be obtained).
- It has the ability to analyse register data in order to obtain a local profile of disability and need.
- It provides ongoing training for health professionals – a team spirit of learning, keeping up to date and seeking continuous improvement.

A difficult problem in defining the ideal service is to determine and provide optimal therapy. There is constant pressure from parents for more therapy input. Understandably, parents feel that more must mean better. The evidence on this point is unhelpful. A disability service can always absorb more physiotherapy, occupational therapy and speech therapy but, even without substantial extra resources, the service can be improved by:

- better definition of therapy goals
- short programmes with defined objectives followed by a period of observation
- more effective liaison with educational services
- better teaching of parents and carers regarding the methods and goals of therapy
- the use of therapy aides
- provision of secretarial and clerical help.

Low-severity, high-prevalence conditions

The ideal model includes effective case finding (using the mechanisms outlined earlier), shared resources and planning with social services and education (since problems often involve more than one of these agencies), and a developmentally oriented day-care and educational system that can meet the needs of all young children and, in particular, those with special needs. In many inner-city areas the needs of ethnic minorities affect service provision; cultural influences and the need to expose young children to English may override other considerations.

Important considerations here include the following.

- Assessment can be but rarely is streamlined. For example, parents of children with speech and language problems may have to attend for a hearing test, a paediatric examination, a speech therapist assessment and a psychological assessment, all on different days and at different venues. A triage approach by experienced speech and language therapists can dramatically reduce waiting lists and identify those children who have a serious problem.
- There is overlap between health and educational services for assessment of educational problems, such as difficulty in learning to read or spell. In some districts such referrals are passed back to the educational psychologist unless there are additional problems (e.g. school refusal, depression, organic deterioration, etc.), but in many places there is no coherent policy.
- Speech and language therapy should not focus solely on one-to-one treatment but should develop a consultative and advisory service, helping parents, nursery and teaching staff to understand the process of language development. Indeed, accumulating evidence suggests that teaching staff about language promotion and pre-literacy skills, as in some Sure-Start programmes, could be a highly cost-effective use of therapists' time.

The constraints on a good or ideal service include the following:

- lack of clear management structure or lines of accountability in a service involving many disciplines and sometimes several trusts
- failure of primary care trusts to define requirements or commission services
- inadequate investment in staff training
- lack of flexibility with regard to methods of service delivery, priorities and boundaries between professions
- lack of clearly articulated objectives of the service as a whole and for each child, making audit impossible
- failure to use knowledge and services that are already available
- difficulty in liaison with senior officers in social services or education
- little opportunity for clinicians to influence overall policy or budgets.

Mild and moderate psychological disorders

A tiered model for dealing with child and adolescent mental health problems, including mild and moderate psychological pathology, psychiatric disorder and mental illness, has been endorsed by a number of bodies, especially the Department of Health and the Health Advisory Service, the latter developing it in detail in the publication *Together We Stand*.[135] It derives from an earlier paper by Hill for a Royal College of Psychiatrists conference.[136] This format is now a recommendation from the Departments of Health and Education as well as the Social Services Inspectorate.[137] It can be realised within the health service as a Child and Adolescent Mental Health Service (CAMHS), and the principle can be further extended across other agencies. Thus there can be an *inter-agency CAMHS*, a child and adolescent mental health service within the NHS including mental health professionals, paediatricians, school nurses and the primary health care team (*health CAMHS*), and a *specialist CAMHS* comprising the upper three tiers and consisting of child and adolescent mental health professionals.[138] This form of organisation has not been scientifically evaluated but came into being as a way of integrating with other agencies and avoiding duplication of clinical work.

Within the recommended framework there is a series of tiers intended to group together services appropriate for clinical problems with different levels of severity. Within the NHS:

- tier 1 is primary health care
- tier 2 consists of child and adolescent mental health professionals working alone
- tier 3 consists of multi-disciplinary teams, most obvious in child and adolescent psychiatric (child guidance, child and family consultation) clinics
- tier 4 comprises highly specialised provision such as child or adolescent psychiatric inpatient units or tertiary referral clinics for rare problems.

Community child health interventions for mild and moderate psychopathology will be linked to tiers 1 and 2. The model does not accommodate community paediatricians straightforwardly. It will depend upon their personal expertise as to whether they are regarded as child mental health professionals working solo and receiving referrals from tier 1 services (as in enuresis clinics or some ADHD screening clinics) or whether they are the first point of contact with NHS services for some children and families with a mental health problem and thus tier 1.

The mental health contributions of health visitors and school nurses are most likely to be in tier 1.

It is generally supposed that tier 1 services will see the largest number of child mental health problems of all tiers and will also be the focus for much preventative work. Nevertheless, the evidence is that outreach from specialist CAMHS into tier 1 to support and train non-mental health professionals is low (only 1% of specialist CAMHS staff time in the Audit Commission survey).[38]

The child mental health worker concept promoted in the first edition of this chapter has been taken up by a number of services, so that some 60% of specialist community CAMHS employ staff with this remit (sometimes given other titles, such as 'mental health practitioners'), most from a nursing background. They typically operate at the interface between tiers 1 and 2. Some have been employed to work in close association with general practice, others from a clinic base.

Historically, local authorities have provided a number of social workers and educational psychologists to NHS CAMHS, but this has been unusual in recent years as these professionals have been directed to other priorities such as child protection and the assessment of special educational needs. The clinical burden has therefore fallen increasingly upon the NHS.

Services promoting the mental health of children are provided by several different agencies, of which health is one. Inter-agency commissioning and planning are required in certain areas, such as children's service plans, but are good practice in any case. This can fruitfully extend to joint commissioning or purchasing, though this alone does not guarantee good practice. The interdependence of social factors, parental well-being and competence, and child psychopathology is well recognised.[139]

Linkage between agencies is currently promoted as national policy. In the field of mild and moderate psychopathology, children's service plans should prove a conduit for joint planning, but this has not yet obviously borne fruit. In parallel, the child protection procedure has developed a model for inter-agency collaboration but the involvement of general practitioners is notoriously patchy. In the face of apparent fragmentation of health services for children generally and strong representations from users, the House of Commons Health Committee advocated a single commissioner for children's services or the formation of a single provider unit for children.[140]

When services are organised according to the tiered approach recommended by the Department of Health, some re-allocation of resource to ensure a viable tier 2 is likely to be necessary. Tier 1 (primary care in NHS terms) will need support from tier 2 professionals as well as freedom to refer to them.

It is not known what the volume of service required at each NHS tier will be. This will depend upon the support provided or constraints experienced by other agencies.

8 Outcome measures

The aim of the CCHS is to promote health and prevent disease, disability and death. Measuring impact depends primarily on epidemiological trends data from routine health information systems or surveys. The only relevant routinely available information is rates of death and of infectious diseases, both of which have shown an impressive decline in recent years. Collection of other relevant information about child health has been hampered by problems related to definitions of normality and levels of severity of disease and disability. This is true of rates of injury, disability, abuse, emotional and behavioural problems, and speech and language delay. All of these are in turn related to lack of agreement amongst policy makers and health professionals about the goal of the NHS.

If health and disease represent a spectrum with well-being at one end and distress due to disease and disability at the other, it will be necessary to define and measure well-being. Development of instruments to measure positive health in children is still at an early stage and has yet to be used on a population basis in the UK. Measurement of outcomes in child health has therefore been restricted to process and quality of service provision, together with measurement of risk factors for future health problems.

Evaluation of the service quality which depends on measures of parent and patient satisfaction will also go some way to measuring how well the services have met emotional as well as health care needs. Surveys of schoolchildren collect rates of smoking, alcohol and drug misuse, healthy eating and exercise participation. Surveys of parents collect rates of breastfeeding and passive smoking.

Support and advice to social services departments

The desired outcome for primary prevention is a fall in the number of abused children, but most programmes intended to have this effect involve development of a close relationship with families. This can heighten awareness of child protection risks, so that prevention programmes can have a paradoxical effect on notifications – a research dilemma that is well recognised.

The immediate outcome in child protection cases is a decision about registration followed by development of a child protection plan. Outcomes are usually specified in terms of process and quality measures. For treatment services, desired outcomes include improved mental health and psychological adjustment in adult life, but these have been addressed only in research studies.

Support to Local Education Authorities

Currently used measures of process and outcome are derived from the data in Table 8. These are mostly disease based. The school health service currently measures and records children's height at school entry. These data could be useful for monitoring health, but at present the data are little used and their accuracy is doubtful. Collection of routine height, weight and BMI data at school entry has been proposed as part of a public health minimum data set. Alternatively, this could be monitored by sampling the population rather than by measuring all children. Height is a robust measure of health, and the gradient between social groups may reflect other socio-economic gradients. The BMI data would be useful for monitoring the current 'epidemic' of obesity. The cost and value of this exercise need further evaluation.

Outcome measures of the contribution made by the health service in respect of the Education Act have not been developed. Whilst evaluation of outcomes is important to inform the development of future policy, it has been considered more relevant to assess performance in terms of process and quality, e.g. completion of medical evidence within the prescribed time frame. No outcome measures have been published relevant to the support of children with special needs in mainstream schools. Reviews of the benefits and disadvantages of fully integrating children with disabilities in the mainstream system have been published. Many of these relate to the emotional impact on the child and the family. Successful maintenance of the child with a disability in mainstream school to the satisfaction of the school, the child and the family might be a successful outcome. However, sometimes a move to a specialist unit would be in the child's best interests, and should not be regarded as a failure of either the health or education services. Thus there are no simple numerical measures, but quality and event monitoring would support a policy of continuous professional learning and improvement. A disproportionate number of children with Statements of Special Educational Need are excluded from school, and a fall in this number might indicate progress.

With the exception of research projects which have aimed to capture aspects of emotional and mental well-being, outcome measurement of school health promotion programmes has been restricted to the collection of data on adolescent health-related lifestyles, e.g. rates of teenage pregnancy, alcohol and drug use, smoking, exercise participation and healthy eating. Whilst these are important risk factors for future diseases, they are not synonymous with health. It has been argued that further development of school health promotion programmes depends on the development of tools which measure well-being.[141] Educational and social outcomes, such as progress through school, the numbers of children dropping out of school or leaving with no formal qualifications, or the number involved with youth offending teams, might also reflect well-being and mental health.

Organisation of neonatal and pre-school childhood screening, immunisation and health education programmes

Monitoring of the outcome of screening programmes will undergo development over the next few years as a result of Government policy. At district level, outcomes are likely to be restricted to measures of performance such as uptake, timeliness, referral rate and false-positive rates. The importance of demonstrating that identification in screening programmes has a positive impact on health overall has been stressed in the literature on screening,[142] but measurement of such outcomes requires research projects and cannot be undertaken on a routine basis.

Immunisation uptake rates are reported each year by immunisation co-ordinators, and the incidence of infectious diseases by consultants in communicable disease control. Districts may be required to report on their performance with regard to TB contact tracing and hepatitis B programme coverage. It has been recommended that breastfeeding rates are monitored regularly, together with passive smoking rates.

Whilst the numbers are too small to demonstrate the effectiveness of the programme at district level, trends in sudden infant death demonstrate the effectiveness of the Back to Sleep campaign at national level. Monitoring of aspects of pre-school children's dietary intake has been undertaken in national surveys, but because of the expense involved is unlikely to be practicable at district level. Some districts are experimenting with developing valid measures of the rates of injury from Accident and Emergency registers.

Organisation and provision of health promotion and preventive services which aim to change the micro-environment and child public health services which aim to influence the macro-environment

The outcome of these services is an improvement in the health of parents and children, and their impact is made primarily though improvement in emotional well-being. Until measures which capture these aspects of health are developed, the outcome can only be measured using disease-specific measures (e.g. emotional and behavioural problems, postnatal depression, speech and language delay, incidence of abuse, postnatal depression). All of these outcomes suffer from problems of definition (*see* above). Since it is such an important risk factor for disease and disability in childhood, the level of income differential in families at either end of the social spectrum would be an important outcome measure of child health advocacy. This may in turn be reflected in class-related outcomes, which currently show marked gradients for injuries, birth weight and height at age five.

Children with a disability

For children with *high-severity, low-prevalence* disabilities, outcome measures which describe changes in their functional ability can rarely be used in routine practice. The most useful outcome measures for local use address service quality, issues of adaptation and participation for the child, and help for the family to deal with their problems and minimise disruption to their lives.

Success in achieving these aims can be assessed:

- by setting up quality standards (for example, *see* Appendix 2)
- by carrying out an interview or questionnaire-based audit to determine consumer satisfaction (although this is difficult and time consuming, it can be a useful way of taking stock of service quality; standardised instruments are preferable[143])
- by assessing coverage, using multiple data sources (health including primary care, voluntary sector, education, social services) to determine how many of the disabled children in a district use the facilities and services available.

Outcome measures also present difficulties when considering *low-severity, high-prevalence* conditions, but process measures describing uptake and attendance, duration of intervention, involvement of carers, effectiveness of triage to ensure optimal use of services and change achieved within each individual child are widely used.

Mild and moderate psychological disorders

The group of problems associated with mild and moderate psychopathology is heterogeneous. Three possible approaches suggest themselves.

- Using a symptomatic rating scale such as the Conners CRS-R.[144] This provides a count of symptoms (complaints by the child and concerns or complaints about them) and some measure of the severity of each individual symptom. However, like many of the rating scales available in the field of child and adolescent mental health, the CRS-R has been designed to focus on psychiatric disorder of greater severity than the mild and moderate psychopathology discussed here. Floor effects are thus likely. Other rating scales such as the CBCL or the SDQ are primarily designed to identify probable caseness in epidemiological prevalence work rather than to detect change, and are likely to be insensitive when used to measure outcome. There is no rating scale which can be generally recommended to detect change related to health care interventions in the field of mild to moderate psychopathology.
- Identifying target problems on an individual basis with the child and parents, and subsequently assessing the impact of an intervention in terms of a Likert scale with agreed anchor points of differing severity.[145] This is labour-intensive, and aims or end-points are likely to vary from one family to another. Nevertheless, it is generally applicable although the reliability between raters in different

domains (general practice, classroom, parent, child, health professional) is low (Hill P, unpublished data). There is no ceiling effect. The implication behind such an approach is that health services are acting as a problem-solving agency. It can be used to obtain a rating from a referrer when the aim of the referral has been solely to provide assessment or consultation to another agency.

- Taking a measure of psychosocial functioning independent of the key clinical problem and assessing the child's functioning on the former. The major instrument for such an approach has been the C-GAS, which requires an assessing professional to allocate a score between 0 and 100 according to a range of suggested anchor points, 100 representing optimal functioning.[146] It is very American in its use of language, and preliminary informal trials have not revealed it to be very popular with UK clinicians. With mild and moderate problems there is the problem of ceiling effects. Nevertheless, it emphasises that services may act to promote mental health as well as solve clinical problems. A UK version, probably simpler in form, would be very welcome.

Assessing outcomes on a large scale is difficult because of the frequent plurality of problems in any one child and the difference in impact of a particular problem in a particular family. There is also the importance of context (facilitative, uninvolved or even opposed parents, schools or other agencies), so that one agency can undermine or amplify work carried out by another. Sometimes the role of services is to slow or arrest decline in functioning rather than restore a symptom-free state. The targets of health service intervention and their mutual priorities are likely to vary between stakeholders. These themes are developed in the paper by Berger *et al.*, reprinted in *Together We Stand*.[135]

Targets

It follows from the above that appropriate targets for the CCHS have yet to be developed and that the service relies on measures which are flawed. For example, falls in the numbers of children on the Child Protection Register could be detected locally or nationally, but are more likely to reflect changes in registration policy than real changes in child care. The same applies to adopted and looked after children. Meanwhile, targets should be set in terms of service quality, coverage and outcomes. High quality of service is best achieved by supporting health professionals, providing regular in-service training and professional development programmes, and supporting those who are caring for very distressed families. It could be argued that the well-being of health professionals who provide these services should be monitored and targeted if found to be poor.

9 Information

The outcomes set out in the previous section suggest the content of a minimum data set to be collected in each district. A core data set of information considered to be of public health importance based on the NHS number has been proposed by the Child Health Informatics Consortium.[147] There would be substantial benefits in a collaborative approach to data handling between health, social services and education, but there are still many obstacles to achieving this. Information on child health inequalities is particularly important, and ways of measuring this are currently under investigation.

Some potentially useful information may be obtained by collaboration with other services. For example, information about the educational and behavioural difficulties in children could be obtained, as from

September 1998, from school entrant baseline testing data. This is collected as a statutory requirement so that the 'value added' offered by each school can be calculated when the next assessment is carried out at the age of seven.[148] Education authorities should be able to provide this data (at least in amalgamated and anonymised format) to the PCT, and this provides useful information about the effectiveness of both the earlier identification and early intervention procedures available for pre-school children. One possible indicator of a successful health-promoting school would be a fall in the number of children out of school, since children who drop out for whatever reason are at high risk of both health problems and educational failure. Early intervention where children are failing in school, or showing a declining attendance record, might if carried out in collaboration with the primary care team have measurable benefits.

Information on the uptake of immunisation is usually reliable for the immunisations given in the first few months of life, but is probably much less reliable for BCG and hepatitis B vaccine. Although the size of the problem for these is very much smaller, high standards are equally important.

Information about child health surveillance uptake is usually collected by general practitioners and health visitors, using carbon copies of standard record pages placed within the personal child health record. These data are collected and aggregated at district level on Child Health Systems which vary from one place to another. Whilst the establishment of these systems is critical for scheduling appointments and chasing up defaulters, lack of epidemiological expertise in the CCHS has meant that many of these data are of dubious quality and underused. Much of the data is potentially of value, and some that might be useful are not currently available, e.g. duration of breastfeeding, depression, injuries, accidents, disabilities or other important health problems.

The principles of risk management should be considered. Although community services are less vulnerable to expensive litigation than departments like obstetrics and orthopaedics, there are nevertheless a number of poorly recognised hazards, and the identification of these highlights areas where quality can be measured.

In order to facilitate comparisons between districts, a list of all child development teams in the UK has been compiled and is available for comparative studies.[149]

A list or register of children with disabilities is kept in most districts but is of variable quality and accessibility. It may be developed in collaboration with educational and/or social services (who are required by the Children Act to maintain a register), though issues of consent and confidentiality increasingly present problems for staff in all agencies. The register records how many children have been seen each year with each diagnostic category, how many with differing levels of disability, and which children are due for review. However, the lack of any nationally agreed system is an obstacle to rational recording and to comparative research, and this needs to be addressed. A list of all equipment and aids supplied (or denied) and of collaborative funding of special school placements and respite care is needed to facilitate budget setting and review.

Many child mental health services have information systems that are downward extensions of adult mental health systems and prove quite inadequate. Correspondingly, paediatric services often have relatively few categories available for psychological problems. Neither derivative is satisfactory. A unified information system is needed which is sensitive to the issues and practice relevant to mild and moderate psychological pathology. The one drawn up by the Association for Child Psychology and Psychiatry[150] has been used in several computerised data sets but has been found to be time-consuming if implemented in full. A common problem is that the data requested by purchasers, provider unit managers and clinicians have not often overlapped, so that a cumbersome total set is the result. Local economy of data entry through the establishment of an agreed minimum set would be appropriate.

10 Research requirements

Most experimental child health promotion research has been carried out in the USA and there is an urgent need for investment in this type of research in the UK. The development of reliable and valid measures of health which capture social, mental and emotional well-being may be a rate-limiting step in health promotion research both for schoolchildren and for parents and children in the pre-school period. Measures are needed which can be collected in self-completion questionnaires for use in trials. Primary health care teams also need a method of data collection to assess their own effectiveness with each individual client. This would be a useful addition to formal randomised trials the results of which are not easy to generalise to everyday practice. Important topics include promotion of mental health, supporting breastfeeding, helping parents to stop smoking, and promoting optimum child development, particularly with regard to language development and behaviour.

More research is needed into the optimum configuration of the health promotion components of the CCHS, including the relative merits of population and high-risk approaches, group approaches vs. one-to-one support and the most efficient use of health professionals and lay staff. The WHO has concluded that RCTs may be inappropriate, misleading and unnecessarily expensive in the evaluation of health promotion interventions.[151] Health promotion research needs investment in units with critical mass and long-term secure funding.

Legislation and central directives may have limited the scope for research on different models of care in some aspects of the CCHS, and arguably as a result may have limited the development of effective services. Policy makers may need to take this potential side-effect into account and draft legislation which enables rather than inhibits research and development. There is a need to research and develop services for secondary and tertiary prevention for child abuse. There is also a need to research the health benefits of the medical contribution to the 'Statementing' of children with special educational needs.

In areas where pre-school health care is poor, or where there are large numbers of newly arrived immigrant or refugee children, the abandonment of routine school-entrant examination might have adverse effects on the health of children. This proposition needs to be examined further with some urgency. It is vital to study not only the number of referrals initiated, but also the extent to which the cases identified have conditions that were not previously suspected, are significant for the individual, and are susceptible to treatment or intervention. Although there is an extensive research literature, there is still much controversy about a number of screening issues in child health, particularly the value of pre-school and school vision screening, hearing and height screening at school entry, and screening for congenital dislocation of the hip and congenital heart disease in infancy. The health benefits of these programmes warrant further research. For rare conditions, a national register would be a valuable aid to research.

Children with a disability

Proposals for research in the field of childhood disability are summarised in Box 10.

Box 10: Research needs in the field of childhood disability.

Basic neuroscience and genetics research	• Inheritance, environment and brain mechanisms in learning disability, autism, speech and language disorders, hearing loss, cerebral palsy, etc.
Clinical research	• Outcome measures and outcomes for therapy services • Effectiveness and cost-effectiveness of new therapies • Role and impact of non-orthodox therapies
Health services research	• Definitions of disability – coding systems and database organisation • Measures of the quality of life for disabled children • Reasons for variability in service provision for disabled children • Optimum staffing levels for child development teams • Relationship between secondary and tertiary disability services • Delivering the service standard set out in the Charter (*see* Appendix 2) – obstacles and costs

Children with mild and moderate psychological disorders

It has been asserted that the major difficulty in this field (as in child and adolescent psychiatric disorder) is the poor level of co-ordination between agencies relevant to child and adolescent mental health, both within the NHS (child psychiatry, child psychology, hospital and community paediatrics, adult psychiatry and primary care) and across health, education, social services, youth justice and the voluntary sector.[152] A number of new Government initiatives are promoting and will promote inter-agency linkage and need evaluative monitoring. The tiered approach provides a potential answer to some of these problems, but its interpretation varies and a comparative evaluation of approaches based on tiered models is required. This might be qualitative in the first instance, and for mild and moderate psychopathology might address the ways of working of tiers 1 and 2 in particular, across NHS specialties and agencies.

The use of problem resolution as a target measure is hampered by comorbidity and Likert scaling, and is confused by differences between raters according to which domain the child is in (school, home, peers, etc.). The development of a children's scale of adaptive functioning which is less complex and less Americanised than the C-GAS (*see* 'Models of care – Mild and moderate psychological disorders' above) is needed.

Appendix 1: Working with non-government organisations in the voluntary or charitable sector

Provision of services

- Mother and toddler groups.
- Drop-in centres for parents with young children.
- Bereavement support: one-to-one and in groups.
- Support for parents of children with a disability.
- Home visiting and befriending.
- Group-based parenting programmes.
- Health visitor, midwife and teacher training.

Benefits of NHS collaboration with voluntary sector

- Services do not suffer from the stigmatisation attached to clinical or social service provision.
- Providers have credibility because of their experience as parents, and can offer practical information and advice on how to cope in a way that may not be easy for professionals.
- Services are in tune with what the consumers want.
- Groups of parents in voluntary organisations are better placed to develop a genuine partnership with professionals.
- Access is allowed to information and insight which otherwise would not be available to professionals.
- Work experience is provided for mothers returning to work, giving them experience and confidence.
- Non-professional services are less expensive than professional services, but the cost of recruiting, vetting and training volunteers can be significant.

Limitations

- Volunteers and voluntary groups are not representative of all children or all shades of opinion.
- Voluntary work can become a crusade or a way for an individual to deal with their own problems.
- Recruitment difficulties – many people undertake voluntary work for a short period of time in order to gain experience and confidence before seeking to re-enter the world of work.
- The cost of recruiting, vetting and training volunteers can be substantial.
- Professionals are often anxious about aspects such as skill, confidentiality and commitment.
- It is difficult for professionals to keep up to date with all the different voluntary groups which may exist in the locality.
- Variations in the number of volunteers available to provide a particular service may mean that some referrals are not taken up, making it less likely that the professionals will make use of the organisation again in the future.

Insecure funding available to voluntary groups – and variation in numbers of volunteers – means that service provision can be erratic. (More permanent financial support would undoubtedly make them more efficient and effective. Often this is a preferable option to providing short-term start-up funding to new organisations.)

Appendix 2: A charter for disabled children and their families

Principles

- The family should feel that they have been listened to and heard, and that their concerns and aspirations have been taken seriously, and that their responsibility to their child is respected.

Referral and follow-up

- There should be a prompt response to the first referral (within one week), and the degree of urgency and parental anxiety should be considered when arranging the first appointment.
- The child should receive either regular medical follow-up or open access to the consultant in the event of new problems.
- There should be arrangements for children with complex medical needs to be seen urgently on request. The family should know whom to contact in the event of new problems.

The diagnosis and the disability

- The process of 'news-breaking' should follow established guidelines, whichever professional undertakes the task. Where necessary, training should be provided. There should be arrangements for an early follow-up appointment and/or home visit, and telephone support should be available.
- The parents and child should know the correct name, label or description for the child's condition, and its prognosis and functional implications.
- Investigations should be carried out according to current best professional practice. Even if no exact diagnosis can be made, the family should know what tests have been done and what the results mean. If the situation changes, any new investigations should be explained.
- The child's future needs (e.g. for care in adolescence and adult life, or for terminal care in the case of progressive disease) should be discussed with the parents and the child as soon as possible. There should be planned handover to a relevant, co-ordinated adult service, in line with the requirements of current legislation.

Treatment and therapy

- If the child takes any medication, the parent should know what, why, for how long and how much. They should have a medication card to summarise complex drug or multiple therapy.
- The family should know what sort of therapy or teaching the child is receiving, what it is intended to achieve and how they can help. There should be defined and achievable goals. The parents and child should understand what system of prioritising need is used by therapists and the reasons for any delays in commencing a treatment programme.
- The family should know what other methods might be offered by others for treating the child's condition (including both orthodox and controversial therapies, and alternative medicine) and why the team/therapists are not using them for the child. They should be aware that some treatments of

dubious efficacy can be disturbing and distressing to children. Families who try other methods should continue to receive support.

Information

- Every family should be offered full information about the child's condition (including implications and prognosis), a meeting with another parent whose child has the same problem, and the name and phone number of the organisation for children with this condition.
- Every family should be offered expert information about the genetic aspects of the child's condition, either by a clinical geneticist or by a well-informed paediatrician. This information should not be omitted even when the condition is thought by the professionals to be non-genetic.

Medical care and support

- The growth of every child should be monitored. Every child should have access to expertise on feeding problems and techniques, and nutritional support.
- Every child should be offered hearing and vision assessments as appropriate.
- Every parent should know about day care (day nurseries, etc.) and respite care (short breaks). There should be a range of respite provision and other relevant local support services.
- Every child should be offered prophylactic dental advice and access to dental specialist services if needed.
- Every parent should know about benefits and the Family Fund.
- Every child with cerebral palsy associated with a risk of hip dislocation and/or scoliosis should receive regular orthopaedic checks and hip and spine X-rays as appropriate.
- Every child should be offered a full immunisation programme unless there are recognised contra-indications.
- Every parent should know about pre-school educational help (home teachers, Portage, etc.), their rights under the Education Act, and the procedures involved with assessment and Statements of Special Educational Need. Limitations in resource provision should be explained. There should be an impartial source of advice on services.
- The family should be provided with all equipment and aids appropriate to the child's needs.
- There should not be undue delays in providing or repairing the equipment. If delay is unavoidable, the family should be kept informed.
- The family should be invited and encouraged to identify other important service needs. They should be able to offer suggestions and there should be a clear complaints procedure.

Appendix 3: Recommended minimum service provision through European countries for children with disability[153]

Philosophy

1 Services should be needs led.
2 Use terms such as 'normalisation' and 'therapy' with care and with adequate explanation.
3 Some services should be available as a basic right and not require validation.

Process

4 Care programmes should be goal orientated and individually adapted.
5 Early identification is the key to early intervention and service availability.
6 Services should be provided by local, well-co-ordinated teams.
7 User input is essential to planning, development and managing services.
8 Appropriate support for behaviour problems should be an integral part of service provision.
9 Disability services must be locally based with ready access to tertiary support.

Structure

10 Children with rare disabling conditions may need considerable tertiary care but should also receive support from a local disability service.
11 Better information on numbers of disabled children and services available is needed at local levels.
12 Integration into mainstream education is to be encouraged where appropriate.
13 Inter-agency collaboration (health, education, social services) is important for providing a comprehensive service.
14 Proper business plans with costings and coverage need to be developed.

Appendix 4: Education Act and Code of Practice

The NHS Act 1977 requires the Secretary of State to provide for the medical and dental inspection of schoolchildren in maintained schools at appropriate intervals, and the Education Reform Act 1988 extended this to include grant-maintained (opt-out) schools. Independent schools should make arrangements with the provider unit ('Child health in the Community'[17] 8:21).

Section 166 of the Education Act 1993 requires health authorities (now PCTs) to comply with requests from Local Education Authorities in respect of children with special educational needs unless, having regard to the resources available to them, it is not reasonable for them to comply with the request.

Negotiating School Health Services and **Nurses and Purchasing: School Nurses in the New Health Service Structure** advise purchasers to consider the pattern of services in schools, paying particular attention to dental care, consent to medical examination, medication in schools, health care needs of children with special needs, independent schools and training.[17]

The Education Act 1993 required the British Secretary of State for Education to publish guidance on good practice for the identification and assessment of children with special educational needs in the Code of Practice, to which all involved must have regard.

The 1993 Education Act developed and extended the **Education Act of 1981**, which in turn was based on the Warnock Report 1978. The 1981 Act had a wide range of recommendations, but the requirement for a formal assessment and the written Statements of Special Educational Need became the prime concern of educational and health services. One of the aims of the 1993 Act was to take note of the lessons learned as a result of experience with the statement process.

Key elements of the 1994 Code of Practice (now superseded by the **Special Educational Needs Code of Practice** 2001; *see* www.dfes.gov.uk/sen/) included the following.

- Early identification of the children who may have special needs and notification to the education service. There should be a named person responsible for liaison with the Local Education Authority.
- Twenty per cent of children may have special educational needs at some point. Identification and intervention have five stages. At stage 1, the teacher reviews the problem with the parents. At stages 2 and 3, advice may be sought from health experts and others. At stages 4 and 5, where formal assessment and written statement, respectively, may take place, health advice is a necessary part of the process.
- The health advice must be submitted within 6 weeks of the request and the formal assessment process must be completed in 26 weeks.
- Annual reviews of children with a Statement of Special Educational Need are statutory. From age 14 onwards there must be a transition plan. The Local Education Authority is required to consult child health services, for the first review after the pupil's 14th birthday and any subsequent annual reviews until the child leaves school. This is good practice for children with disabilities even if they do not have a Statement of Special Educational Need.
- Subsequent legal interpretations of the Code and the law have addressed the problem of providing therapy services such as speech therapy for children with a Statement of Special Educational Need.

In addition, education authorities are encouraged to:

- establish a monitoring group with health and social services
- ensure a named health service contact for each school
- agree a process for specifying and providing equipment (e.g. for seating, mobility and communication)
- have a means of discussing with other agencies pre-school children with special educational needs
- review children placed outside the local authority with involvement of other agencies
- agree a policy on health promotion and sex education for children with special needs.

Appendix 5: The Children Act (1989)

This provides the framework for the care and protection of children. The Act defines children in need as follows.

A child shall be taken to be in need if:
    (a) he is unlikely to achieve or maintain, or to have the opportunity of achieving or maintaining, a reasonable standard of health or development without the provision for him of services by a local authority;
    (b) his health or development is likely to be significantly impaired, or further impaired, without the provision for him of such services;
    (c) he is disabled.

(*See Working Together Under the Children Act 1989*. London: HMSO, 1991.)

Child protection

The health authority (now PCT) must:

- comply with requests for help from a local authority
- identify a senior nurse with a health-visiting qualification as designated senior professional to be a member of the Area Child Protection Committee (ACPC)
- take a strategic lead in inter-agency child protection matters
- ensure that service specifications include child protection
- co-ordinate Part 8 reviews of cases where a child has died or suffered serious harm
- identify a designated doctor for child protection.

Trusts must:

- provide training in child protection
- identify a named nurse and doctor for child protection within the trust.

Commissioners (including primary care groups and trusts) must:

- purchase child protection services
- purchase health-visiting services that fully meet child protection aspects of the health authority (now PCT) service specifications.

Appendix 6: Adoption and fostering

The **Adoption Agencies Regulations 1983**[73] state that at least one registered medical practitioner should be nominated to act as Medical Adviser, to be a member of the adoption panel and to be consulted regarding access to and disclosure of health information. The functions of the adoption panel are to recommend whether adoption is in the child's best interests, whether adoptive applicants are suitable and whether applicants are suitable for particular children.

Over 20 000 babies and children were placed for adoption each year in England and Wales in the early 1970s. This has now fallen to less than one-third of that figure. Half of these are placed with step-parents and the other half to a permanent substitute family as a consequence of neglect, rejection, abuse within the biological family or because of disability and handicap. Thus most adopted children are now not straightforward 'normal' children.

The **Arrangements for Placement of Children Regulations 1991** and the **Review of Children's Placements Regulations 1991**[73] set out the requirements for 'medical examinations with written records of every six months for children under two and thereafter every year, with child's consent'.

(The number of children looked after each year is approximately 50 000, but many are very short term: at any one time the figure is approximately 30 000 [100–200 per 100 000 total population].)

The Utting Report[34] made the following recommendations.

- 'Local authorities must pay particular attention to the educational and health needs of children they look after.'
- 'Local authorities must observe the regulations governing the placement and supervision of children in foster care.'
- 'Local and health authorities should assess and meet the need for treatment of children who have been abused.'

Appendix 7: The health-promoting school

There are three main components in health-promoting school programmes:

- health education – a curriculum aimed at providing new knowledge, challenging existing attitudes and developing skills
- health-enhancing changes to the school ethos and environment – developing policies, improving relationships among and between staff and pupils, and ensuring a healthy physical environment
- involving parents and the wider community in health-promoting initiatives.

The criteria for health-promoting schools in England are:

- active promotion of the self-esteem of all pupils by demonstrating that everyone can make a contribution to the life of the school
- development of good relationships between staff and pupils and among pupils in the daily life of the school
- clarification for staff and pupils of the social aims of the school
- provision of stimulating challenges for all pupils from a wide range of activities
- use of every opportunity to improve the physical environment of the school
- development of good links in and between school, home and community
- development of good links among associated primary and secondary schools to plan a coherent health education curriculum
- active promotion of the health and well-being of the school's staff
- consideration of the role of staff as examples in health-related issues
- consideration of the complementary role of school meals (if provided) in the health education curriculum
- realisation of the potential of specialist services in the community for advice and support in health education
- development of the education potential of school health services beyond routine screening and towards active support for the curriculum.

Appendix 8: Role of the immunisation co-ordinator

- Establish and monitor the information and appointments systems; ensure efforts are made to reach 'difficult' families.
- Make monthly reports of immunisation statistics.
- Ensure that there is continuing education on the subject of immunisation at local level.
- Form an advisory group with members from other disciplines, including community or public health, nursing, general practice, pharmacy, health promotion, etc.
- Monitor cases and outbreaks of infectious disease in collaboration with the CCDC (consultant in communicable disease control).
- Plan campaigns and programmes for the introduction of new vaccines and for changes in the existing protocol of immunisation.
- Ensure the maintenance of the 'cold chain' (i.e. ensuring safe refrigerated transport and storage of delicate vaccines, especially polio vaccine, which is inactivated by heat or sunlight).
- With the CCDC, monitor service provision for BCG, TB contacts and hepatitis B vaccine coverage as well as for the basic vaccine programme.
- Provide advice in cases where doctors and/or parents are doubtful about immunisation or where there are contraindications in a particular case. Many districts provide an immunisation advice clinic.
- Provide training for health visitors to give immunisations themselves. It is useful for health visitors to have this skill, particularly in cases where parents are reluctant to come to clinics.

Appendix 9: Specialist services needed by disabled children

Specialist or service	Examples
Paediatric neurologist: combined clinic, peripatetic service; regional centre for investigations and treatment.	Diagnosis of unusual or obscure neurological disorders causing disability; management of complex epilepsy; botulinum toxin treatment trials, etc.
Clinical genetics: peripatetic or regional centre.	Diagnosis of chromosome disorders, dysmorphic syndromes, genetic counselling. Important whether or not referring clinician thinks child's condition is genetically determined.
Child psychiatry: district service.	Suspected autism, disintegrative psychosis, behavioural problems in disabled child. Referral to specialist centre may be needed for some problems, especially self-injurious behaviour which can be life-threatening.
Clinical psychologist (if not part of CDC team): district service.	Opinion on developmental problems (intellectual assessment, etc.), behaviour problems, parental stress and management problems, family conflict over care of disabled child.
Community mental handicap team (CMHT) (team for people with learning disabilities): district service.	In most districts, children with learning disabilities are cared for by the paediatric services with the support of child psychiatry/psychology; handover to the CMHT may be in the early teens, or at school leaving.
Cardiologist: regional or peripatetic.	Congenital heart defects may be part of range of the child's disabilities.
Orthoptist and ophthalmologist: district, but regional or supra-regional for uncommon conditions.	Eye defects and disorders are more common in children with other disabilities. Complex behavioural problems and developmental setback in blind children need specialised team.
Audiologist: district, but regional or supra-regional for some investigations and for cochlear implant.	A hearing check is vital for all disabled children – multiple impairments are common. Hearing-impaired children need wide range of services.
ENT surgeon: district except for rare or complex problems.	Treatment of glue ear; salivary duct transplantation; laryngeal or tracheal stenosis, especially in prematures.
Paediatric surgeon: supra-district or regional.	Repair of spina bifida, replacement of valves for hydrocephalus, bladder problems, gastrostomies, congenital anomalies.
Paediatric orthopaedic surgeon plus orthotist: supra-district or regional.	Dislocated hips, scoliosis and contractures are common in disabled children. Judgements about surgery are often very complex.
Paediatric neurosurgeon: supra-district or regional.	Spinal problems, e.g. late complications of spina bifida repair. Shunt complications. Congenital anomalies.
Paediatric gastroenterologist and/or surgeon, dietitian, speech therapist: district, but complex disorders clinic supra-district or regional.	Severe feeding and swallowing problems are common in severely physically disabled children; may need tube feeding or gastrostomy. Constipation is common and often intractable.
Dental and orthodontic care: district.	Dental disease is not different in disabled children, but it is harder to assess and treat and many children need specialist expertise.
Wheelchair and seating services: district for most, regional for complex seating.	Some equipment is readily available; a few children need custom-made or specially ordered wheelchairs or seats; bio-engineering service.
Communication aids centres: regional or supra-regional.	Ensure that the correct equipment is purchased, and follow-up must be continued until the child's family and teachers can use it correctly.

Appendix 10: The children's audiology service

Screening and management tiers

- **Level 1 – screening services:** The infant distraction test (IDT) by health visitors; the sweep test used to screen children starting school; neonatal screening.
- **Level 2 – children referred from level 1:** Secondary screening to select children who need a full diagnostic evaluation. May manage children with minor hearing loss, behaviour problems such as inattention, and speech and language impairment; mostly in the 2–4 years age group.
- **Level 3 – full diagnostic and management service:** Hearing-aid provision, syndrome diagnosis, genetic advice, co-ordination of early speech and language therapy, education, psychology, social work, long-term supervision. (*Note*: In some districts, level 2 and level 3 are provided as a combined service.)
- **Level 4 – tertiary services:** Referral for specialised investigation, genetics, cochlear implants, etc.

Changes proposed in the near future

- **Move to universal neonatal screening:** The IDT produces disappointing results; universal neonatal screening is a better investment. If implemented, this would substantially reduce the volume of work at level 2. The cost of neonatal screening is less than the true cost of the health visitor test, and the yield is greater.
- **Standard of service:** Neonatal screening presents a variety of new challenges, and guidelines for a 'Family-Friendly Hearing Service' are being prepared (MRC Institute of Hearing Research, University of Nottingham). Districts will need audiological scientists, technicians and managerial/public health expertise to maintain a high standard of neonatal screening and follow-up. Full evaluation, including genetic studies, for the underlying cause of hearing loss is also vital.
- **Review service for 2–4 years age group:** Experienced speech therapists run triage to sort these referrals, and it is suggested that they could in addition undertake first-level audiology screening and basic psychological assessment.
- **Review school-entrant testing:** The sweep test at school entry detects a large number of children with middle ear disease, but the value of this exercise and the best referral pathway are under scrutiny.

Appendix 11: What primary health care teams could do to improve services for adolescents in primary care and community settings: general principles

- Create a practice profile for 10–18-year-olds using the age/sex register.
- Provide positive information stressing confidentiality (posters, leaflets, reassurance during face-to-face consultation), and confirm that this applies to every member of the practice or clinic.
- Create an environment that is user-friendly to adolescents. This includes the attitudes of staff as well as the physical environment.
- Make sure that teenagers know about the services on offer by publicity through schools, school health staff, or by arranging for teenagers to visit the clinic or health care facility as part of a school personal development programme.
- As children approach puberty, educate parents about the need for children progressively to take responsibility for their own health and health care and encourage them to consult the doctor on their own.
- Offer the freedom to change GPs when a person reaches the age of 16.
- Make use of routine health care opportunities such as immunisation, minor consultations for health problems, or invited routine health checks.
- Provide specific information for parents about health problems of the teenage years.
- Since few doctors have any specific training in communication skills with adolescents, this must be included in GPs' and paediatricians' training programmes and also incorporated in undergraduate teaching.

Appendix 12: Philosophical models of service for disabled children[130]

The expert model

The professionals give information. They inform the parents of the results of the assessment. They assess and treat the child:

- according to their own perceptions
- with minimal negotiation of goals with parents or other carers
- in a place of their choosing.

The expert model is outmoded. It does not allow for the differences between families, nor does it consider the need to relate professional goals to family needs and priorities.

The transplant model

The professionals provide the expertise and teach the parents to carry out particular tasks. In this model it is implicitly assumed that:

- parents know their own child better than anyone else can
- parents are motivated to help their child
- parents have the personal resources to carry out what is required of them
- the professionals will be in charge of the management plan
- the professionals have the ability to communicate the necessary skills to the parents.

The transplant model maintains the dependent role of the family in relation to professional services. It does not address the problem of multiple professional inputs.

The consumer rights model

This model emphasises the parents as consumers and assumes that:

- parents have the right to select services and interventions that they feel are appropriate
- parents will need information in order to make these choices
- parents have the expertise to judge for themselves what is needed in the light of their life situation.

It follows that:

- service packages would need to be tailored to individual family needs
- sometimes the family and the professionals would have different perceptions of the services needed; if this happened, the parents' views would be respected
- negotiation about service provision would be essential
- parents would be part of the management structure of special needs services.

The danger of this model is (in theory at least) that it neglects the child's needs in favour of those of the whole family.

The social network model

This model emphasises the child as a member of a social network and assumes that:

- environmental factors interact with biological disadvantage in complex ways
- under most circumstances, the child's social network is a more powerful factor in influencing development than any professional service
- families may rate factors causing social disadvantage (poor housing, unemployment) as more important than developmental problems
- parents will draw on their social networks for information, ideas and support as much as, or more than, their professional advisers
- families previously labelled as 'difficult' or 'non-compliant' would be regarded as having different priorities
- professional skills would be used to assist the family in setting, adjusting and achieving its priorities for the child.

The empowerment model

This combines features of the consumer rights model and the social network model.

- It emphasises the empowerment of parents, i.e. the aim is to facilitate the parents' ability to make and carry out decisions and actions which they consider to be right for them.
- It aims to build on the strengths of the family rather than its weaknesses.
- It retains the professional role and responsibility to consider the needs of the child and to help parents to consider how these can be met.
- It has implications for the ways in which services are provided and monitored.

References

1 Wallace S, Crown J, Cox A, Berger M. Child and adolescent mental health. In: Stevens A, Raftery J (eds). *Health Care Needs Assessment.* Oxford: Radcliffe Medical Press, 1997, pp. 55–120.

2 Richman N, Stevenson J, Graham P. *Preschool to School: a Behavioural Study.* London: Academic Press, 1982.

3 Bone MMH. *The Prevalence of Disability Amongst Children. 3.* London: HMSO, 1989.

4 World Health Organization Working Group on Health Promotion Evaluation. *Health Promotion Evaluation. Recommendations to policy makers: WHO European Working Group on Health Promotion Evaluation, Brighton 1998.* Copenhagen: World Health Organization, 1998.

5 Stewart-Brown S, Layte R. Emotional health problems are the most important cause of disability in adults of working age: a study in the four counties of the old Oxford Region. *J Epidemiol Community Health* 1997; **51**: 672–5.

6 Bennet P, Murphy S. *Psychology and Health Promotion.* Buckingham: Open University Press, 1997.

7 Murray C, Lopez A. *The Global Burden of Disease.* Harvard: Harvard School of Public Health (on behalf of the World Bank and the World Health Organization), 1996.

8 Graves P, Thomsa C, Mead L. Familial and psychological predictors of cancer. *Cancer Detect Prev* 1991; **15**: 59–64.

9 Caspi A, Harrington H, Moffit T *et al.* Personality differences predict health risk behaviours in young adulthood: evidence from longitudinal study. *J Pers Health Soc Psychol* 1997; **73**: 1052–63.

10 Jenkins S. Prevention. In: Harvey D, Miles M, Smyth D (eds). *Community Child Health and Paediatrics.* Oxford: Butterworth-Heinemann, 1995, pp. 152–7.

11 Beverley D, Ball R, Smith R *et al.* Planning for the future: the experience of implementing a children's day unit in a district general hospital. *Arch Dis Child* 1997; **77**: 287–92.

12 Meates M. Ambulatory paediatric – making a difference. *Arch Dis Child* 1997; **76**: 468–73.

13 McConachie H, Salt A, Chadury Y, McLachlan A, Logan S. How do child development teams work? Findings from a UK national survey. *Child Care Health Dev* 1999; **25**: 157–68.

14 Zahir M, Bennett S. Review of child development teams. *Arch Dis Child* 1994; **70**: 224–8.

15 Scott S, Spender Q, Doolan M, Jacobs B, Aspland H. Multicentre controlled trial of parenting groups for childhood anti-social behaviour in clinical practice. *BMJ* 2001; **323**: 194–8.

16 Rutter M. Connections between child and adolescent psychopathology. *Eur J Child Adolesc Psychiatry* 1996; **5**: 4–7.

17 Power C, Manor O, Fox J. *Health and Class: the early years.* London: Chapman and Hall, 1991.

18 Glozier N, Millar J. *ICIDH-2: the International Classification of Impairments, Activities and Participation.* Geneva: World Health Organization, 1999.

19 Office of Population Censuses and Surveys (OPCS). *Prevalence of Disability Among Children. Volume 3.* London: OPCS, 1989.

20 British Association for Community Child Health and Department of Health. *Disability in Childhood: towards nationally useful definitions. Report of a working group on definitions of disability.* London: British Association for Community Child Health, 1994.

21 Ottenbacher K, Msall M, Lyon N, Duffy L, Granger C, Braun S. Measuring developmental and functional status in children with disabilities. *Dev Med Child Neurol* 1999; **41**: 186–94.

22 Milner J, Bungay C, Jellinek D, Hall D. Needs of disabled children and their families. *Arch Dis Child* 1996; **75**: 399–404.

23 Paterson G, DeBaryshe D, Ramsay E. A developmental perspective on antisocial behaviour. *Am Psychiatry* 1989; **44**: 329–35.

24 Cohen D, Richardson J, LaBree L. Parenting behaviour and the onset of smoking and alcohol use: a longitudinal study. *Pediatrics* 1994; **94**: 368–75.

25 Russek L, Schwartz G. Perceptions of parental caring predict health status in midlife: a 35-year follow-up of the Harvard Mastery of Stress Study. *Psychosom Med* 1997; **59**: 144–9.

26 Barlow J, Stewart-Brown S, Fletcher J. Systematic review of the school entrant medical examination. *Arch Dis Child* 1998; **78**: 301–11.

27 Hall D, Elliman D (eds). *Health for all Children* (4e). Oxford: Oxford University Press, 2003.

28 Roberts I, Kramer M, Suissa S. Does home visiting prevent childhood injuries? A systematic review of randomised controlled trials. *BMJ* 1996; **312**: 29–33.

29 Olds D, Eckenrode J, Henderson C et al. Long-term effects of home nurse visitation on maternal life courses and child abuse and neglect: fifteen-year follow-up of a randomised trial. *JAMA* 1997; **278**: 637–43.

30 Roberts I, Guiseppe C, Ward H. Childhood injuries: extent of the problem, epidemiological trends and costs. *Injury Prev* 1998; **4** (Suppl.): 10–16.

31 Barker M, Power C. Disability in young adults: the role of injuries. *J Epidemiol Community Health* 1993; **47**: 349–54.

32 Woodroffe C, Glickman M, Barker M, Power C. *Children, Teenagers and Health: the key data.* Buckingham: Open University Press, 1993.

33 Health Education Authority. *Today's Young Adults.* London: Health Education Authority, 1992.

34 Utting W. *People Like Us.* London: HMSO, 1997, pp. 81–3.

35 Hill P. Child psychiatry. In: Murray R, Hill P, McGuffin P (eds). *The Essentials of Postgraduate Psychiatry.* Cambridge: Cambridge University Press, 1997.

36 Office for National Statistics (ONS). *Mental Health of Children and Adolescents.* London: ONS, 1999.

37 Davis H, Spurr P. Parent counselling: an evaluation of a community child mental health service. *J Child Psychol Psychiatry* 1998; **39**: 365–76.

38 Audit Commission. *Children in Mind.* Oxford: Audit Commission Publications, 1999.

39 Shaffer D, Gardner A. Behaviour and bladder disturbance of enuretic children: a rational classification of a common disorder. *Dev Med Child Neurol* 1984; **26**: 781–92.

40 Koot H. *The Epidemiology of Child and Adolescent Psychopathology.* Oxford: Oxford University Press, 1992.

41 Millstein S, Litt I. Adolescent health. In: Feldman S, Elliot G (eds). *At the Threshold: the developing adolescent.* Boston, MA: Harvard University Press, 1990.

42 Rutter M, Graham P, Chadwick O, Yule W. Adolescent turmoil: fact or fiction. *J Child Psychol Psychiatry* 1976; **17**: 36–56.

43 Lavigne J, Arend R, Rosenbaum D, Binns H, Christoffel K, Gibbons R. Psychiatric disorders with onset in the pre-school years. 1. Stability of diagnoses. *J Am Acad Child Adolesc Psychiatry* 1998; **37**: 1246–54.

44 Kovacs M, Feinberg T, Crouse-Novak M, Paulaskas S, Pollock M, Finkelstein R. Depressive disorders in childhood. II. A longitudinal study of the risk for a subsequent major depression. *Arch Gen Psychiatry* 1984; **41**: 643–9.

45 Sanderson D. *Cost Analysis of Child Health Surveillance.* York: University of York, Health Economics Consortium, 1998.

46 Cotton L, Brazier J, Marsh P et al. School nursing – costs and potential benefits. *J Adv Nurs* 2000; **31**: 1063–71.

47 Crofts D, Bowns I, Williams T, Rigby A, Haining R, Hall D. Hitting the target – equitable distribution of health visitors across case-loads. *J Public Health Med* 2000; **22**: 295–301.

48 National Commission of Inquiry into the Prevention of Child Abuse. *Childhood Matters.* London: HMSO, 1996.

49 Department of Health. *Working Together to Safeguard Children: a guide to inter-agency working to safeguard and promote the welfare of children.* London: The Stationery Office, 1999.

50 Department of Health and Welsh Office. *Child Protection: clarification of arrangements between the NHS and other agencies.* London: HMSO, 1995.

51 Sanders R, Jackson S, Thomas N. The balance of prevention, investigation and treatment in the management of child protection services. *Child Abuse Neglect* 1996; **20**: 899–906.

52 Meerstadt PWD, Battye D. *Model Business Plan.* London: British Agencies for Adoption and Fostering, 1995.

53 Department of Health. *Quality Protects: transforming children's lives.* London: The Stationery Office, 1998.

54 NHS Executive. *Child Health in the Community: a guide to good practice.* London: Department of Health, 1996.

55 Polnay L. *Health Care Needs of School-Age Children.* London: British Paediatric Association, 1993.

56 Department for Education and Skills. *Special Educational Needs Code of Practice.* London: Department for Education and Skills, 2001.

57 Elkan R, Kendrick D, Hewitt M *et al.* Effectiveness of domiciliary health visiting: a systematic review of international studies and a selective review of the British literature. *Health Technol Assess* 2000; **4**.

58 Frost N, Johnson L, Stein M, Wallis L. *Negotiated Friendship: Home Start and the delivery of family support.* Leicester: Home Start, 1996.

59 Reading R, Allen C. The impact of social inequalities in child health on health visitors' work. *J Public Health Med* 1998; **19**: 424–30.

60 Audit Commission. *Seen But Not Heard.* London: HMSO, 1994.

61 Durlak J, Wells A. Primary prevention mental health programs for children and adolescents: a meta-analytic review. *Am J Community Psychol* 1997; **25**: 115–52.

62 Barlow J, Stewart-Brown S. Behavioural problems and group-based parent education programs. *Dev Behav Pediatrics* 2000; **21**(5): 356–70.

63 Smith C. *Developing Parenting Programmes.* London: National Children's Bureau, 1996.

64 Conroy S, Smith M. *Exploring Infant Health: a review commissioned by the Foundation for the Study of Infant Deaths.* London: Foundation for the Study of Infant Deaths, 1999.

65 Fletcher J, Stewart-Brown S, Barlow J. *Systematic Review of Reviews of the Effectiveness of School-Based Health Promotion.* Oxford: Health Services Research Unit, Oxford University, 1997.

66 Oppong-Odiseng A, Heycock E. Adolescent health services – through their eyes. *Arch Dis Child* 1997; **77**: 115–19.

67 Court F. *Fit for the Future.* London: HMSO, 1976.

68 Bax M, Whitmore K. District handicap teams in England: 1983–8. *Arch Dis Child* 1991; **66**: 656–64.

69 McConachie H, Salt A, Chadury Y, McLachlan A, Logan S. How do child development teams work? Findings from a UK national survey. *Child Care Health Dev* 1999; **23**: 77–86.

70 Yerbury M. Issues in multidisciplinary teamwork for children with disabilities. *Child Care Health Dev* 1997; **23**: 77–86.

71 Cooper P, Murray L. Prediction, detection and treatment of postnatal depression. *Arch Dis Child* 1997; **7**: 97–9.

72 Working Party Report. *Pattern of Medical Services for Children: medical staffing and training.* London: British Medical Association, 1997.

73 Law J, Boyle J, Harris F, Harness A, Nye C. Screening for speech and language delay: a systematic review of the literature. *Health Technol Assess* 1998; **2**.

74 Hall D. Child development teams: are they fulfilling their purpose? *Child Care Health Dev* 1997; **23**: 87–99.

75 Davis A, Bamford J, Wilson I, Ramkalawan T, Forshaw M, Wright S. A critical review of the role of neonatal hearing screening in the detection of congenital hearing impairment. *Health Technol Assess* 1997; **1**.

76 Cameron R. Early intervention for young children with developmental delay: the Portage approach. *Child Care Health Dev* 1997; **23**: 11–27.

77 Marpole S, Reading R. *The Provision of Equipment for Children with Special Needs in Norfolk 1997.* Norwich: Norwich Social Services, 1998.

78 Alexander T. *Family Learning.* London: Demos Arguments Series, 1997.

79 Bowns I, Crofts D, Williams T, Rigby A, Hall D, Haining R. Levels of satisfaction of low-risk mothers with their current health-visiting service. *J Adv Nurs* 2000; **31**: 805–11.

80 Finkelhor D, Berliner L. Research on the treatment of sexually abused children: a review and recommendation. *J Am Acad Child Adolesc Psychiatry* 1995; **34**: 1408–23.

81 Chapman S, Stewart-Brown S. *The School-Entry Health Check: the literature*. Oxford: Health Services Research Unit, 1998.

82 Joint Tuberculosis Committee of the British Thoracic Society. Control and prevention of tuberculosis in the UK: Code of Practice 1994. *Thorax* 1994; **49**: 1193–200.

83 DeBell D, Everett G. *In a Class Apart: a study of school nursing*. Norwich: The Research Centre, City College, 1997.

84 Lightfoot J, Bines W. *The Role of Nursing in Meeting the Health Needs of School-Age Children Outside Hospital. Final report to the Department of Health DH1430*. York: Social Policy Research Unit, University of York, 1996.

85 Snowdon S, Stewart-Brown S. Pre-school vision screening: a systematic review. *Health Technol Assess* 1997; **1**.

86 Pollitt J, Green A, McCabe C *et al*. Neonatal screening for inborn errors of metabolism: cost, yield and outcome. *Health Technol Assess* 1997; **1**.

87 Zeuner D, Ades AE, Karnon J, Brown J, Dezateux C, Anionwu EN. Antenatal and neonatal haemoglobinopathy screening in the UK: review and economic analysis. *Health Technol Assess* 1999; **3**(11).

88 MacMillan H, MacMillan J, Offird D, Griffith L, MacMillan A. Primary prevention of child physical abuse and neglect: a critical review. *J Child Psychol Psychiatry* 1994; **35**: 856.

89 Ciliska D, Hayward S, Thomas H *et al*. A systematic overview of the effectiveness of home visiting as a delivery strategy for public health nursing interventions. *Can J Public Health* 1997; **87**(3): 193–8.

90 Barker WE, Anderson RA, Chalmers C. *Health Trends Over Time and Major Outcomes of the Child Development Programmes*. Bristol: Eastern Health and Social Services Board, Bristol ECDU, 1994.

91 Emond AM, Pollock J, Deare T, Bonnell S, Peters TJ, Harvey L. An evaluation of the First Parent Health Visitor Scheme. *Arch Dis Child* 2002; **86**: 150–7.

92 Johnson Z, Howell F, Molloy B. Community mothers programme: randomised controlled trial of non-professional intervention in parenting. *BMJ* 1993; **306**: 1449–52.

93 Larner M, Halpern R, Harkavy O. *Fair Start for Children: lessons learned from seven demonstration projects*. New Haven, CT: Yale University Press, 1992.

94 Anonymous. Public health implications of childhood behaviour problems and parenting programmes. In: Buchanan A, Hudson B (eds). *Parenting, Schooling and Children's Behaviour: interdisciplinary approaches*. Aldershot: Ashgate Publishing, 1998.

95 Weare K. *The Health-Promoting School: an overview of key concepts, principles and strategies and the evidence for their effectiveness*. London: Routledge, 2000.

96 Elias M, Zins J, Weissberg R *et al. Promoting Social and Emotional Learning*. Alexandria, VA: ASCD, 2000.

97 Jamison J, Ashby P, Hamilton K, Lewis G, MacDonald A, Saunders L. *The Health-Promoting School: final report of the ENHPS evaluation project in England*. London: Health Education Authority, 1998.

98 McPherson A. Primary health care and adolescents. In: Macfarlane A (ed.). *Adolescent Medicine*. London: Royal College of Physicians, 1996, pp. 33–43.

99 NHS Centre for Reviews and Dissemination. Preventing and reducing the adverse effects of unintended teenage pregnancies. *Effect Health Care Bull* 1997; **3**(1): 1–12.

100 Morton R, Benton S, Bower E *et al*. Multi-disciplinary appraisal of the British Institute for Brain-Injured Children. *Dev Med Child Neurol* 1999; **41**: 211–12.

101 Sloper P, Turner S. Determinants of parental satisfaction with disclosure of disability. *Dev Med Child Neurol* 1993; **35**: 816–25.

102 King G, Rosenbaum P, King S. Evaluating family-centred service using a measure of parents' perceptions. *Child Care Health Dev* 1997; **23**: 47–62.

103 Beresford B. Resources and strategies: how parents cope with the care of a disabled child. *J Child Psychol Psychiatry* 1994; **35**: 171–211.

104 Ramchandani P, Wiggs L, Webb V, Stores G. A systematic review of treatments for settling problems and night waking in young children. *BMJ* 2000; **320**: 209–13.

105 Webster-Stratton C, Hollinsworth T, Kolpacoff M. The long-term effectiveness and clinical significance of three cost-effective training programs for families with conduct-problem children. *J Consult Clin Psychol* 1989; **57**: 550–3.

106 Nicol R, Stretch D, Fundudis T. *Preschool Children in Troubled Families*. Chichester: John Wiley & Sons, 1993.

107 Scott G, Richards M. Night waking in infants: effects of providing advice and support for infants. *J Child Psychol Psychiatry* 1990; **31**: 551–67.

108 Simonoff E, Stores G. Controlled trial of trimeprazine tartrate for night waking. *Arch Dis Child* 1987; **62**: 253–7.

109 Miller K, Klauber G. Desmopressin acetate in children with severe primary nocturnal enuresis. *Clin Ther* 1990; **12**: 357–66.

110 Hersov L. Faecal soiling. In: Rutter M, Hersov L, Taylor E (eds). *Child and Adolescent Psychiatry: modern approaches*. Oxford: Blackwell Scientific Publications, 1994, pp. 520–8.

111 Child Psychotherapy Trust. *Is Child Psychotherapy Effective for Children and Young People?* London: Child Psychotherapy Trust, 1998.

112 Weiss B, Catron T, Harris V, Phung T. The effectiveness of traditional child psychotherapy. *J Consult Clin Psychol* 1999; **67**: 82–94.

113 Lask J. Social work in child psychiatry setting. In: Rutter M, Taylor E, Hersov L (eds). *Child and Adolescent Psychiatry: modern approaches*. Oxford: Blackwell Scientific Publications, 1994.

114 Elliot S. A model of multi-disciplinary training in the management of postnatal depression. In: *Postnatal Depression: focus on a neglected issue. Papers from the HVA/NCT National Conference*. London: Health Visitors Association, 1996.

115 Olds D, Henderson C, Chamberlin R, Tatelbaum R. Preventing child abuse and neglect: a randomized trial of nurse home visitation. *Pediatrics* 1986; **78**: 65–78.

116 Cox J, Holden J. *Perinatal Psychiatry: use and abuse of the Edinburgh Postnatal Depression Scale*. London: Gaskell, 1997.

117 Murray L, Cooper P. *Postpartum Depression and Child Development*. New York: Guilford Press, 1997.

118 Cooper P, Murray L. Postnatal depression. *BMJ* 2000; **316**: 1884–6.

119 Appleby L, Warner R, Whitton A, Faragher B. A controlled study of fluoxetine and cognitive-behavioural counselling in the treatment of postnatal depression. *BMJ* 1997; **314**: 932–6.

120 Anonymous. *Health-Visitor-Based Services for Pre-School Children with Behaviour Problems*. London: Association for Child Psychology and Psychiatry, 1990.

121 Child Development Project. *The Child Development Programme*. Bristol: Child Development Unit, University of Bristol, 1984.

122 Marcé Society. *The Emotional Effects of Childbirth. Distance learning course*. Doncaster: H Wharton, 1994.

123 Earle J, Hill P. *Research into Practice: a distance learning pack on child mental health for health visitors*. London: Department of Psychiatry, St George's Hospital Medical School, 1998.

124 Webster Stratton C. Advancing videotape parent training: a comparison study. *J Consult Clin Psychol* 1994; **62**: 583–93.

125 Kazdin A. Psychosocial treatments for conduct disorder in children. *J Child Psychol Psychiatry* 1997; **38**: 161–78.

126 Hill P. Prevention and other public health issues. In: Gelder M, Andreason N, Lopez-Ibor (eds). *New Oxford Textbook of Psychiatry*. Oxford: Oxford University Press, 2000.

127 Aronen E, Kurkel S. Long-term effects of an early home-based intervention. *J Am Acad Child Adolesc Psychiatry* 1996; **35**: 1665–72.

128 Home Office. *Supporting Families*. London: The Stationery Office, 1998.

129 Secretary of State for Education and Employment and Minister of State for Public Health. *Sure Start*. London: DFEE Publications, 1999.

130 Appleton P, Minchom P. Models of parent partnership and child development centres. *Child Care Health Dev* 1991; **17**: 27–38.

131 Appleton P, Boll V, Everett J, Kelly A, Meredith K, Payne T. Beyond child development centres: care coordination for children with disabilities. *Child Care Health Dev* 1997; **23**: 29–40.

132 House of Commons Health Committee. *Health Services for Children and Young People in the Community: home and school.* London: The Stationery Office, 1997.

133 British Paediatric Neurology Association. *Guide for Purchasers of Tertiary Services for Children with Neurological Problems.* London: British Paediatric Neurology Association, 1998.

134 Planck M. *Child Development Centres: teams for mentally handicapped people.* London: Campaign for Mentally Handicapped People, 1982.

135 Health Advisory Service. *Together we Stand.* London: HMSO, 1995.

136 Hill P. Contribution from the child and adolescent psychiatry section. In: Royal College of Psychiatrists (ed.). *Purchasing Psychiatric Care.* London: Royal College of Psychiatrists, 1994.

137 Department of Health and Department for Education. *A Handbook on Child Adolescent Mental Health.* London: HMSO, 1995.

138 Finch J, Hill P, Clegg C. *Standards for Child and Adolescent Mental Health Services.* London: Health Advisory Service and Brighton: Pavilion Publishing, 2000.

139 Campbell S. Behaviour problems in preschool children: a review of recent research. *J Child Psychol Psychiatry* 1995; **36**: 113–49.

140 House of Commons Health Committee. *Child and Adolescent Mental Health.* London: The Stationery Office, 1997.

141 Stewart-Brown S. Evaluating health promotion in schools. In: Rootman I, Goodstadt M, Hyndman B *et al.* (eds). *WHO-Euro Working Group on Health Promotion Evaluation in Health Promotion: principles and perspectives.* Copenhagen: World Health Organization Regional Office for Europe, 2001.

142 Stewart-Brown S, Farmer A. Screening could seriously damage your health. *BMJ* 1997; **314**: 533.

143 King S, Rosenbaum P, King G. *The Measure of Processes of Care (MPOC): a means to assess family-centred behaviours of health care providers.* Hamilton, Ontario: Neurodevelopmental Research Unit, McMaster University, 1995.

144 Conners C. *Conners Rating Scales – revised.* Windsor: NFER, 1998.

145 Berger M, Hill P, Sein E, Thompson M, Verduyn C. *A Proposed Core Dataset for Child and Adolescent Psychology and Psychiatry Services.* London: Association for Child Psychology and Psychiatry, 1993.

146 Shaffer D, Gould M, Brasic G *et al.* A Children's Global Assessment Scale (C-GAS). *Arch Gen Psychiatry* 1983; **40**: 1228–31.

147 Child Health Informatics Consortium. *Monitoring the Health of Our Nation's Children.* Cardiff: Child Health Informatics Consortium with the Royal College of Paediatrics and Child Health, 2000.

148 Qualification and Curriculum Authority (QCA). *The Baseline Assessment Information Pack: preparation for statutory baseline assessment.* London: QCA, 1998.

149 Royal College of Paediatrics and Child Health. *Directory of Child Development Centres.* London: Royal College of Paediatrics and Child Health, 1999.

150 Berger M, Hill P, Walk D. A suggested framework for outcomes in child and adolescent mental health services. In: Williams R, Richardson G (eds). *Together We Stand.* London: HMSO, 1995.

151 World Health Organization European Working Group on Health Promotion Evaluation, Brighton. *Recommendations to Policy Makers.* Copenhagen: World Health Organization, 1998.

152 Mental Health Foundation. *Bright Futures.* London: Mental Health Foundation, 1999.

153 McConachie H, Smyth D, Bax M. Services for children with disabilities in European countries. *Dev Med Child Neurol* 1997; **39** (Suppl. 76): 1–71.

Addendum

Since this chapter was completed, there have been a number of important developments. Of these, the most significant is the publication in April 2003 of the first section of the National Service Framework (NSF) for Children, on acute and hospital services, together with an overview of preliminary proposals regarding other aspects of child health including those covered in this chapter, under the title 'Emerging findings'. These can be obtained via the Department of Health website. The remainder of the NSF is expected to be published in the spring of 2004. Other relevant reports and documents are summarised below.

In January 2003, the fourth edition of *Health For All Children* was published (Oxford: Oxford University Press). This replaces the third edition. It further emphasises the move towards health promotion and community development and expands on several emerging issues such as parent education, parental mental health and substance abuse. There are some revisions to the programme of child health surveillance, setting out various options in anticipation of the NSF. The screening topics are updated in the light of work by the National Screening Committee.

Several Government programmes have continued to grow in size and importance, including Sure Start, Connexions and the Children's Fund. Further details can be obtained from the websites for the DfES and the Children and Young People's Unit, respectively. The Government also published an overarching strategy, *Tomorrow's Future*, in 2001.

The report by Lord Laming on the Victoria Climbié case in 2003 has highlighted the need to improve child protection procedures, and new initiatives are expected soon, including legislation that will be based on the proposals in the Green Paper published in response to Lord Laming's report (*see Keeping Children Safe* and *Every Child Matters*) (www.dfee.gov.uk/cypu); *see also Safeguarding Children*, 2002).

In 2003, the Audit Commission published a review of *Services for Disabled Children* with wide-ranging recommendations for improvements (*see* www.audit-commission.gov.uk).

In 2002, the Royal College of Paediatrics and Child Health published a review entitled *Strengthening the Care of Children in the Community* (*see* www.rcpch.ac.uk).

19 Contraception, Induced Abortion and Fertility Services

Mary W Lyons and John R Ashton

1 Summary

The issues and problems

Planned parenthood is an important and identifiable public health objective that benefits both individuals and the community. It provides individuals with the freedom to engage in a fulfilling and healthy sex life whilst delaying childbearing until such time as optimum conditions for childrearing exist.

For a variety of socio-economic reasons, the average number of years between the onset of sexual activity and childbearing is widening, leading to an increased demand for contraception to prevent unwanted pregnancy during the intervening years.[1,2]

Young women from deprived backgrounds, who already carry a heavier burden of ill-health, are the group most at risk of unintended pregnancy. Although not all unplanned pregnancies result in personal difficulties, the poverty, social exclusion and subsequent ill-health suffered by many teenage mothers and their children serve to widen the health inequalities that often already exist.[3]

Provision of appropriate sex and relationship education and effective services empowers people and can help individuals to make a personal risk–benefit analysis, make informed choices from the contraceptive methods available and become motivated to use them.[4]

At a public health level, contraceptive services are among the most cost-effective, with an estimated cost–benefit ratio of 1:14.[5–8] The cost–benefit ratio for contraception would be even higher if the economic benefits derived from health gains other than unintended pregnancy, such as the avoidance of sexually transmitted diseases, were included.[8]

Almost half of all conceptions in England are thought to be unplanned, and about one in five will be terminated. All contraceptives have a level of failure, and studies suggest that three out of four women seeking a termination were using some form of contraception at the time of conception.[9,10] The demand for abortion services is increasing, but it would be incorrect to assume that this indicates a failure in contraceptive services, since the increase could be due to many other social and physical factors. Even when provision and uptake of contraceptive services are high, there will always be a need for adequate abortion services to cater for contraceptive failures and problems that emerge as pregnancy develops.

Increasing numbers of couples are seeking medical help with fertility problems. It is difficult to know whether this represents a real increase in infertility or an increased demand for services caused by changing expectations of medical interventions to help with fertility problems.[11–13] NHS service provision for infertility varies considerably across the UK. However, the National Institute for Clinical Excellence (NICE) is drawing up clinical guidelines that will have to be implemented in all parts of the NHS in England and Wales to provide an equal level of service across these countries.

Sub-categories

Unlike disease-oriented services, contraceptive, induced abortion and fertility service needs cannot be usefully categorised by aetiology or severity.

Predictors of service need are most usefully categorised by requirements for health services, and these have been described in the three main areas by factors such as age, marital status, social class, gender and special groups. Some or all of these factors determine choice of contraceptive method, as well as demand for abortion and fertility services. Sexually transmitted infections are an important cause of infertility, so sex and relationship education that can help to prevent these infections is considered in this section.

Prevalence and incidence

The greatest demand for contraception, induced abortion and fertility services comes from sexually active women of childbearing age, but an increasing number of men are also requesting contraceptive advice and supplies.

Changes in family structure and the desired number of children affect the level of demand for contraceptive services.

The last 10 years have seen a decline in overall conception rates, but an increase for women aged 35–39 years as more women delay childbearing until later in life.[14,15] The proportion of women who report that they expect either by choice or infertility to remain childless is increasing.

In 1998, for the first time since records began, the proportion of conceptions outside marriage exceeded those within marriage.[15] A considerable proportion of the births to women who were not married were registered by both parents living at the same address, signifying that the absence of marriage is an indicator neither of unplanned pregnancy nor of an unstable environment for the child.

To provide a truly comprehensive sexual health service, commissioners must ensure that the contraceptive, abortion and fertility needs of all sectors of the population, including the disabled, ethnic minorities, and young people in care and institutions, are properly assessed and catered for.

Abortion rates in the UK are comparatively high, and an examination of the situation in other European countries suggests that by improving contraceptive and sex education services, abortion rates could be reduced. Women at both ends of the age spectrum (over 40 and under 16 years) have low conception rates but a high proportion of pregnancies ending in induced abortion. Most abortions (71% in 2000) were carried out on women who were either single, separated, divorced or widowed.[16]

Since a woman's fertility decreases with age, trends towards delaying the age of childbearing are likely to result in the increased prevalence of infertility. This, together with an increase in the prevalence of sexually transmitted infections, particularly chlamydia, coupled with increased expectations of the availability of medical treatment, heralds an increase in demand for fertility services over the next few years.[17,18]

Services available and costs

Contraception

Over half of all women between the ages of 16 and 49 use a non-surgical method of contraception and an estimated 12% have been sterilised.[19] An assortment of providers catering for different sections or groups in the population delivers contraceptive services. Women who use general practitioner services are more likely to be older, married, have had one child and be using oral contraception to space their children. Family planning clinics, including those specialising in the provision of services for teenagers, young women or other groups, provide a more comprehensive range of services and contraceptive methods. Since many unintended pregnancies occur in younger women, commissioners in some areas have allocated considerable funds to the development of services that are acceptable and accessible to teenage girls and boys. Young people report that they are more comfortable using clinics that are tailored to their needs.[20,21]

High-quality sex and relationship education in schools can do much to ensure that young people know how to protect themselves from unintended pregnancy, know where to go for advice and supplies and have the confidence and social skills to negotiate contraceptive use with a partner.

There has been a general trend towards the increased use of condoms, particularly among women under 30. Oral contraceptive use has remained at a similar level overall since 1993, and remains the most popular method for women in their twenties and thirties, although between 1995 and 1998 there was a statistically significant decrease from 29% to 24% in the proportion of women aged 30–34 reporting the pill as their usual form of contraception.[22]

Emergency contraception is a relatively new, but increasingly popular, safe and highly effective method of contraception that can be used after unprotected intercourse or contraceptive failure. In 1998, 10% of women of childbearing age who were not sterilised and were therefore at risk of pregnancy had used emergency contraception at least once in the previous two years.[22]

The average cost to the NHS of first attendance at a family planning clinic is £36, and £29 for a follow-up visit.[23] Costs of services in the independent sector vary. In 1998 an initial visit for a prescription for the contraceptive pill cost from £35. Follow-up visits cost from £20. Female sterilisation cost between £395 and £475, while male sterilisation cost between £150 and £170 (local anaesthetic) and £230 (general anaesthetic). Fitting of an IUCD, including screening, fitting and follow-up visit, cost £110. Emergency contraception cost £20.[24,25]

Induced abortion

Induced abortion accounts for approximately 23% of known conceptions in the general population.

Between 1992 and 1995 the proportion of conceptions terminated by induced abortion was steady. However, in 1996 the number and rate of conceptions and the number of induced abortions, particularly in women aged 20–24, increased. This change in direction appeared to be linked to warnings by the Committee on Safety of Medicines regarding certain new oral contraceptives. Since 1995, abortion rates in all age groups have continued to rise. Some young women in particular seem to have lost confidence in, and have stopped using, oral contraception.[26]

Since 1975, the proportion of abortions carried out during the safest period – before nine weeks' gestation – has gradually increased.

Most abortions are the result of extramarital conceptions. Only about 7.5% of conceptions within marriage result in abortion.

Provision of NHS-funded abortions in England and Wales is variable, with significant differences between regions.

The average cost to the NHS of a termination of pregnancy carried out as a day case is £393 for a surgical and £278 for a medical procedure. Costs rise to £555 for surgical and £478 for medical abortions carried out as elective inpatient procedures, and £614 for surgical and £528 for medical abortions carried out as non-elective procedures.[23]

Induced abortions are a major source of income for the independent sector, with an estimated market of £30 million in 1996. Specialist charitable organisations provide most non-NHS (privately funded) abortions in England and Wales and also provide abortions for the NHS (agency abortions).[27] Abortion costs in the private sector depend on gestational age, but are comparable to NHS costs.

Fertility

For about 70% of infertile couples, preliminary investigations carried out at the primary care level result in a broad diagnosis, and this knowledge makes decisions about treatment and referral more effective.

There is considerable debate surrounding the extent to which the NHS should fund infertility treatments. The ill-health caused by infertility is psychosocial rather than physical, and this means that it does not fit neatly into the medical model of health held by many in the NHS. Infertility as a condition competing for resources is therefore rarely given priority, though the Government accepts that infertility is a legitimate health need.

In the UK, only about 25% of *in-vitro* fertilisation (IVF) treatments are funded by the NHS, and 80% of all licensed treatments that take place, such as IVF, intracytoplasmic sperm injection (ICSI) or donor insemination (DI), take place in the private sector. Each health authority (now PCT) decides how much of its budget to allocate to fertility services, and 25% do not fund IVF at all.

Many clinics that operate under the NHS also offer private treatment to those who can pay. Each institution sets criteria for eligibility for private as well as NHS treatment, and many do not offer treatment to single women or unmarried couples as a matter of policy.

The availability and costs of infertility treatments vary considerably. Donor insemination costs around £150 and IVF upwards of about £2000 per treatment cycle.[28] The average number of treatment cycles per patient was 3 for donor insemination and 1.37 for IVF in 1996.

Effectiveness of services and interventions

Many young people lack the knowledge and social skills to use contraception effectively, which puts them at greater risk of unintended pregnancy. Effective sex and relationship education for young people has the power to increase individual control over fertility by ensuring that should they wish to do so, sexually mature individuals are able to obtain and use contraception. There is considerable debate about what should be taught and the ability of sexual health interventions to change behaviour. The inadequate design of many evaluations of sexual health interventions means that there is lack of clear evidence about what type of intervention can effectively change knowledge, attitudes and behaviour.

Contraceptive services are financially and socially beneficial to an extent that far outweighs their cost. It is cheaper to provide contraceptive services than to cover the costs of induced abortion or child maintenance. Contraceptive services are increasingly regarded by providers as just one part of the comprehensive sexual health service on offer. The wider benefits of contraception in the promotion of sexual health should be considered in future analyses of the cost-effectiveness of services.

Induced abortion is less traumatic psychologically and physically than an unwanted full-term pregnancy and there is low risk of serious complications, provided the referral is not delayed and the procedure is carried out during the early stages of gestation. Surgical abortion is more expensive than medical termination, but remains the most popular method, possibly because the procedure is quicker and only involves one visit to hospital. There is a need for a rigorous economic evaluation of medical abortions.

Fertility treatment services improve quality of life by removing the psychosocial ill-health caused by infertility, but many rely on a high level of technology, are not totally risk-free and are expensive. The effectiveness of services is difficult to quantify as the average success rate of, for example, IVF is 17% per cycle, which although low, appears better when compared to the average monthly chance of conceiving for a fertile couple having regular intercourse, which is only 20–25%. The relatively low level of success of many treatments suggests that adequate funds should therefore be directed towards infertility prevention as a more effective use of resources.

Models of care/recommendation

The ideal model:

- includes a range of complementary services designed to meet contraceptive, abortion, fertility and other sexual needs based on the requirements of the local community
- includes the development of programmes of professional training in sexual health for all service providers
- provides equity of access to services
- targets resources at groups or areas in greatest need within the community
- links into or commissions research into the causes or factors contributing to inequalities in health experienced by the population
- actively seeks feedback from service users and providers on quality and appropriateness of services provided (e.g. the views of pharmacists were sought after the introduction of emergency hormonal contraception under patient group direction by pharmacists in the Manchester, Salford and Trafford as well as Lambeth, Southwark and Lewisham health action zones)[29]
- has input into partnerships delivering sex and relationship education in schools and other institutions
- is based on local data, where all providers agree to a minimum set of indicators.

The national strategy for HIV and sexual health suggests examination of the benefits of more integrated sexual health services, including pilots of one-stop clinics, primary care youth services and primary care teams with a special interest in sexual health.[30]

Outcome measures, audit and targets

National targets, particularly with regard to the reduction in teenage pregnancy rates, have been described in Government documents and are being monitored closely. Routine data can be used to monitor uptake of contraceptive, abortion and fertility services. Service providers are being encouraged to develop local targets to meet the area's needs.

Information and research requirements

Much of the information required to establish need and to evaluate and monitor services is collected, analysed and made available by the Office for National Statistics (ONS). These data would be more useful to commissioners of services if they were available more promptly and were broken down by local area.

Methodologically sound evaluations of the effectiveness, including cost-effectiveness, of different approaches to sex and relationship education, contraceptive advice and specific young people's services are required.

There is a need to develop research methodologies to allow greater understanding of the contribution of both providers and service users to the effectiveness of contraception in normal use.

With the development of an expanded role for nurses in the primary care setting, the cost-effectiveness and quality of contraceptive and other sexual health services provided by trained family planning nurses based in primary care trusts compared to general practitioners and family planning clinics need to be established.

The long-term clinical effectiveness of the levonorgestrel intrauterine system as an alternative to hysterectomy and its cost-effectiveness and acceptability to women need to be established.

2 Introduction and statement of the problem

The foundations for a healthy life start well before birth. Increasing evidence suggests that preconceptual care for mothers, as well as conditions during fetal and the first years of life have consequences likely to affect health throughout childhood and adult life, and subsequently contribute to inequalities in health both nationally and internationally. Children experience the best start in life when the pregnancy that gives them life is both planned for and wanted.[3]

Services should facilitate choice about the number and timing of births and help to reduce the inequalities in health that result from the social, mental and physical problems linked to unintended pregnancy. The aim of commissioners of health services should be to empower people and enable them to enjoy their sexuality without detriment to their health or that of their partner.

Planned parenthood

Planned parenthood provides people with the opportunity to choose to have their children at a propitious time, when their economic, social and psychological environment is such that a child (or further child) will enhance their health and not present an undue burden. Children are an asset both to their parents and the community, and those born as the result of a planned pregnancy are more likely to experience favourable conditions for growth and development that will enable them to achieve their potential. Planned parenthood in a financially and emotionally stable family environment is therefore an important and identifiable public health objective in its own right and a component in any local and national strategy to reduce health inequalities. In his book on the role of medicine published in 1976 McKeown said that he considered the control of fertility to be of paramount importance in the analysis of factors contributing to the improved health enjoyed by people today compared to people of our grandparents' generation.[31]

In developing countries where extreme poverty, malnutrition and infectious diseases are major problems, planned parenthood is key to reducing infant and maternal mortality rates. The same does not hold in developed countries, where health threats tend to be more subtle, with complex social and psychological dimensions.[32,33]

Unplanned pregnancy is more common among sexually active and inexperienced teenagers who lack the skills or the means to avoid the consequences. Teenage pregnancy, particularly in women aged less than 15, is linked to a variety of adverse physical, social, educational and economic circumstances. Teenagers are less likely to use contraception, and when they do use it are less likely to do so effectively. Teenagers who do have a baby are also at greater risk of social exclusion because they are less likely to complete their education and get a good job, and subsequently suffer more from poverty and ill-health throughout life.[3] In Europe in the past and in many countries today, marriage, the onset of sexual relationships and pregnancy closely follow puberty. Amongst the physical and social changes that have affected adolescents between the late nineteenth and mid-twentieth centuries across many European countries, including the UK, is the earlier onset of sexual maturity indicated by a downward trend in the average age of menarche by a year or more and the deferral of childbearing until later in life. (The median menarcheal age appears to have stabilised at around 12 years 11 months.)[1] Due to the earlier onset of physical maturity and increasing participation in employment and higher education, the average young woman will be sexually mature for 15 years or more before contemplating marriage or having children.[2] Hence the increasing call for contraception during this period of women's lives.

Inequalities in health

Within the UK, under-age conception rates show a high degree of correlation with indices of deprivation.[34] There is a fourfold difference in under-16 conceptions between those health authorities (now PCTs) with the highest and lowest indices of deprivation.

The risk of teenage pregnancy increases with a number of factors, such as low educational attainment and poor housing. Particularly at risk are the daughters of teenage mothers, young people either in care or leaving care, school truants and excluded pupils, the homeless and young people who have run away from home.[6] A teenager coming from a financially and emotionally secure background who sees a clear future through education and work has greater motivation to use contraception, and much to lose from an unintended teenage pregnancy and the prospect of a life on welfare benefits.

The risk of unintended pregnancy is higher among girls who engage in intercourse from an early age and there is a link between age at first intercourse, social class, ethnic background and low educational achievement.[3] The risk of becoming a teenage mother is almost 10 times higher for a girl whose family is in social class V (unskilled manual) than for those in social class I (professional).[35] Those from higher social classes and with higher educational qualifications also report experiencing first intercourse at older ages. Table 1 shows that young black people are more likely to have first intercourse under the age of 16 than young white or Asian people.[36]

Table 1: Proportion of young people in each group experiencing first intercourse under the age of 16 years.

	Men	Women
Black	26%	10%
White	19%	8%
Asian	11%	1%

The consequences of teenage pregnancy also reveal health inequalities, as it is associated with increased risk of poor social, economic and health outcomes for both mother and child.[37] The infant mortality rate for babies born to teenage mothers is more than 50% higher than the average (and 40% higher than for manual groups), accounting for almost 400 deaths in 2000 (12% of all infant deaths). The infant mortality rate for babies born to mothers under the age of 18 is more than double the average, and there is also an increased risk of maternal mortality for this group.[38]

Variations in access to services also serve to increase inequalities in health and will be dealt with in discussions about respective services.

Contraception and abortion

At the beginning of the twentieth century the use of contraception was advocated as part of the strategy to reduce the high rates of infant and maternal mortality suffered particularly by the lower-paid working population. More recently the emphasis has been on empowerment and the benefits of providing women with greater choice and control over their fertility, as well as reducing the risk of unhappiness, social exclusion and ill-health that may be experienced as a consequence of unplanned parenthood, especially by young women and their children.[3]

Following campaigning by voluntary organisations and the legalisation of abortion in the 1960s, the early 1970s saw the introduction of free contraception through the NHS. This action was supported by research, which indicated that contraception was cheaper and more desirable than the social and medical costs of unintended pregnancy.

Increasing rates of abortion indicate that the aim for all pregnancies to be planned seems to be far from current social reality. However, even the best contraceptive practice will not eliminate the demand for abortion.

The promotion of sexual health

The promotion of sexual health, and in particular the sexual health of young people, is a key issue in the new public health agenda. Within a holistic framework, good sexual health is an important component of mental and social well-being and includes a capacity to enjoy and express sexuality without guilt or shame, coupled with freedom from disorders that interfere with health.

Most unintended pregnancies occur in the first six months of sexual activity with a new partner when contraception is either not being used or is being used inconsistently. It should therefore be possible to alter this behaviour with appropriate education and advice.[39]

Young people report that they get most information and support from friends and young people's magazines, but that they would like to receive more of their sex education from their parents. Parents tend to have more fears in relation to their daughters' sexual health, e.g. the possibility of becoming pregnant. In practice it is usually only mothers who discuss sex with their children, and they tend to focus on information and advice on the prevention of pregnancy and the needs of girls.[40] Parental discomfort acts as an inhibitory factor during discussions concerning sexuality.[41]

The sexual health needs of boys are not being met adequately – demonstrated amongst other things by an increase in sexually transmitted diseases in young people. Boys appear to be less interested than girls in the biological aspects of sex education. The emphasis on reproduction may reinforce the message that sex education is nothing to do with boys, who may therefore need to be taught in a different way.[42] The reason for focusing on boys' sexual health needs is to increase their confidence and ability to take responsibility for their sexual behaviour.

Wide differences of opinion exist about what constitutes correct or moral sexual behaviour, which makes it difficult to develop a sex and relationship educational programme that does not cause offence. The media, for example, carry sexually exploitative stories, yet decry misconduct and are reluctant to broadcast sexual health promotion messages. High rates of abortion are regarded with disapproval, while single women who choose to have children without the support of a partner are considered irresponsible.

Sex and relationship education in schools aims to promote sexual health by enabling young people to make informed choices about sexual behaviour. It can also help young people to develop the social skills needed to successfully negotiate contraceptive use, protect themselves and avoid premature sexual intercourse. School-based sex and relationship education is variable in quality and has been criticised for providing too little too late, and being too biological.[43] Although it is important to understand the biological side, young people do not engage in sexual intercourse because of a conscious desire to procreate, but rather to indulge their curiosity, assuage natural sexual urges or comply with peer pressure.[3,44] Increased resources and prospects of a real improvement in the quality of sex and relationship education have accompanied Government guidance for schools issued in July 2000. All schools are now required to have a policy that describes what they will teach and against which they can be assessed during an (OFSTED) inspection, but it will take many years for the full benefits of these additional resources to be felt.

A national survey of young people of school age in 1996 found that even though sex and relationship education is the most commonly covered health topic in schools, more than half (54%) of the respondents would have liked more information about sexual health.[45] Up to 94% of parents are in favour of secondary schools providing more sex education.[46,47] The high proportion of young people who are sexually active before the age of 16 years and the high rates of teenage pregnancy and induced abortion indicate that education about sex and relationships needs to be provided well before this age.

Infertility

In contrast to the problem of unintended pregnancy is that of infertility. For the purposes of this chapter infertility is defined as the inability to conceive after 12 months (or more) of intercourse without using contraception. However, this definition is arbitrary and the diagnosis of infertility must be based on the age of the woman and an accurate assessment of fertility in both partners.[48] Infertility is distinguished from impaired fecundity in that infertility relates solely to difficulty in conceiving, whereas impaired fecundity also takes into account difficulties in carrying to term. Infertility can be either primary or secondary. Secondary infertility refers to the inability to become pregnant by women who have previously been pregnant, regardless of outcome.

At the International Conference on Population and Development (ICPD) held in Cairo in 1994 it was asserted that 'Reproductive rights rest on the recognition of the basic right of all couples and individuals to decide freely and responsibly the number, spacing and timing of their children and to have the information and means to do so and the right to attain the highest standard of sexual and reproductive health.' Endorsement of this document by the UK means that the Government has a responsibility to tackle infertility. The Royal College of Obstetricians and Gynaecologists (RCOG) supports this view and has said that 'Infertility is considered to be a disease process worthy of investigation and treatment.'

Infertility affects one in seven couples in the UK, and an increasing number are asking for help with conception.[12,13] Some evidence suggests that rather than demonstrating an increasing prevalence this reflects the higher proportion of couples with fertility problems who are seeking help.[102]

Table 2: Most common fertility problems for which people seek treatment in a year.

Problem	Percentage
Ovulatory failure	27%
Tubal damage	14%
Endometriosis	5%
Male factors	19%
Unexplained	30%
Other	5%

Source: *Effective Health Care* Bulletin No.3, 1992;[129] Male Infertility (Review), *Lancet* 1997[49]

Although significant technological advances in the treatment of infertility have been made in recent years, many treatments, such as *in-vitro* fertilisation (IVF), are expensive, and NHS-funded treatment is restricted. There will always be people who argue that such treatments should not be accorded priority when there are limited funds available for health services. However, this argument dismisses the mental health problems and lack of social well-being experienced by those suffering from infertility.

Approximately 80% of all IVF treatment in the UK is privately funded and there was considerable variation in the extent to which health authorities (now PCTs) funded treatment, with some health authorities not allocating any NHS resources to IVF or other highly technical fertility treatments. The clinical guideline on fertility published by the National Institute for Clinical Excellence covers the range of treatments for subfertility.[50] The clinical criteria to be met to qualify for NHS treatment, such as age of the woman and the number of cycles of IVF treatment to be offered, is also considered. The extent to which infertility treatments should be financed poses a dilemma for the NHS, but it would seem reasonable to limit NHS treatment to those patients likely to achieve a 50% birth rate within a set time limit or number of cycles.[51]

3 Sub-categories

Contraception

Contraceptive advice and prescription-dispensed contraceptive products are available free of charge through general practitioners. Family planning clinics, young people's sexual health services, voluntary organisations such as Brook Advisory Centres, a few hospital-based departments and genito-urinary medicine clinics supply a wide range of contraceptive services and products free of charge. Condoms can also be easily purchased from retail outlets. The most popular forms of contraception used in England and Wales are oral contraceptives, sterilisation and condoms. Men and women's contraceptive preferences change throughout their life cycle, so age and lifestyle are important categories. All methods of contraception have a failure rate, and each has characteristics that make it more or less suitable for different categories of the population.

Induced abortion

The number of notifications of legally induced abortions has increased annually since the implementation of the 1967 Abortion Act, but the proportion of conceptions that end in induced abortion varies by age and marital status. The total annual number of induced abortions has risen from 54 819 in 1969 to 175 542 in 2000.[52] Providing a summary of the need for induced abortion is made difficult by the dynamic nature of the factors involved. An increase in the number of induced abortions over time does not necessarily imply less effective contraceptive use, but may come about as a result of more recent cohorts of teenagers being sexually active at younger ages or from women choosing an abortion rather than continuing the pregnancy when contraception has failed. The number of pregnancies depends on the number in the cohort, their level of sexual activity and their effective fertility, taking account of primary fertility and efficacy of contraception. Therefore age, marital status and social class are the most important sub-categories considered in this section.

Fertility

Fertility problems usually come to light only when people are trying to conceive their first child,[53] and consequently most clinic attendees (70%) suffer from primary infertility, although some women will experience both primary and secondary infertility. Chances of successful IVF treatment depend on maternal age and national trends towards a delay in childbearing increase the likelihood of couples remaining unaware of their fertility problems until such time as treatment is less likely to be effective. Maternal age is therefore an important category in this section.

Studies suggest that the overall prevalence of primary infertility is 16.1% (95% confidence interval 14.6–17.6%), but only approximately half of the women who report infertility ask for medical help. Women from higher social classes are more likely to seek treatment.[11–13] Approximately half of infertile women subsequently become mothers, but only a third of the deliveries are treatment related. Only 3% of women remain involuntarily childless.[11]

4 Prevalence and incidence

Demand for services

The greatest demand for contraceptive, induced abortion and fertility services is from sexually active heterosexual women of childbearing age. However, with improved education, new technological breakthroughs such as the male contraceptive pill and an increased awareness of the risks associated with sexually transmitted infections, the demands upon services from men can be expected to increase. The female population seeking advice and using services will always be smaller than the population of women of childbearing age, particularly at either end of the spectrum. There will always be a proportion of women who are not sexually active, as well as those who are not in heterosexual relationships or are protected by earlier sterilisation, and the proportions in these categories will vary with social change over time.

Conception and contraception

Amongst other things, the demand for contraception will be determined by changes in family structure and the desired number of children, so in this section trends in conceptions will be considered before moving on to examine demand for contraceptive services in more detail.

Age

In England and Wales, there has been a decline in overall conception rates in recent years. Total fertility rate (TFR) in the UK went down from 2.41 in 1976 to 1.69 in 1999.[14] Between 1990 and 1999 the average conception rate per 1000 women decreased from 79.2 to 71.9 in women aged 15–44. Although conception rates remain highest in the 25–29 years age group compared to women of other ages, rates decreased most in this age group (from 138.0 to 119.2) and increased most among women aged 35–39 (from 33.6 to 42.1).[15]

Increasing proportions of women do not have children at all, whether by choice or because of fertility problems. Between 1986 and 1991 the proportion of young women (under 23 years) expecting to remain childless doubled from 5% to 10%.

Older age at first intercourse is associated with higher educational achievement and higher social class.[54] Early age at first intercourse is associated with subsequent poor sexual health status.[55] Results from the National Survey of Sexual Attitudes and Lifestyles (Natsal) carried out between 1999 and 2001 show that the proportion of those aged 16–19 at the time of interview who reported first sexual intercourse at younger than 16 years was 30% for men and 26% for women, and the median age was 16 years. Following a steep decrease in age at first intercourse among women up to and including the 1970s, there is now evidence of stabilisation, and the proportion of women reporting first intercourse before 16 years increased up to but not after the mid-1990s.

Marital status

Marriage is not as popular as it was, and between 1989 and 1999 the proportion of all conceptions taking place within marriage decreased from 57.7% to 48.3%. In 1998, for the first time since records began more conceptions took place outside (51.2%) rather than within marriage (48.8%).[15]

The following data refer to 1999.[34]

The proportion of all conceptions in each age group that took place outside marriage was:

- 93.5% for teenagers
- 71.1% for women under 25 years old
- 43.5% for women aged 25–29 years
- 32.8% for women aged 30–34 years.

Of all the conceptions that took place outside marriage:

- 59.1% resulted in a birth outside marriage
- 5.5% resulted in a birth within marriage
- 35.4% were terminated by abortion.

Of all the conceptions that took place outside marriage:

- 47.6% resulted in a birth registered jointly by both parents
- 11.5% resulted in a birth registered by the mother alone.

Of all births outside marriage, 78% were jointly registered, and of these 74% were registered births to parents living at the same address. This compares to 1985, when 65% of births outside marriage were jointly registered, and of these 72% were registered to parents living at the same address.[53]

Given the social changes indicating that it is now the norm for a single woman to have a baby, there is little to support the notion that an absence of marriage can be regarded as an indicator of either unplanned pregnancy or an unstable environment for a growing child.

Planned and unplanned conceptions

An unintended or unplanned pregnancy is not necessarily unwanted. The differences between an unintended conception that later becomes wanted, a conception that is unplanned and remains unwanted, and a planned conception that later becomes unwanted cannot easily be established, and this difficulty continues to affect research in this area. Almost half of all conceptions in England are reportedly unplanned.[10] Being of Irish or Afro-Caribbean ethnic origin, or living in an area with a high deprivation score, is linked to an increased risk of reported unplanned pregnancy.[56]

Special groups

The demand for contraceptive and sexual health services is influenced by culture, religion, race and personal circumstances. Members of ethnic minorities and people with severe physical disability, learning difficulties or suffering from social and family stress may require special provision. Muslim women, for example, may not be willing to see a male nurse or doctor. Unfortunately, there is little collated information on the nature of the specific wishes for these groups nationally, but commissioners should ensure that adequate assessment is carried out locally to identify requirements.

Induced abortion

In England and Wales, the annual number of notifications of legally induced abortions has changed little over the last 10 years, and the overall induced abortion rate for women resident in England and Wales in 2000 was 13.6 induced abortions per 1000 women aged 14–49 years.[57] The percentage of all conceptions that are terminated by abortion has increased slightly from 19.8% in 1989 to 22.6% in 1999.

Comparison of the rate of legal abortion per 1000 women aged 15–44 in The Netherlands and in England and Wales from 1975 to 1996 shows that The Netherlands rate of abortion has been consistently about half that for England and Wales. In 1996 the abortion rate in The Netherlands for women aged 15–44 was 6.5 per 1000 compared to a rate of 15.6 per 1000 in England and Wales. Analysis of the situation in The Netherlands and Scandinavia suggests that there is considerable scope for reducing the demand for induced abortion in England and Wales through the provision of effective sex education, planned parenthood programmes and related services at primary care trust level.[58]

Age

The total number of known conceptions is calculated by adding together the total number of abortions and of births. Not included are conceptions that lead to spontaneous abortion or miscarriage. The abortion rate for each age group is calculated as a proportion (per 1000) of total women in that age group. Figures for England and Wales (based on population estimates for 2000) show that conception rates remain highest in the 25–29 years age group, but that this group has the second-lowest proportion of conceptions resulting in induced abortion (17.1%). The lowest proportion of conceptions resulting in induced abortions occurs in the 30–34 years age group (14.9%). Women over 40 and under 15 years of age have low conception rates but the highest proportion of pregnancies ending in induced abortion (*see* Table 3).

Table 3: Pregnancy outcome by age in 1999 in England and Wales.

Age (years)	Conception rates (1999) per 1,000 women	Conception rates (1999) per 1,000 women		Proportion (%) of conceptions ending in induced abortion
		Conceptions leading to maternities	Conceptions terminated by abortion	
All ages (15–44)	71.7	55.5	16.2	22.6
Under 16 (13–15)	8.3	3.9	3.8	52.6
Under 18 (15–17)	45.0	25.7	19.4	43.0
Under 20 (15–19)	62.9	38.6	24.3	38.62
0–24	104.9	74.9	29.9	28.5
25–29	119.2	98.3	20.9	17.5
30–34	94.9	80.9	14.0	14.7
35–39	42.1	33.2	8.9	21.2
40 or over (40–44)	9.1	5.7	3.4	37.0

Source: Office for National Statistics (ONS).[15,26]

The epidemiology of induced abortion for different age groups varies, and factors that could affect abortion ratios and rates include:[59]

- lack of confidence in or fear of side-effects of methods of oral contraception
- the effect of adverse economic circumstances such as unemployment on people's ability to cope financially with an unplanned pregnancy
- changes in social values and changes in the level of financial support for single parents
- pressures on service providers to reduce variations in the availability of induced abortion services
- changes in service provision caused by financial constraints in the health service.

Marital status and social class

In 2000, the majority (71%) of the total number of induced abortions in England and Wales were carried out on women who were either single, separated, divorced or widowed. The abortion rate in single women was 24.02 per 1000 women of all ages compared to a rate of 7.29 per 1000 women of all ages who were ever married.[52] A relatively high proportion (33%) of conceptions to married women aged over 40 end in induced abortion, compared to 15% for married women aged 35–39 years and 8% for married women under 20 years of age.

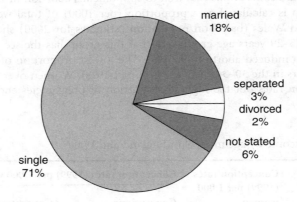

Figure 1: Marital status of women who had abortions in 2000. *Source*: ONS Abortion Statistics 2000.

A study in Liverpool found that high levels of induced abortion and unplanned conceptions among teenagers were associated with high levels of deprivation.[60] However, there are few statistical data available that relate induced abortion levels to social class.

Infertility

Age

The age at which people seek treatment for fertility problems is related to the age at which they first try to conceive. The mean age for childbearing has been steadily increasing. Between 1990 and 2000 the mean age for first birth rose from 25.5 to 27.1 years.[17] Since the risk of infertility increases with age, it can be anticipated that if this trend continues there will be an increasing number of women coming forward experiencing difficulties with conception. The median age at which women seek help with their first episode of infertility is 25.5 years, with 16.9% of women with infertility aged over 30, and 5.7% aged over 35.[11] Unfortunately, the success rate of many infertility treatments decreases with age.

Marital status and social class

The people most frequently referred to specialist centres for treatment of infertility are married or in long-term relationships. The Human Fertilisation and Embryology Act of 1990 states at section 13.(5) that 'A woman shall not be provided with treatment services unless account has been taken of the welfare of any child who may be born as a result of the treatment (including the need of that child for a father), and of any other child who may be affected by the birth.' Therefore the availability and accessibility of fertility services to single people remain limited.

Research suggests that people in lower socio-economic groups are less likely to seek treatment for infertility.[11–13]

Exposure to sexually transmitted infections

Exposure to sexually transmitted infection, and in particular the occurrence of pelvic inflammatory disease in women, is associated with the development of future infertility caused by tubal problems.[61]

The Government's comprehensive national sexual health and HIV strategy proposes an integrated population-based approach to infertility that includes primary prevention through high-quality sex education and easily accessible contraceptive services as well as adequate prompt treatment of sexually transmitted infections at genito-urinary medicine (GUM) clinics and a programme of screening for chlamydia for targeted groups.[30]

GUM clinics have a statutory obligation to make quarterly data returns to the medical officers of their respective jurisdictions and therefore provide the most comprehensive source of data on the epidemiology of sexually transmitted infections. Results from the National Surveys of Sexual Attitudes and Lifestyles reported in the *Lancet*[62] suggest that of those people who had ever had a sexually transmitted infection, 75.6% of men (95% confidence interval 70.9–79.8) and 56.7% of women (95% confidence interval 53.1–60.4) had attended a GUM clinic. This indicates that GUM data provide good indicators of sexual infection in the population, particularly for men.

In the UK in recent years, the number of cases of sexually transmitted infections has increased, particularly among young people. Data show that between 1995 and 2000, uncomplicated gonorrhoea increased by 102% (29% since 1999), genital chlamydia increased by 107% (18% since 1999) and infectious syphilis increased by 145% (57% since 1999).[18] The increases in gonorrhoea and syphilis infections most likely reflect a real increase in prevalence and transmission of the disease. Increases in recorded incidence of chlamydia may also be due to a real increase in prevalence and transmission, but may be due in part to increased awareness and testing as well as the improved sensitivity of tests that are now available. A paper based on results from the National Surveys of Sexual Attitudes and Lifestyles (1999–2001) shows that the prevalence of high-risk sexual behaviours has risen since 1990, so a rise in chlamydia and other sexually transmitted infections would be expected.[63]

Chlamydia trachomatis is the cause of the most frequently transmitted sexual infection in the UK, and between 10% and 30% of women with chlamydia will develop pelvic inflammatory disease, a causal factor in 50% of cases of female infertility.[64,65] Approximately 17% of women with pelvic inflammatory disease will become infertile, and of those women who do conceive 10% will have an ectopic pregnancy.[66]

Three out of four women with tubal infertility are seropositive for chlamydia, compared with only one out of four fertile women.[48]

Chlamydia is the dominant cause of pelvic inflammatory disease, and ectopic pregnancy (the leading cause of maternal death in industrialised countries), tubal factor infertility and chronic pelvic pain are important consequences. Resistance to the recommended antibiotics normally used to treat chlamydia has been recorded and is a potential future problem.

Outside London, the highest infection rates are seen in the North West and Trent (although this may simply reflect provision of diagnostic services). Infection is asymptomatic in up to 70% of women and 50% of men, so a large number of cases are never diagnosed.

The National Surveys of Sexual Attitudes and Lifestyles (1999–2001) confirmed that there is a significant burden of undiagnosed chlamydia in the population, and that prevalence is as high in men as in women. Although a high prevalence of chlamydia infection is seen in people belonging to groups considered to be at 'high risk' for all sexually transmitted infections, there are a considerable number of asymptomatic infections found in people who would not generally be perceived as being at risk.[67–69] More must be done to develop programmes that include men, since chlamydia screening and treatment for men constitute an important infertility prevention strategy for women.[62]

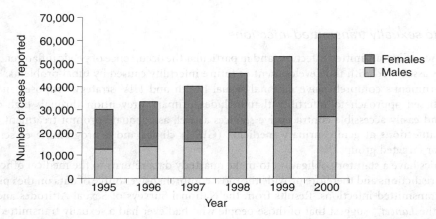

Figure 2: Number of chlamydia cases diagnosed at GUM clinics across England and Wales, 1995–2000.[70]

5 Services available and costs

Contraceptive and related sexual health services

The level of uptake of services in any particular area can be obtained by combining information from Körner records KT31 (the number of women using family planning clinics), general practitioner records of the number of residents currently registered with a general practitioner for contraceptive advice, data from non-NHS providers of contraceptive services in the area, and a survey of clinic attendees to establish the proportion of the latter who are residents of the area.

Trends in the use of contraceptive methods by women aged 16–49 have been monitored since 1986, when questions about contraception were first addressed to all women between these ages through the General Household Survey. Between 1986 and 1998 the proportion of women using some form of contraception ranged from 69% to 73%. Although differences between individual years were statistically significant, overall changes were small and no very clear trends emerge from the data.[19]

Over half of women aged 16–49 years report using a non-surgical method of contraception and an estimated 12% have been sterilised.[19] In 2000, about 1.2 million women and 84 000 men attended a family planning clinic in England.[71]

Family planning clinics, general practices and specific clinics for young people each provide a different range of services and are accessed by and acceptable to different client groups. Primary care trusts (PCTs) commission all contraceptive services at the primary care level. This freedom should encourage the commissioning of innovative, effective and efficient services based on local client need. In the past, several non-governmental organisations devised innovative service models that could be modified for current use by primary care trusts. The Family Planning Association developed a model for community contraceptive services, which recognised the special needs of ethnic minorities, people with physical and/or mental disabilities, younger women, older women and those experiencing fertility problems. The Brook Advisory Centres produced guidelines for the provision of services for young people, and have successfully developed the 'enhanced role for nurses' scheme, which provides training for nurses enabling them to administer oral contraceptives within agreed protocols and without the need for clients to see a doctor.

The level of knowledge of what is available and people's perceptions of how they will be received if they make contact with the service are important determinants of service use. The sex and relationship education provided in schools is particularly important. A person who has received inadequate education will have greater difficulty learning about and accessing services compared to someone who has received a more comprehensive education.

Special groups

Children in care, those frequently absent or excluded from school and those who are homeless have been identified as priority groups for action to reduce unintended conceptions nationally.[3] In 1994, local authorities were looking after 4.5 per 1000 children under 18 years of age. A disproportionate number of these children, many the result of teenage pregnancy, end up as teenage mothers themselves.[17]

General practitioner services

The average size of a general practice population in England and Wales is 5200 patients, with an average of 1888 patients per principal general practitioner, but there are large variations around this mean. About one-third of general practices are single-handed. The remainder are in partnerships of varying size and are more likely to be able to provide a wider range of facilities.[72] Most general practitioners prescribe oral contraceptives, but only a minority provide services for the fitting of intrauterine contraceptive devices (IUCDs) or diaphragms. General practitioners do not generally supply condoms, but they may advise patients to obtain them from family planning clinics or to buy them.[73] The fee for service paid to general practitioners who provide contraceptive prescriptions coupled with the Government desire to develop a wide range of PCT-based services, including cytology screening and recall in general practice, has created incentives to shift provision of contraceptive services from clinics to general practice.[74,75] Compared to clinics, general practitioners tend to offer a more limited variety of methods and be accessed by women who want oral contraceptives, have had at least one child and are spacing their families. In 2000, general practitioners issued about 7.1 million prescriptions for contraceptive pills and prescribed 62 000 IUCDs, 23 000 diaphragms, 874 000 injectable contraceptives, 51 000 spermicides, 5000 implants and 44 000 intra-uterine systems.[71]

Women seek contraceptive advice more often than men. Women who consult their general practitioner are more likely to be older and married or in a stable relationship, to have a child or to be spacing their children, and will probably be prescribed oral contraceptives.[76] For these women, contraceptive advice can be seen as an extension of postnatal care.

General practitioners are not required to undertake specialist training prior to providing basic contraceptive services, and a survey by the Family Planning Association in 1992 found that one in four general practitioners had received no specific training in the provision of contraceptive services.[77] Information is lacking on how many doctors and other members of staff at the primary care level are trained to provide adequate contraceptive services or offer psychosexual counselling and what proportion are willing to refer clients for induced abortion.

In 1993, the Faculty of Family Planning and Reproductive Health Care of the Royal College of Obstetricians and Gynaecologists was set up to maintain and develop standards of care and training and ensure that a high quality of practice is maintained by all providers of family planning and reproductive health care. The College offers a range of training packages, many of which are available to and accessed by general practitioners, but none is compulsory for professional advancement.

Family planning clinics

In 1997, there were 1648 family planning clinics in England and 163 in Wales. On average, 9 out of every 100 women aged 14–49 years use these clinics every year.[78] Far fewer men than women access established contraceptive services, but their numbers are increasing. In 1989–90, there were 32 000 male first contacts with family planning services in England, but by 1999 this had increased to 84 000.[71,79] Over 66 000 men obtained condoms via family planning clinics in 1999–2000, although many more men and women undoubtedly obtained condoms through retail outlets.

Between 1975 and 2000, the proportion of women of childbearing age using family planning clinics fell from 15.8% to 11.5%. However, this figure hides different patterns of service usage among women of different age groups. Young unmarried women are more likely to use specific sexual health clinics or sessions for young people for contraceptive services. In 1975 very few under-16-year-olds attended, but by 2000 it was estimated that over 8.3% of resident females aged 13–15 attended a family planning clinic. From 1975 to the mid-1980s approximately 15% of women aged 16–19 attended a family planning clinic in any one year, but by 2000 this had risen to 23%.[71] Over the same time period, the proportion of women in the 20–34 years age group attending family planning clinics decreased from 21% to only 12%.

Younger teenagers report that they prefer to use clinics or sessions specifically designed for them because they provide improved confidentiality, a better source of advice, a broader choice of contraceptives and are able to provide more time per client than a family doctor. The location, opening times, atmosphere and image influence the acceptability of clinics to young people.[20,21] Young single people also believe that 'family planning' services are targeted towards older people who want children. Therefore services calling themselves 'advisory' or 'sexual health' may be more attractive to young people.[80]

There are 18 Brook Advisory Centres nationally, and in 1996 12% of Brook clients were aged under 16, compared to only 4% five years previously. This increase can be attributed to a commitment by Brook to research the needs and offer appropriate, accessible services to young people. Opening times after school, staff training and liaison with schools and youth projects are some of the reasons for Brook's success in this field of work.[81]

Older women who are experiencing difficulties finding a suitable contraceptive method or who have menopausal problems are more likely to use family planning or Well Woman clinics as a source of information and advice, rather than their family doctor.

Primary methods of contraception

The popularity of different contraceptive methods has varied over time, although the contraceptive pill, surgical sterilisation and the male condom have remained the three most widely used methods. Table 4 shows how usage of the more common contraceptives has varied between 1975 and 2000.

Table 4: Changes in popularity of primary method of contraception (percentage of attendees at family planning clinics) between 1975 and 2000.

	1975	2000
Oral contraceptive (the pill)	70	43
IUCD	20	7
Condom	6	36
Cap/diaphragm	6	2
Depot injection	N/A	6

Source: NHS Contraceptive Services England 1999–2000 (ONS).

No method of contraception can offer 100% protection from pregnancy. Approximately 86% of women of childbearing age would become pregnant within a year if no method of contraception was used. However, many women do not want to become pregnant but are not using contraceptives or are using methods with relatively high rates of failure. Table 5 shows the number of expected pregnancies per year per 100 users for each method of contraception.

Table 5: The number of expected pregnancies per year per 100 users of each method of contraception.

Method	Number of expected pregnancies per year per 100 users*
Oral	3.00
IUCD (copper)	0.40
IUCD (progesterone – T)	2.00
Diaphragm	18.00
Male condom	12.00
Vasectomy	0.04
Tubal ligation	0.17
Withdrawal	20.00
Implant	0.23
None	85.00

* Calculated on average rather than perfect use of the contraceptive method.
Source: *Bandolier* website.[82,83]

There has been a general trend towards the increased use of condoms. Between 1986 and 1995, the proportion of women whose partners used the condom increased from 13% to 18%. There was no further change to this figure between 1995 and the General Household Survey carried out in 1998.[22]

Although 75% of women identified the simultaneous need to protect themselves against sexually transmitted diseases and pregnancy, only 2% were simultaneously using oral contraceptives and condoms.[84]

The reliance by women upon methods such as the IUCD or diaphragm has decreased. IUCDs were used by over 20% of family planning clinic attendees in the late 1970s, but by 2000 they were the primary method for only 7% of those attending. Overall use of the diaphragm rose from 6% in 1975 to 10% in the mid-1980s, but by 2001 had fallen to 1% of attenders.[71]

The relatively new progesterone-based implant 'Norplant' was withdrawn in the UK in 1999, and although another similar brand is available, this method remains unpopular.

Depo Provera and other progesterone-based injectable contraceptives have increased slightly in popularity and are used by about 6% of women attending family planning clinics.

Emergency contraception (also known as postcoital contraception) is a safe and highly effective method of preventing pregnancy after unprotected intercourse or a contraceptive failure such as condom breakage or slippage.[85,86] The General Household Survey first included questions on emergency (postcoital) contraception in 1993. In 1998, 10% of women of childbearing age who were not sterilised and were therefore at risk of pregnancy had used emergency contraception at least once in the two years prior to interview, representing an increase of 3% since 1993. Emergency contraception was most likely to have been used in the past two years by women under 30 years of age, single women (who were twice as likely as other women to have used emergency contraception), women with no children (14%), women with higher levels of educational attainment (12% of those with GCE 'A' levels or above had used this method, compared with 6% of those with no educational qualifications), and women who said they definitely or probably would have (more) children (15%, compared with 6% of those who said they definitely or probably would not). There were no significant differences with regard to the use of emergency contraception between women in manual and non-manual socio-economic situations.

Approximately 800 000 prescriptions for emergency contraception were written in 2000–01. About two-thirds of these were prescribed by general practitioners and a third by family planning clinics. A small minority (about 2%) of women requiring emergency contraception obtained prescriptions from hospital Accident and Emergency departments.[71] A pilot project was started in January 2000 in the Manchester area, and emergency contraception was dispensed free of charge by trained pharmacists following an agreed protocol (patient group direction). In April 200, updated recommendations for clinical practice in emergency contraception were issued by the Faculty of Family Planning and Reproductive Health Care of the Royal College of Obstetricians and Gynaecologists.[87] In January 2001 the progestogen-only emergency contraceptive levonorgestrel was reclassified from a prescription-only medicine to a pharmacy medicine and made available for women aged 16 years or over to buy over the counter at a cost of approximately £20.

Age

The data in Table 6, based on women who attend family planning clinics, show the popularity of different contraceptive methods by age group.

The condom is the most popular method for teenage women, particularly those under the age of 16, whilst the pill is more popular among 20- to 30-year-old women.[71]

Women in younger age groups make less use of contraception and are less likely to use contraception in the initial part of a sexual relationship.[88] First intercourse has been characterised by more planning in recent years and contraception is more likely to be used by either partner when first intercourse is planned.

Between 1989 and 1993, the percentage of women using the pill increased from 22% to 25%, since when it has remained at roughly the same level. However, the proportion of young women using this method is increasing (see Figure 3).

Table 6: Use of different methods of contraception by age group according to first contact with women attending family planning clinics in England in 2000.

Age group (years)	Under 16	16–19	20–24	25–34	35 and over	All ages
Oral	39%	53%	53%	45%	31%	46%
IUCD	0%	1%	3%	10%	18%	7%
Male condom	50%	31%	26%	28%	33%	31%
Female condom			Less than 1% for all age groups			
Cap/diaphragm	0%	0%	0%	2%	4%	1%
Injection	3%	7%	9%	9%	7%	8%
Female sterilisation			Less than 1% for all age groups			
Other methods	7%	7%	6%	5%	4%	6%

Source: NHS contraceptive services in England, 1999–2000 (ONS).

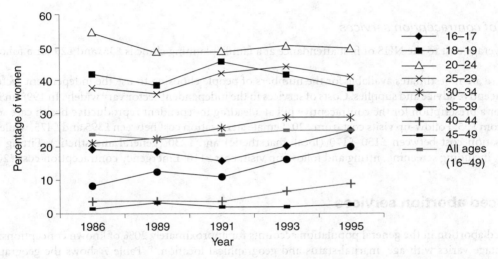

Figure 3: Trends in the proportion of women using the pill as a usual method of contraception by age group, 1986–98. *Source*: General Household Survey, 1998.

The percentage of women aged 35–39 using the pill increased between 1986 and 1995, but this trend was not continued in 1998. Between 1995 and 1998 there was a statistically significant decrease from 29% to 24% in the proportion of women aged 30–34 reporting use of the pill as their usual form of contraception. In other age groups none of the changes between 1995 and 1998 was statistically significant.[22]

Between 1986 and 1998 there was a steady increase in the use of condoms among women under 30 years of age, and a decrease in use among women aged 45–49. In the General Household Survey, women were asked about their use of condoms over the two-year period prior to interview. Among current users of a contraceptive method, 16% reported that they had used condoms as their main method throughout the previous two years, 7% had changed to the condom and were currently using it, and 5% had switched from the condom to some other method. Women aged 25–39 were more likely than those in other age groups to have used the condom as their main method throughout the previous two years. Younger contraceptive users were much more likely than older women to have used the condom at some stage over the past two years.[22]

Among all women aged 16–49, the prevalence of sterilisation as a method of contraception has changed little since 1986. The proportion of women between the ages of 16 and 49 who had been sterilised or relied on their partner's vasectomy to prevent pregnancy was 21% in 1998. However, this broadly stable picture conceals some important variation and opposing trends in different age groups. The use of sterilisation, of self or partner, has declined amongst women aged 30–44, particularly among women in their thirties, and increased among women in their late forties. There are 45% of women in their forties compared to 7% of women aged 25–29 years who are sterilised or reliant on their partner's vasectomy.[22,89]

Marital status

There was no statistically significant difference between the proportion of single women and those who were married or cohabiting who had used condoms throughout the previous two years. Single women were approximately three times more likely than their married or cohabiting counterparts to have changed to the condom from some other method (16% compared with 6%), and they were also twice as likely to have switched from the condom to some other method during the same time period.[22]

Cost of contraception services

The average cost to the NHS of first attendance at a family planning clinic is £36, and £29 for a follow-up visit.[23]

There are no estimates available for the numbers of people choosing to use the independent sector for contraceptive advice and supplies. Costs of services in the independent sector vary widely. In 1998 an initial visit for a prescription for the contraceptive pill at a leading independent reproductive health care service cost from £35. Follow-up visits cost from £20. Female sterilisation cost between £395 and £475, while male sterilisation cost between £150–£170 (local anaesthetic) and £230 (general anaesthetic). Fitting of an IUCD, including screening, fitting and follow-up visit, cost £110. Emergency contraception cost £20.[90,91]

Induced abortion services

Induced abortion in the general population accounts for approximately 20% of known conceptions. This percentage varies with age, marital status and geographical location.[26] Table 7 shows the geographical variation in the numbers and rates of induced abortions performed as well as the different numbers of abortions performed by the NHS, NHS agencies and the independent sector.

Induced abortion rates are at least twice the national average in inner-city areas, so for example, a six-doctor practice in a deprived inner-city area might have to make 50–75 referrals for induced abortion a year, while the number might be less than 20 in a practice of similar size in a prosperous small town.[93]

Between 1992 and 1995 the numbers and rates of conceptions and the proportion of these terminated by induced abortions was steady. In 1996 there was an increase in both the number of conceptions and the rate of conceptions per 1000 women of childbearing age. The abortion rate per 1000 women of childbearing age also increased. This change has been attributed to the 'pill scare' of 1995, which followed a warning from the Committee on Safety of Medicines about certain types of new oral contraceptives which studies had shown might be linked to a slightly increased risk of thrombo-embolic disease.[10] Between 1995 and 1996, the abortion rate among women aged 20–24 increased from 25.7 to 28.5 per 1000 women in this age group, and this was the largest single-year increase observed for any age group over the last 10 years. Abortion rates in all age groups have continued to increase slightly since 1996.[26] Some women and in particular young women seem to have lost confidence in, and have stopped using, oral contraception.

Table 7: Numbers of abortions provided by each sector in each region (England and Wales).

Region	Rates per 1,000 women aged 15–44 years*	NHS	NHS agency	Independent sector	Total
London	28.97	15,829	15,504	18,138	49,471
Northern and Yorkshire	12.84	12,834	1,170	2,399	16,403
Trent	12.97	10,283	1,271	1,820	13,374
North West	14.74	10,118	5,101	4,600	19,819
Eastern	13.18	9,128	2,054	3,255	14,437
South West	12.19	7,823	1,357	2,352	11,532
South East	14.05	7,543	10,080	7,209	24,832
Wales	13.15	4,128	2,202	1,071	7,401
West Midlands	16.32	2,587	10,880	3,942	17,409
Total	16.18	80,273	49,619	44,786	174,678

Source: *Health Statistics Quarterly*, Summer 2001, ONS.
*ONS Abortion Statistics 2000.

In 2000, 88% of terminations were undertaken before 13 weeks' gestation.[92] The proportion of induced abortions carried out before 9 weeks' gestation increased from 34% in 1985 to 43% in 1999, and almost 90% of abortions are carried out within the first 12 weeks of pregnancy. Just 1.5% of all abortions take place after 20 weeks' gestation. In the private sector (non-NHS), most induced abortions (60%) take place before 9 weeks' gestation.

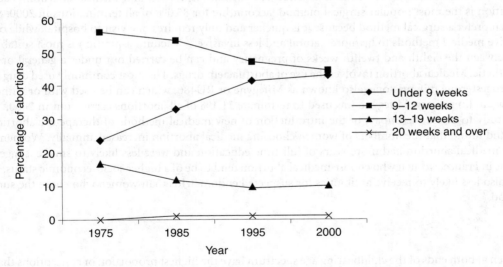

Figure 4: Trends in proportion to total induced abortions carried out according to gestation, 1975–2000. *Source*: ONS Abortion Statistics 1995–2000.

Serious complications of induced abortion are rare. Early termination of pregnancy (under 13 weeks' gestation) results in 2.12 complications per 1000 abortions, compared to 4.59 per 1000 abortions at 13–19 weeks and 9.78 per 1000 abortions if the gestation is over 20 weeks. There are marked differences in the relative risk of complications associated with methods used in the first compared to the second trimester.

Young women are more likely to experience later terminations and therefore suffer a disproportionate increase in the risk of complications.[10,93]

Some of the possible reasons for late abortions include:

- inability to get a hospital appointment earlier in the pregnancy
- the woman may not have realised that she was pregnant (this is more common with young women and women approaching the menopause, both of whom may have infrequent periods)
- very young women may feel unable to cope and hide the pregnancy
- sometimes the pregnancy was originally wanted but the woman's circumstances changed (perhaps because she was abandoned by her partner or found that her parents were unwilling to provide her with a home or any other support)
- fetal abnormality, as many abnormalities cannot be diagnosed early in pregnancy.

The proportion of induced abortions performed before and after 13 weeks varies by region and seems to be related to the level of NHS or NHS agency provision, which ranges from over 85% of local demand in some areas to 63% in others.[16]

Induced abortion has been described as the only acute health service that is not automatically available through the NHS.[94] This is because although on average throughout England and Wales the NHS pays for approximately three-quarters (74.9%) of abortions, there are significant differences between regions. In some areas the NHS pays for more than 90% of abortions, while in others it pays for less than 50%.[95] A survey by the Abortion Law Reform Association in 1996 found factors such as the willingness of key consultants to carry out induced abortions, and that some general practitioners were applying informal means-testing procedures, and were effectively denying some women access to an NHS-funded induced abortion.[96]

The two main methods of induced abortion are vacuum aspiration and medical abortion. Vacuum aspiration is the most popular surgical method, accounting for 85.0% of all terminations in 2000. Some women prefer a surgical method because it is quicker and only requires one visit to hospital, while others perceive medical methods to be more natural and less invasive.[97] Vacuum aspiration is most suitable for use between the eighth and twelfth weeks of pregnancy and can be carried out under a general or local anaesthetic. Medical abortion involves the use of abortifacient drugs. The most commonly used drug is the antiprogesterone mifepristone, also known as Mifegyne or RU486, which can be used with or without a prostaglandin pessary. Mifegyne was used to terminate 11.1% of all abortions carried out in 2000.[52]

A study to assess the impact of the introduction of new medical methods of therapeutic abortion in Scotland found that the numbers of women choosing medical abortion increased annually. Women who chose medical abortion had more years of full-time education and were less likely to smoke, suggesting that, as in France, women who choose medical abortion tend to be of a higher socio-economic status. They were also less likely to receive antibiotics for suspected endometritis than women who chose the surgical method.[97]

Age

Women at both ends of the childbearing age spectrum have the highest proportion of conceptions that are terminated (*see* Table 3). Young women sometimes fail to access an induced abortion because they are not always aware of their pregnancy or are too frightened of the consequences to make their pregnancy known until it is too late.[88] In 1999, among teenagers aged 13–15 years, 52.6% of conceptions were terminated by abortion and for those aged 15–19, 38.6% of conceptions were terminated by abortion. Although the number of conceptions is less for older women, aged 40–44, induced abortion accounted for 37.0% of all conceptions in this age group.[16] However, because of the lower fertility and increased contraceptive efficacy of older women, the actual number of induced abortions per year for women aged 40 and over is small.[10,56] In 2000, there were 5794 induced abortions for women aged 40–44 years and 459 for women aged 45 and over.[26]

Marital status

The majority of induced abortions are the result of extramarital conceptions. About 7.5% of conceptions within marriage will result in an induced abortion, and this proportion is stable nationally.

Cost of induced abortion services

The average cost to the NHS of a termination of pregnancy carried out as a day case is £393 for a surgical procedure and £278 for a medical procedure. Costs rise to £555 for surgical and £478 for medical abortions carried out as elective inpatient procedures, and £614 for surgical and £528 for medical abortions carried out as non-elective procedures.[23]

Induced abortions are a major source of income for the independent sector, with an estimated turnover of £30 million in 1996. The specialist charitable organisations British Pregnancy Advisory Services (BPAS) and Marie Stopes International provide most non-NHS (privately funded) abortions in England and Wales. These organisations also provide abortions for the NHS (agency abortions).[98]

The total cost of an induced abortion at BPAS in 2002 (including assessment, counselling, medical examination, contraceptive advice and post-operative care) is between £315 and £725, depending mainly on gestation. The cost of an early medical abortion up to and including 14 weeks' gestation is £265. Abortions carried out from 15–19 weeks' gestation cost £425 and from 20–24 weeks cost £675. A pregnancy test costs £10. Induced abortions at London units are subject to a £50 supplement. At Marie Stopes International an initial consultation can be booked online and costs £55. An early (up to 9 weeks' gestation) induced medical abortion costs £375 and an early surgical abortion (up to 12 weeks' gestation) costs £345.

The use of private health care facilities is influenced not only by perceptions of the quality of service offered or reduced risk of a breach of confidentiality, but also by access to work-related medical insurance schemes, the ability to afford private medical insurance and personal disposable income. There is wide variation in the proportion of the population in each region covered by private medical insurance or that has access to a non-insured medical expenses scheme, ranging from 20% in the London Metropolitan area to a mere 4% of the population in the North of England in 1996.[98]

A higher proportion of abortions is carried out in the private sector compared to other forms of elective surgery, and this may reflect the lack of a comprehensive, equitable abortion service provided by the NHS. In 1996 a total of 31 000 NHS-funded abortions (19% of total abortions for residents of England and Wales) were performed by the private sector. In stark contrast, an analysis of the distribution of elective surgery (excluding abortion) by funding source and place of treatment (private or NHS hospital) reveals that only 13.4% of all elective inpatient and day surgery nationally, excluding induced abortion, was privately funded (based on 1992–93 data). This difference cannot be accounted for by growth in private medical insurance, which is reported to have remained stagnant throughout the 1990s.[98]

The Birth Control Trust developed a model of care which suggested that, to provide an equitable service, at least 75% of induced abortions in any area should be provided by the NHS, and this recommendation was reinforced in the NHS Plan.[99,74] The ability to offer patients a realistic choice to opt for an NHS abortion should be a recognised objective of service commissioners.[100] In 1995 the Birth Control Trust published guidance for general practitioners outlining the kinds of services that are best able to meet the needs of women.[101]

Fertility services

Approximately 90% of infertile couples who seek help contact their general practitioner in the first instance. Preliminary investigations performed in the primary care setting result in a broad diagnosis in about 70% of patients.[129]

The NHS Executive funded the Royal College of Obstetricians and Gynaecologists to develop guidelines on the investigation and management of infertile couples in primary, secondary and tertiary care. There is no requirement for clinicians to follow these guidelines. However, all parts of the NHS in England and Wales are expected to implement the National Institute for Clinical Excellence clinical guidelines on infertility in full.[102–104]

As of 31 August 2000 there were 116 clinics licensed to carry out various activities as shown in Table 8.

Table 8: Number of Human Fertilisation and Embryology Authority Licensed Clinics.

IVF and donor insemination	75
IVF only	0
Donor insemination only	29
Storage of sperm only	9
Research licences only	3
Total	116

These centres require the services of expert staff, technology and high levels of staff training, and therefore it is probably a function that is best offered on a regional or cross-regional basis.

During the period 1998–99 there were 27 151 patients who received IVF treatment. A total of 35 363 cycles were started, including frozen embryo replacements, of which 30 520 reached embryo transfer. There were 7762 clinical pregnancies (21.9% of treatments started), which led to 6450 live birth events (18.2% of treatments started). The number of conventional IVF cycles (those not involving micro-manipulation) has decreased for the second consecutive year and stands at 86.6% of its peak in 1996–97. Conversely, the number of cycles involving micromanipulation continues to increase, although at a much lower rate than previously (14.4% rise on the 1997–98 figure, compared to 59.8% rise on the 1996–97 figure). The increased use and success of micromanipulation have been behind the rise in the total IVF live birth rate seen since 1993–94, although this now appears to have levelled off. Success with micro-manipulation seems to be higher than with IVF, although this may not be the case when corrected for individual female factors.[105]

Approximately a quarter of all infertile couples will present to secondary care with sperm defects or disorders.[99] As more techniques to address male infertility, such as intracytoplasmic sperm injection (direct injection of a single sperm into the egg), percutaneous epididymal sperm aspiration (recovery of sperm from the epididymis) and testicular sperm aspiration, are developed the demand for donor sperm is likely to decrease. Advances in technology mean that intracytoplasmic sperm injection (ICSI) could benefit up to 13% of couples with male sperm problems,[99] but many couples cannot afford or do not want to accept ICSI.[106]

Cost of fertility services

In the UK only about 25% of IVF treatments are funded by the NHS, and 80% of all licensed treatments that currently take place (IVF, ICSI or DI) take place in the private sector. In the past each health authority (now PCT) decided what funding they would allocate to the treatment of infertility and the types of treatment they would offer, and 25% of health authorities did not fund IVF at all. Many clinics that operate under the NHS and offer treatment free of charge to patients who meet criteria relating to the likelihood of achieving pregnancy also offer private treatment for those who can pay. Criteria for eligibility for both private as well as NHS treatment vary, and many clinics do not offer treatment to single women or unmarried couples as a matter of policy.

The availability and cost of fertility treatment vary considerably. Donor insemination treatment costs around £150 and IVF from about £2000 per treatment cycle.[107] The average number of treatment cycles per patient was 3 for donor insemination and 1.37 for IVF in 1996.

6 Effectiveness of services and interventions

The procedures, approaches and recommendations suggested here have been evaluated using the following scoring system.

Size of effect	
A	The procedure/service has a strong beneficial effect
B	The procedure/service has a moderate beneficial effect
C	The procedure/service has no measurable effect
D	The harms of the procedure/service outweigh its benefits

Quality of evidence	
I-1	Evidence from several consistent or one large randomised controlled trial
I-2	Evidence obtained from at least one properly designed randomised controlled trial
II-1	Evidence obtained from well-designed controlled trials without randomisation, or well-designed cohort or case–control analytical studies
II-2	Evidence obtained from multiple time series with or without the intervention. Dramatic results in uncontrolled experiments (e.g. the results of penicillin treatment in the 1940s) could also be regarded as this type of evidence
III	Opinions of respected authorities, based on clinical experience, descriptive studies, or reports of expert committees
IV	Evidence inadequate and conflicting

Prevention of unintended pregnancy

Many young people lack the knowledge and social skills to use contraception effectively, which puts them at greater risk of unintended pregnancy. Effective sex and relationship education for young people has the power to increase individual control over fertility by ensuring that, should they wish to do so, all sexually mature individuals know how to obtain and use contraception. There is considerable debate about what should be taught and the effectiveness of sexual health interventions. The design of evaluations of sexual health interventions needs to be improved so that reliable evidence of the effectiveness of different approaches to promoting young people's sexual health may be generated. In a review of 270 papers reporting sexual health interventions in the developed world since 1982, 73 reports of evaluations of sexual health interventions examining the effectiveness of these interventions in changing knowledge, attitudes or behavioural outcomes were identified, of which 65 were separate outcome evaluations. Only 12 (18%) of the 65 outcome evaluations were judged to be methodologically sound. Only two of the sound evaluations recorded interventions that were effective in showing an impact on young people's sexual behaviour, and one study actually found that abstinence education encouraged sexual experimentation[108] (level of evidence: A II-1). Despite this lack of positive evidence, there is no evidence that the provision of practical information and contraception leads to increased risk-taking behaviour.[109]

The effectiveness of family planning advice given by general practitioners has not been established, and general practitioners and practice nurses in primary care are not required to have specialist training in the provision of contraceptive counselling or education. However, this is not necessarily a problem, since most women using general practitioner services are older and are more likely to have used contraception before and therefore have less need for explanations and advice.

Nurses working in young people's services have more time per consultation and are more likely to have specialist training in communicating with young people.

Cost-effectiveness of contraceptive services

It has been shown that contraceptive services are financially and socially beneficial to an extent which far outweighs their cost. It is cheaper to provide contraceptive services than induced abortion services and the maintenance of children resulting from unwanted pregnancy. It has been calculated that the total expenditure on contraceptive services represents approximately 0.5% of total public expenditure on health care in the UK and only 3% of total public expenditure on family health services. The cost–benefit ratio of contraception is estimated to be 1:14. Benefits are calculated on the assumption that if contraceptive services were not publicly provided, no method of contraception would be used. On this basis it was estimated that the total direct cost to the NHS averted through the use of contraception services amounted to over £2.5 billion in 1991.[8]

Costs of general practitioner services can only be calculated from data pertaining to an item-for-service fee and from prescription records, and these are incomplete because they do not include provision for consumables and building overheads. No estimates of the number of women who attend both family planning clinics and general practice each year have been made.[8]

As both general practitioners and family planning clinics increasingly regard contraceptive services as one part of their comprehensive sexual health service, the wider benefits of contraception in the promotion of sexual health need to be considered in future analyses of the cost-effectiveness of services.

Contraceptive methods

The effectiveness of contraceptive methods must be balanced against their side-effects and the potential costs that result from contraceptive failure, including costs of induced abortion and pregnancy. Contraceptive use prevents maternal death when compared to no method, and the use of oral contraceptives and barrier methods may avert future deaths by protecting against some cancers and infections (level of evidence: B III). When morbidity and side-effects requiring hospitalisation are considered, IUCDs, oral contraceptives and vasectomy offer health benefits that strongly outweigh the risks associated with their use (level of evidence: A II-1).[110]

A large number of epidemiological studies have investigated the risks to users of combined oral contraceptives. In 1995 the Committee on the Safety of Medicines issued a national warning, based on the findings from large case-controlled studies, that women who used third-generation oral contraceptives containing gestodene or desogestrel were at increased risk of venous thrombo-embolism compared with women who used contraceptives containing levonorgestrel[111,112] (level of evidence: D I-1). A 1997 WHO

Scientific Group Meeting examined the evidence relating to the risks to women of myocardial infarction, ischaemic and haemorrhagic stroke, and venous thrombolic disease.[113] It concluded that any cardiovascular disease incidence or mortality attributable to oral contraceptives is very small if the users do not smoke and do not have other cardiovascular risk factors. However, the already elevated risks of myocardial infarction and stroke among women who smoke or who have high blood pressure are further increased if such women use combined oral contraceptives and, under these circumstances, combined oral contraceptive preparations containing desogestrel and gestodene possibly carry a slightly increased risk of venous thrombo-embolism.

The Cancer and Steroid Hormone Study (CASH) reported that current or former use of oral contraceptives is associated with a slightly increased risk of breast cancer at a younger age – a time when the disease is relatively rare – but with a decrease in likelihood among older women in whom the disease is more common. The use of oral contraception reduces women's risks of ovarian and endometrial cancer. This benefit occurs soon after starting pill use, becomes stronger with duration of use, and persists for many years after use is discontinued.[114] Barrier methods reduce the chance of developing cancer of the cervix associated with infection with human papilloma virus (HPV).[115] Barrier, spermicidal and withdrawal methods are the least effective choices of contraception for women solely concerned with preventing pregnancy (level of evidence: B II-2).

Previous studies of IUCDs have suggested a possible link with tubal infertility. A new study compared women with primary infertility who had tubal occlusion, women with primary infertility who did not have tubal occlusion (infertile controls) and primigravid women (pregnant controls). Information was collected on the women's past use of contraceptives, including copper IUCDs, previous sexual relationships and history of genital tract infections. Compared with infertile women and primigravid women, the relative risk of prior use of the IUCD was similar (1.0 and 0.9, respectively). Tubal infertility was not associated with the duration of IUCD use, the reason for the removal of the IUCD, or the presence or absence of gynaecological problems related to its use. The presence of antibodies to chlamydia was associated with infertility[116] (level of evidence: B II-1). Adequate screening and treatment of sexually transmitted infections, particularly for chlamydia, prior to IUCD insertion reduces the risk of tubal damage and subsequent infertility.

The levonorgestrel intrauterine device (marketed as Mirena) has been developed by Leiras Pharmaceuticals, Turku, Finland and has been available in the UK since May 1996. It is a systemic hormonal contraceptive that releases levonorgestrel 20 micrograms every 24 hours. The device provides fertility control, complete reversibility and convenience, and has a high level of tolerability (level of evidence: A III). It has been shown to reduce menstrual bleeding (level of evidence: A II-1) and therefore may be a particularly useful contraceptive method for women with excessive menstrual bleeding, and has been recommended as an alternative to hysterectomy for fertile women suffering from menorrhagia. An open randomised multi-centre study of women scheduled to undergo hysterectomy for the treatment of excessive menstrual bleeding found that 64% (95% confidence interval: 44–81) of women treated with the levonorgestrel intrauterine device decided to cancel their hysterectomy[117] (level of evidence: A I-2). The cost of the device is currently around £100, which is a fraction of the cost of a hysterectomy, but is 10 times the cost of a copper IUCD. It is therefore a less cost-effective method of contraception compared to the copper IUCD for women without excessive menstrual bleeding.

Induced abortion

Induced abortion is generally less traumatic psychologically and physically than an unwanted full-term pregnancy. The risks of complications such as serious bleeding and infection are minimal if the procedure is performed during the earlier stages of gestation. Complications are related to the method used, which in turn is dependent to some extent on the gestational age of the fetus[118] (level of evidence: A III). An efficient prompt referral system from general practitioner to gynaecologist will help to ensure that women seeking an induced abortion have the lowest possible risk of complications.

Medical abortion

In July 1991, the antiprogestin mifepristone (RU 486) was granted a licence in the UK for the purpose of inducing a medical abortion in the first nine weeks of pregnancy. In combination with a suitable prostaglandin, it has been shown to be an effective and safe alternative to vacuum aspiration[119] (level of evidence: A I). It is most suitable for the first nine weeks of amenorrhoea, but can also be used in the later stages of pregnancy to facilitate the abortion process, reducing both physical and emotional trauma.[120]

Administration of 200 mg oral mifepristone is as effective as 600 mg when each is followed by prostaglandin. Sequential and single-dose regimens have comparable efficacy[99] (level of evidence: A I-2). Methotrexate in combination with misoprostol is more effective than misoprostol alone (level of evidence: A I-2). Misoprostol is more effective when given vaginally than when taken orally. Administration of 800 µg misoprostol 7 days after methotrexate is more effective than the same dose given 3 days after methotrexate (level of evidence: A I).

Complications and short-term psychiatric morbidity associated with medical abortion are similar to those observed in surgical abortion.[121] Medical abortion transfers the workload from medical to nursing staff and, while technically simpler, is logistically more complex than surgical methods. It is a longer process with prolonged bleeding, occasional haemorrhage, higher failure rate, lack of immediate confirmation of success for some patients, and the inconvenience of several visits.[99] No rigorous economic evaluation of the use of medical abortions has taken place.

Fertility treatments

Many couples who experience infertility will eventually conceive without treatment, but despite technological improvements, the outcome for couples who experience infertility for more than three years remains poor. The relatively low level of success of many treatments suggests that attention to infertility prevention is therefore more effective. It has been estimated that the cost of diagnosing and managing genital chlamydia and its complications in the UK would be at least £50 million a year.[68] Yet the Chief Medical Officer's Expert Advisory Group on chlamydia concluded that this infection represents such a big threat to sexual health that there is sufficient evidence to indicate that its effective management would result in considerable health benefits.[66]

Controlled trials have shown that some previously standard treatments for infertility, such as hormonal suppression of endometriosis and clomiphene treatment of women for unexplained infertility of short duration, are ineffective.[122–124] The greatest success in terms of producing live babies has been achieved in the treatment of ovulatory disorders. Tubal problems, even with surgical intervention, continue to have a poor outcome.

The use of clinical guidelines for investigation of a couple presenting in general practice with infertility will produce a more uniform approach to the management of infertility and result in an increase in the proportion of referrals at an appropriate time for treatment[125] (level of evidence: B II-1). To ensure the most effective use of resources, accurate assessment and prompt referral for treatment are needed for women over 35 years of age who have been attempting conception for more than a year.

The Human Fertilisation and Embryology Authority (HFEA), set up in the UK in 1991, ensures that all UK treatment clinics offering *in-vitro* fertilisation (IVF) or donor insemination (DI), or that store eggs, sperm or embryos, conform to high medical and professional standards and are inspected regularly. The

HFEA produces a code of practice that provides clinics with guidelines about the proper conduct of licensed activities. The HFEA also keeps a formal register containing information about donors, treatments and children born from those treatments.

In-vitro fertilisation (IVF), as well as being costly financially, is associated with considerable emotional and some physical risk. IVF involves the collection of eggs and sperm that are mixed outside the body. The pregnancy success rate is improved if women take drugs to stimulate the ovaries to produce several eggs during one cycle. The main risk associated with this is ovarian hyperstimulation (which occurs in 2% of women). The majority of these women have a mild or moderate form of over-response to the drugs, and complain of pain and mild abdominal swelling. In some cases cysts may appear on the ovaries and fluid may collect in the abdominal cavity, causing discomfort. In about 1–2% of cases the ovarian hyperstimulation is severe and the ovaries are very swollen. These complications require urgent hospital admission to restore the fluid balance and monitor progress.

Returning several fertilised eggs to the uterus increases the chance of pregnancy, but increases the risk of multiple pregnancy that in turn increases the risks to the woman's health during pregnancy and may lead to increased risk of premature birth, low birth weight, disability and neonatal death for the babies. Multiple births are also associated with social and financial costs for parents.[126–128] In August 2001 the Human Fertilisation and Embryology Authority announced its decision to reduce the number of embryos that may be transferred in a single IVF treatment cycle from three to two.

The average success rate for IVF is about 17% per treatment cycle, and slightly less (about 12%) for frozen embryo transfer. The chances of success depend on individual circumstances, but decrease with the woman's age. By comparison, the average monthly chance of conceiving for a fertile couple having regular intercourse is 20–25%.

When male-factor defects are the cause of infertility, artificial insemination can be recommended. At present, women under 30 achieve a live birth rate of 10–12% per donor insemination treatment cycle, but this begins to decrease after that age. Women aged 35–39 have a 9% chance of a live birth, and women over 40 have only a 3–4% chance of successful pregnancy for each donor insemination cycle. During the period 1998–99, 4338 patients received treatment involving donor insemination or gamete intrafallopian transport using donated gametes. A total of 11 035 cycles were started, which led to 1332 clinical pregnancies (12.1%) and 1087 live births (9.9%). The number of donor insemination cycles carried out annually has dropped by 57% since the 1992–93 reporting period (from 25 623 to 11 035).[105] Donor insemination is relatively simple and inexpensive, and when provided over 12 cycles can offer about a 50% chance of conception.[99] Therefore donor insemination should remain an integral part of the fertility services. There will also be a small demand for this service from couples where the male partner is HIV-positive and from women without male partners who wish to conceive.

Cost-effectiveness of services is very difficult to estimate, as prices charged do not provide an accurate picture of resource use. A national estimate attributed one-quarter of the costs of fertility services to diagnostic procedures and three-quarters to treatments. As yet there is no existing model of care on which to base exact costing. Cross-subsidisation of services, knock-on antenatal costs and the increased need for neonatal care would all need to be considered for a complete economic evaluation of the service.[129]

7 Models of care/recommendations

The ideal model of service provision includes an adequate range of different but complementary services designed to meet the contraceptive, abortion, fertility and other sexual health needs of the local population. Equity of access to a full range of services should be the central aim of local models of service provision. Resources should be targeted at those groups or areas within populations that are likely to have the greatest need. It is known that communities most at risk of ill-health still tend to experience the least satisfactory access to services – the so-called 'inverse care law'.[130,131] Reasons for differences in uptake of contraception, abortion and fertility services between socio-economic groups and areas of high deprivation should be identified and addressed. Research into the causes or factors contributing to inequalities should be commissioned to inform local Health Improvement Programmes (or equivalent).

The views of service users and providers should be continually sought to evaluate the quality and appropriateness of the current services or when a new or reformed service has been introduced.[29] For example, the Sandyford project in Glasgow is based on a more social model of care and was set up not only to modernise health services but also to tackle the wider determinants in health that affect quality of life. Users' views were an integral part of this project review, and were used to recommend how the project should progress in the future.[132]

Sex and relationship education

The promotion of an informed and positive approach to sexual and reproductive health requires a holistic approach to health and health care provision. Effective education for young people, both boys and girls, is a key component of strategies to increase the proportion of pregnancies that are planned, while reducing the rate of sexually transmitted infections, teenage pregnancies and the need for abortion. The development of partnerships between young people, parents, health and education professionals and other agencies is central to this model.[133]

The promotion of sexual and reproductive health for young people must remain a key factor in all school and other settings, such as young offender institutions and children in care. Local co-operation and co-ordination between health and education professionals is essential to encourage mutual understanding and optimise the available experience, expertise and resources. A partnership approach that involves pupils, parents, teachers, headteachers, governors and relevant outside agencies in the planning, development and evaluation of school and other institutional sexual health policies is needed.

Given that many feel the provision of sex and relationship education is primarily a parental responsibility, education needs to be targeted at a wider audience, not just schools and colleges. Embarrassment and a lack of knowledge leave many parents unable to tackle the subject confidently.

It is recommended that:

- education programmes be developed to help parents provide sex education for their children, including programmes to make fathers more comfortable and able to discuss sexual matters with their sons
- staff who provide information and educational programmes about sexual and reproductive health receive relevant training, not only on issues such as safer sex and methods of contraception, but also on the importance of promoting self-esteem and other social skills (the teenage pregnancy strategy includes provision for an accredited sex and relationship teacher in each school)
- Government guidance about the timing and content of sex and relationship education be followed
- specialist counselling services be made available at a local level for people who have sexual difficulties that are of psychological or emotional origin.

Contraception services

Contraceptive requirements change during a woman's reproductive life cycle. Sexual health clinics that target particular groups, such as young people, should therefore continue to exist alongside general practitioner provision. A model of service provision should be adopted which ensures that services are available for men, young people of both sexes, older women and women who prefer to use their general practitioner. Outreach services should be available for those groups who are excluded, such as the homeless, travellers, those who misuse drugs and commercial sex workers.

The Department of Health's sexual health strategy (2001) suggests that genito-urinary medicine clinics should be developed as the cornerstone for tackling sexually transmitted infections.[30] Since many people from difficult-to-access groups use genito-urinary medicine services, it would be appropriate to use this contact with services as an opportunity to provide contraceptive advice and supplies at the same time. Although some do this already, the role of genito-urinary medicine clinics as providers of more generalised sexual health services such as screening and provision of contraceptive supplies should be encouraged.

As the nature of teenage sexual activity is often unplanned, family planning clinics, general practices and pharmacies need to ensure that staff at all levels are approachable and that they provide clients with accurate information and advice about emergency contraception, and that every effort is made to ensure that emergency contraception is accessible to young people. Targeted sex and relationship education to raise awareness and increase understanding of emergency contraception should be carried out using a range of approaches.

It is recommended that:

- the remit of GUM services be widened so that they develop into holistic sexual health services that are able to provide sexually transmitted infection screening, contraceptive advice and supplies, as well as sexually transmitted infection treatment
- general practitioners who provide a contraceptive service receive appropriate training, so that they are able to offer a wider range of contraceptive methods
- doctors who are unwilling to provide emergency contraceptive services for non-clinical reasons make this known to their patients. In this situation, leaflets and information stating where patients can access emergency contraception services should be made available
- areas with ethnic-minority populations ensure that contraceptive advice is available in the first language of all local people likely to use services
- female doctors be made available on request to all women using contraceptive services, and vice versa for men
- in urban areas with large populations, the development of a dedicated contraceptive and sexual health service for people with physical or learning disabilities be considered. This could be integrated into existing facilities, but providers would require specific training to enable them to develop appropriate expertise and sensitivity when meeting the needs of people who may have single or multiple problems. A domiciliary service may be of great value
- services for travellers be provided within the context of the travellers' culture. For example, it may be advisable for travellers to keep their own records, whether antenatal, contraception or general practice. An outreach service may be needed
- confidentiality assurances be made more explicit and training to raise awareness of the importance of this issue be provided for all, including receptionists and other administrative staff
- contraceptive supplies and advice remain free and be extended to include the provision of condoms by all general practitioner services and the dispensing of over-the-counter emergency contraception by pharmacists

- commissioners and providers of services encourage the extended role of nurses and pharmacists in contraception provision, by supporting increased training of nurses and pharmacists to enable them to dispense contraceptives safely following agreed protocols
- innovative ideas be explored to ensure that condoms are readily available to teenagers who want them[134]
- programmes be developed to encourage boys to take their share of responsibility for contraception. This may include the development of dedicated clinics and educational programmes for boys and young men
- women with menorrhagia be offered the use of a levonorgestrel intrauterine device as an alternative to hysterectomy.

Induced abortion

Commissioners should ensure that a comprehensive and efficient service is provided. It may be appropriate in some areas to commission a large proportion of induced abortions from the private sector. The model adopted depends on the existing level and quality of service provision across the sector within the local area.

Both nationally and locally there is a need to address the wide-ranging differences in the proportion of abortions funded by the NHS. The current level of NHS funding ranges from 92% of abortions in some areas to less than 50% in others. Primary care trusts commissioning abortion services should monitor the age and area of residence of women using the services to identify and address inequalities in access. Whilst some women may decide to use private abortion services by choice, inequality of access, especially in deprived areas, is likely to have a negative impact on the overall physical, mental and social health of young women and their children.

The method of termination should be selected with due regard to clinical suitability and safety, the preferences of the individual woman, the range of services available locally and cost-effectiveness. Day care should be offered whenever this is clinically and socially feasible.

The need for a few late terminations will always exist, and these should be performed in a hospital setting. The service provided to women must be sensitive to their emotional needs and be provided by gynaecologists and nurses who understand and accept the need for this service. As far as possible, women admitted for terminations should be cared for separately from other gynaecological patients.

It is recommended that:

- at least 75% of induced abortions be provided or paid for by the NHS, and the majority take place before nine weeks' gestation. Women should ideally be provided with an appointment for assessment within five days of referral
- counselling be readily available for women who have experienced mental health problems in the past, and are therefore at greater risk of experiencing long-term post-abortion stress.

Fertility services

Infertility should be prevented as far as possible through an integrated and comprehensive sexual health strategy that includes high-quality sexual health education, sexually transmitted infection screening and treatment, and easy access to barrier methods of contraception. The importance and potential of primary prevention of infertility through the effective management of chlamydia infection was detailed in the Chief Medical Officer's Expert Advisory Group on Chlamydia Report. The report recommended opportunistic screening of all sexually active women aged under 25 years, all attendees (both sexes) at genito-urinary medicine clinics, all women seeking terminations and women over 25 years of age with a new partner or who have had two or more partners in the previous 12 months. Pilot chlamydia screening programmes were carried out in the Wirral and in Portsmouth. The pilot programme in the Wirral ran from September 1999 to August 2000, and 6114 women aged 16–24 years were screened for chlamydia using a simple urine test. The pilot programmes showed that:

- selective screening does pick up significant numbers of cases
- very little medical input is required to undertake chlamydia screening using an easily administered urine test
- urine testing for chlamydia is generally acceptable to clients
- opportunistic screening reaches many young people who might otherwise be missed
- the concomitant publicity that the programme attracted served to improve the public profile and understanding of chlamydia as well as other sexual health issues.

Where infertility cannot be prevented, it should be treated. The resources and facilities available for infertility treatment in secondary and tertiary care vary considerably, and depend on local priorities, circumstances and the population served. Even where a dedicated fertility clinic exists, a full range of services may only be cost-effective in the tertiary care setting. The clinical guidelines developed by the National Institute for Clinical Excellence (NICE) for England and Wales include guidance on high-technology treatments such as IVF.

It is recommended that:

- the Royal College of Obstetricians and Gynaecologists guidelines be routinely followed, the appropriateness of referrals from primary to secondary care be monitored and evaluated at local level, and the training needs of local primary care practitioners be addressed
- all clients undergo basic investigations to establish the likely cause of their infertility and assess their prognosis initially in a primary care setting
- a basic minimum set of services be available and the couple always be managed in a dedicated fertility clinic in which there are appropriate facilities and access to trained staff, including doctors, nurses and counsellors. Where specific skills are not available locally, it may be appropriate for health commissioners to seek access to specialist services elsewhere
- commissioners monitor the access to and outcomes of treatment at a local level
- the simultaneous use of both barrier and oral contraceptive methods be monitored, as this would indicate greater awareness of the importance of protection against sexually transmitted infections likely to cause infertility
- a selective screening programme for chlamydia be extended nationally
- local protocols be developed for the testing, management and follow-up of positive chlamydia cases identified through screening, including provision for those people who do not wish to attend a genito-urinary medicine clinic
- equity of access to fertility services be monitored and, where a full range of basic fertility services is not available within the local area, transport be considered to ensure equity of access.

8 Outcome measures, audit and targets

The first time that any health targets were set was in 1992, when sexual health was declared as one of the five key areas in the 'Health of the Nation', the strategy that guided health policy in the UK until 1997, when a new Government came into power.

When the new Government's health policy, *Saving Lives: Our Healthier Nation*, was published in 1999, the key priority areas for action had been reduced to four and sexual health was not included. However, the need to address sexual health was still a priority, and the Social Exclusion Unit's report on teenage pregnancy, published in 1999, set out a national strategy for England. Two key targets were to:

- halve the rate of conceptions among under-19s and set a firmly established downward trend in conception rates for under-16s by 2010
- increase the participation of teenage parents in education and work.

The NHS Plan published in 2000 stated that by 2004 there would be full implementation of the Government's teenage pregnancy strategy, bringing about a 15% reduction in the rate of teenage conceptions, consistent with the longer-term target of reducing the rate of teenage conceptions by half by 2020.

To enable monitoring of these targets, the number of conceptions among girls aged under 18 resident in an area per 1000 girls aged 15–17 years resident in the area was included as one of the NHS performance indicators. However, it is worth mentioning that in the original 1999 document this indicator was based on conceptions in girls under the age of 16 years. The indicator was amended in 2000 to look at conceptions in girls under the age of 18 years, to facilitate monitoring of the Government's goals.

In 2001, the national strategy for sexual health and HIV consultation document was published. This strategy emphasised the Government's belief that the consequences of poor sexual health can be serious, and that unintended pregnancies and sexually transmitted infections can have a long-lasting impact on people's lives. The strategy describes how the Government aims to reduce unintended pregnancy rates and reduce the transmission of HIV and sexually transmitted infections through the modernisation of services and partnership working across a wide range of organisations. Amongst other things, the strategy aims to ensure that the NHS works to improve public health, by emphasising the importance of promoting health and preventing illness, as well as treating problems once they arise.

As well as the national targets found in the NHS Plan, the teenage pregnancy strategy and the national strategy for sexual health and HIV, throughout each document the Government recommends that local targets must be developed.

The setting of targets for local services should be determined by the overall strategic objectives of the services, bearing in mind local need. In every case the objective is to minimise the adverse health consequences of sexual behaviour and to optimise the health and social benefits of a population's sexual expression.

Local targets can therefore relate to inputs and processes such as sex and relationship education, counselling and advisory services, and clinical care. They can also relate to outputs and outcomes such as teenage pregnancy and induced abortion rates, levels of sexually transmitted infection and infertility. Such indicators not only provide good summary measures of the quality of education, accessibility and acceptability of services, but also indicate the level of power that young women have over their sexual and reproductive health. Each locally set target should have a time period for achievement, and be subject to review.

Outcome measures

Routine data can be used to monitor service uptake.

Where routine data are unavailable, contraceptive, induced abortion and fertility services can be monitored through the use of periodic, local community or special group surveys designed to show:

- sexual behaviour and the level of contraceptive use

- uptake of contraceptive provision by general practitioners and other clinics. Preferably, this should be detailed by age and type of contraceptive method chosen rather than just consultation rates per 1000 population. Establishing the proportion of people using both family planning clinics and general practitioner services concurrently would enable a comprehensive assessment of the prevalence of contraceptive use in the area to be calculated
- the extent of planned conceptions.

Services could also be monitored through the use of:

- induced abortion rates, analysed by age, area and social group populations to audit equity of access to services
- surveys that allow service users to indicate their overall satisfaction with the quality of consultations and the extent to which their needs are being met.[135]

For fertility services, the extent to which the guidelines developed by the Royal College of Obstetricians and Gynaecologists are implemented at primary, secondary and tertiary care levels can be used to indicate the appropriateness of referrals from primary to secondary and tertiary care, and should be monitored and evaluated at the primary care trust level. Costs and benefits to health from these services require monitoring. This should include the monitoring of mortality and morbidity experienced by women following clinical procedures, conception and birth, and the proportion of multiple births resulting from assisted conception techniques. Human Fertilisation and Embryology Authority licensed clinics are required to continually monitor and evaluate the services provided.

Sex and relationship education

Appropriate indicators that could be used to set local targets include:

- the proportion of both primary and secondary schools that have established links with local health promotion units, youth advisory or other agencies
- the proportion of schools that have committed themselves to allocating adequate time and training within the school curriculum for sex and relationship education, and have a sex and relationship education policy that reflects the school as a health-promoting environment within the wider community
- the number of teachers who have been specifically trained to provide sex and relationship education and can handle moral and ethical issues sensitively and confidently.

Contraceptive services

Appropriate indicators that could be used to set local targets include:

- the development of a comprehensive range of complementary advisory and clinic services that address the needs of all men and women in the area. This includes men and women of all ages, people with special needs, such as those with learning and physical difficulties, and those in traditionally under-served groups, e.g. prostitutes, drug users and travellers
- a high level of uptake of contraceptive services
- the proportion of family doctors and other professionals providing a contraceptive service who have successfully completed accredited training
- the number of nurses who have completed further training and are willing and able to dispense contraceptives according to agreed protocols

- the number of local pharmacists who have completed further training and are willing and able to dispense emergency contraceptives according to agreed protocols
- the development of strategies to improve awareness and availability of emergency contraception
- inequalities in access to and uptake of services by different groups
- the development of alliances and partnerships between relevant local agencies.

Induced abortion services

Appropriate indicators that could be used to set local targets include:

- the development of strategies to ensure that at least 75% of induced abortions in every area are provided through the NHS
- the proportion of women seeking terminations who are offered appointments within a week of referral for termination
- the proportion of induced abortions provided by the NHS that are carried out by 9 weeks' gestation.

Fertility services

Appropriate indicators that could be used to set local targets include:

- the proportion of people experiencing fertility problems who undergo basic investigations in primary care to establish the likely cause of their infertility and assess their prognosis prior to referral to secondary or tertiary services
- the proportion of people with access to NHS-funded IVF and other specialised treatments at a regional or inter-regional level
- a progressive reduction in sexually transmitted infection rates, especially chlamydia, expressed as 3- or 5-year rolling averages
- an increase in the availability of barrier methods of contraception from general practitioners and other providers
- an increase in the use of barrier methods in the population.

9 Information and research requirements

Much of the crucial information that is required to establish need and to monitor and evaluate services is already collected by the ONS in the form of conception rates, pregnancy rates, induced abortion rates and population data. These data would be of much greater use if they were analysed more rapidly and were made available in relation to a smaller area, such as an electoral ward or primary care trust area.

All providers must fulfil minimum data collection requirements. This means that the information collected in general practice must be improved and made compatible with that collected by family planning clinics and other service providers.

The level and quality of service provision in primary care settings need to be better established, and to provide a comprehensive view of local needs, a minimum data set that enables the quality and equity of access to services to be monitored should be agreed with all service providers.

There is a need to develop methodologies to allow greater understanding of the contribution of both providers and service users to the effectiveness of contraception in normal use. An interesting area of research would be to establish whether there is a gap between the service providers' beliefs about men and women's level of knowledge of the basic biology of reproduction and how contraceptives work and the actual level of understanding among men and women service users. And if a gap exists, it would be useful to know the effect that it has on contraception use.

Methodologically sound evaluations of the effectiveness, including cost-effectiveness, of different approaches to sex and relationship education, contraceptive advice and specific young people's services are required.[136]

With the development of an expanded role for nurses in the primary care setting, the cost-effectiveness and quality of contraceptive and other sexual health services provided by trained family planning nurses based in primary care trusts compared to general practitioners and family planning clinics need to be established.

The long-term clinical effectiveness of the levonorgestrel intrauterine device as an alternative to hysterectomy and the cost-effectiveness and acceptability to women of using this method of contraception need to be established.

The increasing demand for infertility services and the relatively poor outcome of treatment for many suggest that further work is required to estimate the true prevalence and main causes of infertility in the population.

Since a medical abortion is cheaper than a standard surgical procedure, a thorough economic evaluation of the two to help establish reasons for the low uptake of medical abortion is needed.

References

1 Whincup PH, Gilg JA, Odoki K, Taylor SJC, Cook DG. Age of menarche in contemporary British teenagers: survey of girls born between 1982 and 1986. *BMJ* 2001; **322**: 1095–6.

2 Robey B, Rutstein SO, Morris L, Blackburn R. The reproductive revolution: new survey findings. In: *Population Reports 1992*. Series M, No 11. Baltimore, MD: Johns Hopkins University Population Information Program, 1992.

3 The Cabinet Office. *Teenage Pregnancy. A Social Exclusion Unit Report*. London: The Stationery Office, 1999; www.cabinet-office.gov.uk/seu/1999/teenpreg.pdf (accessed on 23 January 2002).

4 Health Education Authority (HEA). *Health Update 4: sexual health*. London: HEA, 1994.

5 Newman M *et al. Contraception and Abortion Services in London: are we missing the need?* The Health of Londoners Project. London: Directorate of Public Health, East London and the City Health Authority, 1997.

6 NHS Centre for Reviews and Dissemination. Preventing and reducing the adverse effects of unintended teenage pregnancies. *Effect Health Care Bull* 1997; **3**(1).

7 Laing WA. *Family Planning: the benefits and costs*. London: Policy Studies Institute, 1982.

8 McGuire A, Hughes D. *The Economics of Family Planning Services: a report prepared for the Contraceptive Alliance*. London: Family Planning Association, 1995.

9 Bodard S, Baldwin B. A survey of women with unplanned pregnancies in Avon, January to March 1994. *Br J Fam Plan* 1996; **22**(1): 42–5.

10 Family Planning Association. *Unplanned Pregnancy*. Factsheet No. 4. London: Family Planning Association, 1997.

11 Gunnell DJ, Ewings P. Infertility prevalence, needs assessment and purchasing. *J Public Health Med* 1994; **16**(1): 29–35.

12 Schmidt L, Munster K. Infertility and the seeking of infertility treatment in a representative population. *Br J Obstet Gynaecol* 1995; **102**: 978–84.

13 Phipps WR. The future of infertility services. *Fertil Steril* 1996; **66**(2): 202–4.

14 Office for National Statistics (ONS). *UK Health Statistics*. London: The Stationery Office, 2001.

15 Office for National Statistics (ONS). *Health Statistics Quarterly. Winter 2001*. London: The Stationery Office, 2001.

16 Office for National Statistics (ONS). Legal abortions in England and Wales, 2000. In: *Health Statistics Quarterly. Summer 2001*. London: The Stationery Office, 2001.

17 Office for National Statistics (ONS). *Social Trends 27*. London: The Stationery Office, 1997.

18 Public Health Laboratory Service, Department of Health, Social Services and Public Safety (Northern Ireland) and The Scottish ISD-(D)-5 Collaborative Group. *Trends in Sexually Transmitted Infections in the UK, 1990–1999*. London: Public Health Laboratory Service, 2000.

19 Office for National Statistics (ONS). *Contraception and Sexual Health 1999. Results of the Omnibus Survey*. London: The Stationery Office, 2001.

20 Health Education Authority (HEA). *Promoting Sexual Health Services to Young People: guidelines for purchasers and providers*. London: HEA, 1996.

21 Jones EF *et al. Teenage Pregnancy in Industrialised Countries*. New Haven, CT: Yale University Press, 1996.

22 Department of Health. *ONS General Household Survey: contraception and sterilisation 2000*; www.doh.gov.uk/ (accessed on 25 January 2002).

23 Department of Health. *The New NHS: reference costs 2001*; www.doh.gov.uk/nhsexec/refcosts.htm (accessed on 30 March 2002).

24 British Pregnancy Advisory Service. *Price List*. London: British Pregnancy Advisory Service (applicable 1 April 1998).

25 Marie Stopes International. *Fees at Marie Stopes*. London: Marie Stopes International, 1998.

26 Office for National Statistics (ONS). *Birth Statistics. FM1 No. 29. Review of the Registrar General on births and patterns of family building in England and Wales, 2000*. London: The Stationery Office, 2001.

27 Laing W. *Laing's Review of Private Healthcare*. London: Laing and Buisson, 1997.

28 Human Fertilisation and Embryology Authority (HFEA). *Human Fertilisation and Embryology Authority Sixth Annual Report 1997*. London: HFEA, 1997.

29 Bissell P, Anderson C, Savage I, Goodyear L. Supplying emergency hormonal contraception through patient group direction: a qualitative study of the views of pharmacists. *Int J Pharm Pract* 2001; **9** (Suppl.): R57.

30 Department of Health. *The National Strategy for Sexual Health and HIV*. London: The Stationery Office, 2001.

31 McKeown T. *The Role of Medicine: dream, mirage or nemesis*. Oxford: Oxford University Press for the Nuffield Provincial Hospitals Trust, 1976.

32 Davies IM. Perinatal and infant deaths: social and biological factors. *Popul Trends* 1980; **19**: 19–21.

33 Ashton JR, Seymour H. *The New Public Health*. Milton Keynes: Open University Press, 1988.

34 Office for National Statistics (ONS). *Conceptions in England and Wales 1996*. London: The Stationery Office, 1998.

35 Department of Health. *Health Minister Welcomes Downward Trend in Teenage Conception Rates*. Press release 2002/0103 following publication of conception statistics for 2000, 28 February 2002; http://tap.ccta.gov.uk/doh/inf (accessed on 26 March 2002).

36 Wellings K, Fields J, Johnson A, Wadsworth J. *Sexual Behaviour in Britain: the National Survey of Sexual Attitudes and Lifestyle*. Harmondsworth: Penguin, 1994.

37 NHS Centre for Reviews and Disseminations, 1997, op. cit.

38 Office for National Statistics (ONS). *Health Statistics Quarterly. Spring 2002*. London: The Stationery Office, 2002.

39 Yoos C. Adolescent cognitive and contraceptive behaviours. *Paediatr Nurs* 1987; **13**(4): 247–50.

40 National Children's Bureau. *Supporting the Needs of Boys and Young Men in Sex and Relationships Education*. Forum Fact Sheet 11. London: Sex Education Forum, 1997.

41 Allen I. *Education in Sex and Personal Relationships*. Research Report No. 665. London: Policy Studies Institute, 1987.

42 National Children's Bureau. *Effective Learning: approaches to teaching sex education*. Forum Fact Sheet 12. London: Sex Education Forum, 1997.

43 Lenderyou G, Ray C (eds). *Let's Hear it for the Boys: supporting sex and relationships education for boys*. London: Sex Education Forum, 1997.

44 Cohen MW. Adolescent sexual activity as an expression of nonsexual needs. *Pediatr Ann* 1995; **24**: 324–9.

45 Turtle J, Jones A, Hickman M. *Young People and Health: the health behaviour of school-aged children. Summary of key findings*. London: Health Education Authority, 1997.

46 Sex Education Forum. *Sex Education Matters*. Forum Fact Sheet 4. London: National Children's Bureau, 1995.

47 National Foundation for Educational Research. *Parents' Views of Health Education. The European Network of Health-Promoting Schools*. London: Health Education Authority, 1997.

48 Healy DL, Trounson AO, Andersen AN. Female infertility: causes and treatment. *Lancet* 1994; **343**: 1539–44.

49 De Krester DM. Male Infertility (review). *Lancet* 1997; **349**: 787–90.

50 National Institute for Clinical Excellence. *Fertility: assessment and treatment for people with fertility problems. Clinical Guideline II.* February 2004. London: NICE.

51 British Fertility Society. *Diagnostic Classification, Basic Diagnostic Procedures and Basic Diagnostic Data Collection.* Dundee: British Fertility Society, 1995.

52 Office for National Statistics (ONS). *Abortion Statistics.* Series AB no. 27. London: The Stationery Office, 2001.

53 Hull MGR *et al.* Population study of causes, treatment and outcome of infertility. *BMJ* 1985; **291**: 1693–7.

54 Wellings K, Nanchahal K, Macdowall W *et al.* Sexual behaviour in Britain: early heterosexual experience. *Lancet* 2001; **358**: 1843–50.

55 Stuart Smith S. Teenage sex. *BMJ* 1996; **312**: 390–1.

56 While AE. The incidence of unplanned and unwanted pregnancies among live births from health visitor records. *Child Care Health Dev* 1990; **16**(4): 219–26.

57 Office for National Statistics (ONS). Legal abortions in England and Wales, 2000. In: *Health Statistics Quarterly. Summer 2001.* London: The Stationery Office, 2001.

58 Alan Guttmacher Institute. *Sharing Responsibility: women, society and abortion worldwide.* Special Report. New York and Washington: Alan Guttmacher Institute, 1999.

59 Ashton JR *et al.* Trends in induced abortion in England and Wales. *J Epidemiol Community Health* 1983; **37**: 105–10.

60 Ubido J, Ashton JR. *Liverpool Planned Parenthood Profile.* Liverpool Public Health Observatory Report No. 4. Liverpool: University of Liverpool, 1991.

61 Adler MW. *ABC of Sexually Transmitted Disease* (3e). London: BMJ Publishing Group, 1995.

62 Fenton KA, Korovessis C, Johnson AM *et al.* Sexual behaviour in Britain: reported sexually transmitted infections and prevalent genital *Chlamydia trachomatis* infection. *Lancet* 2001; **358**: 1851–4.

63 Johnson AM, Mercer CH, Erens B *et al.* Sexual behaviour in Britain: partnerships, practices and HIV risk behaviours. *Lancet* 2001; **358**: 1835–42.

64 Bower H. Britain launches pilot screening programme for chlamydia. *BMJ* 1998; **316**: 1477.

65 Paavonen J. Is screening for *Chlamydia trachomatis* infection cost-effective? *Genitourin Med* 1997; **73**: 103–4.

66 Department of Health. *Summary and Conclusions of Chief Medical Officer's Expert Advisory Group on* Chlamydia trachomatis. London: Department of Health, 1998; www.doh.gov.uk/chlamyd.htm (accessed on 11 January 2002).

67 Simms I *et al.* Epidemiology of genital *Chlamydia trachomatis* in England and Wales. *Genitourin Med* 1997; **73**: 122–6.

68 Stokes T. Screening for chlamydia in general practice: a literature review and summary of the evidence. *J Public Health Med* 1997; **19**(2): 222–32.

69 Dryden MS *et al.* Detection of *Chlamydia trachomatis* in general practice urine samples. *Br J Gen Pract* 1994; **44**: 114–17.

70 Public Health Laboratory Service. *Sexually Transmitted Infections Data from PHLS.* London: Public Health Laboratory Service, 2000; www.phls.org.uk/facts/STI/data_tables/sti_table_chlam1.htm (accessed on 25 January 2002).

71 Office for National Statistics (ONS). *NHS Contraceptive Services, England: 2000–2001.* London: The Stationery Office, 2001.

72 Office for Population Censuses and Surveys (OPCS). *Morbidity Statistics in General Practice. Fourth national study, 1991–1992.* Series MB5 no.3. London: OPCS, 1995.

73 Royal College of Obstetricians and Gynaecologists (RCOG). *Report on the RCOG Working Party on Unplanned Pregnancy.* London: RCOG, 1991.

74 Department of Health. *The NHS Plan: a plan for investment, a plan for reform.* London: The Stationery Office, 2000.

75 Department of Health. *Shifting the Balance of Power Within the NHS. Securing delivery.* London: Department of Health, 2001.

76 Royal College of Obstetricians and Gynaecologists (RCOG). *Report on the RCOG Working Party on Unplanned Pregnancy.* London: RCOG, 1991.

77 Institute of Population Studies. *Sexual Health and Family Planning Services in General Practice.* London: Family Planning Association, 1993.

78 Family Planning Association. *Use of Family Planning Services.* Factsheet No. 2. London: Family Planning Association, 1997.

79 Office for National Statistics (ONS). *NHS Contraceptive Services, England: 1999–2000.* London: The Stationery Office, 2000.

80 Barratt S (ed.). *Health Prospects for Young Citizens of the North West: a Special Report for the Regional Director of Public Health 1998.* Liverpool: Department of Public Health, University of Liverpool, 1998.

81 Brook Advisory Centre. *Annual Report 1995–96.* Liverpool: Brook Advisory Centre, 1996.

82 Trussell J, Leveque JA, Koenig JD. The economic value of contraception: a comparison of 15 methods. *Am J Public Health* 1995; **85**: 494–503; www.jr2.ox.ac.uk/bandolier/band50/b50-3.html#Heading2 (accessed on 25 January 2002).

83 Fotherby K. Twelve years of clinical experience with an oral contraceptive containing 30 µg ethinyloestradiol and 150 µg desogestrel. *Contraception* 1995; **51**: 3–12; www.jr2.ox.ac.uk/bandolier/band50/b50-3.html#Heading2 (accessed on 25 January 2002).

84 Family Planning Association. *Family Planning Services: a model for District Health Authorities.* London: Family Planning Association, 1990.

85 Trussell J, Stewart F. The effectiveness of postcoital hormonal contraception. *Fam Plan Perspect* 1992; **24**: 262–4.

86 Yuzpe A, Kubba A. Postcoital contraception. In: Filshie M, Guillebaud J (eds). *Contraception, Science and Practice.* London: Butterworth, 1989, pp. 126–43.

87 Kubba A, Wilkinson C. *Recommendations for Clinical Practice: emergency contraception.* London: Faculty of Family Planning and Reproductive Health Care of the Royal College of Obstetricians and Gynaecologists, CSC 1/98, valid until 01/2001.

88 Bury J. *Teenage Pregnancy in Britain.* London: Birth Control Trust, 1984.

89 Family Planning Association. *Contraception: patterns of use.* Factsheet No. 5. London: Family Planning Association, 1997.

90 British Pregnancy Advisory Service. *Price List.* London: British Pregnancy Advisory Service (applicable 1 April 1998).

91 Marie Stopes International, 1998, op. cit.

92 Office for National Statistics (ONS). *Abortions in England and Wales, 2000.* London: The Stationery Office (press release September 2001); www.statistics.gov.uk/products/p68.asp (accessed on 16 January 2002).

93 Ashton JR. Components of delay amongst women obtaining termination of pregnancy. *J Biosoc Sci* 1980; **12**: 261–73.

94 Paintin D. *Twenty Questions About Abortion Answered.* London: Birth Control Trust, 1997.

95 British Pregnancy Advisory Service (BPAS); www.bpas.org (accessed on 6 January 2002).

96 Abortion Law Reform Association. *Report on NHS Abortion Services.* London: Abortion Law Reform Association, 1997.

97 Cameron ST *et al.* Impact of the introduction of new medical methods on therapeutic abortions at the Royal Infirmary of Edinburgh. *Br J Obstet Gynaecol* 1996; **103**: 1222–9.

98 Laing W, 1997, op. cit.

99 Department of Health. *Report of the Royal Commission on the National Health Service* (Merrison Report). London: HMSO, 1979.

100 Department of Health. *Working for Patients.* London: HMSO, 1989.

101 Birth Control Trust. *Purchasing Abortion Services: a guide for fundholders.* London: Birth Control Trust, 1995.

102 Royal College of Obstetricians and Gynaecologists. *The Initial Investigation and Management of the Infertile Couple,* 1998; www.rcog.org.uk/guidelines/infertile.html (accessed on 3 January 2002).

103 Royal College of Obstetricians and Gynaecologists. *The Management of Infertility in Secondary Care,* 1998; www.rcog.org.uk/guidelines/secondary.html (accessed on 3 January 2002).

104 Royal College of Obstetricians and Gynaecologists. *The Management of Infertility in Tertiary Care,* 1999; www.rcog.org.uk/guidelines/tertiarycare.html (accessed on 3 January 2002).

105 Human Fertilisation and Embryology Authority (HFEA). *Human Fertilisation and Embryology Authority Annual Report 2000.* London: HFEA, 2001; www.hfea.gov.uk (accessed on 25 January 2002).

106 Personal communication from Michael Hull, Department of Obstetrics and Gynaecology, University of Bristol, 1998.

107 Human Fertilisation and Embryology Authority (HFEA). *Human Fertilisation and Embryology Authority Sixth Annual Report 1997.* London: HFEA, 1997.

108 Oakley A, Fullerton D, Holland J *et al.* Sexual health education interventions for young people: a methodological review. *BMJ* 1995; **310**: 158–62.

109 Kirby D *et al.* School-based programmes to reduce sexual risk behaviours: a review of effectiveness. *Public Health Rep* 1994; **109**(3): 339–61.

110 Harlap S, Kost K, Darroch Forrest J. *Preventing Pregnancy, Protecting Health: a new look at birth control choices in the US.* New York and Washington, DC: Alan Guttmacher Institute, 1991.

111 Jick HJ, Jick SS, Gurewich V, Myers MW, Vasilakis C. Risk of idiopathic cardiovascular death and non-fatal thromboembolism in women using oral contraceptives with differing progestagen components. *Lancet* 1995; **346**: 1589–93.

112 World Health Organization. Collaborative Study of Cardiovascular Disease and Steroid Hormone Contraception. Effect of different progestagens in low-oestrogen oral contraceptives on venous thromboembolic disease. *Lancet* 1995; **346**: 1582–8.

113 World Health Organization. WHO Scientific Group Meeting on Cardiovascular Disease and Steroid Hormone Contraceptives. In: *WHO Weekly Epidemiological Record* No. 48, 28 November 1997, pp. 361–3.

114 Centers for Disease Control, Cancer and Steroid Hormone Study. Oral contraceptive use and the risk of ovarian cancer. *JAMA* 1983; **249**: 1596.

115 Wright NH *et al.* Neoplasia and dysplasia of the cervix uteri and conception: a possible protective effect of the diaphragm. *Br J Cancer* 1978; **38**: 273.

116 Hubacher D, Lara-Ricalde R, Taylor DJ *et al.* Use of copper intrauterine devices and the risk of tubal infertility among nulligravid women. *NEJM* 2001; **345**: 561–7; http://content.nejm.org/ (accessed on 25 January 2002).

117 Lähteenmaki P, Haukkamaa M, Puolakka J *et al.* Open randomised study of use of levonorgestrel-releasing intrauterine system as alternative to hysterectomy. *BMJ* 1998; **316**: 1122–6.

118 Botting B. Trends in abortion. *Popul Trends* 1991; **64**: 19–29.

119 Grimes DA. Medical abortion in early pregnancy: a review of the evidence. *Obstet Gynaecol.* 1997; **89**(5): 790–6.

120 Cabrol D, Dubois C, Cronje H *et al.* Induction of labour with Mifepristone (RU486) in intrauterine fetal death. *Am J Obstet Gynaecol* 1990; **163**: 540–1.

121 Urqhart DR, Templeton AA. Psychiatric morbidity and acceptability following medical and surgical methods of induced abortion. *Br J Obstet Gynaecol* 1991; **98**: 396–9.

122 Vandekerckhove P, O'Donovan PA, Lilford RJ, Harada RW. Infertility treatment: from cookery to science. The epidemiology of randomised controlled trials. *Br J Obstet Gynaecol* 1993; **100**: 1005–36.

123 Hughes EG, Fedorkow DM, Collins JA. A quantitative overview of controlled trials in endometriosis-associated infertility. *Fertil Steril* 1993; **59**: 963–70.

124 Hull MGR. Infertility treatment: relative effectiveness of conventional and assisted conception methods. *Hum Reprod* 1992; **7**: 785–96.

125 Emslie C, Grimshaw J, Templeton A. Do clinical guidelines improve general practice management and referral of infertile couples? *BMJ* 1993; **306**: 1728–31.

126 Human Fertilisation and Embryology Authority (HFEA). *The Patient's Guide to DI and IVF clinics* (3e). London: HFEA, 1997.

127 Garel M *et al.* Psychological consequences of having triplets: a four-year follow-up study. *Fertil Steril* 1997; **67**(6): 1162–5.

128 Doyle P. The outcome of multiple pregnancy. *Hum Reprod* 1996; **11**(Suppl. 4): 110–17.

129 Freemantle N (ed.). The management of subfertility. *Effect Health Care* 1992; **3**.

130 Hart JT. The Inverse Care Law. *Lancet* 1971; **1**: 405–12.

131 Department of Health. *Independent Inquiry into Inequalities in Health Report.* London: The Stationery Office, 1998.

132 Mackenzie M, Lawson L, Mackinnon J. *Evaluation of the Sandyford Initiative: having your voice heard – interim report.* Glasgow: Health Promotion Policy Unit, Department of Public Health, University of Glasgow, 2001.

133 Specialist Health Promotion Service for Central and East Cheshire. *Reducing Teenage Pregnancy in Cheshire: a living resource.* East Cheshire NHS Primary Care Trust; www.healthpromo.org/teenpreg/ (accessed on 20 September 2002).

134 Cossey D. *Teenage Birth Control: the case for the condom.* Liverpool: Brook Advisory Centre, 1979.

135 Smith C. Measuring quality in contraceptive service. *Qual Health Care* 1997; **6**: 59.

136 Medical Foundation for AIDS and Sexual Health. *Using Effectiveness Research to Guide the Development of School Sex Education.* A paper based on a workshop held by the BMA Foundation for AIDS (now known as the Medical Foundation for AIDS and Sexual Health), the Health Education Authority and the Sex Education Forum in early 1996. London: BMA Foundation for AIDS, 1997; www.medfash.org.uk/publications/documents/school_sex_education.htm (accessed on 10 September 2002).

Acknowledgements

We would like to thank Alayne Robin, Regional Sexual Health Co-ordinator, for suggestions and advice, and Sue Waller, Regional Information Research Support Officer, Liverpool John Moores University, for assistance with updating the information in this chapter.

Index